ECONOMICS

For our other contributions to
the next generation:
Catherine, Nicholas and Peter;
and Benjamin, Oliver and Harriet

ECONOMICS

N. Gregory Mankiw and Mark P. Taylor

Australia • Brazil • Japan • Korea • Mexico • Singapore • Spain • United Kingdom • United States

Economics
Second Edition
N. Gregory Mankiw and Mark P. Taylor

Publishing Director: Linden Harris
Publisher: Brendan George
Development Editor: Annabel Ainscow
Editorial Assistant: Helen Green
Content Project Editor: Lucy Arthy
Production Controller: Eyvett Davis
Marketing Manager: Amanda Cheung
Typesetter: MPS Limited, a Macmillan Company
Cover design: Adam Renvoize
Text design: Design Deluxe

This work is adapted from *Economics*, 1st Edition, published by South-Western, a division of Cengage Learning, Inc. © 2008.

British Library Cataloguing-in-Publication Data
A catalogue record for this book is available from the British Library.

ISBN: 13: 978-1-8448-0870-0
ISBN: 10: 1-8448-0870-X

Cengage Learning EMEA
Cheriton House, North Way, Andover, Hampshire SP10 5BE
United Kingdom

Cengage Learning products are represented in Canada by Nelson Education Ltd.

For your lifelong learning solutions, visit
www.cengage.co.uk

Purchase your next print book, e-book or e-chapter at
www.cengagebrain.com

For product information and technology assistance,
contact **emea.info@cengage.com**

For permission to use material from this text or product,
and for permission queries,
email **clsuk.permissions@cengage.com**

Printed by RR Donnelley, China
1 2 3 4 5 6 7 8 9 10 – 13 12 11

BRIEF CONTENTS

CONTENTS

6 Supply, Demand and Government Policies 117

SUPPLY AND DEMAND II: MARKETS AND WELFARE 137

7 Consumers, Producers and the Efficiency of Markets 138

8 Application: The Costs of Taxation 158

9 Application: International Trade 174

THE ECONOMICS OF THE PUBLIC SECTOR 197

10 Externalities 198

11 Public Goods and Common Resources 221

PART 5

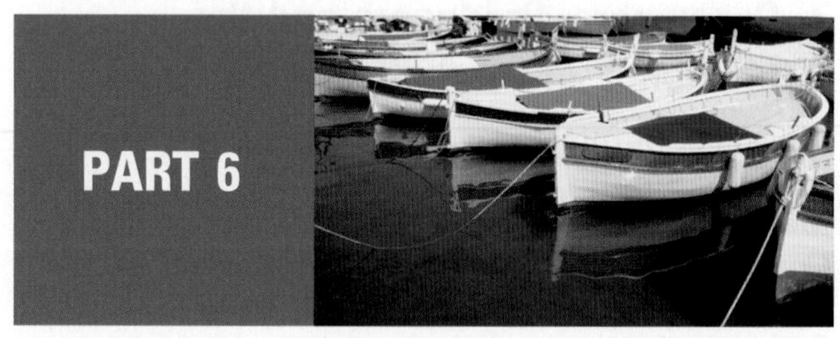
PART 6

PART 7

TOPICS FOR FURTHER STUDY 437

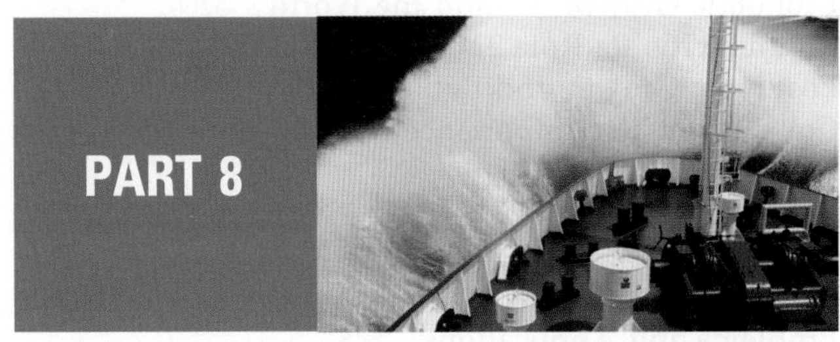

PART 8

THE DATA OF MACROECONOMICS 485

THE REAL ECONOMY IN THE LONG RUN 523

MONEY AND PRICES IN THE LONG RUN 615

THE MACROECONOMICS OF OPEN ECONOMIES 665

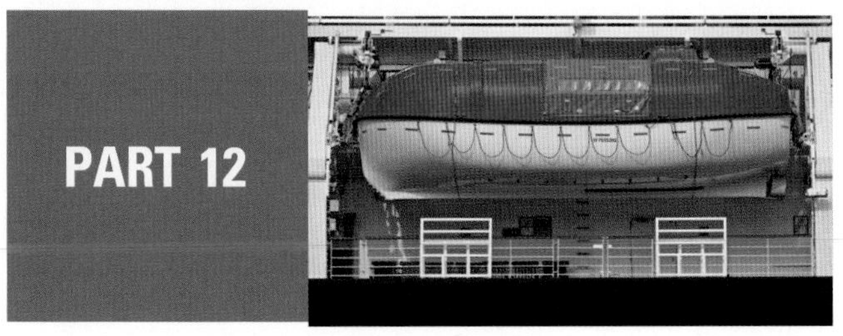

SHORT-RUN ECONOMIC FLUCTUATIONS 705

TOPICS IN INTERNATIONAL FINANCE AND MACROECONOMICS 815

37 THE FINANCIAL CRISIS 816

38 Common Currency Areas and European Monetary Union 840

FINAL THOUGHTS 867

39 Five Debates over Macroeconomic Policy 868

ABOUT THE AUTHORS

AUTHORS:

N. GREGORY MANKIW is Professor of Economics at Harvard University. As a student, he studied economics at Princeton University and the Massachusetts Institute of Technology. As a teacher he has taught macroeconomics, microeconomics, statistics and principles of economics. Professor Mankiw is a prolific writer and a regular participant in academic and policy debates. In addition to his teaching, research and writing, Professor Mankiw has been a research associate of the National Bureau of Economic Research, an advisor to the Federal Reserve Bank of Boston and the Congressional Budget Office. From 2003 to 2005, he served as chairman of the US President's Council of Economic Advisors. Professor Mankiw lives in Wellesley, Massachusetts, with his wife Deborah, their three children and their border terrier Tobin.

MARK P. TAYLOR is Dean of Warwick Business School at the University of Warwick and Professor of International Finance. He obtained his first degree in philosophy, politics and economics from Oxford University and his master's degree in economics from London University, from where he also holds a doctorate in economics and international finance. Professor Taylor has taught economics and finance at various universities (including Oxford, Warwick and New York) and at various levels (including principles courses, advanced undergraduate and advanced postgraduate courses). He has also worked as a senior economist at the International Monetary Fund and at the Bank of England and, before becoming Dean of Warwick Business School, was a managing director at BlackRock, the world's largest financial asset manager, where he worked on international asset allocation based on macroeconomic analysis. His research has been extensively published in scholarly journals and he is today one of the most highly cited economists in the world. Professor Taylor lives with his family in a 15th century farmhouse near Stratford upon Avon, Warwickshire, where he collects clocks and keeps bees.

CONTRIBUTOR:

ANDREW ASHWIN has over 20 years experience as a teacher of economics. He has an MBA and is currently researching for a Ph.D. investigating assessment and the notion of threshold concepts in economics. Andrew is an experienced author writing a number of texts for students at different levels, journal publications related to his Ph.D. research and is currently working on a text on the business environment for undergraduates. Andrew is Chair of Examiners for a major awarding body for business and economics and is Editor of the Economics, Business and Enterprise Association (EBEA) journal. As one of the content editors for Biz/ed (http://www.bized.co.uk), Andrew writes articles and resources on business studies and economics for the website. Andrew lives in Rutland with his wife Sue and their twin sons Alex and Johnny.

'Economics is a study of mankind in the ordinary business of life.' So wrote Alfred Marshall, the great 19th-century British economist, in his textbook, *Principles of Economics*. Although we have learned much about the economy since Marshall's time, this definition of economics is as true today as it was in 1890, when the first edition of his text was published.

Why should you, as a student of the 21st century, embark on the study of economics? Here are three good reasons. The first reason to study economics is that it will help you understand the world in which you live. There are many questions about the economy that might spark your curiosity. Why do airlines charge less for a return ticket if the traveller stays over a Saturday night? Why is Julia Roberts paid so much to star in films? Why are living standards so meagre in many African countries? Why do some countries have high rates of inflation while others have stable prices? Why have some European countries adopted a common currency? These are just a few of the questions that a course in economics will help you answer.

The second reason to study economics is that it will make you a more astute participant in the economy As you go about your life, you make many economic decisions. While you are a student, you decide how many years to stay in full-time education. Once you take a job, you decide how much of your income to spend, how much to save and how to invest your savings. One day you may find yourself running a small business or a large firm, and you will decide what prices to charge for your products. The insights developed in the coming chapters will give you a new perspective on how best to make these decisions. Studying economics will not by itself make you rich, but it will give you some tools that may help in that endeavour if that is what you desire.

The third reason to study economics is that it will give you a better understanding of the potential and limits of economic policy. As a voter, you help choose the policies that guide the allocation of society's resources. When deciding which policies to support, you may find yourself asking various questions about economics. What are the burdens associated with alternative forms of taxation? What are the effects of free trade with other countries? What is the best way to protect the environment? How does the government budget deficit affect the economy? These and similar questions are always on the minds of policy makers.

Thus the principles of economics can be applied in many of life's situations. Whether the future finds you reading the newspaper, running a business or running the country, you will be glad that you studied economics.

FOR WHOM IS THIS BOOK WRITTEN?

It is tempting for professional economists writing a textbook to take the economist's point of view and to emphasize those topics that fascinate them and other economists. We have done our best to avoid that temptation. We have tried to put ourselves in the position of someone seeing economics for the first time. Our goal has been to emphasize the material that *students* should and do find interesting about the study of the economy.

One result is that this book is briefer than many books used to introduce students to economics. Another is that more of this book is devoted to applications and policy – and less to formal economic theory – than is the case with many other books written for an introductory course. Throughout this book we have tried to return to applications and policy questions as often as possible. All the chapters include case studies illustrating how the principles of economics are applied. In addition, 'In the News' boxes offer highlights from news events showing how economic ideas shed light on current issues facing society. After students finish their first course in economics, they should think about news stories from a new perspective and with greater insight.

Something else worth pointing out is that the book has a distinctively European focus. This is not to say that it is an introduction to the economics of the European economy – it is not. Nor does the book ignore the importance of the US economy and the rest of the world – to do so would give a very lopsided view. But what it does attempt to do is to relate economic concepts to an environment that will be familiar and interesting to a European student, and we do examine some important issues relevant specifically to the European economy, such as the single European currency. The case studies and 'In the News' boxes also draw on European material. Since this is a book designed to teach students how to think about the world like an economist, analyses of particular institutional details are necessary primarily in order to illustrate the underlying economic principles, but we have used European institutional examples wherever possible. In some instances we have chosen to focus on a particular economy for reasons of space or clarity of exposition but in this Second Edition we have been able to introduce analysis of other economies as well, for example, in our discussion of the tax system we have covered the UK, South Africa and Germany.

HOW IS THIS BOOK ORGANIZED?

To write a brief and student-friendly book, we had to consider new ways to organize familiar material. What follows is a whirlwind tour of this text. With any textbook, instructors can choose to cover material in different orders; each section in the book does contain chapters that build on previous ones, although but each section can be tackled independently of the others if desired. The tour will, we hope, give instructors some sense of how the pieces fit together.

Introductory Material

Chapter 1, 'Ten Principles of Economics', introduces students to the economists' view of the world. It previews some of the big ideas that recur throughout economics, such as opportunity cost, marginal decision-making, the role of incentives, the gains from trade, and the efficiency of market allocations. Throughout the book, we refer regularly to the *Ten Principles of Economics* introduced in Chapter 1 to remind students that these ideas are the foundation for all economics. An icon in the margin calls attention to these key, interconnected principles.

Chapter 2, 'Thinking Like an Economist', examines how economists approach their field of study. It discusses the role of assumptions in developing a theory and introduces the concept of an economic model. It also discusses the role of economists in making policy. The appendix to this chapter offers a brief refresher course on how graphs are used and how they can be abused.

Chapter 3, 'Interdependence and the Gains from Trade', presents the theory of comparative advantage. This theory explains why individuals trade with their neighbours, as well as why nations trade with other nations. Much of economics is about how market forces coordinate many individual production and consumption decisions. As a starting point for this analysis, students see in this chapter why specialization, interdependence and trade can benefit everyone.

The Fundamental Tools of Supply and Demand

The next three chapters introduce the basic tools of supply and demand. Chapter 4, 'The Market Forces of Supply and Demand', develops the supply curve, the demand curve and the notion of market equilibrium. Chapter 5, 'Elasticity and its Application', introduces the concept of elasticity and uses it to analyse events in three different markets. Chapter 6, 'Supply, Demand and Government Policies', uses these tools to examine price controls, such as rent control, minimum wage laws, and tax incidence.

Chapter 7, 'Consumers, Producers and the Efficiency of Markets', extends the analysis of supply and demand using the concepts of consumer surplus and producer surplus. It begins by developing the link between consumers' willingness to pay and the demand curve, and the link between producers' costs of production and the supply curve. It then shows that the market equilibrium maximizes the sum of the producer and consumer surplus. Thus, students learn early about the efficiency of market allocations.

The next two chapters apply the concepts of producer and consumer surplus to questions of policy. Chapter 8, 'Application: The Costs of Taxation', shows why taxation results in deadweight losses and what determines the size of those losses. Chapter 9, 'Application: International Trade', considers who wins and who loses from international trade and presents the debate over protectionist trade policies.

More Microeconomics

Having examined why market allocations are often desirable, the book then considers how the government can sometimes improve on them. Chapter 10,'Externalities', explains how external effects such as pollution can render market outcomes inefficient and discusses the possible public and private solutions to those inefficiencies. Chapter 11, 'Public Goods and Common Resources', considers the problems that arise when goods, such as national defence, have no market price. Chapter 12, 'The Design of the Tax System', describes how the government raises the revenue necessary to pay for public goods. It presents some institutional background about the UK tax system and an outline of the system in Germany and South Africa for comparison, and then discusses how the goals of efficiency and equity come into play when designing a tax system.

The next five chapters examine firm behaviour and industrial organization. Chapter 13, 'The Costs of Production', discusses what to include in a firm's costs, and it introduces cost curves. Chapter 14, 'Firms in Competitive Markets', analyses the behaviour of price-taking firms and derives the market supply curve. Chapter 15, 'Monopoly', discusses the behaviour of a firm that is the sole seller in its market. It discusses the inefficiency of monopoly pricing, the possible policy responses, and the attempts by monopolies to price discriminate. Chapter 16, 'Monopolistic Competition', looks at behaviour in a market in which many sellers offer similar but differentiated products. It also discusses the debate over the effects of advertising. Chapter 17, 'Oligopoly', covers markets in which there are only a few sellers, using the prisoner's dilemma as the model for examining strategic interaction.

The next three chapters present issues related to labour markets. Chapter 18, 'The Markets for the Factors of Production', emphasizes the link between factor prices and marginal productivity. Chapter 19, 'Earnings and Discrimination', discusses the determinants of equilibrium wages, including compensating differentials, human capital and discrimination. Chapter 20, 'Income Inequality and Poverty', examines the degree of inequality in UK society, alternative views about the government's role in changing the distribution of income and various policies aimed at helping society's poorest members.

The next two chapters present optional material. Chapter 21, 'The Theory of Consumer Choice', analyses individual decision-making using budget constraints and indifference curves. Chapter 22, 'Frontiers of Microeconomics', introduces the topics of asymmetric information, political economy and behavioural economics.

Many instructors may choose to omit all or some of this material. Instructors who do cover these topics may choose to assign these chapters earlier than they are presented in the book, and we have written them to give instructors flexibility.

Macroeconomics

Our overall approach to teaching macroeconomics is to examine the economy in the long run (when prices are flexible) before examining the economy in the short run (when prices are sticky). We believe that this organization simplifies learning macroeconomics for several reasons. Firstly, the classical assumption of price flexibility is more closely linked to the basic lessons of supply and demand, which students have already mastered. Secondly, the classical dichotomy allows the study of the long run to be broken up into several, easily digested pieces. Thirdly, because the business cycle represents a transitory deviation from the economy's long-run growth path, studying the transitory deviations is more natural after the long-run equilibrium is understood. Fourthly, the macroeconomic theory of the short run is more controversial among economists than the macroeconomic theory of the long run. For these reasons, most upper-level courses in macroeconomics now follow this long-run-before-short-run approach; our goal is to offer introductory students the same advantage. There would be nothing to stop lecturers who prefer to approach the short run first from so doing – the book is flexible enough to allow this approach to be adopted.

Returning to the detailed organization, we start the coverage of macroeconomics with issues of measurement. Chapter 23, 'Measuring a Nation's Income', discusses the meaning of gross domestic product and related statistics from the national income accounts. Chapter 24, 'Measuring the Cost of Living', discusses the measurement and use of the consumer price indices.

The next four chapters describe the behaviour of the real economy in the long run. Chapter 25, 'Production and Growth', examines the determinants of the large variation in living standards over time and across countries. Chapter 26, 'Saving, Investment and the Financial System', discusses the types of financial institutions in a modern, advanced economy and examines their role in allocating resources. Chapter 27, 'The Basic Tools of Finance', introduces present value, risk management and asset pricing. Chapter 28, 'Unemployment', considers the long-run determinants of the unemployment rate, including job search, minimum wage laws, the market power of unions and efficiency wages.

Having described the long-run behaviour of the real economy, the book then turns to the long-run behaviour of money and prices. Chapter 29, 'The Monetary System', introduces the economist's concept of money and the role of the central bank in controlling the quantity of money. We also introduce some institutional background on the European Central Bank, the Bank of England and the US Federal Reserve. Chapter 30, 'Money Growth and Inflation', develops the classical theory of inflation and discusses the costs that inflation imposes on a society.

The next two chapters present the macroeconomics of open economies, maintaining the long-run assumptions of price flexibility and full employment. Chapter 31, 'Open-economy Macroeconomics: Basic Concepts', explains the relationship among saving, investment and the trade balance, the distinction between the nominal and real exchange rate, and the theory of purchasing-power parity. Chapter 32, 'A Macroeconomic Theory of the Open Economy', presents a classical model of the international flow of goods and capital. The model sheds light on various issues, including the link between budget deficits and trade deficits and the macroeconomic effects of trade policies.

After developing the long-run theory of the economy in Chapters 25 through to 32, the book turns to explaining short-run fluctuations around the long-run trend. This organization simplifies teaching the theory of short-run fluctuations because, at this point in the course, students have a good grounding in many basic macroeconomic concepts. A new feature of the Second Edition is to start this process by looking at Keynesian economics and introducing the IS-LM model, leading into Chapter 34, which begins with some facts about the business cycle and then develops the 'Aggregate Demand and Aggregate Supply' model. Chapter 35, 'The Influence of Monetary and Fiscal Policy on Aggregate Demand', explains how policy makers can use the tools at their disposal to shift the aggregate demand curve. Chapter 36, 'The Short-run Trade-off between Inflation and Unemployment', explains why policy makers who control aggregate demand face a trade-off between inflation and unemployment. It examines why this trade-off exists in the short run, why it shifts over time, and why it does not exist in the long run.

Chapter 37, 'The Financial Crisis' provides an overview of the main causes of one of the most turbulent economic periods in recent times and introduces some of the key questions facing economists and policy makers in the wake of the crisis.

Chapter 38, 'Common Currency Areas and European Monetary Union', looks at the costs and benefits of adopting a common currency among a group of countries, focusing particularly on European monetary union. In doing so, it draws on many of the tools of macroeconomic analysis that have been introduced in previous chapters in developing the theory of optimum currency areas and applying it to the European case.

The book concludes with Chapter 39, 'Five Debates Over Macroeconomic Policy.' This capstone chapter considers five controversial issues in economics today: the role of information in developing sound policy; the idea of a structural deficit, the importance of balancing the government's budget; the role of regulation in the prevention of future financial crises; and the debate between economists on the importance of demand in recessions and efficient markets. For each issue, the chapter presents both sides of the debate and encourages students to make their own judgements.

LEARNING TOOLS

The purpose of this book is to help students learn the fundamental lessons of economics and to show how such lessons can be applied to the world in which they live. Towards that end, we have used various learning tools that recur throughout the book.

- *Case studies*. Economic theory is useful and interesting only if it can be applied to understanding actual events and policies. This book, therefore, contains numerous case studies that apply the theory that has just been developed.
- *'In the News' boxes*. One benefit that students gain from studying economics is a new perspective and greater understanding about news from around the world. To highlight this benefit, we have incorporated discussions of news events including excerpts from newspaper articles. These articles, together

with our brief introductions, show how basic economic theory can be applied and raise important questions for discussion.

- *'FYI' boxes.* These boxes provide additional material 'for your information'. Some of them offer a glimpse into the history of economic thought. Others clarify technical issues. Still others discuss supplementary topics that instructors might choose either to discuss or skip in their lectures.
- *Definitions of key concepts.* When key concepts are introduced in the chapter, they are presented in **bold** typeface. In addition, their definitions are placed in the margins. This treatment should aid students in learning and reviewing the material.
- *Quick quizzes.* After most major sections, students are offered a 'quick quiz' to check their comprehension of what they have just learned. If students cannot readily answer these quizzes, they should stop and reread material before continuing.
- *Chapter summaries.* Each chapter ends with a brief summary that reminds students of the most important lessons that they have just learned. Later in their study it offers an efficient way to revise for exams.
- *List of key concepts.* A list of key concepts at the end of each chapter offers students a way to test their understanding of the new terms that have been introduced. Page references are included so that students can review the terms they do not understand. All key terms can also be found in the glossary at the end of the book.
- *Questions for review.* At the end of each chapter are questions for review that cover the chapter's primary lessons. Students can use these questions to check their comprehension and to prepare for exams.
- *Problems and applications.* Each chapter also contains a variety of problems and applications that ask students to apply the material they have learned. Some professors may use these questions for homework assignments. Others may use them as a starting point for classroom discussions.

WHAT'S NEW IN THE SECOND EDITION?

One of the most interesting things about economics is that though a science, it is built on shifting sands – dynamic and forever changing. What we understand about human behaviour and the way in which the economy works is constantly being updated to take account of new data and new events. The Second Edition brings you some new, and not so new, thinking to help you understand the debates and dilemmas facing economists and policy makers in making sense of the world. The financial crisis which began to gather pace in 2007 and the subsequent recession have led to a major rethink about some fundamental assumptions in economic theory. The consequences of the crisis have raised new questions for economists as well as challenging some widely held assumptions and beliefs. These topical issues are introduced throughout the book where appropriate to highlight the dynamic nature of the discipline. All chapters have been thoroughly revised and updated with the latest data at the time of writing. The growing influence of behavioural economics is acknowledged throughout the book and attempts have been made to use new case studies and 'In the News' articles to reflect the European focus of the book and the importance of business economics. Together the new and revised chapters provide a range of fascinating new topics to explore. All the issues and economic concepts covered will be familiar to students and provide them with further food for thought in their quest to 'think like an economist'.

WALK THROUGH TOUR

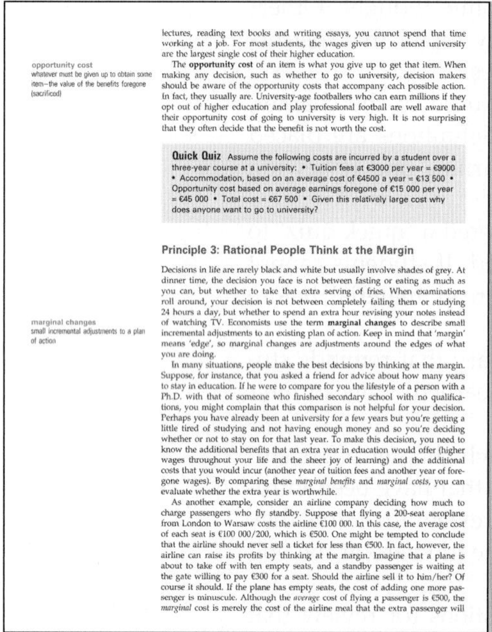

lectures, reading text books and writing essays, you cannot spend that time working at a job. For most students, the wages given up to attend university are the largest single cost of their higher education.

opportunity cost
whatever must be given up to obtain some item–the value of the benefits foregone (sacrificed)

The **opportunity cost** of an item is what you give up to get that item. When making any decision, such as whether to go to university, decision makers should be aware of the opportunity costs that accompany each possible action. In fact, they usually are. University-age footballers who can earn millions if they opt out of higher education and play professional football are well aware that their opportunity cost of going to university is very high. It is not surprising that they often decide that the benefit is not worth the cost.

Quick Quiz Assume the following costs are incurred by a student over a three-year course at a university: • Tuition fees at €3000 per year = €9000 • Accommodation, based on an average cost of €4500 a year = €13 500 • Opportunity cost based on average earnings foregone of €15 000 per year = €45 000 • Total cost = €67 500 • Given this relatively large cost why does anyone want to go to university?

Principle 3: Rational People Think at the Margin

marginal changes
small incremental adjustments to a plan of action

Decisions in life are rarely black and white but usually involve shades of grey. At dinner time, the decision you face is not between fasting or eating as much as you can, but whether to take that extra serving of fries. When examinations roll around, your decision is not between completely failing them or studying 24 hours a day, but whether to spend an extra hour revising your notes instead of watching TV. Economists use the term **marginal changes** to describe small incremental adjustments to an existing plan of action. Keep in mind that 'margin' means 'edge', so marginal changes are adjustments around the edges of what you are doing.

In many situations, people make the best decisions by thinking at the margin. Suppose, for instance, that you asked a friend for advice about how many years to stay in education. If he were to compare for you the lifestyle of a person with a Ph.D. with that of someone who finished secondary school with no qualifications, you might complain that this comparison is not helpful for your decision. Perhaps you have already been at university for a few years but you're getting a little tired of studying and not having enough money and so you're deciding whether or not to stay on for that last year. To make this decision, you need to know the additional benefits that an extra year in education would offer (higher wages throughout your life and the sheer joy of learning) and the additional costs that you would incur (another year of tuition fees and another year of foregone wages). By comparing these *marginal benefits* and *marginal costs*, you can evaluate whether the extra year is worthwhile.

As another example, consider an airline company deciding how much to charge passengers who fly standby. Suppose that flying a 200-seat aeroplane from London to Warsaw costs the airline €100 000. In this case, the average cost of each seat is €100 000/200, which is €500. One might be tempted to conclude that the airline should never sell a ticket for less than €500. In fact, however, the airline can raise its profits by thinking at the margin. Imagine that a plane is about to take off with ten empty seats, and a standby passenger is waiting at the gate willing to pay €300 for a seat. Should the airline sell it to him/her? Of course it should. If the plane has empty seats, the cost of adding one more passenger is minuscule. Although the *average* cost of flying a passenger is €500, the *marginal* cost is merely the cost of the airline meal that the extra passenger will

Quick quizzes are provided at the end of each section and allow students to check their comprehension of what they have just learned.

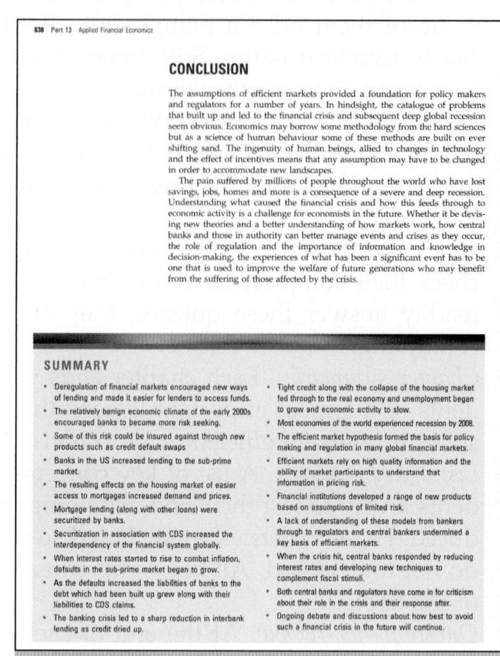

838 Part 13 Applied Financial Economics

CONCLUSION

The assumptions of efficient markets provided a foundation for policy makers and regulators for a number of years. In hindsight, the catalogue of problems that built up and led to the financial crisis and subsequent deep global recession seem obvious. Economics may borrow some methodology from the hard sciences but as a science of human behaviour some of these methods are built on ever shifting sand. The ingenuity of human beings, allied to changes in technology and the effect of incentives means that any assumption may have to be changed in order to accommodate new landscapes.

The pain suffered by millions of people throughout the world who have lost savings, jobs, homes and more is a consequence of a severe and deep recession. Understanding what caused the financial crisis and how this feeds through to economic activity is a challenge for economists in the future. Whether it be devising new theories and a better understanding of how markets work, how central banks and those in authority can better manage events and crises as they occur, the role of regulation and the importance of information and knowledge in decision-making, the experiences of what has been a significant event has to be one that is used to improve the welfare of future generations who may benefit from the suffering of those affected by the crisis.

SUMMARY

- Deregulation of financial markets encouraged new ways of lending and made it easier for lenders to access funds.
- The relatively benign economic climate of the early 2000s encouraged banks to become more risk seeking.
- Some of this risk could be insured against through new products such as credit default swaps
- Banks in the US increased lending to the sub-prime market.
- The resulting effects on the housing market of easier access to mortgages increased demand and prices.
- Mortgage lending (along with other loans) were securitized by banks.
- Securitization in association with CDS increased the interdependency of the financial system globally.
- When interest rates started to rise to combat inflation, defaults in the sub-prime market began to grow.
- As the defaults increased the liabilities of banks to the debt which had been built up grew along with their liabilities to CDS claims.
- The banking crisis led to a sharp reduction in interbank lending as credit dried up.
- Tight credit along with the collapse of the housing market fed through to the real economy and unemployment began to grow and economic activity to slow.
- Most economies of the world experienced recession by 2008.
- The efficient market hypothesis formed the basis for policy making and regulation in many global financial markets.
- Efficient markets rely on high quality information and the ability of market participants to understand that information in pricing risk.
- Financial institutions developed a range of new products based on assumptions of limited risk.
- A lack of understanding of these models from bankers through to regulators and central bankers undermined a key basis of efficient markets.
- When the crisis hit, central banks responded by reducing interest rates and developing new techniques to complement fiscal stimuli.
- Both central banks and regulators have come in for criticism about their role in the crisis and their response after.
- Ongoing debate and discussions about how best to avoid such a financial crisis in the future will continue.

Summaries at the end of each chapter remind students of what they have learned so far, offering a useful way to review for exams.

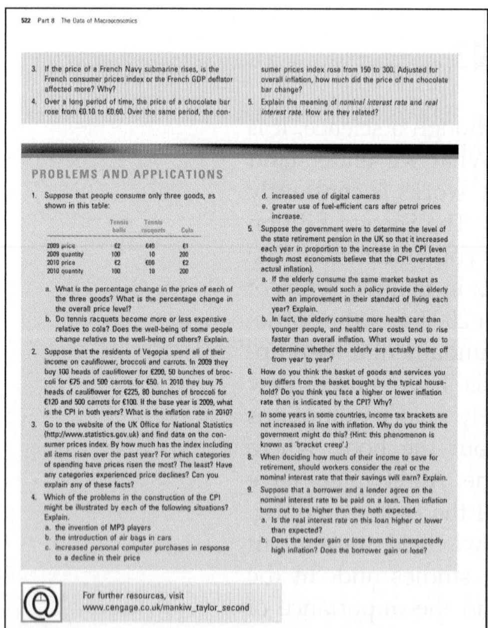

522 Part 8 The Data of Macroeconomics

3. If the price of a French Navy submarine rises, is the French consumer prices index or the French GDP deflator affected more? Why?
4. Over a long period of time, the price of a chocolate bar rose from €0.10 to €0.60. Over the same period, the consumer prices index rose from 150 to 300. Adjusted for overall inflation, how much did the price of the chocolate bar change?
5. Explain the meaning of *nominal interest rate* and *real interest rate*. How are they related?

PROBLEMS AND APPLICATIONS

1. Suppose that people consume only three goods, as shown in this table:

	Tennis balls	Tennis racquets	Cola
2009 price	€2	€40	€1
2009 quantity	100	10	200
2010 price	€2	€60	€2
2010 quantity	100	10	200

   a. What is the percentage change in the price of each of the three goods? What is the percentage change in the overall price level?
   b. Do tennis racquets become more or less expensive relative to cola? Does the well-being of some people change relative to the well-being of others? Explain.

2. Suppose that the residents of Vegopia spend all of their income on cauliflower, broccoli and carrots. In 2009 they buy 100 heads of cauliflower for €200, 50 bunches of broccoli for €75 and 500 carrots for €50. In 2010 they buy 75 heads of cauliflower for €225, 80 bunches of broccoli for €120 and 500 carrots for €100. If the base year is 2009, what is the CPI in both years? What is the inflation rate in 2010?
3. Go to the website of the UK Office for National Statistics (http://www.statistics.gov.uk) and find data on the consumer prices index. By how much has the index including all items risen over the past year? For which categories of spending have prices risen the most? The least? Have any categories experienced price declines? Can you explain any of these facts?
4. Which of the problems in the construction of the CPI might be illustrated by each of the following situations? Explain.
   a. the invention of MP3 players
   b. the introduction of air bags in cars
   c. increased personal computer purchases in response to a decline in their price
   d. increased use of digital cameras
   e. greater use of fuel-efficient cars after petrol prices increase.
5. Suppose the government were to determine the level of the state retirement pension in the UK so that it increased each year in proportion to the increase in the CPI (even though most economists believe that the CPI overstates actual inflation).
   a. If the elderly consume the same market basket as other people, would such a policy provide the elderly with an improvement in their standard of living each year? Explain.
   b. In fact, the elderly consume more health care than younger people, and health care costs tend to rise faster than overall inflation. What would you do to determine whether the elderly are actually better off from year to year?
6. How do you think the basket of goods and services you buy differs from the basket bought by the typical household? Do you think you face a higher or lower inflation rate than is indicated by the CPI? Why?
7. In some years in some countries, income tax brackets are not increased in line with inflation. Why do you think the government might do this? (Hint: this phenomenon is known as 'bracket creep'.)
8. When deciding how much of their income to save for retirement, should workers consider the real or the nominal interest rate that their savings will earn? Explain.
9. Suppose that a borrower and a lender agree on the nominal interest rate to be paid on a loan. Then inflation turns out to be higher than they both expected.
   a. Is the real interest rate on this loan higher or lower than expected?
   b. Does the lender gain or lose from this unexpectedly high inflation? Does the borrower gain or lose?

For further resources, visit www.cengage.co.uk/mankiw_taylor_second

Problems and applications allow students to apply the material they have learned within the chapter. These can also be used for classroom discussions or homework assignments.

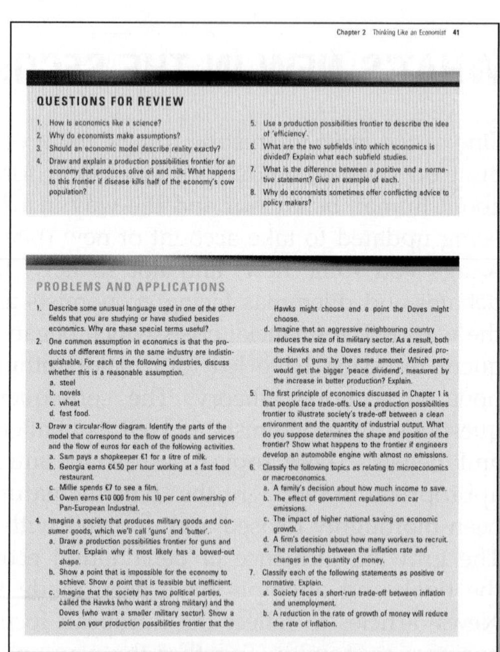

Chapter 2 Thinking Like an Economist 41

QUESTIONS FOR REVIEW

1. How is economics like a science?
2. Why do economists make assumptions?
3. Should an economic model describe reality exactly?
4. Draw and explain a production possibilities frontier for an economy that produces olive oil and milk. What happens to this frontier if disease kills half of the economy's cow population?
5. Use a production possibilities frontier to describe the idea of 'efficiency'.
6. What are the two subfields into which economics is divided? Explain what each subfield studies.
7. What is the difference between a positive and a normative statement? Give an example of each.
8. Why do economists sometimes offer conflicting advice to policy makers?

PROBLEMS AND APPLICATIONS

1. Describe some unusual language used in one of the other fields that you are studying or have studied besides economics. Why are these special terms useful?
2. One common assumption in economics is that the products of different firms in the same industry are indistinguishable. For each of the following industries, discuss whether this is a reasonable assumption.
   a. steel
   b. novels
   c. wheat
   d. fast food.
3. Draw a circular-flow diagram. Identify the parts of the model that correspond to the flow of goods and services and the flow of euros for each of the following activities.
   a. Sam pays a shopkeeper €1 for a litre of milk.
   b. Georgia earns €4.50 per hour working at a fast food restaurant.
   c. Millie spends €7 to see a film.
   d. Owen earns €10 000 from his 10 per cent ownership of Pan-European Industrial.
4. Imagine a society that produces military goods and consumer goods, which we'll call 'guns' and 'butter'.
   a. Draw a production possibilities frontier for guns and butter. Explain why it most likely has a bowed-out shape.
   b. Show a point that is impossible for the economy to achieve. Show a point that is feasible but inefficient.
   c. Imagine that the society has two political parties, called the Hawks (who want a strong military) and the Doves (who want a smaller military sector). Show a point on your production possibilities frontier that the Hawks might choose and a point the Doves might choose.
   d. Imagine that an aggressive neighbouring country reduces the size of its military sector. As a result, both the Hawks and the Doves reduce their desired production of guns by the same amount. Which party would get the bigger 'peace dividend', measured by the increase in butter production? Explain.
5. The first principle of economics discussed in Chapter 1 is that people face trade-offs. Use a production possibilities frontier to illustrate society's trade-off between a clean environment and the quantity of industrial output. What do you suppose determines the shape and position of the frontier? Show what happens to the frontier if engineers develop an automobile engine with almost no emissions.
6. Classify the following topics as relating to microeconomics or macroeconomics.
   a. A family's decision about how much income to save.
   b. The effect of government regulations on car emissions.
   c. The impact of higher national saving on economic growth.
   d. A firm's decision about how many workers to recruit.
   e. The relationship between the inflation rate and changes in the quantity of money.
7. Classify each of the following statements as positive or normative. Explain.
   a. Society faces a short-run trade-off between inflation and unemployment.
   b. A reduction in the rate of growth of money will reduce the rate of inflation.

Questions for review cover each chapter's primary lessons. These can be used to check comprehension and to prepare for exams.

FYI provides additional material 'for your information'; the boxes offer a range of supplementary material, such as a glimpse into the history of economic thought, technical issues and current topics that can be discussed in lectures.

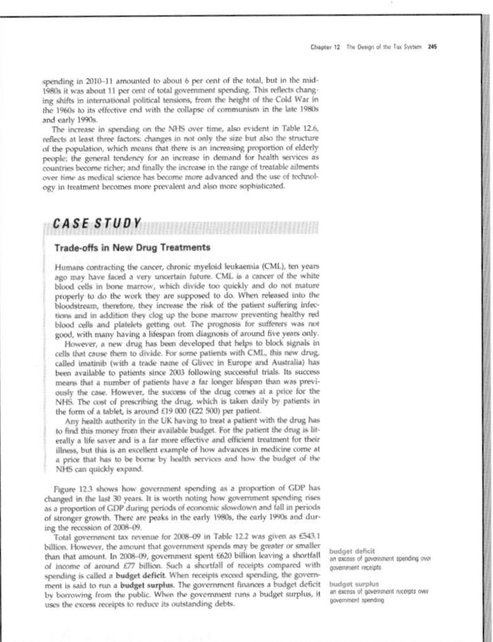

Case studies are provided throughout the text that apply the theory that has been developed to understanding events and policies.

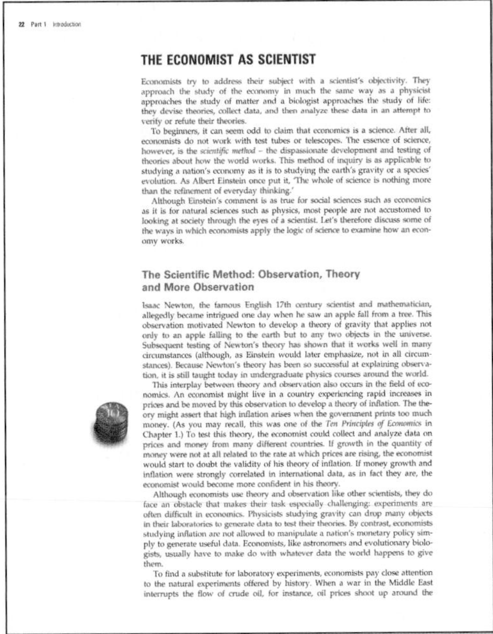

Ten Principles of Economics references within the text are marked by a coin icon in the margin.

'In the News' articles relate key ideas covered in the chapter to topical news events to highlight the application of economic ideas and introduce new angles to consider in topical debates.

Cengage Learning offers various supplements for instructors and students who use this book. These resources are designed to make teaching the principles of economics easy for the instructor and learning them easy for the student.

ABOUT THE WEBSITE

Please visit the *Economics* Second Edition website for all the following material at: www.cengage.co.uk/mankiw_taylor2

For Instructors

Teaching the principles of economics can be a demanding job. The supplements designed for the instructor make the job less difficult. The instructor's supplements have been written by Chris Downs of University College, Chichester and Andrew Ashwin.

- **Instructor's Manual** – a detailed outline of each chapter of the text that provides learning objectives, identifies stumbling blocks that students may face, offers helpful teaching tips and provides suggested in-classroom activities for a more cooperative learning experience. The Instructor's Manual also includes solutions to all of the end-of-chapter exercises, Quick Quizzes, Questions for Review, and Problems and Applications found in the text.
- **PowerPoint Lecture Slides and Exhibit Slides** – instructors can save valuable time as they prepare for classes using these fully adaptable comprehensive lecture presentations with integrated graphs, tables, lists and concepts. A separate exhibit presentation provides instructors with all of the tables and graphs from the main text.
- **ExamView Testbank** – with test generator software included, allows lecturers to create online, paper and local area network (LAN) tests specifically for this book.

For Students

The supplements designed for the student enrich and support the learning experience, providing excellent revision tools and further study opportunities.

- **Learning Objectives** – listed for each chapter, they help the student to monitor their understanding and progress through the book.
- **Exhibit Slides** – provided in PowerPoint, the exhibit presentations provide students with animated figures from the main text.
- **Glossary** – the full glossary of key terms that appears at the end of the book in a downloadable PDF file.
- **Multiple Choice Questions** – test yourself, chapter by chapter.
- **Advanced Critical Thinking Questions –** short scenario-related questions and answers.
- **Discussion Questions –** these can be used to practise and improve your essay-writing skills.

- **Short-answer-questions** – a series of questions requiring some thorough and some more extended writing to assess understanding and application skills.
- **Case studies** – a case study will be available for each chapter focusing on some aspect of the content in the chapter and developing the theory covered, introducing new and relevant research material along with a series of questions to promote thinking and develop writing skills.
- **Practice Questions** – test yourself on a set of questions for each chapter, with the chance to check your answers once you have finished.
- **Internet Activities** – interesting and practical tasks for the student to undertake using internet research linked to the content of each chapter.
- **Maths Workout** – introductory guide and questions on the use of maths in economics related to appropriate topics in relevant chapters.

OTHER SUPPLEMENTARY RESOURCES

Global Economic Watch Cengage Learning's Global Economic Watch is a powerful, continuously updated online resource which stimulates discussion and understanding of the global downturn through articles from leading publications, a real-time database of videos, podcasts and much more.

Aplia Cengage Learning's Aplia is an online homework solution, is dedicated to improving learning by increasing student effort and engagement. Aplia has been used by more than 1 million students at over 1,200 institutions. It offers chapter assignments, tutorials, news analyses, and experiments to make economics relevant and engaging. All assignments are automatically graded, and there are detailed explanations for every question to help students stay focused, alert, and thinking critically.

CourseMate Cengage Learning's CourseMate brings course concepts to life with interactive learning, study and exam preparation tools that support the printed textbook. Watch student comprehension soar as your class works with the printed textbook and the textbook-specific website. CourseMate includes: an interactive eBook; interactive teaching and learning tools including videos, games, quizzes and flashcards (resources are mapped to specific disciplines so the range of resources will vary with each text); Engagement Tracker, a first-of-its-kind tool that monitors student engagement in the course.

For more information about these digital resources, please contact your local Cengage Learning representative.

Virtual Learning Environment All of the web material is available in a format that is compatible with virtual learning environments such as Moodle, Blackboard and WebCT.

TextChoice The home of Cengage Learning's online digital content. It provides the fastest, easiest way for you to create your own learning materials. You may select content from hundreds of our best selling titles to make a custom text.

ACKNOWLEDGEMENTS

The authors would like to thank the following reviewers for their comments.

Robert Ackrill – Nottingham Trent University
Sverrir Arngrimsson – Iceland Engineering College
Michael Artis – European University Institute, Florence
Snæfríður Baldvinsdóttir – Bifrost School of Business, Iceland
Dr John Ball – University of Swansea
Jürgen Bitzer – Free University Berlin
Randy Bootland – Webster University
Phil Bowers – University of Edinburgh
Peter Clarke – University of Lincoln
Paul de Grauwe – Catholic University, Leuven
Julia Darby – University of Strathclyde
Kevin Denny – University College Dublin
Michael Devereux – University of Warwick
Sebastian Dullien – HTW Berlin, University of Applied Sciences
James Duncan – Robert Gordon University
Robert Eastwood – University of Sussex
Peter Else – University of Sheffield
Kirstín Flygenring – Reykjavik University – Iceland
Vanina Farber – Webster University, Geneva Campus
Michael Funke – University of Hamburg – Germany
Heather Gage – University of Surrey
Erich Gundlach – Kiel Institute for World Economics/Helmut-Schmidt University Hamburg
Bjarni Már Gylfason – Commercial College of Iceland
Heinz-Deiter Hardes – University of Trier
Philippe Gugler – University of Fribourg, Switzerland
Bolli Héðinsson – Reykjavik University, Iceland
Andrew Henley – Swansea University
David Higgins – University of York
Hilary Ingham – Lancaster University
Ian Jackson – Staffordshire University
Colin Jennings – University of Strathclyde
Brendan Kennelly – NUI Galway
Xander Koolman – Erasmus University Medical Centre
Richard Ledward – Staffordshire University
Oliver Marnet – University of Aberystwyth
Michael J. McCrostie – University of Buckingham
Lukas Menkhoff – University of Hannover
Jonathan Michie – Director of the Oxford University Department for Continuing Education
Kerry Patterson – University of Reading
Martin Peiz – International University in Germany
Odile Poulsen – University of East Anglia
Tom Segers – Group T Leuven Engineering School
Frank Seitz – Amberg-Weiden University of Applied Sciences
Kunal Sen – University of East Anglia
Lorena Škuflic – University of Zagreb
Tilman Slembeck – University of St. Gallen and Zurich University of Applied Sciences
Ian Smith – University of St. Andrews
Remigiusz Smolinski – Leipzig Graduate School of Management
Frank H. Stephen – Manchester School of Law
Kristian Sund – University of Applied Sciences, Chur
Benjamin Swalens – Vrije Universiteit Brussels
Oliver Taylor – University of Cambridge
Karen Thomas – University of the Free State, South Africa
Elsie Tosi – EAI CERAM, Sophia Antipolis
Jan Janse van Rensburg – University of Pretoria, South Africa
Rolf Weder – University of Basel
Linda Yueh – University of Oxford

1

INTRODUCTION

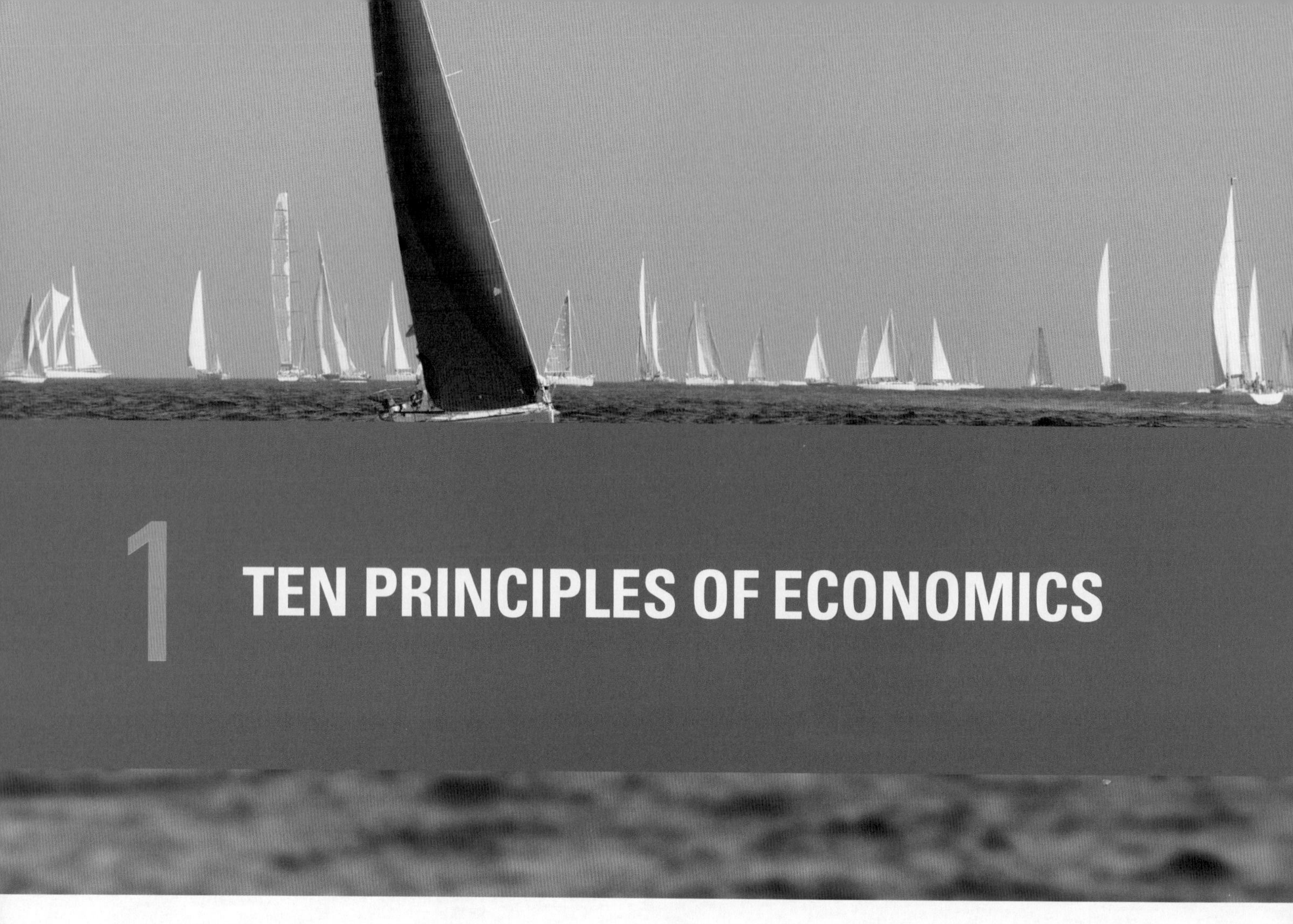

1 TEN PRINCIPLES OF ECONOMICS

The word *economy* comes from the Greek word *oikonomos,* which means 'one who manages a household'. At first, this origin might seem peculiar. But, in fact, households and economies have much in common.

A household faces many decisions. It must decide which members of the household do which tasks and what each member gets in return: Who cooks dinner? Who does the laundry? Who gets the extra slice of cake at tea time? Who chooses what TV programme to watch? In short, the household must allocate its scarce resources among its various members, taking into account each member's abilities, efforts and desires.

Like a household, a society faces many decisions. A society must decide what jobs will be done and who will do them. It needs some people to grow food, other people to make clothing and still others to design computer software. Once society has allocated people (as well as land, buildings and machines) to various jobs, it must also allocate the output of goods and services that they produce. It must decide who will eat caviar and who will eat potatoes. It must decide who will drive a Jaguar and who will take the bus.

scarcity
the limited nature of society's resources

The management of society's resources is important because resources are scarce. **Scarcity** means that society has limited resources and therefore cannot produce all the goods and services people wish to have. Just as a household cannot give every member everything he or she wants, a society cannot give every individual the highest standard of living to which he or she might aspire.

economics
the study of how society manages its scarce resources

Economics is the study of how society manages its scarce resources. In most societies, resources are allocated not by a single central planner but through the combined actions of millions of households and firms. Economists therefore study how people make decisions: how much they work, what they buy, how much they save and how they invest their savings. Economists also study how people interact with one another. For instance, they examine how the multitude of buyers and sellers of a good together determine the price at which the good is sold and the quantity that is sold. Finally, economists analyse forces and trends that affect the economy as a whole, including the growth in average income, the fraction of the population that cannot find work and the rate at which prices are rising.

Although the study of economics has many facets, the field is unified by several central ideas. In the rest of this chapter we look at *Ten Principles of Economics*. Don't worry if you don't understand them all at first, or if you don't find them completely convincing. In the coming chapters we will explore these ideas more fully. The ten principles are introduced here just to give you an overview of what economics is all about. You can think of this chapter as a 'preview of coming attractions'.

HOW PEOPLE MAKE DECISIONS

There is no mystery to what an 'economy' is. Whether we are talking about the economy of a group of countries such as the European Union, or the economy of one particular country, such as the United Kingdom, or of the whole world, an economy is just a group of people interacting with one another as they go about their lives. Because the behaviour of an economy reflects the behaviour of the individuals who make up the economy, we start our study of economics with four principles of individual decision-making.

CASE STUDY

A Decision of Life and Death

Millions of people every day use medicinal drugs for a variety of reasons but mostly because taking them brings some benefit. In some cases, the use of medicinal drugs helps to alleviate relatively mild conditions but for a large number of patients, for example, those suffering from different types of cancer, such drugs can literally mean the difference between life and death. In recent years there have been a large number of drugs developed by companies to help cancer sufferers. The complexity of the illness, however, means that the cost of developing such drugs can be extremely high. In Europe, the European Medicines Agency (EMA) evaluates and supervises medicines for human and animal use. In the UK, the National Institute for Health and Clinical Excellence (NICE) carries out a similar role and licenses drugs for use within the National Health Service (NHS). It has to decide whether to recommend drugs for use within the NHS. It balances out the costs of using a drug against the benefits to patients. It also considers the wider costs and benefits as well. If the costs outweigh the benefits then it may reject the use of the drug under the NHS.

One example of such a rejection occurred in November 2009. The drug in question was called sorafenib or, to give it its brand name, Nexavar. The drug is produced by German pharmaceutical company Bayer and is for treatment of hepatocellular carcinoma (HCC). This is a cancer of the liver, a disease which affects around 3 000 people in the UK every year. Of these, around

600–700 would benefit from the drug; it is not a cure but extends the life of patients for up to six months. Given the life expectancy of patients with this illness, this can be a significant benefit. The prognosis for liver cancer sufferers is poor; 80 per cent die within a year of diagnosis and 95 per cent die within five years.

Despite the benefits, NICE rejected the use of the drug on the NHS because the cost of licensing greatly outweighed the benefits. This was not simply the financial cost of administering the drug, estimated at £3 000 per month, but the wider costs in terms of the benefits to other patients with other illnesses that would have to be foregone. The NHS budget, like most other health budgets across Europe, is limited. Decisions have to be made on who to treat and who not to because resources are scarce in relation to demand. NICE decided that the money that could be spent on sorafenib could be better spent on treating other patients; the value of the benefits to those patients would outweigh the value of the benefits to liver cancer sufferers. Andrew Dillon, chief executive of NICE, said: 'The price being asked by Bayer is simply too high to justify using NHS money which could be spent on better value cancer treatments.'

For liver cancer sufferers the decision by NICE was a major blow. The decision means that some will be deprived of additional months of good quality life which they could have had if they had access to the drug. For other cancer patients, the decision might be good news – it may mean there is more money available to treat them and that money may result in a longer period of good quality life. The decision may seem like a cold and calculating one, but in simple economics terms it makes sense.

Principle 1: People Face Trade-offs

The first lesson about making decisions is summarized in an adage popular with economists: 'There is no such thing as a free lunch'. To get one thing that we like, we usually have to give up another thing that we also like. Making decisions requires trading off one goal against another.

Consider a student who must decide how to allocate her most valuable resource – her time. She can spend all of her time studying economics; she can spend all of her time studying psychology; or she can divide her time between the two fields. For every hour she studies one subject, she gives up an hour she could have used studying the other. And for every hour she spends studying, she gives up an hour that she could have spent in the gym, riding a bicycle, watching TV, napping or working at her part-time job for some extra spending money.

Or consider parents deciding how to spend their family income. They can buy food, clothing or a family holiday. Or they can save some of the family income for retirement or perhaps to help the children buy a house or a flat when they are grown up. When they choose to spend an extra euro on one of these goods, they have one less euro to spend on some other good.

When people are grouped into societies, they face different kinds of trade-offs. The classic trade-off is between 'guns and butter'. The more we spend on national defence (guns) to protect our country from foreign aggressors, the less we can spend on consumer goods (butter) to raise our standard of living at home. Also important in modern society is the trade-off between a clean environment and a high level of income. Laws that require firms to reduce pollution raise the cost of producing goods and services. Because of the higher costs, these firms end up earning smaller profits, paying lower wages, charging higher prices, or some combination of these three. Thus, while pollution regulations give us the benefit of a cleaner environment and the improved levels of health that come with it, they have the cost of reducing the incomes of the firms' owners, workers and customers.

Another trade-off society faces is between efficiency and equity. Efficiency means that society is getting the most it can from its scarce resources. **Equity** means that the benefits of those resources are distributed fairly among society's members. In other words, efficiency refers to the size of the economic cake, and equity refers to how the cake is divided. Often, when government policies are being designed, these two goals conflict.

equity
the property of distributing economic prosperity fairly among the members of society

Consider, for instance, policies aimed at achieving a more equal distribution of economic well-being. Some of these policies, such as the social security system or unemployment insurance, try to help those members of society who are most in need. Others, such as the individual income tax, ask the financially successful to contribute more than others to support the government. Although these policies have the benefit of achieving greater equity, they have a cost in terms of reduced efficiency. When the government redistributes income from the rich to the poor, it reduces the reward for working hard; as a result, people work less and produce fewer goods and services. In other words, when the government tries to cut the economic cake into more equal slices, the cake gets smaller.

Recognizing that people face trade-offs does not by itself tell us what decisions they will or should make. A student should not abandon the study of psychology just because doing so would increase the time available for the study of economics. Society should not stop protecting the environment just because environmental regulations reduce our material standard of living. The poor should not be ignored just because helping them distorts work incentives. Nevertheless, acknowledging life's trade-offs is important because people are likely to make good decisions only if they understand the options that they have available.

Quick Quiz Does the adage 'there is no such thing as a free lunch' simply refer to the fact that someone has to have paid for the lunch to be provided and served? Or does the recipient of the 'free lunch' also incur a cost?

Principle 2: The Cost of Something is What You Give Up to Get It

Because people face trade-offs, making decisions requires comparing the costs and benefits of alternative courses of action. In many cases, however, the cost of some action is not as obvious as it might first appear.

Consider, for example, the decision whether to go to university. The benefit is intellectual enrichment and a lifetime of better job opportunities. But what is the cost? To answer this question, you might be tempted to add up the money you spend on tuition fees, books, room and board. Yet this total does not truly represent what you give up to spend a year at university.

The first problem with this answer is that it includes some things that are not really costs of going to university. Even if you decided to leave full-time education, you would still need a place to sleep and food to eat. Room and board are part of the costs of higher education only to the extent that they are more expensive at university than elsewhere. Indeed, the cost of room and board at your university might be less than the rent and food expenses that you would pay living on your own. In this case, the savings on room and board are actually a benefit of going to university.

The second problem with this calculation of costs is that it ignores the largest cost of a university education – your time. When you spend a year listening to lectures, reading textbooks and writing essays, you cannot spend that time working at a job. For most students, the wages given up to attend university are the largest single cost of their higher education.

opportunity cost
whatever must be given up to obtain some item – the value of the benefits foregone (sacrificed)

The **opportunity cost** of an item is what you give up to get that item. When making any decision, such as whether to go to university, decision makers should be aware of the opportunity costs that accompany each possible action. In fact, they usually are. University-age footballers who can earn millions if they opt out of higher education and play professional football are well aware that their opportunity cost of going to university is very high. It is not surprising that they often decide that the benefit is not worth the cost.

Quick Quiz Assume the following costs are incurred by a student over a three-year course at a university: • Tuition fees at €3 000 per year = €9 000 • Accommodation, based on an average cost of €4 500 a year = €13 500 • Opportunity cost based on average earnings foregone of €15 000 per year = €45 000 • Total cost = €67 500 • Given this relatively large cost why does anyone want to go to university?

Principle 3: Rational People Think at the Margin

Decisions in life are rarely black and white but usually involve shades of grey. At dinner time, the decision you face is not between fasting or eating as much as you can, but whether to take that extra serving of fries. When examinations roll around, your decision is not between completely failing them or studying 24 hours a day, but whether to spend an extra hour revising your notes instead of watching TV. Economists use the term **marginal changes** to describe small incremental adjustments to an existing plan of action. Keep in mind that 'margin' means 'edge', so marginal changes are adjustments around the edges of what you are doing.

marginal changes
small incremental adjustments to a plan of action

In many situations, people make the best decisions by thinking at the margin. Suppose, for instance, that you asked a friend for advice about how many years to stay in education. If he were to compare for you the lifestyle of a person with a Ph.D. with that of someone who finished secondary school with no qualifications, you might complain that this comparison is not helpful for your decision. Perhaps you have already been at university for a few years but you're getting a little tired of studying and not having enough money and so you're deciding whether or not to stay on for that last year. To make this decision, you need to know the additional benefits that an extra year in education would offer (higher wages throughout your life and the sheer joy of learning) and the additional costs that you would incur (another year of tuition fees and another year of foregone wages). By comparing these *marginal benefits* and *marginal costs*, you can evaluate whether the extra year is worthwhile.

As another example, consider an airline company deciding how much to charge passengers who fly standby. Suppose that flying a 200-seat aeroplane from London to Warsaw costs the airline €100 000. In this case, the average cost of each seat is €100 000/200, which is €500. One might be tempted to conclude that the airline should never sell a ticket for less than €500. In fact, however, the airline can raise its profits by thinking at the margin. Imagine that a plane is about to take off with ten empty seats, and a standby passenger is waiting at the gate willing to pay €300 for a seat. Should the airline sell it to him/her? Of course it should. If the plane has empty seats, the cost of adding one more passenger is minuscule. Although the *average* cost of flying a passenger is €500, the *marginal* cost is merely the cost of the airline meal that the extra passenger will consume (which may have gone to waste in any case) and possibly an extremely slight increase in the amount of aircraft fuel used. As long as the standby passenger pays more than the marginal cost, selling him or her a ticket is profitable.

As these examples show, individuals and firms can make better decisions by thinking at the margin. A rational decision maker takes an action if and only if the marginal benefit of the action exceeds the marginal cost.

Principle 4: People Respond to Incentives

Because people make decisions by comparing costs and benefits, their behaviour may change when the costs or benefits change. That is, people respond to incentives. When the price of an apple rises, for instance, people decide to eat more pears and fewer apples because the cost of buying an apple is higher. At the same time, apple orchards decide to hire more workers and harvest more apples, because the benefit of selling an apple is also higher. As we shall see, the effect of price on the behaviour of buyers and sellers in a market – in this case, the market for apples – is crucial for understanding how the economy works.

Public policy makers should never forget about incentives, because many policies change the costs or benefits that people face and, therefore, alter behaviour. A tax on petrol, for instance, encourages people to drive smaller, more fuel-efficient cars. It also encourages people to use public transport rather than drive and to live closer to where they work. If the tax were large enough, people would start driving electric cars.

When policy makers fail to consider how their policies affect incentives, they often end up with results they did not intend. For example, consider public policy regarding motor vehicle safety. Today all cars sold in the European Union have to have seat belts fitted by law (although actual seat belt use – especially by rear-seat passengers – varies widely, with official estimates ranging from about 30 per cent of car occupants in some member states to around 90 per cent in others, notably Sweden).

How does a seat belt law affect car safety? The direct effect is obvious: when a person wears a seat belt, the probability of surviving a major car accident rises. But that's not the end of the story, for the law also affects behaviour by altering incentives. The relevant behaviour here is the speed and care with which drivers operate their cars. Driving slowly and carefully is costly because it uses the driver's time and energy. When deciding how safely to drive, rational people compare the marginal benefit from safer driving to the marginal cost. They drive more slowly and carefully when the benefit of increased safety is high. It is no surprise, for instance, that people drive more slowly and carefully when roads are icy than when roads are clear.

Quick Quiz The emphasis on road safety throughout Europe has increased over the last 25 years. Not only are cars packed with safety technology and devices but roads are also designed to be safer with the use of safety barriers and better road surfaces, for example. Is there a case, therefore, for believing that if people feel that they are safer in their cars there is an incentive to drive faster because the marginal cost is now outweighed by the marginal benefit?

Consider how a seat belt law alters a motorist's cost–benefit calculation. Seat belts make accidents less costly because they reduce the likelihood of injury or death. In other words, seat belts reduce the benefits of slow and careful driving. People respond to seat belts as they would to an improvement in road

© ALLSTAR PICTURE LIBRARY / ALAMY

Music, TV and television producer and executive Simon Cowell understood opportunity cost and incentives. He decided to leave school before completing his post-16 education and is reported to earn in excess of £50 million a year!

conditions – by faster and less careful driving. The end result of a seat belt law, therefore, is a larger number of accidents and so it will affect both motorists and pedestrians. The decline in safe driving has a clear, adverse impact on pedestrians, who are more likely to find themselves in an accident but (unlike the motorists) don't have the benefit of added protection.

At first, this discussion of incentives and seat belts might seem like idle speculation. Yet a 1981 study of seat belt laws in eight European countries commissioned by the UK Department of Transport showed that the laws did appear to have had many of these effects. Similar evidence was also presented in a 1975 study of US seat belt laws by the American economist Sam Peltzman. It does indeed seem that seat belt laws produce both fewer deaths per accident and more accidents. The net result is little change in the number of motorist deaths and an increase in the number of pedestrian deaths.

This is an example of the general principle that people respond to incentives. Many incentives that economists study are more straightforward than those of the car-safety laws. No one is surprised that people drive smaller cars in Europe, where petrol taxes are relatively high, than in the United States, where petrol taxes are lower. Yet, as the seat belt example shows, policies can have effects that are not obvious in advance. When analysing any policy, we must consider not only the direct effects but also the indirect effects that work through incentives. If the policy changes incentives, it will cause people to alter their behaviour.

Quick Quiz List and briefly explain the four principles of individual decision-making.

HOW PEOPLE INTERACT

The first four principles discussed how individuals make decisions. As we go about our lives, many of our decisions affect not only ourselves but other people as well. The next three principles concern how people interact with one another.

Principle 5: Trade Can Make Everyone Better Off

The Americans and the Japanese are often mentioned in the news as being competitors to Europeans in the world economy. In some ways this is true, because American and Japanese firms do produce many of the same goods as European firms. Airbus and Boeing compete for the same customers in the market for aircraft. Toyota and Citroën compete for the same customers in the market for cars.

Yet it is easy to be misled when thinking about competition among countries. Trade between Europe and the United States or between Europe and Japan is not like a sports contest, where one side wins and the other side loses (a zero-sum game). In fact, the opposite is true: trade between two economies can make each economy better off.

To see why, consider how trade affects your family. When a member of your family looks for a job, he or she competes against members of other families who are looking for jobs. Families also compete against one another when they go shopping, because each family wants to buy the best goods at the lowest prices. So, in a sense, each family in the economy is competing with all other families.

Despite this competition, your family would not be better off isolating itself from all other families. If it did, your family would need to grow its own food,

"You'll have to look harder than that to find a job, son."

make its own clothes and build its own home. Clearly, your family gains much from its ability to trade with others. Trade allows each person to specialize in the activities he or she does best, whether it is farming, sewing or home building. By trading with others, people can buy a greater variety of goods and services at lower cost.

Countries as well as families benefit from the ability to trade with one another. Trade allows countries to specialize in what they do best and to enjoy a greater variety of goods and services. The Japanese and the Americans, as well as the Egyptians and the Brazilians, are as much our partners in the world economy as they are our competitors.

Principle 6: Markets Are Usually a Good Way to Organize Economic Activity

The collapse of communism in the Soviet Union and Eastern Europe in the 1980s may be the most important change in the world during the past half century. Communist countries worked on the premise that central planners in the government were in the best position to guide economic activity. These planners decided what goods and services were produced, how much was produced, and who produced and consumed these goods and services. The theory behind central planning was that only the government could organize economic activity in a way that promoted economic well-being for the country as a whole.

Today, most countries that once had centrally planned economies have abandoned this system and are trying to develop market economies. In a **market economy**, the decisions of a central planner are replaced by the decisions of millions of firms and households. Firms decide whom to hire and what to make. Households decide which firms to work for and what to buy with their incomes. These firms and households interact in the marketplace, where prices and self-interest guide their decisions.

market economy
an economy that allocates resources through the decentralized decisions of many firms and households as they interact in markets for goods and services

At first glance, the success of market economies is puzzling. After all, in a market economy, no one is considering the economic well-being of society as a

FYI

Adam Smith and the Invisible Hand

Adam Smith's great work *An Inquiry into the Nature and Causes of The Wealth of Nations* was published in 1776 and is a landmark in economics. In its emphasis on the invisible hand of the market economy, it reflected a point of view that was typical of so-called 'enlightenment' writers at the end of the 18th century – that individuals are usually best left to their own devices, without the heavy hand of government guiding their actions. This political philosophy provides the intellectual basis for the market economy.

Why do decentralized market economies work so well? Is it because people can be counted on to treat one another with love and kindness? Not at all. Here is Adam Smith's description of how people interact in a market economy:

Man has almost constant occasion for the help of his brethren, and it is vain for him to expect it from their benevolence only. He will be more likely to prevail if he can interest their self-love in his favour, and show them that it is for their own advantage to do for him what he requires of them.... It is not from the benevolence of the butcher, the brewer, or the baker that we expect our dinner, but from their regard to their own interest....

Every individual... neither intends to promote the public interest, nor knows how much he is promoting it.... He intends only his own gain, and he is in this, as in many other cases, led by an invisible hand to promote an end which was no part of his intention. Nor is it always the worse for the society that it was no part of it. By pursuing his own interest he frequently promotes that of the society more effectually than when he really intends to promote it.

Smith is saying that participants in the economy are motivated by self-interest and that the 'invisible hand' of the marketplace guides this self-interest into promoting general economic well-being.

Adam Smith

Many of Smith's insights remain at the centre of modern economics. Our analysis in the coming chapters will allow us to express Smith's conclusions more precisely and to analyse fully the strengths and weaknesses of the market's invisible hand.

whole. Free markets contain many buyers and sellers of numerous goods and services, and all of them are interested primarily in their own well-being. Yet, despite decentralized decision-making and self-interested decision makers, market economies have proven remarkably successful in organizing economic activity in a way that promotes overall economic well-being.

In his 1776 book *An Inquiry Into the Nature and Causes of the Wealth of Nations*, the British economist Adam Smith made the most famous observation in all of economics: households and firms interacting in markets act as if they are guided by an 'invisible hand' that leads them to desirable market outcomes. One of our goals in this book is to understand how this invisible hand works its magic. As you study economics, you will learn that prices are the instrument with which the invisible hand directs economic activity. Prices reflect both the value of a good to society and the cost to society of making the good. Because households and firms look at prices when deciding what to buy and sell, they unknowingly take into account the social benefits and costs of their actions. As a result, prices guide these individual decision makers to reach outcomes that, in many cases, maximize the welfare of society as a whole.

There is an important corollary to the skill of the invisible hand in guiding economic activity: when the government prevents prices from adjusting naturally to supply and demand, it impedes the invisible hand's ability to coordinate the millions of households and firms that make up the economy. This corollary explains why taxes adversely affect the allocation of resources: taxes distort prices and thus the decisions of households and firms. It also explains the even greater harm caused by policies that directly control prices, such as rent control. And it also explains the failure of communism. In communist countries, prices were not determined in the marketplace but were dictated by central planners. These planners lacked the information that gets reflected in prices when prices are free to respond to market forces. Central planners failed because they tried to run the economy with one hand tied behind their backs – the invisible hand of the marketplace.

Principle 7: Governments Can Sometimes Improve Market Outcomes

If the invisible hand of the market is so wonderful, why do we need government? One answer is that the invisible hand needs government to protect it. Markets work only if property rights are enforced. A farmer won't grow food if he expects his crop to be stolen, and a restaurant won't serve meals unless it is assured that customers will pay before they leave. We all rely on government-provided police and courts to enforce our rights over the things we produce.

Yet there is another answer to why we need government: although markets are usually a good way to organize economic activity, this rule has some important exceptions. There are two broad reasons for a government to intervene in the economy – to promote efficiency and to promote equity. That is, most policies aim either to enlarge the economic cake or to change the way in which the cake is divided.

Although the invisible hand usually leads markets to allocate resources efficiently, that is not always the case. Economists use the term **market failure** to refer to a situation in which the market on its own fails to produce an efficient allocation of resources. One possible cause of market failure is an **externality**, which is the uncompensated impact of one person's actions on the well-being of a bystander (a third party). For instance, the classic example of an external cost is pollution. Another possible cause of market failure is **market power**, which refers to the ability of a single person (or small group) to unduly influence market prices. For example, if everyone in a remote village in the Scottish Highlands needs water but there is only one well, the owner of the well is not subject to the rigorous competition with which the invisible hand normally keeps self-interest in check. In the presence of externalities or market power, well designed public policy can enhance economic efficiency.

market failure
a situation where scarce resources are not allocated to their most efficient use

externality
the uncompensated impact of one person's actions on the well-being of a bystander (a third party)

market power
the ability of a single economic agent (or small group of agents) to have a substantial influence on market prices

The invisible hand may also fail to ensure that economic prosperity is distributed equitably. A market economy rewards people according to their ability to produce things for which other people are willing to pay. The world's best footballer earns more than the world's best chess player simply because people are willing to pay more to watch football than chess. The invisible hand does not ensure that everyone has sufficient food, decent clothing and adequate health care. Many public policies, such as income tax and the social security system, aim to achieve a more equitable distribution of economic well-being.

To say that the government *can* improve on market outcomes at times does not mean that it always *will*. Public policy is made not by angels but by a political process that is far from perfect. Sometimes policies are designed simply to reward the politically powerful. Sometimes they are made by well intentioned leaders who are not fully informed. One goal of the study of economics is to help you judge when a government policy is justifiable to promote efficiency or equity, and when it is not.

Quick Quiz List and briefly explain the three principles concerning economic interactions.

HOW THE ECONOMY AS A WHOLE WORKS

We started by discussing how individuals make decisions and then looked at how people interact with one another. All these decisions and interactions together make up 'the economy'. The last three principles concern the workings of the economy as a whole. A key concept in this section is **economic growth** – the percentage increase in the number of goods and services produced in an economy over a period of time usually expressed over a quarter and annually.

economic growth
the increase in the amount of goods and services in an economy over a period of time

Principle 8: An Economy's Standard of Living Depends on its Ability to Produce Goods and Services

gross domestic product per head
the market value of all final goods and services produced within a country in a given period of time divided by the population of a country to give a per capita figure

Table 1.1 shows **gross domestic product per head** of the population in a number of selected countries. It is clear that many of the advanced economies have a relatively high income per capita; in the UK it is $35 728 whilst in Germany and France it is $39 442 and $42 092 respectively. In Spain average income is a little lower at $31 142, somewhat higher in Ireland at $51 128, higher still in Switzerland at $66 127 and an enviable $94 418 in Luxembourg. These figures compare with an income per person of about $39 000 in Canada and $46 500 in the United States. But once we move away from the prosperous economies of Western Europe, North America and parts of Asia, we begin to see differences in income and living standards around the world that are quite staggering. For example, in the same year, 2009, average income in Poland was $11 098 almost a third of the level in Spain, while in Argentina it was just $7 508, in India $1 033 and in Ethiopia just $418 – less than one half of a per cent of the annual income per person in Luxembourg. Not surprisingly, this large variation in average income is reflected in various other measures of the quality of life and **standard of living**. Citizens of high-income countries have better nutrition, better health care and longer life expectancy than citizens of low-income countries, as well as more TV sets, more DVD players and more cars.

standard of living
refers to the amount of goods and services that can be purchased by the population of a country. Usually measured by the inflation-adjusted (real) income per head of the population

Changes in the standard of living over time are also large. Over the last 50 years, average incomes in Western Europe and North America have grown at about 2 per cent per year (after adjusting for changes in the cost of living). At this rate, average income doubles every 35 years, and over the last half-century average income in many of these prosperous economies has risen approximately three-fold. On the other hand, average income in Ethiopia rose by only a third over this period – an average annual growth rate of around only 0.5 per cent.

What explains these large differences in living standards among countries and over time? The answer is surprisingly simple. Almost all variation in living standards is attributable to differences in countries' **productivity** – that is, the amount of goods and services produced from each hour of a worker's time. In nations where workers can produce a large quantity of goods and services per unit of time, most people enjoy a high standard of living; in nations where workers are less productive, most people must endure a more meagre existence. Similarly, the growth rate of a nation's productivity determines the growth rate of its average income.

productivity
the quantity of goods and services produced from each hour of a worker's time

The fundamental relationship between productivity and living standards is simple, but its implications are far-reaching. If productivity is the primary determinant of living standards, other explanations must be of secondary importance. For example, it might be tempting to credit trades unions or minimum wage laws for the rise in living standards of European workers over the past 50 years. Yet the real hero of European workers is their rising productivity.

TABLE 1.1

Gross Domestic Product Per Capita, Current Prices, US dollars 2009

Country	GDP per capita
Albania	3 681
Argentina	7 508
Australia	41 982
Azerbaijan	4 864
Bangladesh	559
Belarus	5 122
Brazil	7 737
Canada	39 217
China	3 566
Ethiopia	418
France	42 092
Germany	39 442
Haiti	772
Iceland	36 873
India	1 033
Ireland	51 128
Japan	39 573
Kazakhstan	6 875
Luxembourg	94 418
Mexico	8 040
Norway	76 692
Pakistan	1 017
Paraguay	2 169
Peru	4 377
Poland	11 098
Portugal	20 655
Romania	7 503
Russia	8 874
Saudi Arabia	14 871
South Africa	5 635
Spain	31 142
Sweden	43 147
Switzerland	66 127
Syrian Arab Republic	2 669
Tajikistan	705
Thailand	3 973
United Arab Emirates	46 584
United Kingdom	35 728
United States	46 443
Zimbabwe	303

Source: International Monetary Fund, World Economic Outlook Database, October 2009.

The relationship between productivity and living standards also has profound implications for public policy. When thinking about how any policy will affect living standards, the key question is how it will affect our ability to produce goods and services. To boost living standards, policy makers need to raise productivity by ensuring that workers are well educated, have the tools needed to produce goods and services, and have access to the best available technology.

Principle 9: Prices Rise When the Government Prints Too Much Money

inflation
an increase in the overall level of prices in the economy

In Germany in January 1921, a daily newspaper was priced at 0.30 marks. Less than two years later, in November 1922, the same newspaper was priced at 70 000 000 marks. All other prices in the economy rose by similar amounts. This episode is one of history's most spectacular examples of **inflation**, an increase in the overall level of prices in the economy.

While inflation in Western Europe and North America has been much lower over the last 50 years than that experienced in Germany in the 1920s, inflation has at times been an economic problem. During the 1970s, for instance, the overall level of prices in the UK more than tripled. By contrast, UK inflation from 2000 to 2008 was about 3 per cent per year; at this rate it would take more than 20 years for prices to double. In more recent times, Zimbabwe has experienced German-like hyperinflation. In March 2007 inflation in the African state was reported to be running at 2 200 per cent. That meant that a good priced at the equivalent of €2.99 in March 2006 would be priced at €65.78 just a year later. In July 2008 the government issued a Z$100 billion note. At that time it was just about enough to buy a loaf of bread. Estimates for inflation in Zimbabwe in July 2008 put the rate of growth of prices at 231 000 000 per cent. In January 2009, the

"… but if daddy increased your allowance he'd be hurting the economy by stimulating inflation. You wouldn't want him to do that, would you?"

government issued Z$10, 20, 50 and 100 trillion dollar notes – 100 trillion is 100 followed by 12 zeros. Because high inflation imposes various costs on society, keeping inflation at a low level is a goal of economic policy makers around the world.

What causes inflation? In almost all cases of high or persistent inflation, the culprit turns out to be the same – growth in the quantity of money. When a government creates large quantities of the nation's money, the value of the money falls. In Germany in the early 1920s, when prices were on average tripling every month, the quantity of money was also tripling every month. Although less dramatic, the economic history of other European and North American countries points to a similar conclusion: the high inflation of the 1970s was associated with rapid growth in the quantity of money and the low inflation of the 2000s was associated with slow growth in the quantity of money.

Principle 10: Society Faces a Short-run Trade-off Between Inflation and Unemployment

When the government increases the amount of money in the economy, one result is inflation. Another result, at least in the short run, is a lower level of unemployment. The curve that illustrates this short-run trade-off between inflation and unemployment is called the **Phillips curve**, after the economist who first examined this relationship while working at the London School of Economics.

Phillips curve
a curve that shows the short-run trade-off between inflation and unemployment

The Phillips curve remains a controversial topic among economists, but most economists today accept the idea that society faces a short-run trade-off between inflation and unemployment. This simply means that, over a period of a year or two, many economic policies push inflation and unemployment in opposite directions. Policy makers face this trade-off regardless of whether inflation and unemployment both start out at high levels (as they were in the early 1980s), at low levels (as they were in the late 1990s) or somewhere in between.

The trade-off between inflation and unemployment is only temporary, but it can last for several years. The Phillips curve is, therefore, crucial for understanding many developments in the economy. In particular, it is important for understanding the **business cycle** – the irregular and largely unpredictable fluctuations in economic activity, as measured by the number of people employed or the production of goods and services.

business cycle
fluctuations in economic activity, such as employment and production

TABLE 1.2

Ten Principles of Economics

How people make decisions	1. People face trade-offs
	2. The cost of something is what you give up to get it
	3. Rational people think at the margin
	4. People respond to incentives
How people interact	5. Trade can make everyone better off
	6. Markets are usually a good way to organize economic activity
	7. Governments can sometimes improve market outcomes
How the economy as a whole works	8. A country's standard of living depends on its ability to produce goods and services
	9. Prices rise when the government prints too much money
	10. Society faces a short-run trade-off between inflation and unemployment

Policy makers can exploit the short-run trade-off between inflation and unemployment using various policy instruments. By changing the amount that the government spends, the amount it taxes and the amount of money it prints, policy makers can influence the combination of inflation and unemployment that the economy experiences. Because these instruments of monetary and fiscal policy are potentially so powerful, how policy makers should use these instruments to control the economy, if at all, is a subject of continuing debate.

Quick Quiz List and briefly explain the three principles that describe how the economy as a whole works.

IN THE NEWS

Using Incentives

Policy makers are well aware of the importance of incentives in changing behaviour. The concern over carbon emissions and global warming (despite some questioning the validity of the economics behind some of the predictions that have been made) has meant that governments and the European Union are looking at ways to reduce the reliance on carbon-based energies. In order to change behaviour various policies are adopted to change incentives to achieve the desired outcome. The example in this article highlights a number of the principles referred to in this chapter.

In November 2009, the European Union (EU) issued notice of a new directive in relation to the energy efficiency of newly constructed buildings. The Directive requires member states to plan ahead for the introduction of near zero energy buildings which make use of renewable energy from 2020. The Directive also requires member states to implement targets to the public sector to only use (whether owned or rented) buildings that adhere to near zero energy standards. This means that all members must find ways of converting or refurbishing existing buildings to comply with this standard by the end of 2018.

Such a Directive presents major challenges not only to the public sector in member states but also to the private sector. There are trade-offs in putting in place such plans. It has been reported that around 40 per cent of all energy use is attributable to buildings and that they are responsible for over a third of Europe's CO_2 emissions. Whilst the Directive will cost millions to implement, the trade-off is that savings of €300 [per building] each year in energy bills could result (Principle 1). In addition, the EU says that there will be a boost to the construction and building renovation industry throughout the continent (Principle 5).

After 2020, any new building will have to meet energy efficiency standards set by Brussels. If left to the market, the sort of work envisaged by the EU may not happen – the cost of doing this in relation to the benefits accruing to private individuals would likely be insufficient to encourage individuals to act on their own. So in this case the 'invisible hand' needs some assistance (Principle 7). EU governments are being encouraged to provide a list of incentives which include technical assistance, subsidies, loan schemes, low interest rate deals and other financial assistance to help change the relative costs and benefits (Principle 4). Part of the reason for this was that following the original 2002 Energy Performance of Buildings Directive, progress towards improving standards had been limited largely due to a lack of inspectors qualified to issue certificates, a qualified workforce and ambition. The market, in the eyes of the EU, had failed to bring about the resource allocation they desired.

As a result the introduction of incentives and a restatement of the Directive are designed to bring about that desired resource allocation. Incentives such as subsidies, for example, help reduce the cost to the producer (the building owner in this example) of carrying out the work required to comply with the standards. In diverting resources to this desired outcome the EU believe that it represents a more efficient allocation of resources and therefore has benefits which are wider than just those to the building owner but to society at large. Diverting resources by subsidy has a cost, however. Someone has to pay for the subsidy and this is the EU taxpayer.

The use of taxes for this purpose has an opportunity cost – the value of the benefits that could have accrued from the tax money that could have been used for the next best alternative (Principle 2).

Whenever government intervenes in the market resource allocation is distorted. We saw in Principle 3 that rational people think at the margin and that this margin is associated with the costs and benefits of additional (or fewer) units. When governments intervene in the market with incentives such as those in this example, those marginal costs and benefits are changed and hence rational people respond to those changes and alter their behaviour as a result.

One issue to consider here is the value of the outcomes as a result of these changed behaviours. The EU has stated clearly that it believes there are significant cost savings to be made for all buildings as exemplified above. However, it is sometimes difficult to measure the value of the outcomes of the next best alternative and in addition if the decision to encourage this sort of behaviour is based on inaccurate or inappropriate assumptions, then the outcome may actually lead to an overall cost to society as a whole as opposed to the overall benefit envisaged by the EU.

FYI

How To Read This Book

Economics is fun, but it can also be hard to learn. Our aim in writing this text has been to make it as easy and as much fun as possible. But you, the student, also have a role to play. Experience shows that if you are actively involved as you study this book, you will enjoy a better outcome, both in your exams and in the years that follow. Here are a few tips about how best to read this book.

1. *Summarize, don't highlight.* Running a yellow marker over the text is too passive an activity to keep your mind engaged. Instead, when you come to the end of a section, take a minute and summarize what you have just learnt in your own words, writing your summary in the wide margins we've provided. When you've finished the chapter, compare your summary with the one at the end of the chapter. Did you pick up the main points?
2. *Test yourself.* Throughout the book, Quick Quizzes offer instant feedback to find out if you've learned what you are supposed to. Take the opportunity. Write your answer in the book's margin. The quizzes are meant to test your basic comprehension. If you aren't sure your answer is right, you probably need to review the section.
3. *Practise, practise, practise.* At the end of each chapter, Questions for Review test your understanding, and Problems and Applications ask you to apply and extend the material. Perhaps your lecturer will assign some of these exercises as course-work. If so, do them. If not, do them anyway. The more you use your new knowledge, the more solid it becomes.
4. *Study in groups.* After you've read the book and worked through the problems on your own, get together with other students to discuss the material. You will learn from each other – an example of the gains from trade.
5. *Don't forget the real world.* In the midst of all the numbers, graphs and strange new words, it is easy to lose sight of what economics is all about. The Case Studies and In the News boxes sprinkled throughout this book should help remind you. Don't skip them. They show how the theory is tied to events happening in all of our lives. If your study is successful, you won't be able to read a newspaper again without thinking about supply, demand and the wonderful world of economics.

CONCLUSION

You now have a taste of what economics is all about. In the coming chapters we will develop many specific insights about people, markets and economies. Mastering these insights will take some effort, but it is not an overwhelming task.

The field of economics is based on a few basic ideas that can be applied in many different situations.

Throughout this book we will refer back to the *Ten Principles of Economics* highlighted in this chapter and summarized in Table 1.2. Whenever we do so, an icon will be displayed in the margin, as it is now. But even when that icon is absent, you should keep these building blocks in mind. Even the most sophisticated economic analysis is built using the ten principles introduced here.

SUMMARY

- The fundamental lessons about individual decision-making are that people face trade-offs among alternative goals, that the cost of any action is measured in terms of foregone opportunities, that rational people make decisions by comparing marginal costs and marginal benefits, and that people change their behaviour in response to the incentives they face.
- The fundamental lessons about interactions among people are that trade can be mutually beneficial, that markets are usually a good way of coordinating trade among people, and that the government can potentially improve market outcomes if there is some market failure or if the market outcome is inequitable.
- The fundamental lessons about the economy as a whole are that productivity is the ultimate source of living standards, that money growth is the ultimate source of inflation, and that society faces a short-run trade-off between inflation and unemployment.

KEY CONCEPTS

scarcity, p. 2
economics, p. 2
equity, p. 5
opportunity cost, p. 6
marginal changes, p. 6
market economy, p. 9
market failure, p. 11
externality, p. 11
market power, p. 11
economic growth, p. 12
gross domestic product per head, p. 12
standard of living, p. 12
productivity, p. 12
inflation, p. 14
Phillips curve, p. 15
business cycle, p. 15

QUESTIONS FOR REVIEW

1. Give three examples of important trade-offs that you face in your life.
2. What is the opportunity cost of going to the cinema to see a film?
3. Water is necessary for life. Is the marginal benefit of a glass of water large or small?
4. Why should policy makers think about incentives?
5. Why isn't trade among countries like a game, with some winners and some losers?
6. What does the 'invisible hand' of the marketplace do?
7. Explain the two main causes of market failure and give an example of each.
8. Why is productivity important?
9. What is inflation, and what causes it?
10. How are inflation and unemployment related in the short run?

PROBLEMS AND APPLICATIONS

1. Describe some of the trade-offs faced by each of the following.
   a. A family deciding whether to buy a new car.
   b. A member of the government deciding how much to spend on building a new national football stadium.
   c. A company chief executive officer deciding whether to open a new factory.
   d. A university lecturer deciding how much to prepare for her lecture.
2. You are trying to decide whether to take a holiday. Most of the costs of the holiday (airfare, hotel, foregone wages) are measured in euros, but the benefits of the holiday are psychological. How can you compare the benefits to the costs?
3. You were planning to spend Saturday working at your part-time job, but a friend asks you to go to a football match. What is the true cost of going to the football match? Now suppose that you had been planning to spend the day studying in the library. What is the cost of going to the football match in this case? Explain.
4. You win €1 000 in the EuroMillions Lottery. You have a choice between spending the money now or putting it away for a year in a bank account that pays 5 per cent interest. What is the opportunity cost of spending the €1 000 now?
5. The company that you manage has invested €5 million in developing a new product, but the development is not quite finished. At a recent meeting, your sales people report that the introduction of competing products has reduced the expected sales of your new product to €3 million. If it would cost €1 million to finish development and make the product, should you go ahead and do so? What is the most that you should pay to complete development?
6. Three managers of the Hubble Bubble Magic Potion Company are discussing a possible increase in production. Each suggests a way to make this decision.

   FIRST WITCH: When shall we three meet again? We need to decide how much Magic Potion to produce. Personally, I think we should examine whether our company's productivity – litres of potion per worker per hour – would rise or fall if we increased output.

   SECOND WITCH: We should examine whether our average cost – cost per worker – would rise or fall.

   THIRD WITCH: We should examine whether the extra revenue from selling the additional potion would be greater or smaller than the extra costs.

   Who do you think is right? Why?
7. The social security system provides income for people over the age of 65. If a recipient of social security decides to work and earn some income, the amount he or she receives in social security benefits is typically reduced.
   a. How does the provision of social security affect people's incentive to save while working?
   b. How does the reduction in benefits associated with higher earnings affect people's incentive to work past age 65?
8. Your flatmate is a better cook than you are, but you can clean more quickly than your flatmate can. If your flatmate did all of the cooking and you did all of the cleaning, would your household chores take you more or less time than if you divided each task evenly? Give a similar example of how specialization and trade can make two countries both better off.
9. Suppose the European Union adopted central planning for its economy, and you became the Chief Planner. Among the millions of decisions that you need to make for next year are how many DVDs to produce, what films to record and who should receive the DVDs.
   a. To make these decisions intelligently, what information would you need about the DVD industry? What information would you need about each of the people in the countries making up the European Union?
   b. How would your decisions about DVDs affect some of your other decisions, such as how many DVD players to make or Blu-ray discs to produce? How might some of your other decisions about the economy change your views about DVDs?
10. Explain whether each of the following government activities is motivated by a concern about equity or a concern about efficiency. In the case of efficiency, discuss the type of market failure involved.
    a. Regulating water prices.
    b. Regulating electricity prices.
    c. Providing some poor people with vouchers that can be used to buy food.
    d. Prohibiting smoking in public places.
    e. Imposing higher personal income tax rates on people with higher incomes.
    f. Instituting laws against driving whilst under the influence of alcohol.
11. Discuss each of the following statements from the standpoints of equity and efficiency.
    a. 'Everyone in society should be guaranteed the best health care possible.'

b. 'When workers are laid off, they should be able to collect unemployment benefits until they find a new job.'

12. In what ways is your standard of living different from that of your parents or grandparents when they were your age? Why have these changes occurred?
13. Suppose Europeans decide to save more of their incomes. If banks lend this extra saving to European businesses, which use the funds to build new European factories, how might this lead to faster growth in European productivity? Who do you suppose benefits from the higher productivity? Is society getting a free lunch?
14. Imagine that you are a policy maker trying to decide whether to reduce the rate of inflation in your country. To make an intelligent decision, what would you need to know about inflation, unemployment and the trade-off between them?
15. Look at a newspaper or at the website http://www.economist.com to find three stories about the economy that have been in the news lately. For each story, identify one (or more) of the *Ten Principles of Economics* discussed in this chapter that is relevant, and explain how it is relevant. Also, for each story, look through this book's table of contents and try to find a chapter that might shed light on the news event.

For further resources, visit www.cengage.com/mankiw_taylor2

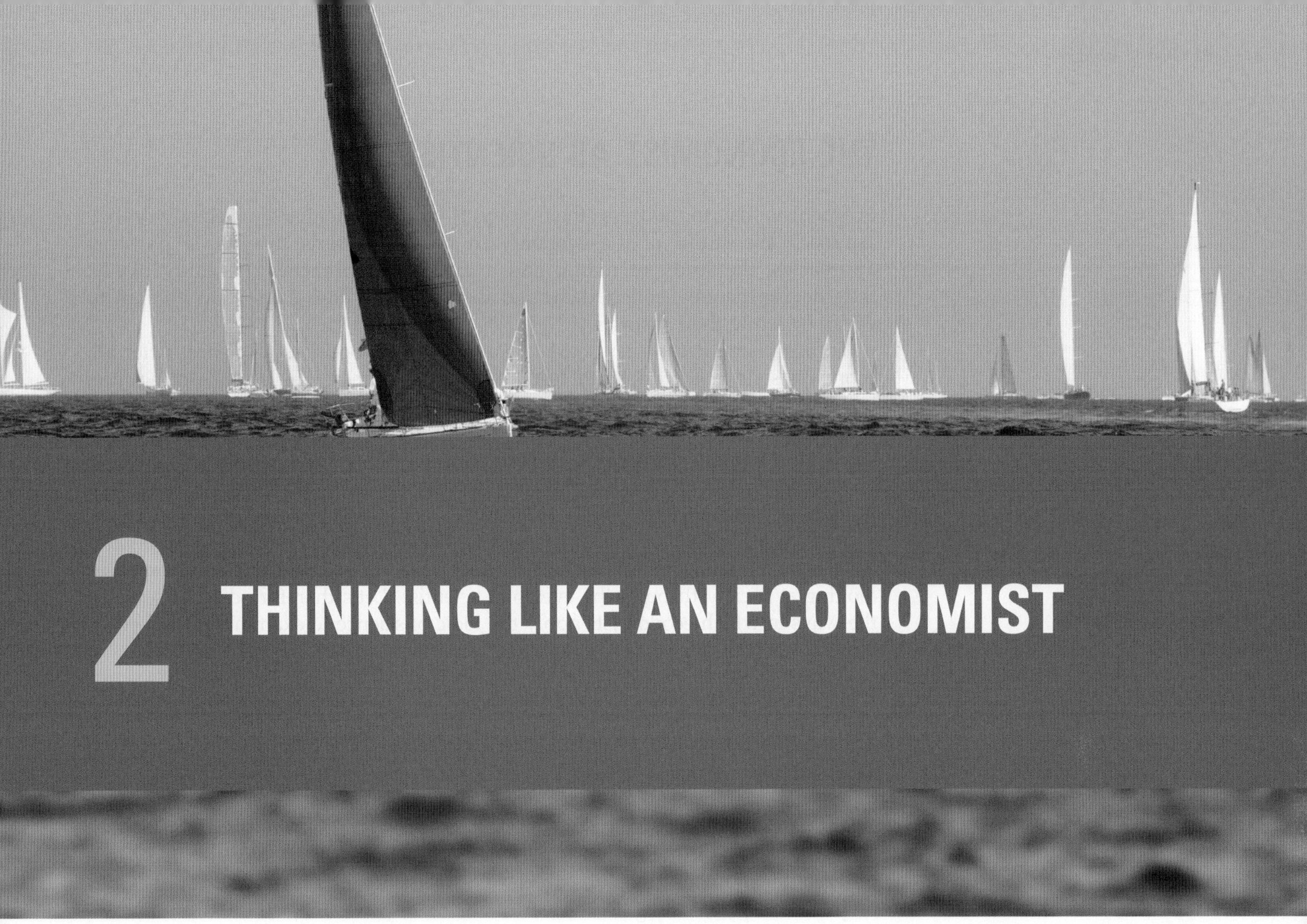

2 THINKING LIKE AN ECONOMIST

Every field of study has its own language and its own way of thinking. Mathematicians talk about axioms, integrals and vector spaces. Psychologists talk about ego, id and cognitive dissonance. Medics talk about dyspnoea, claudication and myocardial infarction. Lawyers talk about venue, torts and promissory estoppel.

Economics is no different. Supply, demand, elasticity, comparative advantage, consumer surplus, deadweight loss – these terms are part of the economist's language. In the coming chapters, you will encounter many new terms and some familiar words that economists use in specialised ways. At first, this new language may seem needlessly arcane. But, as you will see, its value lies in its ability to provide you with a new and useful way of thinking about the world in which you live.

The single most important purpose of this book is to help you learn the economist's way of thinking. Of course, just as you cannot become a mathematician, psychologist, medical doctor or lawyer overnight, learning to think like an economist will take some time. Yet with a combination of theory, case studies and examples of economics in the news, this book will give you ample opportunity to develop and practise this skill.

Before delving into the substance and details of economics, it is helpful to have an overview of how economists approach the world. This chapter, therefore, discusses the field's methodology. What is distinctive about how economists confront a question? What does it mean to think like an economist?

THE ECONOMIST AS SCIENTIST

Economists try to address their subject with a scientist's objectivity. They approach the study of the economy in much the same way as a physicist approaches the study of matter and a biologist approaches the study of life: they devise theories, collect data, and then analyse these data in an attempt to verify or refute their theories.

To beginners, it can seem odd to claim that economics is a science. After all, economists do not work with test tubes or telescopes. The essence of science, however, is the *scientific method* – the dispassionate development and testing of theories about how the world works. This method of inquiry is as applicable to studying a nation's economy as it is to studying the earth's gravity or a species' evolution. As Albert Einstein once put it, 'The whole of science is nothing more than the refinement of everyday thinking.'

Although Einstein's comment is as true for social sciences such as economics as it is for natural sciences such as physics, most people are not accustomed to looking at society through the eyes of a scientist. Let's therefore discuss some of the ways in which economists apply the logic of science to examine how an economy works.

The Scientific Method: Observation, Theory and More Observation

Isaac Newton, the famous English 17th century scientist and mathematician, allegedly became intrigued one day when he saw an apple fall from a tree. This observation motivated Newton to develop a theory of gravity that applies not only to an apple falling to the earth but to any two objects in the universe. Subsequent testing of Newton's theory has shown that it works well in many circumstances (although, as Einstein would later emphasize, not in all circumstances). Because Newton's theory has been so successful at explaining observation, it is still taught today in undergraduate physics courses around the world.

This interplay between theory and observation also occurs in the field of economics. An economist might live in a country experiencing rapid increases in prices and be moved by this observation to develop a theory of inflation. The theory might assert that high inflation arises when the government prints too much money. (As you may recall, this was one of the *Ten Principles of Economics* in Chapter 1.) To test this theory, the economist could collect and analyse data on prices and money from many different countries. If growth in the quantity of money were not at all related to the rate at which prices are rising, the economist would start to doubt the validity of his theory of inflation. If money growth and inflation were strongly correlated in international data, as in fact they are, the economist would become more confident in his theory.

Although economists use theory and observation like other scientists, they do face an obstacle that makes their task especially challenging: experiments are often difficult in economics. Physicists studying gravity can drop many objects in their laboratories to generate data to test their theories. By contrast, economists studying inflation are not allowed to manipulate a nation's monetary policy simply to generate useful data. Economists, like astronomers and evolutionary biologists, usually have to make do with whatever data the world happens to give them.

To find a substitute for laboratory experiments, economists pay close attention to the natural experiments offered by history. When a war in the Middle East interrupts the flow of crude oil, for instance, oil prices shoot up around the world. For consumers of oil and oil products, such an event depresses living standards. For economic policy makers, it poses a difficult choice about how best to respond. But for economic scientists, it provides an opportunity to study the effects of a key natural resource on the world's economies, and this opportunity persists long after the wartime increase in oil prices is over. Throughout this book, therefore, we consider many historical episodes. These episodes are valuable to study because they give us insight into the economy of the past and, more important, because they allow us to illustrate and evaluate economic theories of the present. The study of events and outcomes at different periods of time is called 'intertemporal study'.

The Role of Assumptions

If you ask a physicist how long it would take for a cannonball to fall from the top of the Leaning Tower of Pisa, she will probably answer the question by assuming that the cannonball falls in a vacuum. Of course, this assumption is false. In fact, the building is surrounded by air, which exerts friction on the falling cannonball and slows it down. Yet the physicist will correctly point out that friction on the cannonball is so small in relation to its weight that its effect is negligible. Assuming the cannonball falls in a vacuum greatly simplifies the problem without substantially affecting the answer.

Economists make assumptions for the same reason: assumptions can simplify the complex world and make it easier to understand. To study the effects of international trade, for example, we may assume that the world consists of only two countries and that each country produces only two goods. Of course, the real world consists of dozens of countries, each of which produces thousands of different types of goods. But by assuming two countries and two goods, we can focus our thinking. Once we understand international trade in an imaginary world with two countries and two goods, we are in a better position to understand international trade in the more complex world in which we live.

The art in scientific thinking – whether in physics, biology or economics – is deciding which assumptions to make. Suppose, for instance, that we were dropping a beach ball rather than a cannonball from the top of the building. Our physicist would realize that the assumption of no friction is far less accurate in this case: friction exerts a greater force on a beach ball than on a cannonball because a beach ball is much larger and, moreover, the effects of air friction may not be negligible relative to the weight of the ball because it is so light. The assumption that gravity works in a vacuum may, therefore, be reasonable for studying a falling cannonball but not for studying a falling beach ball.

Similarly, economists use different assumptions to answer different questions. Suppose that we want to study what happens to the economy when the government changes the amount of money in circulation. An important piece of this analysis, it turns out, is how prices respond. Many prices in the economy change infrequently; the prices of magazines and newspapers, for instance, are changed only every few years. Knowing this fact may lead us to make different assumptions when studying the effects of the policy change over different time horizons. For studying the short-run effects of the policy, we may assume that prices do not change much. We may even make the extreme and artificial assumption that all prices are completely fixed. For studying the long-run effects of the policy, however, we may assume that all prices are completely flexible. Just as a physicist uses different assumptions when studying falling cannonballs and falling beach balls, economists use different assumptions when studying the short-run and long-run effects of a change in the quantity of money.

CASE STUDY

Developing Theories in Economics

As in physical sciences, theories are developed in economics to help make predictions. The ways in which these theories develop evolve over time as the scientific method of theory, observation and refinement of the theory continues. As with any science, economics does not have definitive answers to any question, only theories that are developed on the basis of currently known information. In physics, Newtonian laws explained a great deal but were improved by Einstein who opened up new avenues of investigation and challenged existing orthodoxies. Physicists know that Einstein's theories, as remarkable and good as they are, do not represent the whole 'truth' and that if anything his theories raise even more questions than they provide answers. Experiments using the Large Hadron Collider (LHC) are expected to shed more light on our understanding of physics but the cost of finding out this information has not come cheap; estimations put the cost of building the LHC and carrying out the experiments at nearly €4 billion.

In economics the development of theories is no different, but rather than creating new data as is the case with the LHC, we have to rely on observation. Many economic theories are relatively simple in nature but this can hide a number of complexities which may influence outcome and thus the power of the theory to predict and help in the generation of economic policy. Later in this book you will learn about economic growth. Economic growth is the change in the value of output in a country or region over a period of time. At its simplest it measures the amount of goods and services produced in a time period multiplied by the price of those goods and services. Economic growth, as you will see, is crucial to improvements in standards of living around the world. A fundamental question in economics, therefore, is what determines economic growth?

There have been different theories of economic growth put forward over time, one of the most popular has been that advanced by Robert. M. Solow and Trevor Swan in 1956. They identified the rate of human and physical capital and population growth as being key determinants of economic growth. Over the years, economists have looked at other factors that may influence economic growth including the level of macroeconomic stability in an economy (don't worry too much about what this means at this stage, this will become clearer as you read the relevant section of the book), the type of trade policy that exists in a country (is the country outward looking or does it tend to be insular), the nature and quality of institutions and governance (i.e. how effectively the rule of law operates and how well governments are able to control corruption) in the country concerned, the extent to which violence, war and conflict exist in a country, regional characteristics such as whether the country is part of Europe, North America, Asia or sub-Saharan Africa, geographical factors such as physical resource endowments and climate, the extent to which the country is competitive in international markets and internal factors such as the amount of productive land available.

These could all be represented as a simple equation which might look like the following.

$$E = f(SS_1, \text{Me}, \text{Tp}, \text{G}, \text{St}, \text{R}, \text{Gf}, \text{P}, \text{Ic}, \gamma)$$

This simply states that economic growth (E) is dependent on (is a function of) a range of possible factors which are given symbols or letters corresponding to the list given above. In order to influence economic growth, therefore, policy makers would have to find ways of influencing one or more of the factors in the equation to boost economic growth. The problem is, which factors should they focus on? This will depend on a variety of effects, including the resources policy makers have at their disposal, but will also be heavily dependent on which of the factors exerts the most powerful effects. Different economists may place a different reliance on the importance of one or more of these factors and this can significantly influence the outcome.

For example, assume that one economist places a value against each of the factors in the equation as follows:

$$E = f(0.5SS_1, 0.03Me, 0.01Tp, 0.1G, 0.15St, 0.03R, 0.024Gf, 0.06P, 0.08Ic, 0.115\,\gamma)$$

This tells us that the most important factor influencing economic growth is SS_1 the Solow-Swan human/physical capital, population growth. The value assigned to it means that it accounts for half of the determinants of economic growth. This would imply that emphasis might be placed on this factor if policy makers are interested in increasing economic growth. However, the assumptions made in deriving such an equation are varied. Economists will use sophisticated statistical and mathematical techniques in interpreting data to derive such equations and these can all influence the nature of the equation and the value of the theory as a predictor or basis of policy making.

Alin Mirestean and Charalambos Tsangarides[1] looked at the way in which these factors are assessed and arrived at some interesting conclusions which highlight the way in which economists think and work. They applied a different mathematical method of analysing data and found that this method cast doubt on some of the accepted assumptions about the relative value of each factor. Whilst they pointed out that all the factors were clearly important in economic growth, their analysis suggested some had a less important role. They identified four key factors – initial income, investment, population growth and life expectancy – as having the strongest evidence for being important whilst inflation, debt and trade openness were 'strong' factors. They pointed out, however, that their findings did depend to an extent on the type of data set used for the analysis. If 5-year averaged data are used it might give different outcomes to those based on 8-year average data. They conclude that different mathematical methods may give more robust data and may, therefore, be more appropriate in looking at theories of the determinants of economic growth.

[1]Mirestean, A. & Tsangarides, C. (2009) *Growth Determinants Revisited*, IMF Research Department Working Paper: http://www.imf.org/external/pubs/ft/wp/2009/wp09268.pdf accessed 10 December 2009.

Economic Models

Secondary school biology teachers often teach basic anatomy with plastic replicas of the human body. These models have all the major organs – the heart, the liver, the kidneys and so on. The models allow teachers to show their students in a simple way how the important parts of the body fit together. Of course, these plastic models are not actual human bodies, and no one would mistake the model for a real person. These models are stylised, and they omit many details. Yet despite this lack of realism – indeed, because of this lack of realism – studying these models is useful for learning how the human body works.

Economists also use models to learn about the world, but instead of being made of plastic, they are most often composed of diagrams and equations. Like a biology teacher's plastic model, economic models omit many details to allow us to see what is truly important. Just as the biology teacher's model does not include all of the body's muscles and capillaries, an economist's model does not include every feature of the economy.

As we use models to examine various economic issues throughout this book, you will see that all the models are built with assumptions. Just as a physicist begins the analysis of a falling cannonball by assuming away the existence of friction, economists assume away many of the details of the economy that are irrelevant for studying the question at hand. All models – in physics, biology or economics – simplify reality in order to improve our understanding of it.

Another analogy that is useful in thinking about the role of assumptions in economic models has to do with maps. Maps are scaled-down representations of the world, but every map leaves out some features of the real world. Imagine what a map would look like that tried to describe every feature of the area it was supposed to represent: as well as standard features like roads and parks, it would, for example, have to represent all of the buildings, the rooms within the buildings, the furniture within each room, and so on. There would be so much detail that the scale would have to be very large and the map would be very hard to read. Of course, you might say that it would be ridiculous to have so much detail in a map, and you would be right. But how do you decide what details to leave out and what details to leave in? The answer depends on what you plan to do with the map.

Suppose a friend knocks on your door one day and asks whether you can lend her a map of Berlin. In fact, you have three maps that would answer this general description: a road map showing the motorways and main roads going around and through the Berlin area, an A-to-Z street map of Berlin city centre and a U-Bahn metro map showing all of the lines and stations of the metro system. Which should you give her? It all depends on the use to which your friend wants to put the map. If she is planning to travel around Berlin on the metro, a metro map is indispensable. But if she wants to walk from Kurfürstendamm to see the Reichstag building, the metro map will be completely useless – it doesn't have a single street on it (unless the street name happens to coincide with a metro station) and she will need the A-to-Z. On the other hand, if she just wants to drive around the greater Berlin area avoiding the city centre she will need the road map: the other two maps – since they do not show any major roads outside of Berlin city centre – will not help her. Now, each of the maps leaves out certain features of the real world and, as a result, each of them is indispensable for a particular purpose and useless for other purposes.

The same is true of economic models. Becoming a skilled economic modeller involves deciding what features of the real world to try to capture in the model and what features are just so much unnecessary detail. The decision as to which details are necessary to leave in and which details should be left out will depend crucially on the purpose for which you wish to use the model. In our first model of the economy, we shall try to understand in very general terms how the economy works and we shall therefore not try to explain within the model, for example, how firms decide exactly how many workers to employ or households decide how much milk to buy.

Our First Model: The Circular-flow Diagram

The economy consists of millions of people engaged in many activities – buying, selling, working, hiring, manufacturing and so on. To understand how the economy works, we must find some way to simplify our thinking about all these activities. In other words, we need a model that explains, in general terms, how the economy is organised and how participants in the economy interact with one another.

FIGURE 2.1

The Circular Flow

This diagram is a schematic representation of the organization of the economy. Decisions are made by households and firms. Households and firms interact in the markets for goods and services (where households are buyers and firms are sellers) and in the markets for the factors of production (where firms are buyers and households are sellers). The outer set of arrows shows the flow of money, and the inner set of arrows shows the corresponding flow of inputs and outputs.

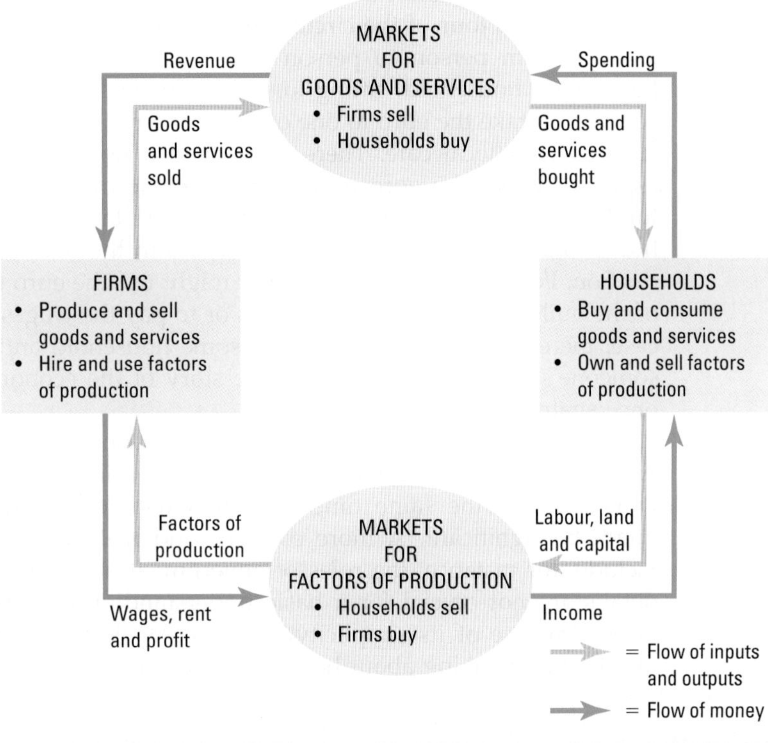

Figure 2.1 presents a visual model of the economy, called a **circular-flow diagram**. In this model, the economy is simplified to include only two types of decision makers – households and firms. Firms produce goods and services using inputs, such as labour, land and capital (buildings and machines). These inputs are called the *factors of production*. Households own the factors of production and consume all the goods and services that the firms produce. (Readers of this book are owners of the factor of production 'labour'. If you are a student then you are seeking to improve the value of this factor so that you can sell it for a higher price!)

circular-flow diagram
a visual model of the economy that shows how money and production inputs and outputs flow through markets among households and firms

Households and firms interact in two types of markets. In the *markets for goods and services*, households are buyers and firms are sellers. In particular, households buy the output of goods and services that firms produce. In the *markets for the factors of production*, households are sellers and firms are buyers. In these markets, households provide the inputs that the firms use to produce goods and services. The circular-flow diagram offers a simple way of organizing all of the economic transactions that occur between households and firms in the **economy**.

economy
a word to describe all the economic activity (buying and selling or transactions) that take place in a country or region

The inner loop of the circular-flow diagram represents the flows of inputs and outputs. The households sell the use of their labour, land and capital to the firms in the markets for the factors of production. The firms then use these factors to produce goods and services, which in turn are sold to households in the markets for goods and services. Hence, the factors of production flow from households to firms, and goods and services flow from firms to households.

The outer loop of the circular-flow diagram represents the corresponding flows of money. The households spend money to buy goods and services from the firms. The firms use some of the revenue from these sales to pay for the factors of production, such as the wages of their workers. What's left is the profit of the firm's owners, who themselves are members of households. Hence, spending on goods and services flows from households to firms, and income in the form of wages, rent and profit flows from firms to households.

Let's take a tour of the circular flow by following a one euro coin as it makes its way from person to person through the economy. Imagine that the euro begins at a household, sitting in, say, your pocket. If you want to buy a cup of coffee, you take the euro to one of the economy's markets for goods and services, such as your local café. There you spend it on your favourite drink: a double espresso. When the euro moves into the café cash register, it becomes revenue for the owner of the café. The euro doesn't stay with the café owner for long, however, because he uses it to buy inputs in the markets for the factors of production. For instance, the café owner might use the euro to pay rent to the owner of the building that the café occupies or to pay the wages of its workers. In either case, the euro enters the income of some household and, once again, is back in someone's pocket. At that point, the story of the economy's circular flow starts once again.

The circular-flow diagram in Figure 2.1 is one simple model of the economy. As such, it is useful for developing some basic ideas as to how the economy works, but at the same time dispenses with details that, for some purposes, might be significant. A more complex and realistic circular-flow model would include, for instance, the roles of government and international trade. Yet these details are not crucial for a basic understanding of how the economy is organised. Because of its simplicity, this circular-flow diagram is useful to keep in mind when thinking about how the pieces of the economy fit together.

Our Second Model: The Production Possibilities Frontier

Most economic models, unlike the purely visual circular-flow diagram, are built using the tools of mathematics. Here we consider one of the simplest such models, called the production possibilities frontier, and see how this model illustrates some basic economic ideas.

Although real economies produce thousands of goods and services, let's imagine an economy that produces only two goods – cars and computers. (Note, as outlined on page 23, we are making an assumption to help simplify the complexity of real economies, just like physicists make assumptions in order to simplify the complex world.) Together the car industry and the computer industry use all of the economy's factors of production. The **production possibilities frontier** is a graph that shows the various combinations of output – in this case, cars and computers – that the economy can possibly produce given the available factors of production and the available production technology that firms can use to turn these factors into output.

production possibilities frontier
a graph that shows the combinations of output that the economy can possibly produce given the available factors of production and the available production technology

Figure 2.2 is an example of a production possibilities frontier. In this economy, if all resources were used in the car industry, the economy would produce 1 000 cars and no computers. If all resources were used in the computer industry, the economy would produce 3 000 computers and no cars. The two end points of the production possibilities frontier represent these extreme possibilities. If the economy were to divide its resources between the two industries, it could produce

FIGURE 2.2

The Production Possibilities Frontier

The production possibilities frontier shows the combinations of output – in this case, cars and computers – that the economy can possibly produce. The economy can produce any combination on or inside the frontier. Points outside the frontier are not feasible given the economy's resources.

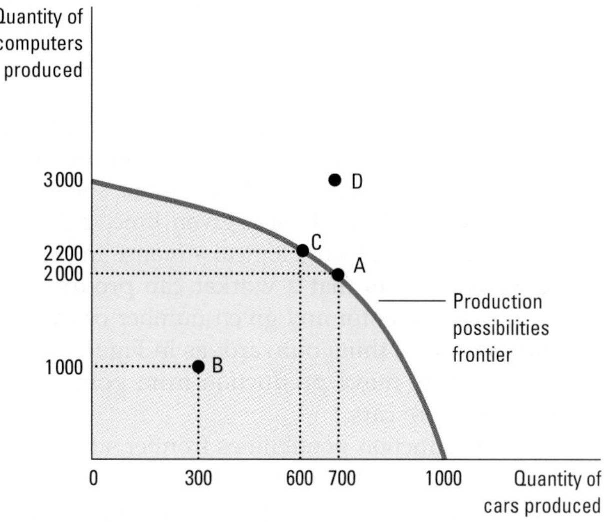

700 cars and 2 000 computers, shown in the figure by point A. By contrast, the outcome at point D is not possible because resources are scarce: the economy does not have enough of the factors of production to support that level of output. In other words, the economy can produce at any point on or inside the production possibilities frontier, but it cannot produce at points outside the frontier.

An outcome is said to be *efficient* if the economy is getting all it can from the scarce resources it has available. Points on (rather than inside) the production possibilities frontier represent efficient levels of production. When the economy is producing at such a point, say point A, there is no way to produce more of one good without producing less of the other. Point B represents an *inefficient* outcome. For some reason, perhaps widespread unemployment, the economy is producing less than it could from the resources it has available: it is producing only 300 cars and 1 000 computers. If the source of the inefficiency were eliminated, the economy could move from point B to point A, increasing production of both cars (to 700) and computers (to 2 000).

One of the *Ten Principles of Economics* discussed in Chapter 1 is that people face trade-offs. The production possibilities frontier shows one trade-off that society faces. Once we have reached the efficient points on the frontier, the only way of getting more of one good is to get less of the other. When the economy moves from point A to point C, for instance, society produces more computers but at the expense of producing fewer cars.

Another of the *Ten Principles of Economics* is that the cost of something is what you give up to get it. This is called the opportunity cost. The production possibilities frontier shows the opportunity cost of one good as measured in terms of the other good. When society reallocates some of the factors of production from the car industry to the computer industry, moving the economy from point A to point C, it gives up 100 cars to get 200 additional computers. In other words, when the economy is at point A, the opportunity cost of 200 computers is 100 cars.

Notice that the production possibilities frontier in Figure 2.2 is bowed outward. This means that the opportunity cost of cars in terms of computers depends on how much of each good the economy is producing. When the economy is using most of its resources to make cars, the production possibilities frontier is quite steep. Because even workers and machines best suited to making computers are being used to make cars, the economy gets a substantial increase in the number of computers for each car it gives up. By contrast, when the economy is using most of its resources to make computers, the production possibilities frontier is quite flat. In this case, the resources best suited to making computers are already in the computer industry, and each car the economy gives up yields only a small increase in the number of computers.

The production possibilities frontier shows the trade-off between the production of different goods at a given time, but the trade-off can change over time. For example, if a technological advance in the computer industry raises the number of computers that a worker can produce per week, the economy can make more computers for any given number of cars. As a result, the production possibilities frontier shifts outward, as in Figure 2.3. Because of this economic growth, society might move production from point A to point E, enjoying more computers and more cars.

The production possibilities frontier simplifies a complex economy to highlight and clarify some basic ideas. We have used it to illustrate some of the concepts mentioned briefly in Chapter 1: scarcity, efficiency, trade-offs, opportunity cost and economic growth. As you study economics, these ideas will recur in various forms. The production possibilities frontier – our second economic model – offers one simple way of thinking about them.

FIGURE 2.3

A Shift in the Production Possibilities Frontier

An economic advance in the computer industry shifts the production possibilities frontier outward, increasing the number of cars and computers the economy can produce.

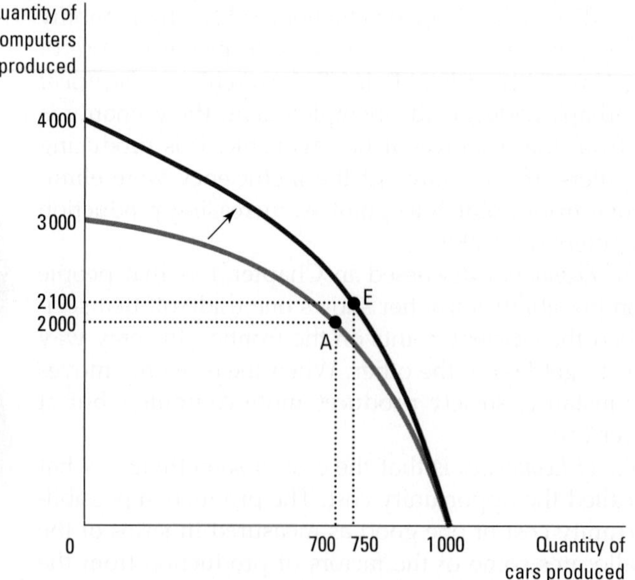

Microeconomics and Macroeconomics

Many subjects are studied on various levels. Consider biology, for example. Molecular biologists study the chemical compounds that make up living things. Cellular biologists study cells, which are made up of many chemical compounds and, at the same time, are themselves the building blocks of living organisms. Evolutionary biologists study the many varieties of animals and plants and how species change gradually over the centuries.

Economics is also studied on various levels. We can study the decisions of individual households and firms. Or we can study the interaction of households and firms in markets for specific goods and services. Or we can study the operation of the economy as a whole, which is just the sum of the activities of all these decision-makers in all these markets.

Since roughly the 1930s, the field of economics has traditionally been divided into two broad subfields. **Microeconomics** is the study of how households and firms make decisions and how they interact in specific markets. **Macroeconomics** is the study of economy-wide phenomena. A microeconomist might study the effects of a congestion tax on the use of cars in central London, the impact of foreign competition on the European car industry or the effects of attending university on a person's lifetime earnings. A macroeconomist might study the effects of borrowing by national governments, the changes over time in an economy's rate of unemployment or alternative policies to raise growth in national living standards.

microeconomics
the study of how households and firms make decisions and how they interact in markets

macroeconomics
the study of economy-wide phenomena, including inflation, unemployment and economic growth

Microeconomics and macroeconomics are closely intertwined. Because changes in the overall economy arise from the decisions of millions of individuals, it is impossible to understand macroeconomic developments without considering the associated microeconomic decisions. For example, a macroeconomist might study the effect of a cut in income tax on the overall production of goods and services in an economy. To analyse this issue, he or she must consider how the tax cut affects the decisions of households concerning how much to spend on goods and services.

Despite the inherent link between microeconomics and macroeconomics, the two fields are distinct. In economics, as in biology, it may seem natural to begin with the smallest unit and build up. Yet doing so is neither necessary nor always the best way to proceed. Evolutionary biology is, in a sense, built upon molecular biology, since species are made up of molecules. Yet molecular biology and evolutionary biology are separate fields, each with its own questions and its own methods. Similarly, because microeconomics and macroeconomics address different questions, they sometimes take quite different approaches and are often taught in separate courses.

Quick Quiz In what sense is economics like a science? • Draw a production possibilities frontier for a society that produces food and clothing. Show an efficient point, an inefficient point and an unfeasible point. Show the effects of a drought. • Define *microeconomics* and *macroeconomics*.

THE ECONOMIST AS POLICY ADVISOR

Often economists are asked to explain the causes of economic events. Why, for example, is unemployment higher for teenagers than for older workers? Sometimes economists are asked to recommend policies to improve economic outcomes. What, for instance, should the government do to improve the economic well-being of teenagers? Can economics shed any light on the problem of non-medicinal drug use? How might economics help in finding solutions to the problems associated with global warming? When economists are trying to explain the world, they are scientists. When they are trying to help improve it, they are policy advisors.

Positive versus Normative Analysis

To help clarify the two roles that economists play, we begin by examining the use of language. Because scientists and policy advisors have different goals, they use language in different ways.

For example, suppose that two people are discussing minimum wage laws. Here are two statements you might hear:

PASCALE: Minimum wage laws cause unemployment.
SOPHIE: The government should raise the minimum wage.

Ignoring for now whether you agree with these statements, notice that Pascale and Sophie differ in what they are trying to do. Pascale is speaking like a scientist: she is making a claim about how the world works. Sophie is speaking like a policy advisor: she is making a claim about how she would like to change the world.

positive statements
claims that attempt to describe the world as it is

normative statements
claims that attempt to prescribe how the world should be

In general, statements about the world are of two types. One type, such as Pascale's, is positive. **Positive statements** are descriptive. They make a claim about how the world *is*. A second type of statement, such as Sophie's, is normative. **Normative statements** are prescriptive. They make a claim about how the world *ought to be*.

A key difference between positive and normative statements is how we judge their validity. We can, in principle, confirm or refute positive statements by examining evidence. An economist might evaluate Pascale's statement by analysing data on changes in minimum wages and changes in unemployment over time. By contrast, evaluating normative statements involves values as well as facts. Sophie's statement cannot be judged using data alone. Deciding what is good or bad policy is not merely a matter of science; it also involves our views on ethics, religion and political philosophy.

Of course, positive and normative statements may be related. Our positive views about how the world works affect our normative views about what policies are desirable. Pascale's claim that the minimum wage causes unemployment, if true, might lead us to reject Sophie's conclusion that the government should raise the minimum wage. Yet our normative conclusions cannot come from positive analysis alone; they involve value judgements as well.

As you study economics, keep in mind the distinction between positive and normative statements. Much of economics just tries to explain how the economy works. Yet often the goal of economics is to improve how the economy works. When you hear economists making normative statements, you know they have crossed the line from scientist to policy advisor.

Economists in Governmental and Supra-governmental Institutions

An old joke about economists concerns the politician who one day said that she would only employ economists with one hand: she was tired of receiving advice of the form, 'On the one hand,…On the other hand….'

Throughout Europe, North America and the world more generally, many government ministries dealing with economic issues – such as a country's finance ministry or Treasury – have large numbers of economists working for them, providing advice on alternative policy measures or forecasts of the economy. In the UK, the Government Economic Service is the biggest single employer of economists, with about 1 000 of them working in 30 government departments and agencies.

The joke about one-handed economists does reflect an element of truth concerning the nature of economic advice – namely that good economic advice is not always straightforward. This tendency is rooted in one of the *Ten Principles of Economics* in Chapter 1: people face trade-offs. Economists are aware that trade-offs are involved in most policy decisions. For example, a policy might, on the one hand, increase efficiency but, on the other hand, reduce equity. It might help future generations but hurt current generations. An economist who says that all policy decisions are easy is an economist not to be trusted.

Economists are also found outside the administrative branch of government. The Bank of England, the institution that implements the UK's monetary policy, employs a large staff of economists to analyse economic developments in the United Kingdom and throughout the world. At the time of writing this chapter, both the Governor and Deputy Governor of the Bank of England were former professors of the London School of Economics, while the President of the German central bank, the Bundesbank, and of the US central bank, the Federal Reserve, were also former professors of economics. Most of the central banks of other European countries also have economic research departments, as do the European Central Bank in Frankfurt and the US Federal Reserve in Washington.

WE HAVE TO MAKE MASSIVE CUTS SO WE CAN REDUCE DEBT... WHICH WILL CUT INTO GROWTH WHICH IS NEEDED SO WE CAN MAKE MASSIVE CUTS....

Economists are also employed to provide advice at the supra-governmental level. The International Monetary Fund, which was created in 1945 to help promote the health of the world economy, employs at its headquarters in Washington DC probably the largest number of economics Ph.D.s based at a single location anywhere in the world, originating from a very large proportion of the 185 countries that make up the IMF's near-global membership. Table 2.1 lists the websites of some of these agencies.

The influence of economists on policy goes beyond their role as advisors: their research and writings often affect policy indirectly. The great British economist John Maynard Keynes offered this observation:

> The ideas of economists and political philosophers, both when they are right and when they are wrong, are more powerful than is commonly understood. Indeed, the world is ruled by little else. Practical men, who believe themselves to be quite exempt from intellectual influences, are usually the slaves of some defunct economist. Madmen in authority, who hear voices in the air, are distilling their frenzy from some academic scribbler of a few years back.

Although these words were written in 1935, they remain true today. Indeed, the 'academic scribbler of a few years back' now influencing public policy is often Keynes himself.

Quick Quiz Give an example of a positive statement and an example of a normative statement. • Name four government departments that regularly rely on advice from economists.

TABLE 2.1

Websites

Here are the websites for a few of the government and supra-governmental agencies that are responsible for collecting economic data and making or advising on economic policy.

European Central Bank	http://www.ecb.int
Organization for Economic Cooperation and Development	http://www.oecd.org
International Monetary Fund	http://www.imf.org
Bank of England	http://www.bankofengland.co.uk
UK Treasury	http://www.hm-treasury.gov.uk
UK Office for National Statistics	http://www.ons.gov.uk
US Federal Reserve Board	http://www.federalreserve.gov

CASE STUDY

Professor Mankiw

Professor Mankiw Goes to Washington

Both of the authors of the textbook you are now reading are university professors. But in the past few years, each of us has had the opportunity to leave the ivory tower and put our economics to the test. One of us, Professor Taylor, went into the world of global finance, while the other, Professor Mankiw, had the opportunity to become the chairman of the US Council of Economic Advisors (CEA) and the US President's chief economist from 2003 to 2005. Here, Professor Mankiw describes what it was like to be the chief economic advisor in one of the world's most powerful economies.

As chair of the CEA, I met with the President about twice a week. Some of these meetings were briefings on the state of the economy; most were discussions of current issues in economic policy. I worked closely with other members of the White House staff to analyse policy options and brief the President on a wide range of topics, such as tax policy, the federal budget, social security and international trade. I also met regularly with economic officials outside the White House, such as the Secretary of the Treasury (the head of the US finance ministry) and the Federal Reserve Chairman (the head of the US central bank) and with leaders of the business community.

For anyone used to the measured pace and quiet reflection of university life, taking such a job is exhilarating. Sitting with the President in his famous Oval Office in the White House, flying on *Air Force One,* and spending the weekend with the President and his aides at his country retreat, Camp David, are unforgettable experiences. Testifying as the President's representative before congressional committees, which include politicians who are usually partisan and sometimes hostile, is also an experience a person does not easily forget – no matter how hard one might try.

During my two years in Washington, I learned a lot about the process by which economic policy is made. It differs in many ways from the idealised policy process assumed in economics textbooks.

Throughout this text, whenever we discuss economic policy, we often focus on one question: What is the best policy for the government to pursue? We act as if policy were set by a benevolent king. Once the king figures out the right policy, he has no trouble putting his ideas into action.

In the real world, figuring out the right policy is only part of a leader's job, sometimes the easiest part. After the President hears from his economic advisers about what policy is best from their perspective, he turns to other advisors for related input. His communications advisors will tell him how best to explain the proposed policy to the public, and they will try to anticipate any misunderstandings that might arise to make the challenge more difficult. His press advisors will tell him how the news media will report on his proposal and what opinions will likely be expressed on the nation's editorial pages. His legislative affairs advisors will tell him how Congress will view the proposal, what amendments members of Congress will suggest, and the likelihood that Congress will pass some version of the President's proposal into law. His political advisors will tell him which groups will organize to support or oppose the proposed policy, how this proposal will affect his standing among different groups in the electorate, and whether it will affect support for any of the President's other policy initiatives. After hearing and weighing all this advice, the President then decides how to proceed.

My two years in Washington were a vivid reminder of an important lesson: making economic policy in a representative democracy is a messy affair – and there are often good reasons presidents (and other politicians) do not advance the policies that economists advocate. Economists offer crucial input into the policy process, but their advice is only one ingredient of a complex recipe.

WHY ECONOMISTS DISAGREE

'If all economists were laid end to end, they would not reach a conclusion.' This witticism from George Bernard Shaw is revealing. Economists as a group are often criticised for giving conflicting advice to policy makers. There are two basic reasons:

- Economists may disagree about the validity of alternative positive theories about how the world works.
- Economists may have different values and, therefore, different normative views about what policy should try to accomplish.

Let's discuss each of these reasons.

Differences in Scientific Judgements

Several centuries ago, astronomers debated whether the earth or the sun was at the centre of the solar system. More recently, meteorologists have debated whether the earth is experiencing global warming and, if so, why. Science is a search for understanding about the world around us. It is not surprising that as the search continues, scientists can disagree about the direction in which truth lies.

Economists often disagree for the same reason. Economics is a young science, and there is still much to be learned. Economists sometimes disagree because they have different beliefs about the validity of alternative theories or about the size of important parameters.

For example, economists disagree about whether the government should levy taxes based on a household's income or based on its consumption (spending). Advocates of a switch from an income tax to a consumption tax believe that the change would encourage households to save more, because income that is saved would not be taxed. Higher saving, in turn, would lead to more rapid growth in productivity and living standards. Advocates of an income tax system believe that household saving would not respond much to a change in the tax laws. These two groups of economists hold different normative views about the tax system because they have different positive views about the responsiveness of saving to tax incentives.

Differences in Values

Suppose that Henrik and Carlos both take the same amount of water from the town well. To pay for maintaining the well, the town imposes a property tax on its residents. Henrik lives in a large house worth €2 million and pays a property tax of €10 000 a year. Carlos owns a small cottage worth €20 000 and pays a property tax of €1 000 a year.

Is this policy fair? If not, who pays too much and who pays too little? Would it be better to replace the tax based on the value of the property with a tax that was just a single payment from everyone living in the town (a poll tax) in return for using the well – say, €1 000 a year? After all, Henrik lives on his own and actually uses much less water than Carlos and the other four alpine pipe players in Carlos's band who live with him and bathe regularly before and after a gig. Would that be a fairer policy?

In the 1980s, when the UK government attempted to replace the system of property tax in the UK with a poll tax, it resulted in riots in Trafalgar Square – many people clearly thought that it was indeed very unfair. There were also a large number of people who thought it a much fairer system than the one which existed at the time. This raises two interesting questions in economics – how do we define words like 'fair' and 'unfair' and who holds the power to influence and make decisions? If the power is in the hands of the anti-poll tax lobby then the policy may be dropped even if it is a much 'fairer' system!

What about replacing the property tax not with a poll tax but with an income tax? Henrik has an income of €100 000 a year so that a 5 per cent income tax would present him with a tax bill of €5 000. Carlos, on the other hand, has an income of only €10 000 a year and so would pay only €500 a year in tax (although his four tenants, who earn about the same, would also have to pay a similar tax bill). Does it matter whether Carlos's low income is due to his decision to pursue a career as an alpine horn player? Would it matter if it were due to a physical disability? Does it matter whether Henrik's high income is due to a large inheritance from his uncle? What if it were due to his willingness to work long hours at a dreary job?

These are difficult questions on which people are likely to disagree. If the town hired two experts to study how the town should tax its residents to pay for the well, we should not be surprised if they offered conflicting advice.

This simple example shows why economists sometimes disagree about public policy. As we learned earlier in our discussion of normative and positive analysis, policies cannot be judged on scientific grounds alone. Economists give conflicting advice sometimes because they have different values. Perfecting the science of economics will not tell us whether it is Henrik or Carlos who pays too much.

Perception versus Reality

Because of differences in scientific judgements and differences in values, some disagreement among economists is inevitable. Yet one should not overstate the amount of disagreement. In many cases, economists do offer a united view.

Table 2.2 contains ten propositions about economic policy. In a survey of economists in business, government and academia, these propositions were endorsed by an overwhelming majority of respondents. Most of these propositions would fail to command a similar consensus among the general public.

TABLE 2.2

Proposition (and Percentage of Economists Who Agree)

Ten propositions about which most economists agree

1. A ceiling on rents reduces the quantity and quality of housing available. (93%)
2. Tariffs and import quotas usually reduce general economic welfare. (93%)
3. Flexible and floating exchange rates offer an effective international monetary arrangement. (90%)
4. Fiscal policy (e.g., tax cut and/or government expenditure increase) has a significant stimulative impact on a less than fully employed economy. (90%)
5. If the government budget is to be balanced, it should be done over the business cycle rather than yearly. (85%)
6. Cash payments increase the welfare of recipients to a greater degree than do transfers-in-kind of equal cash value. (84%)
7. A large government budget deficit has an adverse effect on the economy. (83%)
8. A minimum wage increases unemployment among young and unskilled workers. (79%)
9. The government should restructure the welfare system along the lines of a 'negative income tax'. (79%)
10. Effluent taxes and marketable pollution permits represent a better approach to pollution control than imposition of pollution ceilings. (78%)

Source: Adapted from Richard M. Alston, J.R. Kearl and Michael B. Vaughn, 'Is There Consensus Among Economists in the 1990s?' *American Economic Review* (May 1992): 203–209. Used by permission.

One of the propositions in the table concerns tariffs and import quotas, two policies that restrict trade among nations. For reasons we will discuss more fully in later chapters, almost all economists oppose such barriers to free trade. This, in fact, is one of the major reasons why the European Union was set up and why countries are queuing up to join it: tariffs and quotas are not imposed on trade between EU member countries. Tariffs and quotas *are*, however, often imposed by EU countries on goods coming from outside of the European Union. In the USA, the President and Congress have, over the years, often chosen to restrict the import of certain goods. In 2002, for example, the Bush administration imposed large tariffs on steel to protect domestic steel producers from foreign competition – although they later had to drop the policy when the European Union threatened to retaliate by increasing the tariffs on US goods imported into EU countries from the US. In this case, economists did offer united advice, but policy makers chose to ignore it.

Another of the propositions concerns the imposition of a legal minimum wage – nearly 80 per cent of economists surveyed said that they thought that a minimum wage increases unemployment among unskilled and young workers. Nevertheless, the US and nine European Union countries, including the UK, now have a statutory minimum wage. Of course, these economists were not necessarily *against* the imposition of a minimum wage. Some of them might argue, for example, that while, on the one hand, introducing a minimum wage above a certain level may affect unemployment, on the other hand it may increase the average quality of goods and services produced in the economy by making it harder for producers of low-quality goods and services to compete by keeping wages and prices low, and this may lead to a net benefit to the economy overall. Remember: people face trade-offs.

Table 2.3 shows another aspect of this same idea. This is based on a paper written by Alan Budd, a former Chief Economic Advisor to HM Treasury in the UK and Provost of The Queen's College, Oxford University. The paper appeared in the journal *World Economics* in 2004. This table shows a list of things that Sir Alan thinks that economists know and therefore agree on. Most of these things

TABLE 2.3

What Economists Know

- **Economists know that demand curves slope downwards from left to right.**
  - This suggests that when prices rise, the quantity demanded of a product (under normal circumstances) will fall, and vice versa.
- **Economists know that supply curves slope upwards from left to right.**
  - This suggests that when prices rise, the quantity supplied by producers will also rise and vice versa.
- **Economists know that the proportion of income spent on food falls as income rises.**
  - This is what is referred to as Engel's Law, after the German statistician Ernst Engel. Budd points out that this law applies not only to studies of the differences in the proportion of income spent on food by the rich and the poor, but also over time. When nations go through economic development and become richer, the proportion of national income spent on food falls.
- **Economists know that there are gains from trade to be had when countries or individuals have comparative advantage.**
  - What this means is that one country might be better at producing a number of goods than another. However, if it focuses its attention on producing the good in which it has a comparative advantage, both countries can gain from trade and the world economy will be in a better state. By focusing on production of one good at the expense of others, countries move resources from the production of one good to another. By doing so, the country sacrifices the output of this other good that it could have produced. However, the gains made from shifting resources into production of products in which they are more efficient in production helps to raise total output. A mutually beneficial rate of exchange between the two countries means they both are better off than before.
- **Economists tend to think in terms of general rather than partial equilibrium.**
  - Economies are made up of millions of interrelated markets. Non-economists, argues Budd, tend to see things from a partial equilibrium point of view. In many cases, this view is based around a zero-sum outcome – the benefit received by one party to an economic decision is offset by a negative impact on someone else. Looking at the big picture gives a more accurate understanding of how economies work and what the consequences of economic policy can be.
- **Economists know that sunk costs should not affect pricing decisions.**
  - Sunk costs are those costs have been spent and cannot be recovered or affected by future economic activity. What this means is that the spending on projects like the Olympic Games site in east London and the associated infrastructure will be largely academic. Arguments about how much it will cost to build a new rail link from London to the Channel coast to support the staging of the Games are simply not relevant. What will be important are the ongoing costs of actually running the line and the infrastructure that is built when the Games go ahead, as well as the cost of running the legacy that the Games will leave.
- **There is a difference between what economists know and what non-economists know.**
  - This can be summarized under the heading 'folk economics'. Folk economics is the intuitive understanding that untrained people have about how the economy operates. If you like, this can be seen as being a novice perspective as opposed to an expert one.

    Budd makes an interesting observation here. If you (as a non-physicist) were engaged in conversation with a physicist who tells you about string theory, you are unlikely to interrupt him or her and disagree with what they were telling you. An economist engaged in a discussion about obesity, for example, with a non economist would be far more likely to be questioned about the views being put forward. If I, as an economist, told you, a non-economist, that obesity was caused by the rise in poverty levels in countries, it is likely that there would be some disagreement with my view. In short, economists think in the subject, whereas non-economists do not!

are based on hypotheses that have been tested and observed and which appear to explain key behaviours. It is worth bearing the information in these two tables in mind as you read through the book.

Quick Quiz Why might economic advisors to the government disagree about a question of policy?

Economists as Decision Makers

It could be said that economics is the science of decision-making. The way that economists go about making decisions is a specific one. They will initially try to identify the problem or issue related to the decision, for example, will measures to cut greenhouse gas emissions be efficient or is it worth my while travelling 50 kilometres to redeem a voucher for €50 at a particular store?

The next stage is to look at the costs and benefits involved in the decision. These costs and benefits are not just the private costs and benefits to the individual concerned, however, they will also include the costs and benefits to third parties who are not directly involved in the actual decision. For example, cutting greenhouse gas emissions means that resources will have to be diverted to new ways of production or different ways of producing energy. The private costs will be those borne by the businesses that will have to implement measures to adhere to the limits placed upon them. The social costs might include the impact on local people of the construction of wind farms or new nuclear power stations. If I chose to make the 50-kilometre journey then I would incur travelling costs – petrol, vehicle depreciation and so on as well as the cost in terms of the time I have to give to make the journey. The social costs include the addition to possible road congestion that I add as well as the potential danger to other road users that my being on the road presents.

Having identified the costs and benefits, the economist then seeks to place a value on them in order to get some idea of the relationship between the costs and benefits of making the decision. In some cases, valuing costs and benefits can be easy; in the case of my shopping trip, the benefit is the €50 saved; the costs of petrol used on the journey are easy to calculate. Some costs and benefits are much more difficult to value. The loss of visual amenity for a resident living near a wind turbine or the value of the possible loss of life from a nuclear catastrophe at a power plant may be very difficult to value. Economists have devised ways in which these values can be estimated.

Once the sum of the costs and benefits are calculated, the decision then becomes clearer. If the cost outweighs the benefit then making the decision may be unwise but if the costs are less than the benefits then it may mean the decision is warranted. Policy makers may want to look at the extent to which the costs outweigh the benefit or the benefit outweighs the cost, however. If the benefit to me of going to redeem the voucher is €50 but the cost of making the trip to do so is valued at €49 then it may not be worth my while going, but if the cost were valued at just €10 then my decision may be more obvious.

Every day millions of decisions are made by individuals, businesses and governments. Whilst not every one of these decisions will be made using the exact processes outlined above, economists do make assumptions that humans do behave in a rational way and part of this rational behaviour involves weighing up the costs and benefits of an action.

The Economist as Mathematician

As your course in economics progresses you will have to develop skills in mathematics to help you understand some of the key concepts and methods that economists adopt. If you read academic economics journals you will see examples of how mathematics is used as a tool to help frame and explain hypotheses and theories. The appendix to this chapter provides a brief outline of some important points to learn about graphing. The website will provide more detailed information on the relevance of mathematics to key concepts you will encounter in this book.

LET'S GET GOING

The first two chapters of this book have introduced you to the ideas and methods of economics. We are now ready to get to work. In the next chapter we start learning in more detail the principles of economic behaviour and economic policy.

As you proceed through this book, you will be asked to draw on many of your intellectual skills. You might find it helpful to keep in mind some advice from the great John Maynard Keynes:

> The study of economics does not seem to require any specialised gifts of an unusually high order. Is it not...a very easy subject compared with the higher branches of philosophy or pure science? An easy subject, at which very few excel! The paradox finds its explanation, perhaps, in that the master-economist must possess a rare *combination* of gifts. He must be mathematician, historian, statesman, philosopher – in some degree. He must understand symbols and speak in words. He must contemplate the particular in terms of the general, and touch abstract and concrete in the same flight of thought. He must study the present in the light of the past for the purposes of the future. No part of man's nature or his institutions must lie entirely outside his regard. He must be purposeful and disinterested in a simultaneous mood; as aloof and incorruptible as an artist, yet sometimes as near the earth as a politician.

It is a tall order. But with practice you will become more and more accustomed to thinking like an economist.

SUMMARY

- Economists try to address their subject with a scientist's objectivity. Like all scientists, they make appropriate assumptions and build simplified models in order to understand the world around them. Two simple economic models are the circular-flow diagram and the production possibilities frontier.
- The field of economics is divided into two subfields: microeconomics and macroeconomics. Microeconomists study decision-making by households and firms and the interaction among households and firms in the marketplace. Macroeconomists study the forces and trends that affect the economy as a whole.
- A positive statement is an assertion about how the world *is.* A normative statement is an assertion about how the world *ought to be.* When economists make normative statements, they are acting more as policy advisors than scientists.
- Economists who advise policy makers offer conflicting advice either because of differences in scientific judgements or because of differences in values. At other times, economists are united in the advice they offer, but policy makers may choose to ignore it.

KEY CONCEPTS

circular-flow diagram, p. 27
economy, p. 27
production possibilities frontier, p. 28
microeconomics, p. 31
macroeconomics, p. 31
positive statements, p. 32
normative statements, p. 32

QUESTIONS FOR REVIEW

1. How is economics like a science?
2. Why do economists make assumptions?
3. Should an economic model describe reality exactly?
4. Draw and explain a production possibilities frontier for an economy that produces olive oil and milk. What happens to this frontier if disease kills half of the economy's cow population?
5. Use a production possibilities frontier to describe the idea of 'efficiency'.
6. What are the two subfields into which economics is divided? Explain what each subfield studies.
7. What is the difference between a positive and a normative statement? Give an example of each.
8. Why do economists sometimes offer conflicting advice to policy makers?

PROBLEMS AND APPLICATIONS

1. Describe some unusual language used in one of the other fields that you are studying or have studied besides economics. Why are these special terms useful?
2. One common assumption in economics is that the products of different firms in the same industry are indistinguishable. For each of the following industries, discuss whether this is a reasonable assumption.
   a. steel
   b. novels
   c. wheat
   d. fast food.
3. Draw a circular-flow diagram. Identify the parts of the model that correspond to the flow of goods and services and the flow of euros for each of the following activities.
   a. Sam pays a shopkeeper €1 for a litre of milk.
   b. Georgia earns €4.50 per hour working at a fast food restaurant.
   c. Millie spends €7 to see a film.
   d. Owen earns €10 000 from his 10 per cent ownership of Pan-European Industrial.
4. Imagine a society that produces military goods and consumer goods, which we'll call 'guns' and 'butter'.
   a. Draw a production possibilities frontier for guns and butter. Explain why it most likely has a bowed-out shape.
   b. Show a point that is impossible for the economy to achieve. Show a point that is feasible but inefficient.
   c. Imagine that the society has two political parties, called the Hawks (who want a strong military) and the Doves (who want a smaller military sector). Show a point on your production possibilities frontier that the Hawks might choose and a point the Doves might choose.
   d. Imagine that an aggressive neighbouring country reduces the size of its military sector. As a result, both the Hawks and the Doves reduce their desired production of guns by the same amount. Which party would get the bigger 'peace dividend', measured by the increase in butter production? Explain.
5. The first principle of economics discussed in Chapter 1 is that people face trade-offs. Use a production possibilities frontier to illustrate society's trade-off between a clean environment and the quantity of industrial output. What do you suppose determines the shape and position of the frontier? Show what happens to the frontier if engineers develop an automobile engine with almost no emissions.
6. Classify the following topics as relating to microeconomics or macroeconomics.
   a. A family's decision about how much income to save.
   b. The effect of government regulations on car emissions.
   c. The impact of higher national saving on economic growth.
   d. A firm's decision about how many workers to recruit.
   e. The relationship between the inflation rate and changes in the quantity of money.
7. Classify each of the following statements as positive or normative. Explain.
   a. Society faces a short-run trade-off between inflation and unemployment.
   b. A reduction in the rate of growth of money will reduce the rate of inflation.

c. The European Central Bank should reduce the rate of growth of money.
d. Society ought to require welfare recipients to look for jobs.
e. Lower tax rates encourage more work and more saving.

8. Classify each of the statements in Table 2.2 as positive, normative or ambiguous. Explain.
9. If you were prime minister, would you be more interested in your economic advisors' positive views or their normative views? Why?
10. The *Bank of England Quarterly Bulletin* contains statistical information about the UK economy as well as analysis of current policy issues by the Bank's economic staff. Find a recent copy of this bulletin and read a chapter about an issue that interests you. Summarize the issue discussed and describe the Bank's recommended policy.
11. Who is the current President of the European Central Bank? Who is the current Governor of the Bank of England? Who is the current UK Chancellor of the Exchequer?
12. Would you expect economists to disagree less about public policy as time goes on? Why or why not? Can their differences be completely eliminated? Why or why not?
13. Look up one of the websites listed in Table 2.1. What recent economic trends or issues are addressed there? For further resources, visit www.cengage.co.uk/mankiw_taylor_second

For further resources, visit www.cengage.com/mankiw_taylor2

APPENDIX Graphing: A Brief Review

Many of the concepts that economists study can be expressed with numbers – the price of bananas, the quantity of bananas sold, the cost of growing bananas and so on. Often these economic variables are related to one another. When the price of bananas rises, people buy fewer bananas. One way of expressing the relationships among variables is with graphs.

Graphs serve two purposes. First, when developing economic theories, graphs offer a way to express visually ideas that might be less clear if described with equations or words. Secondly, when analysing economic data, graphs provide a way of finding how variables are in fact related in the world. Whether we are working with theory or with data, graphs provide a lens through which a recognizable forest emerges from a multitude of trees.

Numerical information can be expressed graphically in many ways, just as a thought can be expressed in words in many ways. A good writer chooses words that will make an argument clear, a description pleasing or a scene dramatic. An effective economist chooses the type of graph that best suits the purpose at hand.

In this appendix we discuss how economists use graphs to study the mathematical relationships among variables. We also discuss some of the pitfalls that can arise in the use of graphical methods.

FIGURE 2A.1

Types of Graph

The pie chart in panel (a) shows how UK government expenditure was divided between the major spending categories in 2008 to 2009. The bar graph in panel (b) compares the average income in four countries in 2007. The time-series graph in panel (c) shows the EU unemployment rate for all 27 countries from November 2008 to October 2009.

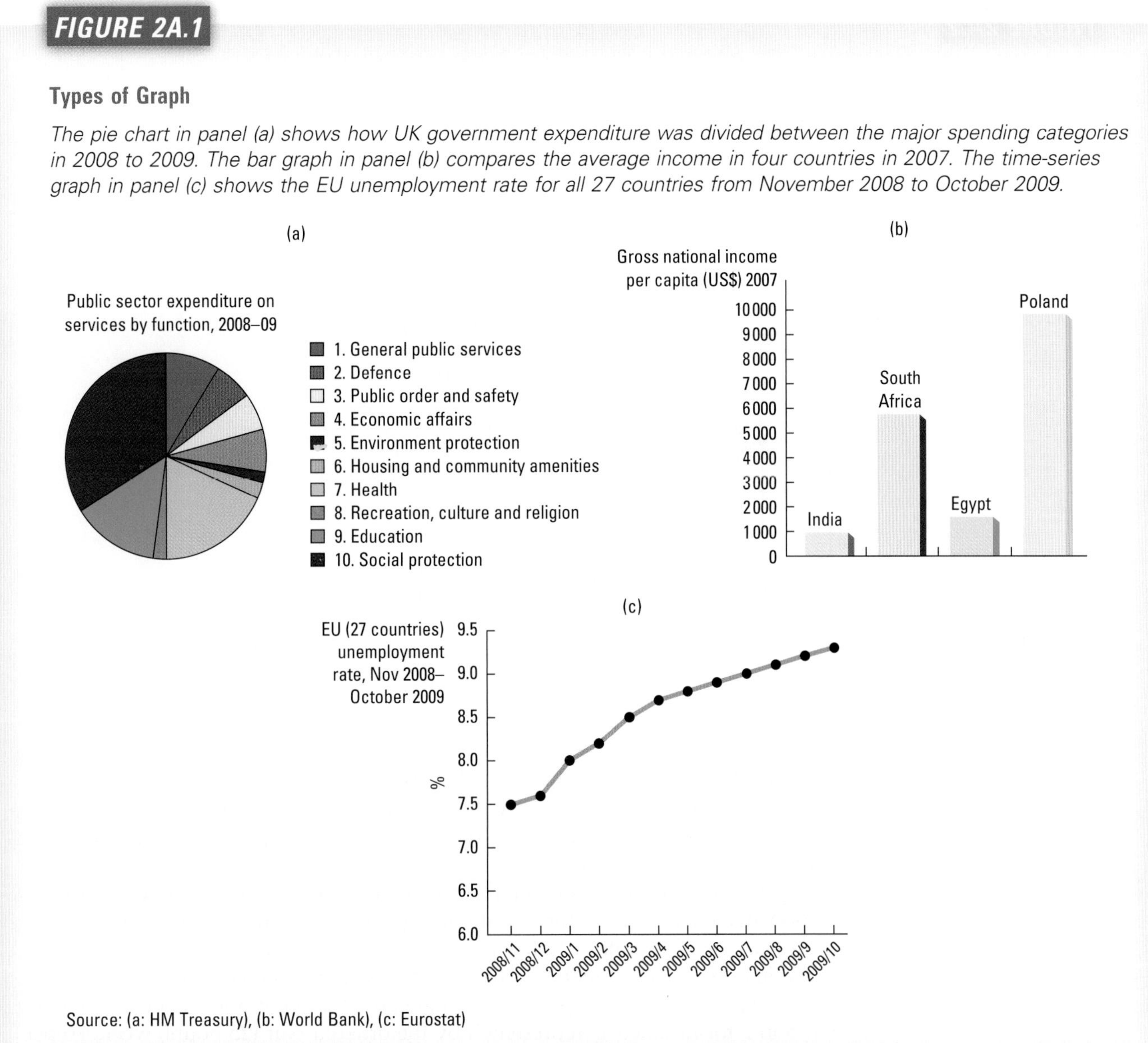

Source: (a: HM Treasury), (b: World Bank), (c: Eurostat)

Graphs of a Single Variable

Three common graphs are shown in Figure 2A.1. The *pie chart* in panel (a) shows how total government expenditure in the UK in 2008–2009 was divided among the major categories such as social protection the National Health Service, education, defence and so on. A slice of the pie represents each category's share of total government expenditure. The *bar graph* in panel (b) compares income per person for four countries in 2007, each expressed in US dollars. The height of each bar represents the average income in each country. The *time-series graph* in panel (c) traces the course of unemployment in the 27 countries of the EU over a year. The height of the line shows the percentage of the workforce that was out of work in each year. You have probably seen similar graphs presented in newspapers and magazines.

Graphs of Two Variables: The Coordinate System

Although the three graphs in Figure 2A.1 are useful in showing how a variable changes over time or across individuals, such graphs are limited in how much

FIGURE 2A.2

Using the Coordinate System

Final examination mark is measured on the vertical axis and study time on the horizontal axis. Albert E., Alfred E. and the other students on their course are represented by various points. We can see from the graph that students who study more tend to get higher marks.

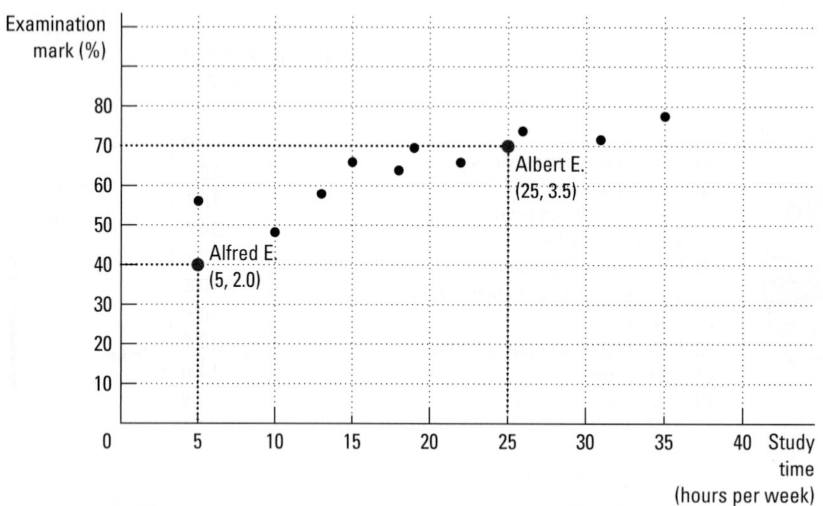

they can tell us. These graphs display information only on a single variable. Economists are often concerned with the relationships between variables. Thus, they need to be able to display two variables on a single graph. The *coordinate system* makes this possible.

Suppose you want to examine the relationship between study time and examination marks. For each student attending your economics lectures, you could record a pair of numbers: hours per week spent studying and marks obtained in the final course examination. These numbers could then be placed in parentheses as an *ordered pair* and appear as a single point on the graph. Albert E. ('Young Einstein'), for instance, is represented by the ordered pair (25 hours/week, 70 per cent examination mark), while his classmate Alfred E. ('What, me worry?') is represented by the ordered pair (5 hours/week, 40 per cent examination mark).

We can graph these ordered pairs on a two-dimensional grid. The first number in each ordered pair, called the *x-coordinate,* tells us the horizontal location of the point. The second number, called the *y-coordinate,* tells us the vertical location of the point. The point with both an x-coordinate and a y-coordinate of zero is known as the *origin.* The two coordinates in the ordered pair tell us where the point is located in relation to the origin: x units to the right of the origin and y units above it.

Figure 2A.2 graphs examination marks against study time for Albert E., Alfred E. and the rest of the students who attended the course. This type of graph is called a *scatterplot* because it plots scattered points. Looking at this graph, we immediately notice that points farther to the right (indicating more study time) also tend to be higher (indicating a better examination result). Because study time and examination mark typically move in the same direction, we say that these two variables have a *positive correlation.* By contrast, if we were to graph time spent partying per week and examination marks, we would probably find that higher party time is associated with lower marks; because these variables typically move in opposite directions, we would call this a *negative correlation.* In either case, the coordinate system makes the correlation between the two variables easy to see.

Curves in the Coordinate System

Students who study more do tend to get higher marks, but other factors also influence a student's marks. Previous preparation is an important factor, for instance, as are talent, attention from teachers and even eating a good breakfast. A scatterplot like Figure 2A.2 does not attempt to isolate the effect that study has on grades from the effects of other variables. Often, however, economists prefer looking at how one variable affects another while holding everything else constant.

To see how this is done, let's consider one of the most important graphs in economics – the *demand curve.* The demand curve traces out the effect of a good's price on the quantity of the good consumers want to buy. Before showing a demand curve, however, consider Table 2A.1, which shows how the number of novels that Pascale buys depends on her income and on the price of novels. When novels are cheap, Pascale buys them in large quantities. As they become more expensive, she borrows books from the library instead of buying them or chooses to go to the cinema instead of reading. Similarly, at any given price, Pascale buys more novels when she has a higher income. That is, when her income increases, she spends part of the additional income on novels and part on other goods.

We now have three variables – the price of novels, income and the number of novels purchased – which is more than we can represent in two dimensions. To put the information from Table 2A.1 in graphical form, we need to hold one of the three variables constant and trace out the relationship between the other two. Because the demand curve represents the relationship between price and quantity demanded, we hold Pascale's income constant and show how the number of novels she buys varies with the price of novels.

Suppose that Pascale's income is €30 000 per year. If we place the number of novels Pascale purchases on the x-axis and the price of novels on they y-axis, we can graphically represent the middle column of Table 2A.1. When the points that represent these entries from the table – (5 novels, €10), (9 novels, €9) and so

TABLE 2A.1

Novels Purchased by Pascale

This table shows the number of novels Pascale buys at various incomes and prices. For any given level of income, the data on price and quantity demanded can be graphed to produce Pascale's demand curve for novels, as shown in Figures 2A.3 and 2A.4.

	Income		
Price	**€20 000**	**€30 000**	**€40 000**
€10	*2 novels*	*5 novels*	*8 novels*
€9	*6*	*9*	*12*
€8	*10*	*13*	*16*
€7	*14*	*17*	*20*
€6	*18*	*21*	*24*
€5	*22*	*25*	*28*
	Demand curve, D_3	*Demand curve,* D_1	*Demand curve,* D_2

FIGURE 2A.3

Demand Curve

The line D_1 shows how Pascale's purchases of novels depend on the price of novels when her income is held constant. Because the price and the quantity demanded are negatively related, the demand curve slopes downward.

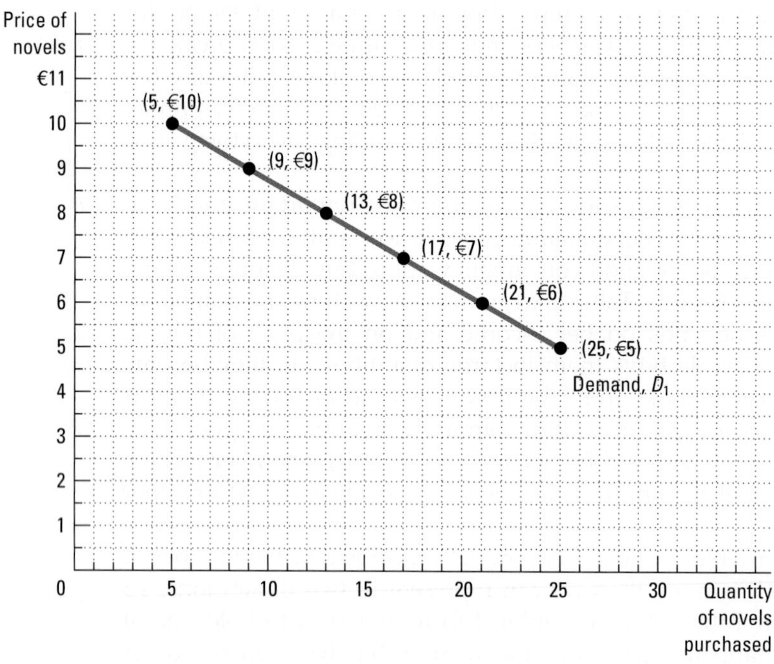

on – are connected, they form a line. This line, pictured in Figure 2A.3, is known as Pascale's demand curve for novels; it tells us how many novels Pascale purchases at any given price. The demand curve is downward sloping, indicating that a higher price reduces the quantity of novels demanded. Because the quantity of novels demanded and the price move in opposite directions, we say that the two variables are *negatively or inversely related.* (Conversely, when two variables move in the same direction, the curve relating them is upward sloping, and we say the variables are *positively related.*)

Now suppose that Pascale's income rises to €40 000 per year. At any given price, Pascale will purchase more novels than she did at her previous level of income. Just as earlier we drew Pascale's demand curve for novels using the entries from the middle column of Table 2A.1, we now draw a new demand curve using the entries from the right-hand column of the table. This new demand curve (curve D_2) is pictured alongside the old one (curve D_1) in Figure 2A.4; the new curve is a similar line drawn farther to the right. We therefore say that Pascale's demand curve for novels *shifts* to the right when her income increases. Likewise, if Pascale's income were to fall to €20 000 per year, she would buy fewer novels at any given price and her demand curve would shift to the left (to curve D_3).

In economics, it is important to distinguish between *movements along a curve* and *shifts of a curve.* As we can see from Figure 2A.3, if Pascale earns €30 000 per year and novels are priced at €8 apiece, she will purchase 13 novels per year. If the price of novels falls to €7, Pascale will increase her purchases of novels to 17 per year. The demand curve, however, stays fixed in the same

FIGURE 2A.4

Shifting Demand Curves

The location of Pascale's demand curve for novels depends on how much income she earns. The more she earns, the more novels she will purchase at any given price, and the further to the right her demand curve will lie. Curve D_1 represents Pascale's original demand curve when her income is €30 000 per year. If her income rises to €40 000 per year, her demand curve shifts to D_2. If her income falls to €20 000 per year, her demand curve shifts to D_3.

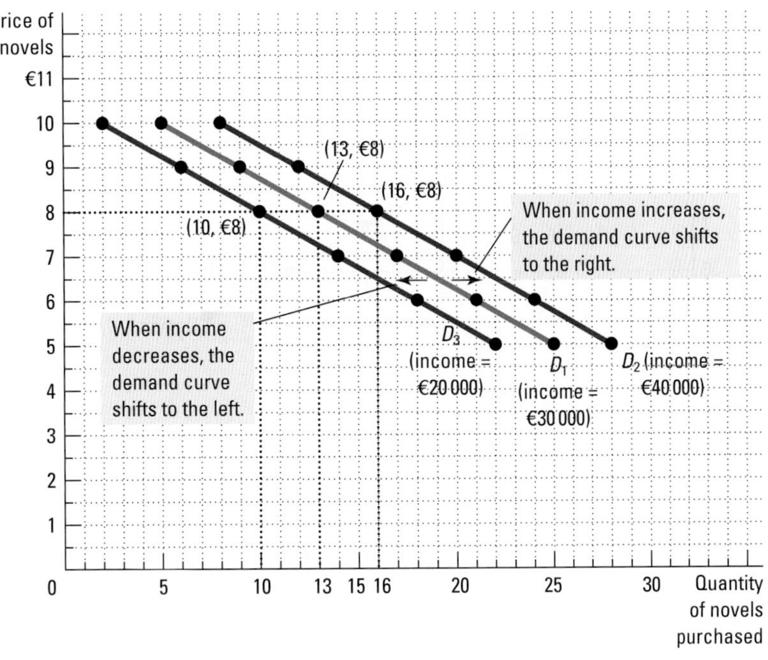

place. Pascale still buys the same number of novels *at each price,* but as the price falls she moves along her demand curve from left to right. By contrast, if the price of novels remains fixed at €8 but her income rises to €40 000, Pascale increases her purchases of novels from 13 to 16 per year. Because Pascale buys more novels *at each price,* her demand curve shifts out, as shown in Figure 2A.4.

There is a simple way to tell when it is necessary to shift a curve. When a variable that is not named on either axis changes, the curve shifts. Income is on neither the *x*-axis nor the *y*-axis of the graph, so when Pascale's income changes, her demand curve must shift. Any change that affects Pascale's purchasing habits, besides a change in the price of novels, will result in a shift in her demand curve. If, for instance, the public library closes and Pascale must buy all the books she wants to read, she will demand more novels at each price, and her demand curve will shift to the right. Or, if the price of going to the cinema falls and Pascale spends more time at the movies and less time reading, she will demand fewer novels at each price, and her demand curve will shift to the left. By contrast, when a variable on an axis of the graph changes, the curve does not shift. We read the change as a movement along the curve.

Slope

One question we might want to ask about Pascale is how much her purchasing habits respond to price. Look at the demand curve pictured in Figure 2A.5. If this curve is very steep, Pascale purchases nearly the same number of novels regardless of whether they are cheap or expensive. If this curve is much flatter, Pascale

FIGURE 2A.5

Calculating the Slope of a Line

To calculate the slope of the demand curve, we can look at the changes in the x*- and* y*-coordinates as we move from the point (21 novels, €6) to the point (13 novels, €8). The slope of the line is the ratio of the change in the* y*-coordinate (−2) to the change in the* x*-coordinate (+8), which equals −1/4.*

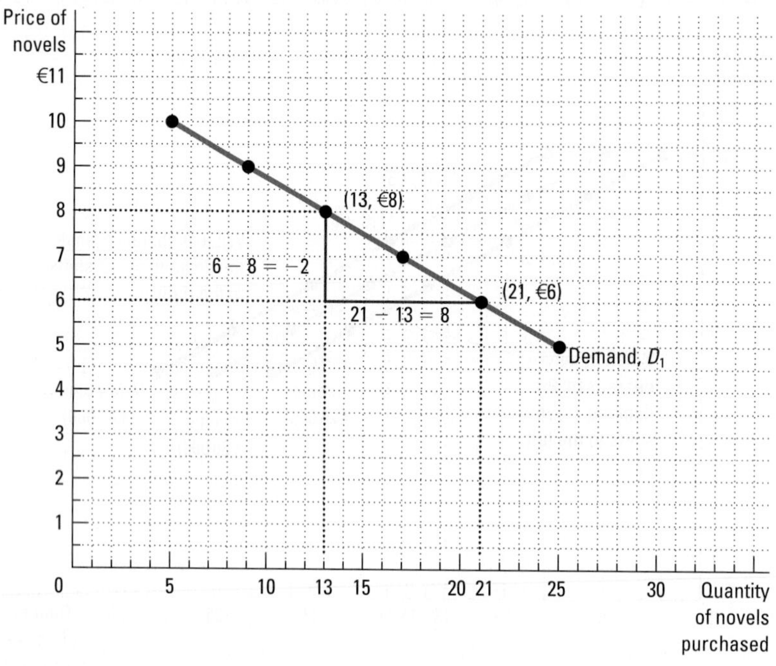

purchases many fewer novels when the price rises. To answer questions about how much one variable responds to changes in another variable, we can use the concept of *slope*.

The slope of a line is the ratio of the vertical distance covered to the horizontal distance covered as we move along the line. This definition is usually written out in mathematical symbols as follows:

$$\text{slope} = \frac{\Delta y}{\Delta x}$$

where the Greek letter Δ (delta) stands for the change in a variable. In other words, the slope of a line is equal to the 'rise' (change in y) divided by the 'run' (change in x). The slope will be a small positive number for a fairly flat upward sloping line, a large positive number for a steep upward sloping line and a negative number for a downward sloping line. A horizontal line has a slope of zero because in this case the y-variable never changes; a vertical line is said to have an infinite slope because the y-variable can take any value without the x-variable changing at all.

What is the slope of Pascale's demand curve for novels? First of all, because the curve slopes down, we know the slope will be negative. To calculate a numerical value for the slope, we must choose two points on the line. With Pascale's income at €30 000, she will purchase 21 novels at a price of €6 or 13 novels at a price of €8. When we apply the slope formula, we are concerned with the change between these two points; in other words, we are concerned with the difference between them, which lets us know that we will have to subtract one set of values from the other, as follows:

$$\text{Slope} = \frac{\Delta y}{\Delta x} = \frac{\text{first } y\text{-coordinate} - \text{second } y\text{-coordinate}}{\text{first } x\text{-coordinate} - \text{second } x\text{-coordinate}} = \frac{6-8}{21-13} = -\frac{2}{8} = -\frac{1}{4}$$

Figure 2A.5 shows graphically how this calculation works. Try computing the slope of Pascale's demand curve using two different points. You should get exactly the same result, –1/4. One of the properties of a straight line is that it has the same slope everywhere. This is not true of other types of curves, which are steeper in some places than in others.

The slope of Pascale's demand curve tells us something about how responsive her purchases are to changes in the price. A small slope (a number close to zero) means that Pascale's demand curve is relatively flat; in this case, she adjusts the number of novels she buys substantially in response to a price change. A larger slope (a number further from zero) means that Pascale's demand curve is relatively steep; in this case, she adjusts the number of novels she buys only slightly in response to a price change.

Cause and Effect

Economists often use graphs to advance an argument about how the economy works. In other words, they use graphs to argue about how one set of events *causes* another set of events. With a graph like the demand curve, there is no doubt about cause and effect. Because we are varying price and holding all other variables constant, we know that changes in the price of novels cause changes in the quantity Pascale demands. Remember, however, that our demand curve came from a hypothetical example. When graphing data from the real world, it is often more difficult to establish how one variable affects another.

The first problem is that it is difficult to hold everything else constant when measuring how one variable affects another. If we are not able to hold variables constant, we might decide that one variable on our graph is causing changes in the other variable when actually those changes are caused by a third *omitted variable* not pictured on the graph. Even if we have identified the correct two variables to look at, we might run into a second problem – *reverse causality*. In other words, we might decide that A causes B when in fact B causes A. The omitted variable and reverse causality traps require us to proceed with caution when using graphs to draw conclusions about causes and effects.

Omitted Variables To see how omitting a variable can lead to a deceptive graph, let's consider an example. Imagine that the government, spurred by public concern about the large number of deaths from cancer, commissions an exhaustive study from Big Brother Statistical Services. Big Brother examines many of the items found in people's homes to see which of them are associated with the risk of cancer. Big Brother reports a strong relationship between two variables: the number of cigarette lighters that a household owns and the probability that someone in the household will develop cancer. Figure 2A.6 shows this relationship.

What should we make of this result? Big Brother advises a quick policy response. It recommends that the government discourages the ownership of cigarette lighters by taxing their sale. It also recommends that the government requires warning labels: 'Big Brother has determined that this lighter is dangerous to your health.'

In judging the validity of Big Brother's analysis, one question is paramount: has Big Brother held constant every relevant variable except the one under

FIGURE 2A.6

Graph With an Omitted Variable

The upward sloping curve shows that members of households with more cigarette lighters are more likely to develop cancer. Yet we should not conclude that ownership of lighters causes cancer, because the graph does not take into account the number of cigarettes smoked.

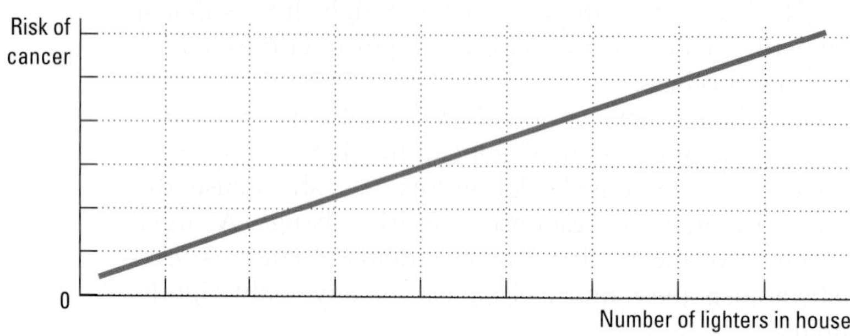

consideration? If the answer is no, the results are suspect. An easy explanation for Figure 2A.6 is that people who own more cigarette lighters are more likely to smoke cigarettes and that cigarettes, not lighters, cause cancer. If Figure 2A.6 does not hold constant the amount of smoking, it does not tell us the true effect of owning a cigarette lighter.

This story illustrates an important principle: when you see a graph being used to support an argument about cause and effect, it is important to ask whether the movements of an omitted variable could explain the results you see.

Reverse Causality Economists can also make mistakes about causality by misreading its direction. To see how this is possible, suppose the Association of European Anarchists commissions a study of crime in Eurovia and arrives at Figure 2A.7, which plots the number of violent crimes per 1 000 people in major Eurovian cities against the number of police officers per 1 000 people. The anarchists note the curve's upward slope and argue that because police increase rather than decrease the amount of urban violence, law enforcement should be abolished.

If we could run a controlled experiment, we would avoid the danger of reverse causality. To run an experiment, we would set the number of police officers in different cities randomly and then examine the correlation between police and crime. Figure 2A.7, however, is not based on such an experiment. We simply observe that more dangerous cities have more police officers. The explanation for this may be that more dangerous cities hire more police. In other words, rather than police causing crime, crime may cause police. Nothing in the graph itself allows us to establish the direction of causality.

It might seem that an easy way to determine the direction of causality is to examine which variable moves first. If we see crime increase and then the police force expand, we reach one conclusion. If we see the police force expand and then crime increase, we reach the other. Yet there is also a flaw with this approach: often people change their behaviour not in response to a change in their present conditions but in response to a change in their *expectations* of future conditions. A city that expects a major crime wave in the future, for instance, might well hire more police now. This problem is even easier to see in the case

FIGURE 2A.7

Graph Suggesting Reverse Causality

The upward sloping curve shows that Eurovian cities with a higher concentration of police are more dangerous. Yet the graph does not tell us whether police cause crime or crime-plagued cities hire more police.

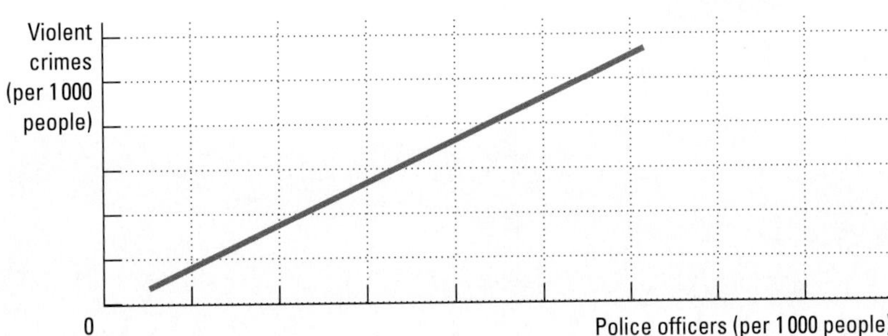

of babies and baby cots. Couples often buy a baby cot in anticipation of the birth of a child. The cot comes before the baby, but we wouldn't want to conclude that the sale of cots causes the population to grow!

There is no complete set of rules that says when it is appropriate to draw causal conclusions from graphs. Yet just keeping in mind that cigarette lighters don't cause cancer (omitted variable) and baby cots do not cause larger families (reverse causality) will keep you from falling for many faulty economic arguments.

3 INTERDEPENDENCE AND THE GAINS FROM TRADE

Consider your typical day. You wake up in the morning and you make yourself some coffee from beans grown in Brazil, or tea from leaves grown in Sri Lanka. Over breakfast, you listen to a radio programme on your radio set made in Japan. You get dressed in clothes manufactured in Thailand. You drive to the university in a car made of parts manufactured in more than a dozen countries around the world. Then you open up your economics textbook written by two authors of whom one lives in the USA and the other lives in England, published by a company located in Hampshire and printed on paper made from trees grown in Finland.

Every day you rely on many people from around the world, most of whom you do not know, to provide you with the goods and services that you enjoy. Such interdependence is possible because people trade with one another. Those people who provide you with goods and services are not acting out of generosity or concern for your welfare. Nor is some government or supra-governmental agency directing them to make products you want and to give them to you. Instead, people provide you and other consumers with the goods and services they produce because they get something in return.

In subsequent chapters we will examine how our economy coordinates the activities of millions of people with varying tastes and abilities. As a starting point for this analysis, here we consider the reasons for economic interdependence. One of the *Ten Principles of Economics* highlighted in Chapter 1 is that trade can make everyone better off. This principle explains why people trade with their neighbours and why nations trade with other nations. In this chapter we examine this principle more closely. What exactly do people gain when they trade with one another? Why do people choose to become interdependent?

A PARABLE FOR THE MODERN ECONOMY

To understand why people choose to depend on others for goods and services and how this choice improves their lives, let's look at a simple economy. Imagine that there are two goods in the world – beef and potatoes. And there are two people in the world – a cattle farmer named Fabia and a market gardener named Marius – each of whom would like to eat both beef and potatoes.

The gains from trade are most obvious if the cattle farmer can produce only meat and the market gardener can produce only potatoes. In one scenario, the farmer and the gardener could choose to have nothing to do with each other. But after several months of eating beef roasted, boiled, fried and grilled, the cattle farmer might decide that self-sufficiency is not all he expected. The market gardener, who has been eating potatoes mashed, fried and baked, would most likely agree. It is easy to see that trade would allow them to enjoy greater variety: each could then have steak and chips.

Although this scene illustrates most simply how everyone can benefit from trade, the gains would be similar if the farmer and the gardener were each capable of producing the other good, but only at great cost. Suppose, for example, that the market gardener is able to rear cattle and produce meat, but that he is not very good at it. Similarly, suppose that the cattle farmer is able to grow potatoes, but that her land is not very well suited for it. In this case, it is easy to see that the gardener and the farmer can each benefit by specializing in what he or she does best and then trading with the other.

The gains from trade are less obvious, however, when one person is better at producing *every* good. For example, suppose that the cattle farmer is better at rearing cattle *and* better at growing potatoes than the market gardener. In this case, should the farmer or gardener choose to remain self-sufficient, or is there still reason for them to trade with each other? To answer this question, we need to look more closely at the factors that affect such a decision.

Production Possibilities

Suppose that the gardener and the farmer each work eight hours a day six days a week (a working week of 48 hours) and take Sunday off. They can spend their time growing potatoes, rearing cattle, or a combination of the two. Table 3.1 shows the amount of time each person takes to produce 1 kilogram of each good. The gardener can produce 1 kilogram of meat in 6 hours and 1 kilogram of potatoes in an hour and a half. The farmer, who is more productive in both

TABLE 3.1

The Production Opportunities of the Gardener and the Farmer

	Time needed to make 1 kg of:		Amount of meat or potatoes produced in 48 hours	
	Meat	Potatoes	Meat	Potatoes
Gardener	6 hrs/kg	1.5 hrs/kg	8 kg	32 kg
Farmer	2 hrs/kg	1 hr/kg	24 kg	48 kg

FIGURE 3.1

The Production Possibilities Frontier

Panel (a) shows the combinations of meat and potatoes that the gardener can produce. Panel (b) shows the combinations of meat and potatoes that the farmer can produce. Both production possibilities frontiers are derived from Table 3.1 and the assumption that the gardener and farmer each work 8 hours a day.

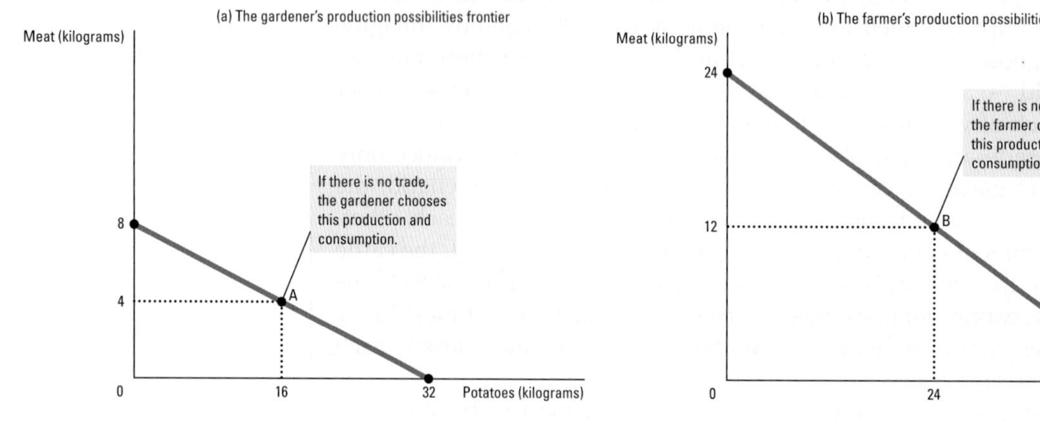

activities, can produce a kilogram of meat in 2 hours and a kilogram of potatoes in 1 hour. The last columns in Table 3.1 show the amounts of meat or potatoes the gardener and farmer can produce in a 48-hour working week, producing only that good.

Panel (a) of Figure 3.1 illustrates the amounts of meat and potatoes that the gardener can produce. If the gardener devotes all 48 hours of his time to potatoes, he produces 32 kilograms of potatoes (measured on the horizontal axis) and no meat. If he devotes all his time to meat, he produces 8 kilograms of meat (measured on the vertical axis) and no potatoes. If the gardener divides his time equally between the two activities, spending 24 hours a week on each, he produces 16 kilograms of potatoes and 4 kilograms of meat. The figure shows these three possible outcomes and all others in between.

This graph is the gardener's production possibilities frontier. As we discussed in Chapter 2, a production possibilities frontier shows the various mixes of output that an economy, or in this case an individual, can produce given existing resources. It illustrates one of the *Ten Principles of Economics* in Chapter 1: people face trade-offs. Here the gardener faces a trade-off between producing meat and producing potatoes. You may recall that the production possibilities frontier in Chapter 2 was drawn bowed out; in that case, the trade-off between the two goods depended on the amounts being produced. Here, however, the gardener's technology for producing meat and potatoes (as summarized in Table 3.1) allows him to switch between one good and the other at a constant rate. If the gardener devotes an extra hour to producing meat he sacrifices potato production. In Chapter 2 we looked at how to calculate the slope of a straight line. In this case increasing meat production by 1 kilogram leads to a sacrifice of 4 kilograms of potatoes. The Δy is 1 kilogram and the Δx is 4 units. The slope is 0.25 which indicates the rate at which potatoes are sacrificed for more meat as more time is devoted to meat production. In this case, the production possibilities frontier is a straight line and so the trade-off is a constant rate. Every extra kilogram of meat produced results in a sacrifice of 4 kilograms of potatoes. The converse of this is that if the gardener switched from meat production to potato production, then every additional 1 kilogram of potatoes produced would involve a trade-off of ¼ kilogram of meat.

Panel (b) of Figure 3.1 shows the production possibilities frontier for the farmer. If the farmer devotes all 48 hours of her working week to potatoes, she produces 48 kilograms of potatoes and no meat. If she devotes all of her time to meat production, she produces 24 kilograms of meat and no potatoes. If the farmer divides her time equally, spending 24 hours a week on each activity, she produces 24 kilograms of potatoes and 12 kilograms of meat. Once again, the production possibilities frontier shows all the possible outcomes. In this case, reducing meat production by one unit means that potato production can increase by 2 units. The slope of this production possibilities frontier is, therefore, 0.5. Conversely, if she devotes more time to producing potatoes then the rate of sacrifice of meat will be 2 kilograms of meat for every 1 kilogram of potatoes.

If the gardener and farmer choose to be self-sufficient, rather than trade with each other, then each consumes exactly what he or she produces. In this case, the production possibilities frontier is also the consumption possibilities frontier. That is, without trade, Figure 3.1 shows the possible combinations of meat and potatoes that the gardener and farmer can each consume.

Although these production possibilities frontiers are useful in showing the trade-offs that the gardener and farmer face, they do not tell us what the gardener and farmer will actually choose to do. To determine their choices, we need to know the tastes of the gardener and the farmer. Let's suppose they choose the combinations identified by points A and B in Figure 3.1: the gardener produces and consumes 16 kilograms of potatoes and 4 kilograms of meat, while the farmer produces and consumes 24 kilograms of potatoes and 12 kilograms of meat.

Specialization and Trade

After several years of feeding her family on combination B, the farmer gets an idea and she goes to talk to the gardener:

FARMER: Marius, have I got a deal for you! I know how to improve life for both of us. I think you should stop producing meat altogether and devote all your time to growing potatoes. According to my calculations, if you devote all of your working week to growing potatoes, you'll produce 32 kilograms of potatoes. If you give me 15 of those 32 kilograms, I'll give you 5 kilograms of meat in return. You will have 17 kilograms of potatoes left to enjoy and also 5 kilograms of meat every week, instead of the 16 kilograms of potatoes and 4 kilograms of meat you now make do with. If you go along with my plan, you'll have more of *both* foods. [To illustrate her point, the farmer shows the gardener panel (a) of Figure 3.2.]

GARDENER: *(sounding sceptical)* That seems like a good deal for me, Fabia, but I don't understand why you are offering it. If the deal is so good for me, it can't be good for you too.

FARMER: Oh, but it is, Marius! Suppose I spend 12 hours a week growing potatoes and 36 hours rearing cattle. Then I can produce 12 kilograms of potatoes and 18 kilograms of meat. You will give me 15 kilograms of your potatoes in exchange for the 5 kilograms of my meat. This means I end up with 27 kilograms of potatoes and 13 kilograms of meat. So I will also be able to consume more of both foods than I do now. [She points out panel (b) of Figure 3.2.]

FIGURE 3.2

How Trade Expands the Set of Consumption Opportunities

The proposed trade between the gardener and the farmer offers each of them a combination of meat and potatoes that would be impossible in the absence of trade. In panel (a), the gardener consumes at point A rather than point A. In panel (b), the farmer consumes at point B* rather than point B. Trade allows each to consume more meat and more potatoes.*

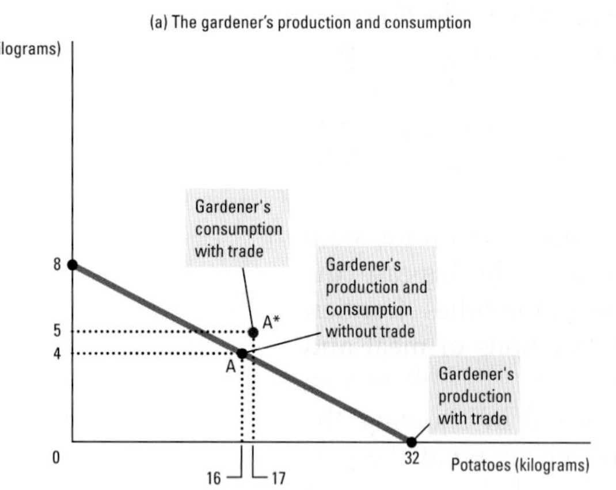

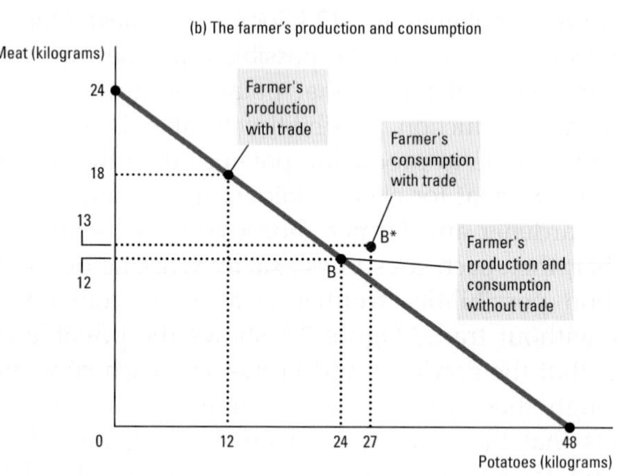

TABLE 3.2

The Gains from Trade: A Summary

	Gardener		Farmer	
	Meat	**Potatoes**	**Meat**	**Potatoes**
Without trade:				
Production and consumption	4 kg	16 kg	12 kg	24 kg
With trade:				
Production	0 kg	32 kg	18 kg	12 kg
Trade	Gets 5 kg	Gives 15 kg	Gives 5 kg	Gets 15 kg
Consumption	5 kg	17 kg	13 kg	27 kg
Gains from trade:				
Increase in consumption	+1 kg	+1 kg	+1 kg	+3 kg

GARDENER: I don't know, Fabia.... This sounds too good to be true.

FARMER: It's really not as complicated as it seems at first. Here – I've summarized my proposal for you in a simple table. [The farmer hands the gardener a copy of Table 3.2.]

GARDENER: *(after pausing to study the table)* These calculations seem correct, but I am puzzled. How can this deal make us both better off?

FARMER: We can both benefit because trade allows each of us to specialize in doing what we do best. You will spend more time growing potatoes and less time rearing cattle. I will spend more time rearing cattle and less time growing potatoes. As a result of specialization and trade, each of us can consume more meat and more potatoes without working any more hours.

Quick Quiz Draw an example of a production possibilities frontier for Hasani, who is stranded on an island after a shipwreck and spends his time gathering coconuts and catching fish. Does this frontier limit Hasani's consumption of coconuts and fish if he lives by himself? Does he face the same limits if he can trade with natives on the island?

THE PRINCIPLE OF COMPARATIVE ADVANTAGE

The farmer's explanation of the gains from trade, though correct, poses a puzzle: if the farmer is better at both rearing cattle and growing potatoes, how can the gardener ever specialize in doing what he does best? The gardener doesn't seem to do anything best. To solve this puzzle, we need to look at the principle of *comparative advantage.*

As a first step in developing this principle, consider the following question: in our example, who can produce potatoes at lower cost – the gardener or the farmer? There are two possible answers, and in these two answers lie the solution to our puzzle and the key to understanding the gains from trade. The slope of the production possibilities frontier discussed above will help us to solve the puzzle.

Absolute Advantage

One way to answer the question about the cost of producing potatoes is to compare the inputs required by the two producers. Economists use the term **absolute advantage** when comparing the productivity of one person, firm or nation to that of another. The producer that requires a smaller quantity of inputs to produce a good is said to have an absolute advantage in producing that good.

absolute advantage
the comparison among producers of a good according to their productivity

In our example, the farmer has an absolute advantage both in producing meat and in producing potatoes, because she requires less time than the gardener to produce a unit of either good. The farmer needs to input only 2 hours in order to produce a kilogram of meat, whereas the gardener needs 6 hours. Similarly, the farmer needs only 1 hour to produce a kilogram of potatoes, whereas the gardener needs 1.5 hours. Based on this information, we can conclude that the farmer has the lower cost of producing potatoes, if we measure cost in terms of the quantity of inputs.

Opportunity Cost and Comparative Advantage

There is another way to look at the cost of producing potatoes. Rather than comparing inputs required, we can compare the opportunity costs. Recall from Chapter 1 that the opportunity cost of some item is what we give up to get that item. In our example, we assumed that the gardener and the farmer each spend 48 hours a week working. Time spent producing potatoes, therefore, takes away from time available for producing meat. As the farmer and gardener reallocate time between producing the two goods, they move along their production possibility frontiers; they give up units of one good to produce units of the other. The

TABLE 3.3

The Opportunity Cost of Meat and Potatoes

	Opportunity cost of:	
	1 kilogram of meat	**1 kilogram of potatoes**
Gardener	4 kg potatoes	0.25 kg meat
Farmer	2 kg potatoes	0.5 kg meat

opportunity cost measures the trade-off between the two goods that each producer faces.

Let's first consider the farmer's opportunity cost. The following analysis confirms our discussion about the slope of the production possibilities frontiers above. According to Table 3.1, producing 1 kilogram of potatoes takes her 1 hour of work. When the farmer spends that 1 hour producing potatoes, she spends 1 hour less producing meat. Because the farmer needs 2 hours to produce 1 kilogram of meat, 1 hour of work would yield ½ kilogram of meat. Hence, the farmer's opportunity cost of producing 1 kilogram of potatoes is ½ kilogram of meat.

Now consider the gardener's opportunity cost. Producing 1 kilogram of potatoes takes him 1½ hours. Because he needs 6 hours to produce 1 kilogram of meat, 1½ hours of work would yield ¼ kilogram of meat. Hence, the gardener's opportunity cost of 1 kilogram of potatoes is ¼ kilogram of meat.

Table 3.3 shows the opportunity costs of meat and potatoes for the two producers. Notice that the opportunity cost of meat is the inverse of the opportunity cost of potatoes. Because 1 kilogram of potatoes costs the farmer ½ kilogram of meat, 1 kilogram of meat costs the farmer 2 kilograms of potatoes. Similarly, because 1 kilogram of potatoes costs the gardener ¼ kilogram of meat, 1 kilogram of meat costs the gardener 4 kilograms of potatoes.

comparative advantage
the comparison among producers of a good according to their opportunity cost

Economists use the term **comparative advantage** when describing the opportunity cost of two producers. The producer who gives up less of other goods to produce good X has the smaller opportunity cost of producing good X and is said to have a comparative advantage in producing it. In our example, the gardener has a lower opportunity cost of producing potatoes than does the farmer: a kilogram of potatoes costs the gardener only ¼ kilogram of meat, while it costs the farmer ½ kilogram of meat. Conversely, the farmer has a lower opportunity cost of producing meat than does the gardener: a kilogram of meat costs the farmer 2 kilograms of potatoes, while it costs the gardener 4 kilograms of potatoes. Thus, the gardener has a comparative advantage in growing potatoes, and the farmer has a comparative advantage in producing meat.

Although it is possible for one person to have an absolute advantage in both goods (as the farmer does in our example), it is impossible for one person to have a comparative advantage in both goods. Because the opportunity cost of one good is the inverse of the opportunity cost of the other, if a person's opportunity cost of one good is relatively high, his opportunity cost of the other good must be relatively low. Comparative advantage reflects the relative opportunity cost. Unless two people have exactly the same opportunity cost, one person will have a comparative advantage in one good, and the other person will have a comparative advantage in the other good.

FYI

The Legacy of Adam Smith and David Ricardo

Economists have long understood the principle of comparative advantage. Here is how the great economist Adam Smith put the argument:

It is a maxim of every prudent master of a family, never to attempt to make at home what it will cost him more to make than to buy. The tailor does not attempt to make his own shoes, but buys them of the shoemaker. The shoemaker does not attempt to make his own clothes but employs a tailor. The gardener attempts to make neither the one nor the other, but employs those different artificers. All of them find it for their interest to employ their whole industry in a way in which they have some advantage over their neighbours, and to purchase with a part of its produce, or what is the same thing, with the price of part of it, whatever else they have occasion for.

This quotation is from Smith's 1776 book *An Inquiry into the Nature and Causes of the Wealth of Nations,* which was a landmark in the analysis of trade and economic interdependence.

Smith's book inspired David Ricardo – an Englishman born of Dutch parents – to become an economist, having already made his fortune as a stockbroker in the City of London. In his 1817 book *Principles of Political Economy and Taxation,* Ricardo developed the principle of comparative advantage, originally put forward by Robert Torrens, a British Army officer and owner of the *Globe* newspaper in 1815, as we know it today. His defence of free trade was not a mere academic exercise. Ricardo put his economic beliefs to work as a member of the British parliament, where he opposed the Corn Laws, which restricted the import of grain.

The conclusions of Adam Smith and David Ricardo on the gains from trade have held up well over time. Although economists often disagree on questions of policy, they are united in their support of free trade. Moreover, the central argument for free trade has not changed much in the past two centuries. Even though the field of economics has broadened its scope and refined its theories since the time of Smith and Ricardo, economists' opposition to trade restrictions is still based largely on the principle of comparative advantage.

David Ricardo

CASE STUDY

Afghanistan and the Opium Trade

In the first decade of the 21st century, troops from a number of nations have been in Afghanistan supporting the government, helping rebuild infrastructure, training Afghan police and troops, and fighting Taliban and insurgent groups who pose a perceived threat to security in the country and beyond. One of the regions where problems have been most acute is Helmand province in the south of the country. There have been considerable losses of civilian and military life in this region and the military struggle has been made all the more difficult by some very real economic issues that have militated against lasting peace in the region.

One of these economic issues relates to the growing of opium poppies. Some 70 per cent of all the opium grown in Afghanistan comes from this province. With opium comes all manner of other problems that have a far reaching impact in many other countries. Opium is the raw material used for heroin and the poppy which produces opium represents a lucrative business for many farmers in the region. There is a very good reason why farmers grow opium – it generates financial returns that are greater than any legal crop. Helmand has a comparative advantage in the production of opium; yields per acre are higher than in other parts of Afghanistan and there is a plentiful supply of relatively cheap labour to help produce and harvest the crop – important given that this is a relatively labour intensive crop to grow.

For farmers in the region, decisions about how to use their land are determined in part by the returns they expect to get from alternative crops that could be grown. Different crops will yield a different value of benefits. The opportunity cost of growing opium is relatively low in that the sacrifice of the value of the benefits foregone of alternatives is low. The sacrifice involved in terms of lost benefits from the movement of resources from producing a legal crop such as wheat, for example, is negligible and so there is a real incentive to produce opium which has high rewards. If the return per acre for growing opium is €150, for example, and that for growing wheat is €25, it does not take an economist to point out that the incentive for growing opium is strong.

It can be argued that growing an illegal crop such as opium also brings with it high risks which would increase the opportunity cost. However, in Helmand this is distorted by the fact that the problems enforcing the rule of law means that the power of the authorities to intervene and punish farmers for growing opium is extremely limited. The protection afforded to farmers by warlords and the network of gangs who stand to benefit from the lucrative trade in opium means that the chances of getting caught and punished are negligible. Only if the law can be enforced and there are real and visible risks to growing an illegal crop will the opportunity cost start to increase and incentives to grow a legal crop start to appear.

This means finding ways of encouraging the growth of legal crops and giving farmers adequate returns that increase the opportunity cost of growing opium. This may be achieved through providing subsidies to farmers to produce legal crops. Subsidies do have to be paid for and the Afghan government would need considerable help to be able to put in place such a solution. One other option that has been suggested involves direct intervention in the market for opium. Under such a scheme the US government, for example, could spend around $2.5 billion in purchasing the opium crop from farmers. Such a price might have to be paid each year but in comparison to the $1 billion it currently pays in trying to eradicate the crop and the $200 billion it has paid out in military operations in Afghanistan, the cost may well be offset by the benefits. There is a trade-off and the trade-off might be worth making! In buying the crop those who rely on it to finance their activities through imposing protection money, taking 'taxes' and so on would be sidelined and the corruption in the Afghan government that has been blamed for being part of the problem would also be marginalized.

Comparative Advantage and Trade

Differences in opportunity cost and comparative advantage create the gains from trade. When each person specializes in producing the good for which he or she has a comparative advantage, total production in the economy rises, and this increase in the size of the economic cake can be used to make everyone better off. In other words, as long as two people have different opportunity costs, each can benefit from trade by obtaining a good at a price that is lower than his or her opportunity cost of that good.

Consider the proposed deal from the viewpoint of the gardener. The gardener gets 5 kilograms of meat in exchange for 15 kilograms of potatoes. In other words, the gardener buys each kilogram of meat for a price of 3 kilograms of potatoes. This price of meat is lower than his opportunity cost for 1 kilogram of meat, which is 4 kilograms of potatoes. Thus, the gardener benefits from the deal because he gets to buy meat at a good price.

Now consider the deal from the farmer's viewpoint. The farmer buys 15 kilograms of potatoes for a price of 5 kilograms of meat. That is, the price of potatoes is ⅓ kilogram of meat. This price of potatoes is lower than her opportunity cost of 1 kilogram of potatoes, which is ½ kilogram of meat. The farmer benefits because she is able to buy potatoes at a good price.

These benefits arise because each person concentrates on the activity for which he or she has the lower opportunity cost: the gardener spends more time growing potatoes, and the farmer spends more time producing meat. As a result, the total production of potatoes and the total production of meat both rise. In our example, potato production rises from 40 to 44 kilograms, and meat production rises from 16 to 18 kilograms. The gardener and farmer share the benefits of this increased production. The moral of the story of the gardener and the farmer should now be clear: *trade can benefit everyone in society because it allows people to specialize in activities in which they have a comparative advantage.*

Quick Quiz Hasani can gather 10 coconuts or catch 1 fish per hour. His new friend, Jacek, can gather 30 coconuts or catch 2 fish per hour. What is Hasani's opportunity cost of catching one fish? What is Jacek's? Who has an absolute advantage in catching fish? Who has a comparative advantage in catching fish?

APPLICATIONS OF COMPARATIVE ADVANTAGE

The principle of comparative advantage explains interdependence and the gains from trade. Because interdependence is so prevalent in the modern world, the principle of comparative advantage has many applications. Here are two examples, one fanciful and one of great practical importance.

Should Ingvar Kamprad Mow his own Lawn?

Ingvar Kamprad is the founder of the retail chain IKEA. He began by selling matches, then fish, Christmas tree decorations, ballpoint pens, pencils and more before establishing IKEA as a global retail business. His talents as an entrepreneur have resulted in a personal fortune estimated at €19 billion. Since 1976 he has lived in a villa in Switzerland. Most likely, he is talented at other activities too. For example, let's imagine that Ingvar Kamprad can mow his lawn faster than anyone else. But just because he *can* mow his lawn fast, does this mean he *should?*

To answer this question, we can use the concepts of opportunity cost and comparative advantage. Let's say that Ingvar Kamprad can mow his lawn in 2 hours. In that same 2 hours he could design a new piece of furniture and earn, say, €10 000. By contrast, Alberto, the boy next door, can mow Ingvar's lawn in 4 hours. In that same 4 hours, he could work at the local McDonald's and earn €20.

In this example, Ingvar's opportunity cost of mowing the lawn is €10 000 and Alberto's opportunity cost is €20. Ingvar has an absolute advantage in mowing lawns because he can do the work in less time. Yet Alberto has a comparative advantage in mowing lawns because he has the lower opportunity cost.

The gains from trade in this example are tremendous. Rather than mowing his own lawn, Ingvar should design the furniture and hire Alberto to mow the lawn. As long as Ingvar pays Alberto more than €20 and less than €10 000, both of them are better off.

Should Countries in Europe Trade with other Countries?

imports
goods produced abroad and purchased for use in the domestic economy

exports
goods produced domestically and sold abroad

Just as individuals can benefit from specialization and trade with one another, as the gardener and farmer did, so can populations of people in different countries. Many of the goods that Europeans enjoy are produced abroad, and many of the goods produced in Europe are sold abroad. Goods produced abroad and purchased for use in the domestic economy are called **imports**. Goods produced domestically and sold abroad are called **exports**.

To see how countries can benefit from trade, suppose there are two countries, Germany and Japan, and two goods, food and cars. Imagine that the two countries produce cars equally well: a German worker and a Japanese worker can each produce 1 car per month. By contrast, because Germany has more land suitable for cultivation, it is better at producing food: a German worker can produce 2 tonnes of food per month, whereas a Japanese worker can produce only 1 tonne of food per month.

The principle of comparative advantage states that each good should be produced by the country that has the smaller opportunity cost of producing that good. Because the opportunity cost of a car is 2 tonnes of food in Germany but only 1 tonne of food in Japan, Japan has a comparative advantage in producing cars. Japan should produce more cars than it wants for its own use and export some of them to Germany. Similarly, because the opportunity cost of a tonne of food is 1 car in Japan but only ½ a car in Germany, Germany has a comparative advantage in producing food. Germany should produce more food than it wants to consume and export some of it to Japan. Through specialization and trade, both countries can have more food and more cars.

In reality, of course, the issues involved in trade among nations are more complex than this simple example suggests, as we will see later in the text. Most important among these issues is that each country has many citizens with different interests. International trade can make some individuals worse off, even as it makes the country as a whole better off. When Germany exports food and imports cars, the impact on a German farmer is not the same as the impact on a German car worker. Yet, contrary to the opinions sometimes voiced by politicians and political commentators, international trade is not like war, in which some countries win and others lose. Trade allows all countries to achieve greater prosperity.

Quick Quiz Suppose that the world's fastest typist happens to be trained in brain surgery. Should he do his own typing or hire a secretary? Explain.

IN THE NEWS

Changing Comparative Advantage

We have seen how economics uses simple examples to highlight key concepts and principles in the subject. The principle of comparative advantage is one such concept. Reality, of course, is quite different not least because the opportunity cost of producing goods and services can change over time and as a result the comparative advantage can also change. This In the News article highlights one example of how this can happen.

The basic principle of the theory of comparative advantage is that a country should focus its resources on production of goods in which the relative opportunity cost is lowest. It means that it is likely to be inefficient for a country like England to devote resources to the production of a good which other countries could produce more efficiently. This might be because the natural climate is more conducive to the production of a particular product.

In the UK, the production of salad crops such as tomatoes, cucumbers and peppers requires certain amounts of light and heat as well as nutrients to produce crops of the right quantity and quality. These crops can be grown in the summer months but in the winter the resources needed to continue production might be seen as too costly. As a result, production of these crops has tended to be seasonal and large quantities of salad crops are imported to maintain year-round supply. Other countries have a comparative advantage in the production of salad crops. It makes sense for them to specialize in production of these crops whilst the UK focuses production on crops in which it has a comparative advantage.

Changes in technology and economies of scale can change the opportunity cost ratios, however, which might make it worthwhile for the UK to devote resources to the production of salad crops. That is exactly what is happening in the south-east corner of England in Kent. Thanet Earth is a development in Birchington, in the east of the county. The development has converted a redundant 91-hectare cauliflower farm into the largest glasshouse complex in the UK. There are seven greenhouses covering an area equivalent to 39 football pitches and a power generation plant that will generate enough electricity to power 50 000 homes. Seven reservoirs have been built to capture the rain from the roofs of the glasshouses, which can store around 65 million gallons of water and over 2 km of new roads have been built.

The Thanet Earth project cost an estimated £80 million and will add 15 per cent to the UK's total salad crop production when it is fully completed. It has been estimated that one of the greenhouses devoted to tomato production will produce 2.5 million tomatoes a week. To get some idea of the scale of production it has been estimated that the new Terminal 5 building at Heathrow would fit twice into one of the greenhouses that has been built! The site is able to generate its own power and the design has focused on ensuring that the green credentials of the site are of the highest standards. The new development shows that the principles of comparative advantage are not set in stone. If technology advances then the relative opportunity costs can be altered. Such changes may warrant resources being transferred to the production of goods that used to be considered economically inefficient. The sheer scale of production will also bring its own benefits in terms of the lower unit costs of production.

There has been an increasing focus on the production of renewable energy in recent years. One common factor in most countries is the existence of wind which can be used to generate energy. However, whilst many countries could think about renewable energy production, some countries are more efficient in the production of such energy than others and as such have a comparative advantage in the production of renewable energy.

One such country is Scotland. It has two features that mark it out as a country that can produce renewable energy: its geographical location and its natural resources. In December 2009, a report, commissioned by the Scottish government and carried out by energy and mining consultants Wood Mackenzie, was published which investigated the possibilities of renewable energy production for the country[1].

The Report identified a number of factors that could encourage the government to shift resources into renewable energy. These included wind, water, the sea and bio-energies as a result of the particular geological features of the country. Scotland also has the potential to store large amounts of carbon dioxide (CO_2) and could utilize the North Sea for a CO_2 infrastructure network. These natural advantages are complemented by the existence of technology and skills developed as a result of the offshore gas and oil industry over the previous 40 years. These technologies and skills could be transferred, says the report, to help develop fledgling renewable energy industries and allow the country to diversify and expand employment opportunities. The report concludes that Scotland has a comparative advantage in a number of renewable energy technologies that it can look to exploit in the coming years.

[1]http://www.scotland.gov.uk/Publications/2009/12/10134807/0 accessed 15 December 2009.

CONCLUSION

The principle of comparative advantage shows that trade can make everyone better off. You should now understand more fully the benefits of living in an interdependent economy. But having seen why interdependence is desirable, you might naturally ask how it is possible. How do free societies coordinate the diverse activities of all the people involved in their economies? What ensures that goods and services will get from those who should be producing them to those who should be consuming them?

In a world with only two people, such as the farmer and the gardener, the answer is simple: these two people can directly bargain and allocate resources between themselves. In the real world with billions of people, the answer is less obvious. We take up this issue in the next chapter, where we see that free societies allocate resources through the market forces of supply and demand.

SUMMARY

- Each person consumes goods and services produced by many other people both in their country and around the world. Interdependence and trade are desirable because they allow everyone to enjoy a greater quantity and variety of goods and services.
- There are two ways to compare the ability of two people in producing a good. The person who can produce the good with the smaller quantity of inputs is said to have an *absolute advantage* in producing the good. The person who has the smaller opportunity cost of producing the good is said to have a *comparative advantage.* The gains from trade are based on comparative advantage, not absolute advantage.
- Trade makes everyone better off because it allows people to specialize in those activities in which they have a comparative advantage.
- The principle of comparative advantage applies to countries as well as to people. Economists use the principle of comparative advantage to advocate free trade among countries.

KEY CONCEPTS

absolute advantage, p. 57
comparative advantage, p. 58
imports, p. 62
exports, p. 62

QUESTIONS FOR REVIEW

1. Explain how absolute advantage and comparative advantage differ.
2. Give an example in which one person has an absolute advantage in doing something but another person has a comparative advantage.
3. Is absolute advantage or comparative advantage more important for trade? Explain your reasoning using the example in your answer to Question 2.
4. Will a nation tend to export or import goods for which it has a comparative advantage? Explain.
5. Why do economists oppose policies that restrict trade among nations?

PROBLEMS AND APPLICATIONS

1. Consider the gardener and the farmer from our example in this chapter. Explain why the gardener's opportunity cost of producing 1 kilogram of meat is 4 kilograms of potatoes. Explain why the farmer's opportunity cost of producing 1 kilogram of meat is 2 kilograms of potatoes.
2. Manuela can read 20 pages of economics in an hour. She can also read 50 pages of sociology in an hour. She spends 5 hours per day studying.
   a. Draw Manuela's production possibilities frontier for reading economics and sociology.
   b. What is Manuela's opportunity cost of reading 100 pages of sociology?
3. UK and Japanese workers can each produce 4 cars a year. A UK worker can produce 10 tonnes of grain a year, whereas a Japanese worker can produce 5 tonnes of grain a year. To keep things simple, assume that each country has 100 million workers.
   a. For this situation, construct a table analogous to Table 3.1.
   b. Graph the production possibilities frontier of the UK and Japanese economies.
   c. For the UK, what is the opportunity cost of a car? Of grain? For Japan, what is the opportunity cost of a car? Of grain? Put this information in a table analogous to Table 3.3.
   d. Which country has an absolute advantage in producing cars? In producing grain?
   e. Which country has a comparative advantage in producing cars? In producing grain?
   f. Without trade, half of each country's workers produce cars and half produce grain. What quantities of cars and grain does each country produce?
   g. Starting from a position without trade, give an example in which trade makes each country better off.
4. Victoria and David share a flat. They spend most of their time studying (of course), but they leave some time for their favourite activities: cooking pizza and making home-brew beer. Victoria takes 4 hours to produce 1 barrel of home-brew and 2 hours to make a pizza. David takes 6 hours to brew 1 barrel of beer and 4 hours to make a pizza.
   a. What is each flatmate's opportunity cost of making a pizza? Who has the absolute advantage in making pizza? Who has the comparative advantage in making pizza?
   b. If Victoria and David trade foods with each other, who will trade away pizza in exchange for home-brew?
   c. The price of pizza can be expressed in terms of barrels of home-brew. What is the highest price at which pizza can be traded that would make both flatmates better off? What is the lowest price? Explain.
5. Suppose that there are 10 million workers in Belgium, and that each of these workers can produce either 2 cars or 30 tonnes of wheat in a year.
   a. What is the opportunity cost of producing a car in Belgium? What is the opportunity cost of producing a tonne of wheat in Belgium? Explain the relationship between the opportunity costs of the two goods.
   b. Draw Belgium's production possibilities frontier. If Belgium chooses to consume 10 million cars, how much wheat can it consume without trade? Label this point on the production possibilities frontier.
   c. Now suppose that the United Kingdom offers to buy 10 million cars from Belgium in exchange for 20 tonnes of wheat per car. If Belgium continues to consume 10 million cars, how much wheat does this deal allow Belgium to consume? Label this point on your diagram. Should Belgium accept the deal?

6. Consider a lecturer who is writing a book. The lecturer can both write the chapters and gather the needed data faster than anyone else at his university. Still, he pays a student to collect data at the library. Is this sensible? Explain.
7. England and Scotland both produce scones and pullovers. Suppose that an English worker can produce 50 scones per hour or 1 pullover per hour. Suppose that a Scottish worker can produce 40 scones per hour or 2 pullovers per hour.
   a. Which country has the absolute advantage in the production of each good? Which country has the comparative advantage?
   b. If England and Scotland decide to trade, which commodity will Scotland trade to England? Explain.
   c. If a Scottish worker could produce only 1 pullover per hour, would Scotland still gain from trade? Would England still gain from trade? Explain.
8. The following table describes the production possibilities of two cities in the country of Footballia:

	Pairs of red socks per worker per hour	Pairs of blue socks per worker per hour
Manchester	3	3
Chelsea	2	1

   a. Without trade, what is the price of blue socks (in terms of red socks) in Manchester? What is the price in Chelsea?
   b. Which city has an absolute advantage in the production of each colour sock? Which city has a comparative advantage in the production of each colour sock?
   c. If the cities trade with each other, which colour sock will each export?
   d. What is the range of prices at which trade can occur?
9. Suppose that all goods can be produced with fewer worker hours in Germany than in Belgium.
   a. In what sense is the cost of all goods lower in Germany than in Belgium?
   b. In what sense is the cost of some goods lower in Belgium?
   c. If Germany and Belgium traded with each other, would both countries be better off as a result? Explain in the context of your answers to parts (a) and (b).
10. Are the following statements true or false? Explain in each case.
   a. 'Two countries can achieve gains from trade even if one of the countries has an absolute advantage in the production of all goods.'
   b. 'Certain very talented people have a comparative advantage in everything they do.'
   c. 'If a certain trade is good for one person, it can't be good for the other one.'

For further resources, visit
www.cengage.com/mankiw_taylor2

2

SUPPLY AND DEMAND I: HOW MARKETS WORK

4 THE MARKET FORCES OF SUPPLY AND DEMAND

When there is a drought in southern Europe, the price of olive oil rises in supermarkets throughout Europe. It is anticipated that the price of hotel accommodation in London and the South East will rise significantly when London hosts the Olympic Games in 2012. When a war breaks out in the Middle East, the price of petrol in Europe rises and the price of a used Mercedes falls. A poor durum wheat harvest leads to a rise in the price of pasta in Italy. What do these events have in common? They all show the workings of supply and demand.

Supply and *demand* are the two words that economists use most often – and for good reason. Supply and demand are the forces that make market economies work. They determine the quantity of each good produced and the price at which it is sold. If you want to know how any event or policy will affect the economy, you must think first about how it will affect supply and demand.

This chapter introduces the theory of supply and demand. It considers how buyers and sellers behave and how they interact with one another. It shows how supply and demand determine prices in a market economy and how prices, in turn, allocate the economy's scarce resources.

MARKETS AND COMPETITION

market
a group of buyers and sellers of a particular good or service

The terms *supply* and *demand* refer to the behaviour of people as they interact with one another in markets. A **market** is a group of buyers and sellers of a particular good or service. The buyers as a group determine the demand for the product, and the sellers as a group determine the supply of the product. Before discussing how buyers and sellers behave, let's first consider more fully what we mean by a 'market' and the various types of markets we observe in the economy.

Competitive Markets

Markets take many forms. Sometimes markets are highly organized, such as the markets for many agricultural commodities and for metals. In these markets, buyers and sellers meet at a specific time and place, where an auctioneer helps set prices and arrange sales.

More often, markets are less organized. For example, consider the market for ice cream in a particular town. Buyers of ice cream do not meet together at any one time. The sellers of ice cream are in different locations and offer somewhat different products. There is no auctioneer calling out the price of ice cream. Each seller posts a price for a cornet of ice cream in their shop, and each buyer decides how much ice cream to buy at each shop.

Even though it is not organized, the group of ice cream buyers and ice cream sellers forms a market. Each buyer knows that there are several sellers from which to choose, and each seller is aware that his product is similar to that offered by other sellers. The price of ice cream and the quantity of ice cream sold are not determined by any single buyer or seller. Rather, price and quantity are determined by all buyers and sellers as they interact in the marketplace.

The market for ice cream, like most markets in the economy, is highly competitive. Competition exists when two or more firms are rivals for customers. Each firm strives to gain the attention and custom of buyers in the market. A **competitive market** is a market in which there are many buyers and many sellers so that each has a negligible impact on the market price. Each seller of ice cream has limited control over the price because other sellers are offering similar products. A seller has little reason to charge less than the going price, and if he or she charges more, buyers will make their purchases elsewhere. Similarly, no single buyer of ice cream can influence the price of ice cream because each buyer purchases only a small amount.

competitive market
a market in which there are many buyers and many sellers so that each has a negligible impact on the market price

In this chapter we examine how buyers and sellers interact in competitive markets. We see how the forces of supply and demand determine both the quantity of the good sold and its price.

Competition: Perfect and Otherwise

We assume in this chapter that markets are *perfectly competitive.* Perfectly competitive markets are defined by two main characteristics: (1) the goods being offered for sale are all the same (homogenous) and as a result buyers have no preference between one seller or another, and (2) the buyers and sellers are so numerous that no single buyer or seller can influence the market price. Because buyers and sellers in perfectly competitive markets must accept the price the market determines, they are said to be *price takers.*

There are some markets in which the assumption of perfect competition applies to a very large degree. In the wheat market, for example, there are thousands of farmers who sell wheat and millions of consumers who use wheat and wheat products. Because no single buyer or seller can influence the price of wheat, each takes the price as given.

Not all goods and services, however, are sold in perfectly competitive markets. Some markets have only one seller, and this seller sets the price. Such a seller is called a *monopoly.* Your local water company, for instance, may be a monopoly. Residents in your area probably have only one water company from which to buy this service.

Some markets fall between the extremes of perfect competition and monopoly. One such market, called an *oligopoly,* has a few sellers that do not always compete aggressively. Airline routes are an example. If a route between two cities is serviced by only two or three carriers, the carriers may avoid rigorous competition so they can keep prices high. Another type of market is *monopolistically or imperfectly competitive;* it contains many sellers but each offers a slightly different product. Because the products are not exactly the same, each seller has some ability to set the price for its own product. An example is the market for magazines. Magazines compete with one another for readers and anyone can enter the market by starting a new one, but each magazine offers different articles and can set its own price.

Despite the diversity of market types we find in the world, we begin by studying perfect competition. Perfectly competitive markets are the easiest to analyse. Moreover, because some degree of competition is present in most markets, many of the lessons that we learn by studying supply and demand under perfect competition apply in more complicated markets as well.

Quick Quiz What is a market? • What are the characteristics of a competitive market?

DEMAND

We begin our study of markets by examining the behaviour of buyers. To focus our thinking, let's keep in mind a particular good ice cream.

The Demand Curve: The Relationship Between Price and Quantity Demanded

quantity demanded
the amount of a good that buyers are willing and able to purchase

law of demand
the claim that, other things equal, the quantity demanded of a good falls when the price of the good rises

demand schedule
a table that shows the relationship between the price of a good and the quantity demanded

The **quantity demanded** of any good is the amount of the good that buyers are willing and able to purchase. As we shall see, many things determine the quantity demanded of any good, but when analysing how markets work, one determinant plays a central role – the price of the good. If the price of ice cream rose to €20 per scoop, you would buy less ice cream. You might buy a frozen ice lolly instead. If the price of ice cream fell to €0.20 per scoop, you would buy more. Because the quantity demanded falls as the price rises and rises as the price falls, we say that the quantity demanded is *negatively related* to the price. This relationship between price and quantity demanded is true for most goods in the economy and, in fact, is so pervasive that economists call it the **law of demand**: other things equal, when the price of a good rises, the quantity demanded of the good falls, and when the price falls, the quantity demanded rises.

The table in Figure 4.1 shows how many cornets of ice cream Sabine is willing and able to buy each month at different prices of ice cream. If ice cream is free, Sabine would be willing to eat 12 cornets. At €0.50 per cornet, Sabine would be willing to buy 10 cornets. As the price rises further, she is willing to buy fewer and fewer cornets. When the price reaches €3.00, Sabine would not be prepared to buy any ice cream at all. This table is a **demand schedule**, a table that shows the relationship between the price of a good and the quantity demanded, holding constant everything else that influences how much consumers of the good want to buy.

The graph in Figure 4.1 uses the numbers from the table to illustrate the law of demand. By convention, the price of ice cream is on the vertical axis, and the

FIGURE 4.1

Sabine's Demand Schedule and Demand Curve

The demand schedule shows the quantity demanded at each price. The demand curve, which graphs the demand schedule, shows how the quantity demanded of the good changes as its price varies. Because a lower price increases the quantity demanded, the demand curve slopes downward.

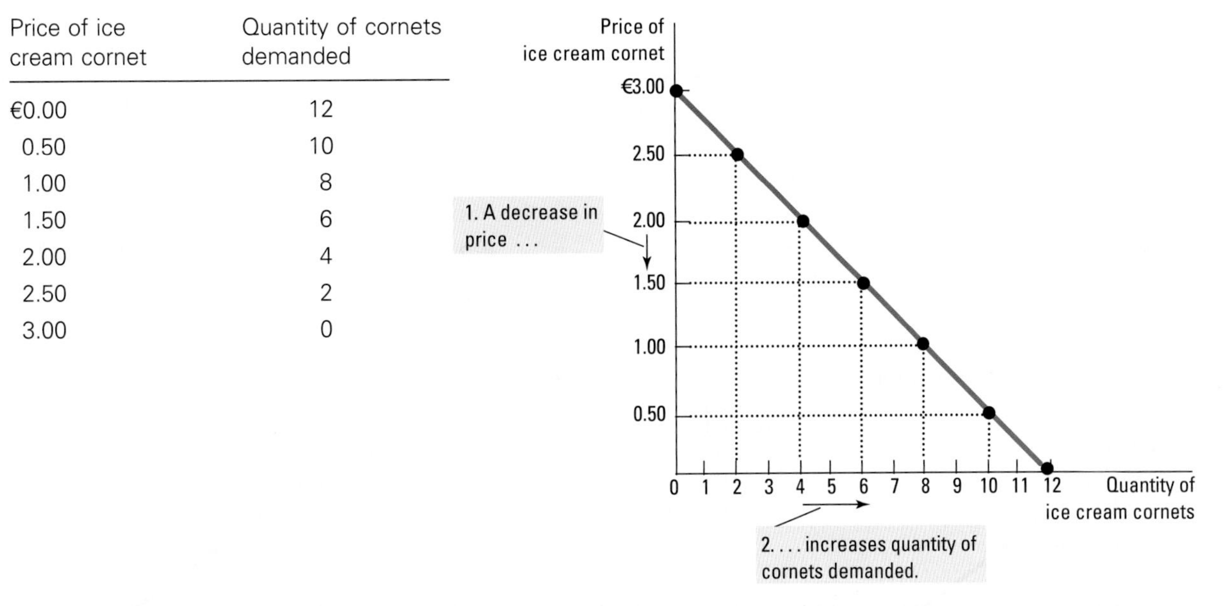

Price of ice cream cornet	Quantity of cornets demanded
€0.00	12
0.50	10
1.00	8
1.50	6
2.00	4
2.50	2
3.00	0

quantity of ice cream demanded is on the horizontal axis. The downward sloping line relating price and quantity demanded is called the **demand curve**.

demand curve
a graph of the relationship between the price of a good and the quantity demanded

Market Demand versus Individual Demand

The demand curve in Figure 4.1 shows an individual's demand for a product. To analyse how markets work, we need to determine the *market demand*, which is the sum of all the individual demands for a particular good or service.

The table in Figure 4.2 shows the demand schedules for ice cream of two individuals – Sabine and Jan. At any price, Sabine's demand schedule tells us how much ice cream she would be willing and able to buy at different prices, and Jan's demand schedule tells us how much ice cream he is willing and able to buy. The market demand at each price is the sum of the two individual demands.

The graph in Figure 4.2 shows the demand curves that correspond to these demand schedules. Notice that we sum the individual demand curves *horizontally* to obtain the market demand curve. That is, to find the total quantity demanded at any price, we add the individual quantities found on the horizontal axis of the individual demand curves. Because we are interested in analysing how markets work, we shall work most often with the market demand curve. The market demand curve shows how the total quantity demanded of a good varies as the price of the good varies, while all the other factors that affect how much consumers want to buy, such as incomes and taste, amongst other things, are held constant.

FIGURE 4.2

Market Demand as the Sum of Individual Demands

The quantity demanded in a market is the sum of the quantities demanded by all the buyers at each price. Thus, the market demand curve is found by adding horizontally the individual demand curves. At a price of €2, Sabine would like to buy 4 ice cream cornets but Jan would only be prepared to buy 3 ice cream cornets. The quantity demanded in the market at this price, therefore, is 7 cornets.

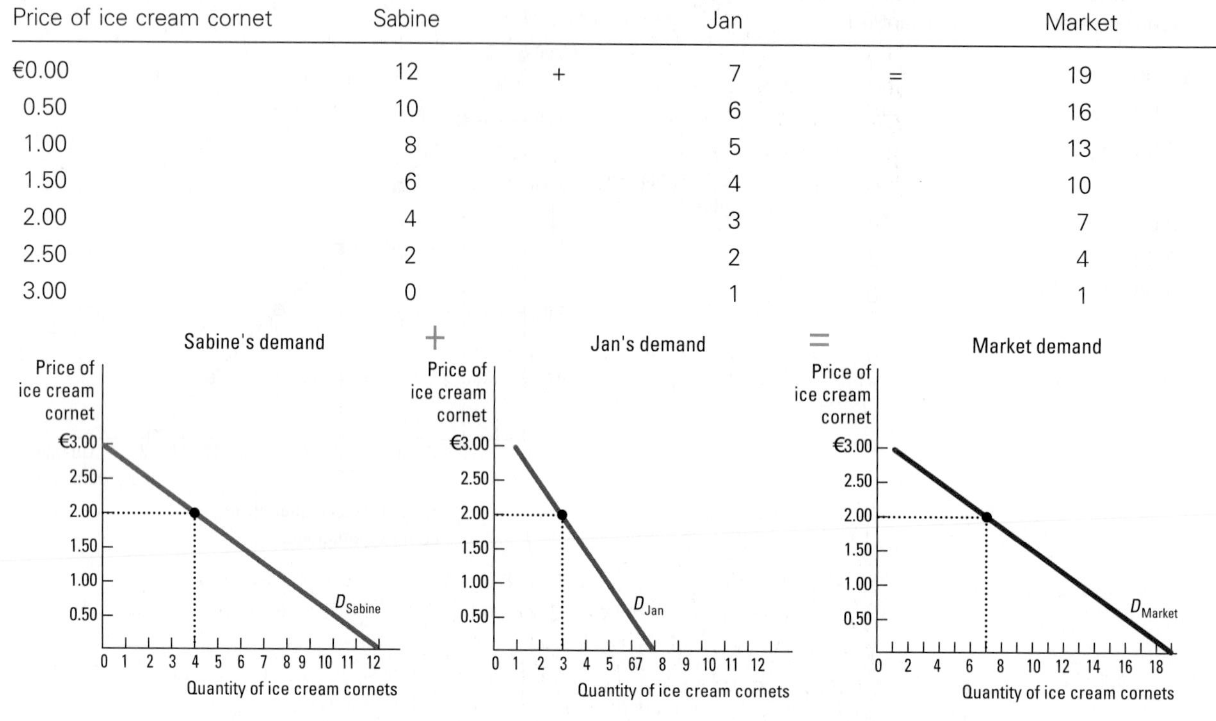

Price of ice cream cornet	Sabine		Jan		Market
€0.00	12	+	7	=	19
0.50	10		6		16
1.00	8		5		13
1.50	6		4		10
2.00	4		3		7
2.50	2		2		4
3.00	0		1		1

Shifts versus Movements along the Demand Curve

One important distinction that must be made is between a shift of the demand curve and a movement along the demand curve. A shift in the demand curve is caused by a factor affecting demand other than a change in price. The factors affecting demand are outlined below. If any of these factors change then the amount consumers wish to purchase changes whatever the price. The shift in the demand curve is referred to as an *increase or decrease in demand.* A movement along the demand curve occurs when there is a change in price. This may occur because of a change in supply conditions. The factors affecting demand are assumed to be held constant. A change in price leads to a movement along the demand curve and is referred to as a *change in quantity demanded.*

Shifts in the Demand Curve

The demand curve for ice cream shows how much ice cream people are willing to buy at any given price, holding constant the many other factors beyond price that influence consumers' buying decisions. As a result, this demand curve need not be stable over time. If something happens to alter the quantity demanded at any given price, the demand curve shifts. For example, suppose European health

FIGURE 4.3

Shifts in the Demand Curve

Any change that raises the quantity that buyers wish to purchase at a given price shifts the demand curve to the right. Any change that lowers the quantity that buyers wish to purchase at a given price shifts the demand curve to the left.

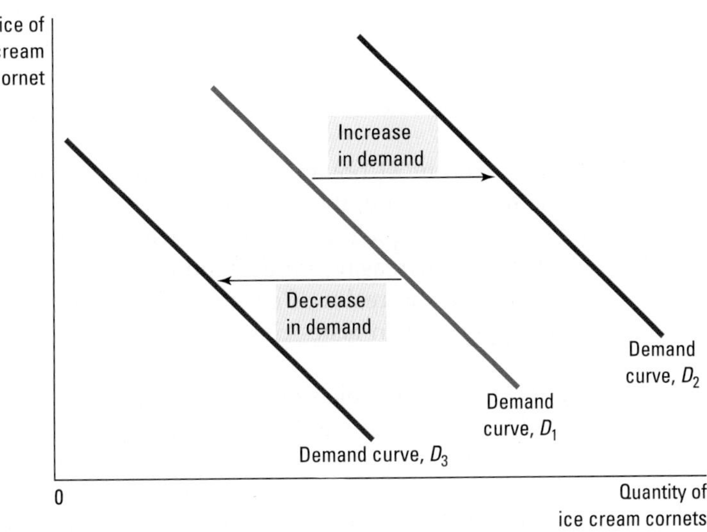

authorities discovered that people who regularly eat ice cream live longer, healthier lives. The discovery would raise the demand for ice cream. At any given price, buyers would now want to purchase a larger quantity of ice cream and the demand curve for ice cream would shift.

Figure 4.3 illustrates shifts in demand. Any change that increases the quantity demanded at every price, such as our imaginary discovery by the European health authorities, shifts the demand curve to the right and is called *an increase in demand.* Any change that reduces the quantity demanded at every price shifts the demand curve to the left and is called *a decrease in demand.*

There are many variables that can shift the demand curve. Here are the most important.

Income What would happen to the demand for ice cream if unemployment increases? Most likely, it would fall because of lower incomes. Lower incomes mean that people have less to spend in total, so they are likely to spend less on some – and probably most – goods. If the demand for a good falls when income falls, the good is called a **normal good**.

normal good
a good for which, other things equal, an increase in income leads to an increase in demand (and vice versa)

Not all goods are normal goods. If the demand for a good rises when income falls, the good is called an **inferior good**. An example of an inferior good might be bus rides. As income falls, people are less likely to buy a car or take a taxi and more likely to take the bus. As income falls, therefore, demand for bus rides tends to increase.

inferior good
a good for which, other things equal, an increase in income leads to a decrease in demand (and vice versa)

Prices of Related Goods Suppose that the price of ice lollies falls. The law of demand says that people will buy more ice lollies. At the same time, people will probably buy less ice cream. Because ice cream and ice lollies are both frozen, sweet confectionary, they satisfy similar desires. When a fall in the price of one good reduces the demand for another good, the two goods are called **substitutes**. Substitutes are often pairs of goods that are used in place of each

substitutes
two goods for which an increase in the price of one leads to an increase in the demand for the other

other, such as beef steak and Wiener schnitzel, pullovers and sweatshirts, and cinema tickets and DVD rentals. The more closely related substitute products are the more effect we might see on demand if the price of one of the substitutes changes.

Now suppose that the price of chocolate flake bars falls. According to the law of demand, people will buy more chocolate flake bars. Yet, in this case, people will buy more ice cream as well, because ice cream and chocolate flake bars are often used together. When a fall in the price of one good raises the demand for another good, the two goods are called **complements**. Complements are often pairs of goods that are used together, such as petrol and cars, computers and software, bread and cheese, strawberries and cream, and bacon and eggs.

complements
two goods for which an increase in the price of one leads to a decrease in the demand for the other (and vice versa).

Tastes The most obvious determinant of demand are tastes and fashions. If people like ice cream, they buy more of it. Economists are increasingly interested in explaining people's tastes. The developments in neuroscience mean that we now have an increasing understanding of why people make decisions and this has come into the realm of economics. This helps economists examine why and what happens when tastes change.

Expectations People's expectations about the future may affect their demand for a good or service today. For example, if people expect to earn a higher income next month, they may be more willing to spend some of their current savings buying ice cream. As another example, if people expect the price of ice cream to fall tomorrow, they may be less willing to buy an ice cream cornet at today's price.

The Size and Structure of the Population A larger population, other things being equal, will mean a higher demand for all goods and services. Changes in the way the population is structured also influences demand. Many European countries have an ageing population and this leads to a change in the demand. Goods and services required by the elderly increase in demand as a result. The demand for retirement homes, insurance policies suitable for elderly drivers and smaller cars may increase as a result.

Summary The demand curve shows what happens to the *quantity demanded* of a good when its price varies, holding constant all the other variables that influence buyers. When one or more of these other variables changes, the demand curve shifts leading to an *increase or decrease in demand*. Table 4.1 lists all the variables that influence how much consumers choose to buy of a good.

TABLE 4.1

Variables That Influence Buyers

This table lists the variables that affect how much consumers choose to buy of any good. Notice the special role that the price of the good plays: a change in the good's price represents a movement along the demand curve, whereas a change in one of the other variables shifts the demand curve.

Variable	A change in this variable . . .
Price	Represents a movement along the demand curve
Income	Shifts the demand curve
Prices of related goods	Shifts the demand curve
Tastes	Shifts the demand curve
Expectations	Shifts the demand curve
Number of buyers	Shifts the demand curve

FIGURE 4.4

Shifts in the Demand Curve versus Movements Along the Demand Curve

If health warnings on cigarette packets convince smokers to smoke less, the demand curve for cigarettes shifts to the left. In panel (a), the demand curve shifts from D_1 *to* D_2*. At a price of €2 per pack, the quantity demanded falls from 20 to 10 cigarettes per day, as reflected by the shift from point A to point B. By contrast, if a tax raises the price of cigarettes, the demand curve does not shift. Instead, we observe a movement to a different point on the demand curve. In panel (b), when the price rises from €2 to €4, the quantity demanded falls from 20 to 12 cigarettes per day, as reflected by the movement from point A to point C.*

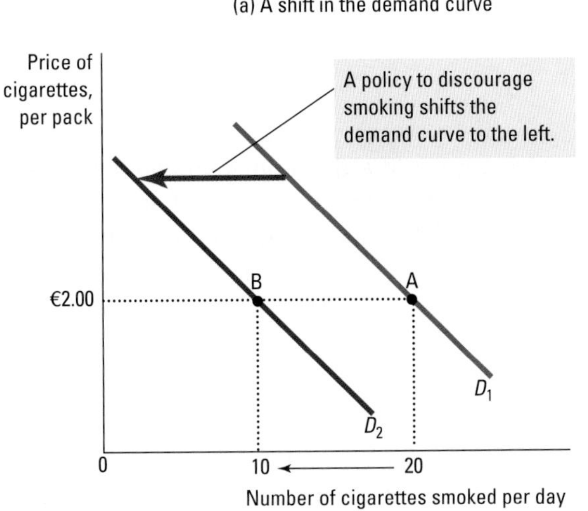

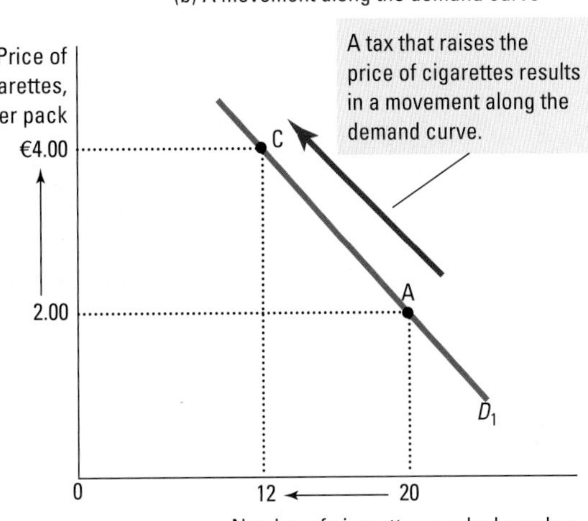

CASE STUDY

Two Ways to Reduce the Quantity of Smoking Demanded

Public policy makers often want to reduce the amount that people smoke. There are two ways that policy can attempt to achieve this goal.

One way to reduce smoking is to shift the demand curve for cigarettes and other tobacco products. Anti-smoking campaigns on television, mandatory health warnings on cigarette packages and the prohibition of cigarette advertising are all policies aimed at reducing the quantity of cigarettes demanded at any given price. If successful, these policies shift the demand curve for cigarettes to the left, as in panel (a) of Figure 4.4.

What is the best way to reduce smoking?

Alternatively, policy makers can try to raise the price of cigarettes. If the government taxes the manufacture of cigarettes, for example, cigarette companies pass much of this tax on to consumers in the form of higher prices. A higher price encourages smokers to reduce the numbers of cigarettes they smoke. In this case, the reduced amount of smoking does not represent a shift in the demand curve. Instead, it represents a movement along the same demand curve to a point with a higher price and lower quantity, as in panel (b) of Figure 4.4.

How much does the amount of smoking respond to changes in the price of cigarettes? Economists have attempted to answer this question by studying what happens when the tax on cigarettes changes. They have found that a 10 per cent increase in the price causes about a 4 per cent reduction in the quantity demanded. Teenagers are found to be especially sensitive to the price of cigarettes: a 10 per cent increase in the price causes about a 12 per cent drop in teenage smoking.

A related question is how the price of cigarettes affects the demand for illicit drugs, such as marijuana. Opponents of cigarette taxes often argue that tobacco and marijuana are substitutes, so that high cigarette prices encourage marijuana use. By contrast, many experts on substance abuse view tobacco as a 'gateway drug' leading the young to experiment with other harmful substances. Most studies of the data are consistent with this view: they find that lower cigarette prices are associated with greater use of marijuana. In other words, tobacco and marijuana appear to be complements rather than substitutes.

Quick Quiz Make up an example of a demand schedule for pizza, and graph the implied demand curve • Give an example of something that would shift this demand curve • Would a change in the price of pizza shift this demand curve?

SUPPLY

We now turn to the other side of the market and examine the behaviour of sellers. Once again, to focus our thinking, let's consider the market for ice cream.

The Supply Curve: The Relationship Between Price and Quantity Supplied

quantity supplied
the amount of a good that sellers are willing and able to sell

The **quantity supplied** of any good or service is the amount that sellers are willing and able to sell. There are many determinants of quantity supplied, but once again price plays a special role in our analysis. When the price of ice cream is high, selling ice cream is profitable, and so the sellers are willing to supply more. Sellers of ice cream work longer hours, buy more ice cream machines and hire extra workers in order to ensure supplies to the market rise. By contrast, when the price of ice cream is low, the business is less profitable, and so sellers are willing to produce less ice cream. At a low price, some sellers may even choose to shut down, and their quantity supplied falls to zero. Because the quantity supplied rises as the price rises and falls as the price falls, we say that the quantity supplied is *positively related* to the price of the good. This relationship between price and quantity supplied is called the **law of supply**: other things equal, when the price of a good rises, the quantity supplied of the good also rises, and when the price falls, the quantity supplied falls as well.

law of supply
the claim that, other things equal, the quantity supplied of a good rises when the price of the good rises

The table in Figure 4.5 shows the quantity, Häagen, an ice cream seller, is willing to supply, at various prices of ice cream. At a price below €1.00 per cornet of ice cream, Häagen does not supply any ice cream at all. As the price rises, he is willing to supply a greater and greater quantity. This is the **supply schedule**, a table that shows the relationship between the price of a good and the quantity supplied, holding constant everything else that influences how much producers of the good want to sell.

supply schedule
a table that shows the relationship between the price of a good and the quantity supplied

The graph in Figure 4.5 uses the numbers from the table to illustrate the law of supply. The curve relating price and quantity supplied is called the **supply curve**. The supply curve slopes upward because, other things equal, a higher price means a greater quantity supplied.

supply curve
a graph of the relationship between the price of a good and the quantity supplied

FIGURE 4.5

Häagen's Supply Schedule and Supply Curve

The supply schedule shows the quantity supplied at each price. This supply curve, which graphs the supply schedule, shows how the quantity supplied of the good changes as its price varies. Because a higher price increases the quantity supplied, the supply curve slopes upward.

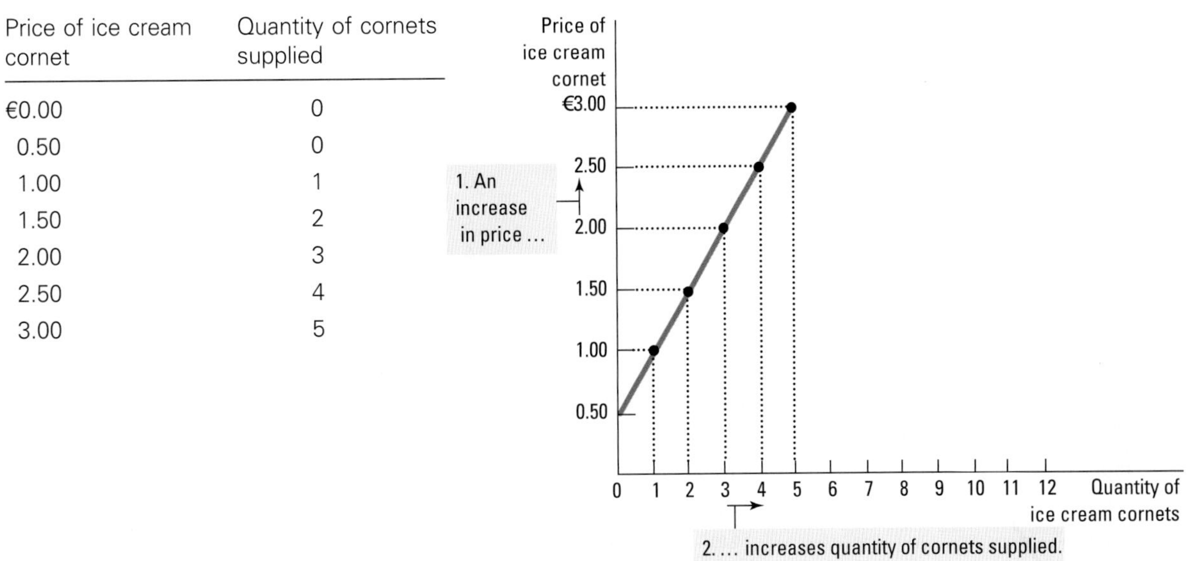

Price of ice cream cornet	Quantity of cornets supplied
€0.00	0
0.50	0
1.00	1
1.50	2
2.00	3
2.50	4
3.00	5

Market Supply versus Individual Supply

Just as market demand is the sum of the demands of all buyers, market supply is the sum of the supplies of all sellers. The table in Figure 4.6 shows the supply schedules for two ice cream producers – Häagen and Dazs. At any price, Häagen's supply schedule tells us the quantity of ice cream Häagen is willing to supply, and Dazs's supply schedule tells us the quantity of ice cream Dazs is willing to supply. The market supply is the sum of the two individual supplies.

The graph in Figure 4.6 shows the supply curves that correspond to the supply schedules. As with demand curves, we sum the individual supply curves *horizontally* to obtain the market supply curve. That is, to find the total quantity supplied at any price, we add the individual quantities found on the horizontal axis of the individual supply curves. The market supply curve shows how the total quantity supplied varies as the price of the good varies.

Shifts versus Movements along the Supply Curve

As noted in our discussion of demand, a distinction that must be made is between a shift in the supply curve and a movement along the supply curve. A shift in the supply curve is caused by a factor affecting supply other than a change in price. The factors affecting supply are outlined below. If any of these factors change then the amount sellers are willing to offer for sale changes whatever the price. The shift in the supply curve is referred to as an *increase or decrease in supply*. A movement along the supply curve occurs when there is a change in price. This may occur because of a change in demand conditions. The factors

FIGURE 4.6

Market Supply as the Sum of Individual Supplies

The quantity supplied in a market is the sum of the quantities supplied by all the sellers at each price. Thus, the market supply curve is found by adding horizontally the individual supply curves. At a price of €2, Häagen is willing to supply 3 ice cream cornets, and Dazs is willing to supply 4 ice cream cornets. The quantity supplied in the market at this price is 7 cornets.

Price of ice cream cornet	Häagen		Dazs		Market
€0.00	0	+	0	=	0
0.50	0		0		0
1.00	1		0		1
1.50	2		2		4
2.00	3		4		7
2.50	4		6		10
3.00	5		8		13

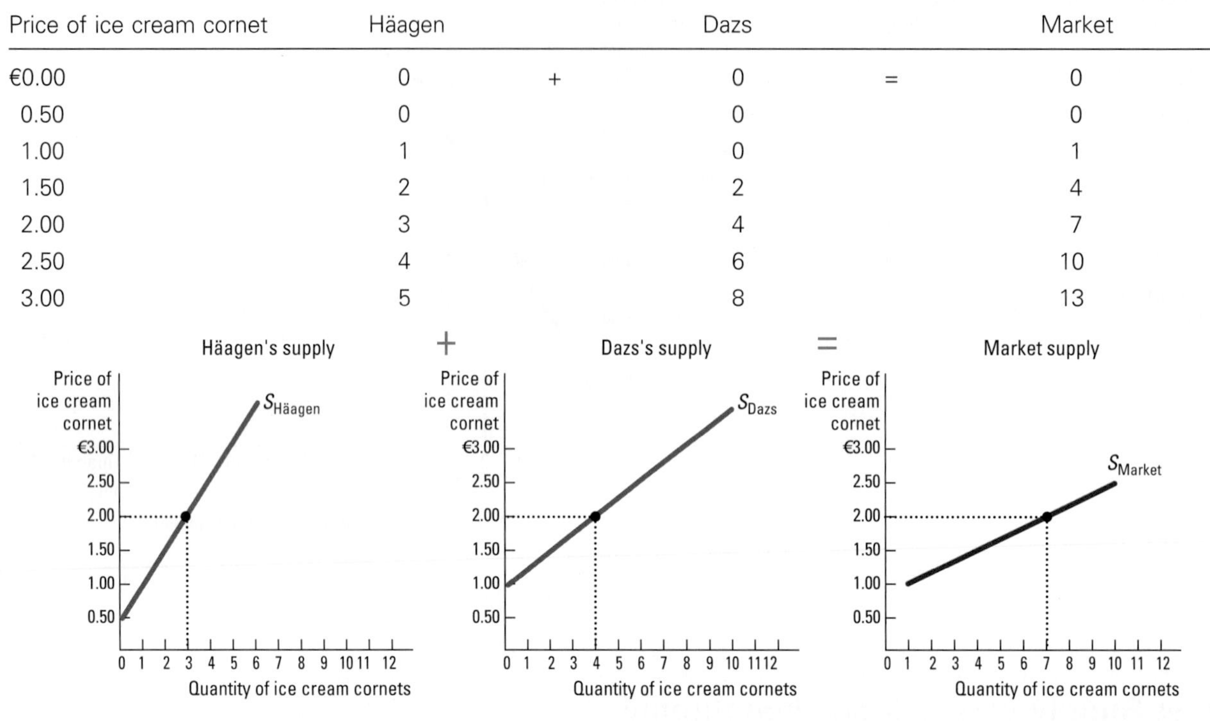

affecting supply are assumed to be held constant. A change in price leads to a movement along the supply curve and is referred to as a *change in quantity supplied.*

Shifts in the Supply Curve

The supply curve for ice cream shows how much ice cream producers are willing to offer for sale at any given price, holding constant all the other factors beyond price that influence producers' decisions about how much to sell. This relationship can change over time, which is represented by a shift in the supply curve. For example, suppose the price of sugar falls. Because sugar is an input into producing ice cream, the fall in the price of sugar makes selling ice cream more profitable. This raises the supply of ice cream: at any given price, sellers are now willing to produce a larger quantity. Thus, the supply curve for ice cream shifts to the right.

Figure 4.7 illustrates shifts in supply. Any change that raises quantity supplied at every price, such as a fall in the price of sugar, shifts the supply curve to the right and is called *an increase in supply*. Similarly, any change that reduces the quantity supplied at every price shifts the supply curve to the left and is called *a decrease in supply*.

FIGURE 4.7

Shifts in the Supply Curve

Any change that raises the quantity that sellers wish to produce at a given price shifts the supply curve to the right. Any change that lowers the quantity that sellers wish to produce at a given price shifts the supply curve to the left.

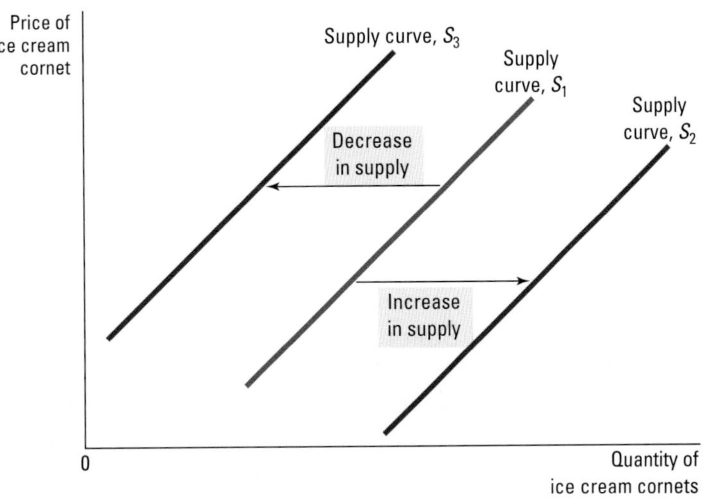

There are many variables that can shift the supply curve. Here are some of the most important.

Input Prices To produce their output of ice cream, sellers use various inputs: cream, sugar, flavouring, ice cream machines, the buildings in which the ice cream is made, and the labour of workers to mix the ingredients and operate the machines. When the price of one or more of these inputs rises, producing ice cream is less profitable and firms supply less ice cream. If input prices rise substantially, some firms might shut down and supply no ice cream at all. If input prices fall for some reason, then production may be more profitable and there is an incentive to supply more at each price. Thus, the supply of a good is negatively related to the price of the inputs used to make the good.

Technology The technology for turning the inputs into ice cream is yet another determinant of supply. Advances in technology increase productivity allowing more to be produced using fewer factor inputs. As a result costs, both total and unit, may fall and supply increases. The invention of the mechanized ice cream machine, for example, reduced the amount of labour necessary to make ice cream. By reducing firms' costs, the advance in technology raised the supply of ice cream.

Expectations The amount of ice cream firms supply today may depend on their expectations of the future. For example, if sellers expect the price of ice cream to rise in the future, they will put some of their current production into storage and supply less to the market today. If there is an expectation of a spell of hot weather then supply may be increased to cater for the expected increase in sales.

TABLE 4.2

Variables That Influence Sellers

This table lists the variables that affect how much producers choose to sell of any good. Notice the special role that the price of the good plays: a change in the good's price represents a movement along the supply curve, whereas a change in one of the other variables shifts the supply curve.

Variable	A change in this variable . . .
Price	Represents a movement along the supply curve
Input prices	Shifts the supply curve
Technology	Shifts the supply curve
Expectations	Shifts the supply curve
Number of sellers	Shifts the supply curve

Number of Sellers Market supply will be affected by the number of firms in the industry. In the 27 EU countries the number of dairy farmers has fallen in the last five years from over 1.56 million to 1.33 million. Output of milk was around 135 million litres in 2010. Unless existing producers are able to expand production, the supply of milk will fall with fewer producers.

Natural/Social Factors There are often many natural or social factors that affect supply. These include such things as the weather affecting crops, natural disasters, pestilence and disease, changing attitudes and social expectations (for example over the production of organic food, the disposal of waste, reducing carbon emissions, ethical supply sourcing and so on) all of which can have an influence on production decisions. Some or all of these may have an influence on the cost of inputs into production.

Summary The supply curve shows what happens to the quantity supplied of a good when its price varies, holding constant all the other variables that influence sellers. When one of these other variables changes, the supply curve shifts. Table 4.2 lists all the variables that influence how much producers choose to sell of a good.

Quick Quiz Make up an example of a supply schedule for pizza, and graph the implied supply curve • Give an example of something that would shift this supply curve • Would a change in the price of pizza shift this supply curve?

SUPPLY AND DEMAND TOGETHER

Having analysed supply and demand separately, we now combine them to see how they determine the quantity of a good sold in a market and its price.

Equilibrium

Figure 4.8 shows the market supply curve and market demand curve together. Equilibrium is defined as a state of rest, a point where there is no force acting for change. Economists refer to supply and demand as being *market forces.* In

FIGURE 4.8

The Equilibrium of Supply and Demand

The equilibrium is found where the supply and demand curves intersect. At the equilibrium price, the quantity supplied equals the quantity demanded. Here the equilibrium price is €2: at this price, 7 ice cream cornets are supplied and 7 ice cream cornets are demanded.

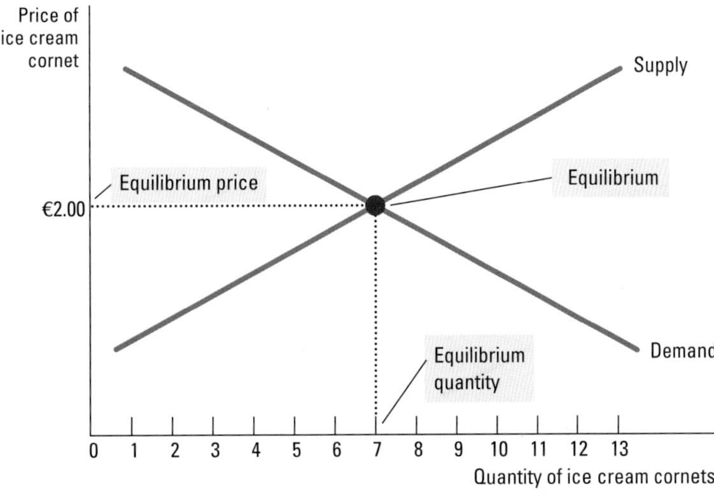

any market the relationship between supply and demand exerts force on price. If supply is greater than demand or vice versa, then there is pressure on price to change. Notice, however, that there is one point at which the supply and demand curves intersect. This point is called the market's **equilibrium**. The price at this intersection is called the **equilibrium price,** and the quantity is called the **equilibrium quantity**. Here the equilibrium price is €2.00 per cornet, and the equilibrium quantity is 7 ice cream cornets.

equilibrium
a situation in which the price has reached the level where quantity supplied equals quantity demanded

equilibrium price
the price that balances quantity supplied and quantity demanded

equilibrium quantity
the quantity supplied and the quantity demanded at the equilibrium price

At the equilibrium price, the quantity of the good that buyers are willing and able to buy exactly balances the quantity that sellers are willing and able to sell. The equilibrium price is sometimes called the *market-clearing price* because, at this price, everyone in the market has been satisfied: buyers have bought all they want to buy, and sellers have sold all they want to sell.

The actions of buyers and sellers naturally move markets towards the equilibrium of supply and demand. To see why, consider what happens when the market price is not equal to the equilibrium price.

Suppose first that the market price is above the equilibrium price, as in panel (a) of Figure 4.9. At a price of €2.50 per cornet, the quantity suppliers would like to sell at this price (10 cornets) exceeds the quantity which buyers are willing to purchase (4 cornets). There is a **surplus** of the good: suppliers are unable to sell all they want at the going price. A surplus is sometimes called a situation of *excess supply*. When there is a surplus in the ice cream market, sellers of ice cream find their freezers increasingly full of ice cream they would like to sell but cannot. They respond to the surplus by cutting their prices. Falling prices, in turn, increase the quantity demanded and decrease the quantity supplied. Prices continue to fall until the market reaches the equilibrium.

surplus
a situation in which quantity supplied is greater than quantity demanded

Suppose now that the market price is below the equilibrium price, as in panel (b) of Figure 4.9. In this case, the price is €1.50 per cornet, and the quantity of the good demanded exceeds the quantity supplied. There is a **shortage** of the good: demanders are unable to buy all they want at the going price. A shortage is

shortage
a situation in which quantity demanded is greater than quantity supplied

FIGURE 4.9

Markets Not in Equilibrium

In panel (a), there is a surplus. Because the market price of €2.50 is above the equilibrium price, the quantity supplied (10 cornets) exceeds the quantity demanded (4 cornets). Suppliers try to increase sales by cutting the price of a cornet, and this moves the price toward its equilibrium level. In panel (b), there is a shortage. Because the market price of €1.50 is below the equilibrium price, the quantity demanded (10 cornets) exceeds the quantity supplied (4 cornets). With too many buyers chasing too few goods, suppliers can take advantage of the shortage by raising the price. Hence, in both cases, the price adjustment moves the market towards the equilibrium of supply and demand.

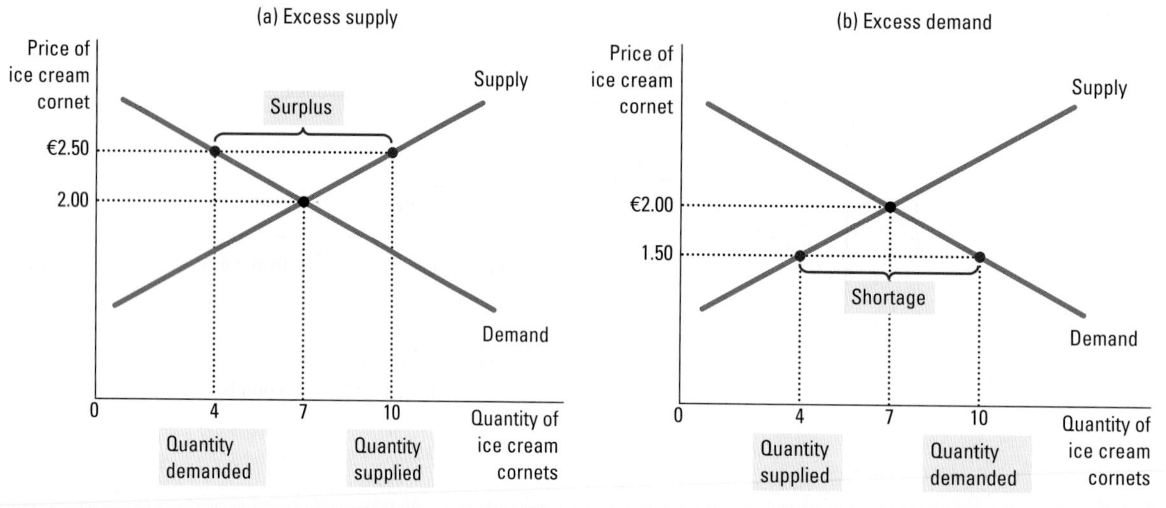

sometimes called a situation of *excess demand*. When a shortage occurs in the ice cream market, buyers have to wait in long queues for a chance to buy one of the few cornets that are available. With too many buyers chasing too few goods, sellers can respond to the shortage by raising their prices without losing sales. As the price rises, quantity demanded falls, quantity supplied rises and the market once again moves toward the equilibrium.

Thus, the activities of the many buyers and sellers automatically push the market price towards the equilibrium price. Once the market reaches its equilibrium, all buyers and sellers are satisfied, and there is no upward or downward pressure on the price. How quickly equilibrium is reached varies from market to market, depending on how quickly prices adjust. In most free markets, surpluses and shortages are only temporary because prices eventually move towards their equilibrium levels (we will see the significance of the word 'free' later in the book). Indeed, this phenomenon is so pervasive that it is called the **law of supply and demand**: the price of any good adjusts to bring the quantity supplied and quantity demanded for that good into balance.

law of supply and demand
the claim that the price of any good adjusts to bring the quantity supplied and the quantity demanded for that good into balance

Three Steps to Analyzing Changes in Equilibrium

So far we have seen how supply and demand together determine a market's equilibrium, which in turn determines the price of the good and the amount of the good that buyers purchase and sellers produce. Of course, the equilibrium price and quantity depend on the position of the supply and demand curves. When some event shifts one of these curves, the equilibrium in the market

FYI

Prices as Signals

Our analysis so far has only brushed the surface of the way markets operate. Economists have conducted extensive research into the nature and determinants of both demand and supply. It is beyond the scope of this book to go into too much detail on these issues but it is useful to have a little bit of background knowledge on this to help understand markets more effectively.

At the heart of research into demand and supply is why buyers and sellers behave as they do. The development of magnetic resonance imaging (MRI) techniques has allowed researchers to investigate how the brain responds to different stimuli when making purchasing decisions (referred to as *neuroeconomics*). As time goes by our understanding of buyer and seller behaviour will improve and theories will have to be adapted to accommodate this new understanding.

However, much of the theory behind how markets work relies on the assumption of rational behaviour defined in terms of humans preferring more to less. The main function of price in a free market is to act as a signal to both buyers and sellers.

For buyers, price tells them something about what they have to give up to acquire the benefits that having the good will confer on them. These benefits are referred to as the *utility* (satisfaction) derived from consumption. If I am willing to pay €10 to go and watch a movie then economists will assume that the value of the benefits I gain from watching the movie is greater than the next best alternative – what else I could have spent my €10 on. Principles 1 and 2 of the *Ten Principles of Economics* state that people face trade-offs and that the cost of something is what you have to give up to acquire it. This is fundamental to the law of demand. At higher prices, the sacrifice being made in terms of the value of the benefits gained from alternatives is greater and so we may be less willing to do so as a result. If the price of a ticket for the movie was €20 then it might have to be a very good movie to persuade us that giving up what else €20 could buy is worth it.

For sellers price acts as a signal in relation to the profitability of production. For most sellers, increasing the amount of a good produced will incur some additional input costs. A higher price is required in order to compensate for the additional cost and to also enable the producer to gain some reward from the risk they are taking in production. That reward is termed *profit.*

If prices are rising in a free market then this acts as a different but related signal to buyers and sellers. Rising prices to a seller means that there is a shortage and thus there is an incentive to expand production because the seller knows that she will be able to sell what she produces. For buyers, a rising price changes the nature of the trade-off they have to face. They will now have to give up more in order to acquire the good and they will have to decide whether the value of the benefits they will gain from acquiring the good is worth the extra price they have to pay.

What we do know is that for both buyers and sellers, there are many complex processes that occur in decision-making. Whilst we do not fully understand all these processes yet, economists are constantly searching for new insights that might help them understand the workings of markets more fully. All of us go through these complex processes every time we make a purchasing decision – although we may not realize it! Having some appreciation of these processes is fundamental to thinking like an economist.

changes. The analysis of such a change is called *comparative statics* because it involves comparing two unchanging situations – an initial and a new equilibrium.

When analysing how some event affects a market, we proceed in three steps. First, we decide whether the event shifts the supply curve, the demand curve or, in some cases, both curves. Secondly, we decide whether the curve shifts to the right or to the left. Thirdly, we use the supply and demand diagram to compare the initial and the new equilibrium, which shows how the shift affects the equilibrium price and quantity. It is important in the analysis that the process by which equilibrium changes is understood and that the changes involved are not instantaneous – some markets will take longer to adjust to changes than others.

TABLE 4.3

A Three-Step Programme for Analysing Changes in Equilibrium

1. Decide whether the event shifts the supply or demand curve (or perhaps both).
2. Decide in which direction the curve shifts.
3. Use the supply and demand diagram to see how the shift changes the equilibrium price and quantity.

Table 4.3 summarizes the three steps. To see how this recipe is used, let's consider various events that might affect the market for ice cream.

Example: A Change in Demand Suppose that one summer the weather is very hot. How does this event affect the market for ice cream? To answer this question, let's follow our three steps.

1. The hot weather affects the demand curve by changing people's taste for ice cream. That is, the weather changes the amount of ice cream that people want to buy at any given price.
2. Because hot weather makes people want to eat more ice cream, the demand curve shifts to the right. Figure 4.10 shows this increase in demand as the shift in the demand curve from D_1 to D_2. This shift indicates that the quantity of ice cream demanded is higher at every price. The shift in demand has led to a shortage of ice creams in the market. At a price of €2.00 buyers now want

FIGURE 4.10

How an Increase in Demand Affects the Equilibrium

An event that raises quantity demanded at any given price shifts the demand curve to the right. The equilibrium price and the equilibrium quantity both rise. Here, an abnormally hot summer causes buyers to demand more ice cream. The demand curve shifts from D_1 to D_2, which causes the equilibrium price to rise from €2.00 to €2.50 and the equilibrium quantity to rise from 7 to 10 cornets.

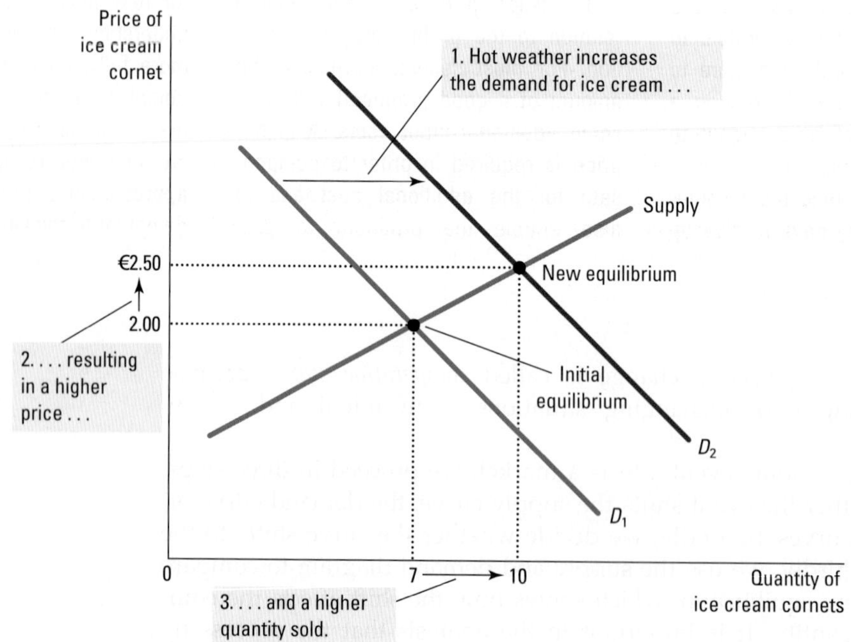

to buy 15 ice creams but sellers are only offering 7 ice creams for sale at this price.

3. As Figure 4.10 shows, the shortage encourages producers to increase the output of ice creams. The additional production incurs extra costs and so a higher price is required to compensate sellers. This raises the equilibrium price from €2.00 to €2.50 and the equilibrium quantity from 7 to 10 cornets. In other words, the hot weather increases the price of ice cream and the quantity of ice cream bought and sold.

"We work on the law of 'supply and demand' - we demand and you supply."

Shifts in Curves versus Movements along Curves Notice that when hot weather drives up the price of ice cream, the quantity of ice cream that firms supply rises, even though the supply curve remains the same. In this case, economists say there has been an increase in 'quantity supplied' but no change in 'supply'.

'Supply' refers to the position of the supply curve, whereas the 'quantity supplied' refers to the amount suppliers wish to sell. In this example, we assumed supply does not change. Instead, the hot weather alters consumers' desire to buy at any given price and thereby shifts the demand curve. The increase in demand causes the equilibrium price to rise. When the price rises, the quantity supplied rises. This increase in quantity supplied is represented by the movement along the supply curve.

To summarize, a shift *in* the supply curve is called a 'change in supply', and a shift *in* the demand curve is called a 'change in demand'. A movement *along* a fixed supply curve is called a 'change in the quantity supplied', and a movement *along* a fixed demand curve is called a 'change in the quantity demanded'.

Example: A Change in Supply Suppose that, during another summer, a hurricane destroys part of the South American sugar cane crop and drives up the world price of sugar. How does this event affect the market for ice cream? Once again, to answer this question, we follow our three steps.

1. The change in the price of sugar, an input into making ice cream, affects the supply curve. By raising the costs of production, it reduces the amount of ice cream that firms produce and sell at any given price. The demand curve does not change because the higher cost of inputs does not directly affect the amount of ice cream households wish to buy.
2. The supply curve shifts to the left because, at every price, the total amount that firms are willing and able to sell is reduced. Figure 4.11 illustrates this decrease in supply as a shift in the supply curve from S_1 to S_2. At a price of €2.00 sellers are now only able to offer 2 ice creams for sale but demand is still 7 ice creams. The shift in supply to the left has created a shortage in the market. Once again, the shortage will create pressure on price to rise as buyers look to purchase ice creams.
3. As Figure 4.11 shows, the shortage raises the equilibrium price from €2.00 to €2.50 and lowers the equilibrium quantity from 7 to 4 cornets. As a result of the sugar price increase, the price of ice cream rises, and the quantity of ice cream bought and sold falls.

Example: A Change in Both Supply and Demand (i) Now suppose that the heat wave and the hurricane occur during the same summer. To analyse this combination of events, we again follow our three steps.

1. We determine that both curves must shift. The hot weather affects the demand curve because it alters the amount of ice cream that households want to buy at any given price. At the same time, when the hurricane drives up sugar prices, it alters the supply curve for ice cream because it changes the amount of ice cream that firms want to sell at any given price.

FIGURE 4.11

How a Decrease in Supply Affects the Equilibrium

An event that reduces quantity supplied at any given price shifts the supply curve to the left. The equilibrium price rises, and the equilibrium quantity falls. Here, an increase in the price of sugar (an input) causes sellers to supply less ice cream. The supply curve shifts from S_1 to S_2, which causes the equilibrium price of ice cream to rise from €2.00 to €2.50 and the equilibrium quantity to fall from 7 to 4 cornets.

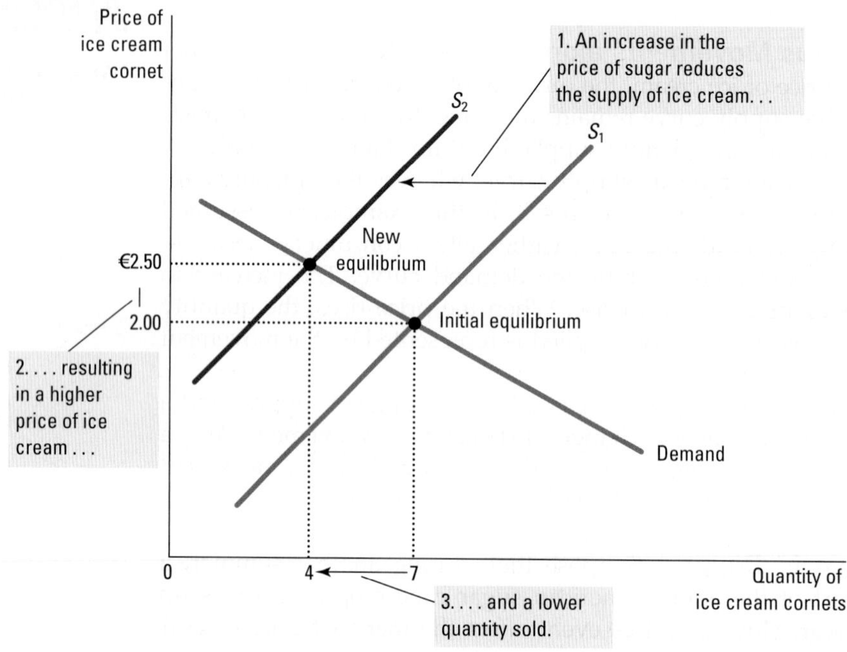

2. The curves shift in the same directions as they did in our previous analysis: the demand curve shifts to the right, and the supply curve shifts to the left. Figure 4.12 illustrates these shifts.
3. As Figure 4.12 shows, there are two possible outcomes that might result, depending on the relative size of the demand and supply shifts. In both cases, the equilibrium price rises. In panel (a), where demand increases substantially while supply falls just a little, the equilibrium quantity also rises. By contrast, in panel (b), where supply falls substantially while demand rises just a little, the equilibrium quantity falls. Thus, these events certainly raise the price of ice cream, but their impact on the amount of ice cream bought and sold is ambiguous (that is, it could go either way).

Example: A Change in Both Supply and Demand (ii) We are now going to look at a slightly different scenario but with both supply and demand increasing together. Assume that forecasters have predicted a heatwave for some weeks. We know that the hot weather is likely to increase demand for ice creams and so the demand curve will shift to the right. However, sellers' expectations that sales of ice creams will increase as a result of the forecasts mean that they take steps to expand production of ice creams. This would lead to a shift of the supply curve

FIGURE 4.12

A Shift in Both Supply and Demand (ii)

Here we observe a simultaneous increase in demand and decrease in supply. Two outcomes are possible. In panel (a), the equilibrium price rises from P_1 to P_2, and the equilibrium quantity rises from Q_1 to Q_2. In panel (b), the equilibrium price again rises from P_1 to P_2, but the equilibrium quantity falls from Q_1 to Q_2.

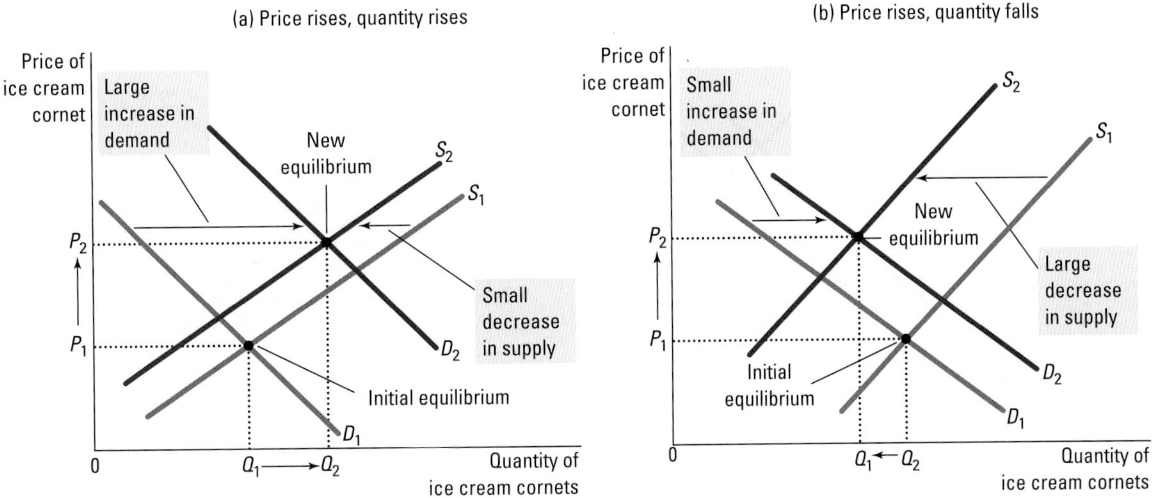

to the right – more ice creams are now offered for sale at every price. To analyse this particular combination of events, we again follow our three steps.

1. We determine that both curves must shift. The hot weather affects the demand curve because it alters the amount of ice cream that households want to buy at any given price. At the same time, the expectations of producers alter the supply curve for ice cream because they change the amount of ice cream that firms want to sell at any given price.
2. Both demand and supply curves shift to the right: Figure 4.13 illustrates these shifts.
3. As Figure 4.13 shows, there are three possible outcomes that might result, depending on the relative size of the demand and supply shifts. In panel (a), where demand increases substantially while supply rises just a little, the equilibrium price and quantity rises. By contrast, in panel (b), where supply rises substantially while demand rises just a little, the equilibrium price falls but the equilibrium quantity rises. In panel (c) the increase in demand and supply are identical and so equilibrium price does not change. Equilibrium quantity will increase, however. Thus, these events have different effects on the price of ice cream although the amount of ice cream bought and sold in each case is higher. In this instance the effect on price is ambiguous.

Summary We have just seen four examples of how to use supply and demand curves to analyse a change in equilibrium. Whenever an event shifts the supply curve, the demand curve, or perhaps both curves, you can use these tools to predict how the event will alter the amount bought and sold in equilibrium and the price at which the good is bought and sold. Table 4.4 shows the predicted outcome for any combination of shifts in the two curves. To make sure you understand how to use the tools of supply and demand, pick a few

FIGURE 4.13

A Shift in both Supply and Demand (ii)

Here, again, we observe a simultaneous increase in demand and supply. Here, three outcomes are possible. In panel (a) the equilibrium price rises from P_1 to P_2 and the equilibrium quantity rises from Q_1 to Q_2. In panel (b), the equilibrium price falls from P_1 to P_2 but the equilibrium quantity rises from Q_1 to Q_2. In panel (c), there is no change to the equilibrium price but the equilibrium quantity rises from Q_1 to Q_2.

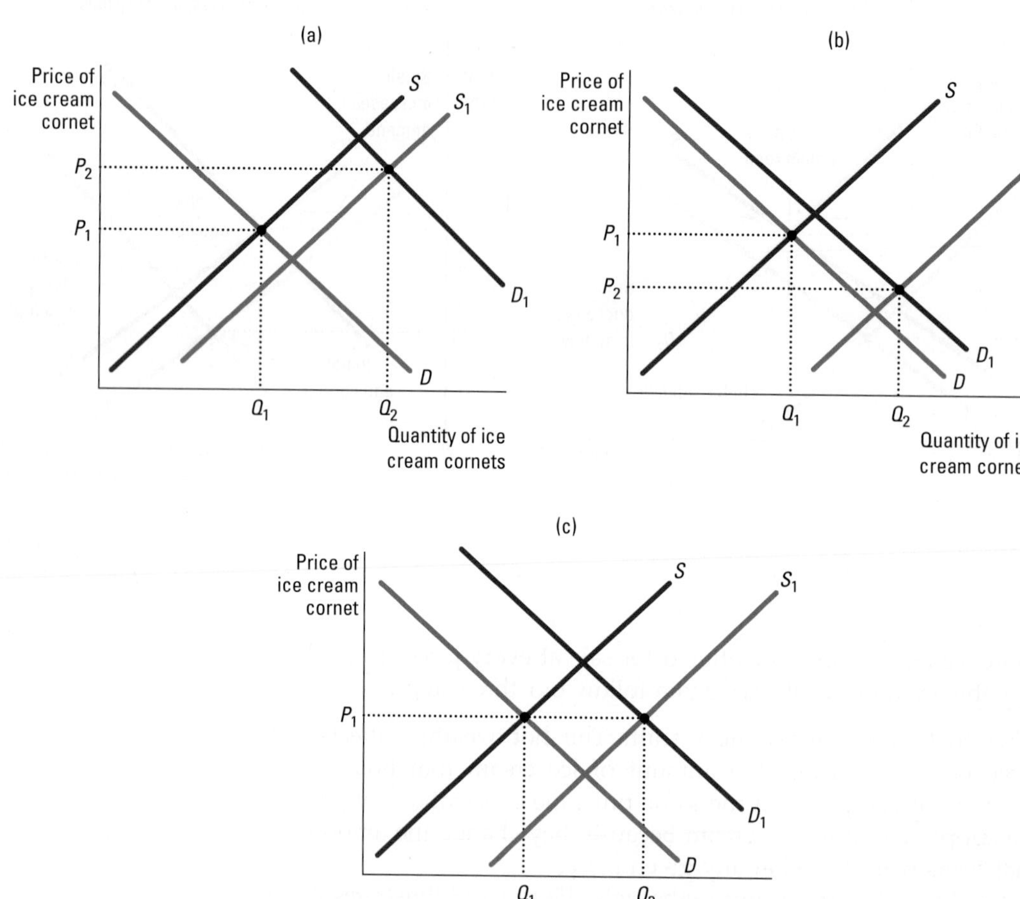

TABLE 4.4

What Happens to Price and Quantity When Supply or Demand Shifts?

As a quick quiz, make sure you can explain each of the entries in this table using a supply and demand diagram.

	No change in supply	**An increase in supply**	**A decrease in supply**
No change in demand	*P* same *Q* same	*P* down *Q* up	*P* up *Q* down
An increase in demand	*P* up *Q* up	*P* ambiguous *Q* up	*P* up *Q* ambiguous
A decrease in demand	*P* down *Q* down	*P* down *Q* ambiguous	*P* ambiguous *Q* down

IN THE NEWS

Markets in Action

We have seen how we can use supply and demand analysis to begin to understand markets. The real world has examples of markets in action every day. This article highlights some examples from early 2010.

Winter 2009–2010 in Europe was a cold one. Large parts of northern Europe 'enjoyed' a white Christmas and extremely low temperatures well into the New Year. In the United States, the east coast suffered heavy snow falls and sub-zero temperatures even reached parts of Florida. The effects on demand and supply of various goods were noticeable.

In the UK, the demand for salt for the roads rose significantly. Local councils found that they ran down supplies as the sub-zero temperatures persisted night after night. The sharp increase in demand for salt led to prices in both Europe and the US rising. One of the major suppliers of rock salt for gritting roads in the UK, Salt Union, for example, worked round the clock to try and meet the demand for salt. The additional cost of the inputs required to work 24 hours a day had to be reflected in the price the company received for its product. The significant rise in demand meant that prices rose. A local government association, the UK Roads Liaison Group, estimated that prices for rock salt were normally between £30 and £40 per ton. As the cold weather continued and the shortage of rock salt got worse, prices rose to between £150 and £200 per ton.

Other businesses also saw changes in demand as a result of the weather. Demand for winter clothing and footwear increased significantly, gas and electricity companies saw demand for energy rising as houses and businesses turned up the thermostats to keep warm and online businesses reported a rise in demand. The explanation was that people were not able to get into work and so tended to sit at home surfing the web and buying goods online! One of the ironic things about this was that sellers had to advise buyers that deliveries of goods might be delayed because of the bad weather.

In many parts of Europe, unseasonably bad weather hit farmers. Parts of southern Europe, normally used to balmy winter weather, suffered snow, ice and frosts which hit crops susceptible to the cold. Analysts were predicting that the bad weather might affect harvests of delicate crops such as soft fruit, citrus fruits and so on and as a result supply would fall. The fall in supply was likely to increase the price of fruit juice by around 2–3 cents a gallon.

In the US, commodity market traders were anticipating that the bad weather would affect the harvest of grain and soya beans. The expectations of a shortage initially drove the price up but a report on harvest levels by the United States Department of Agriculture (USDA) wrong-footed the market. The USDA estimated, in its report published in January 2010, that corn production would rise to 13.151 million bushels (a bushel is around 60 lbs or 27.2 kg), a rise of 230 million bushels on previous estimates. Meanwhile, soya bean output was estimated to rise by 42 million bushels to 3.361 million bushels. The effect of the report was to push soya bean prices down by between 3 and 6 per cent.

entries in this table and make sure you can explain to yourself why the table contains the prediction it does.

Quick Quiz Analyze what happens to the market for pizza if the price of tomatoes rises. • Analyze what happens to the market for pasta if the price of potatoes falls.

CONCLUSION: HOW PRICES ALLOCATE RESOURCES

This chapter has analysed supply and demand in a single market. Although our discussion has centred around the market for ice cream, the lessons learned here apply in most other markets as well. Whenever you go to a shop to buy something, you are contributing to the demand for that item. Whenever you look for a job, you are contributing to the supply of labour services. Because supply and demand are such pervasive economic phenomena, the model of supply and demand is a powerful tool for analysis. We shall be using this model repeatedly in the following chapters.

One of the *Ten Principles of Economics* discussed in Chapter 1 is that markets are usually a good way to organize economic activity. Although it is still too early to judge whether market outcomes are good or bad, in this chapter we have begun to see how markets work. In any economic system, scarce resources have to be allocated among competing uses. Market economies harness the forces of supply and demand to serve that end. Supply and demand together determine the prices of the economy's many different goods and services; prices in turn are the signals that guide the allocation of resources.

For example, consider the allocation of property on the seafront in a seaside resort. Because the amount of this property is limited, not everyone can enjoy the luxury of living by the beach. Who gets this resource? The answer is: whoever is willing and able to pay the price. The price of seafront property adjusts until the quantity of property demanded exactly balances the quantity supplied. Thus, in market economies, prices are the mechanism for rationing scarce resources.

Similarly, prices determine who produces each good and how much is produced. For instance, consider farming. Because we need food to survive, it is crucial that some people work on farms. What determines who is a farmer and who is not? In a free society, there is no government planning agency making this decision and ensuring an adequate supply of food. Instead, the allocation of workers to farms is based on the job decisions of millions of workers. This decentralized system works well because these decisions depend on prices. The prices of food and the wages of farm workers (the price of their labour) adjust to ensure that enough people choose to be farmers.

If a person had never seen a market economy in action, the whole idea might seem preposterous. Economies are large groups of people engaged in many interdependent activities. What prevents decentralized decision-making from degenerating into chaos? What coordinates the actions of the millions of people with their varying abilities and desires? What ensures that what needs to get done does in fact get done? The answer, in a word, is *prices*. If market economies are guided by an invisible hand, as Adam Smith famously suggested, then prices are the baton that the invisible hand uses to conduct the economic orchestra.

SUMMARY

- Economists use the model of supply and demand to analyse competitive markets. In a competitive market, there are many buyers and sellers, each of whom has little or no influence on the market price.
- The demand curve shows how the quantity of a good demanded depends on the price. According to the law of demand, as the price of a good falls, the quantity demanded rises. Therefore, the demand curve slopes downward.
- In addition to price, other determinants of how much consumers want to buy include income, the prices of substitutes and complements, tastes, expectations and the number of buyers. If one of these factors changes, the demand curve shifts.
- The supply curve shows how the quantity of a good supplied depends on the price. According to the law of supply, as the price of a good rises, the quantity supplied rises. Therefore, the supply curve slopes upward.
- In addition to price, other determinants of how much producers want to sell include input prices, technology, expectations, the number of sellers, and natural and social factors. If one of these factors changes, the supply curve shifts.

- The intersection of the supply and demand curves determines the market equilibrium. At the equilibrium price, the quantity demanded equals the quantity supplied.
- The behaviour of buyers and sellers naturally drives markets toward their equilibrium. When the market price is above the equilibrium price, there is a surplus of the good, which causes the market price to fall. When the market price is below the equilibrium price, there is a shortage, which causes the market price to rise.
- To analyse how any event influences a market, we use the supply and demand diagram to examine how the event affects the equilibrium price and quantity. To do this we follow three steps. First, we decide whether the event shifts the supply curve or the demand curve (or both). Secondly, we decide which direction the curve shifts. Thirdly, we compare the new equilibrium with the initial equilibrium.
- In market economies, prices are the signals that guide economic decisions and thereby allocate scarce resources. For every good in the economy, the price ensures that supply and demand are in balance. The equilibrium price then determines how much of the good buyers choose to purchase and how much sellers choose to produce.

KEY CONCEPTS

market, p. 68
competitive market, p. 69
quantity demanded, p. 70
law of demand, p. 70
demand schedule, p. 70
demand curve, p. 71
normal good, p. 73
inferior good, p. 73
substitutes, p. 73
complements, p. 74
quantity supplied, p. 76
law of supply, p. 76
supply schedule, p. 76
supply curve, p. 76
equilibrium, p. 81
equilibrium price,, p. 81
equilibrium quantity, p. 81
surplus, p. 81
shortage, p. 81
law of supply and demand, p. 82

QUESTIONS FOR REVIEW

1. What is a competitive market? Briefly describe the types of markets other than perfectly competitive markets.
2. What determines the quantity of a good that buyers demand?
3. What are the demand schedule and the demand curve, and how are they related? Why does the demand curve slope downward?
4. Does a change in consumers' tastes lead to a movement along the demand curve or a shift in the demand curve? Does a change in price lead to a movement along the demand curve or a shift in the demand curve?
5. Carlos prefers asparagus to spinach. His income declines and as a result he buys more spinach. Is spinach an inferior or a normal good to Carlos? Explain your answer.
6. What determines the quantity of a good that sellers supply?
7. What are the supply schedule and the supply curve, and how are they related? Why does the supply curve slope upward?
8. Does a change in producers' technology lead to a movement along the supply curve or a shift in the supply curve? Does a change in price lead to a movement along the supply curve or a shift in the supply curve?
9. Define the equilibrium of a market. Describe the forces that move a market toward its equilibrium.
10. Cheese and wine are complements because they are often enjoyed together. When the price of wine rises, what happens to the supply, demand, quantity supplied, quantity demanded and the price in the market for cheese?
11. Describe the role of prices in market economies.

PROBLEMS AND APPLICATIONS

1. Explain each of the following statements using supply and demand diagrams.
   a. When there is a drought in southern Europe, the price of olive oil rises in supermarkets throughout Europe.
   b. When the Olympic Games were held in Greece in 2004, the price of hotel rooms in Athens rocketed.
   c. When a war breaks out in the Middle East, the price of petrol in Europe rises and the price of a used Mercedes falls.
2. 'An increase in the demand for mozzarella cheese raises the quantity of mozzarella demanded, but not the quantity supplied.' Is this statement true or false? Explain.
3. Consider the market for large family saloon cars. For each of the events listed here, identify which of the determinants of demand or supply are affected. Also indicate whether demand or supply is increased or decreased. Then show the effect on the price and quantity of large family saloon cars.
   a. People decide to have more children.
   b. A strike by steel workers raises steel prices.
   c. Engineers develop new automated machinery for the production of cars.
   d. The price of estate cars rises.
   e. A stock market crash lowers people's wealth.
4. During the 1990s, technological advances reduced the cost of computer chips. How do you think this affected the market for computers? For computer software? For typewriters?
5. Using supply and demand diagrams, show the effect of the following events on the market for sweatshirts.
   a. A drought in Egypt damages the cotton crop.
   b. The price of leather jackets falls.
   c. All universities require students to attend morning exercise classes in appropriate attire.
   d. New knitting machines are invented.
6. Suppose that in the year 2005 the number of births is temporarily high. How might this baby boom affect the price of baby-sitting services in 2010 and 2020? (Hint: 5-year-olds need babysitters, whereas 15-year-olds can be babysitters.)
7. Vinegar is a complement (as well as a condiment) for chips (at least in the UK and Ireland). If the price of chips rises, what happens to the market for vinegar? For ketchup? For fish? For orange juice?
8. The case study presented in the chapter discussed cigarette taxes as a way to reduce smoking. Now think about the market for cigars.
   a. Are cigars substitutes or complements for cigarettes?
   b. Using a supply and demand diagram, show what happens in the markets for cigars if the tax on cigarettes is increased.
   c. If policy makers wanted to reduce total tobacco consumption, what policies could they combine with the cigarette tax?
9. The market for pizza has the following demand and supply schedules:

Price	Quantity demanded	Quantity supplied
€4	135	26
5	104	53
6	81	81
7	68	98
8	53	110
9	39	121

   Graph the demand and supply curves. What is the equilibrium price and quantity in this market? If the actual price in this market were *above* the equilibrium price, what would drive the market towards the equilibrium? If the actual price in this market were *below* the equilibrium price, what would drive the market towards the equilibrium?
10. Because bacon and eggs are often eaten together, they are complements.
   a. We observe that both the equilibrium price of eggs and the equilibrium quantity of bacon have risen. What could be responsible for this pattern – a fall in the price of chicken feed or a fall in the price of pig feed? Illustrate and explain your answer.
   b. Suppose instead that the equilibrium price of bacon has risen but the equilibrium quantity of eggs has fallen. What could be responsible for this pattern – a rise in the price of chicken feed or a rise in the price of pig feed? Illustrate and explain your answer.
11. Suppose that the price of tickets to see your local football team play at home is determined by market forces. Currently, the demand and supply schedules are as follows:

Price	Quantity demanded	Quantity supplied
€10	50 000	30 000
20	40 000	30 000
30	30 000	30 000
40	20 000	30 000
50	10 000	30 000

   a. Draw the demand and supply curves. What is unusual about this supply curve? Why might this be true?
   b. What are the equilibrium price and quantity of tickets?

c. Your team plans to increase total capacity in its stadium by 5 000 seats next season. What admission price should it charge?

12. An article in *The New York Times* described a successful marketing campaign by the French champagne industry. The article noted that 'many executives felt giddy about the stratospheric champagne prices. But they also feared that such sharp price increases would cause demand to decline, which would then cause prices to plunge.' What mistake are the executives making in their analysis of the situation? Illustrate your answer with a graph.

13. Market research has revealed the following information about the market for chocolate bars: the demand schedule can be represented by the equation $QD = 1\,600 - 300P$, where QD is the quantity demanded and P is the price. The supply schedule can be represented by the equation $QS = 1\,400 + 700P$, where QS is the quantity supplied. Calculate the equilibrium price and quantity in the market for chocolate bars.

14. What do we mean by a perfectly competitive market? Do you think that the example of ice cream used in this chapter fits this description? Is there another type of market that better characterizes the market for ice cream?

For further resources, visit www.cengage.com/mankiw_taylor2

5 ELASTICITY AND ITS APPLICATION

Imagine yourself as a producer of silicon chips for use in personal computers, laptops and a variety of other electronic devices. Because you earn all your income from selling silicon chips, you devote much effort to making your factory as productive as it can be. You monitor how production is organized, staff recruitment and motivation levels, check suppliers for cost effectiveness and quality, and study the latest advances in technology. You know that the more chips you manufacture, the more you will have to sell, and the higher will be your income and your standard of living.

One day a local university announces a major discovery. Scientists have devised a new material to produce chips which would help to increase computing power by 50 per cent. How should you react to this news? Should you use the new material? Does this discovery make you better off or worse off than you were before? In this chapter we will see that these questions can have surprising answers. The surprise will come from applying the most basic tools of economics – supply and demand – to the market for computer chips.

The previous chapter introduced supply and demand. In any competitive market, such as the market for computer chips, the upward sloping supply curve represents the behaviour of sellers, and the downward sloping demand curve represents the behaviour of buyers. The price of the good adjusts to bring the quantity supplied and quantity demanded of the good into balance. To apply this basic analysis to understand the impact of the scientists' discovery, we must first develop one more tool: the concept of *elasticity*. We know from Chapter 4 that when price rises, demand falls and supply rises. What we did not discuss in the chapter was *how far* demand and supply change in response to changes in price. When studying how some event or policy affects a market, we can discuss not only the direction of the effects but their magnitude as well. Elasticity, a measure of how much buyers and sellers respond to changes in market conditions, allows us to analyse supply and demand with greater precision.

THE ELASTICITY OF DEMAND

When we introduced demand in Chapter 4, we noted that consumers usually buy more of a good when its price is lower, when their incomes are higher, when the prices of substitutes for the good are higher or when the prices of complements of the good are lower. Our discussion of demand was qualitative, not quantitative. That is, we discussed the direction in which quantity demanded moves, but not the size of the change. To measure how much consumers respond to changes in these variables, economists use the concept of **elasticity**.

elasticity
a measure of the responsiveness of quantity demanded or quantity supplied to one of its determinants

The Price Elasticity of Demand and its Determinants

The law of demand states that a fall in the price of a good raises the quantity demanded. The **price elasticity of demand** measures how much the quantity demanded responds to a change in price. Demand for a good is said to be *elastic* if the quantity demanded responds substantially to changes in the price. Demand is said to be *inelastic* if the quantity demanded responds only slightly to changes in the price.

price elasticity of demand
a measure of how much the quantity demanded of a good responds to a change in the price of that good, computed as the percentage change in quantity demanded divided by the percentage change in price

The price elasticity of demand for any good measures how willing consumers are to move away from the good as its price rises. Thus, the elasticity reflects the many economic, social and psychological forces that influence consumer tastes. Based on experience, however, we can state some general rules about what determines the price elasticity of demand.

Availability of Close Substitutes Goods with close substitutes tend to have more elastic demand because it is easier for consumers to switch from that good to others. For example, butter and margarine are easily substitutable. A small increase in the price of butter, assuming the price of margarine is held fixed, causes the quantity of butter sold to fall by a relatively large amount. By contrast, because eggs are a food without a close substitute, the demand for eggs is less elastic than the demand for butter.

Necessities versus Luxuries Necessities tend to have inelastic demands, whereas luxuries have elastic demands. People use gas and electricity to heat their homes and cook their food. If the price of gas and electricity rose together, people would not demand dramatically less of them. They might try and be more energy-efficient and reduce their demand a little, but they would still need hot food and warm homes. By contrast, when the price of sailing dinghies rises, the quantity of sailing dinghies demanded falls substantially. The reason is that most people view hot food and warm homes as necessities and a sailing dinghy as a luxury. Of course, whether a good is a necessity or a luxury depends not on the intrinsic properties of the good but on the preferences of the buyer. For an avid sailor with little concern over her health, sailing dinghies might be a necessity with inelastic demand and hot food and a warm place to sleep a luxury with elastic demand.

Definition of the Market The elasticity of demand in any market depends on how we draw the boundaries of the market. Narrowly defined markets tend to have more elastic demand than broadly defined markets, because it is easier to find close substitutes for narrowly defined goods. For example, food, a broad category, has a fairly inelastic demand because there are no good substitutes for food. Ice cream, a narrower category, has a more elastic demand because it is easy to substitute other desserts for ice cream. Vanilla ice cream, a very narrow category, has a very elastic demand because other flavours of ice cream are almost perfect substitutes for vanilla.

Proportion of Income Devoted to the Product Some products have a relatively high price and take a larger proportion of income than others. Buying a new suite of furniture for a lounge, for example, tends to take up a large amount of income whereas buying an ice cream might account for only a tiny proportion of income. If the price of a three-piece suite rises by 10 per cent, therefore, this is likely to have a greater effect on demand for this furniture than a similar 10 per cent increase in the price of an ice cream. The higher the proportion of income devoted to the product the greater the elasticity is likely to be.

Time Horizon Goods tend to have more elastic demand over longer time horizons. When the price of petrol rises, the quantity of petrol demanded falls only slightly in the first few months. Over time, however, people buy more fuel-efficient cars, switch to public transport and move closer to where they work. Within several years, the quantity of petrol demanded falls more substantially. Similarly, if the price of a unit of electricity rises much above an equivalent energy unit of gas, demand may fall only slightly in the short run because many people already have electric cookers or electric heating appliances installed in their homes and cannot easily switch. If the price difference persists over several years, however, people may find it worth their while to replace their old electric heating and cooking appliances with new gas appliances and the demand for electricity will fall.

Computing the Price Elasticity of Demand

Now that we have discussed the price elasticity of demand in general terms, let's be more precise about how it is measured. Economists compute the price elasticity of demand as the percentage change in the quantity demanded divided by the percentage change in the price. That is:

$$\text{Price elasticity of demand} = \frac{\text{Percentage change in quantity demanded}}{\text{Percentage change in price}}$$

For example, suppose that a 10 per cent increase in the price of an ice cream cornet causes the amount of ice cream you buy to fall by 20 per cent. We calculate your elasticity of demand as:

$$\text{Price elasticity of demand} = \frac{20\%}{10\%} = 2$$

In this example, the elasticity is 2, reflecting that the change in the quantity demanded is proportionately twice as large as the change in the price.

Because the quantity demanded of a good is negatively related to its price, the percentage change in quantity will always have the opposite sign to the percentage change in price. In this example, the percentage change in price is a *positive* 10 per cent (reflecting an increase), and the percentage change in quantity demanded is a *negative* 20 per cent (reflecting a decrease). For this reason, price elasticities of demand are sometimes reported as negative numbers. In this book we follow the common practice of dropping the minus sign and reporting all price elasticities as positive numbers. (Mathematicians call this the *absolute value.*) With this convention, a larger price elasticity implies a greater responsiveness of quantity demanded to price.

The Midpoint Method: A Better Way to Calculate Percentage Changes and Elasticities

If you try calculating the price elasticity of demand between two points on a demand curve, you will quickly notice an annoying problem: the elasticity from point A to point B seems different from the elasticity from point B to point A. For example, consider these numbers:

$$\text{Point A:} \quad \text{Price} = €4 \quad \text{Quantity} = 120$$
$$\text{Point B:} \quad \text{Price} = €6 \quad \text{Quantity} = 80$$

Going from point A to point B, the price rises by 50 per cent, and the quantity falls by 33 per cent, indicating that the price elasticity of demand is 33/50, or 0.66. By contrast, going from point B to point A, the price falls by 33 per cent, and the quantity rises by 50 per cent, indicating that the price elasticity of demand is 50/33, or 1.5.

One way to avoid this problem is to use the *midpoint method* for calculating elasticities. The standard way to compute a percentage change is to divide the change by the initial level and multiply by 100. By contrast, the midpoint method computes a percentage change by dividing the change by the midpoint (or average) of the initial and final levels. For instance, €5 is the midpoint of €4 and €6. Therefore, according to the midpoint method, a change from €4 to €6 is considered a 40 per cent rise, because $(6 - 4)/5 \times 100 = 40$. Similarly, a change from €6 to €4 is considered a 40 per cent fall.

Because the midpoint method gives the same answer regardless of the direction of change, it is often used when calculating the price elasticity of demand between two points. In our example, the midpoint between point A and point B is:

$$\text{Midpoint:} \quad \text{Price} = €5 \qquad \text{Quantity} = 100$$

According to the midpoint method, when going from point A to point B, the price rises by 40 per cent, and the quantity falls by 40 per cent. Similarly, when going from point B to point A, the price falls by 40 per cent, and the quantity rises by 40 per cent. In both directions, the price elasticity of demand equals 1.

We can express the midpoint method with the following formula for the price elasticity of demand between two points, denoted (Q_1, P_1) and (Q_2, P_2):

$$\text{Price elasticity of demand} = \frac{(Q_2 - Q_1)/[(Q_2 + Q_1)/2]}{(P_2 - P_1)/[(P_2 + P_1)/2]}$$

The numerator is the percentage change in quantity computed using the midpoint method, and the denominator is the percentage change in price computed using the midpoint method. If you ever need to calculate elasticities, you should use this formula.

In this book, however, we rarely perform such calculations. For most of our purposes, what elasticity represents – the responsiveness of quantity demanded to price – is more important than how it is calculated.

The Variety of Demand Curves

Economists classify demand curves according to their elasticity. Demand is *elastic* when the elasticity is greater than 1, so that quantity changes proportionately more than the price. Demand is *inelastic* when the elasticity is less than 1, so that quantity moves proportionately less than the price. If the elasticity is exactly 1, so that quantity moves the same amount proportionately as price, demand is said to have *unit elasticity.*

Because the price elasticity of demand measures how much quantity demanded responds to changes in the price, it is closely related to the slope of the demand curve. The following rule of thumb (assuming we are using comparable scales on the axes) is a useful guide: the flatter the demand curve that passes through a given point, the greater the price elasticity of demand. The steeper the demand curve that passes through a given point, the smaller the price elasticity of demand.

Figure 5.1 shows five cases. In the extreme case of a zero elasticity shown in panel (a), demand is *perfectly inelastic,* and the demand curve is vertical. In this case, regardless of the price, the quantity demanded stays the same. As the elasticity rises, the demand curve gets flatter and flatter, as shown in panels (b), (c) and (d). At the opposite extreme shown in panel (e), demand is *perfectly elastic.* This occurs as the price elasticity of demand approaches infinity and the demand curve becomes horizontal, reflecting the fact that very small changes in the price lead to huge changes in the quantity demanded.

Finally, if you have trouble keeping straight the terms *elastic* and *inelastic,* here's a memory trick for you: Inelastic curves, such as in panel (a) of Figure 5.1, look like the letter *I.* Elastic curves, as in panel (e), look like the middle bar of the letter *E.* This is not a deep insight, but it might help in your next economics exam.

Total Expenditure, Total Revenue and the Price Elasticity of Demand

total expenditure
the amount paid by buyers, computed as the price of the good times the quantity purchased

total revenue
the amount received by sellers of a good, computed as the price of the good times the quantity sold

When studying changes in supply or demand in a market, two variables we often want to study are **total expenditure** and **total revenue**, the amount paid by buyers and received by sellers of the good. In any market, total revenue received by sellers is $P \times Q$, the price of the good times the quantity of the good sold. Equally, total expenditure is given by the total amount bought multiplied by the price paid. We can show total expenditure graphically, as in Figure 5.2. The height of the box under the demand curve is *P*, and the width is *Q*. The area of this box, $P \times Q$, equals the total expenditure in this market. In Figure 5.2, where $P =$ €4 and $Q = 100$, total expenditure is €4 × 100, or €400.

How does total expenditure change as one moves along the demand curve? The answer depends on the price elasticity of demand. If demand is inelastic, as in Figure 5.3, then an increase in the price causes an increase in total expenditure. Here an increase in price from €1 to €3 causes the quantity demanded to fall only from 100 to 80, and so total expenditure rises from €100 to €240. An increase in price raises $P \times Q$ because the fall in *Q* is proportionately smaller than the rise in *P*.

We obtain the opposite result if demand is elastic: an increase in the price causes a decrease in total expenditure. In Figure 5.4, for instance, when the price rises from €4 to €5, the quantity demanded falls from 50 to 20, and so total expenditure falls from €200 to €100. Because demand is elastic, the reduction in the quantity demanded is so great that it more than offsets the increase in the price. That is, an increase in price reduces $P \times Q$ because the fall in *Q* is proportionately greater than the rise in *P*.

Although the examples in these two figures are extreme, they illustrate a general rule:

- When demand is inelastic (a price elasticity less than 1), price and total expenditure move in the same direction.

FIGURE 5.1

The Price Elasticity of Demand

The price elasticity of demand determines whether the demand curve is steep or flat. Note that all percentage changes are calculated using the midpoint method.

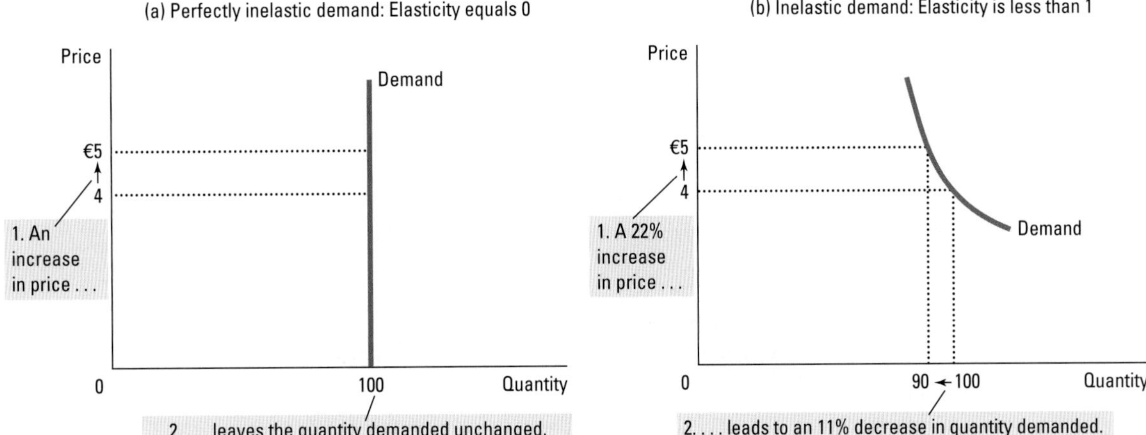

(a) Perfectly inelastic demand: Elasticity equals 0
Price
Demand
€5
4
1. An increase in price . . .
0
100
Quantity
2. . . . leaves the quantity demanded unchanged.
(b) Inelastic demand: Elasticity is less than 1
Price
€5
4
Demand
1. A 22% increase in price . . .
0
90
100
Quantity
2. . . . leads to an 11% decrease in quantity demanded.

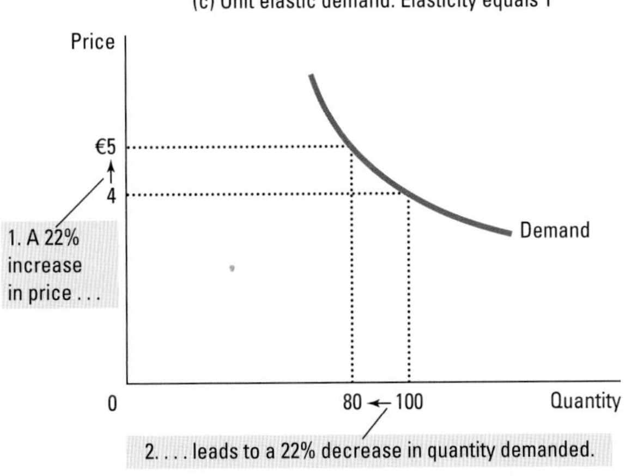

(c) Unit elastic demand: Elasticity equals 1
Price
€5
4
Demand
1. A 22% increase in price . . .
0
80
100
Quantity
2. . . . leads to a 22% decrease in quantity demanded.

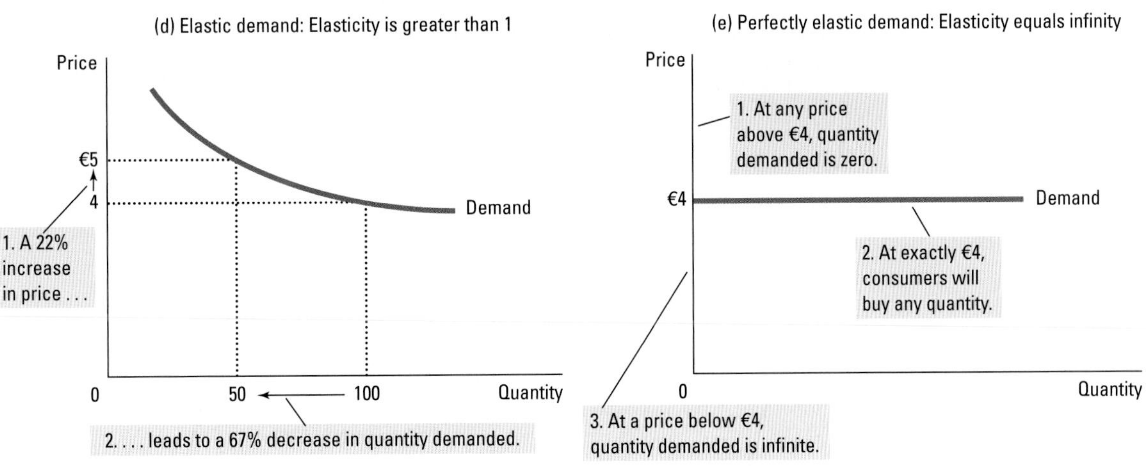

(d) Elastic demand: Elasticity is greater than 1
Price
€5
4
Demand
1. A 22% increase in price . . .
0
50
100
Quantity
2. . . . leads to a 67% decrease in quantity demanded.
(e) Perfectly elastic demand: Elasticity equals infinity
Price
1. At any price above €4, quantity demanded is zero.
€4
Demand
2. At exactly €4, consumers will buy any quantity.
0
Quantity
3. At a price below €4, quantity demanded is infinite.

FIGURE 5.2

Total Expenditure

The total amount paid by buyers, and received as expenditure by sellers, equals the area of the box under the demand curve, P × Q. Here, at a price of €4, the quantity demanded is 100, and total expenditure is €400.

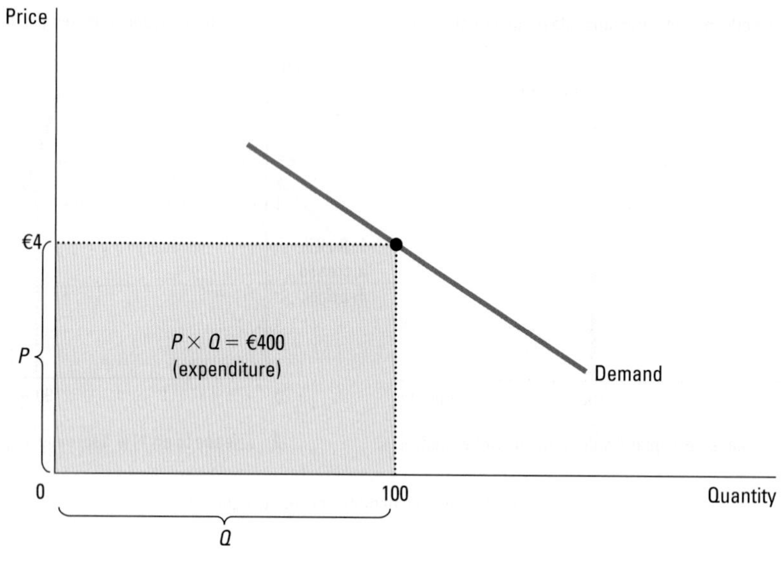

FIGURE 5.3

How Total Expenditure Changes When Price Changes: Inelastic Demand

With an inelastic demand curve, an increase in the price leads to a decrease in quantity demanded that is proportionately smaller. Therefore, total expenditure (the product of price and quantity) increases. Here, an increase in the price from €1 to €3 causes the quantity demanded to fall from 100 to 80, and total expenditure rises from €100 to €240.

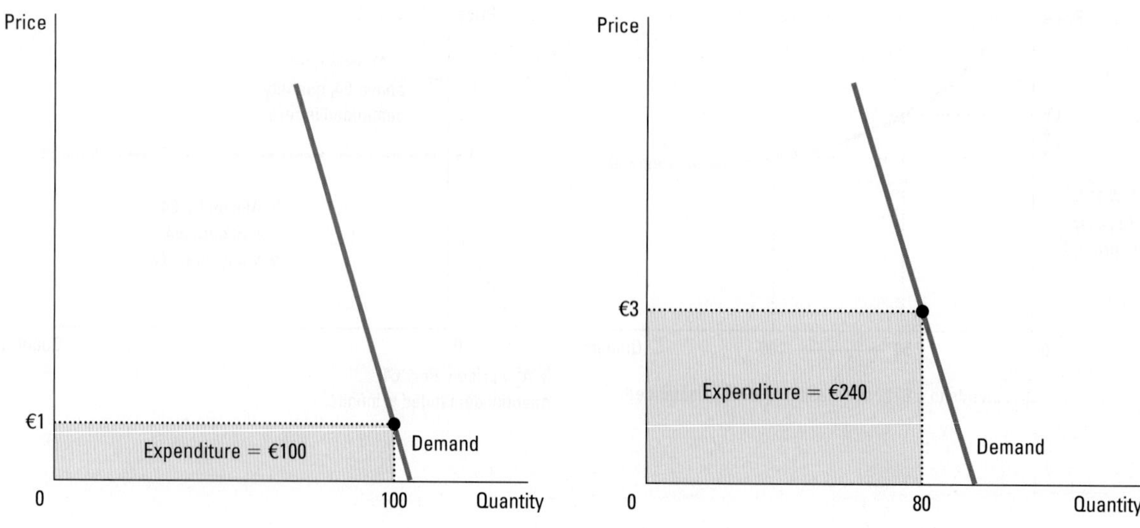

FIGURE 5.4

How Total Expenditure Changes When Price Changes: Elastic Demand

With an elastic demand curve, an increase in the price leads to a decrease in quantity demanded that is proportionately larger. Therefore, total expenditure (the product of price and quantity) decreases. Here, an increase in the price from €4 to €5 causes the quantity demanded to fall from 50 to 20, so total expenditure falls from €200 to €100.

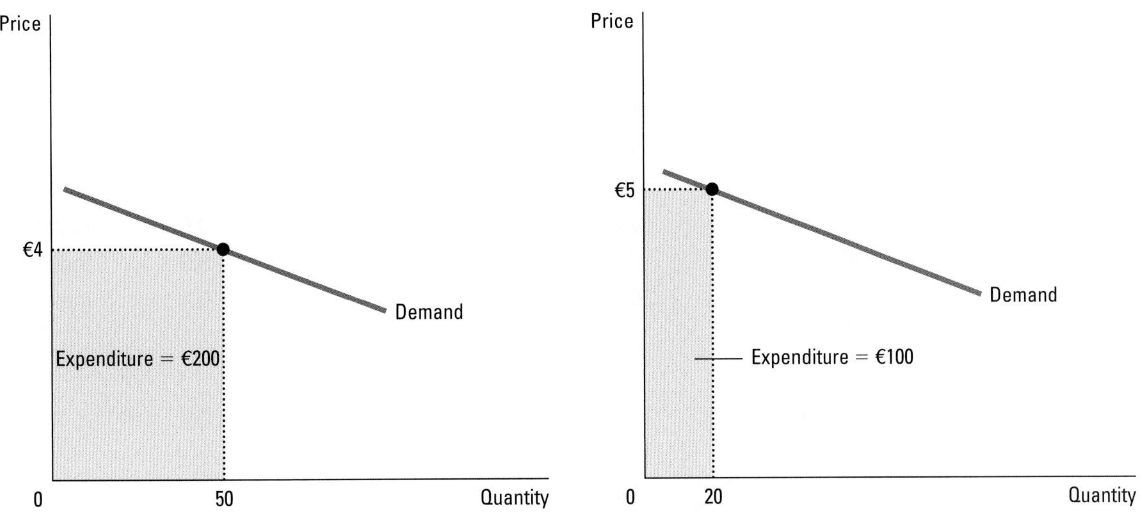

- When demand is elastic (a price elasticity greater than 1), price and total expenditure move in opposite directions.
- If demand is unit elastic (a price elasticity exactly equal to 1), total expenditure remains constant when the price changes.

Elasticity and Total Expenditure along a Linear Demand Curve

Although some demand curves have an elasticity that is the same along the entire curve, this is not always the case. An example of a demand curve along which elasticity changes is a straight line, as shown in Figure 5.5. A linear demand curve has a constant slope. Recall that slope is defined as 'rise over run', which here is the ratio of the change in price ('rise') to the change in quantity ('run'). This particular demand curve's slope is constant because each €1 increase in price causes the same 2-unit decrease in the quantity demanded.

Even though the slope of a linear demand curve is constant, the elasticity is not. The reason is that the slope is the ratio of *changes* in the two variables, whereas the elasticity is the ratio of *percentage changes* in the two variables. You can see this by looking at the table in Figure 5.5, which shows the demand schedule for the linear demand curve in the graph. The table uses the midpoint method to calculate the price elasticity of demand. At points with a low price and high quantity, the demand curve is inelastic. At points with a high price and low quantity, the demand curve is elastic.

The table also presents total expenditure at each point on the demand curve. These numbers illustrate the relationship between total expenditure and elasticity. When the price is €1, for instance, demand is inelastic and a price increase

FIGURE 5.5

Elasticity of a Linear Demand Curve

The slope of a linear demand curve is constant, but its elasticity is not. The demand schedule in the table was used to calculate the price elasticity of demand by the midpoint method. At points with a low price and high quantity, the demand curve is inelastic. At points with a high price and low quantity, the demand curve is elastic.

		Total revenue (Price × Quantity)	Per cent change in price	Per cent change in quantity	Price elasticity	Quantity description
€7	0	€0	15	200	13.0	Elastic
6	2	12	18	67	3.7	Elastic
5	4	20	22	40	1.8	Elastic
4	6	24	29	29	1.0	Unit elastic
3	8	24	40	22	0.6	Inelastic
2	10	20	67	18	0.3	Inelastic
1	12	12	200	15	0.1	Inelastic
0	14	0				

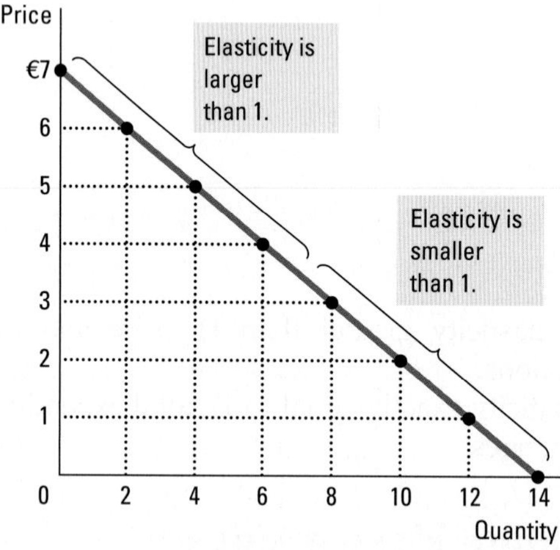

to €2 raises total expenditure. When the price is €5, demand is elastic, and a price increase to €6 reduces total expenditure. Between €3 and €4, demand is exactly unit elastic and total expenditure is the same at these two prices.

CASE STUDY

Putting Bums on Seats!

You are the owner of a coach company running a scheduled bus service between a rural town and surrounding villages. The service runs every two hours between 6am and 8pm. The price passengers pay for a return bus journey is a standard fare priced at €3.00. The maximum capacity of each bus is 80 seats.

You have noticed that the number of passengers on the services is falling and you are considering options to try and increase the demand and fill more seats on each service. You know that price and demand are inversely related and so you are planning on reducing the price to try and encourage more passengers to use your buses. However, a colleague cautions you against doing this until you have thought it through in more detail. She tells you that you need to know a lot more about the price elasticity of demand for the service before making any decision.

You decide to look at the pattern of bus usage throughout the day in a little more detail and also to investigate what substitutes exist for bus travel in the region. Your investigations tell you that the occupancy rate for buses (the proportion of seats taken up by passengers) on buses between the hours of 6am and 8am is around 95 per cent on average. Between 8am and 4pm the occupancy rate falls considerably to only 30 per cent and climbs again to 90 per cent between 4pm and 6pm. After 6pm, the rate falls again to 20 per cent. The substitutes for bus travel in the region are domestic vehicles, taxis and a local train service. The train service, however, would involve most passengers having to make a car journey to the station whereas your bus service does visit more villages and so is more convenient. Taxis are considerably more expensive.

After considering the options open to you and discussing these with your colleague you decide on the following strategy:

- During the hours of 6 am and 8 am and 4 pm and 6.pm, the price of a return ticket will rise by €1.00 to €4.00.
- Between 8 am and 4 pm the price of a return ticket will fall by 50 per cent to €1.50.
- The bus service will stop running after 6.30 pm.

Your colleague advises you to monitor the effect on occupancy rates once the new prices are introduced. After six months you go back to her with your findings. The increase in the ticket price has resulted in a fall in occupancy rates to 90 per cent in the morning and 87 per cent in the afternoon. During the day, the 50 per cent cut in the price has raised the occupancy rate from an average of 30 per cent to 65 per cent. You are very pleased with the results because the total expenditure by passengers on tickets has increased and thus, your total revenue has also risen.

You thank you colleague because without her wisdom you might have made the wrong decision on pricing. You would never have thought that increasing the price could actually be of benefit. Whilst you have fewer bums on seats in the busy period in the morning you have been very successful at increasing occupancy rates during the daytime and the increase in total revenue has been most welcome.

If the price of a bus ticket was higher would the number of passengers decline?

Other Demand Elasticities

In addition to the price elasticity of demand, economists also use other elasticities to describe the behaviour of buyers in a market.

The Income Elasticity of Demand The **income elasticity of demand** measures how the quantity demanded changes as consumer income changes. It is calculated as the percentage change in quantity demanded divided by the percentage change in income. That is,

income elasticity of demand
a measure of how much the quantity demanded of a good responds to a change in consumers' income, computed as the percentage change in quantity demanded divided by the percentage change in income

$$\text{Income elasticity of demand} = \frac{\text{Percentage change in quantity demanded}}{\text{Percentage change in income}}$$

As we discussed in Chapter 4, most goods are *normal goods:* higher income raises quantity demanded. Because quantity demanded and income change in the same direction, normal goods have positive income elasticities. A few goods, such as bus rides, are *inferior goods:* higher income lowers the quantity demanded. Because quantity demanded and income move in opposite directions, inferior goods have negative income elasticities.

Even among normal goods, income elasticities vary substantially in size. Necessities, such as food and clothing, tend to have small income elasticities because consumers, regardless of how low their incomes, choose to buy some of these goods. Luxuries, such as caviar and diamonds, tend to have high income elasticities because consumers feel that they can do without these goods altogether if their income is too low.

cross-price elasticity of demand
a measure of how much the quantity demanded of one good responds to a change in the price of another good, computed as the percentage change in quantity demanded of the first good divided by the percentage change in the price of the second good

The Cross-Price Elasticity of Demand The **cross-price elasticity of demand** measures how the quantity demanded of one good changes as the price of another good changes. It is calculated as the percentage change in quantity demanded of good 1 divided by the percentage change in the price of good 2. That is:

$$\text{Cross-price elasticity of demand} = \frac{\text{Percentage change in quantity demanded of good 1}}{\text{Percentage change in the price of good 2}}$$

Whether the cross-price elasticity is a positive or negative number depends on whether the two goods are substitutes or complements. As we discussed in Chapter 4, substitutes are goods that are typically used in place of one another, such as beef steak and Wiener schnitzel. An increase in the price of beef steak induces people to eat Wiener schnitzel instead. Because the price of beef steak and the quantity of Wiener schnitzel demanded move in the same direction, the cross-price elasticity is positive. Conversely, complements are goods that are typically used together, such as computers and software. In this case, the cross-price elasticity is negative, indicating that an increase in the price of computers reduces the quantity of software demanded. As with price elasticity of demand, cross-price elasticity may increase over time: a change in the price of electricity will have little effect on demand for gas in the short run but much stronger effects over several years.

Quick Quiz Define the price elasticity of demand. • Explain the relationship between total expenditure and the price elasticity of demand.

THE ELASTICITY OF SUPPLY

When we introduced supply in Chapter 4, we noted that producers of a good offer to sell more of it when the price of the good rises, when their input prices fall or when their technology improves. To turn from qualitative to quantitative statements about quantity supplied, we once again use the concept of elasticity.

price elasticity of supply
a measure of how much the quantity supplied of a good responds to a change in the price of that good, computed as the percentage change in quantity supplied divided by the percentage change in price

The Price Elasticity of Supply and its Determinants

The law of supply states that higher prices raise the quantity supplied. The **price elasticity of supply** measures how much the quantity supplied responds to changes in the price. Supply of a good is said to be *elastic* if the quantity supplied responds substantially to changes in the price. Supply is said to be *inelastic* if the quantity supplied responds only slightly to changes in the price.

The price elasticity of supply depends on the flexibility of sellers to change the amount of the good they produce. For example, seafront property has an inelastic supply because it is almost impossible to produce more of it quickly. By contrast, manufactured goods, such as books, cars and television sets, have elastic supplies because the firms that produce them can run their factories longer in response to a higher price.

In most markets, a key determinant of the price elasticity of supply is the time period being considered. Supply is usually more elastic in the long run than in the short run. Over short periods of time, firms cannot easily change the size of their factories to make more or less of a good. Thus, in the short run, the quantity supplied is not very responsive to the price. By contrast, over longer periods, firms can build new factories or close old ones. In addition, new firms can enter a market and old firms can shut down. Thus, in the long run, the quantity supplied can respond substantially to price changes.

Computing the Price Elasticity of Supply

Now that we have some idea about what the price elasticity of supply is, let's be more precise. Economists compute the price elasticity of supply as the percentage change in the quantity supplied divided by the percentage change in the price. That is:

$$\text{Price elasticity of supply} = \frac{\text{Percentage change in quantity supplied}}{\text{Percentage change in price}}$$

For example, suppose that an increase in the price of milk from €2.85 to €3.15 a litre raises the amount that dairy farmers produce from 90 000 to 110 000 litres per month. Using the midpoint method, we calculate the percentage change in price as:

$$\text{Percentage change in price} = (3.15 - 2.85)/3.00 \times 100 = 10\%$$

Similarly, we calculate the percentage change in quantity supplied as:

$$\text{Percentage change in quantity supplied} = (110\,000 - 90\,000)/100\,000 \times 100 = 20\%$$

In this case, the price elasticity of supply is:

$$\text{Price elasticity of supply} = \frac{20\%}{10\%} = 2$$

In this example, the elasticity of 2 reflects the fact that the quantity supplied moves proportionately twice as much as the price.

The Variety of Supply Curves

Because the price elasticity of supply measures the responsiveness of quantity supplied to the price, it is reflected in the appearance of the supply curve (again, assuming we are using similar scales on the axes of diagrams being used). Figure 5.6 shows five cases. In the extreme case of a zero elasticity, as shown in panel (a), supply is *perfectly inelastic* and the supply curve is vertical. In this case, the quantity supplied is the same regardless of the price. As the elasticity rises, the supply curve gets flatter, which shows that the quantity supplied responds more to changes in the price. At the opposite extreme, shown in panel (e), supply is *perfectly elastic*. This occurs as the price elasticity of supply

FIGURE 5.6

The Price Elasticity of Supply

The price elasticity of supply determines whether the supply curve is steep or flat. Note that all percentage changes are calculated using the midpoint method.

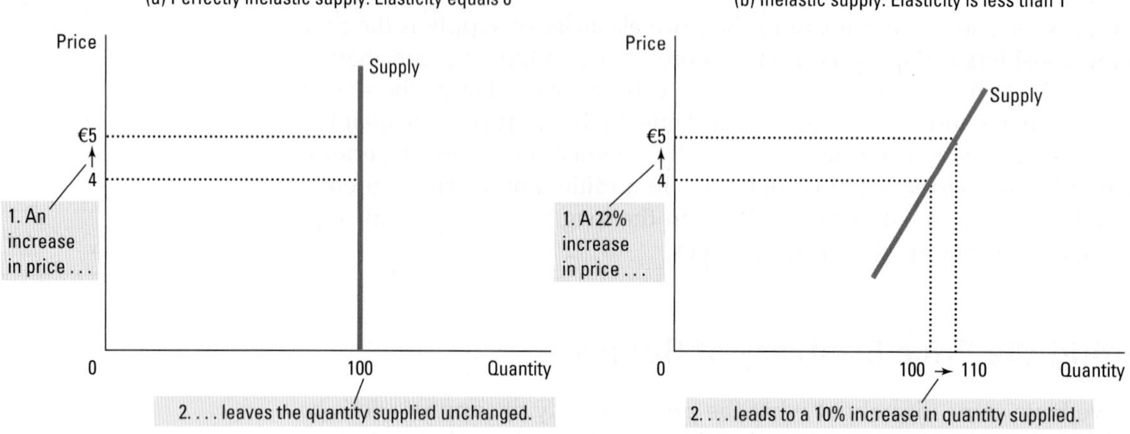

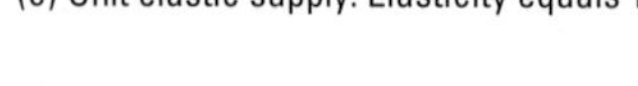

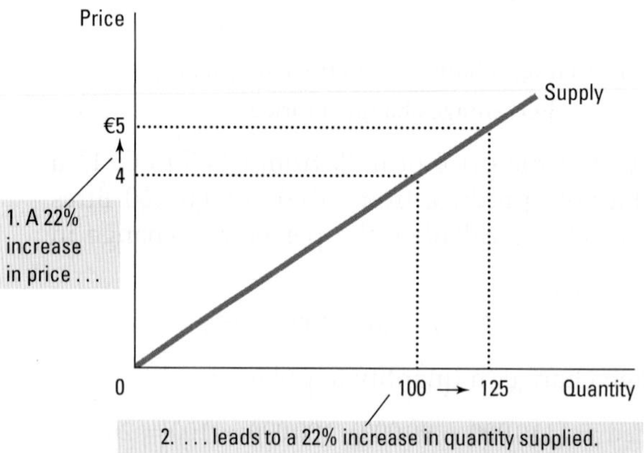

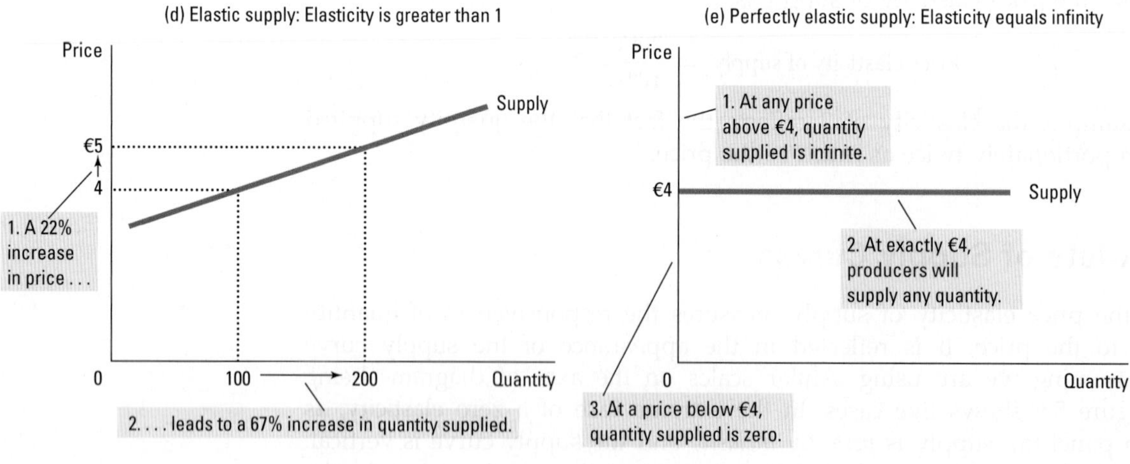

FIGURE 5.7

How the Price Elasticity of Supply Can Vary

Because firms often have a maximum capacity for production, the elasticity of supply may be very high at low levels of quantity supplied and very low at high levels of quantity supplied. Here, an increase in price from €3 to €4 increases the quantity supplied from 100 to 200. Because the increase in quantity supplied of 67 per cent (computed using the midpoint method) is larger than the increase in price of 29 per cent, the supply curve is elastic in this range. By contrast, when the price rises from €12 to €15, the quantity supplied rises only from 500 to 525. Because the increase in quantity supplied of 5 per cent is smaller than the increase in price of 22 per cent, the supply curve is inelastic in this range.

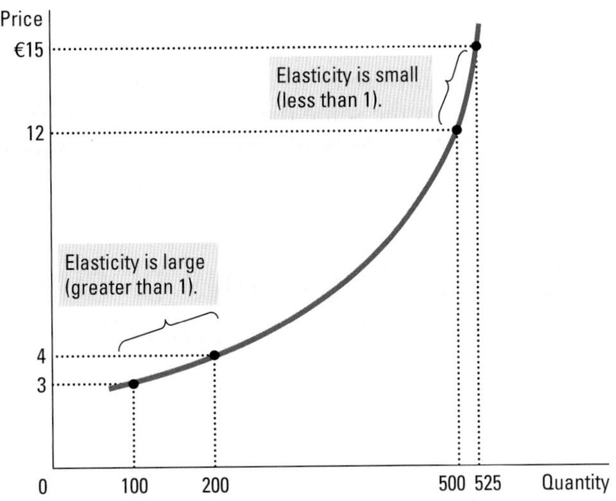

approaches infinity and the supply curve becomes horizontal, meaning that very small changes in the price lead to very large changes in the quantity supplied.

In some markets, the elasticity of supply is not constant but varies over the supply curve. Figure 5.7 shows a typical case for an industry in which firms have factories with a limited capacity for production. For low levels of quantity supplied, the elasticity of supply is high, indicating that firms respond substantially to changes in the price. In this region, firms have capacity for production that is not being used, such as buildings and machinery sitting idle for all or part of the day. Small increases in price make it profitable for firms to begin using this idle capacity. As the quantity supplied rises, firms begin to reach capacity. Once capacity is fully used, increasing production further requires the construction of new factories. To induce firms to incur this extra expense, the price must rise substantially, so supply becomes less elastic.

Figure 5.7 presents a numerical example of this phenomenon. When the price rises from €3 to €4 (a 29 per cent increase, according to the midpoint method), the quantity supplied rises from 100 to 200 (a 67 per cent increase). Because quantity supplied moves proportionately more than the price, the supply curve has elasticity greater than 1. By contrast, when the price rises from €12 to €15 (a 22 per cent increase), the quantity supplied rises from 500 to 525 (a 5 per cent increase). In this case, quantity supplied moves proportionately less than the price, so the elasticity is less than 1.

Quick Quiz Define the price elasticity of supply • Explain why the price elasticity of supply might be different in the long run from in the short run.

Total Revenue and the Price Elasticity of Supply

The principles outlined in the discussion of demand curves and total expenditure by consumers also apply to supply curves. The only difference is that when looked at from the perspective of the seller, changes in sales in relation to changes in price result in changes in total revenue. Total revenue, remember, is calculated by taking the price at which a good is sold and multiplying it by the amount the firm sells. In analysing markets, we will use both demand and supply curves on the same diagram. We will refer to changes in total revenue when looking at the effects of changes in equilibrium conditions but remember that revenue for sellers represents the same identity as expenditure for buyers.

THREE APPLICATIONS OF SUPPLY, DEMAND AND ELASTICITY

Can good news for the computing industry be bad news for computer chip manufacturers? Why do the prices of ski holidays in Europe rise dramatically over public and school holidays? Does drug prohibition increase or decrease drug-related crime? At first, these questions might seem to have little in common. Yet all three questions are about markets and all markets are subject to the forces of supply and demand. Here we apply the versatile tools of supply, demand and elasticity to answer these seemingly complex questions.

Can Good News for the Computer Industry Be Bad News for Chip Makers?

Let's now return to the question posed at the beginning of this chapter: what happens to chip manufacturers and the market for chips when scientists discover a new material for making chips that is more productive than silicon? Recall from Chapter 4 that we answer such questions in three steps. First, we examine whether the supply or demand curve shifts. Secondly, we consider which direction the curve shifts. Thirdly, we use the supply and demand diagram to see how the market equilibrium changes.

This is a situation that is facing chip manufacturers. Scientists are investigating new materials to make computer chips. Such a material may allow the manufacturers to be able to work on building processing power at ever smaller concentrations and increase computing power considerably. In this case, the discovery of the new material affects the supply curve. Because the material increases the amount of computing power that can be produced on each chip, manufacturers are now willing to supply more chips at any given price. In other words, the supply curve for computing power shifts to the right. The demand curve remains the same because consumers' desire to buy chips at any given price is not affected by the introduction of the new material. Figure 5.8 shows an example of such a change. When the supply curve shifts from S_1 to S_2, the quantity of chips sold increases from 100 to 110, and the price of chips falls from €10 per gigabyte to €4 per gigabyte.

FIGURE 5.8

An Increase in Supply in the Market for Computer Chips

When an advance in chip technology increases the supply of chips from S_1 to S_2, the price of chips falls. Because the demand for chips is inelastic, the increase in the quantity sold from 100 to 110 is proportionately smaller than the decrease in the price from €10 to €4. As a result, manufacturers' total revenue falls from €1 000 (€10 × 100) to €440 (€4 × 110).

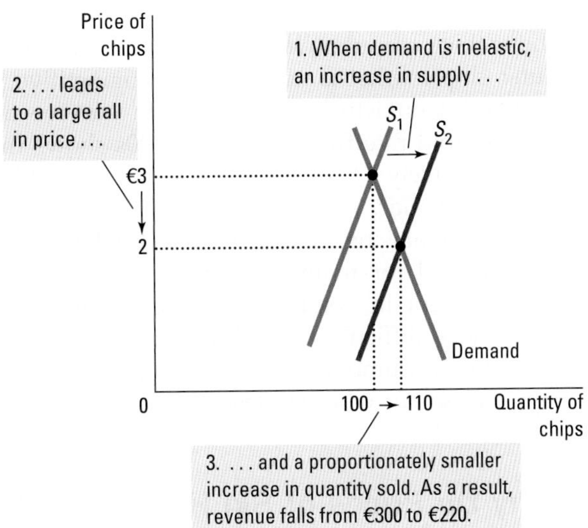

But does this discovery make chip manufacturers better off? As a first stab at answering this question, consider what happens to the total revenue received by chip manufacturers; total revenue is $P \times Q$, the price of each chip times the quantity sold. The discovery affects manufacturers in two conflicting ways. The new material allows manufacturers to produce more chips with greater computing power (Q rises), but now each chip sells for less (P falls).

Whether total revenue rises or falls depends on the elasticity of demand. We can assume that the demand for chips is inelastic, in producing a computer, chips represent a relatively small proportion of the total cost but they also have few good substitutes. When the demand curve is inelastic, as it is in Figure 5.8, a decrease in price causes total revenue to fall. You can see this in the figure: the price of chips falls substantially, whereas the quantity of chips sold rises only slightly. Total revenue falls from €1 000 to €440. Thus, the discovery of the new material lowers the total revenue that chip manufacturers receive for the sale of their products.

If manufacturers are made worse off by the discovery of this new material, why do they adopt it? The answer to this question goes to the heart of how competitive markets work. If each chip manufacturer is a small part of the market for chips, he or she takes the price of chips as given. For any given price of chips, it is better to use the new material in order to produce and sell more chips. Yet when all manufacturers do this, the supply of chips rises, the price falls and manufacturers are worse off.

"WHY DON'T WE JUST KEEP THE LAW OF DEMAND, AND REPEAL THE SUPPLY PART?"

Although this example is only hypothetical, in fact a new material for making computer chips is being investigated. The material is called hafnium and is used in the nuclear industry. In recent years the manufacture of computer chips has changed dramatically. In the early 1990s, prices per megabyte of DRAM (dynamic random access memory) stood at around $55 but fell to under $1 by the early part of the new century. Manufacturers who were first involved in chip manufacture made high profits but as new firms joined the industry, supply increased and as the technology also spread, supply rose and prices fell. The fall in prices led to a number of firms struggling to stay in business. We assumed above that computer chip manufacturers were price takers but in reality the computer chip market is not perfectly competitive. However, the fact that so many smaller manufacturers struggled to survive as chip technology expanded at such a rapid rate from the early 1990s shows that even markets dominated now by a relatively small number of firms exhibit many of the features we have described so far.

When analysing the effects of technology, it is important to keep in mind that what is bad for manufacturers is not necessarily bad for society as a whole. Improvement in computing power technology can be bad for manufacturers who find it difficult to survive unless they are very large, but it represents good news for consumers of this computing power (ultimately the users of PCs, laptops and so on) who pay less for computing.

Why Do Prices of Ski Holidays Differ so Much at Different Times of the Season?

Ski holidays in Europe are becoming ever more popular. There were an estimated 1.3 million people from the UK taking holidays in European ski resorts in 2010. For an increasing number of people the pleasure of a holiday on the slopes is a part of the winter but people also face considerable changes in the prices that they have to pay for their holiday. For example, a quick check of a ski company website for the 2010–11 season revealed the prices shown in Table 5.1 for 7-night ski trips, per person to Austria leaving from London.

There is a considerable variation in the prices that holidaymakers have to pay – £710 being the greatest difference. Prices are particularly high leaving on 26 December and 20 February – why? The reason is that at this time of the season the demand for ski holidays increases dramatically because they coincide with annual holiday periods; 26 December is part of the Christmas holidays and when schoolchildren are also on holiday; 20 February is also a major school holiday for many UK children (although some also have a break which includes or occurs the previous week).

TABLE 5.1

Prices of 7-night Ski holidays in Austria, from London

Departure date	Price per person (£)
5 December 2010	470
26 December 2010	1 000
16 January 2011	650
5 February 2011	670
13 February 2011	720
20 February 2011	1 180
27 February 2011	700

FIGURE 5.9

The Supply of Ski Holidays in Europe

Panel (a) shows the market for ski holidays in off-peak times. The supply curve S_1 is relatively elastic in the short-run. An increase in demand from D_1 to D_2 at this time leads to a relatively small increase in price because the increase can be accommodated by releasing some of the spare capacity that tour operators have. Panel (b) shows the market during peak times. The supply of holidays shown by the curve S_1 is relatively inelastic in the short run. If demand now increases from D_1 to D_2 the result will be a sharp rise in price.

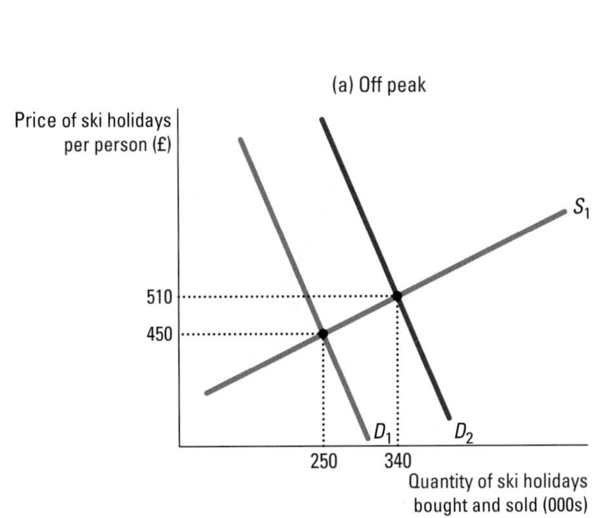

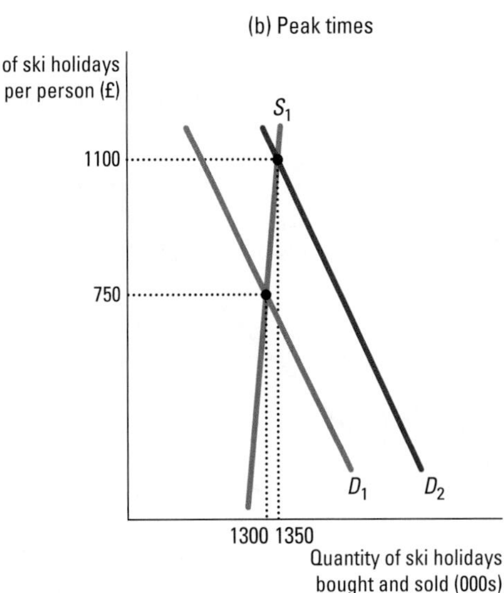

The supply of ski holidays does have a limit – there will be a finite number of accommodation places and passes for ski-lifts and so the elasticity of supply is relatively inelastic (see Figure 5.9). It is difficult for tour operators to increase supply of accommodation or ski-passes easily in the short-run in the face of rising demand at these times. The result is that the increase in demand for ski holidays at these peak times results in prices rising significantly to choke off the excess demand. If holidaymakers are able to be flexible about when they take their holidays then they will be able to benefit from lower prices for the same holiday. Away from these peak periods the demand for ski holidays is lower and so tour operators have spare capacity – the supply curve out of peak times is more elastic in the short run. If there was a sudden increase in demand in early December, for example, then tour operators would have the capacity to accommodate that demand so prices would not rise as much as when that capacity is strictly limited.

Cases for which supply is very inelastic in the short run but more elastic in the long run may see different prices exist in the market. Air and rail travel and the use of electricity may all be examples where prices differ markedly at peak times compared with off peak times because of supply constraints and the ability of firms to be able to discriminate between customers at these times.

Does Drug Prohibition Increase or Decrease Drug-related Crime?

A persistent problem facing society is the use of illegal drugs, such as heroin, cocaine, marijuana and ecstasy. Drug use has several adverse effects. One is that

FIGURE 5.10

Policies to Reduce the Use of Illegal Drugs

Drug prohibition reduces the supply of drugs from S_1 to S_2, as in panel (a). If the demand for drugs is inelastic, then the total amount paid by drug users rises, even as the amount of drug use falls. By contrast, drug education reduces the demand for drugs from D_1 to D_2, as in panel (b). Because both price and quantity fall, the amount paid by drug users falls.

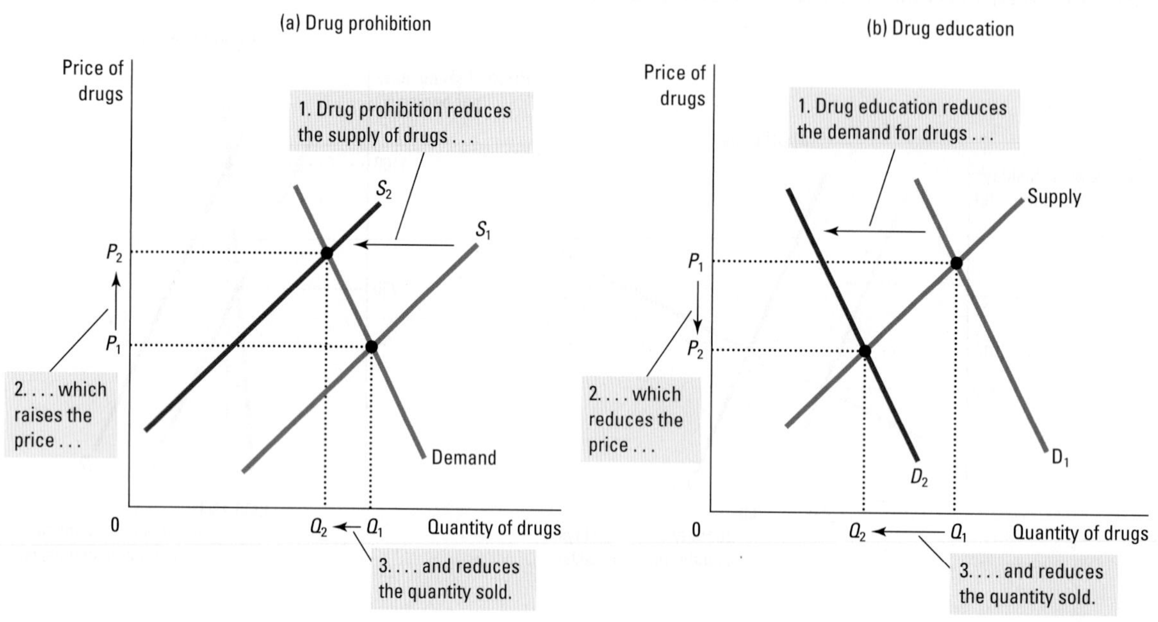

drug dependency can ruin the lives of drug users and their families. Another is that drug addicts often turn to robbery and other violent crimes in order to obtain the money needed to support their habit. To discourage the use of illegal drugs, European governments devote billions of euros each year to reduce the flow of drugs into their countries. Let's use the tools of supply and demand to examine this policy of drug prohibition.

Suppose the government increases the number of undercover police devoted to the war on drugs. What happens in the market for illegal drugs? As is usual, we answer this question in three steps. First, we consider whether the supply or demand curve shifts. Secondly, we consider the direction of the shift. Thirdly, we see how the shift affects the equilibrium price and quantity.

Although the purpose of drug prohibition is to reduce drug use, its direct impact is on the sellers of drugs rather than the buyers. When the government stops some drugs from entering the country and arrests more smugglers, it raises the cost of selling drugs and, therefore, reduces the quantity of drugs supplied at any given price. The demand for drugs – the amount buyers want at any given price – is not changed. As panel (a) of Figure 5.10 shows, prohibition shifts the supply curve to the left from S_1 to S_2 and leaves the demand curve the same. The equilibrium price of drugs rises from P_1 to P_2, and the equilibrium quantity falls from Q_1 to Q_2. The fall in the equilibrium quantity shows that drug prohibition does reduce drug use.

But what about the amount of drug-related crime? To answer this question, consider the total amount that drug users pay for the drugs they buy. Because few drug addicts are likely to break their self-destructive habits in response to a higher price, it is likely that the demand for drugs is inelastic, as it is drawn in the figure. If demand is inelastic, then an increase in price raises total revenue in the drug market. That is, because drug prohibition raises the price of drugs proportionately more than it reduces drug use, it raises the total amount of money that drug users pay for drugs. Addicts who already had to steal to support their habits would have an even greater need for quick cash. Thus, drug prohibition could increase drug-related crime.

Because of this adverse effect of drug prohibition, some analysts argue for alternative approaches to the drug problem. Rather than trying to reduce the supply of drugs, policy makers might try to reduce the demand by pursuing a policy of drug education. Successful drug education has the effects shown in panel (b) of Figure 5.10. The demand curve shifts to the left from D_1 to D_2. As a result, the equilibrium quantity falls from Q_1 to Q_2, and the equilibrium price falls from P_1 to P_2. Total revenue, which is price times quantity, also falls. Thus, in contrast to drug prohibition, drug education can reduce both drug use and drug-related crime.

Advocates of drug prohibition might argue that the effects of this policy are different in the long run from what they are in the short run, because the elasticity of demand may depend on the time horizon. The demand for drugs is probably inelastic over short periods of time because higher prices do not substantially affect drug use by established addicts. But demand may be more elastic over longer periods of time because higher prices would discourage experimentation with drugs among the young and, over time, lead to fewer drug addicts. In this case, drug prohibition would increase drug-related crime in the short run while decreasing it in the long run.

Quick Quiz How might a drought that destroys half of all farm crops be good for farmers? If such a drought is good for farmers, why don't farmers destroy their own crops in the absence of a drought?

IN THE NEWS

Cutting Price in the Console Wars

When firms make pricing decisions, they will have to consider both the short-run and long-run effects, and price elasticity will almost certainly play some part in decision-making. This article looks at pricing of games consoles.

During the summer of 2009 rumours had been circulating suggesting that Sony was planning to cut the price of its PlayStation 3 (PS3) in the face of competition from other games consoles. The market was in a position where there were no plans by any of the main players in the market to release new consoles. As a result, price was being seen as a way in which games console manufacturers might be able to compete for sales. Sony's PS3 has not taken off in the same way as the launch of its previous versions and part of the reason has been the existence of cheaper consoles such as Microsoft's Xbox 360, which retailed upwards of £129 (€150) and Nintendo's Wii, which sold at around £169 (€196). The PS3 was retailing at around the £300 (€350) mark but at a press conference ahead of the Game.Com show in Cologne in August, Sony officials announced that the price would be cut. In Europe the PS3 would sell for €299, £249.99 in the UK and $299 in the US.

A new slimmer version of the PS3, which uses 34 per cent less power and is over a third lighter and around a third smaller was to be released in September. Production of existing PS3 consoles would cease and the price reductions would take place immediately. Part of the reason for the price cut is that figures show it is very effective in generating sales. Sony was hoping that the price elasticity of demand in the short run for the PS3 would be sufficiently elastic to generate increased sales and more than cover the lost revenue resulting from the lower price. In considering the price reduction Sony would have had to consider the reaction of its rivals, Nintendo, manufacturer of the Wii, and Microsoft who make the Xbox 360. In addition, it would be looking at the extent to which these rival products were substitutes to a PS3 in consumers' minds and the role of complements – the various games which users can buy for the console. Analysts suggested that any price cut by Sony would be met with similar tactics from Microsoft and Nintendo. The size of those cuts and whether they will indeed follow suit and when, will influence the size of the effect on sales and thus total revenue for Sony.

Reports in early 2010 suggest that the price cut may have had some effect. In the final five weeks of 2009, Sony announced that it had sold 3.8 million consoles worldwide. This represented an increase of 76 per cent on the equivalent period in 2008.

CONCLUSION

According to an old quip, even a parrot can become an economist simply by learning to say 'supply and demand'. These last two chapters should have convinced you that there is much truth in this statement. The tools of supply and demand allow you to analyse many of the most important events and policies that shape the economy. You are now well on your way to becoming an economist (or, at least, a well educated parrot).

SUMMARY

- The price elasticity of demand measures how much the quantity demanded responds to changes in the price. Demand tends to be more elastic if close substitutes are available, if the good is a luxury rather than a necessity, if the market is narrowly defined or if buyers have substantial time to react to a price change.
- The price elasticity of demand is calculated as the percentage change in quantity demanded divided by the percentage change in price. If the elasticity is less than 1, so that quantity demanded moves proportionately less than the price, demand is said to be inelastic. If the elasticity is greater than 1, so that quantity demanded moves proportionately more than the price, demand is said to be elastic.
- Total revenue, the total amount paid for a good, equals the price of the good times the quantity sold. For inelastic demand curves, total revenue rises as price rises. For elastic demand curves, total revenue falls as price rises.
- The income elasticity of demand measures how much the quantity demanded responds to changes in consumers' income. The cross-price elasticity of demand measures how much the quantity demanded of one good responds to changes in the price of another good.
- The price elasticity of supply measures how much the quantity supplied responds to changes in the price. This elasticity often depends on the time horizon under consideration. In most markets, supply is more elastic in the long run than in the short run.
- The price elasticity of supply is calculated as the percentage change in quantity supplied divided by the percentage change in price. If the elasticity is less than 1, so that quantity supplied moves proportionately less than the price, supply is said to be inelastic. If the elasticity is greater than 1, so that quantity supplied moves proportionately more than the price, supply is said to be elastic.
- The tools of supply and demand can be applied in many different kinds of markets. This chapter uses them to analyse the market for computer chips, the market for ski holidays and the market for illegal drugs.

KEY CONCEPTS

elasticity, p. 95
price elasticity of demand, p. 95
total expenditure, p. 98
total revenue, p. 98
income elasticity of demand, p. 103
cross-price elasticity of demand, p. 104
price elasticity of supply, p. 104

QUESTIONS FOR REVIEW

1. Define the price elasticity of demand and the income elasticity of demand.
2. List and explain some of the determinants of the price elasticity of demand.
3. If the elasticity is greater than 1, is demand elastic or inelastic? If the elasticity equals 0, is demand perfectly elastic or perfectly inelastic?
4. On a supply and demand diagram, show equilibrium price, equilibrium quantity and the total revenue received by producers.
5. If demand is elastic, how will an increase in price change total revenue? Explain.
6. What do we call a good whose income elasticity is less than 0?
7. How is the price elasticity of supply calculated? Explain what this measures.
8. What is the price elasticity of supply of Picasso paintings? (Picasso was a renowned artist who died in 1973.)
9. Is the price elasticity of supply usually larger in the short run or in the long run? Why?
10. In the 1970s, OPEC caused a dramatic increase in the price of oil. In the 1980s, the price of oil fell dramatically. What do you think might have prevented it from maintaining a high price through the 1980s?

PROBLEMS AND APPLICATIONS

1. For each of the following pairs of goods, which good would you expect to have more elastic demand and why?
   a. Required textbooks or mystery novels.
   b. Beethoven recordings or classical music recordings in general.
   c. Heating oil during the next six months or heating oil during the next five years.
   d. Lemonade or water.
2. Suppose that business travellers and holidaymakers have the following demand for airline tickets from Birmingham to Naples:

Price	Quantity demanded (business travellers)	Quantity demanded (holidaymakers)
€150	2 100	1 000
200	2 000	800
250	1 900	600
300	1 800	400

   a. As the price of tickets rises from €200 to €250, what is the price elasticity of demand for (i) business travellers and (ii) holidaymakers? (Use the midpoint method in your calculations.)
   b. Why might holidaymakers have a different elasticity from business travellers?
3. Suppose that your demand schedule for DVDs is as follows:

Price	Quantity demanded (income = €10 000)	Quantity demanded (income = €12 000)
€8	40	50
10	32	45
12	24	30
14	16	20
16	8	12

a. Use the midpoint method to calculate your price elasticity of demand as the price of DVDs increases from €8 to €10 if (i) your income is €10 000, and (ii) your income is €12 000.
b. Calculate your income elasticity of demand as your income increases from €10 000 to €12 000 if (i) the price is €12, and (ii) the price is €16.

4. Xanthe has decided always to spend one-third of her income on clothing.
   a. What is her income elasticity of clothing demand?
   b. What is her price elasticity of clothing demand?
   c. If Xanthe's tastes change and she decides to spend only one-quarter of her income on clothing, how does her demand curve change? What are her income elasticity and price elasticity now?
5. Two drivers – Tom and Jerry – each drive up to a petrol station. Before looking at the price, each places an order. Tom says, 'I'd like 30 litres of petrol.' Jerry says, 'I'd like €30-worth of petrol.' What is each driver's price elasticity of demand?
6. Economists have observed that spending on restaurant meals declines more during economic downturns than does spending on food to be eaten at home. How might the concept of elasticity help to explain this phenomenon?
7. Consider public policy aimed at smoking.
   a. Studies indicate that the price elasticity of demand for cigarettes is about 0.4. If a packet of cigarettes is currently priced at €2 and the government wants to reduce smoking by 20 per cent, by how much should it increase the price?
   b. If the government permanently increases the price of cigarettes, will the policy have a larger effect on smoking one year from now or five years from now?
   c. Studies also find that teenagers have a higher price elasticity than do adults. Why might this be true?
8. Would you expect the price elasticity of *demand* to be larger in the market for all ice cream or the market for vanilla ice cream? Would you expect the price elasticity of *supply* to be larger in the market for all ice cream or the market for vanilla ice cream? Be sure to explain your answers.
9. Pharmaceutical drugs have an inelastic demand, and computers have an elastic demand. Suppose that technological advance doubles the supply of both products (that is, the quantity supplied at each price is twice what it was).
   a. What happens to the equilibrium price and quantity in each market?
   b. Which product experiences a larger change in price?
   c. Which product experiences a larger change in quantity?
   d. What happens to total consumer spending on each product?
10. Seafront properties along the promenade at Brighton on the south coast of England have an inelastic supply, and cars have an elastic supply. Suppose that a rise in population doubles the demand for both products (that is, the quantity demanded at each price is twice what it was).
    a. What happens to the equilibrium price and quantity in each market?
    b. Which product experiences a larger change in price?
    c. Which product experiences a larger change in quantity?
    d. What happens to total consumer spending on each product?
11. Suppose that there is severe flooding in a region in which there is a high concentration of wheat farmers.
    a. Farmers whose crops were destroyed by the floods were much worse off, but farmers whose crops were not destroyed benefited from the floods. Why?
    b. What information would you need about the market for wheat to assess whether farmers as a group were hurt or helped by the floods?
12. Explain why the following might be true: a drought around the world raises the total revenue that farmers receive from the sale of grain, but a drought only in France reduces the total revenue that French farmers receive.
13. Because better weather makes farmland more productive, farmland in regions with good weather conditions is more expensive than farmland in regions with bad weather conditions. Over time, however, as advances in technology have made all farmland more productive, the price of farmland (adjusted for overall inflation) has fallen. Use the concept of elasticity to explain why productivity and farmland prices are positively related across space but negatively related over time.

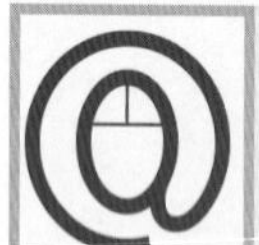

For further resources, visit www.cengage.com/mankiw_taylor2

6 SUPPLY, DEMAND AND GOVERNMENT POLICIES

Economists have two roles. As scientists, they develop and test theories to explain the world around them. As policy advisors, they use their theories to help change the world for the better. The focus of the preceding two chapters has been scientific. We have seen how supply and demand determine the price of a good and the quantity of the good sold. We have also seen how various events shift supply and demand and thereby change the equilibrium price and quantity.

This chapter offers our first look at policy. Here we alalyse various types of government policy using only the tools of supply and demand. As you will see, the analysis yields some surprising insights. Policies often have effects that their architects did not intend or anticipate. One of the *Ten Principles of Economics* is that people respond to incentives. When new policies are introduced they may have good intentions to solve particular problems or help groups of people but new policies also generate new incentives and as a result the consequences may go far beyond those envisaged by the policy makers.

We begin by considering policies that directly control prices. For example, some countries have rent-control laws that dictate a maximum rent that landlords may charge tenants or minimum wage laws that dictate the lowest wage that firms may pay workers. Price controls are usually enacted when policy makers believe that the market price of a good or service is unfair to buyers or sellers. Yet, as we will see, these policies can generate inequities of their own.

After our discussion of price controls, we consider the impact of taxes and subsidies. Policy makers use taxes both to influence market outcomes and to raise revenue for public purposes. Although the prevalence of taxes in a developed economy is obvious, their effects are not. For example, when the government levies a tax on the amount that firms pay their workers, do the firms or the workers bear the burden of the tax? A **subsidy** works almost exactly as the reverse of taxes. They are often used to encourage the supply of a product which is being underproduced and deemed to be in the public interest. In the case of subsidies, someone has to pay for the subsidy, and firms and consumers may benefit in different ways. How taxes and subsidies affect different people and organizations is not at all clear – until we apply the powerful tools of supply and demand.

subsidy
payment to buyers and sellers to supplement income or lower costs and which thus encourages consumption or provides an advantage to the recipient

CONTROLS ON PRICES

To see how price controls affect market outcomes, let's look once again at the market for ice cream. As we saw in Chapter 4, if ice cream is sold in a competitive market free of government regulation, the price of ice cream adjusts to balance supply and demand: at the equilibrium price, the quantity of ice cream that buyers want to buy exactly equals the quantity that sellers want to sell. To be concrete, suppose the equilibrium price is €3 per cornet.

Not everyone may be happy with the outcome of this free market process. Let's say the National Association of Ice Cream Eaters complains that the €3 price is too high for everyone to enjoy a cornet a day (their recommended diet). Meanwhile, the National Organization of Ice Cream Producers complains that the €3 price – the result of 'cut-throat competition' – is too low and is depressing the incomes of its members. Each of these groups lobbies the government to pass laws that alter the market outcome by directly controlling the price of an ice cream cornet.

Of course, because buyers of any good always want a lower price while sellers want a higher price, the interests of the two groups conflict. If the Ice Cream Eaters are successful in their lobbying, the government imposes a legal maximum on the price at which ice cream can be sold. Because the price is not allowed to rise above this level, the legislated maximum is called a **price ceiling** or a price cap. By contrast, if the Ice Cream Makers are successful, the government imposes a legal minimum on the price. Because the price cannot fall below this level, the legislated minimum is called a **price floor**. Let us consider the effects of these policies in turn.

price ceiling
a legal maximum on the price at which a good can be sold

price floor
a legal minimum on the price at which a good can be sold

How Price Ceilings Affect Market Outcomes

When the government, moved by the complaints and campaign contributions of the Ice Cream Eaters, imposes a price ceiling on the market for ice cream, two outcomes are possible. In panel (a) of Figure 6.1, the government imposes a price ceiling of €4 per cornet. In this case, because the price that balances supply and demand (€3) is below the ceiling, the price ceiling is *not binding*. Market forces naturally move the economy to the equilibrium, and the price ceiling has no effect on the price or the quantity sold.

Panel (b) of Figure 6.1 shows the other, more interesting, possibility. In this case, the government imposes a price ceiling of €2 per cornet. Because the equilibrium price of €3 is above the price ceiling, the ceiling is a *binding constraint* on the market. The forces of supply and demand tend to move the price towards the equilibrium price, but when the market price hits the ceiling, it can rise no further. Thus, the market price equals the price ceiling. Given this binding limit on price, incentives change. Some ice cream sellers will not find it profitable to produce ice cream at this price and either cut back production or possibly leave the

FIGURE 6.1

A Market With a Price Ceiling

In panel (a), the government imposes a price ceiling of €4. Because the price ceiling is above the equilibrium price of €3, the price ceiling has no effect, and the market can reach the equilibrium of supply and demand. In this equilibrium, quantity supplied and quantity demanded both equal 100 cornets. In panel (b), the government imposes a price ceiling of €2. Because the price ceiling is below the equilibrium price of €3, the market price equals €2. At this price, 125 cornets are demanded and only 75 are supplied, so there is a shortage of 50 cornets.

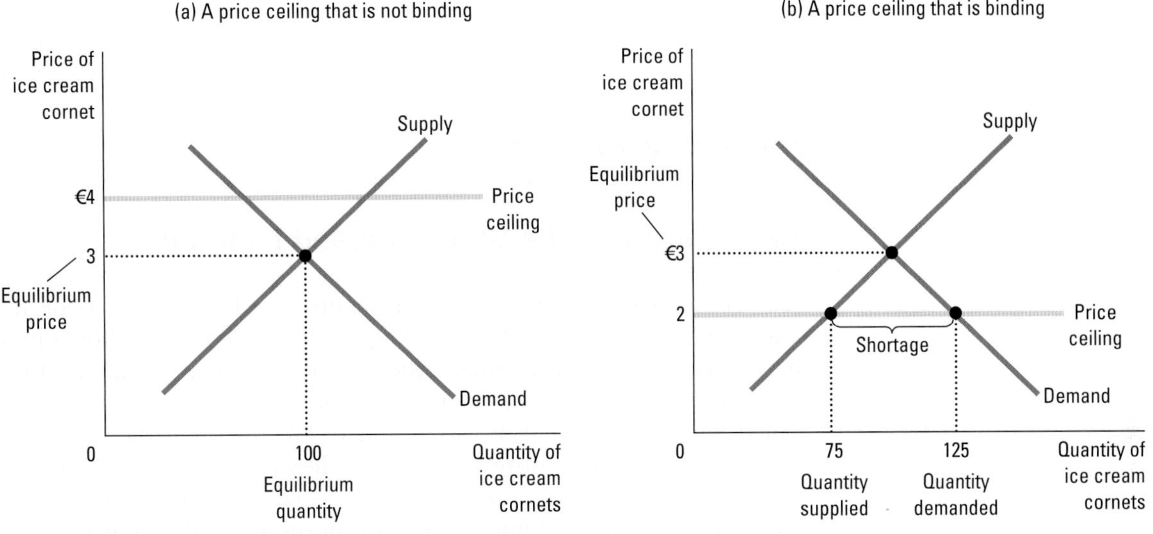

market. Buyers' incentives are different. The lower price means the sacrifice they have to make to buy ice cream is less in terms of alternatives foregone and so are prepared to buy more at the binding price. At this price, the quantity of ice cream demanded (125 cornets in the figure) exceeds the quantity supplied (75 cornets). There is a shortage of ice cream, so some people who want to buy ice cream at the going price are unable to.

When a shortage of ice cream develops because of this price ceiling, some mechanism for rationing ice cream will naturally develop. The mechanism could simply be long queues: buyers who are willing to arrive early and queue get a cornet, while those unwilling to wait do not. Alternatively, sellers could ration ice cream according to their own personal biases, selling it only to friends, relatives, or members of their own racial or ethnic group. Notice that even though the price ceiling was motivated by a desire to help buyers of ice cream, not all buyers benefit from the policy. Some buyers do get to pay a lower price, although they may have to queue a long time to do so, but other buyers cannot get any ice cream at all. In setting policy, the authorities have to consider who gets the benefits and the possible value of these benefits in relation to the cost. The benefit in this case are those buyers who are able to buy ice creams at €2 whereas the cost are those who want to buy ice creams but are unable to do so. There might also be costs in terms of the effect on sellers that has to be taken into consideration. Some sellers may not feel it is worth their while continuing in the market and leave, thus depressing market supply. There will also be the effect on workers and capital which is now taken out of use and will be redundant. To society as a whole there is an opportunity cost of these redundant factor inputs.

This example in the market for ice cream shows a general result: when the government imposes a binding price ceiling on a competitive market, a shortage of the good arises, and sellers must ration the scarce goods among the large number of potential buyers. The rationing mechanisms that develop under price ceilings are rarely desirable. Long queues are inefficient because they waste buyers' time. (The queue may not be a physical one; people may be on a waiting list hoping to hear that the good has become available.) Discrimination according to seller bias is both inefficient (because the good does not necessarily go to the buyer who values it most highly) and potentially unfair. By contrast, the rationing mechanism in a free, competitive market is both efficient and impersonal. When the market for ice cream reaches its equilibrium, anyone who wants to pay the market price can get a cornet. Free markets ration goods with prices.

CASE STUDY

Rent Control in the Short Run and Long Run

It is sometimes argued that governments should help the poor find more affordable housing by placing a ceiling on the rents that landlords may charge their tenants. Economists often criticize rent control, arguing that it is a highly inefficient way to help the poor raise their standard of living. One economist called rent control 'the best way to destroy a city, other than bombing.'

The adverse effects of rent control are less apparent to the general population because these effects occur over many years. In the short run, landlords have a fixed number of housing units (houses and flats) to rent, and they cannot adjust this number quickly as market conditions change. Moreover, the number of people searching for housing in a city may not be highly responsive to rents in the short run because people take time to adjust their housing arrangements. Therefore, the short-run supply and demand for housing are relatively inelastic.

Panel (a) of Figure 6.2 shows the short-run effects of rent control on the housing market. As with any binding price ceiling, rent control causes a shortage. Yet because supply and demand are inelastic in the short run, the initial shortage caused by rent control is small. The primary effect in the short run is to reduce rents.

The long-run story is very different because the buyers and sellers of rental housing respond more to market conditions as time passes – there is an incentive for both buyers and sellers to change their behaviour in response to the changed market conditions. On the supply side, landlords respond to low rents by not building new housing and by failing to maintain existing housing. Some are likely to feel that they are not able to generate any return on investing in improving or maintaining properties because they cannot charge higher prices to compensate for the costs they have incurred. On the demand side, low rents encourage people to find their own housing (rather than living with their parents or sharing with friends) and induce more people to move into a city. Therefore, both supply and demand are more elastic in the long run.

Panel (b) of Figure 6.2 illustrates the housing market in the long run. When rent control depresses rents below the equilibrium level, the quantity of housing units supplied falls substantially, and the quantity of housing units demanded rises substantially. The result is a large shortage of housing.

In cities with rent control, landlords use various mechanisms to ration housing. Some landlords keep long waiting lists. Others give a preference to tenants without children. Still others discriminate on the basis of race.

FIGURE 6.2

Rent Control in the Short Run and in the Long Run

Panel (a) shows the short-run effects of rent control: because the supply and demand for housing units are relatively inelastic, the price ceiling imposed by a rent-control law causes only a small shortage of housing. Panel (b) shows the long-run effects of rent control: because the supply and demand for housing units are more elastic, rent control causes a large shortage.

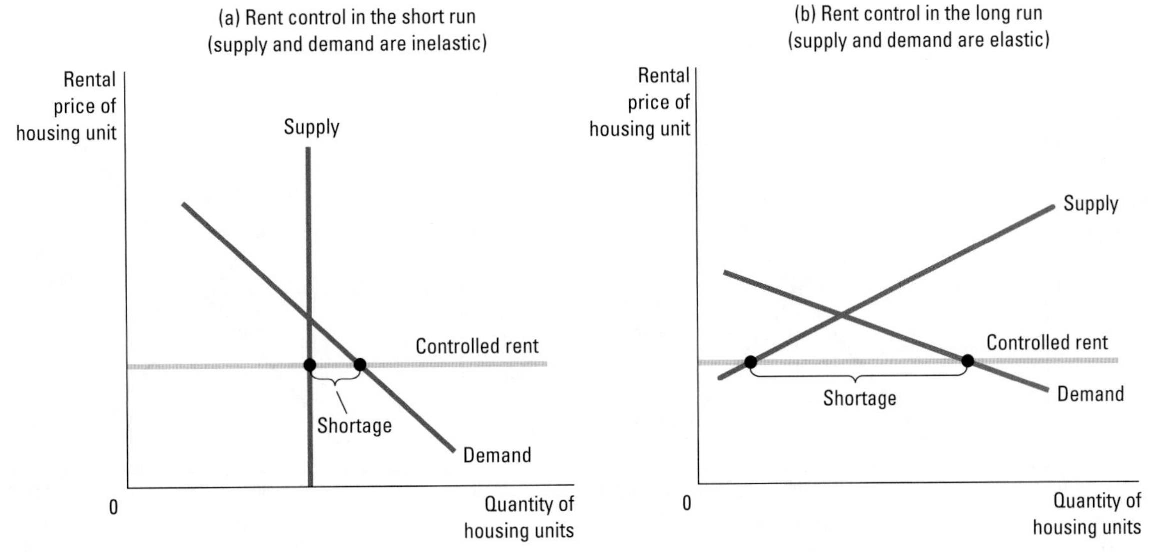

Sometimes, apartments are allocated to those willing to offer under-the-table payments – the so-called 'black market'. In essence, these bribes bring the total price of an apartment (including the bribe) closer to the equilibrium price.

To understand fully the effects of rent control, we need look no further than Principle 4 of the *Ten Principles of Economics* from Chapter 1: people respond to incentives. In free markets, landlords try to keep their buildings clean and safe because desirable apartments command higher prices. By contrast, when rent control creates shortages and waiting lists, landlords lose their incentive to respond to tenants' concerns. Why should a landlord spend his money to maintain and improve his property when people are waiting to get in as it is? In the end, tenants get lower rents, but they also get lower-quality housing.

Policy makers often react to the effects of rent control by imposing additional regulations. For example, there are laws that make racial discrimination in housing illegal and require landlords to provide minimally adequate living conditions. These laws, however, are difficult and costly to enforce. By contrast, when rent control is eliminated and a market for housing is regulated by the forces of competition, such laws are less necessary. In a free market, the price of housing adjusts to eliminate the shortages that give rise to undesirable landlord behaviour.

How Price Floors Affect Market Outcomes

To examine the effects of another kind of government price control, let's return to the market for ice cream. Imagine now that the government is persuaded by the

FIGURE 6.3

A Market With a Price Floor

In panel (a), the government imposes a price floor of €2. Because this is below the equilibrium price of €3, the price floor has no effect. The market price adjusts to balance supply and demand. At the equilibrium, quantity supplied and quantity demanded both equal 100 cornets. In panel (b), the government imposes a price floor of €4, which is above the equilibrium price of €3. Therefore, the market price equals €4. Because 120 cornets are supplied at this price and only 80 are demanded, there is a surplus of 40 cornets.

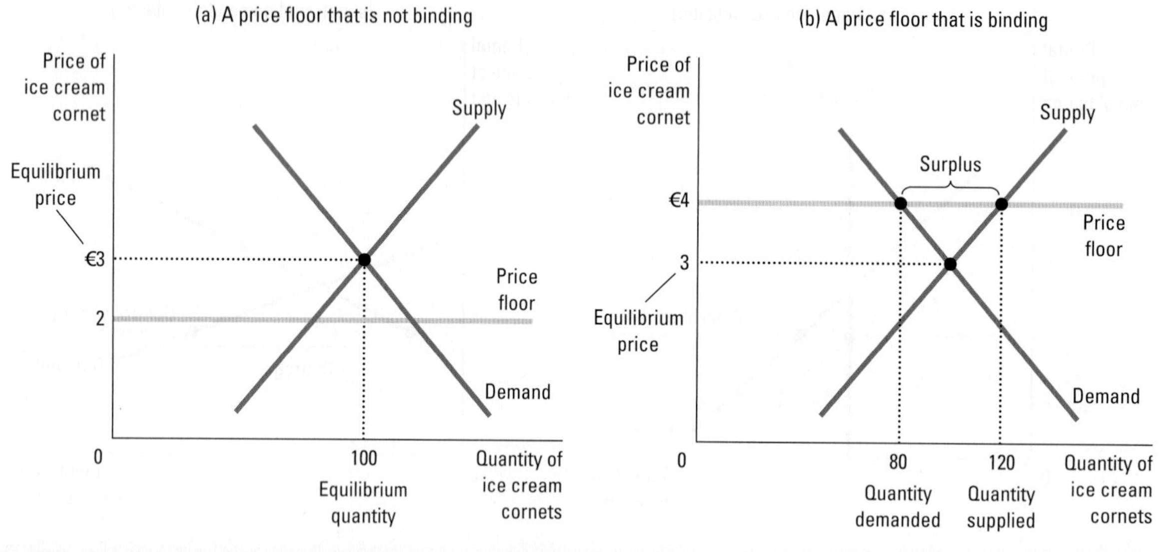

pleas of the National Organization of Ice Cream Producers. In this case, the government might institute a price floor. Price floors, like price ceilings, are an attempt by the government to maintain prices at other than equilibrium levels. Whereas a price ceiling places a legal maximum on prices, a price floor places a legal minimum.

When the government imposes a price floor on the ice cream market, two outcomes are possible. If the government imposes a price floor of €2 per cornet when the equilibrium price is €3, we obtain the outcome in panel (a) of Figure 6.3. In this case, because the equilibrium price is above the floor, the price floor is not binding. Market forces naturally move the economy to the equilibrium, and the price floor has no effect.

Panel (b) of Figure 6.3 shows what happens when the government imposes a price floor of €4 per cornet. In this case, because the equilibrium price of €3 is below the floor, the price floor is a binding constraint on the market. The forces of supply and demand tend to move the price towards the equilibrium price, but when the market price hits the floor, it can fall no further. The market price equals the price floor. At this floor, the quantity of ice cream supplied (120 cornets) exceeds the quantity demanded (80 cornets). Some people who want to sell ice cream at the going price are unable to. Thus, a binding price floor causes a surplus.

Just as price ceilings and shortages can lead to undesirable rationing mechanisms, so can price floors and surpluses. In the case of a price floor, some sellers are unable to sell all they want at the market price. The sellers who appeal to the personal biases of the buyers, perhaps due to racial or familial ties, are better able to sell their goods than those who do not. By contrast, in a free market, the price serves as the rationing mechanism, and sellers can sell all they want at the equilibrium price.

CASE STUDY

The Minimum Wage

An important example of a price floor is the minimum wage. Minimum wage laws dictate the lowest price for labour that any employer may pay. The US and 20 of the 27 European Union countries now have a statutory minimum wage.

To examine the effects of a minimum wage, we must consider the market for labour. Panel (a) of Figure 6.4 shows the labour market, which, like all markets, is subject to the forces of supply and demand. Workers determine the supply of labour, and firms determine the demand. If the government doesn't intervene, the wage normally adjusts to balance labour supply and labour demand.

Panel (b) of Figure 6.4 shows the labour market with a minimum wage. If the minimum wage is above the equilibrium level, as it is here, the quantity of labour supplied exceeds the quantity demanded. The result is unemployment. Thus, the minimum wage raises the incomes of those workers who have jobs, but it lowers the incomes of those workers who cannot find jobs.

To understand fully the minimum wage, keep in mind that the economy contains not a single labour market, but many labour markets for different types of workers. The impact of the minimum wage depends on the skill and experience of the worker. Workers with high skills and much experience are not affected, because their equilibrium wages are well above the minimum. For these workers, the minimum wage is not binding. One would therefore expect a diagram such as that in Panel (b) of Figure 6.4, where the minimum wage is above the equilibrium wage and unemployment results, to apply primarily to the market for low-skilled and teenage labour. Note, however, that the *extent* of the unemployment that results depends upon the elasticities of the supply and demand for labour. In Panel (c) of Figure 6.4 we have redrawn the diagram with a more elastic demand curve for labour and we can see that this results in a higher level of unemployment. It is often argued that the demand for unskilled labour is in fact likely to be highly elastic with respect to the price of labour because employers of unskilled labour, such as fast food restaurants usually face highly price-elastic demand curves for their own product and so cannot easily pass on wage rises in the form of higher prices without seeing their revenue fall.

This is only true, however, if one firm raises its price while others do not. If all fast food companies are forced to raise prices slightly in order to pay the minimum wage to their staff, this may result in a much smaller fall in the demand for the output (e.g. hamburgers) of any one firm. If this is the case, then the imposition of a statutory minimum wage may actually lead to a rightward shift in the segment of the labour demand curve at or above the statutory minimum wage: a firm is able to pay the higher wage without drastically reducing its labour demand because it can pass on the higher wage costs by charging a higher price for its product, safe in the knowledge that other firms in the industry will have to do the same and hence that it will not suffer a dramatic fall in demand for its output. In this case – as in panel (d) of Figure 6.4 – although there is an increase in unemployment relative to the case with no minimum wage, this is mainly because the supply of labour is higher with the minimum wage imposed. This is because some workers will be attracted by the higher wage to enter the labour market – second

FIGURE 6.4

How the Minimum Wage Affects the Labour Market

Panel (a) shows a labour market in which the wage adjusts to balance labour supply and demand. Panel (b) shows the impact of a binding minimum wage. Because the minimum wage is a price floor, it causes a surplus: the quantity of labour supplied exceeds the quantity demanded. The result is unemployment. Panel (c) shows that the more elastic labour demand is, the higher will be ensuing unemployment. In panel (d), because the minimum wage is binding across the whole industry, firms are able to pass a higher proportion of the wage costs onto higher prices without a drastic fall in demand for output, and so the labour demand curve for an individual firm actually shifts to the right at or above the minimum wage, so that the impact on employment is much less.

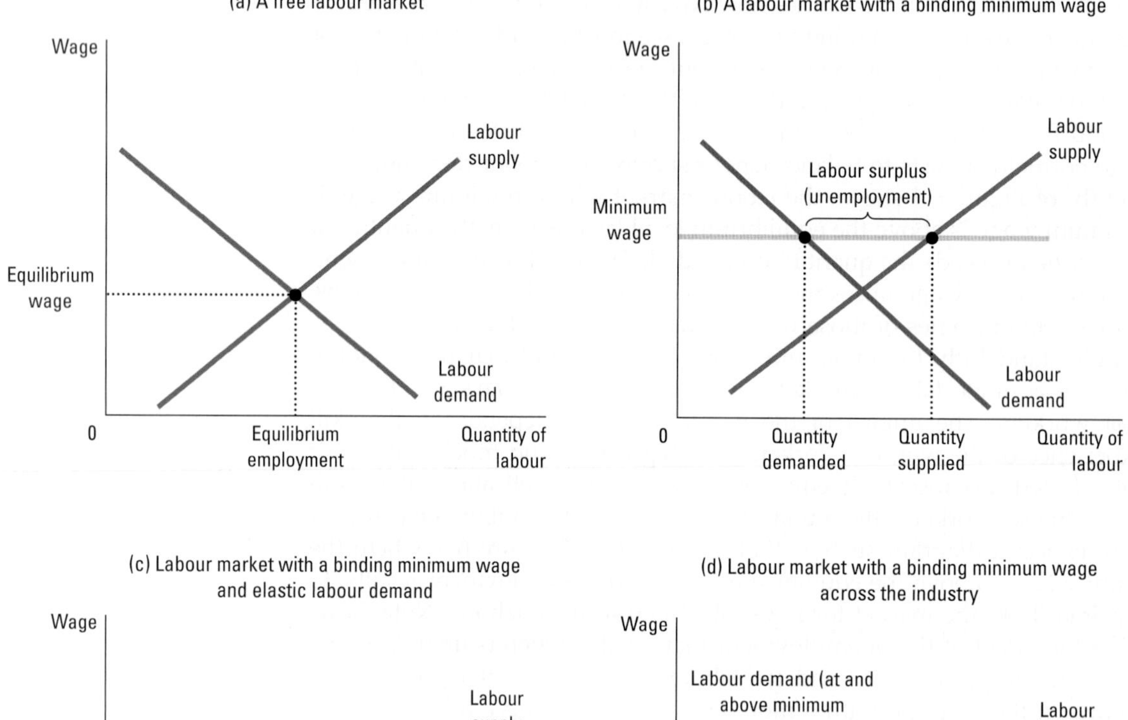

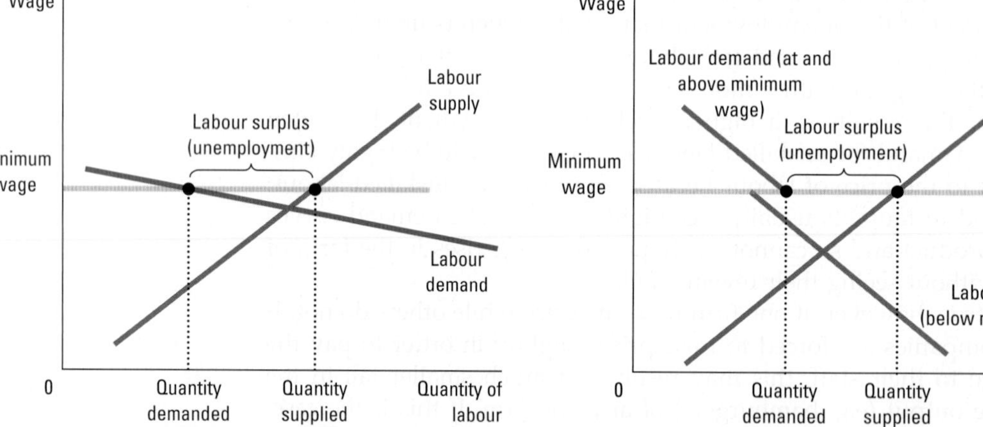

earners, for example, or young people who otherwise would have stayed in full-time education.

Advocates of minimum wage laws view the policy as one way to raise the income of the working poor. They correctly point out that workers who earn the minimum wage can afford only a meagre standard of living. They admit that it may have some adverse effects, including a possible rise in unemployment, but they believe that these effects are small and that, all things considered, a higher minimum wage makes the poor better off. In other words they argue that the value of the benefits of a minimum wage are greater than the value of the costs and so such a policy is worth putting into practice.

Opponents of the minimum wage contend that it is not the best way to combat poverty since it affects only the income of those in employment and may raise unemployment, and because not all minimum wage workers are heads of households trying to help their families escape poverty – some may be second earners or even third earners in relatively well-off households. To decide whether this argument is more powerful than the arguments of the advocates, economists will try and find ways to measure the size of the contrasting effects so that an informed decision can be made with regard to the value of the benefits versus the costs. This is often harder than it may at first appear but is a crucial part of an economist's work.

In short, the effects of the minimum wage on the labour market are complicated. It is one of those cases where there are no clear-cut answers: it all depends on what assumptions you make. At this point you may throw up your hands in despair and ask 'so what's the point of studying economics if it can't tell me one way or the other if introducing a minimum wage benefits the poor or not?' But all our brief economic analysis of the minimum wage has shown is that the issue is very complex: don't shoot the messenger for telling you so. The economist tries to shed light on this complexity so that the costs and benefits of such a policy can be better understood; this is partly why economics is so valuable and so fascinating!

Evaluating Price Controls

One of the *Ten Principles of Economics* discussed in Chapter 1 is that markets are usually a good way to organize economic activity. This principle explains why economists usually oppose price ceilings and price floors. To economists, prices are not the outcome of some haphazard process. Prices, they contend, are the result of the millions of business and consumer decisions that lie behind the supply and demand curves. Prices have the crucial job of balancing supply and demand and, thereby, coordinating economic activity. When policy makers set prices by legal decree, they obscure the signals that normally guide the allocation of society's resources.

Another one of the *Ten Principles of Economics* is that governments can sometimes improve market outcomes. Indeed, policy makers are led to control prices because they view the market's outcome as unfair. Price controls are often aimed at helping the poor. For instance, rent-control laws try to make housing affordable for everyone, and minimum wage laws try to help people escape poverty.

Yet price controls often hurt those they are trying to help. Rent control may keep rents low, but it also discourages landlords from maintaining their buildings and makes housing hard to find in the long run as we have seen. Minimum wage laws may raise the incomes of some workers, but they also cause other workers to be unemployed.

Helping those in need can be accomplished in ways other than controlling prices. For instance, the government can make housing more affordable by paying a fraction of the rent for poor families. Unlike rent control, such rent subsidies do not reduce the quantity of housing supplied and, therefore, do not lead to housing shortages.

Although these alternative policies are often better than price controls, they are not perfect. Rent and wage subsidies cost the government money and, therefore, require higher taxes. As we see in the next section, taxation has costs of its own.

Quick Quiz Define *price ceiling* and *price floor*, and give an example of each. Which leads to a shortage? Which leads to a surplus? Why?

IN THE NEWS

A Price Floor for Alcohol?

Price floors are not only relevant in the case of the labour market. Concerns about the effects of alcohol misuse on health and the economy prompted politicians in Scotland to consider using a price floor as a means of restricting consumption, as highlighted by this article.

Research on industry sales data analysed by the National Health Service in Scotland suggested that adults in the country are drinking the equivalent of 46 bottles of vodka each year. The amount of alcohol consumed by adults has stayed stable since 2005, but at a high level. The findings, published in January 2010 reported that in the year to September 2009 sales averaged 12.2 litres of pure alcohol per person over the age of 18, equivalent to 537 pints or 130 bottles of wine per head of the population. This volume of consumption was above recommended guidelines and amounted to around 25 per cent more than that consumed by individuals in England and Wales.

Would a minimum price on alcohol reduce consumption?

The report served to highlight the concern that politicians and the health community in Scotland have had over alcohol consumption for some time. The Scottish Health Secretary linked the rise in alcohol consumption with a fall in the real price of alcohol. Sales of alcoholic drinks in pubs, clubs and supermarkets had been subject to price discounting; some pubs and clubs had regular price promotions which offered 'two-for-one' drinks or happy hours. Supermarkets had been accused of selling alcohol at very low prices in order to capture sales and market share and all this had helped to make alcohol not only cheaper but more accessible.

The effects on individual health and the economy in terms of lost output because of employee absenteeism, extra policing and alcohol-related crime and violence, not to mention the cost of treating alcohol-related health problems has spurred politicians to try to consider ways to reduce consumption. The report by the Scottish National Health service put the cost to Scotland's economy at £2.25 billion a year. Alcohol-related deaths accounted for around 1 500 lives a year and there are over 42 000 alcohol related hospital discharges every year. Cheap prices have been targeted as being 'public enemy number one' and so policy measures were focused on introducing a price floor on alcohol amongst other measures to try and cut consumption and improve education.

The price floor would seek to put a minimum price on a unit of alcohol (one unit of alcohol is 10ml (1cl) by volume, or 8g by weight, of pure alcohol) above the market price. The aim would be to exploit the law of demand and cut consumption. The Scottish government has cited evidence for the imposition of a price floor from research carried out by the University of Sheffield, published in December 2008. The research suggested that increasing the price of alcohol would lead to a fall in consumption.

The leader of the research, Dr Petra Meier of the university's School of Health and Related Research (ScHARR), said: 'This is the first study to integrate data on alcohol pricing and purchasing patterns, consumption and harm to answer the question of what would happen if government were to introduce different alcohol pricing policies. The results suggest that policies which increase the price of alcohol can bring significant health and social benefits and lead to considerable financial savings in the NHS, criminal justice system and in the workplace.'

The findings suggested that price increases would have to be implemented 'across the board' otherwise consumers would simply find substitutes of cheaper drinks or different places to buy alcohol. The main target of any price increase should be on cheaper drinks which the study suggested tended to be bought by those whose drinking caused the most harm whilst only having a limited effect on more moderate drinkers who tended to buy more expensive drinks. In many cases drinkers are paying less than 40p per unit and there was also plenty of evidence that prices of less than 30p per unit were common. Any minimum price, therefore, would have to be above this level. In September 2010, the Scottish government actually proposed a minimum price of 45p per unit.

The research suggested that as price levels were increased the effect on demand would escalate. At 20p per unit, demand would fall by just 0.1 per cent; at 30p consumption would fall by 0.6 per cent, at 40p demand falls by 2.6 per cent and at 50p, 60p and 70p levels, demand would fall by 6.9 per cent, 12.8 per cent and 18.6 per cent respectively.

TAXES

All governments, whether national or local, use taxes to raise revenue for public projects, such as roads, schools and national defence. Because taxes are such an important policy instrument, and because they affect our lives in many ways, the study of taxes is a topic to which we return several times throughout this book. In this section we begin our study of how taxes affect the economy.

To set the stage for our analysis, imagine that the government decides to hold a national annual ice cream festival – with a parade, fireworks and speeches by leading politicians. To raise revenue to pay for the event, it decides to place a €0.50 tax on the sale of ice cream cornets. When the plan is announced, our two lobbying groups swing into action. The National Organization of Ice Cream Producers claims that its members are struggling to survive in a competitive market, and it argues that *buyers* of ice cream should have to pay the tax. The National Association of Ice Cream Eaters claims that consumers of ice cream are having trouble making ends meet, and it argues that *sellers* of ice cream should pay the tax. The prime minister, hoping to reach a compromise, suggests that half the tax be paid by the buyers and half be paid by the sellers.

To alalyse these proposals, we need to address a simple but subtle question: when the government levies a tax on a good, who bears the burden of the tax – in other words, who actually pays the tax? The people buying the good? The people selling the good? Or, if buyers and sellers share the tax burden, what determines how the burden is divided? Can the government simply legislate the division of the burden, as our prime minister is suggesting, or is the division determined by more fundamental forces in the economy? Economists use the term **tax incidence** to refer to the distribution of a tax burden. As we will see, some surprising lessons about tax incidence arise just by applying the tools of supply and demand.

tax incidence
the manner in which the burden of a tax is shared among participants in a market

How Taxes on Sellers Affect Market Outcomes

Consider a tax levied on sellers of a good. Suppose the government imposes a tax on sellers of ice cream cornets of €0.50 for each cornet they sell. What are the effects of this tax? Again, we apply our three steps.

Step One In this case, the immediate impact of the tax is on the sellers of ice cream. The quantity of ice cream demanded at any given price is the same; thus, the demand curve does not change. By contrast, the tax on sellers makes the ice cream business less profitable at any given price, so it shifts the supply curve.

FIGURE 6.5

A Tax on Sellers

When a tax of €0.50 is levied on sellers, the supply curve shifts up by €0.50 from S_1 *to* S_2*. The equilibrium quantity falls from 100 to 90 cornets. The price that buyers pay rises from €3.00 to €3.30. The price that sellers receive (after paying the tax) falls from €3.00 to €2.80. Even though the tax is levied on sellers, buyers and sellers share the burden of the tax.*

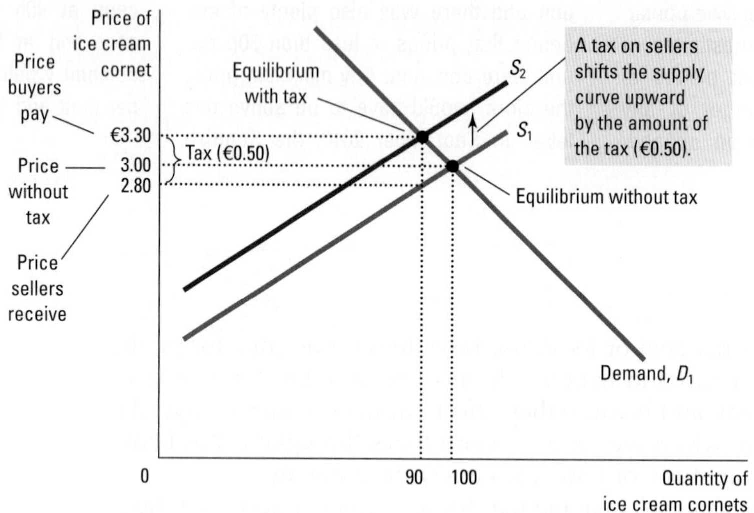

Step Two Because the tax on sellers raises the cost of producing and selling ice cream, it reduces the quantity supplied at every price. The supply curve shifts to the left (or, equivalently, upward).

Once again, we can be precise about the magnitude of the shift. For any market price of ice cream, the effective price to sellers – the amount they get to keep after paying the tax – is €0.50 lower. For example, if the market price of a cornet happened to be €2.00, the effective price received by sellers would be €1.50. Whatever the market price, sellers will supply a quantity of ice cream as if the price were €0.50 lower than it is. Put differently, to induce sellers to supply any given quantity, the market price must now be €0.50 higher to compensate for the effect of the tax. Thus, as shown in Figure 6.5, the supply curve shifts *upward* from S_1 to S_2 by exactly the size of the tax (€0.50).

Step Three Having determined how the supply curve shifts, we can now compare the initial and the new equilibrium. The figure shows that the equilibrium price of ice cream rises from €3.00 to €3.30, and the equilibrium quantity falls from 100 to 90 cornets. Once again, the tax reduces the size of the ice cream market. And once again, buyers and sellers share the burden of the tax. Because the market price rises, buyers pay €0.30 more for each cornet of ice cream than they did before the tax was enacted. Sellers receive a higher price than they did without the tax, but the effective price (after paying the tax) falls from €3.00 to €2.80.

Implications A tax on sellers places a wedge between the price that buyers pay and the price that sellers receive. The wedge between the buyers' price and the sellers' price is the same, and would be the same regardless of whether the tax is levied on buyers or sellers. In reality most governments levy taxes on sellers rather than on buyers, however. The wedge shifts the relative position of the supply and demand curves. In the new equilibrium, buyers and sellers share the burden of the tax.

CASE STUDY

Can the Government Distribute the Burden of a Payroll Tax?

If you have ever received a pay cheque, you probably noticed that taxes were deducted from the amount you earned. In the United Kingdom, one of these taxes is called National Insurance Contributions (NICs). In theory, the UK government uses the revenue from NICs to pay for social security and state pensions (in practice, the money goes into the government coffers without being earmarked for any particular use). NICs are an example of a *payroll tax*, which is a tax on the wages that firms pay their workers. Other European countries have a similar tax with France, Sweden and Slovenia all having a payroll tax.

Who do you think bears the burden of this payroll tax – firms or workers? In fact, if you read official UK government documents, it seems that the burden is split fairly clearly: in 2010–11, for example, average-paid workers paid 11 per cent of their income above a basic level in NICs, while the workers' employer paid 12.8 per cent.

Our analysis of tax incidence, however, shows that politicians cannot so easily dictate the distribution of a tax burden. To illustrate, we can alalyse a payroll tax as merely a tax on a good, where the good is labour and the price is the wage. The key feature of the payroll tax is that it places a wedge between the wage that firms pay and the wage that workers receive. Figure 6.6 shows

FIGURE 6.6

A Payroll Tax

A payroll tax places a wedge between the wage that workers receive and the wage that firms pay. Comparing wages with and without the tax, you can see that workers and firms share the tax burden. This division of the tax burden between workers and firms does not depend on whether the government levies the tax on workers, levies the tax on firms or divides the tax equally between the two groups.

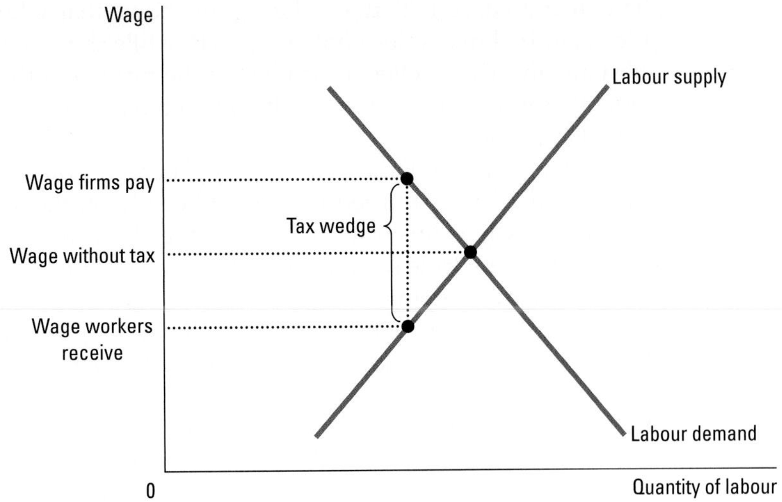

the outcome. When a payroll tax is enacted, the wage received by workers falls, and the wage paid by firms rises. In the end, workers and firms share the burden of the tax, much as the legislation requires. Yet this division of the tax burden between workers and firms has nothing to do with the legislated division. Moreover, the same outcome would prevail if the law levied the entire tax on workers or if it levied the entire tax on firms.

This example shows that the most basic lesson of tax incidence is often overlooked in public debate. Politicians can decide whether a tax comes from the buyer's pocket or from the seller's, but they cannot legislate the true burden of a tax. Rather, tax incidence depends on the forces of supply and demand.

Elasticity and Tax Incidence

When a good is taxed, buyers and sellers of the good share the burden of the tax. But how exactly is the tax burden divided? Only rarely will it be shared equally. To see how the burden is divided, consider the impact of taxation in the two markets in Figure 6.7. In both cases, the figure shows the initial demand curve, the initial supply curve, and a tax that drives a wedge between the amount paid by buyers and the amount received by sellers. (Not drawn in either panel of the figure is the new supply or demand curve. Which curve shifts depends on whether the tax is levied on buyers or sellers. As we have seen, this is irrelevant for the incidence of the tax.) The difference in the two panels is the relative elasticity of supply and demand.

Panel (a) of Figure 6.7 shows a tax in a market with very elastic supply and relatively inelastic demand. That is, sellers are very responsive to changes in the price of the good (so the supply curve is relatively flat), whereas buyers are not very responsive (so the demand curve is relatively steep). When a tax is imposed on a market with these elasticities, the price received by sellers does not fall much, so sellers bear only a small burden. By contrast, the price paid by buyers rises substantially, indicating that buyers bear most of the burden of the tax. Our analysis of elasticity in Chapter 5 should make this something that is not at all surprising. If the price elasticity of demand is low (a steep curve) then demand will fall proportionately less in response to a rise in price – buyers are not very price sensitive. The seller can shift the burden of the tax onto the buyer safe in the knowledge that demand will only fall by a relatively small amount.

Panel (b) of Figure 6.7 shows a tax in a market with relatively inelastic supply and very elastic demand. In this case, sellers are not very responsive to changes in the price (so the supply curve is steeper), while buyers are very responsive (so the demand curve is flatter). The figure shows that when a tax is imposed, the price paid by buyers does not rise much, while the price received by sellers falls substantially. Thus, sellers bear most of the burden of the tax. In this case, sellers know that if they try to pass on the tax to buyers that demand will fall by a relatively large amount.

The two panels of Figure 6.7 show a general lesson about how the burden of a tax is divided: a tax burden falls more heavily on the side of the market that is less elastic. Why is this true? In essence, the elasticity measures the willingness of buyers or sellers to leave the market when conditions become unfavourable. A small elasticity of demand means that buyers do not have good alternatives to consuming this particular good. A small elasticity of supply means that sellers do not have good alternatives to producing this particular good. When the good is taxed, the side of the market with fewer good alternatives cannot easily leave the market and must, therefore, bear more of the burden of the tax.

We can apply this logic to the payroll tax discussed in the previous case study. Most labour economists believe that the supply of labour is much less elastic than the demand. This means that workers, rather than firms, bear most of the burden of any payroll tax, whatever the official split.

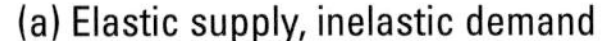

FIGURE 6.7

How the Burden of a Tax Is Divided

In panel (a), the supply curve is elastic and the demand curve is inelastic. In this case, the price received by sellers falls only slightly, while the price paid by buyers rises substantially. Thus, buyers bear most of the burden of the tax. In panel (b), the supply curve is inelastic and the demand curve is elastic. In this case, the price received by sellers falls substantially, while the price paid by buyers rises only slightly. Thus, sellers bear most of the burden of the tax.

(a) Elastic supply, inelastic demand

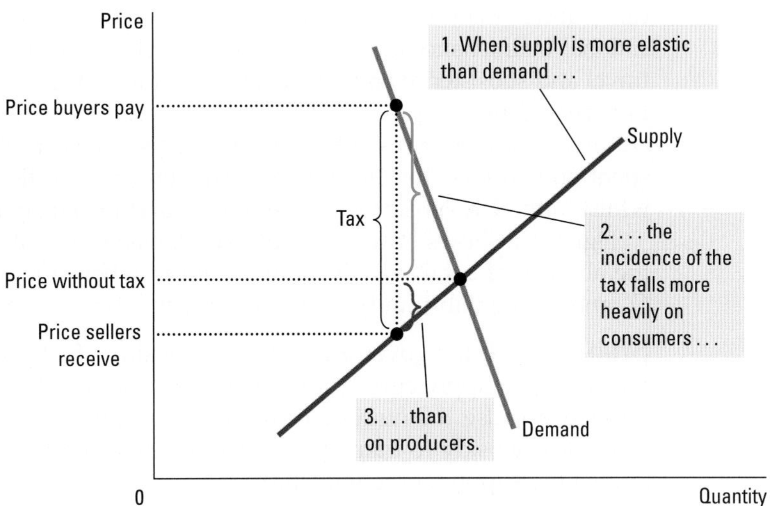

(b) Inelastic supply, elastic demand

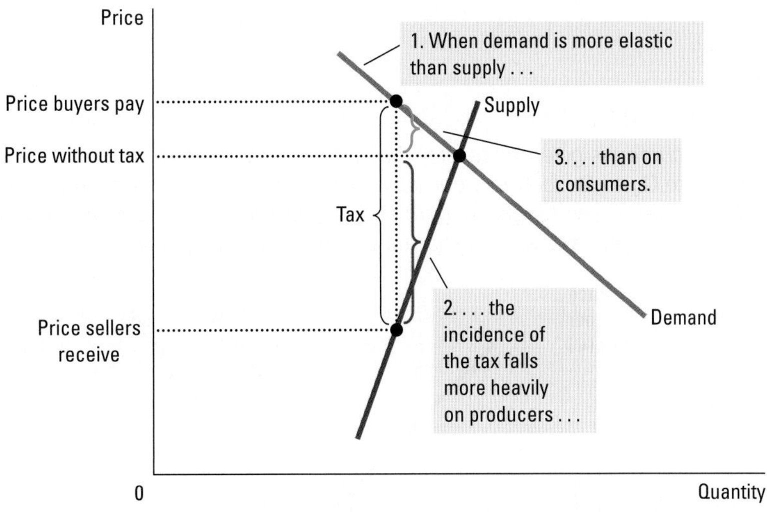

Quick Quiz In a supply and demand diagram, show how a tax on car buyers of €1 000 per car affects the quantity of cars sold and the price of cars. In another diagram, show how a tax on car sellers of €1 000 per car affects the quantity of cars sold and the price of cars. In both of your diagrams, show the change in the price paid by car buyers and the change in price received by car sellers.

How Subsidies Affect Market Outcomes

We mentioned earlier in the chapter that subsidies were the opposite of a tax. Subsidies are levied when governments want to encourage the consumption of a 'good' which they deem is currently underproduced. Subsidies are generally given to sellers and have the effect of reducing the cost of production as opposed to a tax which increases the cost of production. Subsidies exist in a variety of different areas including education, transport, agriculture, regional development, housing and employment.

Subsidies in education help to make the cost of attending college or higher education lower than it would otherwise be; in the UK some students receive an educational maintenance allowance (EMA) which is designed to help them with their travel and subsistence and encourages them to stay on for post-16 education. Most European countries provide subsidies for transport systems and the common agricultural policy oversees subsidies to farmers. In Switzerland some €2.5 billion is spent on subsidies for rail transport, in Germany the figure is nearer to €9 billion whilst in the UK subsidies account for around €3 billion and in France €6.8 billion.

Figure 6.8 shows how a subsidy works using the rail system as an example. In the absence of a subsidy the equilibrium number of journeys bought and sold is Q_e and the equilibrium train ticket for each journey is price P_e.

Step One If the government gives a subsidy of €20 per journey to train operators, it is the supply curve for journeys which is affected; the demand curve is not affected because the number of train journeys demanded at each price stays the same. The subsidy to train operators reduces the cost of providing a train journey and so the supply curve will shift.

Step Two Because the subsidy reduces the cost to the train operators, the supply curve shifts to the right by the amount of the subsidy. If the cost of providing

FIGURE 6.8

A Subsidy on Rail Transport

When a subsidy of €20 per journey is given to sellers, the supply curve shifts to the right by €20 from S_1 to S_2. The equilibrium quantity rises from Q_e to Q_1 journeys per year. The price that buyers pay for a journey falls from €75.00 to €60. The subsidy results in lower prices for passengers and an increased number of journeys available. Even though the subsidy is given to sellers, buyers and sellers share the benefits of the subsidy.

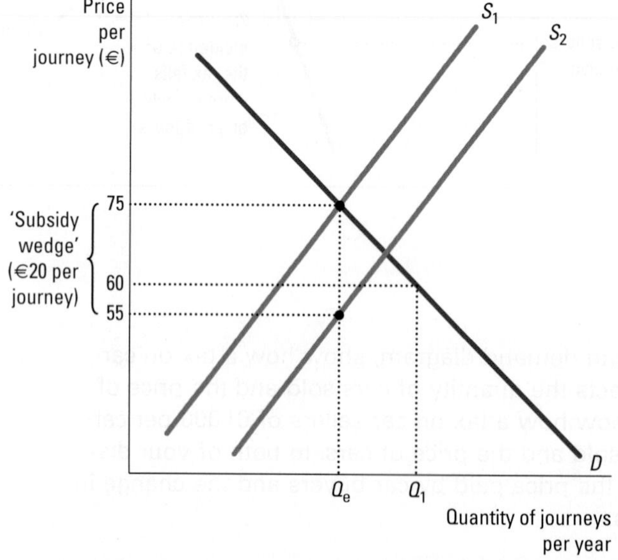

a train journey was an average of €75 and the subsidy was €20 the supply curve would shift so that train operators would now supply train journeys at an effective cost of €20 below the previous cost. They would now be willing to supply more train journeys at every price.

Step Three Comparing the initial and the new equilibrium we can see that the equilibrium price of each train journey is now lower at €60 and the equilibrium number of journeys travelled increases to Q_1. Passengers and train operators both benefit from the subsidy as passengers can obtain train tickets at a lower price than before the subsidy and have more journeys available and sellers receive more revenue than they did before the subsidy allowing them the potential to invest in the service they provide. The precise division of the benefits between buyers and sellers will depend on the relative elasticities of demand and supply.

Implications There is a considerable debate surrounding the value of subsidies. We have seen from the example how price and quantity can be affected following the imposition of a subsidy. In the case of transport, it may have the effect of altering the incentives for people to travel on the train rather than on the roads and so have the benefit of reducing congestion on the roads as well as reducing possible pollution that is associated with road use. In the recent recession some countries introduced subsidies to encourage consumers to trade in their old cars for new ones which helped to boost the European motor industry at a time when it was struggling with a downturn in demand. There are also costs associated with subsidies; for one thing someone has to finance the subsidy and it is often the taxpayer. Subsidies may also encourage firms to overproduce which has a wider effect on the market. Subsidies on commodities such as cotton, bananas and sugar distort the workings of the market and change global comparative advantage. Overproduction leads to excess supply on world markets and drives down prices as well as diverting trade to rich countries who can support producers through subsidies at the expense of poor countries whose producers cannot compete because prices are lower than the free market price. Chapter 7 will provide a further example of how subsidies can affect the efficiency of market outcomes.

CONCLUSION

The economy is governed by two kinds of laws: the laws of supply and demand and the laws enacted by governments. In this chapter we have begun to see how these laws interact. Price controls, taxes and subsidies are common in various markets in the economy, and their effects are frequently debated in the press and among policy makers. Even a little bit of economic knowledge can go a long way towards understanding and evaluating these policies.

In subsequent chapters we shall alalyse many government policies in greater detail. We shall examine the effects of taxation more fully, and we shall consider a broader range of policies than we considered here. Yet the basic lessons of this chapter will not change: when alalysing government policies, supply and demand are the first and most useful tools of analysis.

SUMMARY

- A price ceiling is a legal maximum on the price of a good or service. An example is rent control. If the price ceiling is below the equilibrium price, the quantity demanded exceeds the quantity supplied. Because of the resulting shortage, sellers must in some way ration the good or service among buyers.
- A price floor is a legal minimum on the price of a good or service. An example is the minimum wage. If the price

floor is above the equilibrium price, the quantity supplied exceeds the quantity demanded. Because of the resulting surplus, buyers' demands for the good or service must in some way be rationed among sellers.

- When the government levies a tax on a good, the equilibrium quantity of the good falls. That is, a tax on a market shrinks the size of the market.
- A tax on a good places a wedge between the price paid by buyers and the price received by sellers. When the market moves to the new equilibrium, buyers pay more for the good and sellers receive less for it. In this sense, buyers and sellers share the tax burden. The incidence of a tax (that is, the division of the tax burden) does not depend on whether the tax is levied on buyers or sellers.
- A subsidy given to sellers lowers the cost of production and encourages firms to expand output. Buyers benefit from lower prices.
- The incidence of a tax or subsidy depends on the price elasticities of supply and demand. The burden tends to fall on the side of the market that is less elastic because that side of the market can respond less/more easily to the tax/subsidy by changing the quantity bought or sold.

KEY CONCEPTS

subsidy, p. 118
price ceiling, p. 118
price floor, p. 118
tax incidence, p. 127

QUESTIONS FOR REVIEW

1. Give an example of a price ceiling and an example of a price floor.
2. Which causes a shortage of a good – a price ceiling or a price floor? Which causes a surplus?
3. What mechanisms allocate resources when the price of a good is not allowed to bring supply and demand into equilibrium?
4. Explain why economists usually oppose rent controls.
5. How does a tax imposed on a good with a high price elasticity of demand affect the market equilibrium? Who bears most of the burden of the tax in this instance?
6. How does a subsidy on a good affect the price paid by buyers, the price received by sellers and the quantity bought and sold?
7. What determines how the burden of a tax or a subsidy is divided between buyers and sellers? Why?

PROBLEMS AND APPLICATIONS

1. Lovers of classical music persuade the government to impose a price ceiling of €40 per ticket at classical music concerts. Does this policy get more or fewer people to attend?
2. The government has decided that the free market price of cheese is too low.
   a. Suppose the government imposes a binding price floor in the cheese market. Use a supply and demand diagram to show the effect of this policy on the price of cheese and the quantity of cheese sold. Is there a shortage or surplus of cheese?
   b. Farmers complain that the price floor has reduced their total revenue. Is this possible? Explain.
   c. In response to farmers' complaints, the government agrees to purchase all of the surplus cheese at the price floor. Compared to the basic price floor, who benefits from this new policy? Who loses?

3. A recent study found that the demand and supply schedules for frisbees are as follows:

Price per frisbee	Quantity demanded	Quantity supplied
€11	1 million frisbees	15 million frisbees
10	2	12
9	4	9
8	6	6
7	8	3
6	10	1

What are the equilibrium price and quantity of frisbees?
   a. Frisbee manufacturers persuade the government that frisbee production improves scientists' understanding of aerodynamics and thus is important for national security. The government decides to impose a price floor €2 above the equilibrium price. What is the new market price? How many frisbees are sold?
   b. Irate university students march on the government and demand a reduction in the price of frisbees. The government decides to repeal the price floor and impose a price ceiling €1 below the former price floor. What is the new market price? How many frisbees are sold?
4. Suppose that in the absence of any tax whatsoever, the equilibrium price of beer is €1.50 per litre. Now suppose that the government requires beer drinkers to pay a total tax (sales tax plus alcohol duty) of €0.50 on every litre of beer purchased.
   a. Draw a supply and demand diagram of the market for beer without the tax. Show the price paid by consumers, the price received by producers and the quantity of beer sold. What is the difference between the price paid by consumers and the price received by producers?
   b. Now draw a supply and demand diagram for the beer market with the tax. Show the price paid by consumers, the price received by producers and the quantity of beer sold. What is the difference between the price paid by consumers and the price received by producers? Has the quantity of beer sold increased or decreased?
5. The employment minister wants to raise tax revenue and at the same time make workers better off. A civil servant suggests raising the payroll tax paid by firms and using part of the extra revenue to reduce the payroll tax paid by workers. Would this accomplish the minister's goal?
6. If the government places a €500 tax on luxury cars, will the price paid by consumers rise by more than €500, less than €500 or exactly €500. Explain.
7. The government decides to reduce air pollution by reducing the use of petrol. It imposes €0.50 tax for each litre of petrol sold.
   a. Should it impose this tax on petrol companies or motorists? Explain carefully, using a supply and demand diagram.
   b. If the demand for petrol were more elastic, would this tax be more effective or less effective in reducing the quantity of petrol consumed? Explain with both words and a diagram.
   c. Are consumers of petrol helped or hurt by this tax? Why?
   d. Are workers in the oil industry helped or hurt by this tax? Why?
8. A case study in this chapter discusses the minimum wage law.
   a. Suppose the minimum wage is above the equilibrium wage in the market for unskilled labour. Using a supply and demand diagram of the market for unskilled labour, show the market wage, the number of workers who are employed and the number of workers who are unemployed. Also show the total wage payments to unskilled workers.
   b. Now suppose the minister for employment proposes an increase in the minimum wage. What effect would this increase have on employment? Does the change in employment depend on the elasticity of demand, the elasticity of supply, both elasticities, or neither?
   c. What effect would this increase in the minimum wage have on unemployment? Does the change in unemployment depend on the elasticity of demand, the elasticity of supply, both elasticities, or neither?
   d. If the demand for unskilled labour were inelastic, would the proposed increase in the minimum wage raise or lower total wage payments to unskilled workers? Would your answer change if the demand for unskilled labour were elastic?
9. A subsidy is the opposite of a tax. With a €0.50 tax on the buyers of ice cream cornets, the government collects €0.50 for each cornet purchased; with a €0.50 subsidy for the buyers of ice cream cornets, the government pays buyers €0.50 for each cornet purchased.
   a. Show the effect of a €0.50 per cornet subsidy on the demand curve for ice cream cornets, the effective price paid by consumers, the effective price received by sellers and the quantity of cornets sold.
   b. Do consumers gain or lose from this policy? Do producers gain or lose? Does the government gain or lose?

For further resources, visit www.cengage.com/mankiw_taylor2

3

SUPPLY AND DEMAND II: MARKETS AND WELFARE

7 CONSUMERS, PRODUCERS AND THE EFFICIENCY OF MARKETS

Consumers celebrating Christian festivals like Christmas go to the butcher's shop or the supermarket to buy their turkeys for dinner, and may be disappointed that the price of turkey is as high as it is. At the same time, when farmers bring to market the turkeys they have reared, they wish the price of turkey was even higher. These views are not surprising: buyers always want to pay less and sellers always want to get paid more. But is there a 'right price' for turkey from the standpoint of society as a whole?

In previous chapters we saw how, in market economies, the forces of supply and demand determine the prices of goods and services and the quantities sold. So far, however, we have described the way markets allocate scarce resources without directly addressing the question of whether these market allocations are desirable. In other words, our analysis has been *positive* (what is) rather than *normative* (what should be). We know that the price of turkey adjusts to ensure that the quantity of turkey supplied equals the quantity of turkey demanded. But, at this equilibrium, is the quantity of turkey produced and consumed too small, too large or just right?

welfare economics
the study of how the allocation of resources affects economic well-being

well-being
happiness or satisfaction with life as reported by individuals

In this chapter we take up the topic of **welfare economics**, the study of how the allocation of resources affects economic **well-being**. Economists use the term well-being a good deal and have taken steps to define the term. A UK Treasury Economic Working Paper published in 2008[1] highlighted two main definitions of

[1]Lepper, L. & McAndrew, S. (2008) *Developments in the Economics of Well-being*. Treasury Working Paper number 4. Available at http://www.hm-treasury.gov.uk/d/workingpager4_031108.pdf accessed 21 January 2010.

economic well-being – subjective and objective well-being. Subjective well-being refers to the way in which people evaluate their own happiness. This includes how they feel about work, leisure and their response to the events which occur in their life. Objective well-being refers to measures of the quality of life and uses indicators developed by researchers such as educational attainment, measures of the standard of living, life expectancy and so on. Welfare economics uses some of the microeconomic techniques we have already looked at to estimate **allocative efficiency** – a measure of the utility (satisfaction) derived from the allocation of resources. We have seen how buyers place a value on consumption (which will be discussed in more detail later in the book). Allocative efficiency occurs when the value of the output that firms produce (the benefits to sellers) match the value placed on that output by consumers (the benefit) to buyers.

allocative efficiency
a resource allocation where the value of the output by sellers matches the value placed on that output by buyers

We begin by examining the benefits that buyers and sellers receive from taking part in a market. We then examine how society can make these benefits as large as possible. This analysis leads to a profound conclusion: the equilibrium of supply and demand in a market maximizes the total benefits received by buyers and sellers.

As you may recall from Chapter 1, one of the *Ten Principles of Economics* is that markets are usually a good way to organize economic activity. The study of welfare economics explains this principle more fully. It also answers our question about the right price of turkey: the price that balances the supply and demand for turkey is, in a particular sense, the best one because it maximizes the total welfare of turkey consumers and turkey producers.

CONSUMER SURPLUS

We begin our study of welfare economics by looking at the benefits buyers receive from participating in a market.

Willingness to Pay

Imagine that you own an extremely rare signed copy of Radiohead's album 'The Bends'. Because you are not a Radiohead fan, you decide to sell it. One way to do so is to hold an auction.

Four Radiohead fans show up for your auction: Liam, Paul, Noel and Tony. Each of them would like to own the album, but there is a limit to the amount that each is willing to pay for it. Table 7.1 shows the maximum price that each of the four possible buyers would pay. Each buyer's maximum is called his **willingness to pay**, and it measures how much that buyer values the good. Each buyer would be eager to buy the album at a price less than his willingness to pay, would refuse to buy the album at a price more than his willingness to pay, and would be indifferent about buying the album at a price exactly equal to his willingness to pay.

willingness to pay
the maximum amount that a buyer will pay for a good

TABLE 7.1

Four Possible Buyers' Willingness to Pay

Buyer	Willingness to pay
Liam	€100
Paul	80
Noel	70
Tony	50

To sell your album, you begin the bidding at a low price, say €10. Because all four buyers are willing to pay much more, the price rises quickly. The bidding stops when Liam bids €80 (or slightly more). At this point, Paul, Noel and Tony have dropped out of the bidding because they are unwilling to bid any more than €80. Liam pays you €80 and gets the album. Note that the album has gone to the buyer who values the album most highly.

What benefit does Liam receive from buying the Radiohead album? In a sense, Liam has found a real bargain: he is willing to pay €100 for the album but pays only €80 for it. We say that Liam receives *consumer surplus* of €20. **Consumer surplus** is the amount a buyer is willing to pay for a good minus the amount the buyer actually pays for it. We refer to 'getting a bargain' regularly in everyday language. In economics, a bargain means paying much less for something than we expected or anticipated and as a result we get a greater degree of consumer surplus than we expected.

consumer surplus
a buyer's willingness to pay minus the amount the buyer actually pays

Consumer surplus measures the benefit to buyers of participating in a market. In this example, Liam receives a €20 benefit from participating in the auction because he pays only €80 for a good he values at €100. Paul, Noel and Tony get no consumer surplus from participating in the auction because they left without the album and without paying anything.

Now consider a somewhat different example. Suppose that you had two identical Radiohead albums to sell. Again, you auction them off to the four possible buyers. To keep things simple, we assume that both albums are to be sold for the same price and that no buyer is interested in buying more than one album. Therefore, the price rises until two buyers are left.

In this case, the bidding stops when Liam and Paul bid €70 (or slightly higher). At this price, Liam and Paul are each happy to buy an album and Noel and Tony are not willing to bid any higher. Liam and Paul each receive consumer surplus equal to his willingness to pay minus the price. Liam's consumer surplus is €30 and Paul's is €10. Liam's consumer surplus is higher now than it was previously, because he gets the same album but pays less for it. The total consumer surplus in the market is €40.

Using the Demand Curve to Measure Consumer Surplus

Consumer surplus is closely related to the demand curve for a product. To see how they are related, let's continue our example and consider the demand curve for this rare Radiohead album.

We begin by using the willingness to pay of the four possible buyers to find the demand schedule for the album. The table in Figure 7.1 shows the demand schedule that corresponds to Table 7.1. If the price is above €100, the quantity demanded in the market is 0, because no buyer is willing to pay that much. If the price is between €80 and €100, the quantity demanded is 1, because only Liam is willing to pay such a high price. If the price is between €70 and €80, the quantity demanded is 2, because both Liam and Paul are willing to pay the price. We can continue this analysis for other prices as well. In this way, the demand schedule is derived from the willingness to pay of the four possible buyers.

The graph in Figure 7.1 shows the demand curve that corresponds to this demand schedule. Note the relationship between the height of the demand curve and the buyers' willingness to pay. At any quantity, the price given by the demand curve shows the willingness to pay of the *marginal buyer*, the buyer who would leave the market first if the price were any higher. At a quantity of 4 albums, for instance, the demand curve has a height of €50, the price that Tony (the marginal buyer) is willing to pay for an album. At a quantity of 3 albums, the demand curve has a height of €70, the price that Noel (who is now the marginal buyer) is willing to pay.

FIGURE 7.1

The Demand Schedule and the Demand Curve

The table shows the demand schedule for the buyers in Table 7.1. The graph shows the corresponding demand curve. Note that the height of the demand curve reflects buyers' willingness to pay.

Price	Buyers	Quantity demanded
More than €100	None	0
€80 to €100	Liam	1
€70 to €80	Liam, Paul	2
€50 to €70	Liam, Paul, Noel	3
€50 or less	Liam, Paul, Noel, Tony	4

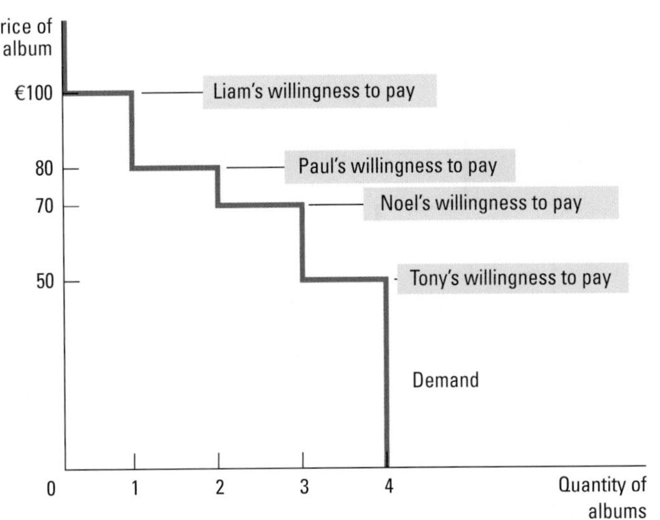

Because the demand curve reflects buyers' willingness to pay, we can also use it to measure consumer surplus. Figure 7.2 uses the demand curve to compute consumer surplus in our example. In panel (a), the price is €80 (or slightly above) and the quantity demanded is 1. Note that the area above the price and below the demand curve equals €20. This amount is exactly the consumer surplus we computed earlier when only 1 album is sold.

Panel (b) of Figure 7.2 shows consumer surplus when the price is €70 (or slightly above). In this case, the area above the price and below the demand curve equals the total area of the two rectangles: Liam's consumer surplus at this price is €30 and Paul's is €10. This area equals a total of €40. Once again, this amount is the consumer surplus we computed earlier.

The lesson from this example holds for all demand curves: the area below the demand curve and above the price measures the consumer surplus in a market. The reason is that the height of the demand curve measures the value buyers place on the good, as measured by their willingness to pay for it. The difference between this willingness to pay and the market price is each buyer's consumer surplus. Thus, the total area below the demand curve and above the price is the sum of the consumer surplus of all buyers in the market for a good or service.

How a Lower Price Raises Consumer Surplus

Because buyers always want to pay less for the goods they buy, a lower price makes buyers of a good better off. But how much does buyers' well-being rise in response to a lower price? We can use the concept of consumer surplus to answer this question precisely.

FIGURE 7.2

Measuring Consumer Surplus with the Demand Curve

In panel (a) the price of the good is €80 and the consumer surplus is €20. In panel (b) the price of the good is €70 and the consumer surplus is €40.

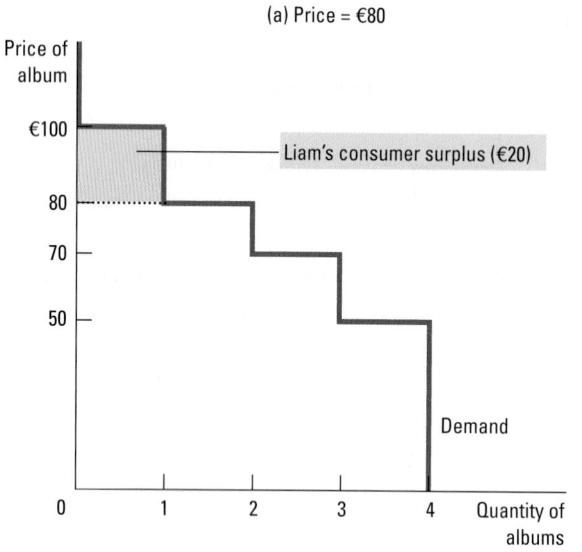

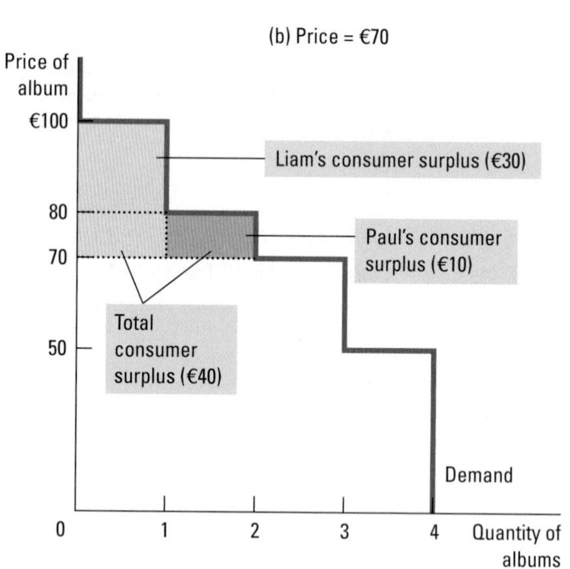

Figure 7.3 shows a typical downward sloping demand curve. Although this demand curve appears somewhat different in shape from the step-like demand curves in our previous two figures, the ideas we have just developed apply nevertheless: consumer surplus is the area above the price and below the demand curve. In panel (a), consumer surplus at a price of P_1 is the area of triangle ABC.

Now suppose that the price falls from P_1 to P_2, as shown in panel (b). The consumer surplus now equals area ADF. The increase in consumer surplus attributable to the lower price is the area BCFD.

This increase in consumer surplus is composed of two parts. First, those buyers who were already buying Q_1 of the good at the higher price P_1 are better off because they now pay less. The increase in consumer surplus of existing buyers is the reduction in the amount they pay; it equals the area of the rectangle BCED. Secondly, some new buyers enter the market because they are now willing to buy the good at the lower price. As a result, the quantity demanded in the market increases from Q_1 to Q_2. The consumer surplus these newcomers receive is the area of the triangle CEF.

What Does Consumer Surplus Measure?

Our goal in developing the concept of consumer surplus is to make normative judgements about the desirability of market outcomes. Now that you have seen what consumer surplus is, let's consider whether it is a good measure of economic well-being.

Imagine that you are a policy maker trying to design a good economic system. Would you care about the amount of consumer surplus? Consumer surplus, the amount that buyers are willing to pay for a good minus the amount they actually pay for it, measures the benefit that buyers receive from a good *as the buyers*

FIGURE 7.3

How the Price Affects Consumer Surplus

In panel (a) the price is P_1, *the quantity demanded is* Q_1 *and consumer surplus equals the area of the triangle* ABC. *When the price falls from* P_1 *to* P_2, *as in panel (b), the quantity demanded rises from* Q_1 *to* Q_2, *and the consumer surplus rises to the area of the triangle* ADF. *The increase in consumer surplus (area* BCFD*) occurs in part because existing consumers now pay less (area* BCED*) and in part because new consumers enter the market at the lower price (area* CEF*).*

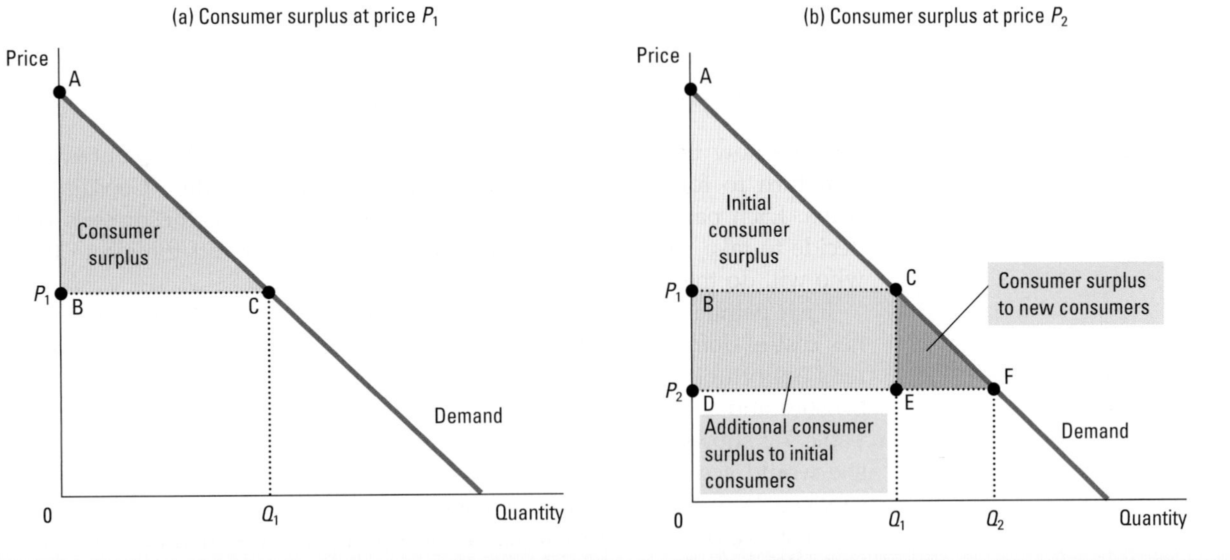

themselves perceive it. Thus, consumer surplus is a good measure of economic well-being if policy makers want to respect the preferences of buyers.

In some circumstances, policy makers might choose not to care about consumer surplus because they do not respect the preferences that drive buyer behaviour. For example, drug addicts are willing to pay a high price for heroin. Yet we would not say that addicts get a large benefit from being able to buy heroin at a low price (even though addicts might say they do). From the standpoint of society, willingness to pay in this instance is not a good measure of the buyers' benefit, and consumer surplus is not a good measure of economic well-being, because addicts are not looking after their own best interests.

In most markets, however, consumer surplus does reflect economic well-being. Economists normally presume that buyers are rational when they make decisions and that their preferences should be respected. In this case, consumers are the best judges of how much benefit they receive from the goods they buy.

Quick Quiz Draw a demand curve for turkey. In your diagram, show a price of turkey and the consumer surplus that results from that price. Explain in words what this consumer surplus measures.

PRODUCER SURPLUS

We now turn to the other side of the market and consider the benefits sellers receive from participating in a market. As you will see, our analysis of sellers' welfare is similar to our analysis of buyers' welfare.

TABLE 7.2

The Costs of Four Possible Sellers

Seller	Cost
Millie	€900
Julie	800
Georgia	600
Nana	500

Cost and the Willingness to Sell

Imagine now that you own a house and you need to get it painted externally. You turn to four sellers of house painting services: Millie, Georgia, Julie and Nana. Each painter is willing to do the work for you if the price is right. You decide to take bids from the four painters and auction off the job to the painter who will do the work for the lowest price.

cost
the value of everything a seller must give up to produce a good

Each painter is willing to take the job if the price she would receive exceeds her **cost** of doing the work. Here the term cost should be interpreted as the painter's opportunity cost: it includes the painter's out-of-pocket expenses (for paint, brushes and so on) as well as the value that the painter places on her own time. Table 7.2 shows each painter's cost. Because a painter's cost is the lowest price she would accept for her work, cost is a measure of her willingness to sell her services. Each painter would be eager to sell her services at a price greater than her cost, would refuse to sell her services at a price less than her cost, and would be indifferent about selling her services at a price exactly equal to her cost.

When you take bids from the painters, the price might start off high, but it quickly falls as the painters compete for the job. Once Nana has bid slightly less than €600 (€599.99), she is the sole remaining bidder. Nana is happy to do the job for this price, because her cost is only €500. Millie, Georgia and Julie are unwilling to do the job for less than €600. Note that the job goes to the painter who can do the work at the lowest cost.

producer surplus
the amount a seller is paid for a good minus the seller's cost

What benefit does Nana receive from getting the job? Because she is willing to do the work for €500 but gets €599.99 for doing it, we say that she receives *producer surplus* of €99.99. **Producer surplus** is the amount a seller is paid minus the cost of production. Producer surplus measures the benefit to sellers of participating in a market.

Now consider a somewhat different example. Suppose that you have two houses that need painting. Again, you auction off the jobs to the four painters. To keep things simple, let's assume that no painter is able to paint both houses and that you will pay the same amount to paint each house. Therefore, the price falls until two painters are left.

In this case, the bidding stops when Georgia and Nana each offer to do the job for a price slightly less than €800 (€799.99). At this price, Georgia and Nana are willing to do the work, and Millie and Julie are not willing to bid a lower price. At a price of €799.99, Nana receives producer surplus of €299.99, and Georgia receives producer surplus of €199.99. The total producer surplus in the market is €499.98.

Using the Supply Curve to Measure Producer Surplus

Just as consumer surplus is closely related to the demand curve, producer surplus is closely related to the supply curve. To see how, let's continue our example.

FIGURE 7.4

The Supply Schedule and the Supply Curve

The table shows the supply schedule for the sellers in Table 7.2. The graph shows the corresponding supply curve. Note that the height of the supply curve reflects sellers' costs.

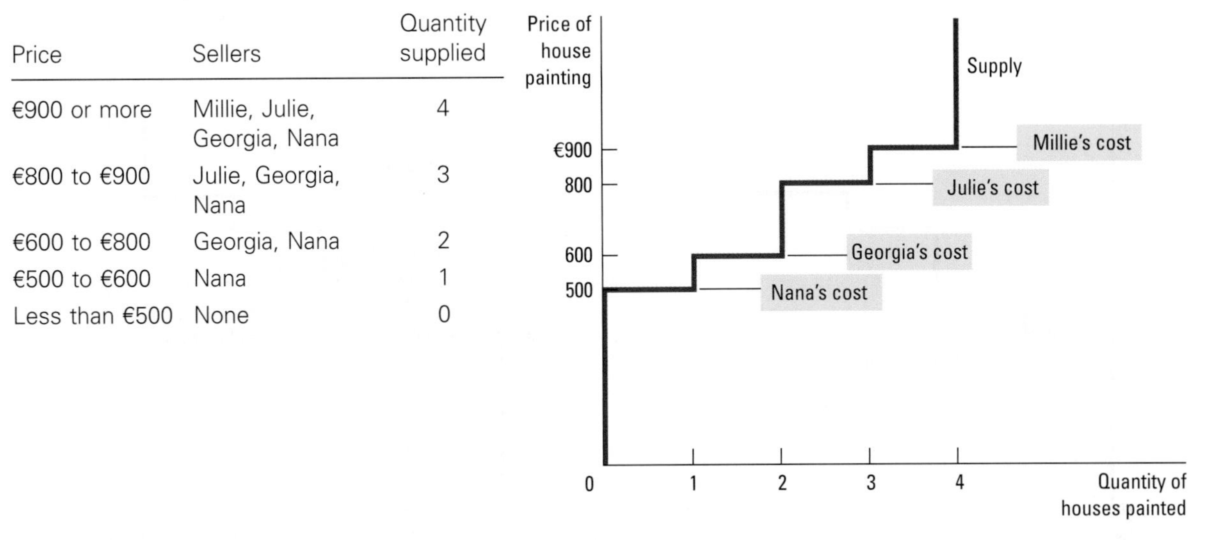

Price	Sellers	Quantity supplied
€900 or more	Millie, Julie, Georgia, Nana	4
€800 to €900	Julie, Georgia, Nana	3
€600 to €800	Georgia, Nana	2
€500 to €600	Nana	1
Less than €500	None	0

We begin by using the costs of the four painters to find the supply schedule for painting services. The table in Figure 7.4 shows the supply schedule that corresponds to the costs in Table 7.2. If the price is below €500, none of the four painters is willing to do the job, so the quantity supplied is zero. If the price is between €500 and €600, only Nana is willing to do the job, so the quantity supplied is 1. If the price is between €600 and €800, Nana and Georgia are willing to do the job, so the quantity supplied is 2, and so on. Thus, the supply schedule is derived from the costs of the four painters.

The graph in Figure 7.4 shows the supply curve that corresponds to this supply schedule. Note that the height of the supply curve is related to the sellers' costs. At any quantity, the price given by the supply curve shows the cost of the *marginal seller,* the seller who would leave the market first if the price were any lower. At a quantity of 4 houses, for instance, the supply curve has a height of €900, the cost that Millie (the marginal seller) incurs to provide her painting services. At a quantity of 3 houses, the supply curve has a height of €800, the cost that Julie (who is now the marginal seller) incurs.

Because the supply curve reflects sellers' costs, we can use it to measure producer surplus. Figure 7.5 uses the supply curve to compute producer surplus in our example. In panel (a) we assume that the price is €600. In this case, the quantity supplied is 1. Note that the area below the price and above the supply curve equals €99.99. This amount is exactly the producer surplus we computed earlier for Nana.

Panel (b) of Figure 7.5 shows producer surplus at a price of €800. In this case, the area below the price and above the supply curve equals the total area of the two rectangles. This area equals €499.99, the producer surplus we computed earlier for Georgia and Nana when two houses needed painting.

The lesson from this example applies to all supply curves: the area below the price and above the supply curve measures the producer surplus in a market.

FIGURE 7.5

Measuring Producer Surplus with the Supply Curve

In panel (a) the price of the good is €600 and the producer surplus is €99.99. In panel (b) the price of the good is €800 and the producer surplus is €499.99.

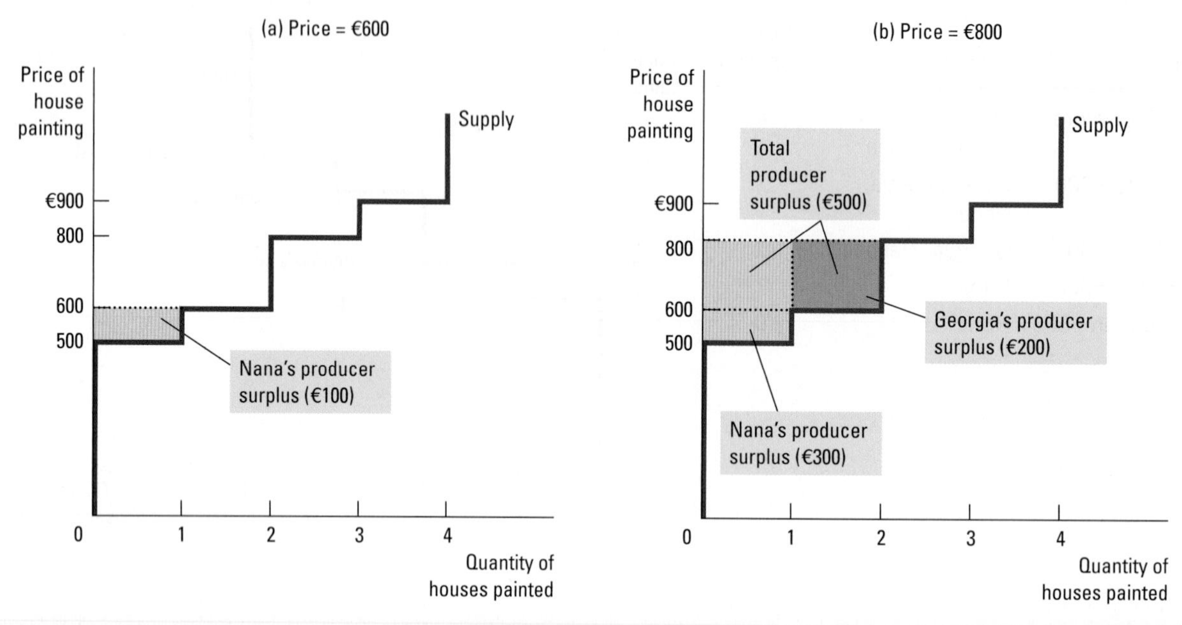

The logic is straightforward: the height of the supply curve measures sellers' costs, and the difference between the price and the cost of production is each seller's producer surplus. Thus, the total area is the sum of the producer surplus of all sellers.

How a Higher Price Raises Producer Surplus

You will not be surprised to hear that sellers always want to receive a higher price for the goods they sell. But how much does sellers' well-being rise in response to a higher price? The concept of producer surplus offers a precise answer to this question.

Figure 7.6 shows a typical upward sloping supply curve. Even though this supply curve differs in shape from the step-like supply curves in the previous figure, we measure producer surplus in the same way: producer surplus is the area below the price and above the supply curve. In panel (a), the price is P_1 and producer surplus is the area of triangle ABC.

Panel (b) shows what happens when the price rises from P_1 to P_2. Producer surplus now equals area ADF. This increase in producer surplus has two parts. First, those sellers who were already selling Q_1 of the good at the lower price P_1 are better off because they now get more for what they sell. The increase in producer surplus for existing sellers equals the area of the rectangle BCED. Secondly, some new sellers enter the market because they are now willing to produce the good at the higher price, resulting in an increase in the quantity supplied from Q_1 to Q_2. The producer surplus of these newcomers is the area of the triangle CEF.

FIGURE 7.6

How the Price Affects Producer Surplus

In panel (a) the price is P_1, the quantity demanded is Q_1 and producer surplus equals the area of the triangle ABC. When the price rises from P_1 to P_2, as in panel (b), the quantity supplied rises from Q_1 to Q_2 and the producer surplus rises to the area of the triangle ADF. The increase in producer surplus (area BCFD) occurs in part because existing producers now receive more (area BCED) and in part because new producers enter the market at the higher price (area CEF).

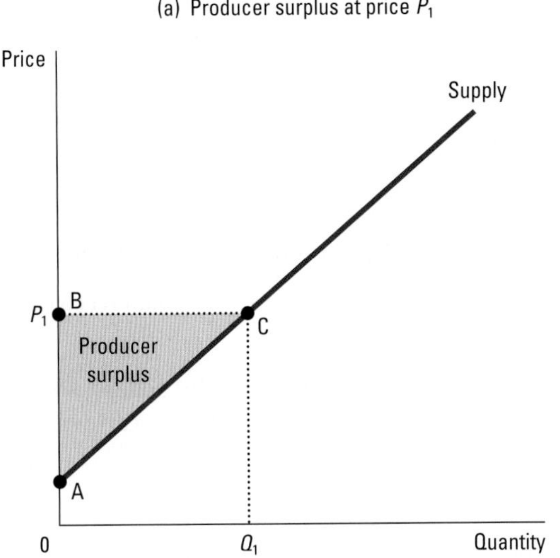

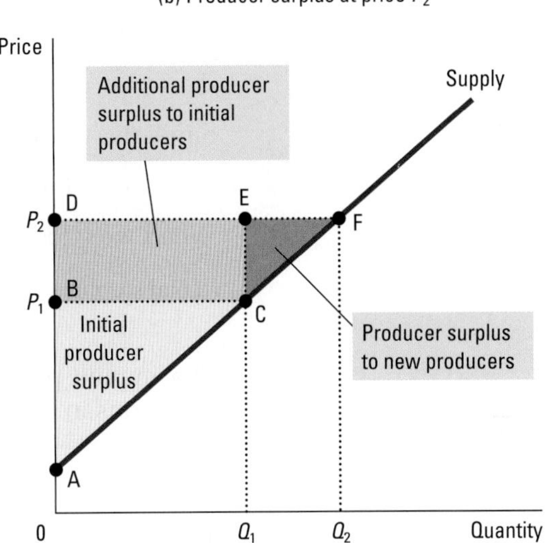

As this analysis shows, we use producer surplus to measure the well-being of sellers in much the same way as we use consumer surplus to measure the well-being of buyers. Because these two measures of economic welfare are so similar, it is natural to use them together. And, indeed, that is exactly what we do in the next section.

Quick Quiz Draw a supply curve for turkey. In your diagram show a price of turkey and the producer surplus that results from that price. Explain in words what this producer surplus measures.

MARKET EFFICIENCY

Consumer surplus and producer surplus are the basic tools that economists use to study the welfare of buyers and sellers in a market. These tools can help us address a fundamental economic question: is the allocation of resources determined by free markets in any way desirable? In other words what evidence is there for allocative efficiency in free markets?

The Benevolent Social Planner

To evaluate market outcomes, we introduce into our analysis a new, hypothetical character, the benevolent social planner – the BSP. The BSP is an omniscient, omnipotent, benign dictator. He wants to maximize the economic well-being of everyone in society. What do you suppose this planner should do? Should he just leave buyers and sellers at the equilibrium that they reach naturally on their own? Or can he increase economic well-being by altering the market outcome in some way?

To answer this question, the planner must first decide how to measure the economic well-being of a society. One possible measure is the sum of consumer and producer surplus, which we call *total surplus.* Consumer surplus is the benefit that buyers receive from participating in a market, and producer surplus is the benefit that sellers receive. It is therefore natural to use total surplus as a measure of society's economic well-being.

To better understand this measure of economic well-being, recall how we measure consumer and producer surplus. We define consumer surplus as:

$$\text{Consumer surplus} = \text{Value to buyers} - \text{Amount paid by buyers}$$

Similarly, we define producer surplus as:

$$\text{Producer surplus} = \text{Amount received by sellers} - \text{Cost to sellers}$$

When we add consumer and producer surplus together, we obtain:

$$\text{Total surplus} = \text{Value to buyers} - \text{Amount paid by buyers} + \text{Amount received by sellers} - \text{Cost to sellers}$$

The amount paid by buyers equals the amount received by sellers, so the middle two terms in this expression cancel each other. As a result, we can write total surplus as:

$$\text{Total surplus} = \text{Value to buyers} - \text{Cost to sellers}$$

Total surplus in a market is the total value to buyers of the goods, as measured by their willingness to pay, minus the total cost to sellers of providing those goods.

efficiency
the property of a resource allocation of maximizing the total surplus received by all members of society

If an allocation of resources maximizes total surplus, we say that the allocation exhibits **efficiency**. If an allocation is not efficient, then some of the gains from trade among buyers and sellers are not being realized. For example, an allocation is inefficient if a good is not being produced by the sellers with lowest cost. In this case, moving production from a high-cost producer to a low-cost producer will lower the total cost to sellers and raise total surplus. Similarly, an allocation is inefficient if a good is not being consumed by the buyers who value it most highly. In this case, moving consumption of the good from a buyer with a low valuation to a buyer with a high valuation will raise total surplus. In Chapter 1, we defined *efficiency* as 'the property of society getting the most it can from its scarce resources'. Now that we have the concept of total surplus, we can be more precise about what we mean by 'getting the most it can'. In this context, society will be getting the most it can from its scarce resources if it allocates them so as to maximize total surplus.

equity
the property of distributing economic prosperity fairly among the members of society

In addition to efficiency, the BSP might also care about **equity** – the property of distributing economic prosperity fairly among the members of society. In essence, the gains from trade in a market are like a cake to be distributed among the market participants. The question of efficiency is whether the cake is as big as possible. The question of equity is whether the cake is divided fairly. Evaluating the equity of a market outcome is more difficult than evaluating the efficiency. Whereas efficiency is an objective goal that can be judged on strictly positive grounds, equity involves normative judgements that go beyond economics and enter into the realm of political philosophy.

In this chapter we concentrate on efficiency as the social planner's goal. Keep in mind, however, that real policy makers often care about equity as well. That is, they care about both the size of the economic cake and how the cake gets sliced and distributed among members of society.

CASE STUDY

Subsidies and Consumer Surplus

In Chapter 6, we introduced the idea of a subsidy. A subsidy is designed to reduce the market price often by giving sellers money which helps to reduce the cost of production. As a result the supply curve shifts to the right and the market equilibrium price will be lower than without the subsidy.

It might be assumed that a lower price would increase the consumer surplus and such an outcome would be desirable for consumers. In the short run this might be the case but markets are dynamic and other factors may affect outcomes and lead to a reduction in the consumer surplus which may bring into question whether the subsidy should be maintained.

To see an example of how this might be the case, we will look at a study carried out by Shahmoradi and Honarvar on the subsidy on gasoline which exists in the Islamic Republic of Iran.[1] The study shows how the existence of a subsidy introduced by the Iranian government on gasoline helps keep the price of driving cars in Iran much lower than the normal free market price. They ask if such a policy increases the welfare of car drivers as measured by consumer surplus.

Figure 7.7 shows how a subsidy would affect the market for gasoline in Iran.

FIGURE 7.7

The Effect of a Subsidy on the Price of Gasoline

In the absence of a subsidy, Iranian drivers would pay the market price of P_{wp} and the quantity Q_1 would be bought and sold. The introduction of a subsidy means that the cost to producers is now lower for each litre of gas they produce and so the supply curve for gas shifts to the right. Car drivers in Iran now pay a price of P_{sub} per litre and the amount bought and sold rises to Q_2. The amount of the subsidy per litre is shown by the vertical distance between the two supply curves.

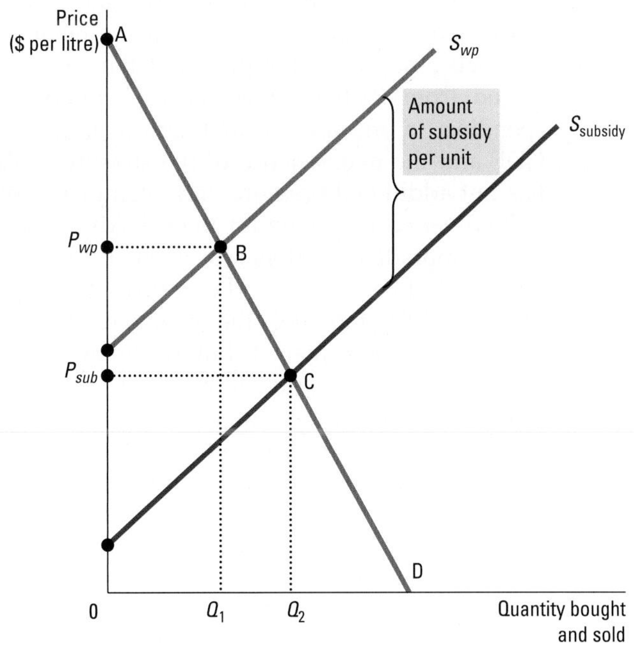

Without the subsidy, car drivers would have to pay the world price for gas, shown as P_{wp} and the amount Q_1 would be purchased. The introduction of the subsidy will shift the supply curve to the right because at each price the cost of producing gas is now cheaper. The result of the subsidy is that car drivers in Iran pay a price of P_{sub} and there is an increase in the amount of gas bought and sold from Q_1 to Q_2.

The welfare benefits to car drivers in Iran is the consumer surplus they gain from the subsidy. Without the subsidy the amount of consumer surplus is given by the area bounded by the triangle ABP_{wp}. After the subsidy is introduced consumer surplus increases as shown by the area bounded by the triangle ACP_{sub}.

The question that Shahmoradi and Honarvar asked was whether the continuation of the policy maintained the level of consumer surplus over time. In the study, the pair identified a number of changes in Iran which have an effect on the success of the policy. Figure 7.7 shows that the quantity demanded of gas increases as a result of the subsidy. But what about the influence of factors affecting demand other than price? Shahmoradi and Honarvar show that the age distribution of the population in Iran is predominantly skewed to the younger end of the population with nearly 50 per cent of the population being 30 years old or younger. This population profile means that the demand for cars has been rising and is likely to continue to rise for some years. In addition, the number of cars available in Iran has increased significantly and so this adds to the demand for gas. As gross domestic product rises and incomes grow, more Iranians can afford cars and so there is a further impetus on demand.

The net result is that these factors combined with the low price of gas has cased demand to rise faster than the capacity of Iran to supply gas for car drivers. Iran is an oil producer but it is increasingly finding it difficult to meet demand (not all oil produced is suitable for gasoline) and so Iran has had to increase imported gas from abroad. Gas consumption has risen by 200 per cent in the last 20 years; in 1986 Iran imported 17 per cent of its gas but by 2005 this had risen to 37 per cent. At the same time, the oil that Iran sells abroad generates export revenue.

For the government the cost of maintaining the subsidy has been rising. Parliament sets the price of gas at the beginning of each year and has been gradually increasing the price but the cost of the subsidy over the ten year period from 1986 is given as $47.7 billion at current prices. Government spending, in one way or another, accounts for around 80 per cent of Iranian GDP and the maintenance of the subsidy in the wake of increasing demand has put additional pressure on government finances. Export revenue has had to be diverted to paying for the subsidy, which has an opportunity cost.

Shahmoradi and Honarvar further show how changes to the price and income elasticity of demand can affect the picture. They estimate that between the years 1988 and 2005, the income elasticity of demand with respect to gas has been greater than 1 but declining. The average income elasticity of demand over the period is put at 1.15 which means that for every 10 per cent increase in income, demand for gas has increased by 15 per cent. Over the same period, Shahmoradi and Honarvar estimate the price elasticity of demand for gas to be inelastic and decreasing. This means that even if parliament increases the price of gas at its annual review the reduction in demand is limited.

Putting all this together, Shahmoradi and Honarvar suggest that the value of consumer surplus expressed in proportion to GDP per capita was around 10 per cent in the late 1980s and early 1990s rising to 20 per cent by 1994. Since that time it has declined to around 5 per cent and is still declining but positive. Such research allows us to be able to make judgements about the allocation of resources and whether the policy represents an efficient allocation. For the Iranian government the cost of maintaining the subsidy seems to be rising but the welfare benefits in terms of the consumer surplus gained by car drivers is falling. One might ask, therefore, whether the Iranian government might re-think the policy and find other ways to improve the welfare of its population.

[1]Shahmoradi, A. & Honarvar, A. (2008). *Gasoline Subsidy and Consumer Surplus* in the Islamic Republic of Iran. In: *OPEC Energy Review.* 32, **3**. 232–245

Evaluating the Market Equilibrium

Figure 7.8 shows consumer and producer surplus when a market reaches the equilibrium of supply and demand. Recall that consumer surplus equals the area above the price and under the demand curve and producer surplus equals the area below the price and above the supply curve. Thus, the total area between the supply and demand curves up to the point of equilibrium represents the total surplus in this market.

Is this equilibrium allocation of resources efficient? Does it maximize total surplus? To answer these questions, keep in mind that when a market is in equilibrium, the price determines which buyers and sellers participate in the market. Those buyers who value the good more than the price (represented by the segment AE on the demand curve) choose to buy the good; those buyers who value it less than the price (represented by the segment EB) do not. Similarly,

FIGURE 7.8

Consumer and Producer Surplus in the Market Equilibrium

Total surplus – the sum of consumer and producer surplus – is the area between the supply and demand curves up to the equilibrium quantity.

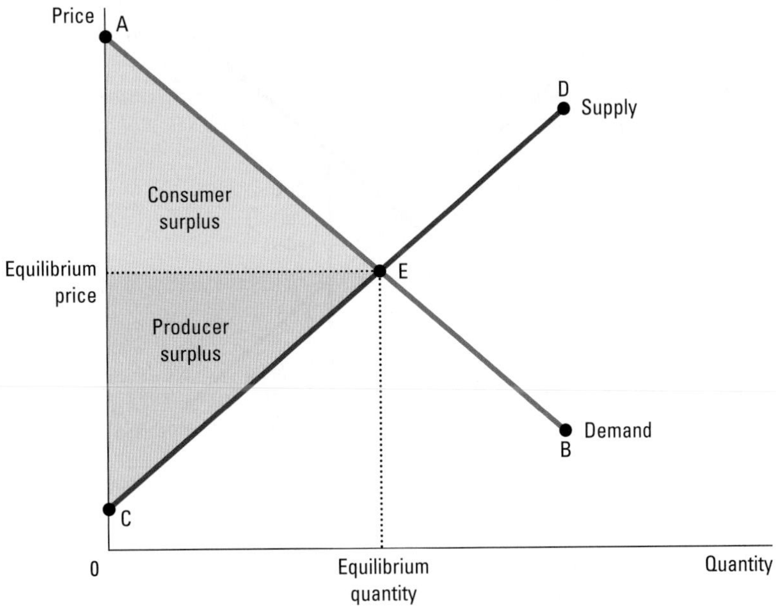

those sellers whose costs are less than the price (represented by the segment CE on the supply curve) choose to produce and sell the good; those sellers whose costs are greater than the price (represented by the segment ED) do not.

These observations lead to two insights about market outcomes:

1. Free markets allocate the supply of goods to the buyers who value them most highly, as measured by their willingness to pay.
2. Free markets allocate the demand for goods to the sellers who can produce them at least cost.

Thus, given the quantity produced and sold in a market equilibrium, the BSP cannot increase economic well-being by changing the allocation of consumption among buyers or the allocation of production among sellers.

But can the BSP raise total economic well-being by increasing or decreasing the quantity of the good? The answer is no, as stated in this third insight about market outcomes:

3. Free markets produce the quantity of goods that maximizes the sum of consumer and producer surplus.

To see why this is true, consider Figure 7.9. Recall that the demand curve reflects the value to buyers and that the supply curve reflects the cost to sellers. At quantities below the equilibrium level, the value to buyers exceeds the cost to sellers. In this region, increasing the quantity raises total surplus, and it continues to do so until the quantity reaches the equilibrium level. Beyond the equilibrium quantity, however, the value to buyers is less than the cost to sellers. Producing more than the equilibrium quantity would, therefore, lower total surplus.

FIGURE 7.9

The Efficiency of the Equilibrium Quantity

At quantities less than the equilibrium quantity, the value to buyers exceeds the cost to sellers. At quantities greater than the equilibrium quantity, the cost to sellers exceeds the value to buyers. Therefore, the market equilibrium maximizes the sum of producer and consumer surplus.

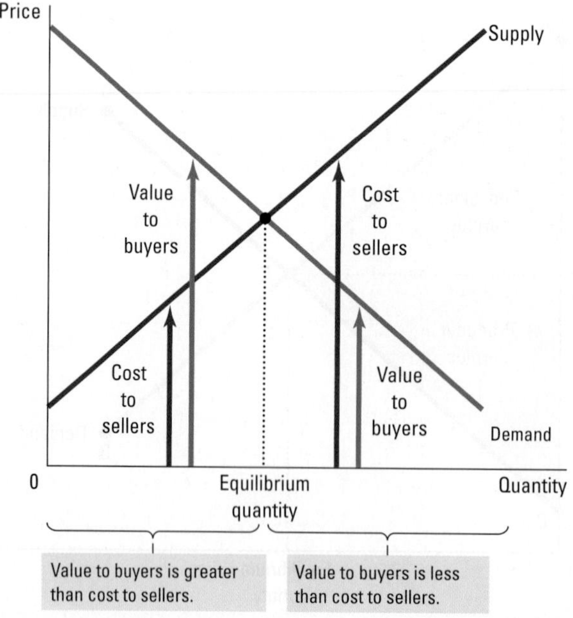

These three insights about market outcomes tell us that the equilibrium of supply and demand maximizes the sum of consumer and producer surplus. In other words, the equilibrium outcome is an efficient allocation of resources. The job of the BSP is, therefore, very easy: he can leave the market outcome just as he finds it. This policy of leaving well enough alone goes by the French expression *laissez-faire,* which literally translated means 'leave them to do'.

We can now better appreciate Adam Smith's invisible hand of the marketplace, which we first discussed in Chapter 1. The BSP doesn't need to alter the market outcome because the invisible hand has already guided buyers and sellers to an allocation of the economy's resources that maximizes total surplus. This conclusion explains why economists often advocate free markets as the best way to organize economic activity.

Quick Quiz Draw the supply and demand for turkey. In the equilibrium, show producer and consumer surplus. Explain why producing more turkey would lower total surplus.

IN THE NEWS

Ticket Touting

To allocate resources efficiently, an economy must get goods to the consumers who value them most highly. Sometimes this job falls to ticket touts.

Ticket Touts – A Much Maligned 'Profession'?

Ticket touts, or scalpers in the United States, are people who try and sell tickets for sporting, public and entertainment events at prices above the face value of the ticket. The issue of ticket touts highlights a number of important points that have been raised in this chapter and in previous chapters where we have been looking at the efficiency of markets. To understand the issues we must look in more detail at what ticket touts do.

There tends to be two distinct groups who may be regarded as touts; one is the individual who may have bought a few tickets to see a concert, for example, but for some reason cannot attend. The individual then makes these tickets available in some way for sale; typically, tickets appear on eBay or other online auction sites. The highest bidder gets the tickets. These people are often not vilified in the same way that 'professional' touts are. This group buy large amounts of tickets when they first go on sale and have no intention of ever going to the event. The purchase they make is simply with the intention of re-selling the tickets to make a profit. This group are often criticized for their mercenary behaviour and are the subject of by-laws, regulation and other regulatory and legal processes.

The next question we have to ask is why ticket touts exist at all? Take the example of a concert tour by the band U2. They announce a gig at the Stade de France in Paris – capacity 80 000; it is their only appearance in France that year. The supply of tickets is perfectly inelastic at 80 000; the promoters know

that demand for tickets is likely to be far in excess of 80 000 but they do not want to set the true market price for the tickets because they do not want to exclude those who may not be able to afford a high price from the chance to see U2. The price of tickets is set at €100 each. At this price demand for tickets far exceeds the available supply – there is a shortage. The concert promoters know that the tickets will have to be rationed in some way, which may be through some sort of first-come-first-served basis. When tickets go on sale they sell out in the first hour.

The market has successfully allocated the tickets but there will be a large number of people who will be left very disappointed by this allocation. Many of these people would have been willing to pay a higher price to get a ticket. In cases of sporting, public and entertainment events, market price is not determined by the actions of millions of buyers and sellers making decisions; promoters of the events will have set a price which may be below the 'natural' equilibrium. Enter the tout. Despite the best efforts of the promoters, touts manage to secure several thousand tickets which they make available for sale. Devoted fans of U2 who were not able to get tickets for whatever reason may be prepared to pay considerably more than €100 to see the band. Most will have some notional upper limit above which they will not be prepared to pay. This may be determined by their income and by their notion of value linked, as we saw in earlier chapters, to the opportunity cost of acquiring the ticket.

Touts will therefore sell tickets to these people at prices in excess of €100. The touts fulfil the function that the market has not done – allocating scarce resources (tickets) according to the value which the buyer places on the ticket. Some fans may pay €200 to get their ticket from a tout and be very happy because they were prepared to pay up to €400 if necessary. They get their ticket and have €200 worth of consumer surplus. The tout gets some producer surplus (€100 assuming they paid the face value for the tickets) and as a result total surplus rises.

The tout does run the risk that they buy a large number of tickets and do not sell them. Outside these sporting and entertainment events one can observe a useful study of markets in action. Two hours before the start of the event touts may be selling tickets at several times the face value; if all the tickets are sold then they are happy and so, presumably, are buyers because they either pay a price equal to the value they place on the ticket or get a ticket at a price below which they were prepared to pay and so gain some consumer surplus. However, if touts find that tickets are not selling then the closer the time comes to the start of the event, prices will start to fall. The seller may even be prepared to suffer a loss to get rid of any tickets left; getting €50 is better than not getting anything at all!

For both buyer and seller, the whole process represents risk; if the buyer waits too long in the hope that they get lower prices they may miss out on the ticket they desire. Equally, if touts hang on to tickets in the hope of securing higher prices they may find they are left with unsold tickets. Both buyers and sellers have to be careful judges of the market in order to make the right decisions for themselves.

The *Financial Times* columnist and respected economist, Samuel Brittan, referred to research carried out by an American economist, Pascal Courty who wrote an article on touts in the *Journal of Economic Perspectives* in Spring 2003. Courty divides the buyers into two groups – the serious fan and the 'busy professional'. The former will be so dedicated that they know when tickets become available and make sure they get in early to get their tickets. The 'busy professionals' do not like to make up their mind too far in advance. If we assume that the dedicated fan gets their tickets on release at face value, the touts will be selling to the 'busy professionals' at above face value prices.

The view that touts fulfil a valuable market function is not held by everyone. Those that really cannot get tickets on release, because they are at work, away, asleep or whatever reason, feel aggrieved that professional touts use their knowledge to acquire tickets with the sole intention of selling them on at a profit. By doing so they 'crowd out' the legitimate buyer from the market. Promoters and governments know that touts are seen as being 'bad' and are going to ever greater lengths to try and make the job of being a tout harder and less profitable. Online ticketing is able to introduce a wide range of electronic monitoring and tagging systems to try and make sure that the buyers are genuine fans who get value for money. Tickets for the World Cup in South Africa in 2010, for the reunion concert of Led Zeppelin at London's O_2 Arena in November 2007, for the series of Michael Jackson concerts prior to his death in 2009, tickets for the Glastonbury music festival in Somerset in the UK and many more, have all tried to make use of sophisticated ordering, distribution and collection systems to prevent touts from 'exploiting' buyers. Despite these best efforts, touts still exist and many found ways around the systems put in place.

The issue raises important questions about efficiency and equity. The general public may believe that touts are unfair and heap vitriol on them; promoters may despise touts because if they are seen to let them get away with the practice they are being unfair to buyers, but there may also be a sneaking suspicion that promoters are jealous of the fact that touts actually sell tickets at nearer the 'true' market price. Economists may point to the fact that few people are willing to pay a price which does not reflect the value they put on the ticket and that even though they pay a higher price than the face value (which, note, is different to the market value) many get considerable consumer surplus. The simple solution would be for promoters to charge the market price in the first place![1]

[1]'Ticket Touts are Good for Spectators' – http://www.samuelbrittan.co.uk/text162_p.html accessed 22 January 2010.

CONCLUSION: MARKET EFFICIENCY AND MARKET FAILURE

This chapter introduced the basic tools of welfare economics – consumer and producer surplus – and used them to evaluate the efficiency of free markets. We showed that the forces of supply and demand allocate resources efficiently. That is, even though each buyer and seller in a market is concerned only about his or her own welfare, they are together led by an invisible hand to an equilibrium that maximizes the total benefits to buyers and sellers.

A word of warning is in order. To conclude that markets are efficient, we made several assumptions about how markets work. When these assumptions do not hold, our conclusion that the market equilibrium is efficient may no longer be true. As we close this chapter, let's consider briefly two of the most important of these assumptions.

First, our analysis assumed that markets are perfectly competitive. In the real world, however, competition is sometimes far from perfect. In some markets a single buyer or seller (or a small group of them) may be able to control market prices. This ability to influence prices is called *market power*. Market power can cause markets to be inefficient because it keeps the price and quantity away from the equilibrium of supply and demand.

Second, our analysis assumed that the outcome in a market matters only to the buyers and sellers in that market. Yet, in the real world, the decisions of buyers and sellers sometimes affect people who are not participants in the market at all. Pollution is the classic example of a market outcome that affects people not in the market. Such side effects, called *externalities,* cause welfare in a market to depend on more than just the value to the buyers and the cost to the sellers. Because buyers and sellers do not take these side effects into account when deciding how much to consume and produce, the equilibrium in a market can be inefficient from the standpoint of society as a whole.

Market power and externalities are examples of a general phenomenon called market failure – the inability of some unregulated markets to allocate resources efficiently. When markets fail, public policy can potentially remedy the problem and increase economic efficiency. Microeconomists devote much effort to studying when market failure is likely and what sorts of policies are best at correcting market failures. As you continue your study of economics, you will see that the tools of welfare economics developed here are readily adapted to that endeavour.

Despite the possibility of market failure, the invisible hand of the marketplace is extraordinarily important. In many markets, the assumptions we made in this chapter work well, and the conclusion of market efficiency applies directly. Moreover, our analysis of welfare economics and market efficiency can be used to shed light on the effects of various government policies. In the next two chapters we apply the tools we have just developed to study two important policy issues – the welfare effects of taxation and of international trade.

SUMMARY

- Consumer surplus equals buyers' willingness to pay for a good minus the amount they actually pay for it, and it measures the benefit buyers get from participating in a market. Consumer surplus can be computed by finding the area below the demand curve and above the price.
- Producer surplus equals the amount sellers receive for their goods minus their costs of production, and it measures the benefit sellers get from participating in a market. Producer surplus can be computed by finding the area below the price and above the supply curve.

- An allocation of resources that maximizes the sum of consumer and producer surplus is said to be efficient. Policy makers are often concerned with the efficiency, as well as the equity, of economic outcomes.
- The equilibrium of supply and demand maximizes the sum of consumer and producer surplus. That is, the invisible hand of the marketplace leads buyers and sellers to allocate resources efficiently.
- Markets do not allocate resources efficiently in the presence of market failures such as market power or externalities.

KEY CONCEPTS

welfare economics, p. 138
well-being, p. 138
allocative efficiency, p. 139
willingness to pay, p. 139
consumer surplus, p. 140
cost, p. 144
producer surplus, p. 144
efficiency, p. 148
equity, p. 148

QUESTIONS FOR REVIEW

1. Explain how buyers' willingness to pay, consumer surplus and the demand curve are related.
2. Explain how sellers' costs, producer surplus and the supply curve are related.
3. In a supply-and-demand diagram, show producer and consumer surplus in the market equilibrium.
4. What is efficiency? Is it the only goal of economic policy makers?
5. What does the invisible hand do?
6. Explain how charging a higher price for tickets for the Wimbledon tennis championships would not only gets rid of queues but also would be a more efficient market allocation.
7. Name two types of market failure. Explain why each may cause market outcomes to be inefficient.

PROBLEMS AND APPLICATIONS

1. An early freeze in Normandy ruins half of the apple harvest. What happens to consumer surplus in the market for apples? What happens to consumer surplus in the market for cider? Illustrate your answers with diagrams.
2. Suppose the demand for French bread rises. What happens to producer surplus in the market for French bread? What happens to producer surplus in the market for flour? Illustrate your answer with diagrams.
3. It is a hot day, and Oliver is thirsty. Here is the value he places on a bottle of water:

Value of first bottle	€7
Value of second bottle	€5
Value of third bottle	€3
Value of fourth bottle	€1

   a. From this information, derive Oliver's demand schedule. Graph his demand curve for bottled water.
   b. If the price of a bottle of water is €4, how many bottles does Oliver buy? How much consumer surplus does Oliver get from his purchases? Show Oliver's consumer surplus in your graph.
   c. If the price falls to €2, how does quantity demanded change? How does Oliver's consumer surplus change? Show these changes in your graph.

4. Ben owns a water pump. Because pumping large amounts of water is harder than pumping small amounts, the cost of producing a bottle of water rises as he pumps more. Here is the cost he incurs to produce each bottle of water:

Cost of first bottle	€1
Cost of second bottle	€3
Cost of third bottle	€5
Cost of fourth bottle	€7

   a. From this information, derive Ben's supply schedule. Graph his supply curve for bottled water.
   b. If the price of a bottle of water is €4, how many bottles does Ben produce and sell? How much producer surplus does Ben get from these sales? Show Ben's producer surplus in your graph.
   c. If the price rises to €6, how does quantity supplied change? How does Ben's producer surplus change? Show these changes in your graph.
5. Consider a market in which Oliver from Problem 3 is the buyer and Ben from Problem 4 is the seller.
   a. Use Ben's supply schedule and Oliver's demand schedule to find the quantity supplied and quantity demanded at prices of €2, €4 and €6. Which of these prices brings supply and demand into equilibrium?
   b. What are consumer surplus, producer surplus and total surplus in this equilibrium?
   c. If Ben produced and Oliver consumed one fewer bottle of water, what would happen to total surplus?
   d. If Ben produced and Oliver consumed one additional bottle of water, what would happen to total surplus?
6. The cost of producing DVD players has fallen over the past few years. Let's consider some implications of this fact.
   a. Use a supply-and-demand diagram to show the effect of falling production costs on the price and quantity of DVD players sold.
   b. In your diagram, show what happens to consumer surplus and producer surplus.
   c. Suppose the supply of DVD players is very elastic. Who benefits most from falling production costs – consumers or producers of DVD players?
7. There are four consumers willing to pay the following amounts for haircuts:

Roberto: €7	Ronaldo: €2	David: €8	Zinadin: €5

There are four haircutting businesses with the following costs:

Firm A: €3	Firm B: €6	Firm C: €4	Firm D: €2

   Each firm has the capacity to produce only one haircut. For efficiency, how many haircuts should be given? Which businesses should cut hair, and which consumers should have their hair cut? How large is the maximum possible total surplus?
8. Suppose a technological advance reduces the cost of making computers.
   a. Use a supply and demand diagram to show what happens to price, quantity, consumer surplus and producer surplus in the market for computers.
   b. Computers and adding machines are substitutes. Use a supply-and-demand diagram to show what happens to price, quantity, consumer surplus and producer surplus in the market for adding machines. Should adding machine producers be happy or sad about the technological advance in computers?
   c. Computers and software are complements. Use a supply-and-demand diagram to show what happens to price, quantity, consumer surplus and producer surplus in the market for software. Should software producers be happy or sad about the technological advance in computers?
   d. Does this analysis help explain why software producer Bill Gates is one of the world's richest men?

For further resources, visit
www.cengage.com/mankiw_taylor2

8 APPLICATION: THE COSTS OF TAXATION

Taxes have been around a long time. In the Bible, for example, we can read how Jesus's parents had to return to Nazareth to be taxed and how, later, Jesus converted a prominent tax collector to become one of his disciples. In the Koran, there are references to *jizya*, which can be translated as the word 'tax'. In the Ottoman Empire *jizya* was a per-capita tax levied on non-Muslim, able-bodied resident males of military age. Since taxes, by definition, are a means of legally extracting money from individuals or organizations, it is not surprising that they have often been a source of heated political debate throughout history. In 1776 the anger of the American colonies over British taxes sparked the American Revolution. More recently, the issue of whether and how tax systems should be harmonized within the European Union has been the source of much debate.

We began our study of taxes in Chapter 6. There we saw how a tax on a good affects its price and the quantity bought and sold and how the forces of supply and demand divide the burden of a tax between buyers and sellers. In this chapter we extend this analysis and look at how taxes affect welfare, the economic well-being of participants in a market.

The effects of taxes on welfare might at first seem obvious. The government imposes taxes in order to raise revenue, and that revenue must come out of someone's pocket. As we saw in Chapter 6, both buyers and sellers are worse off when a good is taxed: a tax raises the price buyers pay and lowers the price sellers receive. Yet to understand fully how taxes affect economic well-being, we must compare the reduced welfare of buyers and sellers to the amount of revenue the government raises. The tools of consumer and producer surplus allow us to make this comparison. The analysis will show that the costs of taxes to buyers and sellers exceeds the revenue raised by the government.

THE DEADWEIGHT LOSS OF TAXATION

In Chapter 6 we looked at the effect of a tax levied on a seller. The same result would be gained, however, if we had analysed the effect of a tax on a buyer – when a tax is levied on buyers, the demand curve shifts downward by the size of the tax; when it is levied on sellers, the supply curve shifts upward by that amount. In either case, when the tax is imposed, the price paid by buyers rises, and the price received by sellers falls. In the end, buyers and sellers share the burden of the tax, regardless of how it is levied.

"DON'T WORRY! SINCE 28% OF MY SALARY GOES TO THE GOVERNMENT, I'VE DECIDED TO WORK 72% OF THE TIME."

Figure 8.1 shows these effects. To simplify our discussion, this figure does not show a shift in either the supply or demand curve, although one curve must shift. Which curve shifts depends on whether the tax is levied on sellers (the supply curve shifts) or buyers (the demand curve shifts). In this chapter, we can simplify the graphs by not bothering to show the shift. The key result for our purposes here is that the tax places a wedge between the price buyers pay and the price sellers receive. Because of this tax wedge, the quantity sold falls below the level that would be sold without a tax. In other words, a tax on a good causes the size of the market for the good to shrink. These results should be familiar from Chapter 6.

How a Tax Affects Market Participants

Now let's use the tools of welfare economics to measure the gains and losses from a tax on a good. To do this, we must take into account how the tax affects buyers, sellers and the government. The benefit received by buyers in a market is

FIGURE 8.1

The Effects of a Tax

A tax on a good places a wedge between the price that buyers pay and the price that sellers receive. The quantity of the good sold falls.

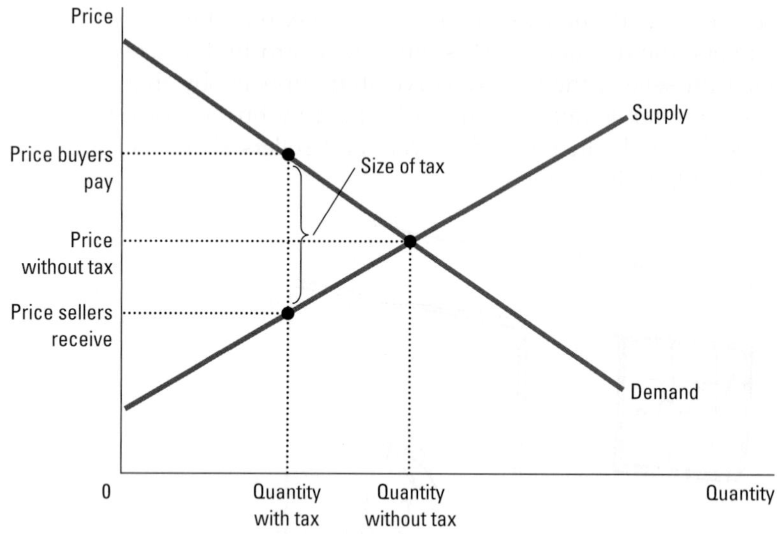

measured by consumer surplus – the amount buyers are willing to pay for the good minus the amount they actually pay for it. The benefit received by sellers in a market is measured by producer surplus – the amount sellers receive for the good minus their costs. These are precisely the measures of economic welfare we used in Chapter 7.

What about the third interested party, the government? If T is the size of the tax and Q is the quantity of the good sold, then the government gets total tax revenue of $T \times Q$. It can use this tax revenue to provide services, such as roads, police and education, or to help the needy. Therefore, to analyse how taxes affect economic well-being, we use tax revenue to measure the government's benefit from the tax. Keep in mind, however, that this benefit actually accrues not to government but to those on whom the revenue is spent.

Figure 8.2 shows that the government's tax revenue is represented by the rectangle between the supply and demand curves. The height of this rectangle is the size of the tax, T, and the width of the rectangle is the quantity of the good sold, Q. Because a rectangle's area is its height times its width, this rectangle's area is $T \times Q$, which equals the tax revenue.

Welfare without a Tax To see how a tax affects welfare, we begin by considering welfare before the government has imposed a tax. Figure 8.3 shows the supply and demand diagram and marks the key areas with the letters A through F.

Without a tax, the price and quantity are found at the intersection of the supply and demand curves. The price is P_1, and the quantity sold is Q_1. Because the demand curve reflects buyers' willingness to pay, consumer surplus is the area between the demand curve and the price, A + B + C. Similarly, because the supply curve reflects sellers' costs, producer surplus is the area between the supply curve and the price, D + E + F. In this case, because there is no tax, tax revenue equals zero.

FIGURE 8.2

Tax Revenue

The tax revenue that the government collects equals T × Q, *the size of the tax* T *times the quantity sold* Q. *Thus, tax revenue equals the area of the rectangle between the supply and demand curves.*

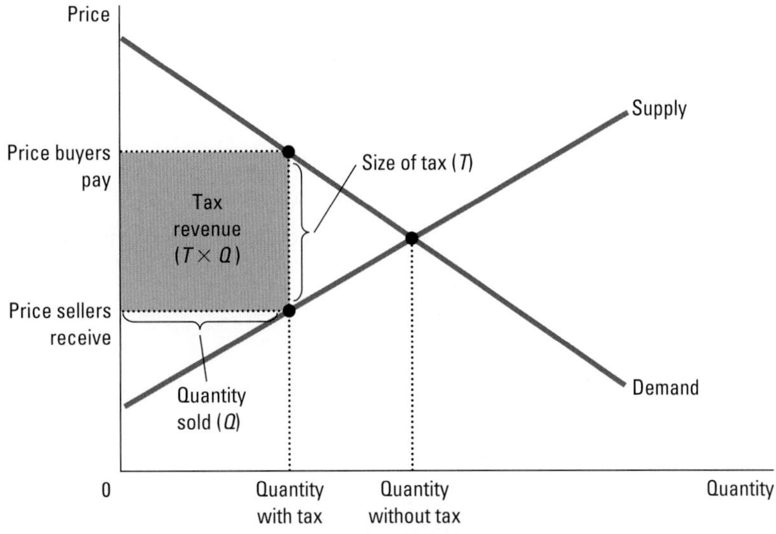

Total surplus – the sum of consumer and producer surplus – equals the area A + B + C + D + E + F. In other words, as we saw in Chapter 7, total surplus is the area between the supply and demand curves up to the equilibrium quantity. The first column of the table in Figure 8.3 summarizes these conclusions.

Welfare with a Tax Now consider welfare after the tax is imposed. The price paid by buyers rises from P_1 to P_B, so consumer surplus now equals only area A (the area below the demand curve and above the buyer's price). The price received by sellers falls from P_1 to P_S, so producer surplus now equals only area F (the area above the supply curve and below the seller's price). The quantity sold falls from Q_1 to Q_2, and the government collects tax revenue equal to the area B + D.

To compute total surplus with the tax, we add consumer surplus producer surplus and tax revenue. Thus, we find that total surplus is area A + B + D + F. The second column of the table provides a summary.

Changes in Welfare We can now see the effects of the tax by comparing welfare before and after the tax is imposed. The third column in the table in Figure 8.3 shows the changes. The tax causes consumer surplus to fall by the area B + C and producer surplus to fall by the area D + E. Tax revenue rises by the area B + D. Not surprisingly, the tax makes buyers and sellers worse off and the government better off.

The change in total welfare includes the change in consumer surplus (which is negative), the change in producer surplus (which is also negative), and the change in tax revenue (which is positive). When we add these three pieces together, we find that total surplus in the market falls by the area C + E. Thus, the losses to buyers and sellers from a tax exceed the revenue raised by the government. The fall in total surplus that results when a tax (or some other policy)

FIGURE 8.3

How a Tax Affects Welfare

A tax on a good reduces consumer surplus (by the area B + C) and producer surplus (by the area D + E). Because the fall in producer and consumer surplus exceeds tax revenue (area B + D), the tax is said to impose a deadweight loss (area C + E).

	Without tax	With tax	Change
Consumer surplus	A + B + C	A	−(B + C)
Producer surplus	D + E + F	F	−(D + E)
Tax revenue	None	B + D	+(B + D)
Total surplus	A + B + C + D + E + F	A + B + D + F	−(C + E)

The area C + E shows the fall in total surplus and is the deadweight loss of the tax.

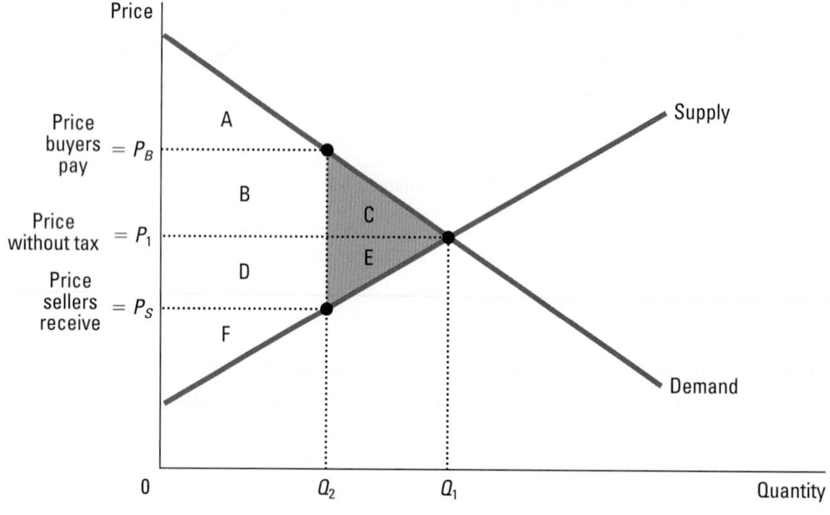

deadweight loss
the fall in total surplus that results from a market distortion, such as a tax

distorts a market outcome is called the **deadweight loss**. The area C + E measures the size of the deadweight loss.

To understand why taxes impose deadweight losses, recall one of the *Ten Principles of Economics* in Chapter 1: people respond to incentives. In Chapter 7 we assumed that markets normally allocate scarce resources efficiently. That is, the equilibrium of supply and demand maximizes the total surplus of buyers and sellers in a market. When a tax raises the price to buyers and lowers the price to sellers, however, it gives buyers an incentive to consume less and sellers an incentive to produce less than they otherwise would. As buyers and sellers respond to these incentives, the size of the market shrinks below its optimum. Thus, because taxes distort incentives, they cause markets to allocate resources inefficiently.

Deadweight Losses and the Gains from Trade

To gain some intuition for why taxes result in deadweight losses, consider an example. Imagine that Carsten cleans Annika's house each week for €100. The opportunity cost of Carsten's time is €80, and the value of a clean house to Annika is €120. Thus, Carsten and Annika each receive a €20 benefit from their deal. The total surplus of €40 measures the gains from trade in this particular transaction.

Now suppose that the government levies a €50 tax on the providers of cleaning services. There is now no price that Annika can pay Carsten that will leave both of them better off after paying the tax. The most Annika would be willing to pay is €120, but then Carsten would be left with only €70 after paying the tax, which is less than his €80 opportunity cost. Conversely, for Carsten to receive his opportunity cost of €80, Annika would need to pay €130, which is above the €120 value she places on a clean house. As a result, Annika and Carsten cancel their arrangement. Carsten goes without the income, and Annika lives in a dirtier house.

The tax has made Carsten and Annika worse off by a total of €40, because they have lost this amount of surplus. At the same time, the government collects no revenue from Carsten and Annika because they decide to cancel their arrangement. The €40 is pure deadweight loss: it is a loss to buyers and sellers in a market not offset by an increase in government revenue. From this example, we can see the ultimate source of deadweight losses: taxes cause deadweight losses because they prevent buyers and sellers from realizing some of the gains from trade.

The area of the triangle between the supply and demand curves (area C + E in Figure 8.3) measures these losses. This loss can be seen most easily in Figure 8.4 by recalling that the demand curve reflects the value of the good to consumers and that the supply curve reflects the costs of producers. When the tax raises the price to buyers to P_B and lowers the price to sellers to P_S, the marginal buyers and sellers leave the market, so the quantity sold falls from Q_1 to Q_2. Yet, as the figure shows, the value of the good to these buyers still exceeds the cost to

FIGURE 8.4

The Deadweight Loss

When the government imposes a tax on a good, the quantity sold falls from Q_1 to Q_2. As a result, some of the potential gains from trade among buyers and sellers do not get realized. These lost gains from trade create the deadweight loss.

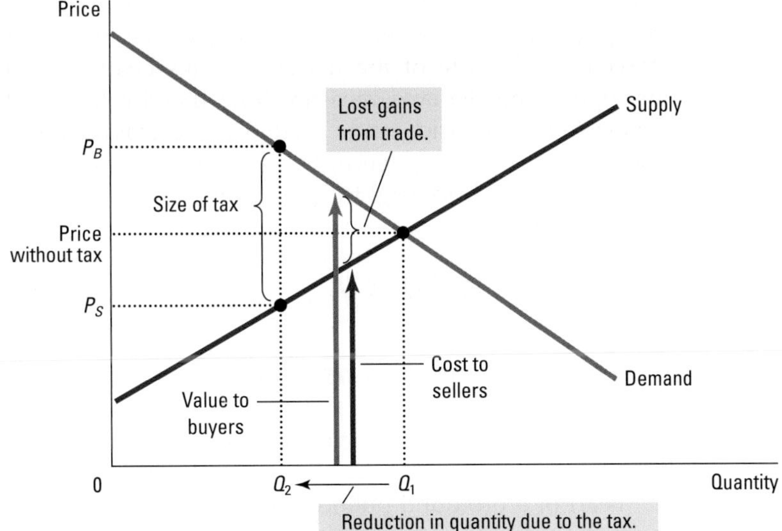

these sellers. As in our example with Carsten and Annika, the gains from trade – the difference between buyers' value and sellers' cost – is less than the tax. Thus, these trades do not get made once the tax is imposed. The deadweight loss is the surplus lost because the tax discourages these mutually advantageous trades.

Quick Quiz Draw the supply and demand curve for ham-and-cheese sandwiches. If the government imposes a tax on sandwiches, show what happens to the quantity sold, the price paid by buyers and the price paid by sellers. In your diagram, show the deadweight loss from the tax. Explain the meaning of the deadweight loss.

THE DETERMINANTS OF THE DEADWEIGHT LOSS

What determines whether the deadweight loss from a tax is large or small? The answer is the price elasticities of supply and demand, which measure how much the quantity supplied and quantity demanded respond to changes in the price.

Let's consider first how the elasticity of supply affects the size of the deadweight loss. In the top two panels of Figure 8.5, the demand curve and the size of the tax are the same. The only difference in these figures is the elasticity of the supply curve. In panel (a), the supply curve is relatively inelastic: quantity supplied responds only slightly to changes in the price. In panel (b), the supply curve is relatively elastic: quantity supplied responds substantially to changes in the price. Notice that the deadweight loss, the area of the triangle between the supply and demand curves, is larger when the supply curve is more elastic.

Similarly, the bottom two panels of Figure 8.5 show how the elasticity of demand affects the size of the deadweight loss. Here the supply curve and the size of the tax are held constant. In panel (c) the demand curve is relatively inelastic, and the deadweight loss is small. In panel (d) the demand curve is more elastic, and the deadweight loss from the tax is larger.

The lesson from this figure is easy to explain. A tax has a deadweight loss because it induces buyers and sellers to change their behaviour. The tax raises the price paid by buyers, so they consume less. At the same time, the tax lowers the price received by sellers, so they produce less. Because of these changes in behaviour, the size of the market shrinks below the optimum. The elasticities of supply and demand measure how much sellers and buyers respond to the changes in the price and, therefore, determine how much the tax distorts the market outcome. Hence, the greater the elasticities of supply and demand, the greater the deadweight loss of a tax.

CASE STUDY

The Deadweight Loss Debate

Supply, demand, elasticity, deadweight loss – all this economic theory is enough to make your head spin. But believe it or not, these ideas go to the heart of a profound political question: how big should the government sector be? The debate hinges on these concepts because the larger the deadweight loss of taxation, the larger the welfare cost of any government expenditure programme such as providing public health services or national defence. If

FIGURE 8.5

Tax Distortions and Elasticities

In panels (a) and (b) the demand curve and the size of the tax are the same, but the price elasticity of supply is different. Notice that the more elastic the supply curve, the larger the deadweight loss of the tax. In panels (c) and (d) the supply curve and the size of the tax are the same, but the price elasticity of demand is different. Notice that the more elastic the demand curve, the larger the deadweight loss of the tax.

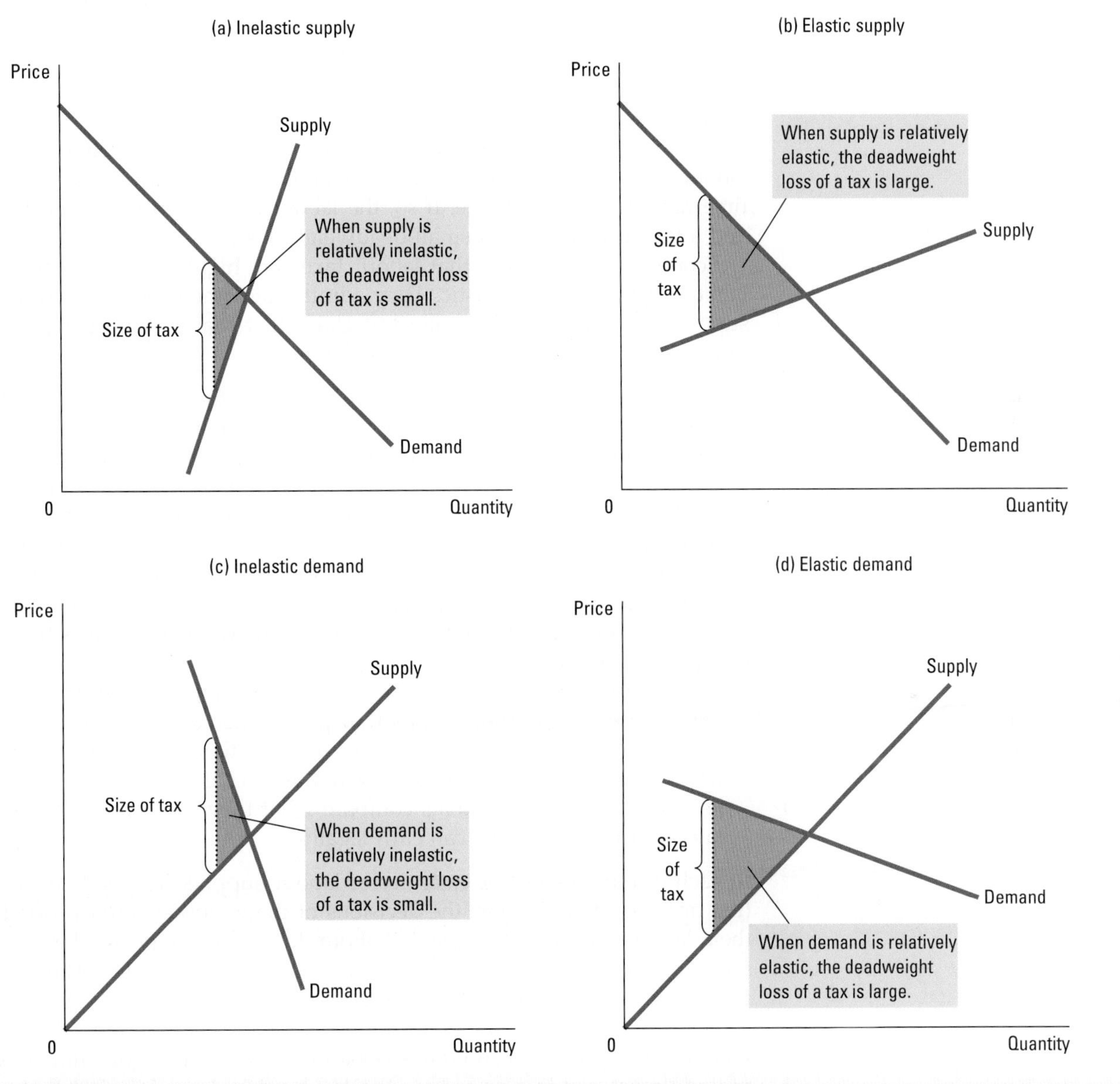

taxation entails large deadweight losses, then these losses are a strong argument for a leaner government that does less and taxes less. But if taxes impose small deadweight losses, then government programmes are less costly than they otherwise might be.

So how big are the deadweight losses of taxation? This is a question about which economists disagree. To see the nature of this disagreement, consider one of the most important taxes in most advanced economies – the tax on labour. In the UK, for example, National Insurance contributions and, to a large extent, income tax are taxes on labour. A labour tax places a wedge between the wage that firms pay and the wage that workers receive. If we add both forms of labour taxes together, the *marginal tax rate* on labour income – the tax on the last pound of earnings – is around 33 per cent for most UK manual workers. In some European countries – particularly Scandinavian countries – the marginal rate is even higher.

Although the size of the labour tax is easy to determine, the deadweight loss of this tax is less straightforward. Economists disagree about whether this 33 per cent labour tax has a small or a large deadweight loss. This disagreement arises because economists hold different views about the elasticity of labour supply.

Economists who argue that labour taxes are not very distorting believe that labour supply is fairly inelastic. Most people, they claim, would work full-time regardless of the wage. If so, the labour supply curve is almost vertical, and a tax on labour has a small deadweight loss.

Economists who argue that labour taxes are highly distorting believe that labour supply is more elastic. They admit that some groups of workers may supply their labour inelastically but claim that many other groups respond more to incentives. Here are some examples:

- Many workers can adjust the number of hours they work – for instance, by working overtime. The higher the wage, the more hours they choose to work.
- Some families have second earners – often married women with children – with some discretion over whether to do unpaid work at home or paid work in the marketplace. When deciding whether to take a job, these second earners compare the benefits of being at home (including savings on the cost of child care) with the wages they could earn.
- Many people can choose when to retire, and their decisions are partly based on the wage. Once they are retired, the wage determines their incentive to work part-time.
- Some people consider engaging in illegal economic activity, such as the drug trade, or working at jobs that pay 'under the table' to evade taxes. Economists call this the *black economy* (or sometimes the underground economy). In deciding whether to work in the black economy or at a legitimate job, these potential criminals compare what they can earn by breaking the law with the wage they can earn legally.

In each of these cases, the quantity of labour supplied responds to the wage (the price of labour). Thus, the decisions of these workers are distorted when their labour earnings are taxed. Labour taxes encourage workers to work fewer hours, second earners to stay at home, the elderly to retire early and the unscrupulous to enter the black economy.

These two views of labour taxation persist to this day. Indeed, whenever you see two political candidates debating whether the government should provide more services or reduce the tax burden, keep in mind that part of the disagreement may rest on different views about the elasticity of labour supply and the deadweight loss of taxation.

Quick Quiz The demand for beer is more elastic than the demand for milk. Would a tax on beer or a tax on milk have larger deadweight loss? Why?

DEADWEIGHT LOSS AND TAX REVENUE AS TAXES VARY

Taxes rarely stay the same for long periods of time. Policy makers are always considering raising one tax or lowering another. Here we consider what happens to the deadweight loss and tax revenue when the size of a tax changes.

Figure 8.6 shows the effects of a small, medium and large tax, holding constant the market's supply and demand curves. The deadweight loss – the reduction in total surplus that results when the tax reduces the size of a market below the optimum – equals the area of the triangle between the supply and demand curves. For the small tax in panel (a), the area of the deadweight loss triangle is quite small. But as the size of a tax rises in panels (b) and (c), the deadweight loss grows larger and larger.

Indeed, the deadweight loss of a tax rises even more rapidly than the size of the tax. The reason is that the deadweight loss is an area of a triangle, and an area of a triangle depends on the *square* of its size. If we double the size of a tax, for instance, the base and height of the triangle double, so the deadweight loss rises by a factor of 4. If we triple the size of a tax, the base and height triple, so the deadweight loss rises by a factor of 9.

The government's tax revenue is the size of the tax times the amount of the good sold. As Figure 8.6 shows, tax revenue equals the area of the rectangle between the supply and demand curves. For the small tax in panel (a), tax revenue is small. As the size of a tax rises from panel (a) to panel (b), tax revenue grows. But as the size of the tax rises further from panel (b) to panel (c), tax revenue falls because the higher tax drastically reduces the size of the market. For a very large tax, no revenue would be raised, because people would stop buying and selling the good altogether.

FIGURE 8.6

Deadweight Loss and Tax Revenue from Three Taxes of Different Size

The deadweight loss is the reduction in total surplus due to the tax. Tax revenue is the amount of the tax times the amount of the good sold. In panel (a) a small tax has a small deadweight loss and raises a small amount of revenue. In panel (b) a somewhat larger tax has a larger deadweight loss and raises a larger amount of revenue. In panel (c) a very large tax has a very large deadweight loss, but because it has reduced the size of the market so much, the tax raises only a small amount of revenue.

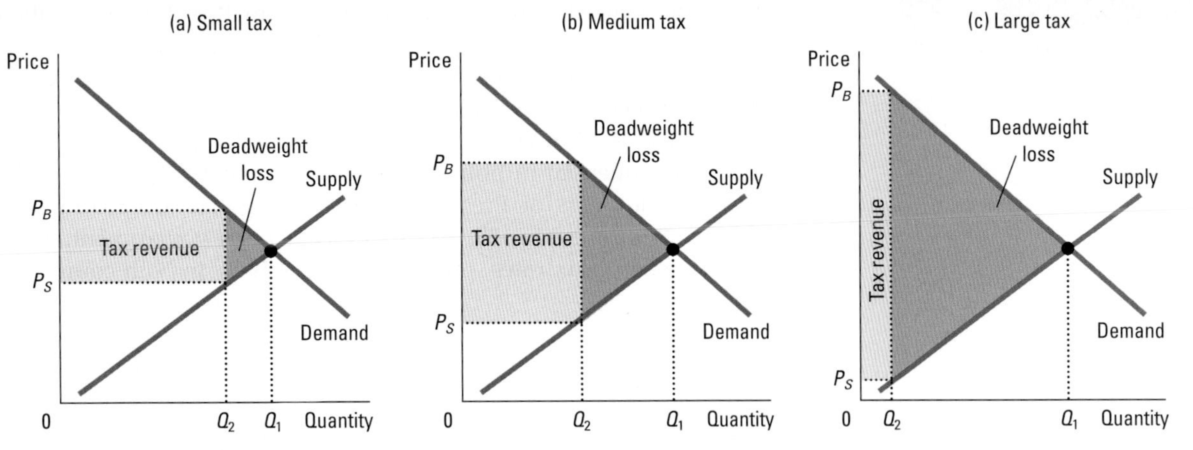

FIGURE 8.7

How Deadweight Loss and Tax Revenue Vary with the Size of a Tax

Panel (a) shows that as the size of a tax grows larger, the deadweight loss grows larger. Panel (b) shows that tax revenue first rises, then falls. This relationship is sometimes called the Laffer curve.

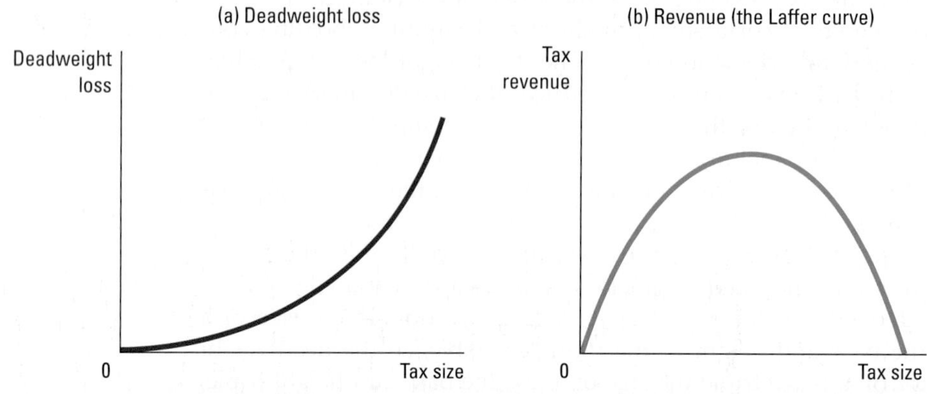

Figure 8.7 summarizes these results. In panel (a) we see that as the size of a tax increases, its deadweight loss quickly gets larger. By contrast, panel (b) shows that tax revenue first rises with the size of the tax; but then, as the tax gets larger, the market shrinks so much that tax revenue starts to fall.

US economist Arthur C. Laffer

CASE STUDY

The Laffer Curve and Supply-Side Economics

One day in 1974, the American economist Arthur Laffer sat in a Washington restaurant with some prominent journalists and politicians. He took out a napkin and drew a figure on it to show how tax rates affect tax revenue. It looked much like panel (b) of our Figure 8.7. Laffer then suggested that the United States was on the downward sloping side of this curve. Tax rates were so high, he argued, that reducing them would actually raise tax revenue.

Most economists were sceptical of Laffer's suggestion. The idea that a cut in tax rates could raise tax revenue was correct as a matter of economic theory, but there was more doubt about whether it would do so in practice. There was little evidence for Laffer's view that tax rates – in the United States or elsewhere – had in fact reached such extreme levels.

Nevertheless, the thinking underlying the *Laffer curve* (as it became known) became very influential in policy circles during the 1980s, particularly in the USA during the years of President Ronald Reagan's administration and in the UK during Prime Minister Margaret Thatcher's government. Tax rates – particularly income tax rates – were cut aggressively in both countries during the 1980s.

In the UK, for example, under Prime Minister Thatcher the top marginal rate of income tax was cut from 83 per cent to 60 per cent in 1980 and then again to 40 per cent in 1988. Economists have, however, found it hard to trace any strong incentive effects of these tax cuts leading to increases in total tax revenue, as the Laffer curve would suggest. A study by the UK Institute for

Fiscal Studies (IFS), for example, concluded that at most about 3 per cent of the increase in tax revenue between 1980 and 1986 could be attributed to the 1980 income tax cut.

In the USA, President Reagan also cut taxes aggressively, but the result was less tax revenue, not more. Revenue from personal income taxes in the United States (per person, adjusted for inflation) fell by 9 per cent from 1980 to 1984, even though average income (per person, adjusted for inflation) grew by 4 per cent over this period. The tax cut, together with policy makers' unwillingness to restrain spending, began a long period during which the US government spent more than it collected in taxes. Throughout Reagan's two terms in office, and for many years thereafter, the US government ran large budget deficits.

Yet Laffer's argument is not completely without merit. Although an overall cut in tax rates normally reduces revenue, some taxpayers at some times may be on the wrong side of the Laffer curve. The idea that cutting taxes can raise revenue may be correct if applied to those taxpayers facing the highest tax rates, but most people face lower marginal rates. Where the *typical* worker is on the top end of the Laffer curve, it may be more appropriate. In Sweden in the early 1980s, for instance, the typical worker faced a marginal tax rate of about 80 per cent. Such a high tax rate provides a substantial disincentive to work. Studies have suggested that Sweden would indeed have raised more tax revenue if it had lowered its tax rates.

Policy makers disagree about these issues in part because they disagree about the size of the relevant elasticities. The more elastic that supply and demand are in any market, the more taxes in that market distort behaviour, and the more likely it is that a tax cut will raise tax revenue. There is no debate, however, about the general lesson: how much revenue the government gains or loses from a tax change cannot be computed just by looking at tax rates. It also depends on how the tax change affects people's behaviour.

Quick Quiz If the government doubles the tax on petrol, can you be sure that revenue from the petrol tax will rise? Can you be sure that the deadweight loss from the petrol tax will rise? Explain.

IN THE NEWS

The Unintended Effects of Taxes

Levying any tax may be done for good reasons but the effects of the tax cannot always be foreseen because it is never easy to predict how incentives will be affected and how behaviour will change as a result. This article highlights such a case.

When the economy is growing strongly governments might want to find ways of making sure that all capacity is fully utilized. One example of such spare capacity is buildings that are lying empty. Having disused shops, offices, industrial or manufacturing facilities is something that the UK government wanted to discourage. In 2006–2007, economic growth was relatively strong, commercial rents were increasing as demand for business property rose. Businesses in the UK have to pay business taxes, specifically a tax on the use of a building for a business. If for some reason the building is not actively being used for business there is some tax relief provided.

In 2007, however, the UK government decided to cut that relief. Prior to the tax change owners of empty business premises paid no tax for the first three months and then 50 per cent thereafter. The aim of this incentive was to give owners of premises the chance to find alternative uses for the building and / or to new tenants. The tax change, which came into effect on 1 April 2008, kept the tax allowance free for the fist three months but thereafter owners were required to pay the full tax. Local government minister Phil Woolas said: 'The reforms will encourage owners of empty properties to bring them back into use, helping to create thriving and vibrant town centres. No-one wants to live or work next to an empty property, and it is frankly daft for the state to subsidize it when commercial rents are so high. That is why a package of reforms that will drive down those rents, encourage business growth, and promote brownfield [former industrial or commercial areas that are not currently being used] development is needed. As well as reforming empty property rates, from last month a new 100% capital allowance is available for the cost of renovating or converting unused businesses in deprived areas.'

The minister was clear on the economic rationale for the tax reforms – provide incentives to get disused buildings back into use, increase the supply of business premises available, drive down rents whilst at the same time giving incentives in the form of capital allowances to encourage renovation. The tax reforms were projected to raise the government around £1.4 billion in tax revenue. Surely a sound policy?

It might have been if economic growth had continued to be strong but the introduction of the tax reforms came at the same time as one of the most severe recessions the UK had witnessed. Bringing disused buildings back into production in a recession was not easy, regardless of the penalty faced for not doing so. The question then arises, how do owners react to the changed circumstances? If they leave their buildings unused then they face a financial penalty in the form of the tax. Trying to bring the building back into use was not an option for many so only one option remained, destroy the building! The cost of demolishing an unused building would have to be factored into the equation but if the cost of demolition was less than the stream of tax payments that have to be made over time then it would be worth doing.

And this is exactly what happened. In Sunderland a business park was demolished after the landlord who owned the land and property, O&H Q7 Ltd., received advice from its agents that the tax liability on the disused buildings was likely to be high. The agents commented: 'The rateable value of the units demolished would have incurred a cost of well over £150 000 per year to our clients, a cost that until then had not been necessary. In demolishing these factory units, we have undoubtedly lost some major assets not just as far as our client is concerned but also as in respect of the City of Sunderland.' This pattern of behaviour was being repeated across many parts of the UK by small and large landlords who owned disused buildings. In addition some construction companies were reported to be leaving sites unfinished rather than incurring the cost of the tax because of the difficulty in the economic climate of the time of letting finished buildings.

The distortions as a result of the policy had some other interesting twists. In the north-east of England, for example, a government agency charged with economic development of the region faced the prospect of having to divert cash it had for regeneration of the area to the Treasury to pay the tax on unused buildings. The buildings concerned were ones that it had taken ownership of and were targeted for regeneration.

The chair of a group representing government backed urban funding councils was quoted as saying: 'There is a lot of pre-emptive demolition going on. This is already having a visual impact – cities are beginning to look like broken teeth.'

CONCLUSION

Taxes, someone once said, are the price we pay for a civilized society. Indeed, our society cannot exist without some form of taxes. We all expect the government to provide us with certain services, such as roads, parks, police and national defence. These public services require tax revenue.

This chapter has shed some light on how high the price of civilized society can be. One of the *Ten Principles of Economics* discussed in Chapter 1 is that markets are usually a good way to organize economic activity. When the government imposes taxes on buyers or sellers of a good, however, society loses some of the benefits of market efficiency. Taxes are costly to market participants not only because taxes transfer resources from those participants to the government, but also because they alter incentives and distort market outcomes. Throughout this chapter we have assumed that the benefit to the government, or more accurately, the third party who receives the benefit of the tax spending, is equal to the tax revenue given by $T \times Q$. This may not always be the case. To get a more accurate analysis of the size of deadweight losses arising from taxes, we may have to find a way to place a value on the benefits of the tax spending. For example, if taxes are spent on improving the road infrastructure there is a benefit to car drivers which may be greater than the tax spending. Calculating the value of these benefits is not easy but has to be carried out to get a more accurate picture of the change in welfare. How the government chooses to spend tax revenue is also a factor to consider. A paper written by Gupta, Verhoeven and Tiongson in 2004[1] entitled 'Public Spending on health care and the Poor' concluded that in 70 developing and transition economies there was evidence to suggest that the impact of public spending on health care on the poor could be substantial in comparison with spending on the non-poor. A 1 per cent increase in public spending on health, for example, reduces child mortality by twice as many deaths amongst the poor as the non-poor and infant mortality rates are similarly affected. This highlights that there are many other factors that may have to be taken into consideration when analysing changes in welfare as a result of taxes.

SUMMARY

- A tax on a good reduces the welfare of buyers and sellers of the good, and the reduction in consumer and producer surplus usually exceeds the revenue raised by the government. The fall in total surplus – the sum of consumer surplus, producer surplus and tax revenue – is called the deadweight loss of the tax.
- Taxes have deadweight losses because they cause buyers to consume less and sellers to produce less, and this change in behaviour shrinks the size of the market below the level that maximizes total surplus. Because the elasticities of supply and demand measure how much market participants respond to market conditions, larger elasticities imply larger deadweight losses.
- As a tax grows larger, it distorts incentives more, and its deadweight loss grows larger. Tax revenue first rises with the size of a tax. Eventually, however, a larger tax reduces tax revenue because it reduces the size of the market.

KEY CONCEPTS

deadweight loss, p. 162

[1]Gupta, S. Verhoeven, M. & Tiongson, E.R. (2004) 'Public Spending on Health Care and the Poor', in Gupta, S. Clements, B., Inchauste, G. (eds), *Helping Countries Develop: The Role of Fiscal Policy*, Washington DC, IMF.

QUESTIONS FOR REVIEW

1. What happens to consumer and producer surplus when the sale of a good is taxed? How does the change in consumer and producer surplus compare to the tax revenue? Explain.
2. Draw a supply and demand diagram with a tax on the sale of the good. Show the deadweight loss. Show the tax revenue.
3. How do the elasticities of supply and demand affect the deadweight loss of a tax? Why do they have this effect?
4. Why do experts disagree about whether labour taxes have small or large deadweight losses?
5. What happens to the deadweight loss and tax revenue when a tax is increased?

PROBLEMS AND APPLICATIONS

1. The market for pizza is characterized by a downward sloping demand curve and an upward sloping supply curve.
   a. Draw the competitive market equilibrium. Label the price, quantity, consumer surplus and producer surplus. Is there any deadweight loss? Explain.
   b. Suppose that the government forces each pizzeria to pay a €11 tax on each pizza sold. Illustrate the effect of this tax on the pizza market, being sure to label the consumer surplus, producer surplus, government revenue and deadweight loss. How does each area compare to the pre-tax case?
   c. If the tax were removed, pizza eaters and sellers would be better off, but the government would lose tax revenue. Suppose that consumers and producers voluntarily transferred some of their gains to the government. Could all parties (including the government) be better off than they were with a tax?
   Explain using the labelled areas in your graph.
2. Evaluate the following two statements. Do you agree? Why or why not?
   a. 'If the government taxes land, wealthy landowners will pass the tax on to their poorer renters.'
   b. 'If the government taxes blocks of flats, wealthy landlords will pass the tax on to their poorer renters.'
3. Evaluate the following two statements. Do you agree? Why or why not?
   a. 'A tax that has no deadweight loss cannot raise any revenue for the government.'
   b. 'A tax that raises no revenue for the government cannot have any deadweight loss.'
4. Consider the market for rubber bands.
   a. If this market has very elastic supply and very inelastic demand, how would the burden of a tax on rubber bands be shared between consumers and producers? Use the tools of consumer surplus and producer surplus in your answer.
   b. If this market has very inelastic supply and very elastic demand, how would the burden of a tax on rubber bands be shared between consumers and producers?
   Contrast your answer with your answer to part (a).
5. Suppose that the government imposes a tax on heating oil.
   a. Would the deadweight loss from this tax likely be greater in the first year after it is imposed or in the fifth year? Explain.
   b. Would the revenue collected from this tax likely be greater in the first year after it is imposed or in the fifth year? Explain.
6. After your economics lecture one day, your friend suggests that taxing food would be a good way to raise revenue because the demand for food is quite inelastic. In what sense is taxing food a 'good' way to raise revenue?
   In what sense is it not a 'good' way to raise revenue?
7. The government places a tax on the purchase of socks.
   a. Illustrate the effect of this tax on equilibrium price and quantity in the sock market. Identify the following areas both before and after the imposition of the tax: total spending by consumers; total revenue for producers; and government tax revenue.
   b. Does the price received by producers rise or fall? Can you tell whether total receipts for producers rise or fall? Explain.
   c. Does the price paid by consumers rise or fall? Can you tell whether total spending by consumers rises or falls? Explain carefully. (Hint: think about elasticity.)

If total consumer spending falls, does consumer surplus rise? Explain.

8. Suppose the government currently raises €100 million through a €0.01 tax on widgets, and another €100 million through a €0.10 tax on gadgets. If the government doubled the tax rate on widgets and eliminated the tax on gadgets, would it raise more money than today, less money or the same amount of money? Explain.
9. In the 1980s the UK government imposed a 'poll tax' that required each person to pay a flat amount to the government independent of his or her income or wealth. What is the effect of such a tax on economic efficiency? What is the effect on economic equity? Do you think this was a popular tax? Explain your answer.
10. This chapter analysed the welfare effects of a tax on a good. Consider now the opposite policy. Suppose that the government *subsidizes* a good: for each unit of the good sold, the government pays €2 to the buyer. How does the subsidy affect consumer surplus, producer surplus, tax revenue and total surplus? Does a subsidy lead to a deadweight loss? Explain.
11. (This problem uses some secondary school algebra and is challenging.) Suppose that a market is described by the following supply and demand equations:

$$Q^S = 2P$$
$$Q^D = 300 - P$$

a. Solve for the equilibrium price and the equilibrium quantity.
b. Suppose that a tax of T is placed on buyers, so the new demand equation is:

$$Q^D = 300 - (P + T).$$

Solve for the new equilibrium. What happens to the price received by sellers, the price paid by buyers and the quantity sold?
c. Tax revenue is $T \times Q$. Use your answer to part (b) to solve for tax revenue as a function of T. Graph this relationship for T between 0 and 300.
d. The deadweight loss of a tax is the area of the triangle between the supply and demand curves. Recalling that the area of a triangle is 1/2 × base × height, solve for deadweight loss as a function of T. Graph this relationship for T between 0 and 300. (Hint: looking sideways, the base of the deadweight loss triangle is T, and the height is the difference between the quantity sold with the tax and the quantity sold without the tax.)
e. The government now levies a tax on this good of €200 per unit. Is this a good policy? Why or why not? Can you propose a better policy?

For further resources, visit www.cengage.com/mankiw_taylor2

9 APPLICATION: INTERNATIONAL TRADE

If you check the labels on the clothes you are now wearing, you will probably find that some of your clothes were made in another country. A century ago the textiles and clothing industry was a major part of the UK and many other European economies. In fact, when Ricardo first developed his argument about the principle of comparative advantage back in the early 19th century, he used an example of cloth being produced in England and wine in Portugal. Portugal still has a comparative advantage in producing wine relative to many countries in the world, but England no longer has a comparative advantage in producing cloth. Faced with foreign competitors that could produce quality goods at low cost, many European firms have found it increasingly difficult to produce and sell textiles and clothing at a profit. As a result, they have laid off their workers and shut down their factories. Today, much of the textiles and clothing that Europeans consume is imported from outside of Europe.

The story of the textiles industry raises important questions for economic policy: how does international trade affect economic well-being? Who gains and who loses from free trade among countries, and how do the gains compare to the losses?

Chapter 3 introduced the study of international trade by applying the principle of comparative advantage. According to this principle, all countries can benefit from trading with one another because trade allows each country to specialize in doing what it does best. But the analysis in Chapter 3 was incomplete. It did not explain how the international marketplace achieves these gains from trade or how the gains are distributed among various economic actors.

We now return to the study of international trade and take up these questions. Over the past several chapters we have developed many tools for analysing how markets work: supply, demand, equilibrium, consumer surplus, producer surplus and so on. With these tools we can learn more about the effects of international trade on economic well-being.

THE DETERMINANTS OF TRADE

Consider the market for olive oil. The olive oil market is well suited to examining the gains and losses from international trade: olive oil is made in many countries around the world, and there is much world trade in olive oil. Moreover, the olive oil market is one in which policy makers often consider (and sometimes implement) trade restrictions to protect domestic olive oil producers from foreign competitors. We examine here the olive oil market in the imaginary country of Isoland.

The Equilibrium Without Trade

As our story begins, the Isolandian olive oil market is isolated from the rest of the world. By government decree, no one in Isoland is allowed to import or export olive oil, and the penalty for violating the decree is so large that no one dares try.

Because there is no international trade, the market for olive oil in Isoland consists solely of Isolandian buyers and sellers. As Figure 9.1 shows, the domestic price adjusts to balance the quantity supplied by domestic sellers and the quantity demanded by domestic buyers. The figure shows the consumer and producer

FIGURE 9.1

The Equilibrium Without International Trade

When an economy cannot trade in world markets, the price adjusts to balance domestic supply and demand. This figure shows consumer and producer surplus in an equilibrium without international trade for the olive oil market in the imaginary country of Isoland.

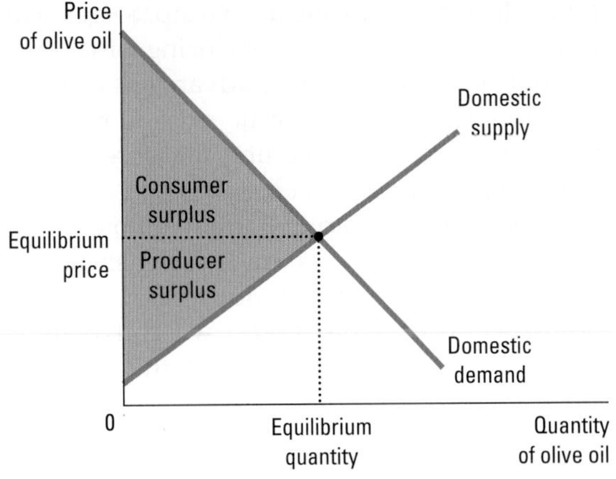

surplus in the equilibrium without trade. The sum of consumer and producer surplus measures the total benefits that buyers and sellers receive from the olive oil market.

Now suppose that, in an election upset, Isoland elects a new president. The president campaigned on a platform of 'change' and promised the voters bold new ideas. Her first act is to assemble a team of economists to evaluate Isolandian trade policy. She asks them to report back on three questions:

- If the government allowed Isolandians to import and export olive oil, what would happen to the price of olive oil and the quantity of olive oil sold in the domestic olive oil market?
- Who would gain from free trade in olive oil and who would lose, and would the gains exceed the losses?
- Should a tariff (a tax on olive oil imports) or an import quota (a limit on olive oil imports) be part of the new trade policy?

After reviewing supply and demand in their favourite textbook (this one, of course), the Isolandian economics team begins its analysis.

The World Price and Comparative Advantage

The first issue our economists take up is whether Isoland is likely to become an olive oil importer or an olive oil exporter. In other words, if free trade were allowed, would Isolandians end up buying or selling olive oil in world markets?

world price
the price of a good that prevails in the world market for that good

To answer this question, the economists compare the current Isolandian price of olive oil with the price of olive oil in other countries. We call the price prevailing in world markets the **world price**. If the world price of olive oil is higher than the domestic price, then Isoland would become an exporter of olive oil once trade is permitted. Isolandian olive oil producers would be eager to receive the higher prices available abroad and would start selling their olive oil to buyers in other countries. Conversely, if the world price of olive oil is lower than the domestic price, then Isoland would become an importer of olive oil. Because foreign sellers offer a better price, Isolandian olive oil consumers would quickly start buying olive oil from other countries.

In essence, comparing the world price and the domestic price before trade indicates whether Isoland has a comparative advantage in producing olive oil. The domestic price reflects the opportunity cost of olive oil: it tells us how much an Isolandian must give up to get one unit of olive oil. If the domestic price is low, the cost of producing olive oil in Isoland is low, suggesting that Isoland has a comparative advantage in producing olive oil relative to the rest of the world. If the domestic price is high, then the cost of producing olive oil in Isoland is high, suggesting that foreign countries have a comparative advantage in producing olive oil.

As we saw in Chapter 3, trade among nations is ultimately based on comparative advantage. That is, trade is beneficial because it allows each nation to specialize in doing what it does best. By comparing the world price and the domestic price before trade, we can determine whether Isoland is better or worse at producing olive oil than the rest of the world.

Quick Quiz The country Autarka does not allow international trade. In Autarka, you can buy a wool suit for 300 grams of gold. Meanwhile, in neighbouring countries, you can buy the same suit for 200 grams of gold. If Autarka were to allow free trade, would it import or export suits? Why?

THE WINNERS AND LOSERS FROM TRADE

To analyse the welfare effects of free trade, the Isolandian economists begin with the assumption that Isoland is a small economy compared with the rest of the world so that its actions have a negligible effect on world markets. The small economy assumption has a specific implication for analysing the olive oil market: if Isoland is a small economy, then the change in Isoland's trade policy will not affect the world price of olive oil. The Isolandians are said to be *price takers* in the world economy. That is, they take the world price of olive oil as given. They can sell olive oil at this price and be exporters, or buy olive oil at this price and be importers.

The small economy assumption is not necessary to analyse the gains and losses from international trade. But the Isolandian economists know from experience (and from reading Chapter 2 of this book) that this assumption greatly simplifies the analysis. They also know that the basic lessons do not change in the more complicated case of a large economy.

The Gains and Losses of an Exporting Country

Figure 9.2 shows the Isolandian olive oil market when the domestic equilibrium price before trade is below the world price. Once free trade is allowed, the domestic price rises to equal the world price. No seller of olive oil would accept less than the world price, and no buyer would pay more than the world price.

With the domestic price now equal to the world price, the domestic quantity supplied differs from the domestic quantity demanded. The supply curve shows the quantity of olive oil supplied by Isolandian sellers. The demand curve shows the quantity of olive oil demanded by Isolandian buyers. Because the domestic quantity supplied is greater than the domestic quantity demanded, Isoland sells olive oil to other countries. Thus, Isoland becomes an olive oil exporter.

FIGURE 9.2

International Trade in an Exporting Country

Once trade is allowed, the domestic price rises to equal the world price. The supply curve shows the quantity of olive oil produced domestically, and the demand curve shows the quantity consumed domestically. Exports from Isoland equal the difference between the domestic quantity supplied and the domestic quantity demanded at the world price.

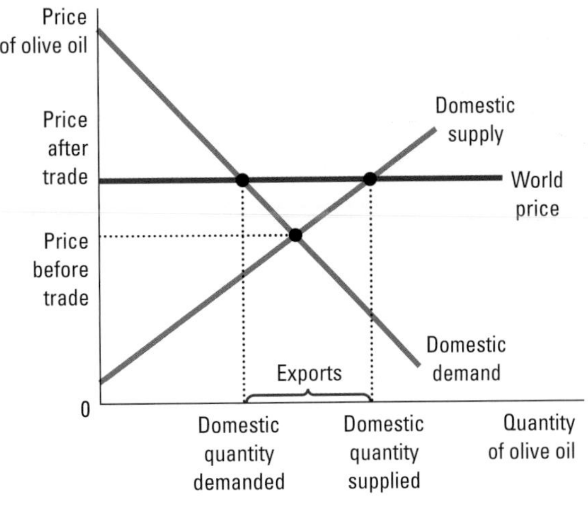

Although domestic quantity supplied and domestic quantity demanded differ, the olive oil market is still in equilibrium because there is now another participant in the market: the rest of the world. One can view the horizontal line at the world price as representing the demand for olive oil from the rest of the world. This demand curve is perfectly elastic because Isoland, as a small economy, can sell as much olive oil as it wants at the world price.

Now consider the gains and losses from opening up trade. Clearly, not everyone benefits. Trade forces the domestic price to rise to the world price. Domestic producers of olive oil are better off because they can now sell olive oil at a higher price, but domestic consumers of olive oil are worse off because they have to buy olive oil at a higher price.

To measure these gains and losses, we look at the changes in consumer and producer surplus, which are shown in the graph and table in Figure 9.3. Before trade is allowed, the price of olive oil adjusts to balance domestic supply and domestic demand. Consumer surplus, the area between the demand curve and the before-trade price, is area A + B. Producer surplus, the area between the supply curve and the before-trade price, is area C. Total surplus before trade, the sum of consumer and producer surplus, is area A + B + C.

After trade is allowed, the domestic price rises to the world price. Consumer surplus is area A (the area between the demand curve and the world price). Producer surplus is area B + C + D (the area between the supply curve and the world price). Thus, total surplus with trade is area A + B + C + D.

FIGURE 9.3

How Free Trade Affects Welfare in an Exporting Country

When the domestic price rises to equal the world price, sellers are better off (producer surplus rises from C *to* B + C + D*), and buyers are worse off (consumer surplus falls from* A + B *to* A*). Total surplus rises by an amount equal to area* D*, indicating that trade raises the economic well-being of the country as a whole.*

	Before trade	After trade	Change
Consumer surplus	A + B	A	− B
Producer surplus	C	B + C + D	+(B + D)
Total surplus	A + B + C	A + B + C + D	+D

The area D shows the increase in total surplus and represents the gains from trade.

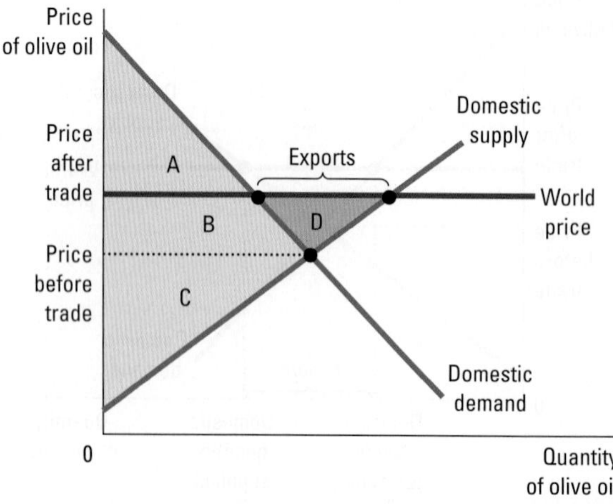

These welfare calculations show who wins and who loses from trade in an exporting country. Sellers benefit because producer surplus increases by the area B + D. Buyers are worse off because consumer surplus decreases by the area B. Because the gains of sellers exceed the losses of buyers by the area D, total surplus in Isoland increases.

This analysis of an exporting country yields two conclusions:

- When a country allows trade and becomes an exporter of a good, domestic producers of the good are better off, and domestic consumers of the good are worse off.
- Trade raises the economic well-being of a nation in the sense that the gains of the winners exceed the losses of the losers.

The Gains and Losses of an Importing Country

Now suppose that the domestic price before trade is above the world price. Once again, after free trade is allowed, the domestic price must equal the world price. As Figure 9.4 shows, the domestic quantity supplied is less than the domestic quantity demanded. The difference between the domestic quantity demanded and the domestic quantity supplied is bought from other countries, and Isoland becomes an olive oil importer.

In this case, the horizontal line at the world price represents the supply of the rest of the world. This supply curve is perfectly elastic because Isoland is a small economy and, therefore, can buy as much olive oil as it wants at the world price.

Now consider the gains and losses from trade. Once again, not everyone benefits. When trade forces the domestic price to fall, domestic consumers are better off (they can now buy olive oil at a lower price), and domestic producers are worse off (they now have to sell olive oil at a lower price). Changes in consumer

FIGURE 9.4

International Trade in an Importing Country

Once trade is allowed, the domestic price falls to equal the world price. The supply curve shows the amount produced domestically, and the demand curve shows the amount consumed domestically. Imports equal the difference between the domestic quantity demanded and the domestic quantity supplied at the world price.

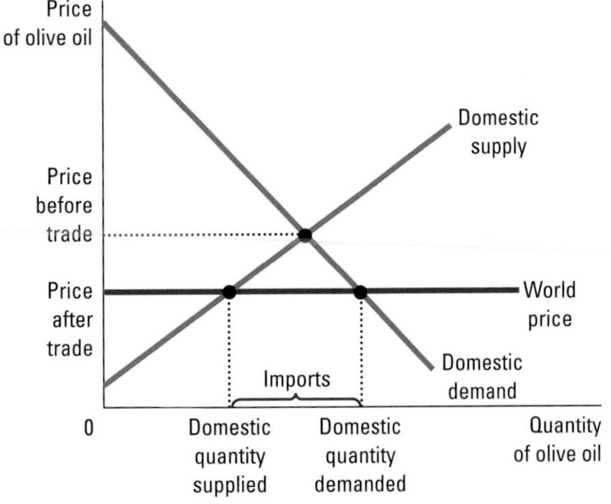

FIGURE 9.5

How Free Trade Affects Welfare in an Importing Country

When the domestic price falls to equal the world price, buyers are better off (consumer surplus rises from A to A + B + D), and sellers are worse off (producer surplus falls from B + C to C). Total surplus rises by an amount equal to area D, indicating that trade raises the economic well-being of the country as a whole.

	Before trade	After trade	Change
Consumer surplus	A	A + B + D	+(B + D)
Producer surplus	B + C	C	− B
Total surplus	A + B + C	A + B + C + D	+D

The area D shows the increase in total surplus and represents the gains from trade.

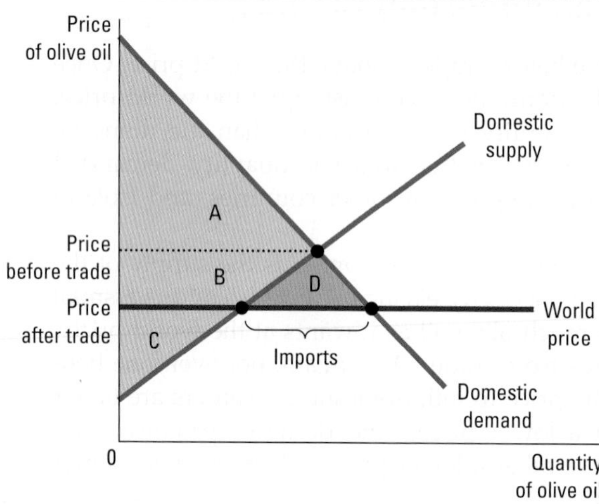

and producer surplus measure the size of the gains and losses, as shown in the graph and table in Figure 9.5. Before trade, consumer surplus is area A, producer surplus is area B + C, and total surplus is area A + B + C. After trade is allowed, consumer surplus is area A + B + D, producer surplus is area C and total surplus is area A + B + C + D.

These welfare calculations show who wins and who loses from trade in an importing country. Buyers benefit because consumer surplus increases by the area B + D. Sellers are worse off because producer surplus falls by the area B. The gains of buyers exceed the losses of sellers, and total surplus increases by the area D.

This analysis of an importing country yields two conclusions parallel to those for an exporting country:

- When a country allows trade and becomes an importer of a good, domestic consumers of the good are better off, and domestic producers of the good are worse off.
- Trade raises the economic well-being of a nation in the sense that the gains of the winners exceed the losses of the losers.

Having completed our analysis of trade, we can better understand one of the *Ten Principles of Economics* in Chapter 1: trade can make everyone better off. If Isoland opens up its olive oil market to international trade the change will create winners and losers, regardless of whether Isoland ends up exporting or importing olive oil.

Notice that in our analysis, we have not made a judgement about the winners and losers – whether the gain to the producers is more valuable than the loss to the consumers. The important issue, from an economic analysis perspective, is the effect on total welfare, which in this case has risen for Isoland. In the real world, policy makers may have to take into consideration the power which resides with different groups. If domestic consumers of olive oil in Isoland had considerable lobbying power compared with olive oil producers then policy decisions may be affected which distort outcomes and reduce total welfare. The effect on consumers, for example, might be limited in comparison with the gains to producers but presenting arguments in this way does not always win political points! This is something that must always be considered because whilst economic analysis may point to a clear policy decision and outcome, there are many other factors that decision makers have to take into account, as exemplified when we look at the arguments for restricting trade on page 189.

In our example, the gains of the winners exceed the losses of the losers, so the winners could compensate the losers and still be better off. In this sense, trade *can* make everyone better off. But *will* trade make everyone better off? Probably not. In practice, compensation for the losers from international trade is rare. Without such compensation, opening up to international trade is a policy that expands the size of the economic cake, whilst perhaps leaving some participants in the economy with a smaller slice.

We can now see why the debate over trade policy is so often contentious. Whenever a policy creates winners and losers, the stage is set for a political battle as outlined above. Nations sometimes fail to enjoy the gains from trade simply because the losers from free trade have more political clout than the winners. The losers lobby for trade restrictions, such as tariffs and import quotas.

The Effects of a Tariff

The Isolandian economists next consider the effects of a **tariff** – a tax on imported goods. The economists quickly realize that a tariff on olive oil will have no effect if Isoland becomes an olive oil exporter. If no one in Isoland is interested in importing olive oil, a tax on olive oil imports is irrelevant. The tariff matters only if Isoland becomes an olive oil importer. Concentrating their attention on this case, the economists compare welfare with and without the tariff.

tariff
a tax on goods produced abroad and sold domestically

The graph in Figure 9.6 shows the Isolandian market for olive oil. Under free trade, the domestic price equals the world price. A tariff raises the price of imported olive oil above the world price by the amount of the tariff. Domestic suppliers of olive oil, who compete with suppliers of imported olive oil, can now sell their olive oil for the world price plus the amount of the tariff. Thus, the price of olive oil – both imported and domestic – rises by the amount of the tariff and is, therefore, closer to the price that would prevail without trade.

The change in price affects the behaviour of domestic buyers and sellers. Because the tariff raises the price of olive oil, it reduces the domestic quantity demanded from Q_1^D to Q_2^D and raises the domestic quantity supplied from Q_1^S to Q_2^S. Thus, the tariff reduces the quantity of imports and moves the domestic market closer to its equilibrium without trade.

Now consider the gains and losses from the tariff. Because the tariff raises the domestic price, domestic sellers are better off, and domestic buyers are worse off. In addition, the government raises revenue. To measure these gains and losses, we look at the changes in consumer surplus, producer surplus and government revenue. These changes are summarized in the table in Figure 9.6.

Before the tariff, the domestic price equals the world price. Consumer surplus, the area between the demand curve and the world price, is area A + B + C + D + E + F. Producer surplus, the area between the supply curve and the world price, is area G. Government revenue equals zero. Total surplus – the sum of consumer

FIGURE 9.6

The Effects of a Tariff

A tariff reduces the quantity of imports and moves a market closer to the equilibrium that would exist without trade. Total surplus falls by an amount equal to area D + F. These two triangles represent the deadweight loss from the tariff.

	Before traiff	After traiff	Change
Consumer surplus	A + B + C + D + E + F	A + B	– (C + D + E +F)
Producer surplus	G	C + G	+ C
Government revenue	None	E	+ E
Total surplus	A + B + C + D + E + F + G	A + B + C + E + G	– (D + F)

The area D + F shows the fall in total surplus and represents the deadweight loss of the tariff.

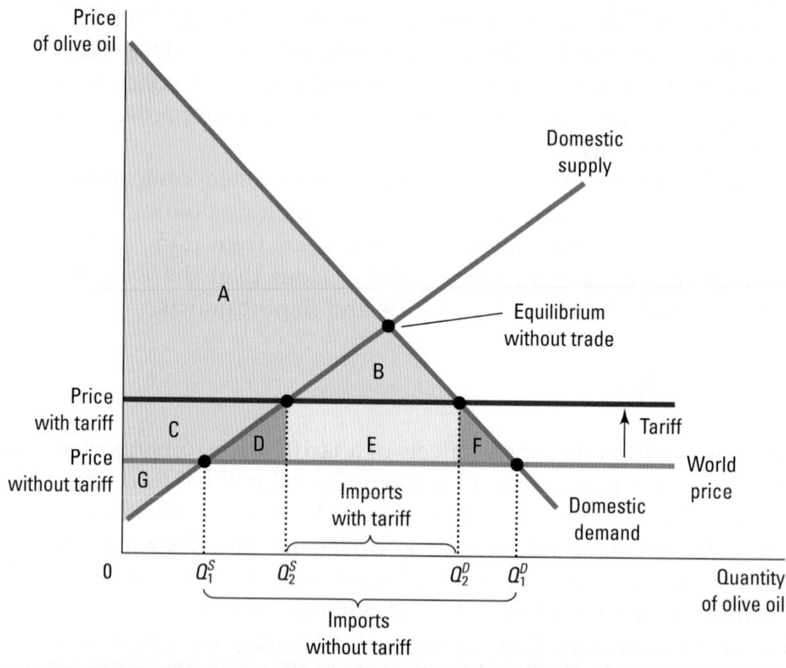

surplus, producer surplus and government revenue – is area A + B + C + D + E + F + G.

Once the government imposes a tariff, the domestic price exceeds the world price by the amount of the tariff. Consumer surplus is now area A + B. Producer surplus is area C + G. Government revenue, which is the quantity of after-tariff imports times the size of the tariff, is the area E. Thus, total surplus with the tariff is area A + B + C + E + G.

To determine the total welfare effects of the tariff, we add the change in consumer surplus (which is negative), the change in producer surplus (positive) and the change in government revenue (positive). We find that total surplus in the market decreases by the area D + F. This fall in total surplus is the *deadweight loss* of the tariff.

A tariff causes a deadweight loss simply because a tariff is a type of tax and follows the same principles as we discussed in Chapter 8. Like most taxes, it distorts incentives and pushes the allocation of scarce resources away from the optimum. In this case, we can identify two effects. First, the tariff on olive oil raises the price of olive oil that domestic producers can charge above the world price and, as a result, encourages them to increase production of olive oil (from Q_1^S to Q_2^S). Second, the tariff raises the price that domestic olive oil buyers have to pay and, therefore, encourages them to reduce consumption of olive oil (from Q_1^D to Q_2^D). Area D represents the deadweight loss from the overproduction of olive oil, and area F represents the deadweight loss from the underconsumption. The total deadweight loss of the tariff is the sum of these two triangles.

The Effects of an Import Quota

The Isolandian economists next consider the effects of an **import quota** – a limit on the quantity of imports. In particular, imagine that the Isolandian government distributes a limited number of import licences. Each licence gives the licence holder the right to import 1 tonne of olive oil into Isoland from abroad. The Isolandian economists want to compare welfare under a policy of free trade and welfare with the addition of this import quota.

import quota
a limit on the quantity of a good that can be produced abroad and sold domestically

The graph and table in Figure 9.7 show how an import quota affects the Isolandian market for olive oil. Because the import quota prevents Isolandians from

FIGURE 9.7

The Effects of an Import Quota

An import quota, like a tariff, reduces the quantity of imports and moves a market closer to the equilibrium that would exist without trade. Total surplus falls by an amount equal to area D + F. These two triangles represent the deadweight loss from the quota. In addition, the import quota transfers E' + E'' to whoever holds the import licences.

	Before quota	After quota	Change
Consumer surplus	A + B + C + D + E' + E'' + F	A + B	– (C + D + E' + E'' + F)
Producer surplus	G	C + G	+ C
Government revenue	None	E' + E''	+(E' + E'')
Total surplus	A + B + C + D + E' + E'' + F + G	A + B + C + E' + E'' + G	– (D + F)

The area D + F shows the fall in total surplus and represents the deadweight loss of the quota.

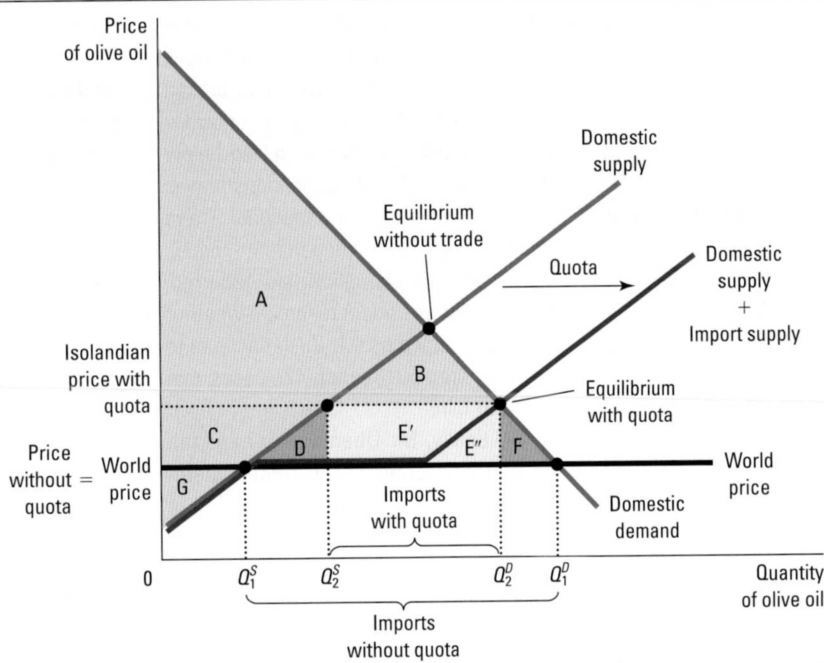

IN THE NEWS

In 2002 economists criticized the US for imposing tariffs on the import of steel, a decision which was later reversed by President Bush in 2003. Whilst Mr Bush was able to show steel producers that he had tried to help them he was also able to claim a victory for free trade in the time it took the World Trade Organization to respond to the accusations that the US move was illegal. So, what lessons have been learned?

Tyred Of Trade?

By succumbing to domestic pressures, America has started an alarming trade row with China.

In raw economic terms Barack Obama's imposition of tariffs on Chinese tyres hardly registers. The number of jobs affected is barely a rounding error in measurements of the mighty American workforce. The cost to consumers is also slight. But in geopolitical terms, it is a whopper. Mr Obama's most overtly protectionist decision so far has triggered a predictably angry reaction from China, which threatened to retaliate against American chickens and car parts and to haul America before the World Trade Organization. The *Global Times*, a newspaper that often reflects the views of hardline nationalists in China, ran a front-page headline saying 'America has erred before the world'.

The decision does come at a risky time. Protectionist actions, in particular against China, have been multiplying in recent years, even within the confines of WTO rules. In November 2008, and April 2009, George Bush and Mr Obama, respectively, on both occasions joined by other leaders of the G20, pledged to 'refrain from raising new barriers to investment or to trade in goods and services'; yet new barriers have steadily increased.

Until now Mr Obama has tried to allay fears that he is a bit of a protectionist by abandoning campaign threats to renegotiate the North American Free-Trade Agreement and to punish China for holding down its currency. He has surrounded himself with mainstream, pro-free-trade economists, watered down (though failed to veto) 'Buy America' provisions in the fiscal stimulus, and opposed carbon tariffs in the cap-and-trade bill now before Congress. Even now Mr Obama insists he is 'committed to pursuing expanded trade and new trade agreements', and this week he defended his action as nothing more than the enforcement of trade laws.

That, however, is a stretch. Mr Obama had no obligation to act. Under the terms of joining the WTO, China gave other countries the right until 2013 to impose temporary 'safeguards' against surges of Chinese imports. In America the relevant law, Section 421 of the Trade Act, does not require proof that China has broken international trade rules against subsidizing or dumping goods (i.e., selling below cost), only that the domestic industry was disrupted. Once the International Trade Commission, an independent panel, says that such disruption has occurred, it is up to the president to decide whether to impose remedies. Mr Bush declined to do so in the four Section 421 cases that came to him.

Politically, Mr Obama may have felt he had little choice. The United Steelworkers union filed the complaint in April 2009 and the law required Mr Obama to decide by September 17th 2009. Having promised repeatedly to enforce trade laws more vigorously than Mr Bush, Mr Obama presumably felt he needed to do something. The economic benefits to those who lobbied for protection, however, are minuscule. Domestic manufacturers have largely abandoned the low-end tyre market. The tariffs, which drop from 35% in the first year to 25% in the third, will mostly divert supply to Mexico, India, Indonesia and Brazil, says Tom Prusa, a Rutgers economist who has done work for tyre companies.

China also bears some blame. American negotiators were ready to withhold the tariffs if China made concessions, but to no avail. Mr Obama's defenders note that China would not have gained entry to the WTO without the 'safeguard' provisions, which bought political support among its trading partners. And voters and Congress might be less likely to support future trade agreements if the safeguards in existing agreements are never used.

Still, Mr Obama's imposition of tariffs will tempt more industries and unions to seek similar relief, and he will have to decide whether this decision is a template or an exception. Other countries, fearing a wave of diverted Chinese imports, could copy America's action. After Mr Bush raised steel tariffs in 2002, half a dozen other countries followed. Under the terms on which China entered the WTO, others can impose safeguards simply because America has. The European Union, however, would struggle to master enough support among its member states.

China itself faces a delicate balancing act. On September 15th 2009 more than 300 of the Communist Party's top officials held a four-day annual meeting in Beijing where, among other things, they were expected to decide whether to give President Hu's presumed successor, Vice-President Xi Jinping, a further boost by making him a deputy commander-in-chief of the armed forces. Succession politics could be complicated by high-level disputes over how to respond to the Americans.

But nor can he let Mr Obama entirely off the hook. Having announced an investigation into America's alleged dumping, it will be hard to back away. Indeed, the spat will awaken unpleasant memories of the controversy over China's accession to the WTO. China agreed to the safeguards clause in 2001 with gritted teeth, in part because its reformists saw WTO entry as a useful tool for encouraging market-oriented reforms. China's prime minister at the time, Zhu Rongji, was subjected to harsh criticism from conservatives at home for pressing so hard for WTO entry. Times are more difficult now than they were back then, so expect a few more fireworks.

Source: 'Playing with fire; The tyre wars.' *The Economist* [US] 19 September 2009: Biz/ed Custom Journals. Web. 2 February 2010. <http://find.galegroup.com/gps/start.do?prodId=IPS&userGroupName=bized>.

buying as much olive oil as they want from abroad, the supply of olive oil is no longer perfectly elastic at the world price. Instead, as long as the price of olive oil in Isoland is above the world price, the licence holders import as much as they are permitted, and the total supply of olive oil in Isoland equals the domestic supply plus the quota amount. That is, the supply curve above the world price is shifted to the right by exactly the amount of the quota. (The supply curve below the world price does not shift because, in this case, importing is not profitable for the licence holders.)

The price of olive oil in Isoland adjusts to balance supply (domestic plus imported) and demand. As the figure shows, the quota causes the price of olive oil to rise above the world price. The domestic quantity demanded falls from Q_1^D to Q_2^D, and the domestic quantity supplied rises from Q_1^S to Q_2^S. Not surprisingly, the import quota reduces olive oil imports.

Now consider the gains and losses from the quota. Because the quota raises the domestic price above the world price, domestic sellers are better off, and domestic buyers are worse off. In addition, the licence holders are better off because they make a profit from buying at the world price and selling at the higher domestic price. To measure these gains and losses, we look at the changes in consumer surplus, producer surplus and licence-holder surplus.

Before the government imposes the quota, the domestic price equals the world price. Consumer surplus, the area between the demand curve and the world price, is area A + B + C + D + E′ + E″ + F. Producer surplus, the area between the supply curve and the world price, is area G. The surplus of licence holders equals zero because there are no licences. Total surplus, the sum of consumer, producer and licence-holder surplus, is area A + B + C + D + E′ + E″ + F + G.

After the government imposes the import quota and issues the licences, the domestic price exceeds the world price. Domestic consumers get surplus equal to area A + B, and domestic producers get surplus equal to area C + G. The licence holders make a profit on each unit imported equal to the difference between the Isolandian price of olive oil and the world price. Their surplus equals this price differential times the quantity of imports. Thus, it equals the area of the rectangle E′ + E″. Total surplus with the quota is the area A + B + C + E′ + E″ + G.

To see how total welfare changes with the imposition of the quota, we add the change in consumer surplus (which is negative), the change in producer surplus (positive) and the change in licence-holder surplus (positive). We find that total surplus in the market decreases by the area D + F. This area represents the deadweight loss of the import quota.

"You drive a Japanese car, drink French wine, eat Chinese food, own an American computer and holiday in Mexico. How can you be AGAINST free trade?!"

This analysis should seem somewhat familiar. Indeed, if you compare the analysis of import quotas in Figure 9.7 with the analysis of tariffs in Figure 9.6, you will see that they are essentially identical. Both tariffs and import quotas raise the domestic price of the good, reduce the welfare of domestic consumers, increase the welfare of domestic producers and cause deadweight losses. There is only one difference between these two types of trade restriction: a tariff raises revenue for the government (area E in Figure 9.6), whereas an import quota creates surplus for licence holders (area E′ + E″ in Figure 9.7).

Tariffs and import quotas can be made to look even more similar. Suppose that the government tries to capture the licence-holder surplus for itself by charging a fee for the licences. A licence to sell 1 tonne of olive oil is worth exactly the difference between the Isolandian price of olive oil and the world price, and the government can set the licence fee as high as this price differential. If the government does this, the licence fee for imports works exactly like a tariff: consumer surplus, producer surplus and government revenue are exactly the same under the two policies.

In practice, however, countries that restrict trade with import quotas rarely do so by selling the import licences. For example, in 1991 the European Union reached an agreement with Japan to 'voluntarily' limit the sale of Japanese cars in member countries of the EU. In this case, the Japanese government allocates the import licences to Japanese firms, and the surplus from these licences (area E′ + E") accrues to those firms. This kind of import quota is, from the standpoint of the welfare of the European Union, strictly worse than an EU tariff on imported cars. Both a tariff and an import quota raise prices, restrict trade and cause deadweight losses, but at least the tariff produces revenue for the European Union rather than for Japanese auto companies. It is perhaps not surprising, therefore, that this arrangement was terminated at the end of 1999.

Although in our analysis so far import quotas and tariffs appear to cause similar deadweight losses, a quota can potentially cause an even larger deadweight loss, depending on the mechanism used to allocate the import licences. Suppose that when Isoland imposes a quota, everyone understands that the licences will go to those who spend the most resources lobbying the Isolandian government. In this case, there is an implicit licence fee – the cost of lobbying. The revenues from this fee, however, rather than being collected by the government, are spent on lobbying expenses. The deadweight losses from this type of quota include not only the losses from overproduction (area D) and underconsumption (area F) but also whatever part of the licence-holder surplus (area E′ + E″) is wasted on the cost of lobbying.

The Lessons for Trade Policy

The team of Isolandian economists can now write to the new president:

Dear Madam President,

You asked us three questions about opening up trade. After much hard work, we have the answers.

Question: If the government allowed Isolandians to import and export olive oil, what would happen to the price of olive oil and the quantity of olive oil sold in the domestic olive oil market?

Answer: Once trade is allowed, the Isolandian price of olive oil would be driven to equal the price prevailing around the world.

If the world price is now higher than the Isolandian price, our price would rise. The higher price would reduce the amount of olive oil Isolandians consume and raise the amount of olive oil that Isolandians produce. Isoland

FYI

Public Choice Theory

There is a branch of economics called public choice theory which looks at the gains and losses associated with lobbying processes like that described in our analysis so far. One of the key concepts of public choice theory is rent seeking. Rent seeking refers to cases where resources are allocated to provide rents (returns) for individuals or groups and where those rents have negative social value.

The following example highlights the issue in relation to arguments for restrictions on imports, relating to labour.

Migrant Workers

The expansion of the EU in 2004 led to the possibility of an increase in the number of workers with free access to enter all EU countries. In the UK, there was much written about immigration into the UK from the new members of the EU. In particular, the number of workers coming into the UK from Poland received widespread press coverage.

Many Polish workers legitimately working in the UK brought with them a high level of skills, motivation, work ethic and expertise. There were plenty of employers willing to testify to the benefits these workers brought to the UK economy. There were some, however, who have expressed deep concern that the flood of migrant workers to the UK was damaging. The argument put forward was that these workers were taking jobs that could be done by UK workers and that they were taking these jobs because they are prepared to work for substantially less than UK workers would be.

In 2007 Bulgaria and Romania became part of the EU. There were fears that the migration seen from Polish workers would be repeated and as a result the government negotiated restrictions on the number of migrant workers who could come to the UK.

In this case, the rents are the wages paid to UK-based workers who get some preference over migrant workers who are now subject to a 'quota'. The costs are that the job concerned could be done by someone from Bulgaria (for example) at a lower wage, as well as to a higher quality with a subsequent benefit to society. The benefits to society as a whole of having migrant workers are subsumed amidst the fear of the effect of the flooding of the labour market with migrant workers.

The public choice theorist would be looking to judge empirically the effects of rent seeking in this case to determine the deadweight loss of the policy decision. The investigation would focus on whether the policy to raise the income of an individual or group (such as domestic-based workers in the UK) and the amount of resources that would be needed to raise that income in comparison to the losses gained by others in society would have an overall negative social impact or not.

would, therefore, become an olive oil exporter. This occurs because, in this case, Isoland would have a comparative advantage in producing olive oil.

Conversely, if the world price is now lower than the Isolandian price, our price would fall. The lower price would raise the amount of olive oil that Isolandians consume and lower the amount of olive oil that Isolandians produce. Isoland would, therefore, become an olive oil importer. This occurs because, in this case, other countries would have a comparative advantage in producing olive oil.

Question: Who would gain from free trade in olive oil and who would lose, and would the gains exceed the losses?

Answer: The answer depends on whether the price rises or falls when trade is allowed. If the price rises, producers of olive oil gain and consumers of olive oil lose. If the price falls, consumers gain and producers lose. In both cases, the gains are larger than the losses. Thus, free trade raises the total welfare of Isolandians.

Question: Should a tariff or an import quota be part of the new trade policy?

Answer: A tariff, like most taxes, has deadweight losses: the revenue raised would be smaller than the losses to the buyers and sellers. In this case, the deadweight losses occur because the tariff would move the economy closer to our current no-trade equilibrium. An import quota works much like a tariff and would cause similar deadweight losses. The best policy, from the standpoint of economic efficiency, would be to allow trade without a tariff or an import quota.

We hope you find these answers helpful as you decide on your new policy.

Your obedient servants,

Isolandian economics team

Quick Quiz Draw the supply and demand curve for wool suits in the country of Autarka. When trade is allowed, the price of a suit falls from 300 to 200 grams of gold. In your diagram, what is the change in consumer surplus, the change in producer surplus and the change in total surplus? How would a tariff on suit imports alter these effects?

FYI

Other Benefits of International Trade

Our conclusions so far have been based on the standard analysis of international trade. As we have seen, there are winners and losers when a nation opens itself up to trade, but the gains to the winners exceed the losses of the losers. Yet the case for free trade can be made even stronger. There are several other economic benefits of trade beyond those emphasized in the standard analysis. Here, in a nutshell, are some of these other benefits:

- *Increased variety of goods.* Goods produced in different countries are not exactly the same. German beer, for instance, is not the same as American beer. Free trade gives consumers in all countries greater variety from which to choose.
- *Lower unit costs through economies of scale.* Some goods can be produced at low unit or average cost only if they are produced in large quantities – a phenomenon called *economies of scale.* A firm in a small country cannot take full advantage of economies of scale if it can sell only in a small domestic market. Free trade gives firms access to larger world markets and allows them to realize economies of scale more fully.
- *Increased competition.* A company shielded from foreign competitors is more likely to have market power, which in turn gives it the ability to raise prices above competitive levels. This is a type of market failure. Opening up trade fosters competition and gives the invisible hand a better chance to work its magic.
- *Enhanced flow of ideas.* The transfer of technological advances around the world is often thought to be linked to international trade in the goods that embody those advances. The best way for a poor, agricultural nation to learn about the computer revolution, for instance, is to buy some computers from abroad, rather than trying to make them domestically.
- *Generates economic growth.* We have seen in Chapter 3 how gains from trade can benefit all countries involved. For poor countries, the increase in output can be a trigger to generating economic growth which may also bring an improvement in the standard of living for its citizens.

Thus, free international trade increases variety for consumers, allows firms to take advantage of economies of scale, makes markets more competitive facilitates the spread of technology and helps generate economic growth. If the Isolandian economists thought these effects were important, their advice to their president would be even more forceful.

THE ARGUMENTS FOR RESTRICTING TRADE

The letter from the economics team persuades the new president of Isoland to consider opening up trade in olive oil. She notes that the domestic price is now high compared to the world price. Free trade would, therefore, cause the price of olive oil to fall and hurt domestic olive oil producers. Before implementing the new policy, she asks Isolandian olive oil companies to comment on the economists' advice.

Not surprisingly, the olive oil companies are opposed to free trade in olive oil. They believe that the government should protect the domestic olive oil industry from foreign competition. Let's consider some of the arguments they might give to support their position and how the economics team would respond.

The Jobs Argument

Opponents of free trade often argue that trade with other countries destroys domestic jobs. In our example, free trade in olive oil would cause the price of olive oil to fall, reducing the quantity of olive oil produced in Isoland and thus reducing employment in the Isolandian olive oil industry. Some Isolandian olive oil workers would lose their jobs.

Yet free trade creates jobs at the same time that it destroys them. When Isolandians buy olive oil from other countries, those countries obtain the resources to buy other goods from Isoland. Isolandian workers would move from the olive oil industry to those industries in which Isoland has a comparative advantage. Although the transition may impose hardship on some workers in the short run, it allows Isolandians as a whole to enjoy a higher standard of living.

Opponents of trade are often sceptical that trade creates jobs. They might respond that *everything* can be produced more cheaply abroad. Under free trade, they might argue, Isolandians could not be profitably employed in any industry. As Chapter 3 explains, however, the gains from trade are based on comparative advantage, not absolute advantage. Even if one country is better than another country at producing everything, each country can still gain from trading with the other. Workers in each country will eventually find jobs in the industry in which that country has a comparative advantage.

The National Security Argument

When an industry is threatened with competition from other countries, opponents of free trade often argue that the industry is vital for national security. Free trade would allow Isoland to become dependent on foreign countries to supply vital resources. If a war later broke out, Isoland might be unable to produce enough to defend itself and remain self-sufficient.

Economists acknowledge that protecting key industries may be appropriate when there are legitimate concerns over national security. Yet they fear that this argument may be used too quickly by producers eager to gain at consumers' expense. Certainly, it is tempting for those in an industry to exaggerate their role in national defence to obtain protection from foreign competition.

The Infant Industry Argument

New industries sometimes argue for temporary trade restrictions to help them get started. After a period of protection, the argument goes, these industries will mature and be able to compete with foreign competitors. Similarly, older industries sometimes argue that they need protection to help them adjust to new conditions. In 2002, for example, when US President George Bush imposed steep tariffs on the import of steel from the European Union, he argued that the industry needed protection in order to be able to afford to pay the pensions and health care costs of its retired workers and while it was going through a period of adjustment in terms of making its production more efficient in order to be able to cope with intense foreign competition.

Economists are often sceptical about such claims. The primary reason is that the infant industry argument is difficult to implement in practice. To apply protection successfully, the government would need to decide which industries will eventually be profitable and decide whether the benefits of establishing these industries exceed the costs to consumers of protection. Yet 'picking winners' is extraordinarily difficult. It is made even more difficult by the political process, which often awards protection to those industries that are politically powerful. And once a powerful industry is protected from foreign competition, the 'temporary' policy is hard to remove.

In addition, many economists are sceptical about the infant industry argument even in principle. Suppose, for instance, that the Isolandian olive oil industry is young and unable to compete profitably against foreign rivals. Yet there is reason to believe that the industry can be profitable in the long run. In this case, the owners of the firms should be willing to incur temporary losses to obtain the eventual profits. Protection is not necessary for an industry to grow. Firms in various industries – such as many internet firms today – incur temporary losses in the hope of growing and becoming profitable in the future. And many of them succeed, even without protection from foreign competition.

The Unfair Competition Argument

A common argument is that free trade is desirable only if all countries play by the same rules. If firms in different countries are subject to different laws and regulations, then it is unfair (the argument goes) to expect the firms to compete in the international marketplace. For instance, suppose that the government of Neighbourland subsidizes its olive oil industry by giving olive oil companies large tax breaks. The Isolandian olive oil industry might argue that it should be protected from this foreign competition because Neighbourland is not competing fairly.

Would it, in fact, hurt Isoland to buy olive oil from another country at a subsidized price? Certainly, Isolandian olive oil producers would suffer, but Isolandian olive oil consumers would benefit from the low price. Moreover, the case for free trade is no different: the gains of the consumers from buying at the low price would exceed the losses of the producers. Neighbourland's subsidy to its olive oil industry may be a bad policy, but it is the taxpayers of Neighbourland who bear the burden. Isoland can benefit from the opportunity to buy olive oil at a subsidized price.

The Protection as a Bargaining Chip Argument

Another argument for trade restrictions concerns the strategy of bargaining. Many policy makers claim to support free trade but, at the same time, argue that trade restrictions can be useful when we bargain with our trading partners. They claim that the threat of a trade restriction can help remove a trade restriction already imposed by a foreign government. For example, Isoland might threaten to impose a tariff on olive oil unless Neighbourland removes its tariff on wheat. If Neighbourland responds to this threat by removing its tariff, the result can be freer trade.

The problem with this bargaining strategy is that the threat may not work. If it doesn't work, the country has a difficult choice. It can carry out its threat and implement the trade restriction, which would reduce its own economic welfare. Or it can back down from its threat, which would cause it to lose prestige in international affairs. Faced with this choice, the country would probably wish that it had never made the threat in the first place.

IN THE NEWS

Economics is a dynamic subject and accepted wisdoms can always be questioned. The belief that free trade makes everyone better off is widely accepted but, as with any theory, needs to be supported by observation and evidence. What happens if observation reveals something contrary to the accepted wisdom?

Economists Rethink Free Trade

It's no wholesale repudiation, to be sure, but something momentous is happening as doubts begin to creep in.

Many ordinary householders have long been suspicious of free trade, seeing it as a destroyer of good-paying jobs. Most economists, though, have told a different story. For them, free trade has been the great unmitigated good, the force that drives a country to shed unproductive industries, focus on what it does best, and create new, higher-skilled jobs that offer better pay than those that are lost. This support of free trade by the academic establishment is a big reason why global leaders are keen to be associated with a free-trade agenda. The experts they consult have always told them that free trade was the best route to ever higher living standards.

But something momentous is happening inside the church of free trade: doubts are creeping in. We're not talking wholesale, dramatic repudiation of the theory. Economists are, however, noting that their ideas can't explain the disturbing stagnation in income that much of the middle class is experiencing. They also fear a protectionist backlash unless more is done to help those who are losing out. 'Previously, you just had extremists making extravagant claims against trade,' says Gary C. Hufbauer, a senior fellow at the Peterson Institute for International Economics. 'Now there are broader questions being raised that would not have been asked 10 or 15 years ago.'

So global leaders may be consulting on trade with experts who feel a lot less confident of the old certainties than they did just a few years ago. From Alan S. Blinder, a former vice-chairman of the Federal Reserve and member of the Council of Economic Advisers in the Clinton Administration, to Dartmouth's Matthew J. Slaughter, an international economist who served on President George W. Bush's CEA, many in the profession are re-evaluating the impact of globalization. They have studied the growth of low-wage work abroad and seen how high-speed telecommunications make it possible to handle more jobs offshore. Now they fear these factors are more menacing than they first thought.

No one is suggesting that trade is bad for countries overall. According to estimates by the Peterson Institute and others, trade and investment liberalization over the past decades have added $500 billion to $1 trillion to annual income in the US, for example.

Yet concern is rising that the gains from free trade may increasingly be going to a small group at the top. For the vast majority of Americans, Dartmouth's Slaughter points out, income growth has all but disappeared in recent years. And it's not just the low-skilled who are getting slammed. Inflation-adjusted earnings have fallen in every educational category other than the 4% who hold doctorates or professional degrees. Such numbers, Slaughter argues, suggest the share of Americans who aren't included in the gains from

trade may be very big. '[That's] a very important change from earlier generations, and it should give pause to people who say they know what's going on,' he says.

Blinder warns the pain may just be starting. Millions of service jobs in the developed world could face competition from workers in India and other low-wage nations. Many of the newly vulnerable will be in skilled fields, such as accounting or research – jobs many global companies will be able to move offshore in ever greater numbers. 'It will be a messy process of adjustment, with a lot of victims along the way,' Blinder says.

In an interview with the *Financial Times* in 2008, Hillary Clinton agreed with economist Paul A. Samuelson's argument that traditional notions of comparative advantage may no longer apply. 'The question of whether spreading globalization and information technology are strengthening or hollowing out our middle class may be the most paramount economic issue of our time,' her chief economic adviser, Gene Sperling, recently wrote. Barack Obama's adviser, the University of Chicago's Austan D. Goolsbee, is not convinced free trade is the culprit behind the squeeze on incomes. But he believes many workers aren't sharing in the gains from open markets and fears a political blowback unless something is done.

What to do? Blinder argues for a big expansion of unemployment insurance and a major overhaul of programmes which are put in place to retrain manufacturing workers whose jobs disappear. More vocational training and wage insurance, which would partially reimburse displaced workers who take new jobs at lower pay, also figure in his proposals.

That's not enough, says Slaughter. He sees a need for some form of income redistribution to spread the gains from free trade to more workers. In a controversial article Slaughter co-wrote in the summer of 2007 for *Foreign Affairs*, he proposed 'A New Deal for Globalization' in which payroll taxes for workers earning below the national median income level would be eliminated. It's one more sign of how far the trade debate has moved.

by Jane Sasseen

Source: Adapted from: http://www.businessweek.com/magazine/content/08_06/b4070032762393.htm Accessed 2 February 2010.

CASE STUDY

Trade Agreements and the World Trade Organization

A country can take one of two approaches to achieving free trade. It can take a *unilateral* approach and remove its trade restrictions on its own. This is the approach that the United Kingdom took in the 19th century and that Chile and South Korea have taken in recent years. Alternatively, a country can take a *multilateral* approach and reduce its trade restrictions while other countries do the same. In other words, it can bargain with its trading partners in an attempt to reduce trade restrictions around the world.

Perhaps the most important example of the multilateral approach is the European Union (EU), which at the time of writing has a total membership of 27 with three candidate countries who have applied to join (Croatia, Turkey and the Former Yugoslav Republic of Macedonia). The EU is an example of a **customs union**. A customs union is a group of countries that agree not to impose any restrictions at all on trade between their own economies, but to impose the same restrictions as one another on goods imported from outside the group.

customs union
a group of countries that agree not to impose any restrictions at all on trade between their own economies, but to impose the same restrictions as one another on goods imported from countries outside the group

Two other examples of the multilateral approach are the North American Free Trade Agreement (NAFTA) – which in 1993 lowered trade barriers among the United States, Mexico and Canada – and the General Agreement on Tariffs and Trade (GATT), which is a continuing series of negotiations among many of the world's countries with the goal of promoting free trade. The United States helped to found GATT after World War II in response to the high tariffs imposed during the Great Depression of the 1930s. Many economists believe that the high tariffs contributed to the economic hardship during that period. GATT has successfully reduced the average tariff among member countries from about 40 per cent after World War II to about 5 per cent today.

The rules established under GATT are now enforced by an international institution called the World Trade Organization (WTO). The WTO was established in 1995 and has its headquarters in Geneva, Switzerland. As of February 2010 148 countries have joined the organization, accounting for about 98 per cent of world trade. Around 30 other nations are negotiating membership to the WTO. The functions of the WTO are to administer trade agreements, provide a forum for negotiations and handle disputes that arise among member countries.

What are the pros and cons of the multilateral approach to free trade? One advantage is that the multilateral approach has the potential to result in freer trade than a unilateral approach because it can reduce trade restrictions abroad as well as at home. If international negotiations fail, however, the result could be more restricted trade than under a unilateral approach.

In addition, the multilateral approach may have a political advantage. In most markets, producers are fewer and better organized than consumers – and thus wield greater political influence. Reducing the Isolandian tariff on olive oil, for example, may be politically difficult if considered by itself. The olive oil companies would oppose free trade, and the users of olive oil who would benefit are so numerous that organizing their support would be difficult. Yet suppose that Neighbourland promises to reduce its tariff on wheat at the same time that Isoland reduces its tariff on olive oil. In this case, the Isolandian wheat farmers, who are also politically powerful, would back the agreement. Thus, the multilateral approach to free trade can sometimes win political support when a unilateral reduction cannot.

Quick Quiz The textile industry of Autarka advocates a ban on the import of wool suits. Describe five arguments its lobbyists might make. Give a response to each of these arguments.

CONCLUSION

Economists and the general public often disagree about free trade. In particular, economists are usually opposed to trade restrictions while the general public often wants to see restrictions on trade in order to 'protect' the domestic economy from 'cut-throat' foreign competition.

To understand better the economists' view of trade, let's continue our parable. Suppose that the country of Isoland ignores the advice of its economics team and decides not to allow free trade in olive oil. The country remains in the equilibrium without international trade.

Then, one day, some Isolandian inventor discovers a new way to make olive oil at very low cost. The process is quite mysterious, however, and the inventor insists on keeping it a secret. What is odd is that the inventor doesn't need any workers or fields to make olive oil. The only input he requires is wheat.

The inventor is hailed as a genius. Because olive oil is used in so many products, the invention lowers the cost of many goods and allows all Isolandians to enjoy a higher standard of living. Workers who had previously produced olive oil do suffer when their factories close, but eventually they find work in other industries. Some become farmers and grow the wheat that the inventor turns into olive oil. Others enter new industries that emerge as a result of higher Isolandian living standards. Everyone understands that the displacement of these workers is an inevitable part of progress.

After several years, a newspaper reporter decides to investigate this mysterious new olive oil process. She sneaks into the inventor's factory and learns that the inventor is a fraud. The inventor has not been making olive oil at all. Instead, he has been smuggling wheat abroad in exchange for olive oil from other countries. The only thing that the inventor had discovered was the gains from international trade.

When the truth is revealed, the government shuts down the inventor's operation. The price of olive oil rises and workers return to jobs in olive oil factories. Living standards in Isoland fall back to their former levels. The inventor is jailed and held up to public ridicule. After all, he was no inventor. He was just an economist.

SUMMARY

- The effects of free trade can be determined by comparing the domestic price without trade to the world price. A low domestic price indicates that the country has a comparative advantage in producing the good and that the country will become an exporter. A high domestic price indicates that the rest of the world has a comparative advantage in producing the good and that the country will become an importer.
- When a country allows trade and becomes an exporter of a good, producers of the good are better off, and consumers of the good are worse off. When a country allows trade and becomes an importer of a good, consumers are better off, and producers are worse off. In both cases, the gains from trade exceed the losses.
- A tariff – a tax on imports – moves a market closer to the equilibrium that would exist without trade and, therefore, reduces the gains from trade. Although domestic producers are better off and the government raises revenue, the losses to consumers exceed these gains.
- An import quota – a limit on imports – has effects that are similar to those of a tariff. Under a quota, however, the holders of the import licences receive the revenue that the government would collect with a tariff.
- There are various arguments for restricting trade: protecting jobs, defending national security, helping infant industries, preventing unfair competition and responding to foreign trade restrictions. Although some of these arguments have some merit in some cases, economists believe that free trade is usually the better policy.

KEY CONCEPTS

world price, p. 176
tariff, p. 181
import quota, p. 183
customs union, p. 192

QUESTIONS FOR REVIEW

1. What does the domestic price that prevails without international trade tell us about a nation's comparative advantage?
2. When does a country become an exporter of a good? An importer?
3. Draw the supply and demand diagram for an importing country. What is consumer surplus and producer surplus before trade is allowed? What is consumer surplus and producer surplus with free trade? What is the change in total surplus?
4. Describe what a tariff is, and describe its economic effects.
5. What is an import quota? Compare its economic effects with those of a tariff.
6. List five arguments often given to support trade restrictions. How do economists respond to these arguments?
7. What is the difference between the unilateral and multilateral approaches to achieving free trade? Give an example of each.

PROBLEMS AND APPLICATIONS

1. France represents a small part of the world apple market.
   a. Draw a diagram depicting the equilibrium in the French apple market without international trade. Identify the equilibrium price, equilibrium quantity, consumer surplus and producer surplus.
   b. Suppose that the world apple price is below the French price before trade, and that the French apple market is now opened to trade. Identify the new equilibrium price, quantity consumed, quantity produced domestically and quantity imported. Also show the change in the surplus of domestic consumers and producers. Has domestic total surplus increased or decreased?
2. The world price of wine is below the price that would prevail in France in the absence of trade.
   a. Assuming that French imports of wine are a small part of total world wine production, draw a graph for the French market for wine under free trade. Identify consumer surplus, producer surplus and total surplus in an appropriate table.
   b. Now suppose that an outbreak of phyloxera (a sap sucking insect which damages grape vines) in California and South America destroys much of the grape harvest there. What effect does this shock have on the world price of wine? Using your graph and table from part (a), show the effect on consumer surplus, producer surplus and total surplus in France. Who are the winners and losers? Is France better or worse off?
3. The world price of cotton is below the no-trade price in country A and above the no-trade price in country B. Using supply and demand diagrams and welfare tables such as those in the chapter, show the gains from trade in each country. Compare your results for the two countries.
4. Suppose that European Union countries impose a common tariff on imported cars to protect the European car industry from foreign competition. Assuming that Europe is a price taker in the world car market, show on a diagram: the change in the quantity of imports, the loss to European consumers, the gain to European car manufacturers, government revenue and the deadweight loss associated with the tariff. The loss to consumers can be decomposed into three pieces: a transfer to domestic producers, a transfer to the government and a deadweight loss. Use your diagram to identify these three pieces.
5. Write a brief essay advocating or criticizing each of the following policy positions.
   a. The government should not allow imports if foreign firms are selling below their costs of production (a phenomenon called 'dumping').
   b. The government should temporarily stop the import of goods for which the domestic industry is new and struggling to survive.
   c. The government should not allow imports from countries with weaker environmental regulations than ours.
6. Suppose that a technological advance in Japan lowers the world price of televisions.
   a. Assume Switzerland is an importer of televisions and there are no trade restrictions. How does the technological advance affect the welfare of Swiss consumers and Swiss producers? What happens to total surplus in Switzerland?
   b. Now suppose that Switzerland has a quota on television imports. How does the Japanese technological advance affect the welfare of Swiss consumers, Swiss producers and the holders of import licences?
7. When the government of Tradeland decides to impose an import quota on foreign cars, three proposals are suggested: (1) Sell the import licences in an auction. (2) Distribute the licences randomly in a lottery. (3) Let people wait in line and distribute the licences on a first-come, first-served basis. Compare the effects of these policies. Which policy do you think has the largest deadweight losses? Which policy has the smallest deadweight losses? Why? (Hint: the government's other ways of raising tax revenue themselves all cause deadweight losses.)
8. (This question is challenging.) Consider a small country that exports steel. Suppose that a 'pro-trade' government decides to subsidize the export of steel by paying a certain amount for each tonne sold abroad. How does this export subsidy affect the domestic price of steel, the quantity of steel produced, the quantity of steel consumed and the quantity of steel exported? How does it affect consumer surplus, producer surplus, government revenue and total surplus? (Hint: the analysis of an export subsidy is similar to the analysis of a tariff.)

9. Examine a trade dispute or trade agreement that has been in the news lately. In this case, who do you think are the winners and losers from free trade? Which group has more political clout? Note: a good place to look for this information is the website of the World Trade Organization (http://www.wto.org).

For further resources, visit www.cengage.com/mankiw_taylor2

4

THE ECONOMICS OF THE PUBLIC SECTOR

10 EXTERNALITIES

Firms that make and sell paper also create, as a by-product of the manufacturing process, a chemical called dioxin. Scientists believe that once dioxin enters the environment it raises the population's risk of cancer, birth defects and other health problems.

Is the production and release of dioxin a problem for society? In Chapters 4 to 9 we examined how markets allocate scarce resources with the forces of supply and demand, and we saw that the equilibrium of supply and demand is typically an efficient allocation of resources. To use Adam Smith's famous metaphor, the 'invisible hand' of the marketplace leads self-interested buyers and sellers in a market to maximize the total benefit that society derives from that market. This insight is the basis for one of the *Ten Principles of Economics* in Chapter 1: markets are usually a good way to organize economic activity. Should we conclude, therefore, that the invisible hand prevents firms in the paper market from emitting too much dioxin?

Markets do many things well, but they do not do everything well. In this chapter we begin our study of another one of the *Ten Principles of Economics:* governments can sometimes improve market outcomes. We examine why markets sometimes fail to allocate resources efficiently, how government policies can potentially improve the market's allocation and what kinds of policies are likely to work best.

The market failures examined in this chapter fall under a general category called *externalities.* An externality arises when a person engages in an activity that influences the well-being of a bystander (a third party) who neither pays nor

© BURAK PEKAKCAN / ISTOCK

receives any compensation for that effect. If the impact on the bystander is adverse, it is called a *negative externality;* if it is beneficial, it is called a *positive externality.*

We have seen how the operation of markets is based on millions of decisions being made by individuals and groups. The invisible hand means that individuals and groups make decisions which are designed to maximize their individual or group welfare. In making these decisions there will be private costs and private benefits. In making a car journey, for example, a person incurs various private costs such as the fuel used in the journey, the wear and tear (depreciation) on the car, the contribution of the vehicle tax and insurance costs related to the journey that the individual has to pay. In using their car the individual also gains a number of private benefits; convenience, warmth, the pleasure of driving, listening to music on the radio, not to mention getting to a destination relatively quickly. However, in making the decision to make the journey the individual may not take into consideration the cost (or benefit) to society that is imposed as a result of that decision. An extra car on the road contributes to congestion, road wear and tear; there are the emissions that the car gives off, the noise pollution and the increased risk of accident which may cause injury or even death to a third party. There may also be some social benefits of the decision; using a car means that there is an extra seat available for someone else to use on public transport, for example.

These social costs are not taken into consideration by the individual as they get into their car. They are costs which have to be borne by a third party. The cost of repairing damaged roads, the cost of dealing with accident and injury, delays caused as a result of congestion, the effects and costs of dealing with pollution and so on, all have to be borne by others – often the taxpayer. Equally, any social benefits arising from the decision are gained by those not party to the initial decision without them having to pay for the benefit derived.

In the presence of externalities, society's interest in a market outcome extends beyond the well-being of buyers and sellers who participate in the market; it also includes the well-being of bystanders who are affected indirectly. Because buyers and sellers neglect the external effects of their actions when deciding how much to demand or supply, the market equilibrium is not efficient when there are externalities. That is, the equilibrium fails to maximize the total benefit to society as a whole. The release of dioxin into the environment, for instance, is a negative externality. Self-interested paper firms will not consider the full cost of the pollution they create and, therefore, will emit too much pollution unless the government prevents or discourages them from doing so.

Externalities come in many varieties, as do the policy responses that try to deal with the market failure. Here are some examples:

- The exhaust from cars is a negative externality because it creates smog that other people have to breathe. Drivers do not take into consideration this externality and so tend to drive too much thus increasing pollution. The government attempts to solve this problem by setting emission standards for cars. It also taxes petrol in order to reduce the amount that people drive.
- Restored historic buildings convey a positive externality because people who walk or drive by them can enjoy their beauty and the sense of history that these buildings provide. Building owners do not get the full benefit of restoration and, therefore, tend to discard older buildings too quickly. Many national governments respond to this problem by regulating the destruction of historic buildings and by providing tax incentives to owners who restore them.
- Barking dogs create a negative externality because neighbours are disturbed by the noise. Dog owners do not bear the full cost of the noise and, therefore, tend to take too few precautions to prevent their dogs from barking. The government may address this problem by making it illegal to 'disturb the peace'.

- Research into new technologies provides a positive externality because it creates knowledge that other people can use. Because inventors cannot capture the full benefits of their inventions, they tend to devote too few resources to research. The government addresses this problem partially through the patent system, which gives inventors an exclusive use over their inventions for a period of time.
- A programme of vaccination against a flu virus protects those who receive it from the risk of contracting the virus. Those who are not vaccinated, however, may receive some benefit too because the prevalence of the virus is lower and so there is a reduced risk that they will contract flu. Health services also benefit because they do not have to devote resources to treating those with flu. Governments encourage flu vaccinations because there are positive benefits to society as a whole.

In each of these cases, some decision maker fails to take account of the external effects of his or her behaviour. The government responds by trying to influence this behaviour to protect the interests of bystanders.

EXTERNALITIES AND MARKET INEFFICIENCY

In this section we use the tools from Chapter 7 to examine how externalities affect economic well-being. The analysis shows precisely why externalities cause markets to allocate resources inefficiently. Later in the chapter we examine various ways in which private actors and public policy makers may remedy this type of market failure.

Welfare Economics: A Recap

We begin by recalling the key lessons of welfare economics from Chapter 7. To make our analysis concrete, we will consider a specific market – the market for aluminium. Figure 10.1 shows the supply and demand curves in the market for aluminium.

As you should recall from Chapter 7, the supply and demand curves contain important information about costs and benefits. The demand curve for aluminium reflects the value of aluminium to consumers, as measured by the prices they are willing to pay. At any given quantity, the height of the demand curve shows the willingness to pay of the marginal buyer. In other words, it shows the value to the consumer of the last unit of aluminium bought. Similarly, the supply curve reflects the costs of producing aluminium. At any given quantity, the height of the supply curve shows the cost of the marginal seller. In other words, it shows the cost to the producer of the last unit of aluminium sold.

In the absence of government intervention, the price adjusts to balance the supply and demand for aluminium. The quantity produced and consumed in the market equilibrium, shown as Q_{MARKET} in Figure 10.1, is efficient in the sense that it maximizes the sum of producer and consumer surplus. That is, the market allocates resources in a way that maximizes the total value to the consumers who buy and use aluminium minus the total costs to the producers who make and sell aluminium.

Negative Externalities

Now let's suppose that aluminium factories emit pollution: for each unit of aluminium produced, a certain amount of a pollutant enters the atmosphere. This

FIGURE 10.1

The Market for Aluminium

The demand curve reflects the value to buyers, and the supply curve reflects the costs of sellers. The equilibrium quantity, Q_{MARKET}, maximizes the total value to buyers minus the total costs of sellers. In the absence of externalities, therefore, the market equilibrium is efficient.

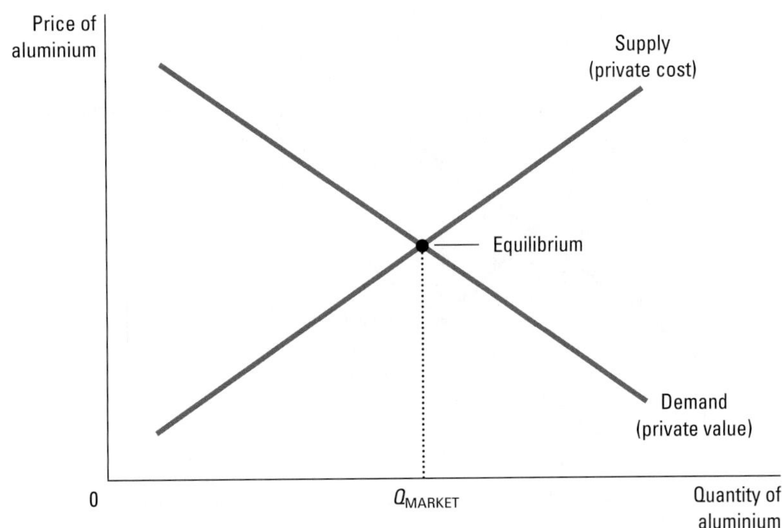

pollutant may pose a health risk for those who breathe the air, it is a negative externality. There is a cost involved in dealing with the effects of the pollutant which may be the health care that those affected have to receive. This cost is not taken into consideration by producers of aluminium who only consider the private costs of production. How does this externality affect the efficiency of the market outcome?

"I've been nominated 'Industrialist of the Year' and the Department of Environment are going to prosecute me for pollution."

Because of the externality, the cost to *society* of producing aluminium is larger than the cost to the aluminium producers. For each unit of aluminium produced, the *social (or external) cost* includes the private costs of the aluminium producers plus the costs to those bystanders affected adversely by the pollution. Figure 10.2 shows the social cost of producing aluminium. The social cost curve is above the supply curve because it takes into account the external costs imposed on society by aluminium producers. At every price the social cost is higher than the private cost so we can say that the social cost curve is the sum of the private costs and the social or external cost. The difference between these two curves reflects the social or external cost of the pollution emitted.

What quantity of aluminium should be produced? To answer this question, we once again consider what a benevolent social planner would do. The planner wants to maximize the total surplus derived from the market – the value to consumers of aluminium minus the cost of producing aluminium. The planner understands, however, that the cost of producing aluminium includes the external costs of the pollution.

The planner would choose the level of aluminium production at which the demand curve crosses the social cost curve. This intersection determines the optimal amount of aluminium from the standpoint of society as a whole. Below this

FIGURE 10.2

Pollution and the Social Optimum

In the presence of a negative externality, such as pollution, the social cost of the good exceeds the private cost. The optimal quantity, $Q_{OPTIMUM}$, is therefore smaller than the equilibrium quantity, Q_{MARKET}.

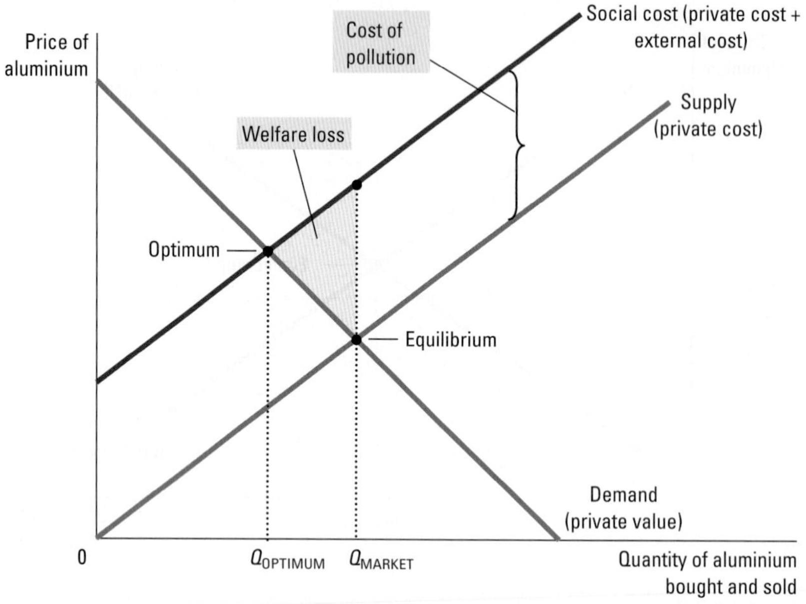

level of production, the value of the aluminium to consumers (as measured by the height of the demand curve) exceeds the social cost of producing it (as measured by the height of the social cost curve). The planner does not produce more than this level because the social cost of producing additional aluminium exceeds the value to consumers.

Note that the equilibrium quantity of aluminium, Q_{MARKET}, is larger than the socially optimal quantity, $Q_{OPTIMUM}$. The reason for this inefficiency is that the market equilibrium reflects only the private costs of production. In the market equilibrium, the marginal consumer values aluminium at less than the social cost of producing it. That is, at Q_{MARKET} the demand curve lies below the social cost curve. Thus, reducing aluminium production and consumption below the market equilibrium level raises total economic well-being. We can measure changes in well-being by the welfare loss associated with different market outcomes. We measure the difference in the value placed on each marginal unit of production of aluminium between $Q_{OPTIMUM}$ and Q_{MARKET} by consumers as shown by the shaded triangle in Figure 10.2.

How can the social planner achieve the optimal outcome? The answer is to somehow force the decision maker to take into consideration some or all of the social costs of the decision. In our example, one way to do this would be to tax aluminium producers for each tonne of aluminium sold. The tax would shift the supply curve for aluminium upward by the size of the tax. If the tax accurately reflected the social cost of the pollution released into the atmosphere, the new supply curve would coincide with the social cost curve. In the new market equilibrium, aluminium producers would produce the socially optimal quantity of aluminium.

The use of such a tax is called **internalizing an externality** because it gives buyers and sellers in the market an incentive to take account of the external effects of their actions. Aluminium producers would, in essence, take the costs of pollution into account when deciding how much aluminium to supply because the tax would make them pay for these external costs. The policy is based on one of the *Ten Principles of Economics:* people respond to incentives. Later in this chapter we consider other ways in which policy makers can deal with externalities.

internalizing an externality altering incentives so that people take account of the external effects of their actions

Positive Externalities

Although some activities impose costs on third parties, others yield benefits. For example, consider education. Education yields positive externalities because a more educated population leads to improved productivity and increases the potential for economic growth, which benefits everyone. Notice that the productivity benefit of education is not necessarily an externality: the consumer of education reaps most of the benefit in the form of higher wages. But if some of the productivity benefits of education spill over and benefit other people, as is the case if economic growth is stimulated, then this effect would count as a positive externality as well.

The analysis of positive externalities is similar to the analysis of negative externalities. As Figure 10.3 shows, the demand curve does not reflect the value to society of the good. The value placed on an activity such as education is valued less by consumers than the total value to society. Because the social value (or external benefit) is greater than the private value, the social value curve lies

FIGURE 10.3

Education and the Social Optimum

In the presence of a positive externality, the social value of the good exceeds the private value. The optimal quantity, $Q_{OPTIMUM}$, is therefore larger than the equilibrium quantity, Q_{MARKET}.

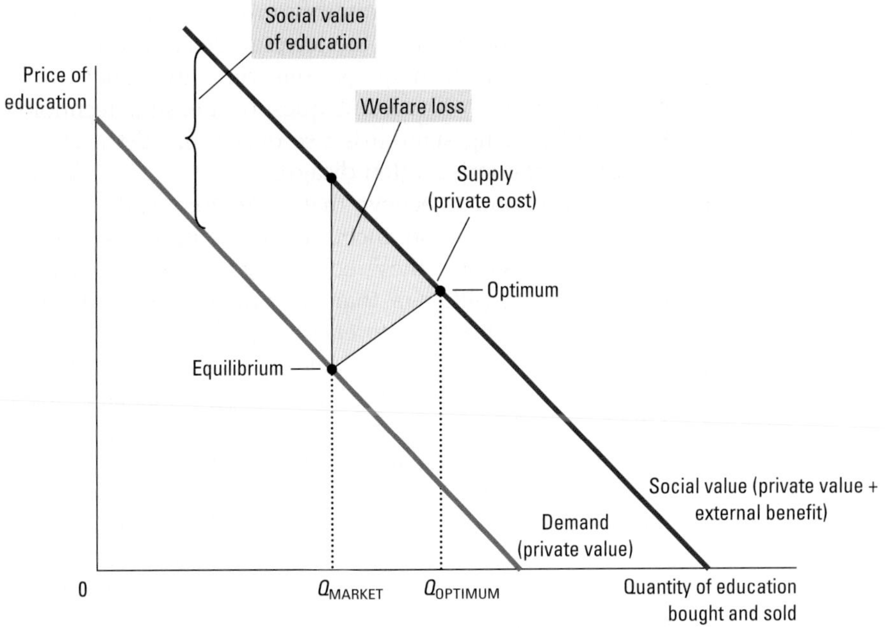

above the demand curve. The social value curve is the private value plus the external benefit to society at each price. At every price the benefit to society is greater than the private benefit, hence the social value curve lies to the right of the private benefit curve. The optimal quantity is found where the social value curve and the supply curve (which represents costs) intersect. Hence, the socially optimal quantity is greater than the quantity determined by the private market.

Once again, the government can correct the market failure by inducing market participants to internalize the externality. The appropriate response in the case of positive externalities is exactly the opposite to the case of negative externalities. To move the market equilibrium closer to the social optimum, a positive externality requires a subsidy. In fact, that is exactly the policy many governments follow by heavily subsidizing education.

To summarize: negative externalities lead markets to produce a larger quantity than is socially desirable. Positive externalities lead markets to produce a smaller quantity than is socially desirable. To remedy the problem, the government can internalize the externality by taxing goods that have negative externalities and subsidizing goods that have positive externalities.

CASE STUDY

Technology Spillovers and Industrial Policy

Consider the market for industrial robots. Robots are at the frontier of a rapidly changing technology. Whenever a firm builds a robot, there is some chance that it will discover a new and better design. This new design will benefit not only this firm but society as a whole because the design will enter society's pool of technological knowledge. This type of positive externality is called a *technology spillover.*

In this case, the government can internalize the externality by subsidizing the production of robots. If the government paid firms a subsidy for each robot produced, the supply curve would shift down by the amount of the subsidy, and this shift would increase the equilibrium quantity of robots. To ensure that the market equilibrium equals the social optimum, the subsidy should equal the value of the technology spillover.

How large are technology spillovers, and what do they imply for public policy? This is an important question because technological progress is the key to why living standards rise over time. Yet it is also a difficult question on which economists often disagree.

Some economists believe that technology spillovers are pervasive and that the government should encourage those industries that yield the largest spillovers. For instance, these economists argue that if making computer chips yields greater spillovers than making fish and chips, then the government should use the tax laws to encourage the production of computer chips relative to the production of fish and chips. Government intervention in the economy that aims to promote technology-enhancing industries is sometimes called *industrial policy.*

In the debate over climate change, some argue that a better way forward for society is to focus efforts on developing new technologies that will reduce our reliance on carbon-based technologies. (Technology, by the way, is defined as the application of knowledge to solve practical problems.) Governments throughout Europe and in the US are providing incentives for the development of so-called 'green technologies'. Some claim that development in this area could bring similar change and benefits to those of the information technology revolution which has taken place over the last 30 years. Key areas of green technology relate to energy production and efficiency, construction, green chemistry (using technologies that reduce or eliminate the use or production of substances that are hazardous or present long-term dangers) and green nanotechnology.

This latter technology involves the use of materials at a minute scale and may also incorporate green chemistry. One area where nanotechnology is being developed is the food industry. The technology could lead to more efficient use of pesticides and fertilizers, improving the safety and viability of genetic engineering, dealing with plant and animal pathogens, enhancing food flavours, removing pathogens from food, increasing output and productivity, improving the safety and efficiency of food packaging, and improving the way humans and animals absorb nutrients. The benefits of this technology are being promoted to the developing world, where there are still millions of people who have to suffer starvation and malnutrition, as well as the developed world.

Other economists are sceptical about industrial policy. Even if technology spillovers are common, the success of an industrial policy requires that the government be able to measure the size of the spillovers from different markets. This measurement problem is difficult at best. Moreover, without precise measurements, the political system may end up subsidizing those industries with the most political clout (remember public choice theory referred to in Chapter 9), rather than those that yield the largest positive externalities.

Another way to deal with technology spillovers is patent protection. The patent laws protect the rights of inventors by giving them exclusive use of their inventions for a period of time. When a firm makes a technological breakthrough, it can patent the idea and capture much of the economic benefit for itself. The patent is said to internalize the externality by giving the firm a **property right** over its invention. If other firms want to use the new technology, they have to obtain permission from the inventing firm and pay it some royalty. Thus, the patent system gives firms a greater incentive to engage in research and other activities that advance technology.

property rights
the exclusive right of an individual, group or organization to determine how a resource is used

Quick Quiz Give an example of a negative externality and a positive externality • Explain why market outcomes are inefficient in the presence of externalities.

PRIVATE SOLUTIONS TO EXTERNALITIES

We have discussed why externalities lead markets to allocate resources inefficiently, but have mentioned only briefly how this inefficiency can be remedied. In practice, both private actors and public policy makers respond to externalities in various ways. All of the remedies share the goal of moving the allocation of resources closer to the social optimum. In this section we examine private solutions.

The Types of Private Solution

Although externalities tend to cause markets to be inefficient, government action is not always needed to solve the problem. In some circumstances, people can develop private solutions.

IN THE NEWS

The concept of externalities has a large range of applications. The models developed in previous chapters relating to the measurement of well-being can be applied to debate a number of perceived problems in society including some issues that arouse a great deal of moral fervour / or anger. This article looks at one of these controversial issues.

Prostitution

In the UK in 2005, a debate at a conference of the nursing profession centred on problems in Liverpool caused by prostitution that have impacts on health and social care needs. The consequences of the existence of prostitution are of direct relevance to nurses not only in the UK but in many parts of Europe, particularly for those who work in major cities. The response of different countries to prostitution allows economists to analyse the externalities, both positive and negative and the associated changes in well-being associated with the practice. The UK government produced a consultation document on prostitution called *Paying the Price* in 2004. The document recognized that the law on prostitution in the UK was 'outdated, confusing and ineffective'. It looked at the possibilities for establishing managed zones for prostitutes to work in and for establishing legalized brothels.

Different laws relating to the practice exist in different European countries and even if it is illegal, governments have to accept that it goes on and that there are social and economic costs that exist. There is evidence that more liberal policies towards prostitution have been successful in The Netherlands, Australia and Germany. By amending legislation, the social costs could be accounted for more effectively and in addition the welfare of those who work in the industry could be more closely monitored and improved.

Some of the problems faced by those who work as prostitutes and the wider implications of this industry raise very important issues. These include drug abuse, child exploitation, crime, and health problems such as sexually transmitted diseases. For those who live near 'red light districts' there are also problems; they have to put up with the girls on the streets and their clients as well as the hangers on in the industry – the pimps and drug dealers who tend to be involved. Would more relaxed laws on prostitution lead to more working girls (and men) being prepared to seek help and advice as a result of removing the fear of prosecution?

Legalizing prostitution, for example, might lead to the externalities being internalized. This means that the external costs (and benefits) of a problem would now be accounted for in decision-making. A prostitute who freely goes to a health clinic for regular check-ups and health advice (because they do not have to fear prosecution) may contribute to the reduction in sexually transmitted diseases which society (the taxpayer in this case) has to pay for through treatment via publicly funded health services. Taking the industry out of the twilight world of criminality would also enable the authorities to monitor what goes on, help reduce the incentives to criminal activity, including drug abuse and child exploitation, have brothels that were subject to minimum standards and regulations and so benefit those who wish to sell and buy these services, as well as releasing public resources such as policing and justice to deal with other criminal activity.

Of course, the problem is that the very idea of selling sex is something that arouses moral indignation. For the economist the job is to try and measure the costs and benefits of different policy options and present these to the policy makers for decision.

Sometimes, the problem of externalities is solved with moral codes and social sanctions. Consider, for instance, why most people do not litter. Although there are laws against littering, these laws are not vigorously enforced. Most people do not litter just because it is the wrong thing to do. Advertising and parental guidance help us to distinguish what society accepts as a norm for behaviour. This moral injunction tells us to take account of how our actions affect other people. In economic terms, it tells us to internalize externalities.

Another private solution to externalities is charities, many of which are established to deal with externalities. For example, Greenpeace, whose goal is to protect the environment, is a non-profit organization funded with private donations. As another example, colleges and universities sometimes receive gifts from alumni, corporations and foundations in part because education has positive externalities for society.

The private market can often solve the problem of externalities by relying on the self-interest of the relevant parties. Sometimes the solution takes the form of integrating different types of business. For example, consider an apple grower and a beekeeper who are located next to each other. Each business confers a positive externality on the other: by pollinating the flowers on the trees, the bees help the orchard produce apples. At the same time, the bees use the nectar they get from the apple trees to produce honey. Nevertheless, when the apple grower is deciding how many trees to plant and the beekeeper is deciding how many bees to keep, they neglect the positive externality. As a result, the apple grower plants too few trees and the beekeeper keeps too few bees. These externalities could be internalized if the beekeeper bought the apple orchard or if the apple grower bought the beehives: both activities would then take place within the same firm, and this single firm could choose the optimal number of trees and bees. Internalizing externalities is one reason that some firms are involved in different types of business.

Another way for the private market to deal with external effects is for the interested parties to enter into a contract. In the foregoing example, a contract between the apple grower and the beekeeper can solve the problem of too few trees and too few bees. The contract can specify the number of trees, the number of bees, and perhaps a payment from one party to the other. By setting the right number of trees and bees, the contract can solve the inefficiency that normally arises from these externalities and make both parties better off. Joint ventures and partnering are good examples of where such contracts can generate positive externalities and improve efficiency.

The Coase Theorem

How effective is the private market in dealing with externalities? A famous result, called the **Coase theorem**, after British economist Ronald Coase, suggests that it can be very effective in some circumstances. According to the Coase theorem, if private parties can bargain *without cost* over the allocation of resources, then the private market will always solve the problem of externalities and allocate resources efficiently.

Coase theorem
the proposition that if private parties can bargain without cost over the allocation of resources, they can solve the problem of externalities on their own

To see how the Coase theorem works, consider an example. Suppose that Sofie owns a dog (a corgi, in fact) named Brandy. Brandy barks and disturbs Lucas, Sofie's neighbour. Sofie gets a benefit from owning the dog, but the dog confers a negative externality on Lucas. Should Sofie be forced to send Brandy to the dogs' home, or should Lucas have to suffer sleepless nights because of Brandy's barking?

Consider first what outcome is socially efficient. A social planner, considering the two alternatives, would compare the benefit that Sofie gets from the dog to the cost that Lucas bears from the barking. If the benefit exceeds the cost, it is efficient for Sofie to keep the dog and for Lucas to live with the barking. Yet if the cost exceeds the benefit, then Sofie should get rid of the dog.

According to the Coase theorem, the private market will reach the efficient outcome on its own. How? Lucas can simply offer to pay Sofie to get rid of the dog. Sofie will accept the deal if the amount of money Lucas offers is greater than the benefit of keeping the dog.

By bargaining over the price, Sofie and Lucas can always reach the efficient outcome. For instance, suppose that Sofie gets a €500 benefit from the dog and Lucas bears an €800 cost from the barking. In this case, Lucas can offer Sofie €600 to get rid of the dog, and Sofie will gladly accept. Both parties are better off than they were before, and the efficient outcome is reached.

It is possible, of course, that Lucas would not be willing to offer any price that Sofie would accept. For instance, suppose that Sofie gets a €1 000 benefit from the dog and Lucas bears an €800 cost from the barking. In this case, Sofie would turn down any offer below €1 000, while Lucas would not offer any amount above €800. Therefore, Sofie ends up keeping the dog. Given these costs and benefits, however, this outcome is efficient.

So far, we have assumed that Sofie has the legal right to keep a barking dog. In other words, we have assumed that Sofie can keep Brandy unless Lucas pays her enough to induce her to give up the dog voluntarily. How different would the outcome be, on the other hand, if Lucas had the legal right to peace and quiet?

According to the Coase theorem, the initial distribution of rights does not matter for the market's ability to reach the efficient outcome. For instance, suppose that Lucas can legally compel Sofie to get rid of the corgi. Although having this right works to Lucas's advantage, it probably will not change the outcome. In this case, Sofie can offer to pay Lucas to allow her to keep the dog. If the benefit of the dog to Sofie exceeds the cost of the barking to Lucas, then Sofie and Lucas will strike a bargain in which Sofie keeps the dog.

Although Sofie and Lucas can reach the efficient outcome regardless of how rights are initially distributed, the distribution of rights is not irrelevant: it determines the distribution of economic well-being. Whether Sofie has the right to a barking dog or Lucas the right to peace and quiet determines who pays whom in the final bargain. But, in either case, the two parties can bargain with each other and solve the externality problem. Sofie will end up keeping the dog only if the benefit exceeds the cost.

To sum up: the Coase theorem says that private economic actors can solve the problem of externalities among themselves. Whatever the initial distribution of rights, the interested parties can always reach a bargain in which everyone is better off and the outcome is efficient.

CASE STUDY

Chewing Gum

Walk down the streets of most towns and cities in Europe, look at the pavements and you will notice lots of black blobs on the floor. This is the remnants of chewing gum, which has been spat out and trodden into the flagstones and tarmac that form our walkways. Local government authorities have long complained about the cost of cleaning up the remains of chewing gum. This is an example of a social cost, a negative externality. One local authority in London points out that cleaning up chewing gum costs them in excess of £100 000 a year. Larger councils in metropolitan areas of the UK experience costs at least twice that amount. It is not only the cost of removing the gum; there is also the effect on energy use. Steam cleaning is a method employed to get rid of gum, but the cost of energy to generate the steam is also significant. In many cases, as with the black blobs, the problem becomes almost impossible to eradicate without very expensive treatments and they remain as a testament to our bad habits.

Whilst it is accepted as a social cost, coming up with a solution does not seem to be easy. One of the issues is who should be responsible for the cost and for solving the problem – should this be an example of the 'polluter pays' principle? In which case, who is the polluter: the chewing gum manufacturer or the individual who uses the chewing gum and then disposes of it in a way that reduces social value?

The industry has been investigating the problem and attempting to develop a gum that is both biodegradable and less sticky. Part of the production process and a key to the success of the gum industry has been the fact that it is stretchy, retains its properties in all conditions and has a long shelf life. Gum is made from synthetic rubber and has various sweeteners and flavourings added. Any change to the product would require significant research and investment by the industry.

Some argue that there is not enough incentive for firms to take research and development seriously and in such cases other strategies need to be adopted. One suggestion is to levy a tax on chewing gum to cover the cost of cleaning it up – 1p per packet has been suggested, but in Ireland a figure of 7p has been reported to be under consideration.

Other suggestions have been spot fines for people who do not dispose of chewing gum properly; educating the public to dispose of gum more responsibly; coating the pavements with a non-stick substance; and having gum boards where users can stick their gum. In one town in southern England a clean-up campaign was followed by the erection of a number of these gum boards – each one collected 1 600 pieces of gum every week and resulted in a lower reported incidence of gum litter on the streets.

In the United States a more radical solution was suggested by one irate commentator. Mark Frauenfelder noted that an industrial chewing gum removal machine was being marketed at $8 000. Frauenfelder noted that this seemed rather steep and that shopping mall and theme park owners could 'simply purchase a gun for less than $100 and shoot the morons who spit their gum on the ground'!

Why Private Solutions Do Not Always Work

Despite the appealing logic of the Coase theorem, private actors on their own often fail to resolve the problems caused by externalities. The Coase theorem applies only when the interested parties have no trouble reaching and enforcing an agreement. In the world, however, bargaining does not always work, even when a mutually beneficial agreement is possible.

Sometimes the interested parties fail to solve an externality problem because of **transaction costs**, the costs that parties incur in the process of agreeing to and following through on a bargain. In our example, imagine that Sofie and Lucas speak different languages so that, to reach an agreement, they will need to hire a translator. If the benefit of solving the barking problem is less than the cost of the translator, Sofie and Lucas might choose to leave the problem unsolved. In more realistic examples, the transaction costs are the expenses not of translators but of the lawyers required to draft and enforce contracts.

transaction costs
the costs that parties incur in the process of agreeing and following through on a bargain

At other times bargaining simply breaks down. The recurrence of wars and labour strikes shows that reaching agreement can be difficult and that failing to reach agreement can be costly. The problem is often that each party tries to hold out for a better deal. For example, suppose that Sofie gets a €500 benefit from the dog, and Lucas bears an €800 cost from the barking. Although it is efficient for

Lucas to pay Sofie to get rid of the dog, there are many prices that could lead to this outcome. Sofie might demand €750, and Lucas might offer only €550. As they haggle over the price, the inefficient outcome with the barking dog persists.

Reaching an efficient bargain is especially difficult when the number of interested parties is large because coordinating everyone is costly. For example, consider a factory that pollutes the water of a nearby lake. The pollution confers a negative externality on the local fishermen. According to the Coase theorem, if the pollution is inefficient, then the factory and the fishermen could reach a bargain in which the fishermen pay the factory not to pollute. If there are many fishermen, however, trying to coordinate them all to bargain with the factory may be almost impossible.

There are two other key reasons why reaching an efficient bargain may not arise: asymmetric information and the assumption of rational behaviour. An example of the former is that Sofie and Lucas may not have perfect knowledge of the costs and benefits to each other of the barking dog. In such situations it becomes very difficult to negotiate an efficient outcome. Both parties have imperfect information about the situation of the other and so incentives may be distorted. Lucas, for example, might exaggerate the cost to him of the barking dog whilst Sofie does the same with regard to the benefits she gets from keeping her dog. The situation is further complicated by the existence of *free riders*. Lucas may not be the only person in the neighbourhood suffering from the barking dog but others may not live directly next to Sofie. These other 'victims' can benefit from any agreement that Sofie and Lucas arrive at but do not pay any of the costs of solving the problem. If Lucas is aware of this then why should he pay the full amount to solve the problem when others will also benefit but not contribute? If all victims think the same way then the problem will remain unsolved and there will be an inefficient outcome.

As regards the assumption of rational behaviour, we assumed that an efficient outcome could be found if Lucas offered €600 for Sofie to get rid of the dog. If Sofie were able to put a price on the value of the dog to her and this was €500, then it would be irrational for her not to accept the money to get rid of the dog. The money could be used to secure something which gave greater value to her than the ownership of the dog. Of course, in real life such rational behaviour may be clouded by all sorts of behavioural and psychological influences that Sofie may not be able to value. The guilt she may feel in getting rid of the dog, the reactions of her friends and family, the sentimental value of the dog to her and so on.

When private bargaining does not work, the government can sometimes play a role. The government is an institution designed for collective action. In the polluting factory example above, the government can act on behalf of the fishermen, even when it is impractical for the fishermen to act for themselves. In the next section, we examine how the government can try to remedy the problem of externalities.

Quick Quiz Give an example of a private solution to an externality. • What is the Coase theorem? • Why are private economic actors sometimes unable to solve the problems caused by an externality?

PUBLIC POLICIES TOWARDS EXTERNALITIES

When an externality causes a market to reach an inefficient allocation of resources, the government can respond in one of two ways. *Command-and-control policies* regulate behaviour directly. *Market-based policies* provide incentives so that private decision makers will choose to solve the problem on their own.

Regulation

The government can remedy an externality by making certain behaviours either required or forbidden. For example, it is a crime in any European country to dump poisonous chemicals into the water supply. In this case, the external costs to society far exceed the benefits to the polluter. The government therefore institutes a command-and-control policy that prohibits this act altogether.

In most cases of pollution, however, the situation is not this simple. Despite the stated goals of some environmentalists, it would be impossible to prohibit all polluting activity. For example, virtually all forms of transport – even the horse – produce some undesirable polluting by-products. But it would not be sensible for the government to ban all transport. Thus, instead of trying to eradicate pollution altogether, society has to weigh the costs and benefits to decide the kinds and quantities of pollution it will allow.

Environmental regulations can take many forms. Sometimes the government may dictate a maximum level of pollution that a factory may emit. Other times the government requires that firms adopt a particular technology to reduce emissions. In all cases, to design good rules, the government regulators need to know the details about specific industries and about the alternative technologies that those industries could adopt. This information is often difficult for government regulators to obtain.

Pigovian Taxes and Subsidies

Instead of regulating behaviour in response to an externality, the government can use market-based policies to align private incentives with social efficiency. For instance, as we saw earlier, the government can internalize the externality by taxing activities that have negative externalities and subsidizing activities that have positive externalities. Taxes enacted to correct the effects of negative externalities are called **Pigovian taxes**, after the English economist Arthur Pigou (1877–1959), an early advocate of their use.

Pigovian tax
a tax enacted to correct the effects of a negative externality

Economists usually prefer Pigovian taxes over regulations as a way to deal with pollution because such taxes can reduce pollution at a lower cost to society. To see why, let us consider an example.

Suppose that two factories – a paper mill and a steel mill – are each dumping 500 tonnes of effluent into a river each year. The government decides that it wants to reduce the amount of pollution. It considers two solutions:

- *Regulation*. The government could tell each factory to reduce its pollution to 300 tonnes of effluent per year.
- *Pigovian tax*. The government could levy a tax on each factory of €50 000 for each tonne of effluent it emits.

The regulation would dictate a level of pollution, whereas the tax would give factory owners an economic incentive to reduce pollution. Which solution do you think is better?

Most economists would prefer the tax. They would first point out that a tax is just as effective as a regulation in reducing the overall level of pollution. The government can achieve whatever level of pollution it wants by setting the tax at the appropriate level. The higher the tax, the larger the reduction in pollution.

Indeed, if the tax is high enough, the factories will close down altogether, reducing pollution to zero.

The reason why economists would prefer the tax is that it reduces pollution more efficiently. The regulation requires each factory to reduce pollution by the same amount, but an equal reduction is not necessarily the least expensive way to clean up the water. It is possible that the paper mill can reduce pollution at lower cost than the steel mill. If so, the paper mill would respond to the tax by reducing pollution substantially to avoid the tax, whereas the steel mill would respond by reducing pollution less and paying the tax.

In essence, the Pigovian tax places a price on the right to pollute. Just as markets allocate goods to those buyers who value them most highly, a Pigovian tax allocates pollution to those factories that face the highest cost of reducing it. Whatever the level of pollution the government chooses, it can achieve this goal at the lowest total cost using a tax.

Economists also argue that Pigovian taxes are better for the environment. Under the command-and-control policy of regulation, the factories have no reason to reduce emission further once they have reached the target of 300 tonnes of effluent. By contrast, the tax gives the factories an incentive to develop cleaner technologies, because a cleaner technology would reduce the amount of tax the factory has to pay.

Pigovian taxes are unlike most other taxes. As we discussed in Chapter 8, most taxes distort incentives and move the allocation of resources away from the social optimum. The reduction in economic well-being – that is, in consumer and producer surplus – exceeds the amount of revenue the government raises, resulting in a deadweight loss. By contrast, when externalities are present, society also cares about the well-being of the bystanders who are affected. Pigovian taxes correct incentives for the presence of externalities and thereby move the allocation of resources closer to the social optimum. Thus, while Pigovian taxes raise revenue for the government, they also enhance economic efficiency.

CASE STUDY

Why Is Petrol Taxed so Heavily?

© WORLDPICS / SHUTTERSTOCK

Petrol tax: payable 24 hours a day.

In European countries, petrol is among the most heavily taxed goods in the economy. In the United Kingdom, for instance, more than three-quarters of what motorists pay for petrol is tax; in Norway it is over 70 per cent, in the Netherlands over 60 per cent, and in Germany and Sweden around 65 per cent.

Why is this tax so common? One possible answer is that tax on petrol is a Pigovian tax aimed at correcting three negative externalities associated with driving:

- *Congestion.* If you have ever been stuck in bumper-to-bumper traffic, you have probably wished that there were fewer cars on the road. A petrol tax keeps congestion down by encouraging people to take public transport, participate in carpools and live closer to work.
- *Accidents.* Whenever a person buys a large car or 4x4 vehicle like a Range Rover, he makes himself safer, but he puts his neighbours at risk. Statistical research has shown that a person driving a typical car is much more likely to die if hit by a 4x4 vehicle than if hit by another car. The petrol tax is an indirect way of making people pay when their large, petrol-thirsty vehicles impose risk on others, which in turn makes them take account of this risk when choosing what vehicle to purchase.

- *Pollution.* The burning of fossil fuels such as petrol increases carbon emissions which, it is argued, are contributing to global warming. Experts disagree about how dangerous this threat is, but there is no doubt that the petrol tax reduces the risk by reducing the use of petrol.

So the tax on petrol, rather than causing deadweight losses like most taxes, actually makes the economy work better. It means less traffic congestion, safer roads and a cleaner environment.

Tradable Pollution Permits

Returning to our example of the paper mill and the steel mill, let us suppose that, despite the advice of its economists, the government adopts the regulation and requires each factory to reduce its pollution to 300 tonnes of effluent per year. Then one day, after the regulation is in place and both mills have complied, the two firms go to the government with a proposal. The steel mill wants to increase its emission of effluent by 100 tonnes. The paper mill has agreed to reduce its emission by the same amount if the steel mill pays it €5 million. Should the government allow the two factories to make this deal?

From the standpoint of economic efficiency, allowing the deal is good policy. The deal must make the owners of the two factories better off, because they are voluntarily agreeing to it. Moreover, the deal does not have any external effects because the total amount of pollution remains the same. Thus, social welfare is enhanced by allowing the paper mill to sell its right to pollute to the steel mill.

The same logic applies to any voluntary transfer of the right to pollute from one firm to another. If the government allows firms to make these deals, it will, in essence, have created a new scarce resource: pollution permits. A market to trade these permits will eventually develop, and that market will be governed by the forces of supply and demand. The invisible hand will ensure that this new market efficiently allocates the right to pollute. The firms that can reduce pollution only at high cost will be willing to pay the most for the pollution permits. The firms that can reduce pollution at low cost will prefer to sell whatever permits they have.

One advantage of allowing a market for pollution permits is that the initial allocation of pollution permits among firms does not matter from the standpoint of economic efficiency. The logic behind this conclusion is similar to that behind the Coase theorem. Those firms that can reduce pollution most easily would be willing to sell whatever permits they get, and those firms that can reduce pollution only at high cost would be willing to buy whatever permits they need. As long as there is a free market for the pollution rights, the final allocation will be efficient whatever the initial allocation.

Although reducing pollution using pollution permits may seem quite different from using Pigovian taxes, in fact the two policies have much in common. In both cases, firms pay for their pollution. With Pigovian taxes, polluting firms must pay a tax to the government. With pollution permits, polluting firms must pay to buy the permit. (Even firms that already own permits must pay to pollute: the opportunity cost of polluting is what they could have received by selling their permits on the open market.) Both Pigovian taxes and pollution permits internalize the externality of pollution by making it costly for firms to pollute.

The similarity of the two policies can be seen by considering the market for pollution. Both panels in Figure 10.4 show the demand curve for the right to pollute. This curve shows that the lower the price of polluting, the more firms will choose to pollute. In panel (a) the government uses a Pigovian tax to set a price for pollution. In this case, the supply curve for pollution rights is perfectly elastic

FIGURE 10.4

The Equivalence of Pigovian Taxes and Pollution Permits

In panel (a) the government sets a price on pollution by levying a Pigovian tax, and the demand curve determines the quantity of pollution. In panel (b) the government limits the quantity of pollution by limiting the number of pollution permits, and the demand curve determines the price of pollution. The price and quantity of pollution are the same in the two cases.

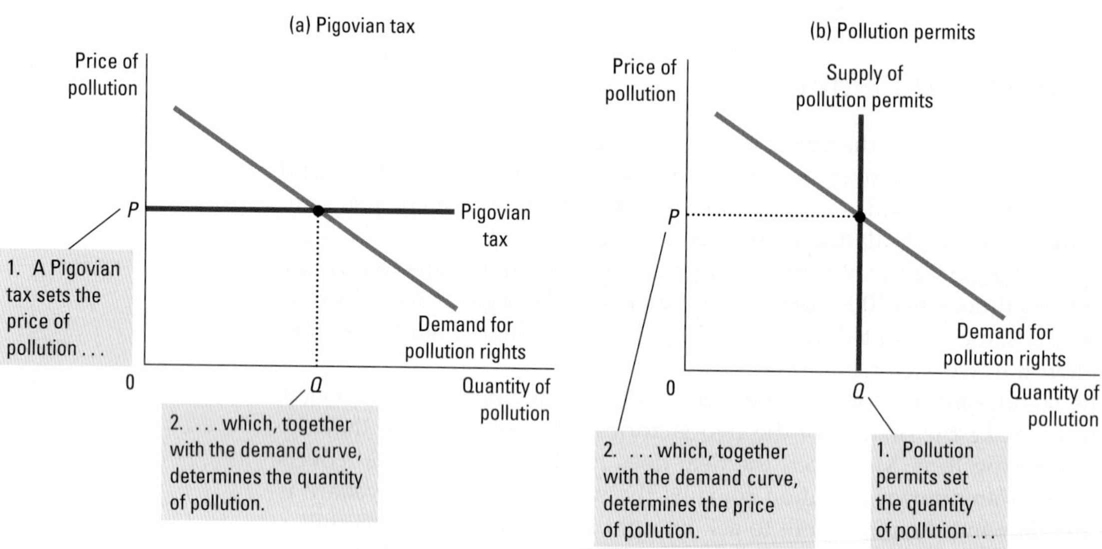

(because firms can pollute as much as they want by paying the tax), and the position of the demand curve determines the quantity of pollution. In panel (b) the government sets a quantity of pollution by issuing pollution permits. In this case, the supply curve for pollution rights is perfectly inelastic (because the quantity of pollution is fixed by the number of permits), and the position of the demand curve determines the price of pollution. Hence, for any given demand curve for pollution, the government can achieve any point on the demand curve either by setting a price with a Pigovian tax or by setting a quantity with pollution permits.

In some circumstances, however, selling pollution permits may be better than levying a Pigovian tax. Suppose the government wants no more than 600 tonnes of effluent to be dumped into the river. But, because the government does not know the demand curve for pollution, it is not sure what size tax would achieve that goal. In this case, it can simply auction off 600 pollution permits. The auction price would yield the appropriate size of the Pigovian tax.

The idea of the government auctioning off the right to pollute may at first sound like a creature of some economist's imagination. And, in fact, that is how the idea began. But a number of governments around the world – in particular the US government – have used such a system as a way to control pollution. In 2002, European Union environment ministers unanimously agreed to set up a market to trade pollution permits for carbon dioxide (CO_2), the main so-called greenhouse gas of concern. Pollution permits, like Pigovian taxes, are increasingly being viewed as a cost-effective way to keep the environment clean.

PUBLIC/PRIVATE POLICIES TOWARDS EXTERNALITIES

Property Rights

In some cases, private solutions to externalities can occur but need some form of legal back-up to be able to work. One such example is the establishment of property rights. In order for any economy to work efficiently, a system of property rights has to be established and understood. This is not as easy as it sounds, however. Property rights grant the exclusive right of an individual, group or organization to determine how a resource is used. The basic theory is this. If you decided to throw a brick through the window of my house I would be well within my rights to expect legal redress. The reason is that you have caused damage to my property and provided I can prove it was you who caused the damage and that I am the legal owner of the house, I can expect compensation, under the law, to put right the damage. This may include replacing the window pane and for any emotional trauma I have experienced.

With things such as rivers, streams, land and air it is less easy to establish who are the legal owners. If some system could be devised whereby the ownership of property could be established then those that cause damage to that property can be brought to book! Extending property rights, therefore, might be one area where externalities can be internalized. For example, if property rights over the air that we breathe can be extended, then any firm polluting that air (in whatever way, noise, smell, smoke, etc.) could face prosecution for doing so. The threat of prosecution is sufficient to act as an incentive to find ways of not polluting the air.

Extension of property rights also means that the owner of the property (which can be intellectual as well as physical) can also exercise the right to sell or share that property if they so wish at some mutually agreeable price. Extending property rights allows individuals, groups and organizations to be able to arrive at efficient solutions. If, for example, an individual was assigned property rights for the air 1 kilometre above their property, then if a nearby factory wanted to pollute that air they would have to enter into negotiations with the houseowner to do so at some mutually agreeable price. The resulting right to pollute could also be sold to another party. A more developed system of property rights can, therefore, improve well-being and it has been identified as playing a crucial role in good governance, particularly relevant for developing countries to be able to attract the sort of inward investment that will help their economies to grow.

There are problems with extending property rights, however. How do we apportion rights to such things as air, the seas, rivers and land? The cost of establishing property rights and getting international agreement on what they entail is considerable and may counteract the social benefits they might provide. If property rights were extended to the volume of air 1 km above a person's property, imagine the complexity of the negotiations that would have to be carried out with any business nearby, or airlines and the military for the right to share that air! Property owners may also have insufficient knowledge about their rights and exactly what they mean; it is also not a costless exercise to prove that property rights have been violated.

In the music industry the complexities of property rights have been the subject of debate and countless lawsuits in recent years. It not only relates to the issues of file sharing, pirating, copying CDs for personal use and downloading but also to the artists themselves and the rights to the music that they have written and performed. Intellectual property law is an incredibly complex area and different countries interpret property rights in different ways making any international agreement even more difficult. Despite the complexities, there have been efforts

IN THE NEWS

The increasing concern over levels of global carbon emissions has prompted governments around the world to look at so-called 'cap and trade' schemes. Markets to trade carbon emission permits have sprung up but whilst the theory may be relatively straighforward, the practice may introduce a number of imperfections that may not result in a socially desirable outcome being reached.

Carbon Trading Permits

The European Union has prided itself on being a leader in setting up carbon trading through the European Trading Scheme (ETS). The EU sets limits on the amount of carbon certain large industries like steel, cement and power generation are allowed to emit over a period of time. Permits are then issued to these industries and they have to work to meet their allowance. If they manage to reduce their carbon emissions below their permitted levels then they can sell the excess permits to others who may have had more difficulty meeting their targets.

Whilst such methods are, in theory, possible solutions to the problem of this type of pollution, the practice has seen different outcomes. The EU was accused of reducing the effectiveness of the system by *giving* permits to industry rather than auctioning them off. As a result there was a surplus of permits on the market and their price dropped. The effectiveness of the emissions trading scheme in reducing carbon emissions and acting as an incentive to producers to find more socially efficient ways of operating was called into question. The end of 2007 brought in the next phase of the scheme and it was hoped that the EU would learn the lessons from its mistakes.

The new limits, set to cover the period between 2008 and 2012, planned to tighten the amount of carbon pollution that can be emitted. In 2007 emissions of carbon were up by 1 per cent. However, the amount of carbon emitted was below targets set by the EU; 1.88 billion tonnes as against a target of 1.90 billion tonnes. It seems that France and Germany had been successful in having emissions below target levels whilst the UK, Spain and Italy were producing above their target levels. The overall figures, however, imply that tougher limits are required and that there would be a surplus of permits on the market, driving down prices.

The new targets set by the EU sought to reduce emissions by 9 per cent between 2008 and 2012. In addition, lessons from the first phase were learned and there was a larger number of permits that had to be bought by industry rather than being given to them. The new targets initially had some effect. The price of permits on the market began to rise. Since the beginning of 2008, when the new targets came into operation, permits were trading above €20 per tonne and analysts were expecting the price to rise further as the year progressed.

However, the recession in 2008 changed things. The global downturn led to a reduction in output and so firms were better able to meet their carbon emission limits. This also meant they were able to sell their permits and so the market saw a significant rise in the supply of permits which pushed down prices from a high of €30 to around €12 per permit. The Climate Change Summit, held in December 2009 in Copenhagen, was supposed to deliver a global agreement on carbon emissions and analysts were anticipating the market for carbon permits to rise significantly as a result of an announcement cutting carbon emissions. The failure to reach any binding agreement at the summit kept the market depressed and by early February 2010, prices were hovering at around €13 per permit.

At this level, the price of a permit does not present a sufficient incentive for firms to invest in technology to reduce carbon emissions. For firms to be prepared to incur the costs of investing in new technologies, the price of carbon permits must be high enough to give an incentive to divert resources to developing more efficient production methods and other technologies such as carbon capture and storage. If the cost of such investment is above the level a firm has to pay for a permit then there is no incentive to invest. Analysts have suggested that prices of permits need to be between €30 and €50 each to begin to have any effect on such investment; at these levels the opportunity cost of buying more permits to emit carbon starts to become too high. The market, it seems, has some way to go before it begins to deliver the social benefits hoped for.

to extend property rights to help bring social benefits. In many parts of Europe, property rights over public spaces such as national parks, rivers and seas have meant that environmental laws can be established and enforced and this has led to an improvement in well-being for millions who are able to use these spaces, enjoy cleaner rivers and exploit the resources of the sea.

Objections to the Economic Analysis of Pollution

Some environmentalists argue that it is in some sense morally wrong to allow anyone to pollute the environment in return for paying a fee. Clean air and clean water, they argue, are fundamental human rights that should not be debased by considering them in economic terms. How can you put a price on clean air and clean water? The environment is so important, they claim, that we should protect it as much as possible, regardless of the cost.

Economists have little sympathy with this type of argument. To economists, good environmental policy begins by acknowledging the first of the *Ten Principles of Economics* in Chapter 1: people face trade-offs. Certainly, clean air and clean water have value. But their value must be compared to their opportunity cost – that is, to what one must give up to obtain them. Eliminating all pollution is impossible. Trying to eliminate all pollution would reverse many of the technological advances that allow us to enjoy a high standard of living. Few people would be willing to accept poor nutrition, inadequate medical care or shoddy housing to make the environment as clean as possible.

Economists argue that some environmental activists hurt their own cause by not thinking in economic terms. A clean environment is a good like other goods. Like all normal goods, it has a positive income elasticity: rich countries can afford a cleaner environment than poor ones and, therefore, usually have more rigorous environmental protection. In addition, like most other goods, clean air and water obey the law of demand: the lower the price of environmental protection, the more the public will want. The economic approach of using pollution permits and Pigovian taxes reduces the cost of environmental protection and should, therefore, increase the public's demand for a clean environment.

Quick Quiz A glue factory and a steel mill emit smoke containing a chemical that is harmful if inhaled in large amounts. Describe three ways the town government might respond to this externality. What are the pros and cons of each of your solutions?

CONCLUSION

The invisible hand is powerful but not omnipotent. A market's equilibrium maximizes the sum of producer and consumer surplus. When the buyers and sellers in the market are the only interested parties, this outcome is efficient from the standpoint of society as a whole. But when there are external effects, such as pollution, evaluating a market outcome requires taking into account the well-being of third parties as well. In this case, the invisible hand of the marketplace may fail to allocate resources efficiently.

In some cases, people can solve the problem of externalities on their own. The Coase theorem suggests that the interested parties can bargain among themselves and agree on an efficient solution. Sometimes, however, an efficient outcome cannot be reached, perhaps because the large number of interested parties makes bargaining difficult.

When people cannot solve the problem of externalities privately, the government often steps in. Yet, even now, society should not abandon market forces entirely. Rather, the government can address the problem by requiring decision makers to bear the full costs of their actions. Pigovian taxes on emissions and pollution permits, for instance, are designed to internalize the externality of pollution. Increasingly, they are being seen as effective policies for those interested in protecting the environment. Market forces, properly redirected, are often the best remedy for market failure.

SUMMARY

- When a transaction between a buyer and seller directly affects a third party, the effect is called an externality. Negative externalities, such as pollution, cause the socially optimal quantity in a market to be less than the equilibrium quantity. Positive externalities, such as technology spillovers, cause the socially optimal quantity to be greater than the equilibrium quantity.
- Those affected by externalities can sometimes solve the problem privately. For instance, when one business confers an externality on another business, the two businesses can internalize the externality by merging. Alternatively, the interested parties can solve the problem by negotiating a contract. According to the Coase theorem, if people can bargain without cost, then they can always reach an agreement in which resources are allocated efficiently. In many cases, however, reaching a bargain among the many interested parties is difficult, so the Coase theorem does not apply.
- When private parties cannot adequately deal with external effects, such as pollution, the government often steps in. Sometimes the government prevents socially inefficient activity by regulating behaviour. At other times it internalizes an externality using Pigovian taxes. Another public policy is to issue permits. For instance, the government could protect the environment by issuing a limited number of pollution permits. The end result of this policy is largely the same as imposing Pigovian taxes on polluters.

KEY CONCEPTS

internalizing an externality, p. 203
property right, p. 205
Coase theorem, p. 207
transaction costs, p. 209
Pigovian taxes, p. 211

QUESTIONS FOR REVIEW

1. Give an example of a negative externality and an example of a positive externality.
2. Use a supply and demand diagram to explain the effect of a negative externality in production.
3. In what way does the patent system help society solve an externality problem?
4. List some of the ways that the problems caused by externalities can be solved without government intervention.
5. Imagine that you are a non-smoker sharing a room with a smoker. According to the Coase theorem, what determines whether your roommate smokes in the room? Is this outcome efficient? How do you and your roommate reach this solution?
6. What are Pigovian taxes? Why do economists prefer them over regulations as a way to protect the environment from pollution?

PROBLEMS AND APPLICATIONS

1. Do you agree with the following statements? Why or why not?
   a. 'The benefits of Pigovian taxes as a way to reduce pollution have to be weighed against the deadweight losses that these taxes cause.'
   b. 'When deciding whether to levy a Pigovian tax on consumers or producers, the government should be careful to levy the tax on the side of the market generating the externality.'
2. Consider the market for fire extinguishers.
   a. Why might fire extinguishers exhibit positive externalities?
   b. Draw a graph of the market for fire extinguishers, labelling the demand curve, the social value curve, the supply curve and the social cost curve.
   c. Indicate the market equilibrium level of output and the efficient level of output. Give an intuitive explanation for why these quantities differ.
   d. If the external benefit is €10 per extinguisher, describe a government policy that would result in the efficient outcome.
3. In many countries, contributions to charitable organizations are deductible from income tax. In what way does this government policy encourage private solutions to externalities?
4. Mick loves playing rock music at high volume. Luciano loves opera and hates rock music. Unfortunately, they are next-door neighbours in an apartment building with paper-thin walls.
   a. What is the externality here?
   b. What command-and-control policy might the landlord impose? Could such a policy lead to an inefficient outcome?
   c. Suppose the landlord lets the tenants do whatever they want. According to the Coase theorem, how might Mick and Luciano reach an efficient outcome on their own? What might prevent them from reaching an efficient outcome?
5. It is rumoured that the Swiss government subsidizes cattle farming, and that the subsidy is larger in areas with more tourist attractions. Can you think of a reason why this policy might be efficient?
6. Greater consumption of alcohol leads to more motor vehicle accidents and, thus, imposes costs on people who do not drink and drive.
   a. Illustrate the market for alcohol, labelling the demand curve, the social value curve, the supply curve, the social cost curve, the market equilibrium level of output and the efficient level of output.
   b. On your graph, shade the area corresponding to the deadweight loss of the market equilibrium. (Hint: the deadweight loss occurs because some units of alcohol are consumed for which the social cost exceeds the social value.) Explain.
7. Many observers believe that the levels of pollution in our economy are too high.
   a. If society wishes to reduce overall pollution by a certain amount, why is it efficient to have different amounts of reduction at different firms?
   b. Command-and-control approaches often rely on uniform reductions among firms. Why are these approaches generally unable to target the firms that should undertake bigger reductions?
   c. Economists argue that appropriate Pigovian taxes or tradable pollution rights will result in efficient pollution reduction. How do these approaches target the firms that should undertake bigger reductions?
8. The Pristine River (or the 'Blue Pristine', as it is affectionately known) has two polluting firms on its banks. European Industrial and Creative Chemicals each dump 100 tonnes of effluent into the river each year. The cost of reducing effluent emissions per tonne equals €10 for European Industrial and €100 for Creative. The government wants to reduce overall pollution from 200 tonnes to 50 tonnes per year.
   a. If the government knew the cost of reduction for each firm, what reductions would it impose to reach its overall goal? What would be the cost to each firm and the total cost to the firms together?
   b. In a more typical situation, the government would not know the cost of pollution reduction at each firm. If the government decided to reach its overall goal by imposing uniform reductions on the firms, calculate the reduction made by each firm, the cost to each firm and the total cost to the firms together.
   c. Compare the total cost of pollution reduction in parts (a) and (b). If the government does not know the cost of reduction for each firm, is there still some way for it to reduce pollution to 50 tonnes at the total cost you calculated in part (a)? Explain.
9. 'A fine is a tax for doing something wrong. A tax is a fine for doing something right.' Discuss.
10. Figure 10.4 shows that for any given demand curve for the right to pollute, the government can achieve the same

outcome either by setting a price with a Pigovian tax or by setting a quantity with pollution permits. Suppose there is a sharp improvement in the technology for controlling pollution.
   a. Using graphs similar to those in Figure 10.4, illustrate the effect of this development on the demand for pollution rights.
   b. What is the effect on the price and quantity of pollution under each regulatory system? Explain.

11. Suppose that the government decides to issue tradable permits for a certain form of pollution.
    a. Does it matter for economic efficiency whether the government distributes or auctions the permits? Does it matter in any other ways?
    b. If the government chooses to distribute the permits, does the allocation of permits among firms matter for efficiency? Does it matter in any other ways?

12. Some people argue that the primary cause of global warming is carbon dioxide, which enters the atmosphere in varying amounts from different countries but is distributed equally around globe within a year. In order to solve this problem, some economists have argued that carbon dioxide emissions should be reduced in countries where the costs are least, with the countries that bear that burden being compensated by the rest of the world.
    a. Why is international cooperation necessary to reach an efficient outcome?
    b. Is it possible to devise a compensation scheme such that all countries would be better off than under a system of uniform emission reductions? Explain.

13. Some people object to market-based policies to reduce pollution, claiming that they place a monetary value on cleaning our air and water. Economists reply that society *implicitly* places a monetary value on environmental clean-up even under command-and-control policies. Discuss why this is true.

14. (This problem is challenging.) There are three industrial firms in Eurovia.

Firm	Initial pollution level	Cost of reducing pollution by 1 unit
A	70 units	€20
B	80	25
C	50	10

The government wants to reduce pollution to 120 units, it gives each firm 40 tradable pollution permits.
    a. Who sells permits and how many do they sell? Who buys permits and how many do they buy? Briefly explain why the sellers and buyers are each willing to do so. What is the total cost of pollution reduction in this situation?
    b. How much higher would the costs of pollution reduction be if the permits could not be traded?

For further resources, visit www.cengage.com/mankiw_taylor2

11 PUBLIC GOODS AND COMMON RESOURCES

An old song lyric maintains that 'the best things in life are free.' A moment's thought reveals a long list of goods that the songwriter could have had in mind. Nature provides some of them, such as rivers, mountains, beaches, lakes and oceans. The government provides others, such as playgrounds, parks and parades. In each case, people do not pay a fee when they choose to enjoy the benefit of the good.

Free goods provide a special challenge for economic analysis. Most goods in our economy are allocated in markets, where buyers pay for what they receive and sellers are paid for what they provide. For these goods, prices are the signals that guide the decisions of buyers and sellers. When goods are available free of charge, however, the market forces that normally allocate resources in our economy are absent.

In this chapter we examine the problems that arise for goods without market prices. Our analysis will shed light on one of the *Ten Principles of Economics* in Chapter 1: governments can sometimes improve market outcomes. When a good does not have a price attached to it, private markets cannot ensure that the good is produced and consumed in the proper amounts. In such cases, government policy can potentially remedy the market failure and raise economic well-being.

THE DIFFERENT KINDS OF GOODS

How well do markets work in providing the goods that people want? The answer to this question depends on the good being considered. As we discussed in Chapter 7, we can rely on the market to provide the efficient number of ice cream cornets: the price of ice cream cornets adjusts to balance supply and demand, and this equilibrium maximizes the sum of producer and consumer surplus. Yet, as we discussed in Chapter 10, we cannot rely on the market to prevent aluminium manufacturers from polluting the air we breathe: buyers and sellers in a market typically do not take account of the external effects of their decisions. Thus, markets work well when the good is ice cream, but they work badly when the good is clean air.

In thinking about the various goods in the economy, it is useful to group them according to two characteristics:

excludability
the property of a good whereby a person can be prevented from using it when they do not pay for it

rivalry
the property of a good whereby one person's use diminishes other people's use

- Is the good **excludable**? Can people who do not pay for the use of a good be prevented from using the good?
- Is the good **rival**? Does one person's use of the good diminish another person's ability to use it?

Using these two characteristics, Figure 11.1 divides goods into four categories:

private goods
goods that are both excludable and rival

1. **Private goods** are both excludable and rival. Consider an ice cream cornet, for example. An ice cream cornet is excludable because it is possible to prevent someone from eating an ice cream cornet – you just don't give it to him. An ice cream cornet is rival because if one person eats an ice cream cornet, another person cannot eat the same cornet. Most goods in the economy are private goods like ice cream cornets. When we analysed supply and demand in Chapters 4, 5 and 6 and the efficiency of markets in Chapters 7, 8 and 9, we implicitly assumed that goods were both excludable and rival.

public goods
goods that are neither excludable nor rival

2. **Public goods** are neither excludable nor rival. That is, people cannot be prevented from using a public good, and one person's use of a public good does not reduce another person's ability to use it. For example, a country's national

FIGURE 11.1

Four Types of Goods

Goods can be grouped into four categories according to two questions: (1) Is the good excludable? That is, can people be prevented from using it? (2) Is the good rival? That is, does one person's use of the good diminish other people's use of it? This diagram gives examples of goods in each of the four categories.

Excludable?	Rival? Yes	Rival? No
Yes	Private goods • Ice cream cornets • Clothing • Congested toll roads	Natural monopolies • The fire service • Cable TV • Uncongested toll roads
No	Common resources • Fish in the ocean • The environment • Congested non-toll roads	Public goods • Flood-control dams • National defence • Uncongested non-toll roads

defence system: it protects all of the country's citizens equally and the fact that one person is being defended does not affect whether or not another citizen is defended.

3. **Common resources** are rival but not excludable. For example, fish in the ocean are a rival good: when one person catches fish, there are fewer fish for the next person to catch. Yet these fish are not an excludable good because, given the vast size of an ocean, it is difficult to stop fishermen from taking fish out of it when, for example, they have not paid for a licence to do so.

common resources
goods that are rival but not excludable

4. When a good is excludable but not rival, it is an example of a *natural monopoly*. For instance, consider fire protection in a small town. It is easy to exclude people from using this good: the fire service can just let their house burn down. Yet fire protection is not rival. Firefighters spend much of their time waiting for a fire, so protecting an extra house is unlikely to reduce the protection available to others. In other words, once a town has paid for the fire service, the additional cost of protecting one more house is small. In Chapter 15 we give a more complete definition of natural monopolies and study them in some detail.

In this chapter we examine goods that are not excludable and, therefore, are available to everyone free of charge: public goods and common resources. As we will see, this topic is closely related to the study of externalities. For both public goods and common resources, externalities arise because something of value has no price attached to it. If one person were to provide a public good, such as a national defence system, other people would be better off, and yet they could not be charged for this benefit. Similarly, when one person uses a common resource, such as the fish in the ocean, other people are worse off, and yet they are not compensated for this loss. Because of these external effects, private decisions about consumption and production can lead to an inefficient allocation of resources, and government intervention can potentially raise economic well-being.

Quick Quiz Define *public goods* and *common resources*, and give an example of each.

PUBLIC GOODS

To understand how public goods differ from other goods and what problems they present for society, let's consider an example: a fireworks display. This good is not excludable because it is impossible to prevent someone from seeing fireworks, and it is not rival because one person's enjoyment of fireworks does not reduce anyone else's enjoyment of them.

The Free Rider Problem

The citizens of a small Spanish town, Hereza, like seeing fireworks on 6 January when Spain celebrates Epiphany. Each of the town's 500 residents places a €10 value on the experience. The cost of putting on a fireworks display is €1 000. Because the €5 000 of benefits exceed the €1 000 of costs, it is efficient for Hereza residents to have a fireworks display on 6 January.

Would the private market produce the efficient outcome? Probably not. Imagine that Conchita, a Hereza entrepreneur, decided to put on a fireworks display.

free rider
a person who receives the benefit of a good but avoids paying for it

Conchita would surely have trouble selling tickets to the event because her potential customers would quickly figure out that they could see the fireworks even without a ticket. Because fireworks are not excludable, people have an incentive to be free riders. A **free rider** is a person who receives the benefit of a good but avoids paying for it.

One way to view this market failure is that it arises because of an externality. If Conchita did put on the fireworks display, she would confer an external benefit on those who saw the display without paying for it. When deciding whether to put on the display, Conchita ignores these external benefits. Even though a fireworks display is socially desirable, it is not privately profitable. As a result, Conchita makes the socially inefficient decision not to put on the display.

Although the private market fails to supply the fireworks display demanded by Hereza residents, the solution to Hereza's problem is obvious: the local government can sponsor a 12th Night celebration. The town council raises revenue by levying taxes on property in the area (in Spain these local property taxes are known as *Impuesto sobre Bienes Inmuebles* (IBI)). Suppose that the council uses this mechanism so as to raise on average an extra €2 from every resident of Hereza and then uses the resulting revenue to hire Conchita to produce the fireworks. Everyone in Hereza is better off by €8 – the €10 in value from the fireworks minus the €2 tax bill. Conchita can help Hereza reach the efficient outcome as a public employee even though she could not do so as a private entrepreneur.

The story of Hereza is simplified, but it is also realistic. In fact, many local councils in Spain do pay for fireworks for festivals, as do local councils in the United Kingdom on 5 November; local governments in France pay for fireworks on 14 July (Bastille Day) and many local governments in the USA pay for fireworks on 4 July (Independence Day). Moreover, the story shows a general lesson about public goods: because public goods are not excludable, the free rider problem prevents the private market from supplying them. The government, however, can potentially remedy the problem. If the government decides that the total benefits exceed the costs, it can provide the public good and pay for it with tax revenue, making everyone better off.

Some Important Public Goods

There are many examples of public goods. Here we consider three of the most important.

National Defence The defence of the country from foreign aggressors is a classic example of a public good. Once the country is defended, it is impossible to prevent any single person from enjoying the benefit of this defence. Moreover, when one person enjoys the benefit of national defence, he does not reduce the benefit to anyone else. Thus, national defence is neither excludable nor rival.

National defence is also one of the most expensive public goods. In the UK in 2008 it accounted for about €39 billion of government expenditure – the fourth largest category (behind social security, the National Health Service and education). In France the defence budget was around €32.5 billion, in Germany, €26 billion and in the United States a massive €502 billion! People disagree about whether these amounts are too small or too large, but almost no one doubts that some government spending on national defence is necessary. Even economists who advocate small government agree that the national defence is a public good the government should provide.

Basic Research The creation of knowledge is a public good. If a mathematician proves a new theorem, the theorem enters the general pool of knowledge that anyone can use without charge. Because knowledge is a public good,

"I just thought of a great new idea that will benefit all mankind. I call it 'TAXES'."

profit-seeking firms tend to free ride on the knowledge created by others and, as a result, devote too few resources to creating new knowledge.

In evaluating the appropriate policy towards knowledge creation, it is important to distinguish general knowledge from specific, technological knowledge. Specific, technological knowledge, such as the invention of a better battery, can be patented. The inventor thus obtains much of the benefit of his invention, although certainly not all of it. By contrast, a mathematician cannot patent a theorem; such general knowledge is freely available to everyone. In other words, the patent system makes specific, technological knowledge excludable, whereas general knowledge is not excludable.

The government tries to provide the public good of general knowledge in various ways. Government agencies such as the UK's Research Councils subsidize basic research in many academic disciplines, including medicine, mathematics, science and even economics. Some people justify government funding of space exploration programmes – for example by public funding of the European Space Agency (ESA) or the US National Aeronautics and Space Administration (NASA) – on the grounds that it adds to society's pool of knowledge. Certainly, many private goods, including bullet-proof vests and the instant drink Tang, an orange flavoured non-carbonated drink the brand name of which is now owned by Kraft, use materials that were first developed or made popular by scientists and engineers trying to land a man on the moon. Determining the appropriate level of governmental support for these endeavours is difficult because the benefits are hard to measure. Moreover, the politicians who appropriate funds for research usually have little expertise in science and, therefore, are not in the best position to judge what lines of research will produce the largest benefits.

Fighting Poverty Many government expenditure programmes are aimed at helping the poor. These anti-poverty programmes are financed by taxes on families that are financially more successful.

Economists disagree among themselves about what role the government should play in fighting poverty. Here we note one important argument: Advocates of anti-poverty programmes claim that fighting poverty is a public good.

Suppose that everyone prefers to live in a society without poverty. Even if this preference is strong and widespread, fighting poverty is not a 'good' that the private market can provide. No single individual can eliminate poverty because the problem is so large. Moreover, private charity is hard pressed to solve the problem: people who do not donate to charity can free ride on the generosity of others. In this case, taxing the wealthy to raise the living standards of the poor can make everyone better off. The poor are better off because they now enjoy a higher standard of living, and those paying the taxes are better off because they enjoy living in a society with less poverty.

The Difficult Job of Cost–Benefit Analysis

So far we have seen that the government provides public goods because the private market on its own will not produce an efficient quantity. Yet deciding that the government must play a role is only the first step. The government must then determine what kinds of public goods to provide and in what quantities.

Suppose that the government is considering a public project, such as building a new motorway or autobahn. To judge whether to build the motorway, it must compare the total benefits of all those who would use it to the costs of building and maintaining it. To make this decision, the government might hire a team of economists and engineers to conduct a study, called a **cost–benefit analysis**, the goal of which is to estimate the total costs and benefits of the project to society as a whole.

cost–benefit analysis
a study that compares the costs and benefits to society of providing a public good

Cost–benefit analysts have a tough job. Because the motorway will be available to everyone free of charge, there is no price with which to judge the value of the motorway. Simply asking people how much they would value the motorway is not reliable: quantifying benefits is difficult using the results from a questionnaire, and respondents have little incentive to tell the truth. Those who would use the motorway have an incentive to exaggerate the benefit they receive to get the motorway built. Those who would be harmed by the motorway have an incentive to exaggerate the costs to them to prevent the motorway from being built.

The efficient provision of public goods is, therefore, intrinsically more difficult than the efficient provision of private goods. Private goods are provided in the market. Buyers of a private good reveal the value they place on it by the prices they are willing to pay. Sellers reveal their costs by the prices they are willing to accept. By contrast, cost–benefit analysts do not observe any price signals when evaluating whether the government should provide a public good. Their findings on the costs and benefits of public projects are, therefore, rough approximations at best.

CASE STUDY

How Much is a Life Worth?

Ask yourself this question: how much would you say a human life is worth? Or put it another way, how much extra, per year, would you be prepared to pay in taxes to save one additional human life? €10, €10 000, €1 000 000? The question is almost impossible to answer, in part because it is so subjective (a normative proposition) and in part because most of us do not have €1 000 000 or anything like that to make the question feasible.

Imagine that you have been elected to serve as a member of your local town council. The town engineer comes to you with a proposal: the town can spend €10 000 to build and operate a traffic light at the intersection of Main Street (the town's busy main road) and Easy Street (the much quieter, leafy road where the stockbrokers live). At present, there are only signs instructing motorists entering Main Street from Easy Street that they must stop and give way to Main Street traffic. The benefit of the traffic light is increased safety. The engineer estimates, based on data from similar intersections, that the traffic light would reduce the risk of a fatal traffic accident over the lifetime of the traffic light from 1.6 to 1.1 per cent. Should you spend the money for the new light?

To answer this question, you turn to cost–benefit analysis. But you quickly run into an obstacle: the costs and benefits must be measured in the same units if you are to compare them meaningfully. The cost is measured in euros, but the benefit – the possibility of saving a person's life – is not directly monetary. To make your decision, you have to put a monetary value on a human life.

At first, you may be tempted to conclude that a human life is priceless. After all, there is probably no amount of money that you could be paid to voluntarily give up your life or that of a loved one. This suggests that a human life has an infinite monetary value.

For the purposes of cost–benefit analysis, however, this answer leads to nonsensical results. If we truly placed an infinite value on human life, we should be placing traffic lights on every street corner. Similarly, we should all be driving large cars with all the latest safety features, instead of smaller ones with fewer safety features. Yet traffic lights are not at every corner, and people sometimes choose to buy small cars without side-impact air bags or antilock brakes. In both our public and private decisions, we are at times willing to risk our lives to save some money.

Once we have accepted the idea that a person's life does have an implicit monetary value, how can we determine what that value is? One approach, sometimes used by courts to award damages in wrongful death suits, is to look at the total amount of money a person would have earned if he or she had lived. This approach was also used by the US government in deciding what amount of damages to award to the families of people killed in the terrorist attack on the World Trade Center in September 2001. Economists are often critical of this approach. It has the bizarre implication that the life of a retired or disabled person has no value. However, the earnings potential idea has been used as one way of measuring the value of a human life.

Health services across Europe have to find some way of making decisions about who to treat and who not to treat because the demand for health services far outstrips supply. The basis for such a decision can be to put an estimate on the contribution the individual might make to society based on their future earning capacity. Take the example of a patient who is 45. In theory that person has another 20 years of work left in them before the normal retirement age. If the average wage is €25 000 per annum, that means that this individual is worth €500 000 to society. If the treatment therefore costs less than €500 000 it could be argued it is worth treating this individual. One method that has been designed to try to come to terms with this is a unit of measurement of the outcome of treatment called quality-adjusted life years (QALYs). The concept was developed by health economics researchers at the University of York in the UK. A QALY gives a measure of the extra quality of life and the number of years of extra life resulting from a treatment.

To create a scale (the measure of health state) that covers the range of outcomes of a treatment (or intervention as it is called), researchers went from 1, the best possible state of health where all normal functions were at the disposal of the patient, to 0, the worst possible health state. Between these two scales (and it may seem rather bizarre) was 'death' – in other words, an intervention could be carried out that results in the death of the patient.

What could be worse than death? This is very much a normative issue but it may be possible to imagine a state of health that exists where a patient suffers intolerable physical and mental pain. Doctors can cite cases where patients are in a state where quality of life is both terrible and permanent and the patient has no feelings other than continuing pain. In such tragic situations, some might view the quality of life as being worse than being dead.

The researchers drew up the grades within this scale based on responses from patients about their preferences for different states of health. The grades within the scale, therefore, allow the user to be able to calculate the number of QALYs gained from a treatment. If treatment of a condition of a 50-year-old patient restores the person to full health and that person's life expectancy is 76, then the treatment will have resulted in 26 QALYs. If the treatment restores the person to a reasonable state of health but with some disabilities, such as some limitations to walking, breathing, sight, hearing or other problems rated on the scale as 0.75, then the number of QALYs would be 0.75 x 26 = 19.5 QALYs.

Having got some indication of an outcome, the cost of providing that outcome can be identified and as a result some measure of the value for money provided by health care treatment can be identified. Assume that the cost of three treatments is as follows:

- The average cost of a primary hip replacement is €4 160.
- The average cost of a heart transplant is €416 500.
- The average cost of treating a patient with an open lower limb fracture or dislocation is €2 521 per fracture.

Let us assume that the following outcomes outlined in Table 11.2 are possible after treating a 40-year-old patient:

TABLE 11.1

Treatment	Cost per patient	Measure of health state	Additional life expectancy	QALY	Cost per QALY
Hip replacement	€4 160	0.95	15	14.25	€291.92
Heart transplant	€16 500	0.83	10	8.3	€1 987.95
Fracture	€2 521	1.00	35	35	€72.03

Predictably the fracture comes out as providing the best value for money because of the amount of years of 'good health' it provides after treatment. We can also deduce from this that the opportunity cost of treating one person with a heart transplant is 6.8 people that could have been given a hip replacement and achieving the same cost per QALY – in other words the cost per outcome.

This system therefore provides the health professionals with some form of measure of the outcome of treatment, its associated cost, comparisons between hospitals and departments and thus the basis for decision-making.

Another way to value human life is to look at the risks that people are voluntarily willing to take and how much they must be paid for taking them. Mortality risk varies across jobs, for example. Construction workers in high-rise buildings face greater risk of death on the job than office workers do. By comparing wages in risky and less risky occupations, controlling for education, experience and other determinants of wages, economists can get some sense about what value people put on their own lives. Studies using this approach conclude that the value of a human life is about €10 million.

Other models look at the individual's willingness to pay to buy an extra year's worth of life or how much someone would be willing to pay to reduce the risk of death. There are inherent problems with all of these models but the essential basis of each of them is the fundamental concept of a trade-off as outlined in Principle 1 of the *Ten Principles of Economics*.

One economist, Orley Ashenfelter, calculated the value of a human life based on an analysis of the effect of a rise in speed limits on US roads. The rise in the speed limit meant that drivers drove slightly faster. This 'led to' a rise in deaths on the roads by 35 per cent. Ashenfelter then compared this to the data from areas where speed limits had not been changed. People in such areas drove slower.

The trade-off occurs between the numbers of hours saved as a result of faster travel against the lives lost as a result. Ashenfelter found that the saving in time was about 45 million hours whereas the increase in the number of deaths was 360. Dividing the two gives an average of 125 000 hours per life. Multiply this figure by the US average wage and he ended up with the figure of $980 000.

One problem with such calculations is that it might assume that everyone's life is of equal value. Treatment given to a 98-year-old may be valued differently compared to a 25-year-old. The question then arises, where do you draw the line? When does someone become too old to treat? Already there have been cases around Europe where doctors have refused to treat patients who have smoked and drank heavily despite repeated warnings because they feel they have brought the problems onto themselves and that the use of public money to treat such people is misdirected.

The basis of such decision-making, therefore, is to find some way in which human life can be valued and then set the benefits (measured by some agreed monetary value) against the costs of achieving the outcome. If the benefits outweigh the cost this provides the basis for making the decision. We can now return to our original example and respond to the town engineer. The traffic light reduces the risk of fatality by 0.5 percentage points. Thus, the expected benefit from having the traffic light is 0.005 × €10 million, or €50 000. This estimate of the benefit well exceeds the cost of €10 000, so you should approve the project.

Quick Quiz What is the free rider problem? • Why does the free rider problem induce the government to provide public goods? • How should the government decide whether to provide a public good?

COMMON RESOURCES

Common resources, like public goods, are not excludable: they are available free of charge to anyone who wants to use them. Common resources are, however, rival: one person's use of the common resource reduces other people's ability to

IN THE NEWS

Every year in Europe there are train accidents. The nature of such accidents often means that loss of life and serious injury are significant. Such accidents feature strongly in the news when they happen and there is invariably much debate following the accidents about improving safety. One of the key questions facing decision makers and those using (and paying) for train journeys is how much they are prepared to pay to improve safety on the railways and how this can be measured.

The Price of Safety

The catalogue of train accidents which occur in Europe builds every year. Many of these accidents lead to loss of life. In 2006, 23 people died and 10 were injured in north-western Germany when an elevated train, travelling at 200 km/h, crashed near Lathen in Lower Saxony; in August 2008, a EuroCity train travelling from Krakow in Poland to the Czech capital Prague crashed killing 7 people and injuring over 70; in July 2009, 22 people died when a train carrying liquefied petroleum gas derailed in Tuscany and exploded causing damage and injury to neighbouring houses. In December 2009 a large number of people were injured in the Croatian capital of Zagreb when a train crashed into barriers at the city's main railway station. In the UK crashes at Paddington in 1999 killed 31 and injured over 500; in Hatfield in 2000 a train crash killed 4 and injured over 100, in North Yorkshire in 2001 10 died and over 80 were injured, in Berkshire 7 died and over 100 were injured in a crash involving a suspected suicide. In Europe every year an average of 100 people are killed in train accidents. As with airplane accidents, the loss of life and injury when such incidents happen tends to be significant and the event high profile.

One of the outcomes of these accidents is calls for policies and procedures to be put in place to improve passenger safety, something which few people would argue with. In the wake of these accidents emotional friends and relatives call for systems to be implemented which will 'ensure that accidents like this will never happen again'. Politicians are often quick to tap into the emotional grief of the situation by promising to ensure that safety procedures are looked at and implemented to reduce the risk. The question has to be asked, is this a sensible promise to make and can it be supported in terms of cost–benefit analysis? In other words, is it worth spending *any* amount of money to bring the risk down to zero? Relatives of those who have died in such accidents are likely to agree that it is and might say the value of their loved one's life is priceless and that no-one else should have to experience the grief they have.

In looking at whether implementing safety systems would reduce the risk of accident is worthwhile, policy makers may conduct a cost–benefit analysis. There are technical features which can be put in place to help reduce the risk of accident on the railways. Two such systems are Automated Train Protection (ATP) and Train Protection Warning Systems (TPWS). On board computers receive information from sensors on the tracks and signalling systems to warn of potential problems allowing the driver to take action. If the driver does not react to the information then the train will automatically be brought to a halt. These systems will reduce the risk of accident but at what cost and can the cost of implementing them be justified?

When deciding whether to introduce additional safety measures, policy makers have to consider a number or factors. What is the risk of an event happening which leads to loss of life? How does this risk compare with other modes of transport (important in justifying any proposed expenditure), does the risk identified justify expenditure to reduce that risk? What is the value of the marginal benefit of reducing the risk compared to the marginal cost?

For example, assume that the risk of death on a train journey was put at

1: 100 000 km. In other words, for every 100 000 kilometres you travel on a train there is a chance you may be involved in an accident which results in your death. Would an individual agree that a reduction of the risk to 1: 50 000 km is a good thing?

Any rational person would agree that the lower the risk the better. One way to reduce the risk would be to implement ATP and TPWS systems on every train and throughout the rail network. The cost of doing this would amount to billions of euros. Ultimately this cost is likely to be passed on to the passenger in the form of higher prices. So, how much is an individual passenger willing to pay in extra fare to reduce the risk (which, remember, we assumed every rational person would agree to). Is paying an extra €5 per journey worth it? What about €10, €20, €100? At what point do passengers believe that the extra price they have to pay for the journey outweighs the benefits of the reduced risk?

These decisions are the sort policy makers have to make and economists can help in providing the data upon which such decisions can be based. Reducing the risk may be desirable but the cost of doing so may be prohibitive. So what is a tolerable risk? In the UK, the Health and Safety Executive (HSE) has devised a tolerability of risk framework (TOR) which was developed in relation to the construction of nuclear power stations, but which can be applied to other situations where risk has to be assessed. This framework was utilized by Professor Andrew Evans, of Imperial College London in a report published by the Royal Academy of Engineering in 2005[1]. The TOR framework ranks risk from 'broadly acceptable' through 'tolerable but must be reduced as low as reasonably practicable' to 'intolerable risk' where the risk cannot be justified. Professor Evans states, 'Individual risk is usually defined as the risk of death per year to a specified or representative individual from a specified activity or hazard.' Tolerable risk for an individual in rail travel is given as 10^{-4} per year. Having established the risk the next stage of a cost–benefit analysis can be undertaken.

Professor Evans notes that calculating these costs and benefits present numerous challenges but must adhere to two principles: '...first, that as far as possible, all costs and benefits, to whomsoever they accrue, should be included; and second, in the context of safety risks, the costs and benefits should be valued as those affected by the risks and costs of reducing them would value them.' Using methods based on these principles, an official value of preventing a fatality is given as £1.31 million (€1.51 million). Implementing automatic train protection was estimated at costing £15 million per prevented fatality (cost per prevented fatality, or CPF). Given that this is significantly higher than the value of preventing a fatality, economists might recommend that such a system was not implemented and that the funds might be better spent elsewhere where the CPF to value ratio is lower and yields a greater benefit than cost. Would you agree?

[1]http://www.raeng.org.uk/news/publications/list/lectures/Lloyds_Safety_Appraisal.pdf

use it. Thus, common resources give rise to a new problem. Once the good is provided, policy makers need to be concerned about how much it is used. This problem is best understood from the classic parable called the **Tragedy of the Commons**.

Tragedy of the Commons
a parable that illustrates why common resources get used more than is desirable from the standpoint of society as a whole

The Tragedy of the Commons

Consider life in a small medieval town. Of the many economic activities that take place in the town, one of the most important is raising sheep. Many of the town's families own flocks of sheep and support themselves by selling the sheep's wool, which is used to make clothing.

As our story begins, the sheep spend much of their time grazing on the land surrounding the town, called the Town Common. No family owns the land. Instead, the town residents own the land collectively, and all the residents are allowed to graze their sheep on it. Collective ownership works well because land is plentiful. As long as everyone can get all the good grazing land they want, the Town Common is not a rival good, and allowing residents' sheep to graze for free causes no problems. Everyone in town is happy.

As the years pass, the population of the town grows, and so does the number of sheep grazing on the Town Common. With a growing number of sheep and a fixed amount of land, the land starts to lose its ability to replenish itself. Eventually, the land is grazed so heavily that it becomes barren. With no grass left on the Town Common, raising sheep is impossible, and the town's once prosperous wool industry disappears and, tragically, many families lose their source of livelihood.

What causes the tragedy? Why do the shepherds allow the sheep population to grow so large that it destroys the Town Common? The reason is that social and private incentives differ. Avoiding the destruction of the grazing land depends on the collective action of the shepherds. If the shepherds acted together, they could reduce the sheep population to a size that the Town Common could support. Yet no single family has an incentive to reduce the size of its own flock because each flock represents only a small part of the problem.

In essence, the Tragedy of the Commons arises because of an externality. When one family's flock grazes on the common land, it reduces the quality of the land available for other families. Because people neglect this negative externality when deciding how many sheep to own, the result is an excessive number of sheep.

If the tragedy had been foreseen, the town could have solved the problem in various ways. It could have regulated the number of sheep in each family's flock, internalized the externality by taxing sheep, or auctioned off a limited number of sheep-grazing permits. That is, the medieval town could have dealt with the problem of overgrazing in the way that modern society deals with the problem of pollution.

In the case of land, however, there is a simpler solution. The town can divide up the land among town families. Each family can enclose its allotment of land with a fence and then protect it from excessive grazing. In this way, the land becomes a private good rather than a common resource. This outcome in fact occurred during the enclosure movement in England in the 17th century.

The Tragedy of the Commons is a story with a general lesson: when one person uses a common resource, he diminishes other people's enjoyment of it. Because of this negative externality, common resources tend to be used excessively. The government can solve the problem by reducing use of the common resource through regulation or taxes. Alternatively, the government can sometimes turn the common resource into a private good.

This lesson has been known for thousands of years. The ancient Greek philosopher Aristotle pointed out the problem with common resources: 'What is common to many is taken least care of, for all men have greater regard for what is their own than for what they possess in common with others.'

Some Important Common Resources

There are many examples of common resources. In almost all cases, the same problem arises as in the Tragedy of the Commons: private decision makers use the common resource too much. Governments often regulate behaviour or impose fees to mitigate the problem of overuse.

Clean Air and Water As we discussed in Chapter 10, markets do not adequately protect the environment. Pollution is a negative externality that can be remedied with regulations or with Pigovian taxes on polluting activities. One can view this market failure as an example of a common-resource problem. Clean air and clean water are common resources like open grazing land, and excessive pollution is like excessive grazing. Environmental degradation is a modern Tragedy of the Commons.

Congested Roads Roads can be either public goods or common resources. If a road is not congested, then one person's use does not affect anyone else. In this case, use is not rival, and the road is a public good. Yet if a road is congested, then use of that road yields a negative externality. When one person drives on the road, it becomes more crowded, and other people must drive more slowly. In this case, the road is a common resource.

One way for the government to address the problem of road congestion is to charge drivers a toll. A toll is, in essence, a Pigovian tax on the externality of congestion. Often, as in the case of local roads, tolls are not a practical solution because the cost of collecting them is too high. Nevertheless, tolls are often charged on stretches of motorways in continental Europe and the USA, and occasionally in the UK (on the M6, for example).

Sometimes congestion is a problem only at certain times of day. If a bridge is heavily travelled only during rush hour, for instance, the congestion externality is larger during this time than during other times of day. The efficient way to deal with these externalities is to charge higher tolls during rush hour. This toll would provide an incentive for drivers to alter their schedules and would reduce traffic when congestion is greatest.

Another policy that responds to the problem of road congestion, discussed in a case study in the previous chapter (page 212–213), is the tax on petrol. Petrol is a complementary good to driving: an increase in the price of petrol tends to reduce the quantity of driving demanded. Therefore, a petrol tax reduces road congestion. A petrol tax, however, is an imperfect solution to road congestion. The problem is that the petrol tax affects other decisions besides the amount of driving on congested roads. For example, the petrol tax discourages driving on non-congested roads, even though there is no congestion externality for these roads.

Fish, Whales and Other Wildlife Many species of animals are common resources. Fish and whales, for instance, have commercial value, and anyone can go to the ocean and catch whatever is available. Each person has little incentive to maintain the species for the next year. Just as excessive grazing can destroy the Town Common, excessive fishing and whaling can destroy commercially valuable marine populations.

The ocean remains one of the least regulated common resources. Two problems prevent an easy solution. First, many countries have access to the oceans, so any solution would require international cooperation among countries that hold different values. Secondly, because the oceans are so vast, enforcing any agreement is difficult. As a result, fishing rights have been a frequent source of international tension among normally friendly countries.

Within the United Kingdom and other European countries, various laws aim to protect fish and other wildlife. For example, the government charges for fishing and hunting licences, and it restricts the lengths of the fishing and hunting seasons. Fishermen are often required to throw back small fish, and hunters can kill only a limited number of animals or shoot certain wild birds such as pheasant or grouse during specified periods of the year. All these laws reduce the use of a common resource and help maintain animal populations.

CASE STUDY

Why the Cow is not Extinct

Throughout history, many species of animals have been threatened with extinction. When Europeans first arrived in North America, more than 60 million buffalo roamed the continent. Yet hunting the buffalo was so popular during the 19th century that by 1900 the animal's population fell to about

"Can the market become my friend too?"

400 before the government stepped in to protect the species. In some African countries today, the elephant faces a similar challenge, as poachers kill the animals for the ivory in their tusks.

Yet not all animals with commercial value face this threat. The cow, for example, is a valuable source of food, but no one worries that the cow will soon be extinct. Indeed, the great demand for beef seems to ensure that the species will continue to thrive.

Why is the commercial value of ivory a threat to the elephant, while the commercial value of beef is a guardian of the cow? The reason is that elephants are a common resource, whereas cows are a private good. Elephants roam freely without any owners. Each poacher has a strong incentive to kill as many elephants as he can find. Because poachers are numerous, each poacher has only a slight incentive to preserve the elephant population. By contrast, cows live on farms that are privately owned. Each farmer takes great effort to maintain the cow population on his farm because he reaps the benefit of these efforts.

Governments have tried to solve the elephant's problem in two ways. Some countries, such as Kenya, Tanzania and Uganda, have made it illegal to kill elephants and sell their ivory. Yet these laws have been hard to enforce, and elephant populations have continued to dwindle. By contrast, other countries, such as Botswana, Malawi, Namibia and Zimbabwe, have made elephants a private good by allowing people to kill elephants, but only those on their own property. Landowners now have an incentive to preserve the species on their own land, and as a result, elephant populations have started to rise. With private ownership and the profit motive now on its side, the African elephant might someday be as safe from extinction as the cow.

Quick Quiz Why do governments try to limit the use of common resources?

CONCLUSION: THE IMPORTANCE OF PROPERTY RIGHTS

In this chapter and the previous one, we have seen there are some 'goods' that the market does not provide adequately. Markets do not ensure that the air we breathe is clean or that our country is defended from foreign aggressors. Instead, societies rely on the government to protect the environment and to provide for the national defence.

Although the problems we considered in these chapters arise in many different markets, they share a common theme. In all cases, the market fails to allocate resources efficiently because *property rights* are not well established. That is, some item of value does not have an owner with the legal authority to control it. For example, although no one doubts that the 'good' of clean air or national defence is valuable, no one has the right to attach a price to it and profit from its use. A factory pollutes too much because no one charges the factory for the pollution it emits. The market does not provide for national defence because no one can charge those who are defended for the benefit they receive.

When the absence of property rights causes a market failure, the government can potentially solve the problem. Sometimes, as in the sale of pollution permits, the solution is for the government to help define property rights and thereby unleash market forces. Other times, as in the restriction on hunting seasons, the solution is for the government to regulate private behaviour. Still other times, as in the provision of national defence, the solution is for the government to supply a good that the market fails to supply. In all cases, if the policy is well planned and well run, it can make the allocation of resources more efficient and thus raise economic well-being.

SUMMARY

- Goods differ in whether they are excludable and whether they are rival. A good is excludable if it is possible to prevent someone from using it. A good is rival if one person's use of the good reduces other people's ability to use the same unit of the good. Markets work best for private goods, which are both excludable and rival. Markets do not work as well for other types of goods.
- Public goods are neither rival nor excludable. Examples of public goods include fireworks displays, national defence and the creation of fundamental knowledge. Because people are not charged for their use of the public good, they have an incentive to free ride when the good is provided privately. Therefore, governments provide public goods, making their decision about the quantity based on cost–benefit analysis.
- Common resources are rival but not excludable. Examples include common grazing land, clean air and congested roads. Because people are not charged for their use of common resources, they tend to use them excessively. Therefore, governments try to limit the use of common resources.

KEY CONCEPTS

excludability, p. 222
rivalry, p. 222
private goods, p. 222
public goods, p. 222
common resources, p. 223
free rider, p. 224
cost–benefit analysis, p. 226
Tragedy of the Commons, p. 231

QUESTIONS FOR REVIEW

1. Explain what is meant by a good being 'excludable'. Explain what is meant by a good being 'rival'. Is a pizza excludable? Is it rival?
2. Define and give an example of a public good. Can the private market provide this good on its own? Explain.
3. What is cost–benefit analysis of public goods? Why is it important? Why is it hard?
4. Define and give an example of a common resource. Without government intervention, will people use this good too much or too little? Why?

PROBLEMS AND APPLICATIONS

1. The text says that both public goods and common resources involve externalities.
   a. Are the externalities associated with public goods generally positive or negative? Use examples in your answer. Is the free market quantity of public goods generally greater or less than the efficient quantity?
   b. Are the externalities associated with common resources generally positive or negative? Use

examples in your answer. Is the free market use of common resources generally greater or less than the efficient use?

2. Think about the goods and services provided by your local government.
   a. Using the classification in Figure 11.1, explain what category each of the following goods falls into:
      - police protection
      - road gritting
      - education
      - rural roads
      - city streets.
   b. Why do you think the government provides items that are not public goods?
3. One of the UK's major broadcasting companies, the British Broadcasting Corporation (BBC) is funded largely by the sale of annual licences. Charles loves watching football matches on TV when the BBC broadcasts them, but he never buys a TV licence.
   a. What name do economists have for Charles?
   b. How can the government solve the problem caused by people like Charles?
   c. Can you think of ways the private market can solve this problem? How does the existence of cable or satellite TV alter the situation?
4. The text states that private firms will not undertake the efficient amount of basic scientific research.
   a. Explain why this is so. In your answer, classify basic research in one of the categories shown in Figure 11.1.
   b. What sort of policy has the United Kingdom adopted in response to this problem?
   c. It is often argued that this policy increases the technological capability of British producers relative to that of foreign firms. Is this argument consistent with your classification of basic research in part (a)? (Hint: can excludability apply to some potential beneficiaries of a public good and not others?)
5. Why is there litter along most major roads but rarely in people's gardens?
6. An *Economist* article (19 March 1994) states: 'In the past decade, most of the rich world's fisheries have been exploited to the point of near-exhaustion.' The article continues with an analysis of the problem and a discussion of possible private and government solutions.
   a. 'Do not blame fishermen for overfishing. They are behaving rationally, as they have always done.' In what sense is 'overfishing' rational for fishermen?
   b. 'A community, held together by ties of obligation and mutual self-interest, can manage a common resource on its own.' Explain how such management can work in principle, and what obstacles it faces in the real world.
   c. 'Until 1976 most world fish stocks were open to all comers, making conservation almost impossible. Then an international agreement extended some aspects of [national] jurisdiction from 12 to 200 miles offshore.' Using the concept of property rights, discuss how this agreement reduces the scope of the problem.
   d. The article notes that many governments come to the aid of suffering fishermen in ways that encourage increased fishing. How do such policies encourage a vicious cycle of overfishing?
   e. 'Only when fishermen believe they are assured a long-term and exclusive right to a fishery are they likely to manage it in the same far-sighted way as good farmers manage their land.' Defend this statement.
   f. What other policies to reduce overfishing might be considered?
7. In a market economy, information about the quality or function of goods and services is a valuable good in its own right. How does the private market provide this information? Can you think of any way in which the government plays a role in providing this information?
8. Do you think the internet is a public good? Why or why not?
9. High-income people are willing to pay more than lower-income people to avoid the risk of death. For example, they are more likely to pay for safety features on cars. Do you think cost–benefit analysts should take this fact into account when evaluating public projects? Consider, for instance, a rich town and a poor town, both of which are considering the installation of a traffic light. Should the rich town use a higher monetary value for a human life in making this decision? Why or why not?

For further resources, visit www.cengage.com/mankiw_taylor2

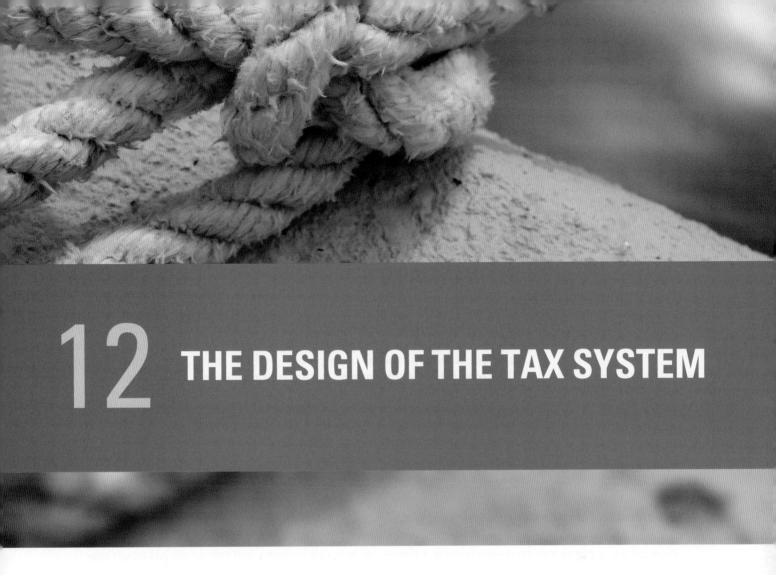

12 THE DESIGN OF THE TAX SYSTEM

Al 'Scarface' Capone, the notorious 1920s Chicago gangster and crime boss, was never convicted for his many violent crimes. Yet eventually he did go to jail – for tax evasion. Capone could, quite literally, get away with murder, but he couldn't get away with not paying his taxes. Taxes are inevitable because we as citizens expect the government to provide us with various goods and services. The previous two chapters have started to shed light on one of the *Ten Principles of Economics* from Chapter 1: the government can sometimes improve market outcomes. When the government remedies an externality (such as air pollution), provides a public good (such as national defence) or regulates the use of a common resource (such as fish in a public lake), it can raise economic well-being. Yet the benefits of government come with costs. For the government to perform these and its many other functions, it needs to raise revenue through taxation.

We began our study of taxation in earlier chapters, where we saw how a tax on a good affects supply and demand for that good. In Chapter 6 we saw that a tax reduces the quantity sold in a market, and we examined how the burden of a tax is shared by buyers and sellers, depending on the elasticities of supply and demand. In Chapter 8 we examined how taxes affect economic well-being. We learned that taxes cause deadweight losses: the reduction in consumer and producer surplus resulting from a tax exceeds the revenue raised by the government.

In this chapter we build on these lessons to discuss the design of a tax system. In particular, we consider the fundamental principles of taxation. Most people agree that taxes should impose as small a cost on society as possible and that the burden of taxes should be distributed fairly. That is, the tax system should be both efficient and equitable. As we will see, however, stating these goals is easier than achieving them.

When thinking about the tax system, it is useful to have in mind some basic facts about a particular tax system and so, for illustrative purposes, we'll start with a financial overview of the UK system. We will then provide some outline details of tax systems in other countries as a means of comparison. The website that accompanies this book will feature tax systems for other major European countries.

A FINANCIAL OVERVIEW OF THE UK GOVERNMENT

How much of the nation's income does the government take as taxes? Figure 12.1 shows UK government spending since 1900 as a percentage of GDP. Figure 12.2 shows UK total managed expenditure (spending by central and local government and public enterprises) as a proportion of GDP since 2000. Figure 12.1 shows that, over time, the government has taken a greater role in the economy. In 1910 government spending was about 15 per cent of total income; in the early years of the 21st century it was around 40 per cent. In other words, as the economy's income has grown, the government has grown even more. Perhaps the most striking feature of Figure 12.1, however, is the role of wars. The 20th century

FIGURE 12.1

UK Government Expenditure as a Percentage of GDP

This figure shows the expenditure of the UK government as a percentage of GDP, which measures the total income in the economy. It shows that the government plays a large role in the UK economy and that its role has grown over time.

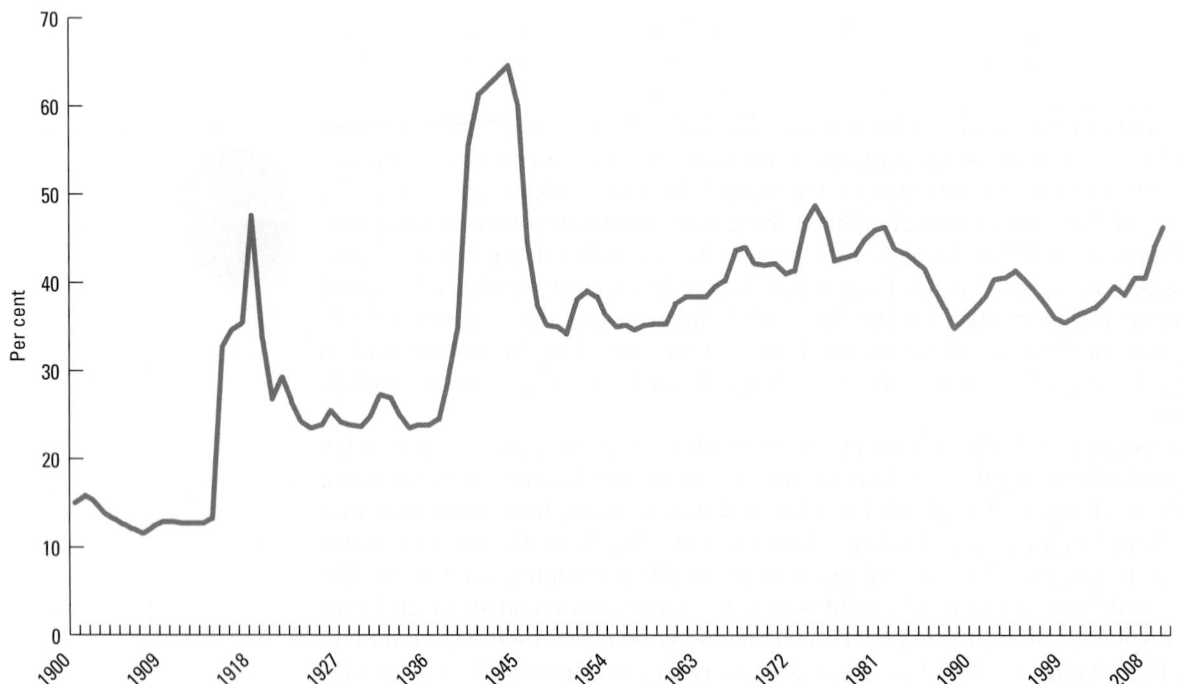

Source: UK Public Spending (http://www.ukpublicspending.co.uk).

FIGURE 12.2

UK Total Managed Expenditure as a Percentage of GDP

This figure shows the expenditure of the UK government as a percentage of GDP. It shows that government expenditure has risen as a percentage of GDP since 2000 and has risen sharply since 2007.

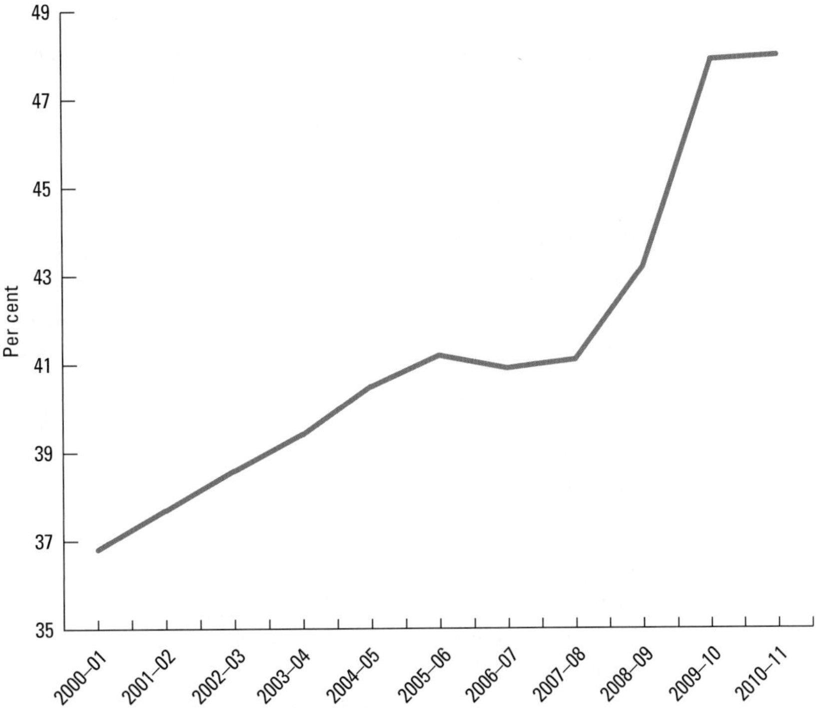

Source: http://www.hm-treasury.gov.uk/d/public_finances_databank.xls accessed 9 February 2010 (Crown Copyright).

began with relatively high spending reflecting the costs of the Boer War. World War I (1914–1918) and World War II (1939–1945) both led to very large increases in public spending. After both of these wars, public spending fell back when hostilities ceased, but to a higher level than before the war. Figure 12.2 shows UK total managed expenditure from 2000 to 2011 (2009–2010 onwards are estimates). It shows how public spending as a proportion of GDP has risen from 36.8 per cent to almost 50 per cent by 2010–2011. Part of the reason for the large rise in expenditure over this period was the recession of 2008–2009. Rising government expenditure was accompanied by falling revenues and so the public deficit widened considerably.

Table 12.1 compares the tax burden for seven major economies – the so-called 'Group of Seven', or G7 – as measured by the total tax revenue as a percentage of the nation's total income in 2008. The overall size of government revenue tells only part of the story, however. Behind the total figures lie thousands of individual decisions about taxes and spending. To understand the government's finances more fully, let's look at how the total breaks down into some broad categories.

Receipts

Table 12.2 shows the sources of UK government revenue in the financial year 2008–09 (in the UK, the tax year or 'fiscal year' runs from the beginning of

TABLE 12.1

Total Tax Revenue as a Percentage of GDP in the G7 Countries, 2008

Country	
Italy	43.2%
France	43.1
Germany	36.4
United Kingdom	35.7
Canada	32.2
Japan	28.3 (2007 figure)
United States	26.9

Source: Reproduced with permission from www.oecd.org

TABLE 12.2

Sources of UK Government Revenue, 2008–09

Tax	Amount (billions £)*	Amount per person (£)*	Percentage of receipts (%)
Personal income tax	153.4	2 498	28.25
National Insurance contributions	96.9	1 578	17.84
Value-added tax	78.4	1 277	14.44
Company taxes	66	1 075	12.15
Other indirect taxes	51.7	842	9.25
Council tax	24.4	397	4.49
Capital taxes	18.8	306	3.46
Other taxes and receipts	53.5	871	9.85
Total	543.1	8 845	100%

Source: HM Treasury, and authors' calculations.
*numbers are rounded up

April). (Here we are defining government in a wide sense to include, for example, local government as well as the central government based in London. Taxes are collected by a government agency, Her Majesty's Revenue and Customs.) Total receipts in 2008–09 were £543 billion and in 2009–10 were estimated to be £498 billion[1].

These numbers are so large that they are hard to comprehend. A billion is one thousand million, or 1 with 9 zeros after it (10^9). To appreciate how large a number this is, imagine counting one digit every second. How long would it take to count to one billion? In one year this constant counting would get you to 31 536 000; it would be another 30 years before you reached one billion!

To bring this astronomical figure down to earth, we can divide it by the size of the UK population, estimated at 61.4 million in an ONS report published in August 2009. We then find that the total of taxes levied amounted to around £8 845 for every man, woman and child in the United Kingdom in 2008–09, falling to around £8 111 in 2009–10.

The largest source of revenue for the government is personal income tax. This represents receipts on a tax on individuals' income from all sources: wages from working, interest on savings, dividends from corporations in which the person owns shares, profits from any small businesses he or she operates, and so on. The individual's tax liability (how much he or she owes) is then based on total income for the year.

[1]http://www.hm-treasury.gov.uk/d/pbr09_chapter1.pdf

TABLE 12.3

UK Income Tax Bands and Rates, 2010–11

This table shows the marginal tax rates for a UK taxpayer under the age of 65. For 2010–11 the personal allowance was £6 475, so that taxable income is any income in excess of this amount. The taxes levied on a taxpayer depend on all the marginal tax rates up to his or her income level. For example, a taxpayer with an income of £34 000 pays nothing on the first £6 475 of income and 20 per cent of the rest. The 10 per cent band is for income from savings only.

Taxable income	Tax rate
Up to £2 440	10%
From £0 to £37 400	20
Over £37 401 – £150 000	40
Over £150 000	50

Source: HM Revenue and Customs. (http://www.hmrc.gov.uk/rates/it.htm)

A person's income tax liability is not simply proportional to their income. Instead, the law requires a more complicated calculation. Taxable income is computed as total income minus a 'personal allowance' – a basic amount of income that is not taxed – and minus certain expenses that policy makers have deemed 'deductible' (such as the costs of operating an office in order to run a small business).

Then the tax liability is calculated from taxable income (income minus personal allowance and deductibles) using a schedule like that shown in Table 12.3 (although the Chancellor of the Exchequer has the power to change this schedule from time to time, and usually does so annually).

This table presents the marginal tax rate – the tax rate applied to each additional amount of income. Because the marginal tax rate rises as income rises, higher income individuals pay a larger percentage of their income in taxes. Note that each tax rate in the table applies only to income within the associated range, not to a person's entire income. For example, in 2009–10, a person with an income of £90 000 a year still paid nothing on the first £6 475 of income and 20 per cent on the next £30 925 before paying 40 per cent on the remainder of income. (We discuss the concept of marginal tax rate more fully later in this chapter.) Note that the UK government introduced a new 50 per cent rate of tax on incomes in excess of £150 000 and set an income limit for tax allowance of £100 000. Incomes in excess of £100 000, therefore, do not qualify for a basic allowance.

Next in importance to the UK government, at around 18 per cent of receipts, are National Insurance contributions. National Insurance contributions, or NICs, are a peculiarity of the UK tax system in that they are part income tax, part payroll tax (a payroll tax is a tax on the wages that a firm pays its workers). NICs work like this: the level of the employee's NICs is based on income, similar to income tax, except that it is usually worked out on weekly rather than annual earnings. The earnings limits and NIC rates for 2010–11 are shown in Table 12.4.

Up to a weekly earned income of £97, nothing is paid. Once a worker earns more than £97 a week, however, he pays 11 per cent of weekly income above £97 and less than £844. On the balance of his weekly earnings in excess of £844 he pays 1 per cent. The payroll tax part of NICs, the employer's NIC, is more straightforward: the employer pays 12.8 per cent of all earnings paid to the employee above £97 a week. These rates will be lower if the worker has 'contracted out' of the state pension scheme (i.e. elected not to receive a state pension).

TABLE 12.4

UK National Insurance Contribution Earnings Limits and Rates, 2010–11

This table shows UK standard rate National Insurance contribution rates in 2010–11. They are worked out on weekly earnings and comprise both an employee's contribution and an employer's contribution. For example, a worker with an income of £950 a week (about £49 400 a year) would pay nothing on the first £97 of weekly income, 11 per cent of what he earned between £97 and £844, and 1 per cent on the remaining £11. In addition, his employer would also have to pay 12.8 per cent of his weekly earnings in excess of £97.

Weekly earnings	Employee's contribution
Up to £97	0%
From £97 to £844	11
Over £844	1

Source: HM Revenue and Customs. http://www.hmrc.gov.uk/rates/nic.htm

NICs are a form of social insurance tax, because a worker's entitlement to certain benefits, such as unemployment benefit and a state pension, depends upon the amount of NICs paid (for this reason they are termed 'contributory' benefits). The revenue from these taxes is paid into a National Insurance fund. A small, fixed proportion of this is allocated to the National Health Service and the remainder is used to fund spending on contributory benefits. However, the link between National Insurance contributions paid and eligibility for benefits is quite weak, and has been getting weaker over time.

Value-added tax, or VAT, comprises about 15 per cent of revenue. VAT is a proportional sales tax, and in the UK is currently levied at three rates; 0 per cent, 5 per cent and 20 per cent of the selling price of a range of goods and services. In November 2008 the government announced that VAT would be temporarily cut from 17.5 per cent to 15 per cent in an attempt to boost consumer spending amidst the recession (at that time VAT was set at 17.5 per cent).

VAT returned to the 17.5 per cent rate on 31 December 2009 and was then increased in January 2011 to 20 per cent. It is called 'value-added' tax because the person producing the good or service is able to deduct any VAT he or she has already paid on goods or services used in producing it before paying the tax bill, so that the tax paid is actually a tax on the value added to the product at each stage of production.

To make this clearer, let's consider an example assuming VAT is set at 20 per cent. Suppose a sculptor wants £800 for a stone sculpture. She will charge £800 plus VAT of £160 (= 20 per cent of £800), or £960 in total. Before paying her VAT bill to HM Revenue and Customs, however, she will deduct from the £160 any VAT she paid in the production of the sculpture. In fact, she bought a block of stone from a local quarry for £200 plus VAT of £40 (= 20 per cent of £200), so she will deduct the £40 VAT she has already paid and send £120 (= £160 – £40) to HM Revenue and Customs. How much VAT will the Revenue and Customs receive in total? They get £40 when the stone is sold to the sculptor; this represents a tax on the value added at this stage of production – digging the stone up from the quarry, where it was worth nothing, and delivering it to the sculptor's studio, where it was worth £200.

Then Revenue and Customs received £120 when the sculptor sold the sculpture. This again represents a tax on the value added at this stage of production: the selling price of £800 minus the cost of marble of £200 equals value added of £600, and 20 per cent of £600 is £120. Adding the £40 the Revenue and Customs received when the block of stone was sold to the sculptor and the £120 they received when the sculptor sold the final sculpture, they have received £160. This is 20 per cent of the total value added in the whole production process – from a value of zero when the stone was in the ground, to £800 when the sculpture was sold (£160 = 20 per cent of £800).

VAT is an example of an **indirect tax**, as opposed to income tax, which is a **direct tax**. A direct tax is levied directly on a person or a company's income or wealth, while an indirect tax is levied on the price of something sold. Other indirect taxes, including taxes on fuel and on cigarettes and alcoholic drinks, account for about 9 per cent of revenue.

indirect tax
a tax that is levied on goods and services bought

direct tax
a tax that is levied directly on a person's income

After VAT, company taxes are next in importance in terms of the percentage of total tax receipts they represent. These include direct taxes such as local taxes levied on the value of a company's buildings, as well as corporation tax, which is a tax on a company's profits. A corporation is a business that is set up as a separate legal entity. The government taxes each corporation based on its profit – the amount the corporation receives for the goods or services it sells minus the costs of producing those goods or services. Notice that corporate profits are, in essence, taxed twice. They are taxed once by corporation tax when the corporation earns the profits; they are taxed a second time by the individual income tax when the corporation uses its profits to pay dividends to its shareholders.

Council taxes, accounting for about 4.5 per cent of total receipts, are local taxes paid by individuals – in the UK, usually levied on the value of residential property owned – in order to finance local amenities such as refuse collection and local roads.

Capital taxes, accounting for about 3.5 per cent of total tax revenue, are composed of inheritance tax, capital gains tax and stamp duty. Inheritance tax is the tax paid by an individual when he or she inherits money or property. Capital gains tax is paid when an individual makes a profit from investments – for example if he or she buys shares in a company and later sells them at a profit, capital gains tax will be payable on that profit. Stamp duty is a tax levied by the government on capital transactions: for example, when a person buys shares in a company or a house to live in, they will normally be liable to pay a certain percentage of the price as stamp duty. (The term 'stamp duty' is a reminder of years gone by when a government official would have used a rubber stamp on the transaction document as proof that the tax had been paid.)

Spending

Table 12.5 shows the spending of the UK government in 2010–11. Total spending in that year was £706.6 billion, or £11 508 per person. This table also shows how the government's spending was divided among major categories.

The largest category in Table 12.5 is social security, which represents transfer payments to the elderly (i.e. pensions) as well as unemployment benefits and other forms of social benefits. (A transfer payment is a government payment not made in exchange for a good or service.) This category is estimated to represent 28 per cent of spending by the UK government in 2010–11.

The second largest category of spending is on the National Health Service. Since 1948, the UK has offered health care to UK residents free at the point of delivery. The term 'free at the point of delivery' is important here. It means that at the time the service is delivered – when you go to see your general practitioner (GP) or you have your appendix taken out in hospital – there is no charge made. At a total cost of £127.2 billion to taxpayers in 2010–11, however, or £2 072 for every man, woman and child in the United Kingdom, it is clear that health care has to be paid for like everything else.

TABLE 12.5

UK Government Spending, 2010–11 (Estimated)

Category	Amount (£ billions)	Amount per person (£)	Percentage of spending %
Social security	197.8	3 221	28
National Health Service	127.2	2 072	18
Education	91.9	1 497	13
Defence	42.4	691	6
Public order and safety	35.3	575	5
Transport	21.2	345	3
Other	190.8	3 107	27
Total	£706.6	£11 508	100%

Source: HM Treasury and authors' calculations.

TABLE 12.6

UK Government Spending as a Percentage of GDP in the Six Main Areas

	1958–59	1978–79	1996–97	2008–09
Social security	6.0%	9.8%	13.1%	11.9%
NHS	3.2	4.4	5.1	7.8
Education	3.3	5.2	4.6	5.7
Defence	6.4	4.5	2.8	2.6
Public order and safety	n/a	1.5	2.0	2.4
Transport	n/a	1.6	1.2	1.5

Source: *A Survey of Public Spending in the UK.* Institute for Fiscal Studies Briefing Note BN43 http://www.ifs.org.uk/bns/bn43.pdf

Next in importance in terms of the amount spent is education, accounting for about £92 billion in 2010–11, or about 13 per cent of total spending. This includes spending on all forms of primary, secondary and higher education, as well as government training programmes.

Expenditure on national defence, weighing in at £42.4 billion, or £691 per person, is the fourth largest individual category. This includes both the salaries of military personnel and purchases of military equipment such as guns, fighter jets and warships.

The fifth category is public order and safety, which includes, for example, the cost of maintaining a police force and a fire service, as well as the criminal justice system. Government spending on transport – for example the cost of maintaining national motorways and the cost of subsidies paid to rail operators for maintaining the rail network – makes up the sixth largest category, at around £21 billion, or some 3 per cent of total spending.

(The category labelled 'other' in Table 12.5 is composed of a range of smaller categories of expenditure, such as environmental protection, housing, culture, science and technology, and agriculture, as well as items such as debt interest.)

In Table 12.6, we show how the main categories of UK government expenditure have changed over time, measured as a percentage of GDP. It is striking how expenditure on social security and the NHS have both increased strongly and steadily over the past four decades, while defence expenditure has shown a steady decline. The decline in defence expenditure is even more marked as a percentage of total government expenditure: as shown in Table 12.5, defence spending in 2010–11 amounted to about 6 per cent of the total, but in the mid-1980s it was about 11 per cent of total government spending. This reflects changing shifts in international political tensions, from the height of the Cold War in the 1960s to its effective end with the collapse of communism in the late 1980s and early 1990s.

The increase in spending on the NHS over time, also evident in Table 12.6, reflects at least three factors: changes in not only the size but also the structure of the population, which means that there is an increasing proportion of elderly people; the general tendency for an increase in demand for health services as countries become richer; and finally the increase in the range of treatable ailments over time as medical science has become more advanced and the use of technology in treatment becomes more prevalent and also more sophisticated.

CASE STUDY

Trade-offs in New Drug Treatments

Humans contracting the cancer, chronic myeloid leukaemia (CML), ten years ago may have faced a very uncertain future. CML is a cancer of the white blood cells in bone marrow, which divide too quickly and do not mature properly to do the work they are supposed to do. When released into the bloodstream, therefore, they increase the risk of the patient suffering infections and in addition they clog up the bone marrow preventing healthy red blood cells and platelets getting out. The prognosis for sufferers was not good, with many having a lifespan from diagnosis of around five years only.

However, a new drug has been developed that helps to block signals in cells that cause them to divide. For some patients with CML, this new drug, called imatinib (with a trade name of Glivec in Europe and Australia) has been available to patients since 2003 following successful trials. Its success means that a number of patients have a far longer lifespan than was previously the case. However, the success of the drug comes at a price for the NHS. The cost of prescribing the drug, which is taken daily by patients in the form of a tablet, is around £19 000 (€22 500) per patient.

Any health authority in the UK having to treat a patient with the drug has to find this money from their available budget. For the patient the drug is literally a life saver and is a far more effective and efficient treatment for their illness, but this is an excellent example of how advances in medicine come at a price that has to be borne by health services and how the budget of the NHS can quickly expand.

Figure 12.3 shows how government spending as a proportion of GDP has changed in the last 30 years. It is worth noting how government spending rises as a proportion of GDP during periods of economic slowdown and fall in periods of stronger growth. There are peaks in the early 1980s, the early 1990s and during the recession of 2008–09.

Total government tax revenue for 2008–09 in Table 12.2 was given as £543.1 billion. However, the amount that government spends may be greater or smaller than that amount. In 2008–09, government spent £620 billion leaving a shortfall of income of around £77 billion. Such a shortfall of receipts compared with spending is called a **budget deficit**. When receipts exceed spending, the government is said to run a **budget surplus**. The government finances a budget deficit by borrowing from the public. When the government runs a budget surplus, it uses the excess receipts to reduce its outstanding debts.

budget deficit
an excess of government spending over government receipts

budget surplus
an excess of government receipts over government spending

FIGURE 12.3

Total Managed Expenditure as a Percentage of GDP

The chart shows changes in total managed expenditure as a percentage of GDP between 1980 and 2010. It shows how government spending is closely linked to the performance of the economy. There are a series of peaks corresponding to periods of recession in the economy.

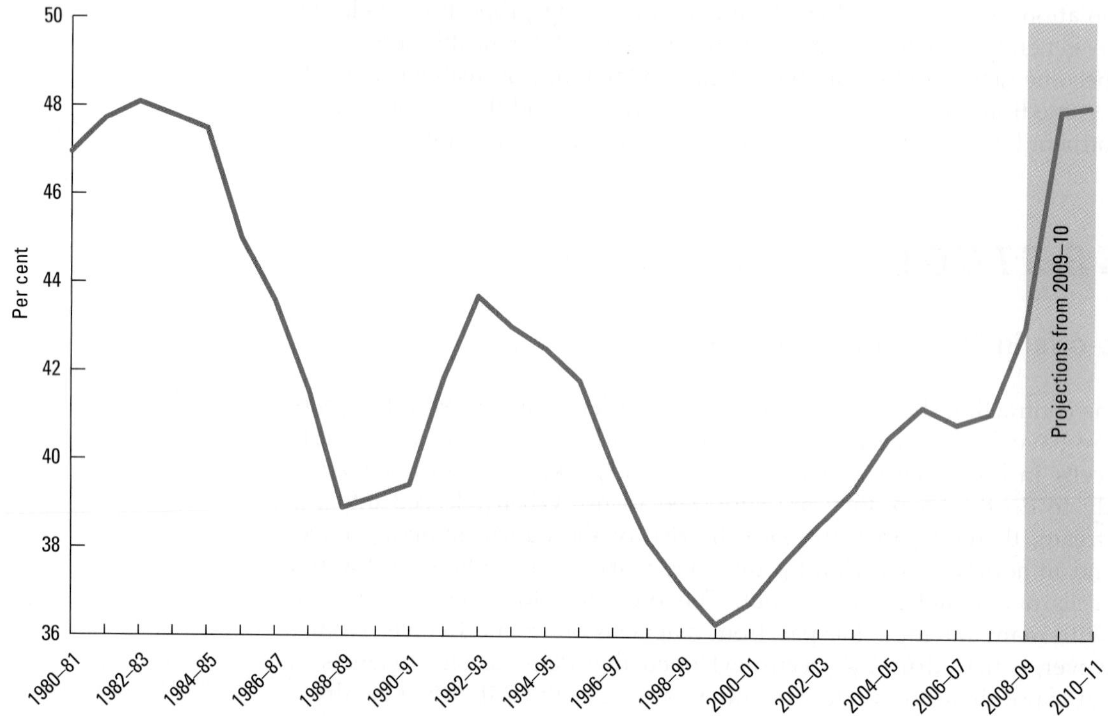

Source: HM Treasury (http://www.hm-treasury.gov.uk/d/public_finances_databank.xls (Crown Copyright)).

Figure 12.4 shows how public sector debt as a percentage of GDP rose sharply in the wake of the recession of 2008–09 and is estimated to rise further until moderating in 2013–14. The impact of recession on the UK economy meant that government tax revenue fell but spending rose (particularly on social security payments). A high proportion of government spending is committed for some years in advance (on ongoing capital projects for example) and as a result the deficit is forecast to get wider.

In the Pre-Budget Report in December 2009, the Chancellor of the Exchequer estimated that the deficit would rise a further £178 billion in 2009–10 before falling back slightly to £174.7 billion in 2010–11. This was based on total managed expenditure being £676 billion against total receipts of £498 billion.

Quick Quiz What are the three most important sources of tax revenue for the UK government? • What are the three most important expenditure categories?

FIGURE 12.4

UK Public Debt as a Percentage of GDP

This figure shows the borrowing of the UK government as a percentage of GDP. It shows that government borrowing rose in the wake of the recession of the early 1990s and then fell back before rising sharply following the recession of 2008–09.

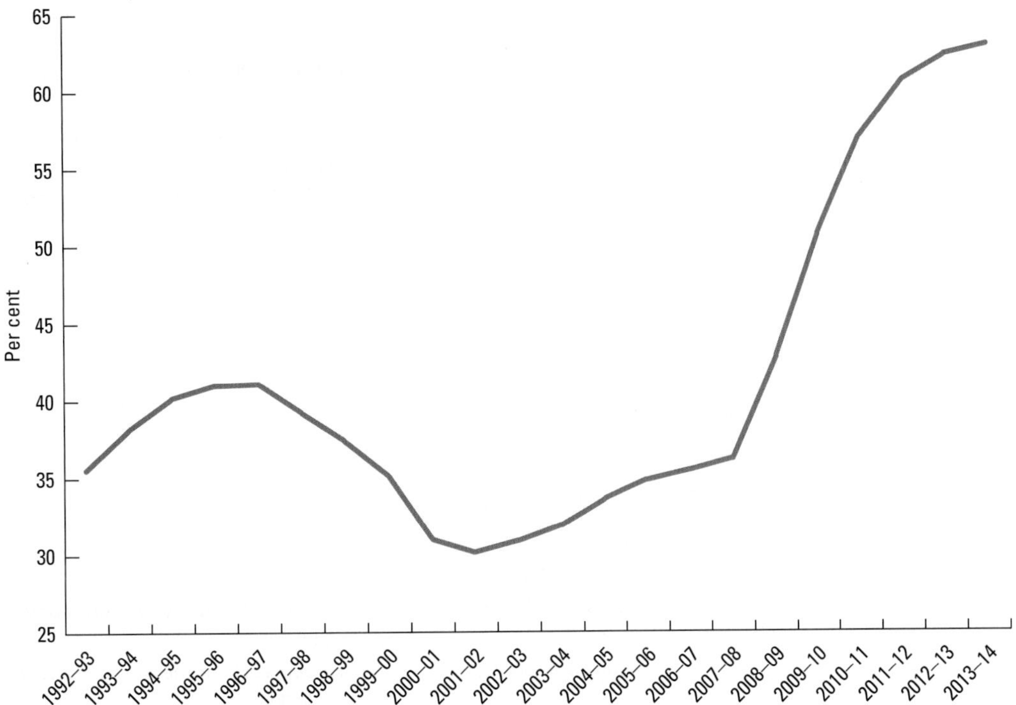

Source: http://www.hm-treasury.gov.uk/d/public_finances_databank.xls accessed 9 February 2010 (Crown Copyright).

TAX SYSTEMS IN OTHER COUNTRIES

Having outlined the tax system in the UK, we will now provide an overview of systems in two other countries. Viewing different tax systems tells us a great deal about the priorities and philosophies that are adopted by other governments with regard to their tax system and allows some comparison of the burden of taxation faced by a country's citizens in relation to others.

South Africa

The main source of tax revenue in South Africa (which has a population of 49.3 million) is income tax. There are a number of taxes levied on individuals and companies that come under the legal definition of income tax. Income tax, therefore, is collected not just from individuals but also from income generated by companies including profit. Income tax is residency based, meaning that if an individual is resident in South Africa they are subject to income tax from all their earnings, both from within South Africa and from without. Non-residents

TABLE 12.7

Income Tax Rates in South Africa

Taxable income (rand)	Rate of tax
0–132 000	18% of each R1
132 000–210 000	R23 760 + 25% of the amount above R132 000
210 000–290 000	R43 260 + 30% of the amount above R210 000
290 001–410 000	R67 260 + 35% of the amount above R290 000
410 001–525 000	R109 260 + 38% of the amount above R410 000
525 001 +	R152 960 + 40% of the amount above R4 525 000

Source: South African Revenue Service.

TABLE 12.8

Turnover Tax Rates for 'Micro-businesses' in South Africa

Taxable turnover (rand)	Rate of tax
0–100 000	0%
100 001–300 000	1%
300 001–500 000	R2 000 + 3% of the amount above R300 000
500 001–750 000	R8 000 + 5% of the amount above R750 000
750 001 +	R20 500 + 7% of the amount above R750 000

Source: South African Revenue Service.

are subject to tax on earnings generated within South Africa. Table 12.7 outlines the tax rates on income.

Corporation tax is one form of income tax levied on companies. In 2008 the government reduced corporation tax from 29 per cent to 28 per cent and there is also a 10 per cent Secondary Tax on Companies (STC) which is payable on net dividends. This was replaced in 2010 by a Dividends Tax. Small businesses are taxed differently: on income up to R54 200 there is a zero rate of tax; a 10 per cent rate on income between R54 201 and R300 000; and on income above R300 000 businesses pay R24 580 plus 28 per cent of the amount over R300 000. So-called 'micro businesses' have to pay a turnover tax levied on their turnover (sales revenue) as outlined in Table 12.8.

Capital gains tax is levied on individuals, companies and trusts at 10 per cent, 14 per cent and 20 per cent respectively. VAT is levied at a rate of 14 per cent on the majority of goods and services (with some exceptions). There are also other taxes on inheritance (called transfer duty), estate duty (at a flat rate of 20 per cent on property), taxes on international air travel, a skills development levy of 1 per cent which is paid by employers on the remuneration paid to employees, and Unemployment Insurance Contributions paid by both employers and employees based on employees' earnings.

TABLE 12.9

South African Government Spending 2008–09

Category	Amount (R billions)	Amount per person (R)	Percentage of spending
General public services	48	974	8.2%
Defence	31	629	5.3
Public order and safety	68	1 340	11.6
Economic affairs	126	2 556	21.5
Environmental protection	5	101	0.8
Housing and community amenities	5	1 318	11.1
Recreation and culture	10	203	1.7
Education	127	2 567	21.7
Social protection	105	2 130	17.9
Total	585	11 827	100%

Source: South Africa Budget 2009; South African Revenue Service.

Total government receipts in 2009–10 were R740.4 billion, with expenditure for the same period at R834.3 billion, giving a budget deficit of R93.9 billion (see Table 12.9 for an analysis of government spending in 2008–09).

Germany

Germany has a population of 82 million. The German tax system has a reputation of being very complex, with legislation around tax involving over 110 laws, 185 forms and some 90 000 policies. It has been reported that administration of the tax system costs €23.7 billion each year, 2.5 per cent of the annual tax yield. In recent years, successive German governments have sought to try and simplify the tax system, the latest reform being in 2008. Being a Federal Republic, taxes are levied by the federal government (*Bund*), the states (*Laender*) and municipalities (*Kommunen*).

For individuals, whether self-employed or in employment, income tax is payable on earnings and if that person is classed as a permanent resident of Germany then they are liable for tax on earnings from overseas as well as from inside Germany. As with South Africa, foreign residents living in Germany are liable for tax on income generated within Germany. Income tax is progressive with rates ranging from 14 per cent to 45 per cent as highlighted in Table 12.10.

In addition to income tax, Germans pay a 5.5 per cent Solidarity Tax, which was levied to help rebuild East Germany after unification of the country in 1991. For many Germans the tax is highly unpopular and it is widely perceived

TABLE 12.10

Income Tax Rates in Germany, 2009

Tax rate (%)	Rate of tax (€)
0	Earnings up to 7 384
14	7 385–52 552
42	52 553–250 400
45	250 401 +

Source: German Federal Ministry of Finance.

TABLE 12.11

Federal Government Spending in Germany, 2009

Category	Amount (€ billions)	Amount per person (€)	Percentage of spending
General public services	54.0	659	17.4%
Health, environment, sport, recreation	1.3	16	0.42
Food, agriculture and forestry water supplies, trade, services	7.4	90	2.4
Economic cooperation and development	6.0	73	1.9
Transport and communications	13.0	158	4.2
Housing, regional planning and local community services	1.9	23	0.6
Commercial enterprises, general real property and capital assets	16.0	195	5.2
Education, training, research and development	15.0	183	4.8
Social security and benefits	153.0	1 866	49.25
General financial management	43.0	524	13.8
Total	310.6	3783	100%

Source: German Federal Ministry of Finance.

that the tax has not done a great deal to improve conditions in the five eastern states and bring them up to the standards of the rest of the country. If an individual is a member of one of the established churches in Germany 8–9 per cent of their income tax is specified as Church Tax.

Corporation tax in Germany was lowered from 25 per cent to 15 per cent as part of the reforms of company tax which came into force on 1 January 2009. However, a business tax is also payable to municipalities ranging from 14 to 17 per cent. When Solidarity Tax is taken into account, the effective corporate tax rate can be as high as 33 per cent. As part of the tax reforms a flat rate of 25 per cent was levied on income derived from capital investments for individuals.

Value-added tax in Germany is 19 per cent although there are some exceptions, including books, magazines and food which are subject to 7 per cent VAT. Government receipts in 2009 totalled €253.8 billion with expenditure for the same period (see Table 12.11) at €310.6 billion, giving a budget deficit of €56.8 billion.

TAXES AND EFFICIENCY

Now that we have seen how governments raise and spend money, let's consider how one might evaluate tax policy. Obviously, the aim of a tax system is to raise revenue for the government. But there are many ways to raise any given amount of money. In designing a tax system, policy makers have two objectives: efficiency and equity.

One tax system is more efficient than another if it raises the same amount of revenue at a smaller cost to taxpayers and the government. What are the costs of taxes to taxpayers? The most obvious cost is the tax payment itself. This transfer of money from the taxpayer to the government is an inevitable feature of any tax system. Yet taxes also impose two other costs, which well designed tax policy tries to avoid or, at least, minimize:

- The deadweight losses that result when taxes distort the decisions that people make.
- The administrative burdens that taxpayers bear as they comply with the tax laws.

An efficient tax system is one that imposes small deadweight losses and small administrative burdens.

Deadweight Losses

One of the *Ten Principles of Economics* is that people respond to incentives, and this includes incentives provided by the tax system. Taxes have the effect of changing people's behaviour. If the government taxes tea, some people will drink less tea and drink more coffee. If the government taxes housing, some people will change behaviour and look to live in smaller houses and spend more of their income on other things. If the government taxes labour earnings, some people will not see additional work as having the same reward and may decide to work less and enjoy more leisure.

Because taxes have the effect of changing behaviour and distorting incentives, they entail deadweight losses. As we first discussed in Chapter 8, the deadweight loss of a tax is the reduction in economic well-being of taxpayers in excess of the amount of revenue raised by the government. The deadweight loss is the inefficiency that a tax creates as people allocate resources according to the tax incentive rather than the true costs and benefits of the goods and services that they buy and sell.

To recall how taxes cause deadweight losses, consider an example. Suppose that Ian places an €8 value on a pizza, and Dawn places a €6 value on it. If there is no tax on pizza, the price of pizza will reflect the cost of making it (including an element of profit). Let's suppose that the price of pizza is €5, so both Ian and Dawn choose to buy one. Both consumers get some surplus of value over the amount paid. Ian gets consumer surplus of €3, and Dawn gets consumer surplus of €1. Total surplus is €4.

Now suppose that the government levies a €2 tax on pizza and the price of pizza rises to €7. Ian still buys a pizza, but now he has consumer surplus of only €1. Dawn now decides not to buy a pizza because its price is higher than its value to her. The government collects tax revenue of €2 on Ian's pizza. Total consumer surplus has fallen by €3 (from €4 to €1). Because total surplus has fallen by more than the tax revenue, the tax has a deadweight loss. In this case, the deadweight loss is €1.

Notice that the deadweight loss comes not from Ian, the person who pays the tax, but from Dawn, the person who doesn't. The reduction of €2 in Ian's surplus exactly offsets the amount of revenue the government collects. The deadweight loss arises because the tax causes Dawn to alter her behaviour. When the tax raises the price of pizza, Dawn is worse off, and yet there is no offsetting revenue to the government. This reduction in Dawn's welfare is the deadweight loss of the tax.

CASE STUDY

Should Income or Consumption Be Taxed?

When taxes induce people to change their behaviour – such as inducing Dawn to buy less pizza – the taxes cause deadweight losses and make the allocation of resources less efficient. As we have already seen, much government revenue comes from personal income tax. In a case study in Chapter 8 we discussed how this tax discourages people from working as hard as they otherwise might. Another inefficiency caused by this tax is that it discourages people from saving.

Consider a person 25 years old who is considering saving €100. If he puts this money in a savings account that earns 8 per cent and leaves it there, he would have €2 172 when he retires at age 65. Yet if the government taxes one quarter of his interest income each year, the effective interest rate is only 6 per cent. After 40 years of earning 6 per cent, the €100 grows to only €1 029, less than half of what it would have been without taxation. Thus, because interest income is taxed, saving is much less attractive.

Some economists advocate eliminating the current tax system's disincentive towards saving by changing the basis of taxation. Rather than taxing the amount of income that people earn, the government could tax the amount that people spend. Under this proposal, all income that is saved would not be taxed until the saving is later spent. This alternative system, called a consumption tax, would not distort people's saving decisions – but it might lead to distortion of their consumption decisions, depending on how and on what the consumption tax was levied.

Administrative Burden

In the UK, anyone paying (or who should pay) the higher rate of income tax at 40 per cent (in 2010–11, those with taxable income of £37 400 or more) is required to fill in a tax return and send it to HM Revenue and Customs (or file it online). This is a long form that Revenue and Customs use to determine tax liability. If you ask the typical person required to do this for an opinion about the tax system, the opinion is unlikely to be favourable. The administrative burden of any tax system is part of the inefficiency it creates. This burden includes not only the time spent filling out forms but also the time spent throughout the year keeping records for tax purposes and the resources the government has to use to enforce the tax laws.

Many taxpayers – especially those in higher tax brackets – hire accountants or tax lawyers to help them with their taxes. These experts in the complex tax laws fill out the tax forms for their clients and help clients arrange their affairs in a way that reduces the amount of taxes owed. This behaviour is avoidance (optimizing your affairs so that you pay as little tax as possible without breaking the law, which is different from tax evasion – i.e. lying about your affairs in order to reduce the amount of tax paid). Tax avoidance is perfectly legal. Tax evasion is illegal, as Scarface Capone discovered.

Critics of the tax system say that these advisors help their clients avoid taxes by abusing some of the detailed provisions of the tax system (or, as it is sometimes termed, the tax code). These detailed provisions are often dubbed 'loopholes'. In some cases, loopholes are government mistakes: they arise from ambiguities or omissions in the tax laws. More often, they arise because the government has chosen to give special treatment to specific types of behaviour. For example, the UK tax system allows money spent on a personal pension plan to be exempt from income tax, up to a certain limit. This is because the government wants to encourage people to save for their retirement.

The resources devoted to complying with the tax laws are a type of deadweight loss. The government gets only the amount of taxes paid. By contrast, the taxpayer loses not only this amount but also the time and money spent documenting, computing and avoiding taxes.

The administrative burden of the tax system could be reduced by simplifying the tax laws. Yet simplification is often politically difficult. Most people are ready to simplify the tax code by eliminating the loopholes that benefit others, yet few are eager to give up the loopholes that they use. In the end, the complexity of tax law results from the political process as various taxpayers with their own special interests lobby for their causes. This process is called 'rent seeking' and is part of a branch of economics called public choice theory (see Chapter 9). Remember that public choice theory is about the analysis of governmental behaviour, and the behaviour of individuals who interact with government.

Marginal Tax Rates versus Average Tax Rates

When discussing the efficiency and equity of income taxes, economists distinguish between two notions of the tax rate: the average and the marginal. The **average tax rate** is total taxes paid divided by total income. The **marginal tax rate** is the extra taxes paid on an additional unit of income. For example, suppose that the government taxes 20 per cent of the first €50 000 of income and 50 per cent of all income above €50 000. Under this tax, a person who earns €60 000 pays tax of €15 000: 20 per cent of the first €50 000 (0.20 × €50 000 = €10 000) plus 50 per cent of the next €10 000 (0.50 × €10 000 = €5 000). For this person, the average tax rate is €15 000/€60 000, or 25 per cent. But the marginal tax rate is 50 per cent. If the taxpayer earned an additional euro of income, that euro would be subject to the 50 per cent tax rate, so the amount the taxpayer would owe to the government would rise by €0.50.

average tax rate
total taxes paid divided by total income

marginal tax rate
the extra taxes paid on an additional unit of income

The marginal and average tax rates each contain a useful piece of information. If we are trying to gauge the sacrifice made by a taxpayer, the average tax rate is more appropriate because it measures the fraction of income paid in taxes. By contrast, if we are trying to gauge how much the tax system distorts incentives, the marginal tax rate is more meaningful. One of the *Ten Principles of Economics* in Chapter 1 is that rational people think at the margin. A corollary to this principle is that the marginal tax rate measures how much the tax system discourages people from working. If you are thinking of working an extra few hours, the marginal tax rate determines how much the government takes of your additional earnings. It is the marginal tax rate, therefore, that determines the deadweight loss of an income tax.

CASE STUDY

Iceland's Natural Experiment

In the 1980s, Iceland changed its tax system in a way that, as a side effect, provided a natural experiment to show how taxes affect an economy. Before the reform, people paid taxes based on their previous year's income. After the reform, people paid taxes based on their current income. Thus, taxes in 1987 were based on 1986 income, but taxes in 1988 were based on 1988 income.

Income earned in 1987 was never taxed. For this one year of transition, the marginal income tax rate fell to zero. As reported in a December 2001 article in the *American Economic Review*, the citizens of Iceland took advantage of this tax holiday. Total hours worked rose by about 3 per cent in 1987 and then fell back to its normal level in 1988. The production of goods and services in 1987 (as measured by real GDP) was 4 per cent higher than the average of the year before and the year after. This episode confirms one of the *Ten Principles of Economics*: people respond to incentives. The fall in the Icelandic marginal tax rate was for one year only, and this fact surely influenced the

response. On the one hand, some people may have put off vacations and worked overtime to take advantage of the temporary incentive. On the other hand, no one would alter career plans and no business would restructure its work environment in response to an incentive that would soon disappear. A permanent change in a marginal tax rate could have either a smaller or a larger incentive effect than a temporary change.

Lump-sum Taxes

lump-sum tax
a tax that is the same amount for every person

Suppose the government imposes a tax of €4 000 on everyone. That is, everyone owes the same amount, regardless of earnings or any actions that a person might take. Such a tax is called a **lump-sum tax**.

A lump-sum tax shows clearly the difference between average and marginal tax rates. For a taxpayer with income of €20 000, the average tax rate of a €4 000 lump-sum tax is 20 per cent; for a taxpayer with income of €40 000, the average tax rate is 10 per cent. For both taxpayers, the marginal tax rate is zero because no tax is owed on an additional unit of income.

A lump-sum tax is the most efficient tax possible. Because a person's decisions do not alter the amount owed, the tax does not distort incentives and, therefore, does not cause deadweight losses. Because everyone can easily compute the amount owed and because there is no benefit to hiring tax lawyers and accountants, the lump-sum tax imposes a minimal administrative burden on taxpayers. If lump-sum taxes are so efficient, why do we rarely observe them in the real world? The reason is that efficiency is only one goal of the tax system. A lump sum tax would take the same amount from the poor and the rich, an outcome most people would view as unfair. To understand the tax systems that we observe, in the next section we consider the other major goal of tax policy – equity.

Quick Quiz What is meant by the efficiency of a tax system? • What can make a tax system inefficient?

TAXES AND EQUITY

In any country, tax policy always generates some of the most heated political debates. The heat is rarely fuelled by questions of efficiency. Instead, it usually arises from disagreements over how the tax burden should be distributed. Of course, if we are to rely on the government to provide some of the goods and services we want, taxes must fall on someone. In this section we consider the equity of a tax system. How should the burden of taxes be divided among the population? How do we evaluate whether a tax system is fair? Everyone agrees that the tax system should be equitable, but there is much disagreement about what equity means and how the equity of a tax system can be judged.

The Benefits Principle

benefits principle
the idea that people should pay taxes based on the benefits they receive from government services

One principle of taxation, called the **benefits principle**, states that people should pay taxes based on the benefits they receive from government services. This principle tries to make public goods similar to private goods. It seems fair that a person who often goes to the cinema pays more in total for cinema tickets than a person who rarely goes. Similarly, a person who gets great benefit from a public good should pay more for it than a person who gets little benefit.

The duty on petrol, for instance, is sometimes justified using the benefits principle, since in some countries, revenues from the tax on petrol are used to build and maintain roads. Because those who buy petrol are the same people who use the roads, this tax might be viewed as a fair way to pay for this government service.

The benefits principle can also be used to argue that wealthy citizens should pay higher taxes than poorer ones. Why? Simply because the wealthy benefit more from public services. Consider, for example, the benefits of police protection from theft. Citizens with much to protect get greater benefit from the police than do those with less to protect. Therefore, according to the benefits principle, the wealthy should contribute more than the poor to the cost of maintaining the police force. The same argument can be used for many other public services, such as fire protection, national defence and the criminal justice system.

It is even possible to use the benefits principle to argue for anti-poverty programmes funded by taxes on the wealthy. As we discussed in Chapter 11, people prefer living in a society without poverty, suggesting that anti-poverty programmes are a public good. If the wealthy place a greater value on this public good than other members of society, perhaps just because the wealthy have more to spend, then, according to the benefits principle, they should be taxed more heavily to pay for these programmes.

The Ability-to-Pay Principle

Another way to evaluate the equity of a tax system is called the **ability-to-pay principle**, which states that taxes should be levied on a person according to how well that person can shoulder the burden. This principle is sometimes justified by the claim that all citizens should make an 'equal sacrifice' to support the government. The magnitude of a person's sacrifice, however, depends not only on the size of his tax payment but also on his income and other circumstances. A €1 000 tax paid by a poor person may require a larger sacrifice than a €10 000 tax paid by a rich one.

ability-to-pay principle
the idea that taxes should be levied on a person according to how well that person can shoulder the burden

The ability-to-pay principle leads to two corollary notions of equity: vertical equity and horizontal equity. **Vertical equity** states that taxpayers with a greater ability to pay taxes should contribute a larger amount. **Horizontal equity** states that taxpayers with similar abilities to pay should contribute the same amount.

vertical equity
the idea that taxpayers with a greater ability to pay taxes should pay larger amounts

horizontal equity
the idea that taxpayers with similar abilities to pay taxes should pay the same amount

Although these notions of equity are widely accepted, applying them to evaluate a tax system is rarely straightforward.

Vertical Equity If taxes are based on ability to pay, then richer taxpayers should pay more than poorer taxpayers. But how much more should the rich pay? Much of the debate over tax policy concerns this question.

Consider the three tax systems in Table 12.12. In each case, taxpayers with higher incomes pay more. Yet the systems differ in how quickly taxes rise with income. The first system is called **a proportional tax** or sometimes a flat tax because all taxpayers pay the same fraction of income. The second system is called **regressive** because high-income taxpayers pay a smaller fraction of their income, even though they pay a larger amount. The third system is called **progressive** because high-income taxpayers pay a larger fraction of their income.

proportional or flat tax
a tax for which high-income and low-income taxpayers pay the same fraction of income

regressive tax
a tax for which high-income taxpayers pay a smaller fraction of their income than do low-income taxpayers

progressive tax
a tax for which high-income taxpayers pay a larger fraction of their income than do low-income taxpayers

Which of these three tax systems is most fair? Sometimes it is argued that a progressive tax system is fairer because richer people pay more tax and they can afford to do so because they are richer. But richer people will also pay more tax than poorer people under a flat tax system or even under a regressive tax system. In fact, there is no obvious answer, and economic theory does not offer any help in trying to find one. Equity, like beauty, is in the eye of the beholder.

TABLE 12.12

Three Tax Systems

	Proportional or flat tax		Regressive tax		Progressive tax	
Income	**Amount of tax**	**Percentage of income**	**Amount of tax**	**Percentage of income**	**Amount of tax**	**Percentage of income**
€50 000	€12 500	25%	€15 000	30%	€10 000	20%
100 000	25 000	25	25 000	25	25 000	25
200 000	50 000	25	40 000	20	60 000	30

Horizontal Equity If taxes are based on ability to pay, then similar taxpayers should pay similar amounts of taxes. But what determines if two taxpayers are similar? Individuals' circumstances can differ in many ways. To evaluate whether a tax system is horizontally equitable, one must determine which differences are relevant for a person's ability to pay and which differences are not.

Suppose Mr Smith and Ms Jones each have an income of €50 000 a year. Mr Smith is unmarried and has no children, but he has an illness that means that he has to employ someone to be with him while he is at work and getting to and from his place of business. This costs him €20 000 a year. Ms Jones is in good health and is a lone parent with a child aged three. Ms Jones has to pay €15 000 a year for child care while she is at work. Would it be fair for Mr Smith and Ms Jones to pay the same tax because they have the same income? Would it be fairer to give Mr Smith a tax break to help him offset the costs of a caring assistant? Would it be fairer to give Ms Jones a tax break to compensate her for the cost of childcare?

There are no easy answers to these questions.

SCHWADRON
"...IN SICKNESS OR HEALTH, INFLATION OR DEFLATION, MARRIAGE TAX CREDIT OR DEBIT..."

Tax Incidence and Tax Equity

Tax incidence – the study of who bears the burden of taxes – is central to evaluating tax equity. As we first saw in Chapter 6, the person who bears the burden of a tax is not always the person who gets the tax bill from the government. Because taxes alter supply and demand, they alter equilibrium prices. As a result, they affect people beyond those who, according to statute, actually pay the tax. When evaluating the vertical and horizontal equity of any tax, it is important to take account of these indirect effects.

Many discussions of tax equity ignore the indirect effects of taxes and are based on what economists mockingly call the flypaper theory of tax incidence. According to this theory, the burden of a tax, like a fly on flypaper, sticks wherever it first lands. This assumption, however, is rarely valid.

For example, a person not trained in economics might argue that a tax on expensive fur coats is vertically equitable because most buyers of furs are wealthy. Yet if these buyers can easily substitute other luxuries for furs, then a tax on furs might only reduce the sale of furs. In the end, the burden of the tax will fall more on those who make and sell furs than on those who buy them. Because most workers who make furs are not wealthy, the equity of a fur tax could be quite different from what the flypaper theory indicates.

CASE STUDY

Who Pays Corporation Tax?

Corporation tax provides a good example of the importance of tax incidence for tax policy. Corporation tax is popular among voters. After all, corporations are not people. Voters are always eager to have their taxes reduced and have some impersonal corporation pick up the tab. In a sense, corporation tax appears to be a tax that is imposed on nobody. No wonder it's popular with policy makers also.

But before deciding that corporation tax is a good way for the government to raise revenue, we should consider who bears the burden of corporation tax. This is a difficult question on which economists disagree, but one thing is certain: *people pay all taxes*. When the government levies a tax on a corporation, the corporation is more like a tax collector than a taxpayer. The burden of the tax ultimately falls on people – the owners, customers or workers of the corporation.

Many economists believe that workers and customers bear much of the burden of corporation tax. To see why, consider an example. Suppose that the government decides to raise the tax on the income earned by car companies. At first, this tax hurts the owners of the car companies who receive less profit. But, over time, these owners will respond to the tax. Because producing cars is less profitable, they invest less in building new car factories. Instead, they invest their wealth in other ways – for example, by buying larger houses or by building factories in other industries or other countries. With fewer car factories, the supply of cars declines, as does the demand for car workers. Thus, a tax on corporations making cars causes the price of cars to rise and the wages of car workers to fall.

Corporation tax shows how dangerous the flypaper theory of tax incidence can be. Corporation tax is popular in part because it appears to be paid by rich corporations. Yet those who bear the ultimate burden of the tax – the customers and workers of corporations – are often not rich. If the true incidence of corporation tax were more widely known, this tax might be less popular among voters – and policy makers.

Workers pay part of corporation tax.

Quick Quiz Explain the benefits principle and the ability-to-pay principle. • What are vertical equity and horizontal equity? • Why is studying tax incidence important for determining the equity of a tax system?

CASE STUDY

Tax Policy – Fair or Foul?

Two years after coming to power in 1997, the then Labour Chancellor of the Exchequer, Gordon Brown, introduced a 10 per cent income tax band. The introduction of the tax was hailed as an incentive to those seeking work to take employment and get off benefits, would help the lower paid and was 'fair'. In 2007, Mr Brown was looking forward to the almost certain possibility that he would become Prime Minister when Tony Blair finally decided to leave office. In his last Budget in this year, Mr Brown announced that the 10p rate of tax was being abolished and that the basic tax rate would be reduced from 22 per cent to 20 per cent. For Mr Brown the move looked to be a popular one; in his Chancellorship he had succeeded in reducing the basic rate from 23 per cent to 20 per cent and analysts viewed the move as a perfect way to start off his impending premiership giving him a large lead over the Conservatives and allowing him to call a quick election to confirm his status as Prime Minister for another five years. Mr Brown, for reasons, ultimately only known to him, decided not to call that election and a year after the announcement of the abolishing of the 10p tax rate he was caught up in a storm of criticism from his own MPs, opposition parties and representatives of the low paid.

Why the furore? Robert Chote from the Institute of Fiscal Studies (IFS) summed the situation up in an article published in April 2008. Under Mr Brown's tax system prior to the announcement, the taxable allowance stood at £5 435; the next £2 230 of tax commanded a 10p rate and the next £32 370 was taxed at 22 per cent. Following the Budget announcement by Mr Brown, the tax allowance stayed at £5 435 and the next £36 000 would be taxed at 20 per cent.

What effect would this have on taxpayers; would it be fairer? Take an example of an individual earning an annual salary of £10 000. Prior to the change this person's tax bill would be:

Tax allowance = £5 435
Taxable income would be £10 000 – £5 435 = £4 565
Of which £2 230 would be taxed at 10 per cent (£223.00)
The remaining £2 335 of taxable income would be taxed at 22 per cent (£513.70)
Total tax paid = £736.70

For an individual earning a salary of £30 000 the situation would be:

Tax allowance = £5 435
Taxable income would be £30 000 – £5 435 = £24 565
Of which £2 230 would be taxed at 10 per cent (£223.00)
The remaining £22 335 of taxable income would be taxed at 22 per cent (£4 913.70)
Total tax paid = £5 136.70

After the 10p rate was abolished and the 20 per cent rate introduced the situation would now be:

On a salary of £10 000:
Tax allowance = £5 435
Taxable income would be £10 000 – £5 435 = £4 565
£4 565 taxed at 20 per cent = £913.00
Total tax paid = £913.00: a net increase in tax paid of £176.30

On a salary of £30 000:
Tax allowance = £5 435
Taxable income would be £30 000 – £5 435 = £24 565
£24 565 taxed at 20 per cent = £4 913.00
Total tax paid = £4 913.00: a net reduction in tax paid of £223.70

Such a simple calculation highlights claims that the abolishing of the 10p rate was hitting the low paid and that the least wealthy people in society were, in effect, subsidizing those who were better off. Chote showed that those on incomes between £5 435 and £19 355 a year would be worse off with those earning £7 755 being the hardest hit with a rise in tax paid of £232.00 a year. Those earning between £19 355 and around £40 000 would gain, however, with someone earning £36 140 benefiting most, being £337 a year better off. The outcry facing Mr Brown, who by now was Prime Minister, and his new Chancellor, Alistair Darling, was significant. The abolishing of the 10p tax was clearly 'unfair' and would hit hardest those it was designed to help; but was it?

This was not the whole story. It seems that the full picture was somehow lost in translation and a party that has been embroiled in accusations of 'spin' clearly did not manage to communicate the big picture very well.

Chote points out that the 2007 Budget was indeed a Budget to help the poor, as claimed by Mr Brown. The abolishing of the 10p tax rate was *one* of the elements of a package that, put together, resulted in winners and losers but led to 'the poorest third of the population emerging as the biggest winners'. Crucial to understanding the issues raised here is being clear about what is meant by 'the poor'. Some people are poor because they are over 65 and have limited income, others because they are single families and have difficulty finding work, others because they are of a particular age with no family but either out of work or in low-paid work, and others because they have low-paid jobs and families to support.

Changes in tax rates are not the only way in which individuals are affected in terms of the tax burden they suffer. In the 2007 Budget, Mr Brown also raised tax allowances for those over 65, increased the child tax credit (a negative tax, in effect, which qualifying individuals can claim if they have a responsibility for at least one child; credits come in the form of a payment from government) and increasing the threshold over which tax credits would not be paid. As a result of these changes, those affected by the abolishing of the 10p tax rate may have lost from that measure but gained from tax credits. Chote pointed out that when all the changes were taken into account the poorest third of the population would have benefited as would the richest third with the remainder being largely unaffected. Any criticism of Mr Brown's tax changes, therefore, might be that he treated different types of poor people differently.

Childless single people under 25 working less than 30 hours a week or who may have relatively high earnings, childless couples and those retiring early are the groups who were likely to lose out as a result of the changes.

The lesson from this case study is that equity and efficiency in the tax system is not as simple as the theory may make it sound. Tax systems in most countries are complex and changes to any system affects different people in different ways. What may look on the surface as a more equitable tax system may in fact have a disproportionate impact on some groups in society who, depending on the 'power' they have, may have problems in getting their plight publicized.

The abolition of the 10p rate caused Mr Brown and Mr Darling considerable problems. The publicity and column inches written on behalf of the 'losers' was such that Mr Darling was forced into announcing measures to compensate those who would lose out from the changes. On 13 May 2008, the government announced that personal tax allowances for 2008–09 would rise by £600 and that there would be a cut in the higher-rate threshold. The cost to the government of these measures was estimated by the IFS at £5.5 billion with £2.6 billion being financed by other tax and spending measures and £2.9 billion from borrowing. The IFS estimated that as a result of the changes, widely reported as a 'climbdown' by the government, 21.3 million families would be better off than before the 13 May announcement but that 900 000 families would still be adversely affected by the cut in the 10p tax rate with around 50 per cent of these being single people under 25.

CONCLUSION: THE TRADE-OFF BETWEEN EQUITY AND EFFICIENCY

Almost everyone agrees that equity and efficiency are the two most important goals of the tax system. But often these two goals conflict. Many proposed changes in the tax laws increase efficiency while reducing equity, or increase equity whilst reducing efficiency. People disagree about tax policy often because they attach different weights to these two goals.

Economics alone cannot determine the best way to balance the goals of efficiency and equity. This issue involves political philosophy as well as economics. But economists do have an important role in the political debate over tax policy: they can shed light on the trade-offs that society faces and can help us avoid policies that sacrifice efficiency without any benefit in terms of equity.

SUMMARY

- Governments raises revenue using various taxes. In many countries, the most important taxes for the government are personal income taxes and social insurance taxes.
- The efficiency of a tax system refers to the costs that it imposes on taxpayers. There are two costs of taxes beyond the transfer of resources from the taxpayer to the government. The first is the distortion in the allocation of resources that arises as taxes alter incentives and behaviour. The second is the administrative burden of complying with the tax laws.
- The equity of a tax system concerns whether the tax burden is distributed fairly among the population. According to the benefits principle, it is fair for people to pay taxes based on the benefits they receive from the government. According to the ability-to-pay principle, it is fair for people to pay taxes based on their capability to handle the financial burden. When evaluating the equity of a tax system, it is important to remember a lesson from the study of tax incidence: the distribution of tax burdens is not the same as the distribution of tax bills.
- When considering changes in the tax laws, policy makers often face a trade-off between efficiency and equity. Much of the debate over tax policy arises because people give different weights to these two goals.

KEY CONCEPTS

indirect tax, p. 243
direct tax, p. 243
budget deficit, p. 245
budget surplus, p. 245
average tax rate, p. 253
marginal tax rate, p. 253
lump-sum tax, p. 254
benefits principle, p. 254
ability-to-pay principle, p. 255
vertical equity, p. 255
horizontal equity, p. 255
proportional or flat tax, p. 255
regressive tax, p. 255
progressive tax, p. 255

QUESTIONS FOR REVIEW

1. Over the past century, has the size of government, as measured by tax receipts or government spending, grown more or less slowly than the rest of the economy? (You can find this out for the country you are studying in by using its national statistics service.)
2. What are the two most important sources of revenue for the government?
3. Explain how corporate profits are taxed twice.
4. Why is the burden of a tax to taxpayers greater than the revenue received by the government?
5. Why do some economists advocate taxing consumption rather than income?
6. Give two arguments why wealthy taxpayers should pay more taxes than poor taxpayers.
7. What is the concept of horizontal equity, and why is it hard to apply?

PROBLEMS AND APPLICATIONS

1. Government spending in most industrialized countries has grown as a share of national income over time. What changes in our economy and our society might explain this trend? Do you expect the trend to continue?
2. In a published source or on the internet, find out whether your government had a budget deficit or surplus last year. What do policy makers expect to happen over the next few years?
3. In many industrialized countries, the elderly population is growing more rapidly than the total population. This is partly because of historical movements in the birth rate ('baby booms') and partly due to the fact that people are now living longer on average. Because the elderly are eligible for state retirement pensions, this places an increasing burden on the working age population to pay for those retirement pensions. Discuss the merits of each of the following proposed policies for dealing with this problem. Which do you think would be the best policy or combination of policies? Explain.
   a. Making exempt from income tax any money paid into a private retirement pension fund.
   b. Making exempt from income tax any money paid into a private retirement pension fund so long as the person involved gives up his or her right to a state pension.
   c. Reducing the amount of state retirement pension by 50 per cent.
   d. Raising the minimum age of retirement from 65 to 70 years of age.
   e. Raising the basic rate of income tax.
   f. Raising the higher rate of income tax.
   g. A drive to increase immigration in order to increase the working age population.
4. Suppose you are a typical person in the UK economy. Refer to Tables 12.3 and 12.4 for income tax and employer's National Insurance contribution rates. How much income tax do you pay if you earn £25 000 a year? How much do you pay in National Insurance contributions? Taking both of these taxes into account, what are your average and marginal tax rates? What happens to your total tax bill and to your average and marginal tax rates if your income rises to £40 000?

5. In the UK, value-added tax is levied at the rate of 20 per cent on most goods and services, although it is not levied on a range of items, such as food, books, and water and sewerage systems. Discuss the merits of this policy. Consider the principles of equity and efficiency.
6. VAT is not levied in the UK on children's clothing but it is levied on adult's clothing. Discuss the merits of this distinction, considering both efficiency and equity.
7. Suppose that the tax system had the following features. Explain how individuals' behaviour is affected.
   a. Contributions to charity are tax-deductible.
   b. Sales of beer are taxed.
   c. Realized capital gains are taxed, but accrued gains are not. (When someone owns a share of stock that rises in value, she has an 'accrued' capital gain. If she sells the share, she has a 'realized' gain.)
8. The tax on cigarettes and other smoking products is very high in many countries (in the UK it is over 80 per cent of the selling price) and has been rising over time. Discuss the merits of this policy, considering the principles of equity and efficiency.
9. Categorize each of the following funding schemes as examples of the benefits principle or the ability-to-pay principle.
   a. Visitors to public museums are required to pay an entrance fee.
   b. Local property taxes support primary and secondary schools.
   c. An airport trust fund collects a tax on each plane ticket sold and uses the money to improve airports and the air traffic control system.
10. Any income tax schedule embodies two types of tax rates – average tax rates and marginal tax rates.
    a. The average tax rate is defined as total taxes paid divided by income. For the proportional tax system presented in Table 12.12, what are the average tax rates for people earning €50 000, €100 000 and €200 000? What are the corresponding average tax rates in the regressive and progressive tax systems?
    b. The marginal tax rate is defined as the extra taxes paid on additional income divided by the increase in income. Calculate the marginal tax rate for the proportional tax system as income rises from €50 000 to €100 000. Calculate the marginal tax rate as income rises from €100 000 to €200 000. Calculate the corresponding marginal tax rates for the regressive and progressive tax systems.
    c. Describe the relationship between average tax rates and marginal tax rates for each of these three systems. In general, which rate is relevant for someone deciding whether to accept a job that pays slightly more than her current job? Which rate is relevant for judging the vertical equity of a tax system?
11. As we noted in the text, the employer's contribution element of UK National Insurance contributions (NICs) are effectively a form of income tax. Consider the figures on tax rates and NIC rates given in Tables 12.3 and 12.4. Work out a complete schedule showing the total amount of tax (income tax and employee's NIC combined) payable on income over all ranges.
12. What is the efficiency justification for taxing consumption rather than income? If your country were to adopt a consumption tax, do you think that would make the tax system more or less progressive? Explain.

For further resources, visit www.cengage.com/mankiw_taylor2

5

FIRM BEHAVIOUR AND THE ORGANIZATION OF INDUSTRY

13 THE COSTS OF PRODUCTION

The economy is made up of thousands of firms that produce the goods and services we enjoy every day: Mercedes Benz produces cars, Miele produce kitchen appliances, and Nestlé produces food and drink. Some firms, such as these three, are large; they employ thousands of workers and have thousands of shareholders who share in the firms' profits. Other firms, such as the local hairdresser's shop or pizzeria, are small; they employ only a few workers and may be owned by a single person or family.

In this chapter and the ones that follow, we examine firm behaviour in more detail. This topic will give you a better understanding of what decisions lie behind the supply curve in a market which we introduced in previous chapters. In addition, it will introduce you to a part of economics called *industrial organization* – the study of how firms' decisions regarding prices and quantities depend on the market conditions they face. The town in which you live, for instance, may have several restaurants but only one water supply company. How does this difference in the number of firms affect the prices in these markets and the efficiency of the market outcomes? The field of industrial organization addresses exactly this question.

Before we turn to these issues, however, we need to discuss the costs of production. All firms, from Air France to your local baker's shop, incur costs as they make the goods and services that they sell. As we will see in the coming chapters, a firm's costs are a key determinant of its production and pricing decisions. In this chapter, we define some of the variables that economists use to measure a firm's costs, and we consider the relationships among them. A word of warning: this topic can seem dry and technical. But it provides a crucial foundation for the fascinating topics that follow.

WHAT ARE COSTS?

We begin our discussion of costs at Hungry Horace's Pizza Factory. Horace, the owner of the firm, buys flour, tomatoes, mozzarella cheese, salami and other pizza ingredients. He also buys the mixers and ovens and hires workers to run this equipment. He then sells the resulting pizzas to consumers. By examining some of the issues that Horace faces in his business, we can learn some lessons about costs that apply to all firms in the economy.

Total Revenue, Total Cost and Profit

We begin with the firm's objective. To understand what decisions a firm makes, we must understand what it is trying to do. It is conceivable that Horace started his firm because of an altruistic desire to provide the world with pizza or, perhaps, out of love for the pizza business. More likely, Horace started his business to make money. Economists often use the assumption that the goal of a firm is to maximize profit. Whilst the extent to which this assumption holds in the real world has been questioned, it is a useful starting point for our analysis.

What is a firm's profit? The amount that the firm receives for the sale of its output (pizzas) is called its total revenue, which we introduced in Chapter 5. The amount that the firm pays to buy inputs (flour, mozzarella cheese, workers, ovens, etc.) is called its **total cost**. Horace's profit is the difference between his total revenue and his total cost. **Profit**, therefore, is a firm's total revenue minus its total cost. That is:

total cost
the market value of the inputs a firm uses in production

profit
total revenue minus total cost

$$\text{Profit} = \text{Total revenue} - \text{Total cost}$$

We can express this in the formula:

$$\Pi = \text{TR} - \text{TC}$$

where Π represents profit.

We will assume that Horace's objective is to make his firm's profit as large as possible – in other words, he wants to maximize profit.

To see how a firm goes about maximizing profit, we must consider fully how to measure its total revenue and its total cost. Total revenue is the easy part: it equals the quantity of output the firm produces times the price at which it sells its output. If Horace produces 10 000 pizzas and sells them at €2 a pizza, his total revenue is €20 000. By contrast, the measurement of a firm's total cost is more subtle and open to different interpretations.

Costs as Opportunity Costs

When measuring costs at Hungry Horace's Pizza Factory, or any other firm, it is important to keep in mind one of the *Ten Principles of Economics* from Chapter 1: the cost of something is what you give up to get it. Recall that the *opportunity cost* of an item refers to all those things that must be forgone to acquire that item. When economists speak of a firm's cost of production, they include the opportunity costs of making its output of goods and services.

A firm's opportunity costs of production are sometimes obvious and sometimes less so. When Horace pays €1 000 for flour, Horace can no longer use that €1 000 to buy something else; he has to sacrifice what else that €1 000 could have purchased. Similarly, when Horace hires workers to make the pizzas, the wages he pays are part of the firm's costs. Because these costs require the firm to pay out some money, they are called **explicit costs**. By contrast, some of a firm's opportunity costs, called **implicit costs,** do not require a cash outlay. Imagine that Horace is skilled with computers and could earn €100 per hour working as a programmer.

explicit costs
input costs that require an outlay of money by the firm

implicit costs
input costs that do not require an outlay of money by the firm

For every hour that Horace works at his pizza factory, he gives up €100 in income, and this forgone income is also classed as part of his costs by an economist.

This distinction between explicit and implicit costs highlights an important difference between how economists and accountants analyse a business. Economists are interested in studying how firms make production and pricing decisions. Because these decisions are based on both explicit and implicit costs, economists include both when measuring a firm's costs. By contrast, accountants have the job of keeping track of the money that flows into and out of firms. As a result, they measure the explicit costs but often ignore the implicit costs.

The difference between economists and accountants is easy to see in the case of Hungry Horace's Pizza Factory. When Horace gives up the opportunity to earn money as a computer programmer, his accountant will not count this as a cost of his pizza business. Because no money flows out of the business to pay for this cost, it never shows up on the accountant's financial statements. An economist, however, will count the foregone income as a cost because it will affect the decisions that Horace makes in his pizza business. This is an important part of thinking like an economist and was highlighted on page 61 in Chapter 3, 'Should Ingvar Kamprad mow his own lawn?' In Horace's case, if the wage as a computer programmer rose from €100 to €500 per hour, the opportunity cost of running his pizza business might now change his decision-making. The opportunity cost of running the business in terms of what Horace is sacrificing in foregone income has risen. Horace might decide he could earn more by closing the business and switching to computer programming.

The Cost of Capital as an Opportunity Cost

An important implicit cost of almost every business is the opportunity cost of the financial capital that has been invested in the business. As we have already noted, economists and accountants treat costs differently, and this is especially true in their treatment of the cost of capital. Suppose, for instance, that Horace used €300 000 of his savings to buy his pizza factory from the previous owner. If Horace had instead left this money deposited in a savings account that pays an interest rate of 5 per cent, he would have earned €15 000 per year (assuming simple interest). To own his pizza factory, therefore, Horace has given up €15 000 a year in interest income. This forgone €15 000 is an implicit opportunity costs of Horace's business. An economist views the €15 000 in interest income that Horace gives up every year as a cost of his business, even though it is an implicit cost. Horace's accountant, however, will not show this €15 000 as a cost because no money flows out of the business to pay for it.

To explore further the difference between economists and accountants, let's change the example slightly. Suppose now that Horace did not have the entire €300 000 to buy the factory but, instead, used €100 000 of his own savings and borrowed €200 000 from a bank at an interest rate of 5 per cent. Horace's accountant, who only measures explicit costs, will now count the €10 000 interest paid on the bank loan every year as a cost because this amount of money now flows out of the firm. By contrast, according to an economist, the opportunity cost of owning the business is still €15 000. The opportunity cost equals the interest on the bank loan (an explicit cost of €10 000) plus the forgone interest on savings (an implicit cost of €5 000).

Economic Profit versus Accounting Profit

economic profit
total revenue minus total cost, including both explicit and implicit costs

Now let's return to the firm's objective – profit. Because economists and accountants measure costs differently, they also measure profit differently. An economist measures a firm's **economic profit** as the firm's total revenue minus all the

FIGURE 13.1

Economists versus Accountants

Economists include all opportunity costs when analysing a firm, whereas accountants measure only explicit costs. Therefore, economic profit is smaller than accounting profit.

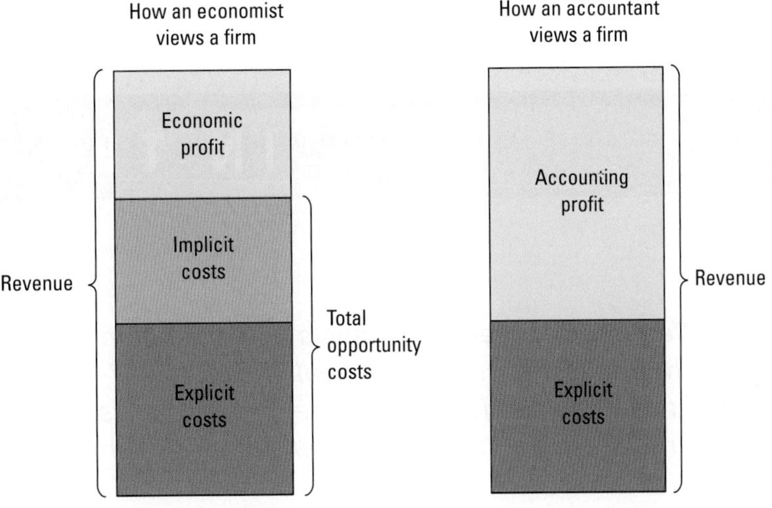

opportunity costs (explicit and implicit) of producing the goods and services sold. An accountant measures the firm's **accounting profit** as the firm's total revenue minus only the firm's explicit costs.

accounting profit
total revenue minus total explicit cost

Figure 13.1 summarizes this difference. Notice that because the accountant ignores the implicit costs, accounting profit is usually larger than economic profit. For a business to be profitable from an economist's standpoint, total revenue must cover all the opportunity costs, both explicit and implicit.

Quick Quiz Richard Collishaw is a farmer who is also a skilled metal worker. He makes unique garden sculptures that could earn him €40 an hour. One day, he spends 10 hours planting €200 worth of seeds on his farm. What opportunity cost has he incurred? What cost would his accountant measure? If these seeds will yield €400 worth of crops, does Richard earn an accounting profit? Does he earn an economic profit? Would you advise Richard to continue as a farmer or switch to metal working?

PRODUCTION AND COSTS

Firms incur costs when they buy inputs to produce the goods and services that they plan to sell. In this section we examine the link between a firm's production process and its total cost. Once again, we consider Hungry Horace's Pizza Factory.

In the analysis that follows, we make an important simplifying assumption: we assume that the size of Horace's factory is fixed and that Horace can vary

the short run
the period of time in which some factors of production cannot be changed

the long run
the period of time in which all factors of production can be altered

the quantity of pizzas produced only by changing the number of workers. This assumption is realistic in **the short run**, but not in **the long run**. That is, Horace cannot build a larger factory overnight, but he can do so within a year or so. This analysis, therefore, should be viewed as describing the production decisions that Horace faces in the short run. We examine the relationship between costs and time horizon more fully later in the chapter.

IN THE NEWS

Interpreting Profit

Our discussion of the difference between economists' interpretation of profit and that of accountants has important implications. The financial crisis of 2007–09 highlighted ways in which definitions of profit can have serious consequences for banks and ultimately for overall economic stability. This article looks at how these interpretations can cause problems for banks and their investors.

Banking Inquiry May Uncover Ponzi Schemes
By Cormac Butler

To the relief of bank shareholders, not to mention the taxpayer, the Irish Central Bank governor Patrick Honohan is about to focus on what caused the banking crisis. He will identify what encouraged bankers to lend vast sums on speculative loss-making transactions.

People assume that high salaries and bonuses are only paid to bankers and traders who make genuine profits and increase shareholder wealth. Wrong. Poorly devised incentive schemes encourage them to ruin shareholder value. The lending to Irish developers is a case in point.

Many apparently successful financial institutions operate a 'Ponzi' scheme – an investment operation that pays returns to separate investors from their own money or money paid by subsequent investors, rather than from any actual profit earned. In this way shareholders have the illusion of profits, allowing bankers to pay themselves lavish incentives. Named after the Italian-American fraudster Charles Ponzi who perfected the scam in the 1920s, Ponzis arise because banks exploit what seems a minor – but is in fact a major – accounting flaw.

Irish banks often use 'loss leader' strategies similar to supermarkets. They offer subsidized loans to build customer relationships or increase market share. Once the door is opened, the bank can then sell more lucrative treasury services. In the same way supermarkets may subsidize the cost of bread in the hope of luring customers to more high-margin product lines. Banks can easily hide the subsidy on the loss leader but supermarkets cannot.

Therefore supermarkets will use the strategy sparingly whereas banks will lend recklessly as long as they can show an accounting profit. For almost 20 years, international banks, hungry for large bonuses, have exploited this flaw. Imagine interest rates are expected to be 4 per cent, 5 per cent and 6 per cent over the next three years. A bank borrowing €1 000 000 would have to pay interest of €150 000 over this period. If the bank used the borrowings to buy a bond which paid interest of 4.6 per cent, the total income from the bond would be only €138 000. There's a shortfall of €12 000, that makes the bond unattractive for the bank's shareholders.

Charles Ponzi

Nevertheless, in the year of purchase, the bank could record an accounting profit of €6 000, from the difference between rates of 4.6 per cent and 4 per cent. Bonuses are often based on just such an accounting profit – yet the banker gets rewarded for destroying shareholder value. Structured product people made millions from the basic accounting flaw above. They developed lethal, leveraged structured products such as 'inverse floaters'. Put simply, with a leverage of say 10, the accounting profit jumps from €6 000 to €60 000 – but the shareholders' loss multiplies to €120 000.

The salespeople learned a lucrative lesson. Many bankers became willing to overpay for dangerous structured products as long as they could record an accounting profit and pay themselves bonuses. New accounting rules eventually curtained 'inverse floater' abuses but – like most badly designed rules – created an even bigger problem. Once the salesmen found bankers were happy to ruin shareholders if they earned a bonus first, they devised complex, lethal securitization portfolios, known now as toxic structured credit products. These produced a high return and therefore, high initial accounting profits.

Yet they were extremely difficult to value. The accounting rules for such risky products are hugely flawed. As the bankers simply didn't care what they were buying, the salesmen packed hundreds of sub-prime – i.e. dodgy – loans into these overpriced structures and still they flew off the shelves. In the same vein, Irish banks queued up to acquire dodgy loans from property developers without any regard for the fact that these loans were overpriced.

Irish banks offered cheap loans to property developers, knowing that they could create an accounting profit but hide losses.

Source: http://www.irishtimes.com/newspaper/opinion/2010/0211/1224264198292.html accessed 23 February 2010.

The Production Function

Table 13.1 shows how the quantity of pizzas Horace's factory produces per hour depends on the number of workers. As you see in the first two columns, if there are no workers in the factory Horace produces no pizzas. When there is 1 worker he produces 50 pizzas. When there are 2 workers he produces 90 pizzas, and so on. Figure 13.2 (panel (a)) presents a graph of these two columns of numbers. The number of workers is on the horizontal axis, and the number of pizzas produced is on the vertical axis. This relationship between the quantity of inputs (workers) and quantity of output (pizzas) is called the **production function**.

production function
the relationship between quantity of inputs used to make a good and the quantity of output of that good

One of the *Ten Principles of Economics* introduced in Chapter 1 is that rational people think at the margin. As we will see in future chapters, this idea is the key to understanding the decision a firm makes about how many workers to hire and how much output to produce. To take a step toward understanding these decisions, the third column in the table gives the marginal product of a worker. The **marginal product** of any input in the production process is the increase in the quantity of output obtained from one additional unit of that input. When the number of workers goes from 1 to 2, pizza production increases from 50 to 90,

marginal product
the increase in output that arises from an additional unit of input

TABLE 13.1

A Production Function and Total Cost: Hungry Horace's Pizza Factory

Number of workers	Output (quantity of pizzas produced per hour)	Marginal product of labour	Cost of factory	Cost of workers	Total cost of inputs (cost of factory + cost of workers)
0	0		€30	€0	€30
1	50	50	30	10	40
2	90	40	30	20	50
3	120	30	30	30	60
4	140	20	30	40	70
5	150	10	30	50	80

FIGURE 13.2

Hungry Horace's Production Function

The production function in panel (a) shows the relationship between the number of workers hired and the quantity of output produced. Here the number of workers hired (on the horizontal axis) is from the first column in Table 13.1, and the quantity of output produced (on the vertical axis) is from the second column. The production function gets flatter as the number of workers increases, which reflects diminishing marginal product. The total cost curve in panel (b) shows the relationship between the quantity of output produced and total cost of production. Here the quantity of output produced (on the horizontal axis) is from the second column in Table 13.1, and the total cost (on the vertical axis) is from the sixth column. The total cost curve gets steeper as the quantity of output increases because of diminishing marginal product.

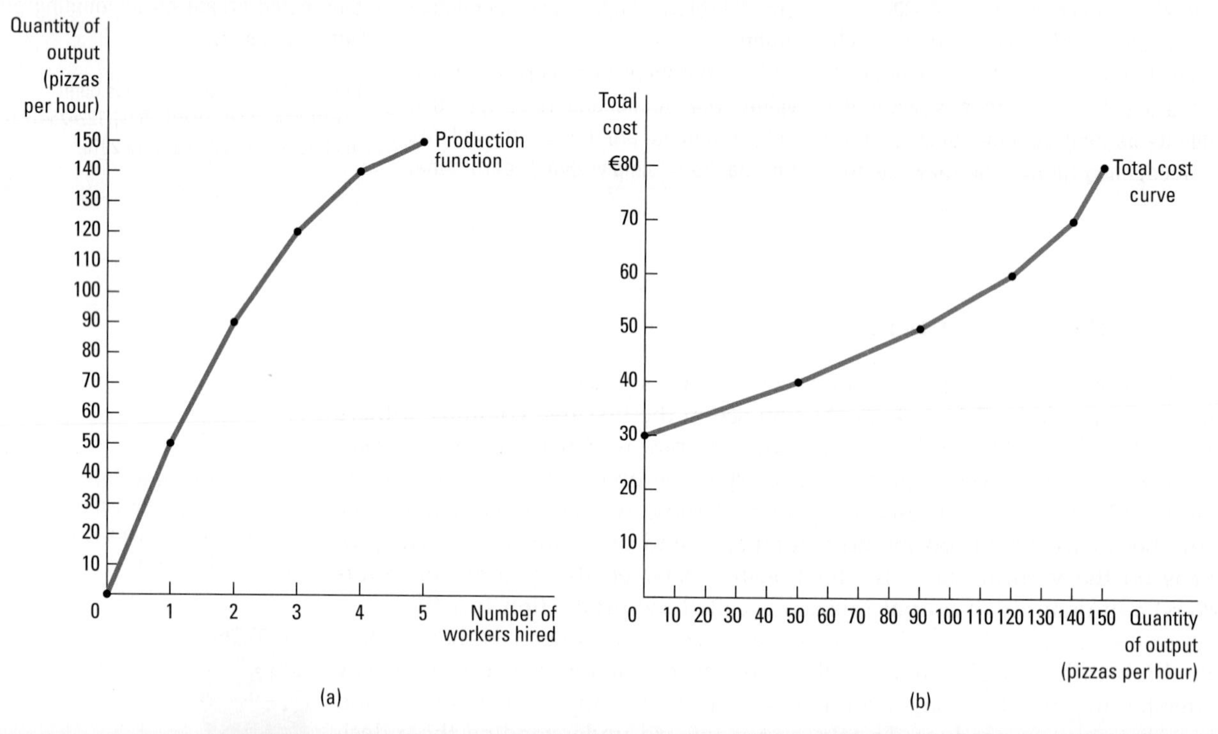

so the marginal product of the second worker is 40 pizzas. And when the number of workers goes from 2 to 3, pizza production increases from 90 to 120, so the marginal product of the third worker is 30 pizzas.

Notice that as the number of workers increases, the marginal product declines. The second worker has a marginal product of 40 pizzas, the third worker has a marginal product of 30 pizzas and the fourth worker has a marginal product of 20 pizzas. This property of the production function is called **diminishing marginal product**. At first, when only a few workers are hired, they have easy access to Horace's kitchen equipment. As the number of workers increases, additional workers have to share equipment and work in more crowded conditions. Hence, as more and more workers are hired, each additional worker contributes less to the production of pizzas.

diminishing marginal product
the property whereby the marginal product of an input declines as the quantity of the input increases

Diminishing marginal product is also apparent in Figure 13.2 (panel (a)). The production function's slope ('rise over run') tells us the change in Horace's output of pizzas ('rise') for each additional input of labour ('run'). That is, the slope of the production function measures the marginal product of a worker. As the number of workers increases, the marginal product declines, and the production function becomes flatter.

From the Production Function to the Total Cost Curve

The last three columns of Table 13.1 are reproduced as a graph in Figure 13.2 (panel (b)) to show Horace's cost of producing pizzas. In this example, the cost of operating the factory is €30 per hour and the cost of a worker is €10 per hour. If Horace hires 1 worker, his total cost is €40. If he hires 2 workers, his total cost is €50, and so on. With this information, the table now shows how the number of workers Horace hires is related to the quantity of pizzas he produces and to his total cost of production.

Our goal in the next several chapters is to study firms' production and pricing decisions. For this purpose, the most important relationship in Table 13.1 is between quantity produced (in the second column) and total costs (in the sixth column). Panel (b) of Figure 13.2 graphs these two columns of data with the quantity produced on the horizontal axis and total cost on the vertical axis. This graph is called the *total cost curve.*

Now compare the total cost curve in panel (b) of Figure 13.2 with the production function in panel (a). These two curves are opposite sides of the same coin. The total cost curve gets steeper as the amount produced rises, whereas the production function gets flatter as production rises. These changes in slope occur for the same reason. High production of pizzas means that Horace's kitchen is crowded with many workers. Because the kitchen is crowded, each additional worker adds less to production, reflecting diminishing marginal product. Therefore, the production function is relatively flat. But now turn this logic around: when the kitchen is crowded, producing an additional pizza requires a lot of additional labour and is thus very costly. Therefore, when the quantity produced is large, the total cost curve is relatively steep.

Quick Quiz If Farmer Schmidt plants no seeds on his farm, he gets no harvest. If he plants 1 bag of seeds he gets 3 tonnes of wheat. If he plants 2 bags he gets 5 tonnes. If he plants 3 bags he gets 6 tonnes. A bag of seeds is priced at €100, and seeds are his only cost. Use these data to graph the farmer's production function and total cost curve. Explain their shapes.

THE VARIOUS MEASURES OF COST

Our analysis of Hungry Horace's Pizza Factory demonstrated how a firm's total cost reflects its production function. From data on a firm's total cost we can derive several related measures of cost which will turn out to be useful when we analyse production and pricing decisions in future chapters. To see how these related measures are derived, we consider the example in Table 13.2 This table presents cost data on Horace's neighbour: Thirsty Virgil's Lemonade Stand.

The first column of the table shows the number of glasses of lemonade that Virgil might produce, ranging from 0 to 10 glasses per hour. The second column shows Virgil's total cost of producing glasses of lemonade. Figure 13.3 plots Virgil's total cost curve. The quantity of lemonade (from the first column) is on the horizontal axis, and total cost (from the second column) is on the vertical axis. Thirsty Virgil's total cost curve has a shape similar to Hungry Horace's. In particular, it becomes steeper as the quantity produced rises, which (as we have discussed) reflects diminishing marginal product.

TABLE 13.2

The Various Measures of Cost: Thirsty Virgil's Lemonade Stand

Quantity of lemonade glasses (per hour)	Total cost	Fixed cost	Variable cost	Average fixed cost	Average variable cost	Average total cost	Marginal cost
0	€3.00	€3.00	€0.00	–	–	–	
1	3.30	3.00	0.30	€3.00	€0.30	€3.30	€0.30
2	3.80	3.00	0.80	1.50	0.40	1.90	0.50
3	4.50	3.00	1.50	1.00	0.50	1.50	0.70
4	5.40	3.00	2.40	0.75	0.60	1.35	0.90
5	6.50	3.00	3.50	0.60	0.70	1.30	1.10
6	7.80	3.00	4.80	0.50	0.80	1.30	1.30
7	9.30	3.00	6.30	0.43	0.90	1.33	1.50
8	11.00	3.00	8.00	0.38	1.00	1.38	1.70
9	12.90	3.00	9.90	0.33	1.10	1.43	1.90
10	15.00	3.00	12.00	0.30	1.20	1.50	2.10

FIGURE 13.3

Thirsty Virgil's Total Cost Curve

Here the quantity of output produced (on the horizontal axis) is from the first column in Table 13.2, and the total cost (on the vertical axis) is from the second column. As in Figure 13.2, the total cost curve gets steeper as the quantity of output increases because of diminishing marginal product.

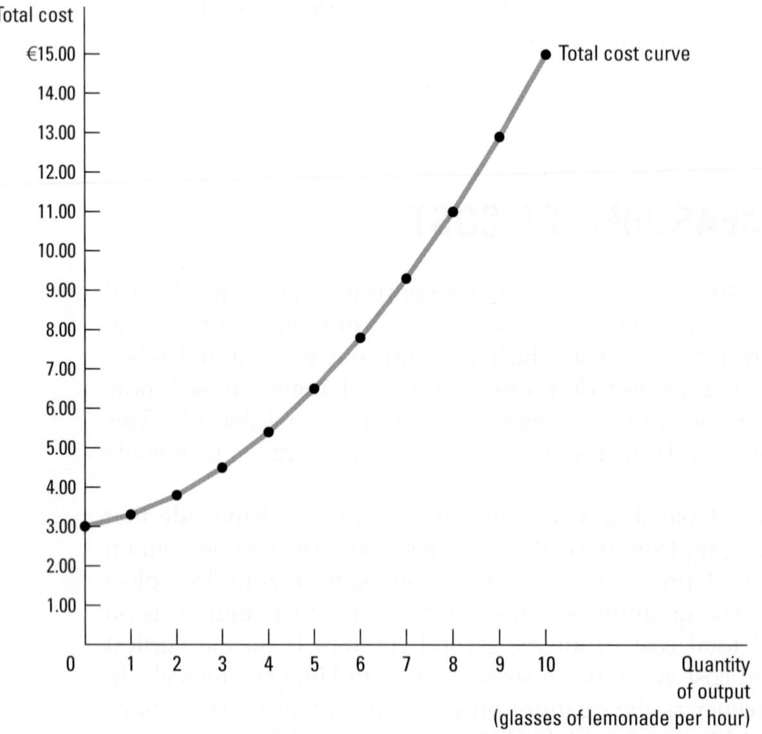

Fixed and Variable Costs

Virgil's total cost can be divided into two types. Some costs, called **fixed costs,** are not determined by the amount of output produced; they can change but not as a result of changes in the amount produced. They are incurred even if the firm produces nothing at all. Virgil's fixed costs include any rent he pays because this cost is the same regardless of how much lemonade Virgil produces. Similarly, if Virgil needs to hire a barman to serve the drinks, regardless of the quantity of lemonade sold, the barman's salary is a fixed cost. The third column in Table 13.2 shows Virgil's fixed cost, which in this example is €3.00.

fixed costs
costs that are not determined by the quantity of output produced

Some of the firm's costs, called **variable costs,** change as the firm alters the quantity of output produced. Virgil's variable costs include the cost of lemons, sugar, paper cups and straws: the more lemonade Virgil makes, the more of these items he needs to buy. Similarly, if Virgil pays his workers overtime to make more lemonade, the wages of these workers are variable costs. The fourth column of the table shows Virgil's variable cost. The variable cost is 0 if he produces nothing, €0.30 if he produces 1 glass of lemonade, €0.80 if he produces 2 glasses and so on.

variable costs
costs that are dependent on the quantity of output produced

A firm's total cost is the sum of fixed and variable costs. In Table 13.2 total cost in the second column equals fixed cost in the third column plus variable cost in the fourth column.

Average and Marginal Cost

As the owner of his firm, Virgil has to decide how much to produce. A key part of this decision is how his costs will vary as he changes the level of production. In making this decision, Virgil might ask his production supervisor the following two questions about the cost of producing lemonade:

- How much does it cost to make the typical glass of lemonade?
- How much does it cost to increase production of lemonade by 1 glass?

Although at first these two questions might seem to have the same answer, they do not. Both answers will turn out to be important for understanding how firms make production decisions.

To find the cost of the typical unit produced, we would divide the firm's total costs by the quantity of output it produces. For example, if the firm produces 2 glasses per hour, its total cost is €3.80, and the cost of the typical glass is €3.80/2, or €1.90. Total cost divided by the quantity of output is called **average total cost**. Because total cost is just the sum of fixed and variable costs, average total cost can be expressed as the sum of average fixed cost and average variable cost. **Average fixed cost** is the fixed cost divided by the quantity of output, and **average variable cost** is the variable cost divided by the quantity of output.

average total cost
total cost divided by the quantity of output

average fixed cost
fixed costs divided by the quantity of output

average variable cost
variable costs divided by the quantity of output

Although average total cost tells us the cost of the typical unit, it does not tell us how much total cost will change as the firm alters its level of production. The last column in Table 13.2 shows the amount that total cost rises when the firm increases production by 1 unit of output. This number is called **marginal cost**. For example, if Virgil increases production from 2 to 3 glasses, total cost rises from €3.80 to €4.50, so the marginal cost of the third glass of lemonade is €4.50 minus €3.80, or €0.70.

marginal cost
the increase in total cost that arises from an extra unit of production

It may be helpful to express these definitions mathematically:

$$\text{Average total cost} = \text{Total cost}/\text{Quantity}$$
$$ATC = TC/Q$$

and

$$\text{Marginal cost} = \text{Change in total cost}/\text{Change in quantity}$$
$$MC = \Delta TC/\Delta Q.$$

Here Δ, the Greek letter delta, represents the change in a variable. These equations show how average total cost and marginal cost are derived from total cost. Average total cost tells us the cost of a typical unit of output if total cost is divided evenly over all the units produced. Marginal cost tells us the increase in total cost that arises from producing an additional unit of output. As we will see more fully in the next chapter, Virgil, our lemonade entrepreneur, will find the concepts of average total cost and marginal cost useful when deciding how much lemonade to produce.

Cost Curves and their Shapes

Just as in previous chapters we found graphs of supply and demand useful when analysing the behaviour of markets, we will find graphs of average and marginal cost useful when analysing the behaviour of firms. Figure 13.4 graphs Virgil's costs using the data from Table 13.2 The horizontal axis measures the quantity the firm produces, and the vertical axis measures marginal and average costs. The graph shows four curves: average total cost *(ATC)*, average fixed cost *(AFC)*, average variable cost *(AVC)*, and marginal cost *(MC)*.

FIGURE 13.4

Thirsty Virgil's Average Cost and Marginal Cost Curves

This figure shows the average total cost (ATC), average fixed cost (AFC) average variable cost (AVC) and marginal cost (MC) for Thirsty Virgil's Lemonade Bar. All of these curves are obtained by graphing the data in Table 13.2. These cost curves show three features that are typical of many firms: (1) Marginal cost rises with the quantity of output. (2) The average total cost curve is U-shaped. (3) The marginal cost curve crosses the average total cost curve at the minimum of average total cost.

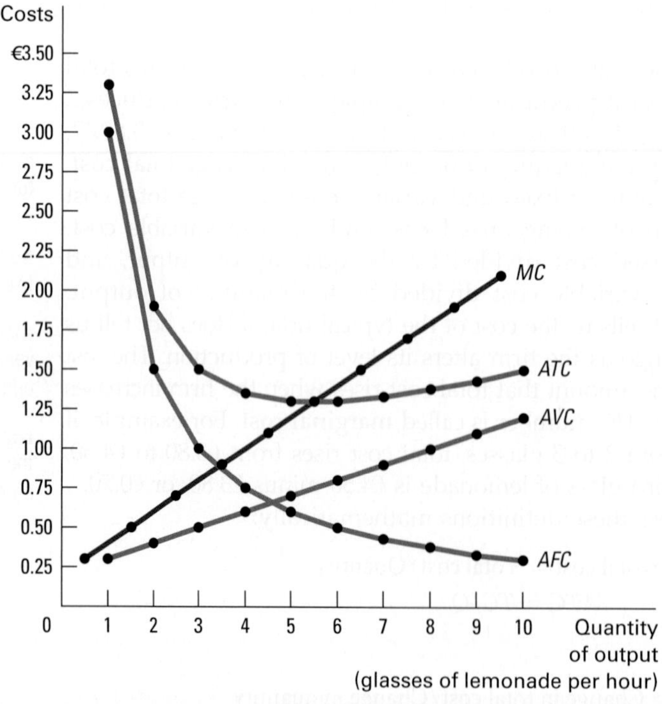

The cost curves shown here for Thirsty Virgil's Lemonade Bar have some features that are common to the cost curves of many firms in the economy. Let's examine three features in particular: the shape of marginal cost, the shape of average total cost, and the relationship between marginal and average total cost.

Rising Marginal Cost Thirsty Virgil's marginal cost rises with the quantity of output produced. This reflects the property of diminishing marginal product. When Virgil is producing a small quantity of lemonade he has few workers and much of his equipment is not being used. Because he can easily put these idle resources to use, the marginal product of an extra worker is large, and the marginal cost of an extra glass of lemonade is small. By contrast, when Virgil is producing a large quantity of lemonade his stand is crowded with workers and most of his equipment is fully utilized. Virgil can produce more lemonade by adding workers, but these new workers have to work in crowded conditions and may have to wait to use the equipment. Therefore, when the quantity of lemonade being produced is already high, the marginal product of an extra worker is low, and the marginal cost of an extra glass of lemonade is large.

U-Shaped Average Total Cost Thirsty Virgil's average total cost curve takes on a U-shape. To understand why this is so, remember that average total cost is the sum of average fixed cost and average variable cost. Average fixed cost always declines as output rises because the fixed cost does not change as output rises and so gets spread over a larger number of units. Average variable cost typically rises as output increases because of diminishing marginal product. Average total cost reflects the shapes of both average fixed cost and average variable cost. As shown in Figure 13.4 at very low levels of output, such as 1 or 2 glasses per hour, average total cost is high because the fixed cost is spread over only a few units. Average total cost then declines as output increases until the firm's output reaches 5 glasses of lemonade per hour, when average total cost falls to €1.30 per glass. When the firm produces more than 6 glasses, average total cost starts rising again because average variable cost rises substantially. If further units of output were produced the average total cost curve would continue to slope upwards giving the typical U-shape referred to.

The bottom of the U-shape occurs at the quantity that minimizes average total cost. This quantity is sometimes called the **efficient scale** of the firm. For Thirsty Virgil, the efficient scale is 5 or 6 glasses of lemonade. If he produces more or less than this amount, his average total cost rises above the minimum of €1.30.

efficient scale
the quantity of output that minimizes average total cost

The Relationship between Marginal Cost and Average Total Cost If you look at Figure 13.4 (or back at Table 13.2) you will see something that may be surprising at first. Whenever marginal cost is less than average total cost, average total cost is falling. Whenever marginal cost is greater than average total cost, average total cost is rising. This feature of Thirsty Virgil's cost curves is not a coincidence from the particular numbers used in the example: it is true for all firms and is a basic mathematical relationship.

To see why, refer to your understanding of averages and consider what happens to average cost as output goes up by one unit. If the cost of the extra unit is above the average cost of units produced up to that point, then it will tend to pull up the new average cost of a unit. If the new unit actually costs less than the average cost of a unit up to that point, it will tend to drag the new average down. But the price of an extra unit is what economists call marginal cost, so what we have just asserted is tantamount to saying that if marginal cost is less than average cost, average cost will be falling; and if marginal cost is above average cost, average cost will be rising.

This relationship between average total cost and marginal cost has an important corollary: the marginal cost curve crosses the average total cost curve at its minimum. Why? At low levels of output, marginal cost is below average total cost, so average total cost is falling. But after the two curves cross, marginal cost rises above average total cost. For the reason we have just discussed, average total cost must start to rise at this level of output. Hence, at this point of intersection the cost of an additional unit is the same as the average and so the average does not change and the point is the minimum of average total cost. As you will see in the next chapter, this point of minimum average total cost plays a key role in the analysis of competitive firms.

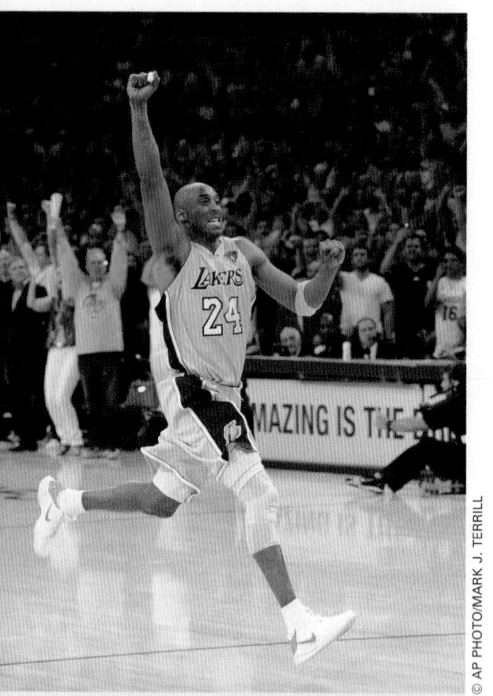

Los Angeles Lakers' star player Kobe Bryant scored an average 29.2 points per game (PPG) in the 2009–2010 season, helping the Lakers to win the season for the second year running.

CASE STUDY

Understanding Averages and Marginal Values

When first encountering average and marginal costs, it can be a little confusing so it is often worth thinking about these values in a different context. Sebastien is an up-and-coming basketball player. In the first 18 games of the season Sebastien has scored a total of 306 points. The average points per game (PPG) at this stage of the season, therefore is 306/18 = 17 points per game. The number of points that Sebastien scores in each successive game is his marginal score. If Sebastien scores 15 points in the 19th game, this is below his average of 17 and his average will fall. If in the next three games he scores 12, 14 and 10 then the marginal points score continues to be below the average and so his average will continue to fall. At the end of the 22nd game he will have scored a total of 357 points and his average will have fallen to 16.2. If in the next four games he scores 20, 18, 22 and 20 points, then each successive game sees his marginal points score being better than his average and so the average will be pulled up. At then end of 26 games, therefore, his total points score will be 437 and his average PPG will have risen to 16.8.

So, if Sebastien marginal points score in each successive game is less than his average, his average will fall but if his marginal points score in each game is more than his average points score then his average will rise. It's the same principle for firms' costs!

Typical Cost Curves

In the examples we have studied so far, the firms exhibit diminishing marginal product and, therefore, rising marginal cost at all levels of output. Yet actual firms are often a bit more complicated than this. In many firms, diminishing marginal product does not start to occur immediately after the first worker is hired. Depending on the production process, the second or third worker might have higher marginal product than the first because a team of workers can divide tasks and work more productively than a single worker. Such firms would first experience increasing marginal product for a while before diminishing marginal product sets in.

The table in Figure 13.5 shows the cost data for such a firm, called Berit's Bagel Bin. These data are used in the graphs. Panel (a) shows how total cost *(TC)* depends on the quantity produced, and panel (b) shows average total cost *(ATC)*, average fixed cost *(AFC)*, average variable cost *(AVC)* and marginal cost *(MC)*. In the range of output from 0 to 4 bagels per hour, the firm experiences

FIGURE 13.5

Berit's Cost Curves

Many firms, like Berit's Bagel Bin, experience increasing marginal product before diminishing marginal product and, therefore, have cost curves shaped like those in this figure. Panel (a) shows how total cost (TC) depends on the quantity produced. Panel (b) shows how average total cost (ATC), average fixed cost (AFC), average variable cost (AVC) and marginal cost (MC) depend on the quantity produced. These curves are derived by graphing the data from the table. Notice that marginal cost and average variable cost fall for a while before starting to rise.

Quantity of bagels (per hour)	Total cost	Fixed cost	Variable cost	Average fixed cost	Average variable cost	Average total cost	Marginal cost
Q	*TC = FC + VC*	*FC*	*VC*	*AFC = FC/Q*	*AVC = VC/Q*	*ATC = TC/Q*	*MC = ΔTC/ΔQ*
0	€2.00	€2.00	€0.00	–	–	–	
1	3.00	2.00	1.00	€2.00	€1.00	€3.00	€1.00
2	3.80	2.00	1.80	1.00	0.90	1.90	0.80
3	4.40	2.00	2.40	0.67	0.80	1.47	0.60
4	4.80	2.00	2.80	0.50	0.70	1.20	0.40
5	5.20	2.00	3.20	0.40	0.64	1.04	0.40
6	5.80	2.00	3.80	0.33	0.63	0.96	0.60
7	6.60	2.00	4.60	0.29	0.66	0.95	0.80
8	7.60	2.00	5.60	0.25	0.70	0.95	1.00
9	8.80	2.00	6.80	0.22	0.76	0.98	1.20
10	10.20	2.00	8.20	0.20	0.82	1.02	1.40
11	11.80	2.00	9.80	0.18	0.89	1.07	1.60
12	13.60	2.00	11.60	0.17	0.97	1.14	1.80
13	15.60	2.00	13.60	0.15	1.05	1.20	2.00
14	17.80	2.00	15.80	0.14	1.13	1.27	2.20

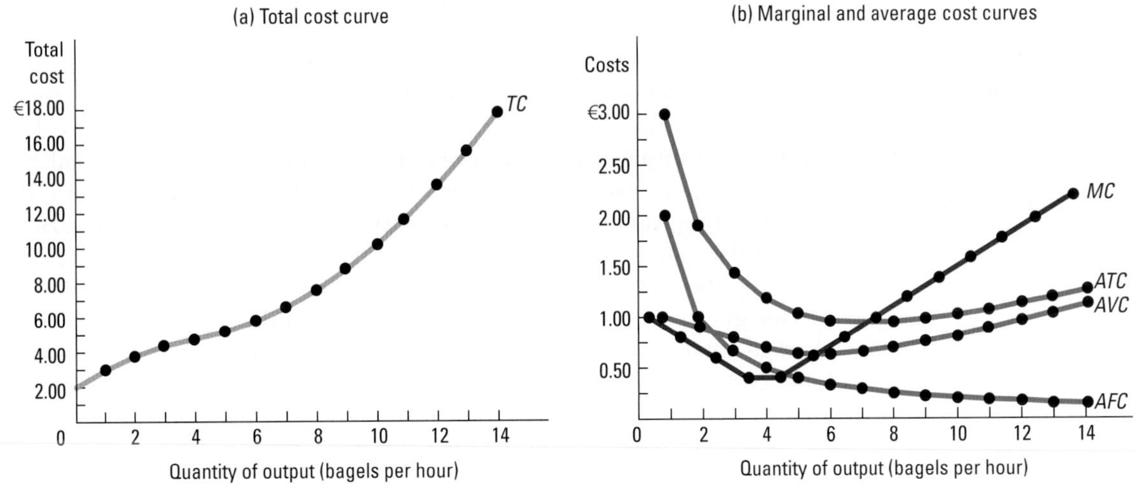

(a) Total cost curve

(b) Marginal and average cost curves

increasing marginal product, and the marginal cost curve falls. After 5 bagels per hour, the firm starts to experience diminishing marginal product, and the marginal cost curve starts to rise. This combination of increasing then diminishing marginal product also makes the average variable cost curve U-shaped.

Despite these differences from our previous example, Berit's cost curves share the three properties that are most important to remember:

- Marginal cost eventually rises with the quantity of output.
- The average total cost curve is U-shaped.
- The marginal cost curve crosses the average total cost curve at the minimum of average total cost.

Quick Quiz Suppose BMW's total cost of producing 4 cars is €225 000 and its total cost of producing 5 cars is €250 000. What is the average total cost of producing 5 cars? What is the marginal cost of the fifth car? • Draw the marginal cost curve and the average total cost curve for a typical firm, and explain why these curves cross where they do.

COSTS IN THE SHORT RUN AND IN THE LONG RUN

We noted at the beginning of this chapter that a firm's costs might depend on the time horizon being examined. Let's discuss more precisely why this might be the case.

The Relationship Between Short-Run and Long-Run Average Total Cost

For many firms, the division of total costs between fixed and variable costs depends on the time horizon. Consider, for instance, a car manufacturer, such as Renault. Over a period of only a few months, Renault cannot adjust the number or sizes of its car factories. The only way it can produce additional cars is to hire more workers at the factories it already has. The cost of these factories is, therefore, a fixed cost in the short run. By contrast, over a period of several years, Renault can expand the size of its factories, build new factories or close old ones. Thus, the cost of its factories is a variable cost in the long run.

Because many decisions are fixed in the short run but variable in the long run, a firm's long-run cost curves differ from its short-run cost curves. Figure 13.6 shows an example. The figure presents three short-run average total cost curves representing the cost structures for a small, medium and large factory. It also presents the long-run average total cost curve. As the firm adjusts the size of the factory to the quantity of production, it moves along the long-run curve, and it is adjusting the size of the factory to the quantity of production.

This graph shows how short-run and long-run costs are related. The long-run average total cost curve is a much flatter U-shape than the short-run average total cost curve. In addition, all the short-run curves lie on or above the long-run curve. These properties arise because firms have greater flexibility in the long run. In essence, in the long run, the firm chooses which short-run curve it wants to use. But in the short run, it has to use whatever short-run curve it chose in the past.

The figure shows an example of how a change in production alters costs over different time horizons. When Renault wants to increase production from 1 000 to 1 200 cars per day, it has no choice in the short run but to hire more workers at its existing medium-sized factory. Because of diminishing marginal product, average total cost rises from €10 000 to €12 000 per car. In the long run, however, Renault can expand both the size of the factory and its workforce, and average total cost returns to €10 000.

FIGURE 13.6

Average Total Cost in the Short and Long Runs

Because fixed costs are variable in the long run, the average total cost curve in the short run differs from the average total cost curve in the long run.

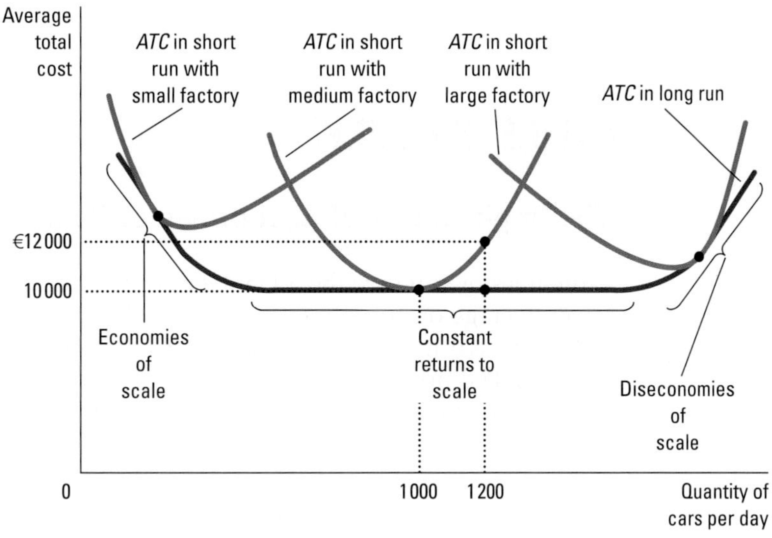

How long does it take for a firm to get to the long run? The answer depends on the firm. It can take a year or longer for a major manufacturing firm, such as a car company, to build a larger factory. By contrast, a person running a newspaper stand might be able to find new premises and expand sales in a matter of weeks or days. There is, therefore, no single answer about how long it takes a firm to adjust its production facilities.

Economies and Diseconomies of Scale

The shape of the long-run average total cost curve conveys important information about the technology for producing a good. When long-run average total cost declines as output increases, there are said to be **economies of scale**. When long-run average total cost rises as output increases, there are said to be **diseconomies of scale**. When long-run average total cost does not vary with the level of output, there are said to be **constant returns to scale**. In this example, Renault has economies of scale at low levels of output, constant returns to scale at intermediate levels of output and diseconomies of scale at high levels of output.

economies of scale
the property whereby long-run average total cost falls as the quantity of output increases

diseconomies of scale
the property whereby long-run average total cost rises as the quantity of output increases

constant returns to scale
the property whereby long-run average total cost stays the same as the quantity of output changes

What might cause economies or diseconomies of scale? Economies of scale often arise because higher production levels allow *specialization* among workers and increases the possibility that technology can be used, which permits each worker to become better at his or her assigned tasks. For instance, modern assembly line production may require fewer workers in relation to the technology used but still produce more cars. If Renault were producing only a small quantity of cars, it could not take advantage of this approach and would have higher average total cost. Diseconomies of scale can arise because of *coordination problems* that are inherent in any large organization. The more cars Renault produces, the more stretched the management team becomes, and the less effective the managers become at keeping costs down.

This analysis shows why long-run average total cost curves are often U-shaped. At low levels of production, the firm benefits from increased size because it can take advantage of greater specialization. Coordination problems, meanwhile, are not yet acute. By contrast, at high levels of production, the benefits of specialization have already been realized, and coordination problems become more severe as the firm grows larger. Thus, long-run average total cost is falling at low levels of production because of increasing specialization and rising at high levels of production because of increasing coordination problems.

CASE STUDY

The Implications of Economies of Scale

Economies of scale are the advantages of large-scale production that result in lower average or unit costs.

Imagine a firm which makes bricks. The current plant has a maximum capacity of 100 000 bricks per week and the total costs are €200 000 per week. The average cost for each brick, therefore, is €2. The firm sets a price of €2.20 per brick giving it a profit margin of €0.20 per brick.

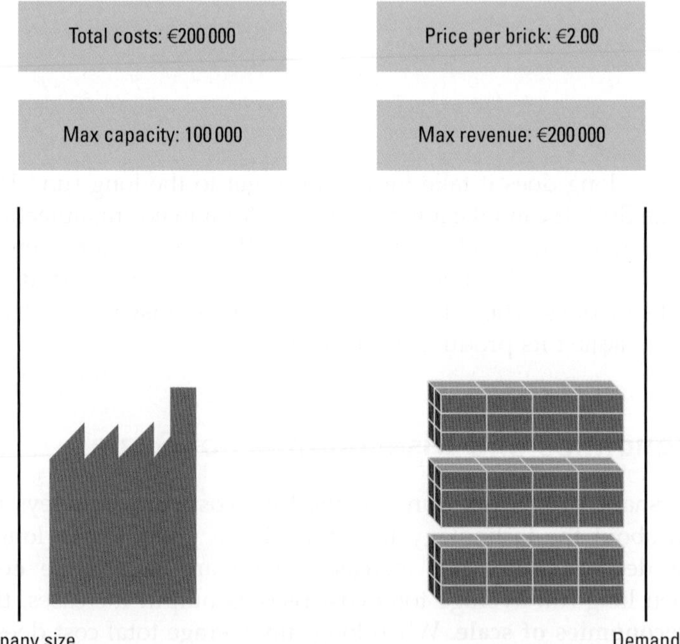

Now imagine that in the long run, the firm expands. It doubles the size of its plant. The total costs, obviously, increase – they are now using more land and putting up more buildings, as well as hiring extra labour and buying more equipment and raw materials. All of this expansion will increase the total cost (although it should be pointed out that such a neat figure is unlikely in real life).

Assume TC is now 350 000 per week. The expansion of the plant means that the firm can double its output so its capacity is now 200 000 bricks per week. The proportionate increase in the total costs is less than the proportionate increase in output. Total costs have risen by €150 000 or 75 per cent and total output by 100 per cent, which means that the average cost per brick is now 1.75 per brick.

TABLE 13.3

The Many Types of Cost: A Summary

Term	Definition	Mathematical description
Explicit costs	Costs that require an outlay of money by the firm	–
Implicit costs	Costs that do not require an outlay of money by the firm	–
Fixed costs	Costs that do not vary with the quantity of output produced	FC
Variable costs	Costs that do vary with the quantity of output produced	VC
Total cost	The market value of all the inputs that a firm uses in production	$TC = FC + VC$
Average fixed cost	Fixed costs divided by the quantity of output	$AFC = FC/Q$
Average variable cost	Variable costs divided by the quantity of output	$AVC = VC/Q$
Average total cost	Total cost divided by the quantity of output	$ATC = TC/Q$
Marginal cost	The increase in total cost that arises from an extra unit of production	$MC = \Delta TC/\Delta Q$

By themselves, of course, a firm's cost curves do not tell us what decisions the firm will make. But they are an important component of that decision, as we will begin to see in the next chapter.

SUMMARY

- One goal of firms is to maximize profit, which equals total revenue minus total cost.
- When analysing a firm's behaviour, it is important to include all the opportunity costs of production. Some of the opportunity costs, such as the wages a firm pays its workers, are explicit. Other opportunity costs, such as the wages the firm owner gives up by working in the firm rather than taking another job, are implicit.
- A firm's costs reflect its production process. A typical firm's production function gets flatter as the quantity of an input increases, displaying the property of diminishing marginal product. As a result, a firm's total cost curve gets steeper as the quantity produced rises.
- A firm's total costs can be divided between fixed costs and variable costs. Fixed costs are costs that are not determined by the quantity of output produced. Variable costs are costs that directly related to the amount produced and so change when the firm alters the quantity of output produced.
- From a firm's total cost, two related measures of cost are derived. Average total cost is total cost divided by the quantity of output. Marginal cost is the amount by which total cost changes if output increases (or decreases) by 1 unit.
- When analysing firm behaviour, it is often useful to graph average total cost and marginal cost. For a typical firm, marginal cost rises with the quantity of output. Average total cost first falls as output increases and then rises as output increases further. The marginal cost curve always crosses the average total cost curve at the minimum of average total cost.
- A firm's costs often depend on the time horizon being considered. In particular, many costs are fixed in the short run but variable in the long run. As a result, when the firm changes its level of production, average total cost may rise more in the short run than in the long run.

KEY CONCEPTS

total cost, p. 265
profit, p. 265
explicit costs, p. 265
implicit costs, p. 265
economic profit, p. 266
accounting profit, p. 267
the short run, p. 268
the long run, p. 268
production function, p. 269
marginal product, p. 269
diminishing marginal product, p. 270
fixed costs, p. 273
variable costs, p. 273
average total cost, p. 273
average fixed cost, p. 273
average variable cost, p. 273
marginal cost, p. 273
efficient scale, p. 275
economies of scale, p. 279
diseconomies of scale, p. 279
constant returns to scale, p. 279

QUESTIONS FOR REVIEW

1. What is the relationship between a firm's total revenue, profit and total cost?
2. Give an example of an opportunity cost that an accountant might not count as a cost. Why would the accountant ignore this cost?
3. What is marginal product, and what does it mean if it is diminishing?
4. Draw a production function that exhibits diminishing marginal product of labour. Draw the associated total cost curve. (In both cases, be sure to label the axes.) Explain the shapes of the two curves you have drawn.
5. Define total cost, average total cost and marginal cost. How are they related?
6. Draw the marginal cost and average total cost curves for a typical firm. Explain why the curves have the shapes that they do and why they cross where they do.
7. How and why does a firm's average total cost curve differ in the short run and in the long run?
8. Define *economies of scale* and explain why they might arise. Define *diseconomies of scale* and explain why they might arise.

PROBLEMS AND APPLICATIONS

1. This chapter discusses many types of costs: opportunity cost, total cost, fixed cost, variable cost, average total cost and marginal cost. Fill in the type of cost that best completes each phrase below:
   a. The true cost of taking some action is its ________.
   b. ________ is falling when marginal cost is below it, and rising when marginal cost is above it.
   c. A cost that does not depend on the quantity produced is a ________.
   d. In the ice cream industry in the short run, ________ includes the cost of cream and sugar, but not the cost of the factory.
   e. Profits equal total revenue minus ________.
   f. The cost of producing an extra unit of output is the ________.
2. Your Aunt Imelda is thinking about opening a pub. She estimates that it would cost €500 000 per year to rent the premises, buy a licence to serve alcohol and to buy in enough Murphy's Irish Stout from the brewery. In addition, she would have to leave her €50 000 per year job as an accountant.
   a. Define opportunity cost.
   b. What is your aunt's opportunity cost of running the pub for a year? If your aunt thought she could sell €510 000 worth of Murphy's in a year, should she open the pub? Explain.
3. Suppose that your university charges you separately for tuition and for room and board.
   a. What is a cost of going to university that is not an opportunity cost?
   b. What is an explicit opportunity cost of going to university?
   c. What is an implicit opportunity cost of going to university?

4. A commercial fisherman notices the following relationship between hours spent fishing and the quantity of fish caught:

Hours	Quantity of fish (in kilograms)
0	0
1	10
2	18
3	24
4	28
5	30

   a. What is the marginal product of each hour spent fishing?
   b. Use these data to graph the fisherman's production function. Explain its shape.
   c. The fisherman has a fixed cost of €10 (his fishing rod). The opportunity cost of his time is €5 per hour. Graph the fisherman's total cost curve. Explain its shape.

5. Clean Sweep is a company that makes brooms and then sells them door-to-door. Here is the relationship between the number of workers and Clean Sweep's output in a given day:

Workers	Output	Marginal product	Average total cost	Marginal cost
0	0			
1	20			
2	50			
3	90			
4	120			
5	140			
6	150			
7	155			

   a. Fill in the column of marginal product. What pattern do you see? How might you explain it?
   b. A worker costs €100 a day, and the firm has fixed costs of €200. Use this information to fill in the column for total cost.
   c. Fill in the column for average total cost. (Recall that $ATC = TC/Q$.) What pattern do you see?
   d. Now fill in the column for marginal cost. (Recall that $MC = \Delta TC/\Delta Q$.) What pattern do you see?
   e. Compare the column for marginal product and the column for marginal cost. Explain the relationship.
   f. Compare the column for average total cost and the column for marginal cost. Explain the relationship.

6. Suppose that you and your roommate have started a bagel delivery service on campus. List some of your fixed costs and describe why they are fixed. List some of your variable costs and describe why they are variable.

7. Consider the following cost information for a pizzeria:

Q (dozens)	Total cost	Variable cost
0	€300	€0
1	350	50
2	390	90
3	420	120
4	450	150
5	490	190
6	540	240

   a. What is the pizzeria's fixed cost?
   b. Construct a table in which you calculate the marginal cost per dozen pizzas using the information on total cost. Also calculate the marginal cost per dozen pizzas using the information on variable cost. What is the relationship between these sets of numbers? Comment.

8. You are thinking about setting up a lemonade bar. The bar itself costs €200 a week to rent. The ingredients for each cup of lemonade cost €0.50.
   a. What is your fixed cost of doing business? What is your variable cost per cup?
   b. Construct a table showing your total cost, average total cost and marginal cost for output levels varying from 0 to 100 litres. (Hint: there are 4 cups in a litre.) Draw the three cost curves.

9. Your cousin Vinnie owns a painting company with fixed costs of €200 and the following schedule for variable costs:

Quantity of houses painted per month	1	2	3	4	5	6	7
Variable costs	€10	€20	€40	€80	€160	€320	€640

   Calculate average fixed cost, average variable cost and average total cost for each quantity. What is the efficient scale of the painting company?

10. Healthy Harry's Juice Bar has the following cost schedules:

Q (vats)	Variable cost	Total cost
0	€0	€30
1	10	40
2	25	55
3	45	75
4	70	100
5	100	130
6	135	165

   a. Calculate average variable cost, average total cost and marginal cost for each quantity.

b. Graph all three curves. What is the relationship between the marginal cost curve and the average total cost curve? Between the marginal cost curve and the average variable cost curve? Explain.

11. Consider the following table of long-run total cost for three different firms:

Quantity	1	2	3	4	5	6	7
Firm A	€60	€70	€80	€90	€100	€110	€120
Firm B	11	24	39	56	75	96	119
Firm C	21	34	49	66	85	106	129

Does each of these firms experience economies of scale or diseconomies of scale?

For further resources, visit www.cengage.com/mankiw_taylor2

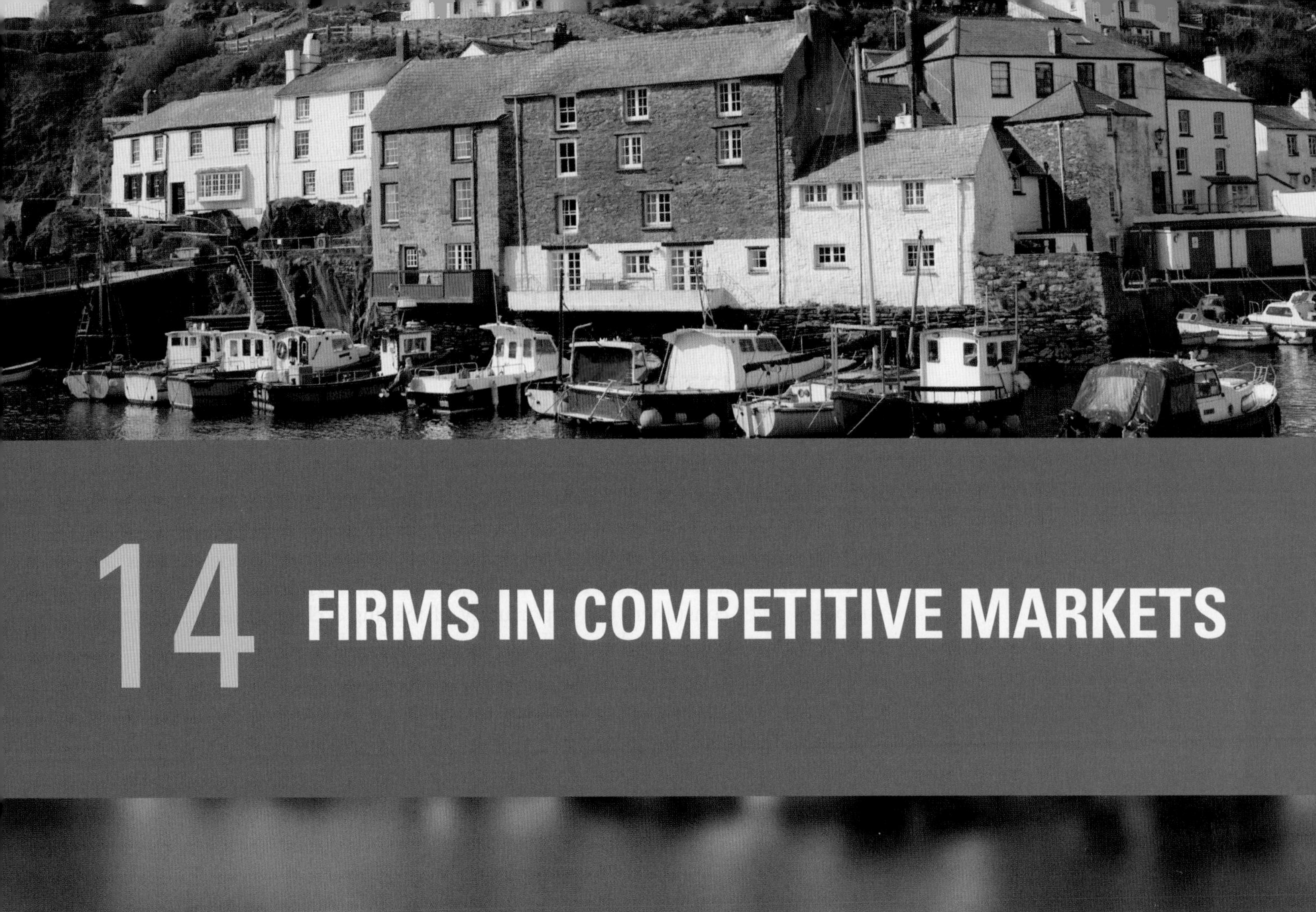

14 FIRMS IN COMPETITIVE MARKETS

If your local petrol station raised the price it charges for petrol by 20 per cent it would see a large drop in the amount of petrol it sold. Its customers would quickly switch to buying their petrol at other petrol stations. By contrast, if your regional water company raised the price of water by 20 per cent, it would see only a small decrease in the amount of water it sold. People might water their lawns less often and buy more water-efficient showers, but they would be hard pressed to reduce water consumption greatly and would be unlikely to find another supplier. The difference between the petrol market and the water market is obvious: there are many firms selling petrol in your area, but there is only one firm selling water. As you might expect, this difference in market structure shapes the pricing and production decisions of the firms that operate in these markets.

In this chapter we examine the behaviour of competitive firms, such as your local petrol station. You may recall that a market is competitive if each buyer and seller is small compared to the size of the market and, therefore, has little ability to influence market prices. By contrast, if a firm can influence the market price of the good it sells, it is said to have *market power*. Later in the book we examine the behaviour of firms with market power, such as your local water company.

Our analysis of competitive firms in this chapter will shed light on the decisions that lie behind the supply curve in a competitive market. Not surprisingly, we will find that a market supply curve is tightly linked to firms' costs of production. (Indeed, this general insight should be familiar to you from our analysis in Chapter 7.) But among a firm's various costs – fixed, variable, average and marginal – which ones are most relevant for its decision about the quantity to supply at any given price? We will see that all these measures of cost play important and interrelated roles.

WHAT IS A COMPETITIVE MARKET?

Our goal in this chapter is to examine how firms make production decisions in competitive markets. As a background for this analysis, we begin by considering what a competitive market is.

The Meaning of Competition

Competition refers to a situation where there are rivals in production who allow the consumer to make a choice. A market in which there is only one supplier has no competition as consumers have no choice but a market where there are many suppliers gives consumers the opportunity of making a choice based on quality, value for money, price and so on. We can summarize the meaning of competition in the following way:

- Where more than one firm offers the same or a similar product there is competition.
- Competition can also manifest itself where substitutes exist: for example, gas and electricity are separate markets but there is the opportunity for consumers to substitute gas cookers for electric ones and so some element of competition exists.
- The closer the degree of substitutability the greater will be the competition that exists.
- Firms may influence the level of competition through the way they build relationships with consumers, encourage purchasing habits, provide levels of customer service and after sales service and so on.

In Chapter 4 we looked at competitive markets. Let us briefly review the lesson on the extreme end of the competitive scale, a *perfectly competitive market*. A competitive market has two characteristics:

- There are many buyers and many sellers in the market.
- The goods offered by the various sellers are largely the same (if identical the goods are described as being 'homogenous'.

As a result of these conditions, the actions of any single buyer or seller in the market have a negligible impact on the market price. Each buyer and seller takes the market price as given.

An example is the market for milk. No single buyer of milk can influence the price of milk because each buyer purchases a small amount relative to the size of the market. Similarly, each seller of milk has limited control over the price because many other sellers are offering milk that is essentially identical. Because each seller can sell all he wants at the going price, he has little reason to charge less, and if he charges more, buyers will go elsewhere. Buyers and sellers in competitive markets must accept the price the market determines and, therefore, are said to be *price takers.*

In addition to the foregoing two conditions for competition, there are two other conditions sometimes thought to characterize perfectly competitive markets:

- Firms can freely enter or exit the market.
- There is a high degree of information available to buyers and sellers in the market.

If, for instance, anyone can decide to start a dairy farm, and if any existing dairy farmer can decide to leave the dairy business, then the dairy industry would satisfy this condition. It should be noted that much of the analysis of competitive firms does not rely on the assumption of free entry and exit because this condition is not necessary for firms to be price takers. But as we will see later in this chapter, entry and exit are often powerful forces shaping the long-run outcome in competitive markets.

The developments in technology now mean that many more people have access to information about firms. Price comparison websites, blogs, review sites and so on mean that it is much easier for consumers to find out about the prices being charged by different firms in a market as well as the sort of service and quality they offer. Firms can also make use of this information and are aware that they are subject to increasing transparency over the way they conduct their business. This can affect their behaviour.

The Revenue of a Competitive Firm

A firm in a competitive market, like most other firms in the economy, tries to maximize profit, which equals total revenue minus total cost. To see how it does this, we first consider the revenue of a competitive firm. To keep matters concrete, let's consider a specific firm: the Grundy Family Dairy Farm.

The Grundy Farm produces a quantity of milk Q and sells each unit at the market price P. The farm's total revenue is $P \times Q$. For example, if a litre of milk sells for €6 and the farm sells 1 000 litres, its total revenue is €6 000.

Because the Grundy Farm is small compared with the world market for milk, it takes the price as given by market conditions. This means, in particular, that the price of milk does not depend on the quantity of output that the Grundy Farm produces and sells. If the Grundys double the amount of milk they produce, the price of milk remains the same, and their total revenue doubles. As a result, total revenue is proportional to the amount of output.

Table 14.1 shows the revenue for the Grundy Family Dairy Farm. The first two columns show the amount of output the farm produces and the price at which it sells its output. The third column is the farm's total revenue. The table assumes that the price of milk is €6 a litre, so total revenue is simply €6 times the number of litres.

TABLE 14.1

Total, Average and Marginal Revenue for a Competitive Firm

Quantity	Price	Total revenue	Average revenue	Marginal revenue
(Q)	(P)	($TR = P \times Q$)	($AR = TR/Q$)	($MR = \Delta TR/\Delta Q$)
1 litre	€6	€6	€6	
2	6	12	6	€6
3	6	18	6	6
4	6	24	6	6
5	6	30	6	6
6	6	36	6	6
7	6	42	6	6
8	6	48	6	6

Just as the concepts of average and marginal were useful in the preceding chapter when analysing costs, they are also useful when analysing revenue. To see what these concepts tell us, consider these two questions:

- How much revenue does the farm receive for the typical litre of milk?
- How much additional revenue does the farm receive if it increases production of milk by 1 litre?

The last two columns in Table 14.1 answer these questions.

average revenue
total revenue divided by the quantity sold

The fourth column in the table shows **average revenue,** which is total revenue (from the third column) divided by the amount of output (from the first column). Average revenue tells us how much revenue a firm receives for the typical unit sold. In Table 14.1, you can see that average revenue equals €6, the price of a litre of milk. This illustrates a general lesson that applies not only to competitive firms but to other firms as well. Total revenue is the price times the quantity ($P \times Q$), and average revenue is total revenue ($P \times Q$) divided by the quantity (Q). Therefore, *for all firms, average revenue equals the price of the good.*

marginal revenue
the change in total revenue from an additional unit sold

The fifth column shows **marginal revenue,** which is the change in total revenue from the sale of each additional unit of output. The sale of one more litre of milk adds €6 to total revenue, therefore the marginal revenue is also €6. In Table 14.1, marginal revenue equals €6, the price of a litre of milk. This result illustrates a lesson that applies only to competitive firms. Total revenue is $P \times Q$, and P is fixed for a competitive firm. Therefore, when Q rises by 1 unit, total revenue rises by P euros. For competitive firms, marginal revenue equals the price of the good.

Quick Quiz When a competitive firm doubles the amount it sells, what happens to the price of its output and its total revenue?

PROFIT MAXIMIZATION AND THE COMPETITIVE FIRM'S SUPPLY CURVE

One goal of a competitive firm is assumed to be maximizing profit, which equals total revenue minus total cost. We have just discussed the firm's revenue, and in the last chapter we discussed the firm's costs. We are now ready to examine how the firm maximizes profit and how that decision leads to its supply curve.

A Simple Example of Profit Maximization

Let's begin our analysis of the firm's supply decision with the example in Table 14.2. In the first column of the table is the number of litres of milk the Grundy Family Dairy Farm produces. The second column shows the farm's total revenue, which is €6 times the number of litres. The third column shows the farm's total cost. Total cost includes fixed costs, which are €3 in this example, and variable costs, which depend on the quantity produced.

The fourth column shows the farm's profit, which is computed by subtracting total cost from total revenue. If the farm produces nothing, it has a loss of €3. If it produces 1 litre, it has a profit of €1. If it produces 2 litres, it has a profit of €4, and so on. To maximize profit, the Grundy Farm chooses the quantity that makes profit as large as possible. In this example, profit is maximized when the farm produces 4 or 5 litres of milk, when the profit is €7.

TABLE 14.2

Profit Maximization: A Numerical Example

Quantity	Total revenue	Total cost	Profit	Marginal revenue	Marginal cost	Change in profit
(Q)	(TR)	(TC)	($TR - TC$)	($MR = \Delta TR/\Delta Q$)	($MC = \Delta TC/\Delta Q$)	($MR - MC$)
0 litres	€0	€3	–€3			
				€6	€2	€4
1	6	5	1			
				6	3	3
2	12	8	4			
				6	4	2
3	18	12	6			
				6	5	1
4	24	17	7			
				6	6	0
5	30	23	7			
				6	7	–1
6	36	30	6			
				6	8	–2
7	42	38	4			
				6	9	–3
8	48	47	1			

There is another way to look at the Grundy Farm's decision: the Grundys can find the profit-maximizing quantity by comparing the marginal revenue and marginal cost from each unit produced. The fifth and sixth columns in Table 14.2 compute marginal revenue and marginal cost from the changes in total revenue and total cost, and the last column shows the change in profit for each additional litre produced. The first litre of milk the farm produces has a marginal revenue of €6 and a marginal cost of €2; hence, producing that litre adds €4 to profit (from –€3 to €1). The second litre produced has a marginal revenue of €6 and a marginal cost of €3, so that litre adds €3 to profit (from €1 to €4). As long as marginal revenue exceeds marginal cost, increasing the quantity produced adds to profit. Since additional production of milk adds to profit it is worth the Grundy Farm producing this extra milk. Once the Grundy Farm has reached 5 litres of milk, however, the situation is very different. The sixth litre would have marginal revenue of €6 and marginal cost of €7, so producing it would reduce profit by €1 (from €7 to €6). It does not make sense for the Grundy Farm to produce the sixth litre and so as a result, the Grundys would not produce beyond 5 litres.

One of the *Ten Principles of Economics* in Chapter 1 is that rational people think at the margin. We now see how the Grundy Family Dairy Farm can apply this principle. If marginal revenue is greater than marginal cost – as it is at 1, 2 or 3 litres – it is worth the Grundys increasing the production of milk; even making a decision to increase production from the third to the fourth litre is worth doing since the MC and MR are the same at this point and as a result the profit level is neither increased nor decreased. If marginal revenue is less than marginal cost – as it is at 5, 6 or 7 litres – the Grundys should decrease production. If the Grundys think at the margin and make incremental adjustments to the level of production, they are naturally led to produce the profit-maximizing quantity.

The Marginal Cost Curve and the Firm's Supply Decision

To extend this analysis of profit maximization, consider the cost curves in Figure 14.1. These cost curves have the three features that, as we discussed in the previous chapter, are thought to describe most firms: the marginal cost curve (*MC*) is upward sloping; the average total cost curve (*ATC*) is U-shaped; and the marginal cost curve crosses the average total cost curve at the minimum of average total cost. The figure also shows a horizontal line at the market price (*P*). The price line is horizontal because the firm is a price taker: the price of the

FIGURE 14.1

Profit Maximization for a Competitive Firm

This figure shows the marginal cost curve (MC), *the average total cost curve* (ATC) *and the average variable cost curve* (AVC). *It also shows the market price* (P), *which equals marginal revenue* (MR) *and average revenue* (AR). *At the quantity* Q_1, *marginal revenue* MR_1 *exceeds marginal cost* MC_1, *so raising production increases profit. At the quantity* Q_2 *marginal cost* MC_2 *is above marginal revenue* MR_2, *so reducing production increases profit. The profit maximizing quantity* Q_{MAX} *is found where the horizontal price line intersects the marginal cost curve.*

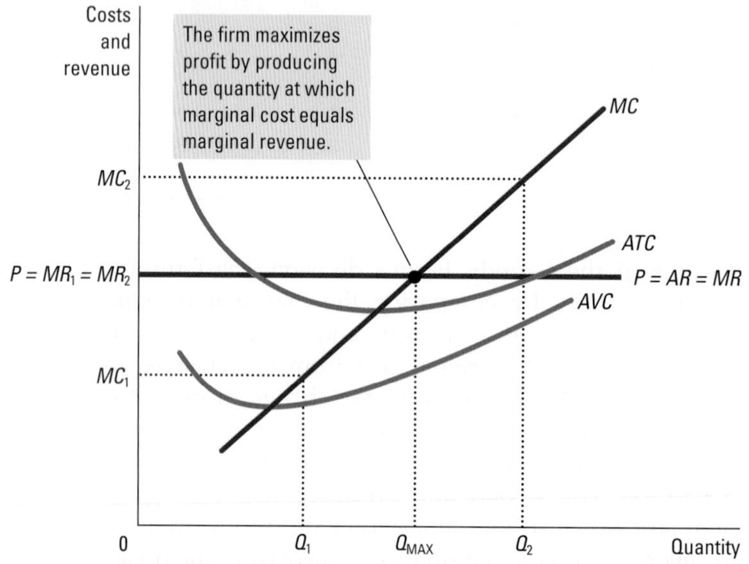

firm's output is the same regardless of the quantity that the firm decides to produce. Keep in mind that, for a competitive firm, the firm's price equals both its average revenue (*AR*) and its marginal revenue (*MR*).

We can use Figure 14.1 to find the quantity of output that maximizes profit. Imagine that the firm is producing at Q_1. At this level of output, marginal revenue is greater than marginal cost. That is, if the firm raised its level of production and sales by 1 unit, the additional revenue (MR_1) would exceed the additional costs (MC_1). Profit, which equals total revenue minus total cost, would increase. Hence, if marginal revenue is greater than marginal cost, as it is at Q_1, the firm can increase profit by increasing production.

A similar argument applies when output is at Q_2. In this case, marginal cost is greater than marginal revenue. If the firm reduced production by 1 unit, the costs saved (MC_2) would exceed the revenue lost (MR_2). Therefore, if marginal revenue is less than marginal cost, as it is at Q_2, the firm can increase profit by reducing production.

Where do these marginal adjustments to level of production end? Regardless of whether the firm begins with production at a low level (such as Q_1) or at a high level (such as Q_2), the firm will eventually adjust production until the quantity produced reaches Q_{MAX}. This analysis shows a general rule for profit maximization: at the profit-maximizing level of output, marginal revenue and marginal cost are exactly equal.

We can now see how the competitive firm decides the quantity of its good to supply to the market. Because a competitive firm is a price taker, its marginal revenue equals the market price. For any given price, the competitive firm's profit-maximizing quantity of output is found by looking at the intersection of

FIGURE 14.2

Marginal Cost as the Competitive Firm's Supply Curve

An increase in the price from P_1 to P_2 leads to an increase in the firm's profit-maximizing quantity from Q_1 to Q_2. Because the marginal cost curve shows the quantity supplied by the firm at any given price, it is the firm's supply curve.

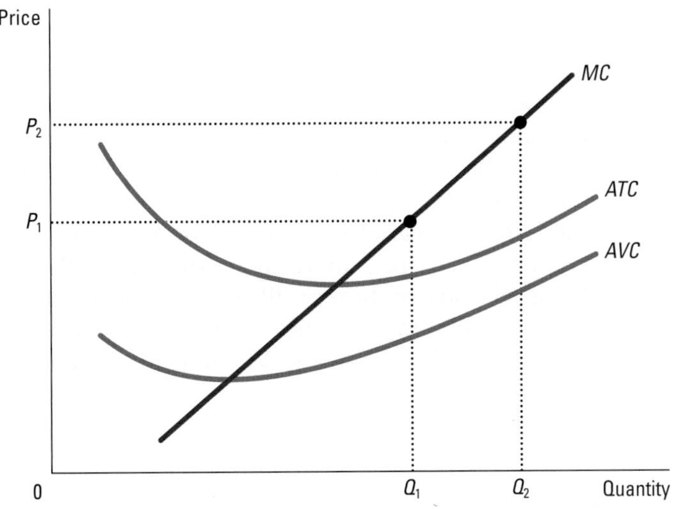

the price with the marginal cost curve. In Figure 14.1, that quantity of output is Q_{MAX}.

Figure 14.2 shows how a competitive firm responds to an increase in the price which may have been caused by a change in global market conditions. Remember that competitive firms are price takers and have to accept the market price for their product. Prices of commodities such as grain, metals, sugar, cotton, coffee, pork bellies, oil and so on are set by organized international markets and so the individual firm has no power to influence price. When the price is P_1, the firm produces quantity Q_1, the quantity that equates marginal cost to the price. Assume that an outbreak of bovine spongiform encephalopathy (BSE) results in the need to slaughter a large proportion of dairy cattle and as a result there is a shortage of milk on the market. When the price rises to P_2, the firm finds that marginal revenue is now higher than marginal cost at the previous level of output, so the firm increases production. The new profit-maximizing quantity is Q_2, at which marginal cost equals the new higher price. In essence, because the firm's marginal cost curve determines the quantity of the good the firm is willing to supply at any price, it is the competitive firm's supply curve.

The Firm's Short-Run Decision to Shut Down

So far we have been analysing the question of how much a competitive firm will produce. In some circumstances, however, the firm will decide to shut down and not produce anything at all.

Here we should distinguish between a temporary shutdown of a firm and the permanent exit of a firm from the market. A *shutdown* refers to a short-run decision not to produce anything during a specific period of time because of current market conditions. *Exit* refers to a long-run decision to leave the market. The short-run and long-run decisions differ because most firms cannot avoid their fixed costs in the short run but can do so in the long run. That is, a firm that shuts down temporarily still has to pay its fixed costs, whereas a firm that exits the market saves both its fixed and its variable costs.

For example, consider the production decision that a farmer faces. The cost of the land is one of the farmer's fixed costs. If the farmer decides not to produce any crops one season, the land lies fallow, and he cannot recover this cost. When making the short-run decision whether to shut down for a season, the fixed cost of land is said to be a *sunk cost*. By contrast, if the farmer decides to leave farming altogether, he can sell the land. When making the long-run decision whether to exit the market, the cost of land is not sunk. (We return to the issue of sunk costs shortly.)

Now let's consider what determines a firm's shutdown decision. If the firm shuts down, it loses all revenue from the sale of its product. At the same time, it saves the variable costs of making its product (but must still pay the fixed costs). Thus, the firm shuts down if the revenue that it would get from producing is less than its variable costs of production; it is simply not worth producing a product which costs more to produce than the revenue generated by its sale. Doing so would reduce profit or make any existing losses even greater.

A little bit of mathematics can make this shutdown criterion more useful. If TR stands for total revenue and VC stands for variable costs, then the firm's decision can be written as:

$$\text{Shut down if } TR < VC$$

The firm shuts down if total revenue is less than variable cost. By dividing both sides of this inequality by the quantity Q, we can write it as:

$$\text{Shut down if } TR/Q < VC/Q$$

Notice that this can be further simplified. TR/Q is total revenue divided by quantity, which is average revenue. As we discussed previously, average revenue for any firm is simply the good's price P. Similarly, VC/Q is average variable cost AVC. Therefore, the firm's shutdown criterion is:

$$\text{Shut down if } P < AVC$$

That is, a firm chooses to shut down if the price of the good is less than the average variable cost of production. This criterion is intuitive: when choosing to produce, the firm compares the price it receives for the typical unit to the average variable cost that it must incur to produce the typical unit. If the price doesn't cover the average variable cost, the firm is better off stopping production altogether. The firm can reopen in the future if conditions change so that price exceeds average variable cost.

We now have a full description of a competitive firm's profit-maximizing strategy. If the firm produces anything, it produces the quantity at which marginal cost equals the price of the good. Yet if the price is less than average variable cost at that quantity, the firm is better off shutting down and not producing anything. These results are illustrated in Figure 14.3. The competitive firm's short-run supply curve is the portion of its marginal cost curve that lies above average variable cost.

Spilt Milk and other Sunk Costs

sunk cost
a cost that has already been committed and cannot be recovered

Sometime in your life you have probably been told, 'Don't cry over spilt milk,' or 'Let bygones be bygones.' These adages hold a deep truth about rational decision making. Economists say that a cost is a **sunk cost** when it has already been committed and cannot be recovered. In a sense, a sunk cost is the opposite of an opportunity cost: an opportunity cost is what you have to give up if you choose to do one thing instead of another, whereas a sunk cost cannot be avoided,

FIGURE 14.3

The Competitive Firm's Short-Run Supply Curve

In the short run, the competitive firm's supply curve is its marginal cost curve (MC) *above average variable cost* (AVC). *If the price falls below average variable cost, the firm is better off shutting down.*

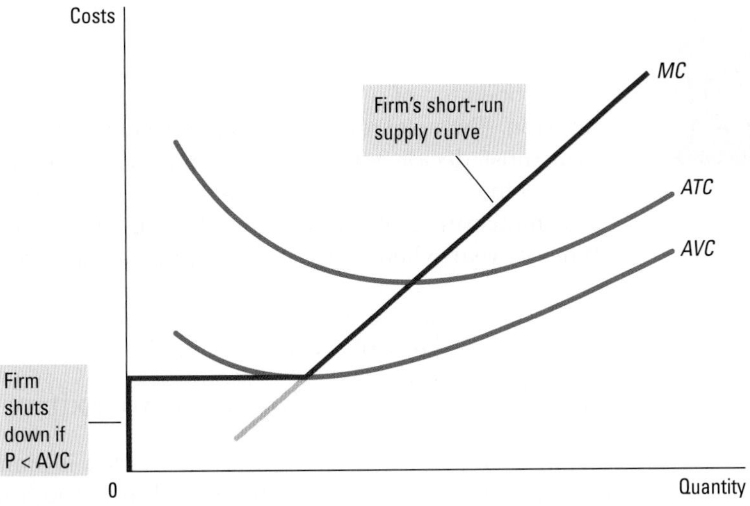

regardless of the choices you make. Because nothing can be done about sunk costs, you can ignore them when making decisions about various aspects of life, including business strategy.

Our analysis of the firm's shutdown decision is one example of the importance of recognizing sunk costs. We assume that the firm cannot recover its fixed costs by temporarily stopping production. As a result, the firm's fixed costs are sunk in the short run, and the firm can safely ignore these costs when deciding how much to produce. The firm's short-run supply curve is the part of the marginal cost curve that lies above average variable cost, and the size of the fixed cost does not matter for this supply decision.

The irrelevance of sunk costs is also important for personal decisions. Imagine, for instance, that you place a €10 value on seeing a newly released film. You buy a ticket for €7, but before entering the cinema you lose the ticket. Should you buy another ticket? Or should you now go home and refuse to pay a total of €14 to see the film? The answer is that you should buy another ticket. The benefit of seeing the film (€10) still exceeds the opportunity cost (the €7 for the second ticket). The €7 you paid for the lost ticket is a sunk cost. As with spilt milk, there is no point in crying about it.

CASE STUDY

Near-empty Restaurants and Off-season Miniature Golf

Have you ever walked into a restaurant for lunch and found it almost empty? Why, you might have asked, does the restaurant even bother to stay open? It might seem that the revenue from the few customers could not possibly cover the cost of running the restaurant.

© ANDREY NIKIFOROV / SHUTTERSTOCK

Staying open can be profitable, even with many tables empty.

In making the decision whether to open for lunch, a restaurant owner must keep in mind the distinction between fixed and variable costs. Many of a restaurant's costs – the rent, kitchen equipment, tables, plates, cutlery and so on – are fixed. Shutting down during lunch would not reduce these costs. In other words, these costs are sunk in the short run. When the owner is deciding whether to serve lunch, only the variable costs – the price of the additional food and the wages of the extra staff – are relevant. The owner shuts down the restaurant at lunchtime only if the revenue from the few lunchtime customers fails to cover the restaurant's variable costs.

An operator of a miniature golf course in a seaside resort faces a similar decision. Because revenue varies substantially from season to season, the firm must decide when to open and when to close. Once again, the fixed costs – the costs of buying the land and building the course – are irrelevant. The miniature golf course should be open for business only during those times of year when its revenue exceeds its variable costs.

The Firm's Long-run Decision to Exit or Enter a Market

The firm's long-run decision to exit the market is similar to its shutdown decision. If the firm exits, it again will lose all revenue from the sale of its product, but now it saves on both fixed and variable costs of production. Thus, the firm exits the market if the revenue it would get from producing is less than its total costs.

We can again make this criterion more useful by writing it mathematically. If *TR* stands for total revenue and *TC* stands for total cost, then the firm's criterion can be written as:

$$\text{Exit if } TR < TC$$

The firm exits if total revenue is less than total cost. By dividing both sides of this inequality by quantity *Q*, we can write it as:

$$\text{Exit if } TR/Q < TC/Q$$

We can simplify this further by noting that *TR*/*Q* is average revenue, which equals the price *P*, and that *TC*/*Q* is average total cost *ATC*. Therefore, the firm's exit criterion is:

$$\text{Exit if } P < ATC$$

That is, a firm chooses to exit if the price of the good is less than the average total cost of production.

A parallel analysis applies to an entrepreneur who is considering starting a firm. The firm will enter the market if such an action would be profitable, which occurs if the price of the good exceeds the average total cost of production. The entry criterion is:

$$\text{Enter if } P > ATC$$

The criterion for entry is exactly the opposite of the criterion for exit.

We can now describe a competitive firm's long-run profit-maximizing strategy. If the firm is in the market, it produces the quantity at which marginal cost equals the price of the good. Yet if the price is less than average total cost at that quantity, the firm chooses to exit (or not enter) the market. These results are illustrated in Figure 14.4. The competitive firm's long-run supply curve is the portion of its marginal cost curve that lies above average total cost.

FIGURE 14.4

The Competitive Firm's Long-Run Supply Curve

In the long run, the competitive firm's supply curve is its marginal cost curve (MC) *above average total cost* (ATC). *If the price falls below average total cost, the firm is better off exiting the market.*

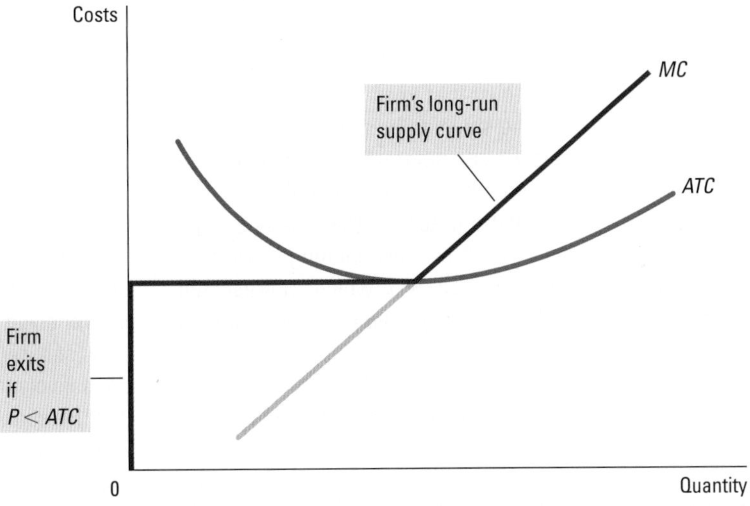

IN THE NEWS

Shutdowns in the Short Run and Long Run

The global economic slowdown of 2008–09 led to many firms having to make difficult decisions about how to respond to falling sales and whether to carry on producing. Many smaller firms were forced to shut down and leave the market but others took different decisions and shut down production operations for a period of time in the hope that economic activity would pick up. This article looks at these two aspects of firms' behaviour.

The economic slowdown left many businesses facing falling sales and thus revenues whilst the opportunity for cutting costs was limited. In the absence of support by the banks due to the credit crunch or only having access to funds at far higher interest rates many firms had to make a painful decision about whether to carry on trading or shut down. Smaller firms tend to face far greater challenges in surviving periods of falling demand than larger firms. Large firms may have large capital assets in the form of buildings, equipment and machinery but in the short run these represent sunk costs and are, therefore, irrelevant to decision-making.

Many smaller firms may be operating at the margin. They are more likely to be in competitive markets and thus have limited opportunities to affect market price and force down supply costs. Many will have been making zero profit and once demand falls and revenue goes down profit levels fall below zero and the firm may have to accept that shut down is the only option and cut its losses; it is better to lose €20 000 than €100 000! In 2008, business failure rates in the UK rose by 30 per cent with 23 879 firms closing over the year. In January 2009, the consultancy and credit checking agency, Experian, reported that 1 418 firms in the UK failed during the month, a 24 per cent fall compared to the same month in 2008. In 2009 the rate of failure continued to slow but the total number of business failures was not expected to peak until 2010.

For larger businesses, the decision may not have been to shut down completely but to cut operations in the short run. An excellent example of this was the motor industry. The European car industry faced a dramatic fall in sales as a result of the recession. In 2010, western European car sales were estimated to be 2.5 million units, a fall of over 60 per cent on the peak of sales in 2007. Particular countries experienced considerable falls in sales. In Iceland car sales fell by 88 per cent in January 2009, in Latvia the fall was 77 per cent and in Ireland, 66 per cent. In Spain car sales fell 41.6 per cent in January 2009 whilst in Italy the fall was 32.6 per cent.

In response to the falling sales a number of the main car manufacturing companies operating in Europe made decisions to shut down production for differing periods from 2008. In the UK, Honda shut down operations for the four months, February to May 2009; Aston Martin shut down over the holiday period at the end of 2008–2009, Vauxhall shut down for 40 days over the same Christmas and New Year period, and Mini ceased production over February 2009 and for two weeks in August that year.

The situation across the rest of Europe was no different. HIS Global Insight reported that the total lost plant-days in the first quarter of 2009 across Europe as a result of firms shutting down production was 950 which represented 1 368 607 lost production units, around a quarter of total European output. Despite the fact that the European economy seemed to have come out of recession in 2009, the forecasts for 2010 were gloomy. In January 2010 Fiat announced that it was closing its production facilities in Italy for two weeks in February because of poor sales the previous month. General Motors announced that it was going to shut down operations completely at its Antwerp factory in Belgium. The company said that the decision had been taken because it needed to reduce its capacity by 20 per cent to take account the new market conditions. If it did not shutdown operations at the plant completely its long-term sustainability and the operations at its other European Vauxhall and Opel plants would be compromised, it said.

Whilst the effect on the workers at car manufacturers across Europe was significant with a large number losing their jobs, the total impact on unemployment was less than some analysts had predicted. One of the explanations was that a temporary shutdown of operations might have meant that workers received lower wages but at least they still retained their jobs. For the firms involved, the plant and equipment may be sunk costs but the skills of the workforce represent an investment and those skills would be needed when demand picked up. The cost of making redundancies and then having to recruit new workers in the event of an upturn can be considerable and so it made sense to retain employees, cut costs during the shutdown but save on the costs of having to recruit at a later stage.

Measuring Profit in Our Graph for the Competitive Firm

As we analyse exit and entry, it is useful to be able to analyse the firm's profit in more detail. Recall that profit equals total revenue (*TR*) minus total cost (*TC*):

$$\text{Profit} = TR - TC$$

We can rewrite this definition by multiplying and dividing the right-hand side by *Q*:

$$\text{Profit} = (TR/Q - TC/Q) \times Q$$

But note that TR/Q is average revenue, which is the price *P*, and TC/Q is average total cost *ATC*. Therefore:

$$\text{Profit} = (P - ATC) \times Q$$

This way of expressing the firm's profit allows us to measure profit in our graphs.

Panel (a) of Figure 14.5 shows a firm earning positive profit. As we have already discussed, the firm maximizes profit by producing the quantity at which price equals marginal cost. Now look at the shaded rectangle. The height of the rectangle is $P - ATC$, the difference between price and average total cost. The width of the rectangle is *Q*, the quantity produced. Therefore, the area of the rectangle is $(P - ATC) \times Q$, which is the firm's profit.

FIGURE 14.5

Profit as the Area Between Price and Average Total Cost

The area of the shaded box between price and average total cost represents the firm's profit. The height of this box is price minus average total cost (P – ATC), and the width of the box is the quantity of output (Q). In panel (a), price is above average total cost, so the firm has positive profit. In panel (b), price is less than average total cost, so the firm has losses.

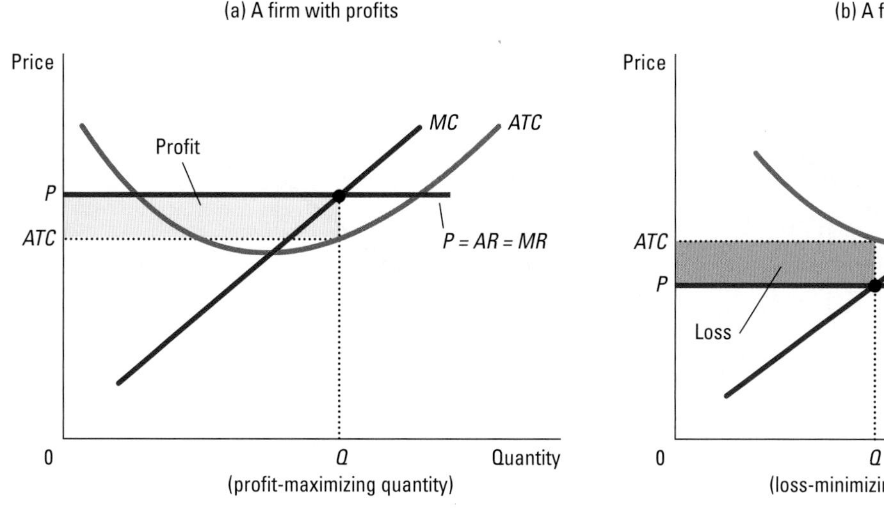

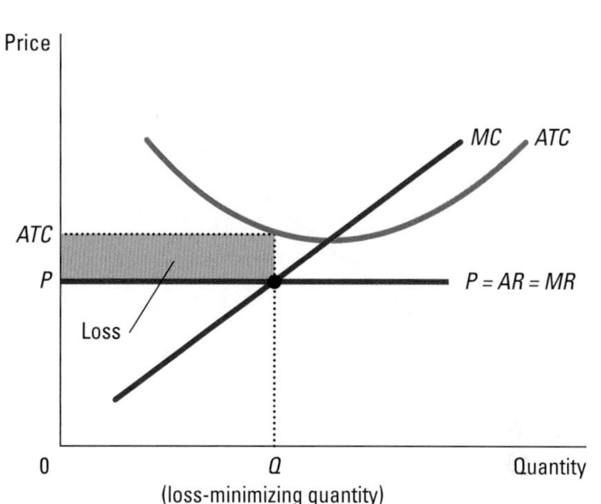

Similarly, panel (b) of this figure shows a firm with losses (negative profit). In this case, maximizing profit means minimizing losses, a task accomplished once again by producing the quantity at which price equals marginal cost. Now consider the shaded rectangle. The height of the rectangle is $ATC - P$, and the width is Q. The area is $(ATC - P) \times Q$, which is the firm's loss. Because a firm in this situation is not making enough revenue to cover its average total cost, the firm would choose to exit the market.

Quick Quiz How does the price faced by a profit-maximizing competitive firm compare to its marginal cost? Explain. • When does a profit-maximizing competitive firm decide to shut down? When does a profit-maximizing competitive firm decide to exit a market?

THE SUPPLY CURVE IN A COMPETITIVE MARKET

Now that we have examined the supply decision of a single firm, we can discuss the supply curve for a market. There are two cases to consider. First, we examine a market with a fixed number of firms. Secondly, we examine a market in which the number of firms can change as old firms exit the market and new firms enter. Both cases are important, for each applies over a specific time horizon. Over short periods of time it is often difficult for firms to enter and exit, so the assumption of a fixed number of firms is appropriate. But over long periods of time, the number of firms can adjust to changing market conditions.

FIGURE 14.6

Market Supply With a Fixed Number of Firms

When the number of firms in the market is fixed, the market supply curve, shown in panel (b), reflects the individual firms' marginal cost curves, shown in panel (a). Here, in a market of 1 000 firms, the quantity of output supplied to the market is 1 000 times the quantity supplied by each firm.

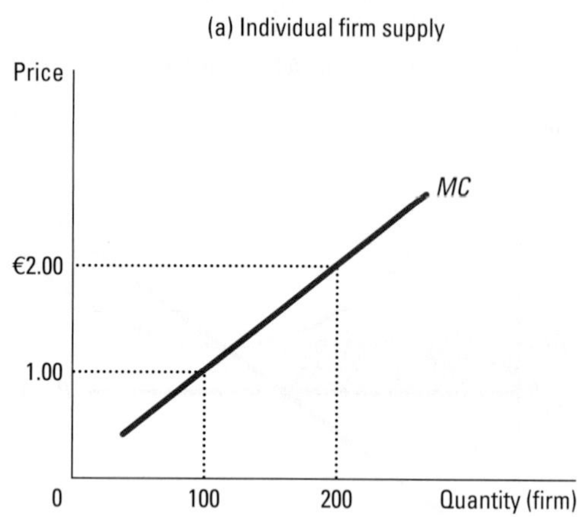

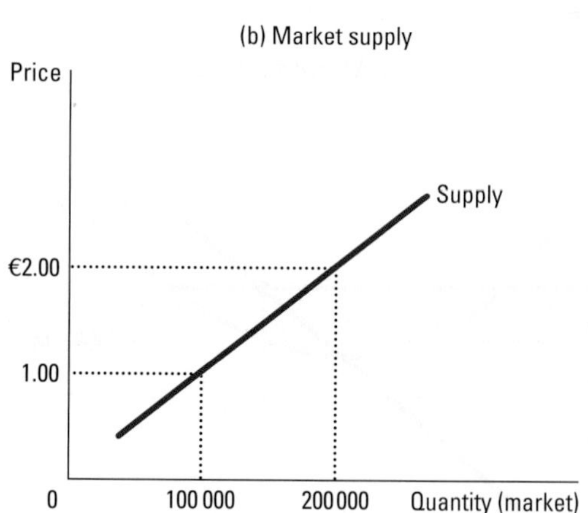

The Short Run: Market Supply with a Fixed Number of Firms

Consider first a market with 1 000 identical firms. For any given price, each firm supplies a quantity of output so that its marginal cost equals the price, as shown in panel (a) of Figure 14.6. That is, as long as price is above average variable cost, each firm's marginal cost curve is its supply curve. The quantity of output supplied to the market equals the sum of the quantities supplied by each of the 1 000 individual firms. Thus, to derive the market supply curve, we add the quantity supplied by each firm in the market. As panel (b) of Figure 14.6 shows, because the firms are identical, the quantity supplied to the market is 1 000 times the quantity supplied by each firm.

The Long Run: Market Supply with Entry and Exit

Now consider what happens if firms are able to enter or exit the market. Let's suppose that everyone has access to the same technology for producing the good and access to the same markets to buy the inputs into production. Therefore, all firms and all potential firms have the same cost curves.

Decisions about entry and exit in a market of this type depend on the incentives facing the owners of existing firms and the entrepreneurs who could start new firms. If firms already in the market are profitable, then new firms will have an incentive to enter the market. This entry will expand the number of firms, increase the quantity of the good supplied, and drive down prices and profits. Conversely, if firms in the market are making losses, then some existing firms will exit the market. Their exit will reduce the number of firms, decrease the quantity of the good supplied, and drive up prices and profits. At the end of this process of entry and exit, firms that remain in the market must be making zero economic profit. Recall that we can write a firm's profits as:

$$\text{Profit} = (P - ATC) \times Q$$

This equation shows that an operating firm has zero profit if and only if the price of the good equals the average total cost of producing that good. If price is above average total cost, profit is positive, which encourages new firms to enter. If price is less than average total cost, profit is negative, which encourages some firms to exit. The process of entry and exit ends only when price and average total cost are driven to equality.

This analysis has a surprising implication. We noted earlier in the chapter that competitive firms produce so that price equals marginal cost. We just noted that free entry and exit forces price to equal average total cost. But if price is to equal both marginal cost and average total cost, these two measures of cost must equal each other. Marginal cost and average total cost are equal, however, only when the firm is operating at the minimum of average total cost. Recall from the preceding chapter that the level of production with lowest average total cost is called the firm's efficient scale. Therefore, the long-run equilibrium of a competitive market with free entry and exit must have firms operating at their efficient scale.

Panel (a) of Figure 14.7 shows a firm in such a long-run equilibrium. In this figure, price P equals marginal cost MC, so the firm is profit-maximizing. Price also equals average total cost ATC, so profits are zero. New firms have no incentive to enter the market, and existing firms have no incentive to leave the market.

From this analysis of firm behaviour, we can determine the long-run supply curve for the market. In a market with free entry and exit, there is only one price consistent with zero profit – the minimum of average total cost. As a result, the long-run market supply curve must be horizontal at this price, as in panel (b) of Figure 14.7. Any price above this level would generate profit, leading to entry

FIGURE 14.7

Market Supply With Entry and Exit

Firms will enter or exit the market until profit is driven to zero. Thus, in the long run, price equals the minimum of average total cost, as shown in panel (a). The number of firms adjusts to ensure that all demand is satisfied at this price. The long-run market supply curve is horizontal at this price, as shown in panel (b).

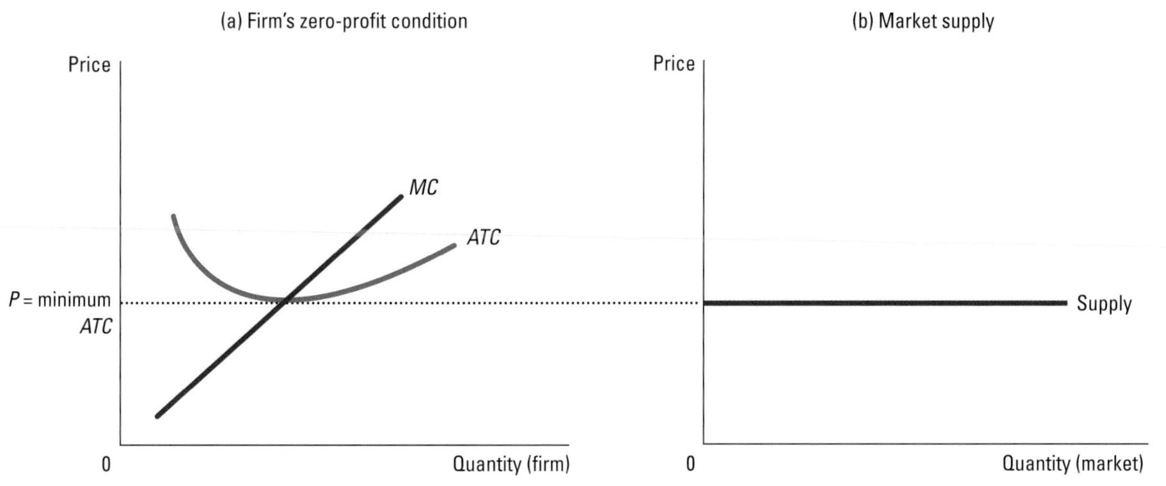

and an increase in the total quantity supplied. Any price below this level would generate losses, leading to exit and a decrease in the total quantity supplied. Eventually, the number of firms in the market adjusts so that price equals the minimum of average total cost, and there are enough firms to satisfy all the demand at this price.

Why Do Competitive Firms Stay in Business If They Make Zero Profit?

"non-profit-making organization."

At first, it might seem odd that competitive firms earn zero profit in the long run. After all, people start businesses to make a profit. If entry eventually drives profit to zero, there might seem to be little reason to stay in business.

To understand the zero-profit condition more fully, recall that profit equals total revenue minus total cost, and that total cost includes all the opportunity costs of the firm. In particular, total cost includes the opportunity cost of the time and money that the firm owners devote to the business. In the zero-profit equilibrium, the firm's revenue must compensate the owners for the time and money that they expend to keep their business going.

Consider an example. Suppose that a farmer had to invest €1 million to open his farm, which otherwise he could have deposited in a bank to earn €50 000 a year in interest. In addition, he had to give up another job that would have paid him €30 000 a year. Then the farmer's opportunity cost of farming includes both the interest he could have earned and the forgone wages – a total of €80 000. This sum must be calculated as part of the farmer's total costs. In some situations zero profit is referred to as **normal profit** – the minimum amount required to keep factor inputs in their current use. Even if his profit is driven to zero, his revenue from farming compensates him for these opportunity costs.

normal profit
the minimum amount required to keep factors of production in their current use

Keep in mind that accountants and economists measure costs differently. As we discussed in the previous chapter, accountants keep track of explicit costs but usually miss implicit costs. That is, they measure costs that require an outflow of money from the firm, but they fail to include opportunity costs of production that do not involve an outflow of money. As a result, in the zero-profit equilibrium, economic profit is zero, but accounting profit is positive. Our farmer's accountant, for instance, would conclude that the farmer earned an accounting profit of €80 000, which is enough to keep the farmer in business. In the short run as we shall see, profit can be above zero or normal profit which is referred to as **abnormal profit**.

abnormal profit
the profit over and above normal profit

A Shift in Demand in the Short Run and Long Run

Because firms can enter and exit a market in the long run but not in the short run, the response of a market to a change in demand depends on the time horizon. To see this, let's trace the effects of a shift in demand. This analysis will show how a market responds over time, and it will show how entry and exit drive a market to its long-run equilibrium.

Suppose the market for milk begins in long-run equilibrium. Firms are earning zero profit, so price equals the minimum of average total cost. Panel (a) of Figure 14.8 shows the situation. The long-run equilibrium is point A, the quantity sold in the market is Q_1, and the price is P_1.

Now suppose scientists discover that milk has miraculous health benefits. As a result, the demand curve for milk shifts outward from D_1 to D_2, as in panel (b). The short-run equilibrium moves from point A to point B; as a result, the quantity rises from Q_1 to Q_2 and the price rises from P_1 to P_2. All of the existing firms

FIGURE 14.8

An Increase in Demand in the Short Run and Long Run

The market starts in a long-run equilibrium, shown as point A in panel (a). In this equilibrium, each firm makes zero profit, and the price equals the minimum average total cost. Panel (b) shows what happens in the short run when demand rises from D_1 to D_2. The equilibrium goes from point A to point B, price rises from P_1 to P_2, and the quantity sold in the market rises from Q_1 to Q_2. Because price now exceeds average total cost, firms make profits, which over time encourage new firms to enter the market. This entry shifts the short-run supply curve to the right from S_1 to S_2 as shown in panel (c). In the new long-run equilibrium, point C, price has returned to P_1 but the quantity sold has increased to Q_3. Profits are again zero, price is back to the minimum of average total cost, but the market has more firms to satisfy the greater demand.

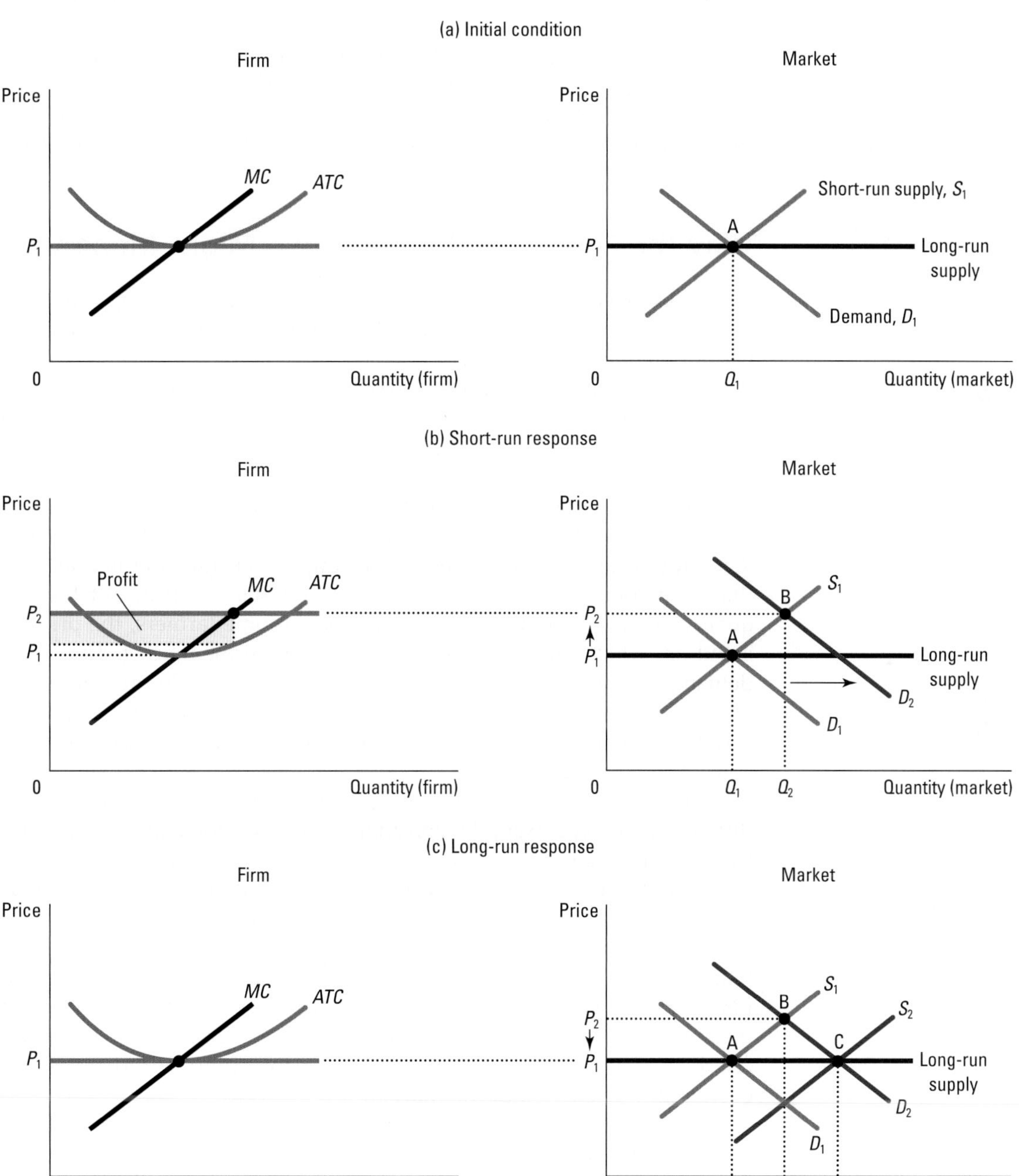

respond to the higher price by raising the amount produced. Because each firm's supply curve reflects its marginal cost curve, how much they each increase production is determined by the marginal cost curve. In the new short-run equilibrium, the price of milk exceeds average total cost, so the firms are making positive profit.

Over time, the profit in this market encourages new firms to enter. Some farmers may switch to milk from other farm products, for example. As the number of firms grows, the short-run supply curve shifts to the right from S_1 to S_2, as in panel (c), and this shift causes the price of milk to fall. Eventually, the price is driven back down to the minimum of average total cost, profits are zero and firms stop entering. Thus, the market reaches a new long-run equilibrium, point C. The price of milk has returned to P_1, but the quantity produced has risen to Q_3. Each firm is again producing at its efficient scale, but because more firms are in the dairy business, the quantity of milk produced and sold is higher.

Why the Long-Run Supply Curve Might Slope Upward

So far we have seen that entry and exit can cause the long-run market supply curve to be horizontal. The essence of our analysis is that there are a large number of potential entrants, each of which faces the same costs. As a result, the long-run market supply curve is horizontal at the minimum of average total cost. When the demand for the good increases, the long-run result is an increase in the number of firms and in the total quantity supplied, without any change in the price.

There are, however, two reasons that the long-run market supply curve might slope upward. The first is that some resources used in production may be available only in limited quantities. For example, consider the market for farm products. Anyone can choose to buy land and start a farm, but the quantity and quality of land is limited. As more people become farmers, the price of farmland is bid up, which raises the costs of all farmers in the market. Thus, an increase in demand for farm products cannot induce an increase in quantity supplied without also inducing a rise in farmers' costs, which in turn means a rise in price. The result is a long-run market supply curve that is upward sloping, even with free entry into farming.

A second reason for an upward sloping supply curve is that firms may have different costs. For example, consider the market for painters. Anyone can enter the market for painting services, but not everyone has the same costs. Costs vary in part because some people work faster than others, use different materials and equipment and because some people have better alternative uses of their time than others. For any given price, those with lower costs are more likely to enter than those with higher costs. To increase the quantity of painting services supplied, additional entrants must be encouraged to enter the market. Because these new entrants have higher costs, the price must rise to make entry profitable for them. Thus, the market supply curve for painting services slopes upward even with free entry into the market.

Notice that if firms have different costs, some firms earn profit even in the long run. In this case, the price in the market reflects the average total cost of the *marginal firm* – the firm that would exit the market if the price were any lower. This firm earns zero profit, but firms with lower costs earn positive profit. Entry does not eliminate this profit because would-be entrants have higher costs than firms already in the market. Higher-cost firms will enter only if the price rises, making the market profitable for them.

Thus, for these two reasons, the long-run supply curve in a market may be upward sloping rather than horizontal, indicating that a higher price is necessary to induce a larger quantity supplied. Nevertheless, the basic lesson about entry and exit remains true. Because firms can enter and exit more easily in the long run than in the short run, the long-run supply curve is typically more elastic than the short-run supply curve.

Quick Quiz In the long run with free entry and exit, is the price in a market equal to marginal cost, average total cost, both, or neither? Explain with a diagram.

CONCLUSION: BEHIND THE SUPPLY CURVE

We have been discussing the behaviour of competitive profit-maximizing firms. You may recall from Chapter 1 that one of the *Ten Principles of Economics* is that rational people think at the margin. This chapter has applied this idea to the competitive firm. Marginal analysis has given us a theory of the supply curve in a competitive market and, as a result, a deeper understanding of market outcomes.

We have learned that when you buy a good from a firm in a competitive market, you can be assured that the price you pay is close to the cost of producing that good. In particular, if firms are competitive and profit-maximizing, the price of a good equals the marginal cost of making that good. In addition, if firms can freely enter and exit the market, the price also equals the lowest possible average total cost of production.

Although we have assumed throughout this chapter that firms are price takers, many of the tools developed here are also useful for studying firms in less competitive markets. In the next chapter we will examine the behaviour of firms with market power. Marginal analysis will again be useful in analysing these firms, but it will have quite different implications.

SUMMARY

- Because a competitive firm is a price taker, its revenue is proportional to the amount of output it produces. The price of the good equals both the firm's average revenue and its marginal revenue.
- To maximize profit, a firm chooses a quantity of output such that marginal revenue equals marginal cost. Because marginal revenue for a competitive firm equals the market price, the firm chooses quantity so that price equals marginal cost. Thus, the firm's marginal cost curve is its supply curve.
- In the short run when a firm cannot recover its fixed costs, the firm will choose to shut down temporarily if the price of the good is less than average variable cost. In the long run when the firm can recover both fixed and variable costs, it will choose to exit if the price is less than average total cost.
- In a market with free entry and exit, profits are driven to zero in the long run. In this long-run equilibrium, all firms produce at the efficient scale, price equals the minimum of average total cost, and the number of firms adjusts to satisfy the quantity demanded at this price.
- Changes in demand have different effects over different time horizons. In the short run, an increase in demand raises prices and leads to profits, and a decrease in demand lowers prices and leads to losses. But if firms can freely enter and exit the market, then in the long run the number of firms adjusts to drive the market back to the zero-profit equilibrium.

KEY CONCEPTS

average revenue, p. 290
marginal revenue, p. 290
sunk cost, p. 294
normal profit, p. 302
abnormal profit, p. 302

QUESTIONS FOR REVIEW

1. What is meant by a competitive firm?
2. Draw the cost curves for a typical firm. For a given price, explain how the firm chooses the level of output that maximizes profit.
3. Under what conditions will a firm shut down temporarily? Explain.
4. Under what conditions will a firm exit a market? Explain.
5. Does a firm's price equal marginal cost in the short run, in the long run, or both? Explain.
6. Does a firm's price equal the minimum of average total cost in the short run, in the long run, or both? Explain.
7. Are market supply curves typically more elastic in the short run or in the long run? Explain.

PROBLEMS AND APPLICATIONS

1. What are the characteristics of a competitive market? Which of the following drinks do you think is best described by these characteristics? Why aren't the others?
   a. tap water
   b. bottled water
   c. cola
   d. beer.
2. Your flatmate's long hours in the chemistry lab finally paid off – she discovered a secret formula that lets people do an hour's worth of studying in 5 minutes. So far, she's sold 200 doses, and faces the following average total cost schedule:

Q	Average total cost
199	€199
200	200
201	201

   If a new customer offers to pay your flatmate €300 for one dose, should she make one more? Explain.
3. The liquorice industry is competitive. Each firm produces 2 million liquorice bootlaces per year. The bootlaces have an average total cost of €0.20 each, and they sell for €0.30.
   a. What is the marginal cost of a liquorice bootlace?
   b. Is this industry in long-run equilibrium? Why or why not?
4. You go out to the best restaurant in town and order a steak tartar dinner for €40. After eating half of the steak tartar, you realize that you are quite full. Your date wants you to finish your dinner, because you can't take it home and because 'you've already paid for it.' What should you do? Relate your answer to the material in this chapter.
5. Alejandro's lawn-mowing service is a profit-maximizing, competitive firm. Alejandro mows lawns for €27 each. His total cost each day is €280, of which €30 is a fixed cost. He mows 10 lawns a day. What can you say about Alejandro's short-run decision regarding shutdown and his long-run decision regarding exit?
6. Consider total cost and total revenue given in the table below:

Quantity	0	1	2	3	4	5	6	7
Total cost	€8	19	110	111	113	119	127	137
Total revenue	0	8	16	24	32	40	48	56

   a. Calculate profit for each quantity. How much should the firm produce to maximize profit?
   b. Calculate marginal revenue and marginal cost for each quantity. Graph them. (Hint: put the points

between whole numbers. For example, the marginal cost between 2 and 3 should be graphed at 2½.) At what quantity do these curves cross? How does this relate to your answer to part (a)?
   c. Can you tell whether this firm is in a competitive industry? If so, can you tell whether the industry is in long-run equilibrium?

7. 'High prices traditionally cause expansion in an industry, eventually bringing an end to high prices and manufacturers' prosperity.' Explain, using appropriate diagrams.

8. Suppose the book-printing industry is competitive and begins in long-run equilibrium.
   a. Draw a diagram describing the typical firm in the industry.
   b. Hi-Tech Printing Company invents a new process that sharply reduces the cost of printing books. What happens to Hi-Tech's profits and the price of books in the short run when Hi-Tech's patent prevents other firms from using the new technology?
   c. What happens in the long run when the patent expires and other firms are free to use the technology?

9. Many small boats are made of fibreglass, which is derived from crude oil. Suppose that the price of oil rises.
   a. Using diagrams, show what happens to the cost curves of an individual boat-making firm and to the market supply curve.
   b. What happens to the profits of boat makers in the short run? What happens to the number of boat makers in the long run?

10. Suppose that the European Union textile industry is competitive, and there is no international trade in textiles. In long-run equilibrium, the price per unit of cloth is €30.
    a. Describe the equilibrium using graphs for the entire market and for an individual producer.
    Now suppose that textile producers in non-EU countries are willing to sell large quantities of cloth in the EU for only €25 per unit.
    b. Assuming that EU textile producers have large fixed costs, what is the short-run effect of these imports on the quantity produced by an individual producer? What is the short-run effect on profits? Illustrate your answer with a graph.
    c. What is the long-run effect on the number of EU firms in the industry?

11. Assume that the gold-mining industry is competitive.
    a. Illustrate a long-run equilibrium using diagrams for the gold market and for a representative gold mine.
    b. Suppose that an increase in jewellery demand induces a surge in the demand for gold. Using your diagrams from part (a), show what happens in the short run to the gold market and to each existing gold mine.
    c. If the demand for gold remains high, what would happen to the price over time? Specifically, would the new long-run equilibrium price be above, below or equal to the short-run equilibrium price in part (b)? Is it possible for the new long-run equilibrium price to be above the original long-run equilibrium price? Explain.

For further resources, visit www.cengage.com/mankiw_taylor2

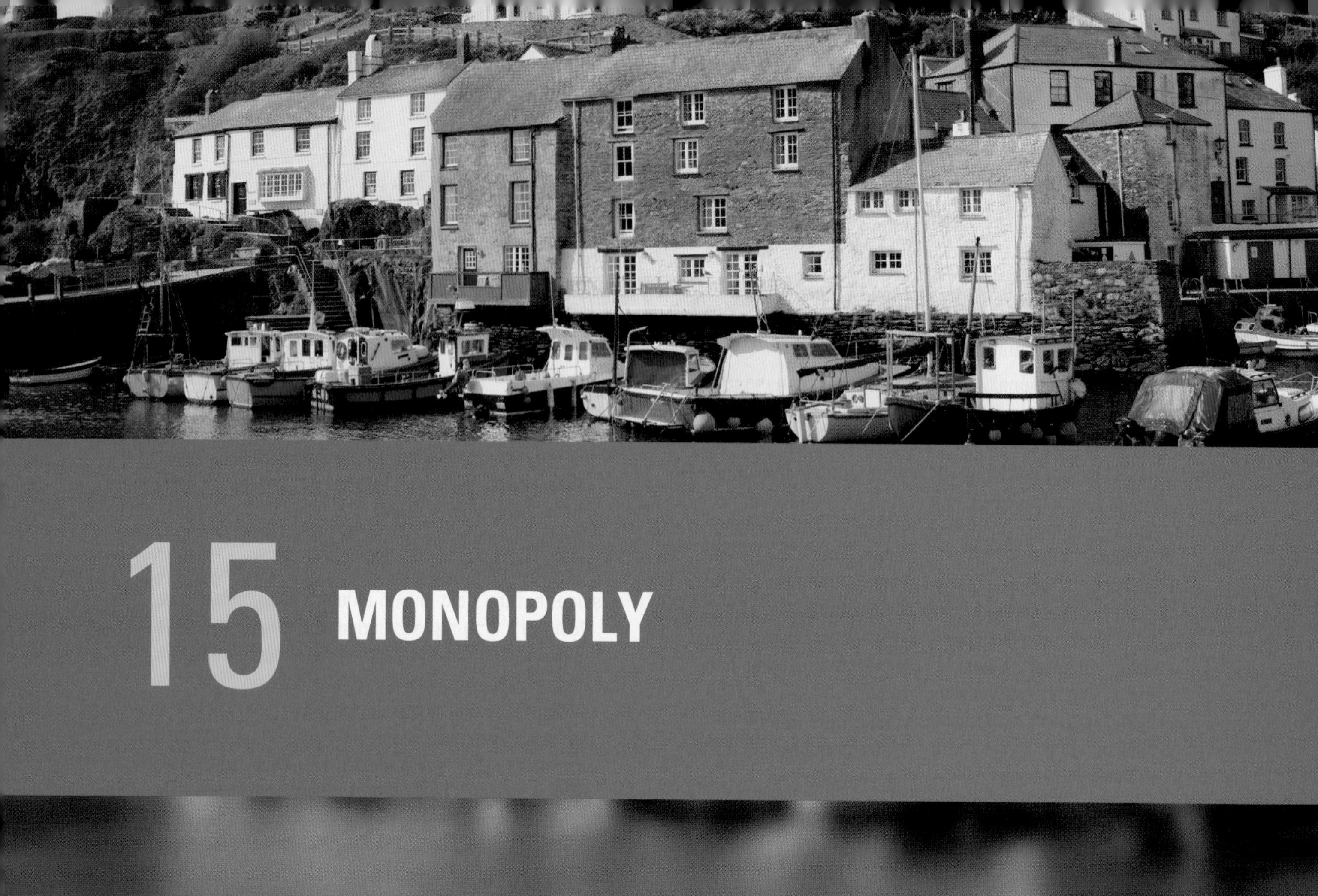

15 MONOPOLY

If you own a personal computer, it probably uses some version of Windows, the operating system sold by the US company, Microsoft Corporation. When Microsoft first designed Windows many years ago, it applied for and received a copyright, first from the US government and then from many of the governments of the world. The copyright gives Microsoft the exclusive right to make and sell copies of the Windows operating system. So if a person wants to buy a copy of Windows, he or she has little choice but to give Microsoft the price that the firm has decided to charge for its product. Windows is the operating system used by over 90 per cent of the PCs in the world (see Figure 15.1). Microsoft is said to have a *monopoly* in the market for Windows.

Microsoft's business decisions are not well described by the model of firm behaviour we developed in the previous chapter. In that chapter we analysed competitive markets in which there are many firms offering essentially identical products, so each firm has little influence over the price it receives. By contrast, a monopoly such as Microsoft has no close competitors and, therefore, can influence the market price of its product. While a competitive firm is a *price taker*, a monopoly firm is a *price maker*.

In this chapter we examine the implications of this market power. We will see that market power alters the relationship between a firm's costs and the price at which it sells its product to the market. A competitive firm takes the price of its output as given by the market and then chooses the quantity it will supply so that price equals marginal cost. By contrast, the price charged by a monopoly exceeds marginal cost. This result is clearly true in the case of Microsoft's Windows. The marginal cost of Windows – the extra cost that Microsoft would

FIGURE 15.1

Computer Operating Systems

A pie chart showing operating system market share; it is clear from the chart that Microsoft's Windows has a majority of the market and can be considered as having considerable monopoly power.

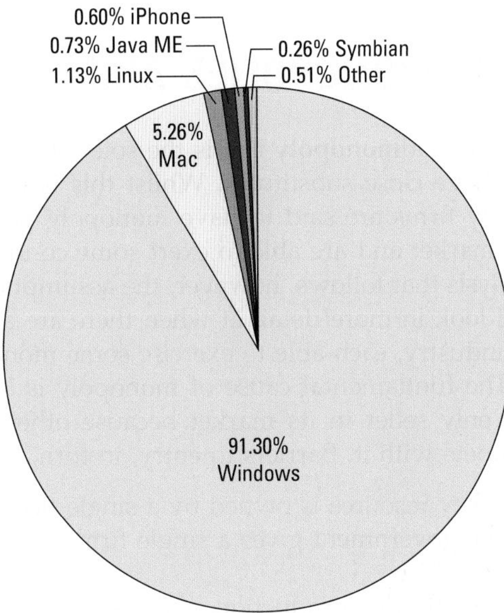

Source: © 2010 http://www.netapplications.com

incur by printing one more copy of the program onto a CD – is only a few euros. The market price of Windows is many times marginal cost.

It is perhaps not surprising that monopolies charge relatively high prices for their products. Customers of monopolies might seem to have little choice but to pay whatever the monopoly charges. But, if so, why is a copy of Windows priced at about €50 and not €500? Or €5 000? The reason, of course, is that if Microsoft set the price that high, fewer people would buy the product. People would buy fewer computers, switch to other operating systems or make illegal copies. Monopolies cannot achieve any level of profit they want because high prices reduce the amount that their customers buy. Although monopolies can control the prices of their goods, their profits are not unlimited.

As we examine the production and pricing decisions of monopolies, we also consider the implications of monopoly for society as a whole. Monopoly firms, like competitive firms, aim to maximize profit. But this goal has very different ramifications for competitive and monopoly firms. As we first saw in Chapter 7, self-interested buyers and sellers in competitive markets are unwittingly led by an invisible hand to promote general economic well-being. By contrast, because monopoly firms are unchecked by competition, the outcome in a market with a monopoly is often not in the best interest of society.

One of the *Ten Principles of Economics* in Chapter 1 is that governments can sometimes improve market outcomes. The analysis in this chapter will shed more light on this principle. As we examine the problems that monopolies raise for society, we will also discuss the various ways in which government policy makers might respond to these problems. The Competition Commission in Europe has been keeping a close eye on Microsoft for some years. Microsoft was accused of preventing fair competition because it bundled its web browser, Internet Explorer (IE), with its Windows operating system (this is known as 'tying'). Companies have complained about the way in which Microsoft allegedly makes it more difficult for other browsers to be interoperable – that is, work within a range of other platforms. The Commission imposed a fine of $1.4 billion in 2008 on Microsoft for breaching EU competition rules. As part of that investigation, the EU insisted that Microsoft made more of its code available to other software manufacturers to ensure greater interoperability. Microsoft had argued that such a move would compromise its security and that the code constituted sensitive commercial information.

WHY MONOPOLIES ARISE

monopoly
a firm that is the sole seller of a product without close substitutes

A firm is a **monopoly** if it is the sole seller of its product and if its product does not have close substitutes. Whilst this is the strict definition of a monopoly, in reality firms are said to have monopoly power if they are a dominant seller in the market and are able to exert some control over the market as a result. In the analysis that follows, however, the assumption is that there is only one seller. We will look in more detail at when there are a small number of dominant firms in an industry, each able to exercise some monopoly power, in Chapter 17.

The fundamental cause of monopoly is *barriers to entry:* a monopoly remains the only seller in its market because other firms cannot enter the market and compete with it. Barriers to entry, in turn, have four main sources:

- A key resource is owned by a single firm.
- The government gives a single firm the exclusive right to produce some good or service.
- The costs of production make a single producer more efficient than a large number of producers.
- A firm is able to gain control of other firms in the market and thus grow in size.

Let's briefly discuss each of these.

Monopoly Resources

The simplest way for a monopoly to arise is for a single firm to own a key resource. For example, consider the market for water in a small town on a remote Scottish island not served by the water company from the mainland. If dozens of town residents on the island have working wells, the competitive model discussed in the preceding chapter describes the behaviour of sellers. As a result, the price of a litre of water is driven to equal the marginal cost of pumping an extra litre. But if there is only one well in town and it is impossible to get water from anywhere else, then the owner of the well has a monopoly on water. Not surprisingly, the monopolist has much greater market power than any single firm in a competitive market. In the case of a necessity like water, the monopolist could command quite a high price, even if the marginal cost is low.

Although exclusive ownership of a key resource is a potential cause of monopoly, in practice monopolies rarely arise for this reason. Actual economies are large, and resources are owned by many people. Indeed, because many goods are traded internationally, the natural scope of their markets is often worldwide. There are, therefore, few examples of firms that own a resource for which there are no close substitutes.

Government-created Monopolies

In many cases, monopolies arise because the government has given one person or firm the exclusive right to sell some good or service. Sometimes the monopoly arises from the sheer political clout of the would-be monopolist. European kings, for example, once granted exclusive business licences to their friends and allies in order to raise money – a highly prized monopoly being the exclusive right to sell and distribute salt in a particular region of Europe. Even today, governments sometimes grant a monopoly (perhaps even to itself) because doing so is viewed to be in the public interest. In Sweden, for example, the retailing of alcoholic beverages is carried out under a state-owned monopoly known as the Systembolaget, because the Swedish government deems it to be in the interests of public health to be able to control directly the sale of alcohol. As a member of the EU, questions have been raised about this policy but Sweden seems keen to maintain its control of alcohol sales. In a recent study commissioned by the Swedish National Institute for Public Health, researchers concluded that if retail alcohol sales were privatized, the net effects on the country would be negative with an increase in alcohol related illness and deaths, fatal accidents, suicides and homicides and a large increase in the number of working days lost to sickness.[1]

The patent and copyright laws are two important examples of how the government creates a monopoly to serve the public interest. When a pharmaceutical company discovers a new drug, it can apply to the government for a patent. If the government deems the drug to be truly original, it approves the patent, which gives the company the exclusive right to manufacture and sell the drug for a fixed number of years – often 20 years. Similarly, when a novelist finishes a book, he can copyright it. The copyright is a government guarantee that no one can print and sell the work without the author's permission. The copyright makes the novelist a monopolist in the sale of his novel.

The effects of patent and copyright laws are easy to see. Because these laws give one producer a monopoly, they lead to higher prices than would occur under competition. But by allowing these monopoly producers to charge higher prices and earn higher profits, the laws also encourage some desirable behaviour. Drug companies are allowed to be monopolists in the drugs they discover in order to encourage research. Authors are allowed to be monopolists in the sale of their books to encourage them to write more and better books.

Thus, the laws governing patents and copyrights have benefits and costs. The benefits of the patent and copyright laws are the increased incentive for creative activity. These benefits are offset, to some extent, by the costs of monopoly pricing, which we examine fully later in this chapter.

Natural Monopolies

An industry is a **natural monopoly** when a single firm can supply a good or service to an entire market at a lower cost than could two or more firms. A natural monopoly arises when there are economies of scale over the relevant range of output. Figure 15.2 shows the average total costs of a firm with economies of scale. In this case, a single firm can produce any amount of output at least cost. That is, for any given amount of output, a larger number of firms leads to less output per firm and higher average total cost.

natural monopoly
a monopoly that arises because a single firm can supply a good or service to an entire market at a smaller cost than could two or more firms

An example of a natural monopoly is the distribution of water. To provide water to residents of a town, a firm must build a network of pipes throughout the town. If two or more firms were to compete in the provision of this service, each firm would have to pay the fixed cost of building a network. Thus, the average total cost of water is lowest if a single firm serves the entire market.

We saw other examples of natural monopolies when we discussed public goods and common resources in Chapter 11. We noted in passing that some goods in the economy are excludable but not rival. An example is a bridge used

[1]Holder, H. (Ed) (2007) *If retail alcohol sales in Sweden were privatized, what would be the potential consequences?* http://www.systembolagetkampanj.se/forskarrapport_en/downloads/Hela_rapporten.pdf

FIGURE 15.2

Economies of Scale as a Cause of Monopoly

When a firm's average total cost curve continually declines, the firm has what is called a natural monopoly. In this case, when production is divided among more firms, each firm produces less, and average total cost rises. As a result, a single firm can produce any given amount at the smallest cost.

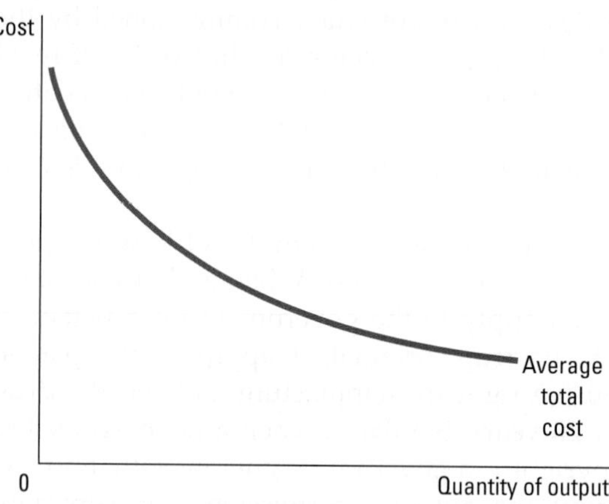

so infrequently that it is never congested. The bridge is excludable because a toll collector can prevent someone from using it. The bridge is not rival because use of the bridge by one person does not diminish the ability of others to use it. Because there is a fixed cost of building the bridge and a negligible marginal cost of additional users, the average total cost of a trip across the bridge (the total cost divided by the number of trips) falls as the number of trips rises. Hence, the bridge is a natural monopoly.

When a firm is a natural monopoly, it is less concerned about new entrants eroding its monopoly power. Normally, a firm has trouble maintaining a monopoly position without ownership of a key resource or protection from the government. The monopolist's profit attracts entrants into the market, and these entrants make the market more competitive. By contrast, entering a market in which another firm has a natural monopoly is unattractive. Would-be entrants know that they cannot achieve the same low costs that the monopolist enjoys because, after entry, each firm would have a smaller piece of the market.

In some cases, the size of the market is one determinant of whether an industry is a natural monopoly. Again, consider a bridge across a river. When the population is small, the bridge may be a natural monopoly. A single bridge can satisfy the entire demand for trips across the river at lowest cost. Yet as the population grows and the bridge becomes congested, satisfying the entire demand may require two or more bridges across the same river. Thus, as a market expands, a natural monopoly can evolve into a competitive market.

External Growth

Many of the largest firms in the world have grown partly through acquisition, merger or takeover of other firms. As they do so, the industry becomes more concentrated; there are fewer firms in the industry. One effect of this is that a firm might be able to develop monopoly power over its rivals and erect barriers to entry to make it harder for new firms to enter. It is for this reason that governments monitor such acquisitions to see if there are implications for competition. In the UK, for example, any merger that gives a firm 25 per cent or more of the market may be investigated to see if the acquisition is in the public interest.

Quick Quiz What are the four reasons that a market might have a monopoly? • Give three examples of monopolies, and explain the reason for each.

HOW MONOPOLIES MAKE PRODUCTION AND PRICING DECISIONS

Now that we know how monopolies arise, we can consider how a monopoly firm decides how much of its product to make and what price to charge for it. The analysis of monopoly behaviour in this section is the starting point for evaluating whether monopolies are desirable and what policies the government might pursue in monopoly markets.

Monopoly versus Competition

The key difference between a competitive firm and a monopoly is the monopoly's ability to influence the price of its output. A competitive firm is small relative to the market in which it operates and, therefore, takes the price of its output as given by market conditions. By contrast, because a monopoly is the sole producer in its market, it can alter the price of its good by adjusting the quantity it supplies to the market.

One way to view this difference between a competitive firm and a monopoly is to consider the demand curve that each firm faces. When we analysed profit maximization by competitive firms in the preceding chapter, we drew the market price as a horizontal line. Because a competitive firm can sell as much or as little as it wants at this price, the competitive firm faces a horizontal demand curve, as in panel (a) of Figure 15.3. In effect, because the competitive firm sells a product with many perfect substitutes (the products of all the other firms in its market), the demand curve that any one firm faces is perfectly elastic.

By contrast, because a monopoly is the sole producer in its market, its demand curve is the market demand curve. Thus, the monopolist's demand curve slopes downward for all the usual reasons, as in panel (b) of Figure 15.3. If the monopolist raises the price of its good, consumers buy less of it. Looked at another way, if the monopolist reduces the quantity of output it sells, the price of its output increases.

The market demand curve provides a constraint on a monopoly's ability to profit from its market power. A monopolist would prefer, if it were possible, to charge a high price and sell a large quantity at that high price. The market demand curve makes that outcome impossible. In particular, the market demand curve describes the combinations of price and quantity that are available to a monopoly firm. By adjusting the quantity produced (or, equivalently, the price charged), the monopolist can choose any point on the demand curve, but it cannot choose a point off the demand curve.

What point on the demand curve will the monopolist choose? As with competitive firms, we assume that the monopolist's goal is to maximize profit.

FIGURE 15.3

Demand Curves for Competitive and Monopoly Firms

Because competitive firms are price takers, they in effect face horizontal demand curves, as in panel (a). Because a monopoly firm is the sole producer in its market, it faces the downward sloping market demand curve, as in panel (b). As a result, the monopoly has to accept a lower price if it wants to sell more output.

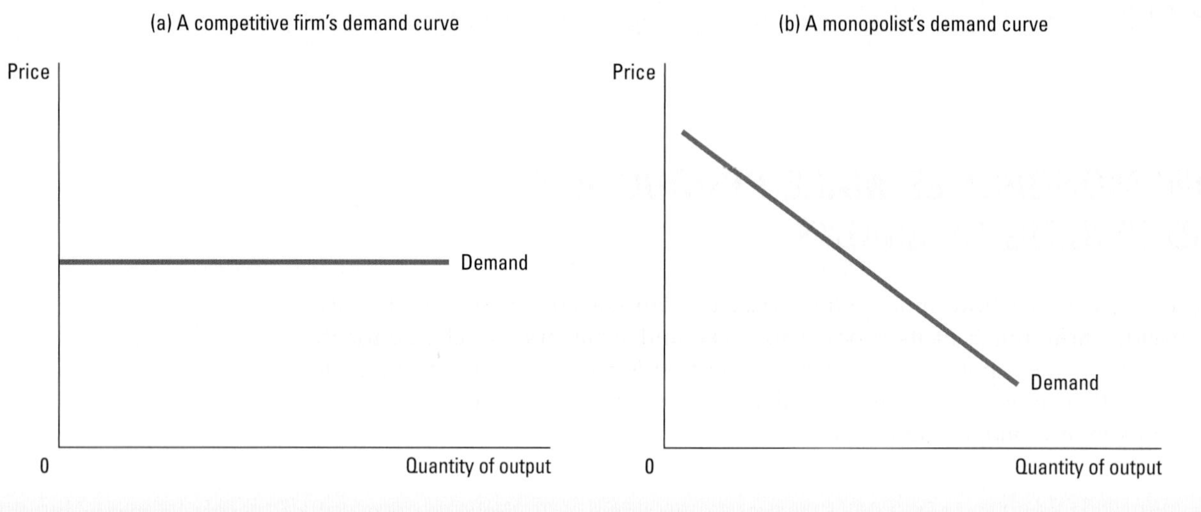

Because the firm's profit is total revenue minus total costs, our next task in explaining monopoly behaviour is to examine a monopolist's revenue.

A Monopoly's Revenue

Consider a town with a single producer of water. Table 15.1 shows how the monopoly's revenue might depend on the amount of water produced.

The first two columns show the monopolist's demand schedule. If the monopolist produces just 1 litre of water, it can sell that litre for €1. If it produces 2 litres, it must lower the price to €0.90 in order to sell both litres. And if it produces 3 litres, it must lower the price to €0.80, and so on. If you graphed these two columns of numbers, you would get a typical downward sloping demand curve.

The third column of the table presents the monopolist's *total revenue.* It equals the quantity sold (from the first column) times the price (from the second column). The fourth column computes the firm's *average revenue,* the amount of revenue the firm receives per unit sold. We compute average revenue by taking the number for total revenue in the third column and dividing it by the quantity of output in the first column. As we discussed in the previous chapter, average revenue always equals the price of the good. This is true for monopolists as well as for competitive firms.

The last column of Table 15.1 computes the firm's *marginal revenue,* the amount of revenue that the firm receives for each additional unit of output. We compute marginal revenue by taking the change in total revenue when output increases by 1 unit. For example, when the firm is producing 3 litres of water it receives total revenue of €2.40. Raising production to 4 litres increases total revenue to €2.80. Thus, marginal revenue is €2.80 minus €2.40, or €0.40.

Table 15.1 shows a result that is important for understanding monopoly behaviour: a monopolist's marginal revenue is always less than the price of its good. For example, if the firm raises production of water from 3 to 4 litres, it will increase total revenue by only €0.40, even though it will be able to sell each litre for €0.70. For a monopoly, marginal revenue is lower than price because a monopoly faces a downward sloping demand curve. To increase the amount sold, a monopoly firm must lower the price of its good. Hence, to sell the fourth litre of water, the monopolist must get less revenue for each of the first three litres.

TABLE 15.1

A Monopoly's Total, Average and Marginal Revenue

Quantity of water	Price	Total revenue	Average revenue	Marginal revenue
(Q)	(P)	$(TR = P \times Q)$	$(AR = TR/Q)$	$(MR = \Delta TR/\Delta Q)$
0 litres	€1.1	€0	–	
1	1.0	1.0	€1	€1
2	0.9	1.8	0.9	0.8
3	0.8	2.4	0.8	0.6
4	0.7	2.8	0.7	0.4
5	0.6	3.0	0.6	0.2
6	0.5	3.0	0.5	0
7	0.4	2.8	0.4	–0.2
8	0.3	2.4	0.3	–0.4

Marginal revenue for monopolies is very different from marginal revenue for competitive firms. When a monopoly increases the amount it sells, it has two effects on total revenue ($P \times Q$):

- *The output effect.* More output is sold, so Q is higher, which tends to increase total revenue.
- *The price effect.* The price falls, so P is lower, which tends to decrease total revenue.

Because a competitive firm can sell all it wants at the market price, there is no price effect. When it increases production by 1 unit, it receives the market price for that unit, and it does not receive any less for the units it was already selling. That is, because the competitive firm is a price taker, its marginal revenue equals the price of its good. By contrast, when a monopoly increases production by 1 unit, it must reduce the price it charges for every unit it sells, and this cut in price reduces revenue on the units it was already selling. As a result, a monopoly's marginal revenue is less than its price.

Figure 15.4 graphs the demand curve and the marginal revenue curve for a monopoly firm. (Because the firm's price equals its average revenue, the demand curve is also the average-revenue curve.) These two curves always start at the same point on the vertical axis because the marginal revenue of the first unit sold equals the price of the good. But thereafter, for the reason we just discussed, the monopolist's marginal revenue is less than the price of the good. Thus, a monopoly's marginal revenue curve lies below its demand curve.

You can see in the figure (as well as in Table 15.1) that marginal revenue can even become negative. Marginal revenue is negative when the price effect on revenue is greater than the output effect. In this case, when the firm produces an

FIGURE 15.4

Demand and Marginal Revenue Curves for a Monopoly

The demand curve shows how the quantity affects the price of the good. The marginal revenue curve shows how the firm's revenue changes when the quantity increases by 1 unit. Because the price on all units sold must fall if the monopoly increases production, marginal revenue is always less than the price.

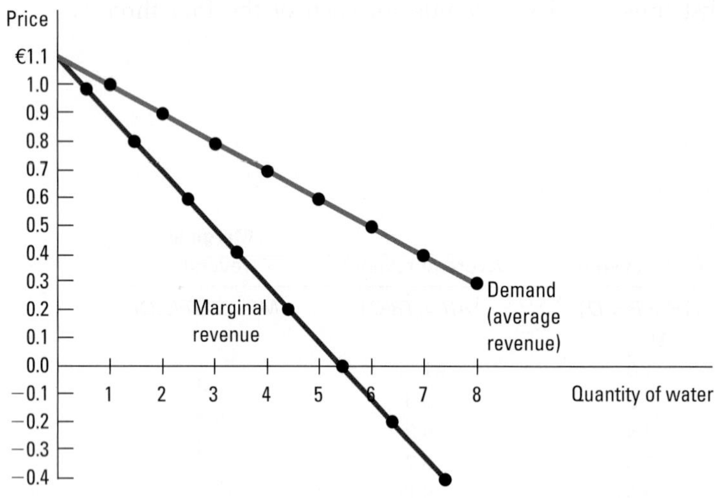

extra unit of output, the price falls by enough to cause the firm's total revenue to decline, even though the firm is selling more units.

Profit Maximization

Now that we have considered the revenue of a monopoly firm, we are ready to examine how such a firm maximizes profit. Recall from Chapter 1 that one of the *Ten Principles of Economics* is that rational people think at the margin. This lesson is as true for monopolists as it is for competitive firms. Here we apply the logic of marginal analysis to the monopolist's decision about how much to produce.

Figure 15.5 graphs the demand curve, the marginal revenue curve and the cost curves for a monopoly firm. All these curves should seem familiar: the demand and marginal revenue curves are like those in Figure 15.4, and the cost curves are like those we encountered in the last two chapters. These curves contain all the information we need to determine the level of output that a profit-maximizing monopolist will choose.

Suppose, first, that the firm is producing at a low level of output, such as Q_1. In this case, marginal cost is less than marginal revenue. If the firm increased production by 1 unit, the additional revenue would exceed the additional costs, and profit would rise. Thus, when marginal cost is less than marginal revenue, the firm can increase profit by producing more units.

A similar argument applies at high levels of output, such as Q_2. In this case, marginal cost is greater than marginal revenue. If the firm reduced production by 1 unit, the costs saved would exceed the revenue lost. Thus, if marginal cost is greater than marginal revenue, the firm can raise profit by reducing production.

In the end, the firm adjusts its level of production until the quantity reaches Q_{MAX}, at which marginal revenue equals marginal cost. Thus, the monopolist's

FIGURE 15.5

Profit Maximization for a Monopoly

A monopoly maximizes profit by choosing the quantity at which marginal revenue equals marginal cost (point A). It then uses the demand curve to find the price that will induce consumers to buy that quantity (point B).

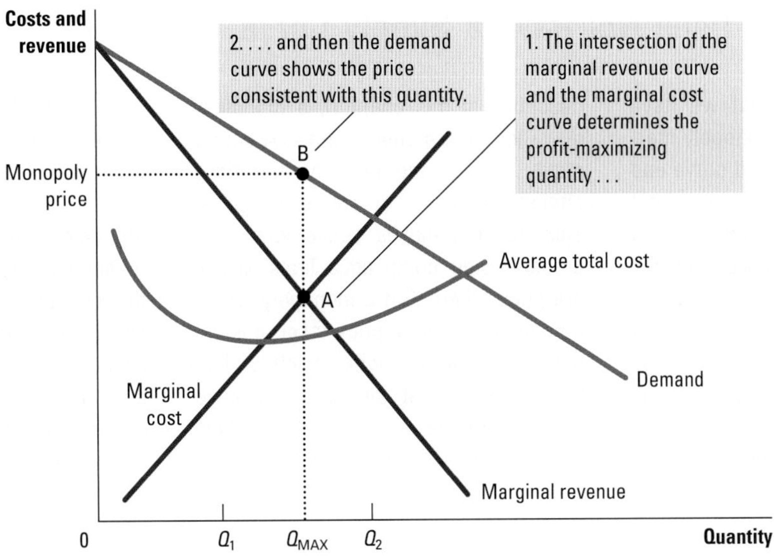

profit-maximizing quantity of output is determined by the intersection of the marginal revenue curve and the marginal cost curve. In Figure 15.5, this intersection occurs at point A.

You might recall from the last chapter that competitive firms also choose the quantity of output at which marginal revenue equals marginal cost. In following this rule for profit maximization, competitive firms and monopolies are alike. But there is also an important difference between these types of firm: the marginal revenue of a competitive firm equals its price, whereas the marginal revenue of a monopoly is less than its price. That is:

$$\text{For a competitive firm}: \; P = MR = MC$$
$$\text{For a monopoly firm}: \; P > MR = MC$$

The equality of marginal revenue and marginal cost at the profit-maximizing quantity is the same for both types of firm. What differs is the relationship of the price to marginal revenue and marginal cost.

How does the monopoly find the profit-maximizing price for its product? The demand curve answers this question because the demand curve relates the amount that customers are willing to pay to the quantity sold. Thus, after the monopoly firm chooses the quantity of output that equates marginal revenue and marginal cost, it uses the demand curve to find the price consistent with that quantity. In Figure 15.5, the profit-maximizing price is found at point B.

We can now see a key difference between markets with competitive firms and markets with a monopoly firm: in competitive markets, price equals marginal cost. In monopolized markets, price exceeds marginal cost. As we will see in a moment, this finding is crucial to understanding the social cost of monopoly.

FYI

Why a Monopoly Does Not Have a Supply Curve

You may have noticed that we have analysed the price in a monopoly market using the market demand curve and the firm's cost curves. We have not made any mention of the market supply curve. By contrast, when we analysed prices in competitive markets beginning in Chapter 4, the two most important words were always *supply* and *demand.*

What happened to the supply curve? Although monopoly firms make decisions about what quantity to supply (in the way described in this chapter), a monopoly does not have a supply curve. A supply curve tells us the quantity that firms choose to supply at any given price. This concept makes sense when we are analysing competitive firms, which are price takers. But a monopoly firm is a price maker, not a price taker. It is not meaningful to ask what such a firm would produce at any price because the firm sets the price at the same time it chooses the quantity to supply.

Indeed, the monopolist's decision about how much to supply is impossible to separate from the demand curve it faces. The shape of the demand curve determines the shape of the marginal revenue curve, which in turn determines the monopolist's profit-maximizing quantity. In a competitive market, supply decisions can be analysed without knowing the demand curve, but that is not true in a monopoly market. Therefore, we never talk about a monopoly's supply curve.

A Monopoly's Profit

How much profit does the monopoly make? To see the monopoly's profit, recall that profit equals total revenue (TR) minus total costs (TC):

$$\text{Profit} = TR - TC$$

We can rewrite this as:

$$\text{Profit} = (TR/Q - TC/Q) \times Q$$

TR/Q is average revenue, which equals the price P, and TC/Q is average total cost ATC. Therefore:

$$\text{Profit} = (P - ATC) \times Q$$

This equation for profit (which is the same as the profit equation for competitive firms) allows us to measure the monopolist's profit in our graph.

Consider the shaded box in Figure 15.6. The height of the box (the segment BC) is price minus average total cost, $P - ATC$, which is the profit on the typical unit sold. The width of the box (the segment DC) is the quantity sold Q_{MAX}. Therefore, the area of this box is the monopoly firm's total profit.

CASE STUDY

Monopoly Drugs versus Generic Drugs

According to our analysis, prices are determined quite differently in monopolized markets from the way they are in competitive markets. A natural place to test this theory is the market for pharmaceutical drugs, because this market takes on both market structures. When a firm discovers a new drug, patent laws give the firm a monopoly on the sale of that drug. But eventually the

FIGURE 15.6

The Monopolist's Profit

The area of the box BCDE *equals the profit of the monopoly firm. The height of the box* (BC) *is price minus average total cost, which equals profit per unit sold. The width of the box* (DC) *is the number of units sold.*

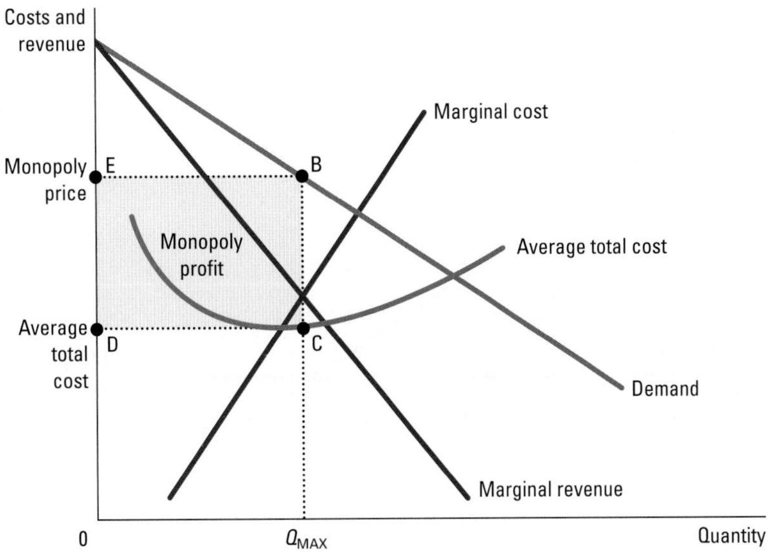

firm's patent runs out, and any company can make and sell the drug. At that time, the market switches from being monopolistic to being competitive.

What should happen to the price of a drug when the patent runs out? Figure 15.7 shows the market for a typical drug. In this figure, the marginal cost of producing the drug is constant. (This is approximately true for many drugs.) During the life of the patent, the monopoly firm maximizes profit by producing the quantity at which marginal revenue equals marginal cost and charging a price well above marginal cost. But when the patent runs out, the profit from making the drug should encourage new firms to enter the market. As the market becomes more competitive, the price should fall to equal marginal cost.

Experience is, in fact, consistent with our theory. When the patent on a drug expires, other companies quickly enter and begin selling so-called generic products that are chemically identical to the former monopolist's brand-name product. And just as our analysis predicts, the price of the competitively produced generic drug is well below the price that the monopolist was charging.

The expiration of a patent, however, does not cause the monopolist to lose all its market power. Some consumers remain loyal to the brand-name drug, perhaps out of fear that the new generic drugs are not actually the same as the drug they have been using for years. As a result, the former monopolist can continue to charge a price somewhat above the price charged by its new competitors.

Quick Quiz Explain how a monopolist chooses the quantity of output to produce and the price to charge.

FIGURE 15.7

The Market for Drugs

When a patent gives a firm a monopoly over the sale of a drug, the firm charges the monopoly price, which is well above the marginal cost of making the drug. When the patent on a drug runs out, new firms enter the market, making it more competitive. As a result, the price falls from the monopoly price to marginal cost.

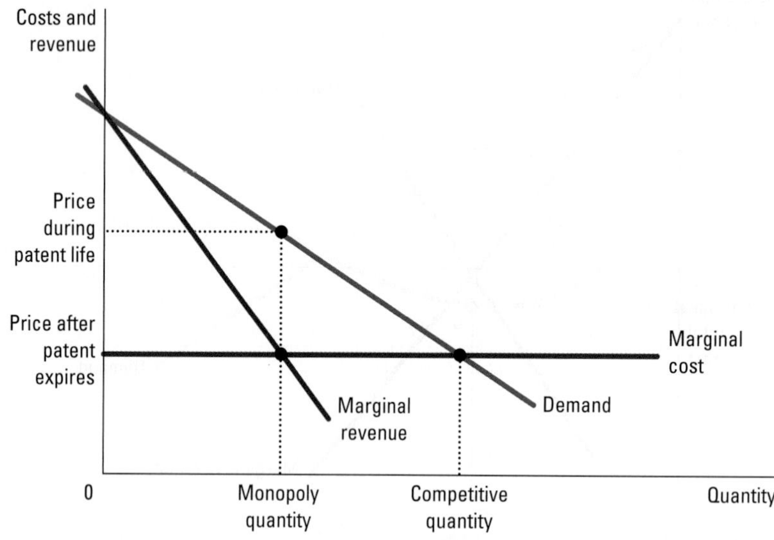

THE WELFARE COST OF MONOPOLY

Is monopoly a good way to organize a market? We have seen that a monopoly, in contrast to a competitive firm, charges a price above marginal cost. From the standpoint of consumers, this high price makes monopoly undesirable. At the same time, however, the monopoly is earning profit from charging this high price. From the standpoint of the owners of the firm, the high price makes monopoly very desirable. Is it possible that the benefits to the firm's owners exceed the costs imposed on consumers, making monopoly desirable from the standpoint of society as a whole?

We can answer this question using the type of analysis we first saw in Chapter 7. As in that chapter, we use total surplus as our measure of economic well-being. Recall that total surplus is the sum of consumer surplus and producer surplus. Consumer surplus is consumers' willingness to pay for a good minus the amount they actually pay for it. Producer surplus is the amount producers receive for a good minus their costs of producing it. In this case, there is a single producer – the monopolist.

You might already be able to guess the result of this analysis. In Chapter 7 we concluded that the equilibrium of supply and demand in a competitive market is not only a natural outcome but a desirable one. In particular, the invisible hand of the market leads to an allocation of resources that makes total surplus as large as it can be. Because a monopoly leads to an allocation of resources different from that in a competitive market, the outcome must, in some way, fail to maximize total economic well-being.

The Deadweight Loss

We begin by considering what the monopoly firm would do if it were run by a benevolent social planner. The social planner cares not only about the profit earned by the firm's owners but also about the benefits received by the firm's consumers. The planner tries to maximize total surplus, which equals producer surplus (profit) plus consumer surplus. Keep in mind that total surplus equals the value of the good to consumers minus the costs of making the good incurred by the monopoly producer.

Figure 15.8 analyses what level of output a benevolent social planner would choose. The demand curve reflects the value of the good to consumers, as measured by their willingness to pay for it. The marginal cost curve reflects the costs of the monopolist. Thus, the socially efficient quantity is found where the demand curve and the marginal cost curve intersect. Below this quantity, the value to consumers exceeds the marginal cost of providing the good, so increasing output would raise total surplus. Above this quantity, the marginal cost exceeds the value to consumers, so decreasing output would raise total surplus.

If the social planner were running the monopoly, the firm could achieve this efficient outcome by charging the price found at the intersection of the demand and marginal cost curves. Thus, like a competitive firm and unlike a profit-maximizing monopoly, a social planner would charge a price equal to marginal

FIGURE 15.8

The Efficient Level of Output

A benevolent social planner who wanted to maximize total surplus in the market would choose the level of output where the demand curve and marginal cost curve intersect. Below this level, the value of the good to the marginal buyer (as reflected in the demand curve) exceeds the marginal cost of making the good. Above this level, the value to the marginal buyer is less than marginal cost.

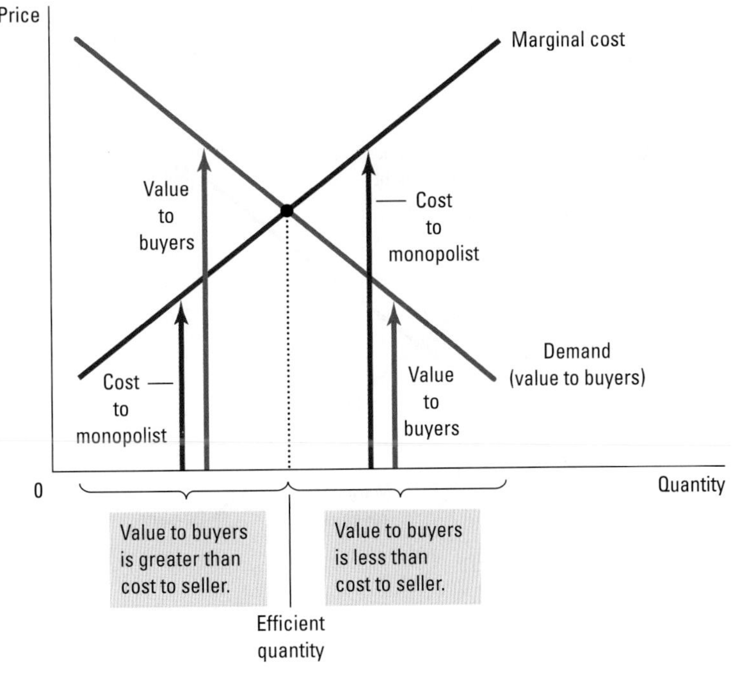

cost. Because this price would give consumers an accurate signal about the cost of producing the good, consumers would buy the efficient quantity.

We can evaluate the welfare effects of monopoly by comparing the level of output that the monopolist chooses to the level of output that a social planner would choose. As we have seen, the monopolist chooses to produce and sell the quantity of output at which the marginal revenue and marginal cost curves intersect; the social planner would choose the quantity at which the demand and marginal cost curves intersect. Figure 15.9 shows the comparison. The monopolist produces less than the socially efficient quantity of output.

We can also view the inefficiency of monopoly in terms of the monopolist's price. Because the market demand curve describes a negative relationship between the price and quantity of the good, a quantity that is inefficiently low is equivalent to a price that is inefficiently high. When a monopolist charges a price above marginal cost, some potential consumers value the good at more than its marginal cost but less than the monopolist's price. These consumers do not end up buying the good. Because the value these consumers place on the good is greater than the cost of providing it to them, this result is inefficient. Thus, monopoly pricing prevents some mutually beneficial trades from taking place.

Just as we measured the inefficiency of taxes with the deadweight loss triangle in Chapter 8, we can similarly measure the inefficiency of monopoly. Figure 15.9 shows the deadweight loss. Recall that the demand curve reflects the value to consumers and the marginal cost curve reflects the costs to the monopoly producer. Thus, the area of the deadweight loss triangle between the demand curve and the marginal cost curve equals the total surplus lost because of monopoly pricing.

The deadweight loss caused by monopoly is similar to the deadweight loss caused by a tax. Indeed, a monopolist is like a private tax collector. As we saw in Chapter 8, a tax on a good places a wedge between consumers' willingness to

FIGURE 15.9

The Inefficiency of Monopoly

Because a monopoly charges a price above marginal cost, not all consumers who value the good at more than its cost buy it. Thus, the quantity produced and sold by a monopoly is below the socially efficient level. The deadweight loss is represented by the area of the triangle between the demand curve (which reflects the value of the good to consumers) and the marginal cost curve (which reflects the costs of the monopoly producer).

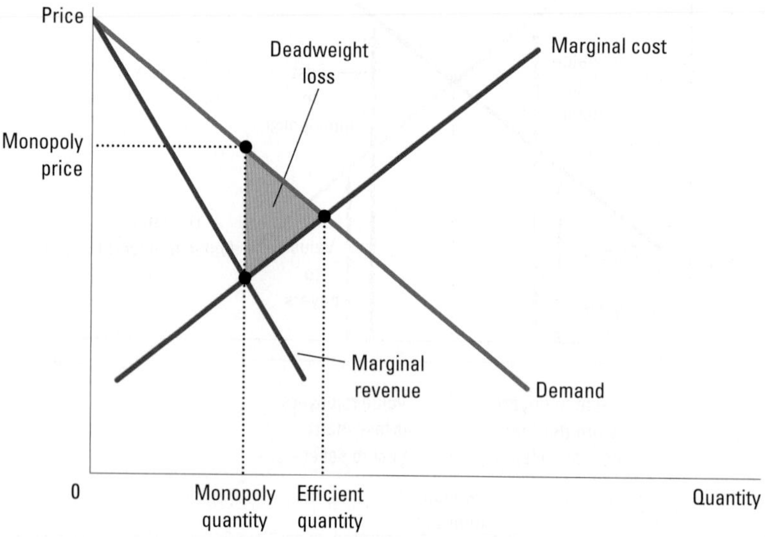

pay (as reflected in the demand curve) and producers' costs (as reflected in the supply curve). Because a monopoly exerts its market power by charging a price above marginal cost, it places a similar wedge. In both cases, the wedge causes the quantity sold to fall short of the social optimum. The difference between the two cases is that the government gets the revenue from a tax, whereas a private firm gets the monopoly profit.

The Monopoly's Profit: A Social Cost?

It is tempting to decry monopolies for 'profiteering' at the expense of the public. And, indeed, a monopoly firm does earn a higher profit by virtue of its market power. According to the economic analysis of monopoly, however, the firm's profit is not in itself necessarily a problem for society.

Welfare in a monopolized market, like all markets, includes the welfare of both consumers and producers. Whenever a consumer pays an extra euro to a producer because of a monopoly price, the consumer is worse off by a euro, and the producer is better off by the same amount. This transfer from the consumers of the good to the owners of the monopoly does not affect the market's total surplus – the sum of consumer and producer surplus. In other words, the monopoly profit itself does not represent a shrinkage in the size of the economic pie; it merely represents a bigger slice for producers and a smaller slice for consumers. Unless consumers are for some reason more deserving than producers – a judgement that goes beyond the realm of economic efficiency – the monopoly profit is not a social problem.

The problem in a monopolized market arises because the firm produces and sells a quantity of output below the level that maximizes total surplus. The deadweight loss measures how much the economic pie shrinks as a result. This inefficiency is connected to the monopoly's high price: consumers buy fewer units when the firm raises its price above marginal cost. But keep in mind that the profit earned on the units that continue to be sold is not the problem. The problem stems from the inefficiently low quantity of output. Put differently, if the high monopoly price did not discourage some consumers from buying the good, it would raise producer surplus by exactly the amount it reduced consumer surplus, leaving total surplus the same as could be achieved by a benevolent social planner.

There is, however, a possible exception to this conclusion. Suppose that a monopoly firm has to incur additional costs to maintain its monopoly position. For example, a firm with a government-created monopoly might need to hire lobbyists to convince lawmakers to continue its monopoly. In this case, the monopoly may use up some of its monopoly profits paying for these additional costs. If so, the social loss from monopoly includes both these costs and the deadweight loss resulting from a price above marginal cost.

Quick Quiz How does a monopolist's quantity of output compare to the quantity of output that maximizes total surplus?

PRICE DISCRIMINATION

So far we have been assuming that the monopoly firm charges the same price to all customers. Yet in many cases firms try to sell the same good to different customers for different prices, even though the costs of producing for the two customers are the same. This practice is called **price discrimination**.

price discrimination
the business practice of selling the same good at different prices to different customers

Before discussing the behaviour of a price-discriminating monopolist, we should note that price discrimination is not possible when a good is sold in a competitive market. In a competitive market, there are many firms selling the same good at the market price. No firm is willing to charge a lower price to any customer because the firm can sell all it wants at the market price. And if any firm tried to charge a higher price to a customer, that customer would buy from another firm. For a firm to price discriminate, it must have some market power.

A Parable about Pricing

To understand why a monopolist would want to price discriminate, let's consider a simple example. Imagine that you are the chief executive officer of Readalot Publishing Company. Readalot's best-selling author has just written her latest novel. To keep things simple, let's imagine that you pay the author a flat €2 million for the exclusive rights to publish the book. Let's also assume – for simplicity – that the cost of printing the book is zero. Readalot's profit, therefore, is the revenue it gets from selling the book minus the €2 million it has paid to the author. Given these assumptions, how would you, as Readalot's CEO, decide what price to charge for the book?

Your first step in setting the price is to estimate what the demand for the book is likely to be. Readalot's marketing department tells you that the book will attract two types of readers. The book will appeal to the author's 100 000 die-hard fans. These fans will be willing to pay as much as €30 for the book. In addition, the book will appeal to about 400 000 less enthusiastic readers who will be willing to pay up to €5 for the book.

What price maximizes Readalot's profit? There are two natural prices to consider: €30 is the highest price Readalot can charge and still get the 100 000 die-hard fans, and €5 is the highest price it can charge and still get the entire market of 500 000 potential readers. It is a matter of simple arithmetic to solve Readalot's problem. At a price of €30, Readalot sells 100 000 copies, has revenue of €3 million, and makes profit of €1 million. At a price of €5, it sells 500 000 copies, has revenue of €2.5 million, and makes profit of €500 000. Thus, Readalot maximizes profit by charging €30 and forgoing the opportunity to sell to the 400 000 less enthusiastic readers.

Notice that Readalot's decision causes a deadweight loss. There are 400 000 readers willing to pay €5 for the book, and the marginal cost of providing it to them is zero. Thus, €2 million of total surplus is lost when Readalot charges the higher price. This deadweight loss is the usual inefficiency that arises whenever a monopolist charges a price above marginal cost.

Now suppose that Readalot's marketing department makes an important discovery: these two groups of readers are in separate markets. All the die-hard fans live in Switzerland and all the other readers live in Turkey. Moreover, it is difficult for readers in one country to buy books in the other. How does this discovery affect Readalot's marketing strategy?

In this case, the company can make even more profit. To the 100 000 Swiss readers, it can charge €30 for the book. To the 400 000 Turkish readers, it can charge €5 for the book (or the Turkish lira equivalent). In this case, revenue is €3 million in Switzerland and €2 million in Turkey, for a total of €5 million. Profit is then €3 million, which is substantially greater than the €1 million the company could earn charging the same €30 price to all customers. Not surprisingly, Readalot chooses to follow this strategy of price discrimination.

Although the story of Readalot Publishing is hypothetical, it describes accurately the business practice of many publishing companies. Textbooks, for example, are often sold at a different price in Europe from in the United States. Even more important is the price differential between hardcover books and paperbacks. When a publisher has a new novel, it initially releases an expensive hardcover edition and later releases a cheaper paperback edition. The difference in price between these two editions far exceeds the difference in printing costs. The publisher's goal is just as in our example. By selling the hardcover to die-hard fans (and libraries) who must have the book as soon as it is published and the paperback to less enthusiastic readers who don't mind waiting, the publisher price discriminates and raises its profit.

The Moral of the Story

Like any parable, the story of Readalot Publishing is stylized. Yet, also like any parable, it teaches some important and general lessons. In this case, there are three lessons to be learned about price discrimination.

The first and most obvious lesson is that price discrimination is a rational strategy for a profit-maximizing monopolist. In other words, by charging different prices to different customers, a monopolist can increase its profit. In essence, a price-discriminating monopolist charges each customer a price closer to his or her willingness to pay than is possible with a single price.

The second lesson is that price discrimination requires the ability to separate customers according to their willingness to pay. In our example, customers were separated geographically. But sometimes monopolists choose other differences, such as age or income, to distinguish among customers. Energy companies are able to discriminate through setting different prices at different times of the day with off-peak usage priced lower than peak time. Similarly, rail companies charge different prices to passengers at certain times of the day with peak travel attracting a much higher price than off-peak travel. Where there is a difference in the price elasticity of demand the monopolist can exploit this and practise price discrimination. Between the hours of 6.00am and 9.30pm on weekday mornings, for example, the price elasticity of demand for rail travel is relatively low whereas between 9.30am and 4.00pm it tends to be relatively high. A higher price can be charged at the peak time but during the off-peak period, the firm may benefit from charging a lower price and encouraging more passengers to travel; the cost of running the train is largely fixed and the marginal cost of carrying an additional passenger is almost zero. Lowering the price, therefore, is a way of utilizing the capacity on the train and adding to profit.

A corollary to this second lesson is that certain market forces can prevent firms from price discriminating. In particular, one such force is *arbitrage*, the process of buying a good in one market at a low price and selling it in another market at a higher price in order to profit from the price difference. In our example, suppose that Swiss bookshops could buy the book in Turkey for €5 and resell it to Swiss readers at a price well below €30. This arbitrage would prevent Readalot from price discriminating because no Swiss resident would buy the book at the higher price. In fact, the increased use of the internet for buying books and other goods through companies like Amazon is likely to affect the ability of companies to price discriminate internationally. Where firms can enforce the division of the market, as in the case of rail fares, it can practise price discrimination. A passenger buying a ticket at off-peak rates is not allowed to travel on a train running during peak periods, and hence arbitrage is circumvented.

The third lesson from our parable is perhaps the most surprising: price discrimination can raise economic welfare. Recall that a deadweight loss arises when Readalot charges a single €30 price, because the 400 000 less enthusiastic readers do not end up with the book, even though they value it at more than its marginal cost of production. By contrast, when Readalot price discriminates, all readers end up with the book, and the outcome is efficient. Thus, price discrimination can eliminate the inefficiency inherent in monopoly pricing.

Note that the increase in welfare from price discrimination shows up as higher producer surplus rather than higher consumer surplus. In our example, consumers are no better off for having bought the book: the price they pay exactly equals the value they place on the book, so they receive no consumer surplus. The entire increase in total surplus from price discrimination accrues to Readalot Publishing in the form of higher profit.

The Analytics of Price Discrimination

Let us consider a little more formally how price discrimination affects economic welfare. We begin by assuming that the monopolist can price discriminate perfectly. *Perfect price discrimination* describes a situation in which the monopolist knows exactly the willingness to pay of each customer and can charge each customer a different price. In this case, the monopolist charges each customer exactly his willingness to pay, and the monopolist gets the entire surplus in every transaction.

Figure 15.10 shows producer and consumer surplus with and without price discrimination. Without price discrimination, the firm charges a single price above marginal cost, as shown in panel (a). Because some potential customers who value the good at more than marginal cost do not buy it at this high price, the monopoly causes a deadweight loss. Yet when a firm can perfectly price discriminate, as shown in panel (b), each customer who values the good at more than marginal cost buys the good and is charged his willingness to pay. All mutually beneficial trades take place, there is no deadweight loss, and the entire

FIGURE 15.10

Welfare With and Without Price Discrimination

Panel (a) shows a monopolist that charges the same price to all customers. Total surplus in this market equals the sum of profit (producer surplus) and consumer surplus. Panel (b) shows a monopolist that can perfectly price discriminate. Because consumer surplus equals zero, total surplus now equals the firm's profit. Comparing these two panels, you can see that perfect price discrimination raises profit, raises total surplus and lowers consumer surplus.

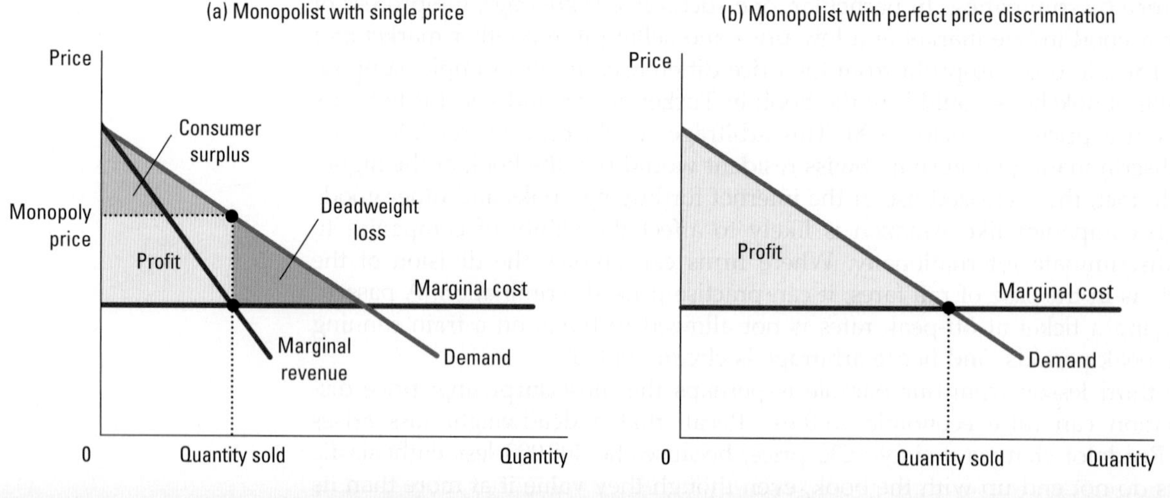

surplus derived from the market goes to the monopoly producer in the form of profit.

In reality, of course, price discrimination is not perfect. Customers do not walk into shops with signs displaying their willingness to pay. Instead, firms price discriminate by dividing customers into groups: young versus old, weekday versus weekend shoppers, Germans versus British, and so on. Unlike those in our parable of Readalot Publishing, customers within each group differ in their willingness to pay for the product, making perfect price discrimination impossible.

How does this imperfect price discrimination affect welfare? The analysis of these pricing schemes is quite complicated, and it turns out that there is no general answer to this question. Compared to the monopoly outcome with a single price, imperfect price discrimination can raise, lower or leave unchanged total surplus in a market. The only certain conclusion is that price discrimination raises the monopoly's profit – otherwise the firm would choose to charge all customers the same price.

Examples of Price Discrimination

Firms use various business strategies aimed at charging different prices to different customers. Now that we understand the economics of price discrimination, let's consider some examples.

Cinema Tickets Many cinemas charge a lower price for children and senior citizens than for other patrons. This fact is hard to explain in a competitive market. In a competitive market, price equals marginal cost, and the marginal cost of providing a seat for a child or senior citizen is the same as the marginal cost of providing a seat for anyone else. Yet this fact is easily explained if cinemas have some local monopoly power and if children and senior citizens have a lower willingness to pay for a ticket. In this case, cinemas raise their profit by price discriminating.

"If we are to reduce prices or leave them the same, may I suggest we raise them first."

Airline Prices Seats on aeroplanes are sold at many different prices. Most airlines charge a lower price for a round-trip ticket between two cities if the traveller stays over a Saturday night. At first this seems odd. Why should it matter to the airline whether a passenger stays over a Saturday night? The reason is that this rule provides a way to separate business travellers and personal travellers. A passenger on a business trip has a high willingness to pay and, most likely, does not want to stay over a Saturday night. By contrast, a passenger travelling for personal reasons has a lower willingness to pay and is more likely to be willing to stay over a Saturday night. Thus, the airlines can successfully price discriminate by charging a lower price for passengers who stay over a Saturday night.

Discount Coupons Many companies offer discount coupons to the public in newspapers and magazines. A buyer simply has to cut out the coupon in order to get €0.50 off his next purchase. Why do companies offer these coupons? Why don't they just cut the price of the product by €0.50?

The answer is that coupons allow companies to price discriminate. Companies know that not all customers are willing to spend the time to cut out coupons. Moreover, the willingness to clip coupons is related to the customer's willingness to pay for the good. A rich and busy executive is unlikely to spend her time cutting discount coupons out of the newspaper, and she is probably willing to pay a higher price for many goods. A person who is unemployed is more likely to clip coupons and has a lower willingness to pay. Thus, by charging a lower price only to those customers who cut out coupons, firms can successfully price discriminate.

Quantity Discounts So far in our examples of price discrimination the monopolist charges different prices to different customers. Sometimes, however, monopolists price discriminate by charging different prices to the same customer for different units that the customer buys. Traditionally, English bakers would give you an extra cake for nothing if you bought 12. While the quaint custom of the 'baker's dozen' (i.e. 13 for the price of 12) is largely a thing of the past, many firms offer lower prices to customers who buy large quantities. This is a form of price discrimination because the customer effectively pays a higher price for the first unit bought than for last. Quantity discounts are often a successful way of price discriminating because a customer's willingness to pay for an additional unit declines as the customer buys more units.

Quick Quiz Give two examples of price discrimination. • How does perfect price discrimination affect consumer surplus, producer surplus and total surplus?

PUBLIC POLICY TOWARDS MONOPOLIES

We have seen that monopolies, in contrast to competitive markets, fail to allocate resources efficiently. Monopolies produce less than the socially desirable quantity of output and, as a result, charge prices above marginal cost. Policy makers in the government can respond to the problem of monopoly in one of four ways, by:

- trying to make monopolized industries more competitive
- regulating the behaviour of the monopolies
- turning some private monopolies into public enterprises
- doing nothing at all.

All industrialized countries have some sort of process for legally prohibiting mergers that are against the public interest.

The earliest moves towards using legal remedies to monopoly power were taken in the US in the late 19th and early 20th centuries, forming the basis of legislation that has become known in the US as the anti-trust laws (in the UK and the rest of Europe, anti-trust law and anti-trust policy are more commonly referred to as competition law and competition policy, although usage of both terms is becoming widespread). The first and most important of the US anti-trust laws was the Sherman Anti-trust Act, which the US Congress passed in 1890 to reduce the market power of the large and powerful 'trusts' or companies that were viewed as dominating the economy at the time. The anti-trust laws give the government various ways to promote competition. For example, a proposed merger between two companies which already have substantial market share would be closely examined by the lawyers and economists in the US Department of Justice, who might well decide that the merger would make the industry in question substantially less competitive and, as a result, would reduce the economic well-being of the country as a whole. If so, the Justice Department would challenge the merger in court, and if the judge agreed, the two companies would not be allowed to merge.

Similarly, in Europe, each country has a competition authority. In the UK it is the Competition Commission; in Germany it is the Federal Cartel Office (*Bundeskartellamt*); in 2009 the French Competition Authority began discharging its regulatory powers following reform of competition regulation; and in Italy the Anti-trust

Authority (*Autorità garante della concorrenza e del mercato*) oversees competition issues. National competition authorities such as these cooperate with each other and with the EU Competition Commission through the European Competition Network (ECN). The aim of the network is to coordinate activities and share information to help enforce EU competition law in member states where the opportunities for cross-border business have increased as the EU has developed and expanded.

Whilst each national country can enforce its own competition legislation, these laws have to be in line with overall EU competition legislation. In the UK, for example, the Competition Act 1998 and the Enterprise Act 2002 both deal with competition issues within the UK but cross-border competition cases would be dealt with under EU law. There are well-defined criteria for deciding whether a proposed merger of companies belonging to more than one European Union country is subject to reference exclusively to the European Commission rather than to national authorities, such as the size of the worldwide or European turnover of the companies in question.

Competition legislation covers three main areas.

- Acting against cartels and cases where businesses engage in restrictive business practices which prevent free trade.
- Banning pricing strategies which are anti-competitive such as price fixing, predatory pricing, price gouging and so on, and through behaviour which might lead to a restriction in competition such as the sharing of information or carving up markets between different firms, rigging bids in tender processes or deliberately restricting production to reduce competition. (See Chapter 17 for more on these two areas.)
- Monitoring and supervising acquisitions and joint ventures

The legislation allows competition authorities the right to fine firms who are found guilty of restricting competition, ordering firms to change behaviour and banning proposed acquisitions. The investigation will consider whether the acquisition, regardless of what size company it produces, is in the public interest. This is in recognition of the fact that companies sometimes merge not to reduce competition but to lower costs through more efficient joint production. These benefits from mergers are often called *synergies.*

Clearly, the government must be able to determine which mergers are desirable and which are not. That is, it must be able to measure and compare the social benefit from synergies to the social costs of reduced competition. In the UK, the Director-General of Fair Trading advises the Secretary of State for Business Innovation and Skills (a government minister) on whether or not a particular merger should be referred for investigation by the Competition Commission – an independent body with members from private industry as well as some academic economists – which then reports its conclusions as to whether the proposed merger is in 'the public interest', so that the minister can then rule on whether to allow or prohibit the merger (although the Secretary of State has the power to – and occasionally does – overrule the recommendations of the Competition Commission).

Regulation

Another way in which the government deals with the problem of monopoly is by regulating the behaviour of monopolists. This solution is common in the case of natural monopolies, such as utility companies like water, gas and electricity companies. These companies are not allowed to charge any price they want. Instead, government agencies regulate their prices.

"You've explained why the merger is good for shareholders, investors and suppliers, the only ones you haven't mentioned are the customers."

FIGURE 15.11

Marginal Cost Pricing For a Natural Monopoly

Because a natural monopoly has declining average total cost, marginal cost is less than average total cost. Therefore, if regulators require a natural monopoly to charge a price equal to marginal cost, price will be below average total cost, and the monopoly will lose money.

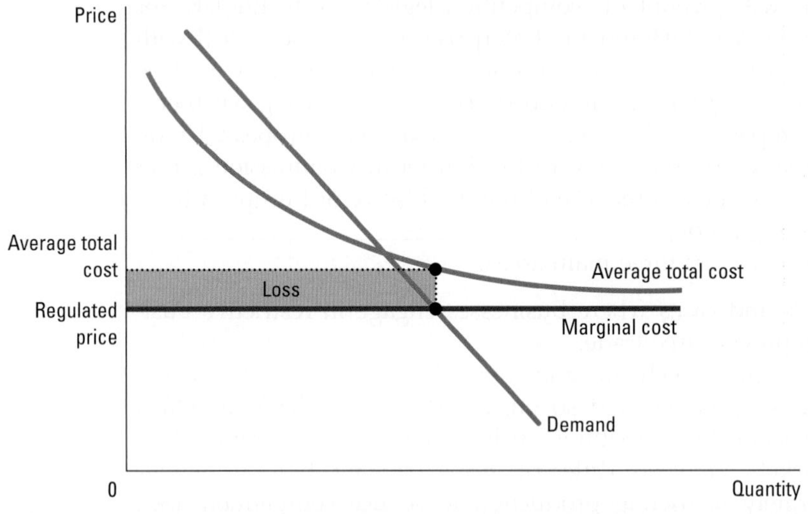

What price should the government set for a natural monopoly? This question is not as easy as it might at first appear. One might conclude that the price should equal the monopolist's marginal cost. If price equals marginal cost, customers will buy the quantity of the monopolist's output that maximizes total surplus, and the allocation of resources will be efficient.

There are, however, two practical problems with marginal-cost pricing as a regulatory system. The first is illustrated in Figure 15.11. Natural monopolies, by definition, have declining average total cost. As we discussed in Chapter 13, when average total cost is declining, marginal cost is less than average total cost. If regulators are to set price equal to marginal cost, that price will be less than the firm's average total cost, and the firm will lose money. Instead of charging such a low price, the monopoly firm would just exit the industry.

Regulators can respond to this problem in various ways, none of which is perfect. One way is to subsidize the monopolist. In essence, the government picks up the losses inherent in marginal-cost pricing. Yet to pay for the subsidy, the government needs to raise money through taxation, which involves its own deadweight losses. Alternatively, the regulators can allow the monopolist to charge a price higher than marginal cost. If the regulated price equals average total cost, the monopolist earns exactly zero economic profit. Yet average-cost pricing leads to deadweight losses, because the monopolist's price no longer reflects the marginal cost of producing the good. In essence, average-cost pricing is like a tax on the good the monopolist is selling.

The second problem with marginal-cost pricing as a regulatory system (and with average-cost pricing as well) is that it gives the monopolist no incentive to reduce costs. Each firm in a competitive market tries to reduce its costs because lower costs mean higher profits. But if a regulated monopolist knows that regulators will reduce prices whenever costs fall, the monopolist will not benefit from lower costs. In practice, regulators deal with this problem by allowing monopolists to keep some of the benefits from lower costs in the form of higher profit, a practice that requires some departure from marginal-cost pricing.

For example, in the UK, utility companies have often been subject to price caps whereby the regulator determines that the real price of the company's product – a kilowatt hour of electricity, for example – should fall by a given number of percentage points each year, reflecting productivity rises. Say, for example, this is 2 per cent. The company would then be allowed to raise its prices each year by the inflation rate *minus* 2 per cent. If the company increases its productivity by, say 4 per cent each year, however (in other words it can produce the same amount of output with 4 per cent less inputs), then in real terms its profits will go up each year. In this way, the system of price caps aims to give natural monopolies the motivation to improve efficiency and productivity that would be supplied by the invisible hand in a competitive market.

Public Ownership

The third policy used by the government to deal with monopoly is public ownership. That is, rather than regulating a natural monopoly that is run by a private firm, the government can run the monopoly itself. An industry owned by the government is called a nationalized industry. This solution is common in many European countries, where the government owns and operates utilities such as the telephone, water and electric companies.

Economists usually prefer private to public ownership of natural monopolies. The key issue is how the ownership of the firm affects the costs of production. Private owners have an incentive to minimize costs as long as they reap part of the benefit in the form of higher profit. If the firm's managers are doing a bad job of keeping costs down, the firm's owners will fire them. By contrast, if the government bureaucrats who run a monopoly do a bad job, the losers are the customers and taxpayers, whose only recourse is the political system. The bureaucrats may become a special interest group and attempt to block cost reducing reforms. Put simply, as a way of ensuring that firms are well run, the voting booth is less reliable than the profit motive.

Doing Nothing

Each of the foregoing policies aimed at reducing the problem of monopoly has drawbacks. As a result, some economists argue that it is often best for the government not to try to remedy the inefficiencies of monopoly pricing. Here is the assessment of economist George Stigler, who won the Nobel Prize for his work in industrial organization, writing in the *Fortune Encyclopedia of Economics:*

> A famous theorem in economics states that a competitive enterprise economy will produce the largest possible income from a given stock of resources. No real economy meets the exact conditions of the theorem, and all real economies will fall short of the ideal economy – a difference called 'market failure.' In my view, however, the degree of 'market failure' for the American economy is much smaller than the 'political failure' arising from the imperfections of economic policies found in real political systems.

As this quotation makes clear, determining the proper role of the government in the economy requires judgements about politics as well as economics.

IN THE NEWS

Monopoly Power and Competition Laws

This article highlights a case where competition authorities are investigating the behaviour of a firm accused of exploiting monopoly power. In this case the firm has a dominant position in the market but is not the only one. Whilst the analysis in this chapter is based on the assumption that there is only one seller in the market, in reality a number of markets have a firm which has a dominant position and can behave as if there is only one seller. In such cases the suspicions of the competition authorities may be aroused.

In February 2010, competition authorities in the European Union (EU) received complaints from three companies, about the search engine giant, Google. The price comparison sites *Foundem*, which is based in the UK and a French search engine site, *ejustice.fr,* claimed that Google is using its dominance in the market to manipulate search results to give more prominence to its own services such as Google Product Search and thus push down competing sites further down the search results. *Ciao! from Bing*, a search engine owned by Microsoft, has filed a complaint with German authorities regarding Google's standard terms and conditions. This was then referred to Brussels and was considered at the same time as the complaints from *Foundem* and *ejustice.fr*.

In the UK, Google has around 90 per cent of the search engine market and globally is estimated to account for over 80 per cent. This, say the complainants, puts Google in a very powerful position. *Foundem* claims that Google uses different algorithms for presenting its own services to that of other sites and as a result is able to create an uneven playing field which raises competition issues. By manipulating search results Google is able to give a greater weighting to its services, for which it receives money, compared to others. *Foundem* was started in 2005 and a spokesperson has said that it encountered problems at an early stage and had its issues with Google resolved in 2009. However, it said that it was acting on behalf of other search firms who may be affected. Microsoft has also commented on the complaint saying that it believes that if there are competition issues as a result of the dominance of one firm over the market then it is right for the EU Commission to investigate. An interesting statement given the dispute between Microsoft and the EU Competition Commission!

Google rejects the claims that it is operating in an anti-competitive manner and has said that it believes it competes fairly in the market. It was notified of the complaints by the Commission and was given time to respond to them. Julia Holtz, a Senior Competition Counsel with Google, presented a robust defence of the company via a corporate blog. In the blog she rather pointedly noted that both *Ciao! from Bing* and *Foundem* have links with Microsoft, the former having been bought by Microsoft in 2008 and the latter as a member of a group called ICOMP, which is partly funded by Microsoft. Holtz says: 'Our algorithms aim to rank first what people are most likely to find useful and we have nothing against vertical search sites.' She went on to say: 'While we will be providing feedback and additional information on these complaints, we are confident that our business operates in the interests of users and partners, as well as in line with European competition law… Though each case raises slightly different issues, the question they ultimately pose is whether Google is doing anything to choke off competition or hurt our users and partners. This is not the case. We always try to listen carefully if someone has a real concern and we work hard to put our users' interests first and to compete fair and square in the market. We believe our business practices reflect those commitments'.

Quick Quiz Describe the ways policy makers can respond to the inefficiencies caused by monopolies. List a potential problem with each of these policy responses.

CONCLUSION: THE PREVALENCE OF MONOPOLY

This chapter has discussed the behaviour of firms that have control over the prices they charge. We have seen that these firms behave very differently from the competitive firms studied in the previous chapter. Table 15.2 summarizes some of the key similarities and differences between competitive and monopoly markets.

From the standpoint of public policy, a crucial result is that monopolists produce less than the socially efficient quantity and charge prices above marginal cost. As a result, they cause deadweight losses. In some cases, these inefficiencies can be mitigated through price discrimination by the monopolist, but at other times they call for policy makers to take an active role.

How prevalent are the problems of monopoly? There are two answers to this question.

In one sense, monopolies are common. Most firms have some control over the prices they charge. They are not forced to charge the market price for their goods, because their goods are not exactly the same as those offered by other firms. A Honda Accord is not the same as a Volkswagen Passat. Ben and Jerry's ice cream is not the same as Wall's. Each of these goods has a downward sloping demand curve, which gives each producer some degree of monopoly power.

Yet firms with substantial monopoly power are quite rare. Few goods are truly unique. Most have substitutes that, even if not exactly the same are very similar. Ben and Jerry can raise the price of their ice cream a little without losing all their sales; but if they raise it very much, sales will fall substantially.

In the end, monopoly power is a matter of degree. It is true that many firms have some monopoly power. It is also true that their monopoly power is usually limited. In these cases, we will not go far wrong assuming that firms operate in competitive markets, even if that is not precisely the case.

TABLE 15.2

Competition versus Monopoly: A Summary Comparison

	Competition	Monopoly
Similarities		
Goal of firms	Maximize profits	Maximize profits
Rule for maximizing	$MR = MC$	$MR = MC$
Can earn economic profits in the short run?	Yes	Yes
Differences		
Number of firms	Many	One
Marginal revenue	$MR = P$	$MR < P$
Price	$P = MC$	$P > MC$
Produces welfare-maximizing level of output?	Yes	No
Entry in long run?	Yes	No
Can earn economic profits in long run?	No	Yes
Price discrimination possible?	No	Yes

SUMMARY

- A monopoly is a firm that is the sole seller in its market. A monopoly arises when a single firm owns a key resource, when the government gives a firm the exclusive right to produce a good, or when a single firm can supply the entire market at a smaller cost than many firms could.
- Because a monopoly is the sole producer in its market, it faces a downward sloping demand curve for its product. When a monopoly increases production by 1 unit, it causes the price of its good to fall, which reduces the amount of revenue earned on all units produced. As a result, a monopoly's marginal revenue is always below the price of its good.
- Like a competitive firm, a monopoly firm maximizes profit by producing the quantity at which marginal revenue equals marginal cost. The monopoly then chooses the price at which that quantity is demanded. Unlike a competitive firm, a monopoly firm's price exceeds its marginal revenue, so its price exceeds marginal cost.
- A monopolist's profit-maximizing level of output is below the level that maximizes the sum of consumer and producer surplus. That is, when the monopoly charges a price above marginal cost, some consumers who value the good more than its cost of production do not buy it. As a result, monopoly causes deadweight losses similar to the deadweight losses caused by taxes.
- Policy makers can respond to the inefficiency of monopoly behaviour in four ways. They can use competition law to try to make the industry more competitive. They can regulate the prices that the monopoly charges. They can turn the monopolist into a government-run enterprise. Or, if the market failure is deemed small compared to the inevitable imperfections of policies, they can do nothing at all.
- Monopolists often can raise their profits by charging different prices for the same good based on a buyer's willingness to pay. This practice of price discrimination can raise economic welfare by getting the good to some consumers who otherwise would not buy it. In the extreme case of perfect price discrimination, the deadweight losses of monopoly are completely eliminated. More generally, when price discrimination is imperfect, it can either raise or lower welfare compared to the outcome with a single monopoly price.

KEY CONCEPTS

monopoly, p. 310

natural monopoly, p. 311

price discrimination, p. 323

QUESTIONS FOR REVIEW

1. Give an example of a government-created monopoly. Is creating this monopoly necessarily bad public policy? Explain.
2. Define natural monopoly. What does the size of a market have to do with whether an industry is a natural monopoly?
3. Why is a monopolist's marginal revenue less than the price of its good? Can marginal revenue ever be negative? Explain.
4. Draw the demand, marginal revenue and marginal cost curves for a monopolist. Show the profit-maximizing level of output. Show the profit-maximizing price.
5. In your diagram from the previous question, show the level of output that maximizes total surplus. Show the deadweight loss from the monopoly. Explain your answer.
6. What gives the government the power to regulate mergers between firms? From the standpoint of the welfare of society, give a good reason and a bad reason that two firms might want to merge.
7. Describe the two problems that arise when regulators tell a natural monopoly that it must set a price equal to marginal cost.
8. Give two examples of price discrimination. In each case, explain why the monopolist chooses to follow this business strategy.

PROBLEMS AND APPLICATIONS

1. A publisher faces the following demand schedule for the next novel of one of its popular authors:

Price (€)	Quantity demanded
€100	0
90	100 000
80	200 000
70	300 000
60	400 000
50	500 000
40	600 000
30	700 000
20	800 000
10	900 000
0	1 000 000

The author is paid €12 million to write the book, and the marginal cost of publishing the book is a constant €110 per book.

a. Compute total revenue, total cost and profit at each quantity. What quantity would a profit-maximizing publisher choose? What price would it charge?
b. Compute marginal revenue. (Recall that $MR = \Delta TR/\Delta Q$.) How does marginal revenue compare to the price? Explain.
c. Graph the marginal revenue, marginal cost and demand curves. At what quantity do the marginal revenue and marginal cost curves cross? What does this signify?
d. In your graph, shade in the deadweight loss. Explain in words what this means.
e. If the author were paid €13 million instead of €12 million to write the book, how would this affect the publisher's decision regarding the price to charge? Explain.
f. Suppose the publisher was not profit-maximizing but was concerned with maximizing economic efficiency. What price would it charge for the book? How much profit would it make at this price?

2. Suppose that a natural monopolist was required by law to charge average total cost. On a diagram, label the price charged and the deadweight loss to society relative to marginal-cost pricing.

3. Consider the delivery of mail. In general, what is the shape of the average total cost curve? How might the shape differ between isolated rural areas and densely populated urban areas? How might the shape have changed over time? Explain.

4. Suppose the Eau de Jeunesse Water Company has a monopoly on bottled water sales in France. If the price of tap water increases, what is the change in Eau de Jeunesse's profit-maximizing levels of output, price and profit? Explain in words and with a graph.

5. A small town is served by many competing supermarkets, which have constant marginal cost.
a. Using a diagram of the market for groceries, show the consumer surplus, producer surplus and total surplus.
b. Now suppose that the independent supermarkets combine into one chain. Using a new diagram, show the new consumer surplus, producer surplus and total surplus. Relative to the competitive market, what is the transfer from consumers to producers? What is the deadweight loss?

6. Guy Rope and his backing group, the Tent Pegs, have just finished recording their latest music CD. Their record company's marketing department determines that the demand for the CD is as follows:

Price (€)	Number of CDs
€24	10 000
22	20 000
20	30 000
18	40 000
16	50 000
14	60 000

The company can produce the CD with no fixed cost and a variable cost of €0.15 per CD.

a. Find total revenue for quantity equal to 10 000, 20 000 and so on. What is the marginal revenue for each 10 000 increase in the quantity sold?
b. What quantity of CDs would maximize profit? What would the price be? What would the profit be?
c. If you were Guy Rope's agent, what recording fee would you advise Guy to demand from the record company? Why?

7. In 1969 the US government charged IBM with monopolizing the computer market. The government argued (correctly) that a large share of all mainframe computers sold in the United States were produced by IBM. IBM argued (correctly) that a much smaller share of the market for *all* types of computers consisted of IBM products. Based on these facts, do you think that the government should have brought a lawsuit against IBM for violating the US anti-trust laws? Explain.

8. A company is considering building a bridge across a river. The bridge would cost €12 million to build and nothing to maintain. The following table shows the company's anticipated demand over the lifetime of the bridge:

Price per crossing (€)	Number of crossings (in thousands)
€8	0
7	100
6	200
5	300
4	400
3	500
2	600
1	700
0	800

   a. If the company were to build the bridge, what would be its profit-maximizing price? Would that be the efficient level of output? Why or why not?
   b. If the company is interested in maximizing profit, should it build the bridge? What would be its profit or loss?
   c. If the government were to build the bridge, what price should it charge for passengers and vehicles to use the bridge? Explain your answer.
   d. Should the government build the bridge? Explain.
9. The Placebo Drug Company holds a patent on one of its discoveries.
   a. Assuming that the production of the drug involves rising marginal cost, draw a diagram to illustrate Placebo's profit-maximizing price and quantity. Also show Placebo's profits.
   b. Now suppose that the government imposes a tax on each bottle of the drug produced. On a new diagram, illustrate Placebo's new price and quantity. How does each compare to your answer in part (a)?
   c. Although it is not easy to see in your diagrams, the tax reduces Placebo's profit. Explain why this must be true.
   d. Instead of the tax per bottle, suppose that the government imposes a tax on Placebo of €110 000 regardless of how many bottles are produced. How does this tax affect Placebo's price, quantity and profits? Explain.
10. Pablo, Dirk and Franz run the only saloon in town. Pablo wants to sell as many drinks as possible without losing money. Dirk wants the saloon to bring in as much revenue as possible. Franz wants to make the largest possible profits. Using a single diagram of the saloon's demand curve and its cost curves, show the price and quantity combinations favoured by each of the three partners. Explain.
11. The Best Computer Company just developed a new computer chip, on which it immediately acquires a patent.
   a. Draw a diagram that shows the consumer surplus, producer surplus and total surplus in the market for this new chip.
   b. What happens to these three measures of surplus if the firm can perfectly price discriminate? What is the change in deadweight loss? What transfers occur?
12. Explain why a monopolist will always produce a quantity at which the demand curve is elastic. (Hint: if demand is inelastic and the firm raises its price, what happens to total revenue and total costs?)
13. Singer Britney Spears has a monopoly over a scarce resource: herself. She is the only person who can produce a Britney Spears concert. Does this fact imply that the government should regulate the prices of her concerts? Why or why not?
14. Napster, the online file-swapping service, originally allowed people to use the internet to download copies of their favourite songs from other people's computers without cost. In what sense did Napster enhance economic efficiency in the short run? In what sense might Napster have reduced economic efficiency in the long run? Why do you think the courts eventually shut Napster down? Do you think this was the right policy?
15. Many schemes for price discriminating involve some cost. For example, discount coupons take up time and resources from both the buyer and the seller. This question considers the implications of costly price discrimination. To keep things simple, let's assume that our monopolist's production costs are simply proportional to output, so that average total cost and marginal cost are constant and equal to each other.
   a. Draw the cost, demand and marginal revenue curves for the monopolist. Show the price the monopolist would charge without price discrimination.
   b. In your diagram, mark the area equal to the monopolist's profit and call it X. Mark the area equal to consumer surplus and call it Y. Mark the area equal to the deadweight loss and call it Z.
   c. Now suppose that the monopolist can perfectly price discriminate. What is the monopolist's profit? (Give your answer in terms of X, Y and Z.)
   d. What is the change in the monopolist's profit from price discrimination? What is the change in total surplus from price discrimination? Which change is larger? Explain. (Give your answer in terms of X, Y and Z.)
   e. Now suppose that there is some cost of price discrimination. To model this cost, let's assume that the monopolist has to pay a fixed cost *C* in order to price

discriminate. How would a monopolist make the decision whether to pay this fixed cost? (Give your answer in terms of X, Y, Z and *C*.)

f. How would a benevolent social planner, who cares about total surplus, decide whether the monopolist should price discriminate? (Give your answer in terms of X, Y, Z and *C*.)

g. Compare your answers to parts (e) and (f). How does the monopolist's incentive to price discriminate differ from the social planner's? Is it possible that the monopolist will price discriminate even though it is not socially desirable?

For further resources, visit www.cengage.com/mankiw_taylor2

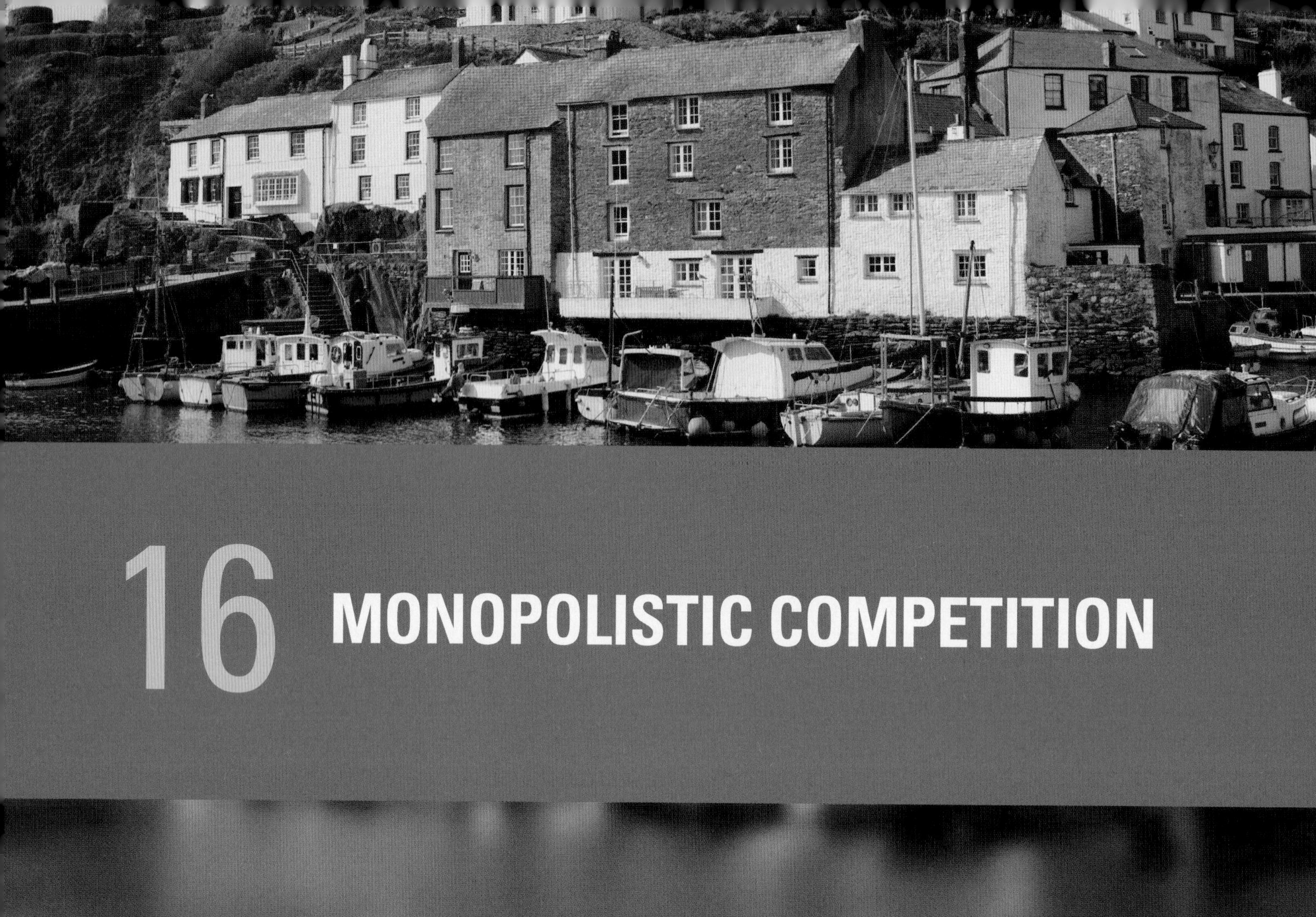

16 MONOPOLISTIC COMPETITION

You walk into a bookshop to buy a book to read during your next summer holiday. On the shop's shelves you find the latest blockbuster crime thriller novel, an interesting looking political novel by a new author, a novel about a thirty-something divorcee trying to build a new life, an intellectual literary novel by a French female author, the autobiography of a former prime minister and many other choices. When you pick out a book and buy it, what kind of market are you participating in?

On the one hand, the market for books seems competitive. As you look over the shelves at your bookshop, you find many authors and many publishers vying for your attention. A buyer in this market has thousands of competing products from which to choose. And because many people are willing to put the time and effort into becoming a writer, there are a lot of people wanting to enter the market. Because of this, the book business is not very profitable. For every highly paid novelist, there are hundreds of struggling ones.

On the other hand, the market for books seems monopolistic. Because each book is unique, publishers have some latitude in choosing what price to charge. The sellers in this market are price makers rather than price takers. And, indeed, the price of books greatly exceeds marginal cost. The price of a typical hardcover novel in the UK, for instance, is about £15, whereas the cost of printing one additional copy of the novel is only a few pounds.

monopolistic competition
a market structure in which many firms sell products that are similar but not identical

In this chapter we examine markets that have some features of competition and some features of monopoly. This market structure is called **monopolistic competition**. Monopolistic competition describes a market with the following attributes:

- *Many sellers.* There are many firms competing for the same group of customers.
- *Product differentiation.* Each firm produces a product that is at least slightly different from those of other firms. The firm is able to have some control over the extent to which it can differentiate its product from its rivals thus reducing the degree of substitutability and garnering an element of customer or brand loyalty. Thus, rather than being a price taker, each firm faces a downward sloping demand curve.
- *Free entry.* Firms can enter (or exit) the market without restriction. Thus, the number of firms in the market adjusts until economic profits are driven to zero.

Table 16.1 lists examples of the types of market with these attributes.

TABLE 16.1

Examples of Markets which Have Characteristics of Monopolistic Competition

Computer games	Vets
Restaurants	Hotel accommodation
Conference organizers	Air conditioning systems
Wedding planners	Pest control
Plumbing	Removal services
Coach hire	Beauty consultants
Funeral directors	Shop fitters
Fabric manufacturers	Waste disposal
Tailors	Dentists
Music teachers	Children's entertainers
Books	Gas engineers
CDs/DVDs	Steel fabricators
Landscape architects	Driving schools
Environmental consultants	Opticians
Furniture manufacturers	Chimney sweeps

Monopolistic competition is a market structure that lies between the extreme cases of competition and monopoly. Under monopolistic competition, there are many sellers, each of which is small compared to the market. A monopolistically competitive market departs from the perfectly competitive ideal because each of the sellers is able to offer a different product by differentiating it in some way from other suppliers.

COMPETITION WITH DIFFERENTIATED PRODUCTS

To understand monopolistically competitive markets, we first consider the decisions facing an individual firm. We then examine what happens in the long run as firms enter and exit the industry. Next, we compare the equilibrium under monopolistic competition to the equilibrium under perfect competition that we examined in Chapter 14. Finally, we consider whether the outcome in a monopolistically competitive market is desirable from the standpoint of society as a whole.

The Monopolistically Competitive Firm in the Short Run

Each firm in a monopolistically competitive market is, in many ways, like a monopoly. Because its product is different from those offered by other firms, it faces a downward sloping demand curve. (By contrast, remember, a perfectly

FIGURE 16.1

Monopolistic Competitors in the Short Run

Monopolistic competitors, like monopolists, maximize profit by producing the quantity at which marginal revenue equals marginal cost. The firm in panel (a) makes a profit because, at this quantity, price is above average total cost. The firm in panel (b) makes losses because, at this quantity, price is less than average total cost.

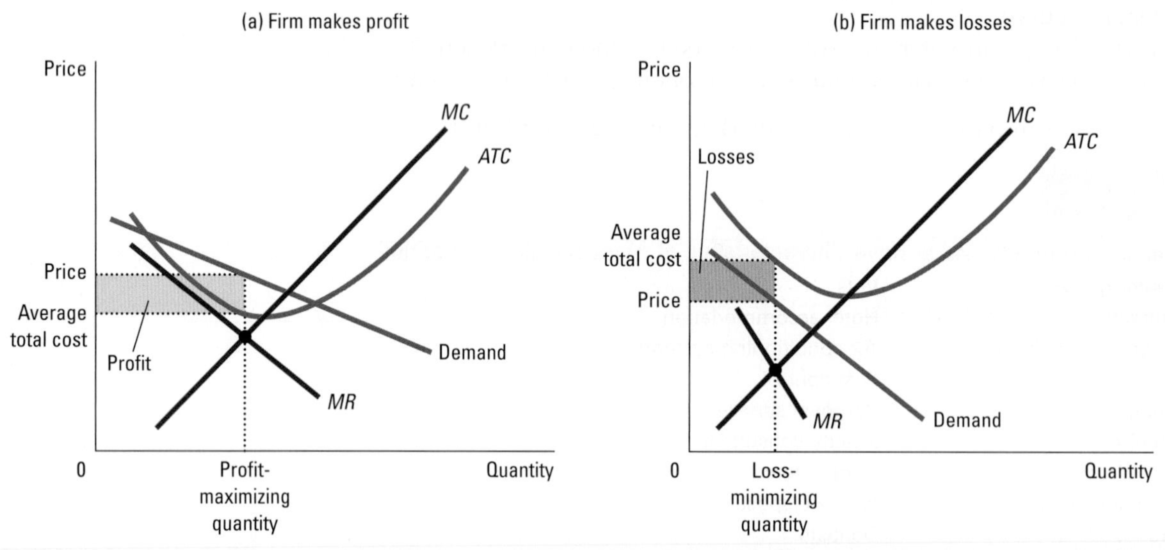

competitive firm faces a horizontal demand curve at the market price.) Thus, the monopolistically competitive firm follows a monopolist's rule for profit maximization: it chooses the quantity at which marginal revenue equals marginal cost and then uses its demand curve to find the price consistent with that quantity.

Figure 16.1 shows the cost, demand and marginal revenue curves for two typical firms, each in a different monopolistically competitive industry. In both panels of this figure, the profit-maximizing quantity is found at the intersection of the marginal revenue and marginal cost curves. The two panels in this figure show different outcomes for the firm's profit. In panel (a), price exceeds average total cost, so the firm makes a profit. In panel (b), price is below average total cost. In this case, the firm is unable to make a positive profit, so the best the firm can do is to minimize its losses.

All this should seem familiar. A monopolistically competitive firm chooses its quantity and price just as a monopoly does. In the short run, these two types of market structure are similar.

The Long-Run Equilibrium

The situations depicted in Figure 16.1 do not last long. When firms are making profits, as in panel (a), new firms have an incentive to enter the market (remember that there is free entry and exit into the market). This entry means that more firms are now offering products for sale in the industry. The increase in supply causes the price received by all firms in the industry to fall. If an existing firm wishes to sell more then it must reduce its price. There are now more substitutes available in the market and so the effect for firms is to shift the demand curve to the left. The effect is that there is an increase in the number of products from

FIGURE 16.2

A Monopolistic Competitor in the Long Run

In a monopolistically competitive market, if firms are making profit, new firms enter and the demand curves for the incumbent firms shift to the left. Similarly, if firms are making losses, old firms exit and the demand curves of the remaining firms shift to the right. Because of these shifts in demand, a monopolistically competitive firm eventually finds itself in the long-run equilibrium shown here. In this long-run equilibrium, price equals average total cost, and the firm earns zero profit.

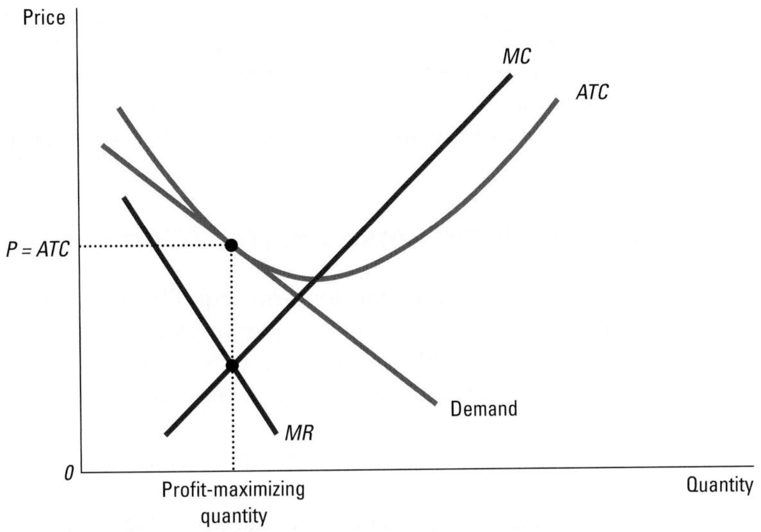

which customers can now choose and, therefore, reduces the demand faced by each firm already in the market. In other words, profit encourages entry, and entry shifts the demand curves faced by the incumbent firms to the left. As the demand for incumbent firms' products falls, these firms experience declining profit.

Conversely, when firms are making losses, as in panel (b), firms in the market have an incentive to exit. As firms exit, the supply will fall and price will rise. There are now fewer substitutes and so customers have fewer products from which to choose. This decrease in the number of firms effectively expands the demand faced by those firms that stay in the market. In other words, losses encourage exit, and exit has the effect of shifting the demand curves of the remaining firms to the right. As the demand for the remaining firms' products rises, these firms experience rising profit (that is, declining losses).

This process of entry and exit continues until the firms in the market are making exactly zero economic profit. Figure 16.2 depicts the long-run equilibrium. Once the market reaches this equilibrium, new firms have no incentive to enter, and existing firms have no incentive to exit.

Notice that the demand curve in this figure just barely touches the average total cost curve. Mathematically, we say the two curves are *tangent* to each other. These two curves must be tangent once entry and exit have driven profit to zero. Because profit per unit sold is the difference between price (found on the demand curve) and average total cost, the maximum profit is zero only if these two curves touch each other without crossing.

To sum up, two characteristics describe the long-run equilibrium in a monopolistically competitive market:

- As in a monopoly market, price exceeds marginal cost. This conclusion arises because profit maximization requires marginal revenue to equal marginal cost and because the downward sloping demand curve makes marginal revenue less than the price.
- As in a competitive market, price equals average total cost. This conclusion arises because free entry and exit drive economic profit to zero.

The second characteristic shows how monopolistic competition differs from monopoly. Because a monopoly is the sole seller of a product without close substitutes, it can earn positive economic profit, even in the long run. By contrast, because there is free entry into a monopolistically competitive market, the economic profit of a firm in this type of market is driven to zero.

Monopolistic versus Perfect Competition

Figure 16.3 compares the long-run equilibrium under monopolistic competition to the long-run equilibrium under perfect competition. (Chapter 14 discussed the equilibrium with perfect competition.) There are two noteworthy differences between monopolistic and perfect competition – excess capacity and the mark-up.

Excess Capacity As we have just seen, entry and exit drive each firm in a monopolistically competitive market to a point of tangency between its demand and average total cost curves. Panel (a) of Figure 16.3 shows that the quantity of

FIGURE 16.3

Monopolistic versus Perfect Competition

Panel (a) shows the long-run equilibrium in a monopolistically competitive market, and panel (b) shows the long-run equilibrium in a perfectly competitive market. Two differences are notable. (1) The perfectly competitive firm produces at the efficient scale, where average total cost is minimized. By contrast, the monopolistically competitive firm produces at less than the efficient scale. (2) Price equals marginal cost under perfect competition, but price is above marginal cost under monopolistic competition.

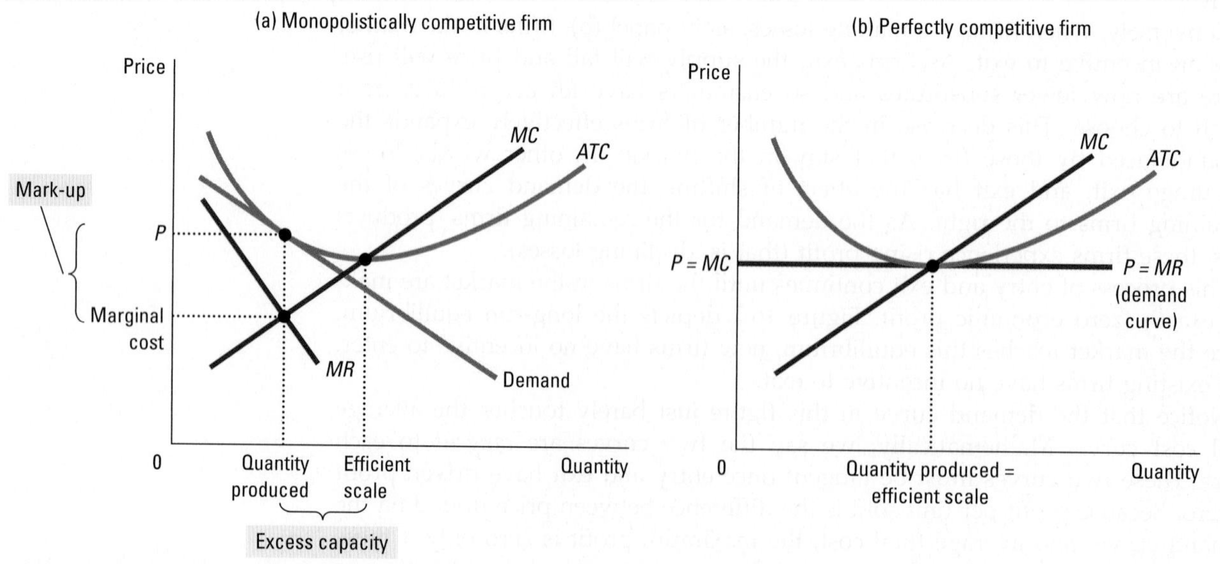

output at this point is smaller than the quantity that minimizes average total cost. Thus, under monopolistic competition, firms produce on the downward sloping portion of their average total cost curves. In this way, monopolistic competition contrasts starkly with perfect competition. As panel (b) of Figure 16.3 shows, free entry in competitive markets drives firms to produce at the minimum of average total cost.

The quantity that minimizes average total cost is called the *efficient scale* of the firm. In the long run, perfectly competitive firms produce at the efficient scale, whereas monopolistically competitive firms produce below this level. Firms are said to have *excess capacity* under monopolistic competition. In other words, a monopolistically competitive firm, unlike a perfectly competitive firm, could increase the quantity it produces and lower the average total cost of production.

Mark-up over Marginal Cost A second difference between perfect competition and monopolistic competition is the relationship between price and marginal cost. For a competitive firm, such as that shown in panel (b) of Figure 16.3, price equals marginal cost. For a monopolistically competitive firm, such as that shown in panel (a), price exceeds marginal cost, because the firm always has some market power.

How is this mark-up over marginal cost consistent with free entry and zero profit? The zero-profit condition ensures only that price equals average total cost. It does *not* ensure that price equals marginal cost. Indeed, in the long-run equilibrium, monopolistically competitive firms operate on the declining portion of their average total cost curves, so marginal cost is below average total cost. Thus, for price to equal average total cost, price must be above marginal cost.

In this relationship between price and marginal cost, we see a key behavioural difference between perfect competitors and monopolistic competitors. Imagine that you were to ask a firm the following question: 'Would you like to see another customer come through your door ready to buy from you at your current price?' A perfectly competitive firm would answer that it didn't care. Because price exactly equals marginal cost, the profit from an extra unit sold is zero. By contrast, a monopolistically competitive firm is always eager to get another customer. Because its price exceeds marginal cost, an extra unit sold at the posted price means more profit. According to an old quip, monopolistically competitive markets are those in which sellers send greetings cards to the buyers.

Monopolistic Competition and the Welfare of Society

Is the outcome in a monopolistically competitive market desirable from the standpoint of society as a whole? Can policy makers improve on the market outcome? There are no simple answers to these questions.

One source of inefficiency is the mark-up of price over marginal cost. Because of the mark-up, some consumers who value the good at more than the marginal cost of production (but less than the price) will be deterred from buying it. Thus, a monopolistically competitive market has the normal deadweight loss of monopoly pricing. We first saw this type of inefficiency when we discussed monopoly in Chapter 15.

Although this outcome is clearly undesirable compared to the first-best outcome of price equal to marginal cost, there is no easy way for policy makers to fix the problem. To enforce marginal-cost pricing, policy makers would need to regulate all firms that produce differentiated products. Because such products are so common in the economy, the administrative burden of such regulation would be overwhelming.

Moreover, regulating monopolistic competitors would entail all the problems of regulating natural monopolies. In particular, because monopolistic competitors are making zero profits already, requiring them to lower their prices to equal marginal cost would cause them to make losses. To keep these firms in business, the government would need to help them cover these losses. Rather than raising taxes to pay for these subsidies, policy makers may decide it is better to live with the inefficiency of monopolistic pricing.

Another way in which monopolistic competition may be socially inefficient is that the number of firms in the market may not be the 'ideal' one. That is, there may be too much or too little entry. One way to think about this problem is in terms of the externalities associated with entry. Whenever a new firm considers entering the market with a new product, it considers only the profit it would make. Yet its entry would also have two external effects:

- *The product-variety externality.* Because consumers get some consumer surplus from the introduction of a new product, entry of a new firm conveys a positive externality on consumers.
- *The business-stealing externality.* Because other firms lose customers and profits from the entry of a new competitor, entry of a new firm imposes a negative externality on existing firms.

Thus, in a monopolistically competitive market, there are both positive and negative externalities associated with the entry of new firms. Depending on which externality is larger, a monopolistically competitive market could have either too few or too many products.

Both of these externalities are closely related to the conditions for monopolistic competition. The product-variety externality arises because a new firm would offer a product different from those of the existing firms. The business-stealing externality arises because firms post a price above marginal cost and, therefore, are always eager to sell additional units. Conversely, because perfectly competitive firms produce identical goods and charge a price equal to marginal cost, neither of these externalities exists under perfect competition.

In the end, we can conclude only that monopolistically competitive markets do not have all the desirable welfare properties of perfectly competitive markets. That is, the invisible hand does not ensure that total surplus is maximized under monopolistic competition. Yet because the inefficiencies are subtle, hard to measure and hard to fix, there is no easy way for public policy to improve the market outcome.

Quick Quiz List the three key attributes of monopolistic competition. • Draw and explain a diagram to show the long-run equilibrium in a monopolistically competitive market. How does this equilibrium differ from that in a perfectly competitive market?

ADVERTISING

It is nearly impossible to go through a typical day in a modern economy without being bombarded with advertising. Whether you are reading a newspaper, watching television or driving down the motorway, some firm will try to convince you to buy its product. Such behaviour is a natural feature of monopolistic competition. When firms sell differentiated products and charge prices above marginal cost, each firm has an incentive to advertise in order to attract more buyers to its particular product.

UK Advertising Spending Share, 2008

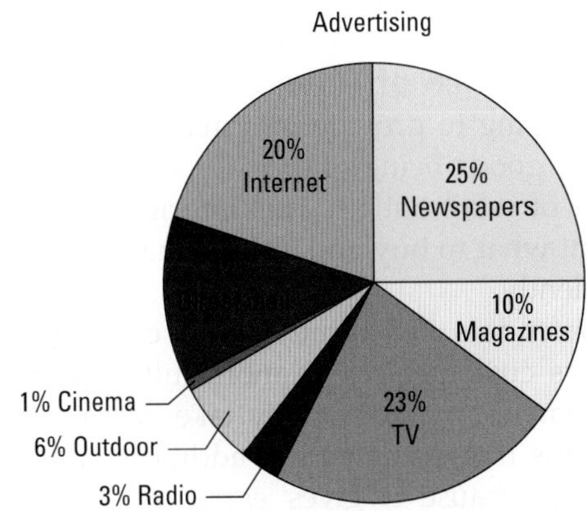

Source: AA's *Quarterly Survey of Advertising Expenditure.*

The amount of advertising varies substantially across products. Firms that sell highly differentiated consumer goods, such as over-the-counter drugs, perfumes, soft drinks, razor blades, breakfast cereals and dog food, typically spend between 10 and 20 per cent of revenue for advertising. Firms that sell industrial products, such as drill presses and communications satellites, typically spend very little on advertising. And firms that sell homogeneous products, such as wheat, peanuts or crude oil, spend nothing at all. In the EU in 2009, spending on online advertising alone was about £14.7 billion.

Advertising takes many forms. Figure 16.4 shows a breakdown of the share of advertising spending in the UK in 2008. Most advertising expenditure in the UK is through newspapers with TV coming a close second. One major change in the way in which firms advertise is the use of the internet. In 2002 around 1 per cent of total advertising spending went on the Internet but this has increased dramatically to 20 per cent by 2008 and is expected to continue to grow.

The Debate over Advertising

Is society wasting the resources it devotes to advertising? Or does advertising serve a valuable purpose? Assessing the social value of advertising is difficult and often generates heated argument among economists. Let's consider both sides of the debate.

The Critique of Advertising Critics of advertising argue that firms advertise in order to manipulate people's tastes. Much advertising is psychological rather than informational. Consider, for example, the typical television advert for some brand of soft drink. The advert most likely does not tell the viewer about the product's price or quality. Instead, it might show a group of happy people at a party on a beach on a beautiful sunny day. In their hands are cans of the soft drink. The goal of the advert is to convey a subconscious (if not subtle) message: 'You too can have many friends and be happy and beautiful, if only you drink our product.' Critics of advertising argue that such an advert creates a desire that otherwise might not exist.

Critics also argue that advertising impedes competition. Advertising often tries to convince consumers that products are more different than they truly are. By increasing the perception of product differentiation and fostering brand loyalty, advertising makes buyers less concerned with price differences among similar goods. With a less elastic demand curve, each firm charges a larger mark-up over marginal cost.

The Defence of Advertising Defenders of advertising argue that firms use advertising to provide information to customers. Advertising conveys the prices of the goods being offered for sale, the existence of new products and the locations of retail outlets. This information allows customers to make better choices about what to buy and, thus, enhances the ability of markets to allocate resources efficiently.

Defenders also argue that advertising fosters competition. Because advertising allows customers to be more fully informed about all the firms in the market, customers can more easily take advantage of price differences. Thus, each firm has less market power. In addition, advertising allows new firms to enter more easily, because it gives entrants a means to attract customers from existing firms.

CASE STUDY

Advertising – What Does it Really Do?

Ask many people the question 'why do firms advertise?' and they are likely to tell you that it is an attempt by firms to try and increase demand for their products or services. If you consider this view intuitively it might make sense but then ask yourself the question, 'how many times have you seen an advert on the TV and then rushed out to buy the product advertised?' The chances are that this has not (consciously) happened very often at all. So if adverts do not make us rush out to buy products what do they do?

Sutherland and Sylvester (2000)[1] argue that it is largely a myth that adverts are designed to persuade us to buy products or services. They point out the following:

> Advertising influences the order in which we evoke or notice the alternatives we consider. This does not feel like persuasion and it is not. It is nevertheless effective. Instead of persuasion and other major effects we should look for 'feathers', or minor effects. These can tip the balance when alternative brands are otherwise equal and, through repetition, can grow imperceptibly by small increments over time.

They liken the effect of advertising to that of watching someone grow up. You know that they are growing but the day-to-day changes in the individual are imperceptible. If you have not seen someone for some time, however, you do tend to notice the difference in their height, shape, features and so on. So it is with many advertising campaigns. The primary aim, they argue, is to generate a series of small effects, which ultimately influence our behaviour and may cause us to view differently the products or the brands that we choose, especially in a crowded marketplace with a large amount of competition.

Exactly how adverts work, therefore, is not easy to quantify. Sutherland and Sylvester suggest that many involved in the advertising industry do not really understand why some adverts seem to work and others don't work anything like as well. It has long been recognized that psychology has a lot to do with advertising. Our understanding of the way the brain works has

© RICHARD LEVINE / ALAMY

been revolutionized by the developments afforded by magnetic resonance imaging (MRI) scans. The advertising industry has not been slow in looking at this technology and its potential for improving the focus and efficiency of advertising.

In essence, this technique looks at the response of the brain to different images and messages. Using MRI techniques, the areas of the brain that respond to different stimuli can be identified. The field developed as a result of work carried out by a neuroscientist called Read Montague. Montague is Professor in the Department of Neuroscience at Baylor College of Medicine in Houston, Texas. He gave a group of individuals two colas, Pepsi and Coke, to taste and asked them to state which they preferred. The respondents did not know that the two colas were in fact Pepsi and Coke. The results were 50:50 for the two products.

However, when the experiment was repeated and the respondents were told what they were drinking, around 75% stated that they preferred Coke. Montague found that brain activity in the medial pre-frontal cortex also showed signs of enhanced activity during the exercise. This area of the brain is associated with higher level thinking. Montague posited that the brain was making an association with the images and messages associated with commercials for Coke that respondents had witnessed over the years. He also suggested that such activity might lead to consumers preferring one product to another, even if there was other evidence to suggest that under normal circumstances, they would not have chosen that product.

[1]Sutherland, M. & Sylvester, A.K. (2000) *Advertising and the Mind of the Consumer: What Works, What Doesn't, and Why.* St Leonards, New South Wales, Allen and Unwin.

Advertising as a Signal of Quality

Many types of advertising contain little apparent information about the product being advertised. Consider a firm introducing a new breakfast cereal. A typical advertisement might have some highly paid actor eating the cereal and exclaiming how wonderful it tastes. How much information does the advertisement really provide?

The answer is: more than you might think. Defenders of advertising argue that even advertising that appears to contain little hard information may in fact tell consumers something about product quality. The willingness of the firm to spend a large amount of money on advertising can itself be a *signal* to consumers about the quality of the product being offered.

Consider the problem facing two firms – Nestlé and Kellogg. Each company has just come up with a recipe for a new breakfast cereal, which it would sell for €3 a box. To keep things simple, let's assume that the marginal cost of making cereal is zero, so the €3 is all profit. Each company knows that if it spends €10 million on advertising, it will get 1 million consumers to try its new cereal. And each company knows that if consumers like the cereal, they will buy it not once but many times.

First consider Nestlé's decision. Based on market research, Nestlé knows that its cereal is only mediocre. Although advertising would sell one box to each of 1 million consumers, the consumers would quickly learn that the cereal is not very good and stop buying it. Nestlé decides it is not worth paying €10 million in advertising to get only €3 million in sales. So it does not bother to advertise. It sends its cooks back to the drawing board to find another recipe.

Kellogg, on the other hand, knows that its cereal is great. Each person who tries it will buy a box a month for the next year. Thus, the €10 million in advertising will bring in €36 million in sales. Advertising is profitable here because

Kellogg has a good product that consumers will buy repeatedly. Thus, Kellogg chooses to advertise.

Now that we have considered the behaviour of the two firms, let's consider the behaviour of consumers. We began by asserting that consumers are inclined to try a new cereal that they see advertised. But is this behaviour rational? Should a consumer try a new cereal just because the seller has chosen to advertise it?

In fact, it may be completely rational for consumers to try new products that they see advertised. In our story, consumers decide to try Kellogg's new cereal because Kellogg advertises. Kellogg chooses to advertise because it knows that its cereal is quite good, while Nestlé chooses not to advertise because it knows that its cereal is only mediocre. By its willingness to spend money on advertising, Kellogg signals to consumers the quality of its cereal. Each consumer thinks, quite sensibly, 'Crikey, if the Kellogg Company is willing to spend so much money advertising this new cereal, it must be really good.'

What is most surprising about this theory of advertising is that the content of the advertisement is irrelevant. Kellogg signals the quality of its product by its willingness to spend money on advertising. (This example is used for illustrative purposes only and is not meant to infer that Nestlé deliberately produces inferior products!)

What the advertisements say is not as important as the fact that consumers know ads are expensive. By contrast, cheap advertising cannot be effective at signalling quality to consumers. In our example, if an advertising campaign cost less than €3 million, both Nestlé and Kellogg would use it to market their new cereals. Because both good and mediocre cereals would be advertised, consumers could not infer the quality of a new cereal from the fact that it is advertised. Over time, consumers would learn to ignore such cheap advertising.

This theory can explain why firms pay celebrities large amounts of money to make advertisements that, on the surface, appear to convey no information at all. The information is not in the advertisement's content, but simply in its existence and expense.

Brand Names

branding
the means by which a business creates an identity for itself and highlights the way in which it differs from its rivals

Advertising is closely related to the existence of **branding**. In many markets, there are two types of firms. Some firms sell products with widely recognized brand names, while other firms sell generic substitutes. For example, in a typical supermarket, you can find Pepsi next to less familiar colas, or Kellogg's cornflakes next to the supermarket's own brand of cornflakes, made for it by an unknown firm. Most often, the firm with the famous brand name spends more on advertising and charges a higher price for its product.

Just as there is disagreement about the economics of advertising, there is disagreement about the economics of brand names and branding. Let's consider both sides of the debate.

Critics of brand names argue that branding causes consumers to perceive differences that do not really exist. In many cases, the generic good is almost indistinguishable from the brand-name good. Consumers' willingness to pay more for the brand-name good, these critics assert, is a form of irrationality fostered by advertising. Economist Edward Chamberlin, one of the early developers of the theory of monopolistic competition, concluded from this argument that brand names were bad for the economy. He proposed that the government discourage their use by refusing to enforce the exclusive trademarks that companies use to identify their products.

More recently, economists have defended brand names as a useful way for consumers to ensure that the goods they buy are of high quality. There are two

FYI

Contestable Markets

Most economics textbooks up to the late 1970s covered market structures ranging from perfect competition from one extreme to monopoly at the other. Changes in the way businesses actually operated in the real world meant that there were some gaps between the theory and the observed behaviour of firms. This led to the development of a new theory which was incorporated into the explanation of market structures. The theory of contestable markets was developed by William J. Baumol, John Panzar and Robert Willig in 1982.

The key characteristic of a perfectly contestable market (the benchmark to explain firms' behaviours) was that firms were influenced by the threat of new entrants into a market. We have seen how, in monopolistically competitive markets, despite the fact that each firm has some monopoly control over its product, the ease of entry and exit means that in the long run profits can be competed away as new firms enter the market. This threat of new entrants may make firms behave in a way that departs from what was assumed to be the traditional goal of firms – to maximize profits. The suggestion by Baumol and colleagues was that firms may deliberately limit profits made to discourage new entrants. The other characteristics of a perfectly contestable market are that there are no barriers to entry or exit and no sunk costs. Profits might be limited by what was termed *entry limit pricing*. This refers to a situation where a firm will keep prices lower than they could be in order to deter new entrants. Similarly, firms may also practise *predatory or destroyer pricing* whereby the price is held below average cost for a period to try and force out competitors or prevent new firms from entering the market. Incumbent firms may be in a position to do this because they may have been able to gain some advantages of economies of scale which new entrants may not be able to exploit.

In a contestable market firms may also erect other artificial barriers to prevent entry into the industry by new firms. Such barriers might include operating at over-capacity, which provides the opportunity to flood the market and drive down price in the event of a threat of entry. Firms will also carry out aggressive marketing and branding strategies to 'tighten' up the market or find ways of reducing costs and increasing efficiency to gain competitive advantage. Searching out sources of competitive advantage was a topic written on extensively by Michael Porter, who defined competitive advantage as being the advantages firms can gain over another which are both distinctive and defensible. These sources are not simply to be found in terms of new product development but through close investigation and analysis of the supply chain, where little changes might make a difference to the cost base of a firm which it can then exploit to its advantage.

Hit-and-run tactics might be evident in a contestable market where firms enter the industry, take the profit and get out quickly (possible because of the freedom of entry and exit). In other cases firms may indulge in what is termed *cream-skimming* – identifying parts of the market that are high in value added and exploiting those markets.

The theory of contestable markets has been widely adopted as a beneficial addition to the theory of the firm and there has been extensive research into its application. There are numerous examples of markets exhibiting contestability characteristics including financial services; airlines, especially flights on domestic routes; the IT industry and in particular internet service providers (ISPs), software and web developers; energy supplies and the postal service.

related arguments. First, brand names provide consumers with *information* which cannot be easily judged in advance of purchase. Second, brand names give firms an *incentive* to meet the needs of consumers, because firms have a financial stake in maintaining the reputation of their brand names. Note that branding does not always equate to high quality. Some firms will happily admit their goods are 'cheap and cheerful' but point out that they provide consumers with value for money. A number of discount stores, for example, expanded during the recession in 2008–09. Firms such as Lidl, Netto, Poundstretcher and Poundland are

"No response - we'll have to use the corporate logo flashcards again"

interested in developing their brand names as much as Armani and Ralph Lauren. Consumers were able to associate the brand name with value for money – important when times are difficult.

To see how these arguments work in practice, consider a famous brand name: Ibis hotels. Imagine that you are driving through an unfamiliar town and you need somewhere to stay for the night. You see a Hotel Ibis and a local hotel next door to it. Which do you choose? The local hotel may in fact offer better accommodation at lower prices, but you have no way of knowing that. In contrast, Hotel Ibis offers a consistent product across many European cities. Its brand name is useful to you as a way of judging the quality of what you are about to buy.

The Ibis brand name also ensures that the company has an incentive to maintain quality. For example, if some customers were to become very ill from bad food served at breakfast at a Hotel Ibis, the news would be disastrous for the company. Ibis would lose much of the valuable reputation that it has built up over the years and, as a result, it would lose sales and profit not just in the hotel that served the bad food but in its many hotels across Europe. By contrast, if some customers were to become ill from bad food served at breakfast in a local hotel, that restaurant might have to close down, but the lost profits would be much smaller. Hence, Ibis has a greater incentive to ensure that its breakfast food is safe.

The debate over brand names thus centres on the question of whether consumers are rational in preferring brand names over generic substitutes. Critics of brand names argue that brand names are the result of an irrational consumer response to advertising. Defenders of brand names argue that consumers have good reason to pay more for brand-name products because they can be more confident in the quality of these products.

Quick Quiz How might advertising make markets less competitive? How might it make markets more competitive? • Give the arguments for and against brand names.

CONCLUSION

Monopolistic competition is true to its name: it is a hybrid of monopoly and competition. Like a monopoly, each monopolistic competitor faces a downward sloping demand curve and, as a result, charges a price above marginal cost. As in a perfectly competitive market, there are many firms, and entry and exit drive the profit of each monopolistic competitor toward zero. Table 16.2 summarizes these lessons.

Because monopolistically competitive firms produce differentiated products, each firm advertises in order to attract customers to its own brand. To some extent, advertising manipulates consumers' tastes, promotes irrational brand loyalty and impedes competition. To a larger extent, advertising provides information, establishes brand names of reliable quality and fosters competition.

The theory of monopolistic competition seems to describe many markets in the economy. It is somewhat disappointing, therefore, that the theory does not yield simple and compelling advice for public policy. From the standpoint of the economic theorist, the allocation of resources in monopolistically competitive markets is not perfect. Yet, from the standpoint of a practical policy maker, there may be little that can be done to improve it.

TABLE 16.2

Monopolistic Competition: Between Perfect Competition and Monopoly

	Market structure		
	Perfect competition	**Monopolistic competition**	**Monopoly**
Features that all three market structures share			
Goal of firms	Maximize profits	Maximize profits	Maximize profits
Rule for maximizing	$MR = MC$	$MR = MC$	$MR = MC$
Can earn economic profits in the short run?	Yes	Yes	Yes
Features that monopoly and monopolistic competition share			
Price taker?	Yes	No	No
Price	$P = MC$	$P > MC$	$P > MC$
Produces welfare-maximizing level of output?	Yes	No	No
Features that perfect competition and monopolistic competition share			
Number of firms	Many	Many	One
Entry in long run?	Yes	Yes	No
Can earn economic profits in long run?	No	No	Yes

IN THE NEWS

The debate over the role of advertising and branding is a complex one with few clear cut answers. If firms see an opportunity to be able to differentiate their products from rivals then advertising and branding may be ways that they can reinforce these differences in the minds of consumers. In some cases, firms may specifically choose to focus on developing the brand because it gives them an advantage in what can be a crowded and often unforgiving market place. This article explains one such example which shows that a focus on the brand can have some benefits to both the business and to consumers.

Innis & Gunn

The brewing industry is dominated by a relatively small number or large firms but for many ordinary consumers the market is one which is characterized by brands with few having any idea (or indeed caring) about which major brewer is behind the brand. Competition between brands is intensive and as the industry has become more and more concentrated, the scope for new firms to enter the market has become increasingly difficult. In addition, the industry has faced challenging times over the past few years. In the UK, rising duties on alcohol, the recession, changes in the way that alcoholic drinks are sold not to mention the concern over alcohol abuse have all conspired to cause commercial difficulties for brewers. The British Beer & Pub Association (BB&PA) has published figures showing that in the first half of 2009, an average of 52 pubs a week closed down – 33 per cent more than the equivalent period in 2008 – and 24 000 jobs were lost in the industry over this time. You might not think that this was an industrial climate to launch a new brewing enterprise but the story of Innis & Gunn shows how even within an industry beset by problems there are entrepreneurial opportunities that can be exploited.

The Innis & Gunn brewery is run by Dougal Sharp. His father, Russell Sharp, led a management buyout of the Caledonian brewery in Edinburgh and Dougal became the head brewer, putting his degree in environmental chemistry to use. Caledonian had been working with whisky producer, William Grant & Sons, and had developed a brew that was used to help the production of whisky in oak casks. The brew flavoured the casks prior to the whisky being put in at which point it was supposed to be drained off and discarded. However, Sharp's attention was brought to the fact that this by-product was actually a tasty beer in its own right. After discussion with Grants it was decided to set up a new company to market the by-product – the birth of Innis & Gunn.

Sharp decided that the focus of the new product would be the brand. By building up the brand other factors such as the location of production could be less of a problem. It means, for example, that it is not essential to have a production facility in Scotland, which could be expensive. This opens up the opportunity for the company to outsource production. The key was to build relationships with suppliers and to make sure those suppliers understood the brand. The firm keeps a close eye on the production process and specifies the ingredients used and the maturation process but another Scottish brewery actually produces the beer. Having sorted out the outsourcing of the brewing, Innis & Gunn were then able to plough their limited funds into promoting the brand. The focus on the brand has been deliberate, therefore, and is designed to try and make the beer synonymous with Scotland in the same way that whisky is.

Since 2004 the business has enjoyed growth of 60 per cent per annum on average and the beer sells around half a million cases each year with revenues of around £5 million. Sharp has a target to break the million case mark in the medium term. Its main sales channel in the UK has been supermarkets and off-licences but it is hoped that this can be broadened to include pubs and possibly a draught version of the beer. It has also been successful in export markets which accounts for around 65 per cent of its revenue. It has become the best selling British bottled beer in terms of value and sales in Canada and in early 2010 the company began to turn its attention to the US market. Prior to the decision to target this new market, sales in the US only accounted for 3 per cent of Innis & Gunn's sales but Sharp noted that the total market for the sort of beer the firm is producing makes up 16 per cent of the US beer market – the so called 'craft beer' segment. The company appointed a dedicated marketing and sales team to the US to try and develop the market all based around the promotion of the brand.

The ability of small and medium-sized enterprises (SMEs) to enter mature markets dominated by larger firms is limited. Few are going to be able to set up full production and distribution facilities to compete with those of their bigger rivals – the cost disadvantages are simply too great. By focusing on the brand the firm can instead develop the demand side of the business by encouraging sales outlets and customers of the quality of the product and driving demand as a result. This type of behaviour is one that provides a different business model to the traditional image of a brewer and is another reminder of how the theory of firms is constantly changing as market structures evolve and businesses change to meet new market conditions.

Source: Adapted from Biz/ed 'In the News'. http://www.bized.co.uk/cgi-bin/chron/chron.pl?id=3559

SUMMARY

- A monopolistically competitive market is characterized by three attributes: many firms, differentiated products and free entry.
- The equilibrium in a monopolistically competitive market differs from that in a perfectly competitive market in two related ways. First, each firm in a monopolistically competitive market has excess capacity. That is, it operates on the downward sloping portion of the average total cost curve. Secondly, each firm charges a price above marginal cost.
- Monopolistic competition does not have all the desirable properties of perfect competition. There is the standard deadweight loss of monopoly caused by the mark-up of price over marginal cost. In addition, the number of firms (and thus the variety of products) can be too large or too small. In practice, the ability of policy makers to correct these inefficiencies is limited.
- The product differentiation inherent in monopolistic competition leads to the use of advertising and brand names. Critics of advertising and brand names argue that firms use them to take advantage of consumer irrationality and to reduce competition. Defenders of advertising and brand names argue that firms use them to inform consumers and to compete more vigorously on price and product quality.

KEY CONCEPTS

monopolistic competition, p. 338

branding, p. 348

QUESTIONS FOR REVIEW

1. Describe the three attributes of monopolistic competition. How is monopolistic competition like monopoly? How is it like perfect competition?
2. Draw a diagram depicting a firm in a monopolistically competitive market that is making profits. Now show what happens to this firm as new firms enter the industry.
3. Draw a diagram of the long-run equilibrium in a monopolistically competitive market. How is price related to average total cost? How is price related to marginal cost?
4. Does a monopolistic competitor produce too much or too little output compared to the most efficient level? What practical considerations make it difficult for policy makers to solve this problem?
5. How might advertising reduce economic well-being? How might advertising increase economic well-being?
6. How might advertising with no apparent informational content in fact convey information to consumers?
7. Explain two benefits that might arise from the existence of brand names.

PROBLEMS AND APPLICATIONS

1. Classify the following markets as perfectly competitive, monopolistic or monopolistically competitive, and explain your answers.
   a. wooden HB pencils
   b. bottled water
   c. copper
   d. local telephone service
   e. strawberry jam
   f. lipstick.
2. What feature of the product being sold distinguishes a monopolistically competitive firm from a monopolistic firm?
3. The chapter states that monopolistically competitive firms could increase the quantity they produce and lower the average total cost of production. Why don't they do so?
4. Sparkle is one firm of many in the market for toothpaste, which is in long-run equilibrium.
   a. Draw a diagram showing Sparkle's demand curve, marginal revenue curve, average total cost curve, and marginal cost curve. Label Sparkle's profit-maximizing output and price.
   b. What is Sparkle's profit? Explain.
   c. On your diagram, show the consumer surplus derived from the purchase of Sparkle toothpaste. Also show the deadweight loss relative to the efficient level of output.
   d. If the government forced Sparkle to produce the efficient level of output, what would happen to the firm? What would happen to Sparkle's customers?
5. Do monopolistically competitive markets typically have the optimal number of products? Explain.
6. The chapter says that monopolistically competitive firms may send greetings cards to their customers. What do they accomplish by this? Explain in words and with a diagram.
7. If you were thinking of entering the ice cream business, would you try to make ice cream that is just like one of the existing (successful) brands? Explain your decision using the ideas of this chapter.
8. Describe three adverts that you have seen on TV. In what ways, if any, were each of these adverts socially useful? In what ways were they socially wasteful? Did the adverts affect the likelihood of your buying the product? Why or why not?

9. For each of the following pairs of firms, explain which firm would be more likely to engage in advertising:
   a. A family-owned farm or a family-owned restaurant.
   b. A manufacturer of forklift trucks or a manufacturer of cars.
   c. A company that invented a very reliable watch or a company that invented a less reliable watch that costs the same amount to make.
10. The makers of *Panadol* pain reliever do a lot of advertising and have very loyal customers. In contrast, the makers of generic paracetamol do no advertising, and their customers shop only for the lowest price. Assume that the marginal costs of *Panadol* and generic paracetamol are the same and constant.
    a. Draw a diagram showing *Panadol*'s demand, marginal revenue and marginal cost curves. Label *Panadol*'s price and mark-up over marginal cost.
    b. Repeat part (a) for a producer of generic paracetamol. How do the diagrams differ? Which company has the bigger mark-up? Explain.
    c. Which company has the bigger incentive for careful quality control? Why?

For further resources, visit www.cengage.com/mankiw_taylor2

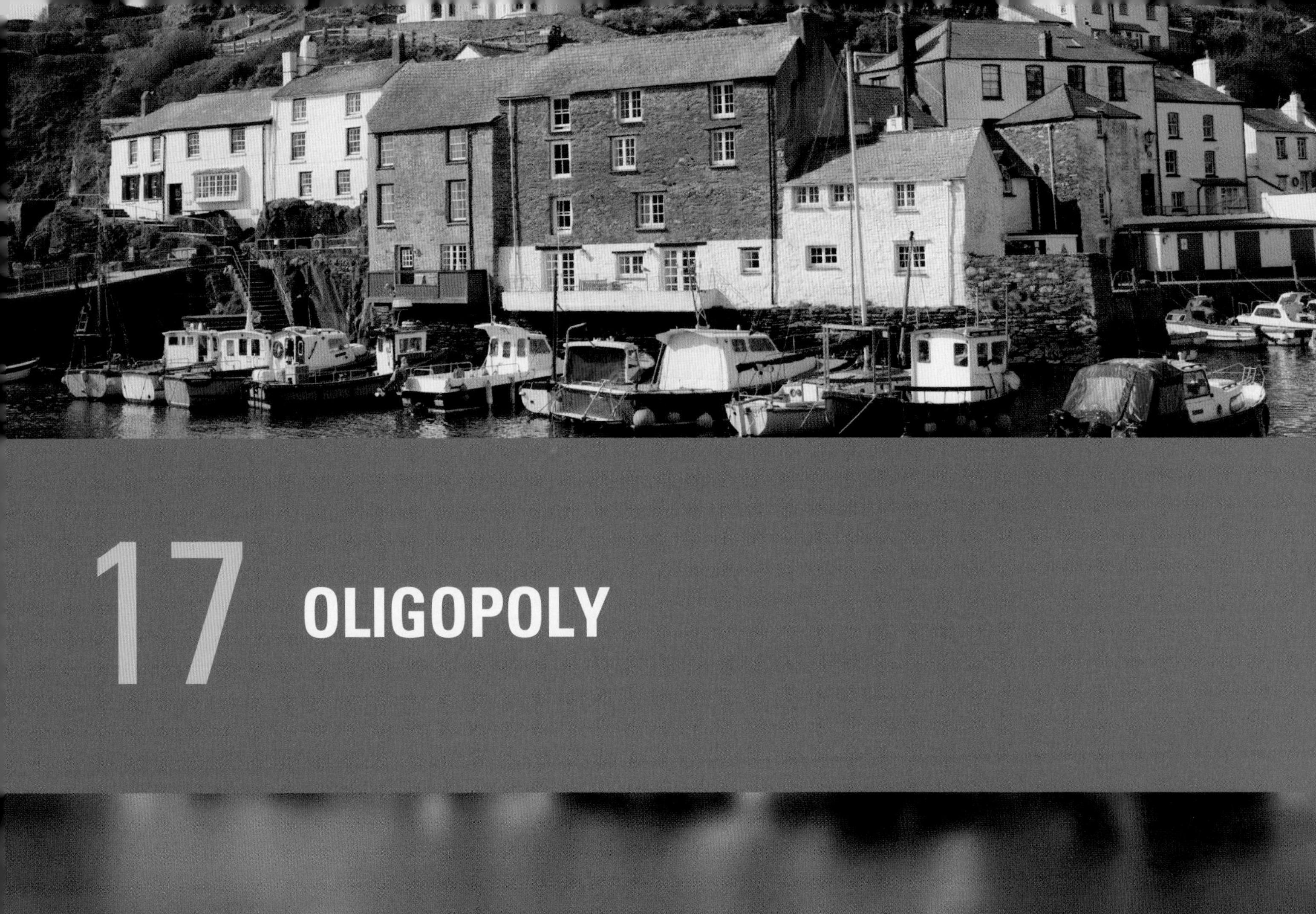

17 OLIGOPOLY

The Europeans love chocolate. The average German eats about 180 62-gram bars of chocolate a year. The Belgians are not far behind at 177 bars, the Swiss around 173 and the British eat around 164 bars per year. There are many firms producing chocolate in Europe including Anthon Berg in Denmark, Camille Bloch, Lindt and Favarger in Switzerland, Guylian and Godiva in Belgium and Hachez in Germany. However, Europeans are likely to find that what they are eating is likely to be made by one of three companies: Cadbury (now owned by US firm Kraft), Mars or Nestlé. These firms dominate the chocolate industry in the European Union. Being so large and dominant they are able to influence the quantity of chocolate bars produced and, given the market demand curve, the price at which chocolate bars are sold.

The previous three chapters discussed three types of market structure. In a competitive market, each firm is so small compared to the market that it cannot influence the price of its product and, therefore, takes the price as given by market conditions. In a monopolized market, a single firm supplies the entire market for a good, and that firm can choose any price and quantity on the market demand curve. In a monopolistic competitive structure, there are many small firms but each is able to differentiate their product in some way and so has some small influence on price.

The European market for chocolate bars fits neither the competitive nor the monopoly model. Competition and monopoly are extreme forms of market structure. Competition occurs when there are many firms in a market offering essentially identical products; monopoly occurs when there is only one firm in a market. It is natural to start the study of industrial organization with these polar cases, for they are the easiest cases to understand. Yet many industries, including the chocolate industry, fall somewhere between these two extremes. Firms in these industries have competitors but, at the same time, do not face so much competition that they are price takers. Economists call this situation *imperfect competition*.

In this chapter we discuss the types of imperfect competition and examine a particular type called *oligopoly*. The essence of an oligopolistic market is that there are only a few sellers. The small number of sellers makes rigorous competition less likely, and it makes strategic interactions among them vitally important. As a result, the actions of any one seller in the market can have a large impact on the profits of all the other sellers. That is, oligopolistic firms are interdependent in a way that competitive firms are not. Our goal in this chapter is to see how this interdependence shapes the firms' behaviour and what problems it raises for public policy.

BETWEEN MONOPOLY AND PERFECT COMPETITION

The cases of perfect competition and monopoly illustrate some important ideas about how markets work. Most markets in the economy, however, include elements of both these cases and, therefore, are not completely described by either of them. The typical firm in the economy faces competition, but the competition is not so rigorous as to make the firm exactly described by the price-taking firm analysed in Chapter 14. The typical firm also has some degree of market power, but its market power is not so great that the firm can be exactly described by the monopoly firm analysed in Chapter 15. In other words, the typical firm in our economy is imperfectly competitive.

There are two types of imperfectly competitive markets. As we saw in Chapter 16, monopolistic competition describes a market structure in which there are many firms selling products that are similar but not identical. An **oligopoly** is a market with only a few sellers, each offering a product similar or identical to the others. One example is the market for chocolate bars. Another is the world market for crude oil: a few countries in the Middle East control much of the world's oil reserves.

oligopoly
competition amongst the few – a market structure in which only a few sellers offer similar or identical products and dominate the market

Figure 17.1 summarizes the four types of market structure. The first question to ask about any market is how many firms there are. If there is only one firm, the market is a monopoly. If there are only a few firms, the market is an oligopoly. If there are many firms, we need to ask another question: do the firms sell identical or differentiated products? If the many firms sell differentiated products, the market is monopolistically competitive. If the many firms sell identical products, the market is perfectly competitive.

Reality, of course, is never as clear-cut as theory. In some cases you may find it hard to decide what structure best describes a market. There is, for instance, no magic number that separates 'few' from 'many' when counting the number of firms. (Do the approximately dozen companies that now sell cars in Europe make this market an oligopoly or more competitive? The answer is open to debate.) Similarly, there is no sure way to determine when products are differentiated and when they are identical. (Are different brands of milk really the same? Again, the answer is debatable.) When analysing actual markets, economists have to keep in mind the lessons learned from studying all types of market structure and then apply each lesson as it seems appropriate.

FIGURE 17.1

The Four Types of Market Structure

Economists who study industrial organization divide markets into four types – monopoly, oligopoly, monopolistic competition and perfect competition.

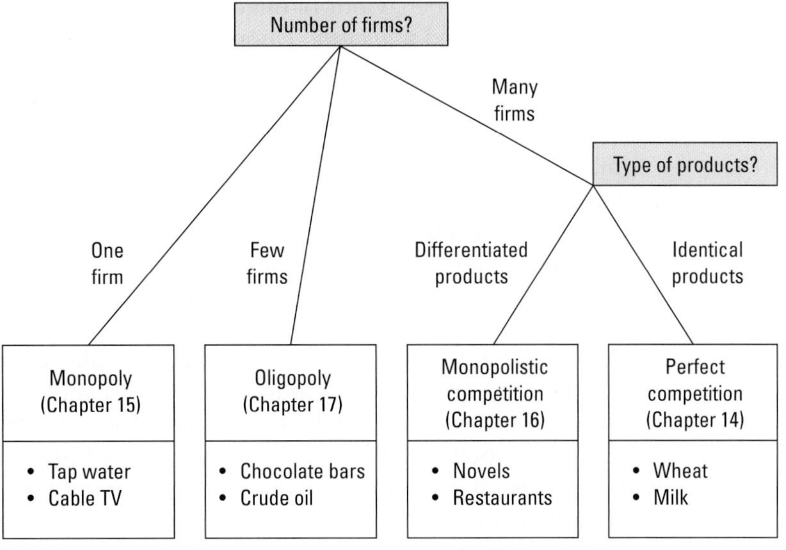

Quick Quiz Define oligopoly and monopolistic competition and give an example of each.

MARKETS WITH ONLY A FEW SELLERS

If a market is dominated by a relatively small number of sellers it is said to be *concentrated*. The *concentration ratio* refers to the proportion of the total market share accounted for by the top *x* number of firms in the industry. For example, a five-firm concentration ratio of 80 per cent means that five firms account for 80 per cent of market share; a three-firm concentration ratio of 72 per cent would indicate that three firms account for 72 per cent of total market sales and so on. There are a number of examples of oligopolistic market structures including brewing, banking, mobile phone networks, the chemical and oil industries, the grocery/supermarket industry, detergents, and entertainment. Note that in each of these industries there might be many sellers in the industry (there are thousands of small independent breweries across Europe, for example) but sales are dominated by a relatively small number of firms. In brewing, the industry is dominated by A-BInBev, Heineken, Carlsberg and SABMiller.

A key feature of oligopoly is the tension that exists between the firms of cooperation and self-interest. The group of oligopolists is best off cooperating and acting like a monopolist – producing a small quantity of output and charging a price above marginal cost. Yet because each oligopolist cares about only its own profit, there are powerful incentives at work that hinder a group of firms from maintaining the monopoly outcome.

A Duopoly Example

To understand the behaviour of oligopolies, let's consider an oligopoly with only two members, called a *duopoly*. Duopoly is the simplest type of oligopoly. Oligopolies with three or more members face the same problems as oligopolies with only two members, so we do not lose much by starting with the case of duopoly.

Imagine a town in which only two residents – Jack and Jill – own wells that produce water safe for drinking. Each Saturday, Jack and Jill decide how many litres of water to pump, bring the water to town, and sell it for whatever price the market will bear. To keep things simple, suppose that Jack and Jill can pump as much water as they want without cost. That is, the marginal cost of water equals zero.

Table 17.1 shows the town's demand schedule for water. The first column shows the total quantity demanded, and the second column shows the price. If the two well owners sell a total of 10 litres of water, water goes for €110 a litre. If they sell a total of 20 litres, the price falls to €100 a litre. And so on. If you graphed these two columns of numbers, you would get a standard downward sloping demand curve.

The last column in Table 17.1 shows the total revenue from the sale of water. It equals the quantity sold times the price. Because there is no cost to pumping water, the total revenue of the two producers equals their total profit.

Let's now consider how the organization of the town's water industry affects the price of water and the quantity of water sold.

Competition, Monopolies and Cartels

Before considering the price and quantity of water that would result from the duopoly of Jack and Jill, let's discuss briefly the two market structures we already understand: competition and monopoly.

TABLE 17.1

The Demand Schedule for Water

Quantity (in litres)	Price	Total revenue (and total profit)
0	€120	€ 0
10	110	1 100
20	100	2 000
30	90	2 700
40	80	3 200
50	70	3 500
60	60	3 600
70	50	3 500
80	40	3 200
90	30	2 700
100	20	2 000
110	10	1 100
120	0	0

Consider first what would happen if the market for water were perfectly competitive. In a competitive market, the production decisions of each firm drive price equal to marginal cost. In the market for water, marginal cost is zero. Thus, under competition, the equilibrium price of water would be zero, and the equilibrium quantity would be 120 litres. The price of water would reflect the cost of producing it, and the efficient quantity of water would be produced and consumed.

Now consider how a monopoly would behave. Table 17.1 shows that total profit is maximized at a quantity of 60 litres and a price of €60 a litre. A profit-maximizing monopolist, therefore, would produce this quantity and charge this price. As is standard for monopolies, price would exceed marginal cost. The result would be inefficient, for the quantity of water produced and consumed would fall short of the socially efficient level of 120 litres.

What outcome should we expect from our duopolists? One possibility is that Jack and Jill get together and agree on the quantity of water to produce and the price to charge for it. Such an agreement among firms over production and price is called **collusion**, and the group of firms acting in unison is called a **cartel**. Once a cartel is formed, the market is in effect served by a monopoly, and we can apply our analysis from Chapter 15. That is, if Jack and Jill were to collude, they would agree on the monopoly outcome because that outcome maximizes the total profit that the producers can get from the market. Our two producers would produce a total of 60 litres, which would be sold at a price of €60 a litre. Once again, price exceeds marginal cost, and the outcome is socially inefficient.

collusion
an agreement among firms in a market about quantities to produce or prices to charge

cartel
a group of firms acting in unison

A cartel must agree not only on the total level of production but also on the amount produced by each member. In our case, Jack and Jill must agree how to split between themselves the monopoly production of 60 litres. Each member of the cartel will want a larger share of the market because a larger market share means larger profit. If Jack and Jill agreed to split the market equally, each would produce 30 litres, the price would be €60 a litre and each would get a profit of €1 800.

The Equilibrium for an Oligopoly

Although oligopolists would like to form cartels and earn monopoly profits, often that is not possible. As we discuss later in this chapter, competition laws prohibit explicit agreements among oligopolists as a matter of public policy. In addition, squabbling among cartel members over how to divide the profit in the market sometimes makes agreement among them impossible. Let's therefore consider what happens if Jack and Jill decide separately how much water to produce.

At first, one might expect Jack and Jill to reach the monopoly outcome on their own, for this outcome maximizes their joint profit. In the absence of a binding agreement, however, the monopoly outcome is unlikely. To see why, imagine that Jack expects Jill to produce only 30 litres (half of the monopoly quantity). Jack would reason as follows:

> I could produce 30 litres as well. In this case, a total of 60 litres of water would be sold at a price of €60 a litre. My profit would be €1 800 (30 litres × €60 a litre). Alternatively, I could produce 40 litres. In this case, a total of 70 litres of water would be sold at a price of €50 a litre. My profit would be €2 000 (40 litres × €50 a litre). Even though total profit in the market would fall, my profit would be higher, because I would have a larger share of the market.

Of course, Jill might reason the same way. If so, Jack and Jill would each bring 40 litres to town. Total sales would be 80 litres, and the price would fall to €40.

Thus, if the duopolists individually pursue their own self-interest when deciding how much to produce, they produce a total quantity greater than the monopoly quantity, charge a price lower than the monopoly price and earn total profit less than the monopoly profit.

Although the logic of self-interest increases the duopoly's output above the monopoly level, it does not push the duopolists to reach the competitive allocation. Consider what happens when each duopolist is producing 40 litres. The price is €40, and each duopolist makes a profit of €1 600. In this case, Jack's self-interested logic leads to a different conclusion:

> Right now my profit is €1 600. Suppose I increase my production to 50 litres. In this case, a total of 90 litres of water would be sold, and the price would be €30 a litre. Then my profit would be only €1 500. Rather than increasing production and driving down the price, I am better off keeping my production at 40 litres.

Nash equilibrium
a situation in which economic actors interacting with one another each choose their best strategy given the strategies that all the other actors have chosen

The outcome in which Jack and Jill each produce 40 litres looks like some sort of equilibrium. In fact, this outcome is called a **Nash equilibrium** (named after economic theorist John Nash, whose life was portrayed in the book, *A Beautiful Mind,* and the film of the same name). A Nash equilibrium is a situation in which economic actors interacting with one another each choose their best strategy given the strategies the others have chosen. In this case, given that Jill is producing 40 litres, the best strategy for Jack is to produce 40 litres. Similarly, given that Jack is producing 40 litres, the best strategy for Jill is to produce 40 litres. Once they reach this Nash equilibrium, neither Jack nor Jill has an incentive to make a different decision.

This example illustrates the tension between cooperation and self-interest. Oligopolists would be better off cooperating and reaching the monopoly outcome. Yet because they pursue their own self-interest, they do not end up reaching the monopoly outcome and maximizing their joint profit. Each oligopolist is tempted to raise production and capture a larger share of the market. As each of them tries to do this, total production rises, and the price falls.

At the same time, self-interest does not drive the market all the way to the competitive outcome. Like monopolists, oligopolists are aware that increases in the amount they produce reduce the price of their product. Therefore, they stop short of following the competitive firm's rule of producing up to the point where price equals marginal cost.

In summary, when firms in an oligopoly individually choose production to maximize profit, they produce a quantity of output greater than the level produced by monopoly and less than the level produced by competition. The oligopoly price is less than the monopoly price but greater than the competitive price (which equals marginal cost).

How the Size of an Oligopoly Affects the Market Outcome

We can use the insights from this analysis of duopoly to discuss how the size of an oligopoly is likely to affect the outcome in a market. Suppose, for instance, that Darby and Joan suddenly discover water sources on their property and join Jack and Jill in the water oligopoly. The demand schedule in Table 17.1 remains the same, but now more producers are available to satisfy this demand. How would an increase in the number of sellers from two to four affect the price and quantity of water in the town?

If the sellers of water could form a cartel, they would once again try to maximize total profit by producing the monopoly quantity and charging the monopoly

FYI

John Nash – A Beautiful Mind

The story of John Nash was dramatized in the film 'A Beautiful Mind' based on a book of the same name by Sylvia Nasar. Nash entered the world of game theory in the late 1940s and 1950s and gained the Nobel Prize for Economics in 1994 for his contribution to the field. (The scene in the film where Nash 'hits' upon his idea based on him and his friends choosing a girl to date is dramatic licence but an interesting way of presenting the theory all the same!) His work has had an impact on all manner of economic and political situations. It is important to remember that Nash was not an economist – he was a mathematician. In fact, Nash only took one course of economics during his undergraduate studies – a course in International Trade – and that was only to fulfil the degree requirements of the course he was on. Nash's ideas, therefore, are purely in the realm of the application of mathematical ideas to a bargaining problem. The application to economics and other areas has been somewhat broader.

At the heart of Nash's ideas were the mix of both cooperative and non-cooperative games. In the former, there are enforceable agreements between players whilst in the latter there are not. The key thing in both cases is that the players in the game know that they cannot predict with any certainty what the other is going to do (exactly the situation facing firms in an oligopolistic market). Equally, they know what *they* want but are aware that all the other players think as they do. It has been referred to as the 'I think he thinks that I think that he thinks that I think…' scenario.

The solutions that Nash derived were based around this thinking, where each player had to try to put him or herself in the position of others. The 'equilibrium' position would be where each player makes a decision which represents the best outcome in response to what other players' decisions are. The definition of a Nash equilibrium is a point where no player can improve their position by selecting any other available strategy whilst others are also playing their best option and not changing their strategies. One of the implications of Nash's work is that cooperation may well be the best option in the long term.

Let us take an example.

Assume there are two firms competing with each other for profits in a market. The two firms have three decisions to make with regard to their pricing strategies. They can choose to set their price at either €10, €20 or €30. The matrix showing the profits made at these different prices is shown in Table 17.2 below.

TABLE 17.2

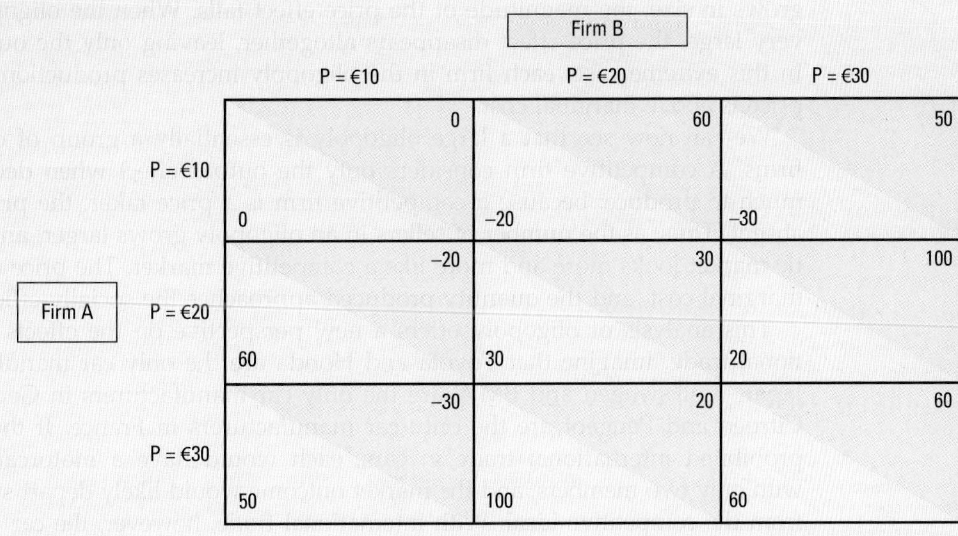

		Firm B		
		P = €10	P = €20	P = €30
Firm A	P = €10	0 0	60 −20	50 −30
	P = €20	−20 60	30 30	100 20
	P = €30	−30 50	20 100	60 60

If we look at the situation when each firm decides to set their price at €30, they both make a profit of €60. This, however, is not a Nash equilibrium, since Firm A could improve its position by reducing its price by €10 to €20, whilst B's strategy remains the same (setting price at €30). In this case, A would now gain a profit of €100 rather than €60.

Let's compare this to the situation where both firms set their price at €10. In this case, if Firm A decided to raise their price to €20, they would be worse off if B continued the strategy of charging €10. In such an instance, A would make a loss of 20. The same position applies to firm B. There is no incentive, therefore, for either firm to change their position; the pay-off of zero profit at a price of €10 represents a Nash equilibrium. Any other pricing decision by either firm would lead to one having an incentive to change its price to gain some advantage.

The work of people like John Nash has opened up new insights into human behaviour and the way in which they interact, make decisions and engage in economic bargaining and activity.

price. Just as when there were only two sellers, the members of the cartel would need to agree on production levels for each member and find some way to enforce the agreement. As the cartel grows larger, however, this outcome is less likely. Reaching and enforcing an agreement becomes more difficult as the size of the group increases.

If the oligopolists do not form a cartel – perhaps because competition laws prohibit it – they must each decide on their own how much water to produce. To see how the increase in the number of sellers affects the outcome, consider the decision facing each seller. At any time, each well owner has the option to raise production by 1 litre. In making this decision, the well owner weighs two effects:

- *The output effect*. Because price is above marginal cost, selling one more litre of water at the going price will raise profit.
- *The price effect*. Raising production will increase the total amount sold, which will lower the price of water and lower the profit on all the other litres sold.

If the output effect is larger than the price effect, the well owner will increase production. If the price effect is larger than the output effect, the owner will not raise production. (In fact, in this case, it is profitable to reduce production.) Each oligopolist continues to increase production until these two marginal effects exactly balance, taking the other firms' production as given.

Now consider how the number of firms in the industry affects the marginal analysis of each oligopolist. The larger the number of sellers, the less concerned each seller is about its own impact on the market price. That is, as the oligopoly grows in size, the magnitude of the price effect falls. When the oligopoly grows very large, the price effect disappears altogether, leaving only the output effect. In this extreme case, each firm in the oligopoly increases production as long as price is above marginal cost.

We can now see that a large oligopoly is essentially a group of competitive firms. A competitive firm considers only the output effect when deciding how much to produce: because a competitive firm is a price taker, the price effect is absent. Thus, as the number of sellers in an oligopoly grows larger, an oligopolistic market looks more and more like a competitive market. The price approaches marginal cost, and the quantity produced approaches the socially efficient level.

This analysis of oligopoly offers a new perspective on the effects of international trade. Imagine that Toyota and Honda are the only car manufacturers in Japan, Volkswagen and BMW are the only car manufacturers in Germany, and Citroën and Peugeot are the only car manufacturers in France. If these nations prohibited international trade in cars, each would have a motorcar oligopoly with only two members, and the market outcome would likely depart substantially from the competitive ideal. With international trade, however, the car market is a

IN THE NEWS

Cement Cartels in South Africa

Firms in oligopolistic markets may recognize that finding a way of colluding with rivals will improve their own position. Sometimes price movements may look suspicious but there may be a perfectly reasonable explanation; in other cases, the movements may be exactly what they seem to be – price-fixing by firms.

There have been concerns about competition in the cement industry in Europe for some time but it seems that it is not only Europe that may have problems in this respect. In June 2009, the South African Competition Commission launched raids on the headquarters of a number of cement producers including Pretoria Portland Cement (PPC) Africa's biggest cement producer, Lafarge Industries South Africa, AfriSam Consortium and Natal Portland Cement. The raids were in relation to suspicions of price fixing in the industry.

The Commission noted that despite changes in input prices and the level of demand, the price of cement from producers in South Africa rose broadly in line every six months. The rise in price, in each case, was far above levels implied by the producer price index (PPI), an indicator of the overall input costs in the South African economy. These price rises for cement have averaged at 6 per cent each time making the annual increases around 12 per cent. It is believed that the allegations, if true, had significantly added to infrastructure costs in South Africa. Such projects were particularly sensitive given the investment in infrastructure in preparation for the World Cup finals, which South Africa hosted in 2010.

The investigations were linked to those being conducted in the European Union (EU) and Brazil and centre on price-fixing, the control or limitation of cement extenders (chemicals or other materials added to slurry to increase the yield) and the abuse of its dominant position in the market by PPC. As a result of the raids and the subsequent investigations, PPC admitted that it had taken part in a cartel of cement companies with the aim of fixing prices. In return for this admission and subsequent help with the Commission's investigation, PPC received some leniency in its treatment.

The investigation, along with costs related to a black empowerment deal, meant that PPC had to post a fall in profits for the financial year of 40 per cent. The empowerment deal is part of the South African government's drive to set quotas for businesses to increase the involvement of blacks in ownership, procurement and employment to better reflect the fact that the majority of the population in the country are black.

world market, and the oligopoly in this example has six members. Allowing free trade increases the number of producers from which each consumer can choose, and this increased competition keeps prices closer to marginal cost. Thus, the theory of oligopoly provides another reason, in addition to the theory of comparative advantage discussed in Chapter 3, why all countries can benefit from free trade.

Quick Quiz If the members of an oligopoly could agree on a total quantity to produce, what quantity would they choose? • If the oligopolists do not act together but instead make production decisions individually, do they produce a total quantity more or less than in your answer to the previous question? Why?

GAME THEORY AND THE ECONOMICS OF COOPERATION

As we have seen, oligopolies would like to reach the monopoly outcome, but doing so requires cooperation, which at times is difficult to maintain. In this section we look more closely at the problems people face when cooperation is desirable but difficult. To analyse the economics of cooperation, we need to learn a little about game theory.

game theory
the study of how people behave in strategic situations

Game theory is the study of how people behave in strategic situations. By 'strategic' we mean a situation in which each person, when deciding what actions to take, must consider how others might respond to that action. Because the number of firms in an oligopolistic market is small, each firm must act strategically. Each firm knows that its profit depends not only on how much it produces but also on how much the other firms produce. In making its production decision, each firm in an oligopoly should consider how its decision might affect the production decisions of all the other firms.

Game theory is not necessary for understanding competitive or monopoly markets. In a competitive market, each firm is so small compared to the market that strategic interactions with other firms are not important. In a monopolized market, strategic interactions are absent because the market has only one firm. But, as we will see, game theory is quite useful for understanding the behaviour of oligopolies.

prisoners' dilemma
a particular 'game' between two captured prisoners that illustrates why cooperation is difficult to maintain even when it is mutually beneficial

A particularly important 'game' is called the **prisoners' dilemma**. This game provides insight into the difficulty of maintaining cooperation. Many times in life, people fail to cooperate with one another even when cooperation would make them all better off. An oligopoly is just one example. The story of the prisoners' dilemma contains a general lesson that applies to any group trying to maintain cooperation among its members.

The Prisoners' Dilemma

The prisoners' dilemma is a story about two criminals who have been captured by the police. Let's call them Mr Green and Mr Blue. The police have enough evidence to convict Mr Green and Mr Blue of a relatively minor crime, illegal possession of a handgun, so that each would spend a year in jail. The police also suspect that the two criminals have committed a jewellery robbery together, but they lack hard evidence to convict them of this major crime. The police question Mr Green and Mr Blue in separate rooms, and they offer each of them the following deal:

> Right now we can lock you up for 1 year. If you confess to the jewellery robbery and implicate your partner, however, we'll give you immunity and you can go free. Your partner will get 20 years in jail. But if you both confess to the crime, we won't need your testimony and we can avoid the cost of a trial, so you will each get an intermediate sentence of 8 years.

If Mr Green and Mr Blue, heartless criminals that they are, care only about their own sentences, what would you expect them to do? Would they confess or remain silent? Figure 17.2 shows their choices. Each prisoner has two strategies: confess or remain silent. The sentence each prisoner gets depends on the strategy he or she chooses and the strategy chosen by his or her partner in crime.

Consider first Mr Green's decision. He reasons as follows:

> I don't know what Mr Blue is going to do. If he remains silent, my best strategy is to confess, since then I'll go free rather than spending a year in

FIGURE 17.2

The Prisoners' Dilemma

In this game between two criminals suspected of committing a crime, the sentence that each receives depends both on his decision whether to confess or remain silent and on the decision made by the other.

Mr Blue's decision		Mr Green's decision: Confess	Mr Green's decision: Remain silent
	Confess	Mr Green gets 8 years / Mr Blue gets 8 years	Mr Green gets 20 years / Mr Blue goes free
	Remain silent	Mr Green goes free / Mr Blue gets 20 years	Mr Green gets 1 year / Mr Blue gets 1 year

jail. If he confesses, my best strategy is still to confess, since then I'll spend 8 years in jail rather than 20. So, regardless of what Mr Blue does, I am better off confessing.

In the language of game theory, a strategy is called a **dominant strategy** if it is the best strategy for a player to follow regardless of the strategies pursued by other players. In this case, confessing is a dominant strategy for Mr Green. He spends less time in jail if he confesses, regardless of whether Mr Blue confesses or remains silent.

dominant strategy
a strategy that is best for a player in a game regardless of the strategies chosen by the other players

Now consider Mr Blue's decision. He faces exactly the same choices as Mr Green, and he reasons in much the same way. Regardless of what Mr Green does, Mr Blue can reduce his time in jail by confessing. In other words, confessing is also a dominant strategy for Mr Blue.

In the end, both Mr Green and Mr Blue confess, and both spend 8 years in jail. Yet, from their standpoint, this is a terrible outcome. If they had *both* remained silent, both of them would have been better off, spending only 1 year in jail on the gun charge. By each pursuing his own interests, the two prisoners together reach an outcome that is worse for each of them.

To see how difficult it is to maintain cooperation, imagine that, before the police captured Mr Green and Mr Blue, the two criminals had made a pact not to confess. Clearly, this agreement would make them both better off *if* they both live up to it, because they would each spend only 1 year in jail. But would the two criminals in fact remain silent, simply because they had agreed to? Once they are being questioned separately, the logic of self-interest takes over and leads them to confess. Cooperation between the two prisoners is difficult to maintain, because cooperation is individually irrational.

Oligopolies as a Prisoner's Dilemma

What does the prisoners' dilemma have to do with markets and imperfect competition? It turns out that the game oligopolists play in trying to reach the

FIGURE 17.3

An Oligopoly Game

In this game between members of an oligopoly, the profit that each earns depends on both its production decision and the production decision of the other oligopolist.

Iran's decision \ Saudi Arabia's decision	High production	Low production
High production	Saudi Arabia gets $40 billion Iran gets $40 billion	Saudi Arabia gets $30 billion Iran gets $60 billion
Low production	Saudi Arabia gets $60 billion Iran gets $30 billion	Saudi Arabia gets $50 billion Iran gets $50 billion

monopoly outcome is similar to the game that the two prisoners play in the prisoners' dilemma.

Consider an oligopoly with two countries, Iran and Saudi Arabia. Both countries sell crude oil. After prolonged negotiation, the countries agree to keep oil production low in order to keep the world price of oil high. After they agree on production levels, each country must decide whether to cooperate and live up to this agreement or to ignore it and produce at a higher level. Figure 17.3 shows how the profits of the two countries depend on the strategies they choose.

Suppose you are the leader of Saudi Arabia. You might reason as follows:

> I could keep production low as we agreed, or I could raise my production and sell more oil on world markets. If Iran lives up to the agreement and keeps its production low, then my country earns profit of $60 billion with high production and $50 billion with low production. In this case, Saudi Arabia is better off with high production. If Iran fails to live up to the agreement and produces at a high level, then my country earns $40 billion with high production and $30 billion with low production. Once again, Saudi Arabia is better off with high production. So, regardless of what Iran chooses to do, my country is better off reneging on our agreement and producing at a high level.

Producing at a high level is a dominant strategy for Saudi Arabia. Of course, Iran reasons in exactly the same way, and so both countries produce at a high level. The result is the inferior outcome (from Iran and Saudi Arabia's standpoint) with low profits for each country.

This example illustrates why oligopolies have trouble maintaining monopoly profits. The monopoly outcome is jointly rational for the oligopoly, but each oligopolist has an incentive to cheat. Just as self-interest drives the prisoners in the prisoners' dilemma to confess, self-interest makes it difficult for the oligopoly to maintain the cooperative outcome with low production, high prices and monopoly profits.

IN THE NEWS

Building in Prices?

Throughout the world, competition authorities are increasingly looking at pricing in markets and uncovering examples of price-fixing. Of course, firms engaging in such activity know that it is illegal and so go to great lengths to try and conceal the collusion. This article looks at an example of price-fixing in the construction industry in the UK and how new techniques are being increasingly deployed to uncover secrets that firms may be trying to hide.

For some years the activities of firms in the construction industry have been under some scrutiny but between 2007 and 2009, competition authorities in the UK looked in more detail at allegations of collusion contrary to competition law. In September 2009, competition authorities handed out hefty fines to a number of construction companies who were charged with breaching competition laws. The fines totalled £129.5 million and the companies concerned included Carillion, the Kier Group and Balfour Beatty. The accusations surround a practice known as 'cover pricing' and related to construction projects on a range of public sector works including a school in Derby and a hospital in Nottingham, both in the Midlands. The OFT looked at contracts over a period from 2000 to 2006 worth £200 million in total. The allegations focused on firms operating in general building work, house construction and commercial and industrial construction both in the public and the private sector.

The investigations centred on the way in which firms bid for and acquired contracts. The authorities were particularly interested in the tendering and bidding process for construction projects for cases of bid rigging cartel activity. This includes cases where a group of firms bid for a construction contract. The bids are supposed to be secret and this is meant to provide the element of competition in the industry. However, there are suggestions that firms were agreeing to carve up the market between themselves. As a result of this they might disclose their intentions to each other so that 'rival' firms would put in bids far higher than the firm who was slated to win the contract. In some cases it is claimed that, because the tender process can be expensive, the 'winning' firm would add on a sum to its bid and use that extra sum is to compensate the 'losers'.

The competition authorities used the latest forensic techniques in their investigation which involved using digital evidence gathering by dissecting files on computers to access information. Firms may have believed that they were able to hide this evidence but these techniques were able to bring to light information that users may have thought was not there. The authorities in the UK also interviewed a number of individuals from the firms concerned. The investigation revealed evidence of bid rigging in thousands of tenders. The total value of these tenders was reported to be around £3 billion.

Many public sector construction projects require companies to be part of an approved list of those allowed to tender. If companies do not tender then they can risk losing their place on this list. In cases where a company may not want the work, possibly because of capacity limitations, tenders may be put in which are way above the budget guidelines in the knowledge that the company concerned will not win the tender but still show that they are 'interested'. For example, a construction project for a new school might have a guide budget of £15 million. Three companies might put in bids but only one is a serious contender. The other two agree to put in bids which are way above the budget limit: for example, one might put in a tender of £20 million and the other of £22 million. The third puts in a tender of £18 million and wins the contract. Such collusion is against competition law.

The authorities also found that not only had collusion occurred but firms had even raised false invoices to distribute some of the surplus tender to other bidders. In the example above, the winning bidder might raise invoices totalling £500 000 each for the other two who did not win. The outcome is an effective sharing out of contracts amongst companies. The competition authorities said that this historic practice had potentially cost the taxpayer millions of pounds. The reason is that winning bids have been higher than would otherwise be the case under true competitive tendering.

Part of the problem is with the system of the way in which such tenders are operated. The assumption is that each firm operates in isolation and that each firm wants to win the tender it has bid for. Based on these twin assumptions, a firm will always try and submit a bid which is the lowest possible for the job in the hope that it will win and thus the taxpayer gets value for money from the process. Where the flaw in the process occurs is the assumption (and, companies might argue the necessity of bidding to stay on the approved tender list) that every bid is a serious one. The outcome is something that game theorists would not be slow to predict.

Source: Adapted from Biz/ed 'In the News'.

Other Examples of the Prisoners' Dilemma

We have seen how the prisoners' dilemma can be used to understand the problem facing oligopolies. The same logic applies to many other situations as well. Here we consider three examples in which self-interest prevents cooperation and leads to an inferior outcome for the parties involved.

Arms Races An arms race is much like the prisoners' dilemma. To see this, consider the decisions of two countries – Iran and Israel – about whether to build new weapons or to disarm. Each country prefers to have more arms than the other because a larger arsenal would give it more influence in world affairs. But each country also prefers to live in a world safe from the other country's weapons.

Figure 17.4 shows the deadly game. If Israel chooses to arm, Iran is better off doing the same to prevent the loss of power. If Israel chooses to disarm, Iran is better off arming because doing so would make it more powerful. For each country, arming is a dominant strategy. Thus, each country chooses to continue the arms race, resulting in the inferior outcome in which both countries are at risk.

Advertising When two firms advertise to attract the same customers, they face a problem similar to the prisoners' dilemma. For example, consider

FIGURE 17.4

An Arms Race Game

In this game between two countries, the safety and power of each country depends on both its decision whether to arm and the decision made by the other country.

Decision of Israel	Decision of Iran: Arm	Decision of Iran: Disarm
Arm	Iran at risk Israel at risk	Iran at risk and weak Israel safe and powerful
Disarm	Iran safe and powerful Israel at risk and weak	Iran safe Israel safe

FYI

Robert J. Aumann and Thomas C. Schelling – Game Theorists who Won the Nobel Prize for Economics

The 2005 Nobel Prize for Economics was awarded to Aumann and Schelling for their work in game theory. Robert J. Aumann was born in Germany in 1930 and has a background in mathematics. His work has been in the field of game theory and specifically the effect of how cooperation can be of benefit as a result of the research he carried out into repeated games. Thomas C. Schelling was born in 1921. His contribution to game theory was set against the backdrop of the Cold War, the tensions between the West and the East and the nuclear arms race. His research on strategies has helped build understanding of conflict and conflict resolution in spheres as diverse as nuclear war and market structure.

Schelling identified two aspects of game theory – non-cooperative game theory and cooperative game theory. Cooperative game theory assumes that there are a set of outcomes or agreements that is known to each player and that each player has preferences over these outcomes. Non-cooperative game theory assumes players have a series of strategies they could use to gain an outcome and that each player has a preference over their desired outcome. The behaviour of firms or individuals might be affected by bargaining which entails some form of conflict of interest but in essence each player will be looking to maximize their returns, whilst knowing at the same time that some agreement is preferable to no agreement at all. In this scenario, how does a player manage to influence the negotiations in order to move towards his or her preferred outcome without upsetting the other players and thus failing to secure any agreement – an outcome which would be disadvantageous to all concerned, including the player?

Schelling proposed that it might be in the interests of the player to worsen his or her own options in order to gain some sort of concession from another player. Where difficulties arise is if both parties to a conflict make commitments that are seen as being irreversible and incompatible. The result could be stalemate and potential serious conflict. The dispute with Iran over its nuclear programme might be looked at in this light.

In most 'game' situations, the protagonists know something about the position of the other – but not everything. However, if there is any perceived chink in the armour of the other player and this is detected by the other, then there is a potential benefit to follow the hard route. This is why this sort of game is referred to as 'chicken' or 'hawk/dove'. Schelling further included other complications to the analysis by looking at how the strategies of each player would change in light of threats and action. Schelling noted that parties will need to recognize that the costs to them of cheating and gaining some short-term benefit (which may be much greater) is far outweighed by the costs to them in the longer term of the destruction of the trust that results from cheating. The relationships between players will need to be assessed in the context of repeated playing of the game over a period of time.

Aumann's most noted contribution is in the field of long-term cooperation around game theory. We have already seen how, in the prisoners' dilemma, the dominant strategy for Mr Green and Mr Blue was to confess. Aumann asked the question about what the equilibrium outcome would be if the game were repeated over and over again, with each prisoner trying to maximize the *average* payoff from each game.

In such a situation, Aumann showed that the equilibrium outcome was to cooperate because any cheating on the agreement in the short term would be punishable by a refusal to cooperate at some point in the future – and both players would know this. Any short-term gains, therefore, are outweighed by longer-term losses. Aumann expressed this through what he referred to as a 'supergame' – that is, looking at the collection of repeated games as a whole game in itself. Aumann's work was extended to look at how groups of players might react in such situations. In a cartel, for example, there is always the tendency or incentive for one firm to break the cartel to seek to gain some advantage in the market. Aumann's work suggested that long-term cooperation could be 'enforced' by the many, against the few who might be seeking to defect.

The work was extended in subsequent research to try to take into account the strategies players might adopt in repeated games with incomplete information. This provides an incentive to players to hide, or seek to conceal, information from their rivals. Firms are very keen to keep their costs to themselves! If one player does manage to access information about their rivals and has some form of strategic advantage therefore, what is the best way to utilize this knowledge? If this situation arose, would playing your hand to gain short-term benefit reveal that you did actually know more than you were letting on? For the player who does not have the information they would like, could they discover anything about the player's position by reviewing the strategies and decisions made by that player in the past? Such scenarios are relevant to the world of financial markets where the issue of insider trading is always something that the authorities are keen to stamp out. The number of people with access to privileged information about market moves, business plans and strategies does mean that there is potential for many decisions that could have long-term implications for the markets and the businesses involved.

Aumann and Schelling's work has a great many applications in everyday life. Trade wars, price wars, negotiations over budgets, wage negotiations, discussions about environmental issues, merger discussions, social policy, monetary policy, fiscal policy, the work of the Competition Commission, EU fisheries debates and oligopolies are just some of the major areas where their work can be applied.

© PAWEL KOPCZYNSKI / REUTERS / CORBIS

Robert J. Aumann (second from right) applauds Thomas C. Schelling as he accepts his Nobel Prize for Economics.

the decisions facing two cigarette companies, Marlboro and Camel. If neither company advertises, the two companies split the market. If both advertise, they again split the market, but profits are lower, since each company must bear the cost of advertising. Yet if one company advertises while the other does not, the one that advertises attracts customers from the other.

Figure 17.5 shows how the profits of the two companies depend on their actions. You can see that advertising is a dominant strategy for each firm. Thus, both firms choose to advertise, even though both firms would be better off if neither firm advertised.

A test of this theory of advertising occurred in many countries during the 1970s and 1980s, when laws were passed in Europe and North America banning cigarette advertisements on television. To the surprise of many observers, cigarette companies did not use their considerable political clout to oppose these bans. When the laws went into effect, cigarette advertising fell and the profits of cigarette companies rose. The television advertising bans did for the cigarette companies what they could not do on their own: they solved the prisoners' dilemma by enforcing the cooperative outcome with low advertising and high profit.

Common Resources In Chapter 11 we saw that people tend to overuse common resources. One can view this problem as an example of the prisoners' dilemma.

Imagine that two oil companies – Shell and BP – own adjacent oil fields. Under the fields is a common pool of oil worth €12 million. Drilling a well to

FIGURE 17.5

An Advertising Game

In this game between firms selling similar products, the profit that each earns depends on both its own advertising decision and the advertising decision of the other firm.

		Marlboro's decision	
		Advertise	Don't advertise
Camel's decision	Advertise	Marlboro gets $3 billion profit Camel gets $3 billion profit	Marlboro gets $2 billion profit Camel gets $5 billion profit
	Don't advertise	Marlboro gets $5 billion profit Camel gets $2 billion profit	Marlboro gets $4 billion profit Camel gets $4 billion profit

recover the oil costs €1 million. If each company drills one well, each will get half of the oil and earn a €5 million profit (€6 million in revenue minus €1 million in costs).

Because the pool of oil is a common resource, the companies will not use it efficiently. Suppose that either company could drill a second well. If one company has two of the three wells, that company gets two-thirds of the oil, which yields a profit of €6 million. The other company gets one-third of the oil, for a profit of €3 million. Yet if each company drills a second well, the two companies again split the oil. In this case, each bears the cost of a second well, so profit is only €4 million for each company.

Figure 17.6 shows the game. Drilling two wells is a dominant strategy for each company. Once again, the self-interest of the two players leads them to an inferior outcome.

The Prisoners' Dilemma and the Welfare of Society

The prisoners' dilemma describes many of life's situations, and it shows that cooperation can be difficult to maintain, even when cooperation would make both players in the game better off. Clearly, this lack of cooperation is a problem for those involved in these situations. But is lack of cooperation a problem from the standpoint of society as a whole? The answer depends on the circumstances.

In some cases, the non-cooperative equilibrium is bad for society as well as the players. In the arms race game in Figure 17.4, both Iran and Israel end up at risk. In the common resources game in Figure 17.6, the extra wells dug by Shell and BP are pure waste. In both cases, society would be better off if the two players could reach the cooperative outcome.

By contrast, in the case of oligopolists trying to maintain monopoly profits, lack of cooperation is desirable from the standpoint of society as a whole. The monopoly outcome is good for the oligopolists, but it is bad for the consumers of the product. As we first saw in Chapter 7, the competitive outcome is best for society because it maximizes total surplus. When oligopolists fail to cooperate, the quantity they produce is closer to this optimal level. Put differently, the

FIGURE 17.6

A Common Resources Game

In this game between firms pumping oil from a common pool, the profit that each earns depends on both the number of wells it drills and the number of wells drilled by the other firm.

BP's decision \ Shell's decision	Drill two wells	Drill one well
Drill two wells	Shell gets €4 million profit; BP gets €4 million profit	Shell gets €3 million profit; BP gets €6 million profit
Drill one well	Shell gets €6 million profit; BP gets €3 million profit	Shell gets €5 million profit; BP gets €5 million profit

invisible hand guides markets to allocate resources efficiently only when markets are competitive, and markets are competitive only when firms in the market fail to cooperate with one another.

Similarly, consider the case of the police questioning two suspects. Lack of cooperation between the suspects is desirable, for it allows the police to convict more criminals. The prisoners' dilemma is a dilemma for the prisoners, but it can be a boon to everyone else.

Why People Sometimes Cooperate

The prisoners' dilemma shows that cooperation is difficult. But is it impossible? Not all prisoners, when questioned by the police, decide to turn in their partners in crime. Cartels sometimes do manage to maintain collusive arrangements, despite the incentive for individual members to defect. Very often, the reason that players can solve the prisoners' dilemma is that they play the game not once but many times.

To see why cooperation is easier to enforce in repeated games, let's return to our duopolists, Jack and Jill. Recall that Jack and Jill would like to maintain the monopoly outcome in which each produces 30 litres, but self-interest drives them to an equilibrium in which each produces 40 litres. Figure 17.7 shows the game they play. Producing 40 litres is a dominant strategy for each player in this game.

Imagine that Jack and Jill try to form a cartel. To maximize total profit they would agree to the cooperative outcome in which each produces 30 litres. Yet, if Jack and Jill are to play this game only once, neither has any incentive to live up to this agreement. Self-interest drives each of them to renege and produce 40 litres.

Now suppose that Jack and Jill know that they will play the same game every week. When they make their initial agreement to keep production low, they can also specify what happens if one party reneges. They might agree, for instance, that once one of them reneges and produces 40 litres, both of them will produce

FIGURE 17.7

Jack and Jill's Oligopoly Game

In this game between Jack and Jill, the profit that each earns from selling water depends on both the quantity he or she chooses to sell and the quantity the other chooses to sell.

Jill's decision \ Jack's decision	Sell 40 litres	Sell 30 litres
Sell 40 litres	Jack gets €1 600 profit; Jill gets €1 600 profit	Jack gets €1 500 profit; Jill gets €2 000 profit
Sell 30 litres	Jack gets €2 000 profit; Jill gets €1 500 profit	Jack gets €1 800 profit; Jill gets €1 800 profit

40 litres forever after. This penalty is easy to enforce, for if one party is producing at a high level, the other has every reason to do the same.

The threat of this penalty may be all that is needed to maintain cooperation. Each person knows that defecting would raise his or her profit from €1 800 to €2 000. But this benefit would last for only one week. Thereafter, profit would fall to €1 600 and stay there. As long as the players care enough about future profits, they will choose to forgo the one-time gain from defection. Thus, in a game of repeated prisoners' dilemma, the two players may well be able to reach the cooperative outcome.

Quick Quiz Tell the story of the prisoners' dilemma. Write down a table showing the prisoners' choices and explain what outcome is likely. • What does the prisoners' dilemma teach us about oligopolies?

PUBLIC POLICY TOWARD OLIGOPOLIES

One of the *Ten Principles of Economics* in Chapter 1 is that governments can sometimes improve market outcomes. The application of this principle to oligopolistic markets is, as a general matter, straightforward. As we have seen, cooperation among oligopolists is undesirable from the standpoint of society as a whole, because it leads to production that is too low and prices that are too high. To move the allocation of resources closer to the social optimum, policy makers should try to induce firms in an oligopoly to compete rather than cooperate. Let's consider how policy makers do this and then examine the controversies that arise in this area of public policy.

Restraint of Trade and Competition Law

One way that policy discourages cooperation is through the common law. Normally, freedom of contract is an essential part of a market economy. Businesses and households use contracts to arrange mutually advantageous trades. In doing this, they rely on the court system to enforce contracts. Yet, for many centuries, courts in Europe and North America have deemed agreements among competitors to reduce quantities and raise prices to be contrary to the public interest. They have therefore refused to enforce such agreements.

Given the long experience of many European countries in tackling abuses of market power, it is perhaps not surprising that competition law is one of the few areas in which the European Union has been able to agree on a common policy. The European Commission can refer directly to the Treaty of Rome to prohibit price-fixing and other restrictive practices such as production limitation, and is especially likely to do so where a restrictive practice affects trade between EU member countries. The EU Competition Commission sets out its role as follows:

> The antitrust area covers two prohibition rules set out in the Treaty on the Functioning of the European Union.
>
> - First, agreements between two or more firms which restrict competition are prohibited by Article 101 of the Treaty, subject to some limited exceptions. This provision covers a wide variety of behaviours. The most obvious example of illegal conduct infringing [the Article] is a cartel between competitors (which may involve price-fixing or market sharing).
> - Second, firms in a dominant position may not abuse that position (Article 102 of the Treaty). This is for example the case for predatory pricing aiming at eliminating competitors from the market.
>
> The Commission is empowered by the Treaty to apply these prohibition rules and enjoys a number of investigative powers to that end (e.g. inspection in business and non business premises, written requests for information, etc). It may also impose fines on undertakings who violate EU antitrust rules. Since 1 May 2004, all national competition authorities are also empowered to apply fully the provisions of the Treaty in order to ensure that competition is not distorted or restricted. National courts may also apply these prohibitions so as to protect the individual rights conferred to citizens by the Treaty.
>
> (Source: http://ec.europa.eu/competition/antitrust/overview_en.html)

Controversies over Competition Policy

Over time, much controversy has centred on the question of what kinds of behaviour competition law should prohibit. Most commentators agree that price-fixing agreements among competing firms should be illegal. Yet competition law has been used to condemn some business practices whose effects are not obvious. Here we consider three examples.

Resale Price Maintenance One example of a controversial business practice is *resale price maintenance,* also called *fair trade.* Imagine that Superduper Electronics sells DVD players to retail stores for €300. If Superduper requires the retailers to charge customers €350, it is said to engage in resale price maintenance. Any retailer that charged less than €350 would have violated its contract with Superduper.

At first, resale price maintenance might seem anti-competitive and, therefore, detrimental to society. Like an agreement among members of a cartel, it prevents the retailers from competing on price. For this reason, the courts have often viewed resale price maintenance as a violation of competition law.

Yet some economists defend resale price maintenance on two grounds. First, they deny that it is aimed at reducing competition. To the extent that Superduper Electronics has any market power, it can exert that power through the wholesale price, rather than through resale price maintenance. Moreover, Superduper has no incentive to discourage competition among its retailers. Indeed, because a cartel of retailers sells less than a group of competitive retailers, Superduper would be worse off if its retailers were a cartel.

Secondly, economists believe that resale price maintenance has a legitimate goal. Superduper may want its retailers to provide customers with a pleasant showroom and a knowledgeable salesforce. Yet, without resale price maintenance, some customers would take advantage of one store's service to learn about the DVD player's special features and then buy the item at a discount retailer that does not provide this service. To some extent, good service is a public good among the retailers that sell Superduper products. As we discussed in Chapter 11, when one person provides a public good, others are able to enjoy it without paying for it. In this case, discount retailers would free ride on the service provided by other retailers, leading to less service than is desirable. Resale price maintenance is one way for Superduper to solve this free-rider problem.

The example of resale price maintenance illustrates an important principle: business practices that appear to reduce competition may in fact have legitimate purposes. This principle makes the application of competition law all the more difficult. The competition authorities in each EU nation under the European Competition Network are in charge of enforcing these laws must determine what kinds of behaviour public policy should prohibit as impeding competition and reducing economic well-being. Often that job is not easy.

Predatory Pricing Firms with market power normally use that power to raise prices above the competitive level. But should policy makers ever be concerned that firms with market power might charge prices that are too low? This question is at the heart of a second debate over competition policy.

Imagine that a large airline, call it Tom Airlines, has a monopoly on some route. Then Jerry Express enters and takes 20 per cent of the market, leaving Tom with 80 per cent. In response to this competition, Tom starts slashing its fares. Some anti-trust analysts argue that Tom's move could be anti-competitive: the price cuts may be intended to drive Jerry out of the market so Tom can recapture its monopoly and raise prices again. Such behaviour is called *predatory pricing*.

Although it is common for companies to complain to the relevant authorities that a competitor is pursuing predatory pricing, some economists are sceptical of this argument and believe that predatory pricing is rarely, and perhaps never, a profitable business strategy. Why? For a price war to drive out a rival, prices have to be driven below cost. Yet if Tom starts selling cheap tickets at a loss, it had better be ready to fly more planes, because low fares will attract more customers. Jerry, meanwhile, can respond to Tom's predatory move by cutting back on flights. As a result, Tom ends up bearing more than 80 per cent of the losses, putting Jerry in a good position to survive the price war. As in the old Tom and Jerry cartoons, the predator suffers more than the prey.

Economists continue to debate whether predatory pricing should be a concern for competition policy makers. Various questions remain unresolved. Is predatory pricing ever a profitable business strategy? If so, when? Are the authorities capable of telling which price cuts are competitive and thus good for consumers and which are predatory? There are no simple answers.

Tying A third example of a controversial business practice is *tying*. Suppose that Makemoney Movies produces two new films – *Spiderman* and *Hamlet*. If

Makemoney offers cinemas the two films together at a single price, rather than separately, the studio is said to be tying its two products.

Some economists have argued that the practice of tying should be banned. Their reasoning is as follows: imagine that *Spiderman* is a blockbuster, whereas *Hamlet* is an unprofitable art film. Then the studio could use the high demand for *Spiderman* to force cinemas to buy *Hamlet.* It seemed that the studio could use tying as a mechanism for expanding its market power.

Other economists are sceptical of this argument. Imagine that cinemas are willing to pay €20 000 for *Spiderman* and nothing for *Hamlet.* Then the most that a cinema would pay for the two films together is €20 000 – the same as it would pay for *Spiderman* by itself. Forcing the cinema to accept a worthless film as part of the deal does not increase the cinema's willingness to pay. Makemoney cannot increase its market power simply by bundling the two films together.

Why, then, does tying exist? One possibility is that it is a form of price discrimination. Suppose there are two cinemas. City Cinema is willing to pay €15 000 for *Spiderman* and €5 000 for *Hamlet.* Country Cinema is just the opposite: it is willing to pay €5 000 for *Spiderman* and €15 000 for *Hamlet.* If Makemoney charges separate prices for the two films, its best strategy is to charge €15 000 for each film, and each cinema chooses to show only one film. Yet if Makemoney offers the two films as a bundle, it can charge each cinema €20 000 for the films. Thus, if different cinemas value the films differently, tying may allow the studio to increase profit by charging a combined price closer to the buyers' total willingness to pay.

Tying remains a controversial business practice. We saw in Chapter 15 how Microsoft had been investigated for 'tying' its internet browser and other software like its Windows Media Player with its Windows operating system and the arguments that the company had put forward in its defence. The argument that tying allows a firm to extend its market power to other goods is not well founded, at least in its simplest form. Yet economists have proposed more elaborate theories for how tying can impede competition. Given our current economic knowledge, it is unclear whether tying has adverse effects for society as a whole.

All the analysis is based on an assumption that rivals may have sufficient information to be able to make a decision and that the decision will be a rational one based on this information. In reality firms do not have perfect information and do not behave rationally. Most firms in oligopolistic markets work very hard to protect sensitive information and only give out what they have to by law. Some information may be given to deliberately obfuscate the situation and hide what their true motives/strategies/tactics are. Economists have tried to include these imperfections into theories. Behavioural economics has become more popular in recent years because it offers some greater insights into the observed behaviour of the real world which often does not conform to the assumptions implied by the assumption of rationality.

Quick Quiz What kind of agreement is illegal for businesses to make?
• Why is competition law controversial?

CONCLUSION

Oligopolies would like to act like monopolies, but self-interest drives them closer to competition. Thus, oligopolies can end up looking either more like monopolies or more like competitive markets, depending on the number of firms in the oligopoly and how cooperative the firms are. The story of the prisoners' dilemma shows why oligopolies can fail to maintain cooperation, even when cooperation is in their best interest.

Policy makers regulate the behaviour of oligopolists through competition law. The proper scope of these laws is the subject of ongoing controversy. Although price fixing among competing firms clearly reduces economic welfare and should be illegal, some business practices that appear to reduce competition may have legitimate if subtle purposes. As a result, policy makers need to be careful when they use the substantial powers of competition law to place limits on firm behaviour.

SUMMARY

- Oligopolists maximize their total profits by forming a cartel and acting like a monopolist. Yet, if oligopolists make decisions about production levels individually, the result is a greater quantity and a lower price than under the monopoly outcome. The larger the number of firms in the oligopoly, the closer the quantity and price will be to the levels that would prevail under competition.
- The prisoners' dilemma shows that self-interest can prevent people from maintaining cooperation, even when cooperation is in their mutual interest. The logic of the prisoners' dilemma applies in many situations, including arms races, advertising, common-resource problems and oligopolies.
- Policy makers use competition law to prevent oligopolies from engaging in behaviour that reduces competition. The application of these laws can be controversial, because some behaviour that may seem to reduce competition may in fact have legitimate business purposes.

KEY CONCEPTS

QUESTIONS FOR REVIEW

1. If a group of sellers could form a cartel, what quantity and price would they try to set?
2. Compare the quantity and price of an oligopoly with those of a monopoly.
3. Compare the quantity and price of an oligopoly with those of a competitive market.
4. How does the number of firms in an oligopoly affect the outcome in its market?
5. What is the prisoners' dilemma, and what does it have to do with oligopoly?
6. Give two examples other than oligopoly to show how the prisoners' dilemma helps to explain behaviour.
7. What kinds of behaviour do the competition laws prohibit?
8. What is resale price maintenance, and why is it controversial?

PROBLEMS AND APPLICATIONS

1. *The Economist* (15 November, 2001) reported that 'OPEC has failed to agree immediate production cuts to shore up oil prices. Afraid of losing market share, it wants non-members, who would also benefit from any price support, to cut output as well. So far, they have refused to agree. If oil prices continue to fall, that would provide relief to the beleaguered world economy, but it might wreak havoc on the finances of OPEC members.'
   a. Why do you suppose OPEC was unable to agree on cutting production?
   b. Why do you think oil-producing non-members refused to cut output?
2. A large share of the world supply of diamonds comes from Russia and South Africa. Suppose that the marginal cost of mining diamonds is constant at €1 000 per diamond, and the demand for diamonds is described by the following schedule:

Price (€)	Quantity
€8 000	5 000
7 000	6 000
6 000	7 000
5 000	8 000
4 000	9 000
3 000	10 000
2 000	11 000
1 000	12 000

   a. If there were many suppliers of diamonds, what would be the price and quantity?
   b. If there were only one supplier of diamonds, what would be the price and quantity?
   c. If Russia and South Africa formed a cartel, what would be the price and quantity? If the countries split the market evenly, what would be South Africa's production and profit? What would happen to South Africa's profit if it increased its production by 1 000 while Russia stuck to the cartel agreement?
   d. Use your answer to part (c) to explain why cartel agreements are often not successful.
3. This chapter discusses companies that are oligopolists in the market for the goods they sell. Many of the same ideas apply to companies that are oligopolists in the market for the inputs they buy. If sellers who are oligopolists try to increase the price of goods they sell, what is the goal of buyers who are oligopolists?
4. Describe several activities in your life in which game theory could be useful. What is the common link among these activities?
5. Suppose that you and a fellow student are assigned a project on which you will receive one combined grade. You each want to receive a good grade, but you also want to do as little work as possible. The decision box and pay-offs are as follows:

		Your decision: Work	Your decision: Shirk
Fellow student's decision	Work	You get A grade, no fun Fellow student gets A grade, no fun	You get B grade, fun Fellow student gets B grade, no fun
	Shirk	You get B grade, no fun Fellow student gets B grade, fun	You get D grade, fun Fellow student gets D grade, fun

   Assume that having fun is your normal state, but having no fun is as unpleasant as receiving a grade that is two letters lower.
   a. Write out the decision box that combines the letter grade and the amount of fun you have into a single pay-off for each outcome.
   b. If neither you nor your fellow student knows how much work the other person is doing, what is the likely outcome? Does it matter whether you are likely to work with this person again? Explain your answer.
6. The chapter states that the ban on cigarette advertising on television which many countries imposed in the 1970s increased the profits of cigarette companies. Could the ban still be good public policy? Explain your answer.
7. Assume that two airline companies decide to engage in collusive behaviour.
   Let's analyse the game between two such companies. Suppose that each company can charge either a high price for tickets or a low price. If one company charges €100, it earns low profits if the other company charges €100 also, and high profits if the other company charges €200. On the other hand, if the company charges €200, it earns very low profits if the other company charges €100, and medium profits if the other company charges €200 also.
   a. Draw the decision box for this game.
   b. What is the Nash equilibrium in this game? Explain.
   c. Is there an outcome that would be better than the Nash equilibrium for both airlines? How could it be achieved? Who would lose if it were achieved?

8. Farmer Jones and Farmer MacDonald graze their cattle on the same field. If there are 20 cows grazing in the field, each cow produces €4 000 of milk over its lifetime. If there are more cows in the field, then each cow can eat less grass, and its milk production falls. With 30 cows on the field, each produces €3 000 of milk; with 40 cows, each produces €2 000 of milk. Cows cost €1 000 apiece.
   a. Assume that Farmer Jones and Farmer MacDonald can each purchase either 10 or 20 cows, but that neither knows how many the other is buying when she makes her purchase. Calculate the pay-offs of each outcome.
   b. What is the likely outcome of this game? What would be the best outcome? Explain.
   c. There used to be more common fields than there are today. Why? (For more discussion of this topic, reread Chapter 11.)
9. Little Kona is a small coffee company that is considering entering a market dominated by Big Brew. Each company's profit depends on whether Little Kona enters and whether Big Brew sets a high price or a low price:

Little Kona \ Big Brew	High price	Low price
Enter	Brew makes €3 million; Kona makes €2 million	Brew makes €1 million; Kona loses €1 million
Don't enter	Brew makes €7 million; Kona makes zero	Brew makes €2 million; Kona makes zero

Big Brew threatens Little Kona by saying, 'If you enter, we're going to set a low price, so you had better stay out.' Do you think Little Kona should believe the threat? Why or why not? What do you think Little Kona should do?

10. Tim and Greg are playing tennis. Every point comes down to whether Greg guesses correctly whether Tim will hit the ball to Greg's left or right. The outcomes are:

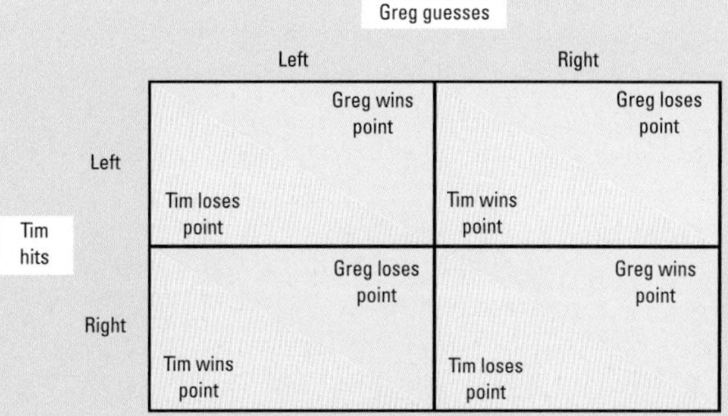

Tim hits \ Greg guesses	Left	Right
Left	Greg wins point; Tim loses point	Greg loses point; Tim wins point
Right	Greg loses point; Tim wins point	Greg wins point; Tim loses point

Does either player have a dominant strategy? If Tim chooses a particular strategy (Left or Right) and sticks with it, what will Greg do? So, can you think of a better strategy for Tim to follow?

For further resources, visit www.cengage.com/mankiw_taylor2

6

THE ECONOMICS OF LABOUR MARKETS

18 THE MARKETS FOR THE FACTORS OF PRODUCTION

When you finish university, your income will be determined largely by what kind of job you take. If you become a professional economist, you will earn more than if you become a petrol station attendant. This fact is not surprising, but it is not obvious why it is true. No law requires that economists be paid more than petrol station attendants. No ethical principle says that economists are more deserving. If you become an academic economist in a university, you will probably earn less than if you become a banker. What then determines which job will pay you the higher wage?

Your income, of course, is a small piece of a larger economic picture. In 2007 the total income of all EU residents was about €12.371 trillion (€12 371 365 000 000). In 2009 the total income of all UK residents was about £140 000 000 000 (£1.4 trillion).

People earned this income in various ways. Workers earned about two-thirds of it in the form of wages and fringe benefits and about 10 per cent of it is income from self-employment. The rest went to landowners and to the owners of *capital* – the economy's stock of equipment and structures – in the form of rent, profit and interest. What determines how much goes to workers? To landowners? To the owners of capital? Why do some workers earn higher wages than others, some landowners higher rental income than others and some capital owners greater profit than others? Why, in particular, do computer programmers earn more than petrol station attendants?

The answers to these questions, like most in economics, hinge on supply and demand. The supply and demand for labour, land and capital determine the

prices paid to workers, landowners and capital owners. To understand why some people have higher incomes than others, therefore, we need to look more deeply at the markets for the services they provide.

This chapter provides the basic theory for the analysis of factor markets. **Factors of production** are the inputs used to produce goods and services. Labour, land and capital are the three most important factors of production. When a computer firm produces a new software program, it uses programmers' time (labour), the physical space on which its offices sit (land), and an office building and computer equipment (capital). Similarly, when a petrol station sells petrol, it uses attendants' time (labour), the physical space (land), and the petrol tanks and pumps (capital).

factors of production
the inputs used to produce goods and services

Although in many ways factor markets resemble the goods markets we have analysed in previous chapters, they are different in one important way: the demand for a factor of production is a *derived demand*. That is, a firm's demand for a factor of production is derived (determined) from its decision to supply a good in another market. The demand for computer programmers is inextricably tied to the supply of computer software, and the demand for petrol station attendants is inextricably tied to the supply of petrol.

The initial analysis will be based on firms operating in a competitive market – both for goods and labour. More will be said on this below but it is also worth remembering that the analysis assumes that labour is free to enter and exit the market and firms are equally free to employ and shed labour at will – in other words people can move into and out of work easily and employers can 'hire and fire' workers when they need to. In reality, of course, there are a number of imperfections in the labour market but our initial analysis serves to act as a benchmark for looking at how labour markets work in reality.

THE DEMAND FOR LABOUR

Labour markets, like other markets in the economy, are governed by the forces of supply and demand. This is illustrated in Figure 18.1. In panel (a) the supply and demand for apples determine the price of apples. In panel (b) the supply and demand for apple pickers determine the price, or wage, of apple pickers.

As we have already noted, labour markets are different from most other markets because labour demand is a derived demand. Most labour services, rather than being final goods ready to be enjoyed by consumers, are inputs into the production of other goods. To understand labour demand, we need to focus on the firms that hire the labour and use it to produce goods for sale. By examining the link between the production of goods and the demand for labour, we gain insight into the determination of equilibrium wages.

The Competitive Profit-maximizing Firm

Let's look at how a typical firm, such as an apple producer, decides the quantity of labour to demand. The firm owns an apple orchard and each week must decide how many apple pickers to hire to harvest its crop. After the firm makes its hiring decision, the workers pick as many apples as they can. The firm then sells the apples, pays the workers, and keeps what is left as profit.

We assume that our firm is *competitive* both in the market for apples (where the firm is a seller) and in the market for apple pickers (where the firm is a buyer). Because there are many other firms selling apples and hiring apple pickers, a single firm has little influence over the price it gets for apples or the wage it pays apple pickers. The firm takes the price and the wage as given by market

FIGURE 18.1

The Versatility of Supply and Demand

The basic tools of supply and demand apply to goods and to labour services. Panel (a) shows how the supply and demand for apples determine the price of apples. Panel (b) shows how the supply and demand for apple pickers determine the wage of apple pickers.

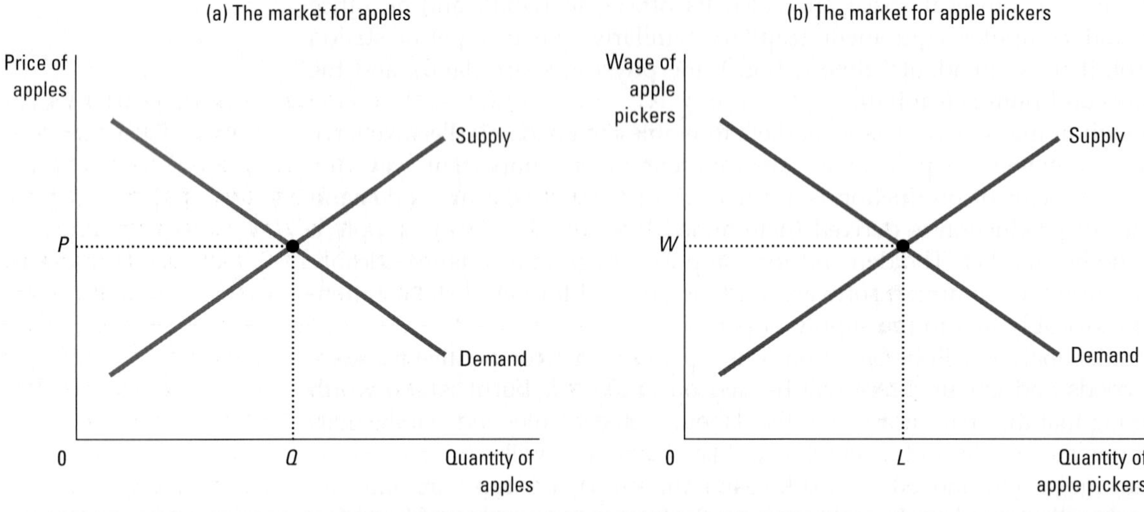

conditions. It only has to decide how many workers to hire and how many apples to sell.

Secondly, we assume that the firm is *profit-maximizing*. Thus, the firm does not directly care about the number of workers it has or the number of apples it produces. It cares only about profit, which equals the total revenue from the sale of apples minus the total cost of producing them. The firm's supply of apples and its demand for workers are derived from its primary goal of maximizing profit.

The Production Function and the Marginal Product of Labour

To make its hiring decision, the firm must consider how the number of apple pickers affects the quantity of apples it can harvest and sell. Table 18.1 gives a numerical example. In the first column is the number of workers. In the second column is the quantity of apples the workers harvest each week.

production function
the relationship between the quantity of inputs used to make a good and the quantity of output of that good

These two columns of numbers describe the firm's ability to produce. As we noted in Chapter 13, economists use the term **production function** to describe the relationship between the quantity of the inputs used in production and the quantity of output from production. Here the 'input' is the apple pickers and the 'output' is the apples. The other inputs – the trees themselves, the land, the firm's trucks and tractors, and so on – are held fixed for now. This firm's production function shows that if the firm hires 1 worker, that worker will pick 1 000 kilos of apples per week. If the firm hires 2 workers, the two workers together will pick 1 800 kilos per week, and so on.

Figure 18.2 graphs the data on labour and output presented in Table 18.1. The number of workers is on the horizontal axis, and the amount of output is on the vertical axis. This figure illustrates the production function.

TABLE 18.1

How the Competitive Firm Decides How Much Labour to Hire

Labour	Output	Marginal product of labour	Value of the marginal product of labour	Wage	Marginal profit
L (number of workers)	*Q* (kilos per week)	*MPL* = $\Delta Q/\Delta L$ (kilos per week)	*VMPL* = *P* × *MPL*	*W*	ΔProfit = *VMPL* – *W*
0	0				
		1 000	€1 000	€500	€500
1	1 000				
		800	800	500	300
2	1 800				
		600	600	500	100
3	2 400				
		400	400	500	–100
4	2 800				
		200	200	500	–300
5	3 000				

FIGURE 18.2

The Production Function

The production function is the relationship between the inputs into production (apple pickers) and the output from production (apples). As the quantity of the input increases, the production function gets flatter, reflecting the property of diminishing marginal product.

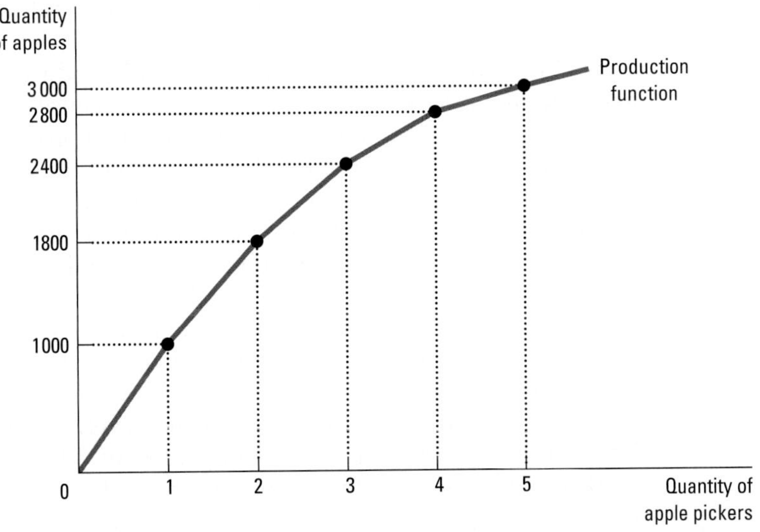

One of the *Ten Principles of Economics* introduced in Chapter 1 is that rational people think at the margin. This idea is the key to understanding how firms decide what quantity of labour to hire. To take a step towards this decision, the third column in Table 18.1 gives the **marginal product of labour**, the increase in the amount of output from an additional unit of labour. When the firm increases the number of workers from 1 to 2, for example, the amount of apples produced rises from 1 000 to 1 800 kilos. Therefore, the marginal product of the second worker is 800 kilos.

marginal product of labour
the increase in the amount of output from an additional unit of labour

Notice that as the number of workers increases, the marginal product of labour declines (remember we are adding more units of a variable factor (labour) to a quantity of fixed factors (land and capital – we are operating in the short run). As you may recall from Chapter 13, this property is called diminishing marginal product. At first, when only a few workers are hired, they pick apples from the best trees in the orchard. As the number of workers increases, additional workers have to pick from the trees with fewer apples. Hence, as more and more workers are hired, each additional worker contributes less to the production of apples. For this reason, the production function in Figure 18.2 becomes flatter as the number of workers rises.

The Value of the Marginal Product and the Demand for Labour

Our profit-maximizing firm is concerned more with money than with apples. As a result, when deciding how many workers to hire, the firm considers how much profit each worker would bring in. Because profit is total revenue minus total cost, the profit from an additional worker is the worker's contribution to revenue minus the worker's wage.

To find the worker's contribution to revenue, we must convert the marginal product of labour (which is measured in kilos of apples) into the *value* of the marginal product (which is measured in euros). We do this using the price of apples. To continue our example, if a kilo of apples sells for €1 and if an additional worker produces 800 kilos of apples, then the worker produces €800 of revenue for the firm.

value of the marginal product
the marginal product of an input times the price of the output

The **value of the marginal product** of any input is the marginal product of that input multiplied by the market price of the output. The fourth column in Table 18.1 shows the value of the marginal product of labour in our example, assuming the price of apples is €1 per kilo. Because the market price is constant for a competitive firm, the value of the marginal product (like the marginal product itself) diminishes as the number of workers rises. Economists sometimes call this column of numbers the firm's *marginal revenue product:* it is the extra revenue the firm gets from hiring an additional unit of a factor of production.

Now consider how many workers the firm will hire. Suppose that the market wage for apple pickers is €500 per week. In this case, as you see in Table 18.1, the first worker that the firm hires is profitable: the first worker yields €1 000 in revenue, or €500 in profit. Similarly, the second worker yields €800 in additional revenue, or €300 in profit. The third worker produces €600 in additional revenue, or €100 in profit. After the third worker, however, hiring workers is unprofitable. The fourth worker would yield only €400 of additional revenue. Because the worker's wage is €500, hiring the fourth worker would mean a €100 reduction in profit. Thus, the firm hires only three workers.

It is instructive to consider the firm's decision graphically. Figure 18.3 graphs the value of the marginal product. This curve slopes downward because the marginal product of labour diminishes as the number of workers rises. The figure also includes a horizontal line at the market wage. To maximize profit, the firm hires workers up to the point where these two curves cross. Below this level of employment, the value of the marginal product exceeds the wage, so hiring another worker would increase profit. Above this level of employment, the value of the marginal product is less than the wage, so the marginal worker is unprofitable. Thus, a competitive, profit-maximizing firm hires workers up to the point where the value of the marginal product of labour equals the wage.

Having explained the profit-maximizing hiring strategy for a competitive firm, we can now offer a theory of labour demand. Recall that a firm's labour demand curve tells us the quantity of labour that a firm demands at any given wage. We

FIGURE 18.3

The Value of the Marginal Product of Labour

This figure shows how the value of the marginal product (the marginal product times the price of the output) depends on the number of workers. The curve slopes downward because of diminishing marginal product. For a competitive, profit-maximizing firm, this value of marginal product curve is also the firm's labour demand curve.

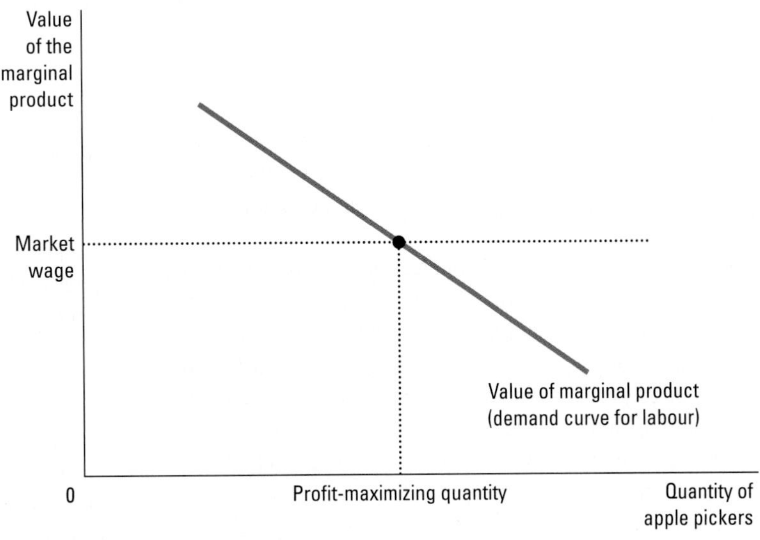

have just seen in Figure 18.3 that the firm makes that decision by choosing the quantity of labour at which the value of the marginal product equals the wage. As a result, the value of marginal product curve is the labour demand curve for a competitive, profit-maximizing firm.

What Causes the Labour Demand Curve to Shift?

The labour demand curve reflects the value of the marginal product of labour. With this insight in mind, let's consider a few of the things that might cause the labour demand curve to shift.

The Output Price The value of the marginal product is marginal product times the price of the firm's output. Thus, when the output price changes, the value of the marginal product changes, and the labour demand curve shifts. An increase in the price of apples, for instance, raises the value of the marginal product of each worker who picks apples and, therefore, increases labour demand from the firms that supply apples. Conversely, a decrease in the price of apples reduces the value of the marginal product and decreases labour demand.

Technological Change Between 2000 and 2008, labour productivity per hour worked in the EU 27 increased by 2.94 per cent[1]. Between 1960 and 2008, the amount of output a typical UK worker produced in an hour rose by around 156 per cent[2]. Why? The most important reason is technological progress: scientists and engineers are constantly figuring out new and better ways of doing

[1]Source: Eurostat (http://epp.eurostat.ec.europa.eu/tgm/table.do?tab=table&init=1&language=en&pcode=tsieb040&plugin=0).

[2]Source: Office for National Statistics (http://www.statistics.gov.uk/statbase/TSDdownload2.asp).

FYI

Input Demand and Output Supply: Two Sides of the Same Coin

In Chapter 14 we saw how a competitive, profit-maximizing firm decides how much of its output to sell: it chooses the quantity of output at which the price of the good equals the marginal cost of production. We have just seen how such a firm decides how much labour to hire: it chooses the quantity of labour at which the wage equals the value of the marginal product. Because the production function links the quantity of inputs to the quantity of output, you should not be surprised to learn that the firm's decision about input demand is closely linked to its decision about output supply. In fact, these two decisions are two sides of the same coin.

To see this relationship more fully, let's consider how the marginal product of labour (*MPL*) and marginal cost (*MC*) are related. Suppose an additional worker costs €500 and has a marginal product of 50 kilos of apples. In this case, producing 50 more kilos costs €500; the marginal cost of a kilo is €500/50, or €10. More generally, if *W* is the wage, and an extra unit of labour produces *MPL* units of output, then the marginal cost of a unit of output is $MC = W/MPL$.

This analysis shows that diminishing marginal product is closely related to increasing marginal cost. When our apple orchard grows crowded with workers, each additional worker adds less to the production of apples (*MPL* falls). Similarly, when the apple firm is producing a large quantity of apples, the orchard is already crowded with workers, so it is more costly to produce an additional kilo of apples (*MC* rises).

Now consider our criterion for profit maximization. We determined earlier that a profit-maximizing firm chooses the quantity of labour so that the value of the marginal product ($P \times MPL$) equals the wage (*W*). We can write this mathematically as:

$$P \times MPL = W$$

If we divide both sides of this equation by *MPL*, we obtain:

$$P = W/MPL$$

We just noted that *W*/*MPL* equals marginal cost *MC*. Therefore, we can substitute to obtain:

$$P = MC$$

This equation states that the price of the firm's output is equal to the marginal cost of producing a unit of output. *Thus, when a competitive firm hires labour up to the point at which the value of the marginal product equals the wage, it also produces up to the point at which the price equals marginal cost.* Our analysis of labour demand in this chapter is just another way of looking at the production decision we first saw in Chapter 14.

things. This has profound implications for the labour market. Technological advance raises the marginal product of labour, which in turn increases the demand for labour. Such technological advance explains persistently rising employment in the face of rising wages: even though UK wages (adjusted for inflation) increased by 120 per cent over these four decades, firms nevertheless increased by 17 per cent the amount of labour they employed.

The Supply of other Factors The quantity available of one factor of production can affect the marginal product of other factors. A fall in the supply of ladders, for instance, will reduce the marginal product of apple pickers and thus the demand for apple pickers. We consider this linkage among the factors of production more fully later in the chapter.

Quick Quiz Define *marginal product of labour* and *value of the marginal product of labour.* • Describe how a competitive, profit-maximizing firm decides how many workers to hire.

THE SUPPLY OF LABOUR

Having analysed labour demand let's turn to the other side of the market and consider labour supply. Here we discuss briefly and informally the decisions that lie behind the labour supply curve.

The Trade-off between Work and Leisure

One of the *Ten Principles of Economics* in Chapter 1 is that people face trade-offs. Probably no trade-off is more obvious or more important in a person's life than the trade-off between work and leisure. The more hours you spend working, the fewer hours you have to watch TV, socialize with friends or pursue your favourite hobby. The trade-off between labour and leisure lies behind the labour supply curve.

Another of the *Ten Principles of Economics* is that the cost of something is what you give up to get it. What do you give up to get an hour of leisure? You give up an hour of work, which in turn means an hour of wages. Thus, if your wage is €15 per hour, the opportunity cost of an hour of leisure is €15. And when you get a pay rise to €20 per hour, the opportunity cost of enjoying leisure goes up.

The labour supply curve reflects how workers' decisions about the labour–leisure trade-off respond to a change in that opportunity cost. An upward sloping labour supply curve means that an increase in the wage induces workers to increase the quantity of labour they supply. Because time is limited, more hours of work means that workers are enjoying less leisure. That is, workers respond to the increase in the opportunity cost of leisure by taking less of it.

It is worth noting that the labour supply curve need not be upward sloping. Imagine you got that raise from €15 to €20 per hour. The opportunity cost of leisure is now greater, but you are also richer than you were before. You might decide that with your extra wealth you can now afford to enjoy more leisure. That is, at the higher wage, you might choose to work fewer hours. If so, your labour supply curve would slope backwards. In Chapter 21, we discuss this possibility in terms of conflicting effects on your labour supply decision (called the income and substitution effects). For now, we ignore the possibility of backward sloping labour supply and assume that the labour supply curve is upward sloping.

What Causes the Labour Supply Curve to Shift?

The labour supply curve shifts whenever people change the amount they want to work at a given wage. Let's now consider some of the events that might cause such a shift.

Changes in Tastes In 1960, 48.7 per cent of women in the UK were employed at paid jobs or looking for work. By 2005, the proportion had risen to 70 per cent. In the EU27, the employment rate for women rose from 54.4 per cent in 2002 to 58.3 per cent in 2007. There are, of course, many explanations for these developments, but one of them is changing tastes, or attitudes toward work. A generation or two ago, it was the norm for women to stay at home while raising children. Today, family sizes are smaller and more mothers choose to work. The result is an increase in the supply of labour.

Changes in Alternative Opportunities The supply of labour in any one labour market depends on the opportunities available in other labour markets. If the wage earned by pear pickers suddenly rises, some apple pickers may choose to switch occupations. The supply of labour in the market for apple pickers falls.

Immigration Movement of workers from region to region, or country to country, is an obvious and often important source of shifts in labour supply. When immigrants move from one European country to another – from Poland to the UK, for instance – the supply of labour in the United Kingdom increases and the supply of labour in Poland contracts. In fact, much of the policy debate about immigration centres on its effect on labour supply and, thereby, equilibrium in the labour market.

Quick Quiz Who has a greater opportunity cost of enjoying leisure – a petrol station attendant or a brain surgeon? Explain. Can this help explain why doctors work such long hours?

EQUILIBRIUM IN THE LABOUR MARKET

So far we have established two facts about how wages are determined in competitive labour markets:

- The wage adjusts to balance the supply and demand for labour.
- The wage equals the value of the marginal product of labour.

At first, it might seem surprising that the wage can do both these things at once. In fact, there is no real puzzle here, but understanding why there is no puzzle is an important step to understanding wage determination.

Figure 18.4 shows the labour market in equilibrium. The wage and the quantity of labour have adjusted to balance supply and demand. When the market is

FIGURE 18.4

Equilibrium in a Labour Market

Like all prices, the price of labour (the wage) depends on supply and demand. Because the demand curve reflects the value of the marginal product of labour, in equilibrium workers receive the value of their marginal contribution to the production of goods and services.

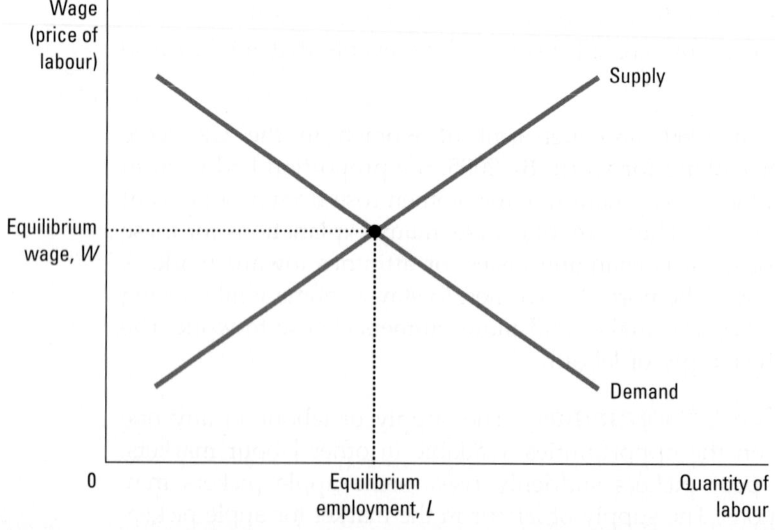

in this equilibrium, each firm has bought as much labour as it finds profitable at the equilibrium wage. That is, each firm has followed the rule for profit maximization: it has hired workers until the value of the marginal product equals the wage. Hence, the wage must equal the value of the marginal product of labour once it has brought supply and demand into equilibrium.

This brings us to an important lesson: any event that changes the supply or demand for labour must change the equilibrium wage and the value of the marginal product by the same amount, because these must always be equal. To see how this works, let's consider some events that shift these curves.

Shifts in Labour Supply

Suppose that immigration increases the number of workers willing to pick apples. As Figure 18.5 shows, the supply of labour shifts to the right from S_1 to S_2. At the initial wage W_1, the quantity of labour supplied now exceeds the quantity demanded. This surplus of labour puts downward pressure on the wage of apple pickers, and the fall in the wage from W_1 to W_2 in turn makes it profitable for firms to hire more workers. As the number of workers employed in each apple orchard rises, the marginal product of a worker falls, and so does the value of the marginal product. In the new equilibrium, both the wage and the value of the marginal product of labour are lower than they were before the influx of new workers.

An episode from Israel illustrates how a shift in labour supply can alter the equilibrium in a labour market. During most of the 1980s, many thousands of Palestinians regularly commuted from their homes in the Israeli-occupied West Bank and Gaza Strip to jobs in Israel, primarily in the construction and

FIGURE 18.5

A Shift in Labour Supply

When labour supply increases from S_1 to S_2, perhaps because of immigration of new workers, the equilibrium wage falls from W_1 to W_2. At this lower wage, firms hire more labour, so employment rises from L_1 to L_2. The change in the wage reflects a change in the value of the marginal product of labour: with more workers, the added output from an extra worker is smaller.

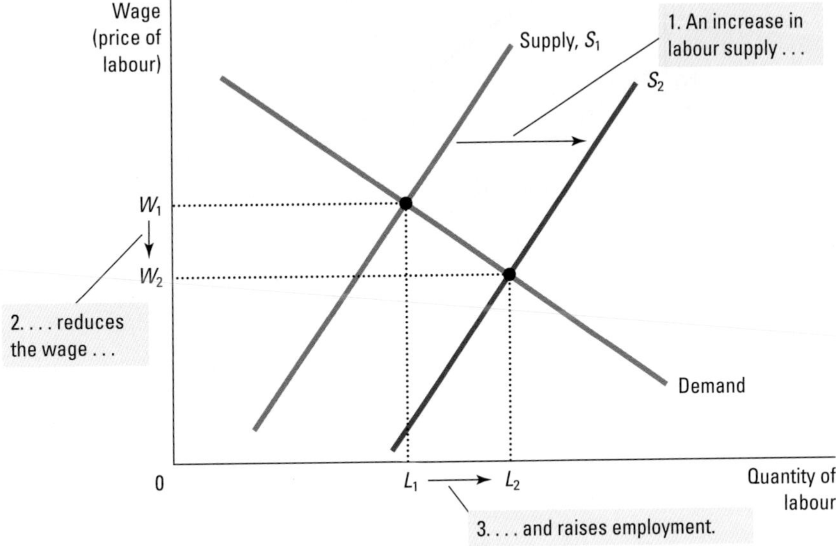

agriculture industries. In 1988, however, political unrest in these occupied areas induced the Israeli government to take steps that, as a by-product, reduced this supply of workers. Curfews were imposed, work permits were checked more thoroughly, and a ban on overnight stays of Palestinians in Israel was enforced more rigorously. The economic impact of these steps was exactly as theory predicts: the number of Palestinians with jobs in Israel fell by half, while those who continued to work in Israel enjoyed wage increases of about 50 per cent. With a reduced number of Palestinian workers in Israel, the value of the marginal product of the remaining workers was much higher.

Shifts in Labour Demand

Now suppose that an increase in the popularity of apples causes their price to rise. This price increase does not change the marginal product of labour for any given number of workers, but it does raise the *value* of the marginal product. With a higher price of apples, hiring more apple pickers is now profitable. As Figure 18.6 shows, when the demand for labour shifts to the right from D_1 to D_2, the equilibrium wage rises from W_1 to W_2, and equilibrium employment rises from L_1 to L_2. Once again, the wage and the value of the marginal product of labour move together.

This analysis shows that prosperity for firms in an industry is often linked to prosperity for workers in that industry. When the price of apples rises, apple producers make greater profit and apple pickers earn higher wages. When the price of apples falls, apple producers earn smaller profit and apple pickers earn lower wages. This lesson is well known to workers in industries with highly volatile prices. Workers in oil fields, for instance, know from experience that their earnings are closely linked to the world price of crude oil.

FIGURE 18.6

A Shift in Labour Demand

When labour demand increases from D_1 to D_2, perhaps because of an increase in the price of the firms' output, the equilibrium wage rises from W_1 to W_2, and employment rises from L_1 to L_2. Again, the change in the wage reflects a change in the value of the marginal product of labour: with a higher output price, the added output from an extra worker is more valuable.

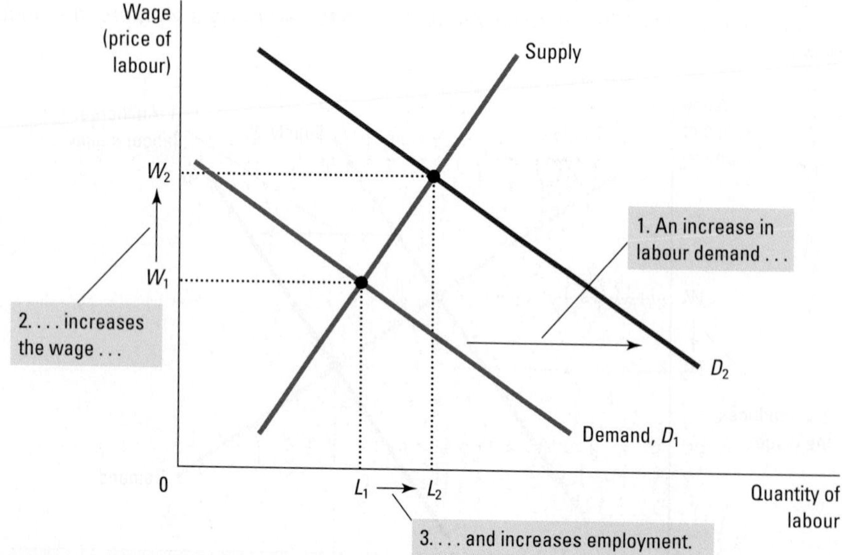

In competitive labour markets, therefore, labour supply and labour demand together determine the equilibrium wage, and shifts in the supply or demand curve for labour cause the equilibrium wage to change. At the same time, profit maximization by the firms that demand labour ensures that the equilibrium wage always equals the value of the marginal product of labour.

CASE STUDY

Productivity and Wages

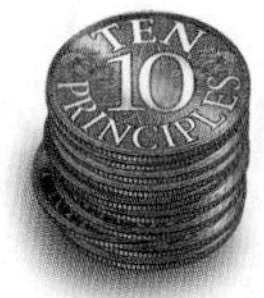

One of the *Ten Principles of Economics* in Chapter 1 is that our standard of living depends on our ability to produce goods and services. We can now see how this principle works in the market for labour. In particular, our analysis of labour demand shows that wages equal productivity as measured by the value of the marginal product of labour. Put simply, highly productive workers are highly paid, and less productive workers are less highly paid.

This lesson is key to understanding why workers today are better off than workers in previous generations. Panel (a) of Figure 18.7 presents some data on growth in productivity in the UK. From 1961 to 2005, productivity as measured by output per worker grew on average at about 2.03 per cent per year. Real wages (that is, wages adjusted for inflation) grew at almost the same rate: 2.0 per cent per year. With a growth rate of close to 2.0 per cent per year, productivity and real wages double about every 35 years.

Table 18.2 shows the rates of growth for the ten-year periods from 1950 to 2000. Notice that from 1971 to 1980 growth in productivity, at 1.80 per cent per year, was slow compared with the period before 1970. Over the period 1990–2000, productivity growth picked up slightly but was still less than in the 1950s and 1960s. There is a similar pattern in productivity growth in the US. The cause of the productivity slowdown in the 1970s is not well understood, but the link between productivity and real wages is exactly as standard theory predicts. The slowdown in productivity growth from 2.7 to 1.8 per cent per year coincided with a slowdown in real wage growth from around 3.0 to 1.5 per cent per year over the period 1973–95, and the growth in productivity over the more recent period of about 1.6 per cent was also reflected in a similar growth rate of real wages of 1.7 per cent per annum. Both theory and history confirm the close connection between productivity and real wages.

In more recent times productivity in the UK fell dramatically as shown in panel (b) of Figure 18.7 This was mainly caused by the financial crisis and the subsequent recession. There is also another reason for the fall in productivity that has been a feature of the recession that occurred. A number of large employers, especially car manufacturers, had long periods where they suspended production. Rather than making workers redundant, however, firms retained staff but paid them a proportion of their normal wage. Many workers were pleased to retain their job even though their wages fell and firms avoided heavy costs in redundancy pay, shutting down factories and having to recruit new labour when the upturn in business eventually occurred. Economists have to be aware, therefore, of new types of behaviour by firms and how this might change theory.

Growth in productivity is measured here as the annualized rate of change in output per worker. Growth in real wages is measured as the annualized change in average wages deflated by the Retail Prices Index. These productivity data measure average productivity – the quantity of output divided by the quantity of labour – rather than marginal productivity, but average and marginal productivity are thought to move closely together.

FIGURE 18.7

UK Labour Productivity, 1961–2005

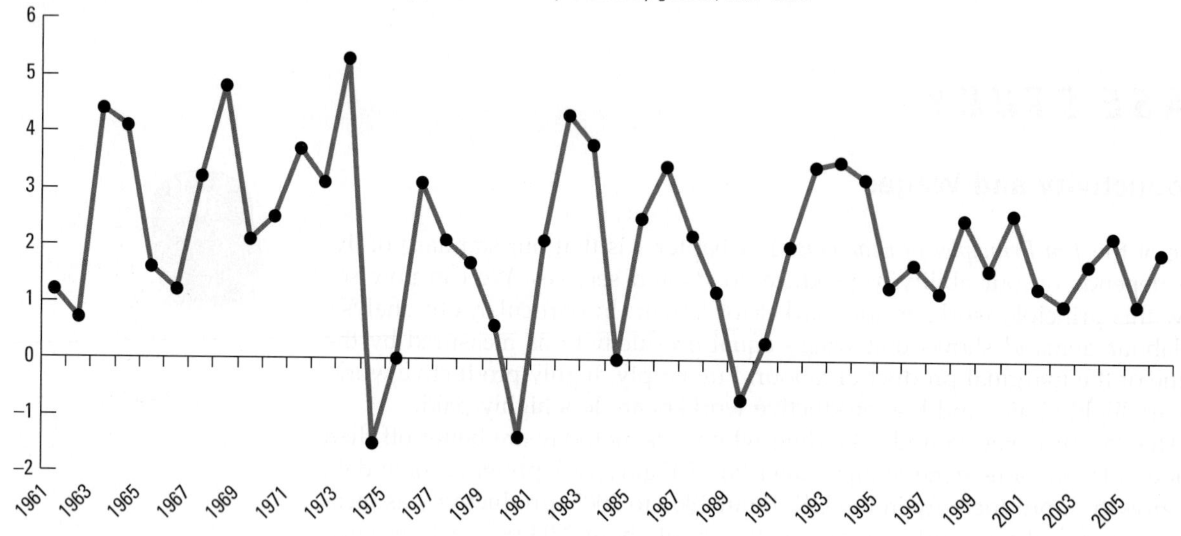

(b) Per cent change, 2004–09

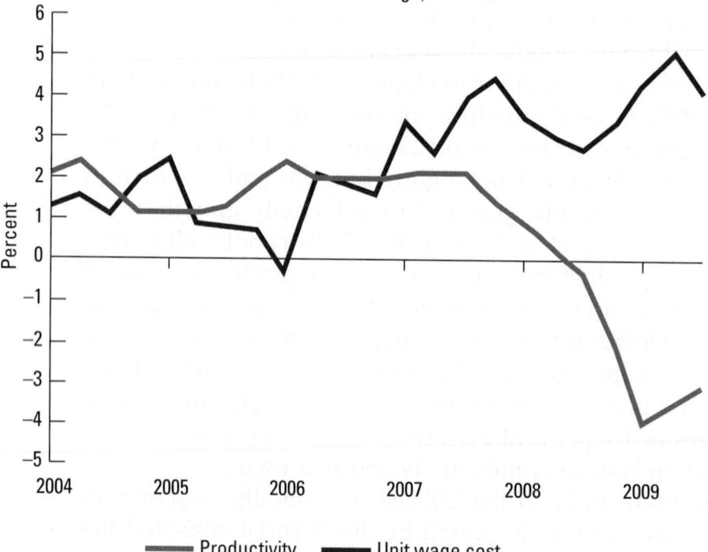

Productivity — Unit wage cost

Source: http://www.statistics.gov.uk/cci/nugget.asp?id=133

TABLE 18.2

Annual Growth in UK Productivity, 1951–2000 (%)

1951–1960	2.3
1961–1970	2.7
1971–1980	1.8
1981–1990	2.0
1991–2000	2.1

FYI

Monopsony

On the preceding pages, we built our analysis of the labour market with the tools of supply and demand. In doing so, we assumed that the labour market was competitive. That is, we assumed that there were many buyers of labour and many sellers of labour, so each buyer or seller had a negligible effect on the wage.

Yet imagine the labour market in a small town dominated by a single large employer. That employer can exert a large influence on the going wage, and it may well use that market power to alter the outcome. Such a market in which there is a single buyer is called a *monopsony*.

A monopsony (a market with one buyer) is in many ways similar to a monopoly (a market with one seller). Recall from Chapter 15 that a monopoly firm produces less of the good than would a competitive firm: by reducing the quantity offered for sale, the monopoly firm moves along the product's demand curve, raising the price and also its profits. Similarly, a monopsony firm in a labour market hires fewer workers than would a competitive firm: by reducing the number of jobs available, the monopsony firm moves along the labour supply curve, reducing the wage it pays and raising its profits. Thus, both monopolists and monopsonists reduce economic activity in a market below the socially optimal level. In both cases, the existence of market power distorts the outcome and causes deadweight losses.

This book does not present the formal model of monopsony because, in the real world, monopsonies are rare although on a small scale, a number of towns in parts of Europe may be highly dependent on a major employer – a motor vehicle manufacturer, a steel works or chocolate manufacturer, for example. In such situations, the analysis may have to be amended to take into consideration the effect that monopoly power of the employer has on the local labour market. In most labour markets, however, workers have many possible employers, and firms compete with one another to attract workers. In this case, the model of supply and demand is the best one to use.

Quick Quiz How does immigration of workers affect labour supply, labour demand, the marginal product of labour and the equilibrium wage?

THE OTHER FACTORS OF PRODUCTION: LAND AND CAPITAL

We have seen how firms decide how much labour to hire and how these decisions determine workers' wages. At the same time that firms are hiring workers, they are also deciding about other inputs to production. For example, our apple-producing firm might have to choose the size of its apple orchard and the number of ladders to make available to its apple pickers. We can think of the firm's factors of production as falling into three categories: labour, land and capital.

Economists use the term **capital** to refer to the stock of equipment and structures used for production – they are not used for their own sake but for what they can contribute to production. The economy's capital represents the accumulation of goods produced in the past that are being used in the present to produce new goods and services. For our apple firm, the capital stock includes the ladders used to climb the trees, the baskets that are used to collect the picked apples, trucks used to transport the apples, the buildings used to store the apples, and even the trees themselves.

capital
the equipment and structures used to produce goods and services

Equilibrium in the Markets for Land and Capital

What determines how much the owners of land and capital earn for their contribution to the production process? Before answering this question, we need to distinguish between two prices: the purchase price and the rental price. The *purchase price* of land or capital is the price a person pays to own that factor of production indefinitely. The *rental price* is the price a person pays to use that factor for a limited period of time. It is important to keep this distinction in mind because, as we will see, these prices are determined by somewhat different economic forces.

Having defined these terms, we can now apply the theory of factor demand that we developed for the labour market to the markets for land and capital. The wage is, after all, simply the rental price of labour. Therefore, much of what we have learned about wage determination applies also to the rental prices of land and capital. As Figure 18.8 illustrates, the rental price of land, shown in panel (a), and the rental price of capital, shown in panel (b), are determined by supply and demand. Moreover, the demand for land and capital is determined just like the demand for labour. That is, when our apple-producing firm is deciding how much land and how many ladders to rent, it follows the same logic as when deciding how many workers to hire. For both land and capital, the firm increases the quantity hired until the value of the factor's marginal product equals the factor's price. Thus, the demand curve for each factor reflects the marginal productivity of that factor.

We can now explain how much income goes to labour, how much goes to landowners and how much goes to the owners of capital. As long as the firms using the factors of production are competitive and profit-maximizing, each factor's rental price must equal the value of the marginal product for that factor: labour, land and capital each earn the value of their marginal contribution to the production process.

FIGURE 18.8

The Markets for Land and Capital

Supply and demand determine the compensation paid to the owners of land, as shown in panel (a), and the compensation paid to the owners of capital, as shown in panel (b). The demand for each factor, in turn, depends on the value of the marginal product of that factor.

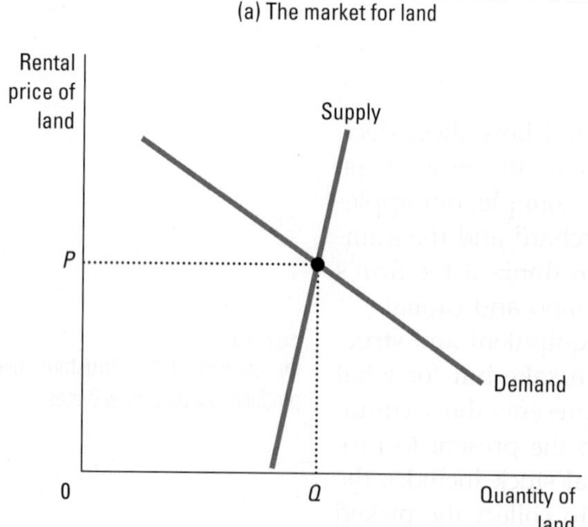

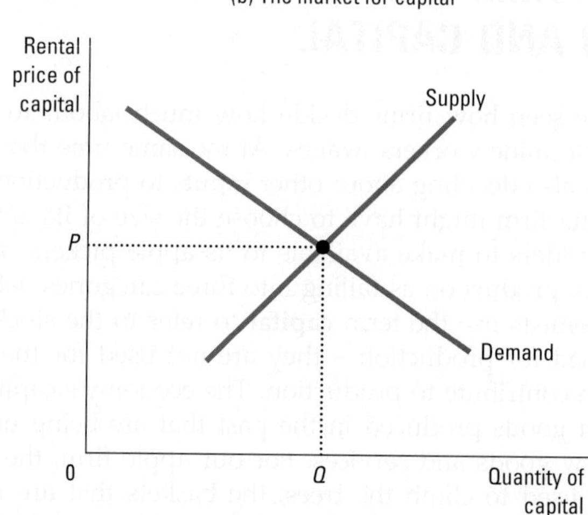

Now consider the purchase price of land and capital. The rental price and the purchase price are obviously related: buyers are willing to pay more for a piece of land or capital if it produces a valuable stream of rental income. And, as we have just seen, the equilibrium rental income at any point in time equals the value of that factor's marginal product. Therefore, the equilibrium purchase price of a piece of land or capital depends on both the current value of the marginal product and the value of the marginal product expected to prevail in the future.

Linkages Among the Factors of Production

We have seen that the price paid to any factor of production – labour, land, or capital – equals the value of the marginal product of that factor. The marginal product of any factor, in turn, depends on the quantity of that factor that is available. Because of diminishing marginal product, a factor in abundant supply has a low marginal product and thus a low price, and a factor in scarce supply has a high marginal product and a high price. As a result, when the supply of a factor falls, its equilibrium factor price rises.

When the supply of any factor changes, however, the effects are not limited to the market for that factor. In most situations, factors of production are used

FYI

What is Capital Income?

Labour income is an easy concept to understand: it is the wages and salaries that workers get from their employers. The income earned by capital, however, is less obvious.

In our analysis, we have been implicitly assuming that households own the economy's stock of capital – equipment, machinery, computers, warehouses and so forth – and rent it to the firms that use it. Capital income, in this case, is the rent that households receive for the use of their capital. This assumption simplified our analysis of how capital owners are compensated, but it is not entirely realistic. In fact, firms usually own the capital they use and, therefore, they receive the earnings from this capital.

These earnings from capital, however, eventually get paid to households. Some of the earnings are paid in the form of interest to those households who have lent money to firms (anyone who has savings in a financial institution, who pays into a pension fund or an insurance policy is indirectly actually lending money to businesses!). Bondholders and bank depositors are two examples of recipients of interest. Thus, when you receive interest on your bank account, that income is part of the economy's capital income.

In addition, some of the earnings from capital are paid to households in the form of dividends. Dividends are payments by a firm to the firm's shareholders. A shareholder is a person who has bought a share in the ownership of the firm and, therefore, is entitled to share in the firm's profits. (This is usually called an equity or, quite simply, a share.)

A firm does not have to pay out all of its earnings to households in the form of interest and dividends. Instead, it can retain some earnings within the firm and use these earnings to buy additional capital. Although these retained earnings do not get paid to the firm's shareholders, the shareholders benefit from them nonetheless. Because retained earnings increase the amount of capital the firm owns, they tend to increase future earnings and, thereby, the value of the firm's equities.

These institutional details are interesting and important, but they do not alter our conclusion about the income earned by the owners of capital. Capital is paid according to the value of its marginal product, regardless of whether this income gets transmitted to households in the form of interest or dividends or whether it is kept within firms as retained earnings.

together in a way that makes the productivity of each factor dependent on the quantities of the other factors available to be used in the production process. As a result, a change in the supply of any one factor alters the earnings of all the factors.

For example, suppose one night lightning strikes the storehouse in which are kept the ladders that the apple pickers use to pick apples from the orchards, and many of the ladders are destroyed in the ensuing fire. What happens to the earnings of the various factors of production? Most obviously, the supply of ladders falls and, therefore, the equilibrium rental price of ladders rises. Those owners who were lucky enough to avoid damage to their ladders now earn a higher return when they rent out their ladders to the firms that produce apples.

Yet the effects of this event do not stop at the ladder market. Because there are fewer ladders with which to work, the workers who pick apples have a smaller marginal product. Thus, the reduction in the supply of ladders reduces the demand for the labour of apple pickers, and this causes the equilibrium wage to fall.

This story shows a general lesson: an event that changes the supply of any factor of production can alter the earnings of all the factors. The change in earnings of any factor can be found by analysing the impact of the event on the value of the marginal product of that factor.

CASE STUDY

The Economics of the Black Death

© PICTORIAL PRESS LTD / ALAMY

Workers who survived the plague were lucky in more ways than one.

In 14th-century Europe, the bubonic plague wiped out about one-third of the population within a few years. This event, called the *Black Death,* provides a grisly natural experiment to test the theory of factor markets that we have just developed. Consider the effects of the Black Death on those who were lucky enough to survive. What do you think happened to the wages earned by workers and the rents earned by landowners?

To answer this question, let's examine the effects of a reduced population on the marginal product of labour and the marginal product of land. With a smaller supply of workers, the marginal product of labour rises. (This is simply diminishing marginal product working in reverse.) Thus, we would expect the Black Death to raise wages.

Because land and labour are used together in production, a smaller supply of workers also affects the market for land, the other major factor of production in medieval Europe. With fewer workers available to farm the land, an additional unit of land produced less additional output. In other words, the marginal product of land fell. Thus, we would expect the Black Death to lower rents.

In fact, both predictions are consistent with the historical evidence. Wages approximately doubled during this period, and rents declined 50 per cent or more. The Black Death led to economic prosperity for the peasant classes and reduced incomes for the landed classes.

Quick Quiz What determines the income of the owners of land and capital? • How would an increase in the quantity of capital affect the incomes of those who already own capital? How would it affect the incomes of workers?

IN THE NEWS

The recession of 2008–09 had a major impact on productivity levels in many European countries, in the US and the Far East. The decline in productivity in different countries is important because it can not only affect standards of living but also international competitiveness. This article looks at the early evidence of changes in productivity at the start of the recession.

Labour Productivity, the Recession and Standards of Living

Europe suffered a slowdown in labour productivity growth in 2007 as measured by growth in output per hour worked, as the business cycle passed its peak and structural reform remained sluggish. The latest annual productivity report from The Conference Board, the international business membership and research organization, shows output per hour worked rose by 1.4 per cent across the 27 European Union states in 2007, down from 1.7 per cent the previous year. It is expected to slow further, to 1.3 per cent, in 2008 in the EU27, and even to 1 per cent in the 'old' 15 member EU. For the second year running, however, Europe performed better than the US, where productivity rose by just 1.1 per cent.

The disappointing European average was the result of weak productivity growth in a number of major economies, including Germany (1 per cent), France (0.6 per cent), Italy (1 per cent) and Spain (0.6 per cent). But it masked some impressive performances, most notably in the UK where productivity rose by 2.9 per cent, making it the top performer among the EU15. Recession concerns and the credit crunch cloud the US economic outlook for 2008, but US productivity growth is expected to accelerate to 1.7 per cent in 2009, while Japan's rate is forecast to pick up to 1.9 per cent.

Despite better European performance in the past two years, the US maintains its productivity edge over the longer term. Innovation is more deeply embedded in the business process in the United States, particularly in service industries. Large investments in information and communications technology (ICT) have gone together with rapid increases in efficiency, which are not found in Europe and Japan. However, Irish labour productivity has been boosted because of the overwhelming dominance of US companies in the Irish economy.

Despite the slow increase in US labour productivity, the level of GDP per hour worked is still among the highest in the advanced economies. In 2007, output per hour worked was US$52.10 – very close to the levels of France, The Netherlands, and Austria, and only significantly behind two smaller economies: Norway ($70.10) and Luxembourg ($70.30). An illustration of the choices that can be made where high levels of labour productivity coincide with low unemployment is provided by Austria and the US. Austria has higher output per worker than the US and similar levels of employment, but its employees work 15 per cent fewer hours a year reducing its GDP per person to 15 per cent below US levels.

Meanwhile, in emerging economies, productivity growth continued to accelerate, topping 8 per cent in the BRIC (Brazil, Russia, India, China) countries on average in 2007, accelerating from 7.5 per cent between 2000 and 2005. There were large differences between the individual economies, however, with China notching up 10.6 per cent growth while Brazil managed just 1.9 per cent. Productivity levels in emerging economies are still very low at between 10 per cent and 40 per cent of the US level. However, as the wage gaps are generally even larger, the labour cost per unit of output provides a cost competitiveness advantage to emerging economies which for manufacturing can be as low as 20 per cent of the US level.

The report warns that advanced economies will need to raise annual productivity growth to well above 2 per cent over the next two decades to maintain current living standards. Given the limits to labour force growth almost everywhere, the onus will be on technology and innovation to drive the growth process. Indeed, one of the most significant changes is the emphasis on innovation-related spending in the emerging world. While expenditure on research and development (R&D) and investment in information and communication technology in emerging economies are still at less than half of the level in advanced economies, the spending gap is narrowing. This reflects a commitment to compete on the basis of innovation capacity not just cost.

Source: http://www.finfacts.com/irelandbusinessnews/publish/article_1012338.shtml and http://www.conference-board.org/pdf_free/Productivity2008Briefing.pdf

CONCLUSION

The theory developed in this chapter is called the *neoclassical theory of distribution*. According to the neoclassical theory, the amount paid to each factor of production depends on the supply and demand for that factor. The demand, in turn, depends on that particular factor's marginal productivity. In equilibrium, each factor of production earns the value of its marginal contribution to the production of goods and services.

The neoclassical theory of distribution is widely accepted. Most economists begin with the neoclassical theory when trying to explain how an economy's income is distributed among the economy's various members. In the following two chapters, we consider the distribution of income in more detail. As you will see, the neoclassical theory provides the framework for this discussion.

Even at this point you can use the theory to answer the question that began this chapter: why are computer programmers paid more than petrol station attendants? It is because programmers can produce a good of greater market value than can a petrol station attendant. People are willing to pay dearly for a good computer game, but they are willing to pay little to have their petrol pumped and their windscreen washed. The wages of these workers reflect the market prices of the goods they produce. If people suddenly got tired of using computers and decided to spend more time driving, the prices of these goods would change, and so would the equilibrium wages of these two groups of workers.

SUMMARY

- The economy's income is distributed in the markets for the factors of production. The three most important factors of production are labour, land and capital.
- The demand for factors, such as labour, is a derived demand that comes from firms that use the factors to produce goods and services. Competitive, profit-maximizing firms hire each factor up to the point at which the value of the marginal product of the factor equals its price.
- The supply of labour arises from individuals' trade-off between work and leisure. An upward sloping labour supply curve means that people respond to an increase in the wage by enjoying less leisure and working more hours.
- The price paid to each factor adjusts to balance the supply and demand for that factor. Because factor demand reflects the value of the marginal product of that factor, in equilibrium each factor is compensated according to its marginal contribution to the production of goods and services.
- Because factors of production are used together, the marginal product of any one factor depends on the quantities of all factors that are available. As a result, a change in the supply of one factor alters the equilibrium earnings of all the factors.

KEY CONCEPTS

factors of production, p. 383
production function, p. 384
marginal product of labour, p. 385
value of the marginal product, p. 386
capital, p. 395

QUESTIONS FOR REVIEW

1. Explain how a firm's production function is related to its marginal product of labour, how a firm's marginal product of labour is related to the value of its marginal product and how a firm's value of marginal product is related to its demand for labour.
2. Give two examples of events that could shift the demand for labour.
3. Give two examples of events that could shift the supply of labour.
4. Explain how the wage can adjust to balance the supply and demand for labour while simultaneously equalling the value of the marginal product of labour.
5. If the population of Norway suddenly grew because of a large immigration, what would you expect to happen to wages? What would happen to the rents earned by the owners of land and capital?

PROBLEMS AND APPLICATIONS

1. Suppose that the government proposes a new law aimed at reducing heath care costs: all citizens are to be required to eat one apple daily.
   a. How would this apple-a-day law affect the demand and equilibrium price of apples?
   b. How would the law affect the marginal product and the value of the marginal product of apple pickers?
   c. How would the law affect the demand and equilibrium wage for apple pickers?
2. Show the effect of each of the following events on the market for labour in the computer manufacturing industry.
   a. The government buys personal computers for all university students.
   b. More university students graduate in engineering and computer science.
   c. Computer firms build new manufacturing factories.
3. Your enterprising uncle opens a sandwich shop that employs 7 people. The employees are paid €6 per hour and a sandwich sells for €13. If your uncle is maximizing his profit, what is the value of the marginal product of the last worker he hired? What is that worker's marginal product?
4. Imagine a firm that hires two types of workers – some with computer skills and some without. If technology advances so that computers become more useful to the firm, what happens to the marginal product of the two types? What happens to equilibrium wages? Explain, using appropriate diagrams.
5. Suppose a harsh winter in Normandy destroys part of the French apple crop.
   a. Explain what happens to the price of apples and the marginal product of apple pickers as a result of the freeze. Can you say what happens to the demand for apple pickers? Why or why not?
   b. Suppose the price of apples doubles and the marginal product falls by 30 per cent. What happens to the equilibrium wage of apple pickers?
   c. Suppose the price of apples rises by 30 per cent and the marginal product falls by 50 per cent. What happens to the equilibrium wage of apple pickers?
6. In recent years, the United Kingdom has experienced a significant inflow of capital in the form of direct investment, especially from the Far East. For example, both Honda and Nissan have built car plants in the United Kingdom.
   a. Using a diagram of the UK capital market, show the effect of this inflow on the rental price of capital in the United Kingdom and on the quantity of capital in use.
   b. Using a diagram of the UK labour market, show the effect of the capital inflow on the average wage paid to UK workers.
7. Suppose that labour is the only input used by a perfectly competitive firm that can hire workers for €150 per day. The firm's production function is as follows:

Days of labour	Units of output
0	0
1	7
2	13
3	19
4	25
5	28
6	29

Each unit of output sells for €110. Plot the firm's demand for labour. How many days of labour should the firm hire? Show this point on your graph.

8. (This question is challenging.) This chapter has assumed that labour is supplied by individual workers acting competitively. In some markets, however, the supply of labour is determined by a union of workers.
   a. Explain why the situation faced by a labour union may resemble the situation faced by a monopoly firm.
   b. The goal of a monopoly firm is to maximize profits. Is there an analogous goal for labour unions?
   c. Now extend the analogy between monopoly firms and unions. How do you suppose that the wage set by a union compares to the wage in a competitive market? How do you suppose employment differs in the two cases?
   d. What other goals might unions have that make unions different from monopoly firms?

For further resources, visit www.cengage.com/mankiw_taylor2

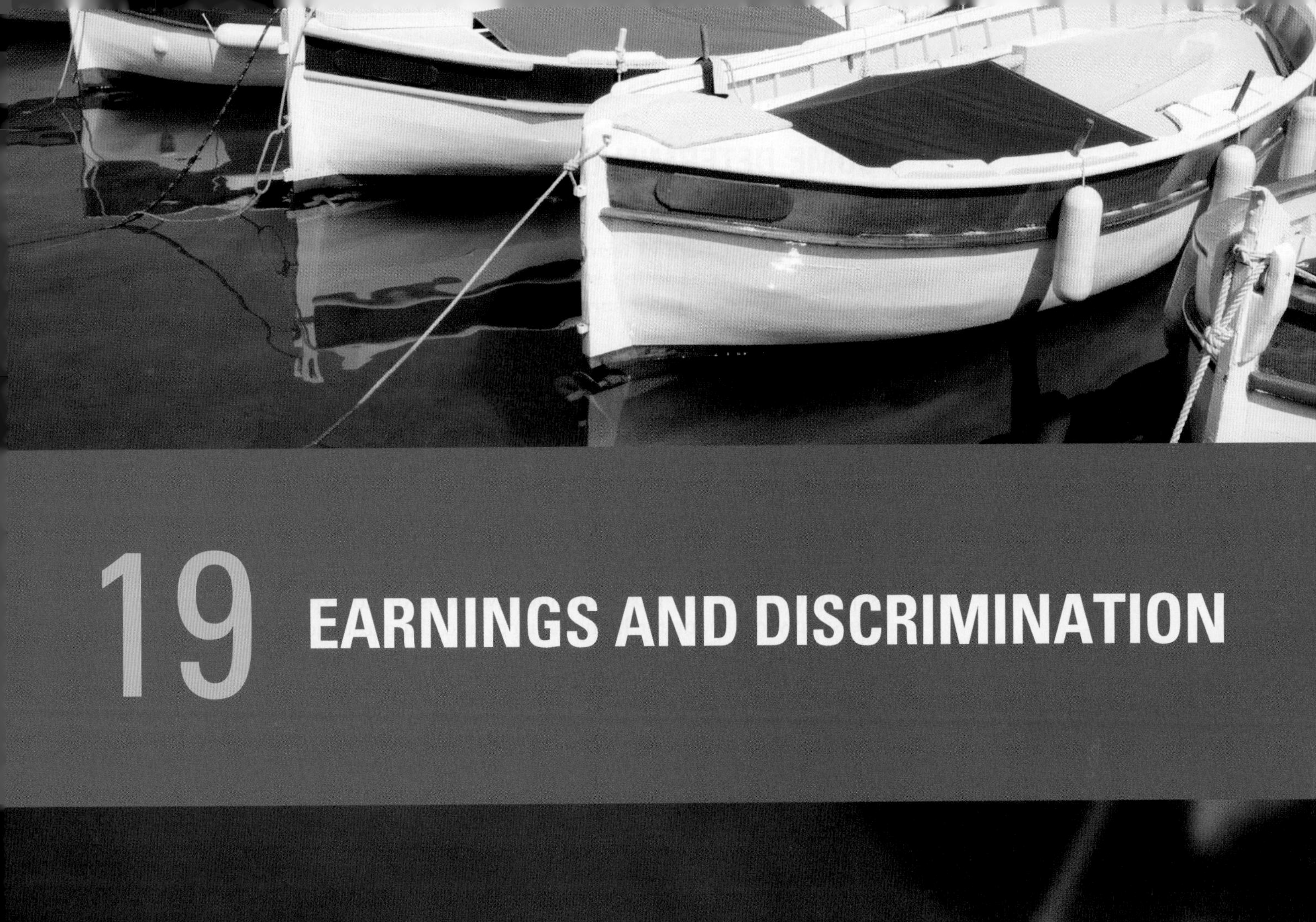

19 EARNINGS AND DISCRIMINATION

In the United Kingdom today, a successful barrister will earn in excess of £200 000 a year, a typical doctor in general practice about £118 000, an experienced secondary school teacher around £35 000 and a bus driver with over ten years experience around £23 000. In Switzerland a long-haul airline pilot with 20 years experience can expect to earn around €157 000 whilst an outsourcing manager is paid around €80 000 and a sales associate around €45 000. These examples illustrate the large differences in earnings that are so common in a modern economy. The differences explain why some people live in large houses, drive expensive cars and go on holiday to exotic places, while other people live in small houses or apartments, take the bus and seldom go abroad for a holiday.

Why do earnings vary so much from person to person? Chapter 18, which developed the basic neoclassical theory of the labour market, offers an answer to this question. There we saw that wages are governed by labour supply and labour demand. Labour demand, in turn, reflects the marginal productivity of labour. In equilibrium, each worker is paid the value of his or her marginal contribution to the economy's production of goods and services.

This theory of the labour market, though widely accepted by economists, is only the beginning of the story. To understand the wide variation in earnings that we observe, we must go beyond this general framework and examine more precisely what determines the supply and demand for different types of labour. That is our goal in this chapter.

SOME DETERMINANTS OF EQUILIBRIUM WAGES

Workers differ from one another in many ways. Jobs also have differing characteristics – both in terms of the wage they pay and in terms of their non-monetary attributes. In this section we consider how the characteristics of workers and jobs affect labour supply, labour demand and equilibrium wages.

Compensating Differentials

When a worker is deciding whether to take a job, the wage is only one of many job attributes that the worker takes into account. Some jobs require few skills, and are 'easy' and safe; others might require considerable skill, experience and may be very dull, whilst others can be very dangerous. The 'better' the job as gauged by these non-monetary characteristics, the more people there are who are willing (and able) to do the job at any given wage. In other words, the supply of labour for jobs requiring few skills or no experience is greater than the supply of labour for highly skilled, and dangerous jobs. As a result, 'good' jobs will tend to have lower equilibrium wages than 'bad' jobs.

For example, imagine you are looking for a summer job at a seaside holiday resort. Two kinds of jobs are available. You can take a job hiring out sunbeds on the beach, or you can take one as a refuse collector. The sunbed attendants take leisurely strolls along the beach during the day and check to make sure the holidaymakers have paid for the hire of their sunbeds. The refuse collectors wake up before dawn to drive dirty, noisy lorries around town to pick up rubbish from households and firms. Which job would you want? Most people would prefer the beach job if the wages were the same. To induce people to become refuse collectors, the town has to offer higher wages to refuse collectors than to sunbed attendants.

compensating differential
a difference in wages that arises to offset the non-monetary characteristics of different jobs

Economists use the term **compensating differential** to refer to a difference in wages that arises from non-monetary characteristics of different jobs. Compensating differentials are prevalent in the economy. Here are some examples:

- Workers who maintain and repair major roads such as motorways, are paid more than other public sector workers who repair roads in towns and cities. This is because the danger level of working on major roads is much higher, not to mention the fact that they often have to work unsociable hours (when drivers are not using the motorways).
- Workers who work night shifts at factories and in other forms of employment such as 24-hour retail outlets are paid more than similar workers who work day shifts. The higher wage compensates them for having to work at night and sleep during the day, a lifestyle that most people find undesirable (and disorientating!).
- University lecturers and professors are on average paid less than lawyers and doctors, who have similar levels of education. Lecturers' lower wages compensate them for the great intellectual and personal satisfaction that their jobs offer. (Indeed, teaching economics is so much fun that it is surprising that economics professors get paid anything at all!)

We're hoping to employ a workaholic for whom job-satisfaction is reward enough.
Meehan

Human Capital

As we discussed in the previous chapter, the word *capital* usually refers to the economy's stock of equipment and structures. The capital stock includes the farmer's tractor, the manufacturer's factory and the teacher's laptop. The essence of capital is that it is a factor of production that itself has been produced.

There is another type of capital that, while less tangible than physical capital, is just as important to the economy's production. **Human capital** is the accumulation of investments in people. The most important type of human capital is education. Like all forms of capital, education represents an expenditure of resources at one point in time to raise productivity in the future. But, unlike an investment in other forms of capital, an investment in education is tied to a specific person, and this linkage is what makes it human capital.

human capital
the accumulation of investments in people, such as education and on-the-job training

Not surprisingly, workers with more human capital on average earn more than those with less human capital. University graduates in Europe and North America, for example, earn almost twice as much as those workers who end their education after secondary school. This large difference tends to be even larger in less developed countries, where educated workers are in scarce supply.

It is easy to see why education raises wages from the perspective of supply and demand. Firms – the demanders of labour – are willing to pay more for the highly educated because highly educated workers have higher marginal products. Workers – the suppliers of labour – are willing to pay the cost of becoming educated only if there is a reward for doing so. In essence, the difference in wages between highly educated workers and less educated workers may be considered a compensating differential for the cost of becoming educated.

Ability, Effort and Chance

Why do football players in the top European leagues such as the English Premiership or the Spanish *La Liga* get paid more than those in the minor leagues? Certainly, the higher wage is not a compensating differential. Playing in the major leagues is associated with more glamour and prestige as well as the, often considerably, higher wages. The major leagues do not necessarily require more years of schooling or more experience. To a large extent, players in the major leagues earn more just because they have greater natural ability.

Natural ability is important for workers in all occupations. Because of heredity and upbringing, people differ in their physical and mental attributes. Some people have physical and mental strength whereas others have less of both. Some people are able to solve complex problems, others less so. Some people are outgoing, others awkward in social situations. These and many other personal characteristics determine how productive workers are and, therefore, play a role in determining the wages they earn.

Closely related to ability is effort. Some people are prepared to put in long hours and considerable effort into their work whereas others are content to do what they are required to do and no more. We should not be surprised to find that those who put in more effort may be more productive and earn higher wages. To some extent, firms reward workers directly by paying people on the basis of what they produce. Salespeople, for instance, are often paid based on a percentage of the sales they make. At other times, greater effort is rewarded less directly in the form of a higher annual salary or a bonus.

Chance also plays a role in determining wages. If a person attended college to learn how to repair televisions with vacuum tubes and then found this skill made obsolete by the invention of solid-state electronics, he or she would end up earning a low wage compared to others with similar years of training. The low wage of this worker is due to chance – a phenomenon that economists recognize but do not shed much light on.

How important are ability, effort and chance in determining wages? It is hard to say, because ability, effort and chance are hard to measure. But indirect evidence suggests that they are very important. When labour economists study wages, they relate a worker's wage to those variables that can be measured – years of schooling, years of experience, age and job characteristics. Although all of these measured variables affect a worker's wage as theory predicts, they account for less than half of the variation in wages in our economy. Because so much of the variation in wages is left unexplained, omitted variables, including ability, effort and chance, must play an important role.

CASE STUDY

© ALLSTAR PICTURE LIBRARY / ALAMY

Brad Pitt: good looks pay.

The Benefits of Beauty

People differ in many ways. One difference is in how attractive they are. Indeed, the idea of beauty is something that is not simply personal – the so-called 'golden ratio' plays a part in our perception of beauty. Those people whose faces and bodies conform most closely to the proportions outlined in the golden ratio are generally seen as being 'beautiful'! Both females and males generally agree that Brad Pitt is a handsome man. In part for this reason, his films attract large audiences. Not surprisingly, the large audiences mean a large income for Mr Pitt.

How prevalent are the economic benefits of beauty? Labour economists Daniel Hamermesh and Jeff Biddle tried to answer this question in a study published in the December 1994 issue of the *American Economic Review*. Hamermesh and Biddle examined data from surveys of individuals in the United States and Canada. The interviewers who conducted the survey were asked to rate each respondent's physical appearance. Hamermesh and Biddle then examined how much the wages of the respondents depended on the standard determinants – education, experience and so on – and how much they depended on physical appearance.

The researchers found that beauty pays. People who are deemed to be more attractive than average earn 5 per cent more than people of average looks. People of average looks earn 5 to 10 per cent more than people considered less attractive than average. Similar results were found for men and women.

What explains these differences in wages? There are several ways to interpret the 'beauty premium.'

One interpretation is that good looks are themselves a type of innate ability determining productivity and wages. Some people are born with the attributes of a film star; other people are not. Good looks are useful in any job in which workers present themselves to the public – such as acting, sales and waiting on tables. In this case, an attractive worker is more valuable to the firm than an unattractive worker. The firm's willingness to pay more to attractive workers reflects its customers' preferences.

A second interpretation is that reported beauty is an indirect measure of other types of ability. How attractive a person appears depends on more than just heredity. It also depends on dress, hairstyle, personal demeanour and other attributes that a person can control. Perhaps a person who successfully projects an attractive image in a survey interview is more likely to be an intelligent person who succeeds at other tasks as well.

A third interpretation is that the beauty premium is a type of discrimination, a topic to which we return later.

An Alternative View of Education: Signalling

Earlier we discussed the human capital view of education, according to which schooling raises workers' wages because it makes them more productive.

Although this view is widely accepted, some economists have proposed an alternative theory, which emphasizes that firms use educational attainment as a way of sorting between high-ability and low-ability workers. According to this alternative view, when people earn a university degree, for instance, they do not become more productive, but they do *signal* their high ability to prospective employers. Because it is easier for high-ability people to earn a university degree than it is for low-ability people, more high-ability people get college degrees. As a result, it is rational for firms to interpret a college degree as a signal of ability.

The signalling theory of education is similar to the signalling theory of advertising discussed in Chapter 16. In the signalling theory of advertising, the advertisement itself contains no real information, but the firm signals the quality of its product to consumers by its willingness to spend money on advertising. In the signalling theory of education, schooling has no real productivity benefit, but the worker signals his innate productivity to employers by his willingness to spend years at school. In both cases, an action is being taken not for its intrinsic benefit but because the willingness to take that action conveys private information to someone observing it.

Thus, we now have two views of education: the human capital theory and the signalling theory. Both views can explain why more educated workers tend to earn more than less educated workers. According to the human capital view, education makes workers more productive; according to the signalling view, education is correlated with natural ability. But the two views have radically different predictions for the effects of policies that aim to increase educational attainment. According to the human capital view, increasing educational levels for all workers would raise all workers' productivity and thereby their wages. According to the signalling view, education does not enhance productivity, so raising all workers' educational levels would not affect wages.

Most likely, the truth lies somewhere between these two extremes. The benefits to education are probably a combination of the productivity enhancing effects of human capital and the productivity revealing effects of signalling. The open question is the relative size of these two effects.

The Superstar Phenomenon

Although most actors earn little and often take jobs as waiters to support themselves, Julia Roberts earns millions of pounds for each film she makes. Similarly, while most people who play tennis do it for free as a hobby, Roger Federer earns millions on the professional circuit. Julia Roberts and Roger Federer are superstars in their fields, and their great public appeal is reflected in astronomical incomes.

Why do Julia Roberts and Roger Federer earn so much? It is not surprising that there are differences in incomes within occupations. Good carpenters earn more than mediocre carpenters, and good plumbers earn more than mediocre plumbers. People vary in ability and effort, and these differences lead to differences in income. Yet the best carpenters and plumbers do not earn the many millions that are common among the best actors and athletes. What explains the difference? To understand the tremendous incomes of Julia Roberts and Roger Federer, we must examine the special features of the markets in which they sell their services. Superstars arise in markets that have two characteristics:

- Every customer in the market wants to enjoy the good supplied by the best producer.
- The good is produced with a technology that makes it possible for the best producer to supply every customer at low cost.

Julia Roberts: popularity + technology = superstar.

If Julia Roberts is the best actor around, then everyone will want to see her next film; seeing twice as many films by an actor half as good is not a good substitute. Moreover, it is *possible* for everyone to enjoy Julia Roberts' acting skills. Because it is easy to make multiple copies of a film, Julia Roberts can provide her service to millions of people simultaneously. Julia Roberts is the top ranking actress by total box office gross of all movies. The 37 movies she has appeared in (at the time of writing) grossed a total of $2 286 622 342, an average of $74.8 million per movie; that's a considerable value of marginal product to the film producers! Similarly, because tennis games are broadcast on television, millions of fans can enjoy the extraordinary athletic skills of Roger Federer.

We can now see why there are no superstar carpenters and plumbers. Other things equal, everyone prefers to employ the best carpenter, but a carpenter, unlike a film actor, can provide his services to only a limited number of customers. Although the best carpenter will be able to command a somewhat higher wage than the average carpenter, the average carpenter will still be able to earn a good living.

IN THE NEWS

The debate over education and its value is a recurring theme in politics, and economics has some contribution to make to the debate. Paying for education represents a significant cost for most economies but part of the justification lies in the benefits that accrue to society as well as the individual. The benefits, however, do vary depending on the individual and the course followed as this article highlights.

A Degree of Value?

If you are reading this book then it is highly likely that you are studying for a degree, possibly in economics but possibly in a number of other disciplines which may require some study of economics. The fact that students with degrees have greater earnings potential than non-graduates is well known and is one of the reasons why people go to university in the first place. In the UK there has been a drive to increase the number of people going to university with the Labour government, who were in power from 1997–2010, having a target of 50 per cent of school leavers going to higher education. This has led to an increase in the number of people gaining degrees. A report by the Organization for Economic Cooperation and Development (OECD) published in September 2009 confirmed that going to university pays dividends in later life. A male student with a university degree can expect to earn $186 000 (gross) more over their lifetime than a male who leaves at the end of secondary school. This is an average across the OECD countries. For females, the average is around $134 000. The US is the country where graduates can expect to earn most with Italy and Portugal also high up on the premium earnings list.

It is not only the individual who benefits, governments do as well. Education is an investment by government and the individual. There are plenty of upfront costs for governments in providing high quality education provision and for the individual continuing in education also means that there are potential earnings foregone whilst studying. The OECD report shows that the average member government will gain a net return of $52 000 in higher tax revenue from an average male student.

The number of people across Europe gaining degrees is increasing. The OECD states that one in three people in OECD countries between the ages of 25 and 34 have a tertiary level qualification and in many countries the increase in those gaining higher education qualifications is increasing. In OECD countries the increase is 4.5 per cent a year between 1998 and 2006 on average but in Ireland, Turkey, Poland, Portugal and Spain the increase has been 7 per cent and more over this period. This may be socially desirable but also presents some problems. In the UK the increasing number of people with degrees means that the job market for graduates is tough. Thirty years ago, having a degree meant an individual was relatively unusual but today the graduate market is saturated and so choice of degree is becoming more important along with the class of degree. It is almost getting to the stage where a postgraduate degree is becoming the norm to help potential employees stand out in the graduate job market!

So what sort of degree should an individual study to give themselves the best chance of getting employment which pays? Yu Zhu of the Economics Department of the University of Kent suggests that the average percentage premium for UK graduates in particular subjects compared to those without a degree but at least two 'A' levels (qualifications which can be gained in the 16–18 age range) varies widely (see Table 19.1). Economics graduates, for example, can gain a premium of 41.6 per cent for males and 68 per cent for females. Other studies show slightly different outcomes but it is clear that certain degrees may be more valuable to future employers if lifetime earnings are anything to go by.

Those studying chemistry and physics, for example, perform well although many do not 'take off' in terms of earnings until after they reach their thirties. Law and management degrees also fare well but medicine may not be as valuable in terms of earnings as other science based degrees partly because the costs of training have to be factored into lifetime earnings. Science-based degrees also have the potential to open up a number of doors for students and, like those who study economics, students may have the ability to transfer a wide range of skills to a variety of different employers and so have the potential to be highly productive to a range of industries.

TABLE 19.1

Average Percentage Premium that Graduates Earned over Those Without a Degree but With Two or More 'A' levels, 1996–2006

Degree subject	Men	Women
Economics	41.6	68.0
Health	39.4	61.8
Business/Management	38.4	53.2
Science	20.6	40.6
Maths/Statistics	34.1	63.9
English	26.9	46.5
Law	37.9	60.7
Education	12.6	52.5
Social science	12.0	35.8
Languages	11.5	45.5
Arts/Humanities	0.4	27.9

Source: Yu Zhu (Department of Economics, Kent University), based on data in the *Labour Force Survey*, HMSO 2007.

Above-Equilibrium Wages: Minimum Wage Laws, Unions and Efficiency Wages

Most analyses of wage differences among workers are based on the equilibrium model of the labour market – that is, wages are assumed to adjust to balance labour supply and labour demand. But this assumption does not always apply. For some workers, wages are set above the level that brings supply and demand into equilibrium. Let's consider three reasons why this might be so.

One reason for above-equilibrium wages is minimum wage laws, as we first saw in Chapter 6. Most workers in the economy are not affected by these laws because their equilibrium wages are well above the legal minimum. But for some workers, especially the least skilled and experienced, minimum wage laws raise wages above the level they would earn in an unregulated labour market.

union
a worker association that bargains with employers over wages and working conditions

A second reason that wages might rise above their equilibrium level is the market power of labour unions. A **union** is a worker association that bargains with employers over wages and working conditions. Unions often raise wages above

strike
the organized withdrawal of labour from a firm by a union

efficiency wages
above-equilibrium wages paid by firms in order to increase worker productivity

the level that would prevail without a union, perhaps because they can threaten to withhold labour from the firm by calling a **strike**. Studies suggest that union workers earn about 10 to 20 per cent more than similar non-union workers.

A third reason for above-equilibrium wages is suggested by the theory of **efficiency wages**. This theory holds that a firm can find it profitable to pay high wages because doing so increases the productivity of its workers. In particular, high wages may reduce worker turnover (hiring and training new workers is an expensive business), increase worker effort, and raise the quality of workers who apply for jobs at the firm. In addition, a firm may feel it has to offer high wages in order to attract and keep the best people – this has been an argument put forward by the banking sector in response to plans by governments in Europe to tax bankers' earning in the wake of the financial crisis. If this theory is correct, then some firms may choose to pay their workers more than they would normally earn.

Above-equilibrium wages, whether caused by minimum wage laws, unions or efficiency wages, have similar effects on the labour market. In particular, pushing a wage above the equilibrium level raises the quantity of labour supplied and reduces the quantity of labour demanded. The result is a surplus of labour, or unemployment. The study of unemployment and the public policies aimed to deal with it is usually considered a topic within macroeconomics, so it goes beyond the scope of this chapter. But it would be a mistake to ignore these issues completely when analysing earnings. Although most wage differences can be understood while maintaining the assumption of equilibrium in the labour market, above-equilibrium wages play a role in some cases.

Quick Quiz Define *compensating differential* and give an example.
• Give two reasons why more educated workers earn more than less educated workers.

THE ECONOMICS OF DISCRIMINATION

discrimination
the offering of different opportunities to similar individuals who differ only by race, ethnic group, sex, age or other personal characteristics

Another source of differences in wages is discrimination. **Discrimination** occurs when the marketplace offers different opportunities to similar individuals who differ only by race, ethnic group, sex, age or other personal characteristics. Discrimination reflects some people's prejudice against certain groups in society. Although discrimination is an emotionally charged topic that often generates heated debate, economists try to study the topic objectively in order to separate myth from reality.

Measuring Labour Market Discrimination

How much does discrimination in labour markets affect the earnings of different groups of workers? This question is important, but answering it is not easy.

There is no doubt that different groups of workers earn substantially different wages. An interesting and particularly striking example of this is in the average amount of money earned by people belonging to different ethnic groups in the United States, as Table 19.2 demonstrates.

The situation in the UK and parts of Europe is not dissimilar. A report published in 2010 by the National Equality Panel[1] showed that inequalities in incomes and earnings are 'high' in Britain compared with other industrialized

[1]Hills, J *et al.* (2010). *An anatomy of economic inequality in the UK.* http://sticerd.lse.ac.uk/dps/case/cr/CASEreport60.pdf

TABLE 19.2

US Median Annual Earnings by Race and Sex

	White	Black	Percentage by which earnings are lower for black workers
Men	$41 982	$32 976	21%
Women	$32 173	$29 680	8%
Percentage by which earnings are lower for women workers	23%	10%	

Note: Earnings data are for the year 2005 and apply to full-time, year-round workers aged 14 and over.
Source: US Bureau of the Census.

countries, and considering figures from 30 years ago. Women, for example, earn 21 per cent less in terms of median hourly pay for all employees and 13 per cent less than men for those working full time. The Report also found that people from non-white ethnic backgrounds are paid less than white British men. Pakistani and Bangladeshi Muslim men and Black African Christian men earn between 13 and 21 per cent less than white British Christian men. Chinese men are one of the highest paid groups in Britain but they are paid 11 per cent less than would be expected given their qualifications. Women from nearly all ethno-religious backgrounds have pay which is anything between a quarter and a third less than their white British Christian male counterparts even with the same qualifications age and in the same occupation, according to the report.

In Germany women earned around 24 per cent less than men in 2009 compared with the European Union average of 18 per cent. Of the 27 member countries of the EU, only in Estonia, the Czech Republic, Austria and The Netherlands is there a higher gender gap in pay in favour of men. Pay differentials between men and women across Europe have hardly changed over the past 15 years according to the European Commission.

Taken at face value, these differentials look like evidence that US, UK and European employers discriminate against those from ethnic minorities and women. Yet there is a potential problem with this inference. Even in a labour market free of discrimination, different people have different wages. People differ in the amount of human capital they have and in the kinds of work they are able and willing to do. The wage differences we observe in the economy are, to some extent, attributable to the determinants of equilibrium wages we discussed in the preceding section. Simply observing differences in wages among broad groups – whites and blacks, men and women – does not prove that employers discriminate.

Consider, for example, the role of human capital. Whether an individual has a degree can account for some of these differences and as we have seen above, the type of degree can also have an impact. White male workers in the United States are about 75 per cent more likely to have a university degree than blacks. Thus, at least some of the difference between the wages of American whites and the wages of American blacks can be traced to differences in educational attainment. Moreover, human capital may be more important in explaining wage differentials than measures of years of schooling suggest. Historically, state schools in predominantly black areas of the United States have been of lower quality – as measured by expenditure, class size and so on – than state schools in predominantly white areas. Similarly, for many years, American schools – in common with European schools – directed girls away from science and mathematics courses, even though these subjects may have had greater value in the marketplace than some of the alternatives. If we could measure the quality as well as the quantity of education, the differences in human capital among these groups would seem even larger. The Federal Bureau of Statistics in Germany points out that gender pay differences in Germany may be due to a number of factors including differences in educational attainment, a high proportion of women work in part-time occupations (69 per cent of employed mothers in 2009) and the type of employment they go into; many of the jobs women enter tend to be low-skill, low-paid jobs.

Human capital acquired in the form of job experience can also help explain wage differences. In particular, women tend to have less job experience on average than men. One reason is that female labour force participation has increased in industrialized economies over the past several decades. Because of this historic change, in both Europe and North America, the average female worker today is younger than the average male worker. In addition, women are more likely to interrupt their careers to raise children. For both reasons, the experience of the average female worker is less than the experience of the average male worker.

Yet another source of wage differences is compensating differentials. Men and women do not always choose the same type of work, and this fact may help explain some of the earnings differential between men and women. For example, women are more likely to be personal assistants or receptionists and men are more likely to be lorry drivers. (Some people would argue that women get 'ushered' into these types of jobs because of stereotypes, but that is not the point here.) The relative wages of personal assistants, receptionists and lorry drivers depend in part on the working conditions of each job. Because these non-monetary aspects are hard to measure, it is difficult to gauge the practical importance of compensating differentials in explaining the wage differences that we observe.

In the end, the study of wage differences among groups does not establish any clear conclusion about the prevalence of discrimination in labour markets. Most economists believe that some of the observed wage differentials are attributable to discrimination, but there is no consensus about how much. The only conclusion about which economists are in consensus is a negative one: because the differences in average wages among groups in part reflect differences in human capital and job characteristics, they do not by themselves say anything about how much discrimination there is in the labour market.

Of course, differences in human capital among groups of workers may themselves reflect discrimination. The less rigorous curriculums historically offered to female students, for instance, can be considered a discriminatory practice. Similarly, the inferior schools historically available to black American students may be traced to prejudice on the part of city councils and school boards. But this kind of discrimination occurs long before the worker enters the labour market. In this case, the disease is political, even if the symptom is economic.

Discrimination by Employers

Let's now turn from measurement to the economic forces that lie behind discrimination in labour markets. If one group in society receives a lower wage than another group, even after controlling for human capital and job characteristics, who is to blame for this differential?

The answer is not obvious. It might seem natural to blame employers for discriminatory wage differences. After all, employers make the hiring decisions that determine labour demand and wages. If some groups of workers earn lower wages than they should, then it seems that employers are responsible. Yet many economists are sceptical of this easy answer. They believe that competitive, market economies provide a natural antidote to employer discrimination. That antidote is called the profit motive.

Imagine an economy in which workers are differentiated by their hair colour. Blondes and brunettes have the same skills, experience and work ethic. Yet, because of discrimination, employers prefer not to hire workers with blonde hair. Thus, the demand for blondes is lower than it otherwise would be. As a result, blondes earn a lower wage than brunettes.

How long can this wage differential persist? In this economy, there is an easy way for a firm to beat out its competitors: it can hire blonde workers. By hiring blondes, a firm pays lower wages and thus has lower costs than firms that hire brunettes. Over time, more and more 'blonde' firms enter the market to take advantage of this cost advantage. The existing 'brunette' firms have higher costs and, therefore, begin to lose money when faced with the new competitors. These losses induce the brunette firms to go out of business. Eventually, the entry of blonde firms and the exit of brunette firms cause the demand for blonde workers to rise and the demand for brunette workers to fall. This process continues until the wage differential disappears.

Put simply, business owners who care only about making money are at an advantage when competing against those who also care about discriminating. As a result, firms that do not discriminate tend to replace those that do. In this way, competitive markets have a natural remedy for employer discrimination.

CASE STUDY

Becker's 'Employer Taste' Model

As you might expect by now, economists have spent some time looking at the economics of discrimination. One important piece of research into this area is from Nobel Prize winner Gary Becker from the University of Chicago, who in 1971 revised his earlier 1957 work on the economics of discrimination. The basis of the employer taste model is that (for whatever reason) some employees will resist working with other employees, possibly because of gender or race. People may, therefore, have a 'taste' for only working with certain groups of people. Those outside this accepted group may end up being disadvantaged as a result.

Assume that a UK firm, which grows asparagus, hires workers to cut the spears. It has a choice of employing locals or migrant workers. Local people have a prejudice against migrant workers for some reason. Our analysis of a competitive firm assumes that workers will be employed up to the point at which the wage equals the marginal revenue product of labour. Assume that both local and migrant workers have the same level of productivity. If the firm has to employ workers at a going wage (which is above the minimum wage) then it may choose not to employ workers from the disadvantaged group because of the preferences of its core workforce. If, however, the firm is able to pay workers from the disadvantaged group lower wages then it faces a trade-off. There is an incentive for it to increase profits by employing these 'disadvantaged' workers – the migrant workers from Europe. If migrant workers were prepared to work for the minimum wage then the firm could lower its costs and increase profit as a result.

A discriminatory firm might employ some migrant workers but would pay these workers a lower wage to avoid upsetting their local workers. This is the 'employer taste' model – discrimination will exist because employers do not employ labour from certain genders, race, etc. unless the workers are prepared to accept lower wages. This discrimination may continue whilst there is some limit to the competition in the labour market – in this case it might be that all firms are prepared to act in the same way.

However, if there were other asparagus farms in the area who were not discriminatory then they might choose to hire all workers at the minimum wage which would increase its overall profits. Such a firm would also employ more workers (remember that the lower the wage rate the more workers a firm is willing to employ). There could be an influx of migrant workers to the area who are willing to take advantage of the jobs available. These non-discriminatory firms could not only produce more output but at a lower wage cost per unit and so make more profit possibly driving out the discriminatory firm from the industry.

In the UK, such a situation has manifested itself in recent years. The extension of membership of the EU in 2004 led to an increase in the number of migrant workers from countries such as Poland, Lithuania and the Czech Republic coming to Britain to find work. Many of these workers appeared willing to take on jobs that paid relatively low wages, such as cutting asparagus spears. In Cambridgeshire in the south-east of England, a large number found work on the farms in the region picking and packing fruit and vegetables. In the town of Wisbech, for example, there are over 2 000 'local' people who are unemployed but there have been around 9 000 migrant workers who have secured jobs in the area – mostly in jobs where the wages are traditionally low.

The sensitivity of the situation in Wisbech with some of the local unemployed blaming migrant workers for their lack of work is difficult. Some employers have been accused of exploiting migrant labour by paying them low wages but some counter that they are paying at least the minimum wage and that they find migrant workers not only willing to work for lower pay but also that their productivity levels are relatively high compared with some 'local' labour. In this case not only are migrant workers prepared to work for lower wages but their marginal product is higher at each price (wage). Some farmers claim that 'local' workers are not prepared to do the sort of work that is available and believe that it is too low paid. It seems that regardless of discrimination, employers are more concerned with getting value for money from their employees and are prepared to put profit before discrimination.

Discrimination by Customers and Governments

Although the profit motive is a strong force acting to eliminate discriminatory wage differentials, there are limits to its corrective abilities. Here we consider two of the most important limits: *customer preferences* and *government policies.*

To see how customer preferences for discrimination can affect wages, consider again our imaginary economy with blondes and brunettes. Suppose that restaurant owners discriminate against blondes when hiring waiters. As a result, blonde waiters earn lower wages than brunette waiters. In this case, a restaurant could open up with blonde waiters and charge lower prices. If customers only cared about the quality and price of their meals, the discriminatory firms would be driven out of business, and the wage differential would disappear.

On the other hand, it is possible that customers prefer being served by brunette waiters. If this preference for discrimination is strong, the entry of blonde restaurants need not succeed in eliminating the wage differential between brunettes and blondes. That is, if customers have discriminatory preferences, a competitive market is consistent with a discriminatory wage differential. An economy with such discrimination would contain two types of restaurants. Blonde restaurants hire blondes, have lower costs and charge lower prices. Brunette restaurants hire brunettes, have higher costs and charge higher prices. Customers who did not care about the hair colour of their waiters would be attracted to the lower prices at the blonde restaurants. Bigoted customers would go to the brunette restaurants. They would pay for their discriminatory preference in the form of higher prices.

Another way for discrimination to persist in competitive markets is for the government to mandate discriminatory practices. If, for instance, the government passed a law stating that blondes could wash dishes in restaurants but could not work as waiters, then a wage differential could persist in a competitive market. The example of segregated buses in the United States in the 1950s and 1960s is one example of government-mandated discrimination. More recently, before South Africa abandoned its system of apartheid, blacks were prohibited from working in some jobs. Discriminatory governments pass such laws to suppress the normal equalizing force of free and competitive markets.

To sum up: competitive markets contain a natural remedy for employer discrimination. The entry into the market of firms that care only about profit tends to eliminate discriminatory wage differentials. These wage differentials persist in competitive markets only when customers are willing to pay to maintain the discriminatory practice or when the government mandates it.

Quick Quiz Why is it hard to establish whether a group of workers is being discriminated against? • Explain how profit-maximizing firms tend to eliminate discriminatory wage differentials. • How might a discriminatory wage differential persist?

CONCLUSION

In competitive markets, workers earn a wage equal to the value of their marginal contribution to the production of goods and services. There are, however, many things that affect the value of the marginal product. Firms pay more for workers who are more talented, more diligent, more experienced and more educated because these workers are more productive. Firms pay less to those workers against whom customers discriminate because these workers contribute less to revenue.

The theory of the labour market we have developed in the last two chapters explains why some workers earn higher wages than other workers. The theory does not say that the resulting distribution of income is equal, fair or desirable in any way. That is the topic we take up in Chapter 20.

SUMMARY

- Workers earn different wages for many reasons. To some extent, wage differentials compensate workers for job attributes. Other things equal, workers in hard, unpleasant jobs get paid more than workers in easy, pleasant jobs.
- Workers with more human capital get paid more than workers with less human capital. The return to accumulating human capital is high and has increased over the past two decades.
- Although years of education, experience and job characteristics affect earnings as theory predicts, there is much variation in earnings that cannot be explained by things that economists can measure. The unexplained variation in earnings is largely attributable to natural ability, effort and chance.
- Some economists have suggested that more educated workers earn higher wages not because education raises productivity but because workers with high natural ability use education as a way to signal their high ability to employers. If this signalling theory is correct, then increasing the educational attainment of all workers would not raise the overall level of wages.

- Wages are sometimes pushed above the level that brings supply and demand into balance. Three reasons for above-equilibrium wages are minimum wage laws, unions and efficiency wages.
- Some differences in earnings are attributable to discrimination on the basis of race, sex or other factors. Measuring the amount of discrimination is difficult, however, because one must correct for differences in human capital and job characteristics.
- Competitive markets tend to limit the impact of discrimination on wages. If the wages of a group of workers are lower than those of another group for reasons not related to marginal productivity, then non-discriminatory firms will be more profitable than discriminatory firms. Profit-maximizing behaviour, therefore, can reduce discriminatory wage differentials. Discrimination persists in competitive markets, however, if customers are willing to pay more to discriminatory firms or if the government passes laws requiring firms to discriminate.

KEY CONCEPTS

compensating differential, p. 404
human capital, p. 405
union, p. 409
strike, p. 410
efficiency wages, p. 410
discrimination, p. 410

QUESTIONS FOR REVIEW

1. Why do coal miners get paid more than other workers with similar amounts of education?
2. In what sense is education a type of capital?
3. How might education raise a worker's wage without raising the worker's productivity?
4. What conditions lead to economic superstars? Would you expect to see superstars in dentistry? In music? Explain.
5. Give three reasons why a worker's wage might be above the level that balances supply and demand.
6. What difficulties arise in deciding whether a group of workers has a lower wage because of discrimination?
7. Do the forces of economic competition tend to exacerbate or ameliorate discrimination on the basis of race?
8. Give an example of how discrimination might persist in a competitive market.

PROBLEMS AND APPLICATIONS

1. University students sometimes work as summer interns for private firms or the government. Many of these positions pay little or nothing.
   a. What is the opportunity cost of taking such a job?
   b. Explain why students are willing to take these jobs.
   c. If you were to compare the earnings later in life of workers who had worked as interns and those who had taken summer jobs that paid more, what would you expect to find?
2. As explained in Chapter 6, a minimum wage law distorts the market for low-wage labour. To reduce this distortion, some economists advocate a two-tiered minimum wage system, with a regular minimum wage for adult workers and a lower, 'sub-minimum' wage for teenage workers. Give two reasons why a single minimum wage might distort the labour market for teenage workers more than it would the market for adult workers.
3. A basic finding of labour economics is that workers who have more experience in the labour force are paid more than workers who have less experience (holding constant the amount of formal education). Why might this be so? Some studies have also found that experience at the

same job (called 'job tenure') has an extra positive influence on wages. Explain.

4. At some universities, economics lecturers receive higher salaries than lecturers in some other fields.
   a. Why might this be true?
   b. Some other universities have a policy of paying equal salaries to lecturers in all fields. At some of these, economics lecturers have lighter teaching loads than lecturers in some other fields. What role do the differences in teaching loads play?
5. Hannah works for Joachim, whom she hates because of his snobbish attitude. Yet when she looks for other jobs, the best she can do is find a job paying €15 000 less than her current salary. Should she take the job? Analyse Hannah's situation from an economic point of view.
6. Imagine that someone were to offer you a choice: you could spend four years studying at the world's best university, but you would have to keep your attendance there a secret. Or you could be awarded an official degree from the world's best university, but you couldn't actually attend (although no one need ever know this). Which choice do you think would enhance your future earnings more? What does your answer say about the debate over signalling versus human capital in the role of education?
7. When recording devices were first invented almost 100 years ago, musicians could suddenly supply their music to large audiences at low cost. How do you suppose this development affected the income of the best musicians? How do you suppose it affected the income of average musicians?
8. When Alan Greenspan (former chairman of the US Federal Reserve) ran an economic consulting firm in the 1960s, he hired primarily female economists. He once told *The New York Times,* 'I always valued men and women equally, and I found that because others did not, good women economists were cheaper than men.' Is Greenspan's behaviour profit-maximizing? Is it admirable or despicable? If more employers were like Greenspan, what would happen to the wage differential between men and women? Why might other economic consulting firms at the time not have followed Greenspan's business strategy?
9. Research into discrimination in US sport found that attendance at some US sports was higher when clubs had a higher proportion of white players than black players and that this may have something to do with the fact that black players earned less than white players. Customer discrimination in sports, therefore, seems to have an important effect on players' earnings. Note that this is possible because sports fans know the players' characteristics, including their race. Why is this knowledge important for the existence of discrimination? Give some specific examples of industries where customer discrimination is and is not likely to influence wages.
10. Suppose that all young women were channelled into careers as secretaries, nurses and teachers; at the same time, young men were encouraged to consider these three careers and many others as well.
    a. Draw a diagram showing the combined labour market for secretaries, nurses and teachers. Draw a diagram showing the combined labour market for all other fields. In which market is the wage higher? Do men or women receive higher wages on average?
    b. Now suppose that society changed and encouraged both young women and young men to consider a wide range of careers. Over time, what effect would this change have on the wages in the two markets you illustrated in part (a)? What effect would the change have on the average wages of men and women?
11. This chapter considers the economics of discrimination by employers, customers and governments. Now consider discrimination by workers. Suppose that some brunette workers did not like working with blonde workers. Do you think this worker discrimination could explain lower wages for blonde workers? If such a wage differential existed, what would a profit-maximizing entrepreneur do? If there were many such entrepreneurs, what would happen over time?

For further resources, visit www.cengage.com/mankiw_taylor2

20 INCOME INEQUALITY AND POVERTY

'The only difference between the rich and other people,' Mary Colum once said to Ernest Hemingway, 'is that the rich have more money.' This may be so but the statement leaves many questions unanswered. The gap between rich and poor is a fascinating and important topic of study – for the very rich, the comfortably rich, for the struggling poor, and indeed for all members of a modern economy. If Hemingway had studied economics, he might have used this reply: 'Yes, but why are they so rich while others are not so rich?'

From the previous two chapters you should have some understanding about why different people have different incomes. A person's earnings depend on the supply and demand for that person's labour, which in turn depend on natural ability, human capital, compensating differentials, discrimination and so on. Labour earnings as measured by employee contributions make up about 53 per cent of total income in the UK economy, around 50 per cent in the Netherlands, 51 per cent in Germany, 56 per cent in Sweden and 48 per cent in the eurozone as a whole[1]. The factors that determine wages are also largely responsible for determining how an economy's total income is distributed among the various members of society. In other words, they determine who is rich and who is poor.

In this chapter we discuss the distribution of income – a topic that raises some fundamental questions about the role of economic policy. One of the *Ten Principles of Economics* in Chapter 1 is that governments can sometimes improve market outcomes. This possibility is particularly important when considering the

[1]Source: Compensation of employees as a proportion of GDP (income approach), http://stats.oecd.org/Index.aspx

distribution of income. The invisible hand of the marketplace acts to allocate resources efficiently, but it does not necessarily ensure that resources are allocated fairly. As a result, many economists – though not all – believe that the government should redistribute income to achieve greater equality. In doing so, however, the government runs into another of the *Ten Principles of Economics:* people face trade-offs. When the government enacts policies to make the distribution of income more equitable, it distorts incentives, alters behaviour and makes the allocation of resources less efficient.

Our discussion of the distribution of income proceeds in three steps. Firstly, we assess how much inequality there is in our society. Secondly, we consider some different views about what role the government should play in altering the distribution of income. Thirdly, we discuss various public policies aimed at helping society's poorest members.

THE MEASUREMENT OF INEQUALITY

We begin our study of the distribution of income by addressing four questions of measurement:

- How much inequality is there in our society?
- How many people live in poverty?
- What problems arise in measuring the amount of inequality?
- How often do people move among income classes?

"And this is for keeping wages down."

These measurement questions are the natural starting point from which to discuss public policies aimed at changing the distribution of income.

European Income Inequality

Imagine that you lined up all the families in the economy according to their annual income. Then you divided the families into groups: the bottom 10 per cent, the next 20 per cent and so on until we got to the top 10 per cent. Table 20.1 shows the income ranges for each of these groups in the United Kingdom in 2008. It also shows the cut-off for the bottom 10 per cent and the top 10 per cent. You can use this table to find where your family lies in the income distribution.

For examining differences in the income distribution over time, economists find it useful to present the income data as in Table 20.2. This table shows the share of total income that each group of families received. In 2008 the bottom fifth of all families received 7.1 per cent of all income, and the top fifth of all families received 43.1 per cent of all income. In other words, even though the top and bottom fifths include the same number of families, the top fifth has over six times as much income as the bottom fifth.

TABLE 20.1

The Distribution of Annual Family Income in the United Kingdom, 2008

10% have income less than:	£ 9 932
30% have income less than:	£15 132
50% have income less than:	£20 436
70% have income less than:	£27 196
90% have income less than:	£41 912

Source: Institute for Fiscal Studies. DWP http://sticerd.lse.ac.uk/dps/case/cr/CASEreport60.pdf

TABLE 20.2

Income Inequality in the United Kingdom

Year	Bottom fifth	Second fifth	Middle fifth	Fourth fifth	Top fifth
2008	7.1%	12.0%	16.1%	21.7%	43.1%
2002	7.5	12.0	16.0	22.0	42.0
1990	7.5	12.0	16.5	22.5	41.5
1979	10.0	14.0	18.0	23.0	35.0

Source: UK Department for Work and Pensions and Department of Social Security: http://research.dwp.gov.uk/asd/hbai/hbai2008/pdf_files/full_hbai09.pdf

Table 20.2 also shows the distribution of income in 1979, 1990 and 2002. The distribution has been quite stable over the period 1990–2008. But comparing the distributions in these years with the distribution in 1979, we can see that UK income inequality increased over the 1980s: the top fifth increased its share by about 7 per cent over that decade and every other fifth decreased its share of total disposable income. In fact, the poorer a group was in relative terms, the more they contributed to the richest group's increased share, with the bottom fifth reducing its share of the total from 10 per cent to 7.1 per cent and the next fifth from 14 to 12 per cent.

In Chapter 19 we discussed some explanations for this recent rise in inequality. Increases in international trade with low-wage countries and changes in technology have tended to reduce the demand for unskilled labour and raise the demand for skilled labour. As a result, the wages of unskilled workers have fallen relative to the wages of skilled workers, and this change in relative wages has increased inequality in family incomes.

How does the amount of inequality in the UK compare with that in the rest of Europe? Data from the European Union Community Statistics on Income and Living Conditions initially compiled in 2005 and revised in 2008, show considerable differences in income inequality between countries in the EU. One immediate point to notice is that average incomes vary, with those countries that used to be part of the Soviet Bloc having the lowest average incomes. Luxembourg has an average income of €29 153, around 5.5 times that of Lithuania (€5 304). Portugal, Greece and Spain all have average incomes between €10 000 and €15 000 whereas the original members of the EU such as France, Italy, Belgium and the Netherlands have average incomes between €15 000 and €20 000. Figure 20.1 shows the income distributions of the countries of the EU. The data bars are marked to show the proportions of each decile (where the population has been divided into ten equal parts). It can be seen that countries like Luxembourg, Italy and Ireland have average incomes in the ninth and tenth deciles, much higher than those of the bottom deciles.

If we look at the wider world, Figure 20.2 compares inequality in 12 countries. The inequality measure is the ratio of the income received by the richest tenth of the population to the income of the poorest tenth. The most equality is found in Japan where the top tenth receives 4.5 times as much income as the bottom tenth. The least equality is found in Brazil, where the top group receives 51.3 times as much income as the bottom group. Although all countries have significant disparities between rich and poor, the degree of inequality varies substantially throughout the world.

Problems in Measuring Inequality

Although data on the income distribution give us some idea about the degree of inequality in our society, interpreting these data is not as straightforward as it

FIGURE 20.1

The Income Distributions of the Countries of the European Union (euros, PPP)

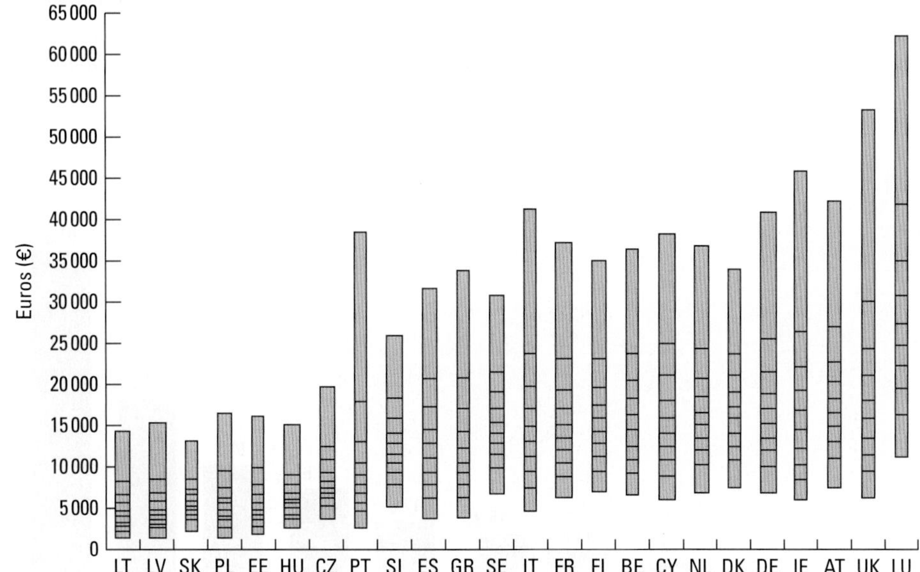

Note: The bottom of the data bars represents the first decile, the top represents the tenth decile and the marks in between show the average incomes of the individual deciles. This data is based on purchasing power parity (PPP) – see Chapter 31.

Source: EU-SILC (2005), recalculations from the 2008 March data release.

might first appear. The data are based on households' annual incomes. What people care about, however, is not their incomes but their ability to maintain a good standard of living. For various reasons, data on the income distribution give an incomplete picture of inequality in living standards. We examine these reasons below.

The Economic Life Cycle Incomes vary predictably over people's lives. A young worker, especially one still engaged in full-time study, has a low income. Income rises as the worker gains maturity and experience, peaks at around age 50, and then falls sharply when the worker retires at around age 65. This regular pattern of income variation is called the **life cycle**.

life cycle
the regular pattern of income variation over a person's life

Because people can borrow and save to smooth out life cycle changes in income, their standard of living in any year depends more on lifetime income than on that year's income. The young often borrow, perhaps to go to university or to buy a house, and then repay these loans later when their incomes rise. People have their highest saving rates when they are middle-aged. Because people can save in anticipation of retirement, the large declines in incomes at retirement need not lead to similar declines in standard of living.

This normal life cycle pattern causes inequality in the distribution of annual income, but it does not represent true inequality in living standards. To gauge the inequality of living standards in our society, the distribution of lifetime incomes is more relevant than the distribution of annual incomes. Unfortunately, data on lifetime incomes are not readily available. When looking at any data on inequality, however, it is important to keep the life cycle in mind. Because a

FIGURE 20.2

Inequality Around the World

This figure shows a measure of inequality: the income (or expenditure) that goes to the richest 10 per cent of the population divided by the income (or expenditure) that goes to the poorest 10 per cent. Among these nations, Japan and Germany have the most equal distribution of economic well-being while South Africa and Brazil have the least equal.

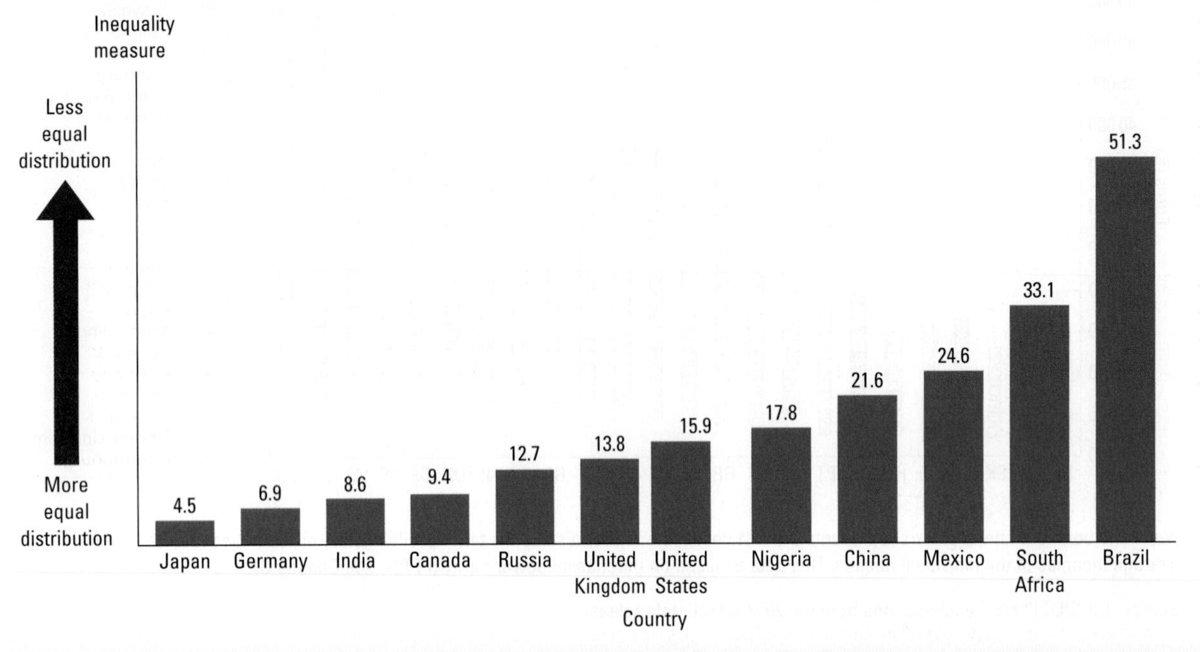

person's lifetime income smoothes out the highs and lows of the life cycle, lifetime incomes are surely more equally distributed across the population than are annual incomes.

Transitory Versus Permanent Income Incomes vary over people's lives not only because of predictable life cycle variation but also because of random and transitory forces. One year a frost kills off the Normandy apple crop and Normandy apple growers see their incomes fall temporarily. At the same time, the Normandy frost drives up the price of apples and English apple growers see their incomes temporarily rise. The next year the reverse might happen.

Just as people can borrow and lend to smooth out life cycle variation in income, they can also borrow and lend to smooth out transitory variation in income. When English apple growers experience a good year, they would be foolish to spend all of their additional income. Instead, they save some of it, knowing that their good fortune is unlikely to persist. Similarly, the Normandy apple growers respond to their temporarily low incomes by drawing down their savings or by borrowing. To the extent that a family saves and borrows to buffer itself from transitory changes in income, these changes do not affect its standard of living. A family's ability to buy goods and services depends largely on its **permanent income**, which is its normal, or average, income.

permanent income
a person's normal income

To gauge inequality of living standards, the distribution of permanent income is more relevant than the distribution of annual income. Although permanent income is hard to measure, it is an important concept. Because permanent income excludes transitory changes in income, permanent income is more equally distributed than is current income.

Economic Mobility

People sometimes speak of 'the rich' and 'the poor' as if these groups consisted of the same families year after year. In fact, this is not at all the case. Economic mobility, the movement of people among income classes, is quite substantial in European and North American economies. Movements up the income ladder can be due to good luck or hard work, and movements down the ladder can be due to bad luck or laziness. Some of this mobility reflects transitory variation in income, while some reflects more persistent changes in income.

Because economic mobility is so great, poverty is a long-term problem for relatively few families. Because it is likely that the temporarily poor and the persistently poor face different problems, policies that aim to combat poverty need to distinguish between these groups.

Another way to gauge economic mobility is the persistence of economic success from generation to generation. Economists who have studied this topic find substantial mobility. If a father earns 20 per cent above his generation's average income, his son will most likely earn 8 per cent above his generation's average income. There is almost no correlation between the income of a grandfather and the income of a grandson. There is much truth to the old saying, 'From shirtsleeves to shirtsleeves in three generations.'

The Poverty Rate

A commonly used gauge of the distribution of income is the poverty rate. The **poverty rate** is the percentage of the population whose family income falls below an absolute level called the **poverty line**. Poverty is a relative concept – one person's poverty is another person's wealthy. A millionaire is wealthy compared to someone earning €50 000 a year but is poor compared to a billionaire! For this reason economists distinguish between absolute and relative poverty. **Absolute poverty** is when individuals do not have access to the basic requirements of life – food, shelter and clothing. **Relative poverty** occurs when individuals are excluded from being able to take part in what are considered the normal, acceptable standards of living in a society.

To get some idea of levels of poverty across different countries, therefore, similar measures have to be used. In Europe the measure for defining the poverty line is set at 60 per cent of the median income. If measuring across Europe, this income has to be equivalized and is called the equivalized household income. If the median income is €20 000 then any family earning less than €12 000 a year would be classed as living in poverty. In the UK there are over 12 million families classed as living in poverty. Figure 20.3 shows poverty rates across European countries in 2000 and 2004. The poverty rate in countries like France, the UK, Germany and Portugal has fallen between these two years but in many countries it has risen. Once again we see the former Soviet states faring badly with the Czech Republic, Hungary, Estonia, Latvia and Poland all seeing an increase in the poverty rate. These latter three countries had poverty rates in excess of 20 per cent in 2004. The recession is likely to have made things worse for many countries as a result of widespread job losses across Europe.

Looking at the poverty rate in addition to other data on inequality is important. We might observe that average incomes have risen over time but not everyone is able to share in the increased prosperity that has occurred. Understanding something of why some people get left behind is crucial to developing policies to support people to help them gain a better standard of living.

poverty rate
the percentage of the population whose family income falls below an absolute level called the poverty line

poverty line
an absolute level of income set by the government below which a family is deemed to be in poverty. In the UK and Europe this is measured by earnings less than 60 per cent of median income

absolute poverty
a level of poverty where an individual does not have access to the basic of life – food, clothing and shelter

relative poverty
a situation where an individual is not able to access what would be considered acceptable standards of living in society

FIGURE 20.3

Poverty rates across European countries in 2000 and 2004

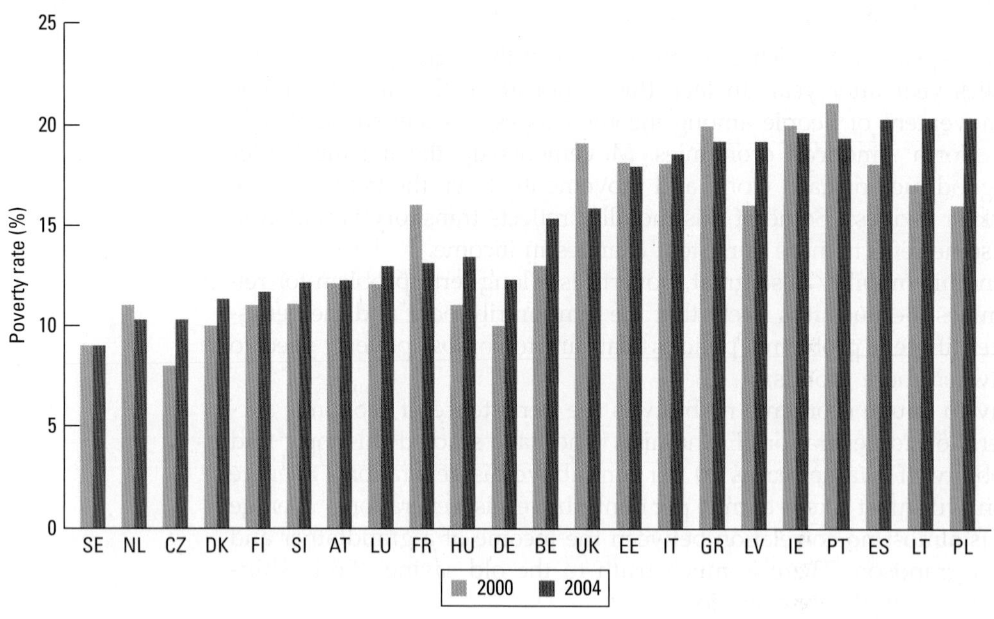

Note: countries are ranked according to year 2004.

Source: ECHP (2000) and EU-SILC (2005) recalculations from the 2008 March data release.

THE POLITICAL PHILOSOPHY OF REDISTRIBUTING INCOME

We have just seen how the economy's income is distributed and have considered some of the problems in interpreting measured inequality. This discussion was *positive* in the sense that it merely described the world as it is. We now turn to the *normative* question facing policy makers: What *should* the government do about economic inequality?

This question is not just about economics. Economic analysis alone cannot tell us whether policy makers *should* try to make our society more egalitarian. Our views on this question are, to a large extent, a matter of political philosophy. Yet because the government's role in redistributing income is central to so many debates over economic policy, here we digress from economic science to consider a bit of political philosophy.

Utilitarianism

utilitarianism
the political philosophy according to which the government should choose policies to maximize the total utility of everyone in society

utility
a measure of happiness or satisfaction

A prominent school of thought in political philosophy is **utilitarianism**. The founders of utilitarianism were the British philosophers Jeremy Bentham (1748–1832) and John Stuart Mill (1806–1873). To a large extent, the goal of utilitarians is to apply the logic of individual decision-making to questions concerning morality and public policy.

The starting point of utilitarianism is the notion of **utility** – the level of happiness or satisfaction that a person receives from his or her circumstances. Utility is a measure of well-being and, according to utilitarians, is the ultimate objective of all public and private actions. The proper goal of the government, they claim, is to maximize the sum of utility of everyone in society.

The utilitarian case for redistributing income is based on the assumption of *diminishing marginal utility*. It seems reasonable that an extra euro of income to a poor person provides that person with more additional utility than does an extra euro to a rich person. In other words, as a person's income rises, the extra well-being derived from an additional euro of income falls. This plausible assumption, together with the utilitarian goal of maximizing total utility, implies that the government should try to achieve a more equal distribution of income.

The argument is simple. Imagine that Dieter and Ernst are the same, except that Dieter earns €80 000 and Ernst earns €20 000. In this case, taking a euro from Dieter to pay Ernst will reduce Dieter's utility and raise Ernst's utility. But, because of diminishing marginal utility, Dieter's utility falls by less than Ernst's utility rises. Thus, this redistribution of income raises total utility, which is the utilitarian's objective.

At first, this utilitarian argument might seem to imply that the government should continue to redistribute income until everyone in society has exactly the same income. Indeed, that would be the case if the total amount of income – €100 000 in our example – were fixed. But, in fact, it is not. Utilitarians reject complete equalization of incomes because they accept one of the *Ten Principles of Economics* presented in Chapter 1: people respond to incentives.

To take from Dieter to pay Ernst, the government must pursue policies that redistribute income, such as the income tax and welfare systems that operate in all industrialized countries. Under these policies, people with high incomes pay high taxes, and people with low incomes receive income transfers. Yet, as we saw in Chapter 8, taxes distort incentives and cause deadweight losses. If the government takes away additional income a person might earn through higher income taxes or reduced transfers, both Dieter and Ernst have less incentive to work hard. As they work less, society's income falls, and so does total utility. The utilitarian government has to balance the gains from greater equality against the losses from distorted incentives. To maximize total utility, therefore, the government stops short of making society fully egalitarian.

A famous parable sheds light on the utilitarian's logic. Imagine that Dieter and Ernst are thirsty travellers trapped at different places in the desert. Dieter's oasis has much water; Ernst's has little. If the government could transfer water from one oasis to the other without cost, it would maximize total utility from water by equalizing the amount in the two places. But suppose that the government has only a leaky bucket. As it tries to move water from one place to the other, some of the water is lost in transit. In this case, a utilitarian government might still try to move some water from Dieter to Ernst, depending on how thirsty Ernst is and how leaky the bucket is. But, with only a leaky bucket at its disposal, a utilitarian government will not try to reach complete equality.

Liberalism

A second way of thinking about inequality might be called **liberalism**. Philosopher John Rawls develops this view in his book *A Theory of Justice*. This book was first published in 1971, and it quickly became a classic in political philosophy.

liberalism
the political philosophy according to which the government should choose policies deemed to be just, as evaluated by an impartial observer behind a 'veil of ignorance'

Rawls begins with the premise that a society's institutions, laws and policies should be just. He then takes up the natural question: how can we, the members of society, ever agree on what justice means? It might seem that every person's point of view is inevitably based on his or her particular circumstances – whether he or she is talented or less talented, diligent or lazy, educated or less educated, born to a wealthy family or a poor one. Could we ever *objectively* determine what a just society would be?

To answer this question, Rawls proposes the following thought experiment. Imagine that before any of us is born, we all get together for a meeting to design the rules that govern society. At this point, we are all ignorant about the station in life each of us will end up filling. In Rawls's words, we are sitting in an 'original position' behind a 'veil of ignorance'. In this original position, Rawls argues, we can choose a just set of rules for society because we must consider how those rules will affect every person. As Rawls puts it, 'Since all are similarly situated and no one is able to design principles to favour his particular conditions, the principles of justice are the result of fair agreement or bargain.' Designing public policies and institutions in this way allows us to be objective about what policies are just.

Rawls then considers what public policy designed behind this veil of ignorance would try to achieve. In particular, he considers what income distribution a person would consider fair if that person did not know whether he or she would end up at the top, bottom or middle of the distribution. Rawls argues that a person in the original position would be especially concerned about the possibility of being at the *bottom* of the income distribution. In designing public policies, therefore, we should aim to raise the welfare of the worst-off person in society. That is, rather than maximizing the sum of everyone's utility, as a utilitarian would do, Rawls would maximize the minimum utility. Rawls's rule is called the **maximin criterion**.

maximin criterion
the claim that the government should aim to maximize the well-being of the worst-off person in society

Because the maximin criterion emphasizes the least fortunate person in society, it justifies public policies aimed at equalizing the distribution of income. By transferring income from the rich to the poor, society raises the well-being of the least fortunate. The maximin criterion would not, however, lead to a completely egalitarian society. If the government promised to equalize incomes completely, people would have no incentive to work hard, society's total income would fall substantially and the least fortunate person would be worse off. Thus, the maximin criterion still allows disparities in income, because such disparities can improve incentives and thereby raise society's ability to help the poor. Nonetheless, because Rawls's philosophy puts weight on only the least fortunate members of society, it calls for more income redistribution than does utilitarianism.

Rawls's views are controversial, but the thought experiment he proposes has much appeal. In particular, this thought experiment allows us to consider the redistribution of income as a form of *social insurance.* That is, from the perspective of the original position behind the veil of ignorance, income redistribution is like an insurance policy. Homeowners buy fire insurance to protect themselves from the risk of their housing burning down. Similarly, when we as a society choose policies that tax the rich to supplement the incomes of the poor, we are all insuring ourselves against the possibility that we might have been a member of a poor family. Because people dislike risk, we should be happy to have been born into a society that provides us this insurance.

It is not at all clear, however, that rational people behind the veil of ignorance would truly be so averse to risk as to follow the maximin criterion. Indeed, because a person in the original position might end up anywhere in the distribution of outcomes, he or she might treat all possible outcomes equally when designing public policies. In this case, the best policy behind the veil of ignorance would be to maximize the average utility of members of society, and the resulting notion of justice would be more utilitarian than Rawlsian.

Libertarianism

libertarianism
the political philosophy according to which the government should punish crimes and enforce voluntary agreements but not redistribute income

A third view of inequality is called **libertarianism**. The two views we have considered so far – utilitarianism and liberalism – both view the total income of society as a shared resource that a social planner can freely redistribute to achieve some social goal. By contrast, libertarians argue that society itself earns no income – only individual members of society earn income. According to libertarians, the government should not take from some individuals and give to others in order to achieve any particular distribution of income.

For instance, philosopher Robert Nozick writes the following in his famous 1974 book *Anarchy, State, and Utopia*:

> We are not in the position of children who have been given portions of pie by someone who now makes last minute adjustments to rectify careless cutting. There is no *central* distribution, no person or group entitled to control all the resources, jointly deciding how they are to be doled out. What each person gets, he gets from others who give to him in exchange for something, or as a gift. In a free society, diverse persons control different resources, and new holdings arise out of the voluntary exchanges and actions of persons.

Whereas utilitarians and liberals try to judge what amount of inequality is desirable in a society, Nozick denies the validity of this very question.

The libertarian alternative to evaluating economic *outcomes* is to evaluate the *process* by which these outcomes arise. When the distribution of income is achieved unfairly – for instance, when one person steals from another – the government has the right and duty to remedy the problem. But, as long as the process determining the distribution of income is just, the resulting distribution is fair, no matter how unequal.

Nozick criticizes Rawls's liberalism by drawing an analogy between the distribution of income in society and the distribution of marks awarded to students taking a course of study. Suppose you were asked to judge the fairness of the marks awarded in the economics course you are now taking. Would you imagine yourself behind a veil of ignorance and choose a marks distribution without knowing the talents and efforts of each student? Or would you ensure that the process of assigning marks to students is fair without regard for whether the resulting distribution is equal or unequal? For the case of course marks at least, the libertarian emphasis on process over outcomes is compelling.

Libertarians conclude that equality of opportunities is more important than equality of incomes. They believe that the government should enforce individual rights to ensure that everyone has the same opportunity to use his or her talents and achieve success. Once these rules of the game are established, the government has no reason to alter the resulting distribution of income.

Libertarian Paternalism

We finally introduce a relatively new concept linked to these philosophies put forward by University of Chicago economists, Richard H. Thaler and Cass R. Sunstein[2]. Libertarian paternalism recognizes that people should be free to choose but that 'choice architects' (the government in the case of making decisions about rectifying inequality) have a legitimate role in trying to influence people's behaviour in order to make their lives longer, healthier and better – improving their utility. Thaler and Sunstein question whether specific policy moves are the best way of changing behaviour to improve utility and whether 'nudges' could achieve the end result whilst retaining the freedom of people to make choices. Nudges relate to details that might often seem insignificant but when paid attention to, can influence the choices people make to 'nudge' them in the direction of improving their own and society's welfare. Their work covers diverse areas but includes savings for pensions and social security systems, both of which have an impact on inequality in society.

[2]Thaler, R. H. & Sunstein C. R. (2009) *Nudge: Improving decisions about health, wealth and happiness.* London, Penguin.

Quick Quiz Franz earns more than Paloma. Someone proposes taxing Franz in order to supplement Paloma's income. How would a utilitarian, a liberal and a libertarian evaluate this proposal?

Policies to Reduce Poverty

As we have just seen, political philosophers and economists hold various views about what role the government should take in altering the distribution of income. Political debate among the larger population of voters reflects a similar disagreement. Despite these continuing debates, however, most people believe that, at the very least, the government should try to help those most in need. According to a popular metaphor, the government should provide a 'safety net' to prevent any citizen from falling too far.

Poverty is one of the most difficult problems that policy makers face. Poor families are more likely than the overall population to experience homelessness, drug dependency, domestic violence, health problems, teenage pregnancy, illiteracy, unemployment and low educational attainment. Members of poor families are both more likely to commit crimes and more likely to be victims of crimes. Although it is hard to separate the causes of poverty from the effects, there is no doubt that poverty is associated with various economic and social ills.

Suppose that you were a policy maker in the government, and your goal was to reduce the number of people living in poverty. How would you achieve this goal? Here we consider some of the policy options that you might consider. Although each of these options does help some people escape poverty, none of them is perfect, and deciding upon the best combination is not easy.

Minimum Wage Laws

Laws setting a minimum wage that employers can pay workers are a perennial source of debate. Advocates view the minimum wage as a way of helping the working poor without any cost to the government. Critics view it as hurting those it is intended to help.

The minimum wage is easily understood using the tools of supply and demand, as we first saw in Chapter 6. For workers with low levels of skill and experience, a high minimum wage forces the wage above the level that balances supply and demand. It therefore raises the cost of labour to firms and reduces the quantity of labour that those firms demand. The result is higher unemployment among those groups of workers affected by the minimum wage. Although those workers who remain employed benefit from a higher wage, those who might have been employed at a lower wage are worse off.

The magnitude of these effects depends crucially on the elasticity of demand. Advocates of a high minimum wage argue that the demand for unskilled labour is relatively inelastic, so that a high minimum wage depresses employment only slightly. Critics of the minimum wage argue that labour demand is more elastic, especially in the long run when firms can adjust employment and production more fully. They also note that many minimum wage workers are teenagers from middle-income families, so that a high minimum wage is imperfectly targeted as a policy for helping the poor.

The effects are also dependent on the degree of substitutability between workers in different industries – the ease with which workers can transfer from one industry to another. Minimum wage laws affect all businesses in all industries in different ways; some industries are not affected greatly by minimum wage laws because they already pay in excess of the minimum wage and so labour market equilibrium is not affected in that particular market. In low-paid industries, such as cleaning, hotel and catering and restaurants, for example, all employers are affected in the same way if they have to increase pay to meet minimum wage laws. As a result no one employer can necessarily gain any advantage over another by paying workers lower wages and thus having lower costs. Whilst minimum wage laws are a contentious issue, it is also a highly complex one requiring detailed analysis and an understanding that the labour market is not simply an amorphous 'one'; it consists of many smaller markets each of which has a varying influence on other markets.

Social Security

One way to raise the living standards of the poor is for the government of a country to supplement their incomes. The primary way in which the government does this is through **social security**. This is a broad term that generally encompasses various government benefits. In the UK, for example, Income Support is paid mainly to poor people who are either lone parents and carers, or incapable of work, or else disabled, tax credits are payments made to those in work and with families but who receive low incomes and have to care for children, while Jobseeker's Allowance is paid to unemployed people who are able and willing to work but temporarily cannot find a job.

social security
government benefits that supplement the incomes of the needy

A common criticism of the social security system is that it may create bad incentives. For example, since a single mother may lose Income Support if she were married to a man who was in work, the Income Support programme may encourage families to break up or encourage illegitimate births. However, governments may introduce other mechanisms to create good incentives. Tax credits, for example, are designed to encourage family members to take paid work in the belief that a person in work, albeit on a low income, is in a better position than one who does not take a job.

How severe are these potential problems with the benefit system? No one knows for sure. Proponents of the benefit system point out that being a poor, single mother is a difficult existence at best, and they are sceptical that many people would be encouraged to pursue such a life if it were not thrust upon them. Moreover, if it can be proved that a person is incapable of work or is disabled, it seems cruel and ridiculous to argue that this is because of the benefits they are receiving. It is often easy, however, for the popular press to portray examples of those who abuse the system; it is important that, as a budding economist, you ask appropriate questions and try to distinguish between fact and opinion in such cases.

Negative Income Tax

Whenever the government chooses a system to collect taxes, it affects the distribution of income. This is clearly true in the case of a progressive income tax, whereby high-income families pay a larger percentage of their income in taxes than do low-income families. Many economists have advocated supplementing the income of the poor using a **negative income tax**. According to this policy, every family would report its income to the government. High-income families would pay a tax based on their incomes. Low-income families would receive a subsidy. In other words, they would 'pay' a 'negative tax'.

negative income tax
a tax system that collects revenue from high-income households and gives transfers to low-income households

For example, suppose the government used the following formula to compute a family's tax liability:

$$\text{Taxes due} = (1/3 \text{ of income}) - €10\,000$$

In this case, a family that earned €60 000 would pay €10 000 in taxes, and a family that earned €90 000 would pay €20 000 in taxes. A family that earned €30 000 would owe nothing. And a family that earned €15 000 would 'owe' –€5 000. In other words, the government would send this family a cheque for €5 000.

Under a negative income tax, poor families would receive financial assistance without having to demonstrate need. The only qualification required to receive assistance would be a low income. Depending on one's point of view, this feature can be either an advantage or a disadvantage. On the one hand, a negative income tax does not encourage illegitimate births and the break-up of families, as critics of the welfare system believe current policy does. On the other hand, a negative income tax would subsidize those who are simply lazy and, in some people's eyes, undeserving of government support.

In-Kind Transfers

Another way to help the poor is to provide them directly with some of the goods and services they need to raise their living standards. For example, charities provide the needy with food, shelter and toys at Christmas. Governments in some countries give poor families vouchers that can be used to buy food or clothing in shops; the shops then redeem the vouchers for money. In the UK, poor people may qualify for free school meals for their children and medical benefits such as free prescriptions, dental treatment and eyesight tests.

in-kind transfers
transfers to the poor given in the form of goods and services rather than cash

Is it better to help the poor with these **in-kind transfers** or with direct cash payments? There is no clear answer.

Advocates of in-kind transfers argue that such transfers ensure that the poor get what they need most. Among the poorest members of society, alcohol and drug addiction is more common than it is in society as a whole. By providing the poor with food and shelter rather than cash, society can be more confident that it is not helping to support such addictions.

Advocates of cash payments, on the other hand, argue that in-kind transfers are inefficient and disrespectful. The government does not know what goods and services the poor need most. Many of the poor are ordinary people down on their luck. Despite their misfortune, they are in the best position to decide how to raise their own living standards. Rather than giving the poor in-kind transfers of goods and services that they may not want, it may be better to give them cash and allow them to buy what they think they need most.

Anti-poverty Policies and Work Incentives

Many policies aimed at helping the poor can have the unintended effect of discouraging the poor from escaping poverty on their own. To see why, consider the following example. Suppose that a family needs an income of €10 000 to maintain a reasonable standard of living. And suppose that, out of concern for the poor, the government promises to guarantee every family that income. Whatever a family earns, the government makes up the difference between that income and €10 000. What effect would you expect this policy to have?

The incentive effects of this policy are obvious: any person who would earn under €10 000 by working has no incentive to find and keep a job. For every euro that the person would earn, the government would reduce the income supplement by one euro. In effect, the government taxes 100 per cent of additional earnings. An effective marginal tax rate of 100 per cent is surely a policy with a large deadweight loss.

The adverse effects of this high effective tax rate can persist over time. A person discouraged from working loses the on-the-job training that a job might offer. In addition, his or her children miss the lessons learned by observing a parent with a full-time job, and this may adversely affect their own ability to find and hold a job.

Although the anti-poverty policy we have been discussing is hypothetical, it is not as unrealistic as it might first appear. In the UK, for example, Income Support

IN THE NEWS

One of the interesting things about economics is that there are diverse views about important issues like poverty that may sometimes raise uncomfortable questions which need to be considered. Appreciating different perspectives is an important part of the economist's toolbox. These two articles are examples of perspectives on poverty, specifically child poverty. The first presents an overview of issues facing policy makers (and shoppers in Europe) on the use of children in Bangladesh to manufacture goods sold in Western markets. The second offers a perspective on ways to help children escape poverty. You should aim to try and understand the perspectives being put forward in each case and ask yourself if an appreciation of these perspectives enables us to arrive at policy decisions which may be more effective in helping improve welfare than those that already exist.

1. Perspectives on Poverty

Many consumers in the developed world are able to go into retail stores and buy clothes at prices that, if time was taken to think about it, are quite remarkable. Access to cheap clothing has become something many almost take for granted. There have been some reports about high profile firms exploiting labour in countries like Bangladesh. These companies tend to respond to these reports swiftly to try and reassure consumers that they do all they can to ensure that ethical guidelines are being adhered to in the factories where their products are manufactured.

Most consumers are probably aware of the ethical issues surrounding the availability of cheap clothing. Most, if asked, would probably not condone the use of child labour and most would also say that wages ought to be fair and working conditions adequate for people who produce the clothes. The problem, of course, is that if steps were taken to improve wages and working conditions then the cost of producing the clothes would increase and the price to consumers is also likely to rise. The question is, to what extent would consumers be willing to pay more for their clothing to ensure improved pay and working conditions for workers in countries like Bangladesh and thus help raise them out of poverty?

There is also another side to the story. In the developed world it is relatively easy to sit back and complain about poor wages and conditions in a country like Bangladesh and deplore the fact that children are used in manufacturing. In the 19th century, children were widely used in industry throughout Europe, often in appalling conditions and subject to considerable danger. Few children had access to education. In Bangladesh today, the situation is much the same. Education is provided by the state for children between the ages of 6 and 10 but there are reports that only half of the children in this age group attend school. Access to education outside this free provision requires payment and many families in Bangladesh cannot afford to educate their children.

Instead, many children have jobs which help to supplement the family income. There was a law, passed in 2006, which is meant to guarantee a fixed salary, holiday entitlement, access to education and compensation in the event of accident. The extent to which this law is observed is open to some debate. The result is that many children will work long hours in difficult conditions and have to forsake education. One of the problems facing Bangladesh in changing the attitudes to this is that many families rely on the incomes of children in the family to help them survive. For consumers in the developed world, the stories of exploitation, danger, hardship and abuse – both physical and sexual – may seem too difficult to accept but for many families in Bangladesh these conditions are a fact of life.

The reports of children working for low wages and in poor conditions raise important questions about the nature of poverty and how to deal with it. What is right and moral may be to prevent children working below a certain age (that, of course, is a subjective opinion) but to achieve this the cycle of poverty needs to be broken. In so doing, children will not have to work to supplement income and if access to education can be widened then this may help future generations. As in 19th century Britain, the process may be a long one before conditions improve for millions in Bangladesh and attitudes will have to change not only in countries like Bangladesh but also in the developed world.

Source: Adapted from http://www.bized.co.uk/cgi-bin/chron/chron.pl?id=3370

2. Economic Truths of Child Labour

Every high street offers us items created by people whose poverty we can barely imagine. The tea in our cups was plucked by some young woman earning pennies in Sri Lanka. Our coffee has similar origins.

Now we are learning that fashionable trainers were crafted by children in grim circumstances in Laos or the Philippines. The International Labour Organization (ILO), an arm of the United Nations, published a report outlining these horrors and urging steps the world should take to suppress child labour. It says that one in six children is at work between their 6th and 17th birthdays. The occurrence of child labour seems a good barometer of local poverty. The ILO's arguments are more than moral outrage – they also say that children are of less economic value without decent schooling.

I don't contest the good intentions of these arguments. I'm sure I'd be pained if I saw children in workshops in Cambodia or Somalia. Yet for the ILO's economic literacy, I give low marks: suppressing child labour would only deepen misery. In its foggy way, the ILO argues parents should be paid the equivalent of their child's market value, replacing the income forfeited if the child attends school instead. It is ambiguous where this money would come from but presumably through taxation of the population – i.e. the parents.

It is easy for us to 'tut' about child labour from our capitalist affluence. If you live in the deeply impoverished nations where markets have been suppressed or deformed, your only asset is your ability to work, and that of your children. Sometimes I find people assume children did nothing more than picnic and play happily until the evil capitalists forced them into the textile mills and down the mines after the Industrial Revolution. The truth is that child labour was the reality of life in all rural economies long before Dickens got on the case of the child chimney sweeps.

It was the rise in capitalism that permitted the extended years of leisure we call education. Working in the newly emerging factories was regarded as a far better option than slaving in the fields – linen was more profitable than turnips. Child labour is not the invention of modern 'globalization'. All farming has always used children. Scotland's school summer holidays exist not so everyone can fly down to the Spanish Costas, but so that children can help with the harvest. To learn rural skills was the reality of education in most of human history. In more urban areas the young would learn other appropriate skills.

I believe that working in scruffy factories in Manila or Nairobi is an opportunity for the people involved. Making fashion garments or chic trainers for eventual sale on Princes Street [*the main shopping area in Edinburgh, the capital of Scotland*] offers far greater benevolence than the humbugging of overseas aid. Aid is famously described as a device by which the poor people in the West fund the rich in the Third World. But free trade in shirts transfers money from the rich of the West to the poor of the East.

US democratic presidential candidates shout at each other about child labour as a malignancy [*something that is evil in nature and has the characteristic of uncontrolled growth*] caused by globalization. Our own politicians are apprehensive about 'asylum seekers', the new euphemism for immigration. Do people try to flock Westwards because of our crazy policies? Or do they look for a solution to the economic problems they have in their own country?

The biggest single preventable cause of poverty is the European Union's agricultural policies. Affluence could spread across the planet if we opened our markets to non-EU foodstuffs. I remain baffled why no Scottish politician campaigns to cut the price of our groceries. Would it not be popular?

I'm not advocating sending any child into dangerous or degrading roles, but I do believe every school could allow pupils to widen their knowledge and experience by participating in local commercial life. It could be fun. It could be life-changing. Many of Scotland's young are held captive in schools that bore and alienate them. All that we seem to accept is newspaper paper rounds and there is even talk in Brussels of banning them. Participating in your community's shops, say, can only widen experience. With regard to student jobs as a degradation, it ought to be part of growing up.

As the economies of Asia accelerate, the number of children working tumbles, as parents prefer to buy education. They know the educated child should earn more and so help the extended family. Self-interest must be a better guide than abstract good intentions from the ILO's office block in Geneva. Next time you are exploring the ever-cheaper wares in your favourite shops, look at the origin labels. The people who produce these items are richer than they would be without production lines nearer their homes.

A pernicious [*having the quality of destroying or being destructive*] argument

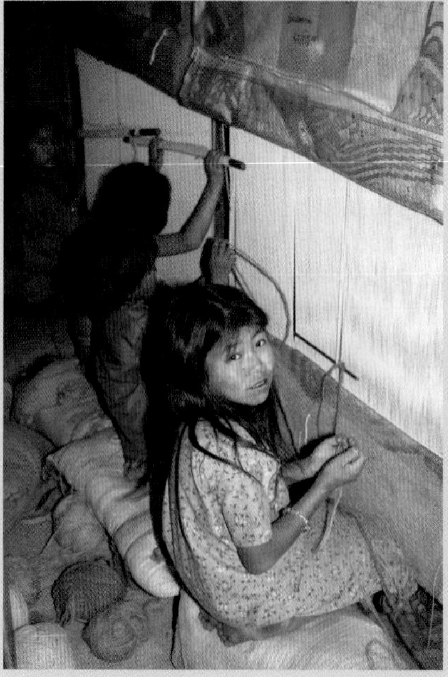

is that children working stop adults earning full wages. This is precisely the economic dunce speak that used to argue a woman's place is in the home. Adam Smith argued that a poor man's poverty can be his asset; he can trade or work his way up. The Third World's great advantage is their relative cheapness. Muddled, if kindly, thinking wants to suppress this. Rich countries should welcome the new nations joining the markets. Child labour will evaporate as prosperity spreads. In the meantime, Scottish pupils might find a day's work far more educational than torture by chalkboard.

Source: Adapted from John Blundell, the Director General of the Institute of Economic Affairs (IEA) (http://www.iea.org.uk). The article originally appeared in *The Scotsman* newspaper on 23 February 2004.

and Housing Benefit (a subsidy to a poor family's rent or mortgage interest payments) are benefits aimed at helping the poor and are tied to family income. As a family's income rises, the family becomes ineligible for these benefits. When all benefits being received are taken together, it is common for families to face effective marginal tax rates that are very high. Sometimes the effective marginal tax rates even exceed 100 per cent, so that poor families are worse off when they earn more: they are caught in a 'poverty trap'. By trying to help the poor, the government discourages those families from working. According to critics of anti-poverty policies, these social security benefits alter work attitudes and create a 'culture of poverty'.

It might seem that there is an easy solution to this problem: reduce benefits to poor families more gradually as their incomes rise. For example, if a poor family loses €0.30 of benefits for every extra €1 it earns, then it faces an effective marginal tax rate of 30 per cent. Although this effective tax reduces work effort to some extent, it does not eliminate the incentive to work completely.

The problem with this solution is that it greatly increases the cost of the social security system. The more gradual the phase-out, the more families are eligible for some level of benefits – and the more the social security system costs. Thus, policy makers face a trade-off between burdening the poor with high effective marginal tax rates and burdening taxpayers with a costly anti-poverty programme.

There are various other ways to try to reduce the work disincentive of anti-poverty programmes, such as stopping or reducing benefits to people who have not found a job within a reasonable period of time or who have turned down job offers for no good reason. In the UK, this kind of reasoning underpins the structure of the benefits paid to the unemployed: unemployed people may be eligible to receive a benefit called Jobseeker's Allowance. To receive the allowance, however, the claimant must be capable of starting work immediately and of actively taking steps to find a job such as attending interviews, writing applications or seeking job information. They must also have a current 'jobseeker's agreement' with the Employment Service, which includes such information as hours available for work, the desired job and any steps that the claimant is willing to take to find work (such as moving to a different town). They must be prepared to work up to 40 hours a week and have a reasonable prospect of finding work (i.e. not place too many restrictions on the type of work they are willing to undertake). If a claimant refuses to take up a job offer without good reason, they may be denied further payments of Jobseeker's Allowance. People aged 18–24 who have been unemployed and claiming Jobseeker's Allowance for six months or more are required to participate in a government scheme designed to get them into work (which includes, for example, a personal advisor on suitable job opportunities) called the New Deal for Young Persons. Those aged 25 or over must participate in a similar programme, called the New Deal 25-Plus programme, if they have been unemployed and claiming Jobseeker's Allowance for 18 months.

Quick Quiz List three policies aimed at helping the poor, and discuss the pros and cons of each.

CONCLUSION

People have long reflected on the distribution of income in society. Plato, the ancient Greek philosopher, concluded that in an ideal society the income of the richest person would be no more than four times the income of the poorest person. Although the measurement of inequality is difficult, it is clear that our society has much more inequality than Plato recommended.

One of the *Ten Principles of Economics* discussed in Chapter 1 is that governments can sometimes improve market outcomes. There is little consensus, however, about how this principle should be applied to the distribution of income. Philosophers and policy makers today do not agree on how much income inequality is desirable, or even whether public policy should aim to alter the distribution of income. Much of public debate reflects this disagreement. Whenever taxes are raised, for instance, politicians argue over how much of the tax hike should fall on the rich, people from the middle-income group, and the poor.

Another of the *Ten Principles of Economics* is that people face trade-offs. This principle is important to keep in mind when thinking about economic inequality. Policies that penalize the successful and reward the unsuccessful reduce the incentive to succeed. Thus, policy makers face a trade-off between equality and efficiency. The more equally the pie is divided, the smaller the pie becomes. This is the one lesson concerning the distribution of income about which almost everyone agrees.

SUMMARY

- Data on the distribution of income show wide disparity in industrialized economies.
- Because in-kind transfers, the economic life cycle, transitory income and economic mobility are so important for understanding variation in income, it is difficult to gauge the degree of inequality in our society using data on the distribution of income in a single year. When these other factors are taken into account, they tend to suggest that economic well-being is more equally distributed than is annual income.
- Political philosophers differ in their views about the role of government in altering the distribution of income. Utilitarians (such as John Stuart Mill) would choose the distribution of income to maximize the sum of utility of everyone in society. Liberals (such as John Rawls) would determine the distribution of income as if we were behind a 'veil of ignorance' that prevented us from knowing our own stations in life. Libertarians (such as Robert Nozick) would have the government enforce individual rights to ensure a fair process but then not be concerned about inequality in the resulting distribution of income.
- Various policies aim to help the poor – minimum wage laws, social security, negative income taxes and in-kind transfers. Although each of these policies helps some families escape poverty, they also have unintended side effects. Because financial assistance declines as income rises, the poor often face effective marginal tax rates that are very high. Such high effective tax rates discourage poor families from escaping poverty on their own.

KEY CONCEPTS

life cycle, p. 421
permanent income, p. 422
poverty rate, p. 423
poverty line, p. 423
absolute poverty, p. 423
relative poverty, p. 423
utilitarianism, p. 424
utility, p. 424
liberalism, p. 425
maximin criterion, p. 426
libertarianism, p. 426
social security, p. 429
negative income tax, p. 429
in-kind transfers, p. 430

QUESTIONS FOR REVIEW

1. How does the extent of income inequality in your country compare to that of other nations around the world?
2. What groups in the population are most likely to live in poverty?
3. When gauging the amount of inequality, why do transitory and life cycle variations in income cause difficulties?
4. How would a utilitarian, a liberal and a libertarian determine how much income inequality is permissible?
5. What are the pros and cons of in-kind (rather than cash) transfers to the poor?
6. Describe how anti-poverty programmes can discourage the poor from working. How might you reduce this disincentive? What are the disadvantages with your proposed policy?

PROBLEMS AND APPLICATIONS

1. Table 20.2 shows that income inequality in the United Kingdom has increased during the past 20 years. Some factors contributing to this increase were discussed in Chapter 19. What are they?
2. Economists often view life cycle variation in income as one form of transitory variation in income around people's lifetime, or permanent, income. In this sense, how does your current income compare to your permanent income? Do you think your current income accurately reflects your standard of living?
3. The chapter discusses the importance of economic mobility.
   a. What policies might the government pursue to increase economic mobility *within* a generation?
   b. What policies might the government pursue to increase economic mobility *across* generations?
   c. Do you think we should reduce spending on social security benefits in order to increase spending on government programmes that enhance economic mobility? What are some of the advantages and disadvantages of doing so?
4. Consider two communities. In one community, ten families have incomes of €100 each and ten families have incomes of €20 each. In the other community, ten families have incomes of €200 each and ten families have incomes of €22 each.
   a. In which community is the distribution of income more unequal? In which community is the problem of poverty likely to be worse?
   b. Which distribution of income would Rawls prefer? Explain.
   c. Which distribution of income do you prefer? Explain.
5. The chapter uses the analogy of a 'leaky bucket' to explain one constraint on the redistribution of income.
   a. What elements of your country's system for redistributing income create the leaks in the bucket? Be specific.
   b. Do you think that people with left-wing political views believe that the bucket used for redistributing income is more or less leaky than it is believed to be by people with more right-wing political views? How does that belief affect their views about the amount of income redistribution that the government should undertake?
6. Suppose there are two possible income distributions in a society of ten people. In the first distribution, nine people would have incomes of €30 000 and one person would have an income of €10 000. In the second distribution, all ten people would have incomes of €25 000.
   a. If the society had the first income distribution, what would be the utilitarian argument for redistributing income?
   b. Which income distribution would Rawls consider more equitable? Explain.
   c. Which income distribution would Nozick consider more equitable? Explain.
7. Suppose that a family's tax liability equalled its income multiplied by one-half, minus €10 000. Under this system, some families would pay taxes to the government, and some families would receive money from the government through a 'negative income tax'.
   a. Consider families with pre-tax incomes of €0, €10 000, €20 000, €30 000, and €40 000. Make a table showing pre-tax income, taxes paid to the government or

money received from the government, and after-tax income for each family.

b. What is the marginal tax rate in this system (i.e. out of every €1 of extra income, how much is paid in tax)? What is the maximum amount of income at which a family *receives* money from the government?

c. Now suppose that the tax schedule is changed, so that a family's tax liability equals its income multiplied by one-quarter, minus €10 000. What is the marginal tax rate in this new system? What is the maximum amount of income at which a family receives money from the government?

d. What is the main advantage of each of the tax schedules discussed here?

8. John and Jeremy are utilitarians. John believes that labour supply is highly elastic, whereas Jeremy believes that labour supply is quite inelastic. How do you suppose their views about income redistribution differ?

9. Do you agree or disagree with each of the following statements? What do your views imply for public policies, such as taxes on inheritance?
   a. 'Every parent has the right to work hard and save in order to give his or her children a better life.'
   b. 'No child should be disadvantaged by the sloth or bad luck of his or her parents.'

For further resources, visit www.cengage.com/mankiw_taylor2

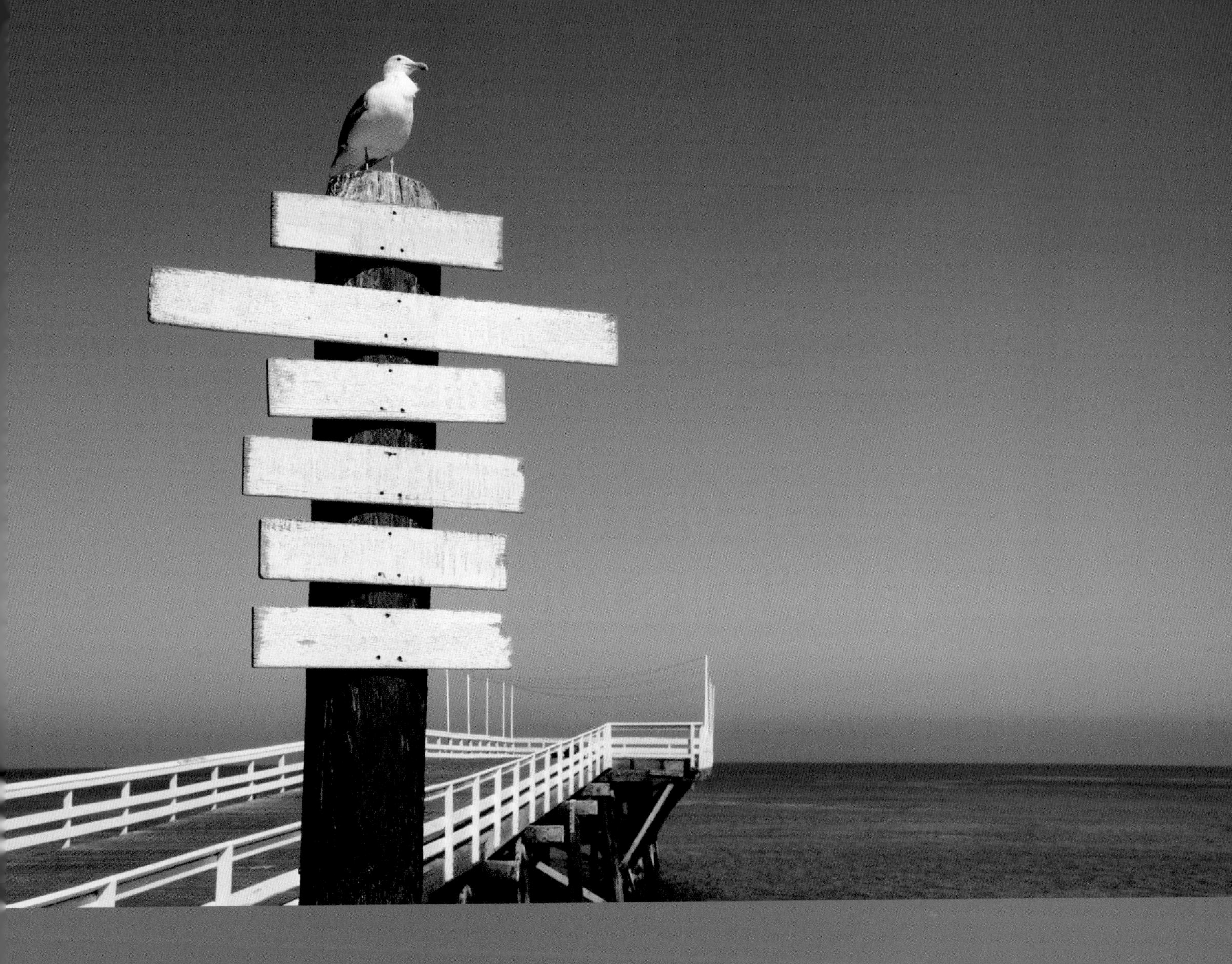

7

TOPICS FOR FURTHER STUDY

21 THE THEORY OF CONSUMER CHOICE

When you walk into a shop, you are confronted with thousands of goods that you might buy. Of course, because your financial resources are limited, you cannot buy everything that you want. The assumption is, therefore, that you consider the prices of the various goods being offered for sale and buy a bundle of goods that, given your resources, best suits your needs and desires.

In this chapter we develop the theory that describes how consumers make decisions about what to buy. So far throughout this book we have summarized consumers' decisions with the demand curve. As we discussed in Chapters 4 through to 7, the demand curve for a good reflects consumers' willingness to pay for it. When the price of a good rises, consumers are willing to pay for fewer units, so the quantity demanded falls. We now look more deeply at the decisions that lie behind the demand curve. The theory of consumer choice presented in this chapter provides a more complete understanding of demand, just as the theory of the competitive firm in Chapter 14 provides a more complete understanding of supply. We will look at the traditional analysis of consumer behaviour and also introduce some ideas that have arisen as a result of more recent research in psychology, which is increasingly being looked at with interest by economists.

One of the *Ten Principles of Economics* discussed in Chapter 1 is that people face trade-offs. The theory of consumer choice examines the trade-offs that people face in their role as consumers. When a consumer buys more of one good, he can afford less of other goods. When he spends more time enjoying leisure and less time working, he has lower income and can afford less consumption. When he spends more of his income in the present and saves less of it, he must accept a lower level of consumption in the future. The theory of consumer choice examines how consumers facing these trade-offs make decisions and how they respond to changes in their environment.

After developing the basic theory of consumer choice, we apply it to three questions about household decisions. In particular, we ask:

- Do all demand curves slope downward?
- How do wages affect labour supply?
- How do interest rates affect household saving?

At first, these questions might seem unrelated. But, as we will see, we can use the theory of consumer choice to address each of them.

THE BUDGET CONSTRAINT: WHAT THE CONSUMER CAN AFFORD

Most people would like to increase the quantity or quality of the goods they consume – to take longer holidays, drive fancier cars or eat at better restaurants. People consume less than they desire because their spending is *constrained,* or limited, by their income. We begin our study of consumer choice by examining this link between income and spending.

To keep things simple, we use a model which examines the decisions facing a consumer who buys only two goods: cola and pizza. Of course, real people buy thousands of different kinds of goods. Yet using this model greatly simplifies the problem without altering the basic insights about consumer choice.

We first consider how the consumer's income constrains the amount he spends on cola and pizza. Suppose that the consumer has an income of €1 000 per month and that he spends his entire income each month on cola and pizza. The price of a litre of cola is €2 and the price of a pizza is €10.

The table in Figure 21.1 shows some of the many combinations of Cola and pizza that the consumer can buy. The first line in the table shows that if the consumer spends all his income on pizza, he can eat 100 pizzas during the month, but he would not be able to buy any cola at all. The second line shows another possible consumption bundle: 90 pizzas and 50 litres of cola. And so on. Each consumption bundle in the table costs exactly €1 000.

The graph in Figure 21.1 illustrates the consumption bundles that the consumer can choose. The vertical axis measures the number of litres of cola, and the horizontal axis measures the number of pizzas. Three points are marked on this figure. At point A, the consumer buys no cola and consumes 100 pizzas. At point B, the consumer buys no pizza and consumes 500 litres of cola. At point C, the consumer buys 50 pizzas and 250 litres of cola. Point C, which is exactly at the middle of the line from A to B, is the point at which the consumer spends an equal amount (€500) on cola and pizza. Of course, these are only three of the many combinations of cola and pizza that the consumer can choose. All the points on the line from A to B are possible. This line, called the **budget constraint**, shows the consumption bundles that the consumer can afford. In this case, it shows the trade-off between cola and pizza that the consumer faces.

budget constraint
the limit on the consumption bundles that a consumer can afford

The slope of the budget constraint measures the rate at which the consumer can trade one good for the other. Recall from the appendix to Chapter 2 that the slope between two points is calculated as the change in the vertical distance divided by the change in the horizontal distance ('rise over run'). From point A to point B, the vertical distance is 500 litres, and the horizontal distance is

FIGURE 21.1

The Consumer's Budget Constraint

The budget constraint shows the various bundles of goods that the consumer can afford for a given income. Here the consumer buys bundles of cola and pizza. The table and graph show what the consumer can afford if his income is €1 000, the price of cola is €2 and the price of pizza is €10.

Litres of cola	Number of pizzas	Spending on cola	Spending on pizza	Total spending
0	100	€0	€1 000	€1 000
50	90	100	900	1 000
100	80	200	800	1 000
150	70	300	700	1 000
200	60	400	600	1 000
250	50	500	500	1 000
300	40	600	400	1 000
350	30	700	300	1 000
400	20	800	200	1 000
450	10	900	100	1 000
500	0	1 000	0	1 000

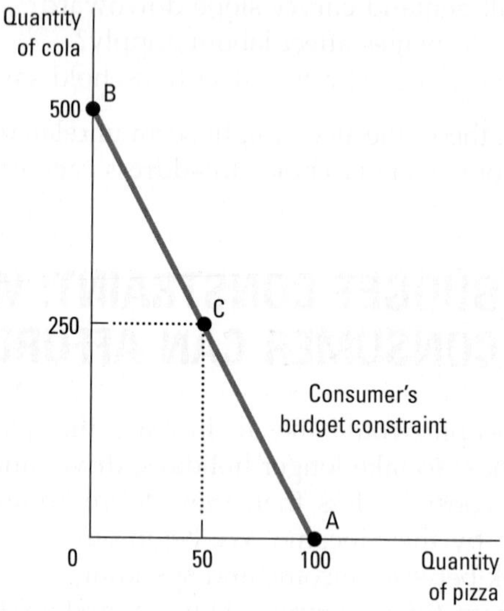

100 pizzas. Because the budget constraint slopes downward, the slope is a negative number – this reflects the fact that to get one extra pizza, the consumer has to *reduce* his consumption of cola by five litres. In fact, the slope of the budget constraint (ignoring the minus sign) equals the *relative price* of the two goods – the price of one good compared to the price of the other. A pizza costs 5 times as much as a litre of cola, so the opportunity cost of a pizza is 5 litres of cola. The budget constraint's slope of 5 reflects the trade-off the market is offering the consumer: 1 pizza for 5 litres of cola.

Quick Quiz Draw the budget constraint for a person with income of €1 000 if the price of cola is €5 and the price of pizza is €10. What is the slope of this budget constraint?

PREFERENCES: WHAT THE CONSUMER WANTS

Our goal in this chapter is to see how consumers make choices. There are two key assumptions that are made about consumers. One is that they have limited incomes but unlimited wants and the second is that they prefer to have more than less. These basic assumptions allow us to investigate behaviour in relation to how a consumer allocates limited income among different preferences. The budget constraint is one piece of the analysis: it shows what combination of goods the consumer can afford given his income and the prices of the goods. The consumer's choices, however, depend not only on his budget constraint but also on his preferences regarding the two goods. Therefore, the consumer's preferences are the next piece of our analysis.

Representing Preferences with Indifference Curves

The consumer's preferences allow him to choose among different bundles of cola and pizza. If you offer the consumer two different bundles, he chooses the bundle that best suits his tastes. If the two bundles suit his tastes equally well, we say that the consumer is *indifferent* between the two bundles.

Just as we have represented the consumer's budget constraint graphically, we can also represent his preferences graphically. We do this with indifference curves. An **indifference curve** shows the bundles of consumption that make the consumer equally happy. In this case, the indifference curves show the combinations of cola and pizza with which the consumer is equally satisfied.

indifference curve
a curve that shows consumption bundles that give the consumer the same level of satisfaction

Figure 21.2 shows two of the consumer's many indifference curves. The consumer is indifferent among combinations A, B and C, because they are all on the same curve. Not surprisingly, if the consumer's consumption of pizza is reduced, say from point A to point B, consumption of cola must increase to keep him equally happy. If consumption of pizza is reduced again, from point B to point C, the amount of cola consumed must increase yet again.

The slope at any point on an indifference curve equals the rate at which the consumer is willing to substitute one good for the other. This rate is called the **marginal rate of substitution** (*MRS*). In this case, the marginal rate of substitution measures how much cola the consumer requires in order to be compensated for a one-unit reduction in pizza consumption. Notice that because the indifference curves are not straight lines, the marginal rate of substitution is not the same at all points on a given indifference curve. The rate at which a consumer is willing to trade one good for the other depends on the amounts of the goods he is already consuming. That is, the rate at which a consumer is willing to trade pizza for cola depends on whether he is hungrier or thirstier, which in turn depends on how much pizza and cola he has.

marginal rate of substitution
the rate at which a consumer is willing to trade one good for another

The consumer is equally happy at all points on any given indifference curve, but he prefers some indifference curves to others. We assume that consumers would rather have more of a good than less of it. Because he prefers more consumption to less, higher indifference curves are preferred to lower ones. In Figure 21.2, any point on curve I_2 is preferred to any point on curve I_1.

FIGURE 21.2

The Consumer's Preferences

The consumer's preferences are represented with indifference curves, which show the combinations of cola and pizza that make the consumer equally satisfied. Because the consumer prefers more of a good, points on a higher indifference curve (I_2 here) are preferred to points on a lower indifference curve (I_1). The marginal rate of substitution (MRS) shows the rate at which the consumer is willing to trade cola for pizza.

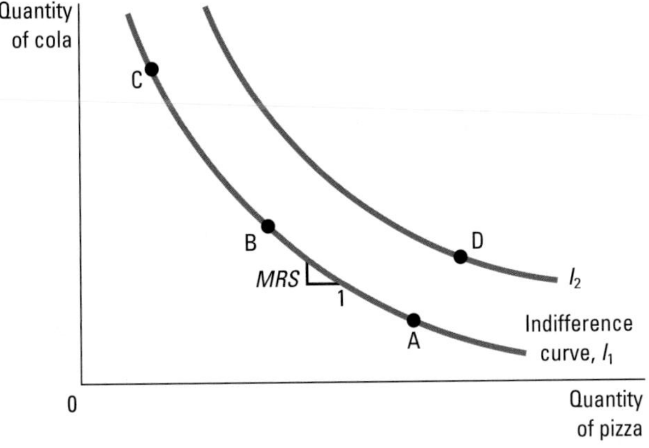

A consumer's set of indifference curves gives a complete ranking of the consumer's preferences. That is, we can use the indifference curves to rank any two bundles of goods. For example, the indifference curves tell us that point D is preferred to point A because point D is on a higher indifference curve than point A. (That conclusion may be obvious, however, because point D offers the consumer both more pizza and more cola.) The indifference curves also tell us that point D is preferred to point C because point D is on a higher indifference curve. Even though point D has less cola than point C, it has more than enough extra pizza to make the consumer prefer it. By seeing which point is on the higher indifference curve, we can use the set of indifference curves to rank any combinations of cola and pizza.

Four Properties of Indifference Curves

Because indifference curves represent a consumer's preferences, they have certain properties that reflect those preferences. Here we consider four properties that describe most indifference curves:

- *Property 1: Higher indifference curves are preferred to lower ones.* Consumers usually prefer more of something to less of it. This preference for greater quantities is reflected in the indifference curves. As Figure 21.2 shows, higher indifference curves represent larger quantities of goods than lower indifference curves. Thus, the consumer prefers being on higher indifference curves.
- *Property 2: Indifference curves are downward sloping.* The slope of an indifference curve reflects the rate at which the consumer is willing to substitute one good for the other. In most cases, the consumer likes both goods. Therefore, if the quantity of one good is reduced, the quantity of the other good must increase in order for the consumer to be equally happy. For this reason, most indifference curves slope downward.
- *Property 3: Indifference curves do not cross.* To see why this is true, suppose that two indifference curves did cross, as in Figure 21.3. Then, because point A is

FIGURE 21.3

The Impossibility of Intersecting Indifference Curves

A situation like this can never happen. According to these indifference curves, the consumer would be equally satisfied at points A, B and C, even though point C has more of both goods than point A.

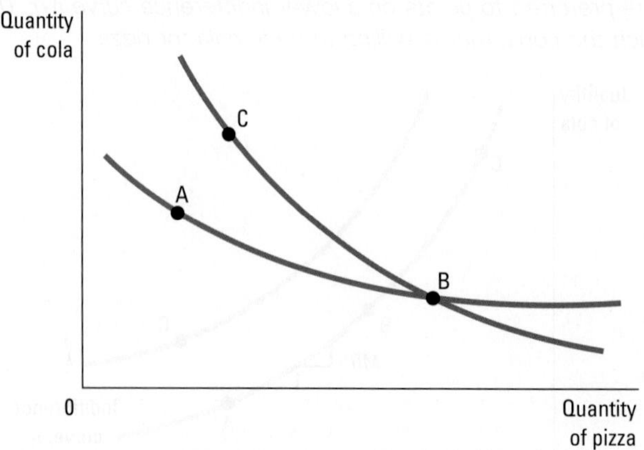

on the same indifference curve as point B, the two points would make the consumer equally happy. In addition, because point B is on the same indifference curve as point C, these two points would make the consumer equally happy. But these conclusions imply that points A and C would also make the consumer equally happy, even though point C has more of both goods. This contradicts our assumption that the consumer always prefers more of both goods to less. This is called the *'axiom of transitivity'*– given any three baskets of goods, if A is preferred to B and B to C then A must be preferred to C. Thus, indifference curves cannot cross.

- *Property 4: Indifference curves are bowed inward.* The slope of an indifference curve is the marginal rate of substitution – the rate at which the consumer is willing to trade off one good for the other. The marginal rate of substitution (*MRS*) usually depends on the amount of each good the consumer is currently consuming. In particular, because people are more willing to trade away goods that they have in abundance and less willing to trade away goods of which they have little, the indifference curves are bowed inward. As an example, consider Figure 21.4. At point A, because the consumer has a lot of cola and only a little pizza, he is very hungry but not very thirsty. To induce the consumer to give up 1 pizza, the consumer has to be given 6 litres of cola: the marginal rate of substitution is 6 litres per pizza. By contrast, at point B, the consumer has little cola and a lot of pizza, so he is very thirsty but not very hungry. At this point, he would be willing to give up 1 pizza to get 1 litre of cola: the marginal rate of substitution is 1 litre per pizza. Thus, the bowed shape of the indifference curve reflects the consumer's greater willingness to give up a good that he already has in large quantity.

FIGURE 21.4

Bowed Indifference Curves

Indifference curves are usually bowed inward. This shape implies that the marginal rate of substitution (MRS) depends on the quantity of the two goods the consumer is consuming. At point A, the consumer has little pizza and much cola, so he requires a lot of extra cola to induce him to give up one of the pizzas: the marginal rate of substitution is 6 litres of cola per pizza. At point B, the consumer has much pizza and little cola, so he requires only a little extra cola to induce him to give up one of the pizzas: the marginal rate of substitution is 1 litre of cola per pizza.

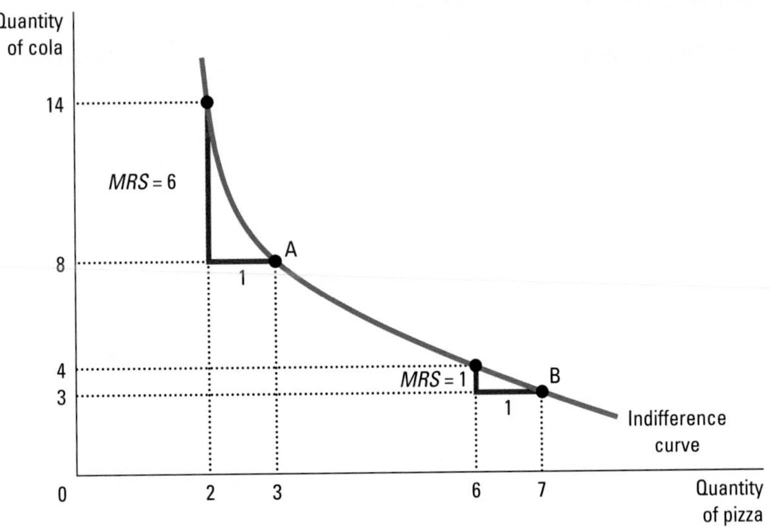

Two Extreme Examples of Indifference Curves

The shape of an indifference curve tells us about the consumer's willingness to trade one good for the other. When the goods are easy to substitute for each other, the indifference curves are less bowed; when the goods are hard to substitute, the indifference curves are very bowed. To see why this is true, let's consider the extreme cases.

Perfect Substitutes Suppose that someone offered you bundles of 50 cent coins and 10 cent coins. How would you rank the different bundles?

Most probably, you would care only about the total monetary value of each bundle. If so, you would judge a bundle based on the number of 50 cent coins plus five times the number of 10 cent coins. In other words, you would always be willing to trade 1 50 cent coin for 5 10 cent coins, regardless of the number of coins in either bundle. Your marginal rate of substitution between 10 cent coins and 50 cent coins would be a fixed number: 5.

We can represent your preferences over 50 cent coins and 10 cent coins with the indifference curves in panel (a) of Figure 21.5. Because the marginal rate of substitution is constant, the indifference curves are straight lines. In this extreme case of straight indifference curves, we say that the two goods are **perfect substitutes**.

perfect substitutes
two goods with straight-line indifference curves

Perfect Complements Suppose now that someone offered you bundles of shoes. Some of the shoes fit your left foot, others your right foot. How would you rank these different bundles?

In this case, you might care only about the number of pairs of shoes. In other words, you would judge a bundle based on the number of pairs you could assemble from it. A bundle of 5 left shoes and 7 right shoes yields only 5 pairs. Getting 1 more right shoe has no value if there is no left shoe to go with it.

FIGURE 21.5

Perfect Substitutes and Perfect Complements

When two goods are easily substitutable, such as 50 cent and 10 cent coins, the indifference curves are straight lines, as shown in panel (a). When two goods are strongly complementary, such as left shoes and right shoes, the indifference curves are right angles, as shown in panel (b).

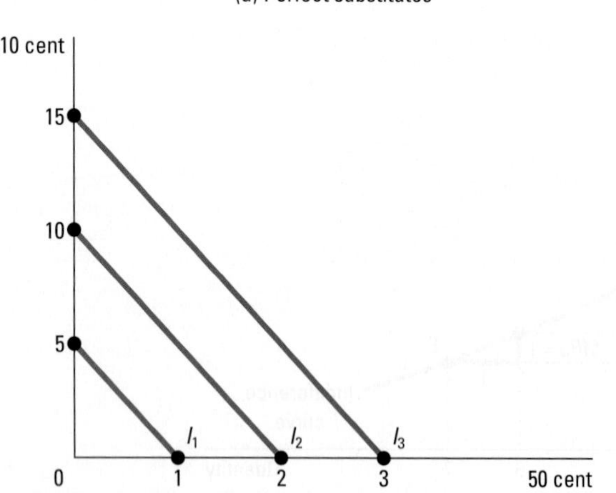

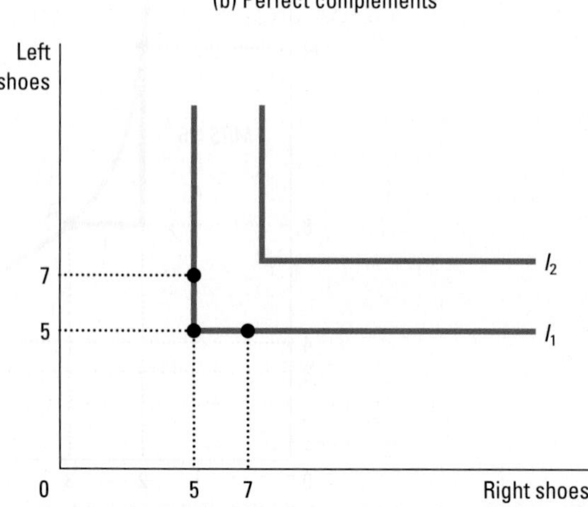

We can represent your preferences for right and left shoes with the indifference curves in panel (b) of Figure 21.5. In this case, a bundle with 5 left shoes and 5 right shoes is just as good as a bundle with 5 left shoes and 7 right shoes. It is also just as good as a bundle with 7 left shoes and 5 right shoes. The indifference curves, therefore, are right angles. In this extreme case of right-angle indifference curves, we say that the two goods are **perfect complements**.

perfect complements
two goods with right-angle indifference curves

In the real world, of course, most goods are neither perfect substitutes (like coins of different denominations) nor perfect complements (like right shoes and left shoes). More typically, the indifference curves are bowed inward, but not so bowed as to become right angles.

Quick Quiz Draw some indifference curves for cola and pizza. Explain the four properties of these indifference curves.

OPTIMIZATION: WHAT THE CONSUMER CHOOSES

The goal of this chapter is to understand how a consumer makes choices. We have the two pieces necessary for this analysis: the consumer's budget constraint and the consumer's preferences. Now we put these two pieces together and consider the consumer's decision about what to buy.

The Consumer's Optimal Choices

Consider once again our cola and pizza example. The consumer would like to end up with the best possible combination of cola and pizza – that is, the combination on the highest possible indifference curve. But the consumer must also end up on or below his budget constraint, which measures the total resources available to him.

Figure 21.6 shows the consumer's budget constraint and three of his many indifference curves. The highest indifference curve that the consumer can reach (I_2 in the figure) is the one that just barely touches the budget constraint. The point at which this indifference curve and the budget constraint touch is called the *optimum*. The consumer would prefer point A, but he cannot afford that point because it lies above his budget constraint. The consumer can afford point B, but that point is on a lower indifference curve and, therefore, provides the consumer less satisfaction. The optimum represents the best combination of consumption of cola and pizza available to the consumer.

Notice that, at the optimum, the slope of the indifference curve equals the slope of the budget constraint. We say that the indifference curve is *tangent* to the budget constraint. The slope of the indifference curve is the marginal rate of substitution between cola and pizza, and the slope of the budget constraint is the relative price of cola and pizza. Thus, the consumer chooses consumption of the two goods so that the marginal rate of substitution equals the relative price.

In Chapter 7 we saw how market prices reflect the marginal value that consumers place on goods. This analysis of consumer choice shows the same result in another way. In making his consumption choices, the consumer takes as given the relative price of the two goods and then chooses an optimum at which his marginal rate of substitution equals this relative price. The relative price is the rate at which the *market* is willing to trade one good for the other, whereas the marginal rate of substitution is the rate at which the *consumer* is willing to

FIGURE 21.6

The Consumer's Optimum

The consumer chooses the point on his budget constraint that lies on the highest indifference curve. At this point, called the optimum, the marginal rate of substitution equals the relative price of the two goods. Here the highest indifference curve the consumer can reach is I_2. The consumer prefers point A, which lies on indifference curve I_3, but the consumer cannot afford this bundle of cola and pizza. In contrast, point B is affordable, but because it lies on a lower indifference curve, the consumer does not prefer it.

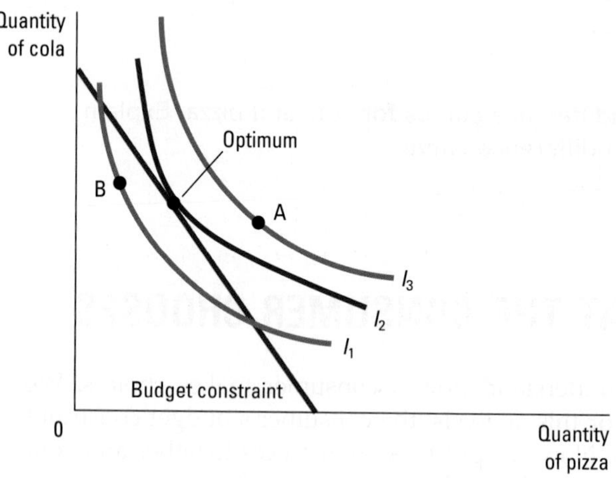

trade one good for the other. At the consumer's optimum, the consumer's valuation of the two goods (as measured by the marginal rate of substitution) equals the market's valuation (as measured by the relative price). As a result of this consumer optimization, market prices of different goods reflect the value that consumers place on those goods.

How Changes in Income Affect the Consumer's Choices

Now that we have seen how the consumer makes the consumption decision, let's examine how consumption responds to changes in income. To be specific, suppose that income increases. With higher income, the consumer can afford more of both goods. The increase in income, therefore, shifts the budget constraint outward, as in Figure 21.7. Because the relative price of the two goods has not changed, the slope of the new budget constraint is the same as the slope of the initial budget constraint. That is, an increase in income leads to a parallel shift in the budget constraint.

The expanded budget constraint allows the consumer to choose a better combination of cola and pizza. In other words, the consumer can now reach a higher indifference curve. Given the shift in the budget constraint and the consumer's preferences as represented by his indifference curves, the consumer's optimum moves from the point labelled 'initial optimum' to the point labelled 'new optimum'.

Notice that in Figure 21.7 the consumer chooses to consume more cola and more pizza. Although the logic of the model does not require increased consumption of both goods in response to increased income, this situation is the most common one. As you may recall from Chapter 4, if a consumer wants

FYI

Utility: An Alternative Way to Describe Preferences and Optimization

We have used indifference curves to represent the consumer's preferences. Another common way to represent preferences is with the concept of *utility.* Utility is an abstract measure of the satisfaction or happiness that a consumer receives from a bundle of goods. Economists say that a consumer prefers one bundle of goods to another if the first provides more utility than the second.

Indifference curves and utility are closely related. Because the consumer prefers points on higher indifference curves, bundles of goods on higher indifference curves provide higher utility. Because the consumer is equally happy with all points on the same indifference curve, all these bundles provide the same utility. You can think of an indifference curve as an 'equal-utility' curve.

The *marginal utility* of any good is the increase in utility that the consumer gets from an additional unit of that good. Most goods are assumed to exhibit *diminishing marginal utility:* the more of the good the consumer already has, the lower the marginal utility provided by an extra unit of that good. Think about it from the point of view of drinking when you are thirsty. If you are very thirsty the value placed on the consumption of the first drink offered is very high (let's give it a value out of 10 – it might, therefore be 10/10). If you are then offered a second drink, it might also give you some utility but chances are the rating you give it will not be as high as the first drink which served to quench that raging thirst (say 9/10). The offer of a third drink might now start to be a little too much. Your thirst has been quenched and whilst you might still drink it the utility ranking is now only 6/10. Each additional drink adds to *total* utility but the *addition* to total utility (marginal utility) is declining.

The marginal rate of substitution between two goods depends on their marginal utilities. For example, if the marginal utility of good X is twice the marginal utility of good Y, then a person would need 2 units of good Y to compensate for losing 1 unit of good X, and the marginal rate of substitution equals 2. More generally, the marginal rate of substitution (and thus the slope of the indifference curve) equals the marginal utility of one good divided by the marginal utility of the other good.

Utility analysis provides another way to describe consumer optimization. Recall that at the consumer's optimum, the marginal rate of substitution equals the ratio of prices. That is:

$$MRS = P_X/P_Y$$

Because the marginal rate of substitution equals the ratio of marginal utilities, we can write this condition for optimization as:

$$MU_X/MU_Y = P_X/P_Y$$

Now rearrange this expression to become:

$$MU_X/P_X = MU_Y/P_Y$$

This equation has a simple interpretation: at the optimum, the marginal utility per euro spent on good X equals the marginal utility per euro spent on good Y. Why? If this equality did not hold, the consumer could increase utility by changing behaviour, switching spending from the good that provided lower marginal utility per euro and more on the good that provided higher marginal utility per euro. This would be the rational thing to do.

When economists discuss the theory of consumer choice, they might express the theory using different words. One economist might say that the goal of the consumer is to maximize utility. Another economist might say that the goal of the consumer is to end up on the highest possible indifference curve. The first economist would conclude that, at the consumer's optimum, the marginal utility per euro is the same for all goods, whereas the second would conclude that the indifference curve is tangent to the budget constraint. In essence, these are two ways of saying the same thing.

more of a good when his income rises, economists call it a normal good. The indifference curves in Figure 21.7 are drawn under the assumption that both cola and pizza are normal goods.

Figure 21.8 shows an example in which an increase in income induces the consumer to buy more pizza but less cola. If a consumer buys less of a good when his income rises, economists call it an inferior good. Figure 21.8 is drawn under the assumption that pizza is a normal good and cola is an inferior good.

FIGURE 21.7

An Increase in Income

When the consumer's income rises, the budget constraint shifts out. If both goods are normal goods, the consumer responds to the increase in income by buying more of both of them. Here the consumer buys more pizza and more cola.

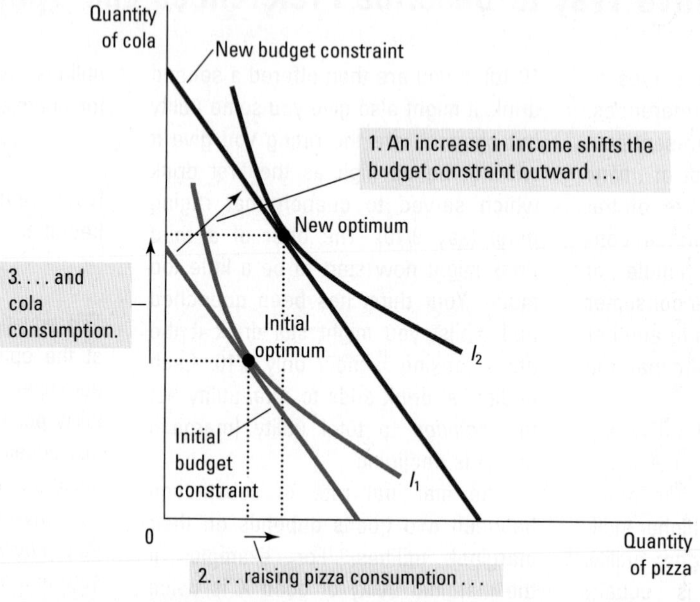

FIGURE 21.8

An Inferior Good

A good is an inferior good if the consumer buys less of it when his income rises. Here cola is an inferior good: when the consumer's income increases and the budget constraint shifts outward, the consumer buys more pizza but less cola.

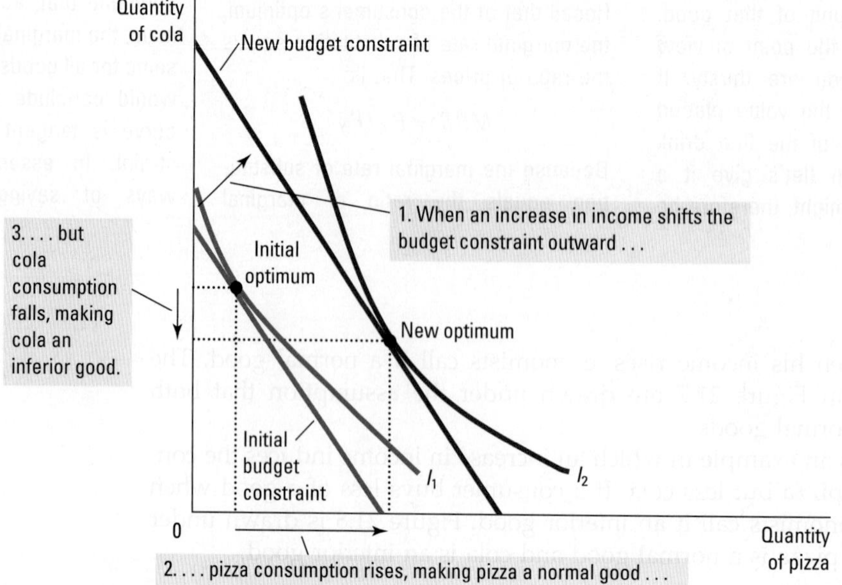

Although most goods are normal goods, there are some inferior goods in the world. One example is bus rides. High-income consumers are more likely to own cars and less likely to ride the bus than low-income consumers. Bus rides, therefore, are an inferior good.

How Changes in Prices Affect the Consumer's Choices

Let's now use this model of consumer choice to consider how a change in the price of one of the goods alters the consumer's choices. Suppose, in particular, that the price of cola falls from €2 to €1 a litre. It is no surprise that the lower price expands the consumer's set of buying opportunities. In other words, a fall in the price of any good causes the budget constraint to pivot. With his available income of €1 000 the consumer can now buy twice as many litres of cola than before but the same amount of pizza. Figure 21.9 shows that point A in the figure stays the same (100 pizzas). Yet if the consumer spends his entire income of €1 000 on cola, he can now buy 1 000 rather than only 500 litres. Thus, the end point of the budget constraint pivots outwards from point B to point D.

Notice that in this case the pivoting of the budget constraint changes its slope. (This differs from what happened previously when prices stayed the same but the consumer's income changed.) As we have discussed, the slope of the budget constraint reflects the relative price of cola and pizza. Because the price of cola has fallen to €1 from €2, while the price of pizza has remained €10, the consumer can now trade a pizza for 10 rather than 5 litres of cola. As a result, the new budget constraint is more steeply sloped.

FIGURE 21.9

A Change in Price

When the price of cola falls, the consumer's budget constraint shifts outward and changes slope. The consumer moves from the initial optimum to the new optimum, which changes his purchases of both cola and pizza. In this case, the quantity of cola consumed rises and the quantity of pizza consumed falls.

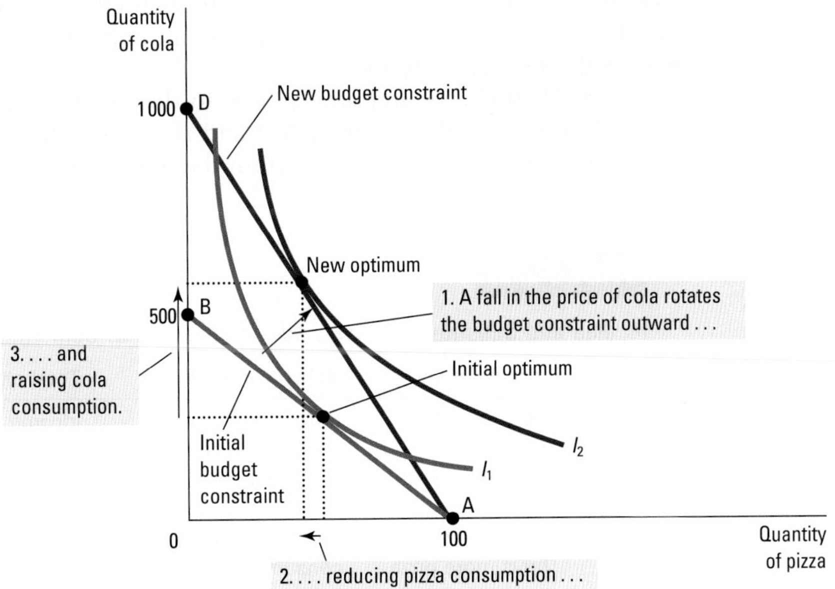

How such a change in the budget constraint alters the consumption of both goods depends on the consumer's preferences. For the indifference curves drawn in this figure, the consumer buys more cola and less pizza.

Income and Substitution Effects

income effect
the change in consumption that results when a price change moves the consumer to a higher or lower indifference curve

substitution effect
the change in consumption that results when a price change moves the consumer along a given indifference curve to a point with a new marginal rate of substitution

The impact of a change in the price of a good on consumption can be decomposed into two effects: an **income effect** and a **substitution effect**. To see what these two effects are, consider how our consumer might respond when he learns that the price of cola has fallen. He might reason in the following ways:

> 'Great news! Now that cola is cheaper, my income has greater purchasing power – my income now buys me more. I am, *in effect*, richer than I was. Because I am richer, I can buy both more cola and more pizza.' (This is the income effect.)
>
> 'Now that the price of cola has fallen, I get more litres of cola for every pizza that I give up. Because pizza is now *relatively* more expensive, I should buy less pizza and more cola.' (This is the substitution effect.)

Which statement do you find more compelling?

In fact, both of these statements make sense. The decrease in the price of cola makes the consumer better off. If cola and pizza are both normal goods, the consumer will want to spread this improvement in his purchasing power over both goods. This income effect tends to make the consumer buy more pizza and more cola. Yet, at the same time, consumption of cola has become less expensive relative to consumption of pizza. This substitution effect tends to make the consumer choose more cola and less pizza.

Now consider the end result of these two effects. The consumer certainly buys more cola, because the income and substitution effects both act to raise purchases of cola. But it is ambiguous whether the consumer buys more pizza, because the income and substitution effects work in opposite directions. This conclusion is summarized in Table 21.1.

We can interpret the income and substitution effects using indifference curves. The income effect is the change in consumption that results from the movement to a higher indifference curve. The substitution effect is the change in consumption that results from being at a point on an indifference curve with a different marginal rate of substitution.

Figure 21.10 shows graphically how to decompose the change in the consumer's decision into the income effect and the substitution effect. When the price of cola falls, the consumer moves from the initial optimum, point A, to the new

TABLE 21.1

Income and Substitution Effects When the Price of Cola Falls

Good	Income effect	Substitution effect	Total effect
Cola	Consumer is richer, so he buys more cola.	Cola is relatively cheaper, so consumer buys more cola.	Income and substitution effects act in same direction, so consumer buys more cola.
Pizza	Consumer is richer, so he buys more pizza.	Pizza is relatively more expensive, so consumer buys less pizza.	Income and substitution effects act in opposite directions, so the total effect on pizza consumption is ambiguous.

FIGURE 21.10

Income and Substitution Effects

The effect of a change in price can be broken down into an income effect and a substitution effect. The substitution effect – the movement along an indifference curve to a point with a different marginal rate of substitution – is shown here as the change from point A to point B along indifference curve I_1. The income effect – the shift to a higher indifference curve – is shown here as the change from point B on indifference curve I_1 to point C on indifference curve I_2.

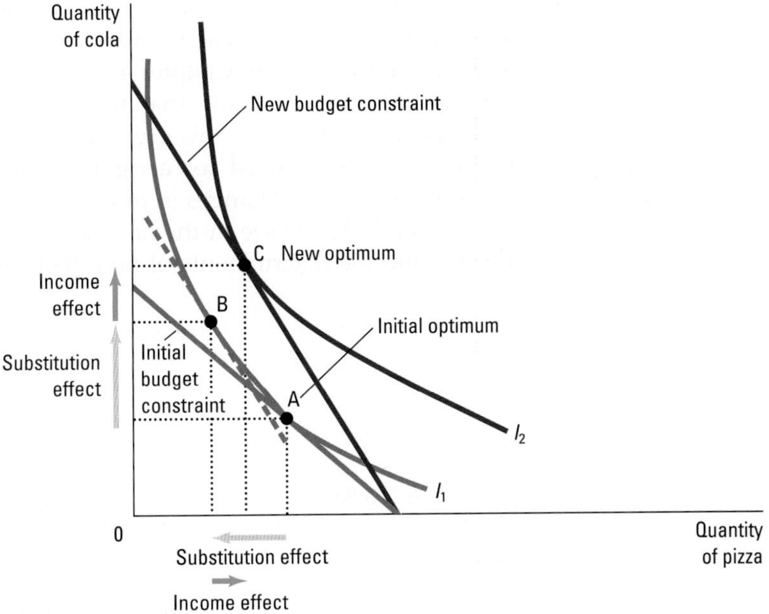

optimum, point C. We can view this change as occurring in two steps. First, the consumer moves *along* the initial indifference curve I_1 from point A to point B. The consumer is equally happy at these two points, but at point B the marginal rate of substitution reflects the new relative price. (The dashed line through point B reflects the new relative price by being parallel to the new budget constraint.) Next, the consumer *shifts* to the higher indifference curve I_2 by moving from point B to point C. Even though point B and point C are on different indifference curves, they have the same marginal rate of substitution. That is, the slope of the indifference curve I_1 at point B equals the slope of the indifference curve I_2 at point C.

Although the consumer never actually chooses point B, this hypothetical point is useful to clarify the two effects that determine the consumer's decision. Notice that the change from point A to point B represents a pure change in the marginal rate of substitution without any change in the consumer's welfare. Similarly, the change from point B to point C represents a pure change in welfare without any change in the marginal rate of substitution. Thus, the movement from A to B shows the substitution effect, and the movement from B to C shows the income effect.

Deriving the Demand Curve

We have just seen how changes in the price of a good alter the consumer's budget constraint and, therefore, the quantities of the two goods that he chooses to buy. The demand curve for any good reflects these consumption decisions. Recall that a demand curve shows the quantity demanded of a good for any given price. We can view a consumer's demand curve as a summary of the optimal decisions that arise from his budget constraint and indifference curves.

For example, Figure 21.11 considers the demand for cola. Panel (a) shows that when the price of a litre falls from €2 to €1, the consumer's budget constraint shifts outward. Because of both income and substitution effects, the consumer increases his purchases of cola from 250 to 750 litres. Panel (b) shows the demand curve that results from this consumer's decisions. In this way, the theory of consumer choice provides the theoretical foundation for the consumer's demand curve, which we first introduced in Chapter 4.

Although it is comforting to know that the demand curve arises naturally from the theory of consumer choice, this exercise by itself does not justify developing the theory. There is no need for a rigorous, analytic framework just to establish that people respond to changes in prices. The theory of consumer choice is, however, very useful. As we see in the next section, we can use the theory to delve more deeply into the determinants of household behaviour.

FIGURE 21.11

Deriving the Demand Curve

Panel (a) shows that when the price of cola falls from €2 to €1, the consumer's optimum moves from point A to point B, and the quantity of cola consumed rises from 250 to 750 litres. The demand curve in panel (b) reflects this relationship between the price and the quantity demanded.

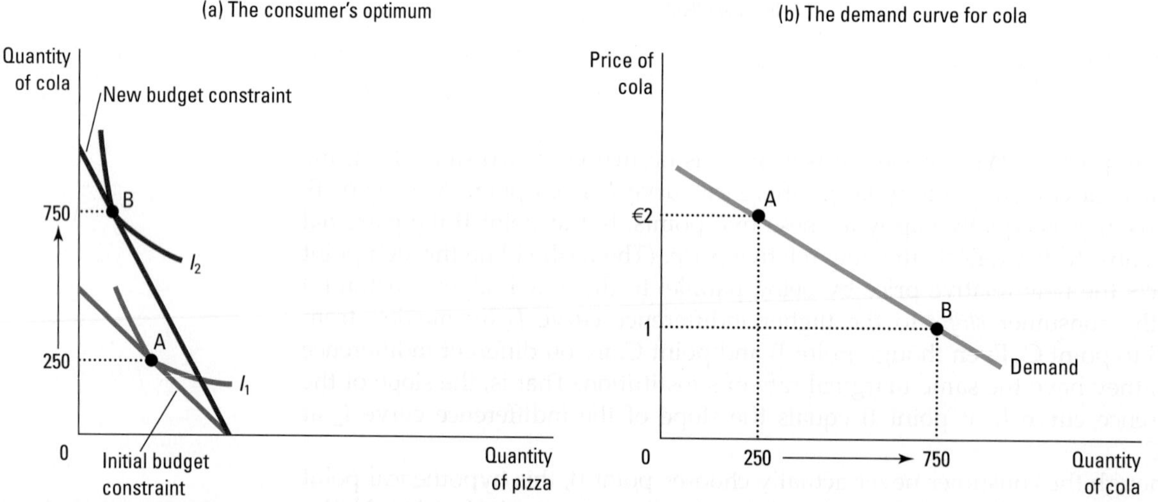

Quick Quiz Draw a budget constraint and indifference curves for cola and pizza. Show what happens to the budget constraint and the consumer's optimum when the price of pizza rises. In your diagram, decompose the change into an income effect and a substitution effect.

THREE APPLICATIONS

Now that we have developed the basic theory of consumer choice, let's use it to shed light on three questions about how the economy works. These three questions might at first seem unrelated. But because each question involves household decision-making, we can address it with the model of consumer behaviour we have just developed.

Do All Demand Curves Slope Downward?

Normally, when the price of a good rises, people buy less of it. Chapter 4 called this usual behaviour the *law of demand.* This law is reflected in the downward slope of the demand curve.

As a matter of economic theory, however, demand curves can sometimes slope upward. In other words, consumers can sometimes violate the law of demand and buy *more* of a good when the price rises. To see how this can happen, consider Figure 21.12. In this example, the consumer buys two goods – meat and potatoes. Initially, the consumer's budget constraint is the line from point A to point B. The optimum is point C. When the price of potatoes rises, the budget constraint shifts inward and is now the line from point A to point D. The optimum is now point E. Notice that a rise in the price of potatoes has led the consumer to buy a larger quantity of potatoes.

Why is the consumer responding in a seemingly perverse way? The reason is that potatoes here are a strongly inferior good. When the price of potatoes rises,

FIGURE 21.12

A Giffen Good

In this example, when the price of potatoes rises, the consumer's optimum shifts from point C *to point* E. *In this case, the consumer responds to a higher price of potatoes by buying less meat and more potatoes.*

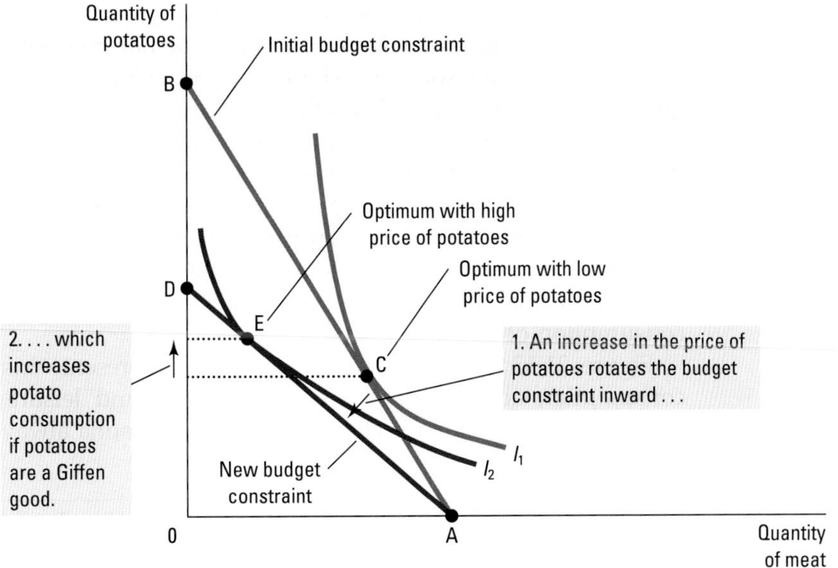

the consumer is poorer. The income effect makes the consumer want to buy less meat and more potatoes. At the same time, because the potatoes have become more expensive relative to meat, the substitution effect makes the consumer want to buy more meat and less potatoes. In this particular case, however, the income effect is so strong that it exceeds the substitution effect. In the end, the consumer responds to the higher price of potatoes by buying less meat and more potatoes.

Giffen good
a good for which an increase in the price raises the quantity demanded

Economists use the term **Giffen good** to describe a good that violates the law of demand. (The term is named after the British economist Robert Giffen, who first noted this possibility.) In this example, potatoes are a Giffen good. Giffen goods are inferior goods for which the income effect dominates the substitution effect. Therefore, they have demand curves that slope upward.

Economists disagree about whether any Giffen good has ever been discovered. Some historians suggest that potatoes were in fact a Giffen good during the Irish potato famine of the 19th century. Potatoes were such a large part of people's diet (historians estimate that the average working man might eat up to fourteen pounds of potatoes a day) that when the price of potatoes rose, it had a large income effect. People responded to their reduced living standard by cutting back on the luxury of meat and buying more of the staple food of potatoes. Thus, it is argued that a higher price of potatoes actually raised the quantity of potatoes demanded.

Whether or not this historical account is true, it is safe to say that Giffen goods are very rare. Some economists, (for example, Dwyer and Lindsey, 1984 and Rosen, 1999) have claimed that a legend has built up around Robert Giffen and that the evidence does not support his idea. Others have suggested that rice and wheat in parts of China might exhibit Giffen qualities. The theory of consumer choice does allow demand curves to slope upward. Yet such occurrences are so unusual that the law of demand is as reliable a law as any in economics.[1,2,3]

How Do Wages Affect Labour Supply?

So far we have used the theory of consumer choice to analyse how a person decides how to allocate his income between two goods. We can use the same theory to analyse how a person decides to allocate his time between work and leisure.

Consider the decision facing Cristina, a freelance software designer. Cristina is awake for 100 hours per week. She spends some of this time enjoying leisure – riding her horse, watching television, studying economics and so on. She spends the rest of this time developing software at her computer. For every hour she spends developing software, she earns €50, which she spends on consumption goods. Thus, her wage (€50) reflects the trade-off Cristina faces between leisure and consumption. For every hour of leisure she gives up, she works one more hour and gets €50 of consumption.

Figure 21.13 shows Cristina's budget constraint. If she spends all 100 hours enjoying leisure, she has no consumption. If she spends all 100 hours working, she earns a weekly consumption of €5 000 but has no time for leisure. If she works a normal 40-hour week, she enjoys 60 hours of leisure and has weekly consumption of €2 000.

Figure 21.13 uses indifference curves to represent Cristina's preferences for consumption and leisure. Here consumption and leisure are the two 'goods' between which Cristina is choosing. Because Cristina always prefers more leisure

[1]Dwyer, G.P. & Lindsay, C.M. (1984) 'Robert Giffen and the Irish Potato'. In *The American Economic Review*, **74**:188–192.

[2]Jensen, R & Miller, N. (2008) 'Giffen Behavior and Subsistence Consumption'. In *American Economic Review*, **97**:1553–1577.

[3]Rosen, S. (1999) 'Potato Paradoxes'. In *The Journal of Political Economy*, **107**:294–213.

FIGURE 21.13

The Work–Leisure Decision

This figure shows Cristina's budget constraint for deciding how much to work, her indifference curves for consumption and leisure, and her optimum.

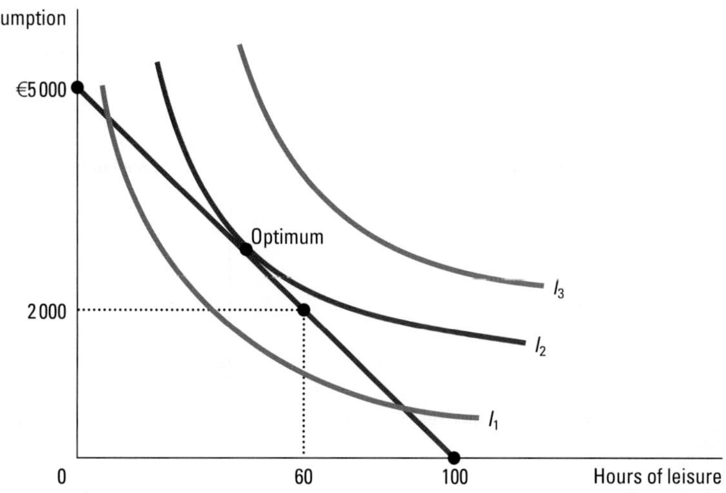

and more consumption, she prefers points on higher indifference curves to points on lower ones. At a wage of €50 per hour, Cristina chooses a combination of consumption and leisure represented by the point labelled 'optimum'. This is the point on the budget constraint that is on the highest possible indifference curve, which is curve I_2.

Now consider what happens when Cristina's wage increases from €50 to €60 per hour. Figure 21.14 shows two possible outcomes. In each case, the budget constraint, shown in the left-hand graph, pivots outward from BC_1 to BC_2. In the process, the budget constraint becomes steeper, reflecting the change in relative price: at the higher wage, Cristina gets more consumption for every hour of leisure that she gives up.

Cristina's preferences, as represented by her indifference curves, determine the resulting responses of consumption and leisure to the higher wage. In both panels, consumption rises. Yet the response of leisure to the change in the wage is different in the two cases. In panel (a), Cristina responds to the higher wage by enjoying less leisure. In panel (b), Cristina responds by enjoying more leisure.

Cristina's decision between leisure and consumption determines her supply of labour because the more leisure she enjoys, the less time she has left to work. In each panel, the right-hand graph in Figure 21.14 shows the labour supply curve implied by Cristina's decision. In panel (a), a higher wage induces Cristina to enjoy less leisure and work more, so the labour supply curve slopes upward. In panel (b), a higher wage induces Cristina to enjoy more leisure and work less, so the labour supply curve slopes 'backward'.

At first, the backward sloping labour supply curve is puzzling. Why would a person respond to a higher wage by working less? The answer comes from considering the income and substitution effects of a higher wage.

Consider first the substitution effect. When Cristina's wage rises, leisure becomes more costly relative to consumption, and this encourages Cristina to substitute consumption for leisure. In other words, the substitution effect induces

FIGURE 21.14

An Increase in the Wage

The two panels of this figure show how a person might respond to an increase in the wage. The graphs on the left show the consumer's initial budget constraint BC_1 *and new budget constraint* BC_2*, as well as the consumer's optimal choices over consumption and leisure. The graphs on the right show the resulting labour supply curve. Because hours worked equal total hours available minus hours of leisure, any change in leisure implies an opposite change in the quantity of labour supplied. In panel (a), when the wage rises, consumption rises and leisure falls, resulting in a labour supply curve that slopes upward. In panel (b), when the wage rises, both consumption and leisure rise, resulting in a labour supply curve that slopes backward.*

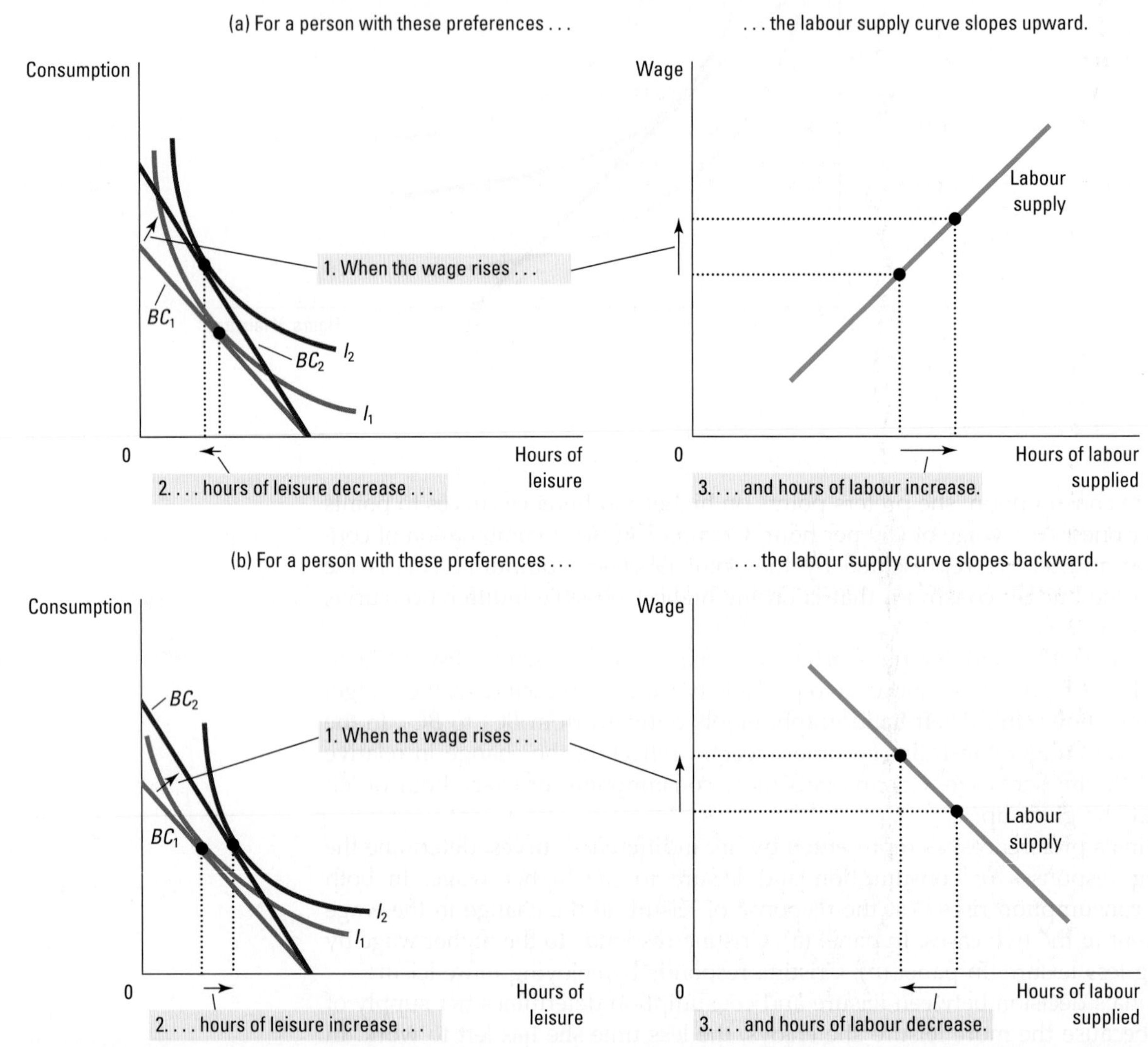

Cristina to work harder in response to higher wages, which tends to make the labour supply curve slope upward.

Now consider the income effect. When Cristina's wage rises, she moves to a higher indifference curve. She is now better off than she was. As long as consumption and leisure are both normal goods, she tends to want to use this increase in well-being to enjoy both higher consumption and greater leisure. In other words, the income effect induces her to work less, which tends to make the labour supply curve slope backward.

In the end, economic theory does not give a clear prediction about whether an increase in the wage induces Cristina to work more or less. If the substitution effect is greater than the income effect for Cristina, she works more. If the income effect is greater than the substitution effect, she works less. The labour supply curve, therefore, could be either upward or backward sloping. This concept has an important application to debates over the effect of tax cuts on work. Some economists argue that cutting taxes encourages people to work more hours because the reward is greater. Such an argument is also used as the basis for supporting an entrepreneurial culture – keep taxes low and this encourages entrepreneurs. Others point out that lower taxes do increase disposable income but workers may now use this higher income to enjoy more leisure and not work additional hours. Having some idea of the relative strength of the income and substitution effects is important in analysing and assessing such policy initiatives.

CASE STUDY

Income Effects on Labour Supply: Historical Trends, Lottery Winners, and the Carnegie Conjecture

The idea of a backward sloping labour supply curve might at first seem like a mere theoretical curiosity, but in fact it is not. Evidence indicates that the labour supply curve, considered over long periods of time, does in fact slope backwards. A hundred years ago many people in Europe and North America worked six days a week. Today five-day working weeks are the norm. At the same time that the length of the working week has been falling, the wage of the typical worker (adjusted for inflation) has been rising.

Here is how economists explain this historical pattern: over time, advances in technology raise workers' productivity and, thereby, the demand for labour. The increase in labour demand raises equilibrium wages. As wages rise, so does the reward for working. Yet rather than responding to this increased incentive by working more, most workers choose to take part of their greater prosperity in the form of more leisure. In other words, the income effect of higher wages dominates the substitution effect.

Further evidence that the income effect on labour supply is strong comes from a very different kind of data: winners of lotteries. Winners of large prizes in the lottery see large increases in their incomes and, as a result, large outward shifts in their budget constraints. Because the winners' wages have not changed, however, the *slopes* of their budget constraints remain the same. There is, therefore, no substitution effect. By examining the behaviour of lottery winners, we can isolate the income effect on labour supply. Nearly all the research on the effects of winning the lottery on labour supply has so far been done in the USA, but the results are striking. Of those winners who win more than $50 000, almost 25 per cent quit working within a year, and another 9 per cent reduce the number of hours they work. Of those winners who win more than $1 million, almost 40 per cent stop working. The income effect on labour supply of winning such a large prize is substantial.

Similar results were found in a study, published in the May 1993 issue of the *Quarterly Journal of Economics*, of how receiving a bequest affects a person's labour supply. The study found that a single person who inherits more than $150 000 is four times as likely to stop working as a single person who inherits less than $25 000. This finding would not have surprised the 19th-century industrialist Andrew Carnegie. Carnegie warned that 'the parent who leaves his son enormous wealth generally deadens the talents and energies of the son, and tempts him to lead a less useful and less worthy life than he otherwise would.' That is, Carnegie viewed the income effect on labour supply to be substantial and, from his paternalistic perspective, regrettable. During his life and at his death, Carnegie gave much of his vast fortune to charity.

How Do Interest Rates Affect Household Saving?

An important decision that every person faces is how much income to consume today and how much to save for the future. We can use the theory of consumer choice to analyse how people make this decision and how the amount they save depends on the interest rate their savings will earn.

Consider the decision facing Emilio, a worker planning ahead for retirement. To keep things simple, let's divide Emilio's life into two periods. In the first period, Emilio is young and working. In the second period, he is old and retired. When young, Emilio earns €100 000. He divides this income between current consumption and saving. When he is old, Emilio will consume what he has saved, including the interest that his savings have earned.

Suppose that the interest rate is 10 per cent. Then for every euro that Emilio saves when young, he can consume €1.10 when old. We can view 'consumption when young' and 'consumption when old' as the two goods that Emilio must choose between. The interest rate determines the relative price of these two goods.

Figure 21.15 shows Emilio's budget constraint. If he saves nothing, he consumes €100 000 when young and nothing when old. If he saves everything, he

FIGURE 21.15

The Consumption–Saving Decision

This figure shows the budget constraint for a person deciding how much to consume in the two periods of his life, the indifference curves representing his preferences, and the optimum.

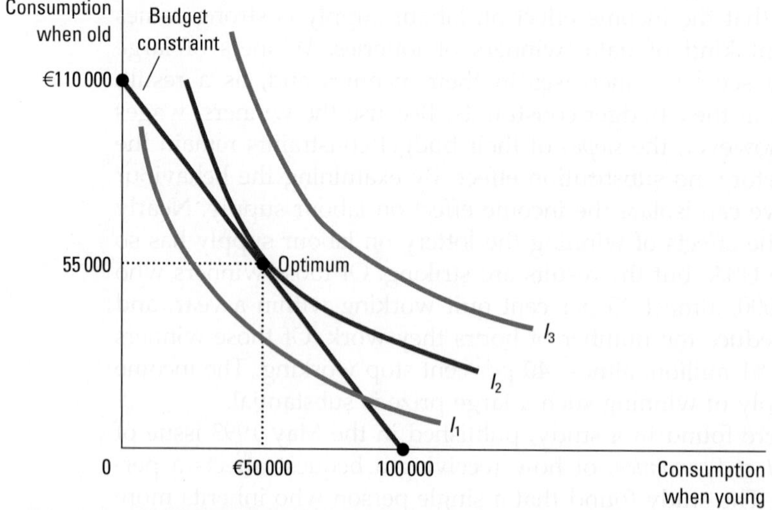

consumes nothing when young and €110 000 when old. The budget constraint shows these and all the intermediate possibilities.

Figure 21.15 uses indifference curves to represent Emilio's preferences for consumption in the two periods. Because Emilio prefers more consumption in both periods, he prefers points on higher indifference curves to points on lower ones. Given his preferences, Emilio chooses the optimal combination of consumption in both periods of life, which is the point on the budget constraint that is on the highest possible indifference curve. At this optimum, Emilio consumes €50 000 when young and €55 000 when old.

Now consider what happens when the interest rate increases from 10 per cent to 20 per cent. Figure 21.16 shows two possible outcomes. In both cases, the budget constraint pivots outward and becomes steeper. At the new higher interest rate, Emilio gets more consumption when old for every euro of consumption that he gives up when young.

The two panels show different preferences for Emilio and the resulting response to the higher interest rate. In both cases, consumption when old rises. Yet the response of consumption when young to the change in the interest rate is different in the two cases. In panel (a), Emilio responds to the higher interest rate by consuming less when young. In panel (b), Emilio responds by consuming more when young.

Emilio's saving, of course, is his income when young minus the amount he consumes when young. In panel (a), consumption when young falls when the interest rate rises, so saving must rise. In panel (b), Emilio consumes more when young, so saving must fall.

FIGURE 21.16

An Increase in the Interest Rate

In both panels, an increase in the interest rate shifts the budget constraint outward. In panel (a), consumption when young falls and consumption when old rises. The result is an increase in saving when young. In panel (b), consumption in both periods rises. The result is a decrease in saving when young.

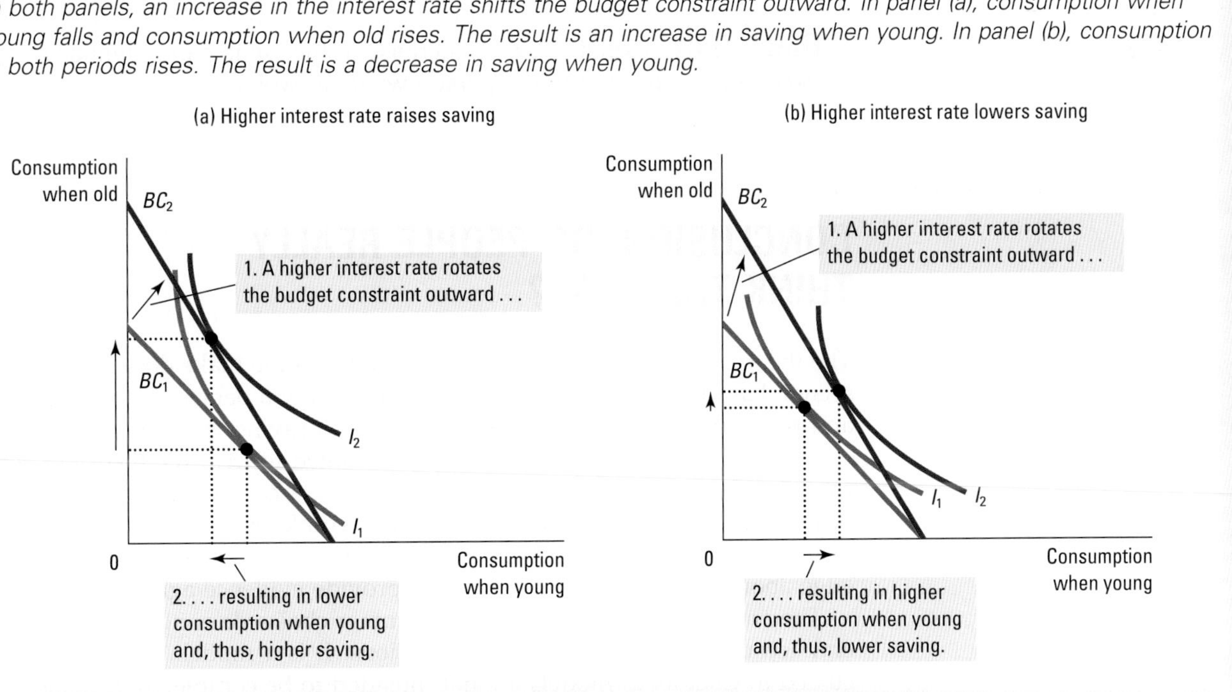

The case shown in panel (b) might at first seem odd: Emilio responds to an increase in the return to saving by saving less. Yet this behaviour is not as peculiar as it might seem. We can understand it by considering the income and substitution effects of a higher interest rate.

Consider first the substitution effect. When the interest rate rises, consumption when old becomes less costly relative to consumption when young. Therefore, the substitution effect induces Emilio to consume more when old and less when young. In other words, the substitution effect induces Emilio to save more.

Now consider the income effect. When the interest rate rises, Emilio moves to a higher indifference curve. He is now better off than he was. As long as consumption in both periods consists of normal goods, he tends to want to use this increase in well-being to enjoy higher consumption in both periods. In other words, the income effect induces him to save less.

The end result, of course, depends on both the income and substitution effects. If the substitution effect of a higher interest rate is greater than the income effect, Emilio saves more. If the income effect is greater than the substitution effect, Emilio saves less. Thus, the theory of consumer choice says that an increase in the interest rate could either encourage or discourage saving.

Although this ambiguous result is interesting from the standpoint of economic theory, it is disappointing from the standpoint of economic policy. It turns out that an important issue in tax policy hinges in part on how saving responds to interest rates. Some economists have advocated reducing the taxation of interest and other capital income, arguing that such a policy change would raise the after-tax interest rate that savers can earn and would thereby encourage people to save more. Other economists have argued that because of offsetting income and substitution effects, such a tax change might not increase saving and could even reduce it. Unfortunately, research has not led to a consensus about how interest rates affect saving. As a result, there remains disagreement among economists about whether changes in tax policy aimed to encourage saving would, in fact, have the intended effect.

Quick Quiz Explain how an increase in the wage can potentially decrease the amount that a person wants to work.

CONCLUSION: DO PEOPLE REALLY THINK THIS WAY?

The theory of consumer choice describes how people make decisions. As we have seen, it has broad applicability. It can explain how a person chooses between cola and pizza, work and leisure, consumption and saving, and so on.

At this point, however, you might be tempted to treat the theory of consumer choice with some scepticism. After all, you are a consumer. You decide what to buy every time you walk into a shop. And you know that you do not decide by writing down budget constraints and indifference curves. Doesn't this knowledge about your own decision-making provide evidence against the theory?

The answer is no. The theory of consumer choice does not try to present a literal account of how people make decisions. It is a model. And, as we first discussed in Chapter 2, models are not intended to be completely realistic.

The best way to view the theory of consumer choice is as a metaphor for how consumers make decisions. No consumer (except an occasional economist) goes through the explicit optimization envisioned in the theory. Yet consumers are aware that their choices are constrained by their financial resources. And, given those constraints, they do the best they can to achieve the highest level of satisfaction. The theory of consumer choice tries to describe this implicit, psychological process in a way that permits explicit, economic analysis. The proof of the pudding is in the eating. And the test of a theory is in its applications. In the last section of this chapter we applied the theory of consumer choice to three practical issues about the economy. If you take more advanced courses in economics, you will see that this theory provides the framework for much additional analysis.

IN THE NEWS

Whilst economists can defend the use of models such as that used in this chapter, they are also aware that new information can also shed light on consumer decision-making. The development of magnetic resonance imaging (MRI) is one example of how economists are able to gain further insights into human behaviour and links with other disciplines, notably psychology, is further extending the frontiers of our understanding.

The Brain and Consumer Choice: Neuroeconomics

Two pieces of research show how the work of psychologists and neuroscientists can help to increase our understanding of the processes involved in decision-making in consumption. In one piece of research, investigators looked at the role played by different areas of the brain in making decisions about investing in financial assets. Researchers also looked at the role of the brain in making purchasing decisions related to preference and price in purchasing chocolate. In both cases, the research was investigating how humans balance out anticipation of the gains and losses that we might get from purchases and whether there was any part of the brain that was associated with being stimulated when faced with the likely gains and losses of a prospective purchase.

The principle behind this investigation was based on the anticipatory effects that occur when faced with a purchasing decision. It is not difficult to conceptualize on a personal level. Think about when you go into a shop or a store and see something you really like. It might be an expensive purchase and you might know that you should not really be thinking of buying it but the item has really caught your attention and you are debating whether to buy it or not.

On the one hand, you know that the price that is being asked represents a loss – the money you will have to give up is an opportunity cost and means you will have to sacrifice other things that it could also buy you. Equally, you also know that owning this item will provide you with some form of gain – utility. When making the purchasing decision, therefore, you are balancing out these competing forces. The brain plays a role in this; there seems to be two main parts of the brain that are involved in such decisions – the nucleus accumbens and the anterior insular. The nucleus accumbens emits two neuro transmitters – dopamine and serotonin. The former is associated with desire and the latter with inhibition. The anterior insula is a part of the brain that has some association with emotional experience and conscious feelings. This will include feelings of pain, anger, happiness, disgust, fear and anger.

The research was relatively complex but the main results from their investigations are given below.

- When making decisions on financial instruments, investors tend not to act rationally. These can be called 'risk-seeking mistakes' and 'risk-aversion mistakes'.
- Activity in the nucleus accumbens has an association with risk-seeking mistakes and risky choices.
- Activity in the anterior insula is associated with risk-aversion mistakes and riskless choices.
- Distinct neural circuits associated with anticipatory affect lead to different types of choices.
- Nucleus accumbens activation represents gain prediction.

►

- Anterior insula activation represents loss prediction.
- Activation of these brain regions can predict decisions to purchase.

In this chapter we looked at a model of consumer behaviour based on a model of rational decision-making – maximizing utility with the constraint of a limited income. However, this might not be the case in reality. The expectations that we might have about a purchase might trigger behavioural or affective (to do with emotions) responses which might influence what we eventually end up buying. The findings might be related to a wide range of decision-making including how we choose to buy insurance and assurance, gambling at casinos, at racing and so on and how we pay for goods and services.

There is a suggestion, for example, that the perceived risk associated with buying goods and services through credit cards is different to that of cash. It has been suggested that we are 'anaesthetized' against the effects of paying. As a result there may be a tendency to overspend when purchasing with credit cards compared to cash. There may also be similar effects going on when people purchase online rather than going to a shop or a store. By understanding how the brain works in this respect, there may be possibilities of building incentives or disincentives to purchase to take account of the way these parts of the brain work.

In making purchasing decisions, we know that there are a number of 'laws' of economics that we might quote. Such 'laws' allow us to be able to make predictions – the very basis of having theories. However, if these laws are based on inaccurate or incomplete knowledge of how humans actually carry out these actions then the model will not be able to be used as a predictive tool.

We assume, for example, that humans are attracted to preferred products (how that preference is generated is another story). We also assume that consumers prefer lower prices than higher prices and that if a price is deemed 'excessive' then we will avoid purchasing the item. Prices represent a potential gain and a potential loss. However, we might view similar losses and gains in different ways. In some cases we might view a loss as being more important than a gain even if they were of equal magnitude. That contradicts the rational approach that characterizes much of economic theory. If our decision-making is being affected by the activation of these distinct neural circuits then the extent to which they are activated might influence our choice. For example, the research cited examples where men were shown pictures of sports cars and other types of car deemed to be less desirable. Viewing sports cars produced a greater degree of brain activity in the mid-brain. Similar results have been obtained in cases where both men and women are shown preferred rather than less preferred drinks, brands of beer and coffee.

If this is the case, then it might suggest that advertising over a long period of time might have significant effects in influencing our choices if it has effects on our perceptions of preferred or non-preferred purchases. What is happening is that the perception of loss and gain is being altered in relation to the price that is being charged.

The second piece of research involves the effect on human behaviour of different emotional states and the effect that hormones play in influencing the brain and human behaviour. In a paper presented to a British Psychological Society (BPS) meeting in April 2009, Professor Karen Pine of the University of Hertfordshire outlined her research findings from a study looking at the link between the menstrual cycle in women and purchasing decisions. Professor Pine's study involved 443 women aged 18 to 50. It appeared to show a link between the stage of the menstrual cycle and purchasing decisions. Of the women in the sample, 153 were in the later stages of their menstrual cycle, known as the luteal phase. Of this group, over 60 per cent said that they had indulged in overspending and had bought items on impulse. The spending, in a small number of cases, was way over normal budgets – some women saying that they had overspent by as much as £250. In many cases, the women said that their purchasing decisions at this time were accompanied by feelings of remorse afterwards.

Professor Pine commented, 'The spending behaviour tends to be a reaction to intense emotions. They are feeling stressed or depressed and are more likely to go shopping to cheer themselves up and using it to regulate their emotions.' The study also found that those women with severe pre-menstrual tension (PMT) displayed more extreme examples of this behaviour.

Part of the explanation for this behaviour is that hormonal changes in women at certain times of the menstrual cycle are associated with changes to the part of the brain that is linked to inhibitions and emotions. It has also been suggested that purchasing decisions may be linked to a desire of women to make themselves look more attractive. There has been other research which has suggested that part of female behaviour is driven by the need to demonstrate their fertility – a throwback to very early days when survival of the species depended in part on the ability to reproduce successfully. Around 14 days before the start of ovulation is a time which sees women increase their spending on items that enhance their attractiveness. These items include make-up, high-heeled shoes and jewellery. Professor Pine has said that her findings are supported by other research which shows a so-called 'ornamental effect' linked to stages in the menstrual cycle.

SUMMARY

- A consumer's budget constraint shows the possible combinations of different goods he can buy given his income and the prices of the goods. The slope of the budget constraint equals the relative price of the goods.
- The consumer's indifference curves represent his preferences. An indifference curve shows the various bundles of goods that make the consumer equally happy. Points on higher indifference curves are preferred to points on lower indifference curves. The slope of an indifference curve at any point is the consumer's marginal rate of substitution – the rate at which the consumer is willing to trade one good for the other.
- The consumer optimizes by choosing the point on his budget constraint that lies on the highest indifference curve. At this point, the slope of the indifference curve (the marginal rate of substitution between the goods) equals the slope of the budget constraint (the relative price of the goods).
- When the price of a good falls, the impact on the consumer's choices can be broken down into an income effect and a substitution effect. The income effect is the change in consumption that arises because a lower price makes the consumer better off. The substitution effect is the change in consumption that arises because a price change encourages greater consumption of the good that has become relatively cheaper. The income effect is reflected in the movement from a lower to a higher indifference curve, whereas the substitution effect is reflected by a movement along an indifference curve to a point with a different slope.
- The theory of consumer choice can be applied in many situations. It can explain why demand curves can potentially slope upward, why higher wages could either increase or decrease the quantity of labour supplied, and why higher interest rates could either increase or decrease saving.

KEY CONCEPTS

budget constraint, p. 439
indifference curve, p. 441
marginal rate of substitution, p. 441
perfect substitutes, p. 444
perfect complements, p. 445
income effect, p. 450
substitution effect, p. 450
Giffen good, p. 454

QUESTIONS FOR REVIEW

1. A consumer has income of €3 000. Wine is priced at €3 a glass and cheese is priced at €6 a kilo. Draw the consumer's budget constraint. What is the slope of this budget constraint?
2. Draw a consumer's indifference curves for wine and cheese. Describe and explain four properties of these indifference curves.

3. Pick a point on an indifference curve for wine and cheese and show the marginal rate of substitution. What does the marginal rate of substitution tell us?
4. Show a consumer's budget constraint and indifference curves for wine and cheese. Show the optimal consumption choice. If the price of wine is €3 a glass and the price of cheese is €6 a kilo, what is the marginal rate of substitution at this optimum?
5. A person who consumes wine and cheese gets a rise, so his income increases from €3 000 to €4 000. Show what happens if both wine and cheese are normal goods. Now show what happens if cheese is an inferior good.
6. The price of cheese rises from €6 to €10 a kilo, while the price of wine remains €3 a glass. For a consumer with a constant income of €3 000, show what happens to consumption of wine and cheese. Decompose the change into income and substitution effects.
7. Can an increase in the price of cheese possibly induce a consumer to buy more cheese? Explain.

PROBLEMS AND APPLICATIONS

1. Jacqueline divides her income between coffee and croissants (both of which are normal goods). An early frost in Brazil causes a large increase in the price of coffee in France.
   a. Show how this early frost might affect Jacqueline's budget constraint.
   b. Show how this early frost might affect Jacqueline's optimal consumption bundle assuming that the substitution effect outweighs the income effect for croissants.
   c. Show how this early frost might affect Jacqueline's optimal consumption bundle assuming that the income effect outweighs the substitution effect for croissants.
2. Compare the following two pairs of goods:
   a. Coke and Pepsi
   b. skis and ski bindings.

   In which case do you expect the indifference curves to be fairly straight, and in which case do you expect the indifference curves to be very bowed? In which case will the consumer respond more to a change in the relative price of the two goods?
3. Eric consumes only cheese and bread.
   a. Could cheese and bread both be inferior goods for Eric? Explain.
   b. Suppose that cheese is a normal good for Eric while bread is an inferior good. If the price of cheese falls, what happens to Eric's consumption of bread? What happens to his consumption of cheese? Explain.
4. Oliver buys only lager and kebabs.
   a. In 2009, Oliver earns €100, lager is priced at €2 a litre and kebabs are priced at €4 each. Draw Oliver's budget constraint.
   b. Now suppose that all prices increase by 10 per cent in 2010 and that Oliver's salary increases by 10 per cent as well. Draw Oliver's new budget constraint. How would Oliver's optimal combination of lager and kebabs in 2010 compare to his optimal combination in 2009?
5. Consider your decision about how many hours to work.
   a. Draw your budget constraint assuming that you pay no taxes on your income. On the same diagram, draw another budget constraint assuming that you pay a 15 per cent tax.
   b. Show how the tax might lead to more hours of work, fewer hours or the same number of hours. Explain.
6. Sarah is awake for 100 hours per week. Using one diagram, show Sarah's budget constraints if she earns €6 per hour, €8 per hour and €10 per hour. Now draw indifference curves such that Sarah's labour supply curve is upward sloping when the wage is between €6 and €8 per hour, and backward sloping when the wage is between €8 and €10 per hour.
7. Draw the indifference curve for someone deciding how much to work. Suppose the wage increases. Is it possible that the person's consumption would fall? Is this plausible? Discuss. (Hint: think about income and substitution effects.)
8. Suppose you take a job that pays €30 000 and set some of this income aside in a savings account that pays an annual interest rate of 5 per cent. Use a diagram with a budget constraint and indifference curves to show how your consumption changes in each of the following situations. To keep things simple, assume that you pay no taxes on your income.
   a. Your salary increases to €40 000.
   b. The interest rate on your bank account rises to 8 per cent.

9. As discussed in the text, we can divide an individual's life into two hypothetical periods: 'young' and 'old'. Suppose that the individual earns income only when young and saves some of that income to consume when old. If the interest rate on savings falls, can you tell what happens to consumption when young? Can you tell what happens to consumption when old? Explain.
10. (This problem is challenging.) The welfare system in industrialized countries provides income to some needy families. Typically, the maximum payment goes to families that earn no income; then, as families begin to earn income, the welfare payment declines gradually and eventually disappears. Let's consider the possible effects of a welfare system on a family's labour supply.
    a. Draw a budget constraint for a family assuming that the welfare system did not exist. On the same diagram, draw a budget constraint that reflects the existence of the welfare system.
    b. Adding indifference curves to your diagram, show how the welfare system could reduce the number of hours worked by the family. Explain, with reference to both the income and substitution effects.
    c. Using your diagram from part (b), show the effect of the welfare system on the well-being of the family.
11. (This problem is challenging.) Suppose that an individual incurred no taxes on the first €10 000 she earned and 15 per cent of any income she earned over €10 000. Now suppose that the government is considering two ways to reduce the tax burden: a reduction in the tax rate and an increase in the amount on which no tax is owed.
    a. What effect would a reduction in the tax rate have on the individual's labour supply if she earned €30 000 to start with? Explain in words using the income and substitution effects. You do not need to use a diagram.
    b. What effect would an increase in the amount on which no tax is owed have on the individual's labour supply? Again, explain in words using the income and substitution effects.
12. (This problem is challenging.) Consider a person deciding how much to consume and how much to save for retirement. This person has particular preferences: her lifetime utility depends on the lowest level of consumption during the two periods of her life. That is, Utility = Minimum {consumption when young, consumption when old}
    a. Draw this person's indifference curves. (Hint: recall that indifference curves show the combinations of consumption in the two periods that yield the same level of utility.)
    b. Draw the budget constraint and the optimum.
    c. When the interest rate increases, does this person save more or less? Explain your answer using income and substitution effects.
13. Economist George Stigler once wrote that, according to consumer theory, 'if consumers do not buy less of a commodity when their incomes rise, they will surely buy less when the price of the commodity rises.' Explain this statement using the concepts of income and substitution effects.

For further resources, visit www.cengage.co.uk/mankiw_taylor2

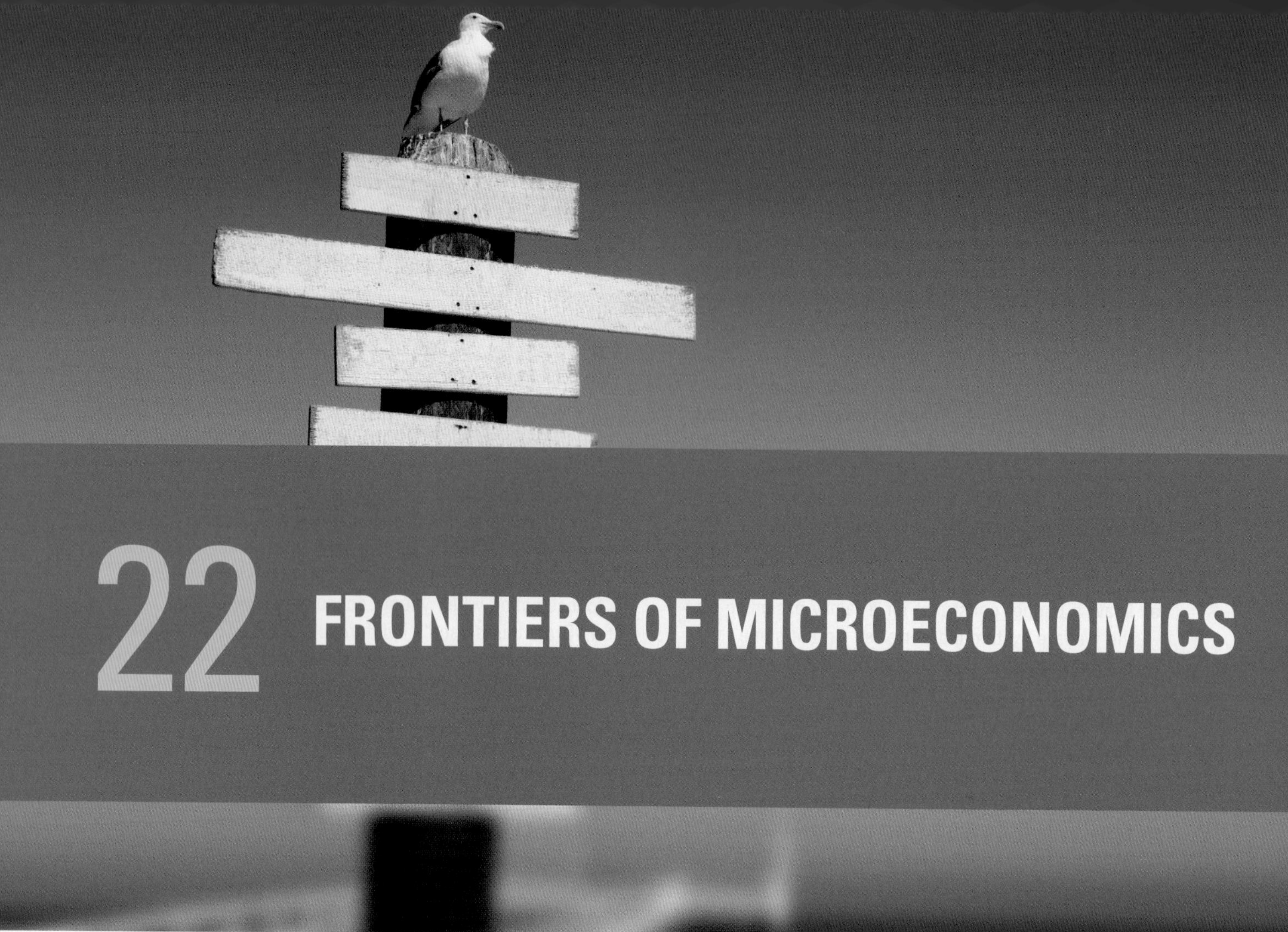

22 FRONTIERS OF MICROECONOMICS

Economics is a study of the choices that people make and the resulting interactions they have with one another. This study has many facets, as we have seen in the preceding chapters. Yet it would be a mistake to think that all the facets we have seen make up a finished jewel, perfect and unchanging. Like all scientists, economists are always on the lookout for new areas to study and new phenomena to explain. This final chapter on microeconomics offers an assortment of three topics at the discipline's frontier to see how economists are trying to expand their understanding of human behaviour and society.

The first topic is the economics of *asymmetric information.* Many times in life, some people are better informed than others, and this difference in information can affect the choices they make and how they deal with one another. Thinking about this asymmetry can shed light on many aspects of the world, from the market for used cars to the custom of gift giving.

The second topic we examine in this chapter is *political economy.* Throughout this book we have seen many examples where markets fail and government policy can potentially improve matters. But 'potentially' is a needed qualifier: whether this potential is realized depends on how well our political institutions work. The field of political economy applies the tools of economics to understand the functioning of government.

The third topic in this chapter is *behavioural economics.* We have already seen at various times in the book so far, how understanding human behaviour helps to explain economic phenomena. This field brings some of the insights from psychology into the study of economic issues. It offers a view of human behaviour that is more subtle and complex than that found in conventional economic theory, but this view may also be more realistic.

This chapter covers a lot of ground. To do so, it offers not a full helping of these three topics but, instead, a taste of each. One goal is to show a few of the directions economists are heading in their effort to expand knowledge of how the economy works. Another goal is to whet your appetite for more courses in economics.

ASYMMETRIC INFORMATION

'I know something you don't know.' This statement is a common taunt among children, but it also conveys a deep truth about how people sometimes interact with one another. Many times in life, one person knows more about what is going on than another. A difference in access to relevant knowledge is called an *information asymmetry*.

Examples abound. A worker knows more than his employer about how much effort he puts into his job. A seller of a used car knows more than the buyer about the car's condition. The first is an example of a *hidden action*, whereas the second is an example of a *hidden characteristic*. In each case, the party in the dark (the employer, the car buyer) would like to know the relevant information, but the informed party (the worker, the car seller) may have an incentive to conceal it.

Because asymmetric information is so prevalent, economists have devoted much effort in recent decades to studying its effects. And, indeed, the 2001 Nobel Prize in economics was awarded to three economists (George Akerlof, Michael Spence and Joseph Stiglitz) for their pioneering work on this topic. Let's discuss some of the insights that this study has revealed.

Hidden Actions: Principals, Agents and Moral Hazard

Moral hazard is a problem that arises when one person, called the **agent**, is performing some task on behalf of another person, called the **principal**. If the principal cannot perfectly monitor the agent's behaviour, the agent tends to undertake less effort than the principal considers desirable and is not fully responsible for the consequences of their actions. The phrase *moral hazard* refers to the risk, or 'hazard', of inappropriate or otherwise 'immoral' behaviour by the agent.

moral hazard
the tendency of a person who is imperfectly monitored to engage in dishonest or otherwise undesirable behaviour

agent
a person who is performing an act for another person, called the principal

principal
a person for whom another person, called the agent, is performing some act

Moral hazard can lead to *adverse selection*. This means that the market process may end up with 'bad' outcomes because of asymmetric information. Adverse selection is a feature of banking, finance and insurance industries. A bank, for example, may set rules and regulations for its accounts which may lead to some customers, who are not very profitable to the bank, adversely selecting the bank – customers the bank would rather not have. In insurance, the person seeking insurance cover has more information about his or her situation than the insurer. A person who knows they are high risk will look to buy insurance but not necessarily divulge the extent of the risk they pose to the insurance company. How does the insurance company distinguish between its high-risk and low-risk customers? The insurance company would rather take on the low-risk customers than the high-risk ones but high-risk customers adversely select the insurance company. In finance, some investment banks have been accused of putting very risky assets into financial products and clients buying these products did not know the full extent of the risk they were buying – clients were dealing with suppliers who they would have been better off not dealing with. In such a situation, the principal tries various ways to encourage the agent to act more responsibly (such as pricing insurance for high-risk customers higher than for low-risk ones).

The employment relationship is the classic example. The employer is the principal, and the worker is the agent. The moral-hazard problem is the temptation of imperfectly monitored workers to shirk their responsibilities. Employers can respond to this problem in various ways:

- *Better monitoring.* Parents hiring nannies or au pairs have been known to plant hidden video cameras in their homes to record the individual's behaviour when the parents are away. The aim is to catch irresponsible behaviour.
- *High wages.* According to *efficiency wages theories* (discussed in Chapter 19), some employers may choose to pay their workers a wage above the level that equilibrates supply and demand in the labour market. A worker who earns an above-equilibrium wage is less likely to shirk, because if he is caught and fired, he might not be able to find another high-paying job.
- *Delayed payment.* Firms can delay part of a worker's compensation, so if the worker is caught shirking and is fired, he suffers a larger penalty. One example of delayed compensation is the year-end bonus. Similarly, a firm may choose to pay its workers more later in their lives. Thus, the wage increases that workers get as they age may reflect not just the benefits of experience but also a response to moral hazard.

These various mechanisms to reduce the problem of moral hazard need not be used alone. Employers can use a combination of them.

Beyond the workplace, there are many other examples of moral hazard. Individuals with insurance cover, be it fire, motor vehicle or medical insurance, may behave differently as a result of having that cover. A motorist, for example, might drive more recklessly in the knowledge that in the event of an accident the cost will be met primarily by the insurance company. Similarly, families choosing to live near a river may benefit from the scenic views but the increased risk of flooding imposes a cost to the insurance company and the government in the event of a serious flood. The financial crisis of 2007–2009 raised the issue of bankers' bonuses. One argument put forward was that banks were acting recklessly in giving large bonuses to workers which encouraged inappropriate and risky investment. Such behaviour was encouraged because bankers 'knew' that governments would step in to prevent banks from failing.

Many regulations are aimed at addressing the problem: an insurance company may require homeowners to buy smoke detectors or pay higher premiums if there is a history of reckless driving (or even refuse to provide insurance cover to the individual), the government may prohibit building homes on land with high risk of flooding and new regulations may be introduced to curb the behaviour of banks. But the insurance company does not have perfect information about how cautious homeowners are, the government does not have perfect information about the risk that families undertake when choosing where to live and regulators do not know fully the risks that bankers take in investment decisions. As a result, the problem of moral hazard persists.

Hidden Characteristics: Adverse Selection and the Lemons Problem

adverse selection
the tendency for the mix of unobserved attributes to become undesirable from the standpoint of an uninformed party

Adverse selection is a problem that arises in markets where one party knows more about the attributes of a good or service being transacted than the other party does. When this occurs the 'selection' of the good or service may be 'adverse' from the standpoint of the uninformed party to the transaction.

The classic example of adverse selection is the market for used cars. Sellers of used cars know their vehicles' defects while buyers often do not. Because owners of the worst cars are more likely to sell them than are the owners of the best cars, buyers are apprehensive about getting a poor car. If you are unlucky enough to buy a poor car, then we might say that you have bought a 'lemon'. This was the term used by Nobel Prize-winner George Akerlof in his famous research article, 'The Market for Lemons'[1]. His co-prize winners in 2001, Joseph Stiglitz and Michael Spence, also used the term in the context of asymmetric information; it comes from the old-fashioned fruit or gambling machines where three wheels spin and come to rest indicating a picture of a fruit that determines the payout; traditionally, a lemon was bad luck, paying out nothing. As a result of this information asymmetry, many people avoid buying vehicles in the used car market. This lemons problem can explain why a used car only a few weeks old sells for thousands of euros less than a new car of the same type. A buyer of the used car might surmise that the seller is getting rid of the car quickly because the seller knows something about it that the buyer does not.

A second example of adverse selection occurs in the labour market. According to another efficiency wage theory, workers vary in their abilities, and they may know their own abilities better than do the firms that hire them. When a firm cuts the wage it pays, the more talented workers are more likely to quit, knowing they are better able to find other employment. Conversely, a firm may choose to pay an above-equilibrium wage to attract a better mix of workers. Or suppose that a firm is not doing so well and needs to cut the wage bill. It can do this either by reducing wages or by keeping wages where they are and laying off workers at random for a few weeks. If it cuts wages, the very best workers will quit, because they know they will be able to find a better job elsewhere. Of course, the better workers who are randomly selected when the firm chooses instead to impose layoffs may also choose to quit and find a steadier job elsewhere. But in this case only *some* of the best workers quit (since not all of them are laid off because workers were chosen randomly) while if the firms cuts wages, *all* of the best workers will quit.

A third example of adverse selection occurs in markets for insurance. For example, buyers of health insurance know more about their own health problems than do insurance companies. Because people with greater hidden health problems are more likely to buy health insurance than are other people, the price of health insurance reflects the costs of a sicker-than-average person. As a result, people in average health may be discouraged from buying health insurance by the high price.

When markets suffer from adverse selection, the invisible hand does not necessarily work its magic. In the used car market, owners of good cars may choose to keep them rather than sell them at the low price that sceptical buyers are willing to pay. In the labour market, wages may be stuck above the level that balances supply and demand, resulting in unemployment. In insurance markets, buyers with low risk may choose to remain uninsured, because the policies they are offered fail to reflect their true characteristics. Advocates of government-provided health insurance sometimes point to the problem of adverse selection as one reason not to trust the private market to provide the right amount of health insurance on its own.

Signalling to Convey Private Information

Although asymmetric information is sometimes a motivation for public policy, it also motivates some individual behaviour that otherwise might be hard to

[1]Akerlof, G. (1970) 'The Market for Lemons: Quality, Uncertainty and the Market Mechanism. *Quarterly Journal of Economics*, **84**:488–500.

signalling
an action taken by an informed party to reveal private information to an uninformed party

explain. Markets respond to problems of asymmetric information in many ways. One of them is **signalling**, which refers to actions taken by an informed party for the sole purpose of credibly revealing his private information.

We have seen examples of signalling in previous chapters. As we saw in Chapter 16, firms may spend money on advertising to signal to potential customers that they have high-quality products. As we saw in Chapter 20, students may earn university degrees in order to signal to potential employers that they are high-ability individuals. Recall that the signalling theory of education contrasts with the human capital theory, which asserts that education increases a person's productivity, rather than merely conveying information about innate talent. These two examples of signalling (advertising, education) may seem very different, but below the surface they are much the same: in both cases, the informed party (the firm, the student) is using the signal to convince the uninformed party (the customer, the employer) that the informed party is offering something of high quality.

What does it take for an action to be an effective signal? Obviously, it must be costly. If a signal were free, everyone would use it, and it would convey no information. For the same reason, there is another requirement: The signal must be less costly, or more beneficial, to the person with the higher-quality product. Otherwise, everyone would have the same incentive to use the signal, and the signal would reveal nothing.

Consider again our two examples. In the advertising case, a firm with a good product reaps a larger benefit from advertising because customers who try the product once are more likely to become repeat customers. Thus, it is rational for the firm with the good product to pay for the cost of the signal (advertising), and it is rational for the customer to use the signal as a piece of information about the product's quality. In the education case, a talented person can get through school more easily than a less talented one. Thus, it is rational for the talented person to pay for the cost of the signal (education), and it is rational for the employer to use the signal as a piece of information about the person's talent.

The world is replete with instances of signalling. Magazine advertisements sometimes include the phrase 'as seen on TV'. Why does a firm selling a product in a magazine choose to stress this fact? One possibility is that the firm is trying to convey its willingness to pay for an expensive signal (a spot on television) in the hope that you will infer that its product is of high quality. For the same reason, graduates of elite universities are always sure to put that fact on their curriculum vitaes.

CASE STUDY

Gifts as Signals

© ISIFA IMAGE SERVICE S.R.O. / ALAMY

"Now we'll see how much he loves me."

A man is debating what to give his girlfriend for her birthday. 'I know,' he says to himself, 'I'll give her cash. After all, I don't know her tastes as well as she does, and with cash, she can buy anything she wants.' But when he hands her the money, she is offended. Convinced he doesn't really love her, she breaks off the relationship. What's the economics behind this story?

In some ways, gift giving is a strange custom. As the man in our story suggests, people typically know their own preferences better than others do, so we might expect everyone to prefer cash to in-kind transfers. If your employer substituted merchandise for your wages, you would likely object to the means of payment. But your reaction is very different when someone who (you hope) loves you does the same thing.

One interpretation of gift giving is that it reflects asymmetric information and signalling. The man in our story has private information that the girlfriend would like to know: does he really love her? Choosing a good gift for her is a signal of his love. Certainly, picking out a gift has the right characteristics to be a signal. It is costly (it takes time), and its cost depends on the private information (how much he loves her). If he really loves her, choosing a good gift is easy because he is thinking about her all the time. If he doesn't love her, finding the right gift is more difficult. Thus, giving a gift that suits the girlfriend is one way for him to convey the private information of his love for her. Giving cash shows that he isn't even bothering to try.

An excellent case in point is Valentine's Day. It is a day when millions of women might be expecting to be sent or be given something that extra bit special as a sign of the love and romance felt by their partner. (Of course, it is not only women who might be expecting such gifts but for the purpose of this case study we will make an assumption that a female is expecting a gift from her male partner.) The two parties to the transaction are the female and the male. The woman, it is assumed, is expecting some show of affection and a sign of the love her partner feels for her and this is manifested in some sort of gift. That gift, we will assume, is the traditional red rose. For the man, the whole issue is quite complex.

On the one hand, he will be faced with the certain knowledge that supply and demand will ensure that the price of roses will be high. He could wait for later in the week and pick up some bargains but that might not go down too well. He therefore has to accept that he will have to buy some roses as a sign of his love and affection. The man might know in his own mind just how much he loves the woman. The woman, on the other hand, is going to base the extent of that love and affection, in part, on the size of the bunch of roses that the man will be expected to give her. This is the asymmetric information. She knows that prices of roses will shoot up on Valentine's Day but that's part of the enjoyment. The bigger the bunch of roses the more the man will have spent and this equates directly to the extent of the love and affection he has for her.

The man is now in a quandary. If he buys a large bunch of roses he knows it will set him back anything between €10 and €100 depending on the number and quality and where they are bought from. Buy them from a supermarket and what does that say for your credibility in the romance stakes? Buy them from a florist and you might get more credibility but the price is likely to be much higher. The credibility is the sign sent to your partner that you went out of your way to find the florist and to choose the flowers, all of which signals your devotion.

The man could choose to be clever and just go for the single red rose – very romantic and perhaps great on any other day, but Valentine's Day? It might backfire horribly. He could go for some other flower but that is not really an option. So how many roses are sufficient to send the right signal about his love? 5, 10, 20? It's a tricky decision.

For all you romantic males out there, a word of advice; when you hand over the roses to your partner, look carefully at her face when she first sees them. If there are slight looks of disappointment then you have got the signal wrong. A broad smile and you can be sure you have reduced the degree of asymmetric information. Or you could have them delivered and have to wait until later to find out if your decision-making was right.

The signalling theory of gift giving is consistent with another observation: people care most about the custom when the strength of affection is most in question. Thus, giving cash to a girlfriend or boyfriend is usually a bad move. But when college students receive a cheque from their parents, they are less often offended. The parents' love is less likely to be in doubt, so the recipient probably won't interpret the cash gift as a signal of lack of affection.

Screening to Induce Information Revelation

When an informed party takes actions to reveal his private information, the phenomenon is called signalling. When an uninformed party takes actions to induce the informed party to reveal private information, the phenomenon is called **screening**.

screening
an action taken by an uninformed party to induce an informed party to reveal information

Some screening is common sense. A person buying a used car may ask that it be checked by a car mechanic before the sale. A seller who refuses this request reveals his private information that the car is a lemon. The buyer may decide to offer a lower price or to look for another car.

Other examples of screening are more subtle. For example, consider a firm that sells car insurance. The firm would like to charge a low premium to safe drivers and a high premium to risky drivers. But how can it tell them apart? Drivers know whether they are safe or risky, but the risky ones won't admit to it. A driver's history is one piece of information (which insurance companies in fact use), but because of the intrinsic randomness of car accidents, history is an imperfect indicator of future risks.

The insurance company might be able to sort out the two kinds of drivers by offering different insurance policies that would induce them to separate themselves. One policy would have a high premium and cover the full cost of any accidents that occur. Another policy would have low premiums but would have, say, a €1 000 excess. (That is, the driver would be responsible for the first €1 000 of damage, and the insurance company would cover the remaining risk.) Notice that the excess is more of a burden for risky drivers because they are more likely to have an accident. Thus, with a large enough excess, the low-premium policy with an excess would attract the safe drivers, while the high-premium policy without an excess would attract the risky drivers. Faced with these two policies, the two kinds of drivers would reveal their private information by choosing different insurance policies.

Asymmetric Information and Public Policy

We have examined two kinds of asymmetric information – moral hazard and adverse selection. And we have seen how individuals may respond to the problem with signalling or screening. Now let's consider what the study of asymmetric information suggests about the proper scope of public policy.

The tension between market success and market failure is central in microeconomics. We learned in Chapter 7 that the equilibrium of supply and demand is efficient in the sense that it maximizes the total surplus that society can obtain in a market. Adam Smith's invisible hand seemed to reign supreme. This conclusion was then tempered with the study of externalities (Chapter 10), public goods (Chapter 11), imperfect competition (Chapters 15 through 17) and poverty (Chapter 20). These examples of market failure showed that government can sometimes improve market outcomes.

The study of asymmetric information gives us new reason to be wary of markets. When some people know more than others, the market may fail to put resources to their best use. People with high-quality used cars may have trouble selling them because buyers will be afraid of getting a lemon. People with few health problems may have trouble getting low-cost health insurance because insurance companies lump them together with those who have significant (but hidden) health problems.

Although asymmetric information may call for government action in some cases, three facts complicate the issue. First, as we have seen, the private market can sometimes deal with information asymmetries on its own using a combination of signalling and screening. Secondly, the government rarely has more information than the private parties. Even if the market's allocation of resources is not first-best, it may be second-best. That is, when there are information asymmetries, policy makers may find it hard to improve upon the market's admittedly imperfect outcome. Thirdly, the government is itself an imperfect institution – a topic we take up in the next section.

Quick Quiz A person who buys a life insurance policy pays a certain amount per year and receives for his family a much larger payment in the event of his death. Would you expect buyers of life insurance to have higher or lower death rates than the average person? How might this be an example of moral hazard? Of adverse selection? How might a life insurance company deal with these problems?

POLITICAL ECONOMY

As we have seen, markets left on their own do not always reach a desirable allocation of resources. When we judge the market's outcome to be either inefficient or inequitable, there may be a role for the government to step in and improve the situation. Yet before we embrace an activist government, we need to consider one more fact: The government is also an imperfect institution. The field of *political economy* (sometimes called the field of *public choice*) applies the methods of economics to study how government works. We have touched upon this concept in Chapters 9, 10 and 12.

The Condorcet Voting Paradox

Most advanced societies rely on democratic principles to set government policy. When a city is deciding between two locations to build a new park, for example, we have a simple way to choose: the majority gets its way. Yet, for most policy issues, the number of possible outcomes far exceeds two. A new park, for instance, could be placed in many possible locations. In this case, as an 18th century French political theorist, the Marquis de Condorcet, famously noted, democracy might run into some problems trying to choose one of the outcomes.

For example, suppose there are three possible outcomes, labelled A, B and C, and there are three voter types with the preferences shown in Table 22.1. The leader of our town council wants to aggregate these individual preferences into preferences for society as a whole. How should he do it?

At first, he might try some pairwise votes (pairwise refers to the process of comparing options in pairs to ascertain which pair is preferred). If he asks voters to choose first between B and C, voter types 1 and 2 will vote for B, giving B the majority. If he then asks voters to choose between A and B, voter types 1 and 3 will vote for A, giving A the majority. Observing that A beats B, and B beats C, the mayor might conclude that A is the voters' clear choice.

But wait: suppose the council leader then asks voters to choose between A and C. In this case, voter types 2 and 3 vote for C, giving C the majority. That is, under pairwise majority voting, A beats B, B beats C, and C beats A. Normally, we expect preferences (as outlined in Chapter 21) to exhibit the axiom of

TABLE 22.1

The Condorcet Paradox

If voters have these preferences over outcomes A, B *and* C, *then in pairwise majority voting,* A *beats* B, B *beats* C, *and* C *beats* A.

	Voter type		
	Type 1	Type 2	Type 3
Percentage of electorate	35	45	20
First choice	A	B	C
Second choice	B	C	A
Third choice	C	A	B

Condorcet paradox
the failure of majority rule to produce transitive preferences for society

transitivity: if A is preferred to B, and B is preferred to C, then we would expect A to be preferred to C. The **Condorcet paradox** is that democratic outcomes do not always obey this property. Pairwise voting might produce transitive preferences for a society, depending on the pattern of individual preferences, but as our example in the table shows, it cannot be counted on to do so.

One implication of the Condorcet paradox is that the order on which things are voted can affect the result. If the council leader suggests choosing first between A and B and then comparing the winner to C, the town ends up choosing C. But if the voters choose first between B and C and then compare the winner to A, the town ends up with A. And if the voters choose first between A and C and then compare the winner to B, the town ends up with B.

There are two lessons to be learned from the Condorcet paradox. The narrow lesson is that when there are more than two options, setting the agenda (that is, deciding the order in which items are voted) can have a powerful impact on the outcome of a democratic election. The broad lesson is that majority voting by itself does not tell us what outcome a society really wants.

Arrow's Impossibility Theorem

Since political theorists first noticed Condorcet's paradox, they have spent much energy studying voting systems and proposing new ones. For example, as an alternative to pairwise majority voting, the leader of the town council could ask each voter to rank the possible outcomes. For each voter, we could give 1 point for last place, 2 points for second to last, 3 points for third to last and so on. The outcome that receives the most total points wins. With the preferences in Table 22.1, outcome B is the winner. (You can do the arithmetic yourself.) This voting method is called a *Borda count,* after the 18th century French mathematician and political scientist who devised it. It is often used in polls that rank sports teams.

Is there a perfect voting system? Economist Kenneth Arrow (the winner of the 1972 Nobel Prize in Economics) took up this question in his 1951 book *Social Choice and Individual Values.* Arrow started by defining what a perfect voting system would be. He assumes that individuals in society have preferences over the various possible outcomes: A, B, C and so on. He then assumes that society wants a voting scheme to choose among these outcomes that satisfies several properties:

- *Unanimity.* If everyone prefers A to B, then A should beat B.
- *Transitivity.* If A beats B, and B beats C, then A should beat C.
- *Independence of irrelevant alternatives.* The ranking between any two outcomes A and B should not depend on whether some third outcome C is also available.

- *No dictators*. There is no person that always gets his way, regardless of everyone else's preferences.

These all seem like desirable properties for a voting system to have. Yet Arrow proved, mathematically and incontrovertibly, that no voting system can satisfy all of these properties. This amazing result is called **Arrow's impossibility theorem**.

Arrow's impossibility theorem
a mathematical result showing that, under certain assumed conditions, there is no scheme for aggregating individual preferences into a valid set of social preferences

The mathematics needed to prove Arrow's theorem is beyond the scope of this book, but we can get some sense of why the theorem is true from a couple of examples. We have already seen the problem with the method of majority rule. The Condorcet paradox shows that majority rule fails to produce a ranking among the outcomes that always satisfies transitivity.

As another example, the Borda count fails to satisfy the independence of irrelevant alternatives. Recall that, using the preferences in Table 22.1, outcome B wins with a Borda count. But suppose that suddenly C disappears as an alternative. If the Borda count method is applied only to outcomes A and B, then A wins. (Once again, you can do the arithmetic on your own.) Thus, eliminating alternative C changes the ranking between A and B. The reason for this change is that the result of the Borda count depends on the number of points that A and B receive, and the number of points depends on whether the irrelevant alternative, C, is also available.

Arrow's impossibility theorem is a deep and disturbing result. It doesn't say that we should abandon democracy as a form of government. But it does say that, no matter what voting scheme society adopts for aggregating the preferences of its members, in some way it will be flawed as a mechanism for social choice.

The Median Voter Is King

Despite Arrow's theorem, voting is how most societies choose their leaders and public policies, often by majority rule. The next step in studying government is to examine how governments run by majority rule work. That is, in a democratic society, who determines what policy is chosen? In some cases, the theory of democratic government yields a surprisingly simple answer.

Let's consider an example. Imagine that society is deciding on how much money to spend on some public good, such as the army or the national parks. Each voter has his own most preferred budget, and he always prefers outcomes closer to his most preferred value to outcomes further away. Thus, we can line up voters from those who prefer the smallest budget to those who prefer the largest. Figure 22.1 is an example. Here there are 100 voters, and the budget size varies from zero to €20 billion. Given these preferences, what outcome would you expect democracy to produce?

According to a famous result called the **median voter theorem**, majority rule will produce the outcome most preferred by the median voter. The *median voter* is the voter exactly in the middle of the distribution. In this example, if you take the line of voters ordered by their preferred budgets and count 50 voters from either end of the line, you will find that the median voter wants a budget of €10 billion. By contrast, the average preferred outcome (calculated by adding the preferred outcomes and dividing by the number of voters) is €9 billion, and the modal outcome (the one preferred by the greatest number of voters) is €15 billion.

median voter theorem
a mathematical result showing that if voters are choosing a point along a line and each voter wants the point closest to his most preferred point, then majority rule will pick the most preferred point of the median voter

The median voter rules the day because his preferred outcome beats any other proposal in a two-way race. In our example, more than half the voters want €10 billion or more, and more than half want €10 billion or less. If someone proposes, say, €8 billion instead of €10 billion, everyone who prefers €10 billion or more will vote with the median voter. Similarly, if someone proposes €12 billion

FIGURE 22.1

The Median Voter Theorem: An Example

This bar chart shows how 100 voters' most preferred budget is distributed over five options, ranging from zero to €20 billion. If society makes its choice by majority rule, the median voter (who here prefers €10 billion) determines the outcome.

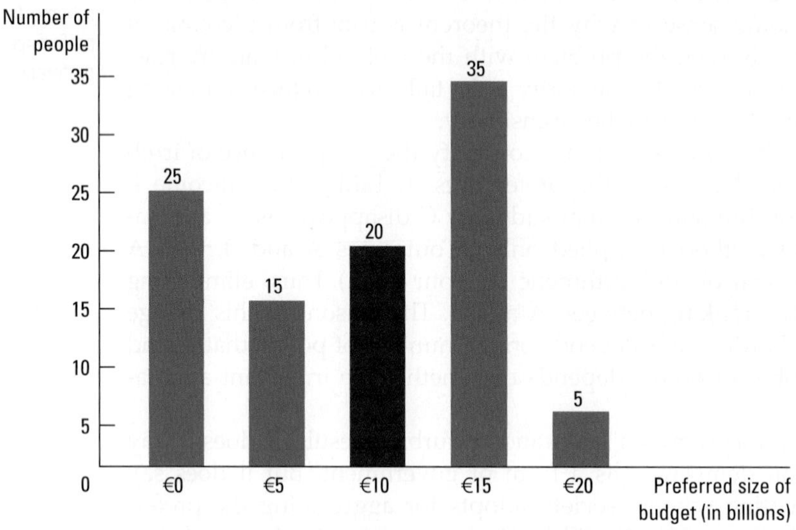

instead of €10 billion, everyone who wants €10 billion or less will vote with the median voter. In either case, the median voter has more than half the voters on his side.

What about the Condorcet voting paradox? It turns out that when the voters are picking a point along a line and each voter aims for his own most preferred point, the Condorcet paradox cannot arise. The median voter's most preferred outcome beats all comers.

One implication of the median voter theorem is that if two political parties are each trying to maximize their chance of election, they will both move their positions toward the median voter. Suppose, for example, that the Red party advocates a budget of €15 billion, while the Blue party advocates a budget of €10 billion. The Red position is more popular in the sense that €15 billion has more proponents than any other single choice. Nonetheless, the Blues get more than 50 per cent of the vote: they will attract the 20 voters who want €10 billion, the 15 voters who want €5 billion and the 25 voters who want zero. If the Reds want to win, they will move their platform toward the median voter. Thus, this theory can explain why the parties in a two-party system (and even in a system where three or four parties dominate the political landscape) are similar to each other: they are both moving towards the median voter.

Another implication of the median voter theorem is that minority views are not given much weight. Imagine that 40 per cent of the population want a lot of money spent on the national parks, and 60 per cent want nothing spent. In this case, the median voter's preference is zero, regardless of the intensity of the minority's view. Such is the logic of democracy. Rather than reaching a compromise that takes into account everyone's preferences, majority rule looks only to the person in the exact middle of the distribution.

Politicians Are People Too

When economists study consumer behaviour, they assume that consumers buy the bundle of goods and services that gives them the greatest level of satisfaction. When economists study firm behaviour, they assume that firms produce the quantity of goods and services that yields the greatest level of profits. What should they assume when they study people involved in the practice of politics?

Politicians also have objectives. It would be nice to assume that political leaders are always looking out for the well-being of society as a whole; that they are aiming for an optimal combination of efficiency and equity. Nice, perhaps, but not realistic. Self-interest is as powerful a motive for political actors as it is for consumers and firm owners. Some politicians are motivated by desire for re-election and are willing to sacrifice the national interest when doing so solidifies their base of voters. Other politicians are motivated by simple greed. If you have any doubt, you should look at the world's poor nations, where corruption and poor governance among government officials is a common impediment to economic development.

This book is not the place to develop a theory of political behaviour. That topic is best left to the political scientists. But when thinking about economic policy, remember that this policy is made not by a benevolent king, but by real people with their own all-too-human desires. Sometimes they are motivated to further the national interest, but sometimes they are motivated by their own political and financial ambitions. We shouldn't be surprised when economic policy fails to resemble the ideals derived in economics textbooks.

Quick Quiz A local district council decides to let the people living in the area vote on how much it should spend on local schools and the resulting student–teacher ratio. A poll finds that 35 per cent of the voters want a ratio of 9:1, 25 per cent want a ratio of 10:1 and 40 per cent want a ratio of 12:1. What outcome would you expect the district to end up with?

BEHAVIOURAL ECONOMICS

Economics is a study of human behaviour, but it is not the only field that can make that claim. The social science of psychology also sheds light on the choices that people make in their lives. The fields of economics and psychology usually proceed independently, in part because they address a different range of questions. But recently a field called *behavioural economics* has emerged in which economists are making use of basic psychological insights. So far in the book we have made reference to a number of instances where behavioural economics has something else to add to our analysis. Let's summarize some of the key insights from behavioural economics here.

People Aren't Always Rational

Economic theory is populated by a particular species of organism, sometimes called *Homo economicus*. Thaler and Sunstein – see Chapter 20 – refer to them as 'econs'. Members of this species are always rational. As managers of firms, they maximize profits. As consumers, they maximize utility (or, equivalently, pick the point on the highest indifference curve). Given the constraints they face, they rationally weigh all the costs and benefits and always choose the best possible course of action.

Real people, however, are *Homo sapiens*. Although in many ways they resemble the rational, calculating people assumed in economic theory, they are far more complex. They can be forgetful, impulsive, confused, emotional and short-sighted. These imperfections of human reasoning are the bread-and-butter of psychologists, but until recently, economists have neglected them.

Herbert Simon, one of the first social scientists to work at the boundary of economics and psychology, suggested that humans should be viewed not as rational maximizers but as *satisficers*. Rather than always choosing the best course of action, they make decisions that are merely good enough. Similarly, other economists have suggested that humans are only 'near rational' or that they exhibit 'bounded rationality'. Bounded rationality is the idea that humans make decisions under the constraints of limited, and sometimes unreliable, information, that they face limits to the amount of information they can process and that they face time constraints in making decisions.

Studies of human decision making have tried to detect systematic mistakes that people make. Here are a few of the findings:

- *People are overconfident.* Imagine that you were asked some numerical questions, such as the number of African countries in the United Nations, the height of the tallest mountain in Europe and so on. Instead of being asked for a single estimate, however, you were asked to give a 90 per cent confidence interval – a range such that you were 90 per cent confident the true number falls within it. When psychologists run experiments like this, they find that most people give ranges that are too small: the true number falls within their intervals far less than 90 per cent of the time. That is, most people are too sure of their own abilities.
- *People give too much weight to a small number of vivid observations.* Imagine that you are thinking about buying a car of brand X. To learn about its reliability, you read *Consumer Reports*, which has surveyed 1 000 owners of car X. Then you run into a friend who owns car X and she tells you that her car is a lemon. How do you treat your friend's observation? If you think rationally, you will realize that she has only increased your sample size from 1 000 to 1 001, which does not provide much new information. In addition, a process called the *reticular activation system* (RAS) works to bring your attention to instances of this car – you will suddenly start to notice more of them. The RAS is an automatic mechanism in the brain that brings relevant information to our attention. Both these effects – your friend's story is so vivid and you have noticed more of these vehicles on the road – mean that you may be tempted to attach a disproportionate weight to them in decision-making.
- *People are reluctant to change their minds.* People tend to interpret evidence to confirm beliefs they already hold. In one study, subjects were asked to read and evaluate a research report on whether capital punishment deters crime. After reading the report, those who initially favoured the death penalty said they were more sure in their view, and those who initially opposed the death penalty also said they were more sure in their view. The two groups interpreted the same evidence in exactly opposite ways.
- *People have a natural tendency to look for examples which confirm their existing view or hypothesis.* Nassim Nicholas Taleb calls this 'naïve empiricism'. People identify, select or observe past instances and quote them as evidence for a viewpoint or hypothesis. For example, every extreme weather event that is reported is selected as evidence of climate change, the fact that the UK enjoyed over a decade of economic growth was evidence that the era of 'boom and bust' had been relegated to the history books or that a rise in the price of petrol of 10 per cent is symptomatic of a broader increase in prices of all goods.
- *People use rules of thumb – heuristics.* When making decisions many people will be influenced by deep-seated rules of thumb or heuristics. There are three main heuristics. *Anchoring* refers to the tendency for people to start with something they are familiar with or know and make decisions or adjustments based

on this anchor. Often these anchors are biased and so the adjustment or decision is flawed in some way. The *availability* heuristic refers to cases where decisions are made based on an assessment of the risks of the likelihood of something happening. If examples readily come to mind as a result of excessive media coverage, for example, decisions may be taken with a skewed assessment of the risks. The third heuristic is *representativeness*. In this instance people tend to make judgements by comparing how representative something is to an image or stereotype that they hold. For example we might judge a person with lots of tattoos and piercings in a negative way or we may have an imperfect understanding of patterns as representations of reality, for example, random events. In many European cities perceptions of the prevalence of certain types of crime do not match the facts. People may be more prepared to pay money to buy a lottery ticket if a close friend has just won a reasonable amount of money on the lottery.

Why, you might ask, is economics built on the rationality assumption when psychology and common sense cast doubt on it? One answer is that the assumption, even if not exactly true, is still a good approximation. For example, when we studied the differences between competitive and monopoly firms, the assumption that firms rationally maximize profit yielded many important and valid insights. Recall from Chapter 2 that economic models are not meant to replicate reality but are supposed to show the essence of the problem at hand as an aid to understanding. When actual observed behaviour differs from the model we can analyse this behaviour to explain what is happening, and why, in relation to the 'benchmark' we have in the model.

Another reason that economists so often assume rationality may be that economists are themselves not rational maximizers. Like most people, they are overconfident, and they are reluctant to change their minds. Their choice among alternative theories of human behaviour may exhibit excessive inertia. Moreover, economists may be content with a theory that is not perfect but is good enough. Indeed, the model of rational man may be the theory of choice for a satisficing social scientist.

People Care about Fairness

Another insight about human behaviour is best illustrated with an experiment called the *ultimatum game*. The game works like this: two volunteers (who are otherwise strangers to each other) are told that they are going to play a game and could win a total of €100. Before they play, they learn the rules. The game begins with a flip of a coin, which is used to assign the volunteers to the roles of player A and player B. Player A's job is to propose a division of the €100 prize (in whole euros) between himself and the other player. After player A makes his proposal, player B decides whether to accept or reject it. If he accepts it, both players are paid according to the proposal. If player B rejects the proposal, both players walk away with nothing. In either case, the game then ends.

Before proceeding, stop and think about what you would do in this situation. If you were player A, what division of the €100 would you propose? If you were player B, what proposals would you accept?

Conventional economic theory assumes in this situation that people are rational wealth-maximizers. This assumption leads to a simple prediction: player A should propose that he gets €99 and player B gets €1, and player B should accept the proposal. After all, once the proposal is made, player B is better off accepting it as long as he gets something out of it (remember, people are assumed to act at the margin – a €1 euro gain is better than nothing). Moreover, because player A knows that accepting the proposal is in player B's interest, player A has no reason to offer him more than €1. In the language of game theory (discussed in Chapter 17), the 99–1 split is the Nash equilibrium.

Yet when experimental economists ask real people to play the ultimatum game, the results are very different from this prediction. People in the role of player B usually reject proposals that give them only €1 or a similarly small amount. Knowing this, people in the role of player A usually propose giving player B much more than €1. Some people will offer a 50–50 split, but it is more common for player A to propose giving player B an amount such as €30 or €40, keeping the larger share for himself. In this case, player B usually accepts the proposal.

What's going on here? The natural interpretation is that people are driven in part by some innate sense of fairness. A 99–1 split seems so wildly unfair to many people that they reject it, even to their own detriment. By contrast, a 70–30 split is still unfair, but it is not so unfair that it induces people to abandon their normal self-interest.

Throughout our study of household and firm behaviour, the innate sense of fairness has not played any role. But the results of the ultimatum game suggest that perhaps it should. For example, in Chapters 18 and 19 we discussed how wages were determined by labour supply and labour demand. Some economists have suggested that the perceived fairness of what a firm pays its workers should also enter the picture. Thus, when a firm has an especially profitable year, workers (like player B) may expect to be paid a fair share of the prize, even if the standard equilibrium does not dictate it. The firm (like player A) might well decide to give workers more than the equilibrium wage for fear that the workers might otherwise try to punish the firm with reduced effort, strikes or even vandalism.

To return to the ultimatum game, do you think that a sense of fairness may have its price? If the players were given, say, €1 000 to divide to the nearest hundred, and player A proposed a split of €900 to him and €100 to player B, do you think that player B would be just as likely to reject the proposal as before? What if the prize money were raised to €1 million, to be divided to the nearest €100 000? The answer may depend on the notion of *framing* – behaviour and decision-making will be dependent on the way decision problems or choices are framed.

People Are Inconsistent over Time

Imagine some dreary task, such as doing your laundry or tidying your room. Now consider the following questions:

1. Would you prefer (A) to spend 50 minutes doing the task immediately or (B) to spend 60 minutes doing the task tomorrow?
2. Would you prefer (A) to spend 50 minutes doing the task in 90 days or (B) to spend 60 minutes doing the task in 91 days?

When asked questions like these, many people choose B to question 1 and A to question 2. When looking ahead to the future (as in question 2), they minimize the amount of time spent on the dreary task. But faced with the prospect of doing the task immediately (as in question 1), they choose to put it off.

In some ways, this behaviour is not surprising: everyone procrastinates from time to time. But from the standpoint of the theory of rational humans, it is puzzling. Suppose that, in response to question 2, a person chooses to spend 50 minutes in 90 days. Then, when the 90th day arrives, we allow him to change his mind. In effect, he then faces question 1, so he opts for doing the task the next day. But why should the mere passage of time affect the choices he makes?

Many times in life, people make plans for themselves, but then they fail to follow through. A smoker promises himself that he will quit, but within a few hours of smoking his last cigarette, he craves another and breaks his promise. A person trying to lose weight promises that he will stop eating chocolate bars, but when he gets to the checkout at the supermarket and sees the tempting array of confectionery next to the cash register, the promise is forgotten. In both cases, the desire for instant gratification induces the decision-maker to abandon his own past plans.

Some economists believe that the consumption–saving decision is an important instance where people exhibit this inconsistency over time. For many people, spending provides a type of instant gratification. Saving, like passing up the cigarette or the dessert, requires a sacrifice in the present for a reward in the distant future. And just as many smokers wish they could quit and many overweight individuals wish they ate less, many consumers wish they saved more.

An implication of this inconsistency over time is that people should try to find ways to commit their future selves to following through on their plans. A smoker trying to quit may throw away his cigarettes, and a person on a diet may put a lock on the refrigerator and ask someone else to do the shopping. What can a person who saves too little do? He should find some way to lock up his money before he spends it. Some personal pension plans do exactly that. A worker can agree to have some money taken out of his salary payment before he ever sees it. The money is placed in an account and invested on his behalf by the pension company. When he retires, he can use the money to fund a pension, but the money can only be used before retirement with a penalty. This is one reason why people take out pension plans: they protect people from their own desires for instant gratification. (Thaler and Sunstein have some interesting perspectives on this very topic, one that is of increasing importance in a world where life expectancy is increasing and where the pressure on pensions is rising as a result.)

Quick Quiz Describe at least three ways in which human decision-making differs from that of the rational individual of conventional economic theory.

IN THE NEWS

In the UK and in Europe, there have been numerous news reports highlighting concerns over the expenses and allowances that elected representatives receive. MEPs and MPs came under heavy criticism for expenses claims made and, in 2009, the British newspapers were full of indignant stories of MPs claiming for moats, duck houses, gardening and even pornographic DVDs! Is moral hazard behind this behaviour?

MPs' and MEPs' Expenses

In May 2009, the British newspaper, *The Daily Telegraph*, published a series of reports on investigations they had carried out over the expenses claimed by members of parliament (MPs). The UK Parliament, like its European equivalent, has rules and regulations governing the claiming of expenses but the revelations seemed to show MPs had been stretching those rules to the very limit. What was revealed shook the confidence in the integrity of MPs and tarnished all, even though many did not abuse the system.

In the UK many MPs need to have a second home in order to carry out their duties in London as opposed to their homes in or around their constituencies. The rules allowed MPs to claim expenses against these second homes but some seemed to have either made claims that might be regarded as fraudulent, such as claiming for mortgage payments when mortgages have been paid off, whilst others have claimed for repairs to swimming pools, garden work, DVD players, coffee makers, trouser presses and toilet seats, amongst other things. The rules allowed MPs to claim up to £20 000 a year and it has been suggested that MPs have been encouraged to claim the full allowance regardless of whether it is appropriate. The public backlash against MPs was substantial; whilst many could see the necessity of having some sort of expenses system the public did not understand how some MPs could justify, on moral grounds, some of the claims they make, which would certainly not apply to 'ordinary' workers.

In Europe there have been similar concerns. In 2008 a report in *The Times* newspaper suggested that a secret inquiry by the European Parliament showed that the annual parliamentary allowance for all 785 MEPs was being abused to the tune of €100 million. Staff, it was claimed, were making claims for employing fictitious staff, unqualified family members and receiving bonuses for Christmas far in excess of their annual salary.

One of the problems facing those charged with regulating the behaviour of elected representatives is asymmetric information – the difference in the information available to the public and to MPs. In this case one party, MPs and MEPs, have more and different information to another party, the public. MPs and MEPs have had the privilege of claiming expenses under a set of rules which few outside the two parliaments understood. It was only through freedom of information legislation, for example, that *The Daily Telegraph* was able to get its information and place it in the public domain. MPs and MEPs, therefore, have been protected from risk and as such have behaved in relation to that protection.

Parties that are insulated from risk tend to behave differently as a result. In this case MPs and MEPs have been insulated from the risk that their claims will be made public and so some have behaved differently than they would if not insulated from risk. This behaviour has been interpreted by the public as being inappropriate and immoral. The agent (MPs and MEPs) may have the incentive to act inappropriately from the viewpoint of the principal (the public). MPs and MEPs have not had to take the consequences and responsibility for their actions and so some may have acted less carefully than they would if those consequences had to be accepted fully by each of them. Any reform to the system, therefore, has to address this fundamental problem and make sure that any new regulatory system addresses the asymmetric information and aligns the interests of MPs and MEPs in legitimately carrying out their duties with what the public see as being fair and equitable.

Source: Adapted from: http://www.bized.co.uk/cgi-bin/chron/chron.pl?id=3361

CONCLUSION

This chapter has examined some of the frontiers of microeconomics. You may have noticed that we have sketched out ideas rather than fully developing them. This is no accident. One reason is that you might study these topics in more detail in advanced courses. Another reason is that these topics remain active areas of research and, therefore, are still being fleshed out.

To see how these topics fit into the broader picture, recall the *Ten Principles of Economics* from Chapter 1. One principle states that markets are usually a good way to organize economic activity. Another principle states that governments can sometimes improve market outcomes. As you study economics, you can more fully appreciate the truth of these principles as well as the caveats that go with them. The study of asymmetric information should make you more wary of market outcomes. The study of political economy should make you more wary of government solutions. And the study of behavioural economics should make you wary of any institution that relies on human decision-making – including both the market and the government.

If there is a unifying theme to these topics, it is that life is messy. Information is imperfect, government is imperfect and people are imperfect. Of course, you knew this long before you started studying economics, but economists need to understand these imperfections as precisely as they can if they are to explain, and perhaps even improve, the world around them.

SUMMARY

- In many economic transactions, information is asymmetric. When there are hidden actions, principals may be concerned that agents suffer from the problem of moral hazard. When there are hidden characteristics, buyers may be concerned about the problem of adverse selection among the sellers. Private markets sometimes deal with asymmetric information with signalling and screening.
- Although government policy can sometimes improve market outcomes, governments are themselves imperfect institutions. The Condorcet paradox shows that majority rule fails to produce transitive preferences for society, and Arrow's impossibility theorem shows that no voting scheme will be perfect. In many situations, democratic institutions will produce the outcome desired by the median voter, regardless of the preferences of the rest of the electorate. Moreover, the individuals who set government policy may be motivated by self-interest rather than the national interest.
- The study of psychology and economics reveals that human decision-making is more complex than is assumed in conventional economic theory. People are not always rational, they care about the fairness of economic outcomes (even to their own detriment), and they can be inconsistent over time.

KEY CONCEPTS

moral hazard, p. 467
agent, p. 467
principal, p. 467
adverse selection, p. 468
signalling, p. 470
screening, p. 472
Condorcet paradox, p. 474
Arrow's impossibility theorem, p. 475
median voter theorem, p. 475

QUESTIONS FOR REVIEW

1. What is moral hazard? List three things an employer might do to reduce the severity of this problem.
2. What is adverse selection? Give an example of a market in which adverse selection might be a problem.
3. Define *signalling* and *screening,* and give an example of each.
4. What unusual property of voting did Condorcet notice?
5. Explain why majority rule respects the preferences of the median voter rather than the average voter.
6. Describe the ultimatum game. What outcome from this game would conventional economic theory predict? Do experiments confirm this prediction? Explain.

PROBLEMS AND APPLICATIONS

1. Each of the following situations involves moral hazard. In each case, identify the principal and the agent, and explain why there is asymmetric information. How does the action described reduce the problem of moral hazard?
   a. Landlords require tenants to pay security deposits.
   b. Firms compensate top executives with options to buy company shares at a given price in the future.
   c. Car insurance companies offer discounts to customers who install anti-theft devices in their cars.
2. Suppose that the Live-Long-and-Prosper Health Insurance Company charges €5 000 annually for a family insurance policy. The company's president suggests that the company raise the annual price to €6 000 in order to increase its profits. If the firm followed this suggestion,

what economic problem might arise? Would the firm's pool of customers tend to become more or less healthy on average? Would the company's profits necessarily increase?

3. The case study in this chapter describes how a boyfriend can signal to a girlfriend that he loves her by giving an appropriate gift. Do you think saying 'I love you' can also serve as a signal? Why or why not?
4. Some AIDS activists believe that health insurance companies should not be allowed to ask applicants if they are infected with the HIV virus that causes AIDS. Would this rule help or hurt those who are HIV-positive? Would it help or hurt those who are not HIV-positive? Would it exacerbate or mitigate the problem of adverse selection in the market for health insurance? Do you think it would increase or decrease the number of people without health insurance? In your opinion, would this be a good policy?
5. The government is considering two ways to help the needy: giving them cash, or giving them free meals at soup kitchens. Give an argument for giving cash. Give an argument, based on asymmetric information, for why the soup kitchen may be better than the cash handout.
6. Ken walks into a restaurant.

   WAITER: Good afternoon, sir. The specials today are roast lamb and baked trout.

   KEN: I'd like the lamb, please.

   WAITER: I almost forgot. We also have lobster thermidor.

   KEN: In that case, I'll have the trout, please.

   What standard property of decision-making is Ken violating? (Hint: reread the section on Arrow's impossibility theorem.) Is Ken necessarily being irrational? (Hint: what information is revealed by the fact that the chef is able to prepare lobster thermidor?)
7. Why might a political party in a two-party system choose not to move towards the median voter? (Hint: think about abstentions from voting and political contributions.)
8. Two ice cream stands are deciding where to locate along a one-mile beach. Each person sitting on the beach buys exactly one ice cream cone per day from the stand nearest to him. Each ice cream seller wants the maximum number of customers. Where along the beach will the two stands locate?

For further resources, visit www.cengage.co.uk/mankiw_taylor2

8

THE DATA OF MACROECONOMICS

23 MEASURING A NATION'S INCOME

When you finish university and start looking for a full-time job, your experience will, to a large extent, be shaped by prevailing economic conditions. In some years, firms throughout the economy are expanding their production of goods and services, employment is rising, and jobs are relatively easy to find. In other years, firms are cutting back on production; employment is declining, and finding a good job takes a long time. Not surprisingly, any university graduate would rather enter the labour force in a year of economic expansion than in a year of economic contraction.

Because the condition of the overall economy profoundly affects all of us, changes in economic conditions are widely reported by the media. Indeed, it is hard to pick up a newspaper without seeing some newly reported statistic about the economy. The statistic might measure the total income of everyone in the economy called gross domestic product (GDP), the rate at which average prices are rising (inflation), the percentage of the labour force that is out of work (unemployment), total spending in shops (retail sales), or the imbalance of trade between the domestic economy and the rest of the world (the trade deficit). All these statistics are *macroeconomic*. Rather than telling us about a particular household or firm, they tell us something about the entire economy.

As you may recall from Chapter 2, economics is divided into two branches: microeconomics and macroeconomics. Microeconomics is the study of how individual households and firms make decisions and how they interact with one another in markets. Macroeconomics is the study of the economy as a whole. The goal of macroeconomics is to explain the economic changes that affect

many households, firms and markets simultaneously. Macroeconomists address diverse questions: why is average income high in some countries while it is low in others? Why do prices rise rapidly in some periods of time while they are more stable in other periods? Why do production and employment expand in some years and contract in others? What, if anything, can the government do to promote rapid growth in incomes, low inflation and stable employment? These questions are all macroeconomic in nature because they concern the workings of the entire economy.

Because the economy as a whole is just a collection of many households and many firms interacting in many markets, microeconomics and macroeconomics are closely linked. The basic tools of supply and demand, for instance, are as central to macroeconomic analysis as they are to microeconomic analysis. Yet studying the economy in its entirety raises some new and intriguing challenges.

In this chapter and the next one, we discuss some of the data that economists and policy makers use to monitor the performance of the overall economy. These data reflect the economic changes that macroeconomists try to explain. This chapter considers *gross domestic product,* or simply GDP, which measures the total income of a nation. GDP is the most closely watched economic statistic because it is thought to be the best single (although not perfect) measure of a society's economic well-being.

THE ECONOMY'S INCOME AND EXPENDITURE

If you were to judge how a person is doing economically, you might first look at his or her income. A person with a high income can more easily afford life's necessities and luxuries. It is no surprise that people with higher incomes enjoy higher standards of living – better housing, better health care, fancier cars, more opulent vacations and so on.

The same logic applies to a nation's overall economy. When judging whether the economy is doing well or poorly, it is natural to look at the total income that everyone in the economy is earning. That is the task of gross domestic product (GDP).

GDP measures two things at once: the total income of everyone in the economy and the total expenditure on the economy's output of goods and services. The reason that GDP can perform the trick of measuring both total income and total expenditure is that these two things are really the same. For an economy as a whole, income must equal expenditure.

Why is this true? An economy's income is the same as its expenditure because every transaction has two parties: a buyer and a seller. Every pound of spending by some buyer is a pound of income for some seller. Suppose, for instance, that Victoria pays David €100 to mow her lawn. In this case, David is a seller of a service, and Victoria is a buyer. David earns €100 and Victoria spends €100. Thus, the transaction contributes equally to the economy's income and to its expenditure. GDP, whether measured as total income or total expenditure, rises by €100.

Another way to see the equality of income and expenditure is with the circular-flow diagram in Figure 23.1. (You may recall this circular-flow diagram from Chapter 2, where it was Figure 2.1.)

You may remember that this is a model which describes all the transactions between households and firms in a simple economy. In this economy, households buy goods and services from firms; these expenditures flow through the markets for goods and services. The firms in turn use the money they receive from sales to pay workers' wages, landowners' rent and firm owners' profit; this income flows through the markets for the factors of production. In this economy, money flows from households to firms and then back to households.

FIGURE 23.1

The Circular-Flow Diagram

Households buy goods and services from firms, and firms use their revenue from sales to pay wages to workers, rent to landowners and profit to firm owners. GDP equals the total amount spent by households in the market for goods and services. It also equals the total wages, rent and profit paid by firms in the markets for the factors of production.

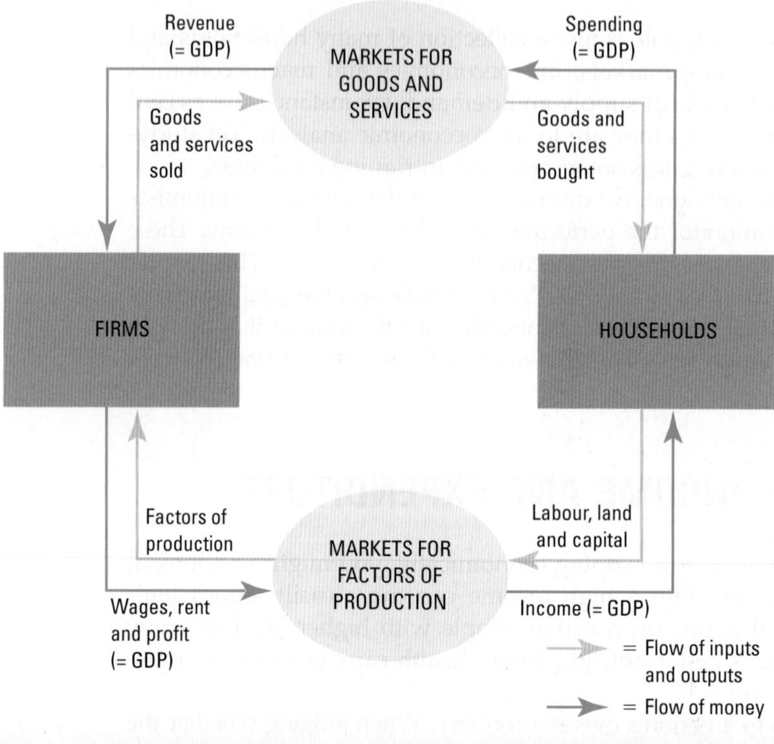

We can compute GDP for this economy in one of two ways: by adding up the total expenditure by households or by adding up the total income (wages, rent and profit) paid by firms. Because all expenditure in the economy ends up as someone's income, GDP is the same regardless of how we compute it.

The actual economy is, of course, more complicated than the one illustrated in Figure 23.1. In particular, households do not spend all of their income. They pay some of it to the government in taxes, and they save some for use in the future. In addition, households do not buy all goods and services produced in the economy. Some goods and services are bought by governments, and some are bought by firms that plan to use them in the future to produce their own output. Some goods are bought from sellers in foreign countries and some domestic products are sold abroad. Yet, regardless of whether a household, government or firm buys a good or service, the transaction has a buyer and seller. Thus, for the economy as a whole, expenditure and income are always the same.

Quick Quiz What two things does gross domestic product measure? How can it measure two things at once?

THE MEASUREMENT OF GROSS DOMESTIC PRODUCT

Now that we have discussed the meaning of gross domestic product in general terms, let's be more precise about how this statistic is measured. Here is a definition of GDP:

- **Gross domestic product (GDP)** is the market value of all final goods and services produced within a country in a given period of time.

gross domestic product (GDP) the market value of all final goods and services produced within a country in a given period of time

This definition might seem simple enough. But, in fact, many subtle issues arise when computing an economy's GDP. Let's therefore consider each phrase in this definition with some care.

'GDP Is the Market Value ...'

You have probably heard the adage, 'You can't compare apples and oranges.' Yet GDP does exactly that. GDP adds together many different kinds of products into a single measure of the value of economic activity. To do this, it uses market prices. Because market prices measure the amount people are willing to pay for different goods, they reflect the value of those goods. If the price of an apple is twice the price of an orange, then an apple contributes twice as much to GDP as does an orange.

'... Of All ...'

GDP tries to be comprehensive. It includes all items produced in the economy and sold legally in markets. GDP measures the market value of not just apples and oranges, but also pears and grapefruit, books and movies, haircuts and health care, and so on.

GDP also includes the market value of the housing services provided by the economy's stock of housing. For rental housing, this value is easy to calculate – the rent equals both the tenant's expenditure and the landlord's income. Yet many people own the place where they live and, therefore, do not pay rent. The government includes this owner-occupied housing in GDP by estimating its rental value. That is, GDP is based on the assumption that the owner, in effect, pays rent to himself, so the rent is included both in his expenditure and in his income.

There are some products, however, that GDP excludes because measuring them is so difficult. GDP excludes most items produced and sold illicitly, such as illegal drugs. It also excludes most items that are produced and consumed at home and, therefore, never enter the marketplace. Vegetables you buy at the greengrocer's shop or the supermarket are part of GDP; vegetables you grow in your garden are not.

These exclusions from GDP can at times lead to paradoxical results. The value of work carried out by house wives and husbands is not included in GDP calculations and neither is the value of child care work carried out by grandparents, for example. In addition, when Eva pays Didi to mow her lawn, that transaction is part of GDP. If Eva were to marry Didi, the situation would change. Even though Didi may continue to mow Eva's lawn, the value of the mowing is now left out of GDP because Didi's service is no longer sold in a market. Thus, when Eva and Didi marry, GDP falls.

'... Final ...'

When a paper company sells paper to a greetings card company, the paper is called an *intermediate good*, and the card is called a *final good*. GDP includes only the value of final goods. The reason is that the value of intermediate goods is already included in the prices of the final goods. Adding the market value of the paper to the market value of the card would be double counting. That is, it would (incorrectly) count the paper twice.

An important exception to this principle arises when an intermediate good is produced and, rather than being used, is added to a firm's inventory of goods to be used or sold at a later date. In this case, the intermediate good is taken to be 'final' for the moment, and its value as inventory investment is added to GDP. When the inventory of the intermediate good is later used or sold, the firm's inventory investment is negative, and GDP for the later period is reduced accordingly.

'... Goods and Services ...'

GDP includes both tangible goods (food, clothing, cars) and intangible services (haircuts, house cleaning, doctor visits). When you (legally) download an album by your favourite band, you are buying a good, and the purchase price is part of GDP. When you pay to hear a concert by the same band, you are buying a service, and the ticket price is also part of GDP.

'... Produced ...'

GDP includes goods and services currently produced. It does not include transactions involving items produced in the past. When Aston Martin produces and sells a new car, the value of the car is included in the GDP of the country in which Aston Martin operates. When one person sells a used car to another person, the value of the used car is not included in GDP.

'... within a Country ...'

GDP measures the value of production within the geographic confines of a country. When an Australian citizen works temporarily in the United Kingdom, his production is part of UK GDP. When a UK citizen owns a factory in Bulgaria, the production at his factory is not part of UK GDP (it's part of Bulgaria's GDP). Thus, items are included in a nation's GDP if they are produced domestically, regardless of the nationality of the producer.

'... in a Given Period of Time.'

GDP measures the value of production that takes place within a specific interval of time. Usually that interval is a year or a quarter (three months). GDP measures the economy's flow of income and expenditure during that interval.

When the government reports the GDP for a quarter, it usually presents GDP 'at an annual rate'. This means that the figure reported for quarterly GDP is the amount of income and expenditure during the quarter multiplied by 4. The government uses this convention so that quarterly and annual figures on GDP can be compared more easily.

In addition, when the government reports quarterly GDP, it presents the data after they have been modified by a statistical procedure called *seasonal adjustment*. The unadjusted data show clearly that the economy produces more goods and services during some times of year than during others. (As you might guess, December's holiday shopping season is a high point in many countries whilst the period before Ramadan is a high point for many Muslim countries.) When monitoring the condition of the economy, economists and policy makers often want to look beyond these regular seasonal changes. Therefore, government statisticians adjust the quarterly data to take out the seasonal cycle. The GDP data reported in the news are always seasonally adjusted.

Now let's repeat the definition of GDP:

- Gross domestic product (GDP) is the market value of all final goods and services produced within a country in a given period of time.

It should be apparent that GDP is a sophisticated measure of the value of economic activity. In advanced courses in macroeconomics you will learn more about the subtleties that arise in its calculation. But even now you can see that each phrase in this definition is packed with meaning.

FYI

Other Measures of Income

When the Office for National Statistics or Eurostat computes the GDP every three months for the UK and the EU respectively, they also compute various other measures of income to arrive at a more complete picture of what's happening in the economy. These other measures differ from GDP by excluding or including certain categories of income. What follows is a brief description of five of these income measures, ordered from largest to smallest, based on the UK.

- *Gross national product (GNP)* is the total income earned by a nation's permanent residents (called *nationals*). It differs from GDP by including income that UK citizens earn abroad and excluding income that foreigners earn in the UK as we saw above. For most countries, including the United Kingdom, domestic residents are responsible for most domestic production, so GDP and GNP are quite close.
- *Net national product (NNP)* is the total income of a nation's residents (GNP) minus losses from depreciation. *Depreciation* is the wear and tear on the economy's stock of equipment and structures, such as lorries rusting and computers becoming obsolete.
- *National income* is the total income earned by a nation's residents in the production of goods and services. It differs from net national product by excluding indirect business taxes (such as sales taxes) and including business subsidies. NNP and national income also differ because of a 'statistical discrepancy' that arises from problems in data collection.
- *Personal income* is the income that households and non-corporate businesses receive. Unlike national income, it excludes *retained earnings*, which is income that corporations have earned but have not paid out to their owners. It also subtracts corporate income taxes and contributions for social insurance. In addition, personal income includes the interest income that households receive from their holdings of government debt and the income that households receive from government transfer programmes, such as welfare and social security payments.
- *Disposable personal income* is the income that households and non-corporate businesses have left after satisfying all their obligations to the government. It equals personal income minus personal taxes and certain non-tax payments (such as parking tickets).

Although the various measures of income differ in detail, they almost always tell the same story about economic conditions. When GDP is growing rapidly, these other measures of income are usually growing rapidly. And when GDP is falling, these other measures are usually falling as well. For monitoring fluctuations in the overall economy, it does not matter much which measure of income we use.

Quick Quiz Which contributes more to GDP – the production of €1 of hamburger or the production of €1 of caviar? Why?

THE COMPONENTS OF GDP

Spending in the economy takes many forms. At any moment, the Müller family may be having lunch in a Munich restaurant; Honda may be building a car factory on the banks of the Rhine; the German Army may be procuring weapons from German arms manufacturers; and a New York investment company may be buying bonds from a German bank. German GDP includes all of these various forms of spending on domestically produced goods and services. Similarly, each country in Europe will monitor the forms of spending and income to arrive at the GDP for that country.

To understand how the economy is using its scarce resources, economists are often interested in studying the composition of GDP among various types of spending. To do this, GDP (which we denote as Y) is divided into four components: consumption (C), investment (I), government purchases (G) and net exports (NX):

$$Y \equiv C + I + G + NX$$

This equation is an *identity* – an equation that must be true by the way the variables in the equation are defined. (That's why we used the three-bar, 'identically equals' symbol, '≡', although for the most part we'll follow normal practice in dealing with identities and use the usual equals sign, '='.) In this case, because each pound or euro of expenditure included in GDP is placed into one of the four components of GDP, the total of the four components must be equal to GDP. Let's look at each of these four components more closely.

Consumption

consumption
spending by households on goods and services, with the exception of purchases of new housing

Consumption is spending by households on goods and services. 'Goods' include household spending on durable goods, such as cars and appliances like washing machines and fridges, and non-durable goods, such as food and clothing. 'Services' include such intangible items as haircuts and medical care. Household spending on education is also included in consumption of services (although one might argue that it would fit better in the next component).

Investment

investment
spending on capital equipment, inventories and structures, including household purchases of new housing

Investment is the purchase of goods that will be used in the future to produce more goods and services. It is the sum of purchases of capital equipment, inventories and structures. Investment in structures includes expenditure on new housing. By convention, the purchase of a new house is the one form of household spending categorized as investment rather than consumption.

As mentioned earlier in this chapter, the treatment of inventory accumulation is noteworthy. When Aston Martin produces a car and, instead of selling it, adds it to its inventory, Aston Martin is assumed to have 'purchased' the car for itself. That is, the national income accountants treat the car as part of Aston Martin's investment spending. (If Aston Martin later sells the car out of inventory, Aston Martin's inventory investment will then be negative, offsetting the positive expenditure of the buyer.) Inventories are treated this way because one aim of GDP is to measure the value of the economy's production, and goods added to inventory are part of that period's production.

Government Purchases

Government purchases include spending on goods and services by local and national governments. It includes the salaries of government workers and spending on public works.

government purchases
spending on goods and services by local, state and national governments

The meaning of 'government purchases' requires a little clarification. When the government pays the salary of an army general, that salary is part of government purchases. But what happens when the government pays a social security benefit to one of the elderly? Such government spending is called a **transfer payment** because it is not made in exchange for a currently produced good or service. Transfer payments alter household income, but they do not reflect the economy's production. (From a macroeconomic standpoint, transfer payments are like negative taxes.) Because GDP is intended to measure income from, and expenditure on, the production of goods and services, transfer payments are not counted as part of government purchases.

transfer payment
a payment for which no good or service is exchanged

Net Exports

Net exports equal the purchases of domestically produced goods by foreigners (exports) minus the domestic purchases of foreign goods (imports). A domestic firm's sale to a buyer in another country, such as the sale of Aston Martin cars to customers in the USA, increases UK net exports.

net exports
spending on domestically produced goods by foreigners (exports) minus spending on foreign goods by domestic residents (imports)

The 'net' in 'net exports' refers to the fact that the value of imports are subtracted from the value of exports. This subtraction is made because imports of goods and services are included in other components of GDP. For example, suppose that a UK household buys a £30 000 car from Volvo, the Swedish car maker. That transaction increases consumption in the UK by £30 000 because car purchases are part of consumer spending in the UK. It also reduces net exports by £30 000 because the car is an import (note it represents an export for Sweden). In other words, net exports include goods and services produced abroad (with a minus sign) because these goods and services are included in consumption, investment and government purchases (with a plus sign). Thus, when a domestic household, firm or government buys a good or service from abroad, the purchase reduces net exports – but because it also raises consumption, investment or government purchases, it does not affect GDP. The above example shows the importance of making sure that we focus on a particular country when discussing imports and exports because of the potential for confusion to arise.

CASE STUDY

The Components of UK GDP

Table 23.1 shows the composition of UK GDP in 2009. In that year, the GDP of the United Kingdom was about £1 267 billion. Dividing this number by the 2008 UK population of about 61.5 million yields GDP per person (sometimes called GDP per capita). We find that in 2009 the income and expenditure of the average Brit was about £20 676.

Consumption made up about 65 per cent of GDP, or £13 439 per person. Investment was £2 895 per person. Government purchases were £4 755 per person. Net exports were –£413 per person. This number is negative because British residents earned less from selling to foreigners than they spent on foreign goods.

These data come from the UK Office of National Statistics and HM Treasury. You can find more recent data on GDP at their websites: www.statistics.gov.uk and http://www.hm-treasury.gov.uk/data. The data for GDP per capita for the EU 27 along with Japan, Switzerland and the Untied States is given in Figure 23.2 to highlight comparisons not only between these and the UK but within the EU and other nations as well.

TABLE 23.1

GDP and its Components

This table shows total GDP for the UK economy in 2009 and the breakdown of GDP among its four components. When reading this table, recall the identity $Y \equiv C + I + G + NX$.

	Total (in billions of pounds)	Per person (in pounds)	Percent of total
Gross domestic product, *Y*	£1 267	£20 676	100%
Consumption, *C*	826	13 439	65
Investment, *I*	183	2 895	14
Government purchases, *G*	288	4 755	23
Net exports, *NX*	–30	–413	–2

Source: UK Office for National Statistics and HM Treasury. Parts may not sum to totals due to rounding.

Quick Quiz List the four components of expenditure. Which is the largest?

REAL VERSUS NOMINAL GDP

As we have seen, GDP measures the total spending on goods and services in all markets in the economy. If total spending rises from one year to the next, one of two things must be true (or a combination of the two): (1) the economy is producing a larger output of goods and services, or (2) goods and services are being sold at higher prices. When studying changes in the economy over time, economists want to separate these two effects. In particular, they want a measure of the total quantity of goods and services the economy is producing that is not affected by changes in the prices of those goods and services.

To do this, economists use a measure called *real GDP.* Real GDP answers a hypothetical question: what would be the value of the goods and services produced this year if we valued these goods and services at the prices that prevailed in some specific year in the past? By evaluating current production using prices that are fixed at past levels, real GDP shows how the economy's overall production of goods and services changes over time.

To see more precisely how real GDP is constructed, let's consider an example.

FIGURE 23.2

GDP per capita in Europe, the US and Japan, 2008

As a means of comparison, the figure shows the GDP per capita in euros for the EU 27 and the United States and Switzerland in 2008. Where an 'X' sits by the country, no data were available.

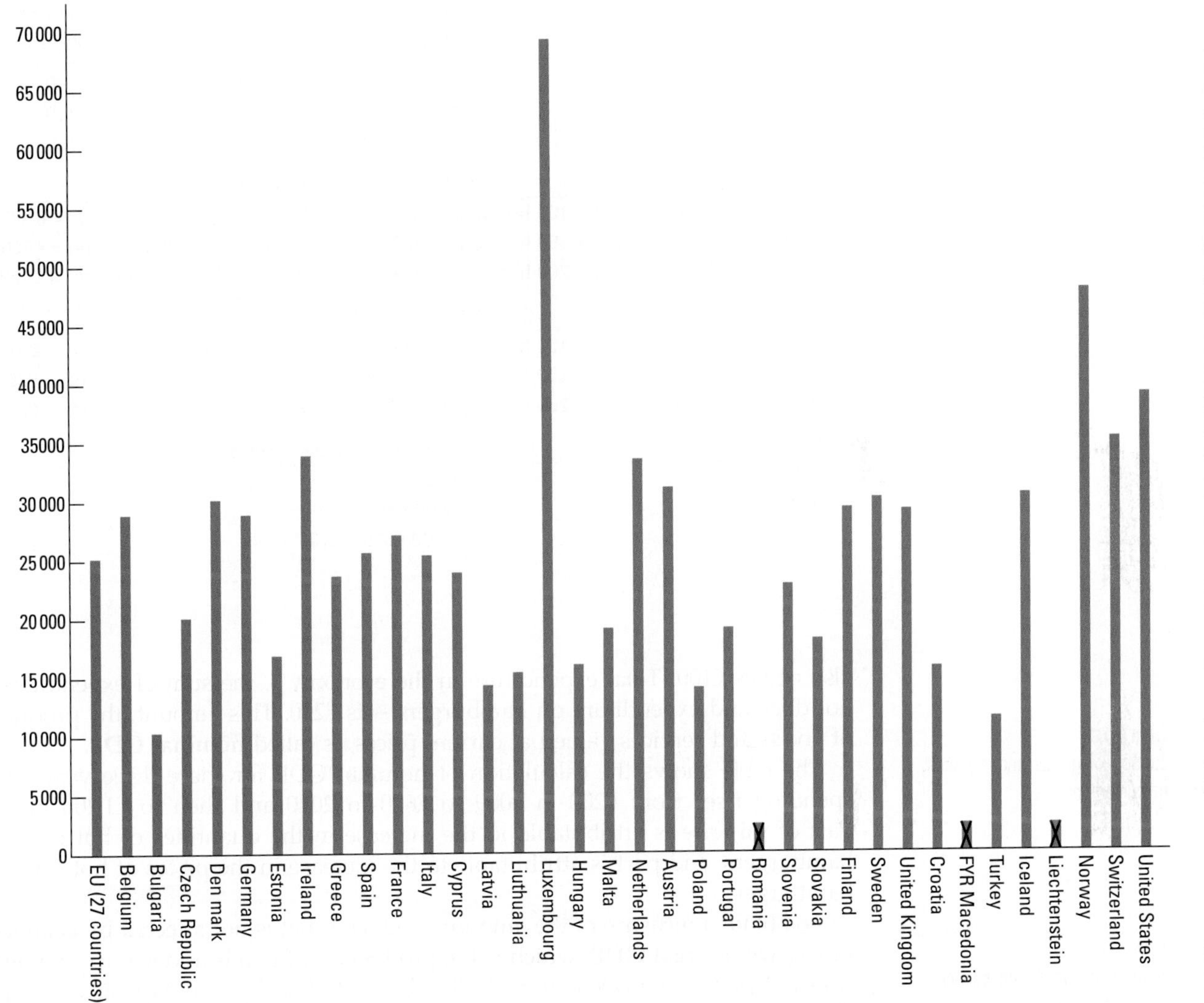

Source: http://epp.eurostat.ec.europa.eu/tgm/graph.do?tab=graph&plugin=0&pcode=tec00001&language=en&toolbox=close

A Numerical Example

Table 23.2 shows some data for an economy that produces only two goods – hot dogs and hamburgers. The table shows the quantities of the two goods produced and their prices in the years 2009, 2010 and 2011.

To compute total spending in this economy, we would multiply the quantities of hot dogs and hamburgers by their prices. In the year 2009, 100 hot dogs are sold at a price of €1 per hot dog, so expenditure on hot dogs equals €100. In the same year, 50 hamburgers are sold for €2 per hamburger, so expenditure on hamburgers

TABLE 23.2

Real and Nominal GDP

This table shows how to calculate real GDP, nominal GDP and the GDP deflator for a hypothetical economy that produces only hot dogs and hamburgers.

Prices and quantities

Year	Price of hot dogs	Quantity of hot dogs	Price of hamburgers	Quantity of hamburgers
2009	€1	100	€2	50
2010	2	150	3	100
2011	3	200	4	150

Year	Calculating nominal GDP
2009	(€1 per hot dog × 100 hot dogs) + (€2 per hamburger × 50 hamburgers) = €200
2010	(€2 per hot dog × 150 hot dogs) + (€3 per hamburger × 100 hamburgers) = €600
2011	(€3 per hot dog × 200 hot dogs) + (€4 per hamburger × 150 hamburgers) = €1 200

Year	Calculating real GDP (base year 2009)
2009	(€1 per hot dog × 100 hot dogs) + (€2 per hamburger × 50 hamburgers) = €200
2010	(€1 per hot dog × 150 hot dogs) + (€2 per hamburger × 100 hamburgers) = €350
2011	(€1 per hot dog × 200 hot dogs) + (€2 per hamburger × 150 hamburgers) = €500

Year	Calculating the GDP deflator
2009	(€200/€200) × 100 = 100
2010	(€600/€350) × 100 = 171
2011	(€1 200/€500) × 100 = 240

also equals €100. Total expenditure in the economy – the sum of expenditure on hot dogs and expenditure on hamburgers – is €200. This amount, the production of goods and services valued at current prices, is called **nominal GDP**.

nominal GDP
the production of goods and services valued at current prices

The table shows the calculation of nominal GDP for these three years. Total spending rises from €200 in 2009 to €600 in 2010 and then to €1 200 in 2011. Part of this rise is attributable to the increase in the quantities of hot dogs and hamburgers, and part is attributable to the increase in the prices of hot dogs and hamburgers.

To obtain a measure of the amount produced that is not affected by changes in prices, we use **real GDP**, which is the production of goods and services valued at constant prices. We calculate real GDP by first choosing one year as a *base year*. We then use the prices of hot dogs and hamburgers in the base year to compute the value of goods and services in all of the years. In other words, the prices in the base year provide the basis for comparing quantities in different years.

real GDP
the production of goods and services valued at constant prices

Suppose that we choose 2009 to be the base year in our example. We can then use the prices of hot dogs and hamburgers in 2009 to compute the value of goods and services produced in 2009, 2010 and 2011. Table 23.2 shows these calculations. To compute real GDP for 2009 we use the prices of hot dogs and hamburgers in 2009 (the base year) and the quantities of hot dogs and hamburgers produced in 2009. (Thus, for the base year, real GDP always equals nominal GDP.) To compute real GDP for 2010, we use the prices of hot dogs and hamburgers in 2009 (the base year) and the quantities of hot dogs and hamburgers produced in 2010. Similarly, to compute real GDP for 2011, we use the prices in 2009 and the quantities in 2011. When we find that real GDP has risen from €200 in 2009 to €350 in 2010 and then to €500 in 2011, we know that the increase is attributable to an increase in the quantities produced, because the prices are being held fixed at base-year levels.

To sum up: nominal GDP uses current prices to place a value on the economy's production of goods and services, while real GDP uses constant base-year prices to place a value on the economy's production of goods and services. Because real GDP is not affected by changes in prices, changes in real GDP reflect only changes in the amounts being produced. Thus, real GDP is a measure of the economy's production of goods and services.

Our goal in computing GDP is to gauge how well the overall economy is performing. Because real GDP measures the economy's production of goods and services, it reflects the economy's ability to satisfy people's needs and desires. Thus, real GDP is a better gauge of economic well-being than is nominal GDP. When economists talk about the economy's GDP, they usually mean real GDP rather than nominal GDP. And when they talk about growth in the economy, they measure that growth as the percentage change in real GDP from one period to another.

The GDP Deflator

As we have just seen, nominal GDP reflects both the prices of goods and services and the quantities of goods and services the economy is producing. In contrast, by holding prices constant at base-year levels, real GDP reflects only the quantities produced. From these two statistics we can compute a third, called the GDP deflator, which reflects the prices of goods and services but not the quantities produced.

The **GDP deflator** is calculated as follows:

GDP deflator
a measure of the price level calculated as the ratio of nominal GDP to real GDP times 100

$$\text{GDP deflator} = (\text{Nominal GDP}=\text{Real GDP}) \times 100$$

Because nominal GDP and real GDP must be the same in the base year, the GDP deflator for the base year always equals 100. The GDP deflator for subsequent years measures the change in nominal GDP from the base year that cannot be attributable to a change in real GDP.

The GDP deflator measures the current level of prices relative to the level of prices in the base year. To see why this is true, consider a couple of simple examples. First, imagine that the quantities produced in the economy rise over time but prices remain the same. In this case, both nominal and real GDP rise together, so the GDP deflator is constant. Now suppose, instead, that prices rise over time but the quantities produced stay the same. In this second case, nominal GDP rises but real GDP remains the same, so the GDP deflator rises as well. Notice that, in both cases, the GDP deflator reflects what's happening to prices, not quantities.

Let's now return to our numerical example in Table 23.2. The GDP deflator is computed at the bottom of the table. For year 2009, nominal GDP is €200, and real GDP is €200, so the GDP deflator is 100. For the year 2010, nominal GDP is €600, and real GDP is €350, so the GDP deflator is 171. Because the GDP deflator rose in year 2010 from 100 to 171, we can say that the price level increased by 71 per cent.

The GDP deflator is one measure that economists use to monitor the average level of prices in the economy. We examine another – the consumer prices index – in the next chapter, where we also describe the differences between the two measures.

Quick Quiz Define real and nominal GDP. Which is a better measure of economic well-being? Why?

FYI

Measuring GDP

We have looked at measuring GDP through income and expenditure methods and said that in theory they are the same. GDP can also be measured by looking at the output method. The price of a product represents the value of the inputs (land, labour and capital) that went into production. At each stage of the production process the value or output can be recorded – the value added. GDP is also a measure of the value of output in the economy. Statistics offices usually classify output according to industry types – construction, agriculture forestry and fisheries, mining, services and so on.

The measure for GDP is essentially what is called a 'volume measure'. In other words, it is measuring 'how much' has been produced. In the UK the ONS has to produce a single measure of GDP and does this by using the three approaches – income, expenditure and output – and balancing the final figure in relation to the three measures. Remember, we said that in theory they should all be the same but the process of collecting information from millions of transactions means that in reality they would never be exact.

Imagine a situation, for example, where someone has some work done on his or her house – say some plastering of a room. The total price for the work paid by the owner of the house might be £1 500 – this should represent the sum of the resources used in the job. The plasterer may declare to Her Majesty's Revenue and Customs (HMRC), that is responsible for collecting UK taxes, that the work represented income of £1 200 (to avoid paying income tax – illegal, but nevertheless it happens!) and the resources used might have included the plasterboard, plaster, electricity, buckets, nails, water, trowels and hawks, the vehicles to get to and from the builders merchants, etc. It is easy to see how, even in such a simple example that it becomes incredibly difficult to keep track of every item involved!

The choice of which base year to use in calculating real GDP is also important. Up until early 2004, the ONS used a method referred to as 'fixed base aggregations'. For example, they might have compared the data using 1995 as the base year. However, as with any statistical data which uses a base year in its compilation, this can lead to inconsistencies in the data because circumstances change. Goods, for example, that were common in 1995 may not exist anymore and there might be some products that were not available at that time – DVDs, for example. In general, the more you can update the base year, the more accurate the statistics will be. Fixed base aggregations in GDP statistics were used as follows. The growth of the different parts of the economy was given weights when trying to arrive at the final figure for GDP. This takes account of their relative importance in the economy and a base year of 1995 was used to help determine these weights. These base years were updated every 5 years but as we have seen, this can lead to problems.

The method known as 'annual chain linking' helps to overcome these problems. Rather than updating the base years every five years, this method does it every year, calculating the prices in previous years' prices (PYPs). In future therefore, you might see GDP tables expressed as 'GDP (CVM)', where CVM means Chained Volume Measures, as opposed to 'GDP in constant prices'. The ONS and other statistical services are constantly looking to update their methods to provide more reliable and accurate data and this is one example of such a revision of methods.

In terms of analysis of the data it should make little difference, but recognizing it enables you to be more confident that the data is more likely to be accurate and reliable compared to the previous measures.

GDP AND ECONOMIC WELL-BEING

Earlier in this chapter, GDP was referred to as the best single measure of the economic well-being of a society. Now that we know what GDP is, we can evaluate this claim.

As we have seen, GDP measures both the economy's total income and the economy's total expenditure on goods and services. Thus, GDP per person tells us the income and expenditure of the average person in the economy. Because most people would prefer to receive higher income and enjoy higher expenditure, GDP per person seems a natural measure of the economic well-being of the average individual.

Yet some people dispute the validity of GDP as a measure of well-being. Surely we should not be obsessed with material things and income? Surely we should value things that are not measured by GDP and that contribute to the quality of life and economic well-being, such as the health of a country's children, or the quality of their education, or even the beauty of the poetry making up our literary heritage.

The answer is that a large GDP does in fact help us to lead a good life. GDP does not measure the health of our children, but nations with larger GDP can afford better health care for their children. GDP does not measure the quality of their education, but nations with larger GDP can afford better educational systems. GDP does not measure the beauty of our poetry, but nations with larger GDP can afford to teach more of their citizens to read and to enjoy poetry. GDP does not take account of our intelligence, integrity, courage or wisdom, but all of these laudable attributes are easier to foster when people are less concerned about being able to afford the material necessities of life. In short, GDP does not directly measure those things that make life worthwhile, but it does measure our ability to obtain the inputs into a worthwhile life.

GDP is not, however, a perfect measure of well-being. Some things that contribute to a good life are left out of GDP. One is leisure. Suppose, for instance, that everyone in the economy suddenly started working every day of the week, rather than enjoying leisure on weekends. More goods and services would be produced, and GDP would rise. Yet, despite the increase in GDP, we should not conclude that everyone would be better off. The loss from reduced leisure would offset the gain from producing and consuming a greater quantity of goods and services.

Because GDP uses market prices to value goods and services, it excludes the value of almost all activity that takes place outside of markets. In particular, GDP omits the value of goods and services produced at home. When a chef prepares a delicious meal and sells it at his restaurant, the value of that meal is part of GDP. But if the chef prepares the same meal for his wife, the value he has added to the raw ingredients is left out of GDP. As we saw above, child care provided in day care centres is part of GDP, whereas child care by parents at home is not. Volunteer work also contributes to the well-being of those in society, but GDP does not reflect these contributions.

Another thing that GDP excludes is the quality of the environment. Imagine that the government eliminated all environmental regulations. Firms could then produce goods and services without considering the pollution they create, and GDP might rise. Yet well-being would most likely fall. The deterioration in the quality of air and water would more than offset the gains from greater production.

GDP also says nothing about the distribution of income. A society in which 100 people have annual incomes of €50 000 has GDP of €5 million and, not surprisingly, GDP per person of €50 000; so does a society in which 10 people earn €500 000 and 90 suffer with nothing at all. Few people would look at those two situations and call them equivalent. GDP per person tells us what happens to the average person, but behind the average lies a large variety of personal experiences.

In the end, we can conclude that GDP is a good measure of economic well-being for most – but not all – purposes. It is important to keep in mind what GDP includes and what it leaves out.

GDP reflects the factory's production, but not the harm that it inflicts on the environment.

CASE STUDY

International Differences in GDP and the Quality of Life

One way to gauge the usefulness of GDP as a measure of economic well-being is to examine international data. Rich and poor countries have vastly different levels of GDP per person. If a large GDP leads to a higher standard of living, then we should observe GDP to be strongly correlated with measures of the quality of life. And, in fact, we do.

Table 23.3 shows 13 of the world's most populous countries ranked in order of GDP per person. The table also shows life expectancy (the expected life span at birth) and literacy (the percentage of the adult population who can read). These data show a clear pattern. In rich countries, such as the United Kingdom, the United States, Japan and Germany, people can expect to live into their late seventies, and almost all of the population can read. In poor countries, such as Nigeria, Bangladesh and Pakistan, people typically live only until their fifties or early sixties, and only about half of the population is literate.

Although data on other aspects of the quality of life are less complete, they tell a similar story. Countries with low GDP per person tend to have more infants with low birth weight, higher rates of infant mortality, higher rates of maternal mortality, higher rates of child malnutrition and less common access to safe drinking water. In countries with low GDP per person, fewer school-age children are actually in school, and those who are in school must learn with fewer teachers per student. These countries also tend to have fewer televisions, fewer telephones, fewer paved roads and fewer households with electricity. International data leave no doubt that a nation's GDP is closely associated with its citizens' standard of living.

TABLE 23.3

GDP, Life Expectancy and Literacy

The table shows GDP per person (measured in US dollars) and two measures of the quality of life for 13 major countries.

Country	Real GDP per person (2006)	Life expectancy	Adult literacy
United States	$44 155	78.1 years	99%
Japan	34 022	82.4	99
Germany	35 270	79.1	99
United Kingdom	38 849	78.8	99
Russia	6 932	66.6	99.6
Mexico	8 051	75.8	91
Brazil	5 659	72.3	88.6
China	2 033	73.1	86
Indonesia	1 634	70.5	90.4
India	816	69.3	59.5
Pakistan	810	64.1	49.9
Bangladesh	429	63.2	43.1
Nigeria	792	46.5	68

Source: Nationmaster.com and OECD.

Quick Quiz Why should policy makers care about GDP?

IN THE NEWS

GDP is one measure of the overall level of economic well-being in an economy. GDP in many European countries has risen markedly over the past 30 years. Does this increase in incomes equate with an increase in happiness? Economists have become increasingly interested in the economics of happiness. The main ideas are discussed below.

The Economics of Happiness

It does appear that, despite the massive increase in wealth, incomes and access to material goods and services, our perception of happiness has not really changed that much. Increased wealth has not brought with it similar increases in happiness. Numerous surveys have highlighted relatively stable rates of 'happiness' in rich countries. Professor Richard Layard, one of a group of economists including Andrew Oswald, Stephen Nickell, Robert Skidelsky, Tim Besley, Will Hutton and those behavioural economists that we have met before in this book, have studied this apparent paradox. Layard[1] states that in relation to Western societies: 'on average, people are no happier than they were fifty years ago.'

Many people perceive January to be a very stressful month. In 2006, a number of newspapers and media organizations ran a story suggesting that 23 January 2006 was going to be the official 'worst day of the year'. How was this arrived at? It appears that someone called Cliff Arnall had devised a formula for calculating it. The formula is: [W + (D – d)] × TQM × NA, where W is the weather, D is debt, T is time since Christmas, Q the time since failing to keep to our New Year's resolutions, M is motivational levels and NA the need to take action.

The formula developed by Cliff Arnall was supposed to make some attempt to quantify a way in which states of happiness (or sadness) can be measured. Its scientific basis has been called into question. Arnall said that it is useful in triggering discussion and debate about what we understand by happiness and to think of ways we can deal with the effects of how we live our lives on our well-being.

What is needed, therefore, is a widely accepted set of criteria that is accepted as constituting happiness. The increased understanding of the brain and neuroscience has helped to shed some light on this but it is a complex area. Psychologists and economists have found that links between how people see their own happiness and other things that might influence such a judgement are statistically strong. This also seems to apply across different countries. As a result, we might be able to conclude that there are a range of factors that can contribute to a definition of happiness; that if you are fortunate enough to find yourself being able to boast having these characteristics or in some cases managing to avoid them then you are more likely to be happy.

Layard identified some key factors that may contribute to 'happiness'. He suggested that some of the factors associated with promoting happiness, include sex, socializing, relaxing, praying, worshipping or meditating, eating, exercising, watching TV and shopping, amongst others.

Other studies have suggested that an individual's level of education, health, whether they are married, single or divorced, the level of income enjoyed, whether they are working/unemployed/retired, their aspirations and whether they have experienced bereavement can all be contributory factors.

From such characteristics, equations to statistically arrive at measures of well-being can be derived. These have been used by both economists and psychologists and have been found to have been surprisingly reliable in statistical terms. One of the leading thinkers on the economics of happiness is Professor Andrew Oswald who is based at the University of Warwick. Oswald offers the following formula:

$$W_{it} = \alpha + \beta x_{it} + \varepsilon_{it}$$

In this formula, W_{it} is the reported well-being of an individual at a particular time period, X represents a collection of variables that are known to be characteristics affecting well-being at a particular time period; these could be economic, such as income, or demographic, such as gender, with various points in between. The final term is an error term, which is used to take into account unobserved factors that may have an impact on the final outcome.

One of the factors above that may be affecting happiness levels more than we might expect is aspirations. You are very likely, whatever your age, to have been regaled by your parents that things were different in their day and that people these days have so much more. That is very true but what might also be the case is that different generations are starting to expect more. If your parents have managed to get to middle age and have a comfortable BMW to drive around in, you might start to expect such a vehicle to be the norm and would hope it might be your first car and so on.

Layard suggests that unhappiness results from society viewing how it is developing in terms of a zero sum game. What he means by this is that we might increasingly view the scramble to gain money and status in terms of a competitive game that has a winner and a loser. If I get a high ranking job with a large salary and lots of status, it means that you somehow lose out – either by not being able to get that same job or in some sort of psychological way. Such a perception of life being a zero sum game is a source of much unhappiness.

If we know something of the factors that can contribute to making someone 'happy' and also that our current measure is not the best at reflecting this, then it makes sense to look elsewhere for a measure of well-being. One such idea is to use something called the Measure of Domestic Progress (MDP). The MDP looks at many of the factors that we might associate with economic growth but takes into consideration the relative effects of economic growth and factors in other things that GDP calculations do not consider. For example, there is an attempt to place a value on the amount of unpaid domestic work that is carried out, which is taken as being a positive factor in contributing to well-being. It also assigns a negative effect to various social and environmental impacts of growth such as pollution, depletion of natural resources and costs of crime and family breakdown.

Other attempts to suggest more effective measures of improvements in well-being include such things as the Measure of Economic Welfare (MEW) developed by James Tobin and William Nordhaus, the Index of Sustainable Economic Welfare and the Genuine Progress Indicator.

It is proving difficult for any of these alternative measures to make a breakthrough and to be accepted in widespread use as a measure of well-being. The problems of attempting to measure subjective human behaviour and expose it to rigorous science are once again proving a challenge to economists. We might think that having some form of 'happiness index' would be a good thing, but if it does not really tell us what we want it to tell us, it is not very useful. There again, GDP figures do not seem to be telling us the whole story either!

[1]Layard, R. (2005) *Happiness: Lessons from a New Science.* London, Penguin.

CONCLUSION

This chapter has discussed how economists measure the total income of a nation. Measurement is, of course, only a starting point. Much of macroeconomics is aimed at revealing the long-run and short-run determinants of a nation's gross domestic product. Why, for example, is GDP higher in the United Kingdom and Japan than in India and Nigeria? What can the governments of the poorest countries do to promote more rapid growth in GDP? Why does GDP in European and North American countries rise rapidly in some years and fall in others? What can policy makers do to reduce the severity of these fluctuations in GDP? These are the questions we will take up shortly.

At this point, it is important to acknowledge the importance of just measuring GDP. We all get some sense of how the economy is doing as we go about our lives. But the economists who study changes in the economy and the policy makers who formulate economic policies need more than this vague sense – they need concrete data on which to base their judgements. Quantifying the behaviour of the economy with statistics such as GDP is, therefore, the first step to developing a science of macroeconomics.

SUMMARY

- Because every transaction has a buyer and a seller, the total expenditure in the economy must equal the total income in the economy.
- Gross domestic product (GDP) measures an economy's total expenditure on newly produced goods and services and the total income earned from the production of these goods and services. More precisely, GDP is the market value of all final goods and services produced within a country in a given period of time.
- GDP is divided among four components of expenditure: consumption, investment, government purchases and net exports. Consumption includes spending on goods and services by households, with the exception of purchases of new housing. Investment includes spending on new equipment and structures, including households' purchases of new housing. Government purchases include spending on goods and services by local, state and central governments. Net exports equal the value of goods and services produced domestically and sold abroad (exports) minus the value of goods and services produced abroad and sold domestically (imports).
- Nominal GDP uses current prices to value the economy's production of goods and services. Real GDP uses constant base-year prices to value the economy's production of goods and services. The GDP deflator – calculated from the ratio of nominal to real GDP – measures the level of prices in the economy.
- GDP is a good measure of economic well-being because people prefer higher to lower incomes. But it is not a perfect measure of well-being. For example, GDP excludes the value of leisure and the value of a clean environment.

KEY CONCEPTS

gross domestic product (GDP), p. 489
consumption, p. 492
investment, p. 492
government purchases, p. 493
transfer payment, p. 493
net exports, p. 493
nominal GDP, p. 496
real GDP, p. 496
GDP deflator, p. 497

QUESTIONS FOR REVIEW

1. Explain why an economy's income must equal its expenditure.
2. Which contributes more to GDP – the production of an economy car or the production of a luxury car? Why?
3. A farmer sells wheat to a baker for €2. The baker uses the wheat to make bread, which is sold for €3. What is the total contribution of these transactions to GDP?
4. Many years ago, Jamanda paid €500 to put together a record collection. Today she sold her albums at a car boot sale for €100. How does this sale affect current GDP?
5. List the four components of GDP. Give an example of each.
6. Why do economists use real GDP rather than nominal GDP to gauge economic well-being?
7. In the year 2010, the economy produces 100 loaves of bread that sell for €2 each. In the year 2011, the economy produces 200 loaves of bread that sell for €3 each. Calculate nominal GDP, real GDP and the GDP deflator for each year. (Use 2010 as the base year.) By what percentage does each of these three statistics rise from one year to the next?
8. Why is it desirable for a country to have a large GDP? Give an example of something that would raise GDP and yet be undesirable.

PROBLEMS AND APPLICATIONS

1. What components of GDP (if any) would each of the following transactions affect? Explain.
   a. A family buys a new refrigerator.
   b. Aunt Jane buys a new house.
   c. Aston Martin sells a DB7 from its inventory.
   d. You buy a pizza.
   e. The government builds a new motorway.
   f. You buy a bottle of Californian wine.
   g. Honda expands its factory in Derby, England.
2. The 'government purchases' component of GDP does not include spending on transfer payments such as social security. Thinking about the definition of GDP, explain why transfer payments are excluded.
3. Why do you think households' purchases of new housing are included in the investment component of GDP rather than the consumption component? Can you think of a reason why households' purchases of new cars should also be included in investment rather than in consumption? To what other consumption goods might this logic apply?
4. As the chapter states, GDP does not include the value of used goods that are resold. Why would including such transactions make GDP a less informative measure of economic well-being?
5. Below are some data from the land of milk and honey.

Year	Price of milk	Quantity of milk (quarts)	Price of honey	Quantity of honey (quarts)
2008	€1	100	€2	50
2009	1	200	2	100
2010	2	200	4	100

   a. Compute nominal GDP, real GDP and the GDP deflator for each year, using 2008 as the base year.
   b. Compute the percentage change in nominal GDP, real GDP and the GDP deflator in 2009 and 2010 from the preceding year. For each year, identify the variable that does not change. Explain in words why your answer makes sense.
   c. Did economic well-being rise more in 2009 or 2010? Explain.
6. If prices rise, people's income from selling goods increases. The growth of real GDP ignores this gain, however. Why, then, do economists prefer real GDP as a measure of economic well-being?
7. Find a newspaper article that reports on the most recent release of data on GDP for the UK or the country in which you are studying. You may be able to obtain this directly from a website of the relevant government department, such as the UK Office of National Statistics at www.statistics.gov.uk or through Eurostat at http://epp.eurostat.ec.europa.eu/portal/page/portal/eurostat/home/. Discuss the recent changes in real and nominal GDP and in the components of GDP.
8. One day Boris the Barber, plc, collects €400 for haircuts. Over this day, his equipment depreciates in value by €50. Of the remaining €350, Boris sends €30 to the government in sales taxes, takes home €220 in wages, and retains €100 in his business to add new equipment in the future. From the €220 that Boris takes home, he pays €70 in income taxes. Based on this information, compute Boris' contribution to the following measures of income.
   a. gross domestic product
   b. net national product
   c. national income
   d. personal income
   e. disposable personal income.
9. Goods and services that are not sold in markets, such as food produced and consumed at home, are generally not included in GDP. Can you think of how this might cause the numbers in the second column of Table 23.3 to be misleading in a comparison of the economic well-being of the United Kingdom and India? Explain.
10. Economists sometimes prefer to use GNP rather than GDP as a measure of economic well-being. Which measure should we prefer if we are analysing the total income of domestic residents? Which measure should we prefer if we are analysing the total amount of economic activity occurring in the economy?
11. The participation of women in many European and North American economies has risen dramatically over the past three decades.

a. How do you think this rise affected GDP?
b. Now imagine a measure of well-being that includes time spent working in the home and taking leisure. How would the change in this measure of well-being compare to the change in GDP?
c. Can you think of other aspects of well-being that are associated with the rise in women's labour-force participation? Would it be practical to construct a measure of well-being that includes these aspects?

For further resources, visit www.cengage.co.uk/mankiw_taylor2

24 MEASURING THE COST OF LIVING

The UK parliament is often referred to as the 'mother of parliaments', by which is meant that it is one of the oldest parliaments and one that has served as a model, to a greater or lesser extent, when parliaments have been established in other countries. The origins of the British parliament, as a meeting place where representatives of the various regions and boroughs throughout the country could influence national policy, can be traced as far back as the early 13th century. It is therefore perhaps strange that members of parliament were paid nothing at all for their trouble until 1911, when they first received a salary of £400 a year. This amount was decreased to £360 in 1931, but has generally increased over time, so that, for example, MPs received £600 in 1937, £6 270 in 1977 and £64 766 in 2009. The 2009 pay doesn't sound too bad (especially as this excludes various allowances to which the MP is also entitled at this time) – it is, after all, over two and a half times what the average bus driver in the UK earns (around £24 000) and double what the average secondary school teacher earns (£32 100). But the pay of £400 a year (about £8 a week) in 1911 seems pretty lousy, and it even went down by 10 per cent over the ensuing 20 years.

But, as everyone knows, the prices of goods and services have also changed over time and have for the most part increased. In 1900, a copy of *The Times* was priced at 1.2p, a pint of beer and milk could be bought for less than 1p and a dozen fresh eggs was 6.9p. In 1930, the average house price was £590; a loaf of bread was around 3p. At the turn of the 21st century, the average level of prices was 66 times the level of 1900. Because prices were so much lower in the early

1900s than they are today, it is not clear whether an MP in 1911 enjoyed a higher or lower standard of living than today's MPs.

In the preceding chapter we looked at how economists use gross domestic product (GDP) to measure the quantity of goods and services that the economy is producing. This chapter examines how economists measure the overall cost of living. To compare an MP's salary of £400 in 1911 to salaries from today, we need to find some way of turning money figures into meaningful measures of purchasing power. That is exactly the job of a statistic called the *consumer prices index.* After seeing how the consumer prices index is constructed, we discuss how we can use such a price index to compare money figures from different points in time.

The consumer prices index is used to monitor changes in the cost of living over time. When the consumer prices index rises, the typical family has to spend more money to maintain the same standard of living. Economists use the term *inflation* to describe a situation in which the economy's overall price level is rising. The *inflation rate* is the percentage change in the price level from the previous period. As we will see in the coming chapters, inflation is a closely watched aspect of macroeconomic performance and is a key variable guiding macroeconomic policy. This chapter provides the background for that analysis by showing how economists measure the inflation rate using the consumer prices index.

THE CONSUMER PRICES INDEX

The **consumer prices index (CPI)** is a measure of the overall prices of the goods and services bought by a typical consumer. This index was adopted as the measure of inflation in the UK to bring it into line with the way inflation is measured in the rest of Europe. Each month, a government bureau – in the UK the Office for National Statistics (ONS) and in Europe, Eurostat – computes and reports the consumer prices index. In this section we discuss how the consumer prices index is calculated and what problems arise in its measurement. We also consider how this index compares to the GDP deflator, another measure of the overall level of prices, which we examined in the preceding chapter.

consumer prices index (CPI)
a measure of the overall prices of the goods and services bought by a typical consumer

How the Consumer Prices Index Is Calculated

When the ONS or Eurostat calculates the consumer prices index and the inflation rate, it uses data on the prices of thousands of goods and services. To see exactly how these statistics are constructed, let's consider a simple economy in which consumers buy only two goods – hot dogs and hamburgers. Table 24.1 shows the five steps that the ONS and Eurostat follow. (We will use the ONS as the base for the example here but the principle applies to the way price changes are measured in Europe as a whole.)

1. *Fix the basket.* The first step in computing the consumer prices index is to determine which prices are most important to the typical consumer. If the typical consumer buys more hot dogs than hamburgers, then the price of hot dogs is more important than the price of hamburgers and, therefore, should be given greater weight in measuring the cost of living. The ONS sets these weights by surveying consumers and finding the basket of goods and services that the typical consumer buys. In the example in the table, the typical consumer buys a basket of 4 hot dogs and 2 hamburgers.
2. *Find the prices.* The second step in computing the consumer prices index is to find the prices of each of the goods and services in the basket for each point in time. The table shows the prices of hot dogs and hamburgers for three different years.

TABLE 24.1

Calculating the Consumer Prices Index and the Inflation Rate: An Example

This table shows how to calculate the consumer prices index and the inflation rate for a hypothetical economy in which consumers buy only hot dogs and hamburgers.

Step 1: Survey consumers to determine a fixed basket of goods

4 hot dogs, 2 hamburgers

Step 2: Find the price of each good in each year

Year	Price of hot dogs	Price of hamburgers
2009	€1	€2
2010	2	3
2011	3	4

Step 3: Compute the cost of the basket of goods in each year

2009	(€1 per hot dog × 4 hot dogs) + (€2 per hamburger × 2 hamburgers) = €8
2010	(€2 per hot dog × 4 hot dogs) + (€3 per hamburger × 2 hamburgers) = €14
2011	(€3 per hot dog × 4 hot dogs) + (€4 per hamburger × 2 hamburgers) = €20

Step 4: Choose one year as a base year (2009) and compute the consumer prices index in each year

2009	(€8/€8) × 100 = 100
2010	(€14/€8) × 100 = 175
2011	(€20/€8) × 100 = 250

Step 5: Use the consumer prices index to compute the inflation rate from previous year

2010	(175 – 100)/100 × 100 = 75%
2011	(250 – 175)/175 × 100 = 43%

3. *Compute the basket's cost.* The third step is to use the data on prices to calculate the cost of the basket of goods and services at different times. The table shows this calculation for each of the three years. Notice that only the prices in this calculation change. By keeping the basket of goods the same (4 hot dogs and 2 hamburgers), we are isolating the effects of price changes from the effect of any quantity changes that might be occurring at the same time.
4. *Choose a base year and compute the index.* The fourth step is to designate one year as the base year, which is the benchmark against which other years are compared. To calculate the index, the price of the basket of goods and services in each year is divided by the price of the basket in the base year, and this ratio is then multiplied by 100. The resulting number is the consumer prices index.

   In the example in the table, the year 2009 is the base year. In this year, the basket of hot dogs and hamburgers costs €8. Therefore, the price of the basket in all years is divided by €8 and multiplied by 100. The consumer prices index is 100 in 2009. (The index is always 100 in the base year.) The consumer prices index is 175 in 2010. This means that the price of the basket in 2010 is 175 per cent of its price in the base year. Put differently, a basket of goods that costs €100 in the base year costs €175 in 2010. Similarly, the consumer prices index is 250 in 2011, indicating that the price level in 2011 is 250 per cent of the price level in the base year.
5. *Compute the inflation rate.* The fifth and final step is to use the consumer prices index to calculate the **inflation rate**, which is the percentage change in the price index from the preceding period. That is, the inflation rate between two consecutive years is computed as follows:

inflation rate
the percentage change in the price index from the preceding period

$$\text{Inflation rate in year 2} = 100 \times (\text{CPI in year 2} - \text{CPI in year 1})/\text{CPI in year 1}$$

In our example, the inflation rate is 75 per cent in 2010 and 43 per cent in 2011.

Although this example simplifies the real world by including only two goods, it shows how the ONS computes the consumer prices index and the inflation rate. The ONS collects and processes data on the prices of thousands of goods and services every month and, by following the five foregoing steps, determines how quickly the cost of living for the typical consumer is rising. When the ONS makes its monthly announcement of the consumer prices index, you can usually hear the number on the evening television news or see it in the next day's newspaper.

In addition to the consumer prices index for the overall economy, the ONS also calculates price indices for the sub-categories of 'goods' and of 'services' separately, as well as the **producer price index**, which measures the change in prices of a basket of goods and services bought by firms rather than consumers. Because firms eventually pass on their costs to consumers in the form of higher consumer prices, changes in the producer price index are often thought to be useful in predicting changes in the consumer prices index.

producer price index
a measure of the change in prices of a basket of goods and services bought by firms

Problems in Measuring the Cost of Living

The goal of the consumer prices index is to measure changes in the cost of living. In other words, the consumer prices index tries to gauge how much incomes must rise in order to maintain a constant standard of living. The consumer prices index, however, is not a perfect measure of the cost of living. Three problems with the index are widely acknowledged but difficult to solve.

The first problem is called *substitution bias.* When prices change from one year to the next, they do not all change proportionately: some prices rise more than others and some prices fall. Consumers respond to these differing price changes by buying less of the goods whose prices have risen by large amounts and by buying more of the goods whose prices have risen less or perhaps even have fallen. That is, consumers substitute towards goods that have become relatively less expensive. If a price index is computed assuming a fixed basket of goods, it ignores the possibility of consumer substitution and, therefore, overstates the increase in the cost of living from one year to the next.

Let's consider a simple example. Imagine that in the base year apples are cheaper than pears, and so consumers buy more apples than pears. When the ONS constructs the basket of goods, it will include more apples than pears. Suppose that next year pears are cheaper than apples. Consumers will naturally respond to the price changes by buying more pears and fewer apples. Yet, when computing the consumer prices index, the ONS uses a fixed basket, which in essence assumes that consumers continue buying the now expensive apples in the same quantities as before. For this reason, the index will measure a much larger increase in the cost of living than consumers actually experience.

The second problem with the consumer prices index is the *introduction of new goods* as highlighted in the following FYI box. When a new good is introduced, consumers have more variety from which to choose. Greater variety, in turn, makes each pound more valuable, so consumers need fewer pounds to maintain any given standard of living. Yet because the consumer prices index is based on a fixed basket of goods and services, it does not reflect this change in the purchasing power of the pound.

Again, let's consider an example. When video players were introduced, consumers were able to watch their favourite films at home. Compared with going to the cinema, the convenience was greater and the cost was less. A perfect cost of

FYI

What Is in the CPI's Basket?

When constructing the consumer prices index, the UK ONS tries to include all the goods and services that the typical consumer buys. Moreover, it tries to weight these goods and services according to how much consumers buy of each item. Every month the ONS collects around 120000 prices of 650 goods and services that are supposed to be representative of the goods and services we use on a regular basis. As buying habits change, the basket of goods and services has to change also. On a regular basis the ONS announces a revision to the basket of goods and services that make up the basis of inflation figures in the UK.

Some goods and services that are not as representative anymore are removed from the basket. In recent years this has included microwave ovens which first made an appearance in the index in the 1980s. They are still popular, say the ONS, but their reliability and the falling prices means that the amount spent on them has reduced and as such they have been removed from the basket. Other items that have dropped out include film for 35mm cameras (the cameras themselves dropped out in 2007), top 40 CD singles and television repair as technology changes the way we live. The ONS says that people prefer to download music rather than buy singles and households tend to replace TVs rather than get them repaired.

The goods and services that have come into the basket are a reflection of the growing 'café culture' in the UK. Muffins have been brought into the basket to represent croissants and cakes that tend to be bought with coffee in cafés. The ONS has also reported that the UK tends to be more health conscious; fruit smoothies are now more popular so they enter the basket as do small fruits such as satsumas and clementines. Perhaps not so healthy are crates of 20 bottles of lager. However, they are now in the basket. The ONS says that the once popular 'stubbie' is now less so and people are tending to buy lager in different ways. Hot rotisserie cooked chickens, Blu-ray discs, bottled rosé wine and MP4 players have also made it into the basket but single cream, imported lamb loin chops and wine boxes have been removed.

Interestingly, whilst we may be downloading more music, the demand for 'classic' albums still exists. In 2008 the ONS noted that 'nostalgic consumption of non-chart "classic" albums by artists such as U2, Pink Floyd and Madonna' is such that it is worthy of a category of its own in the basket and so a new item to represent these was included.

Figure 24.1 shows the breakdown of consumer spending into the major categories of goods and services in 2009. The largest two categories are food and recreation and culture, which includes expenditure on cinema or opera tickets, tickets to football and rugby matches, subscriptions to a gym and so on. which, respectively, make up 22 per cent, and 17 per cent of the typical consumer's budget. Clothing and footwear and furniture and household goods make up 11 per cent each of the budget. The next category, at 8 per cent, is expenditure on restaurants and hotels, followed by transport (6 per cent). This includes spending on cars, petrol, buses and so on. This is followed by spending on housing and household services (5 per cent), alcohol and tobacco (4 per cent), health (3 per cent) and finally education and communication – postal and telephone charges, etc. – (1 per cent each).

Also included in the figure, at 11 per cent of spending, is a category for 'miscellaneous' goods and services. This is a catch-all for things consumers buy that do not naturally fit into the other categories – such as haircuts and funeral expenses.

living index would have reflected the introduction of the video player with a decrease in the cost of living. The consumer prices index, however, did not decrease in response to the introduction of the video player. Eventually, the ONS did revise the basket of goods to include video players, and subsequently the index reflected changes in their prices. But the reduction in the cost of living associated with the initial introduction of the video player never showed up in the index.

The third problem with the consumer prices index is *unmeasured quality change.* If the quality of a good deteriorates from one year to the next, the effective value

FIGURE 24.1

The Typical Basket of Goods and Services (2009)

This figure shows how the typical UK consumer is assumed to divide his spending among various categories of goods and services.

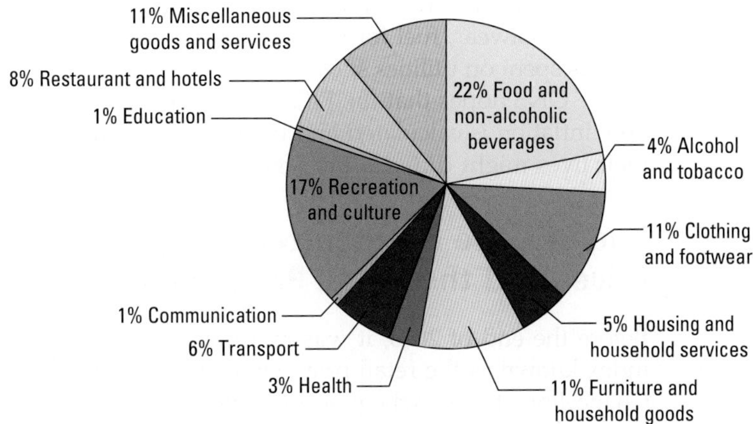

Source: UK Office for National Statistics.

of a pound falls, even if the price of the good stays the same. Similarly, if the quality rises from one year to the next, the effective value of a pound rises. The ONS does its best to account for quality change. When the quality of a good in the basket changes – for example, when a car model has more horsepower or gets better petrol mileage from one year to the next – the ONS adjusts the price of the good to account for the quality change. It is, in essence, trying to compute the price of a basket of goods of constant quality.

To take another example, in 2004 the ONS introduced digital cameras into the CPI for the first time. As well as the problems associated with introducing a new good into the index that we discussed earlier, digital cameras are also subject to very rapid technological progress – features such as zoom and the number of megapixels in the pictures taken keep on improving rapidly. Thus, while the average price of a digital camera might remain the same over a period, the average quality may have risen substantially. The ONS attempts to correct for this by a method known as hedonic quality adjustment. This involves working out the average characteristics (e.g. LCD screen size, number of megapixels, zoom features, etc.) of the average digital camera and adjusting the price when one of these average characteristics increases.

Despite these efforts, changes in quality remain a problem, because quality is so hard to measure.

A final problem with the index is that people may not see the reported CPI measure of inflation as relevant to their particular situation. This is because their spending patterns are individual and might not be typical of the representative pattern on which the official figures are based. For example, if an individual spent a high proportion of their income on fuel and their mortgage, the effect of price rises in gas, electricity, petrol and a rise in mortgage rates would have a disproportionate effect on their own experience of inflation. This different perception of inflation can have an effect on expectations, the importance of which we will see in later chapters.

Because of the different perceptions that people have about inflation and how it affects them, the ONS published a Personal Inflation Calculator (PIC) in 2007. The PIC allows users to be able to input their own details such as what their personal monthly expenditure is, how much they spend on food, meals out, alcohol, clothing and footwear, fuel for transport and so on. In addition, the calculator looks at what is spent on utilities such as water, council tax, vehicles, holidays and housing.

The ONS hopes that the PIC will help people to develop more of an interest in how inflation is calculated and be more aware of how the reality of price rises in their lives might differ to the officially published figures.

The CPI, the Harmonized Index of Consumer Prices and the Retail Prices Index

Before the end of 2003, it was more usual in the UK to measure prices using an index known as the retail prices index (RPI). In December 2003, however, the UK Chancellor of the Exchequer announced that all policy announcements concerning inflation and prices would relate to the CPI rather than the RPI, so that movements in the CPI became the main measure of inflation. What is the difference between the CPI and the RPI and why the switch?

The RPI is a price index constructed in the way described above, and differs from the CPI mainly in the goods and services included in the basket and in the coverage of households. In particular, the CPI excludes a number of items that are included in the RPI, mainly related to housing, such as council tax and house mortgage interest payments. These items are excluded because if council taxes rise or mortgage payments rise because interest rates have risen, then the inflation rate as measured by the RPI will rise even though underlying inflationary pressures in the economy may not have changed. Also, the CPI covers all private households, whereas the RPI excludes the top 4 per cent by income and pensioner households who derive at least three-quarters of their income from state benefits. The CPI also includes the residents of institutional households such as student hostels, and also foreign visitors to the UK. This means that it covers some items that are not in the RPI, such as stockbrokers' fees, university accommodation fees and foreign students' university tuition fees. The two indices also differ in some of the very fine details of the way in which prices are measured (such as allowance for quality adjustment).

What were the reasons for introducing the CPI? One reason is that some economists believe that it is closer to the concept of the overall price level employed in macroeconomic analysis – although others would argue that it may be misleading in the way in which it understates housing costs by excluding mortgage interest payments and council taxes. The main reason for its adoption, however, is that the construction of the CPI is identical to that used in the European Union (EU) to construct price indices for other EU member countries. Because these price indices are harmonized in their construction across countries, they are known in Europe as harmonized indices of consumer prices, or HICPs. This allows direct comparison of inflation rates across EU member states. Such comparisons are not possible using national consumer price indices due to differences in index coverage and construction. The CPI published by the UK Office for National Statistics is in fact the UK HICP.

The HICP has been and will continue to be developed by Eurostat in conjunction with the statistical offices of member states, such as the UK ONS. Its coverage and construction are set out in a series of legally binding EU regulations. The CPI is simply the name for the HICP in the UK.

TABLE 24.2

Inflation Rates Across the European Union (2005 = 100)

Country	HICP in 2010
Austria	108.32
Belgium	110.42
Bulgaria	134.54
Cyprus	109.71
Czech Republic	113.1
Denmark	109.9
Estonia	123.93
Finland	109.53
France	107.34
Germany	107.7
Greece	112.91
Hungary	127.54
Ireland	105.2
Italy	108.3
Latvia	136.12
Lithuania	127.31
Luxembourg	111.66
Malta	108.13
Netherlands	106.55
Poland	114.5
Portugal	106.89
Romania	131.91
Slovakia	111.64
Slovenia	113.61
Spain	110.52
Sweden	110.44
United Kingdom	112.4

Source: Eurostat.

In Table 24.2 we have listed the HICP in 2010 for each of the members of the European Union. Because we know that the price index has been constructed using the same conventions for each country, we can compare the figures directly. The base year is 2005; we can see, therefore, that price rises vary across the EU 27. For example, we can see that the eastern and central European countries that have recently joined the EU have experienced relatively high price rises since 2005 compared with the original members such as France, Italy and Germany. Prices rose in Latvia, Bulgaria and Romania by over 30 per cent since 2005, for example, while Hungary, Estonia and Lithuania, had all experienced price rises greater than 20 per cent over that period. On the other hand, Malta, with price rises of just over 8 per cent since 2005, did as well as Italy and slightly better than Luxembourg, who experienced price rises of 11.6 per cent.

The GDP Deflator versus the Consumer Prices Index

In the preceding chapter, we examined another measure of the overall level of prices in the economy – the GDP deflator. The GDP deflator is the ratio of nominal GDP to real GDP. Because nominal GDP is current output valued at current prices and real GDP is current output valued at base-year prices, the GDP deflator reflects the current level of prices relative to the level of prices in the base year.

Economists and policy makers monitor both the GDP deflator and the consumer prices index to gauge how quickly prices are rising. Usually, these two statistics tell a similar story. Yet there are two important differences that can cause them to diverge.

The first difference is that the GDP deflator reflects the prices of all goods and services *produced domestically,* whereas the consumer prices index reflects the prices of all goods and services *bought by consumers.* For example, suppose that the price of an aeroplane produced by Dassault, a French aerospace firm and sold to the French Air Force rises. Even though the aeroplane is part of GDP in France, it is not part of the basket of goods and services bought by a typical consumer. Thus, the price increase shows up in the GDP deflator for France but not in the consumer prices index.

As another example, suppose that Volvo raises the price of its cars. Because Volvos are made in Sweden, the car is not part of French GDP. But French consumers buy Volvos, and so the car is part of the typical consumer's basket of goods. Hence, a price increase in an imported consumption good, such as a Volvo, shows up in the consumer prices index but not in the GDP deflator.

This first difference between the consumer prices index and the GDP deflator is particularly important when the price of oil changes. Although the United Kingdom does produce some oil, as with all of Europe and also North America, much of the oil used in the UK is imported from the Middle East. As a result, oil and oil products such as petrol and heating oil comprise a much larger share of consumer spending than they do of GDP. When the price of oil rises, the consumer prices index rises by much more than does the GDP deflator.

"When you take out food, energy, taxes, insurance, housing, transportation, healthcare, and entertainment, inflation remained at a 20-year low."

The second and subtler difference between the GDP deflator and the consumer prices index concerns how various prices are weighted to yield a single number for the overall level of prices. The consumer prices index compares the price of a *fixed* basket of goods and services with the price of the basket in the base year. Whilst, as we have seen, the ONS revise the basket of goods on a regular basis, in contrast, the GDP deflator compares the price of *currently produced* goods and services with the price of the same goods and services in the base year. Thus, the group of goods and services used to compute the GDP deflator changes automatically over time. This difference is not important when all prices are changing proportionately. But if the prices of different goods and services are changing by varying amounts, the way we weight the various prices matters for the overall inflation rate.

Figure 24.2 shows the UK inflation rate as measured by both the GDP deflator and the consumer prices index for each year from 1989 until 2009. You can see that sometimes the two measures diverge. In particular, the rates of inflation calculated using the two measures are quite different since 1996, with the GDP deflator recording higher rates of annual increase. They do, however, tend to move together and both record relatively low inflation rates. Figure 24.3 shows the GDP deflator for the EU 27 from 2007 to 2010 as a means of comparison.

Quick Quiz Explain briefly what the consumer prices index is trying to measure and how it is constructed.

FIGURE 24.2

Two Measures of Inflation

This figure shows the UK inflation rate – the percentage change in the level of prices – as measured by the GDP deflator and the consumer prices index using annual data since 1989. Notice that the two measures of inflation generally move together.

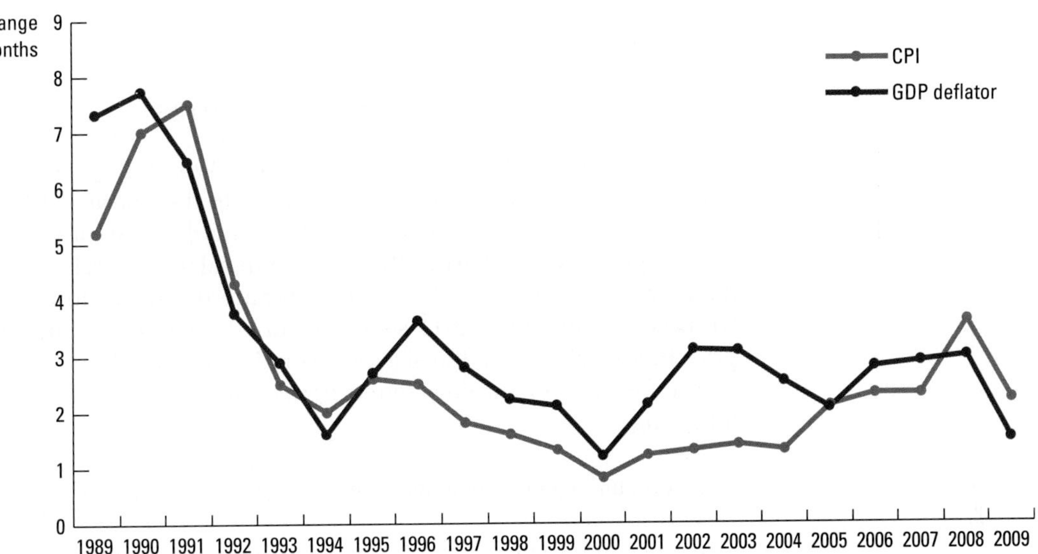

Source: UK Office for National Statistics.

FIGURE 24.3

GDP Deflator (EU 27)

This figure shows the GDP Deflator for the EU 27 countries between 2007 and 2010.

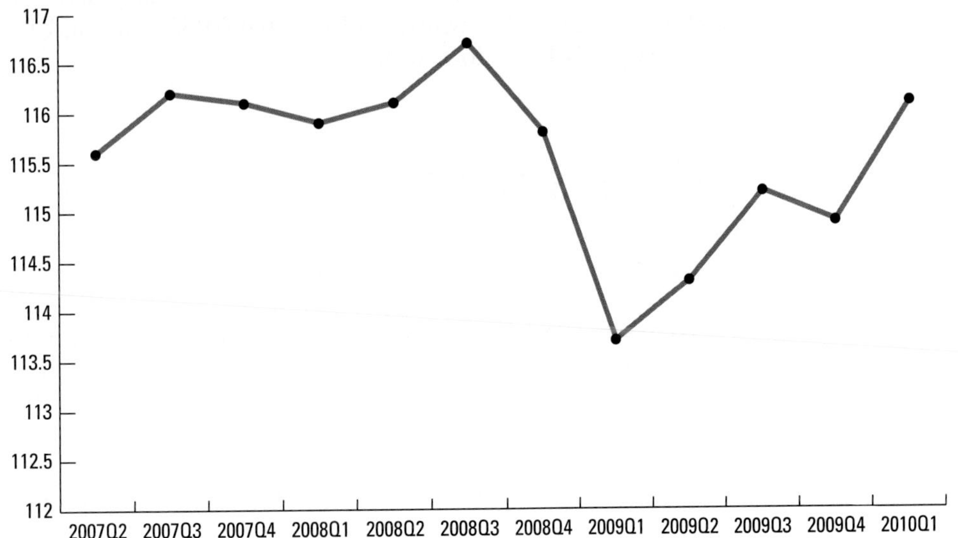

Source: Eurostat.

CORRECTING ECONOMIC VARIABLES FOR THE EFFECTS OF INFLATION

The purpose of measuring the overall level of prices in the economy is to permit comparisons of monetary figures from different points in time. Now that we know how price indices are calculated, let's see how we might use such an index to compare a certain figure from the past to a figure in the present.

Money Figures from Different Times

We first return to the issue of MPs' salary. Was the salary of £400 a year first paid to MPs in 1911 high or low compared to the salaries of today's MPs?

To answer this question, we need to know the level of prices in 1911 and the level of prices today. Part of the increase in salaries merely compensates MPs for the higher level of prices today. To compare the salary to those of today's MPs, we need to inflate the 1911 salary to turn 1911 pounds into today's pounds. A price index determines the size of this inflation correction.

The formula for turning pound figures from *year T* into today's pounds is the following:

$$\text{Amount in today's pounds} = \text{amount in year } T \text{ pounds} \times \frac{\text{Price level today}}{\text{Price level in year } T}$$

A price index such as the CPI measures the price level and determines the size of the inflation correction. Let's apply this formula to MP's wages. Statistics from the ONS[1] show a price index of 9.6 for 1911 and 843.0 for 2009. Thus the overall level of prices has risen by a factor of 87.81 (which equals 843.0/9.6). We can use these numbers to measure MP's salary in 2009 pounds, as follows:

$$\begin{aligned}\text{Salary in 2009 pounds} &= \text{Salary in 1911 pounds} \times \frac{\text{Price level in 2009}}{\text{Price level in 1911}}\\ &= £400 \times \frac{843.0}{9.6}\\ &= £35\,124\end{aligned}$$

We find that the salary paid to an MP in 1911 is equivalent to a salary today of £35 124. This is more than the median annual salary across all occupations in 2009 of £25 428 and is nearly half of what MPs were paid in 2009: £64 766. In that sense, MPs have done well.

CASE STUDY

Adjusting for Inflation: Use the Force

What was the most popular film of all time? The answer might surprise you. Film popularity is usually gauged by worldwide box office receipts. By that measure, as of the end of 2009, *Avatar* (released in 2009) was the number one film of all time, followed by *Titanic* (1993), *Lord of the Rings: Return of the King* (2003), *Pirates of the Caribbean: Dead Man's Chest* (2006) and *The Dark Knight* (2008). But this ranking ignores an obvious but important fact: prices,

[1] http://www.statistics.gov.uk/statbase/TSDdownload2.asp

including those of cinema tickets, have been rising over time. When we correct box office receipts for the effects of inflation, the story is very different.

Table 24.3 shows the top ten films of all time ranked by inflation-adjusted worldwide box office receipts. The original *Star Wars*, released in 1977, moves up to number two, while *The Sound of Music* takes the number three spot and the number one film of all time is *Gone with the Wind*, which was released in 1939 and is well ahead of *Avatar*, which drops down to number nine. In the 1930s, before everyone had televisions in their homes, cinema attendance was about three or four times what it is today. But the films from that era rarely show up in popularity rankings because ticket prices were only a fraction of what they are today. Scarlett and Rhett fare a lot better once we correct for the effects of inflation, as do Mowgli, Balou and King Louie of *The Jungle Book* fame (number ten in the inflation-adjusted list). However, television ownership (indeed multiple television ownership) was widespread by 1977 when *Star Wars* was released, and so the ranking of this film as number two in the inflation-adjusted table perhaps makes Luke Skywalker an even more impressive figure.

Star Wars: the second most popular film in the galaxy.

TABLE 24.3

The Most Popular Films of All Time, Inflation-adjusted

Film	Year of release
1. Gone with the Wind	1939
2. Star Wars	1977
3. The Sound of Music	1965
4. E.T.	1982
5. The Ten Commandments	1956
6. Titanic	1997
7. Jaws	1975
8. Doctor Zhivago	1965
9. Avatar	2009
10. The Jungle Book	1967

Source: *The Movie Times* (http://www.the-movie-times.com/thrsdir/alltime.mv?adjusted+ByAG).

Indexation

As we have just seen, price indices are used to correct for the effects of inflation when comparing monetary figures from different times. This type of correction shows up in many places in the economy. When some money amount is automatically corrected for inflation by law or contract, the amount is said to be **indexed** for inflation.

indexation
the automatic correction of a money amount for the effects of inflation by law or contract

For example, many long-term contracts between firms and unions include partial or complete indexation of the wage to the consumer prices index. Such a provision is called a *cost-of-living allowance,* or COLA. A COLA automatically raises the wage each year based on the consumer prices index or other measure such as the RPI, at a particular point in time.

Income tax brackets – the income levels at which the tax rates change – are also often moved annually in line with inflation, although, in most countries, they are not formally indexed. Indeed, there are many ways in which the tax system is not indexed for inflation, even when perhaps it should be. We discuss these issues more fully when we discuss the costs of inflation later in this book.

Real and Nominal Interest Rates

Correcting economic variables for the effects of inflation is particularly important, and somewhat tricky, when we look at data on interest rates. When you deposit your savings in a bank account, you will earn interest on your deposit. Conversely, when you borrow from a bank in order to buy a car, you will pay interest on the loan. Interest represents a payment in the future for a transfer of money in the past. As a result, interest rates always involve comparing amounts of money at different points in time. To fully understand interest rates, we need to know how to correct for the effects of inflation.

Let's consider an example. Suppose that Carla deposits €1 000 in a bank account that pays an annual interest rate of 10 per cent. After a year passes, Carla has accumulated €100 in interest. Carla then withdraws her €1 100. Is Carla €100 richer than she was when she made the deposit a year earlier?

The answer depends on what we mean by 'richer'. Carla does have €100 more than she had before. In other words, the number of euros has risen by 10 per cent. But if prices have risen at the same time, each euro now buys less than it did a year ago. Thus, her purchasing power has not risen by 10 per cent. If the inflation rate was 4 per cent, then the amount of goods she can buy has increased by only 6 per cent. And if the inflation rate was 15 per cent, then the price of goods has increased proportionately more than the number of euros in her account. In that case, Carla's purchasing power has actually fallen by 5 per cent.

nominal interest rate
the interest rate as usually reported without a correction for the effects of inflation

real interest rate
the interest rate corrected for the effects of inflation

The interest rate that the bank pays is called the **nominal interest rate**, and the interest rate corrected for inflation is called the **real interest rate**. We can write the relationship among the nominal interest rate, the real interest rate and inflation as follows:

$$\text{Real interest rate} = \text{Nominal interest rate} - \text{Inflation rate}$$

The real interest rate is the difference between the nominal interest rate and the rate of inflation. The nominal interest rate tells you how fast the number of pounds or euros in your bank account rises over time. The real interest rate tells you how fast the purchasing power of your bank account rises over time.

Figure 24.4 shows UK real and nominal interest rates since 1975. The nominal interest rate is the interest rate on three-month Treasury bills. The real interest rate is computed by subtracting the annual inflation rate from this nominal interest rate. In this instance we have used the retail prices index as a measure of inflation.

You can see that real and nominal interest rates do not always move together. For example, in the late 1970s, nominal interest rates were high. But because inflation was very high, real interest rates were low. Indeed, in some years, real interest rates were negative, for inflation eroded people's savings more quickly than nominal interest payments increased them. By contrast, in the 1990s, nominal interest rates were low. But because inflation was also low, real interest rates were relatively high. In the coming chapters, when we study the causes and effects of changes in interest rates, it will be important for us to keep in mind the distinction between real and nominal interest rates.

Quick Quiz British Members of Parliament received an annual salary of £360 in 1931, £600 in 1937, £6 270 in 1977 and £57 485 in 2004. With a base year (i.e. CPI of 100) in 1911, the CPI was 151 in 1931, 164 in 1937, 1 335 in 1977 and 5 040 in 2004. How much was MPs' salary worth in each of these years in 2004 pounds?

FIGURE 24.4

Real and Nominal Interest Rates

This figure shows UK nominal and real interest rates using monthly data since 1975. The nominal interest rate is the rate on a three-month Treasury bill. The real interest rate is the nominal interest rate minus the annual inflation rate as measured by the retail price index. Notice that nominal and real interest rates do not always move together.

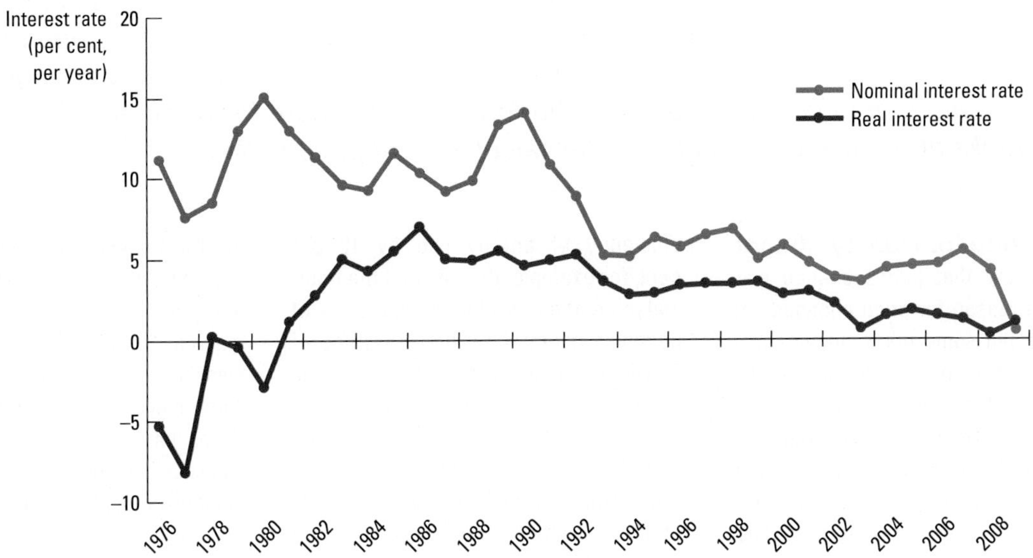

Source: Bank of England and UK Office for National Statistics.

CONCLUSION

Throughout recent history, the real values behind the currencies of most major industrialized countries, such as the pound, euro and dollar, have not been stable. Persistent increases in the overall level of prices in advanced economies such as those of the UK, the other countries of Europe and of the USA have been the norm. Such inflation reduces the purchasing power of each unit of money over time. When comparing figures in monetary or nominal terms from different times, it is important to keep in mind that a pound today is not the same as a pound 20 years ago or, most likely, 20 years from now.

This chapter has discussed how economists measure the overall level of prices in the economy and how they use price indices to correct economic variables for the effects of inflation. This analysis is only a starting point. We have not yet examined the causes and effects of inflation or how inflation interacts with other economic variables. To do that, we need to go beyond issues of measurement. Indeed, that is our next task. Having explained how economists measure macroeconomic quantities and prices in the past two chapters, we are now ready to develop the models that explain long-run and short-run movements in these variables.

IN THE NEWS

Economists and statisticians are always looking to find ways of improving data, which is so crucial to decision-making and policy. Accurate and reliable inflation data is one of the areas that has been subject to considerable review. In particular the issue of how changes in quality affect measures of inflation has been at the forefront of debate for number of years. This article looks at the use of hedonics in the calculation of price indices.

Accounting for Quality Change

We all know that prices change over time. The reason for price changes can be varied but some price changes may reflect improvements in the quality of a product as technology advances ever more rapidly. Does this mean that a TV bought in 2010 for €500 represents better value for money (and therefore a lower price) than one priced at €450 in 2005? Taking into account this issue is the subject of hedonics. Hedonics is a statistical device to account for the changing quality of products when calculating price movements. It has stirred some debate on both sides of the Atlantic. In the United States for example, the *Wall Street Journal* reported on the case of 27 inch TV sets. Tim LaFleur, a commodity specialist for televisions working with the US Bureau of Labor Statistics, the body which compiles CPI data, estimated that the price of a TV set with a nominal price of $329.99 had improved in terms of the quality of the screen, amongst other things, which increased its value by $135. When running the data through a computer programme, LaFleur concluded that the price of the TV had actually fallen by 29 per cent.

There are other aspects to the issue as well. The increasing concern with the effects of humans on the planet means that there is a drive to improve energy efficiency. Developments in technology are also helping to improve health and safety, the improvements in safety records of cars being one example of this. If manufacturers produce a washing machine that improves the efficiency of energy use by 10 per cent, for example, then even if the nominal price of the product rose, the use of hedonics might show that the price of washing machines did not rise at all. Equally if a car is now safer to use and protects the driver and passengers then the value of this is far greater than any increase in price to cover the cost of fitting such features. The adjusted price of the car, therefore, falls.

The ONS has been using hedonics as part of its calculation of price indices since 2004. One news report at the time suggested that the use of hedonics could save the Chancellor around £100 million a year as a result of having to pay less to savers and pensioners. Initially the technique was applied to the RPI relating to digital cameras and computers. It led to a cut in the RPI by around 0.05 per cent, according to the ONS, but this equates to a saving for the government of £50 million in payments to those on index linked benefits, £45 million on interest payments for index linked gilts and further savings on tax allowances which may not be uprated. Whilst the initial introduction of hedonics at the ONS caused a relatively small change in the RPI, there have been suggestions that a wider application of the technique across more goods could reduce the annual rate of inflation by between 0.25 and 0.5 per cent.

There have been concerns expressed, therefore, that the use of this technique presents a distorted picture of how price changes affect the economy. A report published in the US in 1996 suggested that underestimation of the improvements in quality might mean that price indices were overstated by as much as 0.6 per cent per year. There are some concerns, however, that the technique could be exploited for political purposes; whilst hedonics has a firm root in statistical methodology there is some judgement applied about the nature of the quality improvements and there are concerns that these might be used to artificially lower published inflation rates. Given that inflation figures are used to index link certain payments from government and as the basis for wage claims, any depression in the index might be viewed with some suspicion.

Proponents of the use of hedonics argue that far from distorting the picture, the use of the technique gives a far more accurate picture of what is going on in the economy. They point out that bodies such as the Royal Statistical Society make observations on the way the ONS gathers and interprets data and that it is an important way of measuring quality changes in relation to prices. Technology is improving so rapidly that a failure to do so would over inflate prices. They point to the way in which products like digital cameras, mobile phones, TVs and computers have changed in recent years. In many cases, improvements in technology also lead to a reduction in price which will affect price indices. The question is should these price indices be even lower? Take modern laptops which at the time of writing have the computing power to run advanced, high graphics games, have massive memory, roaming internet access, extensive music and video files and are priced at around £700 in comparison to bulky, low graphics, slow machines that basically ran word processing and other office applications but which were priced over £1 000 five years ago? Surely the improvements in speed, quality, capacity and flexibility are worth more to consumers than the reduction in price of £300?

Ultimately the debate comes down to the accuracy of the judgements made by statisticians in being able to accurately account for the improvements in quality of products. If these judgements are accurate and widely accepted then incorporating hedonics into the index could improve its accuracy. If, however, such judgements are subject to political interference then some sections of society could be made worse off.

SUMMARY

- The consumer prices index shows the changes in the prices of a basket of goods and services relative to the prices of the same basket in the base year. The index is used to measure the overall level of prices in the economy. The percentage change in the consumer prices index measures the inflation rate.
- The consumer prices index is an imperfect measure of the cost of living for three reasons. First, it does not take into account consumers' ability to substitute towards goods that become relatively cheaper over time. Secondly, it does not take into account increases in the purchasing power of money due to the introduction of new goods. Thirdly, it is distorted by unmeasured changes in the quality of goods and services. Because of these measurement problems, the CPI overstates true inflation.
- Although the GDP deflator also measures the overall level of prices in the economy, it differs from the consumer prices index because it includes goods and services produced rather than goods and services consumed. As a result, imported goods affect the consumer prices index but not the GDP deflator. In addition, while the consumer prices index uses a fixed basket of goods, the GDP deflator automatically changes the group of goods and services over time as the composition of GDP changes.
- Money figures (e.g. in euros) from different points in time do not represent a valid comparison of purchasing power. To compare a money figure from the past to a money figure today, the older figure should be inflated using a price index.
- Various laws and private contracts use price indices to correct for the effects of inflation.
- A correction for inflation is especially important when looking at data on interest rates. The nominal interest rate is the interest rate usually reported; it is the rate at which the amount of money in a savings account increases over time. In contrast, the real interest rate takes into account changes in the value of the money over time. The real interest rate equals the nominal interest rate minus the rate of inflation.

KEY CONCEPTS

consumer prices index (CPI), p. 507
inflation rate, p. 508
producer price index, p. 509
indexation, p. 517
nominal interest rate, p. 518
real interest rate, p. 518

QUESTIONS FOR REVIEW

1. Which do you think has a greater effect on the consumer prices index: a 10 per cent increase in the price of chicken or a 10 per cent increase in the price of caviar? Why?
2. Describe the three problems that make the consumer prices index an imperfect measure of the cost of living.

3. If the price of a French Navy submarine rises, is the French consumer prices index or the French GDP deflator affected more? Why?
4. Over a long period of time, the price of a chocolate bar rose from €0.10 to €0.60. Over the same period, the consumer prices index rose from 150 to 300. Adjusted for overall inflation, how much did the price of the chocolate bar change?
5. Explain the meaning of *nominal interest rate* and *real interest rate.* How are they related?

PROBLEMS AND APPLICATIONS

1. Suppose that people consume only three goods, as shown in this table:

	Tennis balls	Tennis racquets	Cola
2009 price	€2	€40	€1
2009 quantity	100	10	200
2010 price	€2	€60	€2
2010 quantity	100	10	200

   a. What is the percentage change in the price of each of the three goods? What is the percentage change in the overall price level?
   b. Do tennis racquets become more or less expensive relative to cola? Does the well-being of some people change relative to the well-being of others? Explain.
2. Suppose that the residents of Vegopia spend all of their income on cauliflower, broccoli and carrots. In 2009 they buy 100 heads of cauliflower for €200, 50 bunches of broccoli for €75 and 500 carrots for €50. In 2010 they buy 75 heads of cauliflower for €225, 80 bunches of broccoli for €120 and 500 carrots for €100. If the base year is 2009, what is the CPI in both years? What is the inflation rate in 2010?
3. Go to the website of the UK Office for National Statistics (http://www.statistics.gov.uk) and find data on the consumer prices index. By how much has the index including all items risen over the past year? For which categories of spending have prices risen the most? The least? Have any categories experienced price declines? Can you explain any of these facts?
4. Which of the problems in the construction of the CPI might be illustrated by each of the following situations? Explain.
   a. the invention of MP3 players
   b. the introduction of air bags in cars
   c. increased personal computer purchases in response to a decline in their price
   d. increased use of digital cameras
   e. greater use of fuel-efficient cars after petrol prices increase.
5. Suppose the government were to determine the level of the state retirement pension in the UK so that it increased each year in proportion to the increase in the CPI (even though most economists believe that the CPI overstates actual inflation).
   a. If the elderly consume the same market basket as other people, would such a policy provide the elderly with an improvement in their standard of living each year? Explain.
   b. In fact, the elderly consume more health care than younger people, and health care costs tend to rise faster than overall inflation. What would you do to determine whether the elderly are actually better off from year to year?
6. How do you think the basket of goods and services you buy differs from the basket bought by the typical household? Do you think you face a higher or lower inflation rate than is indicated by the CPI? Why?
7. In some years in some countries, income tax brackets are not increased in line with inflation. Why do you think the government might do this? (Hint: this phenomenon is known as 'bracket creep'.)
8. When deciding how much of their income to save for retirement, should workers consider the real or the nominal interest rate that their savings will earn? Explain.
9. Suppose that a borrower and a lender agree on the nominal interest rate to be paid on a loan. Then inflation turns out to be higher than they both expected.
   a. Is the real interest rate on this loan higher or lower than expected?
   b. Does the lender gain or lose from this unexpectedly high inflation? Does the borrower gain or lose?

For further resources, visit www.cengage.co.uk/mankiw_taylor2

9

THE REAL ECONOMY IN THE LONG RUN

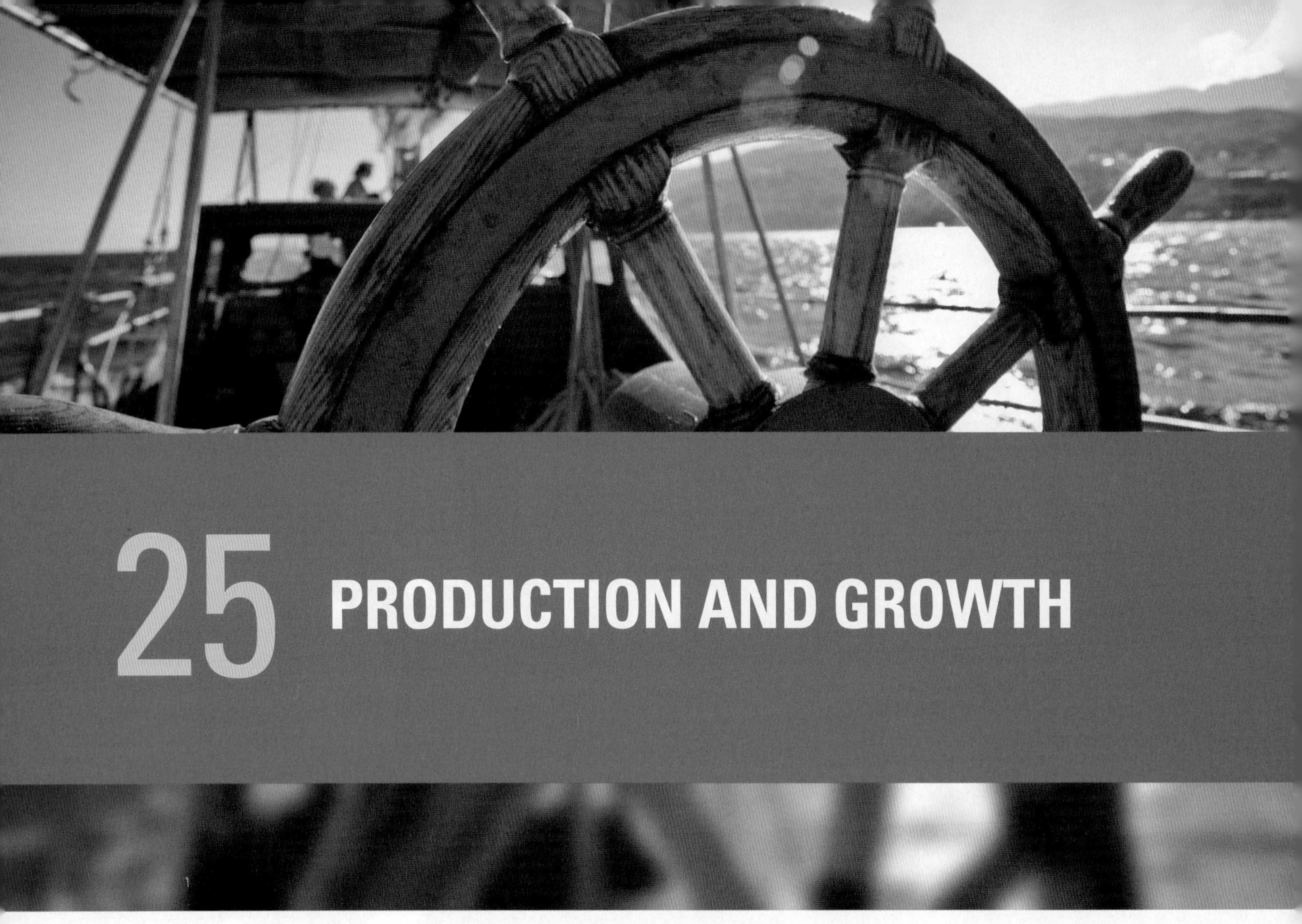

25 PRODUCTION AND GROWTH

When you travel around the world, you see tremendous variation in the standard of living. The average person in a rich country, such as the countries of Western Europe, has an income more than ten times as high as the average person in a poor country, such as India, Indonesia or Nigeria. These large differences in income are reflected in large differences in the quality of life. Richer countries have more cars, more telephones, more televisions, better nutrition, safer housing, better health care and longer life expectancy.

Even within a country, there are large changes in the standard of living over time. In the United Kingdom over the past century or so, average income as measured by real GDP per person has grown by about 1.3 per cent per year. Although 1.3 per cent might seem small, this rate of growth implies that average income doubles about every 50 years. Because of this growth, average UK income today is about four times as high as average income a century ago. As a result, the typical Brit enjoys much greater economic prosperity than did his or her parents, grandparents and great-grandparents. The story is similar for many other European countries. Figure 25.1 shows GDP per person in the EU 27 since 2000. The trend has been upwards until the recession struck but despite this the average person in the EU 27 is still better off in 2010 than they were in 2000.

Growth rates vary substantially from country to country. In some East Asian countries, such as Singapore, South Korea and Taiwan, average income has risen about 7 per cent per year in recent decades. At this rate, average income doubles about every ten years. These countries have, in the length of one generation, gone from being among the poorest in the world to being among the richest.

FIGURE 25.1

EU 27 GDP at Market Prices Purchasing Power Standard Per Capita, 2000–2010

The figure shows GDP per person for the 27 EU countries over the period 2000–2010. Average incomes rose up to 2009 after which the recession led to a fall in GDP per capita.

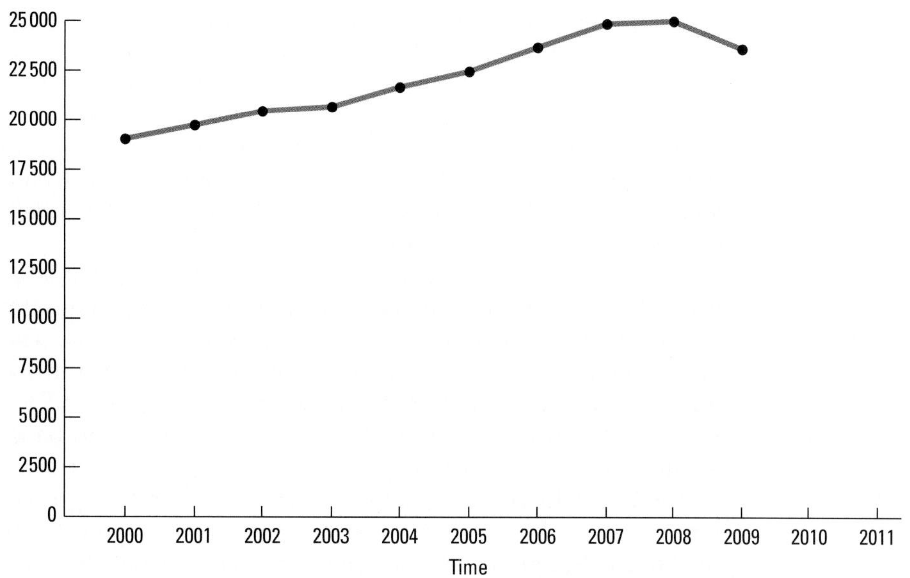

Source: Eurostat: http://epp.eurostat.ec.europa.eu/tgm/graph.do?tab=graph&plugin=0&pcode=tec00001&language=en&toolbox=data

In contrast, in some African countries, such as Chad, Ethiopia and Nigeria, average income has been stagnant for many years.

What explains these diverse experiences? How can the rich countries be sure to maintain their high standard of living? What policies should the poor countries pursue to promote more rapid growth in order to join the developed world? These are among the most important questions in macroeconomics. As the Nobel Prize winning economist Robert Lucas once put it, 'The consequences for human welfare in questions like these are simply staggering: once one starts to think about them, it is hard to think about anything else.'

In the previous two chapters we discussed how economists measure macroeconomic quantities and prices. In this chapter we start studying the forces that determine these variables. As we have seen, an economy's gross domestic product (GDP) measures both the total income earned in the economy and the total expenditure on the economy's output of goods and services. The level of real GDP is a good gauge of economic prosperity, and the growth of real GDP is a good gauge of economic progress. Here we focus on the long-run determinants of the level and growth of real GDP. Later in this book we study the short-run fluctuations of real GDP around its long-run trend.

We proceed here in three steps. Firstly, we examine international data on real GDP per person. These data will give you some sense of how much the level and growth of living standards vary around the world. Secondly, we examine the role of *productivity* – the amount of goods and services produced for each hour of a worker's time. In particular, we see that a nation's standard of living is determined by the productivity of its workers, and we consider the factors that determine a nation's productivity. Thirdly, we consider the link between productivity and the economic policies that a nation pursues.

ECONOMIC GROWTH AROUND THE WORLD

As a starting point for our study of long-run growth, let's look at the experiences of some of the world's economies. Table 25.1 shows data on real GDP per person for 13 countries. For each country, the data cover more than a century of history. The first and second columns of the table present the countries and time periods. (The time periods differ somewhat from country to country because of differences in data availability.) The third and fourth columns show estimates of real GDP per person about a century ago and for a recent year. Because we need to make international comparisons, we need to express the data on income for the various countries in a common currency. Often, economists use the US dollar for this purpose, and in Table 25.1 we have followed suit by expressing all of the income data in dollar terms. We have also adjusted for inflation by reflating the early figures so that they are measured in 2006 dollars.

The data on real GDP per person show that living standards vary widely from country to country. Income per person in the United States, for instance, is about 6 times that in China and about 12 times that in India. The poorest countries have average levels of income that have not been seen in the developed world for many decades. The typical citizen of India in 2006 had less real income than the typical British resident in 1870. The typical person in Bangladesh in 2006 had about two-thirds the real income of a typical American a century ago.

The last column of the table shows each country's growth rate. The growth rate measures how rapidly real GDP per person grew in the typical year. In the United Kingdom, for example, real GDP per person was $4 502 in 1870 and $35580 in 2006. The growth rate was 1.53 per cent per year. This means that if real GDP per person, beginning at $4 502, were to increase by 1.53 per cent for each of 136 years, it would end up at $35 580. Of course, real GDP per person did not actually rise exactly 1.53 per cent every year: some years it rose by more and other years by less. The growth rate of 1.53 per cent per year ignores short-run fluctuations around the long-run trend and represents an average rate of growth for real GDP per person in the United Kingdom over many years.

TABLE 25.1

The Variety of Growth Experiences

Country	Period	Real GDP per person at beginning of period[a]	Real GDP per person at end of period[a]	Growth rate (per year)
Japan	1890–2006	$1 408	$33 150	2.76%
Brazil	1900–2006	729	8 880	2.39
China	1900–2006	670	7 740	2.34
Mexico	1900–2006	1 085	8 810	2.23
Germany	1870–2006	2 045	31 380	2.04
Canada	1870–2006	2 224	34 610	2.04
Argentina	1900–2006	2 147	15 390	1.88
United States	1870–2006	3 752	44 260	1.83
India	1900–2006	632	3 800	1.71
United Kingdom	1870–2006	4 502	35 580	1.53
Indonesia	1900–2006	834	3 950	1.48
Bangladesh	1900–2006	583	2 340	1.32
Pakistan	1900–2006	690	2 500	1.22

[a]Real GDP is measured in 2006 US dollars.
Source: Robert J. Barro and Xavier Sala-i-Martin, *Economic Growth* (New York: McGraw-Hill, 1995), tables 10.2 and 10.3; *World Development Report 2008*, table 1; and authors' calculations.

The countries in Table 25.1 are ordered by their growth rate from the most to the least rapid. Japan tops the list, with a growth rate of 2.76 per cent per year. A hundred years ago, Japan was not a rich country. Japan's average income was only a little higher than Mexico's, and it was well behind Argentina's. To put the issue another way, Japan's income in 1890 was less than in India today. But because of its spectacular growth, Japan is now an economic superpower, with average income more than twice that of Mexico and Argentina and similar to Germany, Canada and the United Kingdom. At the bottom of the list of countries are Bangladesh and Pakistan, which have experienced growth less than 1.4 per cent per year over the past century. As a result, the typical resident of these countries continues to live in abject poverty.

Because of differences in growth rates, the ranking of countries by income changes substantially over time. As we have seen, Japan is a country that has risen relative to others. One country that has fallen behind is the United Kingdom. In 1870, the United Kingdom was the richest country in the world, with average income about 20 per cent higher than that of the United States and more than twice that of Canada. Today, average income in the United Kingdom is 20 per cent below that of the United States and similar to Canada's.

These data show that the world's richest countries have no guarantee that they will stay the richest and that the world's poorest countries are not doomed forever to remain in poverty. But what explains these changes over time? Why do

FYI

Are You Richer Than the Richest Person in the World?

American Heritage magazine once published a list of the richest Americans of all time. The number one spot went to John D. Rockefeller – the oil entrepreneur who lived from 1839 to 1937 and founded Standard Oil, which survives today as Esso (a homonym for the initials of Standard Oil) and Exxon. According to the magazine's calculations, his wealth would today be the equivalent of $200 billion, more than three and a half times that of Carlos Slim Helu, a Telecoms entrepreneur from Mexico who, at the time of writing, was the richest man on the planet with a fortune estimated at $54.5 billion. Helu is the first non-American for 16 years to have this status. Bill Gates ($54 billion) and Warren Buffet ($47.8 billion) are in second and third place respectively. All these three people are very rich by any standards but, in real terms, Rockefeller was richer.

Despite his great wealth, however, Rockefeller did not enjoy many of the conveniences that now we take for granted. He couldn't watch television, play video games, surf the internet or send an e-mail. During the heat of summer, he couldn't cool his home with air-conditioning. For much of his life, he couldn't travel by car or aeroplane, and he couldn't use a telephone to call friends or family. If he became ill, he couldn't take advantage of many medicines, such as antibiotics, that doctors today routinely use to prolong and enhance life.

Now consider: how much money would someone have to pay you to give up for the rest of your life all the modern conveniences that Rockefeller lived without? Would you do it for $200 billion? Perhaps not. And if you wouldn't, is it fair to say that you are better off than John D. Rockefeller, allegedly the richest person of all time?

The preceding chapter discussed how standard price indexes, which are used to compare sums of money from different points in time, fail to fully reflect the introduction of new goods in the economy. As a result, the rate of inflation is overestimated. The flip side of this observation is that the rate of real economic growth is underestimated. Pondering Rockefeller's life shows how significant this problem might be. Because of tremendous technological advances, the average person living in an advanced economy today is arguably 'richer' than the richest person in the world a century ago, even if that fact is lost in standard economic statistics.

FYI

A Picture Is Worth a Thousand Statistics

George Bernard Shaw once said, 'The sign of a truly educated man is to be deeply moved by statistics.' Most of us, however, have trouble being deeply moved by data on GDP – until we see what these statistics represent.

The three photos on these pages show a typical family from each of three countries – the United Kingdom, Mexico and Mali. Each family was photographed outside their home, together with all their material possessions.

These nations have very different standards of living, as judged by these photos, GDP or other statistics.

- The United Kingdom is an advanced economy. In 2006, its GDP per person was $35 580. A negligible share of the population lives in extreme poverty, defined here as less than $2 a day. Educational attainment is high: among children of high school age, 95 per cent are in school. Residents of the United Kingdom can expect to enjoy a long life: the probability of a person surviving to age 65 is 84 per cent for men and 90 per cent for women.
- Mexico is a middle-income country. In 2006, its GDP per person was $11 410. About an eighth of the population lives on less than $2 a day. Among children of high school age, 65 per cent are in school. The probability of a person surviving to age 65 is 76 per cent for men and 84 per cent for women.
- Mali is a poor country. In 2006, its GDP per person was only $1 130. Extreme poverty is the norm: more than half of the population lives on less than $2 per day. Educational attainment in Mali is low: among children of high school age, less than 10 per cent are in school. And life is often cut short: The probability of a person surviving to age 65 is only 44 per cent for men and 54 per cent for women.

Economists who study economic growth try to understand what causes such large differences in the standard of living.

© DAVID REED

A typical family in the United Kingdom

A typical family in Mexico

A typical family in Mali

some countries zoom ahead while others lag behind? These are precisely the questions that we take up next.

Quick Quiz What is the approximate growth rate of real GDP per person in your country? Name a country that has had faster growth and a country that has had slower growth.

There have been a number of theories advanced by economists to explain how economies grow. One of the most famous is that developed by Solow and Swan which was outlined in a case study on page 24 in Chapter 2. You will need to keep in mind that theories of growth are changing as economists carry out more research and have access to more data. The next section will cover the role of productivity in growth which can be referred to as the neoclassical theory of growth. Other theories, such as endogenous growth theory, argue that investment in a nation's human capital will be a key driver of economic growth. The reason being that investment in human capital is more likely to lead to increases in technology which in turn help promote efficiency and increases in productivity. This is the main driver of growth rather than trade. The debates surrounding these different theories are beyond the scope of this book but are something that you need to be aware of and will be covered on the accompanying website to the book.

PRODUCTIVITY: ITS ROLE AND DETERMINANTS

Explaining the large variation in living standards around the world is, in one sense, very easy. As we will see, the explanation can be summarized in a single word – *productivity*. But, in another sense, the international variation is deeply puzzling. To explain why incomes are so much higher in some countries than in others, we must look at the many factors that determine a nation's productivity.

Why Productivity Is So Important

Let's begin our study of productivity and economic growth by developing a simple model based on an individual who finds himself shipwrecked on a desert island, who we will call Fernando. Because Fernando lives alone, he catches his own fish, grows his own vegetables and makes his own clothes. We can think of Fernando's activities – his production and consumption of fish, vegetables and clothing – as being a simple economy. By examining Fernando's economy, we can learn some lessons that also apply to more complex and realistic economies.

What determines Fernando's standard of living? The answer is obvious. If Fernando is good at catching fish, growing vegetables, and making clothes, he lives well. If he is bad at doing these things, he lives poorly. Because Fernando can consume only what he produces, his living standard is tied to his productive ability.

The term productivity refers to the quantity of goods and services that a worker can produce for each hour of work. In the case of Fernando's economy, it is easy to see that productivity is the key determinant of living standards and that growth in productivity is the key determinant of growth in living standards. The more fish Fernando can catch per hour, the more he eats for dinner. If Fernando finds a better place to catch fish, his productivity rises. This increase in productivity makes Fernando better off: he could eat the extra fish, or he could spend less time fishing and devote more time to making other goods he enjoys.

The key role of productivity in determining living standards is as true for nations as it is for Fernando. Recall that an economy's gross domestic product (GDP) measures two things at once: the total income earned by everyone in the economy and the total expenditure on the economy's output of goods and services. The reason why GDP can measure these two things simultaneously is that, for the economy as a whole, they must be equal. Put simply, an economy's income is the economy's output.

Like Fernando, a nation can enjoy a high standard of living only if it can produce a large quantity of goods and services. Western Europeans live better than Nigerians because Western European workers are more productive than Nigerian workers. The Japanese have enjoyed more rapid growth in living standards than Argentineans because Japanese workers have experienced more rapidly growing productivity. Indeed, one of the *Ten Principles of Economics* in Chapter 1 is that a country's standard of living depends on its ability to produce goods and services.

Hence, to understand the large differences in living standards we observe across countries or over time, we must focus on the production of goods and services. But seeing the link between living standards and productivity is only the first step. It leads naturally to the next question: why are some economies so much better at producing goods and services than others?

How Productivity Is Determined

Although productivity is uniquely important in determining Fernando's standard of living, many factors determine Fernando's productivity. Fernando will be better at catching fish, for instance, if he has more fishing rods, if he has been trained in the best fishing techniques, if his island has a plentiful fish supply, and if he invents a better fishing lure. Each of these determinants of Fernando's productivity – which we can call *physical capital, human capital, natural resources* and *technological knowledge* – has a counterpart in more complex and realistic economies. Let's consider each of these factors in turn.

Physical Capital Workers are more productive if they have tools with which to work. The stock of equipment and structures that are used to produce goods and services is called **physical capital**, or just *capital*. For example, when carpenters make furniture, they use saws, lathes and drill presses. More tools allow work to be done more quickly and more accurately. That is, a carpenter with only basic hand tools can make less furniture each week than a carpenter with sophisticated and specialized woodworking equipment.

physical capital
the stock of equipment and structures that are used to produce goods and services

As you may recall from Chapter 2, the inputs used to produce goods and services – labour, capital and so on – are called the *factors of production*. An important feature of capital is that it is a *produced* factor of production. That is, capital is an input into the production process that in the past was an output from the production process. The carpenter uses a lathe to make the leg of a table. Earlier the lathe itself was the output of a firm that manufactures lathes. The lathe manufacturer in turn used other equipment to make its product. Thus, capital is a factor of production used to produce all kinds of goods and services, including more capital.

Human Capital A second determinant of productivity is human capital. Human capital is the economist's term for the knowledge and skills that workers acquire through education, training and experience. Human capital includes the skills accumulated in early childhood programmes, primary school, secondary school, university or college, and on-the-job training for adults in the labour force.

Although education, training and experience are less tangible than lathes, bulldozers and buildings, human capital is like physical capital in many ways. Like physical capital, human capital raises a nation's ability to produce goods and services. Also like physical capital, human capital is a produced factor of production. Producing human capital requires inputs in the form of teachers, lecturers, libraries and student time. Indeed, students can be viewed as 'workers' who have the important job of producing the human capital that will be used in future production.

natural resources
the inputs into the production of goods and services that are provided by nature, such as land, rivers and mineral deposits

Natural Resources A third determinant of productivity is **natural resources**. Natural resources are inputs into production that are provided by nature, such as land, rivers and mineral deposits. Natural resources take two forms: renewable and non-renewable. A forest is an example of a renewable resource. When one tree is cut down, a seedling can be planted in its place to be harvested in the future. Oil is an example of a non-renewable resource. Because oil is produced by nature over many thousands or even millions of years, there is only a limited supply. Once the supply of oil is depleted, it is impossible to create more (at least not for thousands of years).

Differences in natural resources are responsible for some of the differences in standards of living around the world. The historical success of the United States was driven in part by the large supply of land well suited for agriculture. Today, some countries in the Middle East, such as Kuwait and Saudi Arabia, are rich simply because they happen to be on top of some of the largest pools of oil in the world.

Although natural resources can be important, they are not necessary for an economy to be highly productive in producing goods and services. Japan, for instance, is one of the richest countries in the world, despite having few natural resources. International trade makes Japan's success possible. Japan imports many of the natural resources it needs, such as oil, and exports its manufactured goods to economies rich in natural resources.

technological knowledge
society's understanding of the best ways to produce goods and services

Technological Knowledge A fourth determinant of productivity is **technological knowledge** – the understanding of the best ways to produce goods and services. (Technology is defined as the application of knowledge to the environment to enable people to exercise greater control over that environment.) A hundred years ago, most Europeans and North Americans worked on farms, because farm technology required a high input of labour in order to feed the entire population. Today, thanks to advances in the technology of farming, a small fraction of the populations of Western Europe, the USA and Canada can produce enough food to feed their entire population. This technological change made labour available to produce other goods and services.

Technological knowledge takes many forms. Some technology is common knowledge – after it starts to be used by one person, everyone becomes aware of it. For example, once Henry Ford successfully introduced production in assembly lines in the USA, other carmakers and industrial producers throughout the world quickly followed suit. Other technology is proprietary – it is known only by the company that discovers it. Only the Coca-Cola Company, for instance, knows the secret recipe for making its famous soft drink. Still other technology is proprietary for a short time. When a pharmaceutical company discovers a new drug, the patent system gives that company a temporary right to be its exclusive manufacturer. When the patent expires, however, other companies are allowed to make the drug. All these forms of technological knowledge are important for the economy's production of goods and services.

It is worthwhile to distinguish between technological knowledge and human capital. Although they are closely related, there is an important difference.

FYI

The Production Function

Economists often use a *production function* to describe the relationship between the quantity of inputs used in production and the quantity of output from production. For example, suppose Y denotes the quantity of output, L the quantity of labour, K the quantity of physical capital, H the quantity of human capital and N the quantity of natural resources. Then we might write:

$$Y = A\,F(L, K, H, N)$$

where $F(\,)$ is a function that shows how the inputs are combined to produce output. In other words, the quantity of output (Y) is dependent upon the quantity of labour, physical capital, human capital and the quantity of natural resources. A is a variable that reflects the available production technology. As technology improves, A rises, so the economy produces more output from any given combination of inputs.

Many production functions have a property called *constant returns to scale*. If a production function has constant returns to scale, then a doubling of all the inputs causes the amount of output to double as well. Mathematically, we write that a production function has constant returns to scale if, for any positive number x:

$$xY = A\,F(xL, xK, xH, xN)$$

A doubling of all inputs is represented in this equation by $x = 2$. The right-hand side shows the inputs doubling, and the left-hand side shows output doubling.

Production functions with constant returns to scale have an interesting implication. To see what it is, set $x = 1/L$. Then the equation above becomes:

$$Y/L = A\,F(1, K/L, H/L, N/L)$$

Notice that Y/L is output per worker, which is a measure of productivity. This equation says that productivity depends on physical capital per worker (K/L), human capital per worker (H/L), and natural resources per worker (N/L). Productivity also depends on the state of technology, as reflected by the variable A. Thus, this equation provides a mathematical summary of the four determinants of productivity that we have just discussed.

Technological knowledge refers to *society's* understanding about how the world works. Human capital refers to the resources expended transmitting this understanding to the *labour force*. To use a relevant metaphor, knowledge is the quality of society's textbooks, whereas human capital is the amount of time that the population has devoted to reading them. Workers' productivity depends on both the quality of textbooks they have available and the amount of time they have spent studying them.

Quick Quiz List and describe four determinants of a country's productivity.

CASE STUDY

Are Natural Resources a Limit to Growth?

Today the world's population is over 6 billion, about four times what it was a century ago. At the same time, many people are enjoying a much higher standard of living than did their great-grandparents. A perennial debate concerns whether this growth in population and living standards can continue in the future.

Many commentators have argued that natural resources provide a limit to how much the world's economies can grow. At first, this argument might seem hard to ignore. If the world has only a fixed supply of non-renewable natural resources, how can population, production and living standards continue to grow over time? Eventually, won't supplies of oil and minerals start to run out? When these shortages start to occur, won't they stop economic growth and, perhaps, even force living standards to fall?

Despite the apparent appeal of such arguments, most economists are less concerned about such limits to growth than one might imagine. They argue that technological progress often yields ways to avoid these limits. If we compare the economy today to the economy of the past, we see various ways in which the use of natural resources has improved. Modern cars have better petrol mileage. New houses have better insulation and require less energy to heat and cool them. More efficient oil rigs waste less oil in the process of extraction. Recycling allows some non-renewable resources to be reused. The development of alternative fuels, such as ethanol instead of petrol, allows us to substitute renewable for non-renewable resources.

Fifty years ago, some conservationists were concerned about the excessive use of tin and copper. At the time, these were crucial commodities: tin was used to make many food containers, and copper was used to make telephone wire. Some people advocated mandatory recycling and rationing of tin and copper so that supplies would be available for future generations. Today, however, plastic has replaced tin as a material for making many food containers, and telephone calls often travel over fibre-optic cables, which are made from sand. Technological progress has made once-crucial natural resources less necessary.

But are all these efforts enough to permit continued economic growth? One way to answer this question is to look at the prices of natural resources. In a market economy, scarcity is reflected in market prices. If the world were running out of natural resources, then the prices of those resources would be rising over time. But, in fact, the opposite is more nearly true. Natural resource prices exhibit substantial short-run price fluctuations, but over long spans of time, the prices of most natural resources (adjusted for overall inflation) are stable or falling. It appears that our ability to conserve these resources is growing more rapidly than their supplies are dwindling. Market prices give no reason to believe that natural resources are a limit to economic growth.

ECONOMIC GROWTH AND PUBLIC POLICY

So far, we have determined that a society's standard of living depends on its ability to produce goods and services and that its productivity depends on physical capital, human capital, natural resources and technological knowledge. Let's now turn to the question faced by policy makers around the world: what can government policy do to raise productivity and living standards?

The Importance of Saving and Investment

Because capital is a produced factor of production, a society can change the amount of capital it has. If today the economy produces a large quantity of new capital goods, then tomorrow it will have a larger stock of capital and be able to produce more of all types of goods and services. Thus, one way to raise future productivity is to invest more current resources in the production of capital.

One of the *Ten Principles of Economics* presented in Chapter 1 is that people face trade-offs. This principle is especially important when considering the accumulation of capital. Because resources are scarce, devoting more resources to producing capital requires devoting fewer resources to producing goods and services for current consumption. That is, for society to invest more in capital, it must consume less and save more of its current income. The growth that arises from capital accumulation is not a free lunch: it requires that society sacrifice consumption of goods and services in the present in order to enjoy higher consumption in the future.

In the 1930s, the rulers of Russia deliberately diverted resources to the production of capital goods in an attempt to try to catch up with the richer and more industrialized western countries such as Germany, the United States and the United Kingdom. It managed to expand production in core industries such as coal and steel significantly which in turn increased its capacity to produce other capital goods (and military equipment). The trade-off for the Russian people at the time was fewer consumer goods and a harsh life. It could be argued that whilst this represented significant short-term hardship for many of its people, the decision helped Russia to be in a position to fight off the Germans in the Second World War and emerge to be one of the planet's superpowers.

The next chapter examines in more detail how the economy's financial markets coordinate saving and investment. It also examines how government policies influence the amount of saving and investment that takes place. At this point it is important to note that encouraging saving and investment is one way that a government can encourage growth and, in the long run, raise the economy's standard of living.

To see the importance of investment for economic growth, consider Figure 25.2, which displays data on 15 countries. Panel (a) shows each country's growth rate over a 46-year period. The countries are ordered by their average annual growth rates, from most to least rapid. Panel (b) shows the percentage of GDP that each country devotes to investment. The correlation between growth and investment, although not perfect, is strong. Countries that devote a large share of GDP to investment, such as South Korea and Japan, tend to have high growth rates. Countries that devote a small share of GDP to investment, such as Rwanda and Bangladesh, tend to have low growth rates. Studies that examine a more comprehensive list of countries confirm this strong correlation between investment and growth. It should also be noted that the figures can be affected by the starting base; countries such as China now devote over a third of GDP to investment whereas in the early 1960s it hovered between 10.5 per cent and 22.08 per cent.

There is, however, a problem in interpreting these data. As the appendix to Chapter 2 discussed, a correlation between two variables does not establish which variable is the cause and which is the effect. It is possible that high investment causes high growth, but it is also possible that high growth causes high investment. (Or, perhaps, high growth and high investment are both caused by a third variable that has been omitted from the analysis.) The data by themselves cannot tell us the direction of causation. Nevertheless, because capital accumulation affects productivity so clearly and directly, many economists interpret these data as showing that high investment leads to more rapid economic growth.

Diminishing Returns and the Catch-up Effect

Suppose that a government, convinced by the evidence in Figure 25.2, pursues policies that raise the nation's saving rate – the percentage of GDP devoted to saving rather than consumption. What happens? With the nation saving more, fewer resources are needed to make consumption goods, and more resources

FIGURE 25.2

Growth and Investment

Panel (a) shows the growth rate of GDP per person for 15 countries over the period 1961–2007. Panel (b) shows the percentage of GDP that each country devoted to investment over this period. The figure shows that investment and growth are positively correlated.

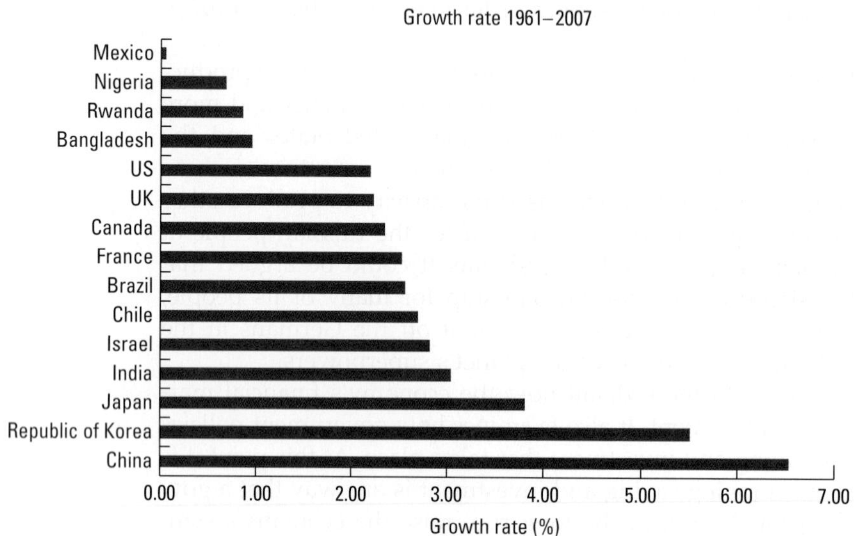

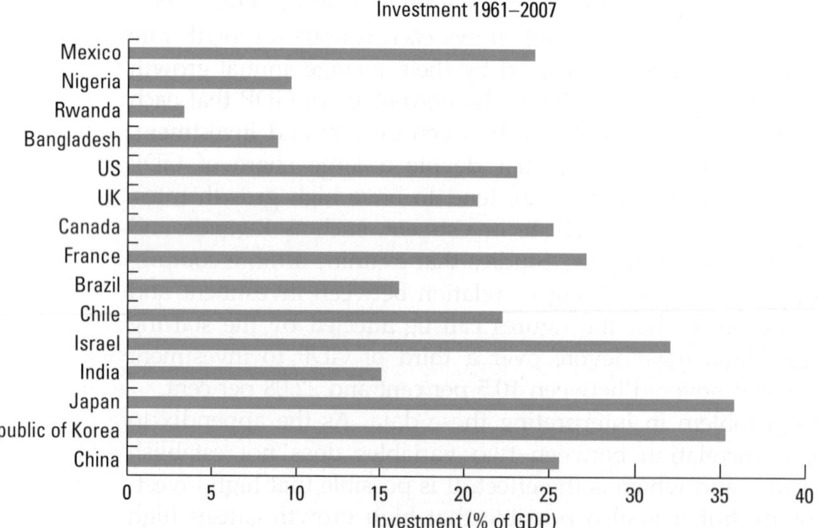

Source: Alan Heston, Robert Summers and Bettina Aten, *Penn World Table* Version 6.3, Center for International Comparisons of Production, Income and Prices at the University of Pennsylvania, August 2009, and authors' calculations.

are available to make capital goods. As a result, the capital stock increases, leading to rising productivity and more rapid growth in GDP. But how long does this higher rate of growth last? Assuming that the saving rate remains at its new higher level, does the growth rate of GDP stay high indefinitely or only for a period of time?

diminishing returns
the property whereby the benefit from an extra unit of an input declines as the quantity of the input increases

The traditional view of the production process is that capital is subject to **diminishing returns**: as the stock of capital rises, the extra output produced

FIGURE 25.3

Illustrating the Production Function

This figure shows how the amount of capital per worker influences the amount of output per worker. Other determinants of output, including human capital, natural resources and technology are held constant. The curve becomes flatter as the amount of capital increases because of diminishing returns to capital.

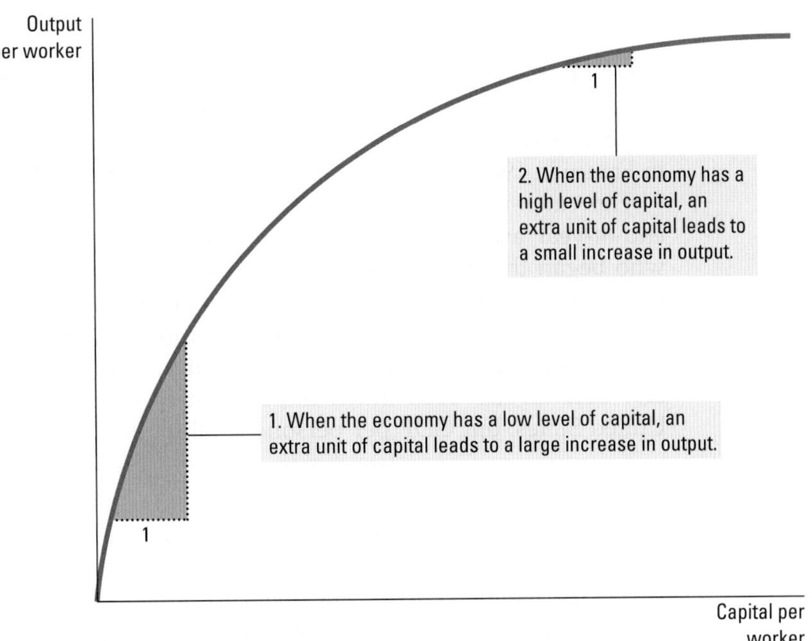

from an additional unit of capital falls. In other words, when workers already have a large quantity of capital to use in producing goods and services, giving them an additional unit of capital increases their productivity only slightly. This is illustrated in Figure 25.3, which shows how the amount of capital per worker determines the amount of output per worker, holding constant all the other determinants of output. Because of diminishing returns, an increase in the saving rate leads to higher growth only for a while. As the higher saving rate allows more capital to be accumulated, the benefits from additional capital become smaller over time, and so growth slows down. In the long run, the higher saving rate leads to a higher level of productivity and income, but not to higher growth in these variables. Reaching this long run, however, can take quite a while. According to studies of international data on economic growth, increasing the saving rate can lead to substantially higher growth for a period of several decades.

The diminishing returns to capital has another important implication: other things equal, it is easier for a country to grow fast if it starts out relatively poor. This effect of initial conditions on subsequent growth is sometimes called the **catch-up effect**. In poor countries, workers lack even the most rudimentary tools and, as a result, have low productivity. Small amounts of capital investment would substantially raise these workers' productivity. By contrast, workers in rich countries have large amounts of capital with which to work, and this partly explains their high productivity. Yet with the amount of capital per worker already so high, additional capital investment has a relatively small effect on productivity. Studies of international data on economic growth confirm this catch-up effect: controlling for other variables, such as the percentage of GDP devoted to investment, poor countries do tend to grow at a faster rate than rich countries.

catch-up effect
the property whereby countries that start off poor tend to grow more rapidly than countries that start off rich

This catch-up effect can help explain some of the puzzling results in Figure 25.2. Over this 46-year period, the Japan invested, on average, over 35 per cent of its GDP, while China invested about 10 per cent less, yet China grew at an average rate 1.7 times the Japanese annual average growth rate of 3.81 per cent. The explanation is the catch-up effect. In 1961 Japan had GDP per person about 15 times that of China, in part because, as stated above, investment in China up to the end of the 1960s had been so low. With a small initial capital stock, the benefits to capital accumulation were much greater in China, and this gave China a higher subsequent growth rate. A similar effect is evident if one compares Brazil and France: both of these countries enjoyed annual average growth rates of about 2.5 per cent over the period, yet France's average investment rate of just over 27 per cent of GDP was almost twice that of Brazil at 16.12 per cent. GDP per person in France in 1961 was over two and a half times that of Brazilian GDP per person.

This catch-up effect shows up in other aspects of life. When a school gives an end-of-year award to the 'Most Improved' student, that student is usually one who began the year with relatively poor performance. Students who began the year not studying find improvement easier than students who always worked hard. Note that it is good to be 'Most Improved,' given the starting point, but it is even better to be 'Best Student'. Similarly, economic growth over the past several decades has been much more rapid in the Republic of Korea than in the United States, but GDP per person is still higher in the United States.

Investment from Abroad

So far we have discussed how policies aimed at increasing a country's saving rate can increase investment and, thereby, long-term economic growth. Yet saving by domestic residents is not the only way for a country to invest in new capital. The other way is investment by foreigners.

Investment from abroad takes several forms. BMW might build a car factory in Portugal. A capital investment that is owned and operated by a foreign entity is called *foreign direct investment.* Alternatively, a German might buy equity in a Portuguese corporation (that is, buy a share in the ownership of the corporation); the Portuguese corporation can use the proceeds from the equity sale to build a new factory. An investment that is financed with foreign money but operated by domestic residents is called *foreign portfolio investment.* In both cases, Germans provide the resources necessary to increase the stock of capital in Portugal. That is, German saving is being used to finance Portuguese investment.

When foreigners invest in a country, they do so because they expect to earn a return on their investment. BMW's car factory increases the Portuguese capital stock and, therefore, increases Portuguese productivity and Portuguese GDP. Yet BMW takes some of this additional income back to Germany in the form of profit. Similarly, when a German investor buys Portuguese equity, the investor has a right to a portion of the profit that the Portuguese corporation earns.

Investment from abroad, therefore, does not have the same effect on all measures of economic prosperity. Recall that gross domestic product (GDP) is the income earned within a country by both residents and non-residents, whereas gross national product (GNP) is the income earned by residents of a country both at home and abroad. When BMW opens its car factory in Portugal, some of the income the factory generates accrues to people who do not live in Portugal. As a result, foreign investment in Portugal raises the income of the Portuguese (measured by GNP) by less than it raises the production in Portugal (measured by GDP).

Nevertheless, investment from abroad is one way for a country to grow. Even though some of the benefits from this investment flow back to the foreign owners, this investment does increase the economy's stock of capital, leading to higher productivity and higher wages. Moreover, investment from abroad is one way for poorer countries to learn the state-of-the-art technologies developed and used in richer countries. For these reasons, many economists who advise governments in less developed economies advocate policies that encourage investment from abroad. Often this means removing restrictions that governments have imposed on foreign ownership of domestic capital.

An organization that tries to encourage the flow of capital to poor countries is the World Bank. This international organization obtains funds from the world's advanced industrialized countries, and uses these resources to make loans to less developed countries so that they can invest in roads, sewage systems, schools and other types of capital. It also offers the countries advice about how the funds might best be used. The World Bank, together with its sister organization, the International Monetary Fund, was set up after World War II. One lesson from the war was that economic distress often leads to political turmoil, international tensions and military conflict. Thus, every country has an interest in promoting economic prosperity around the world. The World Bank and the International Monetary Fund are aimed at achieving that common goal.

Education

Education – investment in human capital – is at least as important as investment in physical capital for a country's long-run economic success. In the developed economies of Western Europe and North America, each extra year of schooling raises a worker's income by about 10 per cent on average. In less developed countries, where human capital is especially scarce, the gap between the wages of educated and uneducated workers is even larger. Thus, one way in which government policy can enhance the standard of living is to provide good schools and to encourage the population to take advantage of them.

Investment in human capital, like investment in physical capital, has an opportunity cost. When students are in school, they forgo the wages they could have earned. In less developed countries, children often drop out of school at an early age, even though the benefit of additional schooling is very high, simply because their labour is needed to help support the family.

Some economists have argued that human capital is particularly important for economic growth because human capital conveys positive externalities. An *externality*, remember, is the effect of one person's actions on the well-being of a bystander. An educated person, for instance, might generate new ideas about how best to produce goods and services. If these ideas enter society's pool of knowledge, so that everyone can use them, then the ideas are an external benefit of education. In this case, the return to schooling for society is even greater than the return for the individual. This argument would justify the large subsidies to human capital investment that we observe in the form of public education.

One problem facing some poor countries is the *brain drain* – the emigration of many of the most highly educated workers to rich countries, where these workers can enjoy a higher standard of living. If human capital does have positive externalities, then this brain drain makes those people left behind poorer than they otherwise would be. This problem offers policy makers a dilemma. On the one hand, rich countries like those of Western Europe and North America have the best systems of higher education, and it would seem natural for poor countries to send their best students abroad to earn higher degrees. On the other hand, those students who have spent time abroad may choose not to return home, and this brain drain will reduce the poor nation's stock of human capital even further.

Health and Nutrition

The term *human capital* usually refers to education, but it can also be used to describe another type of investment in people: expenditures that lead to a healthier population. Other things equal, healthier workers are more productive. The right investments in the health of the population provide one way for a nation to increase productivity and raise living standards.

Economic historian, Robert Fogel, has suggested that a significant factor in long-run economic growth is improved health from better nutrition. He estimates that in Great Britain in 1780 about one in five people were so malnourished that they were incapable of manual labour. Among those who could work, insufficient intake of calories substantially reduced the work effort they could carry out. As nutrition improved so did workers' productivity.

Fogel studies these historical trends in part by looking at the height of the population. Short stature can be an indicator of malnutrition, especially during gestation and the early years of life. Fogel finds that as nations develop economically, people eat more and the population gets taller. From 1775 to 1975, the average caloric intake in Great Britain rose by 26 per cent and the height of the average man rose by 3.6 inches (around 10 cm). Similarly, during the spectacular economic growth in the Republic of Korea from 1962 to 1995, caloric consumption rose by 44 per cent and, average male height rose by 2 inches (5 cm). Of course, a person's height is determined by a combination of genetic predisposition and environment. But because the genetic make-up of a population is slow to change, such increases in average height are likely due to changes in the environment – nutrition being the obvious explanation.

Moreover, studies have found that height is an indicator of productivity. Looking at data on a large number of workers at a point in time, researchers have found that taller workers tend to earn more. Because wages reflect a worker's productivity, this finding suggests that taller workers tend to be more productive. The effect of height on wages is especially pronounced in poorer countries, where malnutrition is a bigger risk.

Fogel won the Nobel Prize in Economics in 1993 for his work in economic history, which includes not only his studies on nutrition but also work on American slavery and the role of the railroads in the development of the American economy. In the lecture he gave when awarded the Prize, he surveyed the evidence on health and economic growth. He concluded that 'improved gross nutrition accounts for roughly 30 per cent of the growth of per capita income in Britain between 1790 and 1980'.

Today malnutrition is fortunately rare in developed nations (obesity is a more widespread problem). But for people in developing nations, poor health and inadequate nutrition remain obstacles to higher productivity and improved living standards. The United Nations estimates that almost a third of the population in sub-Saharan Africa is undernourished.

The causal link between health and wealth runs in both directions. Poor countries are poor, in part, because their populations are not healthy, and their populations are not healthy, in part, because they are poor and cannot afford adequate health care and nutrition. It is a vicious circle. But this fact opens the possibility of a virtuous circle. Policies that lead to more rapid economic growth would naturally improve health outcomes, which in turn would further promote economic growth.

Property Rights, Political Stability and Good Governance

Other ways in which policy makers can foster economic growth is by protecting property rights, promoting political stability and maintaining good governance.

As we first noted when we discussed economic interdependence in Chapter 3, production in market economies arises from the interactions of millions of individuals and firms. When you buy a car, for instance, you are buying the output of a car dealer, a car manufacturer, a steel company, an iron ore mining company and so on. This division of production among many firms allows the economy's factors of production to be used as effectively as possible. To achieve this outcome, the economy has to coordinate transactions among these firms, as well as between firms and consumers. Market economies achieve this coordination through market prices. That is, market prices are the instrument with which the invisible hand of the marketplace brings supply and demand into balance.

An important prerequisite for the price system to work is an economy-wide respect for *property rights.* We covered property rights in Chapters 10 and 11. A mining company will not make the effort to mine iron ore if it expects the ore to be stolen. The company mines the ore only if it is confident that it will benefit from the ore's subsequent sale. For this reason, courts serve an important role in a market economy: they enforce property rights. Through the criminal justice system, the courts discourage direct theft. In addition, through the civil justice system, the courts ensure that buyers and sellers live up to their contracts.

Although those of us in developed countries tend to take property rights for granted, those living in less developed countries understand that lack of property rights can be a major problem. In many countries, the system of justice does not work well. Contracts are hard to enforce, and fraud often goes unpunished. In more extreme cases, the government not only fails to enforce property rights but actually infringes upon them. To do business in some countries, firms are expected to bribe powerful government officials. Such corruption impedes the coordinating power of markets. It also discourages domestic saving and investment from abroad.

One threat to property rights is political instability. When revolutions and coups are common, there is doubt about whether property rights will be respected in the future. If a revolutionary government might confiscate the capital of some businesses, as was often true after communist revolutions, domestic residents have less incentive to save, invest and start new businesses. At the same time, foreigners have less incentive to invest in the country. Even the threat of revolution can act to depress a nation's standard of living. It is no coincidence that countries with a strong military power, who are subject to frequent coups, are ones that are at the bottom of any standard of living league table.

Thus, economic prosperity depends in part on political prosperity. A country with an efficient court system, honest government officials and a stable constitution will enjoy a higher economic standard of living than a country with a poor court system, corrupt officials and frequent revolutions and coups. These are the key features of good governance – the extent to which a country is ruled by sound democracies, where the rule of law, the authority of law, the absence of corruption and independent judicial processes are in existence. If these things are in place then it means that contracts and property rights can be enforced and free markets can operate effectively to allocate scarce resources. Without good governance, many economists believe that economic development will be compromised.

Free Trade

Some of the world's poorest countries have tried to achieve more rapid economic growth by pursuing *inward-oriented policies.* These policies are aimed at raising productivity and living standards within the country by avoiding interaction with the rest of the world. This approach gets support from some domestic firms, which claim that they need protection from foreign competition in order to compete and grow. This infant-industry argument, together with a general distrust of foreigners, has at times led policy makers in less developed countries to impose tariffs and other trade restrictions.

Most economists today believe that poor countries are better off pursuing *outward-oriented policies* that integrate these countries into the world economy. When we studied international trade earlier in the book, we showed how international trade can improve the economic well-being of a country's citizens. Trade is, in some ways, a type of technology. When a country exports wheat and imports steel, the country benefits in the same way as if it had invented a technology for turning wheat into steel. A country that eliminates trade restrictions will, therefore, experience the same kind of economic growth that would occur after a major technological advance.

The adverse impact of inward orientation becomes clear when one considers the small size of many less developed economies. The total GDP of Argentina, for instance, is about that of the South-East of England (if we include London). Imagine what would happen if the South-East were suddenly to declare that it was illegal to trade with anyone beyond the regional boundaries. Without being able to take advantage of the gains from trade, the South-East would need to produce all the goods it consumes. It would also have to produce all its own capital goods, rather than importing state-of-the-art equipment from other cities. Living standards in the South-East would fall immediately, and the problem would probably only get worse over time. This is precisely what happened when Argentina pursued inward-oriented policies throughout much of the 20th century and can also partly explain the economic problems in North Korea which has effectively cut itself off from the rest of the world. By contrast, countries pursuing outward-oriented policies, such as the Republic of Korea, Singapore and Taiwan, have enjoyed high rates of economic growth.

The amount that a nation trades with others is determined not only by government policy but also by geography. Countries with good natural seaports find trade easier than countries without this resource. It is not a coincidence that many of the world's major cities, such as Paris, New York, Hong Kong and London, are located either next to oceans or on the banks of a major river giving easy access for seafaring trade vessels. Similarly, because landlocked countries find international trade more difficult, they tend to have lower levels of income than countries with easy access to the world's waterways.

Research and Development

The primary reason that living standards are higher today than they were a century ago is that technological knowledge has advanced. The telephone, the transistor, the computer, and the internal combustion engine are among the thousands of innovations that have improved the ability to produce goods and services.

Although most technological advance comes from private research by firms and individual inventors, there is also a public interest in promoting these efforts. To a large extent, knowledge is a *public good:* once one person discovers an idea, the idea enters society's pool of knowledge and other people can freely use it (subject to any legal restrictions such as those imposed by intellectual property rights). Just as government has a role in providing a public good such as national defence, it also has a role in encouraging the research and development of new technologies. The governments in most advanced countries do this in a number of ways, for example through science research laboratories owned and funded by the government, or through a system of research grants offered to promising researchers. It may also offer tax breaks and concessions for firms engaging in research and development.

Yet another way in which government policy encourages research is through the patent system. When a person or firm invents a new product, such as a new drug, the inventor can apply for a patent. If the product is deemed truly original, the government awards the patent, which gives the inventor the exclusive right to make the product for a specified number of years. In essence, the patent gives the inventor a property right over his invention, turning his new idea from a public good into a private good. By allowing inventors to profit from their inventions – even if only temporarily – the patent system enhances the incentive for individuals and firms to engage in research.

Population Growth

Economists and other social scientists have long debated how population growth affects a society. The most direct effect is on the size of the labour force: a large population means more workers to produce goods and services. At the same time, it means more people to consume those goods and services. Beyond these obvious effects, population growth interacts with the other factors of production in ways that are less obvious and more open to debate.

Stretching Natural Resources Thomas Robert Malthus (1766–1834), an English minister and early economic thinker, is famous for his book entitled *An Essay on the Principle of Population as It Affects the Future Improvement of Society*. In it, Malthus offered what may be history's most chilling forecast. Malthus argued that an ever increasing population would continually strain society's ability to provide for itself. As a result, mankind was doomed to forever live in poverty.

Malthus's logic was simple. He began by noting that 'food is necessary to the existence of man' and that 'the passion between the sexes is necessary and will remain nearly in its present state'. He concluded that 'the power of population is infinitely greater than the power in the earth to produce subsistence for man'. According to Malthus, the only check on population growth was 'misery and vice'. Attempts by charities or governments to alleviate poverty were counterproductive, he argued, because they merely allowed the poor to have more children, placing even greater strains on society's productive capabilities.

Fortunately, Malthus's dire forecast was far off the mark. Although the world population has increased about six-fold over the past two centuries, living standards around the world are on average much higher. As a result of economic growth, chronic hunger and malnutrition are less common now than they were in Malthus's day. Famines occur from time to time, but they are more often the result of an unequal income distribution or political instability than an inadequate production of food.

Where did Malthus go wrong? He assumed – correctly – that world population would rise exponentially, since as more people are born and survive, more and more people are born as their children, and so on. But he also assumed – incorrectly – that the amount of food produced could rise only linearly, by increasing the amount of land under cultivation with productivity remaining constant. But growth in mankind's ingenuity over the years has offset the effects of a larger population. Pesticides, fertilizers, mechanized farm equipment, new crop varieties and other technological advances that Malthus never imagined have allowed each farmer to feed ever greater numbers of people. Even with more mouths to feed, fewer farmers are necessary because each farmer is so much more productive than Malthus ever imagined.

Thomas Robert Malthus

Diluting the Capital Stock Whereas Malthus worried about the effects of population on the use of natural resources, some modern theories of economic growth emphasize its effects on capital accumulation. According to these theories, high population growth reduces GDP per worker because rapid growth in the number of workers forces the capital stock to be spread more thinly. In other words, when population growth is rapid, each worker is equipped with less capital. A smaller quantity of capital per worker leads to lower productivity and lower GDP per worker.

This problem is most apparent in the case of human capital. Countries with high population growth have large numbers of school-age children. This places a larger burden on the educational system. It is not surprising, therefore, that educational attainment tends to be low in countries with high population growth.

The differences in population growth around the world are large. In developed countries, such as the United States, the United Kingdom and the other countries of Western Europe, the population has risen only about 1 per cent per year in recent decades and is expected to rise even more slowly in the future. In contrast, in many poor African countries, population grows at about 3 per cent per year. At this rate, the population doubles every 23 years. This rapid population growth makes it harder to provide workers with the tools and skills they need to achieve high levels of productivity.

Although rapid population growth is not the main reason that less developed countries are poor, some analysts believe that reducing the rate of population growth would help these countries raise their standards of living. In some countries, this goal is accomplished directly with laws that regulate the number of children families may have. China, for instance, allows only one child per family living in urban areas; couples who violate this rule are subject to substantial fines. (In 2008, the National Population and Family Planning Commission announced that there were no planned changes to the policy for 'at least another decade'.) In countries with greater freedom, the goal of reduced population growth is accomplished less directly by increasing awareness of birth control techniques.

Another way in which a country can influence population growth is to apply one of the *Ten Principles of Economics:* people respond to incentives. Bearing a child, like any decision, has an opportunity cost. When the opportunity cost rises, people will choose to have smaller families. In particular, women with the opportunity to receive good education and desirable employment tend to want fewer children than those with fewer opportunities outside the home. Hence, policies that foster equal treatment of women are one way for less developed economies to reduce the rate of population growth and, perhaps, raise their standards of living.

Promoting Technological Progress Although rapid population growth may depress economic prosperity by reducing the amount of capital each worker has, it may also have some benefits. Some economists have suggested that world population growth has been an engine of technological progress and economic prosperity. The mechanism is simple: if there are more people, then the greater the probability that some of those people will come up with new ideas that will lead to technological progress, which benefits everyone.

Economist Michael Kremer has provided some support for this hypothesis in an article titled 'Population Growth and Technological Change: One Million B.C. to 1990', which was published in the *Quarterly Journal of Economics* in 1993. Kremer begins by noting that over the broad span of human history, world growth rates have increased as world population has. For example, world growth was more rapid when the world population was 1 billion (which occurred around the

IN THE NEWS

Malthus may have first published his essay over 200 years ago but it seems to have an endearing and enduring allure to those who wish to be the prophets of doom. This article looks at how Malthus's ideas still have resonance in some circles.

Malthus, the False Prophet: The Abiding Fallacy of Malthusian Limits

The pessimistic parson and early political economist remains as wrong as ever

Amid an astonishing surge in food prices, which has sparked riots and unrest in many countries and is making even the relatively affluent citizens of America and Europe feel the pinch, faith in the ability of global markets to fill nearly 7 billion bellies is dwindling. Given the fear that a new era of chronic shortages may have begun, it is perhaps understandable that the name of Thomas Malthus is in the air. Yet if his views were indeed now correct, that would defy the experience of the past two centuries.

Malthus first set out his ideas in 1798 in '*An Essay on the Principle of Population*'. This expounded a tragic twin trajectory for the growth of human populations and the increase of food supply. Whereas the natural tendency was for populations to grow without end, food supply would run up against the limit of finite land. As a result, the 'positive checks' of higher mortality caused by famine, disease and war were necessary to bring the number of people back in line with the capacity to feed them.

In a second edition published in 1803, Malthus softened his original harsh message by introducing the idea of moral restraint. Such a 'preventive check', operating through the birth rather than the death rate, could provide a way to counter the otherwise inexorable logic of too many mouths chasing too little food. If couples married late and had fewer children, population growth could be sufficiently arrested for agriculture to cope.

It was the misfortune of Malthus – but the good luck of generations born after him – that he wrote at an historical turning point. His ideas, especially his later ones, were arguably an accurate description of pre-industrial societies, which teetered on a precarious balance between empty and full stomachs. But the industrial revolution, which had already begun in Britain, was transforming the long-term outlook for economic growth. Economies were starting to expand faster than their populations, bringing about a sustained improvement in living standards.

Far from food running out, as Malthus had feared, it became abundant as trade expanded and low-cost agricultural producers like Argentina and Australia joined the world economy. Reforms based on sound political economy played a vital role, too. In particular, the abolition of the Corn Laws in 1846 paved the way for British workers to gain from cheap food imports.

Malthus got his demographic as well as his economic predictions wrong. His assumption that populations would carry on growing in times of plenty turned out to be false. Starting in Europe, one country after another underwent a 'demographic transformation' as economic development brought greater prosperity. Both birth and death rates dropped and population growth eventually started to slow.

The Malthusian heresy re-emerged in the early 1970s, the last time food prices shot up. Then, at least, there appeared to be some cause for demographic alarm. Global population growth had picked up sharply after the Second World War because it took time for high birth rates in developing countries to follow down the plunge in infant-mortality rates brought about by modern medicine. But once again the worries about overpopulation proved mistaken as the 'green revolution' and further advances in agricultural efficiency boosted food supply.

If the world's population growth was a false concern four decades ago, when it peaked at 2 per cent a year, it is even less so now that it has slowed to 1.2 per cent. But even though crude demography is not to blame, changing lifestyles arising from rapid economic growth especially in Asia are a new worry. As the Chinese have become more affluent, they have started to consume more meat, raising the underlying demand for basic food since cattle need more grain to feed than humans. Neo-Malthusians question whether the world can provide 6.7 billion people (rising to 9.2 billion by 2050) with a Western-style diet.

Once again the gloom is overdone. There may no longer be virgin lands to be settled and cultivated, as in the 19th century, but there is no reason to believe that agricultural productivity has hit a buffer. Indeed, one of the main barriers to another 'green revolution' is unwarranted popular worries about genetically modified foods, which are holding back farm output not just in Europe, but in the developing countries that could use them to boost their exports.

▶

Political folly increases in a geometrical ratio

As so often, governments are making matters worse. Food export bans are proliferating. Although these may produce temporary relief for any one country, the more they spread the tighter global markets become. Another wrongheaded policy has been America's subsidy to domestic ethanol production in a bid to reduce dependence on imported oil. This misconceived attempt to grow more fuel rather than to curb demand is expected to gobble up a third of this year's maize (corn) crop.

Although neo-Malthusianism naturally has much to say about food scarcity, the doctrine emerges more generally as the idea of absolute limits on resources and energy, such as the notion of 'peak oil'. Following the earlier scares of the 1970s, oil companies defied the pessimists by finding extra fields, not least since higher prices had spurred new exploration. But even if oil wells were to run dry, economies can still adapt by finding and exploiting other energy sources.

A new form of Malthusian limit has more recently emerged through the need to constrain greenhouse-gas emissions in order to tackle global warming. But this too can be overcome by shifting to a low-carbon economy. As with agriculture, the main difficulty in making the necessary adjustment comes from poor policies, such as governments' reluctance to impose a carbon tax. There may be curbs on traditional forms of growth, but there is no limit to human ingenuity. That is why Malthus remains as wrong today as he was two centuries ago.

Source: Malthus, the false prophet', *The Economist* (US) 17 May 2008 © 2008 The Economist Newspaper Ltd.

year 1800) than it was when the population was only 100 million (around 500 B.C.). This fact is consistent with the hypothesis that having more people induces more technological progress.

Kremer's second piece of evidence comes from comparing regions of the world. The melting of the polar ice caps at the end of the ice age around 10000 B.C. flooded the land bridges and separated the world into several distinct regions that could not communicate with one another for thousands of years. If technological progress is more rapid when there are more people to discover things, then larger regions should have experienced more rapid growth.

According to Kremer, that is exactly what happened. The most successful region of the world in 1500 (when Columbus re-established technological contact) comprised the 'Old World' civilizations of the large Eurasia-Africa region. Next in technological development were the Aztec and Mayan civilizations in the Americas, followed by the hunter-gatherers of Australia, and then the primitive people of Tasmania, who lacked even fire-making and most stone and bone tools.

The smallest isolated region was Flinders Island, a tiny island between Tasmania and Australia. With the smallest population, Flinders Island had the fewest opportunities for technological advance and, indeed, seemed to regress. Around 3000 B.C., human society on Flinders Island died out completely. A large population, Kremer concludes, is a prerequisite for technological advance.

At first sight this conclusion does seem to be at odds with casual empirical observation of the modern world: as we previously noted, in many rich, developed countries population growth has been only about 1 per cent per year in recent decades, while in many poor countries, such as those of sub-Saharan Africa, population growth is much higher. So why doesn't this higher population growth help these poor countries to grow, if Kremer's argument is right? The point is that Kremer was really analysing *world* economic growth, or rather, economic growth in isolated regions of the world. Nowadays, in a very poor country, it is unlikely that technological advances will be made that are not already known in developed countries; the problem is not lack of technological progress but difficulty in applying technology because of the scarcity of human capital and perhaps because of problems arising from political instability and corruption, as we discussed earlier. Moreover, because many talented people from less developed countries tend to emigrate to richer, developed countries where they may work, for example, as scientists or entrepreneurs – a phenomenon we referred to earlier as the *brain drain* – population growth in less developed countries may actually enhance economic growth in developed countries.

Quick Quiz Describe three ways in which a government policy maker can try to raise the growth in living standards in a society. Are there any drawbacks to these policies?

CONCLUSION: THE IMPORTANCE OF LONG-RUN GROWTH

In this chapter we have discussed what determines the standard of living in a nation and how policy makers can endeavour to raise the standard of living through policies that promote economic growth. Most of this chapter is summarized in one of the *Ten Principles of Economics:* a country's standard of living depends on its ability to produce goods and services. Policy makers who want to encourage growth in standards of living must aim to increase their nation's productive ability by encouraging rapid accumulation of the factors of production and ensuring that these factors are employed as effectively as possible.

Economists differ in their views of the role of government in promoting economic growth. At the very least, government can lend support to the invisible hand by maintaining property rights and political stability. More controversial is whether government should target and subsidize specific industries that might be especially important for technological progress. There is no doubt that these issues are among the most important in economics. The success of one generation's policy makers in learning and heeding the fundamental lessons about economic growth determines what kind of world the next generation will inherit.

SUMMARY

- Economic prosperity, as measured by GDP per person, varies substantially around the world. The average income in the world's richest countries is more than ten times that in the world's poorest countries. Because growth rates of real GDP also vary substantially, the relative positions of countries can change dramatically over time.
- The standard of living in an economy depends on the economy's ability to produce goods and services. Productivity, in turn, depends on the amounts of physical capital, human capital, natural resources and technological knowledge available to workers.
- Government policies can try to influence the economy's growth rate in many ways: by encouraging saving and investment, encouraging investment from abroad, fostering education, maintaining property rights and political stability, allowing free trade, promoting the research and development of new technologies, and controlling population growth.
- The accumulation of capital is subject to diminishing returns: the more capital an economy has, the less additional output the economy gets from an extra unit of capital. Because of diminishing returns, higher saving leads to higher growth for a period of time, but growth eventually slows down as the economy approaches a higher level of capital, productivity and income. Also because of diminishing returns, the return to capital is especially high in poor countries. Other things equal, these countries can grow faster because of the catch-up effect.

KEY CONCEPTS

physical capital, p. 531
natural resources, p. 532
technological knowledge, p. 532
diminishing returns, p. 536
catch-up effect, p. 537

QUESTIONS FOR REVIEW

1. What does the level of a nation's GDP measure? What does the growth rate of GDP measure? Would you rather live in a nation with a high level of GDP and a low growth rate, or in a nation with a low level of GDP and a high growth rate?
2. List and describe four determinants of productivity.
3. In what way is a university degree a form of capital?
4. Explain how higher saving leads to a higher standard of living. What might deter a policy maker from trying to raise the rate of saving?
5. Does a higher rate of saving lead to higher growth temporarily or indefinitely?
6. Why would removing a trade restriction, such as a tariff, lead to more rapid economic growth?
7. How does the rate of population growth influence the level of GDP per person?
8. Describe two ways in which the government can try to encourage advances in technological knowledge.

PROBLEMS AND APPLICATIONS

1. Most countries import substantial amounts of goods and services from other countries. Yet the chapter says that a nation can enjoy a high standard of living only if it can produce a large quantity of goods and services itself. Can you reconcile these two facts?
2. List the capital inputs necessary to produce each of the following.
   a. cars
   b. secondary education
   c. air travel
   d. fruit and vegetables.
3. UK income per person today is roughly four times what it was a century ago. Many other countries have also experienced significant growth over that period. What are some specific ways in which your standard of living is likely to differ from that of your great-grandparents?
4. The chapter discusses how employment in developed economies has declined relative to output in the agricultural sector. Can you think of another sector of the economy where the same phenomenon has occurred more recently? Would you consider the change in employment in this sector to represent a success or a failure from the standpoint of society as a whole?
5. Suppose that society decided to reduce consumption and increase investment.
   a. How would this change affect economic growth?
   b. What groups in society would benefit from this change? What groups might be hurt?
6. Societies choose what share of their resources to devote to consumption and what share to devote to investment. Some of these decisions involve private spending; others involve government spending.
   a. Describe some forms of private spending that represent consumption, and some forms that represent investment.
   b. Describe some forms of government spending that represent consumption, and some forms that represent investment.
7. What is the opportunity cost of investing in capital? Do you think a country can 'over-invest' in capital? What is

the opportunity cost of investing in human capital? Do you think a country can 'over-invest' in human capital? Explain.

8. Suppose that a car company owned entirely by South Korean citizens opens a new factory in the north of England.
   a. What sort of foreign investment would this represent?
   b. What would be the effect of this investment on UK GDP? Would the effect on UK GNP be larger or smaller?
9. In the 1980s Japanese investors made significant direct and portfolio investments in the United States. At the time, many Americans were unhappy that this investment was occurring.
   a. In what way was it better for the United States to receive this Japanese investment than not to receive it?
   b. In what way would it have been better still for the US economy if Americans had done this investment?
10. In the countries of South Asia in 1992, only 56 young women were enrolled in secondary school for every 100 young men. Describe several ways in which greater educational opportunities for young women could lead to faster economic growth in these countries.
11. International data show a positive correlation between political stability and economic growth.
    a. Through what mechanism could political stability lead to strong economic growth?
    b. Through what mechanism could strong economic growth lead to political stability?

For further resources, visit
www.cengage.co.uk/mankiw_taylor2

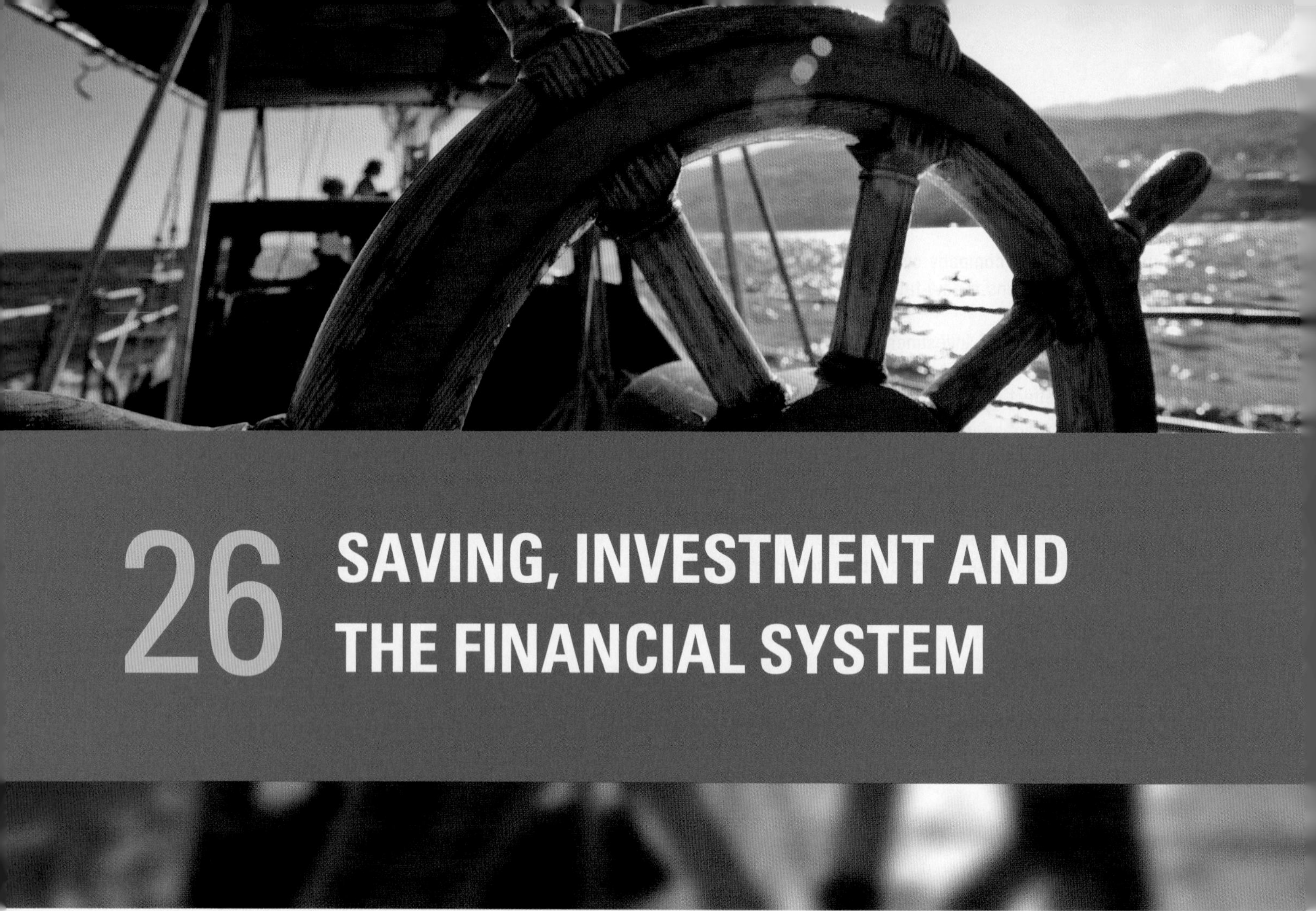

26 SAVING, INVESTMENT AND THE FINANCIAL SYSTEM

Imagine that you have just graduated from university (with a degree in economics, of course) and you decide to start your own business – an economic forecasting firm. Before you make any money selling your forecasts, you have to incur substantial costs to set up your business. You have to buy computers with which to make your forecasts, as well as desks, chairs and filing cabinets to furnish your new office. Each of these items is a type of capital that your firm will use to produce and sell its services.

How do you obtain the funds to invest in these capital goods? Perhaps you are able to pay for them out of your past savings. More likely, however, like most entrepreneurs, you do not have enough money of your own to finance the start of your business. As a result, you have to get the money you need from other sources.

There are various ways for you to finance these capital investments. You could borrow the money, perhaps from a bank or from a friend or relative. In this case, you would promise not only to return the money at a later date but also to pay interest for the use of the money. Alternatively, you could convince someone to provide the money you need for your business in exchange for a share of your future profits, whatever they might happen to be. In either case, your investment in computers and office equipment is being financed by someone else's saving.

financial system
the group of institutions in the economy that help to match one person's saving with another person's investment

The **financial system** consists of those institutions in the economy that help to match one person's saving with another person's investment. As we discussed in the previous chapter, saving and investment are key ingredients to long-run economic growth: when a country saves a large portion of its GDP, more resources are available for investment in capital, and higher capital raises a country's productivity and living standard. The previous chapter, however, did not explain how the economy coordinates saving and investment. At any time, some people want to save some of their income for the future, and others want to borrow in order to finance investments in new and growing businesses. What brings these two groups of people together? (Not physically of course!) What ensures that the supply of funds from those who want to save balances the demand for funds from those who want to invest?

This chapter examines how the financial system works. First, we discuss the large variety of institutions that make up the financial system. Secondly, we discuss the relationship between the financial system and some key macroeconomic variables – notably saving and investment. Thirdly, we develop a model of the supply and demand for funds in financial markets. In the model, the interest rate is the price that adjusts to balance supply and demand. The model shows how various government policies affect the interest rate and, thereby, society's allocation of scarce resources.

FINANCIAL INSTITUTIONS IN THE ECONOMY

At the broadest level, the financial system moves the economy's scarce resources from savers (people who spend less than they earn) to borrowers (people who spend more than they earn). Savers save for various reasons – to help put a child through university in several years or to retire comfortably in several decades. Similarly, borrowers borrow for various reasons – to buy a house in which to live or to start a business with which to make a living. Savers supply their money to the financial system with the expectation that they will get it back with interest at a later date. Borrowers demand money from the financial system with the knowledge that they will be required to pay it back with interest at a later date.

The financial system is made up of various financial institutions that help coordinate savers and borrowers. As a prelude to analysing the economic forces that drive the financial system, let's discuss the most important of these institutions. Financial institutions can be grouped into two categories – financial markets and financial intermediaries. We consider each category in turn.

Financial Markets

Financial markets are the institutions through which a person who wants to save can directly supply funds to a person who wants to borrow. Two of the most important financial markets in advanced economies are the bond market and the stock market.

financial markets
financial institutions through which savers can directly provide funds to borrowers

The Bond Market When BP, the oil company, wants to borrow to finance a major new oil exploration project, it can borrow directly from the public. It does this by selling bonds. A **bond** is a certificate of indebtedness that specifies the obligations of the borrower to the holder of the bond. Put simply, a bond is an IOU. It identifies the time at which the loan will be repaid, called the *date of maturity*, and the rate of interest that will be paid periodically (called the *coupon*) until the loan matures. The buyer of a bond gives his or her money to BP in exchange for this promise of interest and eventual repayment of the amount borrowed (called the *principal*). The buyer can hold the bond until maturity or can sell the bond at an earlier date to someone else.

bond
a certificate of indebtedness

There are literally millions of bonds traded in advanced economies. When large corporations or the national government, or even local governments need to borrow in order to finance the purchase of a new factory, a new jet fighter or a new school, they often do so by issuing bonds. If you look at the *Financial Times* or the business section of any national newspaper, you will find a listing of the prices and interest rates on some of the most important bond issues. Although these bonds differ in many ways, two characteristics of bonds are most important.

The first characteristic is a bond's *term* – the length of time until the bond matures. Some bonds have short terms, such as a few months, while others have terms as long as 30 years. (The British government has even issued a bond that never matures, called a *perpetuity*. This bond pays interest forever, but the principal is never repaid.) The interest rate on a bond depends, in part, on its term. Long-term bonds are riskier than short-term bonds because holders of long-term bonds have to wait longer for repayment of principal. If a holder of a long-term bond needs his money earlier than the distant date of maturity, he has no choice but to sell the bond to someone else, perhaps at a reduced price. To compensate for this risk, long-term bonds usually (but not always) pay higher interest rates than short-term bonds.

The second important characteristic of a bond is its *credit risk* – the probability that the borrower will fail to pay some of the interest or principal. Such a failure to pay is called a *default*. Borrowers can (and sometimes do) default on their loans by declaring bankruptcy. When bond buyers perceive that the probability of default is high, they demand a higher interest rate to compensate them for this risk. Some government bonds are considered a safe credit risk, such as those from Germany, for example, and tend to pay low interest rates. UK government bonds have come to be referred to as *gilt-edged* bonds, or more simply as *gilts*, reflecting that, in terms of credit risk, they are 'as good as gold' (early bond certificates had a gold edge – hence the term 'gilt edged'). In contrast, financially shaky corporations raise money by issuing *junk bonds*, which pay very high interest rates; in recent years some countries' debt has been graded as 'junk'. Buyers of bonds can judge credit risk by checking with various private agencies, such as Standard & Poor's, which rate the credit risk of different bonds. Sometimes, these bonds are referred to euphemistically but less graphically as *below investment grade bonds*.

stock (or share or equity)
a claim to partial ownership in a firm

The Stock Market Another way for BP to raise funds for its oil exploration project is to sell stock in the company. **Stock** represents ownership in a firm and is, therefore, a claim to the profits that the firm makes. For example, if BP sells a total of 1000000 shares of stock, then each share represents ownership of 1/1000000 of the business. A stock is also commonly referred to as a *share* or as an *equity*. In this book, we'll use the terms 'share' and 'stock' (and 'stockholder' and 'shareholder') more or less interchangeably.

The sale of stock to raise money is called *equity finance*, whereas the sale of bonds is called *debt finance*. Although corporations use both equity and debt finance to raise money for new investments, stocks and bonds are very different. The owner of BP shares is a part owner of BP; the owner of a BP bond is a creditor of the corporation. If BP is very profitable, the shareholders enjoy the benefits of these profits, whereas the bondholders get only the interest on their bonds. And if BP runs into financial difficulty, the bondholders are paid what they are due before shareholders receive anything at all. Compared to bonds, stocks offer the holder both higher risk and potentially higher return.

As we noted just now, stocks are also called shares or equities. In the UK bonds are also, confusingly, referred to as 'stock'. This term for government bonds has been in use in England since the late 17th century and is well established. In order to avoid confusion, however, the term is often qualified as *government stock* or *gilt-edged stock*. In general, though, despite the confusing use of language, the term *stock* refers to ownership of a firm.

After a corporation issues stock by selling shares to the public, these shares trade among stockholders on organized stock exchanges. In these transactions, the corporation itself receives no money when its stock changes hands. Most of the world's countries have their own stock exchanges on which the shares of national companies trade.

The prices at which shares trade on stock exchanges are determined by the supply and demand for the stock in these companies. Because stock represents ownership in a corporation, the demand for a stock (and thus its price) reflects people's perception of the corporation's future profitability. When people become optimistic about a company's future, they raise their demand for its stock and thereby bid up the price of a share of stock. Conversely, when people come to expect a company to have little profit or even losses, the price of a share falls.

Various stock indices are available to monitor the overall level of stock prices for any particular stock market. A *stock index* is computed as an average of a group of share prices. Perhaps the most famous stock index is the Dow Jones Industrial Average, which has been computed regularly for the New York Stock Exchange since 1896. It is now based on the prices of the shares of 30 major US companies. Another major index based on a relatively small number of share prices is the Financial Times Stock Exchange (FTSE) 100 Index, which is based on the top 100 companies (according to the total value of their shares) listed on the London Stock Exchange (LSE), while the FTSE All-Share Index is based on all companies listed on the LSE. Indices of prices on the Frankfurt stock market, based on 30 and 100 companies respectively, are the DAX 30 and DAX 100. The NIKKEI 225 (or just plain NIKKEI Index) is based on the largest 225 companies, in terms of market value of shares, traded on the Tokyo Stock Exchange.

Because share prices reflect expected profitability, stock indices are watched closely as possible indicators of future economic conditions.

Financial Intermediaries

Financial intermediaries are financial institutions through which savers can indirectly provide funds to borrowers. The term *intermediary* reflects the role of these institutions in standing between savers and borrowers. Here we consider two of the most important financial intermediaries – banks and investment funds.

financial intermediaries
financial institutions through which savers can indirectly provide funds to borrowers

Banks If the owner of a small supermarket wants to finance an expansion of his business, he probably takes a strategy quite different from BP. Unlike BP, a small businessman would find it difficult to raise funds in the bond and stock markets. Most buyers of stocks and bonds prefer to buy those issued by larger, more familiar companies. The small businessman, therefore, most likely finances his business expansion with a loan from a bank.

Banks are the financial intermediaries with which people are most familiar. A primary function of banks is to take in deposits from people who want to save and use these deposits to make loans to people who want to borrow. Banks pay depositors interest on their deposits and charge borrowers slightly higher interest on their loans. The difference between these rates of interest covers the banks' costs and returns some profit to the owners of the banks.

Besides being financial intermediaries, banks play a second important role in the economy: they facilitate purchases of goods and services by allowing people to write cheques against their deposits, or to use debit cards to transfer money

FYI

How To Read the Newspaper's Stock Market Pages

Many quality daily newspapers include stock market tables, which contain information about recent trading in the shares of several thousand companies. The *Financial Times*, for example, lists detailed information about shares traded on the London Stock Exchange. Here is the kind of information these tables usually provide:

- *Price.* The single most important piece of information about a stock is the price of a share. This is usually the 'last' or 'closing' price, i.e. the price of the last transaction that occurred before the stock exchange closed the previous day. The tables will also tell you the change in the closing price from the closing price of the previous trading day. Many newspapers also give the 'high' and 'low' prices over a given period – the *Financial Times*, for example, lists the highest and lowest closing prices over the previous 52 weeks.
- *Yield.* Corporations pay out some of their profits to their stockholders; this amount is called the dividend. (Profits not paid out are called *retained earnings* and are used by the corporation for additional investment.) Expressing the dividend as a percentage of the stock price gives the dividend yield, often referred to simply as the yield.
- *Price earnings ratio.* A corporation's earnings, or profit, is the amount of revenue it receives for the sale of its products minus its costs of production as measured by its accountants. *Earnings per share* is the company's total earnings divided by the number of shares outstanding. Companies use some of their earnings to pay dividends to shareholders; the rest is kept in the firm to make new investments. The price earnings ratio, often called the *P/E* or *P/E* ratio, is the price of a corporation's stock divided by the amount the corporation earned per share over the past year. Historically, the typical price earnings ratio is about 15. A higher P/E indicates that a corporation's stock is expensive relative to its recent earnings; this might indicate either that people expect earnings to rise in the future or that the stock is overvalued. Conversely, a lower P/E indicates that a corporation's stock is cheap relative to its recent earnings; this might indicate either that people expect earnings to fall or that the stock is undervalued. Note that a high P/E does not mean that you are guaranteed to make money by buying the stock: the higher expected future earnings have already been factored into the higher price (which is why the P/E is high).
- *Volume.* You will usually also find the number of shares sold during the past day of trading, rounded to the nearest thousand. This figure is called the *daily volume* or just plain *volume*.

Below we have shown some of this information for three companies whose shares are traded on the London Stock Exchange – HMV, Unilever and Tesco – as it appeared in the *Financial Times* on Wednesday 7 April 2010. Shares in HMV, for example, closed at 86.20 pence each on the previous trading day (Tuesday 6 April), representing a rise in the price of 1.7 pence over the previous closing price (i.e. on Monday 5 April). The highest closing price of HMV shares over the previous 52 weeks was 159.50 pence, and the lowest 67.60 pence. Expressed as a percentage of the closing price, the dividend last paid on the shares was equal to a yield of 8.6 per cent. HMV's P/E was 7.4, indicating that people probably expect future earnings to fall. This is in contrast to Unilever's P/E of 20.2, which suggests that people expect future earnings to rise for this company. Trading in HMV was relatively light, with 2.4 million shares traded, compared for example to over 33 million shares traded in Tesco.

Why does the newspaper report all these data every day? Many people who invest their savings in stock follow these numbers closely when deciding which shares to buy and sell. In contrast, other shareholders follow a buy-and-hold strategy: they buy the stock of well-run companies, hold it for long periods of time, and do not respond to the daily fluctuations reported in the paper. Whatever their strategy, however, investors will generally want to know whether their share prices have been rising (making them richer) or falling (making them poorer).

			52-Week				
Stock	Price	Change	High	Low	Yield	P/E	Volume (000's)
HMV	86.20	+1.70	159.50	67.60	8.6	7.4	2 443
Tesco	440	+1.50	442.45	321	2.8	18.4	33 331
Unilever	£19.57	+0.18	£20.24	£12.46	3.5	20.2	5 561

Source: *Financial Times*, Wednesday April 7th 2010

electronically from their account to the account of the person or corporation they are buying something from. In other words, banks help create a special asset that people can use as a *medium of exchange.* A medium of exchange is an item that people can easily use to engage in transactions. A bank's role in providing a medium of exchange distinguishes it from many other financial institutions. Stocks and bonds, like bank deposits, are a possible *store of value* for the wealth that people have accumulated in past saving, but access to this wealth is not as easy, cheap and immediate as just writing a cheque or swiping a debit card. For now, we ignore this second role of banks, but we will return to it when we discuss the monetary system later in the book.

Investment Funds A financial intermediary of increasing importance is the investment fund. An **investment fund** is an institution that sells shares to the public and uses the proceeds to buy a selection, or *portfolio,* of various types of shares, bonds, or both shares and bonds. The shareholder of the investment fund accepts all the risk and return associated with the portfolio. If the value of the portfolio rises, the shareholder benefits; if the value of the portfolio falls, the shareholder suffers the loss.

investment fund
an institution that sells shares to the public and uses the proceeds to buy a portfolio of stocks and bonds

The primary advantage of investment funds is that they allow people with small amounts of money to diversify. Buyers of shares and bonds are well advised to heed the adage, 'Don't put all your eggs in one basket.' Because the value of any single stock or bond is tied to the fortunes of one company, holding a single kind of stock or bond is very risky. By contrast, people who hold a diverse portfolio of shares and bonds face less risk because they have only a small stake in each company. Investment funds make this diversification easy. With only a few hundred euros, a person can buy shares in an investment fund and, indirectly, become the part owner or creditor of hundreds of major companies. For this service, the company operating the investment fund charges shareholders a fee, usually between 0.5 and 2.0 per cent of assets each year. Closely related to investment funds are unit trusts, the difference being that when people put money into a unit trust, more 'units' or shares are issued, whereas the only way to buy into an investment fund is to buy existing shares in the fund. For this reason, unit trusts are sometimes referred to as 'open-ended'.

A second advantage claimed by investment fund companies is that investment funds give ordinary people access to the skills of professional money managers. The managers of most investment funds pay close attention to the developments and prospects of the companies in which they buy stock. These managers buy the stock of those companies that they view as having a profitable future and sell the stock of companies with less promising prospects. This professional management, it is argued, should increase the return that investors in investment funds earn on their savings.

"That was when the stock market heard you were retiring, sir."

Financial economists, however, are often sceptical of this second argument. With thousands of money managers paying close attention to each company's prospects, the price of a company's stock is usually a good reflection of the company's true value. As a result, it is hard to 'beat the market' by buying good stocks and selling bad ones. In fact, investment funds called *index funds or tracker trusts* which buy all (or the large majority of) the stocks in a given stock index, perform somewhat better on average than investment funds that take advantage of active management by professional money managers. The explanation for the superior performance of tracker trusts is that they keep costs low by buying and selling very rarely and by not having to pay the salaries of the professional money managers.

Summing Up

An advanced economy contains a large variety of financial institutions. In addition to the bond market, the stock market, banks and investment funds, there are also pension funds, insurance companies and – notably in the UK and the USA – even the local pawnbroker's shop: places where people who might be deemed bad credit risks can borrow money and leave some valuable item such as a watch or a piece of jewellery as security in case the loan is not repaid. Clearly, these institutions differ in many ways. When analysing the macroeconomic role of the financial system, however, it is more important to keep in mind the similarity of these institutions than the differences. These financial institutions all serve the same goal – directing the resources of savers into the hands of borrowers.

Quick Quiz What is stock? What is a bond? How are they different? How are they similar?

credit default swaps (CDS)
a means by which a bondholder can insure against the risk of default

FYI

The financial crisis of 2007–09 brought to light new financial instruments traded in the financial system that may not have been familiar to many ordinary people; indeed, there were some senior bankers who were accused of not fully understanding what they were trading! This FYI gives a brief introduction to two of the main instruments: credit default swaps and collateralized debt obligations.

Credit Default Swaps (CDS)

Whenever a bond is sold there is an associated risk attached to it. In the case of bonds backed by a pool of mortgage debt, the risk is that the mortgage payer defaults on the payment in some way. CDS are a means of insuring against the risk involved. To see how this works let us take an example. Assume a bank has bought a bond in an asset-backed security (in reality of course it might be many bonds) worth \$5 million. The bond has a principal, therefore, of \$5 million. The coupon payment (the interest on the bond) is 10 per cent. The bond is backed by the stream of cash flows being paid by mortgage holders – the underlying asset to the bond. The bondholder knows that there is a risk that some mortgage holders might default and as a result the bond return might also be in default – i.e. it does not pay the coupon or possibly the principal. If the mortgage holders all meet their obligations and pay the money back (the principal) the bank will have earned interest for as long as it held the bond. If the bond was a 10-year bond with a coupon of 10 per cent then the bondholder would have earned a 10 per cent return on the bond for 10 years (\$500 000 per year for 10 years).

The bondholder can go to an insurance company (which could also be another bank or a hedge fund) and take out a policy on the risk. The bank seeking to insure the risk is referred to as the *protection buyer* and the insurance company or other financial institution, the *protection seller*. The policy will agree to restore the bondholder to their original position should the bond default. The bondholder pays the insurance company premiums over the life of the policy, let us assume this is \$500 000 a year over ten years, and in return the insurance company would agree to pay the bondholder \$5 million if the bond defaults in some way during the period of the agreement.

What the bondholder has done is to swap the risk in the bond with the insurance company. In the event of the bond defaulting then the protection seller pays out to the protection buyer. These CDS could also be traded and in many cases the protection buyer might take out a number of such hedges against its risk.

If the bond was subject to default this would trigger a payment called a *credit event*. If a credit event occurs then there are two ways in which the contract could be closed. One was through a physical settlement. In this case the protection buyer would deliver the bond to the seller who would give the buyer the value of the bond, called par. The CDS market expanded rapidly throughout the 'noughties' leading to multiple trading. The holder of the CDS might not actually own the bond in question and so this method of settlement clearly does not work. The growth in the market meant that the number of contracts far outweighed the number of bonds on which they were based. To settle the claims of contract holders through physical means would not be possible. As a consequence, protection sellers undertook to settle the contract claim through cash settlement where the positions were cleared by the transfer of cash.

The protection seller would also have to put up some form of collateral to cover its exposure to the possible default as part of the CDS agreement. The size of the exposure in the example above would be $5 million. This would be part of the contract between the insurance seller and the buyer. The amount of the collateral required would depend on the market value of the bond and the credit rating of the protection seller. The market value of the bond can change because the bondholder can sell their bond.

If a bond associated with a mortgage pool is deemed a higher risk then it may become more difficult to sell it and its price would fall. At a lower price the risk involved for the protection buyer is higher and they can exercise a call (known as a collateral call) on the protection seller to increase the collateral supplied. If, for example, the price of the bond in the example above fell to 40 cents in the dollar, the insurance company would have to find 0.60 x $500000 in additional collateral ($3 million). This process is known as collateral calls. Equally, if the rating of the protection seller is downgraded then the risk to the protection buyer also rises – the seller may be not be able to meet its obligations. Once again, the protection buyer can call the seller to ask for more collateral to be provided. The insurance company would then have to find more funds to top up the collateral it has to provide to reflect the lower value of the bond.

If the seller was unable to meet its obligations at least the buyer would have some protection in the form of the collateral supplied by the seller. If the bond runs its course and matures without any credit event then the collateral is returned to the seller (who also, remember, receives premiums from the buyer). CDS represent sound business principles when the risk of default is very low, which was the case when they were first developed in the late 1990s and when the bonds being insured were corporate bonds with a low risk attached to them. The expansion of CDS presented a different challenge to the financial markets when the housing market collapse occurred from around 2007.

Collateralized Debt Obligations

CDOs are pools of asset-backed securities which are dependent on the value of the asset that backs them up and the stream of income that flows from these assets. Essentially CDOs work in the following way. In setting up a CDO, a manager encourages investors to buy bonds, the funds of which are used to buy pools of debt – mortgage debt. This debt is split and rated according to its risk into tranches, low-risk tranches attract low interest rates whilst the riskier tranches attract higher interest rates. Under *'normal'* circumstances (the relevance of the emphasis will become clear later) the payments by mortgage holders provide sufficient income each month to pay the interest to each of the tranche holders. There is a risk, of course, that some of the mortgage holders in the initial debt could default on payment but historical data enables investors to have some idea of what this risk will be. In the event of default, some of the riskier tranches may not get paid – that is the risk they take and why they get a higher interest rate.

The development of new approaches to risk management enabled these structures to be extended further into second and third 'waves' of securitized debt. Asset managers could buy particular tranches of debt (backed, remember by mortgages ultimately) and mix them with other types of debt and sell them on to other investors. Investors in these higher risk tranches are assured by the ratings on the investment. Calculation of default correlations during this time was relatively low but when times were not *'normal'* the correlations could start to become far more unstable. Problems for CDOs began when holders of sub-prime mortgages began to default on payments. The sub-prime market offered mortgage opportunities to those not traditionally seen as being part of the market and was part of the way in which banks and other lenders sought to increase their lending. Individuals seen as being a relatively low credit risk for mortgage lending were known as the prime market; the term is said to have derived from analogy with the best cuts of meat from an animal. It followed that there was a sub-prime group for whom access to mortgages was altogether more difficult. Some of these people had credit histories that were very poor, some did not have jobs, but in an atmosphere of risk seeking and changed priorities this group provided lenders with a market opportunity because they were willing to pay high rates of interest on their mortgages. At first these defaults might have been 'pin pricks' in the structure but as the number increased the payments to the first tranches began to reduce. Those at the top of the ratings list may have still got paid but the riskier lower tranches began to see their payments dry up. In turn, the asset-backed securities sold in the second and subsequent 'waves' began to see their payments cease and as the sub-prime problem became worse it became clear that it was unlikely that these subsequent 'waves' would not be paid back and were thus worthless. Holders of this debt (including banks, governments and local government around the world) found that they had to write off large assets. The term 'toxic assets' became familiar to many who may never have thought they were affected by high finance. These were mortgage-backed securities and other debt (such as bonds) that are not able to be repaid in many cases because the value of the assets against which they are secured have fallen significantly.

FYI

Dark Pools

Despite having a rather sinister sounding name, dark pools are just an electronic network which puts buyers of shares in touch with sellers. However, the nature of dark pools has raised some concerns and is currently being looked at by the Securities and Exchange Commission (SEC) in the United States. Dark pools are not widespread in the UK and Europe at the time of writing, but are likely to become more significant in the future.

How do dark pools work? Under normal circumstances, trades in shares are carried out via a number of exchanges such as the London and New York stock exchanges. Traders on those exchanges can see who is doing the buying and who is doing the selling. Any transaction that goes through, therefore, can affect the market and traders will be able to amend their positions accordingly. Dark pools allow trades to be carried out anonymously so the trade can go through but no one knows – crucially at the time of the trade – who is doing the buying and selling. Dark pools tend to be used for trades where significant volumes of shares are transacted. The following is an outline of how it works.

Assume an institutional investor, such as a pension fund or insurance company, has $1 billion worth of shares in ExxonMobil that it wants to sell. It knows that if it attempts to trade this amount it is likely to affect the market. Typically, this sort of volume would have to be broken up and sold in chunks. If the price of ExxonMobil shares was currently $500 each, then as the sale progresses, the insurance company would end up with lower prices for the latter chunks of shares than the first lots. The average price it gains from the sale would, therefore, be less than $500 each.

The price would fall because the supply of ExxonMobil shares would be rising, traders would see the trades going through and adjust their positions accordingly. If the insurance company carried out the trade via a dark pool it places the shares into an electronic exchange. In the pool there are buyers and sellers all looking for trades, but anonymously. The use of algorithms to improve the efficiency of the trades in dark pools is common. The algorithm is programmed to search for buyers who want to purchase $1 billion of ExxonMobil shares, for example, and matches the two together. At this point in the trade no-one knows who the traders are. Once the trade is completed then it is announced. The announcement may, or may not, have an effect on the market. The advantage for the pension fund or insurance company is that it completes the trade for the volume of shares it wants to deal and the use of dark pools prevents the market reacting to the sale at the time it is happening and thus affecting the price the seller gets.

There has been some criticism of dark pools mainly because of two key issues. It is feared that dark pools may take too much trade away from traditional exchanges. As they develop, more trading will be conducted in secret and in some cases, even though the trades are announced, the identity of the trader is not revealed. Dark pools may discriminate against individual investors who can be affected by the price changes that result from the activity which they could not foresee because of the very nature of the anonymous transactions.

Despite the criticism, proponents of dark pools point to the efficiency with which they operate and the fact that they help liquidity in the markets. The bank Goldman Sachs has been criticized for its use of dark pools but has defended the practice and suggested that enhanced transparency post-trade is an obvious way to offset concern about secrecy.

SAVING AND INVESTMENT IN THE NATIONAL INCOME ACCOUNTS

Events that occur within the financial system are central to understanding developments in the overall economy. As we have just seen, the institutions that make up this system – the bond market, the stock market, banks and investment funds – have the role of coordinating the economy's saving and investment. And as we saw in the previous chapter, saving and investment are important determinants of long-run growth in GDP and living standards. As a result, macroeconomists need to understand how financial markets work and how various events and policies affect them.

As a starting point for an analysis of financial markets, we discuss in this section the key macroeconomic variables that measure activity in these markets. Our emphasis here is not on behaviour but on accounting. *Accounting* refers to how various numbers are defined and added up. A personal accountant might help an individual add up his income and expenses. A national income accountant does the same thing for the economy as a whole. The national income accounts include, in particular, GDP and the many related statistics.

The rules of national income accounting include several important identities. Recall that an *identity* is an equation that must be true because of the way the variables in the equation are defined. Identities are useful to keep in mind, for they clarify how different variables are related to one another. Here we consider some accounting identities that shed light on the macroeconomic role of financial markets.

Some Important Identities

Recall that gross domestic product (GDP) is both total income in an economy and the total expenditure on the economy's output of goods and services. GDP (denoted as Y) is divided into four components of expenditure: consumption (C), investment (I), government purchases (G), and net exports (NX). We write:

$$Y = C + I + G + NX$$

This equation is an identity because every euro of expenditure that shows up on the left-hand side also shows up in one of the four components on the right-hand side. Because of the way each of the variables is defined and measured, this equation must always hold. Sometimes we make this clear by using an identity sign, with three bars, instead of the usual equals sign with two bars:

$$Y \equiv C + I + G + NX$$

In general, though, we can use the usual equality sign.

In this chapter, we simplify our analysis by assuming that the economy we are examining is closed. A *closed economy* is one that does not interact with other economies. In particular, a closed economy does not engage in international trade in goods and services, nor does it engage in international borrowing and lending. Of course, actual economies are *open economies* – that is, they interact with other economies around the world. Nevertheless, assuming a closed economy is a useful simplification with which we can learn some lessons that apply to all economies. Moreover, this assumption applies perfectly to the world economy (since interplanetary trade is not yet common).

Because a closed economy does not engage in international trade, imports and exports are exactly zero. Therefore, net exports (NX) are also zero. In this case, we can write:

$$Y = C + I + G$$

This equation states that GDP is the sum of consumption, investment and government purchases. Each unit of output sold in a closed economy is consumed, invested or bought by the government.

To see what this identity can tell us about financial markets, subtract C and G from both sides of this equation. We obtain:

$$Y - C - G = I$$

The left-hand side of this equation ($Y - C - G$) is the total income in the economy that remains after paying for consumption and government purchases: this

national saving (saving) the total income in the economy that remains after paying for consumption and government purchases

amount is called **national saving**, or just saving, and is denoted S. Substituting S for $Y - C - G$, we can write the last equation as:

$$S = I$$

This equation states that saving equals investment.

To understand the meaning of national saving, it is helpful to manipulate the definition a bit more. Let T denote the amount that the government collects from households in taxes minus the amount it pays back to households in the form of transfer payments (such as social security payments). We can then write national saving in either of two ways:

$$S = Y - C - G$$

or

$$S = (Y - T - C) + (T - G)$$

These equations are the same, because the two Ts in the second equation cancel each other, but each reveals a different way of thinking about national saving. In particular, the second equation separates national saving into two pieces: private saving $(Y - T - C)$ and public saving $(T - G)$.

private saving the income that households have left after paying for taxes and consumption

public saving the tax revenue that the government has left after paying for its spending

Consider each of these two pieces. **Private saving** is the amount of income that households have left after paying their taxes and paying for their consumption. In particular, because households receive income of Y, pay taxes of T, and spend C on consumption, private saving is $Y - T - C$. **Public saving** is the amount of tax revenue that the government has left after paying for its spending. The government receives T in tax revenue and spends G on goods and services. If T exceeds G, the government runs a budget surplus because it receives more money than it spends. This surplus of $T - G$ represents public saving. If the government spends more than it receives in tax revenue, then G is larger than T. In this case, the government runs a budget deficit, and public saving $T - G$ is a negative number.

Now consider how these accounting identities are related to financial markets. The equation $S = I$ reveals an important fact: for the economy as a whole, saving must be equal to investment. Yet this fact raises some important questions: what mechanisms lie behind this identity? What coordinates those people who are deciding how much to save and those people who are deciding how much to invest? The answer is the financial system. The bond market, the stock market, banks, investment funds, and other financial markets and intermediaries stand between the two sides of the $S = I$ equation. They take in the nation's saving and direct it to the nation's investment.

The Meaning of Saving and Investment

The terms *saving* and *investment* can sometimes be confusing. Most people use these terms casually and sometimes interchangeably. In contrast, the macroeconomists who put together the national income accounts use these terms carefully and distinctly.

Consider an example. Suppose that Rutvij earns more than he spends and deposits his unspent income in a bank or uses it to buy a bond or some stock from a corporation. Because Rutvij's income exceeds his consumption, he adds to the nation's saving. Rutvij might think of himself as 'investing' his money, but a macroeconomist would call Rutvij's act saving rather than investment.

In the language of macroeconomics, investment refers to the purchase of new capital, such as equipment or buildings. When Gerd borrows from the bank to build himself a new house, he adds to the nation's investment. Similarly, when the Schmidt Corporation issues some new shares and uses the proceeds to build a new brass doorknocker factory, it also adds to the nation's investment.

Although the accounting identity $S = I$ shows that saving and investment are equal for the economy as a whole, this does not have to be true for every individual household or firm. Rutvij's saving can be greater than his investment, and he can deposit the excess in a bank. Gerd's saving can be less than his investment, and he can borrow the shortfall from a bank. Banks and other financial institutions make these individual differences between saving and investment possible by allowing one person's saving to finance another person's investment.

Quick Quiz Define private saving, public saving, national saving and investment. How are they related?

THE MARKET FOR LOANABLE FUNDS

Having discussed some of the important financial institutions in the economy and the macroeconomic role of these institutions, we are ready to build a model of financial markets. Our purpose in building this model is to explain how financial markets coordinate the economy's saving and investment. The model also gives us a tool with which we can analyse various government policies that influence saving and investment.

To keep things simple, we assume that the economy has only one financial market, called the **market for loanable funds**. All savers go to this market to deposit their saving, and all borrowers go to this market to get their loans. Thus, the term *loanable funds* refers to all income that people have chosen to save and lend out, rather than use for their own consumption. In the market for loanable funds, there is one interest rate, which is both the return to saving and the cost of borrowing.

market for loanable funds
the market in which those who want to save supply funds and those who want to borrow to invest demand funds

The assumption of a single financial market, of course, is not literally true. As we have seen, the economy has many types of financial institutions. But, as we discussed in Chapter 2, the art in building an economic model is simplifying the world in order to explain it. For our purposes here, we can ignore the diversity of financial institutions and assume that the economy has a single financial market.

Supply and Demand for Loanable Funds

The economy's market for loanable funds, like other markets in the economy, is governed by supply and demand. To understand how the market for loanable funds operates, therefore, we first look at the sources of supply and demand in that market.

The supply of loanable funds comes from those people who have some extra income they want to save and lend out. This lending can occur directly, such as when a household buys a bond from a firm, or it can occur indirectly, such as when a household makes a deposit in a bank, which in turn uses the funds to make loans. In both cases, saving is the source of the supply of loanable funds.

The demand for loanable funds comes from households and firms who wish to borrow to make investments. This demand includes families taking out mortgages

FIGURE 26.1

The Market for Loanable Funds

The interest rate in the economy adjusts to balance the supply and demand for loanable funds. The supply of loanable funds comes from national saving, including both private saving and public saving. The demand for loanable funds comes from firms and households that want to borrow for purposes of investment. Here the equilibrium interest rate is 5 per cent, and €500 billion of loanable funds are supplied and demanded.

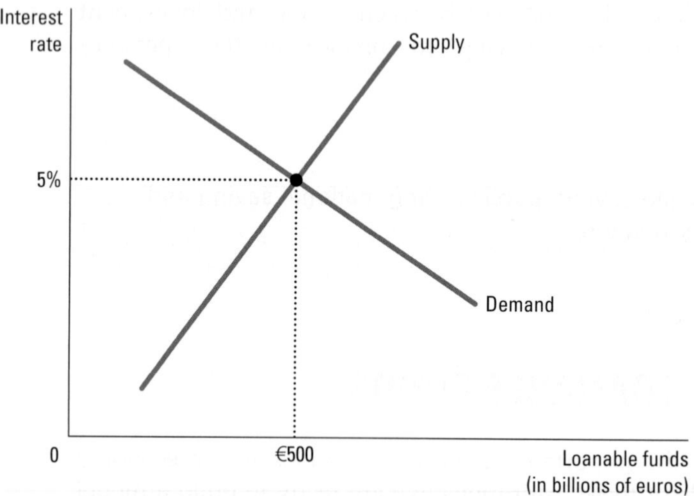

to buy homes. It also includes firms borrowing to buy new equipment or build factories. In both cases, investment is the source of the demand for loanable funds.

The interest rate is the price of a loan. It represents the amount that borrowers pay for loans and the amount that lenders receive on their saving. Because a high interest rate makes borrowing more expensive, the quantity of loanable funds demanded falls as the interest rate rises. Similarly, because a high interest rate makes saving more attractive, the quantity of loanable funds supplied rises as the interest rate rises. In other words, the demand curve for loanable funds slopes downward, and the supply curve for loanable funds slopes upward.

Figure 26.1 shows the interest rate that balances the supply and demand for loanable funds. In the equilibrium shown, the interest rate is 5 per cent, and the quantity of loanable funds demanded and the quantity of loanable funds supplied both equal €500 billion.

The adjustment of the interest rate to the equilibrium level occurs for the usual reasons. If the interest rate was lower than the equilibrium level, the quantity of loanable funds supplied would be less than the quantity of loanable funds demanded. The resulting shortage of loanable funds would encourage lenders to raise the interest rate they charge. A higher interest rate would encourage saving (thereby increasing the quantity of loanable funds supplied) and discourage borrowing for investment (thereby decreasing the quantity of loanable funds demanded). Conversely, if the interest rate was higher than the equilibrium level, the quantity of loanable funds supplied would exceed the quantity of loanable funds demanded. As lenders competed for the scarce borrowers, interest rates would be driven down. In this way, the interest rate approaches the equilibrium level at which the supply and demand for loanable funds exactly balance.

Recall that economists distinguish between the real interest rate and the nominal interest rate. The nominal interest rate is the interest rate as usually reported – the monetary return to saving and cost of borrowing. The real interest rate is the nominal interest rate corrected for inflation; it equals the nominal interest rate minus the inflation rate. Because inflation erodes the value of money over time, the real interest rate more accurately reflects the real return to saving and cost of borrowing. Therefore, the supply and demand for loanable funds depend on the real (rather than nominal) interest rate, and the equilibrium in Figure 26.1 should be interpreted as determining the real interest rate in the economy. For the rest of this chapter, when you see the term *interest rate*, you should remember that we are talking about the real interest rate.

This model of the supply and demand for loanable funds shows that financial markets work much like other markets in the economy. In the market for milk, for instance, the price of milk adjusts so that the quantity of milk supplied balances the quantity of milk demanded. In this way, the invisible hand coordinates the behaviour of dairy farmers and the behaviour of milk drinkers. Once we realize that saving represents the supply of loanable funds and investment represents the demand, we can see how the invisible hand coordinates saving and investment. When the interest rate adjusts to balance supply and demand in the market for loanable funds, it coordinates the behaviour of people who want to save (the suppliers of loanable funds) and the behaviour of people who want to invest (the demanders of loanable funds).

We can now use this analysis of the market for loanable funds to examine various government policies that affect the economy's saving and investment. Because this model is just supply and demand in a particular market, we analyse any policy using the three steps discussed in Chapter 4. Firstly, we decide whether the policy shifts the supply curve or the demand curve. Secondly, we determine the direction of the shift. Thirdly, we use the supply-and-demand diagram to see how the equilibrium changes.

Policy 1: Saving Incentives

One of the *Ten Principles of Economics* in Chapter 1 is that a country's standard of living depends on its ability to produce goods and services. And, as we discussed in the preceding chapter, saving is an important long-run determinant of a nation's productivity. Hence if a country can raise its saving rate, the growth rate of GDP should increase and, over time, the citizens of that country should enjoy a higher standard of living.

Another of the *Ten Principles of Economics* is that people respond to incentives. Many economists have used this principle to suggest that the savings rates in some countries are depressed because of tax laws that discourage saving. Governments collect revenue by taxing income, including interest and dividend income. To see the effects of this policy, consider a 25-year-old who saves €1 000 and buys a 30-year bond that pays an interest rate of 9 per cent. In the absence of taxes, the €1 000 grows to €13 268 when the individual reaches age 55. Yet if that interest is taxed at a rate of, say, 33 per cent, then the after-tax interest rate is only 6 per cent. In this case, the €1 000 grows to only €5 743 after 30 years. The tax on interest income substantially reduces the future pay-off from current saving and, as a result, reduces the incentive for people to save.

In response to this problem, many economists and some politicians have sometimes advocated replacing the current income tax with a consumption tax. Under a consumption tax, income that is saved would not be taxed until the saving is later spent; in essence, a consumption tax is like the value-added tax (VAT) that European countries impose on many goods and services. VAT is an indirect tax, however, levied on a good or service at the time it is purchased by a final consumer, whereas a consumption tax could also be a direct tax levied on an individual by calculating how much consumer expenditure they carried out

FIGURE 26.2

An Increase in the Supply of Loanable Funds

A change in the tax laws to encourage more saving would shift the supply of loanable funds to the right from S_1 to S_2. As a result, the equilibrium interest rate would fall, and the lower interest rate would stimulate investment. Here the equilibrium interest rate falls from 5 per cent to 4 per cent, and the equilibrium quantity of loanable funds saved and invested rises from €500 billion to €600 billion.

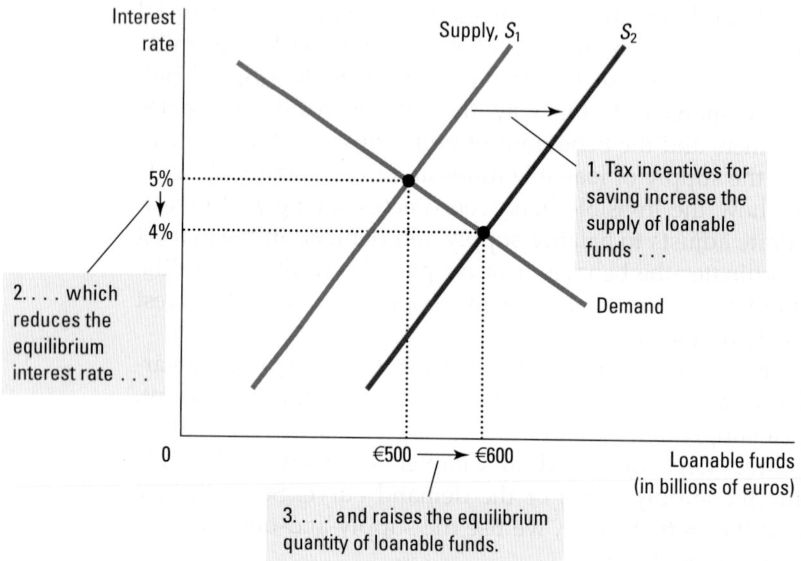

over the year and taxing them on that, perhaps at higher and higher rates as the level of consumer expenditure rises.

A more modest proposal is to expand eligibility for special savings accounts that allow people to shelter some of their saving from taxation. Let's consider the effect of such a saving incentive on the market for loanable funds, as illustrated in Figure 26.2.

First, which curve would this policy affect? Because the tax change would alter the incentive for households to save *at any given interest rate,* it would affect the quantity of loanable funds supplied at each interest rate. Thus, the supply of loanable funds would shift. The demand for loanable funds would remain the same, because the tax change would not directly affect the amount that borrowers want to borrow at any given interest rate.

Secondly, which way would the supply curve shift? Because saving would be taxed less heavily, households would increase their saving by consuming a smaller fraction of their income. Households would use this additional saving to increase their deposits in banks or to buy more bonds. The supply of loanable funds would increase, and the supply curve would shift to the right from S_1 to S_2, as shown in Figure 26.2.

Finally, we can compare the old and new equilibria. In the figure, the increased supply of loanable funds reduces the interest rate from 5 per cent to 4 per cent. The lower interest rate raises the quantity of loanable funds demanded from €500 billion to €600 billion. That is, the shift in the supply curve moves the market equilibrium along the demand curve. With a lower cost of borrowing, households and firms are motivated to borrow more to finance greater investment. Thus, if a reform of the tax laws encouraged greater saving, the result would be lower interest rates and greater investment.

Although this analysis of the effects of increased saving is widely accepted among economists, there is less consensus about what kinds of tax changes should be enacted. Many economists endorse tax reform aimed at increasing saving in order to stimulate investment and growth. Yet others are sceptical that these tax changes would have much effect on national saving. These sceptics also doubt the equity of the proposed reforms. They argue that, in many cases, the benefits of the tax changes would accrue primarily to the wealthy, who are least in need of tax relief.

Policy 2: Investment Incentives

Suppose that the government passed a tax reform aimed at making investment more attractive. In essence, this is what the government does when it institutes an *investment tax credit,* which it does from time to time. An investment tax credit gives a tax advantage to any firm building a new factory or buying a new piece of equipment. Let's consider the effect of such a tax reform on the market for loanable funds, as illustrated in Figure 26.3.

Firstly, would the reform affect supply or demand? Because the tax credit would reward firms that borrow and invest in new capital, it would alter investment at any given interest rate and, thereby, change the demand for loanable funds. By contrast, because the tax credit would not affect the amount that households save at any given interest rate, it would not affect the supply of loanable funds.

Secondly, which way would the demand curve shift? Because firms would have an incentive to increase investment at any interest rate, the quantity of loanable funds demanded would be higher at any given interest rate. Thus, the demand curve for loanable funds would move to the right, as shown by the shift from D_1 to D_2 in the figure.

FIGURE 26.3

An Increase in the Demand for Loanable Funds

If the passage of an investment tax credit encouraged firms to invest more, the demand for loanable funds would increase. As a result, the equilibrium interest rate would rise, and the higher interest rate would stimulate saving. Here, when the demand curve shifts from D_1 to D_2, the equilibrium interest rate rises from 5 per cent to 6 per cent, and the equilibrium quantity of loanable funds saved and invested rises from €500 billion to €600 billion.

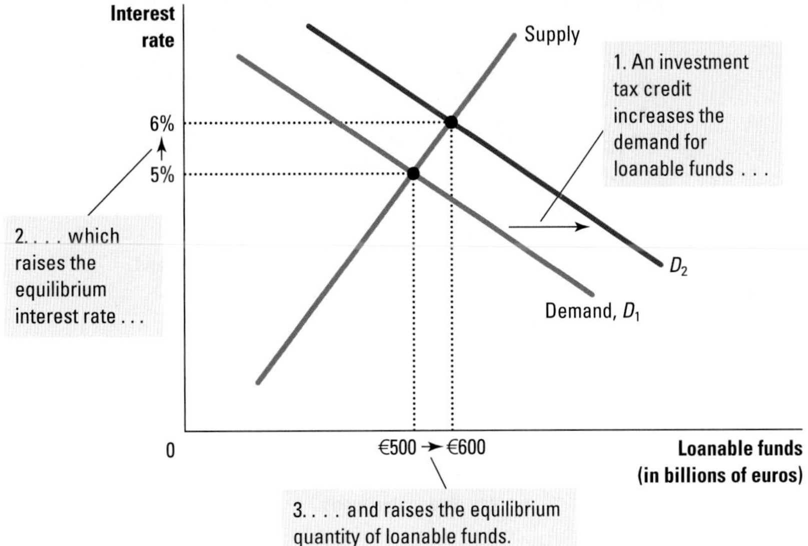

Thirdly, consider how the equilibrium would change. In Figure 26.3, the increased demand for loanable funds raises the interest rate from 5 per cent to 6 per cent, and the higher interest rate in turn increases the quantity of loanable funds supplied from €500 billion to €600 billion, as households respond by increasing the amount they save. This change in household behaviour is represented here as a movement along the supply curve. Thus, if a reform of the tax system encouraged greater investment, the result would be higher interest rates and greater saving.

Policy 3: Government Budget Deficits and Surpluses

A perpetual topic of political debate is the status of the government budget. Recall that a *budget deficit* is an excess of government spending over tax revenue. Governments finance budget deficits by borrowing in the bond market, and the accumulation of past government borrowing is called the *government debt.* A *budget surplus,* an excess of tax revenue over government spending, can be used to repay some of the government debt. If government spending exactly equals tax revenue, the government is said to have a *balanced budget.*

Imagine that the government starts with a balanced budget and then, because of a tax cut or a spending increase, starts running a budget deficit. We can analyse the effects of the budget deficit by following our three steps in the market for loanable funds, as illustrated in Figure 26.4.

First, which curve shifts when the government starts running a budget deficit? Recall that national saving – the source of the supply of loanable funds – is composed of private saving and public saving. A change in the government budget balance represents a change in public saving and, thereby, in the supply of loan-

FIGURE 26.4

The Effect of a Government Budget Deficit

When the government spends more than it receives in tax revenue, the resulting budget deficit lowers national saving. The supply of loanable funds decreases, and the equilibrium interest rate rises. Thus, when the government borrows to finance its budget deficit, it crowds out households and firms who otherwise would borrow to finance investment. Here, when the supply shifts from S_1 to S_2, the equilibrium interest rate rises from 5 per cent to 6 per cent, and the equilibrium quantity of loanable funds saved and invested falls from €500 billion to €300 billion.

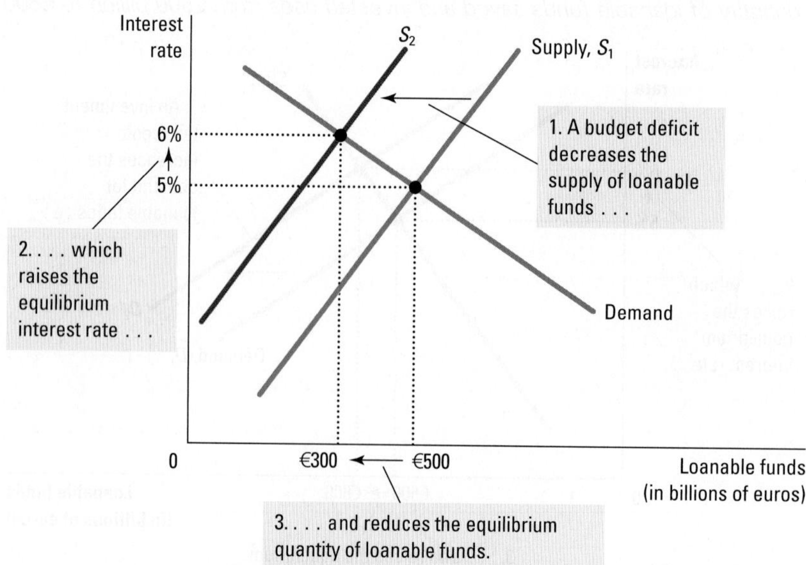

able funds. Because the budget deficit does not influence the amount that households and firms want to borrow to finance investment at any given interest rate, it does not alter the demand for loanable funds.

Secondly, which way does the supply curve shift? When the government runs a budget deficit, public saving is negative, and this reduces national saving. In other words, when the government borrows to finance its budget deficit, it reduces the supply of loanable funds available to finance investment by households and firms. Thus, a budget deficit shifts the supply curve for loanable funds to the left from S_1 to S_2, as shown in Figure 26.4.

Thirdly, we can compare the old and new equilibria. In the figure, when the budget deficit reduces the supply of loanable funds, the interest rate rises from 5 per cent to 6 per cent. This higher interest rate then alters the behaviour of the households and firms that participate in the loan market. In particular, many demanders of loanable funds are discouraged by the higher interest rate. Fewer families buy new homes, and fewer firms choose to build new factories. The fall in investment because of government borrowing is called **crowding out** and is represented in the figure by the movement along the demand curve from a quantity of €500 billion in loanable funds to a quantity of €300 billion. That is, when the government borrows to finance its budget deficit, it crowds out private borrowers who are trying to finance investment.

crowding out
a decrease in investment that results from government borrowing

Thus, the most basic lesson about budget deficits follows directly from their effects on the supply and demand for loanable funds: when the government reduces national saving by running a budget deficit, the interest rate rises and investment falls. Because investment is important for long-run economic growth, government budget deficits reduce the economy's growth rate.

Government budget surpluses work just the opposite way to budget deficits. When government collects more in tax revenue than it spends, its saves the difference by retiring some of the outstanding government debt. This budget surplus, or public saving, contributes to national saving. Thus, a budget surplus increases the supply of loanable funds, reduces the interest rate and stimulates investment. Higher investment, in turn, means greater capital accumulation and more rapid economic growth.

IN THE NEWS

In the wake of the global recession from 2008 to 2009, many governments in Europe were forced to increase borrowing as tax revenue fell and the demands on the public purse grew. Governments have to play by similar rules to others in the market for loanable funds and the bond market, in particular, is a vital source of finance. Running large budget deficits, however, can put additional pressure on these governments to find some way of managing them in the medium to long term. Greece faced particular problems in coping with its budget deficit highlighting the difficulties facing policy makers in keeping public finances under control and the wider effects budget deficits can have on the European economy.

Trichet Says No Special Treatment for Greece

European Central Bank President Jean-Claude Trichet said Greece won't win any special treatment from European officials, increasing pressure on the country to cut the continent's biggest budget deficit. 'No government, no state can expect any special treatment,' he said in Frankfurt in January 2010 when asked about Greece. 'Some governments, one in particular, have very difficult decisions to take.' Greek Prime Minister George Papandreou is struggling to convince investors and other European leaders he can get the deficit under control after rating downgrades last year sparked a rout in the country's bonds. The yield on the 2-year note rose 38 basis points to 3.44 per cent. The premium investors demand to buy those bonds over comparable German debt rose to 234 basis points, the widest spread since 21 December. Trichet spoke after the ECB left its benchmark interest rate unchanged at 1 per cent and signalled he's in no rush to accelerate the withdrawal of emergency policies introduced during the financial crisis.

Trichet's remarks on Greece show that the ECB 'has clearly chosen to maintain its pressure on the Greek government, rather than easing the heightened tensions in bond markets,' Laurent Bilke, a former ECB economist now at Nomura International Plc in London, said in an e-mail. The concern about Greece's ability to tame its deficit is putting the entire euro region 'under great, great pressures,' and threatens to hurt the single currency, [German Chancellor Angela] Merkel said at a private forum. In March the five-year credit default swap, the measurement of the cost of insuring against a Greek default, rose 10 points to 394, the highest in more than two weeks. Fitch Ratings, Moody's Investors Service and Standard & Poor's cut their ratings on Greece in December. That fanned concerns Greek government bonds will be excluded from ECB market operations when collateral rules are returned to pre-crisis levels at the end of this year. 'We will not change our collateral policy for the sake of any particular country,' Trichet said. Greece's record deficit and growing debt, which is set to top 120 per cent of GDP this year, twice the EU limit, have sparked investor concern about a possible default.

It is not just Greece that is a focus of concern. All the 'Pigs' – Portugal, Ireland, Greece and Spain – have found their bonds moving in step, with Greece viewed as a 'bell-wether' for the group. The prices of credit default swaps on Portuguese and Spanish government bonds have reached record highs, while yield spreads between 10-year German bunds and the bonds of other indebted economies have widened further.

Trichet nevertheless today dismissed as an 'absurd hypothesis' the argument that Greece could be forced to exit the euro area. He also played down the importance of Greece's economy on the euro region, which he said represents less than 3 per cent of the bloc's GDP, especially when compared with the size of a US state such as California. Greece deserves the backing of the EU to overcome its financial woes, said Elena Salgado, the finance minister of Spain, which holds the EU's rotating six-month presidency. She travelled to Athens to meet her Greek counterpart George Papaconstantinou. 'It's important that he feels the support from the European Union,' Salgado said in Rome.

In Athens, Papandreou today pledged to 'do whatever it takes' to rein in the budget shortfall and restore confidence in the country's finances when he presented the three-year budget plan. 'Our country can and is obliged to exit as soon as possible this vicious circle of misery,' he said. 'We will not retreat; we will proceed quickly.'

The plan calls for about €10 billion [$14.5 billion] of spending cuts and revenue increases in 2010 to bring the shortfall from 12.7 per cent of output to 8.7 per cent by year-end. That deficit reduction comes as the government forecast that economic growth will contract for a second year in 2010, weighing on revenue. The plan, which was presented to the European Commission in January, included more than €7 billion in revenue-raising measures. Those include some higher taxes and gains from a crackdown on tax evasion and the dodging of social security payments to the pension system. Spending cuts, including trimming benefits to civil servants, were worth €3.6 billion. Trichet said the ECB will study the measures 'carefully.'

Source: 'Trichet says no special treatment for Greece', *Business Week Online* 15 Jan 2010 (Donovan, Jeffrey, and Frances Robinson) © Bloomsberg Business Week

CONCLUSION

'Neither a borrower nor a lender be,' Polonius advises his son in Shakespeare's *Hamlet*. If everyone followed this advice, this chapter would have been unnecessary.

Few economists would agree with Polonius. In our economy, people borrow and lend often, and usually for good reason. You may borrow one day to start your own business or to buy a home. And people may lend to you in the hope that the interest you pay will allow them to enjoy a more prosperous retirement. The financial system has the job of coordinating all this borrowing and lending activity.

In many ways, financial markets are like other markets in the economy. The price of loanable funds – the interest rate – is governed by the forces of supply and demand, just as other prices in the economy are. And we can analyse shifts in supply or demand in financial markets as we do in other markets. One of the *Ten Principles of Economics* introduced in Chapter 1 is that markets are usually a good way to organize economic activity. This principle applies to financial markets as well. When financial markets bring the supply and demand for loanable funds into balance, they help allocate the economy's scarce resources to their most efficient use.

In one way, however, financial markets are special. Financial markets, unlike most other markets, serve the important role of linking the present and the future. Those who supply loanable funds – savers – do so because they want to convert some of their current income into future purchasing power. Those who demand loanable funds – borrowers – do so because they want to invest today in order to have additional capital in the future to produce goods and services. Thus, well functioning financial markets are important not only for current generations but also for future generations who will inherit many of the resulting benefits.

SUMMARY

- The financial system of an advanced economy is made up of many types of financial institutions, such as the bond market, the stock market, banks and investment funds. All of these institutions act to direct the resources of households who want to save some of their income into the hands of households and firms who want to borrow.
- National income accounting identities reveal some important relationships among macroeconomic variables. In particular, for a closed economy, national saving must equal investment. Financial institutions are the mechanism through which the economy matches one person's saving with another person's investment.
- The interest rate is determined by the supply and demand for loanable funds. The supply of loanable funds comes from households who want to save some of their income and lend it out. The demand for loanable funds comes from households and firms who want to borrow for investment. To analyse how any policy or event affects the interest rate, one must consider how it affects the supply and demand for loanable funds.
- National saving equals private saving plus public saving. A government budget deficit represents negative public saving and, therefore, reduces national saving and the supply of loanable funds available to finance investment. When a government budget deficit crowds out investment, it reduces the growth of productivity and GDP.

KEY CONCEPTS

financial system, p. 550
financial markets, p. 551
bond, p. 551
stock (or share or equity), p. 552
financial intermediaries, p. 553
investment fund, p. 555
Credit Default Swaps (CDS), p. 556
national saving (saving), p. 560
private saving, p. 560
public saving, p. 560
market for loanable funds, p. 561
crowding out, p. 567

QUESTIONS FOR REVIEW

1. What is the role of the financial system? Name and describe two markets that are part of the financial system in our economy. Name and describe two financial intermediaries.
2. Why is it important for people who own stocks and bonds to diversify their holdings? What type of financial institution makes diversification easier?
3. What is national saving? What is private saving? What is public saving? How are these three variables related?
4. How do credit default swaps help reduce the risk involved in buying bonds?
5. What is investment? How is it related to national saving?
6. Describe a change in the tax system that might increase private saving. If this policy were implemented, how would it affect the market for loanable funds?
7. What is a government budget deficit? How does it affect interest rates, investment and economic growth?

PROBLEMS AND APPLICATIONS

1. For each of the following pairs, which bond would you expect to pay a higher interest rate? Explain.
   a. A bond of the UK government or a bond of an east European government.
   b. A bond that repays the principal in year 2011 or a bond that repays the principal in year 2031.
   c. A bond from BP or a bond from a software company you run in your garage.
   d. A bond issued by the national government or a bond issued by a local authority.
2. Check a newspaper or the internet for the stock listings of two companies you know something about (perhaps as a customer). What is the price–earnings ratio for each company? Why do you think they differ? If you were to buy one of these shares, which would you choose? Why?
3. What is the difference between gambling at cards or in lotteries or on the race track and gambling in the stock market? What social purpose do you think is served by the existence of the stock market?
4. Declines in share prices are sometimes viewed as harbingers of future declines in real GDP. Why do you suppose that might be true?
5. When the Russian government defaulted on its debt to foreigners in 1998, interest rates rose on bonds issued by many other developing countries. Why do you suppose this happened?
6. Many workers hold large amounts of stock issued by the firms at which they work. Why do you suppose companies encourage this behaviour? Why might a person *not* want to hold stock in the company where he works?
7. Explain the difference between saving and investment as defined by a macroeconomist. Which of the following situations represent investment? Saving? Explain.
   a. Your family takes out a mortgage and buys a new house.
   b. You use your €200 wage payment to buy stock in BP.
   c. Your flatmate earns €100 and deposits it in her account at a bank.
   d. You borrow €1 000 from a bank to buy a car to use in your pizza delivery business.
8. Suppose GDP is €5 trillion, taxes are €1.5 trillion private saving is €0.5 trillion and public saving is €0.2 trillion. Assuming this economy is closed, calculate consumption, government purchases, national saving and investment.
9. Suppose that BP is considering exploring a new oil field.
   a. Assuming that BP needs to borrow money in the bond market to finance the purchase of new oil rigs and drilling machinery, why would an increase in interest rates affect BP's decision about whether to carry out the exploration?
   b. If BP has enough of its own funds to finance the development of the new oil field without borrowing, would an increase in interest rates still affect BP's decision about whether to undertake the new project? Explain.
10. Suppose the government borrows €5 billion more next year than this year.
    a. Use a supply-and-demand diagram to analyse this policy. Does the interest rate rise or fall?
    b. What happens to investment? To private saving? To public saving? To national saving? Compare the size of the changes to the €5 billion of extra government borrowing.

c. How does the elasticity of supply of loanable funds affect the size of these changes?
d. How does the elasticity of demand for loanable funds affect the size of these changes?
e. Suppose households believe that greater government borrowing today implies higher taxes to pay off the government debt in the future. What does this belief do to private saving and the supply of loanable funds today? Does it increase or decrease the effects you discussed in parts (a) and (b)?

11. Over the past 20 years, new computer technology has enabled firms to reduce substantially the amount of inventories they hold for each unit of sales. Illustrate the effect of this change on the market for loanable funds. (Hint: expenditure on inventories is a type of investment.) What do you think has been the effect on investment in factories and equipment?
12. 'Some economists worry that the ageing populations of industrial countries are going to start running down their savings just when the investment appetite of emerging economies is growing' (*The Economist*, 6 May 1995). Illustrate the effect of these phenomena on the world market for loanable funds.
13. This chapter explains that investment can be increased both by reducing taxes on private saving and by reducing the government budget deficit.
    a. Why is it difficult to implement both of these policies at the same time?
    b. What would you need to know about private saving in order to judge which of these two policies would be a more effective way to raise investment?
14. Should the market for CDS be regulated? Explain the reasoning for your answer.
15. Explain why the fact that new market products such as CDOs were developed in the early part of this century had an impact on their longer-term viability.

For further resources, visit
www.cengage.co.uk/mankiw_taylor_2

27 THE BASIC TOOLS OF FINANCE

At some point in your life, you will have to deal with the economy's financial system. You will deposit your savings in a bank account, or you will take out a mortgage to buy a house. After you take a job, you will decide whether to invest your retirement account in company shares, bonds or other financial instruments (or you may buy a personal pension and let the pension company do this for you). You may try to put together your own share portfolio, and then you will have to decide between betting on established companies or newer ones. You will have to take out assurance and insurance policies to cover various risks such as death, fire and theft to property, vehicle insurance and so on. And whenever you watch the evening news, you will hear reports about whether the stock market is up or down, together with the attempts to explain why the market behaves as it does.

If you reflect for a moment on the many financial decisions you will make through your life, you will see two related elements in almost all of them – time and risk. As we saw in the preceding chapter, the financial system coordinates the economy's saving and investment. Thus, it concerns decisions we make today that will affect our lives in the future. But the future is unknown. When a person decides to allocate some saving, or a firm decides to undertake an investment, the decision is based on a guess (albeit an often informed guess) about the likely future result – but the actual result could end up being very different.

finance
the field of economics that studies how people make decisions regarding the allocation of resources over time and the handling of risk

This chapter introduces some tools that help us understand the decisions that people make as they participate in financial markets. The field of **finance** – a sub-discipline of economics – develops these tools in great detail, and you may choose to take courses that focus on this topic. But because the financial system is so important to the functioning of the economy, many of the basic insights of finance are central to understanding how the economy works. The tools of finance may also help you think through some of the decisions that you will make in your own life.

This chapter takes up three topics. First, we discuss how to compare sums of money at different points in time. Secondly, we discuss how to manage risk. Thirdly, we build on our analysis of time and risk to examine what determines the value of an asset, such as a share of stock.

PRESENT VALUE: MEASURING THE TIME VALUE OF MONEY

Imagine that someone offered to give you €100 today or €100 in ten years. Which would you choose? This is an easy question. Getting €100 today is better, because you can always deposit the money in a bank, still have it in ten years, and earn interest on the €100 along the way. The lesson: money today is more valuable than the same amount of money in the future.

Now consider a harder question: imagine that someone offered you €100 today or €200 in ten years. Which would you choose? To answer this question, you need some way to compare sums of money from different points in time. Economists do this with a concept called *present value.* The **present value** of any future sum of money is the amount today that would be needed, at current interest rates, to produce that future sum.

present value
the amount of money today that would be needed to produce, using prevailing interest rates, a given future amount of money

To learn how to use the concept of present value, let's work through a couple of simple examples.

Question: If you put €100 in a bank account today, how much will it be worth in N years? That is, what will be the **future value** of this €100?

future value
the amount of money in the future that an amount of money today will yield, given prevailing interest rates

Answer: Let's use r to denote the interest rate expressed in decimal form (so an interest rate of 5 per cent means $r = 0.05$). Suppose that interest is paid annually and that the interest paid remains in the bank account to earn more interest – a process called **compounding**. Then the €100 will become:

compounding
the accumulation of a sum of money in, say, a bank account, where the interest earned remains in the account to earn additional interest in the future

$(1 + r) \times €100$ after one year

$(1 + r) \times (1 + r) \times €100$ after two years

$(1 + r) \times (1 + r) \times (1 + r) \times €100$ after three years

$(1 + r)^N \times €100$ after N years

For example, if we are investing at an interest rate of 5 per cent for 10 years, then the future value of the €100 will be $(1.05)^{10} \times €100$, which is €163.

Question: Now suppose you are going to be paid €200 in N years. What is the *present value* of this future payment? That is, how much would you have to deposit in a bank right now to yield €200 in N years?

Answer: To answer this question, just turn the previous answer on its head. In the first question, we computed a future value from a present value by *multiplying* by the factor $(1 + r)^N$. To compute a present value from a future value, we *divide* by the factor $(1 + r)^N$. Thus, the present value of €200 in N years is $€200/(1 + r)^N$. If that amount is deposited in a bank today, after N years it would become $(1 + r)^N \times [€200/(1 + r)^N]$, which is €200. For instance, if the interest rate is 5 per cent, the present value of €200 in ten years is $€200/(1.05)^{10}$, which is €123.

This illustrates the general formula: if r is the interest rate, then an amount X to be received in N years has present value of $X/(1 + r)^N$.

Let's now return to our earlier question: should you choose €100 today or €200 in 10 years? We can infer from our calculation of present value that if the interest rate is 5 per cent, you should prefer the €200 in ten years. The future €200 has a present value of €123, which is greater than €100. You are better off waiting for the future sum.

Notice that the answer to our question depends on the interest rate. If the interest rate were 8 per cent, then the €200 in ten years would have a present value of €200/(1.08)^{10}, which is only €93. In this case, you should take the €100 today. Why should the interest rate matter for your choice? The answer is that the higher the interest rate, the more you can earn by depositing your money at the bank, so the more attractive getting €100 today becomes.

The concept of present value is useful in many applications, including the decisions that companies face when evaluating investment projects. For instance, imagine that Citroën is thinking about building a new car factory. Suppose that the factory will cost €100 million today and will yield the company €200 million in ten years. Should Citroën undertake the project? You can see that this decision is exactly like the one we have been studying. To make its decision, the company will compare the present value of the €200 million return to the €100 million cost.

The company's decision, therefore, will depend on the interest rate. If the interest rate is 5 per cent, then the present value of the €200 million return from the factory is €123 million, and the company will choose to pay the €100 million cost. By contrast, if the interest rate is 8 per cent, then the present value of the return is only €93 million, and the company will decide to forgo the project. Thus, the concept of present value helps explain why investment – and thus the quantity of loanable funds demanded – declines when the interest rate rises.

FYI

The Magic of Compounding and the Rule of 70

Suppose you observe that one country has an average growth rate of 1 per cent per year while another has an average growth rate of 3 per cent per year. At first, this might not seem like a big deal. What difference can 2 per cent make?

The answer is, a big difference. Even growth rates that seem small when written in percentage terms seem large after they are compounded for many years.

Consider an example. Suppose that two economics graduates – Milton and Maynard – both take their first jobs at the age of 22 earning €20 000 a year. Milton lives in an economy where all incomes grow at 1 per cent per year, while Maynard lives in one where incomes grow at 3 per cent per year. Straightforward calculations show what happens. Forty years later, when both are 62 years old, Milton earns €30 000 a year, while Maynard earns €65 000. Because of that difference of 2 percentage points in the growth rate, Maynard's salary is more than twice Milton's.

An old rule of thumb, called the *rule of 70*, is helpful in understanding growth rates and the effects of compounding. According to the rule of 70, if some variable grows at a rate of *x* per cent per year, then that variable doubles in approximately 70/*x* years. In Milton's economy, incomes grow at 1 per cent per year, so it takes about 70 years for incomes to double. In Maynard's economy, incomes grow at 3 per cent per year, so it takes about 70/3, or 23, years for incomes to double.

The rule of 70 applies not only to a growing economy but also to a growing savings account. Suppose a rich relative leaves you €10 000 in their will when you are 25 years old. You are inclined to spend it on a luxury cruise, but then you remember studying this chapter and you decide to invest the money for your retirement in 40 years' time. If this money earns around 7 per cent per year – just 7 cents for every euro invested – then it will double in value every 10 years. When you retire aged 65, your nest egg will have grown to about €160 000!

As these examples show, growth rates and interest rates compounded over many years can lead to some spectacular results. That is probably why Albert Einstein once called compounding 'the greatest mathematical discovery of all time.'

Here is another application of present value: suppose you win the Euro Millions Lottery and you are given a choice between €20 000 a year for 50 years (totalling €1 000 000) or an immediate payment of €400 000. Which would you choose? To make the right choice, you need to calculate the present value of the stream of payments. After performing 50 calculations similar to those above (one calculation for each payment) and adding up the results, you would learn that the present value of this million-euro prize at a 7 per cent interest rate is only €276 000. You are better off picking the immediate payment of €400 000. The million euros may seem like more money, but the future cash flows, once discounted to the present, are worth far less.

Quick Quiz The interest rate is 7 per cent. What is the present value of €150 to be received in ten years?

MANAGING RISK

Life is full of gambles. When you go skiing, you risk breaking your leg in a fall. When you cycle to work or university, you risk being knocked off your bike by a car. When you put some of your savings in the stock market, you risk a fall in prices. The rational response to this risk is not necessarily to avoid it at any cost, but to take it into account in your decision-making. Let's consider how a person might do that.

Risk Aversion

risk averse
exhibiting a dislike of uncertainty

Most people are **risk averse**. This means more than simply people dislike bad things happening to them. It means that they dislike bad things more than they like comparable good things. (This is also reflected in *loss aversion* – research suggests that losing something makes people twice as miserable as gaining something makes them happy!)

For example, suppose a friend offers you the following opportunity. He will flip a coin. If it comes up heads, he will pay you €1 000. But if it comes up tails, you will have to pay him €1 000. Would you accept the bargain? You wouldn't if you were risk averse, even though the probability of winning is the same as the probability of losing. For a risk-averse person, the pain from losing the €1 000 would exceed the gain from winning €1 000.

Economists have developed models of risk aversion using the concept of *utility,* which is a person's subjective measure of well-being or satisfaction. Every level of wealth provides a certain amount of utility, as shown by the utility function in Figure 27.1. But the function exhibits the property of diminishing marginal utility: the more wealth a person has, the less utility he gets from an additional euro. Thus, in the figure, the utility function gets flatter as wealth increases. Because of diminishing marginal utility, the utility lost from losing the €1 000 bet is more than the utility gained from winning it. As a result, people are risk averse.

Risk aversion provides the starting point for explaining various things we observe in the economy. Let's consider three of them: insurance, diversification and the risk–return trade-off.

The Markets for Insurance

One way to deal with risk is to buy insurance. The general feature of insurance contracts is that a person facing a risk pays a fee to an insurance company, which

FIGURE 27.1

The Utility Function

This utility function shows how utility, a subjective measure of satisfaction, depends on wealth. As wealth rises, the utility function becomes flatter, reflecting the property of diminishing marginal utility. Because of diminishing marginal utility, a €1 000 loss decreases utility by more than a €1 000 gain increases it.

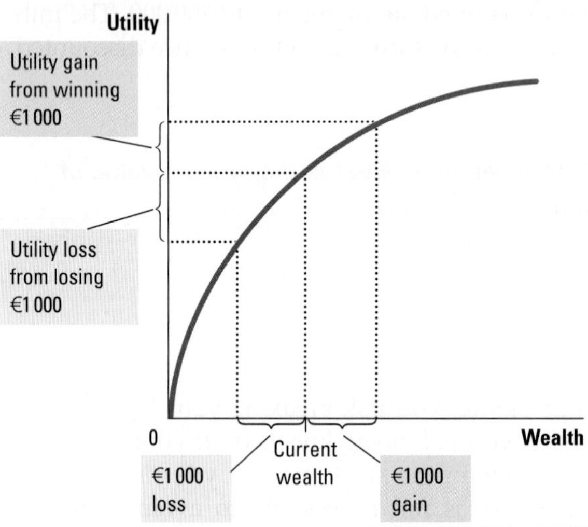

in return agrees to accept all or part of the risk. There are many types of insurance. Car insurance covers the risk of your being in a car accident, fire insurance covers the risk that your house will burn down, and life assurance covers the risk that you will die and leave your family without your income. There is also insurance against the risk of living too long and running out of money: for a fee paid today, an insurance company will pay you an *annuity* – a regular income every year until you die (otherwise known as a pension).

In a sense, every insurance contract is a gamble. It is possible that you will not be in a car accident or that your house will not burn down. In most years, you will pay the insurance company the premium and get nothing in return except peace of mind. Indeed, the insurance company is counting on the fact that most people will not make claims on their policies; otherwise, it couldn't pay out the large claims to those few who are unlucky and still stay in business.

From the standpoint of the economy as a whole, the role of insurance is not to eliminate the risks inherent in life but to spread them around more efficiently. Consider fire insurance, for instance. Owning fire insurance does not reduce the risk of losing your home in a fire. But if that unlucky event occurs, the insurance company compensates you. The risk, rather than being borne by you alone, is shared among the thousands of insurance company shareholders. Because people are risk averse, it is easier for 10 000 people to bear 1/10 000 of the risk than for one person to bear the entire risk himself.

The markets for insurance suffer from two types of problems outlined in Chapter 22 that impede their ability to spread risk. One problem is *adverse selection:* a high-risk person is more likely to apply for insurance than a low-risk person. A second problem is *moral hazard:* after people buy insurance, they have less incentive to be careful about their risky behaviour. Insurance companies are aware of these problems, and the price of insurance reflects the actual risks that the insurance company will face after the insurance is bought. The high price of

FYI

Pricing Risk

We have seen how bond issues are a means by which firms can borrow money. The buyer has to have confidence that they will get their money back and also receive an appropriate reward for lending the money in the first place. There is a risk involved that the issuer will not be able to pay back the money and that risk is associated with a probability. If the issuer is very sound then the probability of default may be zero but if extremely weak then the probability is closer to 1. We saw in Chapter 26 how financial markets now deal in pools of debt (collections of different types of loans sold to an investor). As debt is pooled the outcomes become more varied. In any given pool of mortgage debt, for example, there will be some borrowers who will default and not be able to pay off their mortgages – possibly because of family bereavement or loss of their job. Other mortgage holders may look to pay off their mortgages early, some may move house and thus settle their mortgage, some will increase monthly payments or pay lump sums to help reduce the repayment period of their mortgage and so on. Assessing probabilities with such a wide range of outcomes becomes difficult.

The risk involved with such debt is therefore difficult to assess with any certainty. However, investors want to price risk as part of their decision-making so that they can judge the value of an asset. If an asset is very risky then the returns expected will be higher and vice versa. In order to have an efficient market, that risk has to be priced and the information on which the risk is based has to be reliable, accurate – and understood.

Let's consider an example. In your class there may be a number of students that you associate with every day. Take any one individual and we can identify a number of 'risks' for that person. For example, there is a risk that the individual:

- fails their exams and has to leave the course
- will be involved in a car crash
- will travel on an aircraft more than five times a year
- may get mugged
- may get swine flu.

What are the chances of these events happening? The analysis of such outcomes is what actuaries in the insurance industry have to do. An estimate of the probability of such events happening can be derived from analysis of data, specifically historical data. It is possible, therefore, to gather data on the average 19-year-old student coming from a particular area and with a particular background and use this data to arrive at the probability of the event occurring. Historical data tell us, for example that young people aged between 18 and 24 are more likely to be mugged than the elderly, despite popular perception. If we are able to identify these probabilities then they can be priced. Securities can be issued based on the chances of these things happening – the more likely the event to occur, the higher the price and vice versa.

Whilst it may be possible to identify probabilities for an individual it may be more problematic when looking at relationships between individuals. For example, if person x fails their exams what is the probability that you will also fails your exams? If that individual gets swine flu what are the chances that you also get swine flu? In both cases the probability might depend on your relationship with that person. If you spend a lot of time with that person then it may be that you share similar distractions – going out every night instead of studying, skipping lectures to play pool and so on. If this were the case then the probability of you also failing your exams and getting swine flu might be high but if you have no relationship at all then the chance of you sharing bad habits which lead you to also failing your exams are lower. However, given that you share some time with that person in a lecture hall or seminar room, for example, might mean that the probability of also getting swine flu is relatively high.

Looking at such relationships involves the concept of correlation. If person x is involved in a car crash (and you were not in the car with them) what is the chance of you also being involved in a car crash? The chances are the correlation is very low; the probability of you both getting mugged is higher regardless of the relationship between you and so there will be a stronger correlation in this instance. The correlation is likely to become more and more unstable the more variables are introduced (number of students in this example). In the case of pools of debt, the same problems arise and the efficiency of the information on which investors are basing their decision becomes ever more complex; probabilities become very difficult to assess and therefore to price.

Actuaries have been studying these types of correlations for some years. Issuing life assurance involves a risk.

Life assurance means that the event covered – the death of an individual – will occur at some point in the future (unlike insurance where the event might never happen). The job of the actuary is to provide information to the insurer on the chances of death occurring under different situations. Where information becomes available which indicates risk factors change, actuaries have to incorporate these into models to help insurers price the risk adequately (i.e. set the premiums for the policy). In the 1980s much work was done on studying a phenomenon known as stress cardiomyopathy, a condition for which in the wake of some exceptional emotional trauma, the human brain releases chemicals into the bloodstream that leads to a weakening of the heart and an increased chance of death. The condition has been referred to as a 'broken heart' because it seemed to manifest itself in particular where one partner died soon after the death of the other. Studies showed[1] that following the death of a female partner, a male was over six times more likely to die than normal and women more than twice as likely. The conclusion for the insurance industry is to take such information and build it into the pricing of offering joint-life policies.

[1]Spreeuw, J & Wang, X. (2008). *'Modelling the short-term dependence between two remaining lifetimes'.* http://bunhill.city.ac.uk/research/cassexperts.nsf/RecentPublications?ReadForm&parentunid=80257346003B633B80256D0300537941&form=RecentPublications accessed 15 October 2009.

insurance is why some people, especially those who know themselves to be low-risk, decide against buying insurance and, instead, endure some of life's uncertainty on their own.

Diversification of Idiosyncratic Risk

In 2009 thousands of investors lost their savings as a result of fraud committed by former stock broker Bernard Madoff in the United States. The fraud, known as a Ponzi scheme, involved Madoff taking money from investors on the promise of high returns through a supposedly sophisticated trading and hedging strategy with little apparent risk to the investor. Madoff did not invest the money he received but instead relied on attracting new investors whose money was used to pay existing investors and hence maintain the fraud. Madoff eventually received a prison sentence of 150 years for crimes such as serious fraud, lying to federal securities regulators and money laundering. The saddest part of the story, however, involved the thousands of investors. The estimated value of the fraud was some $65 billion. Some of the victims were wealthy film stars but there were also many who had saved hard for their future and charities, all of whom lost their life savings. At least two suicides have been linked with the fraud.

If there is one piece of practical advice that finance offers to risk-averse people, it is this: 'Don't put all your eggs in one basket.' You may have heard this before, but finance has turned this traditional wisdom into a science. It goes by the name **diversification**.

diversification
the reduction of risk achieved by replacing a single risk with a large number of smaller unrelated risks

The market for insurance is one example of diversification. Imagine a town with 10000 homeowners, each facing the risk of a house fire. If someone starts an insurance company and each person in town becomes both a shareholder and a policyholder of the company, they all reduce their risk through diversification. Each person now faces 1/10000 of the risk of 10000 possible fires, rather than the entire risk of a single fire in his own home. Unless the entire town catches fire at the same time, the downside that each person faces is much smaller.

When people use their savings to buy financial assets, they can also reduce risk through diversification. A person who buys stock in a company is placing a bet on the future profitability of that company. That bet is often quite risky because companies' fortunes are hard to predict. Microsoft evolved from a start-up by some geeky teenagers to one of the world's most valuable companies in only a

FIGURE 27.2

Diversification Reduces Risk

This figure shows how the risk of a portfolio, measured here with a statistic called standard deviation, depends on the number of shares in the portfolio. The investor is assumed to put an equal percentage of his portfolio in each of the shares. Increasing the number of shares reduces the amount of risk in a stock portfolio, but it does not eliminate it.

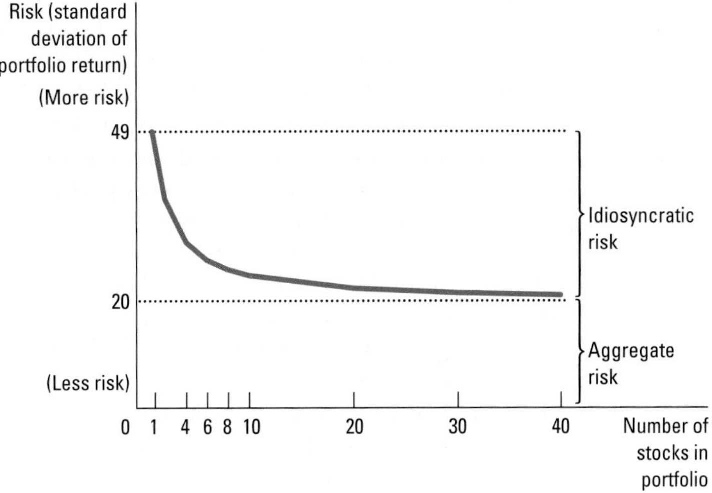

Source: Adapted from Meir Statman, 'How Many Stocks Make a Diversified Portfolio?' *Journal of Financial and Quantitative Analysis 22* (September 1987): 353–364. Reprinted by permission of School of Business Administration/University of Washington.

few years; Enron, a former US energy company which became insolvent with the loss of millions to investors and the jobs of workers because of fraud, went from one of the world's most respected companies to an almost worthless one in only a few months. Fortunately, a shareholder need not tie his own fortune to that of any single company. Risk can be reduced by placing a large number of small bets, rather than a small number of large ones.

Figure 27.2 shows how the risk of a portfolio of shares depends on the number of shares in the portfolio. Risk is measured here with a statistic called *standard deviation,* which you may have learned about in a mathematics or statistics course. Standard deviation measures the volatility of a variable – that is, how much the variable is likely to fluctuate. The higher the standard deviation of a portfolio's return, the more volatile and riskier it is.

The figure shows that the risk of a stock portfolio reduces substantially as the number of shares increase. For a portfolio with single share, the standard deviation is 49 per cent. Going from 1 share to 10 shares eliminates about half the risk. Going from 10 to 20 shares reduces the risk by another 13 per cent. As the number of shares continues to increase, risk continues to fall, although the reductions in risk after 20 or 30 shares are small.

Notice that it is impossible to eliminate all risk by increasing the number of stocks or shares in the portfolio. Diversification can eliminate **idiosyncratic risk** – the uncertainty associated with the specific companies. But diversification cannot eliminate **aggregate risk** – the uncertainty associated with the entire economy, which affects all companies. For example, when the economy goes into a recession, most companies experience falling sales, reduced profit and low stock returns. Diversification reduces the risk of holding stocks, but it does not eliminate it.

idiosyncratic risk
risk that affects only a single economic actor

aggregate risk
risk that affects all economic actors at once

CASE STUDY

The Quants and Zero Risk

Having an economics degree may give you an advantage in the employment stakes but many financial institutions have also found highly skilled mathematicians and physicists extremely useful. They became known as 'the quants.' One such 'quant' was David Li, a talented mathematician who worked on quantitative analysis at the Wall Street investment bank J.P. Morgan Chase. In 2000 he had a paper published in the *Journal of Fixed Income* entitled 'On Default Correlation: A Copula Function Approach'.

Li had some background in actuarial science as well as business and in his role within J.P. Morgan Chase, he was part of a growing number of highly qualified mathematical and statistical individuals being employed by financial institutions to identify risk and find ways of reducing it to a minimum – if not eliminating it totally. The basis behind this 'quantitative finance' was that the market could be beaten. What quantitative finance provided was the possibility of improved information that enabled decision-makers to invest with significantly reduced risk.

The basis of Li's paper in 2000 focused on the problems of probabilities and correlation of events. For example, a company in the south-west of England sources animal hide and processes it into a range of different quality leather for sale to manufacturers of leather products. It sources its hides from a company in Kenya. Analysis of data can give reasonably reliable estimates of the probability of both these businesses' chances of failure. The probability of the UK company failing might be 0.3 and the probability of the Kenyan company failing, 0.4. However, given the relationship between the two, if the Kenyan company did fail then there is a relatively high probability that the UK company might also fail if it cannot source the same high-quality hides elsewhere quickly. The correlation between the two companies failing, therefore, is quite high.

What is the correlation between the chances of the UK company failing and an Icelandic tourism operator also failing? Intuition might suggest that the correlation would be weak given the fact that the two companies are operating in different markets and are not related. However, they may be related by the fact that they have both acquired loans from a bank based in Germany. If that bank suffered problems then the chance of the two companies failing would be relatively high. Li attempted to apply his skills to the effect of the default of one business on another. If this could be modelled then it could help decision-makers to reduce the risk of investing.

One of the statistical devices used for modelling linked events is a copula. The chances of two or more events occurring together can be modelled through the use of a copula which produces a distribution. The specific distribution that Li used was a Gaussian Copula, which to many students is the familiar 'bell curve' given by a normal distribution. Li looked at the probability of any two or more elements in a pool of debt defaulting and his formula showed that this was equal to the normal distribution (the copula) times the probabilities of the time taken for the elements to default (referred to as survival times) multiplied by a correlation constant. The survival time aspect of the formula was derived from Li's knowledge of the work of actuaries in looking at survival rates of partners following the death of one of them. In this scenario events (in this case death) tend to an average and, as mentioned earlier, in this scenario there are certainties – death will occur at some point in the future. With assets the outcomes were not so clear cut and while Li's formula looked 'elegant' it was not able to take into account the range and randomness of events which were not so clear cut. Indeed, Li appeared to recognize (as any goods scientist would claim to do) that his formula did have limitations. In 2005, he is quoted as saying 'Very few people understand the essence of the model'.

For those in the financial world, the model was useful in that it appeared to be able to reduce risk to a 'simple' number and thus help price that risk. It told decision-makers what effect the default of one company might have on another regardless of the knowledge of either company. Li's formula gained some currency in financial markets to the extent that ratings agencies such as Moody's and Standard & Poor's incorporated it into their methodology. In particular the formula could be used to assess risk on collateralized debt obligations (CDOs).

Li's formula may have provided investors with new information which they could use to factor in when making decisions – it became part of the set of 'relevant generally available information'. The problem was that despite having this information, those using it may not have fully understood the information which they were exploiting. The whole point of employing top-ranked mathematicians, statisticians and physicists in the world of finance since the latter part of the 1990s was that their skills were very special – it was simply not something that anybody else but these brilliant minds could do; if it had have been possible then others would have done it!

The problem of employing such minds to try and beat the market is that the new information they bring to the market is highly technical, is based on assumptions that are standard in science but which are recognized in that discipline as 'provisional' and that any theory or model is simply there to be taken apart and either destroyed or improved upon. The information we now have on the financial crisis, some of the causes of which were laid at the feet of these 'quants', is something that markets can now factor into decision-making. There are a great many things in economics that can be modelled and mathematics can be very useful in helping to provide the means to analyse and to predict, but ultimately economics is about human behaviour. Despite such rigorous analysis, the old adage about baskets and eggs still applies!

The Trade-off between Risk and Return

One of the *Ten Principles of Economics* in Chapter 1 is that people face trade-offs. The trade-off that is most relevant for understanding financial decisions is the trade-off between risk and return.

As we have seen, there are risks inherent in holding shares, even in a diversified portfolio. But risk-averse people are willing to accept this uncertainty because they are compensated for doing so. Historically, shares have offered much higher rates of return than alternative financial assets, such as bonds and bank savings accounts. Over the past two centuries, stocks have offered an average real return of about 8 per cent per year, while short-term government bonds paid a real return of only 3 per cent per year.

When deciding how to allocate their savings, people have to decide how much risk they are willing to undertake to earn the higher return. Figure 27.3 illustrates the risk–return trade-off for a person choosing to allocate his portfolio between two asset classes:

- The first asset class is a diversified group of risky stocks, with an average return of 8 per cent and a standard deviation of 20 per cent. (You may recall from mathematics or statistics courses that a normal random variable stays within two standard deviations of its average about 95 per cent of the time. Thus while actual returns are centred around 8 per cent, they typically vary from a gain of 48 per cent to a loss of 32 per cent.)

- The second asset class is a safe alternative. With a return of 3 per cent and a standard deviation of zero. The safe alternative can be either a bank savings account or a government bond.

FIGURE 27.3

The Trade-off Between Risk and Return

When people increase the percentage of their savings that they have invested in shares, they increase the average return they can expect to earn, but they also increase the risks they face.

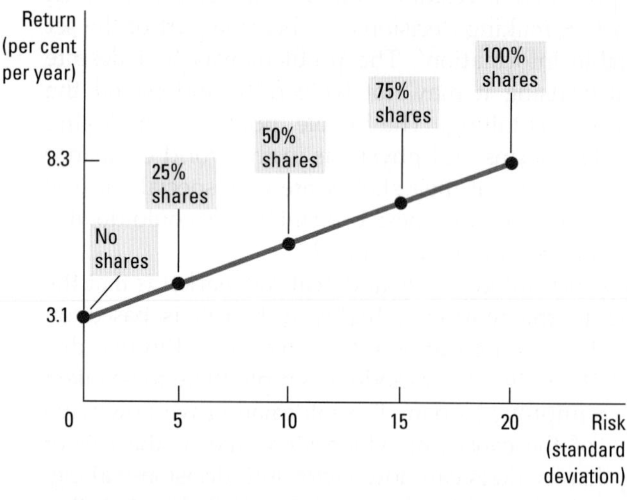

Each point in this figure represents a particular allocation of a portfolio between risky shares and the safe asset. The figure shows that the more a person puts into stock, the greater is both the risk and the return.

Acknowledging the risk–return trade-off does not, by itself, tell us what a person should do. The choice of a particular combination of risk and return depends on a person's risk aversion, which reflects a person's own preferences. But it is important for shareholders to realize that the higher average return that they enjoy comes at the price of higher risk.

Quick Quiz Describe three ways that a risk-averse person might reduce the risk she faces.

ASSET VALUATION

Now that we have developed a basic understanding of the two building blocks of finance – time and risk – let's apply this knowledge. This section considers a simple question: what determines the price of a share of stock? Like most prices, the answer is supply and demand. But that is not the end of the story. To understand share prices, we need to think more deeply about what determines a person's willingness to pay for a share of stock.

Fundamental Analysis

Let's imagine that you have decided to put 60 per cent of your savings into company shares and, to achieve diversification, you have decided to buy 20 different shares. If you open up the *Financial Times*, you will find thousands of shares listed. How should you pick the 20 for your portfolio?

When you buy company shares, you are buying shares in a business. When deciding which businesses you want to own, it is natural to consider two things: the value of the business and the price at which the shares are being sold. If the price is less than the value, the stock is said to be *undervalued*. If the price is more than the value, the stock is said to be *overvalued*. If the price and the value are equal, the stock is said to be *fairly valued*. When choosing 20 stocks for your portfolio, you should prefer undervalued stocks. In these cases, you are getting a bargain by paying less than the business is worth.

This is easier said than done. Learning the price is easy: you can just look it up in the newspaper. Determining the value of the business is the hard part. The term **fundamental analysis** refers to the detailed analysis of a company to determine its value. Many financial sector firms hire stock price analysts to conduct such fundamental analysis and offer advice about which stocks to buy.

fundamental analysis
the study of a company's accounting statements and future prospects to determine its value

The value of a stock to a shareholder is what he gets out of owning it, which includes the present value of the stream of dividend payments and the final sale price. Recall that *dividends* are the cash payments that a company makes to its shareholders. A company's ability to pay dividends, as well as the value of the stock when the shareholder sells his shares, depends on the company's ability to earn profits. Its profitability, in turn, depends on a large number of factors – the demand for its product, how much competition it faces, how much capital it has in place, whether its workers are unionized, how loyal its customers are, what kinds of government regulations and taxes it faces, and so on. The job of fundamental analysts is to take all these factors into account to determine how much a share of stock in the company is worth.

If you want to rely on fundamental analysis to pick a stock portfolio, there are three ways to do it. One way is to do all the necessary research yourself, by reading through companies' annual reports and so forth. A second way is to rely on the advice of financial analysts. A third way is to buy into an investment fund, which has a manager (sometimes called a fund manager) who conducts fundamental analysis and makes the decision for you.

The Efficient Markets Hypothesis

There is another way to choose 20 shares for your portfolio: pick them randomly by, for instance, putting the stock pages of the *Financial Times* on your notice board and throwing darts at the page. This may sound crazy, but there is reason to believe that it won't lead you too far astray. That reason is called the **efficient markets hypothesis**.

efficient markets hypothesis
the theory that asset prices reflect all publicly available information about the value of an asset

To understand this theory, the starting point is to acknowledge that each company listed on a major stock exchange is followed closely by many fund managers, such as the individuals who run investment funds. Every day, these managers monitor news stories and conduct fundamental analysis to try to determine the fund's value. Their job is to buy a share when its price falls below its value, and to sell it when its price rises above its value.

The second piece to the efficient markets hypothesis is that the equilibrium of supply and demand sets the market price. This means that, at the market price, the number of shares being offered for sale exactly equals the number of shares that people want to buy. In other words, at the market price, the number of people who think the share is overvalued exactly balances the number of people who think it's undervalued. As judged by the typical person in the market, all shares are fairly valued all the time.

informationally efficient
reflecting all available information in a rational way

According to this theory, the stock market is **informationally efficient**: It reflects all available information about the value of the asset. Share prices change when information changes. When the good news about the company's prospects become public, the value and the stock price both rise. When the company's prospects deteriorate, the value and price both fall. But at any moment in time, the market price is the best guess of the company's value based on available information.

random walk
the path of a variable whose changes are impossible to predict

One implication of the efficient markets hypothesis is that stock prices should follow a **random walk**. This means that changes in stock prices are impossible to predict from available information. If, based on publicly available information, a person could predict that a stock price would rise by 10 per cent tomorrow, then the stock market must be failing to incorporate that information today. According to this theory, the only thing that can move stock prices is news that changes the market's perception of the company's value. But news must be unpredictable – otherwise, it wouldn't really be news. For the same reason, changes in stock prices should be unpredictable.

If the efficient markets hypothesis is correct, then there is little point in spending many hours studying the business page to decide which 20 shares to add to your portfolio. If prices reflect all available information, no stock is a better buy than any other. The best you can do is buy a diversified portfolio.

CASE STUDY

Efficient Markets Hypothesis: Dead and Buried or Just Resting?

Any theory is a framework for analysing the world and which allows us to be able to make predictions. Theories are subject to testing and can be found to be inaccurate, limited in understanding or just plain wrong! One of the problems with economic theories, unlike those of the hard sciences, is that they are not easily testable in a laboratory environment where experiments can be repeated in order to establish the reliability or otherwise of a theory. Economic theories are used as the basis for policy making and if a theory is inaccurate or unreliable then policies and decisions can be undermined. The assumption of efficient markets and the belief that markets self-correct and revert to reflect true market value was the basis of the regulatory framework that underpinned the financial system in most major centres of the world.

The efficient markets hypothesis (EMH) suggests that it is impossible to predict future movements in asset prices based on an analysis of past events – the idea of the 'random walk'. If information became available today that allowed an investor to predict a rise in price of an asset at some future point in time then the market would be failing to incorporate that information into decision-making. The market price of the asset would undervalue it and as we have already stated, if an asset's price is undervalued there is a rational incentive to buy it. If an investor knew the price of an asset was going to rise at some point in the future, and assuming that humans prefer more than less and seek out the best returns, it would be a rational decision to buy the asset in anticipation of the rise in price.

New information comes out all the time, of course, but to the extent that this information really is new, it is unpredictable. In hindsight it always seems that we could have foreseen events after they have arisen; a chain of causality can invariably be established. However, if humans were able to predict future events with any certainty or predict the news it would not be news, by definition!

Much of the above reasoning, however, is based on the principle of rational behaviour. The question raised in the wake of the financial crisis was the extent to which the 'bubbles' which occurred in asset prices represented rational behaviour as opposed to a herd mentality or mass psychology as proposed by the Yale economist Robert Shiller and Richard Thaler at the University of Chicago, who are leading behavioural economists. The existence of speculative bubbles suggests that markets react to what Alan Greenspan called 'irrational exuberance' and what Keynes referred to as 'animal spirits'. In speculative bubbles, asset prices rise, not because of the stream of income that flows from them and the price when sold, but solely because of an expectation of what others will think the asset will be worth in the future. It is worth pausing on this for a moment, because there is a subtle difference between valuing an assert based on fundamental analysis – the present value of future dividends – and valuing it based on an assumption that people will bid up the price *regardless of expected future dividends*. It is when the price gets detached from the fundamentals and starts to be contingent only on what everyone in the market expects everyone else will think that a bubble starts to form.

Keynes believed that, given the fact that most investors would sell shares they own at some point in the future, it was not unreasonable to have some concern about others' valuation of that asset. Such views could lead to irrational waves of optimism and pessimism. The EMH is based on an assumption that there are a sufficient number of people in the market who act rationally to counter the few that do not.

Central to the EMH is the role of information. Information is necessary to value anything, to enable the valuer to make judgements. This information could include data of different kinds. It might include statistical data based on historical records or on reliable forecasting techniques; data can be gained from official statements from a business, from trends, market research, financial audits, analyst reports on the business in relation to its market and the economy, from government and its agencies on economic performance, from other specialist market analysts such as Mintel and Experian, representatives of retail trades and so on. In valuing the price of an asset, therefore, the assumption is that the market is informationally efficient in that it reflects all available information about the value of that asset.

The extent to which this assumption can be accepted is open to question. Access to information and the speed at which information travels is now greater than ever before. Despite the growth in technology, information transfer is not instantaneous nor is it assimilated and understood by all at the same speed and with the same depth. There is, therefore, a time lag involved with information transfer. As we have seen above, if individuals are able to exploit that time lag they can use this to their advantage to make profits; this is the basis of arbitrage. A conclusion from this might be that EMH implies that markets will clear and that most of the time, or on average that they are efficient. The remaining time periods, when they are not efficient, may be where problems can arise.

A belief in the fundamentals of EMH led even revered financial luminaries such as the former US Federal Reserve Chairman Alan Greenspan to have to admit that he may have been wrong in some of his assumptions.

In testimony given to the Committee of Government Oversight and Reform in the US on 23 October 2008, Greenspan said:

> ...those of us who have looked to the self-interest of lending institutions to protect shareholders' equity (myself especially) are in a state of shocked disbelief. Such counterparty surveillance is a central pillar of our financial markets' state of balance. If it fails, as occurred this year, market stability is undermined.
>
> In response to a further question from Committee Chairman, Henry Waxman, who asked:
>
> You found that your view of the world, your ideology, was not right, it was not working?
>
> Greenspan replied:
>
> That's precisely the reason I was shocked because I'd been going for forty years or so with considerable evidence that it was working exceptionally well.

Information may be widely available and extensive but it does not mean that it is always understood. Decision-makers may have access to a wide range of information but some vital part of that information may be missed if understanding is not complete. Greenspan alluded to this in his testimony. Information may not only be misunderstood but also be partial; gathering information requires some investment in terms of research (information gathering and processing) on the part of decision-makers and this investment can be expensive. In any decision-making, therefore, research costs have to be built in. One very good example of this principle will be considered in the next section. It looks at the way in which information can be made available to decision-makers, can be used and exploited but without critical acceptance may provide the basis for erroneous judgements, as we saw in our outline of the role of 'the quants'.

Faith in markets is fundamental to economic growth in most of the world and the financial crisis of 2007–09 has shaken this faith to the core. There have been many who have consigned EMH to the 'dustbin of history' but there are others that suggest that the events since the early 2000s are testament to the robustness of EMH – that the market cannot be beaten and that attempts to try and do so will ultimately fail. The development of sophisticated information to try and beat the market is one example of how this has happened. The use of such techniques to make 'superrational' valuations of assets is impossible, its supporters would argue.

What may come out of the analysis of the financial crisis is a better understanding of how markets work, especially in a rapidly changing world. The assumptions that have been made about how markets work, the variables that are considered, the effect of external shocks and the extent to which humans may act irrationally, are risk seeking or risk averse and more, may all be revisited, revised and re-interpreted. Ultimately we may be in a better position to understand the complexity of markets but to arrive at the conclusion that our understanding and our mastery is complete is akin to a pronouncement by physicists that they understand every aspect of the physical world and the universe; in short it is not going to happen!

The conclusion is, therefore, that the EMH has been found wanting. Some have suggested an alternative and referred to the idea of American 20th-century economists, Hyman Minsky and Irving Fisher, of the financial instability hypothesis (FIH). This suggests that the idea that markets always move to an equilibrium position and remain in that position pending some external shock may have some resonance in commodities or goods markets but that financial markets are not subject to the same forces. Minsky and Fisher argue that financial markets create their own internal forces which create periods of asset inflation and credit expansion. This will be followed by contraction in credit and asset deflation. Financial markets, they conclude, are not self-optimizing or stable and far from allocating resources efficiently the outcome may be sub-optimal. Minsky suggests that some of these internal forces relate to the lack of supply of assets which drive demand in those markets. For example, the lack of supply of housing drives demand for housing and forces prices upwards creating a bubble. Changing asset prices (such as houses) in turn act as a driver for demand for those assets. If house prices are rising quickly there is an incentive for buyers to want to get into the market quickly to avoid having to pay higher prices and also to benefit from rising prices once they have purchased. This simply fuels demand further in the face of limited supply and so drives price up higher.

Maybe the last word on this issue can be with Burton G. Malkiel from Princeton[1] who, in a paper in 2003, concluded:

> As long as stock markets exist, the collective judgment of investors will sometimes make mistakes. Undoubtedly, some market participants are demonstrably less then rational. As a result, pricing irregularities and predictable patterns in stock returns can appear over time and even persist for short periods. Moreover, the market cannot be perfectly efficient or there would be no incentive for professionals to uncover the information that gets so quickly reflected in market prices, a point stressed by Grossman and Stiglitz (1980). Undoubtedly, with the passage of time and with the increasing sophistication of our databases and empirical techniques, we will document further apparent departures from efficiency and further patterns in the development of stock returns.
>
> But I suspect that the end result will not be an abandonment of the belief of many in the profession that the stock market is remarkably efficient in its utilization of information. Periods such as 1999 where 'bubbles' seem to have existed, at least in certain sectors of the market, are fortunately the exception rather than the rule. Moreover, whatever patterns or irrationalities in the pricing of individual stocks that have been discovered in a search of historical experience are unlikely to persist and will not provide investors with a method to obtain extraordinary returns. If any $100 bills are lying around the stock exchanges of the world, they will not be there for long.

[1]Malkiel, B.G. (2003). 'The Efficient Market Hypothesis and its Critics'. CEPS Working Paper no 91. http://www.princeton.edu/~ceps/workingpapers/91malkiel.pdf – accessed 3 October 2009.

Market Irrationality

The efficient markets hypothesis assumes that people buying and selling stock rationally process the information they have about the stocks' underlying value. But is the stock market really that rational? Or do share prices sometimes deviate from reasonable expectations of their true value?

There is a long tradition suggesting that fluctuations in share prices are partly psychological. In the 1930s, British economist John Maynard Keynes suggested that asset markets are driven by the 'animal spirits' of investors – irrational waves of optimism and pessimism. Alan Greenspan's reference to 'irrational exuberance' became popular in describing stock market behaviour, especially when it was used as the title of a book on stock market behaviour by Robert Shiller that successfully predicted a large fall in US stock prices. Nevertheless, whether the exuberance of stock markets in the USA and around the world in the 1990 and the middle of the noughties was irrational given the information available at the time remains debatable.

Sustained and sometimes rapid rises in stock prices are sometimes called speculative bubbles, since often the price rise comes to an end and share prices fall abruptly, just as a soap bubble will rise and rise until it suddenly bursts. The possibility of such speculative bubbles arises in part because the value of a share to a stockholder depends not only on the stream of dividend payments but also on the final sale price of the share. Thus, a person might be willing to pay more than a stock is worth today if he expects another person to pay even more for it tomorrow. When you evaluate a stock, you have to estimate not only the value of the business but also what other people will think the business is worth in the future.

There is much debate among economists about whether departures from rational pricing are important or rare. Believers in market irrationality point out (correctly) that the stock market often moves in ways that are hard to explain on the basis of news that might alter a rational valuation. We have already described a number of examples where disciplines such as biology and psychology are helping to contribute to our understanding of human behaviour. The growth in 'neuroeconomics' (see Chapters 2 and 21) is one example of where such information is helping to push the boundaries of our understanding and is being applied to finance. Believers in the efficient markets hypothesis point out (correctly) that it is impossible to know the correct, rational valuation of a company, so one should not quickly jump to the conclusion that any particular valuation is irrational. Moreover, if the market were irrational, a rational person should be able to take advantage of this fact; yet, as the previous case study discussed, beating the market is nearly impossible.

Quick Quiz Investors sometimes refer to 'highly respected' companies as 'blue chip companies'. These are usually large, national or multinational corporations with a reputation for high-quality management or products. Examples of blue chip companies quoted on the London Stock Exchange would be Rolls-Royce, Unilever and BP. According to the efficient markets hypothesis, if you restrict your stock portfolio to blue chip companies, would you earn a better than average return? Explain.

FYI

Keynes's View of Stock Markets

As well as being the most influential economist of the 20th century, Keynes was also a successful stock market investor and considerably enriched his college in Cambridge by managing its investment portfolio. Yet his opinion of professional investment managers was notoriously low. In his *Treatise on Money* (1930), he wrote:

... the vast majority of those who are concerned with the buying and selling of securities know almost nothing whatever about what they are doing. They do not possess even the rudiments of what is required for a valid judgment, and are the prey of hopes and fears easily aroused by

transient events and as easily dispelled. This is one of the odd characteristics of the capitalist system under which we live, which, when we are dealing with the real world, is not to be overlooked.

Keynes was not known for his modesty, but, even so, one suspects that he may have been overstating his case somewhat for the sake of emphasis. In *The General Theory of Employment, Interest and Money* (1936), he sketched out a more balanced view that amounts to a simple theory of speculative bubbles in a very famous passage in which he compares the stock market to a beauty contest:

... professional investment may be likened to those newspaper competitions in which the competitors have to pick out the six prettiest faces from a hundred photographs, the prize being awarded to the competitor whose choice most nearly corresponds to the average preferences of the competitors as a whole; so that each competitor has to pick, not those faces which he himself finds prettiest, but those which he thinks likeliest to catch the fancy of the other competitors, all of whom are looking at the problem from the same point of view. It is not a case of choosing those which, to the best of one's judgment, are really the prettiest, nor even those which average opinion genuinely thinks the prettiest. We have reached the third degree where we devote our intelligences to anticipating what average opinion expects the average opinion to be.

For these reasons, a person who believes that departures from rational pricing are the rule rather than the exception in the stock market are sometimes referred to as having a Keynesian view of financial markets.

CONCLUSION

This chapter has developed some of the basic tools that people should (and often do) use as they make financial decisions. The concept of present value reminds us that a pound in the future is less valuable than a pound today, and it gives us a way to compare sums of money at different points in time. The theory of risk management reminds us that the future is uncertain and that risk-averse people can take precautions to guard against this uncertainty. The study of asset valuation tells us that the stock price of any company should reflect its expected future profitability.

Although most of the tools of finance are well established, there is more controversy about the validity of the efficient markets hypothesis and whether stock prices are, in practice, rational estimates of a company's true worth. Rational or not, the large movements in stock prices that we observe have important macroeconomic implications. Stock market fluctuations often go hand in hand with fluctuations in the economy more broadly. We will look at the stock market again when we study economic fluctuations later in the book.

SUMMARY

- Because savings can earn interest, a sum of money today is more valuable than the same sum of money in the future. A person can compare sums from different times using the concept of present value. The present value of any future sum is the amount that would be needed today, given prevailing interest rates, to produce that future sum.
- Because of diminishing marginal utility, most people are risk averse. Risk-averse people can reduce risk using insurance, through diversification, and by choosing a portfolio with lower risk and lower return.
- The value of an asset, such as a share of stock, equals the present value of the cash flows the owner of the share will receive, including the stream of dividends and the final sale price. According to the efficient markets hypothesis, financial markets process available information rationally, so a stock price always equals the best estimate of the value of the underlying business. Some economists question the efficient markets hypothesis, however, and believe that irrational psychological factors also influence asset prices.

KEY CONCEPTS

finance, p. 572
present value, p. 573
future value, p. 573
compounding, p. 573
risk averse, p. 575
diversification, p. 578
idiosyncratic risk, p. 579
aggregate risk, p. 579
fundamental analysis, p. 583
efficient markets hypothesis, p. 583
informationally efficient, p. 584
random walk, p. 584

QUESTIONS FOR REVIEW

1. The interest rate is 7 per cent. Use the concept of present value to compare €200 to be received in 10 years and €300 to be received in 20 years.
2. What benefit do people get from the market for insurance? What two problems impede the insurance company from working perfectly?
3. What is diversification? Does a shareholder get more diversification going from 1 to 10 stocks or going from 100 to 120 stocks?
4. Comparing company shares and government bonds, which has more risk? Which pays a higher average return?
5. What factors should a stock analyst think about in determining the value of a share of stock?
6. Describe the efficient markets hypothesis, and give a piece of evidence consistent with this theory.
7. Explain the view of those economists who are sceptical of the efficient markets hypothesis.

PROBLEMS AND APPLICATIONS

1. About 400 years ago, Native Americans sold the island of Manhattan for $24. If they had invested this money at an interest rate of 7 per cent per year, how much would they have today?
2. A company has an investment project that would cost €10 million today and yield a pay off of €15 million in four years.
   a. Should the firm undertake the project if the interest rate is 11 per cent? 10 per cent? 9 per cent? 8 per cent?
   b. Can you figure out the exact cut-off for the interest rate between profitability and non-profitability?
3. For each of the following kinds of insurance, give an example of behaviour that can be called *moral hazard* and another example of behaviour that can be called *adverse selection.*
   a. health insurance
   b. car insurance.
4. Imagine that you intend to buy a portfolio of ten shares with some of your savings. Should the shares be of companies in the same industry? Should the shares be of companies located in the same country? Explain.
5. For which kind of stock would you expect to pay the higher average return: stock in an industry that is very sensitive to economic conditions (such as a car manufacturer) or stock in an industry that is relatively insensitive to economic conditions (such as a water company). Why?
6. A company faces two kinds of risk. An idiosyncratic risk is that a competitor might enter its market and take some of its customers. An aggregate risk is that the economy might enter a recession, reducing sales. Which of these two risks would more likely cause the company's shareholders to demand a higher return? Why?
7. You have two flatmates who invest in the stock market.
   a. One flatmate says she buys stock only in companies that everyone believes will experience big increases in profits in the future. How do you suppose the price–earnings ratio of these companies compares to the price–earnings ratio of other companies? What

might be the disadvantage of buying stock in these companies?

b. Another flatmate says she only buys stock in companies that are cheap, which she measures by a low price–earnings ratio. How do you suppose the earnings prospects of these companies compare to those of other companies? What might be the disadvantage of buying stock in these companies?

8. When company executives buy and sell stock based on private information they obtain as part of their jobs, they are engaged in *insider trading.*

   a. Give an example of inside information that might be useful for buying or selling stock.
   b. Those who trade shares based on inside information usually earn very high rates of return. Does this fact violate the efficient market hypothesis?
   c. Insider trading is illegal. Why do you suppose that is?

9. Financial markets in the early years of the 21st century were heavily influenced by the work of quantitative analysts ('quants') who looked at ways to reassess the pricing of risk. Discuss some of the advantages and disadvantages of pricing risk using mathematics and mathematical models.

For further resources, visit www.cengage.co.uk/mankiw_taylor2

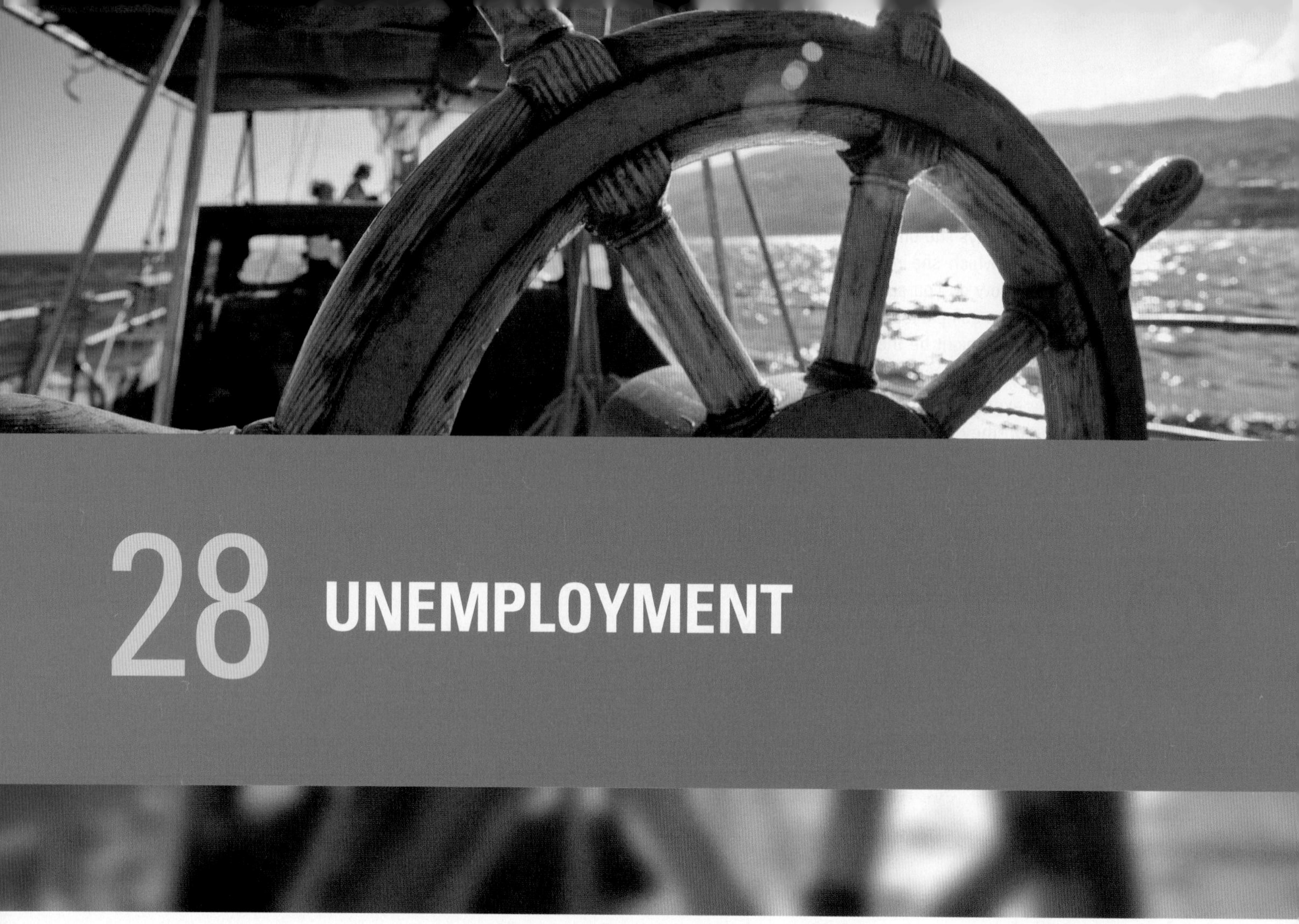

28 UNEMPLOYMENT

Losing a job can be the most distressing economic event in a person's life. Most people rely on their labour earnings to maintain their standard of living, and many people get from their work not only income but also a sense of personal accomplishment. A job loss means a lower living standard in the present, anxiety about the future and reduced self-esteem. It is not surprising, therefore, that politicians campaigning for office often speak about how their proposed policies will help create jobs.

In previous chapters we have seen some of the forces that determine the level and growth of a country's standard of living. A country that saves and invests a high fraction of its income, for instance, enjoys more rapid growth in its capital stock and its GDP than a similar country that saves and invests less. An even more obvious determinant of a country's standard of living is the amount of unemployment it typically experiences. People who would like to work but cannot find a job are not contributing to the economy's production of goods and services. Although some degree of unemployment is inevitable in a complex economy with thousands of firms and millions of workers, the amount of unemployment varies substantially over time and across countries. When a country keeps its workers as fully employed as possible, it achieves a higher level of GDP than it would if it left many of its workers standing idle.

This chapter begins our study of unemployment. The problem of unemployment is usefully divided into two categories – the long-run problem and the short-run problem. The economy's *natural rate of unemployment* refers to the amount of unemployment that the economy normally experiences. *Cyclical unemployment* refers to the year-to-year fluctuations in unemployment around its natural rate, and it is closely associated with the short-run ups and downs of economic activity. Cyclical unemployment has its own explanation, which we defer until we study short-run economic fluctuations later in this book. In this chapter we discuss the determinants of an economy's natural rate of unemployment. As we will see, the designation *natural* does not imply that this rate of unemployment is desirable. Nor does it imply that it is constant over time or impervious to economic policy. It merely means that this unemployment does not go away on its own, even in the long run.

We begin the chapter by looking at some of the relevant facts that describe unemployment. In particular, we examine three questions: how does the government measure the economy's rate of unemployment? What problems arise in interpreting the unemployment data? How long are the unemployed typically without work?

We then turn to the reasons why economies always experience some unemployment and the ways in which policy makers can help the unemployed. We discuss four explanations for the economy's natural rate of unemployment: job search, minimum wage laws, unions and efficiency wages. As we will see, long-run unemployment does not arise from a single problem that has a single solution. Instead, it reflects a variety of related problems. As a result, there is no easy way for policy makers to reduce the economy's natural rate of unemployment and, at the same time, to alleviate the hardships experienced by the unemployed.

IDENTIFYING UNEMPLOYMENT

We begin this chapter by examining more precisely what the term *unemployment* means. We consider how governments measure unemployment, what problems arise in interpreting the unemployment data, how long the typical spell of unemployment lasts and why there will always be some people unemployed.

What is Unemployment?

The answer to this question may seem obvious: an unemployed person is someone who does not have a job. But as economists we need to be precise and careful in our definitions of economic categories. If you are in full-time education, for example, you do not have a full-time job in the usual sense of the word, i.e. you are not in full-time paid employment. And there is a good reason: you are studying. Hence you are not available for work. What if you were not a student but were suffering from some long-term illness that meant that you were unfit for work. Again, although you would not have a job, we would not say that you were unemployed because you would not be available for work. From these two examples, it seems clear that we need to qualify our original definition of an unemployed person as 'someone who does not have a job' to 'someone who does not have a job and who is available for work'.

But we still need to be clear as to what we mean by 'available for work'. Suppose you were not in full-time employment and were looking for a job and I offered you a job as my research assistant for €1 a day. Would you take it? If we ignore for a moment the complication that economic research is so interesting that it is its own reward, you would probably not take the job because the wage rate offered is so low. At another extreme, suppose you won so much money on the Euro Millions Lottery that you decided you would leave university and live off your winnings for the rest of your life. Would you be unemployed? No, because you would still be unavailable for work, no matter what wage rate you were offered. Thus, being unemployed also depends upon whether you are willing to work (whether you are 'available for work') at going wage rates.

We are now in a position to give a more precise definition of what it means to be unemployed: the number unemployed in an economy is the number of people of working age who are able and available for work at current wage rates and who do not have a job.

Normally, economists find it more convenient to speak of the *unemployment rate*. This expresses the number unemployed as a percentage of the *labour force*, which in turn can be defined as the total number of people who could possibly be employed in the economy at any given point in time. If you think about it, this must be equal to the total number of people who are employed plus the total number of people who are unemployed.

How Is Unemployment Measured?

How do government agencies go about measuring the unemployment rate in the economy? There are two basic ways.

The Claimant Count One simple way is to count the number of people who, on any given day, are claiming unemployment benefit payments from the government – the so-called *claimant count*. Since a government agency is paying out the benefits, it will be easy to gather data on the number of claimants. The government also has a good idea of the total labour force in employment, since it is receiving income tax payments from them. Adding to this the number of unemployment benefit claimants is a measure of the total labour force, and expressing the claimant count as a proportion of the labour force is a measure of the unemployment rate.

Since the government already has all the data necessary to compute the unemployment rate based on the claimant count, it is relatively cheap and easy to do. Unfortunately, there are a number of important drawbacks with the claimant count method.

One obvious problem is that it is subject to changes in the rules the government applies for eligibility to unemployment benefit. Suppose the government gets tougher and changes the rules so that few people are now entitled to unemployment benefit. The claimant count will go down and so will the measured unemployment rate, even though there has been no change in the number of people with or without work! The opposite would happen if the government became more lenient and relaxed the rules so that more people became eligible.

As it happens, governments do often change the rules on unemployment benefit eligibility. In the UK, for example, there have been about 30 changes to the eligibility rules over the past 25 years, all but one of which have reduced the claimant count and so reduced the unemployment rate based on this measure. The following are examples of categories of people who are excluded from the UK claimant count: people over the age of 55 who are without a job; those on government training programmes (largely school-leavers who have not found a job); anyone looking for part-time work; and people who have left the workforce for a while and now wish to return to employment (for example women who have raised a family). Many – if not all – of the people in these categories would be people who do not have a job, are of working age and are able and available for work at current wage rates; yet they would be excluded from measured unemployment in the UK using the claimant count method.

Labour Force Surveys The second, and probably more reliable method of measuring unemployment is through the use of surveys – in other words, going out and asking people questions – based on an accepted definition of unemployment. Questions then arise as to whom to speak to, how often (since surveys use up resources and are costly) and what definition of unemployment to use. Although the definition of unemployment that we developed earlier seems reasonable enough, the term 'available for work at current wage rates' may be too loose for this purpose. In the UK and many other countries, the government carries out Labour Force Surveys based on the standardized definition of unemployment from the International Labour Office, or ILO. The ILO definition of an unemployed person is someone who is without a job and who is willing to start work within the next two weeks and either has been looking for work within the past four weeks or was waiting to start a job.

The Labour Force Survey is carried out quarterly in the UK and throughout Europe. The surveys are published in different languages but scrutinized by statisticians to ensure comparability between the surveys carried out in each member state. In the UK, the survey is based on a sample of about 60 000 households. Based on the answers to survey questions, the government places each adult (aged 16 and older) in each surveyed household into one of three categories:

- employed
- unemployed
- not in the labour force (or 'economically inactive').

A person is considered employed if he or she spent some of the previous week working at a paid job. A person is unemployed if he or she fits the ILO definition of an unemployed person. A person who fits neither of the first two categories, such as a full-time student, homemaker or retiree, is not in the labour force (or, to use ILO terminology, is economically inactive). Figure 28.1 shows this breakdown for the UK in the spring of 2010. The total adult population (those over 16) was around 51.4 million. The population of working age (those aged between 16 and 64) was approximately 39.9 million.

FIGURE 28.1

Breakdown of the UK Adult Population in 2010

The UK Office for National Statistics divides the adult working population (those aged 16–64) into three categories: employed, unemployed and economically inactive. The labour force is made up of people who are either employed or unemployed (the economically active).

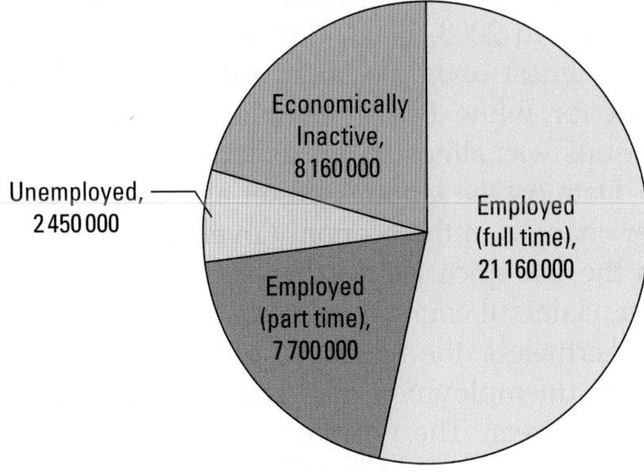

Source: UK Office for National Statistics, *Labour Market Statistics*, March 2010.

Once the government has placed all the individuals covered by the survey in a category, it computes various statistics to summarize the state of the labour market. The **labour force** is defined as the sum of the employed and the unemployed:

labour force
the total number of workers, including both the employed and the unemployed

Labour force = Number of employed + Number of unemployed

Then the **unemployment rate** can be measured as the percentage of the labour force that is unemployed:

unemployment rate
the percentage of the labour force that is unemployed

Unemployment rate = (Number of unemployed/Labour force) × 100

The government computes unemployment rates for the entire adult population and for more narrowly defined groups – men, women, youths and so on.

The same survey results are used to produce data on labour force participation. The **labour force participation rate** measures the percentage of the total adult population of the country that is in the labour force:

labour force participation rate (or economic activity rate)
the percentage of the adult population that is in the labour force

Labour force participation rate = (Labour force/Adult population) × 100

This statistic tells us the fraction of the population that has chosen to participate in the labour market. The labour force participation rate, like the unemployment rate, is computed both for the entire adult population and for more specific groups.

To see how these data are computed, consider the UK figures for spring 2010. According to the *Labour Market Statistics*, 28.86 million people were employed and 2.45 million people were unemployed. The labour force was:

Labour force = 28.86 + 2.45 = 31.31 million

The unemployment rate was:

Unemployment rate = (2.45/31.31)×100 = 8 per cent

Because the adult population (the number of people aged 16 and over) was 51.4 million, the labour force participation rate was:

Labour force participation rate = (31.31/51.4) × 100 = 61 per cent

Hence, in spring 2010, just under two-thirds of the UK adult population were participating in the labour market, and 8 per cent of those labour market participants were without work.

Figure 28.2 shows some statistics on UK unemployment for various groups within the population, broken down by ethnicity, also collected by the ONS. A number of points are worth noting. First – and perhaps most striking – unemployment rates for people from non-white ethnic groups were higher than those for white people. Secondly, unemployment rates among ethnic groups vary widely. In 2008, Black Caribbean people, closely followed by Bangladeshis had the highest unemployment rate in the UK at around 15 per cent – three times that for white British people. The unemployment rate for all ethnic minority groups was almost twice as high as for whites.

Data on the labour market also allow economists and policy makers to monitor changes in the economy over time. Figure 28.3 shows the unemployment rate in the UK since 1971, calculated using the claimant count. As we discussed earlier, claimant count figures are less reliable than the Labour Force Survey figures. Nevertheless, the figure is useful in demonstrating that the economy always has some unemployment and that the amount changes – often considerably – from year to year. The normal rate of unemployment, around which the unemployment rate fluctuates is called the **natural rate of unemployment** and the deviation of unemployment from its natural rate is called **cyclical unemployment**. Figure 28.3 shows that the economy always has some unemployment; a trend line has been added to give some indication of the natural rate of unemployment.

natural rate of unemployment
the normal rate of unemployment around which the unemployment rate fluctuates

cyclical unemployment
the deviation of unemployment from its natural rate

FIGURE 28.2

The Labour Market Experience of Different Groups

The ONS breaks down unemployment rates by ethnicity.

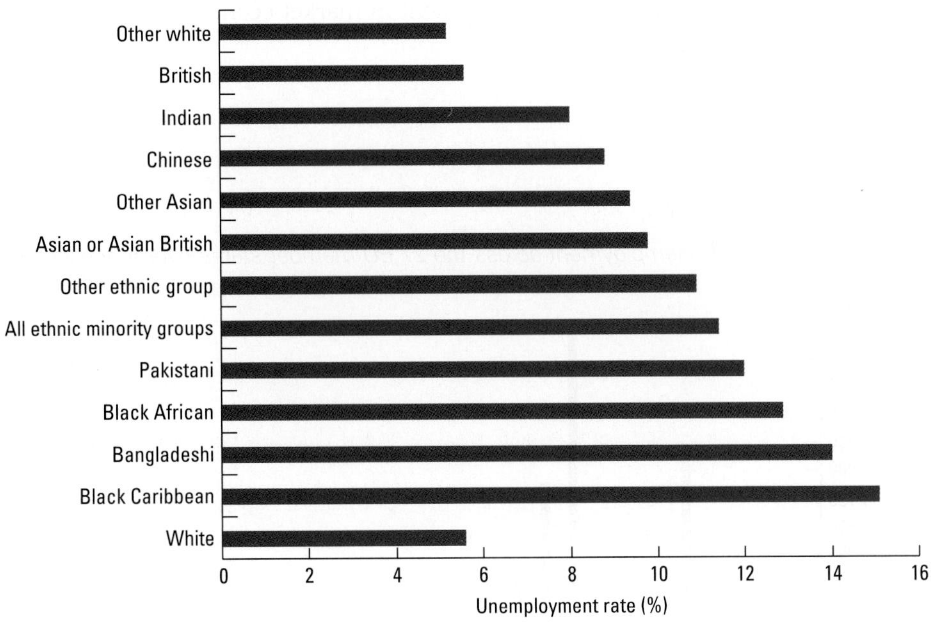

Source: UK Office for National Statistics.

FIGURE 28.3

UK Unemployment Rate Since 1971

This graph uses annual data on the unemployment rate to show the fraction of the labour force without a job, calculated by the LFS definition. A trend line has been added to show the natural rate of unemployment, the normal level of unemployment around which the unemployment rate fluctuates.

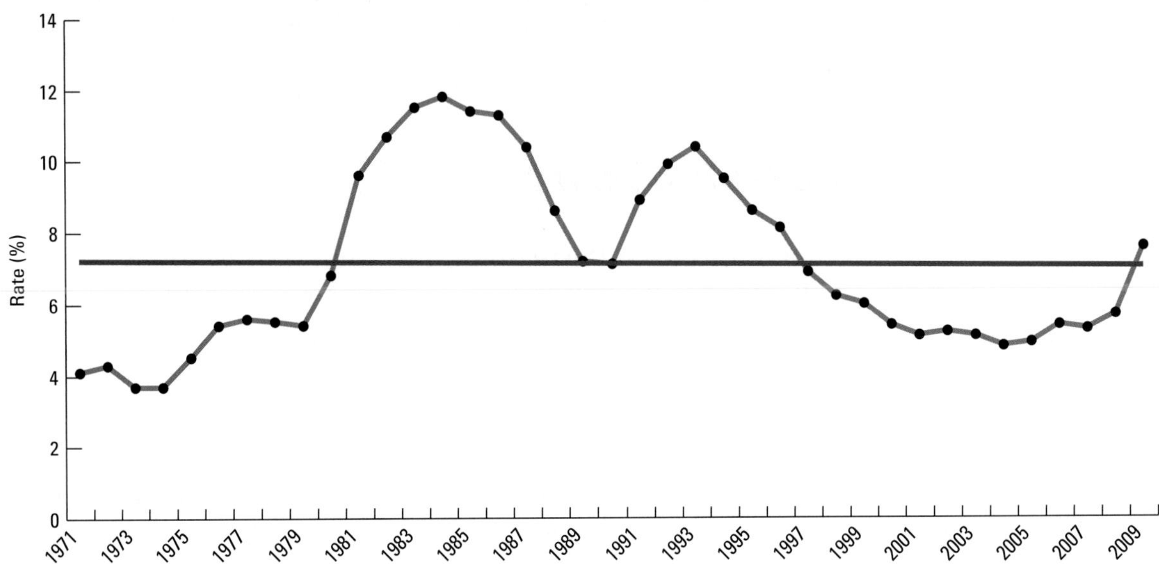

Source: UK Office for National Statistics.

Looking at figures for Europe we can see that there are different levels of unemployment across the EU. Figure 28.4 shows a snapshot of unemployment in the EU at the end of 2009. Later in this book we discuss short-run economic fluctuations, including the year-to-year fluctuations in unemployment. In the rest of this chapter, however, we ignore the short-run fluctuations and examine why there is always some unemployment in market economies.

FIGURE 28.4

EU Unemployment – December 2009

This graph shows the levels of unemployment across the 27 EU member states over a twelve month period.

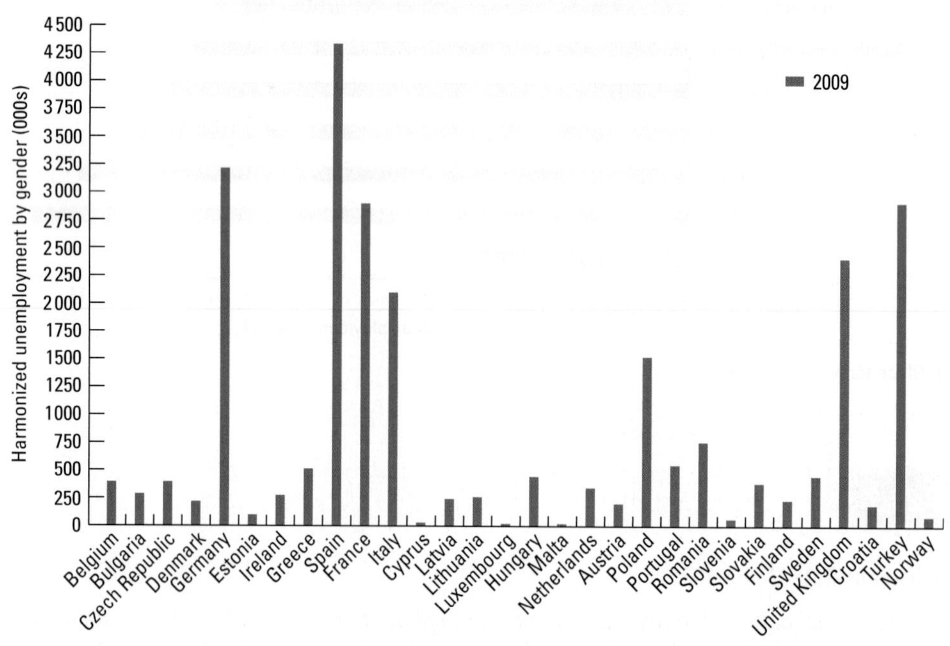

Source: Eurostat.

CASE STUDY

Labour Force Participation of Men and Women in the EU Economy

Women's role in society has changed dramatically over the past century in all of the advanced economies of the world. Social commentators have pointed to many causes for this change. In part, it is attributable to new technologies, such as the washing machine, clothes dryer, refrigerator, freezer and dishwasher, which have reduced the amount of time required to complete routine household tasks. In part, it is attributable to improved birth control, which has reduced the number of children born to the typical family. And, of course, this change in women's role is also partly attributable to changing political and social attitudes. Together these developments have had a profound impact on society in general and on the economy in particular.

Nowhere is that impact more obvious than in data on labour force participation – even in data covering just the last 20 years. Looking at the labour force participation rates of adult men and women in the European Union, the employment rates for young persons and men aged 25–54 remained stable over the period 2000–2008 but the number of older women in employment rose from 27.4 per cent to 36.9 per cent. The employment rate for women aged between 25 and 54 rose by 6 per cent during this time to around 72 per cent. For women in the 15–64 age group across the EU 27, the employment rate was around 59 per cent in 2008 whereas for men it was 73 per cent. One of the explanations for this gender gap is that it is wider in older persons, a reflection of past traditions when women tended not to enter employment and remain in the home and now find it harder to gain employment. In 2000, the European Council held in Lisbon, Portugal, set various goals in relation to employment and the economy. One of these goals included raising the employment rate for women to 60 per cent by 2010. In 2008, 59.1 per cent of working-age women were in work an expansion of over 5 per cent since 2000. Participation rates vary considerably across the EU with over 81 per cent of the working-age population active in the labour market in Denmark but only 59 per cent in Malta. Over 50 per cent of the EU 27 have participation rates in excess of 70 per cent but Poland, Hungary, Romania and Italy have rates less than 65 per cent. The variation between men and women is also marked. The participation rate of women in 2008 was below 64 per cent compared to 78 per cent for men. The Nordic and Baltic states tend to have narrower gaps whereas Malta, Greece and Italy have very wide gaps between participation rates for men and women.

The increase in women's labour force participation is easy to understand, but there are also changes in male participation rates. Young men now tend to stay in education longer than in previous generations; older men now tend to retire earlier and live longer. Thirdly, with more women employed, more fathers now stay at home to raise their children. Full-time students, retirees and stay-at-home fathers are all counted as out of the labour force. Of course, women are also tending to stay in education longer than their mothers and grandmothers, and also to live longer, so the rise in the female participation rate over the period is all the more striking.

How Long Are the Unemployed without Work?

In judging how serious the problem of unemployment is, one question to consider is whether unemployment is typically a short-term or long-term condition. If unemployment is short term, one might conclude that it is not a big problem. Workers may require a few weeks between jobs to find the openings that best suit their tastes and skills. Yet if unemployment is long term, one might conclude that it is a serious problem. Workers unemployed for many months are more likely to suffer economic and psychological hardship.

Because the duration of unemployment can affect our view about how big a problem it is, economists have devoted much energy to studying data on the duration of unemployment spells. In this work, they have uncovered a result that is important, subtle and seemingly contradictory: most spells of unemployment are short, and most unemployment observed at any given time is long term.

To see how this statement can be true, consider an example. Suppose that you visited the government's unemployment office every week for a year to survey the unemployed. Each week you find that there are four unemployed workers. Three of these workers are the same individuals for the whole year, while the fourth person changes every week. Based on this experience, would you say that unemployment is typically short term or long term?

Some simple calculations help answer this question. In this example, you meet a total of 55 unemployed people; 52 of them are unemployed for 1 week, and 3 are unemployed for the full year. This means that 52/55, or 95 per cent, of unemployment spells end in 1 week. Thus, most spells of unemployment are short. Yet consider the total amount of unemployment. The 3 people unemployed for 1 year (52 weeks) make up a total of 156 weeks of unemployment. Together with the 52 people unemployed for 1 week, this makes 208 weeks of unemployment. In this example, 156/208, or 75 per cent, of unemployment is attributable to those individuals who are unemployed for a full year. Thus, most unemployment observed at any given time is long term.

This subtle conclusion implies that economists and policy makers must be careful when interpreting data on unemployment and when designing policies to help the unemployed. Most people who become unemployed will soon find jobs. Yet most of the economy's unemployment problem is attributable to the relatively few workers who are jobless for long periods of time.

Why Are There Always Some People Unemployed?

We have discussed how the government measures the amount of unemployment, the problems that arise in interpreting unemployment statistics, and the findings of labour economists on the duration of unemployment. You should now have a good idea about what unemployment is.

This discussion, however, has not explained why economies experience unemployment. In most markets in the economy, prices adjust to bring quantity supplied and quantity demanded into balance. In an ideal labour market, wages would adjust to balance the quantity of labour supplied and the quantity of labour demanded. This adjustment of wages would ensure that all workers are always fully employed.

Of course, reality does not resemble this ideal. There are always some workers without jobs, even when the overall economy is doing well. In other words, the unemployment rate never falls to zero; instead, it fluctuates around the natural rate of unemployment. To understand this natural rate, the remaining sections in the chapter examine the reasons why actual labour markets depart from the ideal of full employment.

To preview our conclusions, we will find that there are four ways to explain unemployment in the long run. The first explanation is that it takes time for workers to search for the jobs that are best suited for them. The unemployment that results from the process of matching workers and jobs is sometimes called **frictional unemployment**, and it is often thought to explain relatively short spells of unemployment.

frictional unemployment
unemployment that results because it takes time for workers to search for the jobs that best suit their tastes and skills

The next three explanations for unemployment suggest that the number of jobs available in some labour markets may be insufficient to give a job to everyone who wants one. This occurs when the quantity of labour supplied exceeds the quantity demanded. Unemployment of this sort is sometimes called **structural unemployment**, and it is often thought to explain longer spells of unemployment. As we will see, this kind of unemployment results when wages are, for some reason, set above the level that brings supply and demand into equilibrium. We will examine three possible reasons for an above-equilibrium wage: minimum wage laws, unions and efficiency wages.

structural unemployment
unemployment that results because the number of jobs available in some labour markets is insufficient to provide a job for everyone who wants one

Quick Quiz How is the unemployment rate measured? • How might the unemployment rate overstate the amount of joblessness? How might it understate it?

In Chapter 33 we will introduce the ideas of John Maynard Keynes whose ideas on unemployment changed the nature of economics. Since the 1930s there has been an ongoing debate in economics about the principal causes of unemployment and the extent to which these causes stem from the supply side of the economy or the demand side. That debate has continued and has been brought into sharper focus with the rise in unemployment in many European countries and the United States during the fist decade of the new century. Policies designed to improve the workings of the supply side of the economy which includes cutting taxes, investing in training an education, changing the benefits system and improving incentives to get work have to be viewed alongside those which affect the level of aggregate demand in the economy. In essence, the debate centres on the extent to which unemployment is cyclical or structural – the latter accounting for the level of unemployment not due to changes in the economic cycle. As we build the theoretical building blocks of macroeconomics it must be remembered that policies to cut unemployment still deeply divide opinion in the economics profession.

JOB SEARCH

One reason why economies always experience some unemployment is job search. **Job search** is the process of matching workers with appropriate jobs. If all workers and all jobs were the same, so that all workers were equally well suited for all jobs, job search would not be a problem. Laid-off workers would quickly find new jobs that were well suited for them. But, in fact, workers differ in their tastes and skills, jobs differ in their attributes, and information about job candidates and job vacancies is disseminated slowly among the many firms and households in the economy.

job search
the process by which workers find appropriate jobs given their tastes and skills

Why Some Frictional Unemployment Is Inevitable

Frictional unemployment is often the result of changes in the demand for labour among different firms. When consumers decide that they prefer Brand X to Brand Y, the company producing Brand X increases employment, and the other firm lays off workers. The former Brand Y workers must now search for new jobs, and the Brand X producer must decide which new workers to hire for the various jobs that have opened up. The result of this transition is a period of unemployment.

Similarly, because different regions of the country produce different goods, employment can rise in one region while it falls in another. Consider, for instance, what happens when the world price of oil falls. Firms extracting oil from the fields below the North Sea, off the coast of Scotland, respond to the lower price by cutting back on production and employment. At the same time, cheaper petrol stimulates car sales, so car manufacturing firms in northern and central England raise production and employment. Changes in the composition of demand among industries or regions are called *sectoral shifts*. Because it takes time for workers to search for jobs in the new sectors, sectoral shifts temporarily cause unemployment.

Frictional unemployment is inevitable simply because the economy is always changing. In 1960, manufacturing as a percentage of GDP was 38 per cent in the UK; it now accounts for around 15 per cent. The number of people employed in manufacturing in 1960 was around 9 million compared to about 3 million today. The gross value added by industry (where gross value added is defined as the value of newly generated goods and services) in the EU 27 (which includes manufacturing) fell from 23.1 per cent in 1998 to 18.1 per cent in 2009. Even

Germany, traditionally heavily reliant on industry for its export earnings, has seen the value added by industry fall from 25.3 per cent in 1998 to 22 per cent in 2009. On the other hand, business services and finance contributed only about 3 per cent of UK GDP in the mid-1950s but contribute more than a quarter today. The EU 27 has seen gross value added by business activities and financial services increasing from 25.1 per cent of GDP in 1998 to 29.1 per cent in 2009. In Latvia the transition has been significant with an increase from 15.1 per cent in 1998 to 26.7 per cent by 2009. As these transitions take place, jobs are created in some firms and destroyed in others. The end result of this process has been higher productivity and higher living standards. But, along the way, workers in declining industries found themselves out of work and searching for new jobs.

In addition to the effects of sectoral shifts on unemployment, workers will leave their jobs sometimes because they realize that the jobs are not a good match for their tastes and skills and they wish to look for a better job. Many of these workers, especially younger ones, find new jobs at higher wages, although given the vast improvements in information technology in recent years (especially the internet) it is likely that many people search for new jobs without actually quitting their current job. Nevertheless, this churning of the labour force is normal in a well functioning and dynamic market economy, and the result is some amount of frictional unemployment.

Public Policy and Job Search

Even if some frictional unemployment is inevitable, the precise amount is not. The faster information spreads about job openings and worker availability, the more rapidly the economy can match workers and firms. The internet, for instance, may help facilitate job search and reduce frictional unemployment. In addition, public policy may play a role. If policy can reduce the time it takes unemployed workers to find new jobs, it can reduce the economy's natural rate of unemployment.

Government policies try to facilitate job search in various ways. One way is through government-run employment agencies or job centres, which give out information about job vacancies. Another way is through public training schemes, which aim to ease the transition of workers from declining to growing industries and to help disadvantaged groups escape poverty. Advocates of these policies believe that they make the economy operate more efficiently by keeping the labour force more fully employed, and that they reduce the inequities inherent in a constantly changing market economy.

Critics of these policies question whether the government should get involved with the process of job search. They argue that it is better to let the private market match workers and jobs. In fact, most job search in the economy takes place without intervention by the government. Newspaper advertisements, internet job sites, head-hunters and word of mouth all help spread information about job openings and job candidates. Similarly, much worker education is done privately, either through schools or through on-the-job training. These critics contend that the government is no better – and most likely worse – at disseminating the right information to the right workers and deciding what kinds of worker training would be most valuable. They claim that these decisions are best made privately by workers and employers.

unemployment insurance
a government programme that partially protects workers' incomes when they become unemployed

Unemployment Insurance

One government policy that increases the amount of frictional unemployment, without intending to do so, is **unemployment insurance** (or, as it is called in the UK, national insurance). This policy is designed to offer workers partial protection against job loss. The unemployed who quit their jobs, were fired for just cause or who have just entered the labour force are not eligible. Benefits are paid only to the unemployed who were laid off because their previous employers no longer needed their skills.

While unemployment insurance reduces the hardship of unemployment, it is argued that it can also increase the amount of unemployment. This explanation is based on one of the *Ten Principles of Economics* in Chapter 1: people respond to incentives. Because unemployment benefits stop when a worker takes a new job, the unemployed, it is argued, devote less effort to job search and are more likely to turn down unattractive job offers. In addition, because unemployment insurance makes unemployment less onerous, workers are less likely to seek guarantees of job security when they negotiate with employers over the terms of employment. However, research on unemployment insurance in Europe gives a different perspective. In a paper by Konstantinos Tatsiramos[1] the benefits to workers searching for jobs and receiving unemployment insurance is greater than the costs:

> This paper provides evidence on the effect of unemployment benefits on unemployment and employment duration in Europe, using individual data from the European Community Household Panel for eight countries. Even if receiving benefits has a direct negative effect increasing the duration of unemployment spells, there is also a positive indirect effect of benefits on subsequent employment duration. This indirect effect is pronounced in countries with relatively generous benefit systems, and for recipients who have remained unemployed for at least six months. In terms of the magnitude of the effect, recipients remain employed on average two to four months longer than non-recipients. This represents a ten to twenty per cent increase relative to the average employment duration, compensating for the additional time spent in unemployment.

The effect of unemployment insurance is likely to be related to the way the scheme is designed and operated. In one US study, when unemployed workers applied to collect unemployment insurance benefits, some of them were randomly selected and offered each a $500 bonus if they found new jobs within 11 weeks. This group was then compared with a control group not offered the incentive. The average spell of unemployment for the group offered the bonus was 7 per cent shorter than the average spell for the control group. This experiment shows that the design of the unemployment insurance system influences the effort that the unemployed devote to job search.

Several other studies examined search effort by following a group of workers over time. Unemployment insurance benefits, rather than lasting forever, usually run out after six months or a year. These studies found that when the unemployed become ineligible for benefits, the probability of their finding a new job rises markedly. Thus, receiving unemployment insurance benefits does reduce the search effort of the unemployed.

Even though unemployment insurance reduces search effort and raises unemployment, we should not necessarily conclude that the policy is a bad one. The policy does achieve its primary goal of reducing the income uncertainty that workers face. In addition, when workers turn down unattractive job offers, they have the opportunity to look for jobs that better suit their tastes and skills. Some economists have argued that unemployment insurance improves the ability of the economy to match each worker with the most appropriate job.

---

[1]Tatsiramos, K. (2006) *Unemployment Insurance in Europe: Unemployment Duration and Subsequent Employment Stability*. Institute for the Study of Labor Discussion Paper no. 2280.

IN THE NEWS

We have mentioned Richard Thaler and Cass Sunstein on several occasions in this book. Thaler and Sunstein developed the idea of 'nudges' – ways of focusing attention on relatively small details to change people's behaviour in a desired way. Their ideas have widespread application and with the rise in global unemployment following the recession, the subject of unemployment insurance has been reviewed in the context of 'nudges' as this blog outlines.

Rethinking Unemployment Insurance

With millions more people across Europe and North America unemployed compared with the start of the year, unemployment insurance has returned to the forefront as a public policy issue. Most of the talk has been about extending unemployment benefits. It may be time, though, for lawmakers to engage in a more comprehensive reform debate – one that includes a proposal by Jeff Kling to alter the structure of unemployment insurance in such a way that recognizes the psychology of losing a job and strengthens the incentives for returning to work.

Kling's revenue-neutral proposal would reform unemployment insurance by shifting government resources toward protection against especially damaging long stretches of unemployment or permanent effects of job loss, such as lifetime wage reductions. Laid-off workers can remain unemployed for long stretches for two major reasons, one economic and one psychological. 1) They simply cannot find work; 2) They refuse to take lower paying jobs thinking they can find a new one that pays as much as their last.

To create an incentive for workers to clear the psychological hurdle, Kling proposes setting up temporary earnings replacement accounts (TERA) to improve the protection against the effects of long-term unemployment and permanent wage-reduction. The account would be funded by the workers themselves during more prosperous times, and drawn from during periods of distress. Workers could also borrow against the account from future earnings. During periods of unemployment or lower-wage jobs, workers would draw funds from both their unemployment account and more traditional unemployment insurance (UI), which would result in a broader safety net from a similar government budget. While the unemployment accounts would be funded by workers, the unemployment insurance would be funded by firms, as it is currently.

In comparison with UI, use of TERAs should reduce the average amount of time that people spend out of work. Use of TERAs instead of UI increases the price for additional unemployment (at least among those who do not expect to retire with an unpaid loan), because TERA withdrawals would need to be repaid from future income. As a result, the introduction of TERAs may reduce the overall duration of unemployment by 5 to 10 per cent.

The duration of unemployment would also be affected by the availability of wage-loss insurance. Individuals considering a job offering a wage below their insured wage level would be more likely to accept it, since the hourly rate of pay would be augmented by wage loss insurance payments. Making work more rewarding should reduce the tendency of some people to become discouraged and to remain unemployed or even stop looking for work. This reduced duration of unemployment is unlikely to be associated with workers taking jobs too rapidly, rather than waiting more patiently for a more productive job match.

Kling makes the argument that his proposal will actually reduce temporary layoffs by 10–15 per cent and permanent layoffs by an unspecified amount. How? By forcing firms to bear the costs of unemployment. Under the current unemployment insurance system, firms make payments to the government to cover payments. Kling proposes that firms contribute to government coffers for wage-loss insurance, repayment insurance, assistance on earnings and replacement accounts for those with lower wages. Since the proposal is revenue neutral, the total costs to these forms of insurance would be the same as they are now. But Kling proposes raising the taxable earnings base to a real value of $90 000 (in some states in the USA it is currently below $10 000), cutting the overall unemployment insurance payroll tax rate and lowering the minimum amounts that firms must pay. The result, Kling says, would be a tighter linkage between layoffs and direct firm costs. Intra-firm subsidies for unemployment insurance would thus be reduced.

In addition, since most employees who become unemployed would bear the costs of unemployment benefits directly, they would be much more likely to voice strong opposition to temporary layoffs than they are under UI when they receive payments with no corresponding future obligations. Firms in industries with frequent temporary layoffs would be pressured by the labour market to raise wages in order to continue to attract workers who, under the proposal, would be self-insuring income loss during layoff through savings and borrowing.

Here is one more reason why individuals might be more likely to return to work faster under Kling's plan. Recent research by economist Raj Chetty argues unemployment insurance raises some problems of moral hazard, but that equally serious effects come from something he calls the 'liquidity effect'. In essence, unemployment benefits allow an individual to remain out of work longer since they have enough cash-on-hand to survive. But if workers have to use the money they saved themselves through their earnings replacement accounts to fund their short-term unemployment, they could be more motivated to find a job. Certainly more motivated than if the entire insurance check was coming out of some other taxpayer's pocket.

Source: Adapted from: http://nudges.wordpress.com/2008/12/10/rethinking-unemployment-insurance-part-i/ and http://nudges.wordpress.com/2008/12/16/rethinking-unemployment-insurance-part-ii/ accessed 9 April 2009.

The study of unemployment insurance shows that the unemployment rate is an imperfect measure of a nation's overall level of economic well-being. Most economists agree that eliminating unemployment insurance would reduce the amount of unemployment in the economy. Yet economists disagree on whether economic well-being would be enhanced or diminished by this change in policy.

Quick Quiz How would an increase in the world price of oil affect the amount of frictional unemployment? Is this unemployment undesirable? What public policies might affect the amount of unemployment caused by this price change?

MINIMUM WAGE LAWS

Having seen how frictional unemployment results from the process of matching workers and jobs, let's now examine how structural unemployment results when the number of jobs is insufficient for the number of workers.

To understand structural unemployment, we begin by reviewing how unemployment arises from minimum wage laws. Although minimum wages are not the predominant reason for unemployment in an economy, they have an important effect on certain groups with particularly high unemployment rates. Moreover, the analysis of minimum wages is a natural place to start because, as we will see, it can be used to understand some of the other reasons for structural unemployment.

Figure 28.5 reviews the basic economics of a minimum wage. When a minimum wage law forces the wage to remain above the level that balances supply and demand, it raises the quantity of labour supplied and reduces the quantity of labour demanded compared to the equilibrium level. There is a surplus of labour. Because there are more workers willing to work than there are jobs, some workers are unemployed.

Because we discussed minimum wage laws in Chapter 6, we will not discuss them further here. It is, however, important to note why minimum wage laws are not a predominant reason for unemployment: most workers in the economy have wages well above the legal minimum. Minimum wage laws are binding most often for the least skilled and least experienced members of the labour force, such as teenagers. It is only among these workers that minimum wage laws explain the existence of unemployment.

FIGURE 28.5

Unemployment From a Wage Above the Equilibrium Level

In this labour market, the wage at which supply and demand balance is W_E. At this equilibrium wage, the quantity of labour supplied and the quantity of labour demanded both equal L_E. By contrast, if the wage is forced to remain above the equilibrium level, perhaps because of a minimum wage law, the quantity of labour supplied rises to L_S, and the quantity of labour demanded falls to L_D. The resulting surplus of labour, L_S–L_D, represents unemployment.

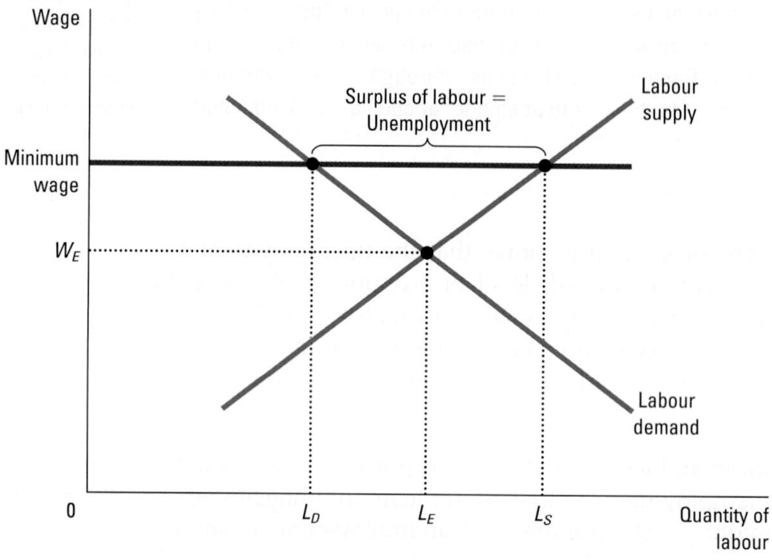

Although Figure 28.5 is drawn to show the effects of a minimum wage law, it also illustrates a more general lesson: if the wage is kept above the equilibrium level for any reason, the result is unemployment. Minimum wage laws are just one reason why wages may be 'too high'. In the remaining two sections of this chapter, we consider two other reasons why wages may be kept above the equilibrium level – unions and efficiency wages. The basic economics of unemployment in these cases is the same as that shown in Figure 28.5, but these explanations of unemployment can apply to many more of the economy's workers.

At this point, however, we should stop and notice that the structural unemployment that arises from an above-equilibrium wage is, in an important sense, different from the frictional unemployment that arises from the process of job search. The need for job search is not due to the failure of wages to balance labour supply and labour demand. When job search is the explanation for unemployment, workers are *searching* for the jobs that best suit their tastes and skills. By contrast, when the wage is above the equilibrium level, the quantity of labour supplied exceeds the quantity of labour demanded, and workers are unemployed because they are *waiting* for jobs to open up.

Quick Quiz Draw the supply curve and the demand curve for a labour market in which the wage is fixed above the equilibrium level. Show the quantity of labour supplied, the quantity demanded and the amount of unemployment.

UNIONS AND COLLECTIVE BARGAINING

A union is a worker association that bargains with employers over wages and working conditions. Union density measures the proportion of the workforce that is unionized, excluding people who cannot, for legal or other reasons, be members of a union – for example, members of the armed forces. Broadly speaking, this amounts to expressing the number of union members as a proportion of civilian employees plus the unemployed. In the UK in 2006, union density was 28.4 per cent, and has been steadily falling since 1995 when it stood at around 32.4 per cent and an even greater marked fall from the beginning of the 1980s, when it was over 50 per cent. In other European countries there is a similar trend of falling union density. In Germany density has fallen from 25.3 per cent in 1999 to 19.9 per cent in 2007, in the Netherlands the fall has been from 24.6 per cent to 19.8 per cent and in Hungary from 26.1 per cent to 16.9 per cent in the same period. However, there are exceptions with countries like Finland, Denmark, Iceland and Sweden having stable densities between 74 per cent and almost 86 per cent. In the United States, by comparison, density is around 12 per cent and in Australia 18.5 per cent (figures for 2007).

The Economics of Unions

A union is a type of cartel. Like any cartel, a union is a group of sellers acting together in the hope of exerting their joint market power. Workers in a union act as a group when discussing their wages, benefits and working conditions with their employers. The process by which unions and firms agree on the terms of employment is called **collective bargaining**.

collective bargaining
the process by which unions and firms agree on the terms of employment

When a union bargains with a firm, it asks for higher wages, better benefits and better working conditions than the firm would offer in the absence of a union. If the union and the firm do not reach agreement, the union can take various steps to put pressure on employers to come to an agreement including working to rule (doing only what is agreed in the contract of employment) and as a last resort organizing a withdrawal of labour from the firm, called a strike. Because a strike reduces production, sales and profit, a firm facing a strike threat is likely to agree to pay higher wages than it otherwise would. Economists who study the effects of unions typically find that union workers earn significantly more than similar workers who do not belong to unions.

When a union raises the wage above the equilibrium level, it raises the quantity of labour supplied and reduces the quantity of labour demanded, resulting in unemployment. Those workers who remain employed are better off, but those who were previously employed and are now unemployed are worse off. Indeed, unions are often thought to cause conflict between different groups of workers – between the *insiders* who benefit from high union wages and the *outsiders* who do not get the union jobs.

The outsiders can respond to their status in one of two ways. Some of them remain unemployed and wait for the chance to become insiders and earn the high union wage. Others take jobs in firms that are not unionized. Thus, when unions raise wages in one part of the economy, the supply of labour increases in other parts of the economy. This increase in labour supply, in turn, reduces wages in industries that are not unionized. In other words, workers in unions reap the benefit of collective bargaining, while workers not in unions bear some of the cost.

The role of unions in the economy depends in part on the laws that govern union organization and collective bargaining. Normally, explicit agreements among members of a cartel are illegal. If firms that sell a common product were to agree to set a high price for that product, they would generally be held to be in breach of competition law and the government would prosecute these firms in the civil and criminal courts. In contrast, unions are given exemption from these laws in the belief that workers need greater market power as they bargain with employers.

Legislation affecting the market power of unions is a perennial topic of political debate. Members of parliament sometime debate *right-to-work laws,* which give workers in a unionized firm the right to choose whether to join the union. In the absence of such laws, unions can insist during collective bargaining that firms make union membership a requirement for employment.

Are Unions Good or Bad for the Economy?

Economists disagree about whether unions are good or bad for the economy as a whole. Let's consider both sides of the debate.

Critics of unions argue that unions are merely a type of cartel. When unions raise wages above the level that would prevail in competitive markets, they reduce the quantity of labour demanded, cause some workers to be unemployed and reduce the wages in the rest of the economy. The resulting allocation of labour is, critics argue, both inefficient and inequitable. It is inefficient because high union wages reduce employment in unionized firms below the efficient, competitive level. It is inequitable because some workers benefit at the expense of other workers.

Advocates of unions contend that unions are a necessary antidote to the market power of the firms that hire workers. In some regions where one particular company is the dominant employer, if workers do not accept the wages and working conditions that the firm offers, they may have little choice but to move or stop working. In the absence of a union, therefore, the firm could use its market power to pay lower wages and offer worse working conditions than would prevail if it had to compete with other firms for the same workers. In this case, a union may balance the firm's market power and protect the workers from being at the mercy of the firm owners.

Advocates of unions also claim that unions are important for helping firms respond efficiently to workers' concerns. Whenever a worker takes a job, the worker and the firm must agree on many attributes of the job in addition to the wage: hours of work, overtime, holidays, sick leave, health benefits, promotion schedules, job security and so on. By representing workers' views on these issues, unions allow firms to provide the right mix of job attributes. In many countries unions have now taken on additional roles in supporting workers with respect to offering legal support in the event of an individual dispute at work, advice on pensions, financial services such as insurance and support for those who have been injured or disabled at work and have to retire early. Even if unions have the adverse effect of pushing wages above the equilibrium level and causing unemployment, they have the benefit of helping firms keep a happy and productive workforce.

"Of course in those days there were no problems with unions."

In the end, there is no consensus among economists about whether unions are good or bad for the economy. Like many institutions, their influence is probably beneficial in some circumstances and adverse in others.

Quick Quiz How does a union in the car industry affect wages and employment at Ford and Nissan plants in the UK? How might it affect wages and employment in other industries?

THE THEORY OF EFFICIENCY WAGES

A fourth reason why economies always experience some unemployment – in addition to job search, minimum wage laws and unions – is suggested by the theory of efficiency wages which we outlined in Chapter 19. According to this theory, firms operate more efficiently if wages are above the equilibrium level. Therefore, it may be profitable for firms to keep wages high even in the presence of a surplus of labour.

In some ways, the unemployment that arises from efficiency wages is similar to the unemployment that arises from minimum wage laws and unions. In all three cases, unemployment is the result of wages above the level that balances the quantity of labour supplied and the quantity of labour demanded. Yet there is also an important difference. Minimum wage laws and unions prevent firms from lowering wages in the presence of a surplus of workers. Efficiency wage theory states that such a constraint on firms is unnecessary in many cases because firms may be better off keeping wages above the equilibrium level.

Why should firms want to keep wages high? This decision may seem odd at first, for wages are a large part of firms' costs. Normally, we expect profit-maximizing firms to want to keep costs – and therefore wages – as low as possible. The novel insight of efficiency wage theory is that paying high wages might be profitable because they might raise the efficiency of a firm's workers.

There are several types of efficiency wage theory. Each type suggests a different explanation for why firms may want to pay high wages. Let's now consider four of these types.

Worker Health

The first and simplest type of efficiency wage theory emphasizes the link between wages and worker health. Better paid workers eat a more nutritious diet, and workers who eat a better diet are healthier and more productive. A firm may find it more profitable to pay high wages and have healthy, productive workers than to pay lower wages and have less healthy, less productive workers.

This type of efficiency wage theory is not relevant for firms in rich countries such as the United Kingdom. In these countries, the equilibrium wages for most workers are well above the level needed for an adequate diet. Firms are not concerned that paying equilibrium wages would place their workers' health in jeopardy.

This type of efficiency wage theory is more relevant for firms in less developed countries where inadequate nutrition is a more common problem. Unemployment is high in the cities of many poor African countries, for example. In these countries, firms may fear that cutting wages would, in fact, adversely influence their workers' health and productivity. In other words, concern over nutrition may explain why firms do not cut wages despite a surplus of labour.

Worker Turnover

A second type of efficiency wage theory emphasizes the link between wages and worker turnover. Workers quit jobs for many reasons – to take jobs in other firms, to move to other parts of the country, to leave the labour force and so on. The frequency with which they quit depends on the entire set of incentives they face, including the benefits of leaving and the benefits of staying. The more a firm pays its workers, the less often its workers will choose to leave. Thus, a firm can reduce turnover among its workers by paying them a high wage.

Why do firms care about turnover? The reason is that it is costly for firms to hire and train new workers. Moreover, even after they are trained, newly hired workers are not as productive as experienced workers. Firms with higher turnover, therefore, will tend to have higher production costs. Firms may find it profitable to pay wages above the equilibrium level in order to reduce worker turnover.

Worker Effort

A third type of efficiency wage theory emphasizes the link between wages and worker effort. In many jobs, workers have some discretion over how hard to work. As a result, firms monitor the efforts of their workers, and workers caught shirking their responsibilities can be disciplined and possibly dismissed. But not all shirkers are caught immediately because monitoring workers is costly and imperfect. A firm can respond to this problem by paying wages above the equilibrium level. High wages make workers more eager to keep their jobs and, thereby, give workers an incentive to put forward their best effort.

This particular type of efficiency wage theory is similar to the old Marxist idea of the 'reserve army of the unemployed'. Marx thought that employers benefited from unemployment because the threat of unemployment helped to discipline those workers who had jobs. In the worker effort variant of efficiency wage theory, unemployment fills a similar role. If the wage were at the level that balanced supply and demand, workers would have less reason to work hard because if they were fired, they could quickly find new jobs at the same wage. Therefore, firms raise wages above the equilibrium level, causing unemployment and providing an incentive for workers not to shirk their responsibilities.

Worker Quality

A fourth and final type of efficiency wage theory emphasizes the link between wages and worker quality. When a firm hires new workers, it cannot perfectly gauge the quality of the applicants. By paying a high wage, the firm attracts a better pool of workers to apply for its jobs.

To see how this might work, consider a simple example. Waterwell Company owns one well and needs one worker to pump water from the well. Two workers, Jekyll and Hyde, are interested in the job. Jekyll, a proficient worker, is willing to work for €10 per hour. Below that wage, he would rather start his own lawn-mowing business. Hyde, a complete incompetent, is willing to work for anything above €2 per hour. Below that wage, he would rather sit on the beach. Economists say that Jekyll's *reservation wage* – the lowest wage he would accept – is €10, and Hyde's reservation wage is €2.

What wage should the firm set? If the firm were interested in minimizing labour costs, it would set the wage at €2 per hour. At this wage, the quantity of workers supplied (one) would balance the quantity demanded. Hyde would take the job, and Jekyll would not apply for it. Yet suppose Waterwell knows that only one of these two applicants is competent, but it does not know whether it is Jekyll or Hyde. If the firm hires the incompetent worker, he may damage the well, causing the firm huge losses. In this case, the firm has a better strategy than paying the equilibrium wage of €2 and hiring Hyde. It can offer €10 per hour, inducing both Jekyll and Hyde to apply for the job. By choosing randomly between these two applicants and turning the other away, the firm has a 50:50 chance of hiring the competent one. By contrast, if the firm offers any lower wage, it is sure to hire the incompetent worker.

This story illustrates a general phenomenon. When a firm faces a surplus of workers, it might seem profitable to reduce the wage it is offering. But by reducing the wage, the firm induces an adverse change in the mix of workers. In this case, at a wage of €10, Waterwell has two workers applying for one job. But if Waterwell responds to this labour surplus by reducing the wage, the competent worker (who has better alternative opportunities) will not apply. Thus, it is profitable for the firm to pay a wage above the level that balances supply and demand.

Quick Quiz Give four explanations for why firms might find it profitable to pay wages above the level that balances quantity of labour supplied and quantity of labour demanded.

CONCLUSION

In this chapter we discussed the measurement of unemployment and the reasons why economies always experience some degree of unemployment. We have seen how job search, minimum wage laws, unions and efficiency wages can all help explain why some workers do not have jobs. Which of these four explanations for the natural rate of unemployment are the most important? Unfortunately, there is no easy way to tell. Economists differ in which of these explanations of unemployment they consider most important.

The analysis of this chapter yields an important lesson: although the economy will always have some unemployment, its natural rate is not immutable. Many events and policies can change the amount of unemployment the economy typically experiences. As the information revolution changes the process of job search, as government adjusts the minimum wage, as workers form or quit unions, and as firms alter their reliance on efficiency wages, the natural rate of unemployment evolves. Unemployment is not a simple problem with a simple solution. But how we choose to organize our society can profoundly influence how prevalent a problem it is.

SUMMARY

- The unemployment rate is the percentage of those who would like to work who do not have jobs. The government calculates this statistic monthly based on a survey of thousands of households.
- The unemployment rate is an imperfect measure of joblessness. Some people who call themselves unemployed may actually not want to work, and some people who would like to work have left the labour force after an unsuccessful search.
- In many advanced economies, most people who become unemployed find work within a short period of time. Nevertheless, most unemployment observed at any given time is attributable to the few people who are unemployed for long periods of time.
- One reason for unemployment is the time it takes for workers to search for jobs that best suit their tastes and skills. Unemployment insurance is a government policy that, while protecting workers' incomes, increases the amount of frictional unemployment.
- A second reason why an economy may always have some unemployment is if there is a minimum wage that exceeds the wage that would balance supply and demand for the workers who are eligible for the minimum wage. By raising the wage of unskilled and inexperienced workers above the equilibrium level, minimum wage laws raise the quantity of labour supplied and reduce the quantity demanded. The resulting surplus of labour represents unemployment.

- A third reason for unemployment is the market power of unions. When unions push the wages in unionized industries above the equilibrium level, they create a surplus of labour.
- A fourth reason for unemployment is suggested by the theory of efficiency wages. According to this theory, firms find it profitable to pay wages above the equilibrium level. High wages can improve worker health, lower worker turnover, increase worker effort and raise worker quality.

KEY CONCEPTS

labour force, p. 596
unemployment rate, p. 596
labour force participation rate, p. 596
natural rate of unemployment, p. 596
cyclical unemployment, p. 596
frictional unemployment, p. 600
structural unemployment, p. 600
job search, p. 601
unemployment insurance, p. 602
collective bargaining, p. 607

QUESTIONS FOR REVIEW

1. How do national statistical offices compute the labour force, the unemployment rate and the labour force participation rate?
2. Is unemployment typically short term or long term? Explain.
3. Why is frictional unemployment inevitable? How might the government reduce the amount of frictional unemployment?
4. Are minimum wage laws a better explanation for structural unemployment among teenagers or among university graduates? Why?
5. How do unions affect the natural rate of unemployment?
6. What claims do advocates of unions make to argue that unions are good for the economy?
7. Explain four ways in which a firm might increase its profits by raising the wages it pays.

PROBLEMS AND APPLICATIONS

1. According to the UK Office for National Statistics, in the summer of 2010, of all adult people, 28 980 000 were employed, 1 116 000 were unemployed and around 10 904 000 were not in the labour force. How big was the labour force? What was the labour force participation rate? What was the unemployment rate?
2. Go to the website of the UK Office for National Statistics (http://www.statistics.gov.uk) or the statistics office for the country where you are studying. What is the national unemployment rate right now? Find the unemployment rate for the demographic group that best fits a description of you (for example, based on age, sex and ethnic group). Is it higher or lower than the national average? Why do you think this is so?
3. According to the Labour Force Survey, between 2003 and 2008, total UK employment increased by around 1.25 million workers, but the number of unemployed workers increased by 287 000.
   a. How are these numbers consistent with each other?
   b. In some cases, there can be an increase in the number of people employed but the number of unemployed people declines by a smaller amount. Why might one expect a reduction in the number of people counted as unemployed to be smaller than the increase in the number of people employed?
4. Are the following workers more likely to experience short-term or long-term unemployment? Explain.

a. A construction worker laid off because of bad weather.
b. A manufacturing worker who loses her job at a plant in an isolated area.
c. A bus industry worker laid off because of competition from the railway.
d. A short-order cook who loses his job when a new restaurant opens across the street.
e. An expert welder with little formal education who loses her job when the company installs automatic welding machinery.

5. Using a diagram of the labour market, show the effect of an increase in the minimum wage on the wage paid to workers, the number of workers supplied, the number of workers demanded and the amount of unemployment.
6. Do you think that firms in small towns or in cities have more market power in hiring? Do you think that firms generally have more market power in hiring today than 50 years ago, or less? How do you think this change over time has affected the role of unions in the economy? Explain.
7. Consider an economy with two labour markets, neither of which is unionized. Now suppose a union is established in one market.
   a. Show the effect of the union on the market in which it is formed. In what sense is the quantity of labour employed in this market an inefficient quantity?
   b. Show the effect of the union on the non-unionized market. What happens to the equilibrium wage in this market?
8. It can be shown that an industry's demand for labour will become more elastic when the demand for the industry's product becomes more elastic. Let's consider the implications of this fact for the UK car industry and for the Transport and General Workers' Union (T&G) – the main labour union for UK car workers.
   a. What happened to the elasticity of demand for British cars when the Japanese developed a strong car industry? What happened to the elasticity of demand for UK car workers? Explain.
   b. As the chapter explains, a union generally faces a trade-off in deciding how much to raise wages, because a bigger increase is better for workers who remain employed but also results in a greater reduction in employment. How did the rise in car imports from Japan affect the wage – employment trade-off faced by the T&G?
   c. Do you think the growth of the Japanese car industry increased or decreased the gap between the competitive wage and the wage chosen by the T&G? Explain.
9. Some workers in the economy are paid a flat salary and some are paid by commission. Which compensation scheme would require more monitoring by supervisors? In which case do firms have an incentive to pay more than the equilibrium level (as in the worker effort variant of efficiency wage theory)? What factors do you think determine the type of compensation firms choose?
10. (This problem is challenging.) Suppose that the government passes a law requiring employers to provide employees some benefit (such as a guaranteed pension) that raises the cost of an employee by €4 per hour.
    a. What effect does this new law have on the demand for labour? (In answering this and the following questions, be quantitative when you can.)
    b. If employees place a value on this benefit exactly equal to its cost, what effect does the new law have on the supply of labour?
    c. If the wage is free to balance supply and demand, how does this law affect the wage and the level of employment? Are employers better or worse off? Are employees better or worse off?
    d. If a minimum wage law prevents the wage from balancing supply and demand, how does the new law affect the wage, the level of employment and the level of unemployment? Are employers better or worse off? Are employees better or worse off?
    e. Now suppose that workers do not value the benefit arising from the new law at all. How does this alternative assumption change your answers to parts (b), (c) and (d) above?

For further resources, visit www.cengage.co.uk/mankiw_taylor2

10

MONEY AND PRICES IN THE LONG RUN

29 THE MONETARY SYSTEM

When you walk into a restaurant to buy a meal, you receive something of value: the enjoyment of the food together with the experience of eating the meal in a pleasant environment and being waited upon. To pay for this service, you might hand the restaurateur several pieces of brightly coloured paper decorated with strange symbols, buildings and maps of Europe (or even a portrait of a monarch). Or you might hand him a small, rectangular piece of coloured plastic with a magnetic strip and a small computer chip set into it, which the restaurateur will later return to you. You might even hand him a single piece of paper with the name of a bank and your signature. Whether you pay by cash, debit card, credit card or cheque, the restaurateur is happy to work hard to satisfy your gastronomic desires either in exchange for pieces of paper that, in and of themselves, are worthless, or in exchange for borrowing an equally worthless small piece of plastic from you for a few minutes.

To anyone who has lived in a modern economy, this social custom is not at all odd. Even though paper money has no intrinsic value, the restaurateur is confident that, in the future, some third person will accept it in exchange for something that the restaurateur does value. And that third person is confident that some fourth person will accept the money, with the knowledge that yet a fifth person will accept the money … and so on. To the restaurateur and to other people in our society, your cash represents a claim to goods and services in the future. If you paid by debit card, the restaurateur is happy because he knows that money has been transferred more or less instantly to his bank account from your bank account, and the figures on his bank balance also represent a claim to goods and services produced by the economy. Similarly, if you paid by cheque, he knows that money will be transferred between accounts as soon as the cheque is processed – usually within a few days. If you paid with a credit card, he knows that his account has been credited with the money that you have borrowed on the credit card in order to pay the restaurant bill.

The social custom of using money for transactions is extraordinarily useful in a large, complex society. Imagine, for a moment, that there was no item in the economy widely accepted in exchange for goods and services. People would have to rely on barter – the exchange of one good or service for another – to obtain the things they need. To get your restaurant meal, for instance, you would have to offer the restaurateur something of immediate value. You could offer to wash some dishes, clean his car or give him the secret recipe for your family's favourite dish. An economy that relies on barter will have trouble allocating its scarce resources efficiently. In such an economy, trade is said to require the *double coincidence of wants* – the unlikely occurrence that two people each have a good or service that the other wants.

The existence of money makes trade easier. The restaurateur does not care whether you can produce a valuable good or service for him. He is happy to accept your money, knowing that other people will do the same for him. Such a convention allows trade to be roundabout. The restaurateur accepts your money and uses it to pay his chef; the chef uses her salary to send her child to the crèche; the crèche uses this money to pay a teacher; and the teacher hires you to child-mind when he goes to the cinema on a Saturday evening. As money flows from person to person in the economy, it facilitates production and trade, thereby allowing each person to specialize in what he or she does best and raising everyone's standard of living.

In this chapter we begin to examine the role of money in the economy. We discuss what money is, the various forms that money takes, how the banking system helps create money, and how the central bank controls the quantity of money in circulation. Because money is so important in the economy, we devote much effort in the rest of this book to learning how changes in the quantity of money affect various economic variables, including inflation, interest rates, production and employment. Consistent with our long-run focus in the previous three chapters, in the next chapter we will examine the long-run effects of changes in the quantity of money. The short-run effects of monetary changes are a more complex topic, which we will take up later in the book. This chapter provides the background for all of this further analysis.

THE MEANING OF MONEY

What is money? This might seem like an odd question. When you read that Mark Zuckerberg, one of the co-founders of Facebook, is a billionaire and has a lot of money, you know what that means: he is so rich that he can buy almost anything he wants. In this sense, the term money is used to mean wealth.

Economists, however, use the word in a more specific sense: **money** is the set of assets in the economy that people regularly use to buy goods and services from other people. The cash in your wallet is money because you can use it to buy a meal at a restaurant or a shirt at a clothes shop. By contrast, if you happened to own part of Facebook, as Mark Zuckerberg does, you would be wealthy, but this asset is not considered a form of money. You could not buy a meal or a shirt with this wealth without first obtaining some cash. According to the economist's definition, money includes only those few types of wealth that are regularly accepted by sellers in exchange for goods and services.

money
the set of assets in an economy that people regularly use to buy goods and services from other people

The Functions of Money

Money has three functions in the economy: it is a medium of exchange, a unit of account and a store of value. These three functions together distinguish money from other assets in the economy, such as stocks, bonds, residential property and art. Let's examine each of these functions of money in turn.

medium of exchange
an item that buyers give to sellers when they want to purchase goods and services

A **medium of exchange** is an item that buyers give to sellers when they purchase goods and services. When you buy a shirt at a clothes shop, the shop gives you the shirt and you give the shop your money. This transfer of money from buyer to seller allows the transaction to take place. When you walk into a shop, you are confident that the shop will accept your money for the items it is selling because money is the commonly accepted medium of exchange.

unit of account
the yardstick people use to post prices and record debts

store of value
an item that people can use to transfer purchasing power from the present to the future

liquidity
the ease with which an asset can be converted into the economy's medium of exchange

A **unit of account** is the yardstick people use to post prices and record debts. When you go shopping, you might observe that a shirt is priced at €20 and a ham-and-cheese sandwich at €2. Even though it would be accurate to say that the price of a shirt is 10 sandwiches and the price of a sandwich is 1/10 of a shirt, prices are never quoted in this way. Similarly, if you take out a loan in euros from a bank, the size of your future loan repayments will be measured in euros, not in a quantity of goods and services. When we want to measure and record economic value, we use money as the unit of account.

A **store of value** is an item that people can use to transfer purchasing power from the present to the future. When a seller accepts money today in exchange for a good or service, that seller can hold the money and become a buyer of another good or service at another time. Of course, money is not the only store of value in the economy, for a person can also transfer purchasing power from the present to the future by holding other assets. The term *wealth* is used to refer to the total of all stores of value, including both money and non-monetary assets.

© PETER BARRITT / ALAMY

A Rembrandt painting: expensive to sell, expensive to buy.

Economists use the term **liquidity** to describe the ease with which an asset can be converted into the economy's medium of exchange. Because money is the economy's medium of exchange, it is the most liquid asset available. Other assets vary widely in their liquidity. Most stocks and bonds can be sold easily with small cost, so they are relatively liquid assets. By contrast, selling a car or a Rembrandt painting requires more time and effort, so these assets are less liquid.

When people decide in what form to hold their wealth, they have to balance the liquidity of each possible asset against the asset's usefulness as a store of value. Money is the most liquid asset, but it is far from perfect as a store of value. When prices rise, the value of money falls. In other words, when goods and services become more expensive, each euro or pound in your wallet can buy less. This link between the price level and the value of money will turn out to be important for understanding how money affects the economy.

The Kinds of Money

commodity money
money that takes the form of a commodity with intrinsic value

When money takes the form of a commodity with intrinsic value, it is called **commodity money**. The term *intrinsic value* means that the item would have value even if it were not used as money. One example of commodity money is gold. Gold has intrinsic value because it is used in industry and in the making of jewellery. Although today we no longer use gold as money, historically gold has been a common form of money because it is relatively easy to carry, measure, and verify for impurities. When an economy uses gold as money (or uses paper money that is convertible into gold on demand), it is said to be operating under a *gold standard*.

Although gold has, historically, been the most common form of commodity money, other commodity monies have been used from time to time. For example, in the hyperinflation in Zimbabwe in the early 2000s the country's people began to lose faith in the Zimbabwean dollar; people began to trade goods and services with one another using cigarettes as the store of value, unit of account and medium of exchange.

Money without intrinsic value is called **fiat money**. A fiat is simply an order or decree, and fiat money is established as money by government decree. For example paper euros are able to circulate as legal tender in 16 European countries because the governments of those countries have decreed that the euro be valid currency in each of their economies.

fiat money
money without intrinsic value that is used as money because of government decree

Although governments are central to establishing and regulating a system of fiat money (by prosecuting counterfeiters, for example), other factors are also required for the success of such a monetary system. To a large extent, the acceptance of fiat money depends as much on expectations and social convention as on government decree. Zimbabweans preferred to accept cigarettes (or American dollars) in exchange for goods and services, because they were more confident that these alternative monies would be accepted by others in the future.

Money in the Economy

As we will see, the quantity of money circulating in the economy, called the money stock, has a powerful influence on many economic variables. But before we consider why that is true, we need to ask a preliminary question: what is the quantity of money? In particular, suppose you were given the task of measuring how much money there is in the economy of a country like the United Kingdom, or in the economies of the 16 countries that make up the euro area. What would you include in your measure?

The most obvious asset to include is **currency** – the paper notes and metal coins in the hands of the public. Currency is clearly the most widely accepted medium of exchange in a modern economy. There is no doubt that it is part of the money stock.

currency
the paper banknotes and coins in the hands of the public

Yet currency is not the only asset that you can use to buy goods and services. Most businesses also accept payment by debit card, which allows money to be transferred electronically between your current account and the current account of the business. Another, more old fashioned way of transferring money between current accounts is to write a personal cheque, and personal cheques are indeed still widely accepted as a means of payment (though rapidly being replaced by debit cards).

So is a debit card or a cheque money? Not really – it is the bank account on which the cheque or debit card draws which contains the money. A debit card is just a *means* of transferring money between accounts. The same is true of a cheque. Although a cheque may seem to be similar in some ways to paper money – it is also written on paper and is made out for a certain sum of money – it is only accepted by a business because it is a *means* of transferring money from your bank account to his.

What about credit cards? We need to think about these even more carefully, because credit cards are not really a method of payment but a method of *deferring* payment. When you buy a meal with a credit card, the bank that issued the card pays the restaurant what it is due – you have effectively borrowed from the bank. At a later date, you will have to repay the bank (perhaps with interest). When the time comes to pay your credit card bill, you will probably do so by direct transfer from your current account (or possibly by writing a cheque against your current account). The balance in this current account is part of the economy's stock of money. Notice that credit cards are very different from debit cards, which automatically withdraw funds from a bank account to pay for items bought. Why does the restaurateur accept payment by credit card? Because he gets his money immediately by having his bank account credited for the price of the meal even though you do not have to pay the credit card company back immediately. Again, however, it is the underlying movement in the restaurateur's bank balance that matters.

CASE STUDY

Local Currencies

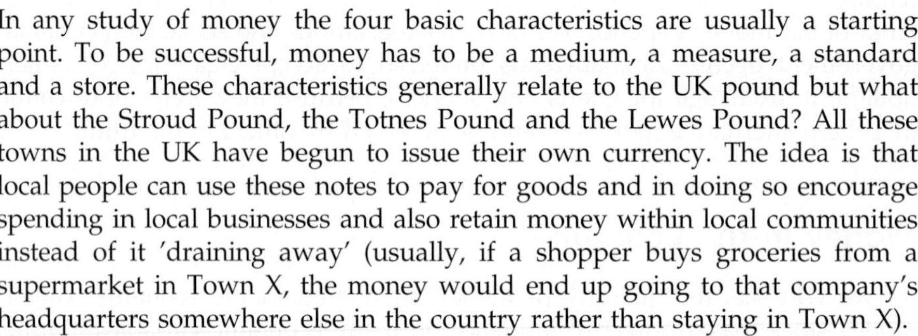

Local currencies can fulfil many of the requirements of national currencies

© PHILLIP WILLS / ALAMY

In any study of money the four basic characteristics are usually a starting point. To be successful, money has to be a medium, a measure, a standard and a store. These characteristics generally relate to the UK pound but what about the Stroud Pound, the Totnes Pound and the Lewes Pound? All these towns in the UK have begun to issue their own currency. The idea is that local people can use these notes to pay for goods and in doing so encourage spending in local businesses and also retain money within local communities instead of it 'draining away' (usually, if a shopper buys groceries from a supermarket in Town X, the money would end up going to that company's headquarters somewhere else in the country rather than staying in Town X).

Organizers of these local currencies issue local pounds which are backed by equivalent sterling deposits in a special bank account. Local people are then encouraged to buy the local currency and use it when they shop. To make it work, local businesses have to be encouraged to accept the notes in transactions; the more people become involved the more successful the scheme becomes. In Stroud, a town in Gloucestershire in the south Midlands, shoppers and traders can join the scheme by paying a small fee (which helps cover costs of administering the currency) and then exchange their sterling for Stroud Pounds. They can then use the currency with participating shops and traders. To encourage users to spend their pounds, the currency loses 3 per cent of its value every six months. Users can maintain its value by buying a stamp which they affix to the note. Without this stamp traders will not accept the currency and so there is an incentive for people to use them before the date on which the value goes down. New notes issued after a certain date will have the stamps already attached.

The success of these schemes is varied. One of the biggest problems is getting enough people to have trust in the system to start it working. In other words, the key function of the notes being accepted as a means of exchange is crucial. If people see the scheme as merely a gimmick or if they find that they cannot use the currency widely enough then it is not likely to take off. Traders can exchange pounds for sterling at a published exchange rate. In Stroud there are over £3 500 worth of pounds in circulation and in Totnes and Lewes, where the schemes have been running for longer, the local pound continues to generate interest from local shoppers and traders.

Source: Adapted from Biz/ed In the News. http://www.bized.co.uk/cgi-bin/chron/chron.pl?id=3565

Thus, although a debit card, a cheque and a credit card can each be used to settle the restaurant bill, none of them are money – they are each a method of transferring money between bank accounts. In the case of a debit card or a cheque, money is transferred from your account to the restaurateur's account more or less immediately or with a very short lag. In the case of a credit card, the restaurateur gets his money in his account more or less immediately and you will then have to settle up with the bank issuing the credit card later by drawing on your bank account. In every case, the true movement in money occurs when bank balances change.

Wealth held in your current account is almost as convenient for buying things as wealth held in your wallet. To measure the money stock, therefore, you might want to include **demand deposits** – balances in bank accounts that depositors can access *on demand* simply by using their debit card or writing a cheque. Once you start to consider balances in current accounts as part of the money stock, you are led to consider the large variety of other accounts that people hold at banks and other financial institutions. Bank depositors usually cannot write cheques or use their debit cards against the balances in their savings accounts, but they can (mostly) easily transfer funds from savings into current accounts. In addition, depositors in money market funds can often write cheques and use debit cards against their balances. Thus, these other accounts should plausibly be counted as part of the money stock.

demand deposits
balances in bank accounts that depositors can access on demand by using a debit card or writing a cheque

In a complex economy, it is in general not easy to draw a line between assets that can be called 'money' and assets that cannot. The coins in your pocket are clearly part of the money stock, and your Rembrandt painting clearly is not, but there are many assets in between these extremes for which the choice is less clear. Therefore, various measures of the money stock are available for advanced economies. Figure 29.1 shows the three most important measures for the euro area, designated M1 (a 'narrow' measure), M2 (an 'intermediate' measure) and M3 (a 'broad' measure). Each of these measures uses a slightly different criterion for distinguishing between monetary and non-monetary assets. In the UK, the most widely observed measures of the money stock are M0 (a narrower measure than the European M1 and corresponding to notes and coins in circulation plus bankers' balances held with the Bank of England) and M4 (a broad measure, similar – but not identical to – the European M3).

FIGURE 29.1

Three Measures of the Money Stock for the Euro Area

The three measures of euro area money stock are M1 *(a 'narrow' monetary aggregate that comprises currency in circulation and overnight deposits),* M2 *(an 'intermediate' monetary aggregate that comprises M1 plus deposits with an agreed maturity of up to two years and deposits redeemable at notice of up to three months) and* M3 (a 'broad' monetary aggregate that comprises M2 plus repurchase agreements, money market fund shares and units as well as debt securities with a maturity of up to two years). *This figure shows the size of each measure in January 2010.*

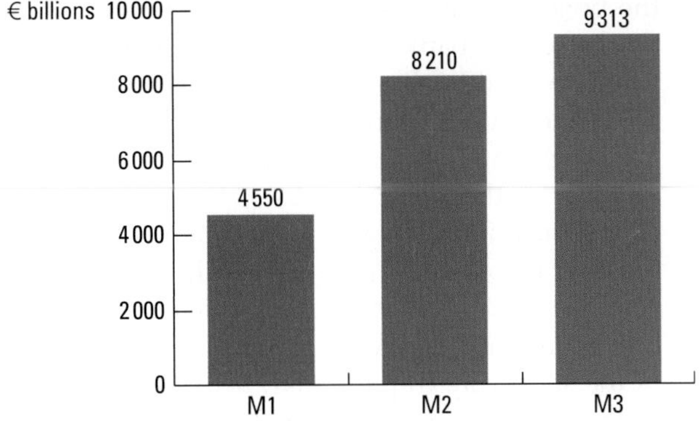

Source: ECB; figures relate to January 2010.

For our purposes in this book, we need not dwell on the differences between the various measures of money. The important point is that the money stock for an advanced economy includes not just currency but also deposits in banks and other financial institutions that can be readily accessed and used to buy goods and services.

Quick Quiz List and describe the three functions of money.

THE ROLE OF CENTRAL BANKS

central bank
an institution designed to regulate the quantity of money in the economy

money supply
the quantity of money available in the economy

Whenever an economy relies on a system of fiat money–as all modern advanced economies do – some agency must be responsible for regulating the system. This agency is generally known as the **central bank** – an institution designed to regulate the quantity of money made available in the economy, called the **money supply**. Two of the most important central banks in Europe are the European Central Bank and the Bank of England. Other major central banks around the world include the US central bank – the Federal Reserve – and the Bank of Japan. We'll take a closer look at the European Central Bank, the Bank of England and the Federal Reserve in a moment. Before then, however, we can look at some features of central banks in general.

monetary policy
the set of actions taken by the central bank in order to affect the money supply

The central bank of an economy has the power to increase or decrease the amount of currency in that economy. The set of actions taken by the central bank in order to affect the money supply is known as **monetary policy**. In simple metaphorical terms, you can imagine the central bank printing up banknotes and dropping them by helicopter. Similarly, you can imagine the central bank using a giant vacuum cleaner to suck banknotes out of people's wallets. Although in practice the central bank's methods for changing the money supply are more complex and subtle than this, the helicopter-vacuum metaphor is a good first approximation to the meaning of monetary policy.

open-market operations
the purchase and sale of non-monetary assets from and to the banking sector by the central bank

We discuss later in this chapter how the central bank actually changes the money supply, but it is worth noting here that an important tool that the central bank can use is **open-market operations** – the purchase and sale of non-monetary assets from and to the banking sector. For example, if the central bank decides to increase the money supply, it can do this by creating currency and using it to buy bonds from the public in the bond market. After the purchase, the extra currency is in the hands of the public. Thus, an open-market purchase of bonds by the central bank increases the money supply. Conversely, if the central bank decides to decrease the money supply, it can do this by selling bonds from its portfolio to the public. After the sale, the currency it receives for the bonds is out of the hands of the public. Thus an open-market sale of bonds by the central bank decreases the money supply.

The central bank of an economy is an important institution because changes in the money supply can profoundly affect the economy. One of the *Ten Principles of Economics* in Chapter 1 is that prices rise when too much money is printed. Another of the *Ten Principles of Economics* is that society faces a short-run trade-off between inflation and unemployment. The power of the central bank rests on these principles. For reasons we discuss more fully in the coming chapters, the central bank's policy decisions have an important influence on the economy's rate of inflation in the long run and the economy's employment and production in the short run. In particular, because of the link between the amount of money in the economy and the inflation rate (the rate of increase of prices), the central bank is often seen as the guardian of price stability in a modern economy and at least two of the central banks we shall look at are specifically charged with the duty to maintain inflation at or near an inflation target – a policy we'll discuss more fully in the coming chapters. To be precise, the central bank should perhaps be thought of as the guardian of inflation stability, rather than price stability, since even with a constant, low rate of inflation, prices are by definition rising. Still, if inflation is low and stable, prices might be said to be rising in a stable fashion – and in any case, this usage is now well established, so we'll follow suit.

Now let's take a closer look at three important central banks.

FYI

Quantitative Easing

During the financial crisis of 2007–09, central banks adopted new tactics to try and support the economy. One of the methods adopted was an Asset Purchasing Facility (APF) or quantitative easing (QE). In the UK the Bank of England cut interest rates to 0.5 per cent and in the US rates fell to a target of between 0 and 0.25 per cent. Having effectively exhausted the use of lowering the price of money in the economy, central banks have looked at affecting the supply of money as part of their armoury in triggering economic activity. QE was the method adopted by the UK (authority to carry out QE was given in January 2009 although the first purchase was 11 March 2009) and the US (from March 2009). The Federal Reserve said that it intended to spend $1 trillion on its QE programme, the Bank of England spent £200 billion. In September 2010 the Federal Reserve announced that it would consider increasing the facility if economic growth was slow and warranted it. By that time its facility had grown to $2.3 trillion.

The purpose of QE is to put banks in a better position to be able to lend and in so doing help to boost demand. All banks have accounts at the Bank of England, which are classed as 'reserves'. The process of QE involves the central bank buying assets from private sector institutions. These might include banks, pension funds and insurance companies. The type of assets purchased varies from bonds and gilt-edged stock to commercial paper (short-term promissory notes issued by companies with a maturity ranging up to 270 days but with an average of 30 days), equities and possibly toxic assets. When the central bank buys assets, these reserves increase.

In buying these assets, the central bank is effectively increasing the amount of money in the accounts of those who sell these assets. The purpose of the policy is to encourage banks and other financial institutions, who are the recipients of this additional money, to lend it out to businesses and consumers thus stimulating demand. An example may serve to help understand the process. Assume a bank has £1 billion worth of gilt-edged stock. It decides that it wants to sell £500 million worth. The Bank of England announces that it intends to purchase gilts at an auction and sets a specific date for the auction (normally a Monday and Wednesday each week for a specified period of time). The process takes place via what is called a 'reverse auction'. Rather than the buyer putting in bids for what they would be willing to pay for the item, the seller submits an electronic bid to the Bank stating what they would like to sell and at what price they would be willing to sell at. The Bank itself has a specified amount that it intends to buy at that time and the bids coming in from banks and other institutions may mean that the auction is oversubscribed (i.e. more bids to sell are received than the Bank intends to buy) and as a result the Bank is able to select which offers it will accept and at what price.

Assume our bank has been successful in its bid. It transfers the gilts to the Bank of England and in return receives a credit for £500 million. It can use this £500 million to lend to businesses for investment into equipment and machinery and consumers for mortgages or personal loans for cars, students loans, new furniture and so on. The additional spending on investment and consumer goods helps boost aggregate demand and so trigger economic growth. Given that the central bank is actively participating in the bond market we can also expect some effects through this market action. Remember from Chapter 26, companies use the bond market as a means of raising funds. Over a period of time these bonds will mature and firms may issue new bonds to replace them. These new bond issues may have different coupon rates to existing ones depending on current conditions in the bond market. Assume that a company has issued a ten-year bond with a coupon, on issue, of 5 per cent. The price at which the bond sells on the market will not necessarily be the same as its par value (what it was originally issued at). The ratio of coupon in relation to the price

▶

gives investors the yield (Yield = coupon/price). For example, if the company issues a €100 bond, with a coupon (interest) rate of 5 per cent, the yield will also be 5 per cent. However, if demand for this bond rises then its price may rise (to €105 for example) and as a result the yield will fall (5 per cent/105 = 4.76 per cent). There is an inverse relationship between bond prices and yield.

If the central bank intervenes to buy bonds the supply of bonds will fall and bond prices will rise. As bond prices rise, yields fall. If our company now issues a new bond it can offer that bond at a lower coupon (there is no incentive not to buy it since buying existing bonds does not give any better return). Using the example above, if our company wanted to issue a new bond to replace the matured €100 bond, then it could offer the bond at a coupon of 4.76 per cent (or slightly higher) and have every chance of raising the finance. For the company it is now raising funds at 4.76 per cent rather than 5 per cent. This means that firms are now able to borrow at cheaper rates. The rise in price of gilts and subsequent fall in yields reduces the spread (the difference between the interest rate on borrowed money and the return on the gilt). As the spread falls there is more incentive for the bank to look for improved returns elsewhere and it is hoped that it will consider lending to consumers and businesses (who may have been seen as being too risky previously) because the return is now greater.

QE, therefore, works in a variety of ways to influence incentives as highlighted in Principle 4 of the *Ten Principles of Economics*. In essence, therefore, the principle of QE is simple; the acid test is whether it works or not. The central bank is in a position to monitor the effects of the process as it collects data about money flows in the economy, the effect on the money supply, credit flows in corporate markets, interest rates on different types of lending (for example on mortgages) and the amount and type of lending taking place. The type of debt bought by the central bank is critical to the success of the policy. Given the situation that many banks found themselves in as a result of the financial crisis, it was possible that if the central bank focused its purchases of assets from these institutions, then rather than lending out the money again and freeing up credit markets, banks may simply have used the receipts to build up their balance sheets. As a result the effect would be weaker than planned. The Bank of England has said that it is aware of this potential problem and so has targeted its purchases from 'the wider economy' rather than just from banks.

Some commentators have suggested that the policy would be more successful if the central bank bought toxic assets off banks rather than gilts since the burden of these types of assets is one of the key reasons why credit markets had been so tight. Central banks and analysts will be looking carefully to see whether there are signs that the money supply is expanding in the way that they hoped and that this translates to increased spending in the real economy. The Bank of England has admitted that it was difficult to know whether QE would work or how long it would take to see any measurable effects. Mervyn King [Governor of the Bank of England] initially suggested that it would take at least nine months to see any noticeable impact and, of course, it would also be highly dependent on the amount of the facility. In the UK, the Bank of England originally set a figure of £75 billion but had the authority from the government to spend up to £150 billion. Three months after its first purchase, it announced it was increasing the level to £125 billion and then in August 2009 a further increase of £50 billion to £175 billion. The Bank expected to complete the purchase of assets to this level by the end of November 2009 and at its November meeting gained authorization from the government to increase the asset purchasing facility to £200 billion which it completed in January 2010.

In an interview with the *Financial Times*[1], Paul Fisher, Executive Director for Markets at the Bank of England, dubbed 'Mr QE' by the newspaper, was confident that QE was beginning to have an effect but noted that the short-term impact on economic activity may be limited because of the way QE works through the system:

> *...one of the ways that QE is working is in stimulating demand for corporate bonds, so large corporates have been borrowing more in the capital markets and using it to repay bank debt; so the outcome from that is that bank lending would be lower than otherwise. Now, that is helpful because it's helping both the banks and the corporates to repair their balance sheets. But there may have been some expectation on the part of commentators that bank lending would rise as a result of QE. And eventually it would because you are putting the banks in a better position and the corporates in a better position for future lending, but the short-term impact goes the other way.*

[1] http://www.ft.com/cms/s/0/64f03818-b8fd-11de-98ee-00144feab49a.html

THE EUROPEAN CENTRAL BANK AND THE EUROSYSTEM

European Central Bank (ECB) the overall central bank of the 16 countries comprising the European Monetary Union

The **European Central Bank** (ECB), located in Frankfurt, Germany, was officially created on 1 June 1998 as a number of European countries had decided that they wished to enter European Monetary Union (EMU) and have the same currency – the euro – circulating among them. We'll discuss the pros and cons of monetary union in a later chapter. For now, though, we just note that if a group of countries has the same currency, then it makes sense for the countries in the group to have a common monetary policy, and the ECB was set up for precisely this purpose. There were originally 11 countries making up the euro area: Belgium, Germany, Spain, France, Ireland, Italy, Luxembourg, the Netherlands, Austria, Portugal and Finland. By 2010, there were 16 countries, the new additions being Greece, Cyprus, Slovakia, Slovenia and Malta.

The primary objective of the ECB is to promote price stability throughout the euro area and to design and implement monetary policy that is consistent with this objective. The ECB operates with the assistance of the national central banks in each of the euro area countries, such as the Banque de France, the Banca d'Italia, the Bank of Greece and the German Bundesbank. The network made up of the ECB together with the 16 euro area national central banks is termed the **Eurosystem**.

Eurosystem
the system made up of the ECB plus the national central banks of each of the 16 countries comprising the European Monetary Union

The implementation of monetary policy by the ECB is under the control of the Executive Board, which comprises the President and Vice-President of the ECB and four other people of high standing in the banking profession. While the Executive Board – as the name suggests – is responsible for *executing* monetary policy, the monetary policy of the ECB is actually designed by the Governing Council, which comprises the whole of the Executive Board plus the governors of the national central banks in the Eurosystem (22 people in total). The Governing Council, which meets twice a month in Frankfurt, is the most important decision-making body of the ECB and decides, for example, on the level of the ECB's key interest rate, the refinancing rate. The Governing Council also decides how to interpret its duty to achieve price stability. In October 1998 it agreed that price stability should be defined as a 'year-on-year increase in prices of less than 2 per cent as measured by the annual change in a harmonized index of consumer prices throughout the euro area'. A problem with this definition of price stability, however, is that 'less than 2 per cent' is a little vague – an annual inflation rate of 1 per cent and an annual inflation rate of 0 per cent are both less than 2 per cent. In fact, some people were worried that the ECB might even aim for falling prices or negative inflation in order to achieve its target of less than 2 per cent. As we discuss more fully in the coming chapters, this would tend sharply to reduce output and employment in the economy, especially in the short to medium run. In May 2003, therefore, the Governing Council confirmed its official definition thus:

> *in the pursuit of price stability, it aims to maintain inflation rates below but close to 2 per cent over the medium term.*

An important feature of the ECB and of the Eurosystem in general is its independence. When performing Eurosystem-related tasks, neither the ECB, nor a national central bank, nor any member of their decision-making bodies is allowed to seek or take instructions from any external body, including any member governments or any European Union institutions.

The President of the ECB and other members of the Executive Board are appointed for a minimum non-renewable term of office of eight years (although a system of staggered appointments was used for the first Executive Board for members other than the President in order to ensure continuity) and the governors of the 16 national central banks in the Eurosystem are appointed for a minimum renewable term of office of five years.

THE BANK OF ENGLAND

The **Bank of England** was founded in 1694, although it is not the oldest European central bank (the Swedish Riksbank was founded in 1668). Arguably the most significant event in the Bank of England's 300-year history was when the

Bank of England
the central bank of the United Kingdom

UK government granted it independence in the setting of interest rates in 1997, which was formalized in an Act of Parliament in 1998. The important body within the Bank that makes the decision on the level at which to set the Bank's key interest rate, the repo rate, is the Monetary Policy Committee (MPC). The MPC consists of the Governor and two Deputy Governors of the Bank of England, two other members appointed by the Bank after consultation with the Chancellor of the Exchequer (the UK finance minister) and four other members appointed by the Chancellor. The Governor and the two Deputy Governors serve five-year renewable terms of office, while other MPC members serve three-year renewable terms. The MPC meets monthly and its interest rate decision is announced immediately after the meeting.

Like the ECB, one of the Bank of England's primary duties is to deliver price stability. Also in common with the ECB, it enjoys independence in the setting of monetary policy – and in particular interest rates – in order to achieve the objective of price stability. Unlike the ECB, however, the Bank of England does not have the freedom to define for itself precisely what 'price stability' means in this context. This is done by the UK government and, in particular, by the Chancellor of the Exchequer. In fact, the 1998 Bank of England Act requires that the Chancellor write to the Governor of the Bank of England once a year to specify what price stability is to be defined as. Currently, the inflation target of 2 per cent is expressed in terms of an annual rate of inflation based on the consumer prices index (CPI). If the target is missed by more than 1 percentage point on either side, i.e. if the annual rate of CPI inflation is more than 3 per cent or less than 1 per cent, the Governor of the Bank of England must write an open letter to the Chancellor explaining the reasons why inflation has increased or fallen to such an extent and what the Bank proposes to do to ensure inflation comes back to the target.

In changes made to financial regulation in the UK in June 2010, the Chancellor of the Exchequer announced that the Bank of England would have new responsibilities focusing on monetary policy and financial stability. The new system led to the Bank of England getting additional responsibilities for financial stability, macro-prudential supervision and oversight of micro-prudential supervision. These regulatory functions are overseen by four main groups, the Prudential Regulatory Authority (not its final name) which is responsible for day-to-day supervision of bank safety and soundness (micro-prudential policy), the Financial Policy Committee, charged with preventing credit and asset bubbles and overall financial stability, the Economic Crime Agency, focusing on serious economic crime such as corporate fraud, market-fixing and insider trading and the Consumer Protection and Markets Authority which manages protection of investors, market supervision and regulation and the conduct of banks and financial services. A Banking Commission was also created to look at ways to reduce systemic risk in the banking system and to investigate the possibility of splitting the retail and investment divisions of banks.

THE FEDERAL RESERVE SYSTEM

Federal Reserve (Fed) the central bank of the United States

The US **Federal Reserve** was created in 1913. The Fed is run by its Board of Governors, which has seven members appointed by the US president. Six of the governors have 14-year terms to give them independence from short-term political pressures when they formulate monetary policy, although the Chairman has a four-year term.

The Federal Reserve System is made up of the Federal Reserve Board in Washington, D.C., and 12 regional Federal Reserve Banks located in major cities around the USA.

At the Federal Reserve, monetary policy is made by the Federal Open Market Committee (FOMC). The FOMC meets about every six weeks in Washington, DC, to discuss the condition of the economy and consider changes in monetary policy, including the setting of its key interest rate, the discount rate. The FOMC is made up of the seven members of the Board of Governors and five of the 12 regional bank presidents. All 12 regional presidents attend each FOMC meeting, but only five get to vote. The five with voting rights rotate among the 12 regional presidents over time. The President of the New York Fed always gets a vote, however, because New York is the traditional financial centre of the US economy and because all Fed open-market operations are conducted at the New York Fed's trading desk.

Quick Quiz If the central bank wants to increase the supply of money, how may it do so?

"YOU WANT A LOAN, YOU SAY? HA, HA, THAT'S A GOOD ONE!... WHERE IN THE WORLD DID YOU HEAR THAT BANKS MADE LOANS?!"

BANKS AND THE MONEY SUPPLY

So far we have introduced the concept of 'money' and discussed how the central bank controls the supply of money by buying and selling government bonds and other assets in open-market operations. Although this explanation of the money supply is correct, it is not complete. In particular, it omits the central role that banks play in the monetary system.

Recall that the amount of money you hold includes both currency (the banknotes in your wallet and coins in your pocket) and demand deposits (the balance in your current account). Because demand deposits are held in banks, the behaviour of banks can influence the quantity of demand deposits in the economy and, therefore, the money supply. This section examines how banks affect the money supply and how they complicate the central bank's job of controlling the money supply.

The Simple Case of 100 Per Cent Reserve Banking

To see how banks influence the money supply, it's useful to imagine first a world without any banks at all. In this simple world, currency is the only form of money. To be concrete, let's suppose that the total quantity of currency is €100. The supply of money is, therefore, €100.

Now suppose that someone opens a bank, appropriately called First European Bank. First European Bank is only a depository institution – that is, it accepts deposits but does not make loans. The purpose of the bank is to give depositors a safe place to keep their money. Whenever a person deposits some money, the bank keeps the money in its vault until the depositor comes to withdraw it or writes a cheque against his or her balance. Deposits that banks have received but have not lent out are called **reserves**. In this imaginary economy, all deposits are held as reserves, so this system is called 100 per cent reserve banking.

reserves
deposits that banks have received but have not loaned out

We can express the financial position of First European Bank with a T-account, which is a simplified accounting statement that shows changes in a bank's assets and liabilities. Here is the T-account for First European Bank if the economy's entire €100 of money is deposited in the bank:

FIRST EUROPEAN BANK

Assets		Liabilities	
Reserves	€100.00	Deposits	€100.00

On the left-hand side of the T-account are the bank's assets of €100 (the reserves it holds in its vaults). On the right-hand side of the T-account are the bank's liabilities of €100 (the amount it owes to its depositors). Notice that the assets and liabilities of First European Bank exactly balance.

Now consider the money supply in this imaginary economy. Before First European Bank opens, the money supply is the €100 of currency that people are holding. After the bank opens and people deposit their currency, the money supply is the €100 of demand deposits. (There is no longer any currency outstanding, for it is all in the bank vault.) Each deposit in the bank reduces currency and raises demand deposits by exactly the same amount, leaving the money supply unchanged. Thus, *if banks hold all deposits in reserve, banks do not influence the supply of money.*

Money Creation With Fractional-reserve Banking

Eventually, the bankers at First European Bank may start to reconsider their policy of 100 per cent reserve banking. Leaving all that money sitting idle in their vaults seems unnecessary. Why not use some of it to make loans? Families buying houses, firms building new factories and students at university would all be happy to pay interest to borrow some of that money for a while. Of course, First European Bank has to keep some reserves so that currency is available if depositors want to make withdrawals. But if the flow of new deposits is roughly the same as the flow of withdrawals, First European needs to keep only a fraction of its deposits in reserve. Thus, First European adopts a system called **fractional-reserve banking**.

fractional-reserve banking
a banking system in which banks hold only a fraction of deposits as reserves

reserve ratio
the fraction of deposits that banks hold as reserves

The fraction of total deposits that a bank holds as reserves is called the **reserve ratio**. This ratio is determined by a combination of government regulation and bank policy. As we discuss more fully later in the chapter, both the European Central Bank and the US Federal Reserve place a minimum on the amount of reserves that banks hold, called a *reserve requirement* (although, unusually among central banks, the Bank of England does not impose reserve requirements). In addition, banks may hold reserves above the legal minimum, called *excess reserves*, so they can be more confident that they will not run short of cash. Even when there are no minimum reserve requirements at all (as in the UK), banks will set their own reserve ratio at which they deem it is prudent to operate. For our purpose here, we just take the reserve ratio as given and examine what fractional-reserve banking means for the money supply.

Let's suppose that First European has a reserve ratio of 10 per cent. This means that it keeps 10 per cent of its deposits in reserve and lends out the rest. Now let's look again at the bank's T-account:

FIRST EUROPEAN BANK

Assets		Liabilities	
Reserves	€10.00	Deposits	€100.00
Loans	€90.00		

First European still has €100 in liabilities because making the loans did not alter the bank's obligation to its depositors. But now the bank has two kinds of assets: it has €10 of reserves in its vault, and it has loans of €90. (These loans are liabilities of the people taking out the loans but they are assets of the bank making the loans, because the borrowers will later repay the bank.) In total, First European's assets still equal its liabilities.

Once again consider the supply of money in the economy. Before First European makes any loans, the money supply is the €100 of deposits in the bank. Yet when First European makes these loans, the money supply increases. The depositors still have demand deposits totalling €100, but now the borrowers hold €90 in currency.

The money supply (which equals currency plus demand deposits) equals €190. Thus, *when banks hold only a fraction of deposits in reserve, banks create money.*

At first, this creation of money by fractional-reserve banking may seem too good to be true because it appears that the bank has created money out of thin air. To make this creation of money seem less miraculous, note that when First European Bank lends out some of its reserves and creates money, it does not create any wealth (wealth, as a concept, is a 'stock' as opposed to a flow). Loans from First European give the borrowers some currency and thus the ability to buy goods and services. Yet the borrowers are also taking on debts, so the loans do not make them any richer. In other words, as a bank creates the asset of money, it also creates a corresponding liability for its borrowers. At the end of this process of money creation, the economy is more liquid in the sense that there is more of the medium of exchange, but the economy is no wealthier than before.

The Money Multiplier

The creation of money does not stop with First European Bank. Suppose the borrower from First European uses the €90 to buy something from someone who then deposits the currency in Second European Bank. Here is the T-account for Second European Bank:

SECOND EUROPEAN BANK

Assets		Liabilities	
Reserves	€9.00	Deposits	€90.00
Loans	€81.00		

After the deposit, this bank has liabilities of €90. If Second European also has a reserve ratio of 10 per cent, it keeps assets of €9 in reserve and makes €81 in loans. In this way, Second European Bank creates an additional €81 of money. If this €81 is eventually deposited in Third European Bank, which also has a reserve ratio of 10 per cent, this bank keeps €8.10 in reserve and makes €72.90 in loans. Here is the T-account for Third European Bank:

THIRD EUROPEAN BANK

Assets		Liabilities	
Reserves	€8.10	Deposits	€81.00
Loans	€72.90		

The process goes on and on. Each time that money is deposited and a bank loan is made, more money is created. How much money is eventually created in this economy? Let's add it up:

Original deposit	= € 100.00
First European lending	= € 90.00 [= .9 × €100.00]
Second European lending	= € 81.00 [= .9 × €90.00]
Third European lending	= € 72.90 [= .9 × €81.00]
.	.
.	.
.	.
Total money supply	= €1 000.00

It turns out that even though this process of money creation can continue forever, it does not create an infinite amount of money. If you laboriously add the infinite

money multiplier
the amount of money the banking system generates with each unit of reserves

sequence of numbers in the foregoing example, you find the €100 of reserves generates €1 000 of money. The amount of money the banking system generates with each euro of reserves is called the **money multiplier**. In this imaginary economy, where the €100 of reserves generates €1 000 of money, the money multiplier is 10. It is important to remember that there is no new cash being created in this process – banks do not print more notes and press more coins. Most transactions in modern economies are simply 'book entries'; when you get a bank statement telling you that there is a balance of €1 500 in your current account there is not a box with this sum of money stored somewhere in the bank's vault. However, the banking system is such that we have trust that if we did wish to withdraw all that money in cash the bank would have sufficient funds to be able to meet our demand. This is where a 'run on banks' causes so many problems; if a large number of account holders all wanted to withdraw their money as cash the bank is unlikely to have the funds to give to everyone and it would effectively be 'bankrupt'.

What determines the size of the money multiplier? It turns out that the answer is simple: the money multiplier is the reciprocal of the reserve ratio. If R is the reserve ratio for all banks in the economy, then each euro of reserves generates $1/R$ euros of money. In our example, $R = 1/10$, so the money multiplier is 10.

This reciprocal formula for the money multiplier makes sense. If a bank holds €1 000 in deposits, then a reserve ratio of 1/10 (10 per cent) means that the bank must hold €100 in reserves. The money multiplier just turns this idea around: if the banking system as a whole holds a total of €100 in reserves, it can have only €1 000 in deposits. In other words, if R is the ratio of reserves to deposits at each bank (that is, the reserve ratio), then the ratio of deposits to reserves in the banking system (that is, the money multiplier) must be $1/R$.

This formula shows how the amount of money banks create depends on the reserve ratio. If the reserve ratio were only 1/20 (5 per cent), then the banking system would have 20 times as much in deposits as in reserves, implying a money multiplier of 20. Each euro of reserves would generate €20 of money. Similarly, if the reserve ratio were 1/5 (20 per cent), deposits would be 5 times reserves, the money multiplier would be 5, and each euro of reserves would generate €5 of money. Thus, the higher the reserve ratio, the less of each deposit banks lend out, and the smaller the money multiplier. In the special case of 100 per cent reserve banking, the reserve ratio is 1, the money multiplier is 1, and banks do not make loans or create money.

The Central Bank's Tools of Monetary Control

As we have already discussed, the central bank is responsible for controlling the supply of money in the economy. Now that we understand how fractional-reserve banking works, we are in a better position to understand how the central bank carries out this job. Because banks create money in a system of fractional-reserve banking, the central bank's control of the money supply is indirect. When the central bank decides to change the money supply, it must consider how its actions will work through the banking system.

In general, a central bank has three main tools in its monetary toolbox: open-market operations, the refinancing rate and reserve requirements.

Open-market Operations We introduced the idea of open-market operations earlier through two simple examples. Let's look at these again. If the central bank wants to increase the money supply, it can create currency and use it to buy bonds from the public in the bond market. After the purchase, the extra currency is in the hands of the public. Thus, an open-market purchase of bonds by the central bank increases the money supply. If, on the other hand, the central bank wants to decrease the money supply, it can sell bonds from its portfolio to the public. After the sale, the currency it receives for the bonds is out of the hands of the public. Thus an open-market sale of bonds by the central bank decreases the money supply. To be precise, the open-market operations discussed in these simple examples are called **outright open-market operations**, because they each involve an outright sale or purchase of non-monetary assets to or from the banking sector without a corresponding agreement to reverse the transaction at a later date.

outright open-market operations
the outright sale or purchase of non-monetary assets to or from the banking sector by the central bank without a corresponding agreement to reverse the transaction at a later date

The Refinancing Rate The central bank of an economy will set an interest rate at which it is willing to lend to commercial banks on a short-term basis. As we shall see, the name of this interest rate differs across central banks, although in general in this book we'll follow the practice of the European Central Bank and refer to it as the refinancing rate.

The way in which the central bank lends to the banking sector is through a special form of open-market operations. In the previous paragraph we discussed the use of *outright* open-market operations. Although outright open-market operations have traditionally been used by central banks to regulate the money supply, central banks nowadays more often use a slightly more sophisticated form of open-market operations that involves buying bonds or other assets from banks and at the same time agreeing to sell them back later. When it does this, the central bank has effectively made a loan and taken the bonds or other assets as collateral or security on the loan. The central bank will have a list of eligible assets that it will accept as collateral – 'safe' assets such as government bonds or assets issued by large corporations, on which the risk of default by the issuer is negligible. The interest rate that the central bank charges on the loan is the refinancing rate. Because the central bank has bought the assets but the seller has agreed to buy them back later at an agreed price, this kind of open-market operation is often called a **repurchase agreement** or 'repo' for short. To see how central bank's use repos as a means of controlling the money supply and how this is affected by the refinancing rate, we need to look a little more closely at the way commercial banks lend money to one another and borrow from the central bank.

repurchase agreement (repo)
the sale of a non-monetary asset together with an agreement to repurchase it at a set price at a specified future date

As we discussed earlier, banks need to carry enough reserves to cover their lending and will generally aim for a certain ratio of reserves to deposits, known as the reserve ratio. The minimum reserve ratio may be set by the central bank, but even if it isn't, banks will still have a reserve ratio that they consider prudent. Now, because deposits and withdrawals at banks can fluctuate randomly, some banks may find that they have an excess of reserves one day (i.e. their reserve ratio is above the level the bank considers prudent or above the minimum reserve ratio, or both), while other banks may find that they are short of reserves and their reserve ratio is too low. Therefore, the commercial banks in an economy will generally lend money to one another on a short-term basis – overnight to a couple of weeks – so that banks with excess reserves can lend them to banks who have inadequate reserves to cover their lending. This market for short-term reserves is called the **money market**. If there is a *general* shortage of liquidity in the money market (because the banks together have done a lot of lending), then the short-term interest rate at which they lend to one another will begin to rise, while it will begin to fall if there is excess liquidity among banks. The central bank closely monitors the money market and may intervene in it in order to affect the supply of liquidity to banks, which in turn affects their lending and hence affects the money supply.

money market
the market in which the commercial banks lend money to one another on a short-term basis

Suppose, for example, that there is a shortage of liquidity in the market because the banks have been increasing their lending and they need to increase their reserves. A commercial bank may then attempt to obtain liquidity from the central bank by selling assets to the central bank and at the same time agreeing to purchase them back a short time later. As we said before, in this type of open-market operation the central bank effectively lends money to the bank and takes the assets as collateral on the loan. Because the commercial bank is legally bound to repurchase the assets at a set price, this is called a 'repurchase agreement' and the difference between the price the bank sells the assets to the central bank and the price at which it agrees to buy them back, expressed as an annualized percentage of the selling price, is called the repurchase or repo rate by the Bank of England and the refinancing rate by the European Central Bank. The ECB's **refinancing rate** is thus the rate at which it will lend to the banking sector of the euro area, while the **repo rate** is the rate at which the Bank of England lends short term to the UK banking sector.

refinancing rate
the interest rate at which the European Central Bank lends on a short-term basis to the euro area banking sector

repo rate
the interest rate at which the Bank of England lends on a short-term basis to the UK banking sector

In the example given, the central bank added liquidity to the banking system by lending reserves to banks. This would have the effect of increasing the money supply. Because the loans made through open-market operations are typically very short term, with a maturity of at most two weeks, however, the banks are constantly having to repay the loans and borrow again, or 'refinance' the loans. If the central bank wants to mop up liquidity it can simply decide not to renew some of the loans. In practice, however, the central bank will set a reference rate of interest – the Bank of England's repo rate or the ECB's refinancing rate – and will conduct open-market operations, adding to or mopping up liquidity, close to this reference rate.

In the USA the interest rate at which the Federal Reserve lends to the banking sector (corresponding to the ECB's refinancing rate or the Bank of England's repo rate) is called the **discount rate**.

discount rate
the interest rate at which the Federal Reserve lends on a short-term basis to the US banking sector

Now we can see why the setting of the central bank's refinancing rate is the key instrument of monetary policy. If the central bank raises the refinancing rate, commercial banks will try and rein in their lending rather than borrow reserves from the central bank, and so the money supply will fall. If the central bank lowers the refinancing rate, banks will feel freer to lend, knowing that they will be able to borrow more cheaply from the central bank in order to meet their reserve requirements, and so the money supply will tend to rise.

Reserve Requirements The central bank may also influence the money supply with **reserve requirements**, which are regulations on the minimum amount of reserves that banks must hold against deposits. Reserve requirements influence how much money the banking system can create with each euro of reserves. An increase in reserve requirements means that banks must hold more reserves and, therefore, can lend out less of each euro that is deposited; as a result, it raises the reserve ratio, lowers the money multiplier and decreases the money supply. Conversely, a decrease in reserve requirements lowers the reserve ratio, raises the money multiplier and increases the money supply.

reserve requirements
regulations on the minimum amount of reserves that banks must hold against deposits

Central banks have traditionally tended to use changes in reserve requirements only rarely because frequent changes would disrupt the business of banking. When the central bank increases reserve requirements, for instance, some banks find themselves short of reserves, even though they have seen no change in deposits. As a result, they have to curtail lending until they build their level of reserves to the new required level.

In fact, the Bank of England no longer sets minimum reserve requirements at all. The European Central Bank does set minimum reserve requirements, but it applies them to the average reserve ratio over a specified period rather than at a single point in time. It does this to stop the amount of lending fluctuating wildly, in order to maintain stability in the money market. Hence, the ECB uses reserve requirements in order to maintain stability in the money market rather than as an instrument of policy by which to increase or decrease the money supply. Following the financial crisis negotiations have taken place on improving banks' reserves to avoid the problems faced during the crisis. The so-called Basel III negotiations between 27 countries set new reserve requirements in September

2010. The new rules will come into force in 2013 and then be phased in over a period of six years. The regulations mean that banks will have to have higher reserves to support lending; for every €50 of lending banks will have to have €3.50 of reserves compared to €1 prior to the Basel III agreement. This obviously more than triples the amount of reserves that banks will have to keep. If banks do not adhere to the new regulations then they risk seeing the authorities placing restrictions on their activities including paying out dividends to shareholders and bonuses to staff.

Problems in Controlling the Money Supply

Through the setting of its refinancing rate and the associated open-market operations, the central bank can exert an important degree of control over the money supply. Yet the central bank's control of the money supply is not precise. The central bank must wrestle with two problems, each of which arises because much of the money supply is created by the system of fractional-reserve banking.

The first problem is that the central bank does not control the amount of money that households choose to hold as deposits in banks. The more money households deposit, the more reserves banks have, and the more money the banking system can create. And the less money households deposit, the less reserves banks have, and the less money the banking system can create. To see why this is a problem, suppose that one day people begin to lose confidence in the banking system and, therefore, decide to withdraw deposits and hold more currency. When this happens, the banking system loses reserves and creates less money. The money supply falls, even without any central bank action.

The second problem of monetary control is that the central bank does not control the amount that bankers choose to lend. When money is deposited in a bank, it creates more money only when the bank lends it out. Because banks can choose to hold excess reserves instead, the central bank cannot be sure how much money the banking system will create. For instance, suppose that one day bankers become more cautious about economic conditions and decide to make fewer loans and hold greater reserves. In this case, the banking system creates less money than it otherwise would. Because of the bankers' decision, the money supply falls.

Hence, in a system of fractional-reserve banking, the amount of money in the economy depends in part on the behaviour of depositors and bankers. Because the central bank cannot control or perfectly predict this behaviour, it cannot perfectly control the money supply.

Quick Quiz Describe how banks create money. • If the ECB wanted to use all three of its policy tools to decrease the money supply, what would it do?

CASE STUDY

The Changed Nature of Banking

A traditional view of banking is closely allied with the idea of prudence. Being prudent may make for safe banking but it does not necessarily satisfy the demands of shareholders for ever larger profits. In the latter part of the 1990s and through to 2008, banks broadened the scope of their activities to generate higher profits. The financial crisis of 2007–2009 was due, in part, to banks taking on riskier activities and an increasingly blurred demarcation from a bank's retail and wholesale operations. We have seen how financial institutions used 'quants' to try and reduce risk. This was part of the process that led to the growth of sub-prime lending. With the benefit of hindsight it might seem rather foolish for anyone, let alone a bank, to have contemplated lending money to people with bad credit histories and low incomes.

The growth in the housing market during this period along with the changes brought about by deregulation of financial markets in North America, Europe and the UK created the circumstances which allowed banks and other mortgage lenders to expand the amount of loans they made. Under 'traditional' lending regimes banks would have had to have set aside reserves to cover the loans that they had made. That assumes, of course, that such loans appeared on the bank's balance sheet. Innovation in the financial services industry and deregulation coupled with some ingenious thinking by the quants led to ways being developed which allowed banks to lend funds without it appearing on their balance sheets and as a result they were able to off-load the risk to others as well as allow more and more lending to be possible.

In the example given on page 628 reserves were assumed to be 10 per cent. Banks do not simply wait for deposits to be made and then use those deposits as reserves against loan multiples. Banks want to make loans as this is one key way in which they can make profits. If they want to increase lending, therefore, they have to attract sufficient deposits to provide the reserves needed. For example, assume a bank wants to increase lending by £1 billion. It knows that it has to have cash reserves to cover such lending of €100 million (10 per cent of €1 billion). If it set reserves lower, say at 8 per cent, then it would only have to attract €80 million in deposits. The bank therefore has to manage the risks inherent in its balance sheet. It has to make sure that any loan defaults are not more than the amount it has in reserve. Under normal circumstances it will have to market its services and products aggressively in order to attract deposits of €100 million. In doing so it will have to offer more attractive interest rates and this will cut the profitability of its loans.

However, if the bank can make €1 billion of loans without the loans appearing on its balance sheet then it does not have to attract the deposits to act as reserves. These off-balance sheet loans attract income in the form of interest and fees. The result is a greater capacity for lending whilst increasing potential profits for the bank. Banks found that they could put together collections of debt and sell them on. These parcels of debt did have risk attached to them but this risk could be reduced by taking out credit default swaps. This securitization of assets represented one of the innovations in banking that grew with the expansion of sub-prime lending. The basis of the process lay in the fact that the assets involved generated cash flows over a period of time. Securitization takes loans off the balance sheet and so the bank does not have to set aside reserves to cover those loans. This means that the bank has more scope for increasing lending. Assume a bank has agreed to lend 1 000 individuals mortgages for property with each individual borrowing $100 000. The bank is known as the *originator*. These mortgages could be bundled up to form $1 billion worth of debt. Mathematicians analyse the debt and make an assessment that the debt has a 1 per cent chance of default. That is to say, of the 1 000 individuals associated with this debt, 10 are likely to default at some point over the lifetime of the debt. The bank can present the debt package to a credit rating agency and, given the limited risk involved as a result of the pooling of the debt, is able to access a favourable credit rating.

Having secured an appropriate credit rating for the package of debt the bank then sets up what is called a *special purpose vehicle* or SPV. The establishment of an SPV allows the bank to separate its financial obligations. Rather than buyers of the debt having a claim on the bank as a whole in case of default, the setting up of an SPV means that the investor has a claim against the SPV but not the bank. Equally the investor has the right to receive payments first by dealing with an SPV. The SPV buys the collection of debt and will sell it to investors which may be other banks and financial institutions. The funds raised by the SPV allow it to be able to buy the debt from the bank. The SPV will issue bonds for this purpose. For the prospective investor the bond is associated with the stream of cash flows from the package of loans which also have a high rate of interest attached to them. Given that the debt package has been given a high credit rating, the risk associated with the investment is considered relatively low. The investor is protected by the value of the underlying assets. If there was a default on any of the loans the bank had the option of seizing the properties which are the security for the original loan.

The SPV will issue bonds for a total value lower than the package of debt. The difference is the first-loss position of the originator (the bank in this example). The aim is to ensure that the potential loss on the pool of debt is not greater than the difference between the total value of the pool and the value of the bonds issued to sell on the debt. In our example, the pool of debt, the collection of mortgages, is worth $1 billion. The SPV will receive the mortgage payments and uses the cash flows to pay the bond interest and the principal. The debt is sold by the SPV for $950 million – the difference, therefore being $50 million. Analysis shows that the likely default losses on this package of debt would be no more than $30 million. This means that the cash inflows from mortgage owners is sufficient to pay the investors their money back – $950 million This represents a 3 per cent loss rate based on the total value of the debt package.

The SPV issues shares in itself and, therefore, becomes a subsidiary company of the bank (or originator) with its own legal status. Shares may be bought by the originator and by other parties in the financial community. The attraction of doing so is that the SPV generates high returns based on the flow of cash of the underlying asset (the mortgage). The benefit of setting up an SPV for the bank is that it transfers liabilities to the SPV and therefore these do not appear on its balance sheet. As a result the bank does not have to set aside reserves to cover these loans and this leaves it free to increase lending or engage in deals which further expand its earnings and profits. Such activity may include providing finance for acquisitions or making loans to hedge funds. The setting up of an SPV also protects investors. If the bank (which originated the debt) fails then creditors of the bank (those to whom the bank owes money) cannot make any claim against investors given that the SPV is a separate legal entity. Equally, if the SPV fails in some way then the investor does not have recourse to any claim against the bank or the originator. The bank can also earn commission on the sale of the debt to the SPV.

The issue of bonds by the SPV would be in bundles, called *tranches*, which reflect different levels of risk. Given these different levels of risk, different types of investors would be attracted for any particular tranche. Each tranche might relate to the maturity date of the mortgages in the pool or be associated with a different rate of interest, but typically in sub-prime securitization there were six tranches (known as '6-pack deals'). Each tranche can be sold separately and much of this bundled debt could be 'insured' using CDS.

The global nature of the financial system meant that what was created was a complex web of financial transactions that built high levels of interdependence amongst those involved but where few had any real knowledge of the extent of this interdependence. In essence, the whole structure of mortgage lending was dependent on the ability of those who had taken out mortgages (including sub-prime) to be able to pay the principal and interest on their loans. When the number of borrowers defaulting on their repayments started to rise in the middle of the 2000s, the structure began to become unstable and the full extent of the interdependence began to reveal itself.

Mortgages with rates that can change are referred to as variable rate or adjustable rate mortgages. Most of these mortgages are linked not simply to central bank base rate but to 'LIBOR', the London Interbank Offered Rate, which is a benchmark set of interest rates which determine other interest rates in the economy and is the rate at which banks will lend to each other in the London money markets. In the United States around $350 trillion of loans are based on LIBOR.

Each morning the British Bankers' Association gets quotes from 16 major banks on the rates at which they are prepared to borrow 10 currencies with 15 different maturities. These maturities are the spot/overnight next (i.e. for loans made today and repaid tomorrow), 1 week, 2 weeks, 1 month, 2 months and so on up to a maximum of 12 months. Whilst 10 currencies are quoted, the four main ones are the dollar, British pound, euro and Japanese yen.

The quotes are ranked in order of size and an average of the middle two quantities taken to give the LIBOR for that currency. The details are published at 11.30am every morning and form the basis of short-term lending. If LIBOR rates rise then adjustable rate mortgages that are tied to it also rise. Some 73 per cent of adjustable rate sub-prime mortgages in the US were based on six-month LIBOR and not the Federal Funds rate in the period April–September 2007.

From around 2005, central banks began pushing up interest rates to counter inflationary pressures. As interest rates rose, borrowers, especially those on sub-prime mortgages, began to feel the pressure and reports of the number of defaults on sub-prime loans began to rise. Once mortgage defaults began to rise to alarming numbers the number of financial institutions affected and their exposure became clearer. The whole edifice was based on the expectation that the underlying assets would continue to generate the income stream over time – in other words, that the very large majority of mortgage holders would continue to pay their monthly mortgage repayments. As mortgage rates rose borrowers found it increasingly difficult to meet their monthly payments.

If mortgage payers default on loans then banks who lent money to SPVs can call in that debt. Banks who set up the SPV may then have to take the assets of the SPV back onto its balance sheet. This not only limits their ability to lend further because they now have to put aside reserves to cover these liabilities which are now on their balance sheet, but they may also have to write down the value of the assets, further damaging their balance sheet and ability to lend. Every day, banks have obligations to meet – loans they have taken out that need paying off, interest payments, CDS that mature, bonds that need to be paid, etc. They must have sufficient liquid funds to be able to meet these obligations. Many banks borrow the funds they need from the interbank market. As the sub-prime market collapsed, the exposure to bad debt started to become more obvious and a number of banks reported significant write-downs and losses. Confidence in the banking system, so important to its functioning, began to fall. Banks were not sure of their own exposure to these bad debts (referred to as **toxic debt**) and so were also unsure about the extent of other banks' exposure. Interbank lending began to become much

toxic debt
mortgage-backed securities and other debt (such as bonds) that are not able to be repaid in many cases because the value of the assets against which they are secured have fallen significantly

tighter as banks were unwilling to lend to each other and they also faced the task of trying to shore up their own balance sheets.

A significant proportion of the funds that banks borrow is from each other. As mentioned above, the rate at which they borrow from each other is LIBOR. Under normal circumstances, the difference between bank rate and LIBOR is small and stable. In times when credit is scarce, the supply of loans falls and as a result the price rises. Between March 2008 and October 2008 LIBOR rose sharply. Central banks around the world responded to the tightness in the credit market, now termed the 'credit crunch', by cutting interest rates and injecting funds in to the markets. It took until June 2008 for LIBOR gradually to fall back to the Fed Funds level, reflecting the continued tightness in the credit market. Accessing credit was, therefore, far more expensive and limited in nature and the higher price of borrowing was passed onto the consumer – individuals and businesses. As business loans are less easy to obtain or more expensive, businesses find it difficult to manage their cash flow and insolvency can result.

In August 2008, the problems facing banks began to mount. In March of that year the US investment bank Bear Stearns' exposure to sub-prime markets led it to seek support from the Fed; a year before New Century Financial had sought protective bankruptcy and needed financial assistance. Other banks with a heavy exposure to sub-prime began to announce losses and write-downs only to have to issue worse revised figures a short time later. Bear Stearns was rescued by being acquired by JP Morgan Chase. In the UK, Northern Rock suffered a run on its assets as account holders queued to get their money before the bank collapsed – the first run on a UK bank for more than a hundred years. The UK government had to step in to take Northern Rock into public hands and nationalize it.

In the US, it became obvious that two of the major players in the mortgage market, the Federal National Mortgage Association, commonly known as 'Fannie Mae', and the Federal Home Loan Mortgage Corporation, known as 'Freddie Mac', were facing deep financial problems. Their business involved buying mortgages from lenders and then selling on the debt to investors. They effectively guaranteed the borrowing for millions of mortgage owners and accounted for around half of the US mortgage market which was worth $12 trillion. Such was their importance that the US authorities stepped in to support them. As in the UK with Northern Rock, the US government announced in early September 2008 that it was going to take temporary ownership of the two companies to save them from collapse. If the two had become insolvent, house prices in the US, which were falling at rates of around 15 per cent in some areas, would have been likely to have fallen even further, and a larger number of people would have fallen into negative equity. It was estimated at the time that up to around 10 per cent of US homeowners were facing difficulties in meeting their mortgage payments, and risked having their homes repossessed.

CONCLUSION

In *Le Bourgeois Gentilhomme*, a play by the French playwright Molière, a character called Monsieur Jourdain finds out what prose is and then exclaims, 'Good heavens! For more than forty years I have been speaking prose without knowing it!' In the same way, newcomers to economics may sometimes be surprised to find that they have been participating in the monetary system of their economy for years without realizing it. Ever since you got your first pocket money you have been using fiat money. Ever since you got your first bank account you have been participating in fractional-reserve banking and the creation of money. Whenever we buy or sell anything, we are relying on the extraordinarily useful social convention called 'money'. Now that we know what money is and what determines its supply, we can discuss how changes in the quantity of money affect the economy. We begin to address that topic in the next chapter.

SUMMARY

- The term *money* refers to assets that people regularly use to buy goods and services.
- Money serves three functions. As a medium of exchange, it provides the item used to make transactions. As a unit of account, it provides the way in which prices and other economic values are recorded. As a store of value, it provides a way of transferring purchasing power from the present to the future.
- Commodity money, such as gold, is money that has intrinsic value: it would be valued even if it were not used as money. Fiat money, such as paper euros or pounds, is money without intrinsic value: it would be worthless if it were not used as money.
- In an advanced economy, money takes the form of currency and various types of bank deposits, such as current accounts.
- A central bank is an institution designed to regulate the quantity of money in an economy.
- The European Central Bank is the overall central bank for the 16 countries participating in European Monetary Union. The Eurosystem is made up of the European Central Bank plus the corresponding 16 national central banks.
- The UK central bank is the Bank of England. It was granted independence in the setting of interest rates in 1997.
- The US central bank is the Federal Reserve.
- Central banks control the money supply primarily through the refinancing rate and the associated open-market operations. An increase in the refinancing rate means that it is more expensive for banks to borrow from the central bank on a short-term basis if they are short of reserves to cover their lending, and so they will tend to reduce their lending and the money supply will contract. Conversely, a reduction in the refinancing rate will tend to expand the money supply.
- The central bank can also use outright open-market operations to affect the money supply: a purchase of government bonds and other assets from the banking sector increases the money supply, and the sale of assets decreases the money supply. The central bank can also expand the money supply by lowering minimum reserve requirements and it can contract the money supply by raising minimum reserve requirements.
- When banks lend out some of their deposits, they increase the quantity of money in the economy. Because banks may choose to hold excess reserves, they can affect the supply of money beyond the control of the central bank. When households deposit money in banks, banks can use these deposits to create money. But the central bank cannot control exactly how much money that households wish to deposit. Because of these two factors, the central bank's control of the money supply is imperfect.
- A bank run occurs when depositors suspect that a bank may go bankrupt and, therefore, 'run' to the bank to withdraw their deposits. Many countries have a system of deposit insurance and central banks are lenders of last resort so bank runs can be managed more effectively.

KEY CONCEPTS

money, p. 617
medium of exchange, p. 618
unit of account, p. 618
store of value, p. 618
liquidity, p. 618
commodity money, p. 618
fiat money, p. 619
currency, p. 619
demand deposits, p. 621
central bank, p. 622
money supply, p. 622
monetary policy, p. 622
open-market operations, p. 622
European Central Bank (ECB), p. 624
Eurosystem, p. 625
Bank of England, p. 625
Federal Reserve (Fed), p. 626
reserves, p. 627
fractional-reserve banking, p. 628
reserve ratio, p. 628
money multiplier, p. 630
outright open-market operations, p. 631
repurchase agreement (repo), p. 631
money market, p. 631
refinancing rate, p. 632
repo rate, p. 632
discount rate, p. 632
reserve requirements, p. 632
toxic debt, p. 636

QUESTIONS FOR REVIEW

1. What distinguishes money from other assets in the economy?
2. What is commodity money? What is fiat money? Which kind do we use?
3. What are demand deposits, and why should they be included in the stock of money?
4. Who is responsible for setting monetary policy at the European Central Bank? How is this group chosen?
5. Who is responsible for setting monetary policy at the Bank of England? How is this group chosen?
6. If the central bank wants to increase the money supply with outright open-market operations, what does it do?
7. Why don't banks hold 100 per cent reserves? How is the amount of reserves banks hold related to the amount of money the banking system creates?
8. What is the refinancing rate? What happens to the money supply when the European Central Bank raises its refinancing rate?
9. What are reserve requirements? What happens to the money supply when the ECB raises reserve requirements?
10. Why can't central banks control the money supply perfectly?

PROBLEMS AND APPLICATIONS

1. Which of the following are money in the UK economy? Which are not? Explain your answers by discussing each of the three functions of money.
   a. a UK penny
   b. a euro
   c. a Picasso painting
   d. a plastic credit card.
2. What characteristics of an asset make it useful as a medium of exchange? As a store of value?
3. Suppose that someone in one of the euro area countries discovered an easy way to counterfeit €100 banknotes. How would this development affect the monetary system of the euro area? Explain.
4. Your uncle repays a €100 loan from Tenth European Bank (TEB) by writing a €100 cheque from his TEB current account. Use T-accounts to show the effect of this transaction on your uncle and on TEB. Has your uncle's wealth changed? Explain.

5. Beleaguered European Bank (BEB) holds €250 million in deposits and maintains a reserve ratio of 10 per cent.
   a. Show a T-account for BEB.
   b. Now suppose that BEB's largest depositor withdraws €10 million in cash from her account. If BEB decides to restore its reserve ratio by reducing the amount of loans outstanding, show its new T-account.
   c. Explain what effect BEB's action will have on other banks.
   d. Why might it be difficult for BEB to take the action described in part (b)? Discuss another way for BEB to return to its original reserve ratio.
6. You take €100 you had kept under your pillow and deposit it in your bank account. If this €100 stays in the banking system as reserves and if banks hold reserves equal to 10 per cent of deposits, by how much does the total amount of deposits in the banking system increase? By how much does the money supply increase?
7. The European Central Bank conducts a €10 million open market purchase of eligible assets from the banking sector. If the required reserve ratio is 10 per cent, what is the largest possible increase in the money supply that could result? Explain. What is the smallest possible increase? Explain.
8. Suppose that the T-account for First European Bank is as follows:

Assets		Liabilities	
Reserves	€100 000	Deposits	€500 000
Loans	€400 000		

   a. If the ECB requires banks to hold 5 per cent of deposits as reserves, how much in excess reserves does First European now hold?
   b. Assume that all other banks hold only the required amount of reserves. If First European decides to reduce its reserves to only the required amount, by how much would the economy's money supply increase?
9. Suppose that the reserve requirement for current deposits is 10 per cent and that banks do not hold any excess reserves.
   a. If the ECB decides not to renew €1 million of loans it previously made to the euro area banking sector, what is the effect on the economy's reserves and money supply?
   b. Now suppose the ECB lowers the reserve requirement to 5 per cent, but banks choose to hold another 5 per cent of deposits as excess reserves. Why might banks do so? What is the overall change in the money multiplier and the money supply as a result of these actions?
10. Assume that the banking system has total reserves of €100 billion. Assume also that required reserves are 10 per cent of current deposits, and that banks hold no excess reserves and households hold no currency.
    a. What is the money multiplier? What is the money supply?
    b. If the ECB now raises required reserves to 20 per cent of deposits, what is the change in reserves and the change in the money supply?
11. (This problem is challenging.) The economy of Elmendyn contains 2000 €1 coins.
    a. If people hold all money as currency, what is the quantity of money?
    b. If people hold all money as demand deposits, and banks maintain 100 per cent reserves, what is the quantity of money?
    c. If people hold equal amounts of currency and demand deposits, and banks maintain 100 per cent reserves, what is the quantity of money?
    d. If people hold all money as demand deposits, and banks maintain a reserve ratio of 10 per cent, what is the quantity of money?
    e. If people hold equal amounts of currency and demand deposits, and banks maintain a reserve ratio of 10 per cent, what is the quantity of money?
12. A bank bundles up €1 billion of mortgage debt with a forecast default ratio of 5 per cent. The debt is sold via an SPV to a group of investors for €800 million.
    a. The group of investors wish to reduce their risk. Explain how a credit default swap with an insurance company might help them to do this.
    b. There is a credit event and the original debt suffers a default ratio of 50 per cent. Explain how the originator and the investors might be affected by such an event.
13. Is the emphasis on purchasing gilts in the Bank of England's asset purchase programme misguided? Explain.
14. To what extent is quantitative easing inflationary?

For further resources, visit www.cengage.co.uk/mankiw_taylor2

30 MONEY GROWTH AND INFLATION

In 1930, the Lyons Maid company produced choc ices – which they described as chocolate-coated vanilla and coffee flavoured ice cream bars – which were sold in UK confectionery shops for two old pence. Given that before the UK currency was decimalized in 1970 there were 240 old pence to the pound, this means that £1 would have bought you 120 choc ices in 1930. Today, a Wall's 'Chunky' choc ice – basically a chocolate-coated vanilla flavoured ice cream bar – is priced at about 70p, so £1 today will buy you only 1.4 choc ices. This represents quite a substantial price rise.

You are probably not surprised at the increase in the price of ice cream. In advanced economies, most prices tend to rise over time. This increase in the overall level of prices is called *inflation.* Inflation may seem natural and inevitable to a person who has grown up in an advanced economy in Western Europe or North America at the end of the 20th century, but in fact it is not inevitable at all. There were long periods in the 19th century during which, in some economies, most prices fell – a phenomenon called *deflation.*

Although inflation has been the norm in more recent history, there has been substantial variation in the rate at which prices rise. Inflation in the UK during the late 1990s and the first half of the 2000s was low and stable at round 2 per cent or so. However, in the mid-1970s, annual UK inflation, as measured by increases in the retail prices index, exceeded 20 per cent.

International data show an even broader range of inflation experiences. Germany after World War I experienced a spectacular example of inflation. The price of a newspaper rose from 0.3 marks in January 1921 to 70 000 000 marks less than two years later. Other prices rose by similar amounts. An extraordinarily high rate of inflation such as this is called *hyperinflation.* The German hyperinflation had such an adverse effect on the German economy that it is often viewed as one contributor to the rise to power of the National Socialists (Nazis) and, as a result, World War II. Over the past 50 years, with this episode still in mind, German policy makers have been extraordinarily averse to inflation, and Germany has had much lower inflation than most other countries of the world.

In more recent times there have been episodes of hyperinflation in the former Yugoslavia and in Zimbabwe. Inflation in Yugoslavia ran at 5 quadrillion per cent (5 with 15 zeros after it) between October 1993 and January 1995. In January 2009, the Zimbabwean authorities announced that inflation had reached 231 000 000 per cent in June 2008. What that means is that a product (say a loaf of bread) priced at Z$1 in June 2007 would have a price tag of Z$2.31 million in June 2008. However, the prices of some goods rose by considerably more. The Zimbabwean central bank reported that some goods on the black market had risen by 70 000 000 per cent. Laundry soap was one of the goods that had risen by this much, but cooking oil also rose by 60 000 000 per cent and sugar by 36 000 000 per cent. Inflation made almost every Zimbabwean a billionaire. Unskilled workers earned around Z$200 000 000 000 a month – at the time, equivalent to about US$10. In July 2008 the government issued a Z$100 billion note. If you had one it would just about have got you a loaf of bread.

What determines whether an economy experiences inflation and, if so, how much? This chapter answers the question by developing the quantity theory of money. Chapter 1 summarized this theory as one of the *Ten Principles of Economics:* prices rise when the government prints too much money. This insight has a long and venerable tradition among economists. The quantity theory was discussed by the famous 18th-century British philosopher and economist David Hume and was advocated in the latter part of the 20th century by the prominent American economist Milton Friedman. This theory of inflation can explain both moderate inflations, such as those experienced in the United States, and hyperinflations, such as those outlined above.

FYI

Milton Friedman 1912–2006

Economist Milton Friedman died in the United States at the age of 94 in November 2006. Friedman won the Nobel Prize for economics in 1976 and was most famous for his work on free market economics and monetarism. Friedman was Professor of Economics at the University of Chicago for over 30 years. The theories and views he established became part of the 'Chicago School' and a number of his ideas and theories were worked on and developed by his students.

Friedman's view that the money supply was an important factor in the determination of income and inflation encapsulated the free market monetarist approach to economics that dominated the governments of both Margaret Thatcher in the UK and Ronald Reagan in the US in the 1980s. The influence he had on policy making in the latter part of the 20th century has been put on a par by some with the influence Keynes had in the first half of that century.

Friedman's economics also extended to other subject areas including home schooling and drugs and prostitution. In the latter two cases he advocated decriminalizing both as a means of dealing with them more effectively. He was also very much in support of deregulation and the privatization movement that was evident in the UK in the 1980s and 1990s. His underpinning philosophy was a belief in the power of the market to allocate scarce resources effectively.

After developing a theory of inflation, we turn to a related question: why is inflation a problem? At first glance, the answer to this question may seem obvious: inflation is a problem because people don't like it. In the 1970s, when the United Kingdom (along with many other economies) was experiencing a relatively high rate of inflation, opinion polls placed inflation as the most important issue facing the nation.

But what, exactly, are the costs that inflation imposes on a society? The answer may surprise you. Identifying the various costs of inflation is not as straightforward as it first appears. As a result, although all economists decry hyperinflation, some economists argue that the costs of moderate inflation are not nearly as large as the general public believes.

THE CLASSICAL THEORY OF INFLATION

We begin our study of inflation by developing the quantity theory of money. This theory is often called 'classical' because it was developed by some of the earliest thinkers about economic issues back in the 18th century such as David Hume, who are often referred to as the 'classical economists'. Most economists today rely on this theory to explain the long-run determinants of the price level and the inflation rate.

The Level of Prices and the Value of Money

Suppose over some period of time we observe a ten-fold increase in the price of an ice cream. What conclusion should we draw from the fact that people are willing to give up so much more money in exchange for an ice cream? It is possible that people have come to enjoy ice cream more. Yet, even if people's enjoyment of ice cream has increased, a large amount of the price rise is probably due to the fact that, over time, the money used to buy ice cream has become less valuable. Indeed, the first insight about inflation is that it is more about the value of money (the goods and services any given amount of money can be exchanged for) than about the value of goods.

This insight helps point the way towards a theory of inflation. When the consumer prices index and other measures of the price level rise, commentators are often tempted to look at the many individual prices that make up these price indices: 'The CPI rose by 3 per cent last month, led by a 20 per cent rise in the price of coffee and a 30 per cent rise in the price of electricity.' Although this approach does contain some interesting information about what's happening in the economy, it also misses a key point: inflation is an economy-wide phenomenon that concerns, first and foremost, the value of the economy's medium of exchange.

The economy's overall price level can be viewed in two ways. So far, we have viewed the price level as the price of a basket of goods and services. When the price level rises, people have to pay more for the goods and services they buy. Alternatively, we can view the price level as a measure of the value of money. A rise in the price level means a lower value of money because each unit of money now buys a smaller quantity of goods and services.

It may help to express these ideas mathematically. Suppose P is the price level as measured, for instance, by the consumer prices index or the GDP deflator. Then P measures the number of euros needed to buy a basket of goods and services. Now turn this idea around: the quantity of goods and services that can be bought with €1 equals $1/P$. In other words, if P is the price of goods and services measured in terms of money, $1/P$ is the value of money measured in terms of goods and services. Thus, when the overall price level rises, the value of money falls. We gave an example of this in relation to choc ices above.

"It's inflation, Miss Borgia – Too much money chasing too few poisons."

Money Supply, Money Demand and Monetary Equilibrium

What determines the value of money? The answer to this question, like many in economics, is supply and demand. Just as the supply and demand for bananas determines the price of bananas, the supply and demand for money determines the value of money. Thus, our next step in developing the quantity theory of money is to consider the determinants of money supply and money demand.

First consider money supply. In the preceding chapter we discussed how the central bank, together with the banking system, determines the supply of money. When the central bank sells bonds in open-market operations, it receives money in exchange and contracts the money supply. When the central bank buys government bonds, it pays out money and expands the money supply. In addition, if any of this money is deposited in banks which then hold them as reserves, the money multiplier swings into action, and these open-market operations can have an even greater effect on the money supply. For our purposes in this chapter, we ignore the complications introduced by the banking system and simply take the quantity of money supplied as a policy variable that the central bank controls.

Now consider money demand. Most fundamentally, the demand for money reflects how much wealth people want to hold in liquid form. Many factors influence the quantity of money demanded. The amount of currency that people hold in their wallets, for instance, depends on how much they rely on credit cards and on whether an automatic cash dispenser is easy to find. And, as we will emphasize in Chapter 35, the quantity of money demanded depends on the interest rate that a person could earn by using the money to buy an interest-bearing bond rather than leaving it in a wallet or low-interest checking account.

Although many variables affect the demand for money, one variable stands out in importance: the average level of prices in the economy. People hold money because it is the medium of exchange. Unlike other assets, such as bonds or stocks, people can use money to buy the goods and services on their shopping lists. How much money they choose to hold for this purpose depends on the prices of those goods and services. The higher prices are, the more money the typical transaction requires, and the more money people will choose to hold in their wallets and bank accounts. That is, a higher price level (a lower value of money) increases the quantity of money demanded.

What ensures that the quantity of money the central bank supplies balances the quantity of money people demand? The answer, it turns out, depends on the time horizon being considered. Later in this book we will examine the short-run answer, and we will see that interest rates play a key role. In the long run, however, the answer is different and much simpler. *In the long run, the overall level of prices adjusts to the level at which the demand for money equals the supply.* Figure 30.1 illustrates this idea. The horizontal axis of this graph shows the quantity of money. The left-hand vertical axis shows the value of money $1/P$, and the right-hand vertical axis shows the price level P. Notice that the price level axis on the right is inverted: a low price level is shown near the top of this axis, and a high price level is shown near the bottom. This inverted axis illustrates that when the value of money is high (as shown near the top of the left axis), the price level is low (as shown near the top of the right axis).

The two curves in this figure are the supply and demand curves for money. The supply curve is vertical because the central bank has fixed the quantity of money available. The demand curve for money is downward sloping, indicating that when the value of money is low (and the price level is high), people demand

FIGURE 30.1

How the Supply and Demand for Money Determine the Equilibrium Price Level

The horizontal axis shows the quantity of money. The left vertical axis shows the value of money, and the right vertical axis shows the price level. The supply curve for money is vertical because the quantity of money supplied is fixed by the central bank. The demand curve for money is downward sloping because people want to hold a larger quantity of money when each euro buys less. At the equilibrium, point A, the value of money (on the left axis) and the price level (on the right axis) have adjusted to bring the quantity of money supplied and the quantity of money demanded into balance.

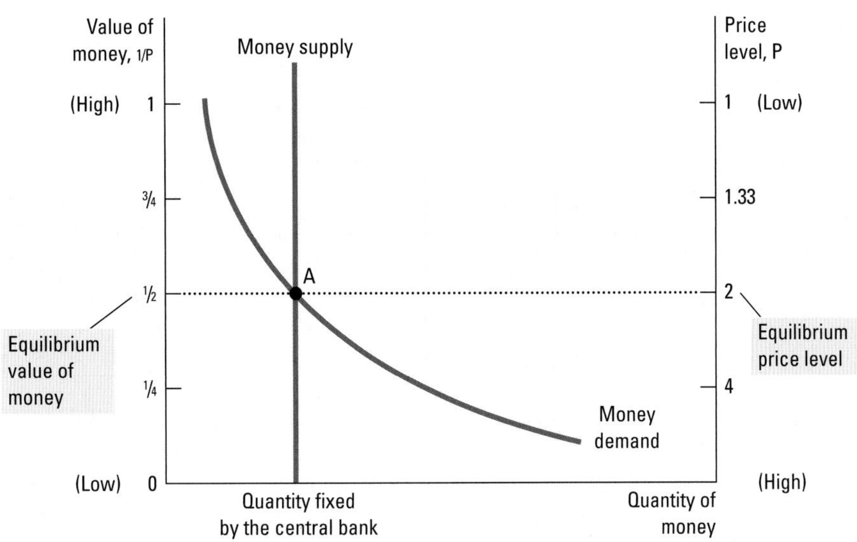

a larger quantity of it to buy goods and services. At the equilibrium, shown in the figure as point A, the quantity of money demanded balances the quantity of money supplied. This equilibrium of money supply and money demand determines the value of money and the price level.

To summarize, if the price level is above the equilibrium level, people will want to hold more money than the central bank has created, so the price level must fall to balance supply and demand. If the price level is below the equilibrium level, people will want to hold less money than the central bank has created, and the price level must rise to balance supply and demand. At the equilibrium price level, the quantity of money that people want to hold exactly balances the quantity of money supplied by the central bank.

The Effects of a Monetary Injection

Let's now consider the effects of a change in monetary policy. To do so, imagine that the economy is in equilibrium and then, suddenly, the central bank doubles the supply of money by printing large amounts of money and dropping it around the country from helicopters (this analogy was first drawn by Milton Friedman and later echoed by the Federal Reserve chair, at the time of writing, Ben Bernanke, which earned him the nickname 'Helicopter Ben'). Or, less dramatically and more realistically, the central bank could inject money into the economy by buying some government bonds from the public in open-market operations. What happens after such a monetary injection? How does the new equilibrium compare to the old one?

FIGURE 30.2

An Increase in the Money Supply

When the central bank increases the supply of money, the money supply curve shifts from MS_1 *to* MS_2*. The value of money (on the left axis) and the price level (on the right axis) adjust to bring supply and demand back into balance. The equilibrium moves from point A to point B. Thus, when an increase in the money supply makes euros more plentiful, the price level increases, making each euro less valuable.*

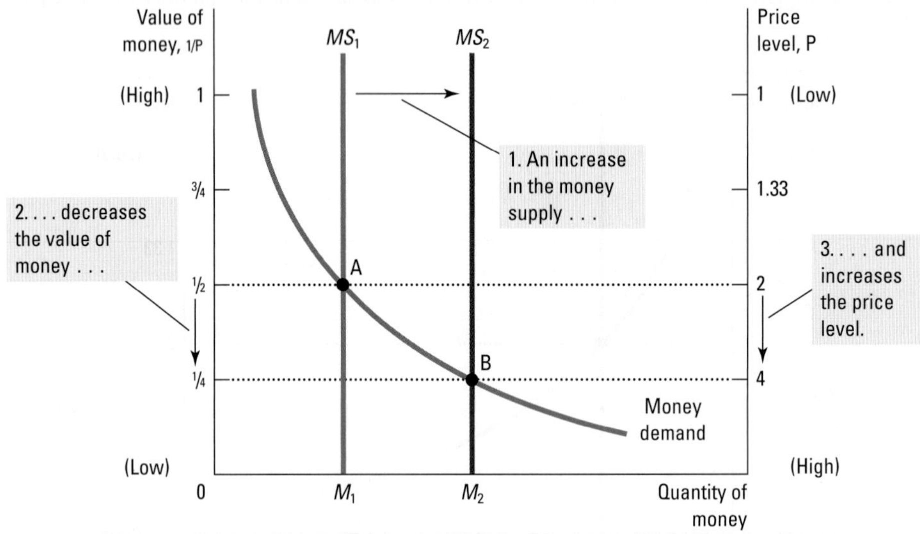

Figure 30.2 shows what happens. The monetary injection shifts the supply curve to the right from MS_1 to MS_2, and the equilibrium moves from point A to point B. As a result, the value of money (shown on the left axis) decreases from ½ to ¼, and the equilibrium price level (shown on the right axis) increases from 2 to 4. In other words, when an increase in the money supply makes euros more plentiful, the result is an increase in the price level that makes each euro less valuable.

This explanation of how the price level is determined and why it might change over time is called the **quantity theory of money**. According to the quantity theory, the quantity of money available in the economy determines the value of money, and growth in the quantity of money is the primary cause of inflation. As Milton Friedman once put it, 'Inflation is always and everywhere a monetary phenomenon.'

quantity theory of money
a theory asserting that the quantity of money available determines the price level and that the growth rate in the quantity of money available determines the inflation rate

A Brief Look at the Adjustment Process

So far we have compared the old equilibrium and the new equilibrium after an injection of money. How does the economy get from the old to the new equilibrium? A complete answer to this question requires an understanding of short-run fluctuations in the economy, which we examine later in this book. Yet, even now, it is instructive to consider briefly the adjustment process that occurs after a change in money supply.

The immediate effect of a monetary injection is to create an excess supply of money. Before the injection, the economy was in equilibrium (point A in Figure 30.2). At the prevailing price level, people had exactly as much money as they wanted. But after the helicopters drop the new money and people pick it up off the streets, people have more euros in their wallets than they need to buy goods and services. At the prevailing price level, the quantity of money supplied now exceeds the quantity demanded.

People try to get rid of this excess supply of money in various ways. They might buy goods and services with their excess holdings of money. Or they might use this excess money to make loans to others by buying bonds or by depositing the money in a bank savings account (remember the relationship between saving and investment outlined in Chapter 25). These loans allow other people to buy goods and services. In either case, the injection of money increases the demand for goods and services.

The economy's ability to supply goods and services, however, has not changed. As we saw in the chapter on production and growth, the economy's output of goods and services is determined by the available labour, physical capital, human capital, natural resources and technological knowledge. None of these is altered by the injection of money.

Thus, the greater demand for goods and services causes the prices of goods and services to increase. The increase in the price level, in turn, increases the quantity of money demanded because people are using more euros for every transaction. Eventually, the economy reaches a new equilibrium (point B in Figure 30.2) at which the quantity of money demanded again equals the quantity of money supplied. In this way, the overall price level for goods and services adjusts to bring money supply and money demand into balance.

The Classical Dichotomy and Monetary Neutrality

We have seen how changes in the money supply lead to changes in the average level of prices of goods and services. How do these monetary changes affect other important macroeconomic variables, such as production, employment, real wages and real interest rates? This question has long intrigued economists. Indeed, the great classical economist and philosopher David Hume wrote about it in the 18th century. The answer we give today owes much to Hume's analysis.

Hume and his contemporaries suggested that all economic variables should be divided into two groups. The first group consists of **nominal variables** – variables measured in monetary units. The second group consists of **real variables** – variables measured in physical units. For example, the income of corn farmers is a nominal variable because it is measured in euros, whereas the quantity of corn they produce is a real variable because it is measured in kilos. Similarly, nominal GDP is a nominal variable because it measures the euro value of the economy's output of goods and services; real GDP is a real variable because it measures the total quantity of goods and services produced and is not influenced by the current prices of those goods and services. This separation of variables into these groups is now called the **classical dichotomy**. (A *dichotomy* is a division into two groups, and *classical* refers to the earlier economic thinkers or classical economists.)

nominal variables
variables measured in monetary units

real variables
variables measured in physical units

classical dichotomy
the theoretical separation of nominal and real variables

Application of the classical dichotomy is somewhat tricky when we turn to prices. Prices in the economy are normally quoted in terms of money and, therefore, are nominal variables. For instance, when we say that the price of corn is €2 a kilo or that the price of wheat is €1 a kilo, both prices are nominal variables. But what about a *relative* price – the price of one thing compared to another? In our example, we could say that the price of a kilo of corn is two kilos of wheat. Notice that this relative price is no longer measured in terms of money. When comparing the prices of any two goods, the euro signs cancel, and the resulting number is measured in physical units. The lesson is that money prices (e.g. in pounds, euros or dollars) are nominal variables, whereas relative prices are real variables.

This lesson has several important applications. For instance, the real wage (the money wage adjusted for inflation) is a real variable because it measures the rate at which the economy exchanges goods and services for each unit of labour. Similarly, the real interest rate (the nominal interest rate adjusted for inflation) is a real variable because it measures the rate at which the economy exchanges goods and services produced today for goods and services produced in the future.

Why bother separating variables into these two groups? Hume suggested that the classical dichotomy is useful in analysing the economy because different forces influence real and nominal variables. In particular, he argued, nominal variables are heavily influenced by developments in the economy's monetary system, whereas the monetary system is largely irrelevant for understanding the determinants of important real variables.

Notice that Hume's idea was implicit in our earlier discussions of the real economy in the long run. In previous chapters, we examined how real GDP, saving, investment, real interest rates and unemployment are determined without any mention of the existence of money. As explained in that analysis, the economy's production of goods and services depends on productivity and factor supplies, the real interest rate adjusts to balance the supply and demand for loanable funds, the real wage adjusts to balance the supply and demand for labour, and unemployment results when the real wage is for some reason kept above its equilibrium level. These important conclusions have nothing to do with the quantity of money supplied.

Changes in the supply of money, according to Hume, affect nominal variables but not real variables. When the central bank doubles the money supply, the price level doubles, the euro wage doubles, and all other euro values double. Real variables, such as production, employment, real wages and real interest rates, are unchanged. This irrelevance of monetary changes for real variables is called **monetary neutrality**.

monetary neutrality
the proposition that changes in the money supply do not affect real variables

An analogy sheds light on the meaning of monetary neutrality. Recall that, as the unit of account, money is the yardstick we use to measure economic transactions. When a central bank doubles the money supply, all prices double, and the value of the unit of account falls by half. A similar change would occur if a European Union directive reduced the definition of the metre from 100 to 50 centimetres: as a result of the new unit of measurement, all *measured* distances (nominal variables) would double, but the *actual* distances (real variables) would remain the same. The euro, like the metre, is merely a unit of measurement, so a change in its value should not have important real effects.

Is this conclusion of monetary neutrality a realistic description of the world in which we live? The answer is, not completely. A change in the length of the metre from 100 to 50 centimetres would not matter much in the long run, but in the short run it would certainly lead to confusion and various mistakes. Similarly, most economists today believe that over short periods of time – within the span of a year or two – there is reason to think that monetary changes do have important effects on real variables. Hume himself also doubted that monetary neutrality would apply in the short run. (We will turn to the study of short-run non-neutrality later in the book, and this topic will shed light on the reasons why central banks change the supply of money over time.)

Most economists today accept Hume's conclusion as a description of the economy in the long run. Over the course of a decade, for instance, monetary changes have important effects on nominal variables (such as the price level) but only negligible effects on real variables (such as real GDP). When studying long-run changes in the economy, the neutrality of money offers a good description of how the world works.

Velocity and the Quantity Equation

We can obtain another perspective on the quantity theory of money by considering the following question: how many times per year is the typical €1 coin used to pay for a newly produced good or service? The answer to this question is given by a variable called the **velocity of money**. In physics, the term *velocity* refers to the speed at which an object travels. In economics, the velocity of money refers to the speed at which money changes hands as it moves around the economy.

velocity of money
the rate at which money changes hands

To calculate the velocity of money, we divide the nominal value of output (nominal GDP) by the quantity of money. If P is the price level (the GDP deflator), Y the quantity of output (real GDP) and M the quantity of money, then velocity is:

$$V = (P \times Y)/M$$

To see why this makes sense, imagine a simple economy that produces only pizza. Suppose that the economy produces 100 pizzas in a year, that a pizza sells for €10, and that the quantity of money in the economy is €50, made up of fifty €1 coins. Then the velocity of money is:

$$V = (€10 \times 100)/€50$$
$$= 20$$

In this economy, people spend a total of €1 000 per year on pizza. For this €1 000 of spending to take place with only €50 of money, each euro coin must be spent (i.e. change hands) on average 20 times per year.

With slight algebraic rearrangement, this equation can be rewritten as:

$$M \times V = P \times Y$$

This equation states that the quantity of money (M) times the velocity of money (V) equals the price of output (P) times the amount of output (Y). It is called the **quantity equation** because it relates the quantity of money (M) to the nominal value of output ($P \times Y$). The quantity equation (which is an identity or a truism) shows that an increase in the quantity of money in an economy must be reflected in one of the other three variables: the price level must rise, the quantity of output must rise or the velocity of money must fall.

quantity equation
the equation $M \times V = P \times Y$, which relates the quantity of money, the velocity of money, and the currency value of the economy's output of goods and services

We now have all the elements necessary to explain the equilibrium price level and inflation rate. Here they are:

1. The velocity of money is relatively stable over time.
2. Because velocity is stable, when the central bank changes the quantity of money (M), it causes proportionate changes in the nominal value of output ($P \times Y$).
3. The economy's output of goods and services (Y) is primarily determined by factor supplies (labour, physical capital, human capital and natural resources) and the available production technology. In particular, because money is neutral, money does not affect output.
4. With output (Y) determined by factor supplies and technology, when the central bank alters the money supply (M) and induces proportional changes in the nominal value of output ($P \times Y$), these changes are reflected in changes in the price level (P).
5. Therefore, when the central bank increases the money supply rapidly, the result is a high rate of inflation.

These five steps are the essence of the quantity theory of money.

CASE STUDY

Money and Prices during Four Hyperinflations

Although earthquakes can wreak havoc on a society, they have the beneficial by-product of providing much useful data for seismologists. These data can shed light on alternative theories and, thereby, help society predict and deal

FIGURE 30.3

Money and Prices During Four Hyperinflations

This figure shows the quantity of money and the price level during four hyperinflations. (Note that these variables are graphed on logarithmic scales. This means that equal vertical distances on the graph represent equal percentage changes in the variable.) In each case, the quantity of money and the price level move closely together. The strong association between these two variables is consistent with the quantity theory of money, which states that growth in the money supply is the primary cause of inflation.

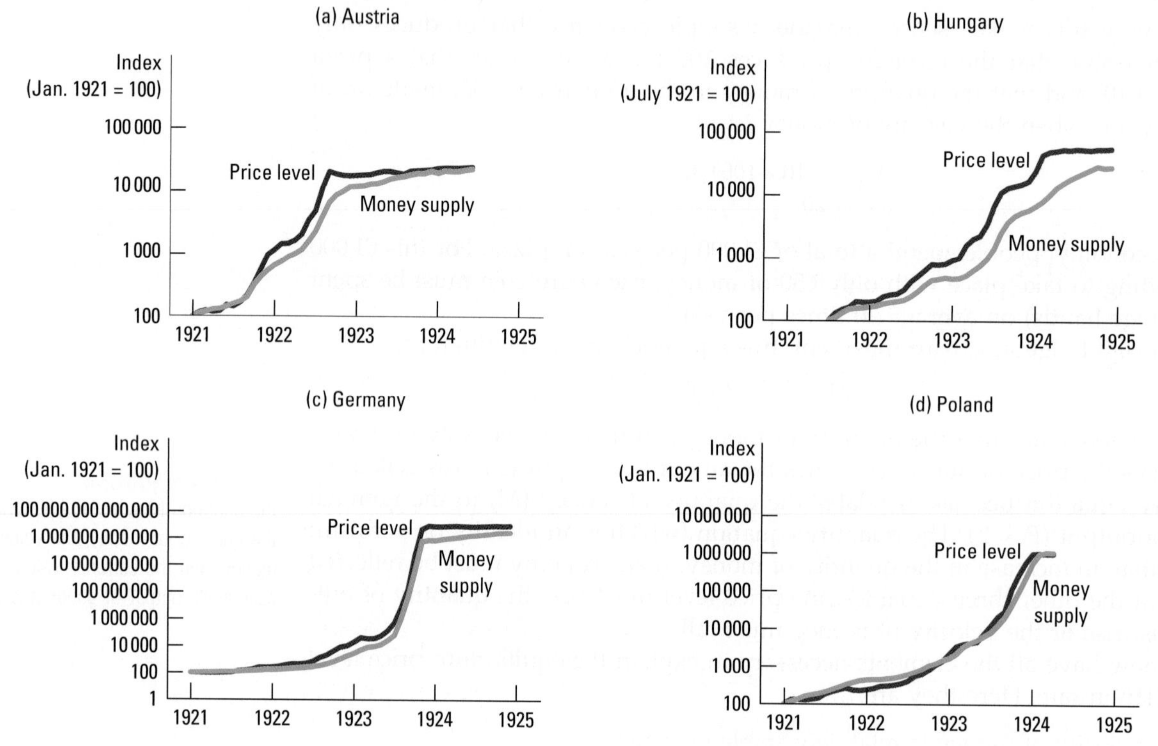

Source: Adapted from Thomas J. Sargent, 'The End of Four Big Inflations,' in Robert Hall, ed., *Inflation* (Chicago: University of Chicago Press, 1983), pp. 41–93. Reprinted with permission.

with future threats. Similarly, hyperinflations offer monetary economists a natural experiment they can use to study the effects of money on the economy.

Hyperinflations are interesting in part because the changes in the money supply and price level are so large. Indeed, hyperinflation is generally defined as inflation that exceeds 50 per cent per month. This means that the price level increases more than 100-fold over the course of a year.

The data on hyperinflation show a clear link between the quantity of money and the price level. Figure 30.3 graphs data from four classic hyperinflations that occurred during the 1920s in Austria, Hungary, Germany and Poland. Each graph shows the quantity of money in the economy and an index of the price level. The slope of the money line represents the rate at which the quantity of money was growing, and the slope of the price line represents the inflation rate. The steeper the lines, the higher the rates of money growth or inflation.

Notice that in each graph the quantity of money and the price level are almost parallel. In each instance, growth in the quantity of money is moderate at first, and so is inflation. But over time, the quantity of money in the economy starts growing faster and faster. At about the same time, inflation also takes off. Then when the quantity of money stabilizes, the price level also stabilizes. These episodes illustrate well one of the *Ten Principles of Economics*: prices rise when the government prints too much money.

The Inflation Tax

If inflation is so easy to explain, why do countries experience hyperinflation? That is, why do the central banks of these countries choose to print so much money that its value is certain to fall rapidly over time?

The answer is that the governments of these countries are using money creation as a way to pay for their spending. When the government wants to build roads, pay salaries to police officers, or give transfer payments to the poor or elderly, it first has to raise the necessary funds. Normally, the government does this by levying taxes, such as income and sales taxes, and by borrowing from the public by selling government bonds. Yet the government can also pay for spending by simply printing the money it needs.

When the government raises revenue by printing money, it is said to levy an **inflation tax**. The inflation tax is not exactly like other taxes, however, because no one receives a bill from the government for this tax. Instead, the inflation tax is more subtle. When the government prints money, the price level rises, and the euros in your wallet are less valuable. Thus, the inflation tax is like a tax on everyone who holds money. It is even, roughly speaking, a progressive tax in the sense we discussed in Chapter 12, since the richer you are, the more money you are likely to hold and therefore the more the inflation tax will affect you.

inflation tax
the revenue the government raises by creating money

The importance of the inflation tax varies from country to country and over time. In the early 21st century, most advanced economies have been enjoying very low rates of inflation, so that the inflation tax has been a trivial source of revenue for the government, amounting to only a few per cent of government revenue. In the four hyperinflations of the 1920s we discussed earlier, and in various Latin American countries during the 1970s and 1980s, the inflation tax would have been quite considerable.

Nearly all hyperinflations follow the same pattern: the government has high spending, limited ability to borrow, inadequate tax revenue (perhaps because the level of income in the economy is low, or there is widespread tax evasion or a poorly developed tax system, or a combination of all these factors), and as a result, it turns to the printing press to pay for its spending. The massive increases in the quantity of money lead to massive inflation. The inflation ends when the government institutes fiscal reforms – such as cuts in government spending – that eliminate the need for the inflation tax.

As the economist John Maynard Keynes once pointed out, the temptation to just print money to pay for government spending through the inflation tax may be hard for a government to resist in such circumstances: 'The burden of the tax is well spread, cannot be evaded, costs nothing to collect, and falls, in a rough sort of way, in proportion to the wealth of the victim. No wonder its superficial advantages have attracted Ministers of Finance.' Of course, Keynes also recognized the great damage that high inflation can do to an economy, which is why he referred to the advantages of an inflation tax as 'superficial'.

The Fisher Effect

According to the principle of monetary neutrality, an increase in the rate of money growth raises the rate of inflation but does not affect any real variable. An important application of this principle concerns the effect of money on interest rates. Interest rates are important variables for macroeconomists to understand because they link the economy of the present and the economy of the future through their effects on saving and investment.

To understand the relationship between money, inflation and interest rates, recall the distinction between the nominal interest rate and the real interest rate introduced in Chapter 24.

The *nominal interest rate* is the interest rate you hear about at your bank. If you have a savings account, for instance, the nominal interest rate tells you how fast the number of euros in your account will rise over time. The *real interest rate* corrects the nominal interest rate for the effect of inflation in order to tell you how fast the purchasing power of your savings account will rise over time. The real interest rate is the nominal interest rate minus the inflation rate:

$$\text{Real interest rate} = \text{Nominal interest rate} - \text{Inflation rate}$$

For example, if the bank posts a nominal interest rate of 7 per cent per year and the inflation rate is 3 per cent per year, then the real value of the deposits grows by 4 per cent per year.

We can rewrite this equation to show that the nominal interest rate is the sum of the real interest rate and the inflation rate:

$$\text{Nominal interest rate} = \text{Real interest rate} + \text{Inflation rate}$$

This way of looking at the nominal interest rate is useful because different economic forces determine each of the two terms on the right-hand side of this equation. As we discussed earlier in the book, the supply and demand for loanable funds determine the real interest rate. And, according to the quantity theory of money, growth in the money supply determines the inflation rate.

Let's now consider how the growth in the money supply affects interest rates. In the long run over which money is neutral, a change in money growth should not affect the real interest rate. The real interest rate is, after all, a real variable. For the real interest rate not to be affected, the nominal interest rate must adjust one-for-one to changes in the inflation rate. Thus, when the central bank increases the rate of money growth, the result is both a higher inflation rate and a higher nominal interest rate. This adjustment of the nominal interest rate to the inflation rate is called the **Fisher effect**, after the American economist Irving Fisher (1867–1947), who first studied it.

Fisher effect
the one-for-one adjustment of the nominal interest rate to the inflation rate

Keep in mind that our analysis of the Fisher effect has maintained a long-run perspective. The Fisher effect does not hold in the short run to the extent that inflation is unanticipated. A nominal interest rate is a payment on a loan, and it is typically set when the loan is first made. If inflation catches the borrower and lender by surprise, the nominal interest rate they set will fail to reflect the rise in prices. To be precise, the Fisher effect states that the nominal interest rate adjusts to expected inflation. Expected inflation moves with actual inflation in the long run but not necessarily in the short run.

The Fisher effect is crucial for understanding changes over time in the nominal interest rate. Figure 30.4 shows the nominal interest rate and the inflation rate in the UK economy since 1975. The close association between these two variables is clear. The nominal interest rate tends to rise when inflation rises and fall when inflation falls. This is true both in high-inflation periods, such as during the late 1970s and the late 1980s, as well as during low-inflation periods, such as the period since the mid-1990s.

Quick Quiz The government of a country increases the growth rate of the money supply from 5 per cent per year to 50 per cent per year. • What happens to prices? • What happens to nominal interest rates? • Why might the government be doing this?

FIGURE 30.4

The UK Nominal Interest Rate and the Inflation Rate

This figure uses annual data since 1976 to show the nominal interest rate on three-month UK Treasury bills (measured as the annual average rate of discount) and the inflation rate (as measured by the retail prices index). The close association between these two variables is evidence for the Fisher effect: when the inflation rate rises, so does the nominal interest rate.

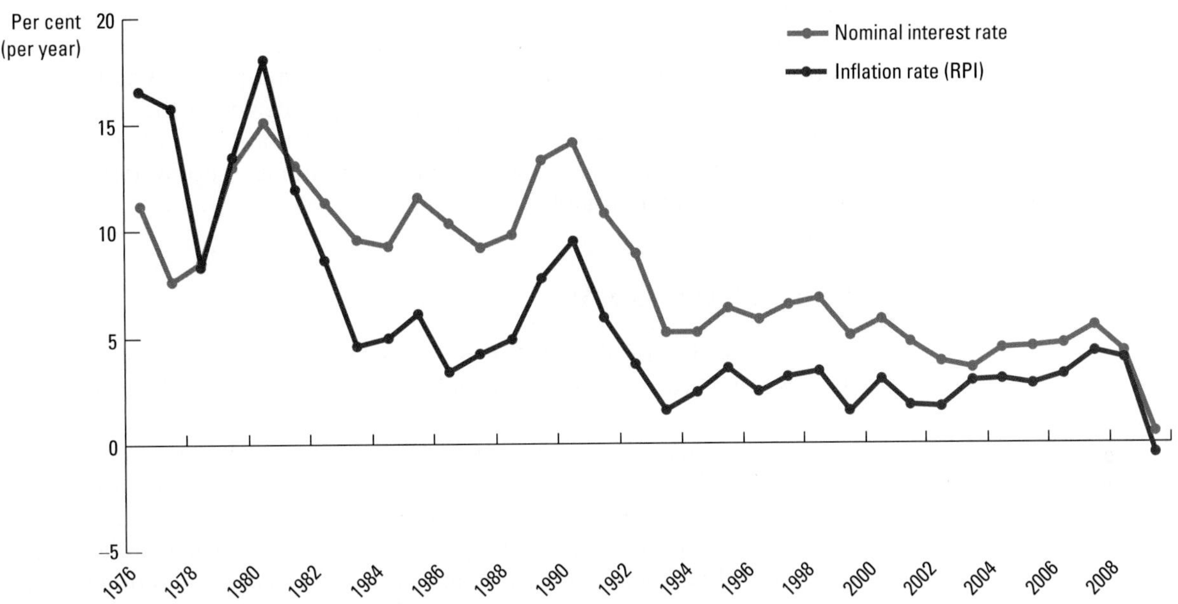

Source: Bank of England and UK Office for National Statistics.

THE COSTS OF INFLATION

In the mid-1970s, when the UK inflation rate reached a peak of about 24 per cent a year, inflation dominated debates over economic policy. And even though inflation was low during the 1990s, it remained a closely watched macroeconomic variable.

Inflation is closely watched and widely discussed because it is thought to be a serious economic problem. But is that true? And if so, why?

A Fall in Purchasing Power? The Inflation Fallacy

If you ask the typical person why inflation is bad, he will tell you that the answer is obvious: Inflation robs him of the purchasing power of his hard-earned money. When prices rise, each euro of income buys fewer goods and services. Thus, it might seem that inflation directly lowers living standards.

Yet further thought reveals a fallacy in this answer. When prices rise, buyers of goods and services pay more for what they buy. At the same time, however, sellers of goods and services get more for what they sell. Because most people earn their incomes by selling their services, such as their labour, inflation in incomes goes hand in hand with inflation in prices. *Thus, inflation does not in itself reduce people's real purchasing power.*

People believe the inflation fallacy because they do not appreciate the principle of monetary neutrality. A worker who receives an annual rise of 10 per cent in her salary tends to view that rise as a reward for her own talent and effort. When an inflation rate of 6 per cent reduces the real value of that pay rise to only 4 per cent, the worker might feel that she has been cheated of what is rightfully her due. In fact, as we discussed in the chapter on production and growth, real incomes are determined by real variables, such as physical capital, human capital, natural resources, and the available production technology. Nominal incomes are determined by those factors and the overall price level. If the central bank were to succeed in lowering the inflation rate from 6 per cent to zero, our worker's annual rise would fall from 10 per cent to 4 per cent. She might feel less robbed by inflation, but her real income would not rise more quickly.

If nominal incomes tend to keep pace with rising prices, why then is inflation a problem? It turns out that there is no single answer to this question. Instead, economists have identified several costs of inflation. Each of these costs shows some way in which persistent growth in the money supply does, in fact, have some effect on real variables.

Shoeleather Costs

As we have discussed, inflation is like a tax on the holders of money. The tax itself is not a cost to society: it is only a transfer of resources from households to the government. Yet most taxes give people an incentive to alter their behaviour to avoid paying the tax, and this distortion of incentives causes deadweight losses for society as a whole. Like other taxes, the inflation tax also causes deadweight losses because people waste scarce resources trying to avoid it.

How can a person avoid paying the inflation tax? Because inflation erodes the real value of the money in your wallet, you can avoid the inflation tax by holding less money. One way to do this is to go to the bank more often. For example, rather than withdrawing €200 every four weeks, you might withdraw €50 once a week. By making more frequent trips to the bank, you can keep more of your wealth in your interest-bearing savings account and less in your wallet, where inflation erodes its value.

shoeleather costs
the resources wasted when inflation encourages people to reduce their money holdings

The cost of reducing your money holdings is called the **shoeleather cost** of inflation because making more frequent trips to the bank causes your shoes to wear out more quickly. Of course, this term is not to be taken literally: the actual cost of reducing your money holdings is not the wear and tear on your shoes but the time and convenience you must sacrifice to keep less money on hand than you would if there were no inflation – it is in effect a *transaction cost,* the opportunity cost of carrying out the trips to the bank.

The shoeleather costs of inflation may seem trivial. And, in fact, they are in countries experiencing only moderate inflation. But this cost is magnified in countries experiencing hyperinflation (see the In the News article on Zimbabwe on page 658). In conditions of hyperinflation, shoeleather costs can be substantial. With a high inflation rate, individuals do not have the luxury of holding the local money as a store of value. Instead, they are forced to convert the domestic currency quickly into goods or into another currency, often the US dollar, which offer a more stable store of value. The time and effort that individuals expend to reduce their money holdings are a waste of resources. If monetary authorities pursued a low-inflation policy, individuals would be happy to hold the domestic currency, and they could put time and effort to more productive use.

Menu Costs

Most firms do not change the prices of their products every day. Instead, firms often announce prices and leave them unchanged for weeks, months or even years.

Firms change prices infrequently because there are costs involved in changing prices. Costs of price adjustment are called **menu costs**, a term derived from a restaurant's cost of printing a new menu. Menu costs include the cost of deciding on new prices, the cost of printing new price lists and catalogues, the cost of sending these new price lists and catalogues to dealers and customers, the cost of advertising the new prices, and even the cost of dealing with customer annoyance over price changes.

menu costs
the costs of changing prices

Inflation increases the menu costs that firms must bear. In an economy with low inflation of just a few percentage points a year, annual price adjustment is an appropriate business strategy for many firms. But when high inflation makes firms' costs rise rapidly, annual price adjustment is impractical. During hyperinflations, for example, firms must change their prices daily or even more often just to keep up with all the other prices in the economy. At the height of the German hyperinflation in the 1920s, people eating in restaurants would sometimes insist on paying the bill at the beginning of the meal rather than at then end, because the price of the food would rise while they were eating!

Relative Price Variability and the Misallocation of Resources

Suppose that the Eatabit Eatery prints a new menu with new prices every January and then leaves its prices unchanged for the rest of the year. If there is no inflation, Eatabit's relative prices – the prices of its meals compared with other prices in the economy – would be constant over the course of the year. By contrast, if the inflation rate is 12 per cent per year, Eatabit's relative prices will automatically fall by 1 per cent each month. The restaurant's relative prices (that is, its prices compared with others in the economy) will be high in the early months of the year, just after it has printed a new menu, and low in the later months. And the higher the inflation rate, the greater is this automatic variability. Thus, because prices change only once in a while, inflation causes relative prices to vary more than they otherwise would.

Why does this matter? The reason is that market economies rely on relative prices to allocate scarce resources. Consumers decide what to buy by comparing the quality and prices of various goods and services. Through these decisions, they determine how the scarce factors of production are allocated among industries and firms. When inflation distorts relative prices, consumer decisions are distorted, and markets are less able to allocate resources to their best use.

Inflation-induced Tax Distortions

Almost all taxes distort incentives, cause people to alter their behaviour, and lead to a less efficient allocation of the economy's resources. Many taxes, however, become even more problematic in the presence of inflation. The reason is that politicians often fail to take inflation into account when writing the tax laws. Economists who have studied the tax system conclude that inflation tends to raise the tax burden on income earned from savings.

One example of how inflation discourages saving is the tax treatment of *capital gains* – the profits made by selling an asset for more than its purchase price. Suppose that in 1990 you used some of your savings to buy stock in Microsoft Corporation for €10 and that in 2010 you sold the stock for €50. According to the tax system, you have earned a capital gain of €40, which you must include in your income when computing how much income tax you owe. But suppose the overall price level doubled from 1990 to 2010. In this case, the €10 you invested in

1990 is equivalent (in terms of purchasing power) to €20 in 2010. When you sell your Microsoft shares for €50, you have a real gain (an increase in purchasing power) of only €30. The tax system, however, does not take account of inflation and assesses you a tax on a gain of €40. Thus, inflation exaggerates the size of capital gains and inadvertently increases the tax burden on this type of income.

Another example is the tax treatment of interest income. The income tax treats the *nominal* interest earned on savings as income, even though part of the nominal interest rate merely compensates for inflation. To see the effects of this policy, consider the numerical example in Table 30.1. The table compares two economies, both of which tax interest income at a rate of 25 per cent. In economy A, inflation is zero, and the nominal and real interest rates are both 4 per cent. In this case, the 25 per cent tax on interest income reduces the real interest rate from 4 per cent to 3 per cent. In economy B, the real interest rate is again 4 per cent, but the inflation rate is 8 per cent. As a result of the Fisher effect, the nominal interest rate is 12 per cent. Because the income tax treats this entire 12 per cent interest as income, the government takes 25 per cent of it, leaving an after-tax nominal interest rate of only 9 per cent and an after-tax real interest rate of only 1 per cent. In this case, the 25 per cent tax on interest income reduces the real interest rate from 4 per cent to 1 per cent. Because the after-tax real interest rate provides the incentive to save, saving is much less attractive in the economy with inflation (economy B) than in the economy with stable prices (economy A).

The taxes on nominal capital gains and on nominal interest income are two examples of how the tax system interacts with inflation. There are many others. Because of these inflation-induced tax changes, higher inflation tends to discourage people from saving. Recall that the economy's saving provides the resources for investment, which in turn is a key ingredient to long-run economic growth. Thus, when inflation raises the tax burden on saving, it tends to depress the economy's long-run growth rate. There is, however, no consensus among economists about the size of this effect.

One solution to this problem, other than eliminating inflation, is to index the tax system. That is, the tax laws could be rewritten to take account of the effects of inflation. In the case of capital gains, for example, the tax code could adjust the purchase price using a price index and assess the tax only on the real gain. In the case of interest income, the government could tax only real interest income by excluding that portion of the interest income that merely compensates for inflation.

TABLE 30.1

How Inflation Raises the Tax Burden on Saving

In the presence of zero inflation, a 25 per cent tax on interest income reduces the real interest rate from 4 per cent to 3 per cent. In the presence of 8 per cent inflation, the same tax reduces the real interest rate from 4 per cent to 1 per cent.

	Economy A (price stability)	Economy B (inflation)
Real interest rate	4%	4%
Inflation rate	0	8
Nominal interest rate (real interest rate + inflation rate)	4	12
Reduced interest due to 25 per cent tax (.25 × nominal interest rate)	1	3
After-tax nominal interest rate (.75 × nominal interest rate)	3	9
After-tax real interest rate (after-tax nominal interest rate – inflation rate)	3	1

In an ideal world, tax laws would be written so that inflation would not alter anyone's real tax liability. In the world in which we live, however, tax laws are far from perfect. More complete indexation would probably be desirable, but it would further complicate a tax system that many people already consider too complex.

Confusion and Inconvenience

Imagine that we took a poll and asked people the following question: 'This year the metre is 100 centimetres. How long do you think it should be next year?' Assuming we could get people to take us seriously, they would tell us that the metre should stay the same length – 100 centimetres. Anything else would just complicate life needlessly.

What does this finding have to do with inflation? Recall that money, as the economy's unit of account, is what we use to quote prices and record debts. In other words, money is the yardstick with which we measure economic transactions. The job of the central bank is a little like the job of the government department that deals with weights and measurements, i.e. to ensure the reliability of a commonly used unit of measurement. When the central bank increases the money supply and creates inflation, it erodes the real value of the unit of account.

It is difficult to judge the costs of the confusion and inconvenience that arise from inflation. Earlier we discussed how the tax system incorrectly measures real incomes in the presence of inflation. Similarly, accountants incorrectly measure firms' earnings when prices are rising over time. Because inflation causes money at different times to have different real values, computing a firm's profit – the difference between its revenue and costs – is more complicated in an economy with inflation. Therefore, to some extent, inflation makes investors less able to sort out successful from unsuccessful firms, which in turn impedes financial markets in their role of allocating the economy's saving to alternative types of investment.

A Special Cost of Unexpected Inflation: Arbitrary Redistributions of Wealth

So far, the costs of inflation we have discussed occur even if inflation is steady and predictable. Inflation has an additional cost, however, when it comes as a surprise. Unexpected inflation redistributes wealth among the population in a way that has nothing to do with either merit or need. These redistributions occur because many loans in the economy are specified in terms of the unit of account – money.

Consider an example. Suppose that Lars, a student takes out a €20 000 loan at a 7 per cent interest rate from Bigbank to attend university. In ten years the loan will have to be repaid. After his debt has compounded for ten years at 7 per cent, Lars will owe Bigbank €40 000. The real value of this debt will depend on inflation over the decade. If Lars is lucky, the economy will have hyperinflation. In this case, wages and prices will rise so high that Lars will be able to pay the €40 000 debt out of pocket change. In contrast, if the economy goes through a major deflation, then wages and prices will fall, and Lars will find the €40 000 debt a greater burden than he anticipated.

This example shows that unexpected changes in prices redistribute wealth among debtors and creditors. A hyperinflation enriches Lars at the expense of Bigbank because it diminishes the real value of the debt; Lars can repay the loan in less valuable euros than he anticipated. Deflation enriches Bigbank at Lars' expense because it increases the real value of the debt; in this case, Lars has to repay the loan in more valuable euros than he anticipated. If inflation were predictable, then Bigbank and Lars could take inflation into account when setting the nominal interest rate. (Recall the Fisher effect.) But if inflation is hard to predict, it imposes risk on Lars and Bigbank that both would prefer to avoid.

This cost of unexpected inflation is important to consider together with another fact: inflation is especially volatile and uncertain when the average rate of inflation is high. This is seen most simply by examining the experience of different countries. Countries with low average inflation, such as Germany in the late 20th century, tend to have stable inflation. Countries with high average inflation, such as many countries in Latin America, tend also to have unstable inflation. There are no known examples of economies with high, stable inflation. This relationship between the level and volatility of inflation points to another cost of inflation. If a country pursues a high-inflation monetary policy, it will have to bear not only the costs of high expected inflation but also the arbitrary redistributions of wealth associated with unexpected inflation.

IN THE NEWS

The most recent example of hyperinflation was in Zimbabwe. The causes have been much the same as those bouts of hyperinflation experienced in other countries and the effects on the people of that country similarly distressing.

Zimbabwe: A Worthless Currency

With prices doubling every few days, Zimbabweans spent huge amounts of time and energy preventing their meagre cash resources from completely evaporating. Trying to catch up with galloping hyperinflation running at 2.2 million per cent a year and at least four times faster in reality, the central bank has been printing ever bigger denominations. But it is outrun by galloping prices: at last count, the most valuable banknote available was for 50 billion Zimbabwean dollars, now worth barely 70 American cents on the black market, and the stock of Zimbabwean dollars is dwindling. Local cash could become scarcer still, now that the German company that was providing Zimbabwe with paper to print its banknotes has cancelled its contract; the Zimbabwean monetary authorities are likely to turn to a less specialized supplier. Meanwhile, people do not even bother to pick up notes of hundreds of thousands on the pavements of Harare, the capital. At independence in 1980, the Zimbabwe dollar was more valuable than the American greenback.

It may seem odd that the local currency is still used at all. From Z$25 billion to the American dollar at the beginning of this month, the cash exchange rate had jumped threefold within a fortnight. In restaurants or shops, prices are still quoted in local currency but revised several times a day. Salaries are paid in Zimbabwean dollars, still the only legal tender. A minibus driver taking commuters into Harare every day still charges his clients in Zimbabwe dollars – but at a higher price on the evening trip home – and changes his local notes into hard currency three times a day. The local money is losing its relevance.

Zimbabweans spend their local dollars as fast as possible or change them into hard currency on the black market. A parallel system is thriving in back offices and parking lots. Ronald was a civil servant but became a money dealer about a year ago to feed his family. He now makes about $100 a month, whereas his former colleagues earn the equivalent of less than $2 a month, enough to buy two loaves of bread. On a recent trip, this correspondent changed money from a central-bank employee running an illegal foreign-exchange business in his own office.

With a strict daily limit (currently less than $1.40) on bank withdrawals, people shun banks as much as possible and are returning to a cash economy. Petrol and rents are now charged mainly in American dollars or South African rand, but since some landlords have been taken to court, rents are increasingly often paid for in groceries. People buying overpriced cooking oil or sugar on the black market, since those items have long vanished from shops due to official price controls, are charged more if they pay in local dollars. Petrol coupons have become a virtual currency.

John Robertson, a local economist, reckons that the informal economy has probably become larger than the formal one. Though estimates are fuzzy, he believes that money sent by Zimbabweans abroad to friends and relatives at home, which used barely to register on Zimbabwe's foreign-exchange radar screen, now accounts for probably a third or so of the country's foreign-exchange inflows.

Turning to foreign exchange or barter is what you would expect in countries that have had inflation of more than a few hundred per cent a year. At the height of its inflation crisis, shops in Argentina were no longer able to price their goods. In some cases, Peruvians started using lavatory paper, then in short supply, as currency. But Zimbabwe holds the dubious distinction of being the only country in the world today that is suffering from hyperinflation: that is, prices are increasing by more than 50 per cent a month. It has not yet reached Hungary's level after the second world war, when inflation peaked at 42 quadrillion per cent a month. But it could yet get there.

In May, the central bank decided to let the exchange rate, until then fixed at a grossly overvalued rate of Z$30 000 to the American greenback, float on the interbank market. For a short while, the rate settled at a level close to the black market's. But very few ordinary people can obtain foreign exchange from banks; most still use the black market to get rid of their Zimbabwean dollars. So the legal and parallel rates have again grown apart. People sending money or groceries to relatives in Zimbabwe still use informal channels.

Hyperinflation can usually be tamed within a few months, provided authorities stop spending money they do not have and no longer turn to printing presses to cover for it. But the damage lingers for years. Argentines held about 60 per cent of their bank deposits in foreign exchange three years after the high inflation of the late 1980s was over, compared with less than 10 per cent before the crisis. In Peru and Bolivia, over 80 per cent of bank deposits were held in hard currency three years after the countries' inflation crises.

Reform will eventually come and prices will stabilize in Zimbabwe, especially if President Robert Mugabe is replaced; but the local dollar will never be the same. Some people have suggested that a reformed Zimbabwe should become part of the rand zone, but so far neither the South Africans nor Zimbabwe's battered opposition have sounded keen on the idea.

Source: 'Zimbabwe: A worthless currency.' *The Economist* [US] 19 July 2008 © 2008 Economist Newspaper Ltd.

The Price of Ice Cream

To return to our starting point – an important discussion of the value of ice cream – how does the price of the 1930 choc ice compare to one you could buy today? Remember that in the 1930s you could have bought 120 choc ices for a pound. Earlier in the book we examined how economists measure the inflation rate as the percentage change in the consumer prices index, the GDP deflator, or some other index of the overall price level. These price indices show that, over the past 70 years or so, UK prices have risen on average about 5 per cent per year. Accumulated over so many years, a 5 per cent annual inflation rate leads to something like a 30-fold increase in the price level, so that £1 in 1930s money is equivalent to about £30 in today's money. With a small amount of mental arithmetic, we can see that the price of a Lyons Maid choc ice in the 1930s would be about 25p in today's money. The retail price of about 70p for a Wall's 'Chunky' choc ice nowadays therefore represents a substantial real increase in the price of a chocolate-coated ice cream bar, even allowing for the possibility of higher quality. Perhaps people have indeed come to enjoy ice cream more.

Quick Quiz List and describe six costs of inflation.

IN THE NEWS

The majority of this chapter has focused on inflation – a period of generally rising prices. Economists generally see some inflation in the economy as being desirable (provided it is stable and manageable). The opposite of inflation is deflation where the price level actually falls – not to be confused with a slowdown in the rate of growth of prices. It might sound intuitive that falling prices would be a good thing but that is not necessarily the case as this article highlights.

Deflation

The post-war period saw unprecedented economic growth in Japan as it grew to become the second biggest economy in the world. Its methods and models were copied and applied in most Western economies; they looked enviously at the consistently high levels of productivity and quality of goods coming out of Japan as its exports flooded the globe.

In the last 15 years, however, the Japanese economy has suffered a number of problems, not least a prolonged recession and deflation. Corporate profits have been low and wage levels falling as business tries to adjust to the new market situation. The result of this is that there is little growth, little incentive to invest, low levels of spending and an increased likelihood of rising unemployment.

Some inflation in any economy is seen as being desirable because it is a sign that demand is present, that there is a reason to produce and invest and that there will be reward to be gained from enterprise. For a number of years in the first decade of the 21st century, interest rates remained at zero in an effort to help stimulate consumer spending. As with any price in any market, the function of the interest rate is to act as a signal and as such provide incentives that allocate scarce resources. When interest rates are zero, there is very little incentive for institutions to lend money; for businesses it might be good news if money can be raised so cheaply for investment but then again, what is there to invest in? Part of the deflation problem in Japan is that consumers were not spending at the levels that would provide a reason for investing in new capacity. Why spend or invest today when you expect prices to be cheaper tomorrow?

Like melting ice caps, or a drunk and disorderly nun, there is something deeply unsettling about the spectacle of money behaving badly. It is a phenomenon we associate with stricken places or remote times – Zimbabwe, with its trillion dollar notes, or Weimar Germany, where shoppers pushed wheelbarrows filled with worthless Reichsmarks. Hyperinflation, when prices rise uncontrollably, is easy to grasp, if alarming to contemplate. But since last year British money has begun to succumb to a new and unfamiliar malady, a ghostly, stealthy affliction that, in its chilly way, can be just as catastrophic.

The UK Retail Price Index fell to 0.1 per cent in February 2009, its lowest in 49 years. This is further confirmation of what many economists regarded as inevitable at the time – a slide into deflation, when prices shrink over time. The last serious case was the Great Depression, so few people under 80 have any experience of living with deflation. But in the ten years up to 2005, 130 million Japanese did, and so did I. It is a curious and deceptive experience in which one superficially delightful fact – that everything is getting cheaper – numbs you to the crippling damage being suffered by the economy and the country as a whole.

I arrived in Tokyo in 1995 in the understanding that I was moving to the richest and most expensive city in the history of the world. This had been true in the late 1980s, when Japan's bubble economy was at its most inflated, and extravagant stories still circulated about those days.

Someone had calculated that the vast park surrounding the Imperial Palace was worth more as real estate than the entire state of California. It was said that a 10 000-yen note, folded as tight as could be and dropped on to the pavement of central Tokyo, would not be enough to buy the square inch of land it covered. In contrast to the rest of Asia, it was American and European tourists, not the locals, who looked shabby and impoverished. Nervously, I braced myself for life in an inflationary inferno.

By the time I arrived the fires were going out. Much of the bank lending on which the bubble was based, it became clear, would never be repaid. The banks stopped lending and, a decade and half before Europe and the US, Tokyo experienced its own credit crunch. Bankruptcies and restructuring increased, and with them came mass job losses such as the Japanese salaryman had never known before. There was suicide and depression, and neat tent villages of homeless people began to appear in parks and along riverbanks. But for those who kept their jobs, and were not burdened with debt and property – people like me, for example – it was a time of strange, weightless prosperity.

I moved into my present home, a small two-bedroomed flat, in 1999. In the morning I made a 20-minute journey to work on the subway. At lunchtime, I enjoyed a piece of grilled fish and bowl of rice, and in the evening a plate of pasta and a bottle of wine. Once in a while I would drunkenly yodel David Bowie songs in my local karaoke parlour. In ten years, none of these expenses increased significantly, if at all.

My rent today is the same, to the yen, as it was when I moved in. Certain prices positively fell during the decade – including karaoke, golf and the cost of lunch in fast-food restaurants after a vicious price war between McDonald's and its great Japanese competitor, the splendidly named MosBurger.

Apart from an effective freeze on the price of everyday goods, new areas of retail opened up. 'Hundred-yen shops' opened, selling cheap food, drinks, make-up and toys for what was then the equivalent of 50p – bargains in a country formerly famous for its love of top-end luxury. Barbers offered cut-price 1 000-yen haircuts. To one who had grown up with the idea that things get somewhat more expensive – gradually, manageably – over time, to experience the opposite was almost exhilarating. But as fun as it was for people like me, for Japan as a whole it was devastating.

The destruction wrought by deflation is less obvious and dramatic than hyperinflation, but it penetrates deep. The most obvious effect is to reduce household spending. If prices are coming down month by month, why hurry to buy a new iPod, fridge or car? Why not wait until it becomes cheaper still – particularly if the value of your home is falling and you are worried about losing your job?

But if people are not buying, less is made and sold. Shops and factories close and jobs are lost. The value of property falls along with everything else, and borrowers default on their mortgages, threatening lenders. And as the number of people with money shrinks, prices are lowered even farther still in an effort to encourage spending.

Hard times can bring long-term benefits, such as healthier banks and fitter and more efficient companies which, having ridden out the storm, find their competitors destroyed. But a deflationary dive is painfully difficult to pull out of. In Japan's case at least, the problem often seemed to lie not so much in the realm of economic policy making as in mass psychology.

In the late 1980s Japan was a self-confident and aggressive global player, confidently buying up iconic foreign properties such as the Columbia film studio and the Rockefeller Centre, and threatening to overtake the US as the world's biggest economy. It entered the new millennium in a funk of hesitation and self-doubt from which it still has not recovered.

Deflation is to inflation what hypothermia is to a raging fever. It chills people as well as economies and slows their vital systems. It gets into the heart as well as the head – and cheap noodles, haircuts and karaoke are no consolation at all.

Source: 'Price cuts are cold comfort in deflation's chill; I enjoyed the cheap noodles and karaoke but in Japan the downward spiral penetrated deep into the national psyche.' *The Times* [London, England] 18 February 2009 © The Times and 18th February 2009 Nisyndication.com.

CONCLUSION

This chapter discussed the causes and costs of inflation. The primary cause of inflation is simply growth in the quantity of money. When the central bank creates money in large quantities, the value of money falls quickly. To maintain stable prices, the central bank must maintain strict control over the money supply.

The costs of inflation are more subtle. They include shoeleather costs, menu costs, increased variability of relative prices, unintended changes in tax liabilities, confusion and inconvenience, and arbitrary redistributions of wealth. Are these costs, in total, large or small? All economists agree that they become huge during hyperinflation. But their size for moderate inflation – when prices rise by less than 10 per cent per year – is more open to debate.

Although this chapter presented many of the most important lessons about inflation, the discussion is incomplete. When the central bank reduces the rate of money growth, prices rise less rapidly, as the quantity theory suggests. Yet as the economy makes the transition to this lower inflation rate, the change in monetary policy will have disruptive effects on production and employment. That is, even though monetary policy is neutral in the long run, it has profound effects on real variables in the short run. Later in this book we will examine the reasons for short-run monetary non-neutrality in order to enhance our understanding of the causes and costs of inflation.

SUMMARY

- The overall level of prices in an economy adjusts to bring money supply and money demand into balance. When the central bank increases the supply of money, it causes the price level to rise. Persistent growth in the quantity of money supplied leads to continuing inflation.
- The principle of monetary neutrality asserts that changes in the quantity of money influence nominal variables but not real variables. Most economists believe that monetary neutrality approximately describes the behaviour of the economy in the long run.
- A government can pay for some of its spending simply by printing money. When countries rely heavily on this 'inflation tax,' the result is hyperinflation.
- One application of the principle of monetary neutrality is the Fisher effect. According to the Fisher effect, when the inflation rate rises, the nominal interest rate rises by the same amount, so that the real interest rate remains the same.
- Many people think that inflation makes them poorer because it raises the cost of what they buy. This view is a fallacy, however, because inflation also raises nominal incomes.
- Economists have identified six costs of inflation: shoeleather costs associated with reduced money holdings; menu costs associated with more frequent adjustment of prices; increased variability of relative prices; unintended changes in tax liabilities due to non-indexation of the tax system; confusion and inconvenience resulting from a changing unit of account; and arbitrary redistributions of wealth between debtors and creditors. Many of these costs are large during hyperinflation, but the size of these costs for moderate inflation is less clear.

KEY CONCEPTS

quantity theory of money, p. 646
nominal variables, p. 647
real variables, p. 647
classical dichotomy, p. 647
monetary neutrality, p. 648
velocity of money, p. 649
quantity equation, p. 649
inflation tax, p. 651
Fisher effect, p. 652
shoeleather cost, p. 654
menu costs, p. 655

QUESTIONS FOR REVIEW

1. Explain how an increase in the price level affects the real value of money.
2. According to the quantity theory of money, what is the effect of an increase in the quantity of money?
3. Explain the difference between nominal and real variables, and give two examples of each. According to the principle of monetary neutrality, which variables are affected by changes in the quantity of money?
4. In what sense is inflation like a tax? How does thinking about inflation as a tax help explain hyperinflation?

5. According to the Fisher effect, how does an increase in the inflation rate affect the real interest rate and the nominal interest rate?
6. What are the costs of inflation? Which of these costs do you think are most important for your economy?
7. If inflation is less than expected, who benefits – debtors or creditors? Explain.

PROBLEMS AND APPLICATIONS

1. Suppose that this year's money supply is €500 billion, nominal GDP is €10 trillion and real GDP is €5 trillion.
   a. What is the price level? What is the velocity of money?
   b. Suppose that velocity is constant and the economy's output of goods and services rises by 5 per cent each year. What will happen to nominal GDP and the price level next year if the central bank keeps the money supply constant?
   c. What money supply should the central bank set next year if it wants to keep the price level stable?
   d. What money supply should the central bank set next year if it wants inflation of 10 per cent?
2. Suppose that changes in bank regulations expand the availability of credit cards, so that people need to hold less cash.
   a. How does this event affect the demand for money?
   b. If the central bank does not respond to this event, what will happen to the price level?
   c. If the central bank wants to keep the price level stable, what should it do?
3. It is often suggested that central banks should try to achieve zero inflation. If we assume that velocity is constant, does this zero inflation goal require that the rate of money growth equal zero? If yes, explain why. If no, explain what the rate of money growth should equal.
4. The economist John Maynard Keynes wrote: 'Lenin is said to have declared that the best way to destroy the capitalist system was to debauch the currency. By a continuing process of inflation, governments can confiscate, secretly and unobserved, an important part of the wealth of their citizens.' Justify Lenin's assertion.
5. Suppose that a country's inflation rate increases sharply. What happens to the inflation tax on the holders of money? Why is wealth that is held in savings accounts *not* subject to a change in the inflation tax? Can you think of any way in which holders of savings accounts are hurt by the increase in the inflation rate?
6. Hyperinflations are extremely rare in countries whose central banks are independent of the rest of the government. Why might this be so?
7. Let's consider the effects of inflation in an economy composed only of two people: Toto, a bean farmer, and Dorothy, a rice farmer. Toto and Dorothy both always consume equal amounts of rice and beans. In year 2009, the price of beans was €1, and the price of rice was €3.
   a. Suppose that in 2010 the price of beans was €2 and the price of rice was €6. What was inflation? Was Toto better off, worse off or unaffected by the changes in prices? What about Dorothy?
   b. Now suppose that in 2010 the price of beans was €2 and the price of rice was €4. What was inflation? Was Toto better off, worse off or unaffected by the changes in prices? What about Dorothy?
   c. Finally, suppose that in 2010 the price of beans was €2 and the price of rice was €1.50. What was inflation? Was Toto better off, worse off or unaffected by the changes in prices? What about Dorothy?
   d. What matters more to Toto and Dorothy – the overall inflation rate or the relative price of rice and beans?
8. If the tax rate is 40 per cent, compute the before-tax real interest rate and the after-tax real interest rate in each of the following cases.
   a. The nominal interest rate is 10 per cent and the inflation rate is 5 per cent.
   b. The nominal interest rate is 6 per cent and the inflation rate is 2 per cent.
   c. The nominal interest rate is 4 per cent and the inflation rate is 1 per cent.
9. What are your shoeleather costs of going to the bank? How might you measure these costs in euros? How do you think the shoeleather costs of the head of your university or college differ from your own?
10. Recall that money serves three functions in the economy. What are those functions? How does inflation affect the ability of money to serve each of these functions?
11. Suppose that people expect inflation to equal 3 per cent, but in fact prices rise by 5 per cent. Describe how this unexpectedly high inflation rate would help or hurt the following:
    a. the government
    b. a homeowner with a fixed-rate mortgage

   c. a union worker in the second year of a labour contract
   d. a retired person who has invested their savings in government bonds.

12. Explain one harm associated with unexpected inflation that is *not* associated with expected inflation. Then explain one harm associated with both expected and unexpected inflation.
13. Explain whether the following statements are true, false or uncertain.
   a. 'Inflation hurts borrowers and helps lenders, because borrowers must pay a higher rate of interest.'
   b. 'If prices change in a way that leaves the overall price level unchanged, then no one is made better or worse off.'
   c. 'Inflation does not reduce the purchasing power of most workers.'

For further resources, visit www.cengage.co.uk/mankiw_taylor2

11

THE MACROECONOMICS OF OPEN ECONOMIES

31 OPEN-ECONOMY MACROECONOMICS: BASIC CONCEPTS

When you next buy some fruit in the supermarket, the chances are that you will have a choice between a domestically produced fruit – perhaps apples – and fruit produced abroad, such as mangoes or bananas. When you take your next holiday, you may consider spending it in one of the cultural capitals of Europe or taking a trip to Disney World in Florida. When you start saving for your retirement, you may choose between a unit trust that buys mainly shares in domestic companies or one that buys shares of US or Japanese companies instead. In all of these cases, you are participating not just in the economy of your own country but in economies around the world.

There are clear benefits to being open to international trade: trade allows people to produce what they produce best and to consume the great variety of goods and services produced around the world. Indeed, one of the *Ten Principles of Economics* highlighted in Chapter 1 is that trade can make everyone better off. As we saw in Chapter 3, international trade can raise living standards in all countries by allowing each country to specialize in producing those goods and services in which it has a comparative advantage.

So far our development of macroeconomics has largely ignored the economy's interaction with other economies around the world. For most questions in macroeconomics, international issues are peripheral. For instance, when we discussed the natural rate of unemployment in Chapter 28 and the causes of inflation in Chapter 30, the effects of international trade could safely be ignored. Indeed, to keep their analysis simple, macroeconomists often assume a **closed economy** – an economy that does not interact with other economies.

closed economy
an economy that does not interact with other economies in the world

© ALEKSANDAR VRZALSKI / ISTOCK

Yet some new macroeconomic issues arise in an **open economy** – an economy that interacts freely with other economies around the world. This chapter and the next one, therefore, provide an introduction to open-economy macroeconomics. We begin in this chapter by discussing the key macroeconomic variables that describe an open economy's interactions in world markets. You may have noticed mention of these variables – exports, imports, the trade balance and exchange rates – when reading the newspaper or watching the evening news. Our first job is to understand what these data mean. In the next chapter we develop a model to explain how these variables are determined and how they are affected by various government policies.

open economy
an economy that interacts freely with other economies around the world

THE INTERNATIONAL FLOWS OF GOODS AND CAPITAL

An open economy interacts with other economies in two ways: it buys and sells goods and services in world product markets, and it buys and sells capital assets such as stocks and bonds in world financial markets. Here we discuss these two activities and the close relationship between them.

The Flow of Goods and Services: Exports, Imports and Net Exports

As we first noted in Chapter 3, exports are domestically produced goods and services that are sold abroad, and imports are foreign-produced goods and services that are sold domestically. When Lloyd's of London insures a building in New York, it is paid an insurance premium for this service by the owner of the building. The sale of the insurance service provided by Lloyd's is an export for the United Kingdom and an import for the United States. When Volvo, the Swedish car manufacturer, makes a car and sells it to a Swiss resident, the sale is an import for the Switzerland and an export for Sweden.

The net exports of any country are the value of its exports minus the value of its imports. The sale of insurance services abroad by Lloyd's raises UK net exports, and the Volvo sale reduces Swiss net exports. Because net exports tell us whether a country is, in total, a seller or a buyer in world markets for goods and services, net exports are also called the **trade balance**. If net exports are positive, exports are greater than imports, indicating that the country sells more goods and services abroad than it buys from other countries. In this case, the country is said to run a **trade surplus**. If net exports are negative, exports are less than imports, indicating that the country sells fewer goods and services abroad than it buys from other countries. In this case, the country is said to run a **trade deficit**. If net exports are zero, its exports and imports are exactly equal, and the country is said to have **balanced trade**.

trade balance
the value of a nation's exports minus the value of its imports; also called net exports

trade surplus
an excess of exports over imports

trade deficit
an excess of imports over exports

balanced trade
a situation in which exports equal imports

In the next chapter we develop a theory that explains an economy's trade balance, but even at this early stage it is easy to think of many factors that might influence a country's exports, imports and net exports. Those factors include the following:

- The tastes of consumers for domestic and foreign goods.
- The prices of goods at home and abroad.
- The exchange rates at which people can use domestic currency to buy foreign currencies.
- The incomes of consumers at home and abroad.

- The cost of transporting goods from country to country.
- The policies of the government towards international trade.

As these variables change over time, so does the amount of international trade.

FIGURE 31.1

The Increasing Openness of the World Economy

The figure shows, for the period 1950–2008, an index of world merchandise exports from all countries in the world, as well as an index of total world GDP, each set equal to 100 in 2000. With total exports as a measure of world trade, we can see that trade has grown substantially in the last 50 years, in fact about 3.75 times as fast as world output. This shows the increasing importance of international trade and finance in the world economy.

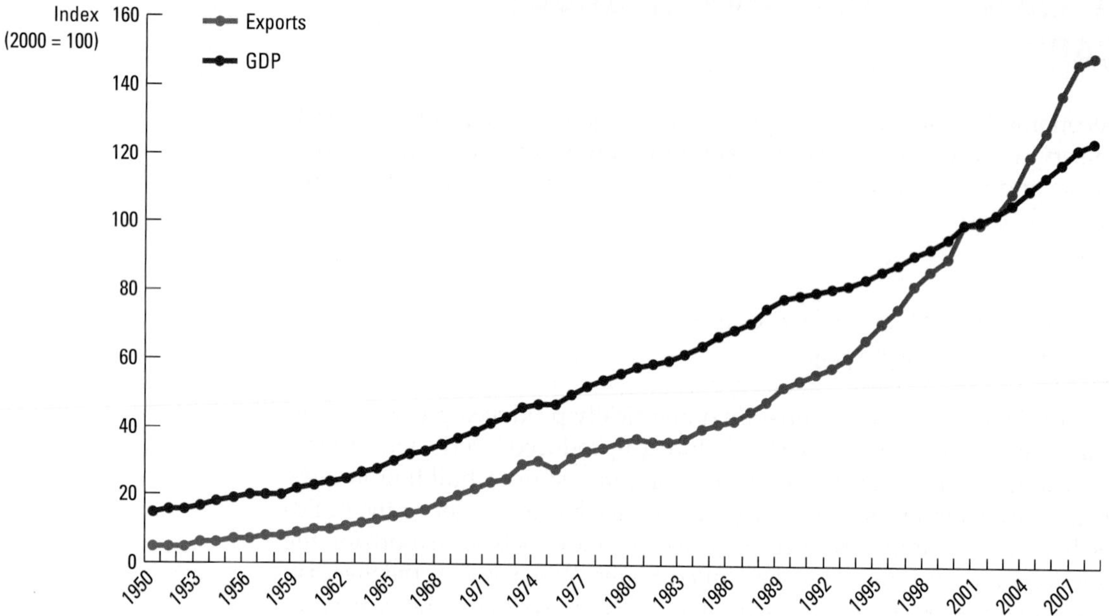

Source: World Trade Organization.

CASE STUDY

The Increasing Openness of the World Economy

Perhaps the most dramatic change in the world economy over the past five decades has been the increasing importance of international trade and finance. This change is illustrated in Figure 31.1, which shows an index of the total real value of goods and services exported from all countries in the world, with 2000 as the base year, as well as an index of world real GDP, also with 2000 as the base year. (We have only shown total world exports, because exports from one country must be imports to another, so that at the world level the total value of exports must be the same as the total value of imports.) World real GDP has grown impressively over the past 50 years or so: the index of real output has risen by a factor of over eight, from 15 in 1950 to 124 in 2008. But growth in international trade, as measured by exports, has been nothing less than spectacular: the index of world exports has risen by a factor of almost 30 between 1950 and 2008. Data from the

World Trade Organization show that world exports move in tandem with GDP growth and invariably exceeds it. Growth in world trade, it says, is associated with an even higher growth in international trade.

This increase in international trade is partly due to improvements in transportation. In 1950 the average merchant ship carried less than 10 000 tons of cargo; today, many ships carry more than 100 000 tons. The long-distance jet was introduced in 1958, and the wide-body jet in 1967, making air transport far cheaper. Because of these developments, goods that once had to be produced locally can now be traded around the world. Cut flowers, for instance, are now grown and sold thousands of miles apart. Fresh fruits and vegetables that can grow only in summer in Europe can now be consumed here in winter as well, because they can be shipped from countries in the southern hemisphere, so Europeans can enjoy cherries and strawberries from Chile all through the winter.

The increase in international trade has also been influenced by advances in telecommunications, which have allowed businesses to reach overseas customers more easily. For example, the first transatlantic telephone cable was not laid until 1956. As recently as 1966, the technology allowed only 138 simultaneous conversations between North America and Europe. Today, communications satellites permit more than 1 million conversations to occur at the same time.

Technological progress has also fostered international trade by changing the kinds of goods that economies produce. When bulky raw materials (such as steel) and perishable goods (such as foodstuffs) were a large part of the world's output, transporting goods was often costly and sometimes impossible. By contrast, goods produced with modern technology are often light and easy to transport. Consumer electronics, for instance, have low weight for every euro of value, which makes them easy to produce in one country and sell in another (think about products like the iPod nano, for example).

National and international trade policies have also been a factor in increasing international trade. As we discussed earlier in this book, economists have long believed that free trade between countries is mutually beneficial. Over time, policy makers around the world have come to accept these conclusions. International agreements, such as the General Agreement on Tariffs and Trade (GATT), have gradually lowered tariffs, import quotas and other trade barriers. The pattern of increasing trade illustrated in Figure 31.1 is a phenomenon that most economists and policy makers endorse and encourage.

The Flow of Financial Resources: Net Capital Outflow

So far we have been discussing how residents of an open economy participate in world markets for goods and services. In addition, residents of an open economy participate in world financial markets. A UK resident with £20 000 could use that money to buy a car from BMW, but he could instead use that money to buy stock in the German BMW corporation. The first transaction would represent a flow of goods, whereas the second would represent a flow of capital.

The term **net capital outflow** refers to the purchase of foreign assets by domestic residents minus the purchase of domestic assets by foreigners. (It is sometimes called *net foreign investment*.) When a UK resident buys shares in BMW, the purchase raises UK net capital outflow. When a Japanese resident buys a bond issued by the UK government, the purchase reduces UK net capital outflow.

net capital outflow
the purchase of foreign assets by domestic residents minus the purchase of domestic assets by foreigners

Recall that the flow of capital abroad takes two forms. If the French car manufacturer Renault opens up a factory in Romania, that is an example of foreign *direct investment*. Alternatively, if a French citizen buys shares in a Romanian company that is an example of *foreign portfolio investment*. In the first case, the French owner is actively managing the investment, whereas in the second case the French owner has a more passive role. In both cases, French residents are buying assets located in another country, so both purchases increase French net capital outflow.

We develop a theory to explain net capital outflow in the next chapter. Here, let's consider briefly some of the more important variables that influence net capital outflow:

- The real interest rates being paid on foreign assets.
- The real interest rates being paid on domestic assets.
- The perceived economic and political risks of holding assets abroad.
- The government policies that affect foreign ownership of domestic assets.

For example, consider German investors deciding whether to buy Mexican government bonds or German government bonds. (Recall that a bond is, in effect, an IOU of the issuer.) To make this decision, German investors compare the real interest rates offered on the two bonds. The higher a bond's real interest rate, the more attractive it is. While making this comparison, however, German investors must also take into account the risk that one of these governments might *default* on its debt (that is, not pay interest or principal when it is due), as well as any restrictions that the Mexican government has imposed, or might impose in the future, on foreign investors in Mexico.

The Equality of Net Exports and Net Capital Outflow

We have seen that an open economy interacts with the rest of the world in two ways – in world markets for goods and services and in world financial markets. Net exports and net capital outflow each measure a type of imbalance in these markets. Net exports measure an imbalance between a country's exports and its imports. Net capital outflow measures an imbalance between the amount of foreign assets bought by domestic residents and the amount of domestic assets bought by foreigners.

An important but subtle fact of accounting states that, for an economy as a whole, these two imbalances must offset each other. That is, net capital outflow (*NCO*) always equals net exports (*NX*):

$$NCO = NX$$

This equation holds because every transaction that affects one side of this equation must also affect the other side by exactly the same amount. This equation is an *identity* – an equation that must hold because of the way the variables in the equation are defined and measured.

To see why this accounting identity is true, consider an example. Suppose that BP sells some aircraft fuel to a Japanese airline. In this sale, a UK company (BP) gives aircraft fuel to a Japanese company, and a Japanese company gives yen to a UK company. Notice that two things have occurred simultaneously. The United Kingdom has sold to a foreigner some of its output (the fuel), and this sale increases UK net exports. In addition, the United Kingdom has acquired some foreign assets (the yen), and this acquisition increases UK net capital outflow.

Although BP most probably will not hold on to the yen it has acquired in this sale, any subsequent transaction will preserve the equality of net exports and net capital outflow. For example, BP may exchange its yen for pounds with a UK investment fund that wants the yen to buy shares in Sony Corporation, the Japanese maker of consumer electronics. In this case, BP's net export of aircraft fuel equals the investment fund's net capital outflow in Sony shares. Hence, *NX* and *NCO* rise by an equal amount.

Alternatively, BP may exchange its yen for pounds with another UK company that wants to buy computers from Toshiba, the Japanese computer maker. In this case, UK imports (of computers) exactly offset UK exports (of aircraft fuel). The sales by BP and Toshiba together affect neither UK net exports nor UK net capital outflow. That is, *NX* and *NCO* are the same as they were before these transactions took place.

The equality of net exports and net capital outflow follows from the fact that every international transaction is an exchange. When a seller country transfers a good or service to a buyer country, the buyer country gives up some asset to pay for this good or service. The value of that asset equals the value of the good or service sold. When we add everything up, the net value of goods and services sold by a country (*NX*) must equal the net value of assets acquired (*NCO*). The international flow of goods and services and the international flow of capital are two sides of the same coin.

Saving and Investment, and their Relationship to the International Flows

A nation's saving and investment are, as we have seen in earlier chapters, crucial to its long-run economic growth. Let's therefore consider how these variables are related to the international flows of goods and capital as measured by net exports and net capital outflow. We can do this most easily with the help of some simple mathematics.

As you may recall, the term *net exports* first appeared earlier in the book when we discussed the components of gross domestic product. The economy's gross domestic product (*Y*) is divided among four components: consumption (*C*), investment (*I*), government purchases (*G*), and net exports (*NX*). We write this as:

$$Y = C + I + G + NX$$

Total expenditure on the economy's output of goods and services is the sum of expenditure on consumption, investment, government purchases and net exports. Because each pound or euro of expenditure is placed into one of these four components, this equation is an accounting identity: it must be true because of the way the variables are defined and measured.

Recall that national saving is the income of the nation that is left after paying for current consumption and government purchases. National saving (*S*) equals $Y - C - G$. If we rearrange the above equation to reflect this fact, we obtain:

$$Y = C + G + I + NX$$
$$S = I + NX$$

Because net exports (*NX*) also equal net capital outflow (*NCO*), we can write this equation as:

$$\begin{array}{ccccc} S & = & I & + & NCO \\ \text{Saving} & = & \begin{array}{c}\text{Domestic} \\ \text{investment}\end{array} & + & \begin{array}{c}\text{Net capital} \\ \text{outflow}\end{array} \end{array}$$

This equation shows that a nation's saving must equal its domestic investment plus its net capital outflow. In other words, when UK citizens save a pound of their income for the future, that pound can be used to finance accumulation of domestic capital or it can be used to finance the purchase of capital abroad.

This equation should look somewhat familiar. Earlier in the book, when we analysed the role of the financial system, we considered this identity for the special case of a closed economy. In a closed economy, net capital outflow is zero ($NCO = 0$), so saving equals investment ($S = I$). In contrast, an open economy has two uses for its saving: domestic investment and net capital outflow.

As before, we can view the financial system as standing between the two sides of this identity. For example, suppose the Smith family decides to save some of its income for retirement. This decision contributes to national saving, the left-hand side of our equation. If the Smiths deposit their saving in an investment fund, the fund may use some of the deposit to buy shares issued by BP, which uses the proceeds to build an oil refinery in Aberdeen. In addition, the investment fund may use some of the Smiths' deposit to buy shares issued by Toyota, which uses the proceeds to build a factory in Osaka. These transactions show up on the right-hand side of the equation. From the standpoint of UK accounting, the BP expenditure on a new oil refinery is domestic investment, and the purchase of Toyota stock by a UK resident is net capital outflow. Thus, all saving in the UK economy shows up as investment in the UK economy or as UK net capital outflow.

Summing Up

Table 31.1 summarizes many of the ideas presented so far in this chapter and will be important for Chapter 33 later. It describes the three possibilities for an open economy: a country with a trade deficit, a country with balanced trade and a country with a trade surplus.

Consider first a country with a trade surplus. By definition, a trade surplus means that the value of exports exceeds the value of imports. Because net exports are exports minus imports, net exports (NX) are greater than zero. As a result, income ($Y = C + I + G + NX$) must be greater than domestic spending ($C = I + G$). But if Y is more than $C + I + G$, then $Y - C - G$ must be more than I. That is, saving ($S = Y - C - G$) must exceed investment. Because the country is saving more than it is investing, it must be sending some of its saving abroad. That is, the net capital outflow must be greater than zero.

The converse logic applies to a country with a trade deficit. By definition, a trade deficit means that the value of exports are less than the value of imports. Because net exports are exports minus imports, net exports (NX) are negative. Thus, income ($Y = C + I + G + NX$) must be less than domestic spending ($C + I + G$). But if Y is less than $C + I + G$, then $Y - C - G$ must be less than I. That is, saving must be less than investment. The net capital outflow must be negative.

A country with balanced trade is between these cases. Exports equal imports, so net exports are zero. Income equals domestic spending, and saving equals investment. The net capital outflow equals zero.

TABLE 31.1

International Flows of Goods and Capital: Summary

This table shows the three possible outcomes for an open economy.

Trade deficit	Balanced trade	Trade surplus
Exports < Imports	Exports = Imports	Exports > Imports
Net exports < 0	Net exports = 0	Net exports > 0
$Y < C + I + G$	$Y = C + I + G$	$Y > C + I + G$
Saving < Investment	Saving = Investment	Saving > Investment
Net capital outflow < 0	Net capital outflow = 0	Net capital outflow > 0

Quick Quiz Define net exports and net capital outflow. • Explain how they are related.

THE PRICES FOR INTERNATIONAL TRANSACTIONS: REAL AND NOMINAL EXCHANGE RATES

So far we have discussed measures of the flow of goods and services and the flow of capital across a nation's border. In addition to these quantity variables, macroeconomists also study variables that measure the prices at which these international transactions take place. Just as the price in any market serves the important role of coordinating buyers and sellers in that market, international prices help coordinate the decisions of consumers and producers as they interact in world markets. Here we discuss the two most important international prices – the nominal and real exchange rates.

Nominal Exchange Rates

The **nominal exchange rate** is the rate at which a person can trade the currency of one country for the currency of another. For example, if you go to a bank, you might see a posted exchange rate of 125 yen per euro. If you give the bank one euro, it will give you 125 Japanese yen; and if you give the bank 125 Japanese yen, it will give you one euro. (In fact, the bank will post slightly different prices for buying and selling yen. The difference gives the bank some profit for offering this service. For our purposes here, we can ignore these differences.)

nominal exchange rate
the rate at which a person can trade the currency of one country for the currency of another

An exchange rate can always be expressed in two ways. If the exchange rate is 125 yen per euro, it is also 1/125 (= 0.01) euro per yen. If a euro is worth £0.88, a pound is worth 1/0.88 (= 1.136) euros. This can be source of confusion, and there is no real hard and fast convention that people use. For example, it is customary to quote the US dollar–pound exchange rate as dollars per pound, e.g. $1.50 if 1 pound exchanges for 1.50 dollars. On the other hand, the pound–euro exchange rate can be quoted either way, as pounds per euro or euros per pound. In this book we shall for the most part think of the exchange rate as being the quantity of foreign currency that exchanges for one unit of domestic currency, or the foreign price of a unit of domestic currency. For example, if we are thinking of the UK as the domestic economy and the USA as the foreign economy, then the exchange rate is $1.90 per pound. If we are thinking of, say, Germany as the domestic economy, then we could express the exchange rate as dollars per euro, e.g. $1.33 dollars per euro.

If the exchange rate changes so that a euro buys more of another currency, that change is called an **appreciation** of the euro. If the exchange rate changes so that a euro buys less of another currency, that change is called a **depreciation** of the euro. For example, when the exchange rate rises from 125 to 127 yen per euro, the euro is said to appreciate. At the same time, because a Japanese yen now buys less of the European currency, the yen is said to depreciate. When the exchange rate falls from 125 to 123 yen per euro, the euro is said to depreciate, and the yen is said to appreciate. (It is sometimes helpful to think how much of the domestic currency an individual has to give up to get the required amount of the foreign currency and vice versa.)

appreciation
an increase in the value of a currency as measured by the amount of foreign currency it can buy

depreciation
a decrease in the value of a currency as measured by the amount of foreign currency it can buy

At times you may have heard the media report that the pound or the euro is either 'strong' or 'weak'. These descriptions usually refer to recent changes in the nominal exchange rate. When a currency appreciates, it is said to *strengthen* because it can then buy more foreign currency. Similarly, when a currency depreciates, it is said to *weaken*. If the individual gets more of the foreign currency in exchange for the same amount of the domestic currency, the domestic currency is stronger. If the individual has to give up more of the domestic currency to get the same amount of the foreign currency then the domestic currency is weaker.

For any currency, there are many nominal exchange rates. The euro can be used to buy US dollars, Japanese yen, British pounds, Mexican pesos and so on. When economists study changes in the exchange rate, they often use indices that average these many exchange rates. Just as the consumer price index turns the many prices in the economy into a single measure of the price level, an exchange rate index turns these many exchange rates into a single measure of the international value of the currency. So when economists talk about the euro or the pound appreciating or depreciating, they often are referring to an exchange rate index that takes into account many individual exchange rates.

CASE STUDY

Cross-border Shopping

Changes in exchange rates create different incentives and as we know from Principle 4 of the *Ten Principles of Economics,* people respond to incentives. The political situation in Ireland presents a particularly interesting case study in how changes in exchange rates can have very different effects on people and businesses.

The exchange rate between the pound and the euro had changed significantly between 2007 and 2008. This led to some strange goings-on in the Irish Republic and Northern Ireland. The change in the exchange rate meant that those living in the Republic of Ireland were benefiting from the fall in the value of sterling. In 2007, a euro was worth around 70p; by the end of 2008 £1 bought almost €1 and many shops and stores in border towns in Northern Ireland were offering shoppers parity.

The movements in the exchange rate led to queues of people crossing the border from the Republic to buy a whole range of goods including food and alcohol in the North. Some stores in the North said that one in three of their customers were from the Republic. The benefit to those from the Republic was clear. A good priced at £100 in December 2007 would have required those in the Republic giving up around €142. In December 2008, they only had to give up €100.

Whilst stores in Northern border towns were experiencing a mini-boom in sales, those in the Republic fared quite differently. Many complained that they were suffering as a result of the fall in the exchange rate and the flight to the North exacerbated the recession that the Irish economy was experiencing. Members of the Irish government criticized shoppers for cashing in on the exchange rate and pointed out that the taxes being paid by shoppers in the North went to the UK government and not the Irish government.

For many shoppers such an appeal fell on deaf ears. The incentives to cross the border and shop were far greater than any emotional appeal to support the Irish economy!

Real Exchange Rates

real exchange rate
the rate at which a person can trade the goods and services of one country for the goods and services of another

The **real exchange rate** is the rate at which a person can trade the goods and services of one country for the goods and services of another. For example, suppose that you go shopping and find that a kilo of Swiss cheese is twice as expensive as a kilo of English cheddar cheese. We would then say that the real exchange rate is a ½ kilo of Swiss cheese per kilo of English cheese. Notice that, like the nominal exchange rate, we express the real exchange rate as units of the foreign item per unit of the domestic item. But in this instance the item is a good rather than a currency.

Real and nominal exchange rates are closely related. To see how, consider an example. Suppose that a kilo of British wheat sells for £1, and a kilo of European wheat sells for €3. What is the real exchange rate between British and European wheat? To answer this question, we must first use the nominal exchange rate to convert the prices into a common currency. If the nominal exchange rate is €2 per pound, then a price for British wheat of £1 per kilo is equivalent to €2 per kilo. European wheat, however, sells for €3 a kilo, so British wheat is only ⅔ as expensive as European wheat. The real exchange rate is ⅔ of a kilo of European wheat per kilo of British wheat.

We can summarize this calculation for the real exchange rate with the following formula, where we are measuring the exchange rate as the amount of foreign currency needed to buy 1 unit of domestic currency:

$$\text{Real exchange rate} = \frac{(\text{Nominal exchange rate} \times \text{Domestic price})}{(\text{Foreign price})}$$

Using the numbers in our example, the formula applies as follows:

$$\text{Real exchange rate} = \frac{(\text{2 Euros per pound}) \times (\text{£1 per kilo of UK wheat})}{\text{€3 per kilo of European wheat}}$$

$$= \text{⅓ kilo of European wheat per kilo of UK wheat}$$

Thus, the real exchange rate depends on the nominal exchange rate and on the prices of goods in the two countries measured in the local currencies.

Why does the real exchange rate matter? As you might guess, the real exchange rate is a key determinant of how much a country exports and imports. For example, when a British bread company is deciding whether to buy British or European wheat to make into flour and use in making its bread, it will ask which wheat is cheaper. The real exchange rate gives the answer. As another example, imagine that you are deciding whether to take a holiday in the Dordogne, France, or in Cancun, Mexico. You might ask your travel agent the price of a hotel room in the Dordogne (measured in euros), the price of a hotel room in Cancun (measured in pesos) and the exchange rate between pesos and euros. If you decide where to go on holiday by comparing costs, you are basing your decision on the real exchange rate.

When studying an economy as a whole, macroeconomists focus on overall prices rather than the prices of individual items. That is, to measure the real exchange rate, they use price indices, such as the consumer prices index, which measure the price of a basket of goods and services. By using a price index for a UK or European basket (P), a price index for a foreign basket (P^*) and the nominal exchange rate between the UK pound or euro and foreign currencies (e = foreign currency per pound), we can compute the overall real exchange rate between the United Kingdom or Europe and other countries as follows:

$$\text{Real exchange rate} = (e \times P)/P^*$$

This real exchange rate measures the price of a basket of goods and services available domestically relative to a basket of goods and services available abroad.

As we examine more fully in the next chapter, a country's real exchange rate is a key determinant of its net exports of goods and services. A depreciation (fall) in the real exchange rate of the euro means that EU goods have become cheaper relative to foreign goods. This change encourages consumers both at home and abroad to buy more EU goods and fewer goods from other countries. As a result, EU exports rise and EU imports fall, and both of these changes raise EU net exports. Conversely, an appreciation (rise) in the euro real exchange rate means that EU goods have become more expensive compared to foreign goods, so EU net exports fall. It is important to remember that whilst we are talking about the prices of exports and imports changing, the domestic price for these goods and services may not change. For example, a French wine producer may have wine for sale priced at €10 per bottle. If the exchange rate between the euro and the UK pound is £1 = €1.2 then a UK buyer of wine will have to give up £8.33 to buy a bottle of wine. If the UK exchange rate appreciates to £1 = €1.4 then the UK buyer now has to give up only £7.14 to buy the bottle of wine. The euro price of the wine has not changed but to the UK buyer the price has fallen. Equally, if the pound exchange rate depreciated from £1 = €1.2 to £1 = €1.00 then the UK buyer would now have to give up £10 to buy the wine. Again, the euro price of the wine has not changed but the price to the UK buyer has risen because the exchange rate between the pound and the euro has changed.

Quick Quiz Define nominal exchange rate and real exchange rate, and explain how they are related. • If the nominal exchange rate goes from 100 to 120 yen per euro, has the euro appreciated or depreciated?

A FIRST THEORY OF EXCHANGE RATE DETERMINATION: PURCHASING POWER PARITY

Exchange rates vary substantially over time. In 1970, one UK pound could buy 2.4 US dollars (i.e. the pound–dollar exchange rate was $2.40), but in 1985 the pound was only worth about half this amount of dollars (the exchange rate was about $1.25), in March 2008 one pound could buy over $2 but by March 2010 the rate stood at £1 = $1.50. So over this 40-year period, the pound first almost halved in value from $2.40 to $1.25 and then increased by over 50 per cent from $1.25 to over $2. On the other hand, if we consider the value of the US dollar against the German and Italian currencies, we see that in 1970, a US dollar could be used to buy 3.65 German marks or 627 Italian lira, while in 1998, as both Germany and Italy were getting ready to adopt the euro as their common currency, a US dollar bought 1.76 German marks or 1 737 Italian lira. In other words, over this period the value of the dollar fell by more than half compared to the mark, while it more than doubled compared to the lira.

What explains these large changes? Economists have developed many models to explain how exchange rates are determined, each emphasizing just some of the many forces at work. Here we develop the simplest theory of exchange rates, called purchasing power parity. This theory states that a unit of any given currency should be able to buy the same quantity of goods in all countries. Many economists believe that **purchasing power parity** describes the forces that determine exchange rates in the long run. We now consider the logic on which this long-run theory of exchange rates is based, as well as the theory's implications and limitations.

purchasing power parity
a theory of exchange rates whereby a unit of any given currency should be able to buy the same quantity of goods in all countries

The Basic Logic of Purchasing Power Parity

The theory of purchasing power parity is based on a principle called the *law of one price*. This law asserts that a good must sell for the same price in all locations. Otherwise, there would be opportunities for profit left unexploited. For example, suppose that coffee beans sold for less in Munich than in Frankfurt. A person could buy coffee in Munich for, say, €4 a kilo and then sell it in Frankfurt for €5 a kilo, making a profit of €1 per kilo from the difference in price. The process of taking advantage of differences in prices in different markets is called *arbitrage*. In our example, as people took advantage of this arbitrage opportunity, they would increase the demand for coffee in Munich and increase the supply in Frankfurt. The price of coffee would rise in Munich (in response to greater demand) and fall in Frankfurt (in response to greater supply). This process would continue until, eventually, the prices were the same in the two markets.

Now consider how the law of one price applies to the international marketplace. If a euro (or any other currency) could buy more coffee in Germany than in Japan, international traders could profit by buying coffee in Germany and selling it in Japan. This export of coffee from Germany to Japan would drive up the German price of coffee and drive down the Japanese price. Conversely, if a euro could buy more coffee in Japan than in Germany, traders could buy coffee in Japan and sell it in Germany. This import of coffee into Germany from Japan would drive down the German price of coffee and drive up the Japanese price. In the end, the law of one price tells us that a euro must buy the same amount of coffee in all countries.

This logic leads us to the theory of purchasing power parity. According to this theory, a currency must have the same purchasing power in all countries. That is, a euro must buy the same quantity of goods in Germany and Japan, and a Japanese yen must buy the same quantity of goods in Japan as in Germany. Indeed, the name of this theory describes it well. *Parity* means equality, and *purchasing power* refers to the value of money. *Purchasing power parity* states that a unit of all currencies must have the same real value in every country.

Implications of Purchasing Power Parity

What does the theory of purchasing power parity say about exchange rates? It tells us that the nominal exchange rate between the currencies of two countries depends on the price levels in those countries. If a euro buys the same quantity of goods in Germany (where prices are measured in euros) as in Japan (where prices are measured in yen), then the number of yen per euro must reflect the prices of goods in Germany and Japan. For example, if a kilo of coffee is priced at 500 yen in Japan and €5 in Germany, then the nominal exchange rate must be 100 yen per euro (500 yen/€5 = 100 yen per euro). Otherwise, the purchasing power of the euro would not be the same in the two countries.

To see more fully how this works, it is helpful to use just a little mathematics. Think of Germany as the home or domestic economy. Suppose that P is the price of a basket of goods in Germany (measured in euros), P^* is the price of a basket of goods in Japan (measured in yen), and e is the nominal exchange rate (the number of yen needed to buy one euro). Now consider the quantity of goods a euro can buy at home (in Germany) and abroad. At home, the price level is P, so the purchasing power of €1 at home is $1/P$. Abroad, a euro can be exchanged into e units of foreign currency, which in turn have purchasing power e/P^*. For the purchasing power of a euro to be the same in the two countries, it must be the case that:

$$1/P = e/P^*$$

With rearrangement, this equation becomes:

$$1 = eP/P^*$$

Notice that the left-hand side of this equation is a constant, and the right-hand side is the real exchange rate. Thus, if the purchasing power of the euro is always the same at home and abroad, then the real exchange rate – the relative price of domestic and foreign goods – cannot change.

To see the implication of this analysis for the nominal exchange rate, we can rearrange the last equation to solve for the nominal exchange rate:

$$e = P^*/P$$

That is, the nominal exchange rate equals the ratio of the foreign price level (measured in units of the foreign currency) to the domestic price level (measured in units of the domestic currency). According to the theory of purchasing power parity, the nominal exchange rate between the currencies of two countries must reflect the different price levels in those countries.

A key implication of this theory is that nominal exchange rates change when price levels change. As we saw in the preceding chapter, the price level in any country adjusts to bring the quantity of money supplied and the quantity of money demanded into balance. Because the nominal exchange rate depends on the price levels, it also depends on the money supply and money demand in each country. When a central bank in any country increases the money supply and causes the price level to rise, it also causes that country's currency to depreciate relative to other currencies in the world. In other words, when the central bank prints large quantities of money, that money loses value both in terms of the goods and services it can buy and in terms of the amount of other currencies it can buy.

We can now attempt to answer the question that began this section. For example, why did the UK pound lose value compared to the US dollar between 1970 and 1985? A good deal of the answer certainly relates to differences in inflation between the two countries. Between 1970 and 1985, the USA pursued, on average, a less inflationary monetary policy than the United Kingdom. Average price inflation in the UK over these 15 years was very high – about 10.5 per cent a year, while in the United States it was only about 6.5 per cent a year on average. This meant that between 1970 and 1985 the UK price level rose an average of 4 per cent a year faster than the US price level. As UK prices rose relative to US prices, the value of the pound fell relative to the dollar.

What about the movements in the exchange rate between the Italian lira and the dollar or the German mark and the dollar? Again, in large measure these movements reflect the relative stance of monetary policy in the countries concerned: Germany pursued a less inflationary monetary policy than the United States, and Italy pursued a more inflationary monetary policy. From 1970 to 1998, inflation in the United States was about 5.3 per cent per year on average. By contrast, average inflation was 3.5 per cent in Germany and 9.6 per cent in Italy. As US prices rose relative to German prices, the value of the dollar fell relative to the mark. Similarly, as US prices fell relative to Italian prices, the value of the dollar rose relative to the lira.

common currency area
a geographical area, possibly covering several countries, in which a common currency is used

Germany and Italy are now part of a **common currency area**, and the common currency is the euro. This means that the two countries share a single monetary policy and that the inflation rates in the two countries will be closely linked. But the historical lessons of the lira and the mark will apply to the euro as well. Whether the UK pound or the US dollar buy more or fewer euros 20 years from now than they do today depends on whether the European Central Bank produces more or less inflation in Europe than the Bank of England does in the United Kingdom or the Federal Reserve does in the United States.

CASE STUDY

The Nominal Exchange Rate During a Hyperinflation

Macroeconomists can only rarely conduct controlled experiments. Most often, they must glean what they can from the natural experiments that history

FIGURE 31.2

Money, Prices and the Nominal Exchange Rate during the German Hyperinflation

This figure shows the money supply, the price level and the exchange rate (measured as US cents per mark) for the German hyperinflation from January 1921 to December 1924. Notice how similarly these three variables move. When the quantity of money started growing quickly, the price level followed and the mark depreciated relative to the dollar. When the German central bank stabilized the money supply, the price level and exchange rate stabilized as well.

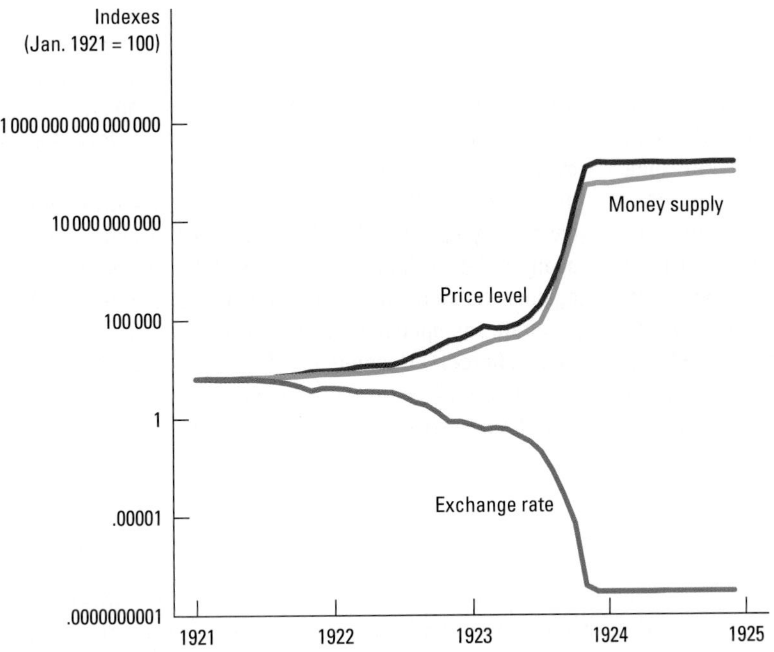

Source: Adapted from Thomas J. Sargent, 'The End of Four Big Inflations,' in Robert Hall, ed., *Inflation* (Chicago: University of Chicago Press, 1983), pp. 41–93. Reprinted with permission.

gives them. One natural experiment is hyperinflation – the high inflation that arises when a government turns to the printing press to pay for large amounts of government spending. Because hyperinflations are so extreme, they illustrate some basic economic principles with clarity.

Consider the German hyperinflation of the early 1920s. Figure 31.2 shows the German money supply, the German price level and the nominal exchange rate (measured as US cents per German mark) for that period. Notice that these series move closely together. When the supply of money starts growing quickly, the price level also takes off and the German mark depreciates. When the money supply stabilizes, so does the price level and the exchange rate.

The pattern shown in this figure appears during every hyperinflation. It leaves no doubt that there is a fundamental link among money, prices and the nominal exchange rate. The quantity theory of money discussed in the previous chapter explains how the money supply affects the price level. The theory of purchasing power parity discussed here explains how the price level affects the nominal exchange rate.

FYI

Purchasing Power Standard (PPS)

If you look at statistics produced by Eurostat, the EU's statistical office, you are likely to see data expressed in *purchasing power standard (PPS)*. This is an extension of the PPP idea but applied to the EU. PPS is an artificial currency which expresses the purchasing power of the EU 27 against the euro. In theory, therefore, one PPS would buy the same amount of goods in each EU country and so 1PPS = €1. In reality there will be price differences between European countries so different amounts of euro will be needed to buy the same goods and services in different countries. PPS takes account of these differences. The PPS is found by taking any national economic aggregate, such as GDP, for example, and dividing by its PPP. Thus PPPs can be seen as the exchange rate of the PPS against the euro and allows for more accurate comparisons between data from different EU countries. The PPS for the EU 27 as a whole would be 100. If GDP per capita was expressed in PPS, then any figure above 100 would show GDP per capita in that country above the EU 27 average and any figure below 100 would indicate GDP per capita below the EU average. In 2008, Switzerland had GDP per capita at 141 and Norway was 177 in 2009, both considerably higher than the EU 27 average whereas Portugal and Malta both had GDP per capita of 78 in 2009, well below the EU 27 average.

Limitations of Purchasing Power Parity

Purchasing power parity provides a simple model of how exchange rates are determined. For understanding many economic phenomena, the theory works well. In particular, it can explain many long-term trends, such as the examples discussed earlier. It can also explain the major changes in exchange rates that occur during hyperinflations.

Yet the theory of purchasing power parity is not completely accurate. That is, exchange rates do not always move to ensure that a euro has the same real value in all countries all the time. There are two reasons why the theory of purchasing power parity does not always hold in practice.

The first reason is that many goods are not easily traded. Imagine, for instance, that haircuts are more expensive in Paris than in New York. International travellers might avoid getting their haircuts in Paris, and some haircutters might move from New York to Paris. Yet such arbitrage would probably be too limited to eliminate the differences in prices. Thus, the deviation from purchasing power parity might persist, and a euro (or dollar) would continue to buy less of a haircut in Paris than in New York.

The second reason that purchasing power parity does not always hold is that even tradable goods are not always perfect substitutes when they are produced in different countries. For example, some consumers prefer German cars, and others prefer Japanese cars. Moreover, consumer tastes can change over time. If German cars suddenly become more popular, the increase in demand will drive up the price of German cars compared to Japanese cars. But despite this difference in prices in the two markets, there might be no opportunity for profitable arbitrage because consumers do not view the two cars as equivalent.

Thus, both because some goods are not tradable and because some tradable goods are not perfect substitutes with their foreign counterparts, purchasing power parity is not a perfect theory of exchange rate determination. For these reasons, real exchange rates fluctuate over time. Nonetheless, the theory of purchasing power parity does provide a useful first step in understanding exchange rates. The basic logic is persuasive: as the real exchange rate drifts from the level predicted by purchasing power parity, people have greater incentive to move goods across national borders. Even if the forces of purchasing power parity do not completely fix the real exchange rate, they provide a reason to expect that changes in the real exchange rate are most often small or temporary. As a result, large and persistent movements in nominal exchange rates typically reflect changes in price levels at home and abroad.

CASE STUDY

The Hamburger Standard

When economists apply the theory of purchasing power parity to explain exchange rates, they need data on the prices of a basket of goods available in different countries. One analysis of this sort is conducted by *The Economist*. This newspaper occasionally collects data on a basket of goods consisting of 'two all-beef patties, special sauce, lettuce, cheese, pickles, onions, on a sesame seed bun.' It's called the 'Big Mac' and is sold by McDonald's around the world.

Once we have the prices of Big Macs in two countries denominated in the local currencies, we can compute the exchange rate predicted by the theory of purchasing power parity. The predicted exchange rate is the one that makes the price of the Big Mac the same in the two countries. For instance, if the price of a Big Mac is $2 in the United States and 200 yen in Japan, purchasing power parity would predict an exchange rate of 100 yen per dollar.

How well does purchasing power parity work when applied using Big Mac prices? Here are some examples from 2007, when the price of a Big Mac was $3.41 in the United States:

Country	Price of a Big Mac	Predicted exchange rate	Actual exchange rate
Euro area	3.06 euros	0.90 euros/US$	0.74 euros/US$
United Kingdom	1.99 pounds	0.58 pound/US$	0.50 pound/US$
Sweden	33 kronor	10.1 kronor/US$	7.4 kronor/US$
South Korea	2900 won	850 won/US$	923 won/US$
Japan	280 yen	82 yen/US$	122 yen/US$
Mexico	28 pesos	9.7 pesos/US$	6.8 pesos/US$
Venezuela	7400 bolivar	2170 bolivar/US$	2147 bolivar/US$

You can see that the predicted and actual exchange rates are not exactly the same. After all, international arbitrage in Big Macs is not easy. Yet the two exchange rates are usually not that far apart.

Purchasing power parity is not a precise theory of exchange rates (and Big Mac purchasing power parity even less so) and for some countries it does not always work well (it always tends to do badly, for example, for Scandinavian countries), but nevertheless it often provides a reasonable first approximation.

In the USA the price of a Big Mac is $3; in Japan it is 264 yen.

Quick Quiz Over the past 20 years, Venezuela has had high inflation and Japan has had low inflation. What do you predict has happened to the number of Venezuelan bolivars a person can buy with a Japanese yen?

IN THE NEWS

The Big Mac Index

The 'Big Mac Index' is reviewed on a regular basis. These two articles show that sometimes the Index can give a pretty good indication that purchasing powers are in line whereas at other times there appears to be a greater divergence. This would imply that there are other factors, in addition to the ones mentioned in the text, which might be influencing relative prices in different countries and the exchange rates between those countries.

---

16 July 2008

Ever since the credit storms first broke last August, the prices of stocks, bonds, gold and other investment assets have been blown this way and that. Currencies have been pushed around too. Did this buffeting bring them any closer to their underlying fair value? Not according to the Big Mac Index, our light-hearted guide to exchange rates. Many currencies look more out of whack than in July 2007, when we last compared burger prices.

Only a handful of currencies are close to their Big Mac PPP. Of the seven currencies that make up the Federal Reserve's major-currency index, only one (the Australian dollar) is within 10 per cent of its fair value. Most of the rest look expensive. The euro is overvalued by a massive 50 per cent. The British pound, Swedish krona, Swiss franc and Canadian dollar are also trading well above their burger benchmark. All are more overvalued against the dollar than a year ago. Only the Japanese yen, undervalued by 27 per cent, could be considered a snip.

The dollar still buys a lot of burger in the rest of Asia too. The Singapore dollar is undervalued by 18 per cent and the South Korean won by 12 per cent. The currencies of less well-off Asian countries, such as Indonesia, Malaysia and Thailand, look even cheaper. China's currency is among the most undervalued, though a bit less so than a year ago.

The angrier type of China-basher might conclude that the yuan should revalue so that it is much closer to its burger standard. But care needs to be taken when drawing hard conclusions from fast-food prices. PPP measures show where currencies should end up in the long run. Prices vary with local costs, such as rents and wages, which are lower in poor countries, as well as with the price of ingredients that trade across borders. For this reason, PPP is a more reliable comparison for the currencies of economies with similar levels of income.

For all these caveats, more sophisticated analyses come to broadly similar conclusions to our own. John Lipsky, number two at the IMF, said this week that the euro is above the fund's medium-term valuation benchmark. China's currency is 'substantially undervalued' in the IMF's view. The dollar is sandwiched in between. The big drop in the greenback's value since 2002 has left it 'close to its medium-term equilibrium level', said Mr Lipsky.

Source: Adapted from: 'The Big Mac Index: Sandwiched.' *The Economist* [US] 26 July 2008 © The Economist Newspaper Ltd.

18 July 2009

When demand is scarce and jobs are being lost, no one relishes a strong currency. A country with an uncompetitive exchange rate will struggle to sell its wares abroad and will also cede its home market to foreign firms. A weak exchange rate, by contrast, encourages consumers to switch from pricey imports to cheaper home-produced goods and services. So which countries has the foreign-exchange market blessed with a cheap currency, and which has it burdened with a dear one?

The dollar buys the most burger in Asia. A Big Mac is priced at 12.5 yuan in China, which is $1.83 at today's exchange rate, around half its price in America. Other Asian currencies, such as the Malaysian ringgit and Thai bhat, look similarly undervalued. Businesses based in continental Europe have most to be cheesed off about. The Swiss franc remains one of the world's dearest currencies. The euro is almost 30 per cent overvalued on the burger gauge. Denmark and Sweden look even less competitive.

On the basis of comparing currencies between countries with similar incomes, the markets have been kindest to British exporters. A year ago the pound was overvalued by more than a quarter on the Big Mac gauge. Now it is close to its fair value against the dollar and looks cheap against the euro. That shift has upset some other EU countries that had relied on selling to spendthrift British consumers. But after years of struggling with an overvalued currency, British firms will feel they deserve a little mercy.

Source: 'Cheesed off; The Big Mac index.' *The Economist* [US] 18 July 2009 © The Economist Newspaper Ltd.

CONCLUSION

The purpose of this chapter has been to develop some basic concepts that macroeconomists use to study open economies. You should now understand why a nation's net exports must equal its net capital outflow, and why national saving must equal domestic investment plus net capital outflow. You should also understand the meaning of the nominal and real exchange rates, as well as the implications and limitations of purchasing power parity as a theory of how exchange rates are determined.

The macroeconomic variables defined here offer a starting point for analszing an open economy's interactions with the rest of the world. In the next chapter we develop a model that can explain what determines these variables. We can then discuss how various events and policies affect a country's trade balance and the rate at which nations make exchanges in world markets.

SUMMARY

- Net exports are the value of domestic goods and services sold abroad minus the value of foreign goods and services sold domestically. Net capital outflow is the acquisition of foreign assets by domestic residents minus the acquisition of domestic assets by foreigners. Because every international transaction involves an exchange of an asset for a good or service, an economy's net capital outflow always equals its net exports.
- An economy's saving can be used either to finance investment at home or to buy assets abroad. Thus, national saving equals domestic investment plus net capital outflow.
- The nominal exchange rate is the relative price of the currency of two countries, and the real exchange rate is the relative price of the goods and services of two countries. When the nominal exchange rate changes so that each unit of domestic currency buys more foreign currency, the domestic currency is said to *appreciate* or *strengthen.* When the nominal exchange rate changes so that each unit of domestic currency buys less foreign currency, the domestic currency is said to *depreciate* or *weaken.*
- According to the theory of purchasing power parity, a unit of currency should be able to buy the same quantity of goods in all countries. This theory implies that the nominal exchange rate between the currencies of two countries should reflect the price levels in those countries. As a result, countries with relatively high inflation should have depreciating currencies, and countries with relatively low inflation should have appreciating currencies.

KEY CONCEPTS

QUESTIONS FOR REVIEW

1. Define net exports and net capital outflow. Explain how and why they are related.
2. Explain the relationship between saving, investment and net capital outflow.
3. If a Japanese car is priced at 500 000 yen, a similar German car is priced at €10 000, and a euro can buy 100 yen, what are the nominal and real exchange rates?
4. Describe the economic logic behind the theory of purchasing power parity.
5. If the European Central Bank started printing large quantities of euros, what would happen to the number of Japanese yen a euro could buy?

PROBLEMS AND APPLICATIONS

1. How would the following transactions affect UK exports, imports and net exports?
   a. A British art lecturer spends the summer touring museums in Italy.
   b. Students in Paris flock to see the latest Royal Shakespeare Company perform *King Lear* on tour.
   c. The British art lecturer buys a new Volvo.
   d. A student in Munich buys a Manchester United official team shirt (in Munich).
   e. A British citizen goes to Calais for the day to stock up on cheap wine.
2. International trade in each of the following products has increased over time. Suggest some reasons why this might be so.
   a. wheat
   b. banking services
   c. computer software
   d. automobiles.
3. Describe the difference between foreign direct investment and foreign portfolio investment. Who is more likely to engage in foreign direct investment – a corporation or an individual investor? Who is more likely to engage in foreign portfolio investment?
4. How would the following transactions affect UK net capital outflow? Also, state whether each involves direct investment or portfolio investment.
   a. A British mobile telephone company establishes an office in the Czech Republic.
   b. A US company's pension fund buys shares in BP.
   c. Toyota expands its factory in Derby, England.
   d. A London-based investment trust sells its Volkswagen shares to a French investor.
5. Holding national saving constant, does an increase in net capital outflow increase, decrease or have no effect on a country's accumulation of domestic capital?
6. The business section of most major newspapers contains a table showing exchange rates amongst many countries, as does *The Economist*. Find such a table (or find *The Economist* table on their website) and use it to answer the following questions.
   a. Does this table show nominal or real exchange rates? Explain.
   b. What are the exchange rates between the euro and the UK pound, and between the UK pound and the US dollar? Calculate the exchange rate between the euro and the dollar.
   c. If UK inflation exceeds European inflation over the next year, would you expect the UK pound to appreciate or depreciate relative to the euro?
7. Would each of the following groups be happy or unhappy if the euro appreciated? Explain.
   a. US pension funds holding French government bonds.
   b. German manufacturing industries.
   c. Australian tourists planning a trip to Europe.
   d. A British firm trying to purchase property overseas.
8. What is happening to the Swiss real exchange rate in each of the following situations? Explain.
   a. The Swiss nominal exchange rate is unchanged, but prices rise faster in Switzerland than abroad.
   b. The Swiss nominal exchange rate is unchanged, but prices rise faster abroad than in Switzerland.
   c. The Swiss nominal exchange rate declines, and prices are unchanged in Switzerland and abroad.
   d. The Swiss nominal exchange rate declines, and prices rise faster abroad than in Switzerland.

9. List three goods for which the law of one price is likely to hold, and three goods for which it is not. Justify your choices.
10. A can of lemonade is priced at €0.75 in Europe and 12 pesos in Mexico. What would the peso–euro exchange rate be if purchasing power parity holds? If a monetary expansion caused all prices in Mexico to double, so that lemonade rose to 24 pesos, what would happen to the peso–euro exchange rate?
11. Assume that American rice sells for $1 a kilo, Japanese rice sells for 160 yen a kilo, and the nominal exchange rate is 80 yen per dollar.
    a. Explain how you could make a profit from this situation. What would be your profit per kilo of rice? If other people exploit the same opportunity, what would happen to the price of rice in Japan and the price of rice in the United States?
    b. Suppose that rice is the only commodity in the world. What would happen to the real exchange rate between the United States and Japan?
12. A case study in the chapter analysed purchasing power parity for several countries using the price of Big Macs. Here are data for a few more countries:

Country	Price of a Big Mac	Predicted exchange rate	Actual exchange rate
Indonesia	14 550 rupiah	? rupiah/$	9267 rupiah/$
Hungary	536 forints	? forints/$	188 forints/$
Czech Republic	57.10 korunas	? korunas/$	23.31 korunas/$
Canada	3.20 C$	? C$/$	1.23 C$/$

    a. For each country, compute the predicted exchange rate of the local currency per euro. (Recall that the US price of a Big Mac was $3.) How well does the theory of purchasing power parity explain exchange rates?
    b. According to purchasing power parity, what is the predicted exchange rate between the Hungarian forint and the Canadian dollar? What is the actual exchange rate?

For further resources, visit www.cengage.co.uk/mankiw_taylor2

32 A MACROECONOMIC THEORY OF THE OPEN ECONOMY

Over the past two decades, the United Kingdom and United States have persistently imported more goods and services than they have exported. That is, UK and US net exports have been negative. Japan and Germany, on the other hand, have persistently exported more than they have imported.

Imagine that you are the British prime minister or the US president and you want to end the trade deficits in your country. What should you do? Should you try to limit imports, perhaps by imposing a quota on the import of cars from Japan or Germany? Or should you try to influence the country's trade deficit in some other way?

To understand what factors determine a country's trade balance and how government policies can affect it, we need a macroeconomic theory of the open economy. The preceding chapter introduced some of the key macroeconomic variables that describe an economy's relationship with other economies – including net exports, net capital outflow, and the real and nominal exchange rates. This chapter develops a model that identifies the forces that determine these variables and shows how these variables are related to one another.

To develop this macroeconomic model of an open economy, we build on our previous analysis in two important ways. First, the model takes the economy's GDP as given. We assume that the economy's output of goods and services, as measured by real GDP, is determined by the supplies of the factors of production and by the available production technology that turns these inputs into output. Secondly, the model takes the economy's price level as given. We assume that the price level adjusts to bring the supply and demand for money into balance.

In other words, this chapter takes as a starting point the lessons learned in Chapters 25 and 30 about the determination of the economy's output and price level.

The goal of the model in this chapter is to highlight the forces that determine the economy's trade balance and exchange rate. In one sense, the model is simple: it applies the tools of supply and demand to an open economy. Yet the model is also more complicated than others we have seen because it involves looking simultaneously at two related markets – the market for loanable funds and the market for foreign currency exchange. After we develop this model of the open economy, we use it to examine how various events and policies affect the economy's trade balance and exchange rate. We shall then be able to determine the government policies that are most likely to reverse trade deficits.

SUPPLY AND DEMAND FOR LOANABLE FUNDS AND FOR FOREIGN CURRENCY EXCHANGE

To understand the forces at work in an open economy, we focus on supply and demand in two markets. The first is the market for loanable funds, which coordinates the economy's saving, investment and the flow of loanable funds abroad (called the net capital outflow). The second is the market for foreign currency exchange, which coordinates people who want to exchange the domestic currency for the currency of other countries. In this section we discuss supply and demand in each of these markets. In the next section we put these markets together to explain the overall equilibrium for an open economy.

The Market for Loanable Funds

When we first analysed the role of the financial system in Chapter 26, we made the simplifying assumption that the financial system consists of only one market, called the *market for loanable funds*. All savers go to this market to deposit their saving and all borrowers go to this market to get their loans. In this market, there is one interest rate, which is both the return to saving and the cost of borrowing.

To understand the market for loanable funds in an open economy, the place to start is the identity discussed in the preceding chapter:

$$S = I + NCO$$

$$\text{Saving} = \text{Domestic investment} + \text{Net capital outflow}$$

Whenever a nation saves some of its income, it can use that money to finance the purchase of domestic capital or to finance the purchase of an asset abroad. The two sides of this identity represent the two sides of the market for loanable funds. The supply of loanable funds comes from national saving (S). The demand for loanable funds comes from domestic investment (I) and net capital outflow (NCO). Note that the purchase of a capital asset adds to the demand for loanable funds, regardless of whether that asset is located at home or abroad. Because net capital outflow can be either positive or negative, it can either add to or subtract from the demand for loanable funds that arises from domestic investment.

As we learned in Chapter 26, the quantity of loanable funds supplied and the quantity of loanable funds demanded depend on the real interest rate. A higher real interest rate encourages people to save and, therefore, raises the quantity of loanable funds supplied. A higher interest rate also makes borrowing to finance capital projects more costly; thus, it discourages investment and reduces the quantity of loanable funds demanded.

In addition to influencing national saving and domestic investment, the real interest rate in a country affects that country's net capital outflow. To see why, consider two investment funds – one in the United Kingdom and one in Germany – deciding whether to buy a UK government bond or a German government bond. The investment funds would make this decision in part by comparing the real interest rates in the United Kingdom and Germany. When the UK real interest rate rises, the UK bond becomes more attractive to both investment funds. Thus, an increase in the UK real interest rate discourages Brits from buying foreign assets and encourages people living in other countries to buy UK assets. For both reasons, a high UK real interest rate reduces UK net capital outflow.

We represent the market for loanable funds on the familiar supply-and-demand diagram in Figure 32.1. As in our earlier analysis of the financial system, the supply curve slopes upward because a higher interest rate increases the quantity of loanable funds supplied, and the demand curve slopes downward because a higher interest rate decreases the quantity of loanable funds demanded. Unlike the situation in our previous discussion, however, the demand side of the market now represents the behaviour of both domestic investment and net capital outflow. That is, in an open economy, the demand for loanable funds comes not only from those who want loanable funds to buy domestic capital goods but also from those who want loanable funds to buy foreign assets.

The interest rate adjusts to bring the supply and demand for loanable funds into balance. If the interest rate were below the equilibrium level, the quantity of loanable funds supplied would be less than the quantity demanded. The resulting shortage of loanable funds would push the interest rate upward. Conversely, if the interest rate were above the equilibrium level, the quantity of

FIGURE 32.1

The Market for Loanable Funds

The interest rate in an open economy, as in a closed economy, is determined by the supply and demand for loanable funds. National saving is the source of the supply of loanable funds. Domestic investment and net capital outflow are the sources of the demand for loanable funds. At the equilibrium interest rate, the amount that people want to save exactly balances the amount that people want to borrow for the purpose of buying domestic capital and foreign assets.

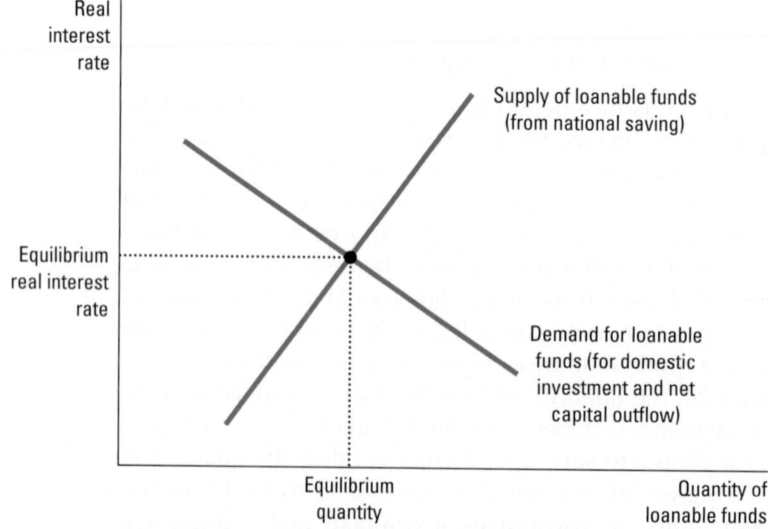

loanable funds supplied would exceed the quantity demanded. The surplus of loanable funds would drive the interest rate downward. At the equilibrium interest rate, the supply of loanable funds exactly balances the demand. That is, at the equilibrium interest rate, the amount that people want to save exactly balances the desired quantities of domestic investment and net capital outflow.

The Market for Foreign Currency Exchange

The second market in our model of the open economy is the market for foreign currency exchange. Let's think of the UK as the domestic economy. Participants in this market trade UK pounds in exchange for foreign currencies. To understand the market for foreign currency exchange, we begin with another identity from the last chapter:

$$\begin{array}{ccc} NCO & = & NX \\ \text{Net capital outflow} & = & \text{Net exports} \end{array}$$

This identity states that the imbalance between the purchase and sale of capital assets abroad (*NCO*) equals the imbalance between exports and imports of goods and services (*NX*). For example, when the German economy is running a trade surplus ($NX > 0$), foreigners are buying more German goods and services than German residents are buying foreign goods and services. What are the Germans doing with the foreign currency they are getting from this net sale of goods and services abroad? They must be buying foreign assets, so German capital is flowing abroad ($NCO > 0$). Conversely, if Switzerland is running a trade deficit ($NX < 0$), the Swiss are spending more on foreign goods and services than they are earning from selling abroad. Some of this spending must be financed by selling Swiss assets abroad, so foreign capital is flowing into Switzerland ($NCO < 0$).

Our model of the open economy treats the two sides of this identity as representing the two sides of the market for foreign currency exchange. Net capital outflow represents the quantity of pounds supplied for the purpose of buying foreign assets. For example, when a UK investment fund wants to buy a Japanese government bond, it needs to change pounds into yen, so it supplies pounds in the market for foreign currency exchange. Net exports represent the quantity of pounds demanded for the purpose of buying UK net exports of goods and services. For example, when a Japanese airline wants to buy aircraft fuel produced by BP, it needs to change its yen into pounds, so it demands pounds in the market for foreign currency exchange.

What price balances the supply and demand in the market for foreign currency exchange? The answer is the real exchange rate. As we saw in the preceding chapter, the real exchange rate is the relative price of domestic and foreign goods and, therefore, is a key determinant of net exports. When the UK real exchange rate appreciates, UK goods become more expensive relative to foreign goods, making UK goods less attractive to consumers abroad (exports would rise) and foreign goods more attractive to domestic consumers (imports would rise). For both reasons, net UK exports fall. Hence, an appreciation of the real exchange rate reduces the quantity of pounds demanded in the market for foreign currency exchange.

Figure 32.2 shows supply and demand in the market for foreign currency exchange. The demand curve slopes downward for the reason we just discussed: a higher real exchange rate makes UK goods more expensive and reduces the quantity of pounds demanded to buy those goods. The supply curve is vertical because the quantity of pounds supplied for net capital outflow does not depend on the real exchange rate. (As discussed earlier, net capital outflow depends on the real interest rate. When discussing the market for foreign currency exchange, we take the real interest rate and net capital outflow as given.)

FIGURE 32.2

The Market for Foreign Currency Exchange

The real exchange rate is determined by the supply and demand for foreign currency exchange. The supply of pounds to be exchanged into foreign currency comes from net capital outflow. Because net capital outflow does not depend on the real exchange rate, the supply curve is vertical. The demand for pounds comes from net exports. Because a lower real exchange rate stimulates net exports (and thus increases the quantity of pounds demanded to pay for these net exports), the demand curve is downward sloping. At the equilibrium real exchange rate, the number of pounds people supply to buy foreign assets exactly balances the number of pounds people demand to buy net exports.

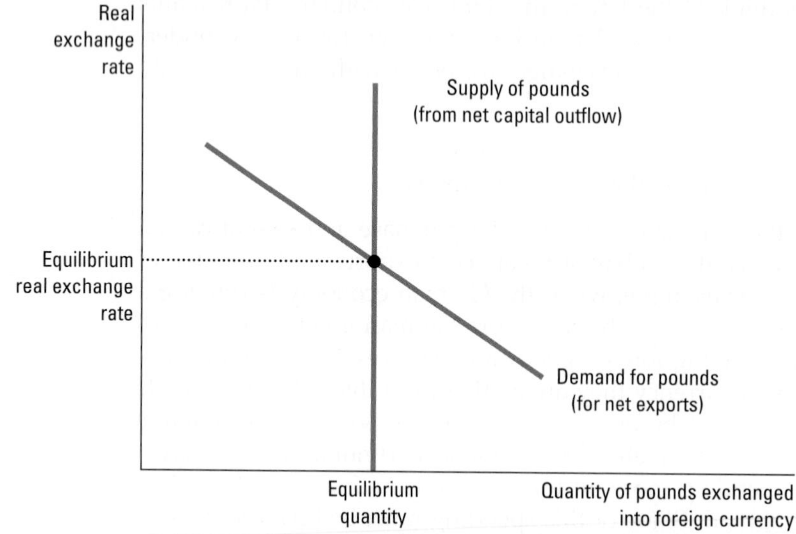

The real exchange rate adjusts to balance the supply and demand for pounds just as the price of any good adjusts to balance supply and demand for that good. If the real exchange rate were below the equilibrium level, the quantity of pounds supplied would be less than the quantity demanded. The resulting shortage of pounds would push the value of the pound upward. Conversely, if the real exchange rate were above the equilibrium level, the quantity of pounds supplied would exceed the quantity demanded. The surplus of pounds would drive the value of the pound downward. At the equilibrium real exchange rate, the demand for pounds by non-UK residents arising from the UK net exports of goods and services exactly balances the supply of pounds from UK residents arising from UK net capital outflow.

At this point, it is worth noting that the division of transactions between 'supply' and 'demand' in this model is somewhat artificial. In our model, net exports are the source of the demand for pounds, and net capital outflow is the source of the supply. Thus, when a UK resident imports a car made in Japan, our model treats that transaction as a decrease in the quantity of pounds demanded (because net exports fall) rather than an increase in the quantity of pounds supplied. Similarly, when a Japanese citizen buys a UK government bond, our model treats that transaction as a decrease in the quantity of pounds supplied (because net capital outflow falls) rather than an increase in the quantity of pounds demanded. This use of language may seem somewhat unnatural at first, but it will prove useful when analysing the effects of various policies.

Quick Quiz Describe the sources of supply and demand in the market for loanable funds and the market for foreign currency exchange.

FYI

Purchasing Power Parity as a Special Case

An alert reader of this book might ask: why are we developing a theory of the exchange rate here? Didn't we already do that in the preceding chapter?

As you may recall, the preceding chapter developed a theory of the exchange rate called purchasing power parity. This theory asserts that a euro (or any other currency) must buy the same quantity of goods and services in every country. As a result, the real exchange rate is fixed, and all changes in the nominal exchange rate between two currencies reflect changes in the price levels in the two countries.

The model of the exchange rate developed here is related to the theory of purchasing power parity. According to the theory of purchasing power parity, international trade responds quickly to international price differences. If goods were cheaper in one country than in another, they would be exported from the first country and imported into the second until the price difference disappeared. In other words, the theory of purchasing power parity assumes that net exports are highly responsive to small changes in the real exchange rate. If net exports were in fact so responsive, the demand curve in Figure 32.2 would be horizontal.

Thus, the theory of purchasing power parity can be viewed as a special case of the model considered here. In that special case, the demand curve for foreign currency exchange, rather than being downward sloping, is horizontal at the level of the real exchange rate that ensures parity of purchasing power at home and abroad. That special case is a good place to start when studying exchange rates, but it is far from the end of the story.

This chapter, therefore, concentrates on the more realistic case in which the demand curve for foreign currency exchange is downward sloping. This allows for the possibility that the real exchange rate changes over time, as in fact it sometimes does in the real world.

EQUILIBRIUM IN THE OPEN ECONOMY

So far we have discussed supply and demand in two markets – the market for loanable funds and the market for foreign currency exchange. Let's now consider how these markets are related to each other.

Net Capital Outflow: The Link Between the Two Markets

We begin by recapping what we've learned so far in this chapter. We have been discussing how the economy coordinates four important macroeconomic variables: national saving (S), domestic investment (I), net capital outflow (NCO) and net exports (NX). Keep in mind the following identities:

$$S = I + NCO$$

and

$$NCO = NX$$

In the market for loanable funds, supply comes from national saving, demand comes from domestic investment and net capital outflow, and the real interest rate balances supply and demand. In the market for foreign currency exchange, supply comes from net capital outflow, demand comes from net exports, and the real exchange rate balances supply and demand.

FIGURE 32.3

How Net Capital Outflow Depends on the Interest Rate

Because a higher domestic real interest rate makes domestic assets more attractive, it reduces net capital outflow. Note the position of zero on the horizontal axis: net capital outflow can be positive or negative. A negative value of net capital outflow means that the economy is experiencing a net inflow of capital.

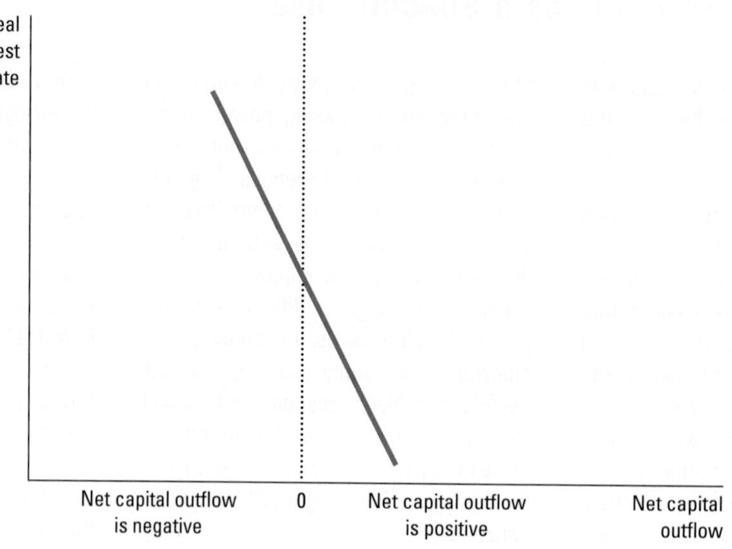

Net capital outflow is the variable that links these two markets. In the market for loanable funds, net capital outflow is a piece of demand. A person who wants to buy an asset abroad must finance this purchase by obtaining resources in the market for loanable funds. In the market for foreign currency exchange, net capital outflow is the source of supply. A person who wants to buy an asset in another country must supply pounds in order to exchange them for the currency of that country.

The key determinant of net capital outflow, as we have discussed, is the real interest rate. When the UK interest rate is high, owning UK assets is more attractive, and UK net capital outflow is low. Figure 32.3 shows this negative relationship between the interest rate and net capital outflow. This net capital outflow curve is the link between the market for loanable funds and the market for foreign currency exchange.

Simultaneous Equilibrium in Two Markets

We can now put all the pieces of our model together in Figure 32.4. This figure shows how the market for loanable funds and the market for foreign currency exchange jointly determine the important macroeconomic variables of an open economy.

Panel (a) of the figure shows the market for loanable funds (taken from Figure 32.1). As before, national saving is the source of the supply of loanable funds. Domestic investment and net capital outflow are the source of the demand for loanable funds. The equilibrium real interest rate (r_1) brings the quantity of

FIGURE 32.4

The Real Equilibrium in an Open Economy

In panel (a), the supply and demand for loanable funds determine the real interest rate. In panel (b), the interest rate determines net capital outflow, which provides the supply of pounds in the market for foreign currency exchange. In panel (c), the supply and demand for pounds in the market for foreign currency exchange determine the real exchange rate.

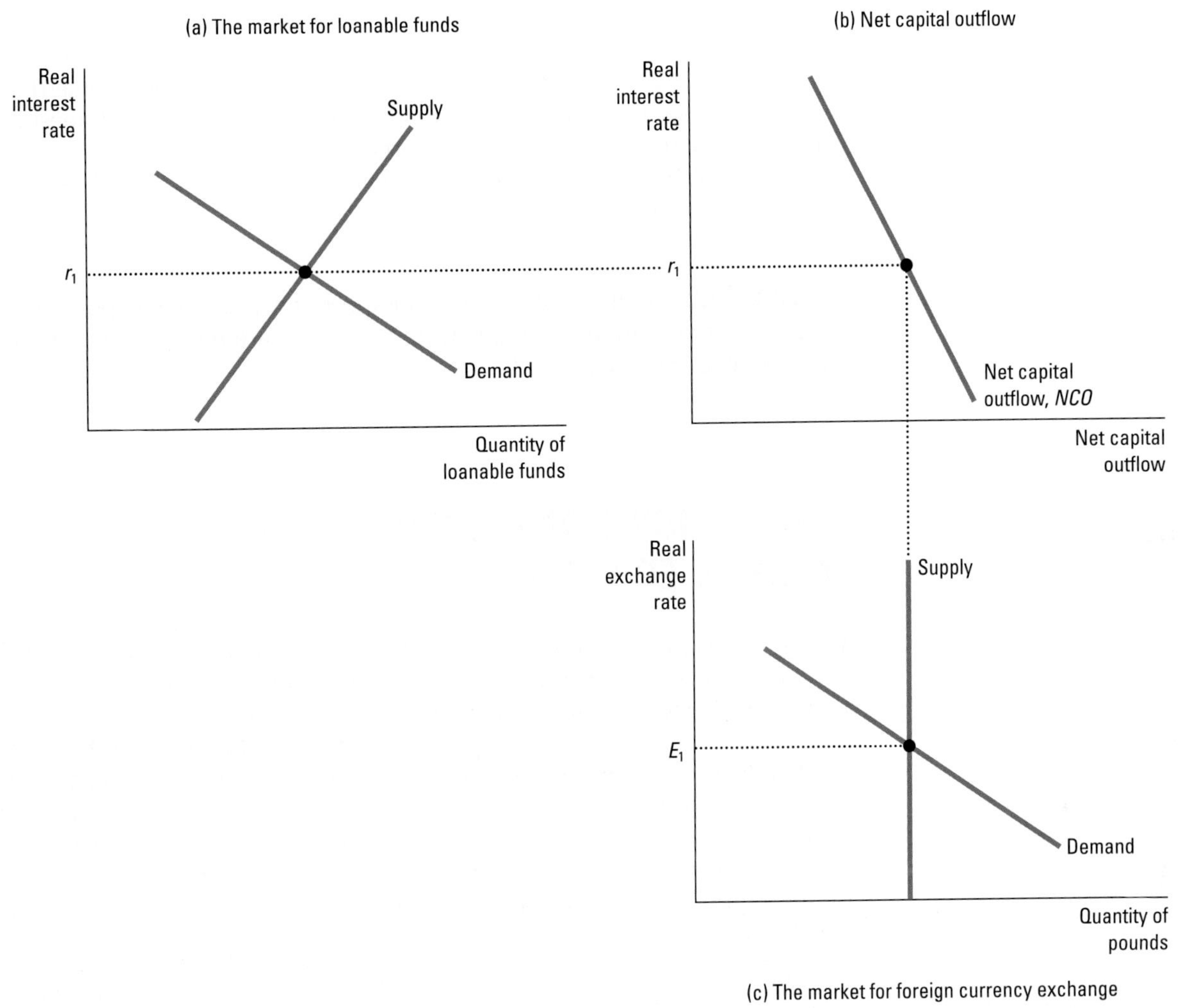

loanable funds supplied and the quantity of loanable funds demanded into balance.

Panel (b) of the figure shows net capital outflow (taken from Figure 32.3). It shows how the interest rate from panel (a) determines net capital outflow. A higher interest rate at home makes domestic assets more attractive, and this in turn reduces net capital outflow. Therefore, the net capital outflow curve in panel (b) slopes downward.

Panel (c) of the figure shows the market for foreign currency exchange (taken from Figure 32.2). Because foreign assets must be purchased with foreign currency, the quantity of net capital outflow from panel (b) determines the supply of pounds to be exchanged into foreign currencies. The real exchange rate does not affect net capital outflow, so the supply curve is vertical. The demand for pounds comes from net exports. Because a depreciation of the real exchange rate increases net exports, the demand curve for foreign currency exchange slopes downward. The equilibrium real exchange rate (E_1) brings into balance the quantity of pounds supplied and the quantity of pounds demanded in the market for foreign currency exchange.

The two markets shown in Figure 32.4 determine two relative prices – the real interest rate and the real exchange rate. The real interest rate determined in panel (a) is the price of goods and services in the present relative to goods and services in the future. The real exchange rate determined in panel (c) is the price of domestic goods and services relative to foreign goods and services. These two relative prices adjust simultaneously to balance supply and demand in these two markets. As they do so, they determine national saving, domestic investment, net capital outflow and net exports. In a moment, we will use this model to see how all these variables change when some policy or event causes one of these curves to shift.

Quick Quiz In the model of the open economy just developed, two markets determine two relative prices. • What are the markets? • What are the two relative prices?

HOW POLICIES AND EVENTS AFFECT AN OPEN ECONOMY

Having developed a model to explain how key macroeconomic variables are determined in an open economy, we can now use the model to analyse how changes in policy and other events alter the economy's equilibrium. As we proceed, keep in mind that our model is just supply and demand in two markets – the market for loanable funds and the market for foreign currency exchange. When using the model to analyse any event, we can apply the three steps outlined in Chapter 4. First, we determine which of the supply and demand curves the event affects. Secondly, we determine which way the curves shift. Thirdly, we use the supply-and-demand diagrams to examine how these shifts alter the economy's equilibrium.

Government Budget Deficits

When we first discussed the supply and demand for loanable funds earlier in the book, we examined the effects of government budget deficits, which occur when government spending exceeds government revenue. Because a government budget deficit represents *negative* public saving, it reduces national saving (the sum of public and private saving). Thus, a government budget deficit reduces the supply of loanable funds, drives up the interest rate and crowds out investment.

Now let's consider the effects of a budget deficit in an open economy. First, which curve in our model shifts? As in a closed economy, the initial impact of the budget deficit is on national saving and, therefore, on the supply curve for loanable funds. Secondly, which way does this supply curve shift? Again as in a closed economy, a budget deficit represents *negative* public saving, so it reduces national saving and shifts the supply curve for loanable funds to the left. This is shown as the shift from S_1 to S_2 in panel (a) of Figure 32.5.

FIGURE 32.5

The Effects of a Government Budget Deficit

If the French government runs a budget deficit, it reduces the supply of loanable funds from S_1 to S_2 in panel (a). The interest rate rises from r_1 to r_2 to balance the supply and demand for loanable funds. In panel (b), the higher interest rate reduces net capital outflow. Reduced net capital outflow, in turn, reduces the supply of euros in the market for foreign currency exchange from S_1 to S_2 in panel (c). This fall in the supply of euros causes the real exchange rate to appreciate from E_1 to E_2. The appreciation of the exchange rate pushes the trade balance towards deficit.

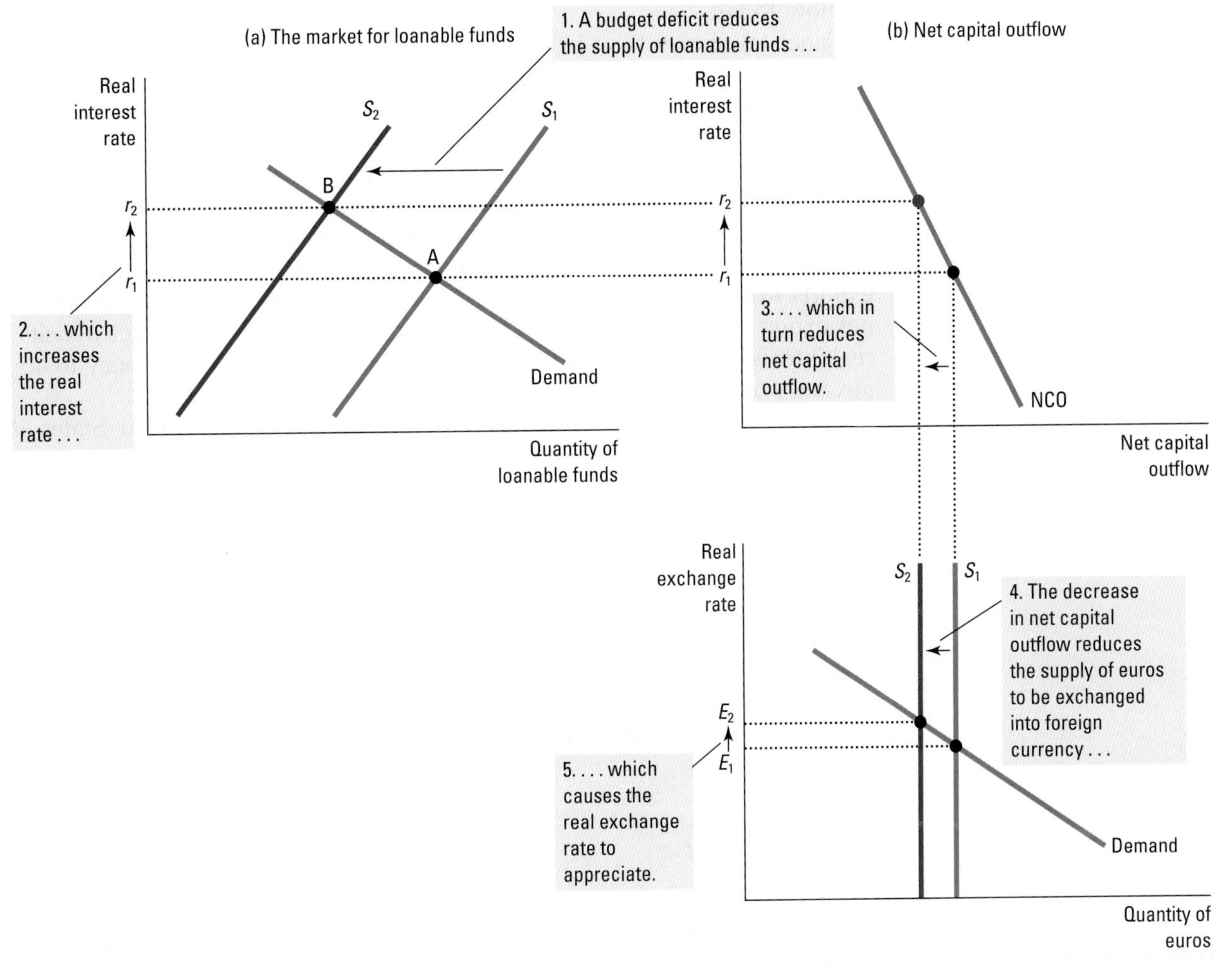

Our third and final step is to compare the old and new equilibria. Panel (a) shows the impact of a French budget deficit on the French market for loanable funds. With fewer funds available for borrowers in France financial markets, the interest rate rises from r_1 to r_2 to balance supply and demand. Faced with a higher interest rate, borrowers in the market for loanable funds choose to borrow less. This change is represented in the figure as the movement from point A to point B along the demand curve for loanable funds. In particular, households and firms reduce their purchases of capital goods. As in a closed economy, budget deficits crowd out domestic investment.

In an open economy, however, the reduced supply of loanable funds has additional effects. Panel (b) shows that the increase in the interest rate from r_1 to r_2 reduces net capital outflow. (This fall in net capital outflow is also part of the decrease in the quantity of loanable funds demanded in the movement from point A to point B in panel (a).) Because saving kept at home now earns higher rates of return, investing abroad is less attractive, and domestic residents buy fewer foreign assets. Higher interest rates also attract foreign investors, who want to earn the higher returns on French assets. Thus, when budget deficits raise interest rates, both domestic and foreign behaviour cause French net capital outflow to fall.

Panel (c) shows how budget deficits affect the market for foreign currency exchange. Because net capital outflow is reduced, people need less foreign currency to buy foreign assets, and this induces a leftward shift in the supply curve for euros from S_1 to S_2. The reduced supply of euros causes the real exchange rate to appreciate from E_1 to E_2. That is, the euro becomes more valuable compared to foreign currencies. This appreciation, in turn, makes French goods more expensive compared to foreign goods. Because people both at home and abroad switch their purchases away from the more expensive French goods, exports from France fall, and imports into France rise. For both reasons, French net exports fall. Hence, in an open economy, government budget deficits raise real interest rates, crowd out domestic investment, cause the currency to appreciate and push the trade balance toward deficit.

An important example of this lesson occurred in the United States in the 1980s, shortly after a new president was elected. The new president had been elected on a platform of cutting taxes and US fiscal policy changed dramatically. The US government enacted large cuts in taxes, but they did not cut government spending by nearly as much, so the result was a large budget deficit. Our model of the open economy predicts that such a policy should lead to a trade deficit, and in fact it did.

The budget deficit and trade deficit are so closely related in both theory and practice that, especially when they are both large, they are often referred to by the nickname of the *twin deficits.* We should not, however, view these twins as identical, for many factors beyond fiscal policy can influence the trade deficit.

Trade Policy

trade policy
a government policy that directly influences the quantity of goods and services that a country imports or exports

A **trade policy** is a government policy that directly influences the quantity of goods and services that a country imports or exports. Trade policy takes various forms. One common trade policy is a *tariff,* a tax on imported goods. Another is an *import quota,* a limit on the quantity of a good that can be produced abroad and sold domestically. Trade policies are common throughout the world, although sometimes they are disguised. For example, before 2000 there was an understanding between Japan and the European Union that Japan would voluntarily limit its sales of cars into the UK, France, Italy, Portugal and Spain to a maximum of 1.1 million (excluding cars produced at factories owned by Japanese companies but located within the European Union). These so-called 'voluntary export restrictions' are not really voluntary and, in essence, are a form of import quota.

Let's consider the macroeconomic impact of trade policy. Suppose that the European car industry, concerned about competition from Japanese car makers, convinces the European Union (EU) to impose a quota on the number of cars that can be imported from Japan into the EU. In making their case, lobbyists for the car industry assert that the trade restriction would improve the overall EU trade balance. Are they right? Our model, as illustrated in Figure 32.6, offers an answer.

FIGURE 32.6

The Effects of an Import Quota

When the EU imposes a quota on the import of Japanese cars, nothing happens in the market for loanable funds in panel (a) or to net capital outflow in panel (b). The only effect is a rise in net exports (exports minus imports) for any given real exchange rate. As a result, the demand for euros in the market for foreign currency exchange rises, as shown by the shift from D_1 *to* D_2 *in panel (c). This increase in the demand for euros causes the value of the euro to appreciate from* E_1 *to* E_2*. This appreciation of the euro tends to reduce net exports, offsetting the direct effect of the import quota on the trade balance.*

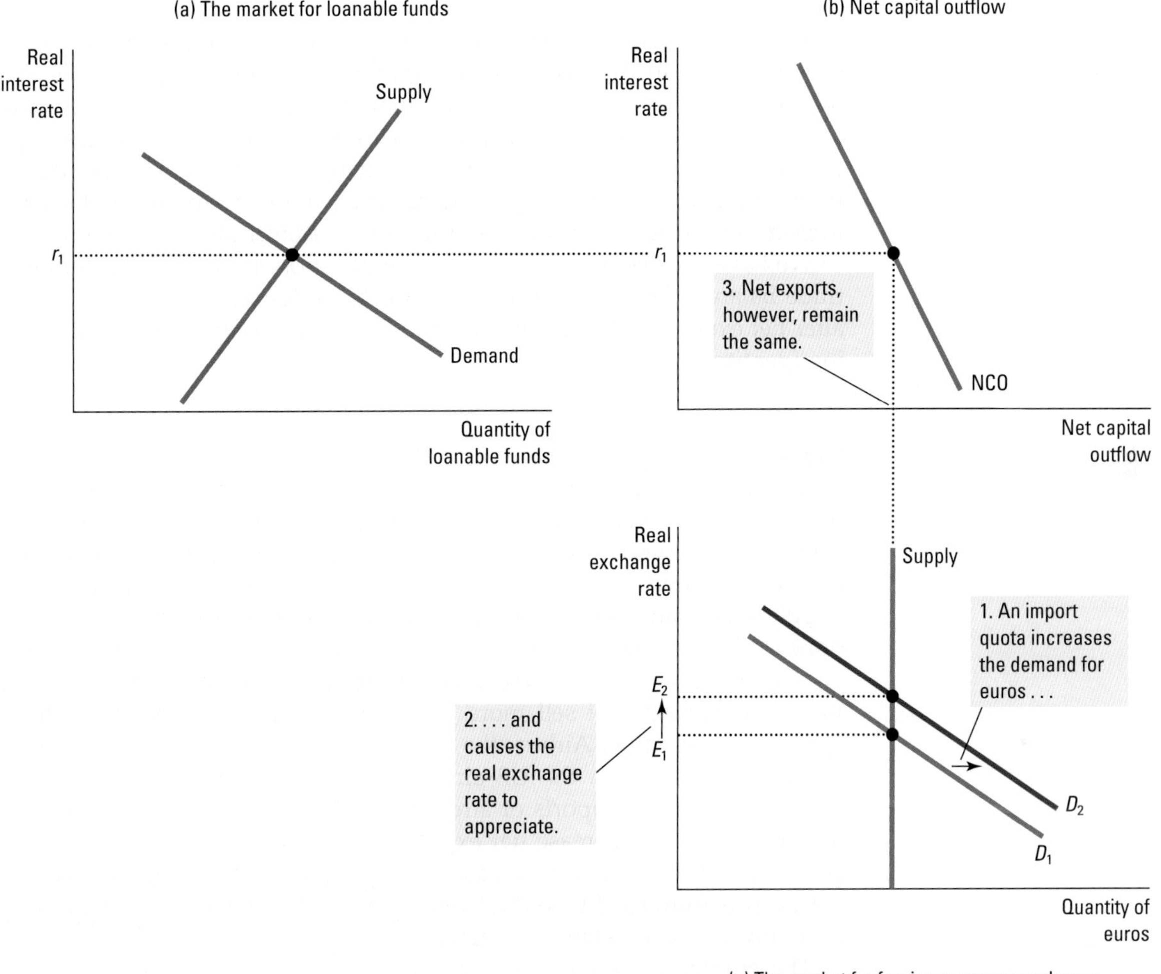

The first step in analysing the trade policy is to determine which curve shifts. The initial impact of the import restriction is, not surprisingly, on imports. Because net exports equal exports minus imports, the policy also affects net exports. And because net exports are the source of demand for euros in the market for foreign currency exchange, the policy affects the demand curve in this market.

The second step is to determine which way this demand curve shifts. Because the quota restricts the number of Japanese cars sold in the EU, it reduces imports at any given real exchange rate. Net exports, which equal exports minus imports, will therefore *rise* for any given real exchange rate. Because non-Europeans need euros to buy EU net exports, there is an increased demand for euros in the market for foreign currency exchange. This increase in the demand for euros is shown in panel (c) of Figure 32.6 as the shift from D_1 to D_2.

The third step is to compare the old and new equilibria. As we can see in panel (c), the increase in the demand for euros causes the real exchange rate to appreciate from E_1 to E_2. Because nothing has happened in the market for loanable funds in panel (a), there is no change in the real interest rate. Because there is no change in the real interest rate, there is also no change in net capital outflow, shown in panel (b). And because there is no change in net capital outflow, there can be no change in net exports, even though the import quota has reduced imports.

The reason why net exports can stay the same while imports fall is explained by the change in the real exchange rate: when the euro appreciates in value in the market for foreign currency exchange, European goods become more expensive relative to non-European goods. This appreciation encourages imports and discourages exports – and both of these changes work to offset the direct increase in net exports due to the import quota. In the end, an import quota reduces both imports and exports, but net exports (exports minus imports) are unchanged.

We have thus come to a surprising implication: trade policies do not affect the trade balance. That is, policies that directly influence exports or imports do not alter net exports. This conclusion seems less surprising if one recalls the accounting identity:

$$NX = NCO = S - I$$

Net exports equal net capital outflow, which equals national saving minus domestic investment. Trade policies do not alter the trade balance because they do not alter national saving or domestic investment. For given levels of national saving and domestic investment, the real exchange rate adjusts to keep the trade balance the same, regardless of the trade policies the government puts in place.

Although trade policies do not affect a country's overall trade balance, these policies do affect specific firms, industries and countries. When the EU imposes an import quota on Japanese cars, European carmakers have less competition from abroad and will sell more cars. At the same time, because the euro has appreciated in value, Airbus, the European aircraft maker, will find it harder to compete with Boeing, the US aircraft maker. European exports of aircraft will fall, and European imports of aircraft will rise. In this case, the import quota on Japanese cars will increase net exports of cars and decrease net exports of aeroplanes. In addition, it will increase net exports from the EU to Japan and decrease net exports from the EU to the United States. The overall trade balance of the EU economy, however, stays the same.

The effects of trade policies are, therefore, more microeconomic than macroeconomic. Although advocates of trade policies sometimes claim (incorrectly) that these policies can alter a country's trade balance, they are usually more motivated by concerns about particular firms or industries. One should not be surprised, for instance, to hear an executive from BMW advocating import quotas for Japanese cars. Economists almost always oppose such trade policies. Free trade allows economies to specialize in doing what they do best, making residents of all countries better off. Trade restrictions interfere with these gains from trade and, thus, reduce overall economic well-being.

Political Instability and Capital Flight

In 1994 political instability in Mexico, including the assassination of a prominent political leader, made world financial markets nervous. People began to view

Mexico as a much less stable country than they had previously thought. They decided to pull some of their assets out of Mexico in order to move these funds to 'safe haven' countries in Western Europe and, in particular, the United States. Such a large and sudden movement of funds out of a country is called **capital flight**. To see the implications of capital flight for the Mexican economy, we again follow our three steps for analysing a change in equilibrium, but this time we apply our model of the open economy from the perspective of Mexico rather than the European Union.

capital flight
a large and sudden reduction in the demand for assets located in a country

Consider first which curves in our model capital flight affects. When investors around the world observe political problems in Mexico, they decide to sell some of their Mexican assets and use the proceeds to buy US and Western European assets. This act increases Mexican net capital outflow and, therefore, affects both markets in our model. Most obviously, it affects the net capital outflow curve, and this in turn influences the supply of pesos in the market for foreign currency exchange. In addition, because the demand for loanable funds comes from both domestic investment and net capital outflow, capital flight affects the demand curve in the market for loanable funds.

Now consider which way these curves shift. When net capital outflow increases, there is greater demand for loanable funds to finance these purchases of capital assets abroad. Thus, as panel (a) of Figure 32.7 shows, the demand curve for loanable funds shifts to the right from D_1 to D_2. In addition, because net capital outflow is higher for any interest rate, the net capital outflow curve also shifts to the right from NCO_1 to NCO_2, as in panel (b).

To see the effects of capital flight on the economy, we compare the old and new equilibria. Panel (a) of Figure 32.7 shows that the increased demand for loanable funds causes the interest rate in Mexico to rise from r_1 to r_2. Panel (b) shows that Mexican net capital outflow increases. (Although the rise in the interest rate does make Mexican assets more attractive, this only partly offsets the impact of capital flight on net capital outflow.) Panel (c) shows that the increase in net capital outflow raises the supply of pesos in the market for foreign currency exchange from S_1 to S_2. That is, as people try to get out of Mexican assets, there is a large supply of pesos to be converted into dollars and euros. This increase in supply causes the peso to depreciate from E_1 to E_2. Thus, capital flight from Mexico increases Mexican interest rates and decreases the value of the Mexican peso in the market for foreign currency exchange. This is exactly what was observed in 1994. From November 1994 to March 1995, the interest rate on short-term Mexican government bonds rose from 14 per cent to 70 per cent, and the peso depreciated in value from 29 to 15 US cents per peso.

These price changes that result from capital flight influence some key macroeconomic quantities. The depreciation of the currency makes exports cheaper and imports more expensive, pushing the trade balance towards surplus. At the same time, the increase in the interest rate reduces domestic investment, which slows capital accumulation and economic growth.

Although capital flight has its largest impact on the country from which capital is fleeing, it also affects other countries. When capital flows out of Mexico into the United States, for instance, it has the opposite effect on the US economy as it has on the Mexican economy. In particular, the rise in Mexican net capital outflow coincides with a fall in US net capital outflow. As the peso depreciates in value and Mexican interest rates rise, the dollar appreciates in value and US interest rates fall. The size of this impact on the US economy is small, however, because the economy of the United States is so large compared to that of Mexico.

The events that we have been describing in Mexico could happen to any economy in the world, and in fact they do from time to time. In 1997, the world learned that the banking systems of several Asian economies, including Thailand, South Korea and Indonesia, were at or near the point of bankruptcy, and this

FIGURE 32.7

The Effects of Capital Flight

If people decide that Mexico is a risky place to keep their savings, they will move their capital to safer havens such as the United States, resulting in an increase in Mexican net capital outflow. Consequently, the demand for loanable funds in Mexico rises from D_1 to D_2, as shown in panel (a), and this drives up the Mexican real interest rate from r_1 to r_2. Because net capital outflow is higher for any interest rate, that curve also shifts to the right from NCO_1 to NCO_2 in panel (b). At the same time, in the market for foreign currency exchange, the supply of pesos rises from S_1 to S_2, as shown in panel (c). This increase in the supply of pesos causes the peso to depreciate from E_1 to E_2, so the peso becomes less valuable compared to other currencies.

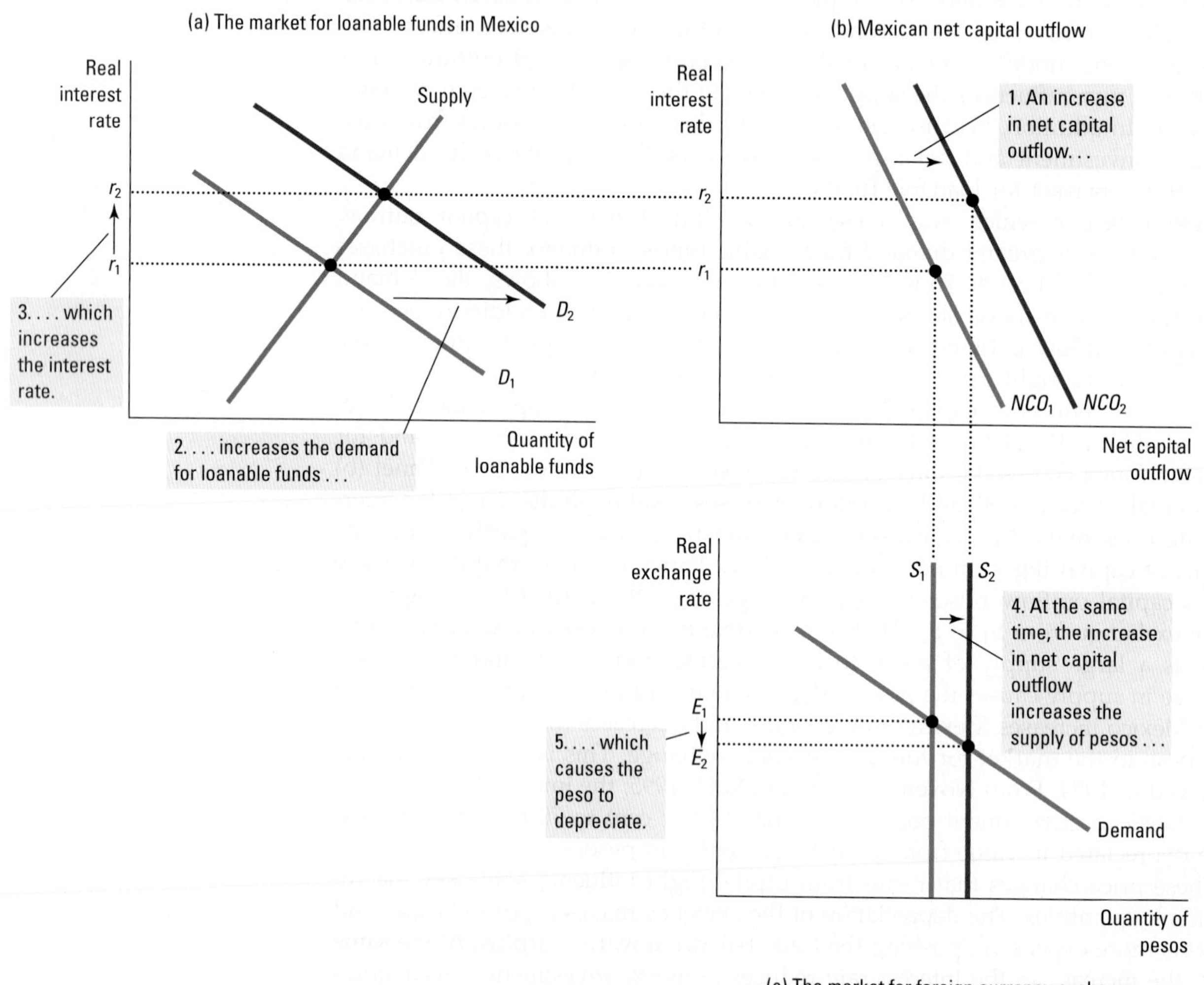

news induced capital to flee from these nations. In 1998, the Russian government defaulted on its debt, inducing international investors to take whatever money they could and run. A similar (but more complicated) set of events unfolded in Argentina in 2002. More recent examples include Venezuela where citizens have moved capital out of the country to protect it from being taken by the country's leader, Hugo Chavez. Some estimates put the extent of the capital flight at $36 billion between 2003 and 2007 alone. In each of these cases of capital flight, the results were much as our model predicts: rising interest rates and a falling currency.

IN THE NEWS

Capital flight is a problem that can continue to hit countries when bad news strikes. In the wake of the financial crisis 2007–2009, the Greek government found itself with a massive fiscal deficit. This was a particularly interesting problem because not only was there a fear that the Greek government might not be able to meet its debt obligations, it was also a member of the eurozone. As a result of the debt crisis, the euro fell in value and interest rates in Greece also rose significantly.

Greek wealth finds a home in London

Greeks taking fright at the fiscal crisis enveloping the debt-stricken country are snapping up properties in Britain as part of a desperate flight of capital. British homeowners may still worry about the resilience of the British economy but from Athens it appears as a relative haven and prime real estate in London, the traditional home of Greece's wealthy shipping community, is being bought at an unprecedented rate by rich Greeks desperate to transfer their bank deposits. The land grab has astounded estate agents, with many referring to the new homebuyers as "cash Greeks" because of their willingness to part with large sums of money in record time to secure £1m-plus properties.

"They are all cash buyers, serious players who are only interested in the high-end market around Regent's Park, Mayfair and Marylebone," said Panos Koutsoyiannakis at the central London estate agents Fraser & Co. "The other day I had one come in who said 'I don't have a budget'. Another bought a two-bedroom flat for £1.6m and didn't bat an eyelid. They're closing deals in record time with many not wanting to even take out a survey."

Koutsoyiannakis should know. As a Greek Australian, it is he, more often than not, who is called upon to screen clients. In recent months, he said, Athenian investors have deluged estate agencies on Baker Street, where his own office is located. "Normally," said Koutsoyiannakis, "you'll get a Greek inquiring about property every two to three months. Recently, we've had up to 15 a week and some even laugh about taking the money out because of the crisis." Many want to buy properties and put them in their children's names as a way of diversifying assets, he said. "There are nine estate agents on our block and when we bump into each other or meet to swap keys we talk about how it's no longer the Arabs but the Greeks who are rocking up wanting to buy, well, anything really."

Historically, Greece's super-wealthy elite has kept its holdings in bank accounts overseas, with Switzerland and Luxembourg among the favoured destinations. Shipping remains one of the top contributors to the country's €240bn (£210bn) economy with shipowners – who first made fortunes running the British naval blockade in the Napoleonic wars – long settling in the UK where their vast fortunes have enabled them to acquire some of London's finest properties, send their offspring to some of the best schools and even bankroll their favourite politicians.

Sir Stelios Hadji-Ioannou, who founded the budget airline easyJet with £1m given to him by his shipowner father, is among the many Greek and Greek-Cypriots who moved to London partly because they like it – and partly because they consider it Europe's natural entrepreneurial hub. But with the sector also losing its preferential tax status in the City of London, a growing number of the community had increasingly returned to Greece. Following the precarious drachma's consignment to the dustbin of history when Athens joined the eurozone in 2001, many transferred their wealth to Greece as well. Much of that money - though certainly not all – is estimated to be among the €10bn believed to have been removed from Greek banks in the first two months of the year (2010).

The outflow, which has underscored fears of bankruptcy among Greeks, also followed a threat by the socialist government to raid millions of local bank accounts as part of a determined drive at revenue collection. In an eerie replay of the mass flight of money abroad in the run-up to Argentina's defaulting on its debt in 2002, vast sums are also said to have been transferred to Greek-owned banks in Cyprus, mostly by corporate companies fearing the knock-on effects of the financial turmoil. "I have even heard of savers moving their money out of accounts into bank safety deposit boxes," said Yannis Stournaras, who heads the Foundation for Economic and Industrial Research.

"But I have also heard that the situation is not alarmist because a lot of the money has gone to buy Greek bonds and has been kept in the Greek banking system. We're not talking about a run on the banks," he said. Nevertheless, the financial sector is clearly feeling the pinch of the debt crisis. Last week, the Greek finance minister, George Papaconstantinou, announced that four of the country's largest lenders had asked for government support to offset the mass exodus of funds. The banks are expected to be given up to €17bn in loan guarantees as part of a €28bn package passed by the previous conservative government to ensure capital and liquidity during the global credit crunch.

The cash exodus has infuriated ordinary Greeks, who have seen their incomes slashed by up to 30%. With the country embroiled in its first recession in 15 years and the effects of the socialist government's draconian austerity package beginning to be felt, the empty cafes, restaurants and shops are redolent of a place starved of cash – a far cry from the posh streets of London where Greece's rich are flocking to in a determined effort to escape the crisis lapping the shores of their own country.

Source: 'Debt crisis: Greek wealth finds a home in London: As Athens desperately tries to raise revenue, the rich are transferring cash to Britain.' *Guardian* [London, England] 14 Apr. 2010. (Contributor Helena Smith) © Guardian News & Media Ltd 2010

Quick Quiz Suppose that Europeans decided to spend a smaller fraction of their incomes. • What would be the effect on saving, investment, interest rates, the real exchange rate and the trade balance in the European Union?

CONCLUSION

Historically, international trade has always played a very important role in most European economies. In the past two centuries or so, international finance has also become increasingly important. The typical modern European country consumes a high proportion of goods produced abroad and exports a significant amount of its output to other European countries and to countries outside Europe. In addition, through investment funds and other financial institutions, Europeans borrow and lend in world financial markets, as indeed do the citizens of all advanced industrialized economies. Even the US economy, which has traditionally been thought of as importing and exporting only a tiny fraction of its GDP, has become increasingly open in recent years, and policy debates over the US current account deficit have become the norm.

It is clear, therefore, that a proper understanding of macroeconomics requires a study of the workings of the open economy. This chapter has provided a basic model for thinking about the macroeconomics of open economies.

SUMMARY

- To analyse the macroeconomics of open economies, two markets are central – the market for loanable funds and the market for foreign currency exchange. In the market for loanable funds, the interest rate adjusts to balance the supply of loanable funds (from national saving) and the demand for loanable funds (from domestic investment and net capital outflow). In the market for foreign currency exchange, the real exchange rate adjusts to balance the supply of domestic currency (for net capital outflow) and the demand for domestic currency (for net exports). Because net capital outflow is part of the demand for loanable funds and provides the supply of domestic currency for foreign currency exchange, it is the variable that connects these two markets.
- A policy that reduces national saving, such as a government budget deficit, reduces the supply of loanable funds and drives up the interest rate. The higher interest rate reduces net capital outflow, which reduces the supply of domestic currency in the market for foreign currency exchange. The domestic currency appreciates, and net exports fall.

- Although restrictive trade policies, such as tariffs or quotas on imports, are sometimes advocated as a way to alter the trade balance, they do not necessarily have that effect. A trade restriction increases net exports for a given exchange rate and, therefore, increases the demand for the domestic currency in the market for foreign currency exchange. As a result, the domestic currency appreciates in value, making domestic goods more expensive relative to foreign goods. This appreciation offsets the initial impact of the trade restriction on net exports.
- When investors change their attitudes about holding assets of a country, the ramifications for the country's economy can be profound. In particular, political instability can lead to capital flight, which tends to increase interest rates and cause the currency to depreciate.

KEY CONCEPTS

trade policy, p. 696

capital flight, p. 699

QUESTIONS FOR REVIEW

1. Describe supply and demand in the market for loanable funds and the market for foreign currency exchange. How are these markets linked?
2. Why are budget deficits and trade deficits sometimes called the twin deficits?
3. Suppose that a textile workers' union encourages people to buy only European-made clothes. What would this policy do to the EU overall trade balance and the real exchange rate? What is the impact on the European textile industry? What is the impact on the European car industry?
4. What is capital flight? When a country experiences capital flight, what is the effect on its interest rate and exchange rate?

PROBLEMS AND APPLICATIONS

1. Japan generally runs a significant trade surplus. Do you think this is most related to high foreign demand for Japanese goods, low Japanese demand for foreign goods, a high Japanese saving rate relative to Japanese investment, or structural barriers against imports into Japan? Explain your answer.
2. An article in *The New York Times* (14 April 1995) regarding a decline in the value of the dollar reported that 'the president was clearly determined to signal that the United States remains solidly on a course of deficit reduction, which should make the dollar more attractive to investors.' Would deficit reduction in fact raise the value of the dollar? Explain.
3. Suppose that the government passes an investment tax credit, which subsidizes domestic investment. How does this policy affect national saving, domestic investment, net capital outflow, the interest rate, the exchange rate and the trade balance?
4. In the 1980s there was a rise in the US trade deficit due largely to the rise in the US budget deficit. On the other hand, some commentators in the popular press claim that the increased US trade deficit resulted from a decline in the quality of US products relative to foreign products.
   a. Assume that US products did decline in relative quality during the 1980s. How did this affect net exports *at any given exchange rate?*
   b. Use a three-panel diagram to show the effect of this shift in net exports on the US real exchange rate and trade balance.

   c. Is the claim in the popular press consistent with the model in this chapter? Does a decline in the quality of US products have any effect on standards of living for US residents? (Hint: when US residents sell goods to non-US residents, what do they receive in return?)
5. Explain in words why European *export* industries would benefit from a reduction in restrictions on *imports* into the European Union.
6. Suppose the French suddenly develop a strong taste for British wine. Answer the following questions in words and using a diagram.
   a. What happens to the demand for pounds in the market for foreign currency exchange?
   b. What happens to the value of pounds in the market for foreign currency exchange?
   c. What happens to the quantity of UK net exports?
7. Suppose your country is running a trade deficit and you hear your trade minister on the radio, saying: 'The trade deficit must be reduced, but import quotas only annoy our trading partners. If we subsidize our exports instead, we can reduce the deficit by increasing our competitiveness.' Using a three-panel diagram, show the effect of an export subsidy on net exports and the real exchange rate. Do you agree with the trade minister?
8. Suppose that real interest rates increase across Europe. Explain how this development will affect US net capital outflow. Then explain how it will affect US net exports by using a formula from the chapter and by using a diagram. What will happen to the US real interest rate and real exchange rate?
9. Suppose that Germans decide to increase their saving.
   a. If the elasticity of German net capital outflow with respect to the real interest rate is very high, will this increase in private saving have a large or small effect on German domestic investment?
   b. If the elasticity of German exports with respect to the real exchange rate is very low, will this increase in private saving have a large or small effect on the German real exchange rate?
10. Over the past decade, some of Japanese saving has been used to finance American investment. That is, the Japanese have been buying American capital assets.
   a. If the Japanese decided they no longer wanted to buy US assets, what would happen in the US market for loanable funds? In particular, what would happen to US interest rates, US saving and US investment?
   b. What would happen in the market for foreign currency exchange? In particular, what would happen to the value of the pound and the US trade balance?
11. In 1998 the Russian government defaulted on its debt payments, leading investors worldwide to raise their preference for US government bonds, which are considered very safe. What effect do you think this 'flight to safety' had on the US economy? Be sure to note the impact on national saving, domestic investment, net capital outflow, the interest rate, the exchange rate and the trade balance.
12. Suppose that US investment funds suddenly decide to invest more in the European Union.
   a. What happens to EU net capital outflow, EU saving and EU domestic investment?
   b. What is the long-run effect on the EU capital stock?
   c. How will this change in the capital stock affect the European labour market? Does this US investment in the EU make European workers better off or worse off?
   d. Do you think this will make US workers better off or worse off? Can you think of any reason why the impact on US citizens generally may be different from the impact on US workers?

For further resources, visit www.cengage.co.uk/mankiw_taylor2

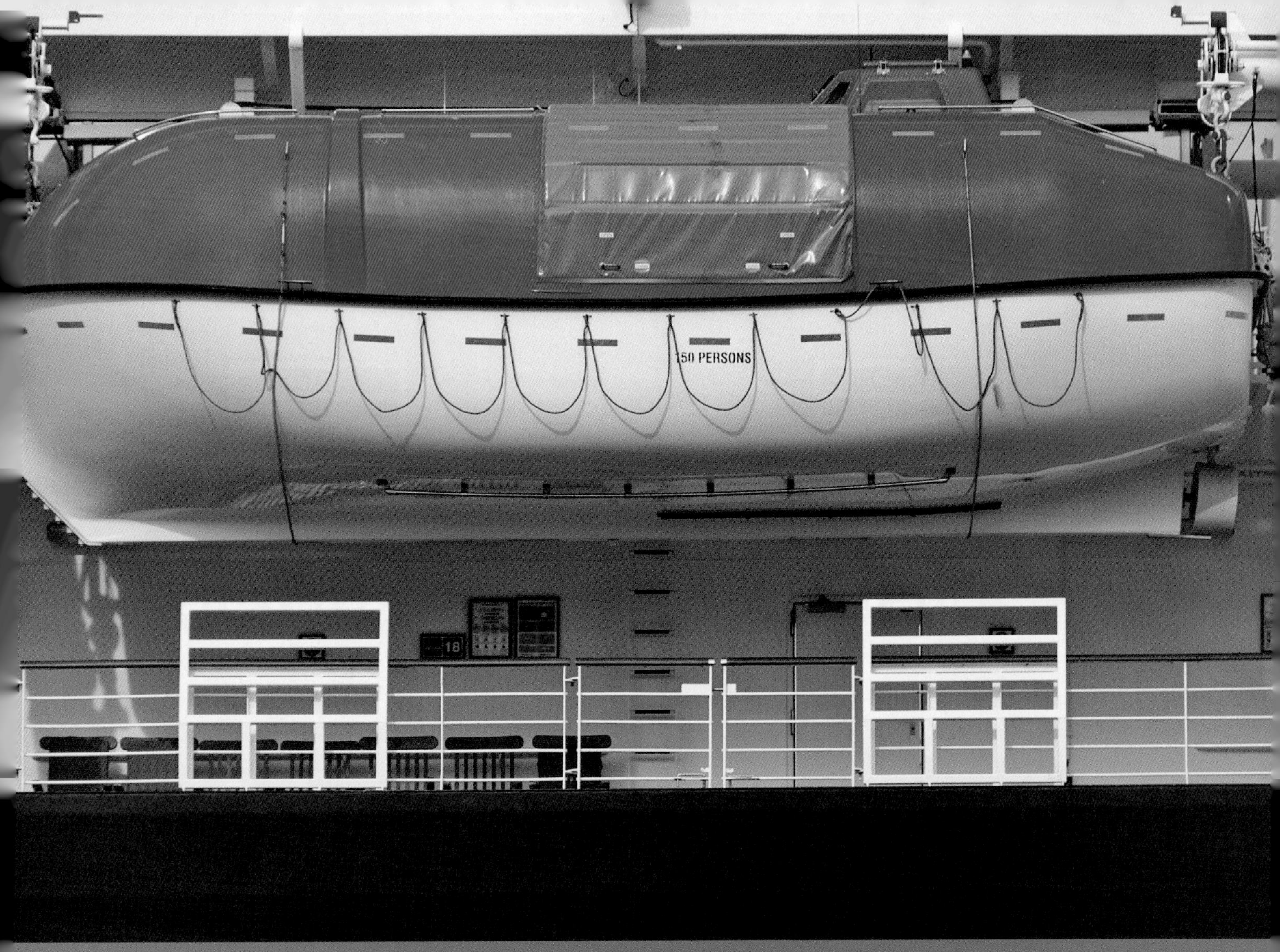

12

SHORT-RUN ECONOMIC FLUCTUATIONS

33 KEYNES AND IS-LM ANALYSIS

The next four chapters will cover different aspects of macroeconomic policy, in particular, the role of fiscal and monetary policy. The framework for analysing the effects of these two policies is developed through a series of steps leading to the model of aggregate demand and aggregate supply.

In 1936, economist John Maynard Keynes published a book entitled *The General Theory of Employment, Interest and Money*, which attempted to explain short-run economic fluctuations in general and the Great Depression in particular. Keynes' primary message was that recessions and depressions can occur because of inadequate aggregate demand for goods and services. Keynes had long been a critic of classical economic theory – the theory we examined earlier in the book – because it could explain only the long-run effects of policies. A few years before offering The General Theory, Keynes had written the following about classical economics: 'The long run is a misleading guide to current affairs. In the long run we are all dead. Economists set themselves too easy, too useless a task if in tempestuous seasons they can only tell us that when the storm is long past, the ocean will be flat.'

Keynes' message was aimed at policy makers as well as economists. As the world's economies suffered with high unemployment, Keynes advocated policies to increase aggregate demand, including government spending on public works. Keynes argued for the necessity of short-run interventions in the economy. He argued that such intervention could lead to improvements in the economy that would be beneficial rather than waiting for the long run equilibrium to establish itself – hence the famous quote about the 'long-run'.

The focus on monetary and supply-side policy as the main ways of controlling the economy in most developed countries in Europe had largely consigned Keynesian demand management to the economic history books. However, the financial crisis and subsequent recession of 2007–09 has reignited the debate about the role of Keynesian economics in macro policy. Keynes' contribution to economic thinking is widely acknowledged and it is valuable to have some insight into Keynesian economics. This chapter will begin this process.

John Maynard Keynes

THE KEYNESIAN CROSS

Classical economics placed a fundamental reliance on the efficiency of markets and the assumption that they would clear. At a macro level, this meant that if the economy was in disequilibrium and unemployment existed, wages and prices would adjust to bring the economy back into equilibrium at full employment. Full employment is defined as a point where those people who want to work at the going market wage level are able to find a job. Any unemployment that did exist would be classed as voluntary unemployment. The experience of the Great Depression of the 1930s brought the classical assumptions under closer scrutiny; the many millions suffering from unemployment could not all be volunteering to not take jobs at the going wage rates so some must, therefore, be involuntarily unemployed.

Fundamental to Keynesian analysis is the distinction between *planned* and *actual* decisions by households and firms. **Planned spending, saving or investment** refers to the desired or intended actions of firms and households. A publisher may plan to sell 100 000 copies of a textbook in the first three months of the year, an individual may plan to go on holiday to Turkey in the summer and to save up to finance the trip, a person may intend to save €1 000 over the year to pay for a wedding next year.

planned spending, saving or investment
the desired or intended actions of households and firms

actual spending, saving or investment
the realized or *ex post* outcome resulting from actions of households and firms

Actual spending, saving or investment refers to the realized, *ex post* (after the event) outcome. The publisher may only sell 80 000 copies in the first three months and so has a build-up of stock of 20 000 more than planned; the holiday-maker may fall ill and so is unable to go on holiday and so actual consumption is lower than planned (whereas actual saving is more than planned) and the plans for saving for the wedding may be compromised by the need to spend the money on repairing a house damaged by a flood.

Planned and actual outcomes might be very different as briefly outlined above. As a result Keynes argued that there was no reason why equilibrium national income would coincide with full employment output. Wages and prices might not adjust in the short run (so called sticky wages and prices, which we will revisit in Chapter 34) and so the economy could be at a position where the level of demand in the economy was insufficient to bring about full employment. The mass unemployment of the 1930s could be alleviated, he argued, by governments intervening in the economy to manage demand to achieve the desired level of employment.

It is useful at this point to refer back to the circular flow of income described in Chapter 2. Households and firms, remember, interact in the market for goods and services and in the factor market. Recall also the identity given in Chapter 31 which described how a country's gross domestic product (national income, Y) is divided among four components, i.e. consumption spending, investment spending, spending by government and net exports – the difference between the funds received from selling exports minus the expenditure on imports. Figure 33.1 summarizes this analysis.

In panels (a) and (b), the 45° line connects all points where consumption spending would be equal to national income. This line can be thought of as the equivalent of the capacity of the economy – the aggregate supply (AS) curve. The economy is in equilibrium where the $C + I + G + (X - M)$ line cuts the 45° line at Y_1 initially. In panel (a) the equilibrium is less than that required to give full

FIGURE 33.1

Deflationary and Inflationary Gaps

The 45° line shows all the points where consumption spending equals income. The vertical intercept of the expenditure line shows autonomous expenditure. The economy is in equilibrium where the expenditure line, C + I + G + (X – M), cuts the 45° line. In panel (a) this equilibrium is lower than full employment output (Y_f) at Y_1 – there is insufficient demand to maintain full employment output. The government would need to shift the expenditure line up to C + I + G + (X – M)$_1$ to eliminate the deflationary gap as shown. In panel (b) the equilibrium is higher than full employment output – the economy does not have the capacity to meet demand. In this case the government needs to shift the C + I + G + (X – M) line down to C + I + G + (X – M)$_2$ to eliminate the inflationary gap.

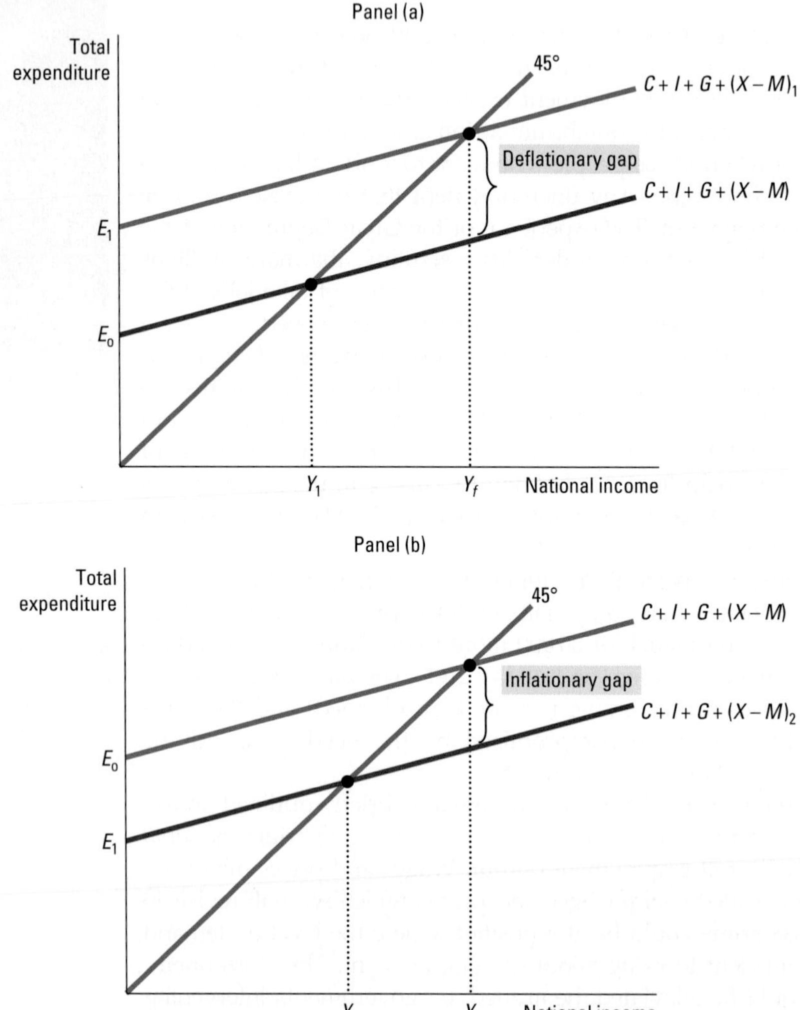

employment output (Y_f). At this equilibrium there is spare capacity in the economy and unemployment will rise. The difference between full employment output and the expenditure required to meet it is termed the *deflationary gap*. In panel (b) equilibrium is above full employment output and in this case the economy does not have the capacity to meet the demand. This will trigger inflationary pressures in the economy. The difference between full employment output and the expenditure line here is called the *inflationary gap*. To eradicate these gaps governments can influence the components of aggregate demand through both fiscal and monetary policy to bring about an equilibrium that is closer to the desired full employment output.

THE MULTIPLIER EFFECT

When a government makes a purchase, say a contract for €10 billion to build three new nuclear power generating stations, that purchase has repercussions. The immediate impact of the higher demand from the government is to raise employment and profits at the construction company (which we shall call Nucelec). Nucelec, in turn, has to buy resources from other contractors to carry out the job and so these suppliers also experience an increase in orders. Then, as the workers see higher earnings and the firm owners see higher profits, they respond to this increase in income by raising their own spending on consumer goods. As a result, the government purchase from Nucelec raises the demand for the products of many other firms in the economy. Because each euro spent by the government can raise the aggregate demand for goods and services by more than a euro, government purchases are said to have a **multiplier effect** on aggregate demand.

multiplier effect
the additional shifts in aggregate demand that result when expansionary fiscal policy increases income and thereby increases consumer spending

This multiplier effect continues even after this first round. When consumer spending rises, the firms that produce these consumer goods hire more people and experience higher profits. Higher earnings and profits stimulate consumer spending once again, and so on. Thus, there is positive feedback as higher demand leads to higher income, which in turn leads to even higher demand. Once all these effects are added together, the total impact on the quantity of goods and services demanded can be much larger than the initial impulse from higher government spending.

This multiplier effect arising from the response of consumer spending can be strengthened by the response of investment to higher levels of demand. For instance, Nucelec might respond to the higher demand for building services by buying more cranes and other mechanized building equipment. In this case, higher government demand spurs higher demand for investment goods. This positive feedback from demand to investment is sometimes called the *investment accelerator.*

CASE STUDY

The Accelerator Principle

The accelerator principle relates the *rate of change* of aggregate demand to the *rate of change* in investment. To produce goods, a firm needs equipment. Imagine that a machine is capable of producing 1 000 DVDs per week. Demand for DVDs is currently 800. A rise in demand for DVDs of up to 200 is capable of being met without any further investment in new machinery. However, if the rate of growth of demand continues to rise, it may be necessary to invest in a new machine.

Imagine that in year 1, demand for DVDs rises by 10 per cent to 880. The business can meet this demand through existing equipment. In year 2, demand increases by 20 per cent and is now 1 056. The existing capacity of the machine means that this demand cannot be met but the shortage is only 56 units so the firm decides that it might increase price rather than invest in a new machine. In year 3, demand rises by a further 25 per cent. Demand is now 1 320 but the machine is only capable of producing a maximum of 1 000 DVDs. The firm decides to invest in a new machine. The manufacturers of the new machine will therefore see a rise in their order books as a result of the increase in demand. An increase in demand of 25 per cent has led to an 'accelerated' rise in investment of 100 per cent. Investment is a component of aggregate demand and so economists are interested in the way investment adjusts to changes in demand in the economy. As this brief example shows, the relationship between an increase in demand and an increase in investment is not a simple one.

A Formula for the Spending Multiplier

A little algebra permits us to derive a formula for the size of the multiplier effect that arises from consumer spending. An important number in this formula is the *marginal propensity to consume* (*MPC*) – the fraction of extra income that a household consumes rather than saves. For example, suppose that the marginal propensity to consume is ¾. This means that for every extra pound or euro that a household earns, the household spends ¾ of it and saves ¼. The marginal propensity to save is the fraction of extra income that a household saves rather than consumes. With an *MPC* of ¾, when the workers and owners of Nucelec earn £10 billion from the government contract, they increase their consumer spending by ¾ × £10 billion, or £7.5 billion. (You should see from the above that the $MPC + MPS = 1$. The formula below can also be expressed in terms of the MPS as a result.)

To gauge the impact on aggregate demand of a change in government purchases, we follow the effects step-by-step. The process begins when the government spends £10 billion, which implies that national income (earnings and profits) also rises by this amount. This increase in income in turn raises consumer spending by $MPC \times$ £10 billion, which in turn raises the income for the workers and owners of the firms that produce the consumption goods. This second increase in income again raises consumer spending, this time by $MPC \times (MPC \times$ £10 billion). These feedback effects go on and on.

To find the total impact on the demand for goods and services, we add up all these effects:

Change in government purchases	=	£10 billion
First change in consumption	=	$MPC \times$ £10 billion
Second change in consumption	=	$MPC^2 \times$ £10 billion
Third change in consumption	=	$MPC^3 \times$ £10 billion
•		•
•		•
•		•
Total change in demand	=	$(1 + MPC + MPC^2 + MPC^3 = \ldots)$ × £10 billion

Here, '…' represents an infinite number of similar terms. Thus, we can write the multiplier as follows:

$$\text{Multiplier} = 1 + MPC + MPC^2 + MPC^3 + \ldots$$

This multiplier tells us the demand for goods and services that each pound of government purchases generates.

To simplify this equation for the multiplier, recall from your school algebra that this expression is an infinite geometric series. For x between –1 and +1:

$$1 + x + x^2 + x^3 + \ldots = 1/(1 - x)$$

In our case, $x = MPC$. Thus:

$$\text{Multiplier} = 1/(1 - MPC)$$

We have said that the $MPC + MPS = 1$ so the multiplier can also be expressed as:

$$\text{Multiplier} = 1/MPS$$

For example, if *MPC* is ¾, the multiplier is 1/(1 – ¾), which is 4. In this case, the £10 billion of government spending generates £40 billion of demand for goods and services.

This formula for the multiplier shows an important conclusion: the size of the multiplier depends on the marginal propensity to consume. While an *MPC* of ¾ leads to a multiplier of 4, an *MPC* of ½ leads to a multiplier of only 2. Thus, a larger *MPC* means a larger multiplier. To see why this is true, remember that the multiplier arises because higher income induces greater spending on consumption. The larger the *MPC* is, the greater is this induced effect on consumption, and the larger is the multiplier.

Other Applications of the Multiplier Effect

Because of the multiplier effect, a euro of government purchases can generate more than a euro of aggregate demand. The logic of the multiplier effect, however, is not restricted to changes in government purchases. Instead, it applies to any event that alters spending on any component of GDP – consumption, investment, government purchases or net exports.

For example, suppose that a recession overseas reduces the demand for German net exports by €1 billion. This reduced spending on German goods and services depresses German national income, which reduces spending by German consumers. If the marginal propensity to consume is ¾ and the multiplier is 4, then the €1 billion fall in net exports means a €4 billion contraction in aggregate demand.

As another example, suppose that a stock market boom increases households' wealth and stimulates their spending on goods and services by €2 billion. This extra consumer spending increases national income, which in turn generates even more consumer spending. If the marginal propensity to consume is ¾ and the multiplier is 4, then the initial impulse of €2 billion in consumer spending translates into an €8 billion increase in aggregate demand.

The multiplier is an important concept in macroeconomics because it shows how the economy can amplify the impact of changes in spending. A small initial change in consumption, investment, government purchases or net exports can end up having a large effect on aggregate demand and, therefore, on the economy's production of goods and services.

Another important concept in this analysis is that of **autonomous expenditure** – spending which does not depend on income – government spending being a key element of this expenditure. The amount spent in each successive 'round' of spending is termed *induced expenditure.* The multiplier showed how the eventual change in income would be determined by the size of the marginal propensity to consume (MPC) and the marginal propensity to save (MPS) – the proportion of an extra €1 spent or saved by consumers. The higher the MPC the greater the multiplier effect.

autonomous expenditure spending which is not dependent on income

However, in an open economy with government, any extra €1 is not simply either spent or saved, some of the extra income may be spent on imported goods and services or go to the government in taxation. These are all classed as withdrawals from the circular flow of income. Withdrawals (*W*) from the circular flow are classed as endogenous as they are directly related to changes in income. There are also injections to the circular flow of income. Governments receive tax revenue but use it to spend on the goods and services they provide for citizens, firms earn

IN THE NEWS

Tax Changes and Marginal Propensities

Changes in tax have different effects depending on a variety of factors. One of the important factors is the marginal propensity to consume (MPC) and its converse, the marginal propensity to save (MPS). Reductions in income tax rates or personal allowances that put more money into people's pockets are likely to lead to an increase in consumption with a resulting effect on aggregate demand. The problem for policy makers is estimating the MPC and MPS in judging the extent of the impact on aggregate demand, as these two related stories highlight.

In September 2008, 22 million UK taxpayers looked forward to receiving an extra £60 in their pay packet and a further £10 per month for the remainder of the financial year, making earners a total of £120 better off. The tax rebate came following the furore over the abolition of the 10p tax band by Gordon Brown in his last Budget as Chancellor before becoming Prime Minister. The next Chancellor, Alistair Darling, was forced into the rebate after it was accepted that low paid workers might be affected adversely by the move to abolish the 10p rate. The total impact of the rebate was to inject around £2.7 billion into the economy over the fiscal year.

Earlier in 2008, the US federal government organized a cash giveaway totalling $150 billion in an effort to inject some life into the economy. This was to be done by sending US citizens cheques of up to $1 200 per household. US citizens earning at least $3 000 but less than $75 000 a year received the cheques and children got $300. The aim was to put money in the hands of 'those who will spend it immediately' and thus help to provide a boost to consumption to offset the effects of the economic slowdown.

In both cases it might be expected that there would be an injection into the economy and a rise in aggregate demand through increased consumer spending. The size of the effect, however, depended upon what households chose to do with the rebate. Some would spend the money and some would save it. The marginal propensity to consume (MPC) measures the proportion of every extra £1 or $1 that is spent by consumers. If the MPC was 0.8 then for every extra £1 or $1 received 80p or 80 cents would be spent and the remainder saved. If this was the case then the effect on consumption in the UK could be expected to be an initial £2.16 billion (i.e. 0.8 times £2.7 billion) and in the US, $120 billion (or 0.8 times $150 billion).

However, if people received the extra money but decided to save a higher proportion of it then the effect on consumption would be much less and thus the effect on aggregate demand would be lower. If the MPC was jus 0.4 then the impact in the UK would only be £1.08 billion and in the US, $60 billion. The size of MPC is therefore a crucial factor to take into consideration with any fiscal stimulus – regardless of why that stimulus came about.

Different income groups also tend to have different MPCs; those on lower incomes tend to have higher MPCs and so it may not simply be a case of creating a fiscal stimulus; who that stimulus is aimed at might be an important consideration for policy makers. In a period of economic downturn it might be expected that people would be only too willing to spend any extra income they received but this may not always be the case. People may use the 'windfall' to pay off debt or save the money for unforeseen events – not unreasonable in an unstable economic climate. But of course if the MPS is high, the MPC must be low. There was some evidence in the United States that the MPS was relatively high, so the impact on the economy in terms of the fiscal boost was less than that for which the federal government might have hoped. The UK rebate was not strictly part of government plans to kick-start the economy, but it would have had some sort of impact and the Treasury would have looked at the size of the effect with interest.

revenue from selling goods abroad (exports) and firms, as we have seen, use savings as a source of funds to borrow for investment. Injections into the circular flow are exogenous – they are not related to the level of output or income – and are investment (I), government spending (G) and export earnings (X).

The slope of the expenditure line, therefore, will be dependent on how much of each extra €1 is withdrawn. There will be a marginal propensity to taxation (*MPT*), a marginal propensity to import (*MPM*) in addition to the *MPS*. Collectively these are referred to as the *marginal propensity to withdraw (MPW)*. The multiplier (*k*) would be expressed as:

$$k = \frac{1}{MPS + MPT + MPM}$$

Or:

$$k = \frac{1}{MPW}$$

The *MPW* will reduce the value of the multiplier and thus the impact on national income. In equilibrium, planned withdrawals would equal planned injections:

$$\text{Planned S} + \text{T} + \text{M} = \text{Planned I} + \text{G} + \text{X}$$

At this point all the output being produced by the economy would be 'bought' by households and firms. However, if actual withdrawals are greater than planned injections then the economy would be experiencing a deficiency in demand. For example, assume that equilibrium output is €100 billion. Planned withdrawals amount to €60 billion. If this planned withdrawal level is not 'bought' by governments, firms and foreigners (i.e. planned injections) then firms will build up stocks and plan to cut back on output in the next period. This leads to a fall in income and as withdrawals are endogenous, planned withdrawals for the next period will fall. The process will continue until planned withdrawals equal planned injections once again and the economy is in equilibrium.

In situations where the economy is experiencing such demand deficiency, the government can budget for a deficit (i.e., spend more than it receives in tax revenue by borrowing or cutting taxes) to boost spending in the economy. It could also influence monetary policy to cut the cost of borrowing and so boost investment; there may also have been an incentive to find ways of boosting exports or cutting imports through imposing various trade barriers and offering export subsidies. However, the emphasis was primarily on fiscal policy which was something that the government could have a direct influence over and whose effect was more immediate. The multiplier process meant that the increase in government spending did not need to be as high as the size of the inflationary or deflationary gap. The steeper the slope of the expenditure line the greater the size of the multiplier, as shown in Figure 33.2.

The Keynesian cross as it is known, gives us a picture of the economy in short run equilibrium. (Note, if you access a copy of Keynes' *General Theory* you might be surprised to see a complete absence of Keynesian cross diagrams. The use of these diagrams to explain Keynesian ideas were developed by later economists to help portray Keynes' ideas.) In equilibrium, planned expenditure (*E*), ($C + I + G + (X - M)$ equals actual income (GDP or national income (*Y*)), ($E = Y$). This equilibrium is referred to as equilibrium in the goods market. We have also seen, in Chapter 24, how equilibrium in the money market is given by the intersection of the demand for money and the supply of **real money balances**. The goods market and the money market are both interrelated with the linking factor being the interest rate. Following Keynes' analysis of the goods market and the money market (via the liquidity preference theory which we will look at in more detail in Chapter 35), Nobel Prize winning economist John Hicks developed a theory that described the links between the two and showed how changes in both fiscal and monetary policy could be analysed. The framework for this analysis is known as the IS-LM model.

real money balances
what money can actually buy given the ratio of the money supply to the price level M/P

FIGURE 33.2

The Slope of the Expenditure Line and Changes in Autonomous Expenditure

Panel (a) shows a relatively shallow expenditure line which would mean that the marginal propensity to withdraw would be high and the value of the multiplier was relatively low. The impact on national income (ΔY) of a change in government spending (ΔG) would be more limited in comparison to the effect as shown in panel (b) where the expenditure line is much steeper reflecting a higher value of the multiplier where the MPW was relatively low. In this case it takes a smaller rise in government spending to achieve the same increase in national income.

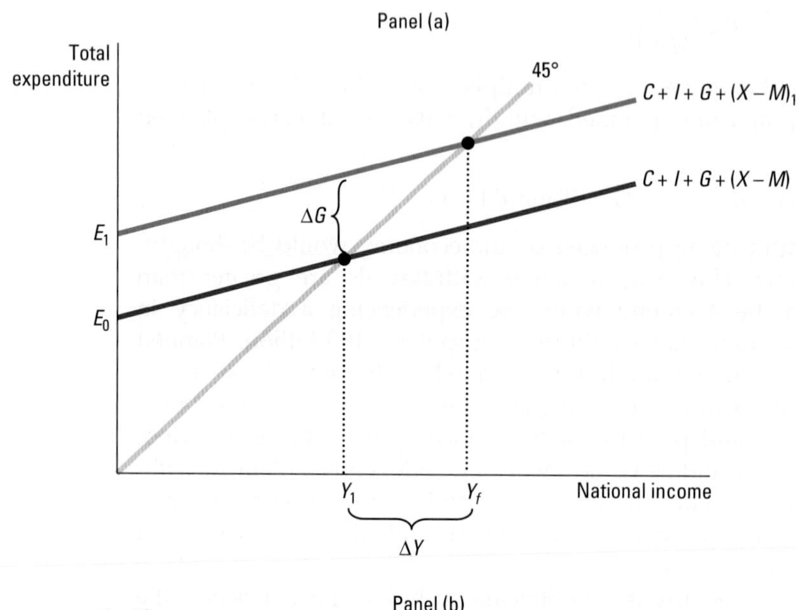

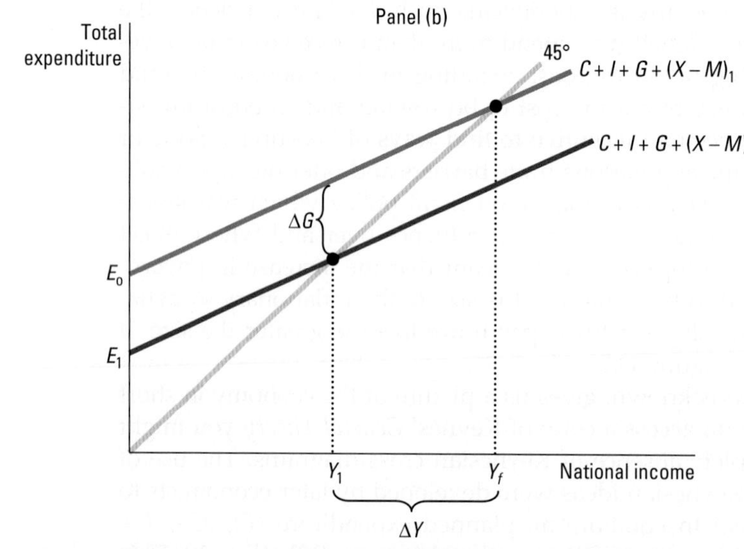

THE IS AND LM CURVES

IS-LM describes equilibrium in two markets and together determines *general equilibrium* in the economy. General equilibrium in the economy occurs at the point where the goods market and money market are both in equilibrium at a particular interest rate and level of income. The remainder of this chapter will provide an introduction to the IS-LM model. The model forms the basis of many intermediate courses in macroeconomics although some have argued that it is now outdated and fails to represent how the modern economy works. We will look at an alternative representation of the model that seeks to take into account such objections.

Regardless of the view about the model, it does represent a useful way of understanding how the goods and money markets interact and as an exercise in analytical thinking is helpful in seeing the effects of monetary and fiscal policy on the macroeconomy.

IS stands for Investment and Saving; LM stands for Liquidity and Money. The thing linking these two markets is the rate of interest (i). The IS curve shows the relationship between the interest rate and level of income (Y) in the goods market. In Figure 33.3, panel (a) shows the Keynesian cross diagram from Figure 33.2 with equilibrium point a where the expenditure line $C + I + G + (X - M)$ crosses the 45° line. Panel (b) shows the IS curve. On the vertical axis is the rate of interest and on the horizontal axis is output (national income). The equilibrium point in panel (a) is associated with a rate of interest i_1. This is plotted as point a on panel (b). If interest rates fall then the expenditure line shifts upwards to the left and there will be a new equilibrium point b where the expenditure line $C + I + G + (X - M)_1$ crosses the 45° line. This is plotted on panel (b) showing the equilibrium of the goods market at a lower interest rate associated with a higher level of national income. If we connect these two points we get the IS curve. The curve connects all possible points of equilibrium in the goods market associated with a particular interest rate and level of national income.

The IS curve shows an inverse relationship between the interest rate and output – a fall in interest rates leads to a rise in income and vice versa. The rise in income will be dependent on the size of the interest rate change and the size of the multiplier. The slope of the IS curve is determined by the responsiveness of consumption and investment ($C + I$) to changes in interest rates. This is important because it leads to different outcomes; where economists tend to disagree is the *extent* to which $C + I$ are responsive to changes in interest rates rather than any disagreement about the fundamental relationship. The more responsive $C + I$ are, the flatter the IS curve. Shifts in the IS curve come about as a result of changes in autonomous expenditure. If, for example, government spending rises this occurs independent of any change in interest rates. A rise in autonomous spending would be associated with a shift in the IS curve to the right – the prevailing interest rate would now be associated with a higher level of income. Equally, if autonomous spending fell then the IS curve would shift to the left showing a lower level of income at the prevailing interest rate.

The LM curve shows all points where the money market is in equilibrium given a combination of the rate of interest and national income. In Figure 33.4, panel (a) shows the money market with the demand for money inversely related to the interest rate. The money supply is shown as a vertical line and it is assumed that the money supply is fixed by the central bank. Equilibrium in the money market is where the demand for money D_m intersects the money supply curve, M_s at interest rate i_1 and a quantity of real money balances (M). This equilibrium point a is plotted on the LM curve as shown. Increases in income will have an effect on the demand for money and assuming the money supply is fixed, will affect the equilibrium interest rate. Assume that national income rises; the demand for money curve in panel (a) would shift to the right to D_{m1} indicating that the public wish to hold higher money balances at all interest rates. At the prevailing interest rate the demand for money is now higher than the supply of money and so the interest rate would rise. The new equilibrium in the money market b is plotted on the LM diagram, If we connect the two points we get the LM curve. The LM curve plots all combinations of interest rates and national income where the money market is in equilibrium.

The LM curve has a positive slope showing that an increase in income is associated with an increase in the interest rate and vice versa. The slope of the LM

FIGURE 33.3

The IS Curve

The IS curve is derived from the Keynesian cross diagram and shows all possible points of equilibrium in the goods market associated with a particular interest rate and level of income. In panel (a) initial equilibrium is where the C + I + G + (X – M) *line crosses the 45° line at point a. This point is plotted on the IS curve as point a. An increase in* C + I + G + (X – M) *to* C + I + G + (X – M)$_1$ *shows a new equilibrium point in the goods market, b, which is plotted on the IS curve. These two points are connected to form the IS curve.*

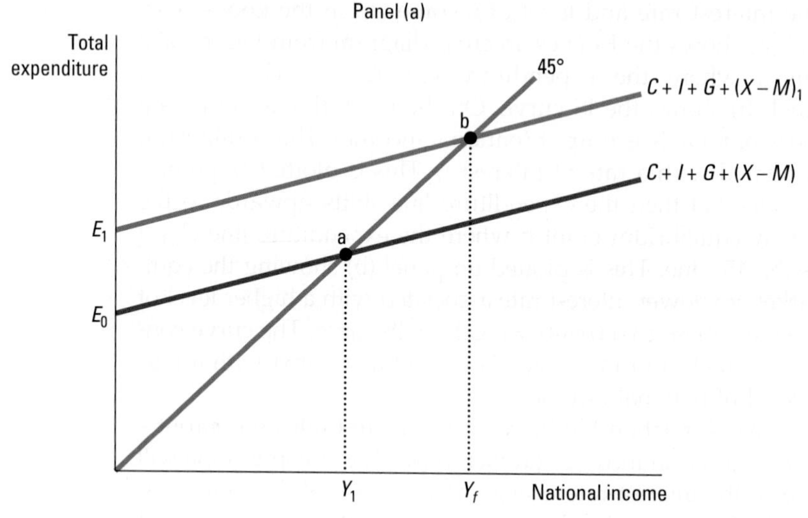

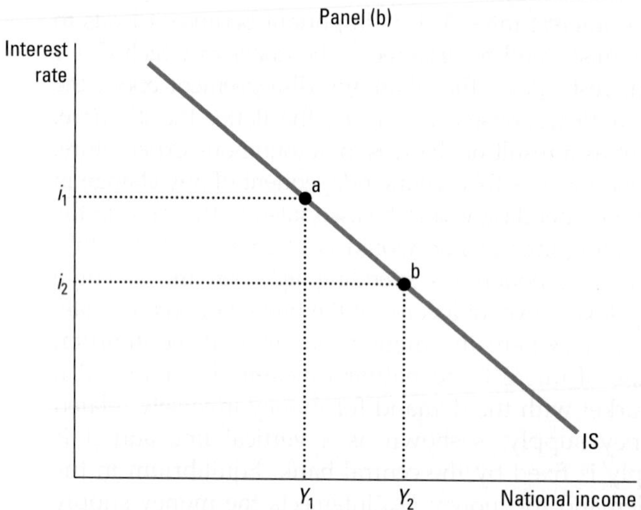

curve will be dependent on the responsiveness of the demand for money to changes in interest rates. Again, the extent of this relationship is often a point of disagreement amongst economists. The LM curve can shift if the central bank expands or contracts the money supply (we will say more about how this might happen later in the chapter). Assuming income is held constant, a rise in the money supply (say) will cause interest rates to fall and a new equilibrium will be reached at a given level of income. This would be associated with a shift of the LM curve downwards to the right showing a new combination of income and interest rate at which the money market is in equilibrium.

FIGURE 33.4

The LM Curve

The LM curve shows all points where the money market is in equilibrium given a combination of the rate of interest and national income. In panel (a), the money market is in equilibrium where the demand for money (D_m) equals the supply of money (MS) at point a. This point is plotted on the LM curve in panel (b). An increase in the demand for money causes a shift of the curve to the right to D_{m1} with a new equilibrium point of b. This is plotted on panel (b) and the points connected to form the LM curve.

Panel (a)

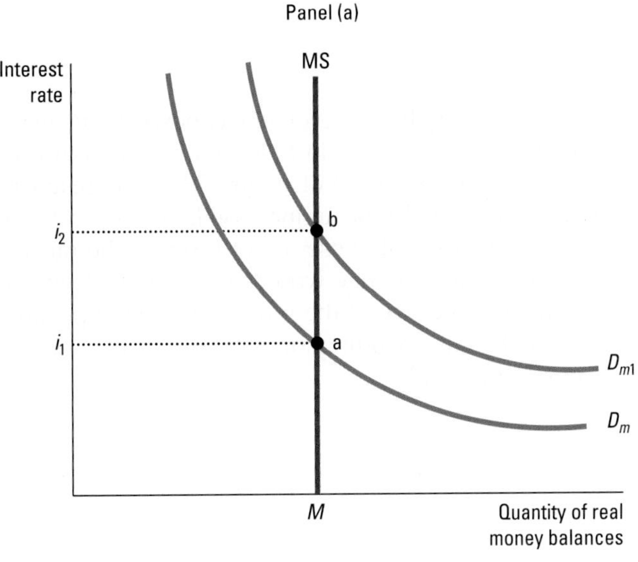

Panel (b)

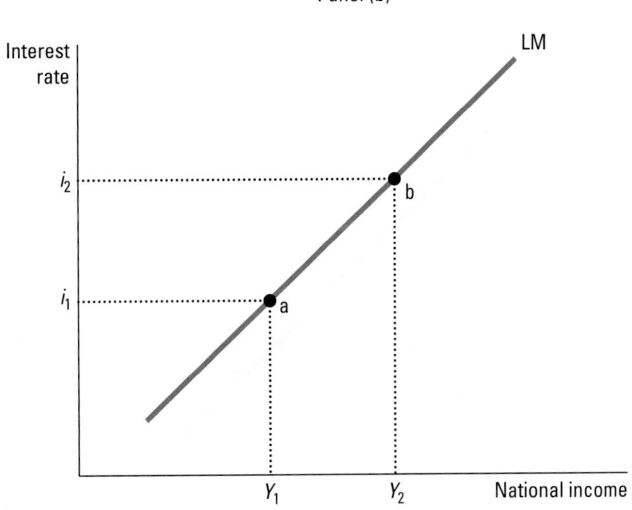

GENERAL EQUILIBRIUM USING THE IS-LM MODEL

Equilibrium is found where the IS curve intersects the LM curve. Remember that any point on either curve describes a point of equilibrium in the goods market and the money market at a rate of interest and level of national income. In Figure 33.5, the point where the IS curve intersects the LM curve gives a point where both markets are in equilibrium at an interest rate i_e and a level of national income Y_e.

Hence, it follows that at this point planned expenditure equals actual expenditure ($E = Y$), and the demand for money = supply of money ($D_m = S_m$).

Having established this general equilibrium, we can use the model to analyse the impact of fiscal and monetary policy changes in an attempt to stabilize the economy and how these two policies are interrelated. Further analysis of both policies will be covered in the next chapter but this uses our model of IS-LM. The detail of IS-LM analysis is beyond the scope of this book, being found in most intermediate courses in macroeconomics. However, the remainder of this chapter will introduce some of the key implications of the model.

Fiscal Policy

Assume that the government chooses to increase spending to boost economic activity. This increase in autonomous expenditure shifts the IS curve to the right as shown in panel (a) of Figure 33.6. The result is that national income will rise but there will also be an increase in interest rates. A similar outcome would occur if the government chose to cut taxes as the means of boosting the economy. The result of either policy would be dependent on the marginal propensity to withdraw and the size of the multiplier. The opposite would occur if the government chose to cut spending or increase taxes – national income and interest rates would both fall.

FIGURE 33.5

General Equilibrium

Equilibrium in the economy is found where the IS curve intersects with the LM curve. At this point the both the goods market and the money market are in equilibrium at a particular interest rate (i_e) and level of national income (Y_e).

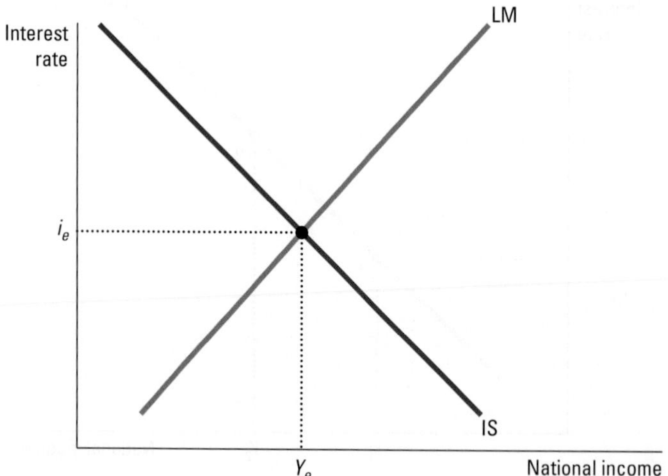

Monetary Policy

If the central bank decided to expand the money supply the LM curve would shift to the right to LM_1 as shown in Panel (b) of Figure 33.6. The new equilibrium would lead to a lower interest rate and a higher level of national income. The reverse outcome would occur if the central bank tightened monetary policy by reducing the money supply.

FIGURE 33.6

The Effects of Fiscal and Monetary Policy

In panel (a) a rise in government spending shifts the IS curve to the right resulting in a new equilibrium with a higher interest rate and level of national income. In panel (b) an increase in the money supply would shift the LM curve to the right and a new equilibrium would result in a lower interest rate and higher level of national income.

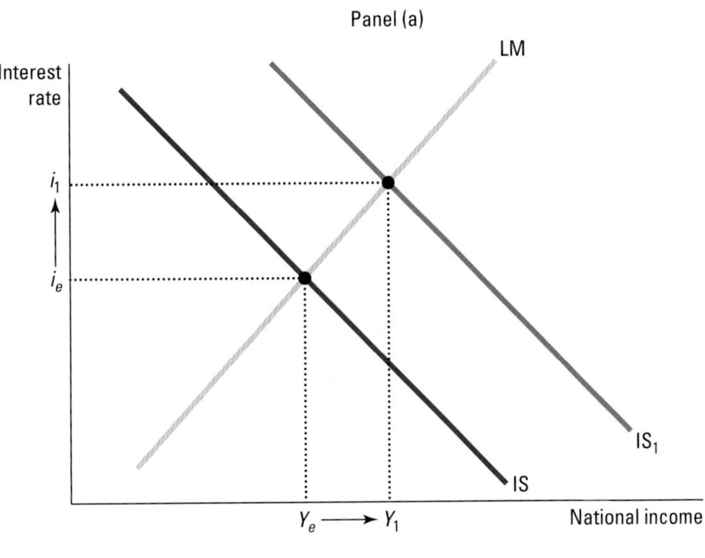

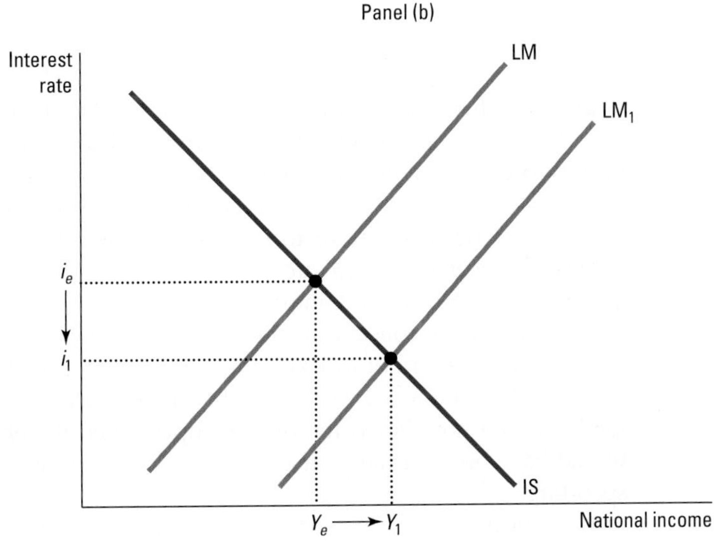

In reality, central banks do not act totally in isolation of government even if they are independent. Central banks will be aware of what governments are doing as outlined in the section, The Case for an Active Stabilization Policy in Chapter 35. This presents a model to analyse the response of the central bank. The Bank of England, European Central Bank and the Federal Reserve have a responsibility to maintain price stability and this may be presented in the form of a target for inflation. Central banks will be monitoring the effect of fiscal policy changes on the economy and how these changes might affect inflationary pressures. These inflationary pressures can be influenced by the central bank's control over short-term interest rates through the rate at which it lends to the

FIGURE 33.7

Maintaining Interest Rates Constant Following a Rise in the IS Curve

A shift in the IS curve to the right would, without central bank action, lead to a rise in the interest rate and in national income. If the central bank wants to maintain the interest rate it must increase the money supply and shift the LM curve to the right. The result would be to maintain the interest rate at i_e *but the increase in national income would be greater than if the central bank had not acted.*

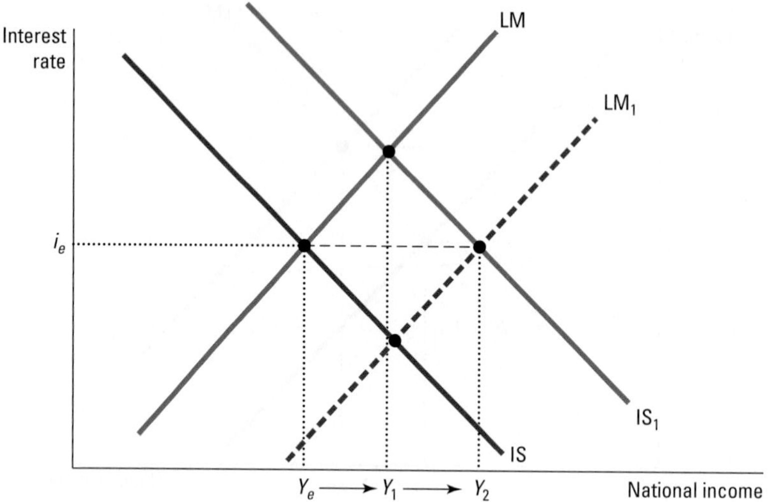

financial system. Governments may wish to implement fiscal policy with the aim of influencing unemployment, for example. The policy may have effects on inflationary pressures which the central bank wants to nullify.

Let us assume that the government reduces taxation to encourage more people to take jobs in the economy or to increase spending through consumers having more disposable income. The IS curve would shift to the right as shown in Figure 33.7 and national income and interest rates would rise. If the central bank wants to keep interest rates constant it must expand the money supply. By doing so the LM curve shifts to the right to LM_1, national income would rise further than if the central bank had not acted to Y_2 and the interest rate will remain at its initial level. If the bank had not altered the money supply then the effects of the reduction in tax would have been partially offset by a rise in interest rates which would have curbed spending.

If government had increased taxes then the IS curve would shift to the left and both national income and interest rates would fall. If the central bank wants to keep interest rates constant it must reduce the money supply and the result would be that the fall in national income would be compounded. If the central bank wanted to avoid this outcome then it could expand the money supply and interest rates would fall. This would help to offset the shift in the IS curve and reduce the impact on national income.

FROM IS-LM TO AGGREGATE DEMAND

It is a short step from using this model to the aggregate demand and aggregate supply model that we will use to analyse changes in the economy later in the book. Remember that the supply of real money balances is what money can actually buy given by M, the money supply divided by P, the price level (M/P). A higher price level causes a fall in the supply of real money balances which in turn shifts the LM curve to the left. The result is that interest rates rise and national income falls. The aggregate demand curve plots the relationship between national income and the price level. If we assume the price level remains constant, a change in national income in the IS-LM model will result in a shift in the aggregate demand curve.

This short analysis of changes in fiscal and monetary policy helps to highlight a number of important issues that you may start to consider as your study of economics moves to the next level. The effects of changes in fiscal and monetary policy are dependent on a number of factors related to the slope of the IS and LM curves, their relative position and how far each shifts in response to changes in policy. It is entirely possible that a change in fiscal policy can be countered by a change in monetary policy that leaves national income unchanged. The potential outcomes are many and economists try to pinpoint more accurately what changes will mean for the economy as a whole of any such changes. This means conducting research to quantify such changes. The outcome of such research will be dependent on the value of variables that economists input into their models and as has already been stated, most economists agree on the fundamentals of the model but disagree on the relative strength of factors affecting the variables in the model.

One example of how the model has developed is the role which microeconomic analysis plays in understanding the macroeconomy. Some economists argue that micro principles cannot be divorced from the macroeconomy. We saw in Chapter 3 how changing economic conditions may lead to wages and prices adjusting at different rates and slowly as a result. If national income falls, for example, then the assumption might be that prices and wages in the economy would also fall to help bring markets back into equilibrium. As we will see in the next chapter, changes in wages and prices (sticky wages and prices theory) may lag behind the reduction in economic activity as firms may be forced into trying to maintain cash flow rather than seeking to expand market share. As prices are sticky, sales fall and firms cut back output which further impacts on economic activity. Price stickiness seemed to be counter to the prevailing assumption about rational behaviour. Professor Mankiw was one of the economists who helped to reconcile the idea of sticky prices and menu costs with rational behaviour in his paper 'Small menu costs and large business cycles: A macroeconomic model of monopoly' published in 1985. The debate over IS-LM has continued and has generated large amounts of valuable and interesting research which has helped build our understanding of the economy as a whole. It still has its critics, however.

Indeed, one such disagreement focuses on a central assumption of the model itself. Some higher education institutions have questioned the value of teaching IS-LM at all because they argue that the world is now a very different place to the one Hicks knew back in the 1930s when he first developed Keynes' ideas. One of the major criticisms is that central banks no longer control the money supply but instead set interest rates. Setting interest rates is seen as leading to more stable economic conditions than policies targeting the money supply. Chapter 36 will highlight how government attempts to control the money supply in the UK in the 1980s were largely unsuccessful. Targeting the interest rate is seen as being easier.

However, it is also important to have a basic understanding of how central bank operations work when setting interest rates. You may read in the newspapers or see on TV an announcement that the ECB or the Bank of England has increased or cut interest rates and it may be tempting to think that the central bank simply tells the financial system that they will have to pay more or less to borrow funds. The reality is that an announcement about changes in interest rates is matched by instructions to the central bank's bond traders to conduct open-market operations to bring about the desired interest rate announced. If interest rates are reduced, the central bank's traders will be instructed to buy bonds. Banks and financial institutions who sell these bonds will receive funds in return which will effectively expand the money supply. This in turn shifts the LM curve to the right and so interest rates fall. If the central bank increases interest rates the opposite occurs; traders will be instructed to sell bonds and thus take funds out of the banking system, reducing the money supply. The LM curve shifts to the left and interest rates rise.

One of Professor Mankiw's close colleagues, David Romer (indeed they are more than simply colleagues given that each was best man at the other's wedding) has suggested an approach termed the IS-MP model which attempts to build on the IS-LM model to reflect how central banks and the economy work today. The assumption in the model is that central banks adjust the money supply as outlined above to generate the interest rate that they want. The interest rate is adjusted in accordance with the inflation target that the central bank is working with or, as is the case with the Bank of England, has been set by the government. In the IS-LM model the money supply is assumed to be exogenous (determined by factors outside the model). In the IS-MP model, the monetary policy reaction function is exogenous. Romer assumes that when output rises, the central bank increases interest rates to dampen inflationary pressures and reduces interest rates when output falls to maintain the price level at its target. National income is a positive function of the interest rate, therefore. Romer plots this upward sloping relationship as the MP curve. The MP function is assumed to be exogenous but in reality both the money supply and the MP function can and do change in response to economic activity and events.

The MP function, therefore, takes into account the fact that central banks now target inflation and set interest rates to achieve this goal rather than simply assuming government (or a central bank) sets the money supply and that interest rates adjust to balance this supply of money with the demand for money. Crucially, Romer suggests that changes in inflation can cause a shift of the MP curve. If the central bank increases interest rates the money supply will fall which will affect the price level and expectations on inflation. Equally if the central bank cuts interest rates the money supply will rise and expectations on inflation will also change as a result. It is at this point where the micro element of the analysis takes on some importance. Expectations of price changes may not match the reality because of the extent of price stickiness. If we assume that prices are completely sticky (i.e. the price level is fixed) it will not change when the money supply changes. Expectations on inflation will, therefore, be zero. If the money supply rises then the supply of real money balances (defined by M/P) also rises and is greater than the demand for real money balances. As the money market is now out of equilibrium we might expect the interest rate to fall but it could also be that the level of income could rise or a combination of the two might occur. There will be a movement along the IS curve and a fall in interest rates will be accompanied by a rise in national income. This implies that the central bank can directly control the real interest rate by adjusting money supply appropriately to achieve the interest rate it desires.

If prices adjusted instantaneously then a change in the money supply would not affect the supply of real money balances because the ratio M/P would hold as before at the rate of interest and level of income; in other words the money market would remain in equilibrium. There would be no movement along the IS curve and the central bank would not be able to affect the real interest rate.

In reality prices are not fixed but the speed with which prices adjust to changes in economic conditions will vary – some will adjust relatively quickly, others will take much longer and will be sticky. These sticky prices will influence the ratio of the money supply to the price level (the supply of real money balances) and so there may be some expectations of inflation which will exist in the economy because M will rise by a greater proportion than P. An increase in the money supply will raise expected inflation and vice versa. If prices are sticky then an increase in the nominal money supply will cause the money market to move out of equilibrium but expected inflation will affect the real interest rate. The nominal interest rate may have to be higher as a result.

The extent to which prices are sticky, therefore, has an important influence on the way in which a central bank can influence the interest rate to achieve its inflation targets. Such an analysis raises interesting questions when interest rates are reduced as was the case in response to the financial crisis and the global recession in 2008–09. We have noted how the UK, Europe and the US saw their central banks reducing interest rates to historically low levels. To reduce interest rates the central bank instructs its traders to buy bonds and the money supply will rise. Increases in the money supply may be associated with an increase in the price level as noted in Principle 9 of the *Ten Principles of Economics*. In times where economic activity is restrained, expectations of inflation may remain subdued and the money market may remain out of equilibrium as a result. The reason is that at these low interest rates people are willing to hold a greater amount of real money balances without any change in interest rate or output – after all the interest rate cannot fall much further. This is the *liquidity trap* which is outlined in the In the News article in Chapter 34 and which may imply that monetary policy can have little effect on stimulating economic growth.

Quick Quiz Draw diagrams to show the effect on interest rates and the level of national income of: (a) a decision by the government to raise taxes to cut a public deficit and (b) a decision by a central bank to increase interest rates.

CONCLUSION

There is still much debate on the value and relevance of the IS-LM model. What is not in much doubt is that an understanding of the relationship between the goods market and the money market is a useful way of developing a broader understanding of analysing the economy as a whole. This short introduction to such analysis provides some pointers to the IS-LM model and to some of the issues that economists are debating. Depending on the university that you attend, a greater or lesser emphasis may be placed on the IS-LM model. Having some awareness of the model does help to develop a focus on the important connections between the money supply, interest rates and economic activity.

SUMMARY

- Keynes developed *The General Theory* as a response to the mass unemployment which existed in the 1930s.
- He advocated governments intervene to boost demand through influencing aggregate demand.
- The Keynesian cross diagram shows how the economy can be in equilibrium when $E = Y$.
- This equilibrium may not be sufficient to deliver full employment output and so the government can attempt to boost demand to help achieve full employment.
- John Hicks developed Keynes' ideas in the form of the IS-LM model which shows general equilibrium in the economy.

- The IS (investment–saving) curve shows all points of equilibrium in the goods market at a particular interest rate and level of national income.
- The LM (liquidity–money supply) curve shows points where the money market is in equilibrium at particular rates of interest and level of national income.
- General equilibrium occurs where the IS curve intersects the LM curve. At this interest rate and level of national income both the goods market and money market are in equilibrium.
- Fiscal policy and monetary policy can cause shifts in the IS and LM curves bringing about new equilibrium positions. The outcome will depend on a variety of factors including the response of consumption and investment to changes in interest rates and the public's response to holding monetary balances as a result of a change in interest rates.
- There have been criticisms that the IS-LM model does not represent the way monetary policy is conducted in modern economies.
- Economists have developed new models to incorporate the changes in policy.

KEY CONCEPTS

Planned spending, saving or investment, p. 707
Actual spending, saving or investment, p. 707
multiplier effect, p. 709
autonomous expenditure, p. 711
real money balances, p. 713

QUESTIONS FOR REVIEW

1. Distinguish between planned expenditure and actual expenditure.
2. Draw a Keynesian cross diagram to show the effects of a rise in autonomous expenditure on an economy operating below full employment output.
3. Explain how the marginal propensity to withdraw affects the outcome of a rise in autonomous expenditure.
4. Use diagrams to describe how the IS and LM curves are derived.
5. Using the IS-LM model, explain the effect on the economy of a reduction in autonomous expenditure resulting from a cut in public spending by the government.
6. A central bank wishes to reduce inflationary expectations by increasing interest rates. Use the IS-MP model to analyse the effect on the economy of such a move.

PROBLEMS AND APPLICATIONS

1. What, according to Keynes, was the main reason why recessions and depressions occurred? As a result of identifying this key reason, what did Keynes suggest was an appropriate policy repose?
2. Distinguish between planned spending and actual spending.
3. Explain, using an appropriate diagram, how a deflationary gap can occur and how this gap can be eliminated.
4. Suppose economists observe that an increase in government spending of €10 billion raises the total demand for goods and services by €30 billion.

a. If these economists ignore the possibility of crowding out, what would they estimate the marginal propensity to consume (*MPC*) to be?
b. Now suppose the economists allow for crowding out. Would their new estimate of the *MPC* be larger or smaller than their initial one? Explain your answer.

5. Suppose the government reduces taxes by €2 billion, that there is no crowding out, and that the marginal propensity to consume is 0.75.
   a. What is the initial effect of the tax reduction on aggregate demand?
   b. What additional effects follow this initial effect? What is the total effect of the tax cut on aggregate demand?
   c. How does the total effect of this €2 billion tax cut compare to the total effect of a €2 billion increase in government purchases? Why?
6. Assume the economy is in equilibrium. Analyse the effect of a cut in autonomous expenditure on economic activity and the level of unemployment. You should use a diagram to help illustrate your answer.
7. What does the IS curve show? What does the LM curve show?
8. What determines the slope of the IS curve? What determines the slope of the LM curve? In relation to your answer to these questions, explain why these determinants can be a source of disagreement amongst economists?
9. Explain the principle of general equilibrium.
10. Use IS-LM analysis to explain the following:
    a. The government institutes significant cuts in public expenditure.
    b. The central bank institutes an asset purchasing facility which expands the money supply by €300 billion.
    c. The central bank fears that inflationary pressures are rising and increases interest rates.
    d. The government increases taxation to try and reduce a large budget deficit.
11. Explain how the aggregate demand curve is derived from the IS-LM model.
12. Assume that a period of deflation leads to a rise in the supply of real money balances. Explain the effect of this change on the economy using the IS-LM model and then what effect it would have on aggregate demand and why.
13. What is the main difference between the IS-LM model and David Romer's IS-MP model? Do you think that Romer's model is more representative of the way modern economies operate? Explain.
14. Do you think that Keynes' ideas still have some relevance today? Explain.

For further resources, visit www.cengage.co.uk/mankiw_taylor2

34 AGGREGATE DEMAND AND AGGREGATE SUPPLY

economic activity the amount of buying and selling (transactions) that take place in an economy over a period of time

recession a period of declining real incomes and rising unemployment. The technical definition gives recession occurring after two successive quarters of negative economic growth

depression a severe recession

Economic activity fluctuates from year to year. In most years, the production of goods and services rises. Because of increases in the labour force, increases in the capital stock and advances in technological knowledge, the economy can produce more and more over time. This growth allows everyone to enjoy a higher standard of living. On average over the past 50 years, the production of the UK economy as measured by real GDP has grown by about 2 per cent per year.

In some years, however, this normal growth does not occur. Firms find themselves unable to sell all of the goods and services they have to offer, so they cut back on production. Workers are laid off, unemployment rises and factories are left idle. With the economy producing fewer goods and services, real GDP and other measures of income fall. Such a period of falling incomes and rising unemployment is called a **recession** if it is relatively mild and a **depression** if it is more severe.

What causes short-run fluctuations in economic activity? What, if anything, can public policy do to prevent periods of falling incomes and rising unemployment? When recessions and depressions occur, how can policy makers reduce their length and severity? These are the questions that we take up now.

The variables that we study are largely those we have already seen in previous chapters. They include GDP, unemployment and the price level. Also familiar are the policy instruments of government spending, taxes, and the money supply and interest rates. What differs from our earlier analysis is the time horizon. So far, our focus has been on the behaviour of the economy in the long run.

Our focus now is on the economy's short-run fluctuations around its long-run trend.

Although there remains some debate among economists about how to analyse short-run fluctuations, most economists use the *model of aggregate demand and aggregate supply.* Learning how to use this model for analysing the short-run effects of various events and policies is the primary task ahead. This chapter introduces the model's two key elements – the aggregate demand curve and the aggregate supply curve. But before turning to the model, let's look at the facts.

THREE KEY FACTS ABOUT ECONOMIC FLUCTUATIONS

Short-run fluctuations in economic activity occur in all countries and in all times throughout history. As a starting point for understanding these year-to-year fluctuations, let's discuss some of their most important properties.

Fact 1: Economic Fluctuations are Irregular and Unpredictable

Fluctuations in the economy are often called *the business cycle.* As this term suggests, economic fluctuations correspond to changes in business conditions. When real GDP grows rapidly, business is good. During such periods of economic expansion, firms find that customers are plentiful and that profits are growing. On the other hand, when real GDP falls during recessions, businesses have trouble. During such periods of economic contraction, many firms experience declining sales and dwindling profits.

The term *business cycle* is somewhat misleading, however, because it seems to suggest that economic fluctuations follow a regular, predictable pattern. In fact, economic fluctuations are not at all regular, and they are almost impossible to predict with much accuracy. Panel (a) of Figure 34.1 shows the real GDP of the UK economy since 1971. Whilst this seems to show GDP rising fairly steadily over the period (apart from the latter part of 2008) if we looked in more detail at the figures on a quarter-by-quarter basis we would be able to see that the path of GDP is not always smooth. If we define a recession as occurring when real GDP falls for two successive quarters, then a study of GDP data reveals five recessions over this whole period: one from late 1973 until mid-1974, one from mid-1975 until the end of 1975, one from the beginning of 1980 until mid-1981, one from about the third quarter of 1990 until the end of 1991 and, finally, the end of 2008 into 2009. Sometimes the recessions are close together, as in the 1970s. Sometimes the economy goes many years without a recession. From the end of 1991 to 2008, the UK economy had not suffered a recession at all.

Fact 2: Most Macroeconomic Quantities Fluctuate Together

Real GDP is the variable that is most commonly used to monitor short-run changes in the economy because it is the most comprehensive measure of economic activity. Real GDP measures the value of all final goods and services produced within a given period of time. It also measures the total income (adjusted for inflation) of everyone in the economy.

FIGURE 34.1

A Look at Short-run Economic Fluctuations

This figure shows real GDP in panel (a), investment spending in panel (b) and the unemployment rate in panel (c) for the UK economy since 1971. Notice that real GDP and investment spending tend to rise and fall together, while unemployment goes in the opposite direction.

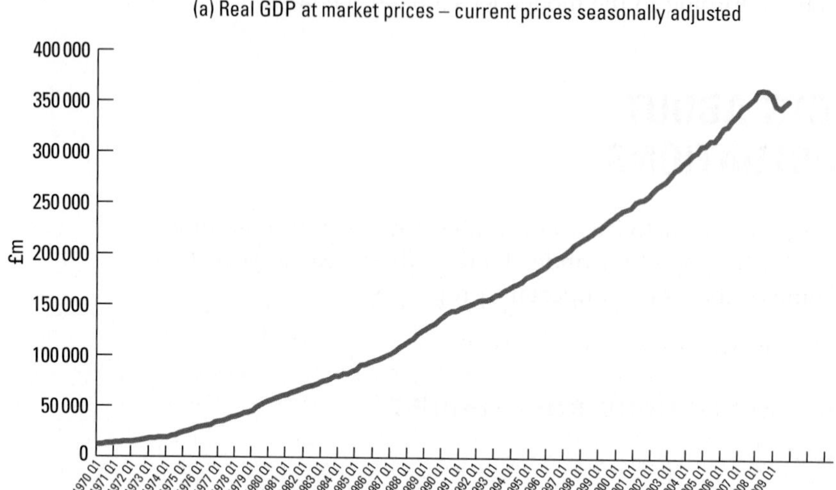

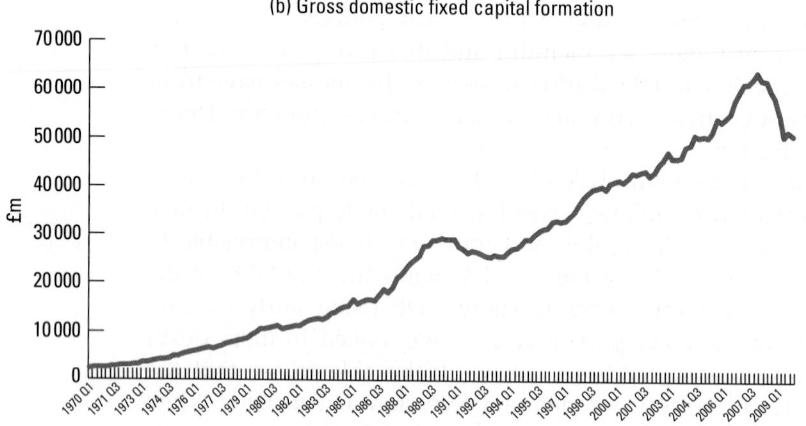

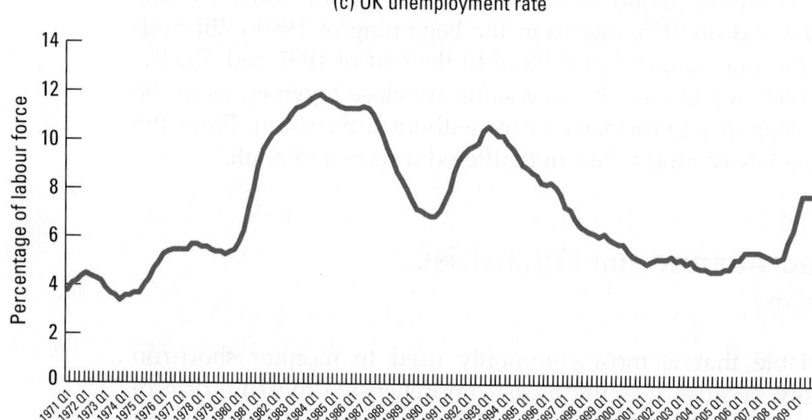

Source: UK Office for National Statistics.

It turns out, however, that for monitoring short-run fluctuations, it does not really matter which measure of economic activity one looks at. Most macroeconomic variables that measure some type of income, spending or production fluctuate closely together. When real GDP falls in a recession, so do personal income, corporate profits, consumer spending, investment spending, industrial production, retail sales, home sales, auto sales and so on. Because recessions are economy-wide phenomena, they show up in many sources of macroeconomic data.

CASE STUDY

The Business Cycle: Not What it Seems?

Finn E. Kydland and Edward C. Prescott won the Nobel Prize for Economics in 2004. Kydland and Prescott's work centred on the debate surrounding the changes in economic activity over a period of time. Traditional economics and business textbooks refer to 'business cycles' and imply that the behaviour of economies follows some sort of pattern in which real growth fluctuates around its trend. The trend in this instance can be regarded as the expected rate of growth in economic activity over a period of time regardless of any interference from government or outside agencies. Thus, in theory, if the economy were just allowed to go its own way, there would be a gradual upward trend. This can also be thought of as potential growth or the potential capacity (aggregate supply (AS)) of the economy.

Kydland and Prescott refer to the work of Robert Solow, himself a Nobel Prize winner in Economics, who developed a theory of economic growth that has come to be used widely in relation to developing countries. This theory suggested that real output per worker and the stock of real capital grow at a mainly constant rate, that the capital to output ratio has no systematic trend and profit in relation to capital has a broadly horizontal trend.

The question they were interested in was not measuring business cycles but focusing on the *pattern of* output and employment around the trend and asking why this seemed to happen in a repeated fashion over time. Many textbooks explain the business cycle in terms of four phases. The term 'cycle' implies a 'what goes around comes around' type of approach to an economy. Such a view of cycles implies an almost inevitable trend where growth turns into boom, which in turn leads to the start of decline that leads to recession before the process begins again. However, Kydland and Prescott do not see cycles in this way. Instead they prefer to use a generally agreed scientific definition of 'cycles' that makes reference to a point of departure – in this case the trend of economic growth. Kydland and Prescott refer to these recurrent departures as 'deviations'.

They argue that business cycles must be seen as periodic deviations from trend growth and that we cannot view business cycles as inevitable or evolutionary. As such the explanation for a downturn in economic activity cannot, in itself, be found in the reasons why growth occurred in the first place. Equally, the seeds of an expansion in growth are not to be found in a recession.

In analysing the behaviour of these deviations from trend they sought to challenge a number of economic myths that had grown up around business cycles. For example, in times of economic downturn the expectation would be that the price level would fall and in times of strong economic growth it would be anticipated that prices would rise. This relationship is referred to as *'procyclical'*. In a downturn, the theory would suggest that firms will seek to reduce prices to encourage sales and are prevented from increasing prices to improve margins because of the lack of demand. Similarly, in times of economic growth, firms experience rising demand and possibly wage and other costs. They are able to increase prices to improve margins without too much damage to business because of the strong growth in demand.

Kydland and Prescott argued that in fact, price showed a counter-cyclical behaviour – when economic growth slowed down, prices rose and when economic growth was strong, prices fell. They further argued that there are other myths surrounding business cycles. These include the idea that real wages fall as growth increases and vice versa (or are not related to the business cycle) and that the money supply was an important factor in leading economic growth.

Price procyclicality is important because if we are looking for the causes of changes in economic activity as a whole, we would presume to be looking for something fairly major as being the cause – large price rises, for example, or shocks caused by changes in things like the money supply. If price procyclicality is a myth then research into the causes of changes in cycles might be misguided. Think of it in terms of a thermometer in a room. The thermometer tells us what the temperature of the room is but is not a cause of the temperature. Looking at the properties of the thermometer to explain the temperature of the room would lead us down the wrong path.

Kydland and Prescott argue that an important factor in explaining business cycles is the decisions people make about how they devote their time between leisure (non-market activities) and income-earning activities. After analysing the factors that may influence business cycles they come to the following conclusions:

- Aggregate hours worked (a measure of labour input) is strongly correlated with changes in GNP. The problem with this is that the contributions to GNP for all workers are considered the same. Kydland and Prescott point out that the contribution by the hours worked by a brain surgeon is not the same as that of a porter in a hospital. With some consideration of this, Kydland and Prescott conclude that real wages are more procyclical and something which traditional literature on business cycles would not suggest.
- The capital stock is largely unrelated to real GNP but is closely correlated if a time lag of about one year is included.
- With regard to the factors affecting aggregate demand – consumption, investment and government spending – Kydland and Prescott report that consumption and investment are highly procyclical whereas government spending does not seem to be correlated with growth.
- They also comment that imports are procyclical as are exports but with a six-month to a year time lag.
- Labour and capital income is strongly procyclical.
- They find no evidence that narrow money (M1) leads the business cycle. In other words they do not find evidence that a rise in M1 will lead to a spurt in growth.
- Credit arrangements are likely to play a significant role in future analysis of business cycle theory.
- The price level is counter-cyclical.

Kydland and Prescott's work has important implications for economic research in that it challenges the traditional method of analysing economic data. They are suggesting that in order to look at what might be happening in economics it might be necessary to look at factors other than those that simply describe the data.

This emphasis on the quantitative features rather than qualitative features (what it tells us rather than what we think it might signify) has been a feature of a re-assessment of statistical analysis in economics particularly the analysis of time series data. What do long-term time series tell us in relation to short-term series?

Their work led to the development of the *rational expectations school* of thought. This school believes that individuals will react to changes in economic policy that might affect the success of that policy. For example, if individuals believe that the government, for example, is intending to restrict the rate of growth of wages in the public sector as a means of putting pressure on private sector pay to be curbed, they may adapt their behaviour to reduce spending in anticipation of that fact that their incomes will not rise as much as they might have hoped. This will therefore have an impact on the economy as a whole different to that which the government might have hoped from the policy.

The notion of 'real business cycles' therefore does not view a recession as a 'failure' in the economy nor might a boom also be seen as a failure. How many times do we see politicians complaining about the 'bad old days of boom and bust'? Kydland and Prescott see business cycles as explanations of shock to the economy that are understandable reactions rather than failures.

Their work tends to dismiss the 'sticky prices' explanation for a slowdown in growth, it also might reject the mismatch between investment and consumption and the monetarist argument of market failure in price signals. Instead they look at real shocks to the economy and the adjustment process to those shocks, which could last for some time after the shock. Essentially, Kydland and Prescott argued that business cycles could occur perfectly naturally within a competitive environment despite the implication in traditional theory that perfect competition would not result in long periods of unemployment, for example.

Kydland and Prescott's work has been criticized by other economists and the global recession of 2008–2009 has led to a reassessment of thinking about recessions, business cycles and ways of dealing with these economic problems. This serves to remind us that there is still much to learn and understand about the way the economy works and this case study presents just one interpretation in the evolution of thinking about economics.

Source: Adapted from http://www.bized.co.uk/learn/economics/nobel/2004.htm

MORRIS

"I've learnt not to worry."

IN THE NEWS

'Bad Times, Good Times'

When the economy goes into a recession economic variables such as employment, inflation and economic growth also fall. Most of these falls are regarded as 'bad' news but there might also be some good news associated with recession.

In the first edition of this book, an In the News article looked at how the US recession in 2001 led to a reduction in the amount of garbage being discarded by residents in Chicago. The article showed how during periods of growth increases in the amount of household refuse disposed of rose by between 2 per cent and 10 per cent across 23 north-western suburbs but dropped 6 per cent as the economy started to slow down. Has this trend been repeated in the most recent recession of 2008–09?

It seems as though it has. Reports from Long Island in New York suggest that residential and commercial refuse was 17 per cent lower in January 2009 than during the same period in 2008 and that waste from construction and demolition was down by over two-fifths. In the north-western state of Oregon officials from the Department of Environmental Quality reported that per capita refuse levels fell by 9 per cent in 2008. This figure was the highest since statistics began in the region in 1992. Officials in Oregon also recorded a fall in construction-related debris similar to the experience of the Long Island case.

The reason for the fall in the amount of refuse generated has been put down to the fact that residents are spending less and thus generating less refuse. In good times, consumers may purchase new furniture and white goods, which each generate significant amounts of packaging, in addition to the amount of food that they buy. During times of economic slowdown. Spending on goods which have a relatively high income elasticity of demand tends to fall, resulting in a reduction in associated waste. The recession of 2008–09 was rooted in the collapse of the housing market and this was the main cause of the fall in construction waste. If houses and office blocks are not being built in the volumes that had been the case then the amount of waste will consequently be less.

The global decline in economic activity led to a fall in industrial output. This in turn led to a fall in carbon dioxide (CO_2) emissions. In September 2009, the International Energy Agency prepared an interim report ahead of the publication of the *World Energy Outlook* in November 2009 which suggested that CO_2 emissions had fallen between 2008 and 2009 further than in any year since 1969. One of the main reasons given by the IEA was the fall in output as well as the postponement or abandonment of plans by some countries to build coal-fired power stations, which also contribute to carbon emissions.

Although many macroeconomic variables fluctuate together, they fluctuate by different amounts. In particular, as panel (b) of Figure 34.1 shows, investment spending varies greatly over the business cycle. Even though investment averages about one-seventh of GDP, declines in investment account for about two-thirds of the declines in GDP during recessions. In other words, when economic conditions deteriorate, much of the decline is attributable to reductions in spending on new factories, housing and inventories.

Fact 3: As Output Falls, Unemployment Rises Changes in the economy's output of goods and services are strongly correlated with changes in the economy's utilization of its labour force. In other words, when real GDP declines the rate of unemployment rises. This fact is hardly surprising: when firms choose to produce a smaller quantity of goods and services, they lay off workers, expanding the pool of unemployed. However, there is generally a time-lag between any downturn in economic activity and a rise in unemployment and vice versa. Even when positive growth resumes, therefore, unemployment is likely to continue to rise for some time afterwards. Unemployment is referred to as a 'lagged indicator'

Panel (c) of Figure 34.1 shows the unemployment rate in the UK economy since 1971. The figure shows clearly the impact of recessions on unemployment. In each of the recessions, the unemployment rate rises substantially.

Quick Quiz List and discuss three key facts about economic fluctuations.

EXPLAINING SHORT-RUN ECONOMIC FLUCTUATIONS

Describing the patterns that economies experience as they fluctuate over time is easy. Explaining what causes these fluctuations is more difficult. Indeed, compared to the topics we have studied in previous chapters, the theory of economic fluctuations remains controversial. In this chapter and the next two chapters, we develop the model that most economists use to explain short-run fluctuations in economic activity.

How the Short Run Differs from the Long Run

In previous chapters we developed theories to explain what determines most important macroeconomic variables in the long run. Chapter 25 explained the level and growth of productivity and real GDP. Chapters 26 and 27 explained how the financial system works and how the real interest rate adjusts to balance saving and investment. Chapter 28 explained why there is always some unemployment in the economy. Chapters 29 and 30 explained the monetary system and how changes in the money supply affect the price level, the inflation rate and the nominal interest rate. Chapters 31 and 32 extended this analysis to open economies in order to explain the trade balance and the exchange rate.

All of this previous analysis was based on two related ideas – the classical dichotomy and monetary neutrality. Recall that the classical dichotomy is the separation of variables into real variables (those that measure quantities or relative prices) and nominal variables (those measured in terms of money). According to classical macroeconomic theory, changes in the money supply affect nominal variables but not real variables. As a result of this monetary neutrality, Chapters 25 through 28 were able to examine the determinants of real variables (real GDP, the real interest rate and unemployment) without introducing nominal variables (the money supply and the price level).

Do these assumptions of classical macroeconomic theory apply to the world in which we live? The answer to this question is of central importance to understanding how the economy works: most economists believe that classical theory describes the world in the long run but not in the short run. Beyond a period of several years, changes in the money supply affect prices and other nominal variables but do not affect real GDP, unemployment or other real variables. When studying year-to-year changes in the economy, however, the assumption of monetary neutrality is no longer appropriate. Most economists believe that, in the short run, real and nominal variables are highly intertwined. In particular, changes in the money supply can temporarily push output away from its long-run trend.

To understand the economy in the short run, therefore, we need a new model. To build this new model, we rely on many of the tools we have developed in previous chapters, but we have to abandon the classical dichotomy and the neutrality of money.

The Basic Model of Economic Fluctuations

Our model of short-run economic fluctuations focuses on the behaviour of two variables. The first variable is the economy's output of goods and services, as measured by real GDP. The second variable is the overall price level, as measured by the CPI or the GDP deflator. Notice that output is a real variable, whereas the price level is a nominal variable. Hence, by focusing on the relationship between these two variables, we are highlighting the breakdown of the classical dichotomy.

We analyse fluctuations in the economy as a whole with the **model of aggregate demand and aggregate supply**, which is illustrated in Figure 34.2. On the vertical axis is the overall price level in the economy. On the horizontal axis is the overall quantity of goods and services. The **aggregate demand curve** shows the quantity of goods and services that households, firms and the government want to buy at each price level. The **aggregate supply curve** shows the quantity of goods and services that firms produce and sell at each price level. According to this model, the price level and the quantity of output adjust to bring aggregate demand and aggregate supply into balance.

It may be tempting to view the model of aggregate demand and aggregate supply as nothing more than a large version of the model of market demand

model of aggregate demand and aggregate supply
the model that most economists use to explain short-run fluctuations in economic activity around its long-run trend

aggregate demand curve
a curve that shows the quantity of goods and services that households, firms and the government want to buy at each price level

aggregate supply curve
a curve that shows the quantity of goods and services that firms choose to produce and sell at each price level

FIGURE 34.2

Aggregate Demand and Aggregate Supply

Economists use the model of aggregate demand and aggregate supply to analyse economic fluctuations. On the vertical axis is the overall level of prices. On the horizontal axis is the economy's total output of goods and services. Output and the price level adjust to the point at which the aggregate supply and aggregate demand curves intersect.

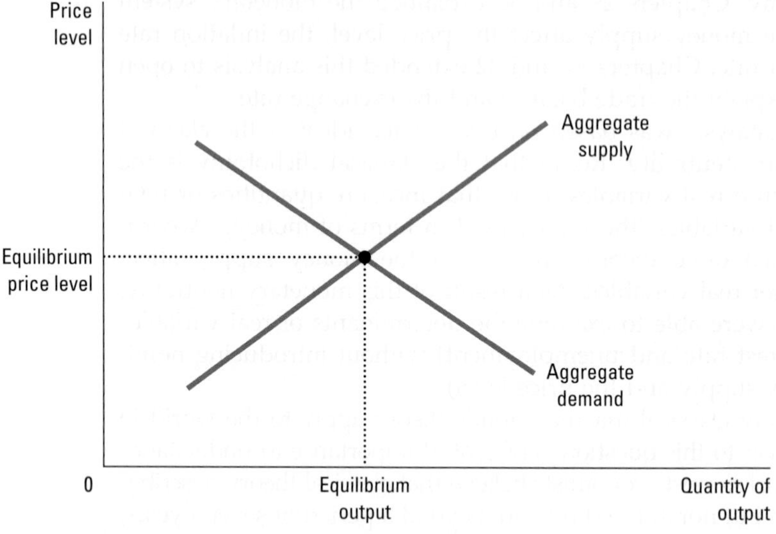

and market supply, which we introduced in Chapter 4. Yet in fact this model is quite different. When we consider demand and supply in a particular market – ice cream, for instance – the behaviour of buyers and sellers depends on the ability of resources to move from one market to another. When the price of ice cream rises, the quantity demanded falls because buyers will use their incomes to buy products other than ice cream. Similarly, a higher price of ice cream raises the quantity supplied because firms that produce ice cream can increase production by hiring workers away from other parts of the economy. This *microeconomic* substitution from one market to another is impossible when we are analysing the economy as a whole. After all, the quantity that our model is trying to explain – real GDP – measures the total quantity produced in all of the economy's markets. To understand why the aggregate demand curve is downward sloping and why the aggregate supply curve is upward sloping, we need a *macroeconomic* theory. Developing such a theory is our next task.

Quick Quiz How does the economy's behaviour in the short run differ from its behaviour in the long run? • Draw the model of aggregate demand and aggregate supply. What variables are on the two axes?

THE AGGREGATE DEMAND CURVE

The aggregate demand curve tells us the quantity of all goods and services demanded in the economy at any given price level. As Figure 34.3 illustrates, the aggregate demand curve is downward sloping. This means that, other things equal, a fall in the economy's overall level of prices (from, say, P_1 to P_2) tends to raise the quantity of goods and services demanded (from Y_1 to Y_2).

FIGURE 34.3

The Aggregate Demand Curve

A fall in the price level from P_1 to P_2 increases the quantity of goods and services demanded from Y_1 to Y_2. There are three reasons for this negative relationship. As the price level falls, real wealth rises, interest rates fall and the exchange rate depreciates. These effects stimulate spending on consumption, investment and net exports. Increased spending on these components of output means a larger quantity of goods and services demanded.

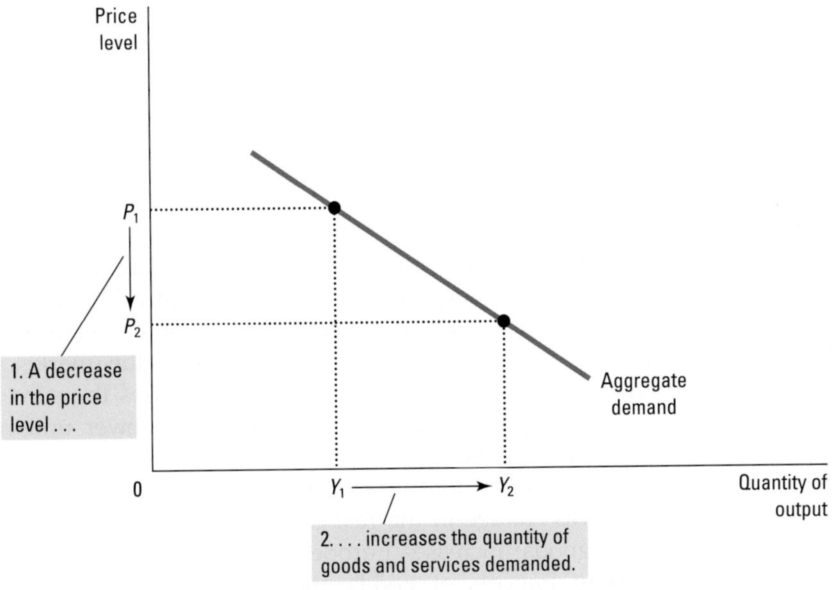

Why the Aggregate Demand Curve Slopes Downward

Why does a fall in the price level raise the quantity of goods and services demanded? To answer this question, it is useful to recall that GDP (which we denote as *Y*) is the sum of consumption (*C*), investment (*I*), government purchases (*G*) and net exports (*NX*):

$$Y = C + I + G + NX$$

Each of these four components contributes to the aggregate demand for goods and services. For now, we assume that government spending is fixed by policy. The other three components of spending – consumption, investment and net exports – depend on economic conditions and, in particular, on the price level. To understand the downward slope of the aggregate demand curve, therefore, we must examine how the price level affects the quantity of goods and services demanded for consumption, investment and net exports.

The Price Level and Consumption: The Wealth Effect Consider the money that you hold in your wallet and your bank account. The nominal value of this money is fixed, but its real value is not. When prices fall, this money is more valuable because then it can be used to buy more goods and services. Thus, a decrease in the price level makes consumers wealthier, which in turn encourages them to spend more. The increase in consumer spending means a larger quantity of goods and services demanded.

The Price Level and Investment: The Interest Rate Effect As we discussed in Chapter 30, the price level is one determinant of the quantity of money demanded. The lower the price level, the less money households need to hold to buy the goods and services they want. When the price level falls, therefore, households try to reduce their holdings of money by lending some of it out. For instance, a household might use its excess money to buy interest-bearing bonds. Or it might deposit its excess money in an interest-bearing savings account, and the bank would use these funds to make more loans. In either case, as households try to convert some of their money into interest-bearing assets, they drive down interest rates. (See Chapter 26, Figure 26.2.) Lower interest rates, in turn, encourage borrowing by firms that want to invest in new factories and equipment and by households who want to invest in new housing. Thus, a lower price level reduces the interest rate, encourages greater spending on investment goods, and thereby increases the quantity of goods and services demanded.

The Price Level and Net Exports: The Exchange Rate Effect As we have just discussed, a lower price level lowers the interest rate. In response, some investors will seek higher returns by investing abroad. For instance, as the interest rate on European government bonds falls, an investment fund might sell European government bonds in order to buy US government bonds. As the investment fund tries to convert its euros into dollars in order to buy the US bonds, it increases the supply of euros in the market for foreign currency exchange. The increased supply of euros causes the euro to depreciate relative to other currencies. Because each euro buys fewer units of foreign currencies, non-European goods (i.e. imports) become more expensive to European residents but exporters find that foreign buyers get more euros for each unit of their currency. This change in the real exchange rate (the relative price of domestic and foreign goods) increases European exports of goods and services and decreases European imports of goods and services. Net exports, which equal exports minus imports, also increase. Thus, when a fall in the European price level causes European interest rates to fall, the real value of the euro falls, and this depreciation stimulates European net exports and thereby increases the quantity of goods and services demanded in the European economy.

Summary There are, therefore, three distinct but related reasons why a fall in the price level increases the quantity of goods and services demanded: (1) Consumers are wealthier, which stimulates the demand for consumption goods. (2) Interest rates fall, which stimulates the demand for investment goods. (3) The exchange rate depreciates, which stimulates the demand for net exports. For all three reasons, the aggregate demand curve slopes downward.

It is important to keep in mind that the aggregate demand curve (like all demand curves) is drawn holding 'other things equal'. In particular, our three explanations of the downward sloping aggregate demand curve assume that the money supply is fixed. That is, we have been considering how a change in the price level affects the demand for goods and services, holding the amount of money in the economy constant. As we will see, a change in the quantity of money shifts the aggregate demand curve. At this point, just keep in mind that the aggregate demand curve is drawn for a given quantity of money.

Why the Aggregate Demand Curve Might Shift

The downward slope of the aggregate demand curve shows that a fall in the price level raises the overall quantity of goods and services demanded. Many other factors, however, affect the quantity of goods and services demanded at a given price level. When one of these other factors changes, the aggregate demand curve shifts.

Let's consider some examples of events that shift aggregate demand. We can categorize them according to which component of spending is most directly affected.

Shifts Arising from Consumption Suppose people suddenly become more concerned about saving for retirement and, as a result, reduce their current consumption. Because the quantity of goods and services demanded at any price level is lower, the aggregate demand curve shifts to the left. Conversely, imagine that a stock market boom makes people wealthier and less concerned about saving. The resulting increase in consumer spending means a greater quantity of goods and services demanded at any given price level, so the aggregate demand curve shifts to the right.

Thus, any event that changes how much people want to consume at a given price level shifts the aggregate demand curve. One policy variable that has this effect is the level of taxation. When the government cuts taxes, it encourages people to spend more, so the aggregate demand curve shifts to the right. When the government raises taxes, people cut back on their spending and the aggregate demand curve shifts to the left.

Shifts Arising from Investment Any event that changes how much firms want to invest at a given price level also shifts the aggregate demand curve. For instance, imagine that the computer industry introduces a faster line of computers, and many firms decide to invest in new computer systems. Because the quantity of goods and services demanded at any price level is higher, the aggregate demand curve shifts to the right. Conversely, if firms become pessimistic about future business conditions, they may cut back on investment spending, shifting the aggregate demand curve to the left.

Tax policy can also influence aggregate demand through investment. As we saw in Chapter 26, an investment tax credit (a tax rebate tied to a firm's investment spending) increases the quantity of investment goods that firms demand at any given interest rate. It therefore shifts the aggregate demand curve to the right. The repeal of an investment tax credit reduces investment and shifts the aggregate demand curve to the left.

Another policy variable that can influence investment and aggregate demand is the money supply. As we discuss more fully in the next chapter, an increase in the money supply lowers the interest rate in the short run. This makes borrowing less costly, which stimulates investment spending and thereby shifts the aggregate demand curve to the right. Conversely, a decrease in the money supply raises the interest rate, discourages investment spending, and thereby shifts the aggregate demand curve to the left. Many economists believe that changes in monetary policy have been an important source of shifts in aggregate demand in most developed economies at some points in their history.

CASE STUDY

Value-added Tax and Consumption

In the Pre-Budget Report in November 2008, the UK Chancellor of the Exchequer announced a decision to cut the rate of value-added tax (VAT) from 17.5 per cent to 15 per cent from 1 December 2008. It was initially met with some scepticism by commentators. The idea was that the cut, which lasted until January 2010, would boost spending and help to get the economy moving again. The question was always how far the cut would go in persuading people to spend money and thus help to shift the aggregate demand curve to the right. Lower priced items would not benefit from much of a change in price – assuming that retailers passed on the cut to customers – and for higher priced goods, would the cut in price be sufficient to tempt consumers to part with their money at a time when confidence was low?

A report by the Centre for Economics and Business Research (CEBR) suggests that the cut had some effect. The CEBR reported in April 2009 that there had been a noticeable effect on consumer spending since the cut. It estimated that the reduction resulted in around £2.1 billion worth of extra sales, and that the effect had been 'immediate'. It derived this figure from looking at annual retail sales growth which rose by 1.6 per cent in November to 2.6 per cent in December and 3.2 per cent in January, before slowing slightly to 3 per cent in February. It further suggested that retail sales would be £8–9 billion higher for the year than they would have been without the cut.

In June 2010, the new UK government announced that VAT would be increased to 20 per cent from 17.5 per cent in January 2011. The increase was designed to help boost tax revenue to help counter a rising budget deficit. Critics of this move argued that such a rise would stifle the fragile economic recovery but there was some expectation that sales would see a boost in the run up to the increase.

Source: Adapted from http://www.bized.co.uk/cgi-bin/chron/chron.pl?id=3337

Shifts Arising from Government Purchases The most direct way that policy makers shift the aggregate demand curve is through government purchases. For example, suppose the government decides to reduce purchases of new weapons systems. Because the quantity of goods and services demanded at any price level is lower, the aggregate demand curve shifts to the left. Conversely, if the government starts building more motorways, the result is a greater quantity of goods and services demanded at any price level, so the aggregate demand curve shifts to the right.

Shifts Arising from Net Exports Any event that changes net exports for a given price level also shifts aggregate demand. For instance, when the US experiences a recession, it buys fewer goods from Europe. This reduces European net exports and shifts the aggregate demand curve for the European economy to the left. When the US recovers from its recession, it starts buying European goods again, shifting the aggregate demand curve to the right.

Net exports sometimes change because of movements in the exchange rate. Suppose, for instance, that international speculators bid up the value of the euro in the market for foreign currency exchange. This appreciation of the euro would make goods produced in the Euro Area more expensive compared to foreign goods, which would depress net exports and shift the aggregate demand curve to the left. Conversely, a depreciation of the euro stimulates net exports and shifts the Euro Area aggregate demand curve to the right.

Summary In the next chapter we analyse the aggregate demand curve in more detail. There we examine more precisely how the tools of monetary and fiscal policy can shift aggregate demand and whether policy makers should use these tools for that purpose. At this point, however, you should have some idea about why the aggregate demand curve slopes downward and what kinds of events and policies can shift this curve. Table 34.1 summarizes what we have learned so far.

Quick Quiz Explain the three reasons why the aggregate demand curve slopes downward. • Give an example of an event that would shift the aggregate demand curve. Which way would this event shift the curve?

TABLE 34.1

The Aggregate Demand Curve: Summary

Why does the aggregate demand curve slope downward?

1. *The wealth effect:* A lower price level increases real wealth, which encourages spending on consumption.
2. *The interest-rate effect:* A lower price level reduces the interest rate, which encourages spending on investment.
3. *The exchange-rate effect:* A lower price level causes the real exchange rate to depreciate, which encourages spending on net exports.

Why might the aggregate demand curve shift?

1. *Shifts arising from consumption:* An event that makes consumers spend more at a given price level (a tax cut, a stock market boom) shifts the aggregate demand curve to the right. An event that makes consumers spend less at a given price level (a tax hike, a stock market decline) shifts the aggregate demand curve to the left.
2. *Shifts arising from investment:* An event that makes firms invest more at a given price level (optimism about the future, a fall in interest rates due to an increase in the money supply) shifts the aggregate demand curve to the right. An event that makes firms invest less at a given price level (pessimism about the future, a rise in interest rates due to a decrease in the money supply) shifts the aggregate demand curve to the left.
3. *Shifts arising from government purchases:* An increase in government purchases of goods and services (greater spending on defence or motorway construction) shifts the aggregate demand curve to the right. A decrease in government purchases on goods and services (a cutback in defence or motorway spending) shifts the aggregate demand curve to the left.
4. *Shifts arising from net exports:* An event that raises spending on net exports at a given price level (a boom overseas, an exchange rate depreciation) shifts the aggregate demand curve to the right. An event that reduces spending on net exports at a given price level (a recession overseas, an exchange rate appreciation) shifts the aggregate demand curve to the left.

THE AGGREGATE SUPPLY CURVE

The aggregate supply curve tells us the total quantity of goods and services that firms produce and sell at any given price level. Unlike the aggregate demand curve, which is always downward sloping, the aggregate supply curve shows a relationship that depends crucially on the time horizon being examined. In the long run, the aggregate supply curve is vertical, whereas in the short run, the aggregate supply curve is upward sloping. To understand short-run economic fluctuations, and how the short-run behaviour of the economy deviates from its long-run behaviour, we need to examine both the long-run aggregate supply curve and the short-run aggregate supply curve.

Why the Aggregate Supply Curve is Vertical in the Long Run

What determines the quantity of goods and services supplied in the long run? We implicitly answered this question earlier in the book when we analysed the process of economic growth. In the long run, an economy's production of goods and services (its real GDP) depends on its supplies of labour, capital and natural resources, and on the available technology used to turn these factors of production into goods and services. Because the price level does not affect these long-run determinants of real GDP, the long-run aggregate supply curve is vertical, as in Figure 34.4. In other words, in the long run, the economy's labour, capital, natural resources and technology determine the total quantity of goods and services supplied, and this quantity supplied is the same regardless of what the price level happens to be.

The vertical long-run aggregate supply curve is, in essence, just an application of the classical dichotomy and monetary neutrality. As we have already discussed, classical macroeconomic theory is based on the assumption that real variables do not depend on nominal variables. The long-run aggregate supply curve is consistent with this idea because it implies that the quantity of output (a real variable) does not depend on the level of prices (a nominal variable). As noted earlier, most economists believe that this principle works well when studying the economy over a period of many years, but not when studying year-to-year changes. Thus, the aggregate supply curve is vertical only in the long run.

One might wonder why supply curves for specific goods and services can be upward sloping if the long-run aggregate supply curve is vertical. The reason is that the supply of specific goods and services depends on *relative prices* – the prices of those goods and services compared to other prices in the economy. For example, when the price of ice cream rises, holding other prices in the economy constant, there is an incentive for suppliers of ice cream to increase their production by taking labour, milk, chocolate and other inputs away from the production of other goods, such as frozen yoghurt. By contrast, the economy's overall production of goods and services is limited by its labour, capital, natural resources and technology. Thus, when all prices in the economy rise together, there is no change in the overall quantity of goods and services supplied because relative prices and thus incentives have not changed.

FIGURE 34.4

The Long-run Aggregate Supply Curve

In the long run, the quantity of output supplied depends on the economy's quantities of labour, capital and natural resources and on the technology for turning these inputs into output. The quantity supplied does not depend on the overall price level. As a result, the long-run aggregate supply curve is vertical at the natural rate of output.

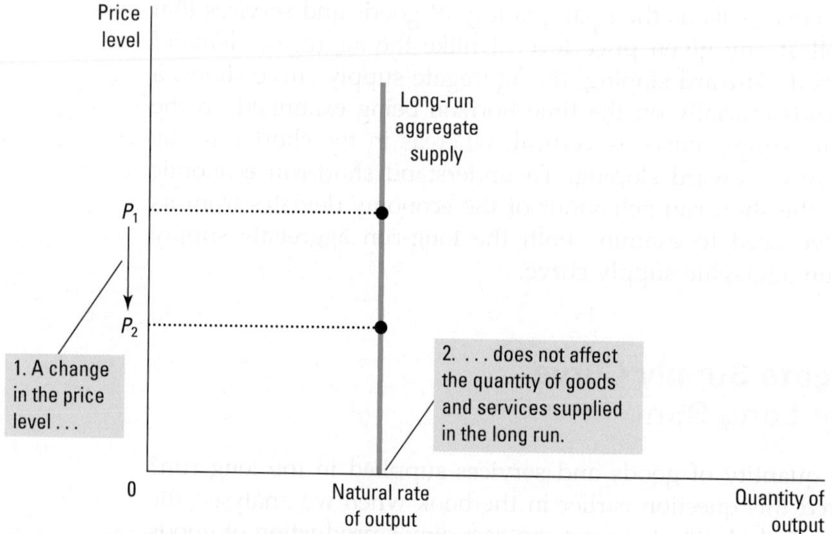

Why the Long-run Aggregate Supply Curve Might Shift

The position of the long-run aggregate supply curve shows the quantity of goods and services predicted by classical macroeconomic theory. This level of production is sometimes called *potential output* or *full-employment output.* To be more accurate, we call it the **natural rate of output** because it shows what the economy produces when unemployment is at its natural, or normal, rate. The natural rate of output is the level of production towards which the economy gravitates in the long run.

natural rate of output
the output level in an economy when all existing factors of production (land, labour, capital and technology resources) are fully utilized and where unemployment is at its natural rate

Any change in the economy that alters the natural rate of output shifts the long-run aggregate supply curve. Because output in the classical model depends on labour, capital, natural resources and technological knowledge, we can categorize shifts in the long-run aggregate supply curve as arising from these sources.

Shifts Arising from Labour Imagine that an economy experiences an increase in immigration from abroad. Because there would be a greater number of workers, the quantity of goods and services supplied would increase. As a result, the long-run aggregate supply curve would shift to the right. Conversely, if many workers left the economy to go abroad, the long-run aggregate supply curve would shift to the left.

The position of the long-run aggregate supply curve also depends on the natural rate of unemployment, so any change in the natural rate of unemployment shifts the long-run aggregate supply curve. For example, if the government were to raise the minimum wage substantially, the natural rate of unemployment would rise, and the economy would produce a smaller quantity of goods and services. As a result, the long-run aggregate supply curve would shift to the left. Conversely, if a reform of the unemployment insurance system were to encourage unemployed workers to search harder for new jobs, the natural rate of unemployment would fall, and the long-run aggregate supply curve would shift to the right.

Shifts Arising from Capital An increase in the economy's capital stock increases productivity and, thereby, the quantity of goods and services supplied. As a result, the long-run aggregate supply curve shifts to the right. Conversely, a decrease in the economy's capital stock decreases productivity and the quantity of goods and services supplied, shifting the long-run aggregate supply curve to the left.

Notice that the same logic applies regardless of whether we are discussing physical capital or human capital. An increase either in the number of machines or in the number of university degrees will raise the economy's ability to produce goods and services. Thus, either would shift the long-run aggregate supply curve to the right.

Changes in oil production are one source of macroeconomic fluctuations.

Shifts Arising from Natural Resources An economy's production depends on its natural resources, including its land, minerals and weather. A discovery of a new mineral deposit shifts the long-run aggregate supply curve to the right. A change in weather patterns that makes farming more difficult shifts the long-run aggregate supply curve to the left.

In many countries, important natural resources are imported from abroad. A change in the availability of these resources can also shift the aggregate supply curve. As we discuss later in this chapter, events occurring in the world oil market have historically been an important source of shifts in aggregate supply.

Shifts Arising from Technological Knowledge Perhaps the most important reason that the economy today produces more than it did a generation ago is that our technological knowledge has advanced. The invention of the computer, for instance, has allowed us to produce more goods and services from any given amounts of labour, capital and natural resources. As a result, it has shifted the long-run aggregate supply curve to the right.

Although not literally technological, there are many other events that act like changes in technology. As Chapter 9 explains, opening up international trade has effects similar to inventing new production processes, so it also shifts the long-run aggregate supply curve to the right. Conversely, if the government passed new regulations preventing firms from using some production methods, perhaps because they were too dangerous for workers, the result would be a leftward shift in the long-run aggregate supply curve.

Summary The long-run aggregate supply curve reflects the classical model of the economy we developed in previous chapters. Any policy or event that raised real GDP in previous chapters can now be viewed as increasing the quantity of goods and services supplied and shifting the long-run aggregate supply curve to the right. Any policy or event that lowered real GDP in previous chapters can now be viewed as decreasing the quantity of goods and services supplied and shifting the long-run aggregate supply curve to the left.

A New Way to Depict Long-run Growth and Inflation

Having introduced the economy's aggregate demand curve and the long-run aggregate supply curve, we now have a new way to describe the economy's long-run trends. Figure 34.5 illustrates the changes that occur in the economy from decade to decade. Notice that both curves are shifting. Although there are many forces that govern the economy in the long run and can in principle cause such shifts, the two most important in practice are technology and monetary policy. Technological progress enhances the economy's ability to produce goods and services, and this continually shifts the long-run aggregate supply curve to the right. At the same time, because the central bank increases the money supply over time, the aggregate demand curve also shifts to the right. As the figure illustrates, the result is trend growth in output (as shown by increasing Y) and continuing inflation (as shown by increasing P). This is just another way of representing the classical analysis of growth and inflation we conducted in Chapters 25 and 30.

The purpose of developing the model of aggregate demand and aggregate supply, however, is not to dress our long-run conclusions in new clothing. Instead, it is to provide a framework for short-run analysis, as we will see in a moment. As we develop the short-run model, we keep the analysis simple by not showing the continuing growth and inflation depicted in Figure 34.5. But always remember that long-run trends provide the background for short-run fluctuations. Short-run fluctuations in output and the **price level** should be viewed as deviations from the continuing long-run trends.

price level
the price of a basket of goods and services measured as the weighted arithmetic average of current prices

Why the Aggregate Supply Curve Slopes Upward in the Short Run

We now come to the key difference between the economy in the short run and in the long run: the behaviour of aggregate supply. As we have already discussed, the long-run aggregate supply curve is vertical. By contrast, in the short run, the aggregate supply curve is upward sloping, as shown in Figure 34.6. That is, over

FIGURE 34.5

Long-run Growth and Inflation in the Model of Aggregate Demand and Aggregate Supply

As the economy becomes better able to produce goods and services over time, primarily because of technological progress, the long-run aggregate supply curve shifts to the right. At the same time, as the central bank increases the money supply, the aggregate demand curve also shifts to the right. In this figure, output grows from Y_{1990} to Y_{2000} and then to Y_{2010}, and the price level rises from P_{1990} to P_{2000} and then to P_{2010}. Thus, the model of aggregate demand and aggregate supply offers a new way to describe the classical analysis of growth and inflation.

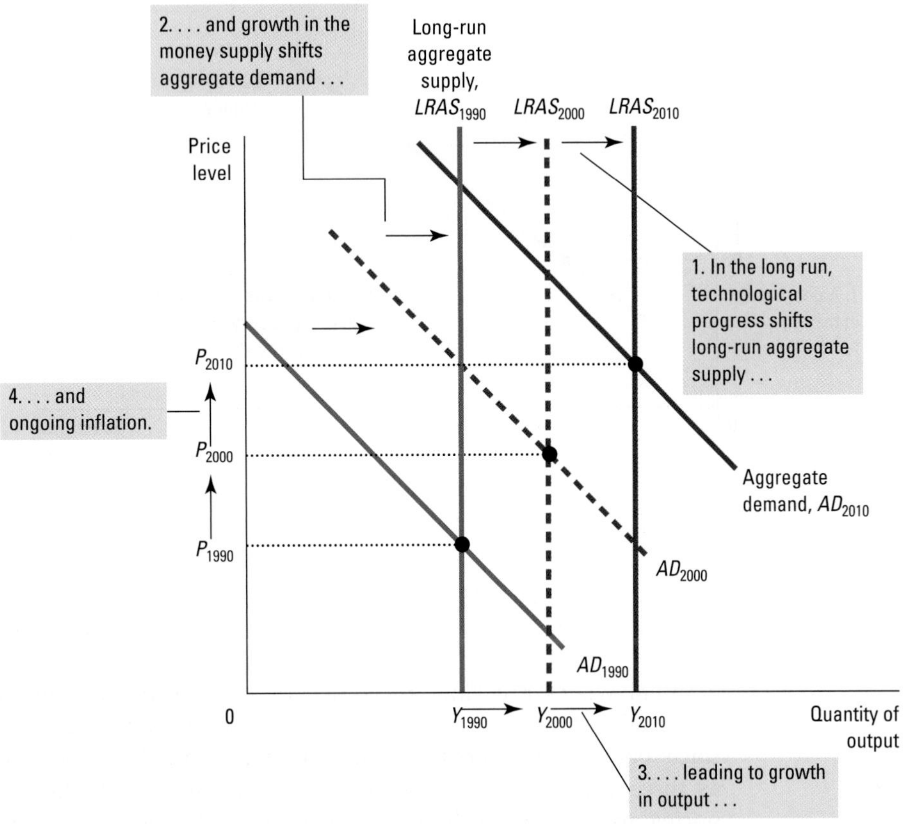

a period of a year or two, an increase in the overall level of prices in the economy tends to raise the quantity of goods and services supplied, and a decrease in the level of prices tends to reduce the quantity of goods and services supplied.

What causes this positive relationship between the price level and output? Macroeconomists have proposed three theories for the upward slope of the short-run aggregate supply curve. In each theory, a specific market imperfection causes the supply side of the economy to behave differently in the short run than it does in the long run. Although each of the following theories will differ in detail, they share a common theme: the quantity of output supplied deviates from its long-run, or 'natural' level when the price level deviates from the price level that people expected to prevail. When the price level rises above the expected level, output rises above its natural rate, and when the price level falls below the expected level, output falls below its natural rate.

The Sticky Wage Theory The first and simplest explanation of the upward slope of the short-run aggregate supply curve is the sticky wage theory. According to this theory, the short-run aggregate supply curve slopes upward because

FIGURE 34.6

The Short-run Aggregate Supply Curve

In the short run, a fall in the price level from P_1 to P_2 reduces the quantity of output supplied from Y_1 to Y_2. This positive relationship could be due to sticky wages, sticky prices or misperceptions. Over time, wages, prices and perceptions adjust, so this positive relationship is only temporary.

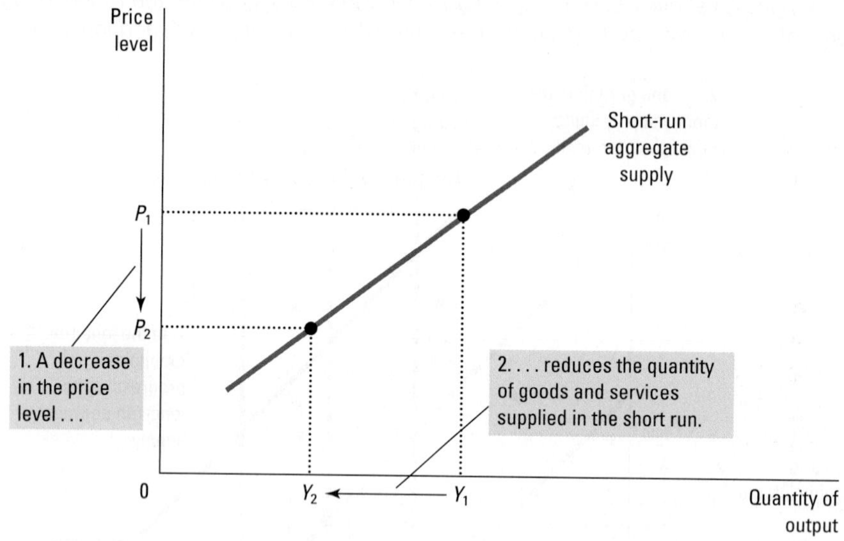

nominal wages are slow to adjust, or are 'sticky', in the short run. To some extent, the slow adjustment of nominal wages is attributable to long-term contracts between workers and firms that fix nominal wages, sometimes for as long as three years. In addition, this slow adjustment may be attributable to social norms and notions of fairness that influence wage setting and that change only slowly over time.

To see what sticky nominal wages mean for aggregate supply, imagine that a firm has agreed in advance to pay its workers a certain nominal wage based on what it expected the price level to be. If the price level P falls below the level that was expected and the nominal wage remains stuck at W, then the real wage W/P rises above the level the firm planned to pay. Because wages are a large part of a firm's production costs, a higher real wage means that the firm's real costs have risen. The firm responds to these higher costs by hiring less labour and producing a smaller quantity of goods and services. In other words, because wages do not adjust immediately to the price level, a lower price level makes employment and production less profitable, so firms reduce the quantity of goods and services they supply.

The Sticky Price Theory Some economists have advocated another approach to the short-run aggregate supply curve, called the sticky-price theory. As we just discussed, the sticky-wage theory emphasizes that nominal wages adjust slowly over time. The sticky-price theory emphasizes that the prices of some goods and services also adjust sluggishly in response to changing economic conditions. This slow adjustment of prices occurs in part because there are costs to adjusting prices, called *menu costs* as we saw in Chapter 30. These menu costs include the cost of printing and distributing price lists or mail-order catalogues and the time required to change price tags. As a result of these costs, prices as well as wages may be sticky in the short run.

To see the implications of sticky prices for aggregate supply, suppose that each firm in the economy announces its prices in advance based on the economic conditions it expects to prevail. Then, after prices are announced, the economy experiences an unexpected contraction in the money supply, which (as we have learned) will reduce the overall price level in the long run. Although some firms reduce their prices immediately in response to changing economic conditions, other firms may not want to incur additional menu costs and, therefore, may temporarily lag behind. Because these lagging firms have prices that are too high, their sales decline. Declining sales, in turn, cause these firms to cut back on production and employment. In other words, because not all prices adjust instantly to changing conditions, an unexpected fall in the price level leaves some firms with higher-than-desired prices, and these higher-than-desired prices depress sales and induce firms to reduce the quantity of goods and services they produce.

The Misperceptions Theory A third approach to the short-run aggregate supply curve is the misperceptions theory. According to this theory, changes in the overall price level can temporarily mislead suppliers about what is happening in the individual markets in which they sell their output. As a result of these short-run misperceptions, suppliers respond to changes in the level of prices, and this response leads to an upward sloping aggregate supply curve.

To see how this might work, suppose the overall price level falls below the level that people expected. When suppliers see the prices of their products fall, they may mistakenly believe that their *relative* prices have fallen. For example, wheat farmers may notice a fall in the price of wheat before they notice a fall in the prices of the many items they buy as consumers. They may infer from this observation that the reward to producing wheat is temporarily low, and they may respond by reducing the quantity of wheat they supply. Similarly, workers may notice a fall in their nominal wages before they notice a fall in the prices of the goods they buy. They may infer that the reward to working is temporarily low and respond by reducing the quantity of labour they supply. In both cases, a lower price level causes misperceptions about relative prices, and these misperceptions induce suppliers to respond to the lower price level by decreasing the quantity of goods and services supplied.

Summary There are three alternative explanations for the upward slope of the short-run aggregate supply curve: (1) sticky wages, (2) sticky prices and (3) misperceptions. Economists debate which of these theories is correct, and it is very possible each contains an element of truth. For our purposes in this book, the similarities of the theories are more important than the differences. All three theories suggest that output deviates from its natural rate when the price level deviates from the price level that people expected. We can express this mathematically as follows:

$$\begin{array}{c}\text{Quantity}\\\text{of output}\\\text{supplied}\end{array} = \begin{array}{c}\text{Natural}\\\text{rate of}\\\text{output}\end{array} + a\left(\begin{array}{c}\text{Actual}\\\text{price}\\\text{level}\end{array} - \begin{array}{c}\text{Expected}\\\text{price}\\\text{level}\end{array}\right)$$

where a is a number that determines how much output responds to unexpected changes in the price level.

Notice that each of the three theories of short-run aggregate supply emphasizes a problem that is likely to be only temporary. Whether the upward slope of the aggregate supply curve is attributable to sticky wages, sticky prices or misperceptions, these conditions will not persist forever. Eventually, as people adjust their expectations, nominal wages adjust, prices become unstuck and misperceptions are corrected. In other words, the expected and actual price levels are equal in the long run, and the aggregate supply curve is vertical rather than upward sloping.

Why the Short-run Aggregate Supply Curve Might Shift

The short-run aggregate supply curve tells us the quantity of goods and services supplied in the short run for any given level of prices. We can think of this curve as similar to the long-run aggregate supply curve but made upward sloping by the presence of sticky wages, sticky prices and misperceptions. Thus, when thinking about what shifts the short-run aggregate supply curve, we have to consider all those variables that shift the long-run aggregate supply curve plus a new variable – the expected price level – that influences sticky wages, sticky prices and misperceptions.

Let's start with what we know about the long-run aggregate supply curve. As we discussed earlier, shifts in the long-run aggregate supply curve normally arise from changes in labour, capital, natural resources or technological knowledge. These same variables shift the short-run aggregate supply curve. For example, when an increase in the economy's capital stock increases productivity, both the long-run and short-run aggregate supply curves shift to the right. When an increase in the minimum wage raises the natural rate of unemployment, both the long-run and short-run aggregate supply curves shift to the left.

The important new variable that affects the position of the short-run aggregate supply curve is people's expectation of the price level. As we have discussed, the quantity of goods and services supplied depends, in the short run, on sticky wages, sticky prices and misperceptions. Yet wages, prices and perceptions are set on the basis of expectations of the price level. So when expectations change, the short-run aggregate supply curve shifts.

To make this idea more concrete, let's consider a specific theory of aggregate supply – the sticky wage theory. According to this theory, when workers and firms expect the price level to be high, they are more likely to negotiate high nominal wages. High wages raise firms' costs and, for any given actual price level, reduce the quantity of goods and services that firms supply. Thus, when the expected price level rises, wages are higher, costs increase, and firms supply a smaller quantity of goods and services at any given actual price level. Thus, the short-run aggregate supply curve shifts to the left. Conversely, when the expected price level falls, wages are lower, costs decline, firms increase production at any given price level, and the short-run aggregate supply curve shifts to the right.

A similar logic applies in each theory of aggregate supply. The general lesson is the following: an increase in the expected price level reduces the quantity of goods and services supplied and shifts the short-run aggregate supply curve to the left. A decrease in the expected price level raises the quantity of goods and services supplied and shifts the short-run aggregate supply curve to the right. As we will see in the next section, this influence of expectations on the position of the short-run aggregate supply curve plays a key role in reconciling the economy's behaviour in the short run with its behaviour in the long run. In the short run, expectations are fixed, and the economy finds itself at the intersection of the aggregate demand curve and the short-run aggregate supply curve. In the long run, expectations adjust, and the short-run aggregate supply curve shifts. This shift ensures that the economy eventually finds itself at the intersection of the aggregate demand curve and the long-run aggregate supply curve.

TABLE 34.2

The Short-Run Aggregate Supply Curve: Summary

Why does the short-run aggregate supply curve slope upward?

1. *The sticky wage theory:* An unexpectedly low price level raises the real wage, which causes firms to hire fewer workers and produce a smaller quantity of goods and services.
2. *The sticky price theory:* An unexpectedly low price level leaves some firms with higher-than-desired prices, which depresses their sales and leads them to cut back production.
3. *The misperceptions theory:* An unexpectedly low price level leads some suppliers to think their relative prices have fallen, which induces a fall in production.

Why might the short-run aggregate supply curve shift?

1. *Shifts arising from labour:* An increase in the quantity of labour available (perhaps due to a fall in the natural rate of unemployment) shifts the aggregate supply curve to the right. A decrease in the quantity of labour available (perhaps due to a rise in the natural rate of unemployment) shifts the aggregate supply curve to the left.
2. *Shifts arising from capital:* An increase in physical or human capital shifts the aggregate supply curve to the right. A decrease in physical or human capital shifts the aggregate supply curve to the left.
3. *Shifts arising from natural resources:* An increase in the availability of natural resources shifts the aggregate supply curve to the right. A decrease in the availability of natural resources shifts the aggregate supply curve to the left.
4. *Shifts arising from technology:* An advance in technological knowledge shifts the aggregate supply curve to the right. A decrease in the available technology (perhaps due to government regulation) shifts the aggregate supply curve to the left.
5. *Shifts arising from the expected price level:* A decrease in the expected price level shifts the short-run aggregate supply curve to the right. An increase in the expected price level shifts the short-run aggregate supply curve to the left.

You should now have some understanding about why the short-run aggregate supply curve slopes upward and what events and policies can cause this curve to shift. Table 34.2 summarizes our discussion.

Quick Quiz Explain why the long-run aggregate supply curve is vertical. • Explain three theories for why the short-run aggregate supply curve is upward sloping.

TWO CAUSES OF ECONOMIC FLUCTUATIONS

Now that we have introduced the model of aggregate demand and aggregate supply, we have the basic tools we need to analyse fluctuations in economic activity. In particular, we can use what we have learned about aggregate demand and aggregate supply to examine the two basic causes of short-run fluctuations.

To keep things simple, we assume the economy begins in long-run equilibrium, as shown in Figure 34.7. Equilibrium output and the price level are determined by the intersection of the aggregate demand curve and the long-run aggregate supply curve, shown as point A in the figure. At this point, output is

FIGURE 34.7

The Long-run Equilibrium

The long-run equilibrium of the economy is found where the aggregate demand curve crosses the long-run aggregate supply curve (point A). When the economy reaches this long-run equilibrium, wages, prices and perceptions will have adjusted so that the short-run aggregate supply curve crosses this point as well.

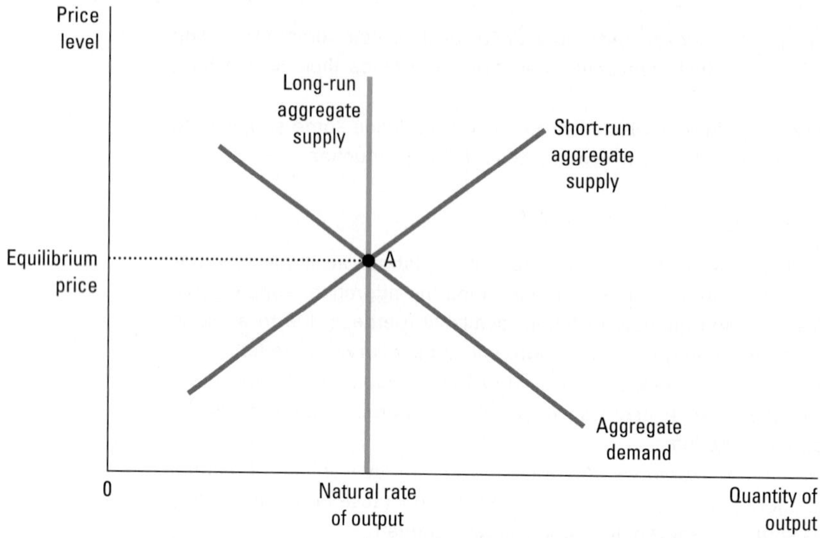

at its natural rate. The short-run aggregate supply curve passes through this point as well, indicating that wages, prices and perceptions have fully adjusted to this long-run equilibrium. That is, when an economy is in its long-run equilibrium, wages, prices and perceptions must have adjusted so that the intersection of aggregate demand with short-run aggregate supply is the same as the intersection of aggregate demand with long-run aggregate supply.

The Effects of a Shift in Aggregate Demand

Suppose that for some reason a wave of pessimism suddenly overtakes the economy. The cause might be a government scandal, a crash in the stock market or the outbreak of war overseas. Because of this event, many people lose confidence in the future and alter their plans. Households cut back on their spending and delay major purchases, and firms put off buying new equipment.

What is the impact of such a wave of pessimism on the economy? Such an event reduces the aggregate demand for goods and services. That is, for any given price level, households and firms now want to buy a smaller quantity of goods and services. As Figure 34.8 shows, the aggregate demand curve shifts to the left from AD_1 to AD_2.

In this figure we can examine the effects of the fall in aggregate demand. In the short run, the economy moves along the initial short-run aggregate supply curve AS_1, going from point A to point B. As the economy moves from point A to point B, output falls from Y_1 to Y_2, and the price level falls from P_1 to P_2. The falling level of output indicates that the economy is in a recession. Although not shown in the figure, firms respond to lower sales and production by reducing employment. Thus, the pessimism that caused the shift in aggregate demand is,

FIGURE 34.8

A Contraction in Aggregate Demand

A fall in aggregate demand, which might be due to a wave of pessimism in the economy, is represented with a leftward shift in the aggregate demand curve from AD_1 to AD_2. The economy moves from point A to point B. Output falls from Y_1 to Y_2, and the price level falls from P_1 to P_2. Over time, as wages, prices and perceptions adjust, the short-run aggregate supply curve shifts to the right from AS_1 to AS_2, and the economy reaches point C, where the new aggregate demand curve crosses the long-run aggregate supply curve. The price level falls to P_3, and output returns to its natural rate, Y_1.

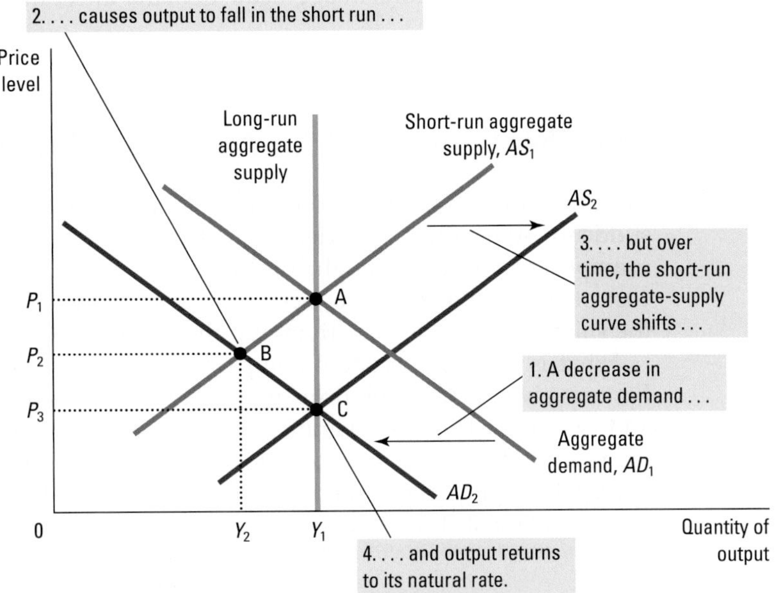

to some extent, self-fulfilling: pessimism about the future leads to falling incomes and rising unemployment.

What should policy makers do when faced with such a recession? One possibility is to take action to increase aggregate demand. As we noted earlier, an increase in government spending or an increase in the money supply would increase the quantity of goods and services demanded at any price and, therefore, would shift the aggregate demand curve to the right. If policy makers can act with sufficient speed and precision, they can offset the initial shift in aggregate demand, return the aggregate demand curve back to AD_1, and bring the economy back to point A. (The next chapter discusses in more detail the ways in which monetary and fiscal policy influence aggregate demand, as well as some of the practical difficulties in using these policy instruments.)

Even without action by policy makers, the recession will remedy itself over a period of time. Because of the reduction in aggregate demand, the price level falls. Eventually, expectations catch up with this new reality, and the expected price level falls as well. Because the fall in the expected price level alters wages, prices and perceptions, it shifts the short-run aggregate supply curve to the right from AS_1 to AS_2 in Figure 34.8. This adjustment of expectations allows the economy over time to approach point C, where the new aggregate demand curve (AD_2) crosses the long-run aggregate supply curve.

In the new long-run equilibrium, point C, output is back to its natural rate. Even though the wave of pessimism has reduced aggregate demand, the price level has fallen sufficiently (to P_3) to offset the shift in the aggregate demand curve. Thus, in the long run, the shift in aggregate demand is reflected fully in the price level and not at all in the level of output. In other words, the long-run effect of a shift in aggregate demand is a nominal change (the price level is lower) but not a real change (output is the same).

To sum up, this story about shifts in aggregate demand has two important lessons:

- In the short run, shifts in aggregate demand cause fluctuations in the economy's output of goods and services.
- In the long run, shifts in aggregate demand affect the overall price level but do not affect output.

The Effects of a Shift in Aggregate Supply

Imagine once again an economy in its long-run equilibrium. Now suppose that suddenly some firms experience an increase in their costs of production. For example, bad weather might destroy some agricultural crops, driving up the cost of producing food products. Or a war in the Middle East might interrupt the shipping of crude oil, driving up the cost of producing oil products.

What is the macroeconomic impact of such an increase in production costs? For any given price level, firms now want to supply a smaller quantity of goods and services. Thus, as Figure 34.9 shows, the short-run aggregate supply curve shifts to the left from AS_1 to AS_2. (Depending on the event, the long-run aggregate supply curve might also shift. To keep things simple, however, we will assume that it does not.)

FIGURE 34.9

An Adverse Shift in Aggregate Supply

When some event increases firms' costs, the short-run aggregate supply curve shifts to the left from AS_1 to AS_2. The economy moves from point A to point B. The result is stagflation: output falls from Y_1 to Y_2, and the price level rises from P_1 to P_2.

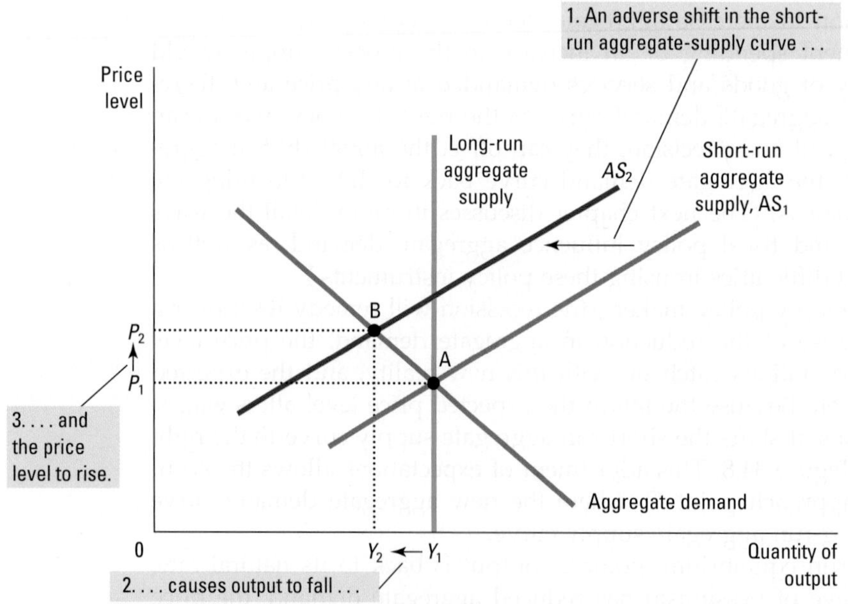

In this figure we can trace the effects of the leftward shift in aggregate supply. In the short run, the economy moves along the existing aggregate demand curve, going from point A to point B. The output of the economy falls from Y_1 to Y_2, and the price level rises from P_1 to P_2. Because the economy is experiencing both *stagnation* (falling output) and *inflation* (rising prices), such an event is sometimes called **stagflation**.

stagflation
a period of falling output and rising prices

What should policy makers do when faced with stagflation? There are no easy choices. One possibility is to do nothing. In this case, the output of goods and services remains depressed at Y_2 for a while. Eventually, however, the recession will remedy itself as wages, prices and perceptions adjust to the raise production costs. A period of low output and high unemployment, for instance, puts downward pressure on workers' wages. Lower wages, in turn, increase the quantity of output supplied. Over time, as the short-run aggregate supply curve shifts back toward AS_1, the price level falls, and the quantity of output approaches its natural rate. In the long run, the economy returns to point A, where the aggregate demand curve crosses the long-run aggregate supply curve. This is the view that believers of free markets might adopt.

Alternatively, policy makers who control monetary and fiscal policy might attempt to offset some of the effects of the shift in the short-run aggregate supply curve by shifting the aggregate demand curve. This possibility is shown in Figure 34.10. In this case, changes in policy shift the aggregate demand curve to the right from AD_1 to AD_2 – exactly enough to prevent the shift in aggregate supply from affecting output. The economy moves directly from point A to point C. Output remains at its natural rate, and the price level rises from P_1 to P_3. In this case, policy makers are said to *accommodate* the shift in aggregate supply because they allow the increase in costs to permanently affect the level of prices. This intervention by policy makers would be

FIGURE 34.10

Accommodating an Adverse Shift in Aggregate Supply

Faced with an adverse shift in aggregate supply from AS_1 to AS_2, policy makers who can influence aggregate demand might try to shift the aggregate demand curve to the right from AD_1 to AD_2. The economy would move from point A to point C. This policy would prevent the supply shift from reducing output in the short run, but the price level would permanently rise from P_1 to P_3.

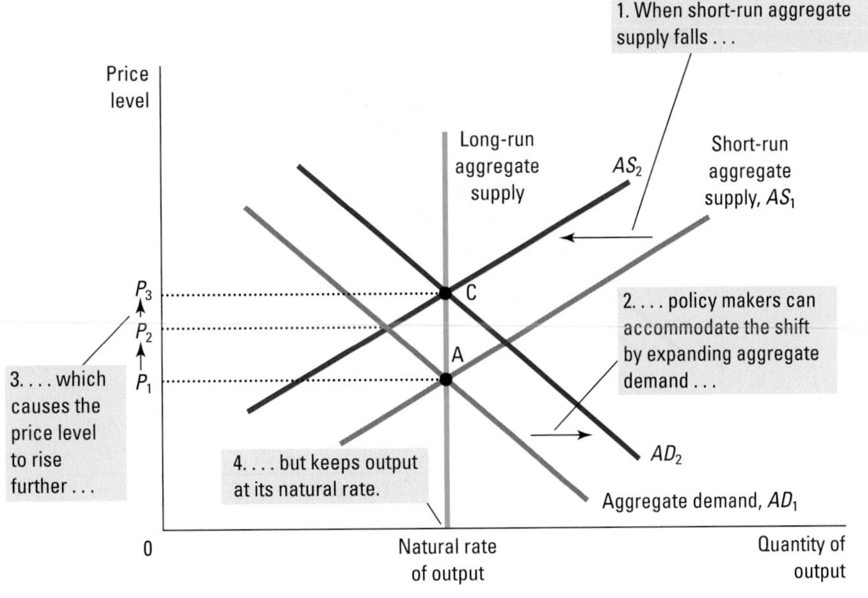

seen as being desirable by supporters of Keynes. These different views on policy action form a key aspect of the debate between economists about action in the face of short-run fluctuations in economic activity. We revisit this debate in Chapter 39.

To sum up, this story about shifts in aggregate supply has two important lessons:

- Shifts in aggregate supply can cause stagflation – a combination of recession (falling output) and inflation (rising prices).
- Policy makers who can influence aggregate demand cannot offset both of these adverse effects simultaneously.

Quick Quiz Suppose that the election of a popular prime minister suddenly increases people's confidence in the future. Use the model of aggregate demand and aggregate supply to analyse the effect on the economy.

CASE STUDY

The Aggregate Demand and Aggregate Supply Model

The events of 2007–09 provide a very good framework for applying the model of aggregate demand and aggregate supply covered in the text. The figures given below have been rounded but are reasonably accurate in relation to what actually happened.

Let us start by assuming that the European economy was in equilibrium in March 2007. Figure 34.11 gives the equilibrium price level at 2.0 per cent and the natural rate of unemployment at 7 per cent. At this time the rate of

FIGURE 34.11

Aggregate Demand and Aggregate Supply

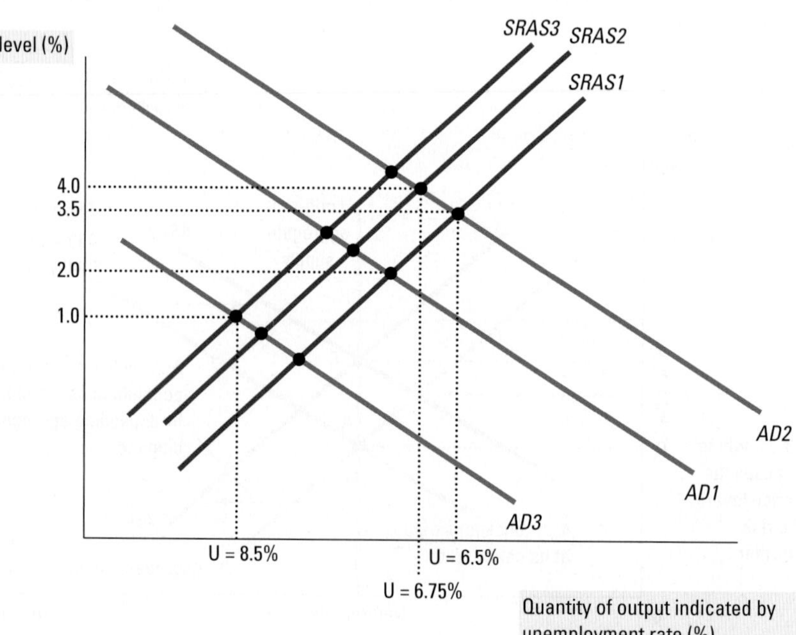

growth of wages, consumption expenditure and investment are strong. We would expect this to cause a shift in aggregate demand to the right (*AD2*). There is a movement along the *SRAS1* curve leading to a rise in the price level to 3.5 per cent and an increase in the level of output. This equates with a fall in the rate of unemployment to 6.5 per cent by May 2008.

The average wage increases in the Euro Area reflects the relatively buoyant economic conditions and stands at 4 per cent. The increase in the price level along with the relatively high wage costs means higher costs for businesses. This is exacerbated by the increase in oil and gas prices. Oil prices reached a peak of $147 a barrel in July 2008 and wholesale gas prices increased by around 80 per cent between 2007 and 2008. The increase in costs causes the *SRAS* curve to shift to the left (*SRAS2*) and the movement along the *AD2* curve leaves us with a further rise in the price level to 4.0 per cent and a slight rise in unemployment (as output falls) of 6.75 per cent.

The increase in inflation prompts the ECB to increase interest rates from 4.0 per cent to 4.5 per cent. Almost at the same time the effects of the sub-prime mortgage collapse begin to take effect on the real economy. Construction is one of the first industries to be hit but this is followed by the motor industry, manufacturing and in services as firms either cut back output or are forced out of business. Remember that wage rates had been rising relatively strongly but firms are now starting to feel the effect of the fall in demand but wages remain sticky. For many firms, wage costs are relatively high in the face of falling demand and now form a higher proportion of costs. Some firms, especially in the automotive industry, responded to the slowdown in economic activity by ceasing production. Some closed for an extended period over Christmas 2008, others shut down operations 1 week each month and others shut down for up to two months. The combined effect of the increase in interest rates and the economic slowdown is to push the *AD* curve to the left – a quite marked shift to *AD3*. The effect of sticky wages and cuts in production is to push the *SRAS* curve even further to the left. The effect of this is to force down the price level and to increase unemployment even further. The rate of growth of prices now starts to fall back to 1.0 per cent and unemployment rises to 8.5 per cent. The time frame considered does not allow expectations to fully adjust to the new circumstances hence we have not included a LRAS curve, which would be in a position where unemployment is at its natural rate of 7 per cent.

The analysis uses a simple model to highlight what we might expect as a result of the changes witnessed. The effects could be made more accurate, of course, by using a mathematical model and inputting more accurate data into the *AD* and *AS* equations. The analysis above assumes, for example, that the elasticity of both *AS* and *AD* do not change but in reality this is unlikely to be the case. The *AS* and *AD* curves could become more inelastic as firms and consumers find it more difficult to respond to changes in the price level and the shocks that occur.

CONCLUSION

This chapter has achieved two goals. First, we have discussed some of the important facts about short-run fluctuations in economic activity. Secondly, we have introduced a basic model to explain those fluctuations, called the model of aggregate demand and aggregate supply. We continue our study of this model in the next chapter in order to understand more fully what causes fluctuations in the economy and how policy makers might respond to these fluctuations.

SUMMARY

- All societies experience short-run economic fluctuations around long-run trends. These fluctuations are irregular and largely unpredictable. When recessions do occur, real GDP and other measures of income, spending and production fall, and unemployment rises.
- Economists analyse short-run economic fluctuations using the model of aggregate demand and aggregate supply. According to this model, the output of goods and services and the overall level of prices adjust to balance aggregate demand and aggregate supply.
- The aggregate demand curve slopes downward for three reasons. First, a lower price level raises the real value of households' money holdings, which stimulates consumer spending. Secondly, a lower price level reduces the quantity of money households' demand; as households try to convert money into interest-bearing assets, interest rates fall, which stimulates investment spending. Thirdly, as a lower price level reduces interest rates, the local currency depreciates in the market for foreign currency exchange, which stimulates net exports.
- Any event or policy that raises consumption, investment, government purchases or net exports at a given price level increases aggregate demand. Any event or policy that reduces consumption, investment, government purchases or net exports at a given price level decreases aggregate demand.
- The long-run aggregate supply curve is vertical. In the long run, the quantity of goods and services supplied depends on the economy's labour, capital, natural resources and technology, but not on the overall level of prices.
- Three theories have been proposed to explain the upward slope of the short-run aggregate supply curve. According to the sticky wage theory, an unexpected fall in the price level temporarily raises real wages, which induces firms to reduce employment and production. According to the sticky price theory, an unexpected fall in the price level leaves some firms with prices that are temporarily too high, which reduces their sales and causes them to cut back production. According to the misperceptions theory, an unexpected fall in the price level leads suppliers to mistakenly believe that their relative prices have fallen, which induces them to reduce production. All three theories imply that output deviates from its natural rate when the price level deviates from the price level that people expected.
- Events that alter the economy's ability to produce output, such as changes in labour, capital, natural resources or technology, shift the short-run aggregate supply curve (and may shift the long-run aggregate supply curve as well). In addition, the position of the short-run aggregate supply curve depends on the expected price level.
- One possible cause of economic fluctuations is a shift in aggregate demand. When the aggregate demand curve shifts to the left, for instance, output and prices fall in the short run. Over time, as a change in the expected price level causes wages, prices and perceptions to adjust, the short-run aggregate supply curve shifts to the right, and the economy returns to its natural rate of output at a new, lower price level.
- A second possible cause of economic fluctuations is a shift in aggregate supply. When the aggregate supply curve shifts to the left, the short-run effect is falling output and rising prices – a combination called stagflation. Over time, as wages, prices and perceptions adjust, the price level falls back to its original level, and output recovers.

KEY CONCEPTS

QUESTIONS FOR REVIEW

1. Name two macroeconomic variables that decline when the economy goes into a recession. Name one macroeconomic variable that rises during a recession.
2. Draw a diagram with aggregate demand, short-run aggregate supply and long-run aggregate supply. Be careful to label the axes correctly.
3. List and explain the three reasons why the aggregate demand curve is downward sloping.
4. Explain why the long-run aggregate supply curve is vertical.
5. List and explain the three theories for why the short-run aggregate supply curve is upward sloping.
6. What might shift the aggregate demand curve to the left? Use the model of aggregate demand and aggregate supply to trace through the effects of such a shift.
7. What might shift the aggregate supply curve to the left? Use the model of aggregate demand and aggregate supply to trace through the effects of such a shift.

PROBLEMS AND APPLICATIONS

1. Why do you think that investment is more variable over the business cycle than consumer spending? Which category of consumer spending do you think would be most volatile: durable goods (such as furniture and car purchases), non-durable goods (such as food and clothing) or services (such as haircuts and medical care)? Why?
2. Suppose that the economy is in a long-run equilibrium.
   a. Use a diagram to illustrate the state of the economy. Be sure to show aggregate demand, short-run aggregate supply and long-run aggregate supply.
   b. Now suppose that a financial crisis causes aggregate demand to fall. Use your diagram to show what happens to output and the price level in the short run. What happens to the unemployment rate?
   c. Use the sticky wage theory of aggregate supply to explain what will happen to output and the price level in the long run (assuming there is no change in policy). What role does the expected price level play in this adjustment? Be sure to illustrate your analysis with a graph.
3. Explain whether each of the following events will increase, decrease or have no effect on long-run aggregate supply.
   a. The country experiences a wave of immigration.
   b. The government raises the minimum wage above the national average wage level.
   c. A war leads to the destruction of a large number of factories.
4. In Figure 34.8, how does the unemployment rate at points B and C compare to the unemployment rate at point A? Under the sticky wage explanation of the short-run aggregate supply curve, how does the real wage at points B and C compare to the real wage at point A?
5. Explain why the following statements are false.
   a. 'The aggregate demand curve slopes downward because it is the horizontal sum of the demand curves for individual goods.'
   b. 'The long-run aggregate supply curve is vertical because economic forces do not affect long-run aggregate supply.'
   c. 'If firms adjusted their prices every day, then the short run aggregate supply curve would be horizontal.'
   d. 'Whenever the economy enters a recession, its long run aggregate supply curve shifts to the left.'
6. For each of the three theories for the upward slope of the short-run aggregate supply curve, carefully explain the following.
   a. How the economy recovers from a recession and returns to its long-run equilibrium without any policy intervention.
   b. What determines the speed of that recovery?
7. Suppose the central bank expands the money supply, but because the public expects this action, it simultaneously raises its expectation of the price level. What will happen to output and the price level in the short run? Compare this result to the outcome if the central bank expanded the money supply but the public didn't change its expectation of the price level.
8. Suppose that the economy is currently in a recession. If policy makers take no action, how will the economy evolve over time? Explain in words and using an aggregate demand/aggregate supply diagram.

9. Suppose workers and firms suddenly believe that inflation will be quite high over the coming year. Suppose also that the economy begins in long-run equilibrium, and the aggregate demand curve does not shift.
   a. What happens to nominal wages? What happens to real wages?
   b. Using an aggregate demand/aggregate supply diagram, show the effect of the change in expectations on both the short-run and long-run levels of prices and output.
   c. Were the expectations of high inflation accurate? Explain.
10. Explain whether each of the following events shifts the short-run aggregate supply curve, the aggregate demand curve, both, or neither. For each event that does shift a curve, use a diagram to illustrate the effect on the economy.
   a. Households decide to save a larger share of their income.
   b. Cattle farmers suffer a prolonged period of foot-and-mouth disease which cuts average cattle herd sizes by 80 per cent.
   c. Increased job opportunities overseas cause many people to leave the country.
11. For each of the following events, explain the short run and long-run effects on output and the price level, assuming policy makers take no action.
   a. The stock market declines sharply, reducing consumers' wealth.
   b. The government increases spending on national defence.
   c. A technological improvement raises productivity.
   d. A recession overseas causes foreigners to buy fewer domestic goods.
12. Suppose that firms become very optimistic about future business conditions and invest heavily in new capital equipment.
   a. Use an aggregate demand/aggregate supply diagram to show the short-run effect of this optimism on the economy. Label the new levels of prices and real output. Explain, in words, why the aggregate quantity of output supplied changes.
   b. Now use the diagram from part (a) to show the new long-run equilibrium of the economy. (For now, assume there is no change in the long-run aggregate supply curve.) Explain, in words, why the aggregate quantity of output demanded changes between the short run and the long run.
   c. How might the investment boom affect the long-run aggregate supply curve? Explain.

For further resources, visit www.cengage.co.uk/mankiw_taylor2

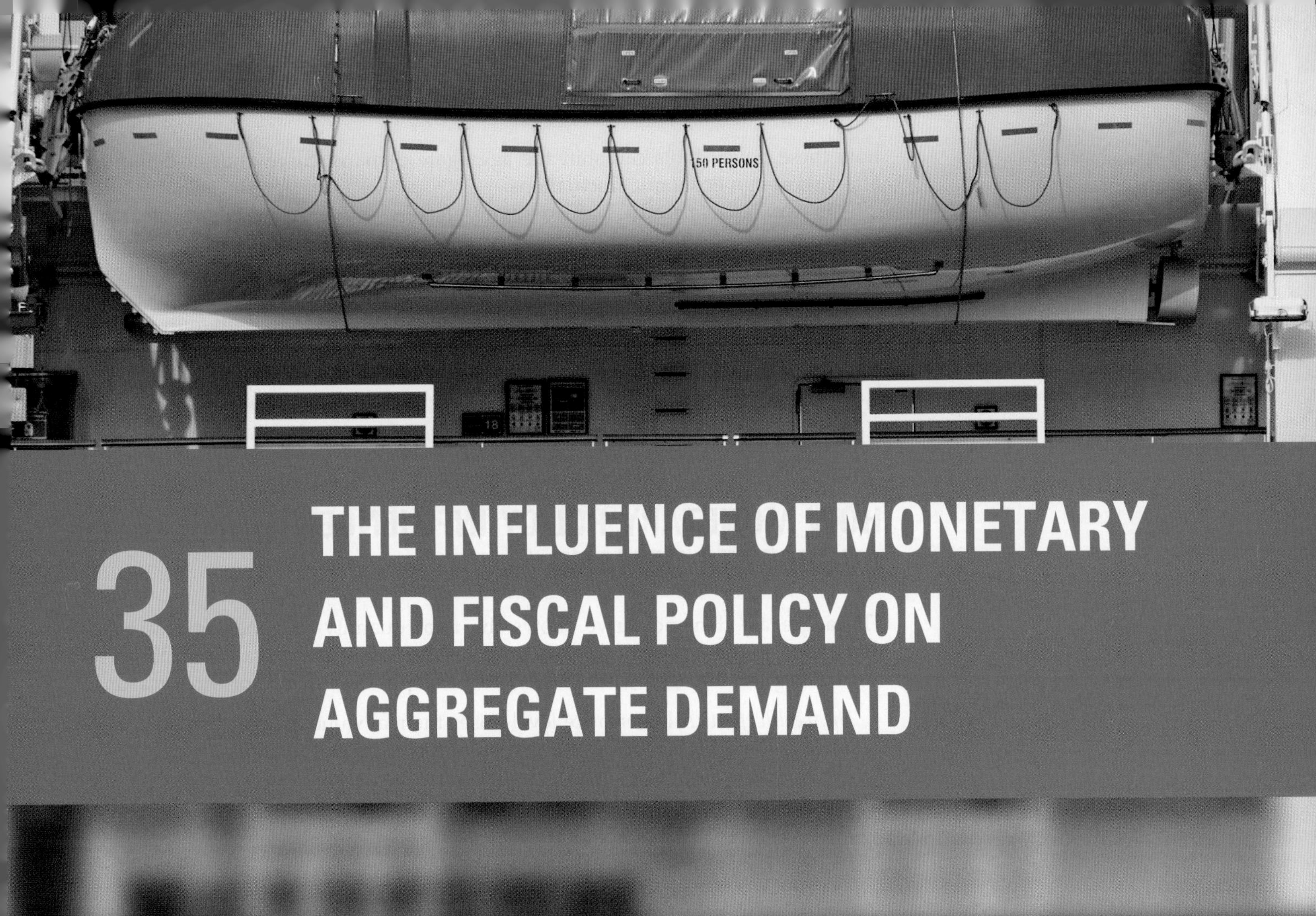

35 THE INFLUENCE OF MONETARY AND FISCAL POLICY ON AGGREGATE DEMAND

Imagine that you are a member of the Bank of England's Monetary Policy Committee (MPC), which sets UK monetary policy. You observe that the Chancellor of the Exchequer has announced in his Budget speech that he is going to cut government spending. How should the MPC respond to this change in fiscal policy? Should it reduce interest rates (and so allow the money supply to expand faster), raise interest rates or leave interest rates the same?

To answer this question, you need to consider the impact of monetary and fiscal policy on the economy. In the preceding chapter we saw how to explain short-run economic fluctuations using the model of aggregate demand and aggregate supply. When the aggregate demand curve or the aggregate supply curve shifts, the result is fluctuations in the economy's overall output of goods and services and in its overall level of prices. As we noted in the previous chapter, monetary and fiscal policy can each influence aggregate demand. Thus, a change in one of these policies can lead to short-run fluctuations in output and prices. Policy makers will want to anticipate this effect and, perhaps, adjust the other policy in response.

In this chapter we examine in more detail how the tools of monetary and fiscal policy influence the position of the aggregate demand curve. We have previously discussed the long-run effects of these policies. In Chapters 25 and 26 we saw how fiscal policy affects saving, investment and long-run economic growth. In Chapters 29 and 30 we saw how the central bank controls the money supply and how the money supply affects the price level in the long run. We now see how these policy tools can shift the aggregate demand curve and, in doing so, affect short-run economic fluctuations.

As we have already learned, many factors influence aggregate demand besides monetary and fiscal policy. In particular, desired spending by households and firms determines the overall demand for goods and services. When desired spending changes, aggregate demand shifts. If policy makers do not respond, such shifts in aggregate demand cause short-run fluctuations in output and employment. As a result, monetary and fiscal policy makers sometimes use the policy levers at their disposal to try to offset these shifts in aggregate demand and thereby stabilize the economy. Here we discuss the theory behind these policy actions and some of the difficulties that arise in using this theory in practice.

HOW MONETARY POLICY INFLUENCES AGGREGATE DEMAND

The aggregate demand curve shows the total quantity of goods and services demanded in the economy for any price level. As you may recall from the preceding chapter, the aggregate demand curve slopes downward for three reasons:

- *The wealth effect.* A lower price level raises the real value of households' money holdings, and higher real wealth stimulates consumer spending.
- *The interest rate effect.* A lower price level lowers the interest rate as people try to lend out their excess money holdings, and the lower interest rate stimulates investment spending.
- *The exchange rate effect.* When a lower price level lowers the interest rate, investors move some of their funds overseas and cause the domestic currency to depreciate relative to foreign currencies. This depreciation makes domestic goods cheaper compared to foreign goods and, therefore, stimulates spending on net exports.

These three effects should not be viewed as alternative theories. Instead, they occur simultaneously to increase the quantity of goods and services demanded when the price level falls and to decrease it when the price level rises.

Although all three effects work together in explaining the downward slope of the aggregate demand curve, they are not of equal importance. Because money holdings are a small part of household wealth, the wealth effect is the least important of the three. Whether or not the exchange rate effect is important depends upon the degree of openness of the economy. For a relatively closed economy like the USA, for example, because exports and imports represent only a small fraction of US GDP, the exchange rate effect is not very large. In the UK and most other European economies, however, the economy is much more open in the sense that imports and exports represent a much larger fraction of total GDP, so that the exchange rate effect will be more important. However, the exchange rate effect is probably secondary to the interest rate effect even in relatively open economies, for two reasons. First, the interest rate effect impacts immediately upon the whole economy, affecting consumers, homebuyers and firms across the board, while the loss of competitiveness that is part of the exchange rate effect impacts only upon traded goods, and affects mainly firms producing tradable goods and consumers buying tradable goods. Secondly, many of the countries of Europe have a common currency – the euro – which they share with many of their major trading partners, so that the exchange rate effect is muted.

theory of liquidity preference
Keynes' theory that the interest rate adjusts to bring money supply and money demand into balance

To understand how policy influences aggregate demand, therefore, we shall examine the interest rate effect in more detail. Here we develop a theory of how the interest rate is determined, called the **theory of liquidity preference**, which was originally developed by John Maynard Keynes in the 1930s. After we develop this theory, we use it to understand the downward slope of the aggregate demand curve and how monetary policy shifts this curve. By shedding new light on the aggregate demand curve, the theory of liquidity preference expands our understanding of short-run economic fluctuations.

The Theory of Liquidity Preference

In his classic book, *The General Theory of Employment, Interest and Money,* John Maynard Keynes proposed the theory of liquidity preference to explain what factors determine the economy's interest rate. The theory is, in essence, just an application of supply and demand. According to Keynes, the interest rate adjusts to balance the supply and demand for money. We introduced some elements of the theories covered here in Chapter 33 as part of the IS-LM model.

You may recall that economists distinguish between two interest rates: the *nominal interest rate* is the interest rate as usually reported, and the *real interest rate* is the interest rate corrected for the effects of inflation. Which interest rate are we now trying to explain? The answer is both. In the analysis that follows, we hold constant the expected rate of inflation. (This assumption is reasonable for studying the economy in the short run, as we are now doing.) Thus, when the nominal interest rate rises or falls, the real interest rate that people expect to earn rises or falls as well. For the rest of this chapter, when we refer to changes in the interest rate, you should envision the real and nominal interest rates moving in the same direction.

Let's now develop the theory of liquidity preference by considering the supply and demand for money and how each depends on the interest rate.

Money Supply The first element of the theory of liquidity preference is the supply of money. As we first discussed in Chapter 29, the money supply is controlled by the central bank, such as the Bank of England, the European Central Bank or the US Federal Reserve. The central bank can alter the money supply by changing the quantity of reserves in the banking system through the purchase and sale of government bonds in outright open-market operations. When the central bank buys government bonds, the money it pays for the bonds is typically deposited in banks, and this money is added to bank reserves. When the central bank sells government bonds, the money it receives for the bonds is withdrawn from the banking system, and bank reserves fall. These changes in bank reserves, in turn, lead to changes in banks' ability to make loans and create money. In addition to these open-market operations, the central bank can alter the money supply by changing reserve requirements (the amount of reserves banks must hold against deposits) or the refinancing rate (the interest rate at which banks can borrow reserves from the central bank).

These details of monetary control are important for the implementation of central bank policy, and we discussed them in detail in Chapter 29, but they are not crucial in this chapter. Our goal here is to examine how changes in the money supply affect the aggregate demand for goods and services. For this purpose, we can ignore the details of how central bank policy is implemented and simply assume that the central bank controls the money supply directly. In other words, the quantity of money supplied in the economy is fixed at whatever level the central bank decides to set it.

Because the quantity of money supplied is fixed by central bank policy, it does not depend on other economic variables. In particular, it does not depend on the interest rate. Once the central bank has made its policy decision, the quantity of

FIGURE 35.1

Equilibrium in the Money Market

According to the theory of liquidity preference, the interest rate adjusts to bring the quantity of money supplied and the quantity of money demanded into balance. If the interest rate is above the equilibrium level (such as at r_1), the quantity of money people want to hold (M_1^d) is less than the quantity the central bank has created, and this surplus of money puts downward pressure on the interest rate. Conversely, if the interest rate is below the equilibrium level (such as at r_2), the quantity of money people want to hold (M_2^d) is greater than the quantity the central bank has created, and this shortage of money puts upward pressure on the interest rate. Thus, the forces of supply and demand in the market for money push the interest rate towards the equilibrium interest rate, at which people are content holding the quantity of money the central bank has created.

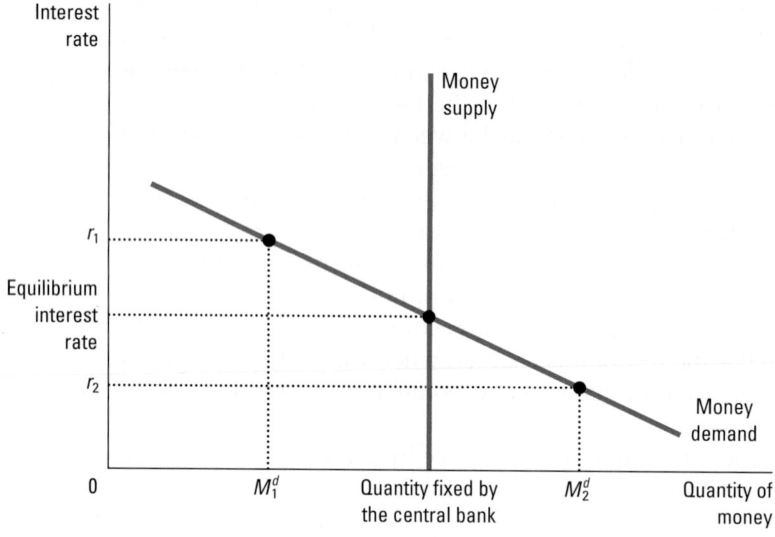

money supplied is the same, regardless of the prevailing interest rate. We represent a fixed money supply with a vertical supply curve in Figure 35.1.

Money Demand The second element of the theory of liquidity preference is the demand for money. As a starting point for understanding money demand, recall that any asset's *liquidity* refers to the ease with which that asset is converted into the economy's medium of exchange. Money is the economy's medium of exchange, so it is by definition the most liquid asset available. The liquidity of money explains the demand for it: people choose to hold money instead of other assets that offer higher rates of return because money can be used to buy goods and services.

Although many factors determine the quantity of money demanded, the one emphasized by the theory of liquidity preference is the interest rate. The reason is that the interest rate is the opportunity cost of holding money. That is, when you hold wealth as cash in your wallet, instead of as an interest-bearing bond or bank account, you forgo the benefits of the interest you could have earned (the opportunity cost). An increase in the interest rate raises the opportunity cost of holding money. There is an incentive, therefore for people to exchange cash holdings for interest-bearing deposits and this, as a result, reduces the quantity of money demanded. A decrease in the interest rate reduces the opportunity cost of holding money. The cost of the benefits forgone are not as high so there is more incentive to hold money as cash and as a result the quantity demanded increases. Thus, as shown in Figure 35.1, the money demand curve slopes downward.

Equilibrium in the Money Market According to the theory of liquidity preference, the interest rate adjusts to balance the supply and demand for money. There is one interest rate, called the *equilibrium interest rate,* at which the quantity of money demanded exactly balances the quantity of money supplied. If the interest rate is at any other level, people will try to adjust their portfolios of assets and, as a result, drive the interest rate toward the equilibrium.

For example, suppose that the interest rate is above the equilibrium level, such as r_1 in Figure 35.1. In this case, the quantity of money that people want to hold, M^d_1, is less than the quantity of money that the central bank has supplied. Those

FYI

Interest Rates in the Long Run and the Short Run

At this point, we should pause and reflect on a seemingly awkward embarrassment of riches. It might appear as if we now have two theories for how interest rates are determined. Chapter 26 said that the interest rate adjusts to balance the supply of and demand for loanable funds (that is, national saving and desired investment). By contrast, we just established here that the interest rate adjusts to balance the supply and demand for money. How can we reconcile these two theories?

To answer this question, we must again consider the differences between the long-run and short-run behaviour of the economy. Three macroeconomic variables are of central importance: the economy's output of goods and services, the interest rate and the price level. According to the classical macroeconomic theory we developed in Chapters 25, 26 and 30, these variables are determined as follows:

1. *Output* is determined by the supplies of capital and labour and the available production technology for turning capital and labour into output. (We call this the natural rate of output.)
2. For any given level of output, the *interest rate* adjusts to balance the supply and demand for loanable funds.
3. The *price level* adjusts to balance the supply and demand for money. Changes in the supply of money lead to proportionate changes in the price level.

These are three of the essential propositions of classical economic theory. Most economists believe that these propositions do a good job of describing how the economy works *in the long run.*

Yet these propositions do not hold in the short run. As we discussed in the preceding chapter, many prices are slow to adjust to changes in the money supply; this is reflected in a short-run aggregate supply curve that is upward sloping rather than vertical. As a result, the overall price level cannot, by itself, balance the supply and demand for money in the short run. This stickiness of the price level forces the interest rate to move in order to bring the money market into equilibrium. These changes in the interest rate, in turn, affect the aggregate demand for goods and services. As aggregate demand fluctuates, the economy's output of goods and services moves away from the level determined by factor supplies and technology.

For issues concerning the short run, then, it is best to think about the economy as follows:

1. The *price level* is stuck at some level (based on previously formed expectations) and, in the short run, is relatively unresponsive to changing economic conditions.
2. For any given price level, the *interest rate* adjusts to balance the supply and demand for money.
3. The level of *output* responds to the aggregate demand for goods and services, which is in part determined by the interest rate that balances the money market.

Notice that this precisely reverses the order of analysis used to study the economy in the long run.

Thus, the different theories of the interest rate are useful for different purposes. When thinking about the long-run determinants of interest rates, it is best to keep in mind the loanable funds theory. This approach highlights the importance of an economy's saving propensities and investment opportunities. By contrast, when thinking about the short-run determinants of interest rates, it is best to keep in mind the liquidity preference theory. This theory highlights the importance of monetary policy.

people who are holding the surplus of money will try to get rid of it by buying interest-bearing bonds or by depositing it in an interest-bearing bank account. Because bond issuers and banks prefer to pay lower interest rates, they respond to this surplus of money by lowering the interest rates they offer. As the interest rate falls, people become more willing to hold money until, at the equilibrium interest rate, people are happy to hold exactly the amount of money the central bank has supplied.

Conversely, at interest rates below the equilibrium level, such as r_2 in Figure 35.1, the quantity of money that people want to hold, M_2^d, is greater than the quantity of money that the central bank has supplied. As a result, people try to increase their holdings of money by reducing their holdings of bonds and other interest-bearing assets. As people cut back on their holdings of bonds, bond issuers find that they have to offer higher interest rates to attract buyers. Thus, the interest rate rises and approaches the equilibrium level.

The Downward Slope of the Aggregate Demand Curve

Having seen how the theory of liquidity preference explains the economy's equilibrium interest rate, we now consider its implications for the aggregate demand for goods and services. As a warm-up exercise, let's begin by using the theory to re-examine a topic we already understand – the interest rate effect and the downward slope of the aggregate demand curve. In particular, suppose that the overall level of prices in the economy rises. What happens to the interest rate that balances the supply and demand for money, and how does that change affect the quantity of goods and services demanded?

As we discussed in Chapter 30, the price level is one determinant of the quantity of money demanded. At higher prices, more money is exchanged every time a good or service is sold. As a result, people will choose to hold a larger quantity of money. That is, a higher price level increases the quantity of money demanded for any given interest rate. Thus, an increase in the price level from P_1 to P_2 shifts the money demand curve to the right from MD_1 to MD_2, as shown in panel (a) of Figure 35.2.

Notice how this shift in money demand affects the equilibrium in the money market. For a fixed money supply, the interest rate must rise to balance money supply and money demand. The higher price level has increased the amount of money people want to hold and has shifted the money demand curve to the right. Yet the quantity of money supplied is unchanged, so the interest rate must rise from r_1 to r_2 to discourage the additional demand.

This increase in the interest rate has ramifications not only for the money market but also for the quantity of goods and services demanded, as shown in panel (b). At a higher interest rate, the cost of borrowing and the return to saving are greater. Fewer households choose to borrow to buy a new house, and those who do buy smaller houses, so the demand for residential investment falls. Fewer firms choose to borrow to build new factories and buy new equipment, so business investment falls. Thus, when the price level rises from P_1 to P_2, increasing money demand from MD_1 to MD_2 and raising the interest rate from r_1 to r_2, the quantity of goods and services demanded falls from Y_1 to Y_2.

Hence, this analysis of the interest rate effect can be summarized in three steps: (1) A higher price level raises money demand. (2) Higher money demand leads to a higher interest rate. (3) A higher interest rate reduces the quantity of goods and services demanded. Of course, the same logic works in reverse as well: a lower price level reduces money demand, which leads to a lower interest rate, and this in turn increases the quantity of goods and services demanded. The end result of this analysis is a negative relationship between the price level and

FIGURE 35.2

The Money Market and the Slope of the Aggregate Demand Curve

An increase in the price level from P_1 to P_2 shifts the money demand curve to the right, as in panel (a). This increase in money demand causes the interest rate to rise from r_1 to r_2. Because the interest rate is the cost of borrowing, the increase in the interest rate reduces the quantity of goods and services demanded from Y_1 to Y_2. This negative relationship between the price level and quantity demanded is represented with a downward sloping aggregate demand curve, as in panel (b).

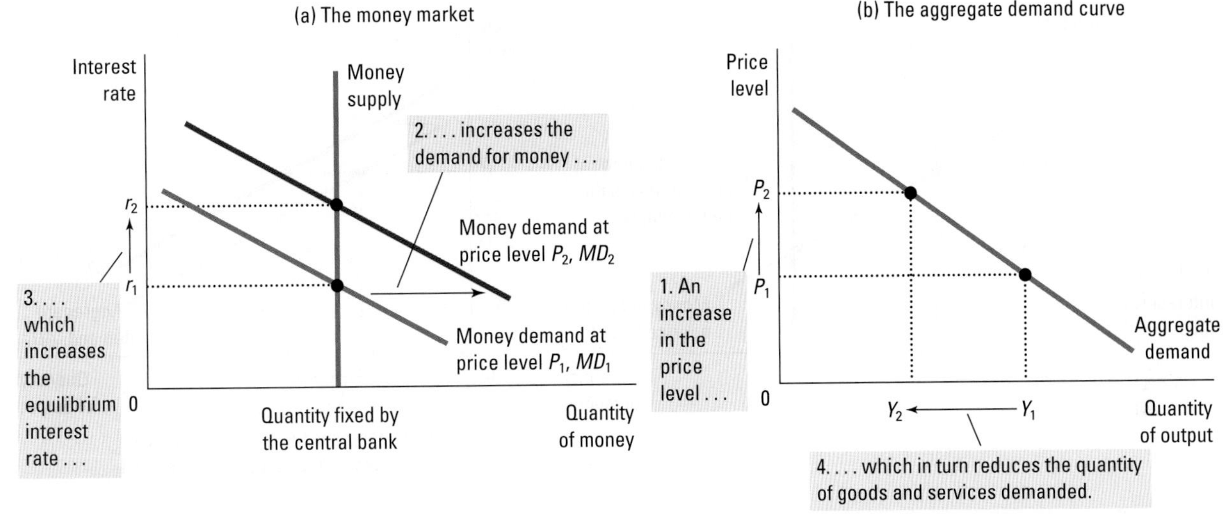

the quantity of goods and services demanded, which is illustrated with a downward sloping aggregate demand curve.

Changes in the Money Supply

So far we have used the theory of liquidity preference to explain more fully how the total quantity demanded of goods and services in the economy changes as the price level changes. That is, we have examined movements along the downward sloping aggregate demand curve. The theory also sheds light, however, on some of the other events that alter the quantity of goods and services demanded. Whenever the quantity of goods and services demanded changes *for a given price level,* the aggregate demand curve shifts.

One important variable that shifts the aggregate demand curve is monetary policy. To see how monetary policy affects the economy in the short run, suppose that the central bank increases the money supply by buying government bonds in open-market operations. (Why the central bank might do this will become clear later after we understand the effects of such a move.) Let's consider how this monetary injection influences the equilibrium interest rate for a given price level. This will tell us what the injection does to the position of the aggregate demand curve.

As panel (a) of Figure 35.3 shows, an increase in the money supply shifts the money-supply curve to the right from MS_1 to MS_2. Because the money demand curve has not changed, the interest rate falls from r_1 to r_2 to balance money supply and money demand. That is, the interest rate must fall to induce people to hold the additional money that the central bank has created.

FIGURE 35.3

A Monetary Injection

In panel (a), an increase in the money supply from MS_1 to MS_2 reduces the equilibrium interest rate from r_1 to r_2. Because the interest rate is the cost of borrowing, the fall in the interest rate raises the quantity of goods and services demanded at a given price level from Y_1 to Y_2. Thus, in panel (b), the aggregate demand curve shifts to the right from AD_1 to AD_2.

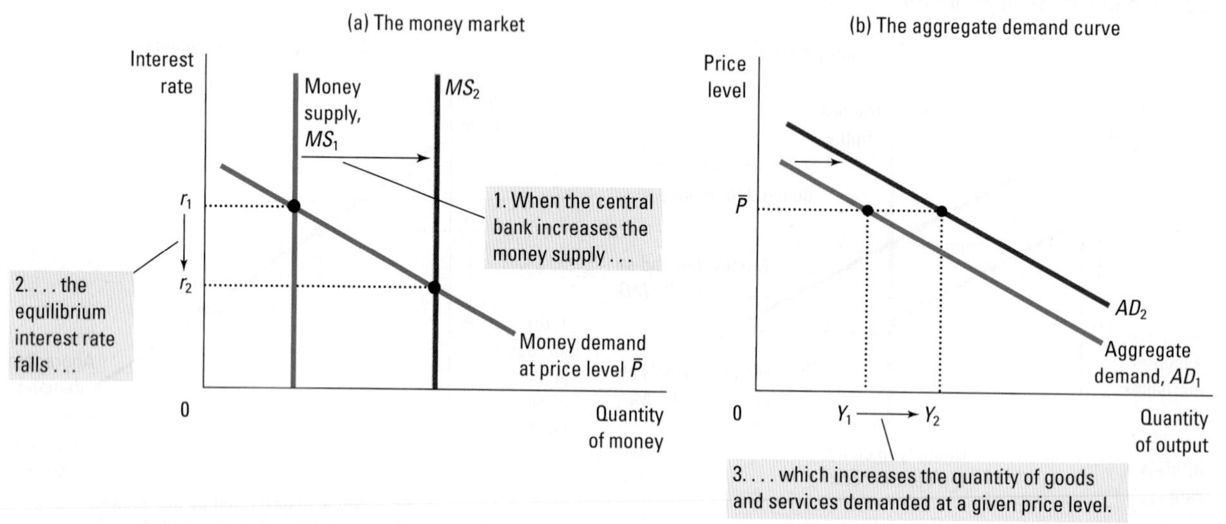

Once again, the interest rate influences the quantity of goods and services demanded, as shown in panel (b) of Figure 35.3. The lower interest rate reduces the cost of borrowing and the return to saving. Households buy more and larger houses, stimulating the demand for residential investment. Firms spend more on new factories and new equipment, stimulating business investment. As a result, the quantity of goods and services demanded at a given price level $\bar{P}$, rises from Y_1 to Y_2. Of course, there is nothing special about $\bar{P}$: the monetary injection raises the quantity of goods and services demanded at every price level. Thus, the entire aggregate demand curve shifts to the right.

To sum up: when the central bank increases the money supply, it leads to a fall in the interest rate and increases the quantity of goods and services demanded for any given price level, shifting the aggregate demand curve to the right. Conversely, when the central bank contracts the money supply, the interest rate rises to bring the money market into equilibrium and reduces the quantity of goods and services demanded for any given price level, shifting the aggregate demand curve to the left.

The Role of Interest Rates

Our discussion so far in this chapter has treated the money supply as the central bank's policy instrument. When the central bank buys government bonds in open-market operations, it increases the money supply and expands aggregate demand. When the central bank sells government bonds in open-market operations, it decreases the money supply and contracts aggregate demand.

Often, however, discussions of central bank policy treat the interest rate, rather than the money supply, as the central bank's policy instrument. Indeed, as we discussed in Chapter 29, in recent years many of the major central banks, including the Bank of England, the European Central Bank and the US Federal Reserve, have conducted policy by setting the interest rate at which they will lend to the banking sector – the refinancing rate for the European Central Bank, the repurchase or 'repo' rate for the Bank of England, and the discount rate for the Federal Reserve (you may wish to review the definitions of these terms on pages 630–632).

The central bank's decision to set interest rates rather than target a certain level (or rate of growth) of the money supply does not fundamentally alter our analysis of monetary policy. The theory of liquidity preference illustrates an important principle: monetary policy can be described either in terms of the money supply or in terms of the interest rate. When the central bank sets a target for the refinancing rate of, say, x per cent, the central bank's bond traders are told: 'Conduct whatever open-market operations are necessary to ensure that the equilibrium interest rate equals x per cent.' In other words, when the central bank sets a target for the interest rate, it commits itself to adjusting the money supply in order to make the equilibrium in the money market hit that target.

As a result, changes in monetary policy can be viewed either in terms of a changing target for the interest rate or in terms of a change in the money supply. As noted in Chapter 29, when you read in the newspaper that the central bank has lowered interest rates, you should understand that this occurs only because the central bank's bond traders are doing what it takes to make it happen. If interest rates have been lowered, then the central bank's bond traders will have bought government bonds, and this purchase increases the money supply and lowers the equilibrium interest rate (just as in Figure 35.3).

The lessons from all this are quite simple: changes in monetary policy that aim to expand aggregate demand can be described either as increasing the money supply or as lowering the interest rate. Changes in monetary policy that aim to contract aggregate demand can be described either as decreasing the money supply or as raising the interest rate.

"Gerald, is that a fixed-rate scowl, or is it adjustable to the current interest rate?"

CASE STUDY

Why Central Banks Watch the Stock Market (and Vice Versa)

'Irrational exuberance.' That was how former US Federal Reserve Chairman Alan Greenspan once described the booming stock market of the late 1990s. He was right that the market was exuberant: average stock prices increased about four-fold during that decade. And perhaps it was even irrational: in 2001 and 2002 the stock market took back some of these large gains, as stock prices experienced a pronounced decline.

Regardless of how we view the booming market, it does raise an important question: how should the central bank respond to stock market fluctuations? The central bank has no reason to care about stock prices in themselves, but it does have the job of monitoring and responding to developments in the overall economy, and the stock market is a piece of that puzzle. When the stock market booms, households become wealthier, and this increased wealth stimulates consumer spending. In addition, a rise in stock prices makes it more attractive for firms to sell new shares of stock, and this stimulates investment spending. For both reasons, a booming stock market expands the aggregate demand for goods and services.

As we discuss more fully later in the chapter, one of the central bank's goals is to stabilize aggregate demand, for greater stability in aggregate demand means greater stability in output and the price level. To do this, the central bank might respond to a stock market boom by keeping the money supply lower and interest rates higher than it otherwise would. The contractionary effects of higher interest rates would offset the expansionary effects of higher stock prices. In fact, this analysis does describe central bank behaviour: real interest rates were kept high by historical standards during the 'irrationally exuberant' stock market boom of the late 1990s.

The opposite occurs when the stock market falls. Spending on consumption and investment declines, depressing aggregate demand and pushing the economy towards recession. To stabilize aggregate demand, the central bank needs to increase the money supply and lower interest rates. And, indeed, that is what it typically does.

Figures 35.4 and 35.5 highlight this clearly. The decline in the FTSE 100 from January 2000 to April/May 2003 is mirrored by a fall in the Bank of England's Base Rate from 6.0 per cent to 3.75 per cent. As the market rose to early January 2008, so the interest rate gradually increased to 5.75 per cent. The financial crisis saw the FTSE 100 fall sharply in 2008 and into 2009 and Bank Rate was also cut dramatically. Historically this has also been the case. For example, on Monday 19 October 1987, stock prices in most of the major industrialized economies plummeted. The New York stock market fell by 22.6 per cent – at that time the biggest one-day drop in history – and the value of quoted shares on the London Stock Exchange fell by £50 billion as the *Financial Times* 30-share index dived 10 per cent. The debate over the cause of the crash continued for many years after the event but economists have never agreed on a single factor that ushered in 'Black Monday'. By the end of October, stock prices in Australia had fallen 41.8 per cent, in Canada 22.5 per cent, in Hong Kong 45.8 per cent and in the United Kingdom by 26.4 per cent. The reaction of monetary policy makers in most of these countries was to reduce interest rates and allow the money supply to expand in order to offset the contractionary effects of the reduction in wealth on aggregate demand.

FIGURE 35.4

FTSE 100 Index Opening Prices, 2000–09

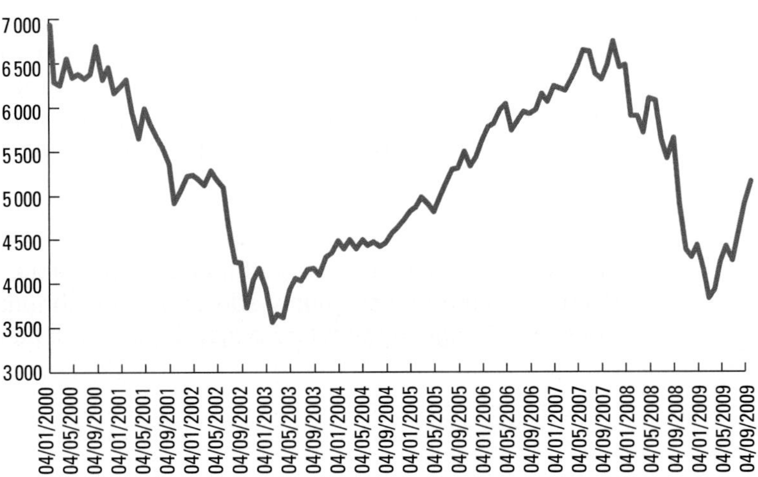

Source: London Stock Exchange.

FIGURE 35.5

Bank of England Base Rate, 2000–09

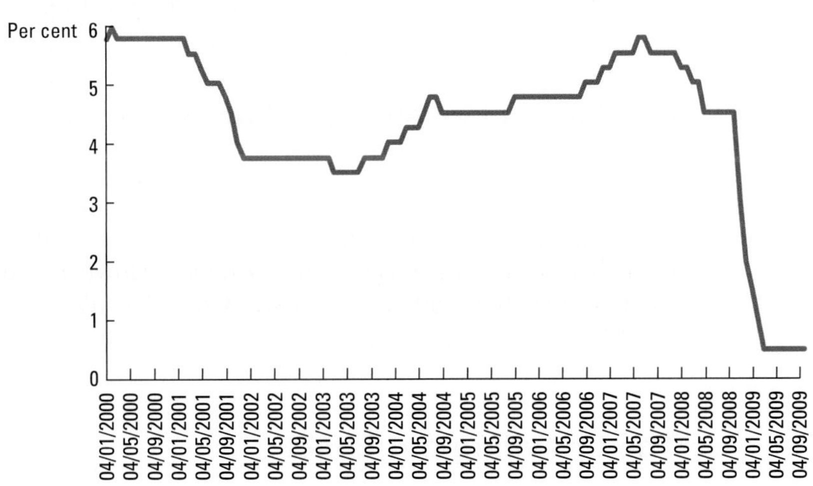

Source: Bank of England.

In the United States, the crash in the stock market caused by the terrorist attacks of 9/11 led to the Fed cutting interest rates. It also cut rates in response to the economic crisis that precipitated a stock market collapse in the late 1990s after the hedge fund Long Term Capital Management became exposed following the Russian government's default on its debt, generating substantial turmoil in financial markets.

While the central bank keeps an eye on the stock market, stock market participants also keep an eye on the central bank. Because the central bank can influence interest rates and economic activity, it can alter the value of stocks. For example, when the central bank raises interest rates by reducing the money supply, it makes owning stocks less attractive for two reasons. First, a higher interest rate means that bonds, the alternative to stocks, are earning a higher return. Secondly, the central bank's tightening of monetary policy risks causing a slowdown in economic activity, which reduces profits. As a result, stock prices often fall when the central bank raises interest rates.

Quick Quiz Use the theory of liquidity preference to explain how a decrease in the money supply affects the equilibrium interest rate. How does this change in monetary policy affect the demand curve?

HOW FISCAL POLICY INFLUENCES AGGREGATE DEMAND

The government can influence the behaviour of the economy not only with monetary policy but also with fiscal policy. Fiscal policy refers to the government's choices regarding the overall level of government purchases or taxes. Earlier in the book we examined how fiscal policy influences saving, investment and growth in the long run. In the short run, however, the primary effect of fiscal policy is on the aggregate demand for goods and services.

Changes in Government Purchases

We saw in Chapter 33 that changes in autonomous spending can have an effect on the level of spending in the economy which is greater than the initial injection. The multiplier effect means that aggregate demand will shift by a larger amount than the increase in government spending. However, the crowding-out effect suggests that the shift in aggregate demand could be *smaller* than the initial injection.

The Crowding-out Effect

While an increase in government purchases stimulates the aggregate demand for goods and services, it also causes the interest rate to rise, and a higher interest rate reduces investment spending and chokes off aggregate demand. The reduction in aggregate demand that results when a fiscal expansion raises the interest rate is called the **crowding-out effect**.

crowding-out effect
the offset in aggregate demand that results when expansionary fiscal policy raises the interest rate and thereby reduces investment spending

To see why crowding out occurs, let's consider what happens in the money market when the government invests in nuclear power stations from Nucelec. As we have discussed, this increase in demand raises the incomes of the workers and owners of this firm (and, because of the multiplier effect, of other firms as well). As incomes rise, households plan to buy more goods and services and, as

FIGURE 35.6

The Crowding-out Effect

Panel (a) shows the money market. When the government increases its purchases of goods and services, the resulting increase in income raises the demand for money from MD_1 to MD_2, and this causes the equilibrium interest rate to rise from r_1 to r_2. Panel (b) shows the effects on aggregate demand. The initial impact of the increase in government purchases shifts the aggregate demand curve from AD_1 to AD_2. Yet, because the interest rate is the cost of borrowing, the increase in the interest rate tends to reduce the quantity of goods and services demanded, particularly for investment goods. This crowding out of investment partially offsets the impact of the fiscal expansion on aggregate demand. In the end, the aggregate demand curve shifts only to AD_3.

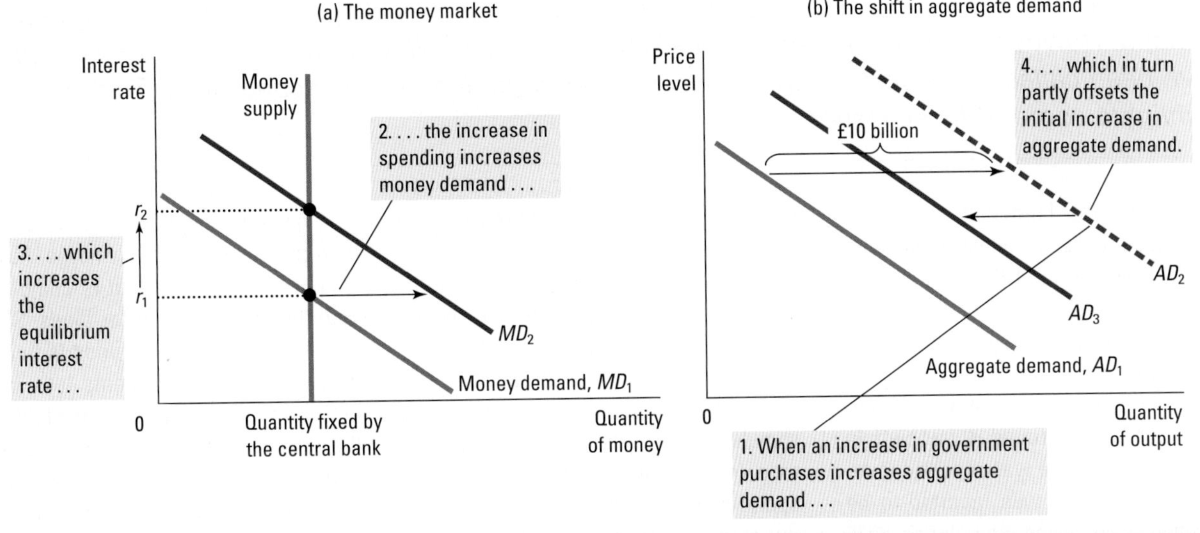

a result, choose to hold more of their wealth in liquid form. That is, the increase in income caused by the fiscal expansion raises the demand for money.

The effect of the increase in money demand is shown in panel (a) of Figure 35.6. Because the central bank has not changed the money supply, the vertical supply curve remains the same. When the higher level of income shifts the money demand curve to the right from MD_1 to MD_2, the interest rate must rise from r_1 to r_2 to keep supply and demand in balance.

The increase in the interest rate, in turn, reduces the quantity of goods and services demanded. In particular, because borrowing is more expensive, the demand for residential and business investment goods declines. That is, as the increase in government purchases increases the demand for goods and services, it may also crowd out investment. This crowding-out effect partially offsets the impact of government purchases on aggregate demand, as illustrated in panel (b) of Figure 35.6. The initial impact of the increase in government purchases is to shift the aggregate demand curve from AD_1 to AD_2, but once crowding out takes place, the aggregate demand curve drops back to AD_3.

To sum up: when the government increases its purchases by £10 billion, the aggregate demand for goods and services could rise by more or less than £10 billion, depending on whether the multiplier effect or the crowding-out effect is larger.

IN THE NEWS

Fiscal Stimulus

During periods of economic downturn there are calls for governments to step in to help to cushion the worst effects of the slowdown. The global recession of 2008–09 saw governments around the world making announcements of fiscal stimulus packages to help boost aggregate demand. However, the benefits of such packages and even whether they amount to a stimulus, have been called into question and aroused much debate amongst economists. The following highlights some of these issues.

In late 2008 the European Union (EU) announced a fiscal stimulus package of €200 billion; in the UK the Chancellor of the Exchequer had to admit that government borrowing might reach £175 billion and be 79 per cent of GDP in 2013–14. In India public debt as a component of GDP is around 80 per cent; in the US the package was reported to be $800 billion. China was reported to be injecting $586 billion and Japan $275 billion. On the one hand critics were arguing that such packages were not enough to bridge the output gap that had widened in most economies. In the US, for example, the gap between potential and actual GDP was estimated by some economists at around $2 trillion. Other criticisms of fiscal stimulus packages suggested that they were not really what they seemed to be and if they were then they would not bring the benefits that were claimed for them because of crowding out.

For example, in a study of the EU stimulus package in February 2009, David Saha and Jakob von Weizsäcker said, 'It should be recognized that the likely real impact on aggregate demand in the near future may well be more limited than suggested by the headline figures'[1]. In their analysis of the fiscal stimulus in Italy, announced as €80 billion, Saha and Weizsäcker conclude that the stimulus was not a stimulus at all but a fiscal tightening amounting to €0.3 billion. In parts of Europe there were concerns that any major fiscal stimulus package would put pressure on the public debt and affect the stability of the euro around which so much of the future prosperity of the EU lies.

One of the concerns about any fiscal stimulus is the extent to which it creates 'real wealth'. Governments may spend more money but on what? If the money is spent on public works – the building of new schools, hospitals, roads and so on, then surely this would boost aggregate demand? To an extent it would but how is this additional spending to be financed? To raise the money governments will either have to tax its citizens more or increase borrowing as in the case of the UK, for example. Additional spending on the construction of a new road may put money into the pockets of construction companies and its workers, but to fund this the government has to tax other wealth producers thus offsetting some of the benefits of the stimulus. If the spending goes on additional benefits for those who become unemployed then critics argue that the government is not contributing to wealth creation; these individuals may be supported in times of hardship and may spend their benefits on food and other goods but they are not actually generating any wealth in return for the benefits they receive.

If governments have to borrow more then crowding out may emerge. In this scenario the government is competing with the private sector for funds. Since the supply of loanable funds is finite it follows that if governments take more of these funds there is less available for the private sector. If it is also assumed that the private sector uses such investment funds more efficiently than the public sector then not only do fiscal stimulus packages crowd out private investment they divert investment funds to less productive uses.

Whilst this view is widely accepted, there are those that suggest that extraordinary times call for extraordinary action. One such proponent of this view is Paul Krugman, the Nobel Prize winning Princeton University economist. Krugman argued that the depth of the financial crisis and global recession between 2007 and 2009 was such that a fiscal stimulus was necessary to get out of a liquidity trap and far from crowding out, fiscal stimuli would lead to 'crowding in'. A liquidity trap occurs when monetary policy is insufficient to generate the economic stimulus necessary to get out of recession. In the US and the UK, for example, interest rates were lowered by the Fed and the Bank of England to near zero, the Bank of Japan's key interest rate stood at 0.1 per cent in August 2009 whilst the ECB had rates at 1 per cent.

Krugman argued that private investment is a function of the state of the economy and, given the depth of the global recession, investment had plummeted. Investment, therefore, in this situation is more responsive to product demand than to the rate of interest. If governments applied appropriate fiscal stimuli then this would improve the state of the economy and thus encourage private sector investment. As private sector investment increases then this improves the productive potential and helps bring economies out of recession. Far from crowding out, Krugman argues, the fiscal stimulus would lead to crowding in.

Critics of this view suggest that increased government spending will crowd out private investment to an extent and so any fiscal stimulus has to take into account the loss of the benefits of that private investment in assessing the success of such a policy. The success of a stimulus package in putting economies on a sounder footing and bringing benefits to future generations would be highly dependent on the type of spending carried out by governments worldwide. Spending on new schools and transport infrastructure may improve the future productive potential of the economy. However, the issue of rent seeking and log rolling have to be taken into consideration. Rent seeking occurs where decisions are made leading to resource allocation that maximizes the benefit to the decision-maker at the expense of another party or parties. Log rolling is where decisions may be made on resource allocation to projects that have less importance, in return for the support of the interested party in other decision-making areas. In both cases, it is argued that resource allocation is not as efficient as that carried out by the private sector and this has to be taken into consideration in assessing the benefits of public sector spending as a result of any stimulus package.

[1]http://aei.pitt.edu/10549/01/UPDATED-SIZE-OF-STIMULUS-FINAL.pdf accessed 6 October 2009.

Changes in Taxes

The other important instrument of fiscal policy, besides the level of government purchases, is the level of taxation. When the government cuts personal income taxes, for instance, it increases households' take-home pay. Households will save some of this additional income, but they will also spend some of it on consumer goods. Because it increases consumer spending, the tax cut shifts the aggregate demand curve to the right. Similarly, a tax increase depresses consumer spending and shifts the aggregate demand curve to the left.

The size of the shift in aggregate demand resulting from a tax change is also affected by the multiplier and crowding-out effects. When the government cuts taxes and stimulates consumer spending, earnings and profits rise, which further stimulates consumer spending. This is the multiplier effect. At the same time, higher income leads to higher money demand, which tends to raise interest rates. Higher interest rates make borrowing more costly, which reduces investment spending. This is the crowding-out effect. Depending on the size of the multiplier and crowding-out effects, the shift in aggregate demand could be larger or smaller than the tax change that causes it.

In addition to the multiplier and crowding-out effects, there is another important determinant of the size of the shift in aggregate demand that results from a tax change: households' perceptions about whether the tax change is permanent or temporary. For example, suppose that the government announces a tax cut of €1 000 per household. In deciding how much of this €1 000 to spend, households must ask themselves how long this extra income will last. If households expect the tax cut to be permanent, they will view it as adding substantially to their financial resources and, therefore, increase their spending by a large amount. In this case, the tax cut will have a large impact on aggregate demand. By contrast, if households expect the tax change to be temporary, they will view it as adding only slightly to their financial resources and, therefore, will increase their spending by only a small amount. In this case, the tax cut will have a small impact on aggregate demand.

FYI

How Fiscal Policy Might Affect Aggregate Supply

So far our discussion of fiscal policy has stressed how changes in government purchases and changes in taxes influence the quantity of goods and services demanded. Most economists believe that the short-run macroeconomic effects of fiscal policy work primarily through aggregate demand. Yet fiscal policy can potentially also influence the quantity of goods and services supplied.

For instance, consider the effects of tax changes on aggregate supply. One of the *Ten Principles of Economics* in Chapter 1 is that people respond to incentives. When the government cuts tax rates, workers keep more of each pound they earn, so they have a greater incentive to work and produce goods and services. If they respond to this incentive, the quantity of goods and services supplied will be greater at each price level, and the aggregate supply curve will shift to the right. Some economists, called *supply-siders,* have argued that the influence of tax cuts on aggregate supply is very large. Indeed, some supply-siders claim the influence is so large that a cut in tax rates will actually increase tax revenue by increasing worker effort. Most economists, however, believe that the supply-side effects of tax cuts are much smaller.

Like changes in taxes, changes in government purchases can also potentially affect aggregate supply. Suppose, for instance, that the government increases expenditure on a form of government-provided capital, such as roads. Roads are used by private businesses to make deliveries to their customers; an increase in the quantity of roads increases these businesses' productivity. Hence, when the government spends more on roads, it increases the quantity of goods and services supplied at any given price level and, thus, shifts the aggregate supply curve to the right. This effect on aggregate supply is probably more important in the long run than in the short run, however, because it would take some time for the government to build the new roads and put them into use.

Quick Quiz Suppose that the government reduces spending on motorway construction by €1 billion. Which way does the aggregate demand curve shift? Explain why the shift might be larger than €1 billion. Explain why the shift might be smaller than €1 billion.

USING POLICY TO STABILIZE THE ECONOMY

We have seen how monetary and fiscal policy can affect the economy's aggregate demand for goods and services. These theoretical insights raise some important policy questions: should policy makers use these instruments to control aggregate demand and stabilize the economy? If so, when? If not, why not?

The Case for an Active Stabilization Policy

Let's return to the question that began this chapter: when the government reduces its spending, how should the central bank respond? As we have seen, government spending is one determinant of the position of the aggregate demand curve. When the government cuts spending, aggregate demand will fall, which will depress production and employment in the short run. If the central bank wants to prevent this adverse effect of the fiscal policy, it can act to expand aggregate demand by increasing the money supply. A monetary expansion would reduce interest rates, stimulate investment spending and expand aggregate demand. If monetary policy responds appropriately, the combined changes in monetary and fiscal policy could leave the aggregate demand for goods and services unaffected.

This analysis is exactly the sort followed by the members of the policy-setting committees of central banks like the Bank of England, the European Central Bank and the Federal Reserve. They know that monetary policy is an important determinant of aggregate demand. They also know that there are other important determinants as well, including fiscal policy set by the government, and so they will watch debates over fiscal policy with a keen eye.

This response of monetary policy to the change in fiscal policy is an example of a more general phenomenon: the use of policy instruments to stabilize aggregate demand and, as a result, production and employment. Economic stabilization has been seen as an explicit or implicit goal of government macroeconomic policy in European and North American economies since the end of World War II. In the UK, for example, this view was embodied in a government White Paper, published in 1944, which explicitly stated: 'The Government accepts as one of their primary aims and responsibilities the maintenance of a high and stable level of employment after the War.' In the USA, similar sentiments were embodied in the Employment Act of 1946. This explicit recognition by governments of their responsibility to stabilize the economy, has two implications. The first, more modest, implication is that the government should avoid being a cause of economic fluctuations itself. Thus, most economists advise against large and sudden changes in monetary and fiscal policy, for such changes are likely to cause fluctuations in aggregate demand. Moreover, when large changes do occur, it is important that monetary and fiscal policy makers be aware of and respond to the other's actions.

The second, more ambitious, implication of this explicit admission of responsibility – and one that was especially dominant in the first 30 years after the end of World War II – was that the government should respond to changes in the private economy in order to stabilize aggregate demand. Before proceeding further in this discussion, it is as well to take a step back and ask why it was that there was this explicit admission of government responsibility for macroeconomic stabilization at this point in history. There are two reasons. First, policy makers remembered the misery of the Great Depression before the war, and were keen to avoid a recurrence not only because of the misery involved for millions of people but also because of the political effects of economic depression which were associated with a rise in extremism. Poverty was directly linked with the rise of extremism and political instability. As the war ended, therefore, they wanted to look forward to a better world in which governments could help avoid major recessions and the associated political instability. Secondly, however, the war ended less than ten years after the publication of Keynes' *The General Theory of Employment, Interest and Money*, which has been one of the most influential books ever written about economics. In it, Keynes emphasized the key role of aggregate demand in explaining short-run economic fluctuations. Keynes claimed that the government should actively stimulate aggregate demand when aggregate demand appeared insufficient to maintain production at its full-employment level.

Keynes (and his many followers) argued that aggregate demand fluctuates because of largely irrational waves of pessimism and optimism. He used the term 'animal spirits' to refer to these arbitrary changes in attitude. When pessimism reigns, households reduce consumption spending, and firms reduce investment spending. The result is reduced aggregate demand, lower production and higher unemployment. Conversely, when optimism reigns, households and firms increase spending. The result is higher aggregate demand, higher production and inflationary pressure. Notice that these changes in attitude are, to some extent, self-fulfilling.

In principle, the government can adjust its monetary and fiscal policy in response to these waves of optimism and pessimism and, thereby, stabilize the

IN THE NEWS

Fiscal Policy in South Africa

The use of macroeconomic policies to help boost economic activity has been a feature of developed economies for many years. In emerging economies structural issues make the appropriate use of such policies even more important. In South Africa the considerable structural difficulties that are the legacy of Apartheid have meant that attempts by post-Apartheid governments have faced considerable challenges. This article highlights the fact that macroeconomic policies take time to work and that a country like South Africa not only faces structural difficulties but also the vagaries of swings in the economic cycle.

In September 2009, the International Monetary Fund (IMF) released a report on the performance of the South African economy. Its summary conclusions were that the country needed to boost spending to obviate the recession but at the same time be mindful of the potential inflationary effects of so doing. Global recession has affected South Africa although its banking system has not been as exposed to the global financial crisis as some countries have been. However, the government estimated that tax revenue would be around R60 billion ($7.9 billion) lower than forecast which would lead to a widening of the budget deficit to 3.8 per cent of GDP.

One of the problems for the South African government is the high level of unemployment. In 2009 the rate of unemployment stood at 23.6 per cent and the government has a target of reducing that rate to 14 per cent by 2014. However, this target may not be met given the global economic slowdown. The South African economy grew at an average rate of around 4 per cent between 1999 and 2007; the government had targeted growth at 6 per cent in order to reach its unemployment target. South Africa, however, has not been immune to the global downturn and after minimal growth in quarter three 2008, the economy slipped into negative growth in quarter four 2008 and quarter one 2009 (Figure 35.7). At the same time, however, the country had an inflation rate of 6.7 per cent in July 2009 – above the 3–6 per cent target rate which the South African Reserve Bank (SARB) is working towards.

The recession in South Africa means that the government faces difficult decisions if it wants to maintain progress in removing the structural barriers to reducing unemployment. One major plus for the country is that the banking system remained reasonably stable amidst the global banking crisis. Most South African banks had not borrowed excessively to finance lending and had only limited exposure to overseas assets and as a result the degree of support required by its central bank was minimal. The SARB loosened monetary policy in the latter part of 2008 resulting in a total cut of some 5 per cent by August 2009, to 7 per cent. The challenge for the government is to counter the economic downturn and maintain the progress it has made in reducing unemployment (a 5 per cent reduction between 2004 and 2007).

In February 2009, the then South African Finance Minister, Trevor Manuel, announced that the government would spend R787 billion on infrastructure projects. Within the budget Mr Manuel allocated resources to spending on public transport, road and rail networks, school buildings, health facilities, water systems, power generation and telecommunications systems. The aim was to improve the productive capacity of the economy for the future but also to cushion the economy from the worst of the recession. Manuel's successor, Pravin Gordhan, said in September 2009: 'Our fiscal expansion is having a positive effect on our economic performance. In particular, the acceleration of infrastructure spending is contributing to both greater long-term capacity and short-term employment creation. These measures have not offset the full effect of the decline in… demand, but the situation would have been far worse had we firstly not anticipated the crisis, and secondly not acted as boldly as we have.'

The IMF supported the fiscal stimulus and its annual report on the South African economy implied that the expansion of the budget deficit was desirable given the economic circumstances. However, it also noted that plans must be put in place to enable the government to cut back on the deficit from 2011 in order to keep plans for controlling inflation on target. 'The immediate challenge is supporting domestic demand with well-calibrated counter-cyclical macroeconomic policies, while preserving price and external stability,' it said.

FIGURE 35.7

South Africa's Annualized Growth Rate in the Seasonally Adjusted Real Value Added at Basic Prices of (a) All Industries and (b) Non-Primary Industries

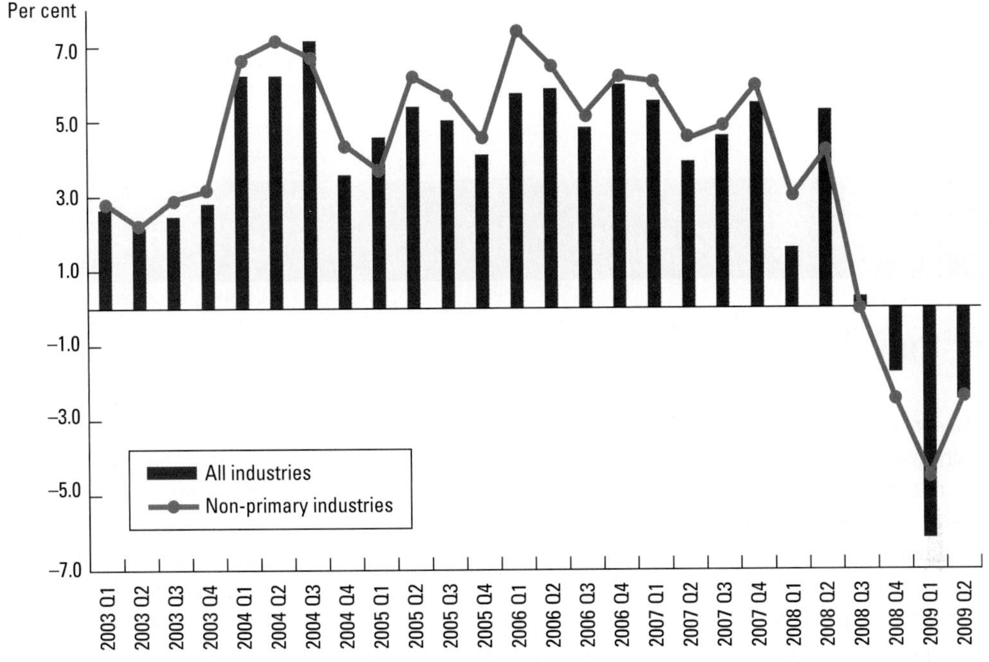

Source: Statistics South Africa; StatsOnline.

Source: http://www.oldmutual.co.za/markets/south-african-budget-2009/budget-speech-transcript.aspx – Budget Speech; http://www.imf.org/external/pubs/ft/scr/2009/cr09273.pdf – South Africa: 2009 Article IV Consultation – Staff Report; Staff Statement and Supplement; Public Information Notice on the Executive Board Discussion; and Statement by the Executive Director for South Africa.

economy. For example, when people are excessively pessimistic, the central bank can expand the money supply to lower interest rates and expand aggregate demand. When they are excessively optimistic, it can contract the money supply to raise interest rates and dampen aggregate demand.

The Case Against an Active Stabilization Policy

Some economists argue that the government should avoid active use of monetary and fiscal policy to try to stabilize the economy. They claim that these policy instruments should be set to achieve long-run goals, such as rapid economic growth and low inflation, and that the economy should be left to deal with short-run fluctuations on its own. Although these economists may admit that monetary and fiscal policy can stabilize the economy in theory, they doubt whether it can do so in practice.

The primary argument against active monetary and fiscal policy is that the effects of these policies may be to a large extent uncertain both in terms of magnitude and timing. As we have seen, monetary policy works by changing interest rates. This can have strong and rapid effects on consumer spending if (as in the United Kingdom) a large number of people are buying their house with a mortgage loan on which the interest rate can vary according to market interest rates: quite simply, if interest rates go up, then mortgage payments go up and people have less money to spend. On the other hand, if people have mortgages on which the interest rate is fixed for one or more years ahead (as is usually the case in the USA, and as is increasingly the case in the UK), then the interest rate change will only affect mortgage payments with a very long lag. And if most people live in rented accommodation (as is the case in most of the countries of

FYI

The Taylor Rule

In 1993, John Taylor, an economist at Stanford University in the United States, spent some time observing the behaviour of the Federal Reserve's Federal Open Market Committee (FOMC). Taylor's observations led him to put forward what has become known as the *Taylor Rule* which has been an influential idea since it was published. For many economists, interest has centred on the extent to which the rule is followed in interest rate decision-making around the world, if at all. John Taylor was observing the US economy and the work of the FOMC. Inflation in the US had come under a far greater degree of control in the 1980s when the FOMC was headed by Paul Volcker. Part of Taylor's conclusion was that the FOMC had reacted more aggressively to inflation than had occurred before 1979. His observations led to the notion of the interest rate-setting body 'leaning into the wind' when it comes to inflation. By this he meant being willing to raise rates more significantly in response to an inflation threat than had been the case prior to 1979.

Taylor suggested that the pattern of FOMC behaviour with regard to interest rates during the period 1979–92 could be expressed as a formula – the 'rule'. This formula, given below, has been simplified but in essence captures the main flavour of his original work.

$$r = p + 0.5y + 0.5(p - 2) + 2$$

In this formula, the following variables are expressed:

r = the short-term interest rate in percentage terms per annum
p = the rate of inflation over the previous four quarters measured as the GDP deflator
y = the difference between real GDP from potential output (the 'output gap').

Taylor made a number of assumptions about the US economy in this formula. He assumed that there was a target level of inflation, which he put at 2 per cent. He also made an assumption that the equilibrium real interest rate was also 2 per cent. The formula offers a rule or guide to policy makers about what the level of interest rates should be if there is a target for inflation of 2 per cent. In effect, interest rates can be set in response to the deviation of inflation from the target and the deviation of real output from potential output. It suggests that the response to inflation or output being off-target should be met with a more aggressive response to monetary policy – this is the so-called 'leaning into the wind'.

Suppose, for example, that the output gap was zero – that actual GDP was at its potential level – but that inflation was currently 5 per cent, 3 per cent above the assumed target level of 2 per cent. Then the *Taylor rule* would suggest that the central bank should aim to set the short-term interest rate at 8.5 per cent, corresponding to a real rate of interest of 8.5 – 5 = 3.5 per cent. If, however, GDP was, say, 2 per cent below its potential level, so that there was a an output gap of –2 per cent, then the *Taylor rule* would suggest setting the nominal interest rate a little lower, at 7.5 per cent.

How accurate is the *Taylor rule?* Studies have shown that a number of countries seem to have patterns of interest rates that follow the *Taylor rule* relatively closely. In reality, Taylor and other researchers appreciated that decision-makers could not stick rigidly to such a rule because sometimes circumstances might dictate the need to apply discretion. Such circumstances might be, for example, when the World Trade Centre was attacked in 2001, the intervention in Iraq or the financial crisis of 2008–09. Taylor argued that whilst a rule gave a guideline to policy makers, it also implied that any deviation from the rule had to be explained through a coherent and well-argued case and that such a discipline was helpful to overall monetary policy decisions. The *Taylor rule* has provided researchers with a great deal of impetus to look at the whole way in which monetary policy decisions are arrived at. It also gives the financial markets the opportunity to be able to second guess the decision-making of central banks and factor this into their thinking. In times of financial crisis, however, the rule may be jettisoned in favour of a more pragmatic approach to policy.

continental Europe) then a rise in interest rates will have no strong effects through this channel at all. In all cases, however, the interest rate rise will still clearly affect consumer spending because buying goods on credit (e.g. with a credit card) will be more expensive. The net effect on consumer spending may, therefore, be hard to predict, especially in terms of its timing.

Monetary policy can also affect aggregate demand through its influence on investment spending. But many firms make investment plans far in advance. Thus, most economists believe that it takes at least six months for changes in monetary policy to have much effect on output and employment. Most central banks readily admit that changes in interest rates can take up to eighteen months to work their way through the economy. Moreover, once these effects occur, they can last for several years.

Critics of stabilization policy argue that because of these uncertain lags, the central bank should not try to fine-tune the economy. They claim that the central bank often reacts too late to changing economic conditions and, as a result, ends up being a cause of, rather than a cure for, economic fluctuations. These critics advocate a passive monetary policy, such as slow and steady growth in the money supply.

Fiscal policy may also work with a lag. Of course, the impact of a change in government spending is felt as soon as the change takes place and cuts in direct and indirect taxation can feed through into the economy quickly. However, considerable time may pass between the decision to adopt a government spending programme and its implementation. In the UK, for example, the government has often tended to undershoot on its planned spending, partly because of problems in attracting sufficient extra staff into key public services such as transport, education and health. At the same time, announcements about changes to income taxes (both personal and corporate) tend to occur months (and sometimes years) before implementation. In the intervening time period, households and businesses factor in the impending changes into their behaviour and so the effects are uncertain.

These lags in monetary and fiscal policy are a problem in part because economic forecasting is so imprecise. If forecasters could accurately predict the condition of the economy a year in advance, then monetary and fiscal policy makers could look ahead when making policy decisions. In this case, policy makers could stabilize the economy despite the lags they face. Decisions are made, in part, on the basis of existing statistical data which is fed into models. That data can be inaccurate and subject to revision. In March 2010, for example, the Office for National Statistics in the UK revised its data on economic growth for the fourth quarter of the year for the second time. In January 2010, fourth quarter GDP had been reported at 0.1 per cent suggesting the economy had come out of recession but that growth was very weak. In early March this figure was revised to 0.3 per cent and in late March revised again to 0.4 per cent. In June 2010 the ONS had to postpone publication of further revised figures because of errors in calculation which raised concern about the accuracy of previous GDP data. Without accurate and up-to-date information, the outcome from modelling can vary considerably. In practice, however, major recessions and depressions arrive without much advance warning. The best policy makers can do at any time is to respond to economic changes as they occur.

Automatic Stabilizers

All economists – both advocates and critics of stabilization policy – agree that the lags in implementation render policy less useful as a tool for short-run stabilization. The economy would be more stable, therefore, if policy makers could find a way to avoid some of these lags. In fact, they have. **Automatic stabilizers** are changes in fiscal policy that stimulate aggregate demand when the economy goes into a recession without policy makers having to take any deliberate action.

automatic stabilizers
changes in fiscal policy that stimulate aggregate demand when the economy goes into a recession, without policy makers having to take any deliberate action

The most important automatic stabilizer is the tax system. When the economy goes into a recession, the amount of taxes collected by the government falls automatically because almost all taxes are closely tied to economic activity and because in many countries income taxes are progressive. This means that as economic activity increases an increasing proportion of income is paid in tax and vice versa. Income tax depends on households' incomes and corporation tax depends on firms' profits. Because incomes and profits both fall in a recession, the government's tax revenue falls as well. Taxes are a withdrawal from the circular flow which has the effect of dampening the level of aggregate demand. If tax revenues are lower it means that consumers have more disposable income to spend on consumption and businesses on investment. If economic activity increases then tax revenues will rise. These automatic tax changes either stimulate or dampen aggregate demand and, thereby, reduces the magnitude of economic fluctuations.

Government spending also acts as an automatic stabilizer. In particular, when the economy goes into a recession and workers are laid off, more people apply for state unemployment benefits, welfare benefits and other forms of income support. Extra spending on benefits and the welfare system helps to provide a cushion against too large a fall in economic activity. This increase in government spending stimulates aggregate demand at exactly the time when aggregate demand is insufficient to maintain full employment. However, it must be taken into consideration that in order to finance this additional spending (at a time when tax revenue is falling) governments may have to borrow. This additional borrowing can put upward pressure on interest rates and dampen the overall effect.

Automatic stabilizers are generally not sufficiently strong to prevent recessions completely. Nevertheless, without these automatic stabilizers, output and employment would probably be more volatile than they are. For this reason, most economists would not favour a policy of always running a balanced budget, as some politicians have proposed. When the economy goes into a recession, taxes fall, government spending rises, and the government's budget moves toward deficit. If the government faced a strict balanced-budget rule, it would be forced to look for ways to raise taxes or cut spending in a recession. In other words, a strict **balanced budget** rule would eliminate the automatic stabilizers inherent in our current system of taxes and government spending and would, in effect, be an 'automatic destabilizer'.

balanced budget
where the total sum of money received by a government in tax revenue and interest is equal to the amount it spends, including on any debt interest owing

Quick Quiz Suppose a wave of negative 'animal spirits' overruns the economy, and people become pessimistic about the future. • What happens to aggregate demand? • If the central bank wants to stabilize aggregate demand, how should it alter the money supply? • If it does this, what happens to the interest rate? • Why might the central bank choose not to respond in this way?

CONCLUSION

Before policy makers make any change in policy, they need to consider all the effects of their decisions. Earlier in the book we examined classical models of the economy, which describe the long-run effects of monetary and fiscal policy. There we saw how fiscal policy influences saving, investment and long-run growth, and how monetary policy influences the price level and the inflation rate.

In this chapter we examined the short-run effects of monetary and fiscal policy. We saw how these policy instruments can change the aggregate demand for goods and services and, thereby, alter the economy's production and employment in the short run. When the government reduces spending in order to balance the budget, it needs to consider both the long-run effects on saving and growth and the short-run effects on aggregate demand and employment. When the central bank reduces the growth rate of the money supply, it must take into account the long-run effect on inflation as well as the short-run effect on production. In the next chapter we discuss the transition between the short run and the long run more fully, and we see that policy makers often face a trade-off between long-run and short-run goals.

SUMMARY

- In developing a theory of short-run economic fluctuations, Keynes proposed the theory of liquidity preference to explain the determinants of the interest rate. According to this theory, the interest rate adjusts to balance the supply and demand for money.
- An increase in the price level raises money demand and increases the interest rate that brings the money market into equilibrium. Because the interest rate represents the cost of borrowing, a higher interest rate reduces investment and, thereby, the quantity of goods and services demanded. The downward sloping aggregate demand curve expresses this negative relationship between the price level and the quantity demanded.
- Policy makers can influence aggregate demand with monetary policy. An increase in the money supply reduces the equilibrium interest rate for any given price level. Because a lower interest rate stimulates investment spending, the aggregate demand curve shifts to the right. Conversely, a decrease in the money supply raises the equilibrium interest rate for any given price level and shifts the aggregate demand curve to the left.
- Policy makers can also influence aggregate demand with fiscal policy. An increase in government purchases or a cut in taxes shifts the aggregate demand curve to the right. A decrease in government purchases or an increase in taxes shifts the aggregate demand curve to the left.
- When the government alters spending or taxes, the resulting shift in aggregate demand can be larger or smaller than the fiscal change. The multiplier effect tends to amplify the effects of fiscal policy on aggregate demand. The crowding-out effect tends to dampen the effects of fiscal policy on aggregate demand.
- Because monetary and fiscal policy can influence aggregate demand, the government sometimes uses these policy instruments in an attempt to stabilize the economy. Economists disagree about how active the government should be in this effort. According to advocates of active stabilization policy, changes in attitudes by households and firms shift aggregate demand; if the government does not respond, the result is undesirable and unnecessary fluctuations in output and employment. According to critics of an active stabilization policy, monetary and fiscal policy work with such long lags that attempts at stabilizing the economy often end up being destabilizing.

KEY CONCEPTS

theory of liquidity preference, p. 758
crowding-out effect, p. 768
automatic stabilizers, p. 777
balanced budget, p. 778

QUESTIONS FOR REVIEW

1. What is the theory of liquidity preference? How does it help explain the downward slope of the aggregate demand curve?
2. Use the theory of liquidity preference to explain how a decrease in the money supply affects the aggregate demand curve.
3. The government spends €500 million to buy police cars. Explain why aggregate demand might increase by more than €500 million. Explain why aggregate demand might increase by less than €500 million.
4. Suppose that survey measures of consumer confidence indicate a wave of pessimism is sweeping the country. If policy makers do nothing, what will happen to aggregate demand? What should the government do if it wants to stabilize aggregate demand? If the government does nothing, should the central bank stabilize aggregate demand? If so, how?
5. Give an example of a government policy that acts as an automatic stabilizer. Explain why this policy has this effect.

PROBLEMS AND APPLICATIONS

1. Explain how each of the following developments would affect the supply of money, the demand for money and the interest rate. Illustrate your answers with diagrams.
   a. The central bank's bond traders buy bonds in open-market operations.
   b. An increase in credit card availability reduces the cash people hold.
   c. The central bank reduces banks' reserve requirements.
   d. Households decide to hold more money to use for holiday shopping.
   e. A wave of optimism boosts business investment and expands aggregate demand.
   f. An increase in oil prices shifts the short-run aggregate supply curve to the left.
2. Suppose banks install automatic teller machines on every street corner and, by making cash readily available, reduce the amount of money people want to hold.
   a. Assume the central bank does not change the money supply. According to the theory of liquidity preference, what happens to the interest rate? What happens to aggregate demand?
   b. If the central bank wants to stabilize aggregate demand, how should it respond?
3. Consider two policies – a tax cut that will last for only one year, and a tax cut that is expected to be permanent. Which policy will stimulate greater spending by consumers? Which policy will have the greater impact on aggregate demand? Explain.
4. The economy is in a recession with high unemployment and low output.
   a. Use a graph of aggregate demand and aggregate supply to illustrate the current situation. Be sure to include the aggregate demand curve, the short-run aggregate supply curve, and the long-run aggregate supply curve.
   b. Identify an open-market operation that would restore the economy to its natural rate.
   c. Use a graph of the money market to illustrate the effect of this open-market operation. Show the resulting change in the interest rate.
   d. Use a graph similar to the one in part (a) to show the effect of the open-market operation on output and the price level. Explain in words why the policy has the effect that you have shown in the graph.
5. In the early 1980s banks in many countries began to pay interest on current accounts.
   a. If we define money to include current accounts, what effect did this legislation have on money demand? Explain.
   b. If the central bank had maintained a constant money supply in the face of this change, what would have happened to the interest rate? What would have happened to aggregate demand and aggregate output?
   c. If the central bank had maintained a constant market interest rate (the interest rate on non-monetary assets) in the face of this change, what change in the money supply would have been necessary? What would have happened to aggregate demand and aggregate output?

6. This chapter explains that expansionary monetary policy reduces the interest rate and thus stimulates demand for investment goods. Explain how such a policy also stimulates the demand for net exports.
7. Suppose government spending increases. Would the effect on aggregate demand be larger if the central bank took no action in response, or if the central bank were committed to maintaining a fixed interest rate? Explain.
8. In which of the following circumstances is expansionary fiscal policy more likely to lead to a short-run increase in investment? Explain.
   a. When the investment accelerator is large, or when it is small?
   b. When the interest sensitivity of investment is large, or when it is small?
9. Assume the economy is in a recession. Explain how each of the following policies would affect consumption and investment. In each case, indicate any direct effects, any effects resulting from changes in total output, any effects resulting from changes in the interest rate and the overall effect. If there are conflicting effects making the answer ambiguous, say so.
   a. An increase in government spending.
   b. A reduction in taxes.
   c. An expansion of the money supply.
10. For various reasons, fiscal policy changes automatically when output and employment fluctuate.
    a. Explain why tax revenue changes when the economy goes into a recession.
    b. Explain why government spending changes when the economy goes into a recession.
    c. If the government was to operate under a strict balanced-budget rule, what would it have to do in a recession? Would that make the recession more or less severe?
11. Recently, some members of the legislature have proposed a law that would make price stability the sole goal of monetary policy. Suppose such a law were passed.
    a. How would the central bank respond to an event that contracted aggregate demand?
    b. How would the central bank respond to an event that caused an adverse shift in short-run aggregate supply?
    c. In each case, is there another monetary policy that would lead to greater stability in output?
12. Go to the website of the Bank of England, http://www.bankofengland.co.uk, and download the latest *Inflation Report*. What does it say about the state of the economy and recent decisions about monetary policy? Now go the website of the European Central Bank, http://www.ecb.int. Find a recent report on monetary policy in the Euro Area. What does it say about the state of the Euro Area economy and recent decisions about monetary policy?
13. Some economists have proposed that central banks should use the following rule for choosing its target interest rate (r): $r = 2\% + p + 1/2\ (y - y^*)/y^* + 1/2\ (p - p^*)$, where p is the average of the inflation rate over the past year, y is real GDP as recently measured, y^* is an estimate of the natural rate of output and p^* is the central bank's target rate of inflation.
    a. Explain the logic that might lie behind this rule for setting interest rates. Would you support the use of this rule?
    b. Some economists advocate such a rule for monetary policy but believe p and y should be the *forecasts* of future values of inflation and output. What are the advantages of using forecasts instead of actual values? What are the disadvantages?

For further resources, visit www.cengage.co.uk/mankiw_taylor2

36 THE SHORT-RUN TRADE-OFF BETWEEN INFLATION AND UNEMPLOYMENT

Two closely watched indicators of economic performance in any advanced economy are inflation and unemployment. When the government agency responsible for producing national statistics releases data on these variables, policy makers are eager to hear the news. Sometimes commentators add together the inflation rate and the unemployment rate to produce a *misery index,* which purports to measure the health of the economy.

How are these two measures of economic performance related to each other? Earlier in the book we discussed the long-run determinants of unemployment and the long-run determinants of inflation. We saw that the natural rate of unemployment depends on various features of the labour market, such as minimum wage laws, the market power of unions, the role of efficiency wages and the effectiveness of job search. By contrast, the inflation rate depends primarily on growth in the money supply, which a nation's central bank controls. In the long run, therefore, inflation and unemployment are largely unrelated problems.

In the short run, just the opposite is true. One of the *Ten Principles of Economics* discussed in Chapter 1 is that society faces a short-run trade-off between inflation and unemployment. If monetary and fiscal policy makers expand aggregate demand and move the economy up along the short-run aggregate supply curve, they can lower unemployment for a while, but only at the cost of higher inflation. If policy makers contract aggregate demand and move the economy down the short-run aggregate supply curve, they can lower inflation, but only at the cost of temporarily higher unemployment.

In this chapter we examine this trade-off more closely. The relationship between inflation and unemployment is a topic that has attracted the attention of some of the most important economists of the last half century. The best way to understand this relationship is to see how thinking about it has evolved over time.

THE PHILLIPS CURVE

'Probably the single most important macroeconomic relationship is the Phillips curve.' These are the words of economist George Akerlof from the lecture he gave when he received the Nobel Prize for Economics in 2001. The *Phillips curve* is the short-run relationship between inflation and unemployment.

Origins of the Phillips Curve

In 1958, a New Zealand economist working at the London School of Economics, A.W. Phillips, published an article in the British journal *Economica* that would make him famous. The article was entitled 'The Relationship Between Unemployment and the Rate of Change of Money Wages in the United Kingdom, 1861–1957.' In it, Phillips showed a negative correlation between the rate of unemployment and the rate of inflation. That is, Phillips showed that years with low unemployment tend to have high inflation, and years with high unemployment tend to have low inflation. (Phillips examined inflation in nominal wages rather than inflation in prices, but for our purposes that distinction is not important. These two measures of inflation usually move together.) Phillips concluded that two important macroeconomic variables – inflation and unemployment – were linked in a way that economists had not previously appreciated.

Although Phillips's discovery was based on data for the United Kingdom, researchers quickly extended his finding to other countries. Two years after Phillips published his article, economists Paul Samuelson and Robert Solow published an article in the *American Economic Review* called 'Analytics of Anti-inflation Policy' in which they showed a similar negative correlation between inflation and unemployment in data for the United States. They reasoned that this correlation arose because low unemployment was associated with high aggregate demand, which in turn puts upward pressure on wages and prices throughout the economy. Samuelson and Solow dubbed the negative association between inflation and unemployment the **Phillips curve**. Figure 36.1 shows an example of a Phillips curve like the one found by Samuelson and Solow.

Phillips curve
a curve that shows the short-run trade-off between inflation and unemployment

As the title of their paper suggests, Samuelson and Solow were interested in the Phillips curve because they believed that it held important lessons for policy makers. In particular, they suggested that the Phillips curve offers policy makers a menu of possible economic outcomes. By altering monetary and fiscal policy to influence aggregate demand, policy makers could choose any point on this curve. Point A offers high unemployment and low inflation. Point B offers low unemployment and high inflation. Policy makers might prefer both low inflation and low unemployment, but the historical data as summarized by the Phillips curve indicate that this combination is impossible. According to Samuelson and Solow, policy makers face a trade-off between inflation and unemployment, and the Phillips curve illustrates that trade-off.

Aggregate Demand, Aggregate Supply and the Phillips Curve

The model of aggregate demand and aggregate supply provides an easy explanation for the menu of possible outcomes described by the Phillips curve. The

FIGURE 36.1

The Phillips Curve

The Phillips curve illustrates a negative association between the inflation rate and the unemployment rate. At point A, inflation is low and unemployment is high. At point B, inflation is high and unemployment is low.

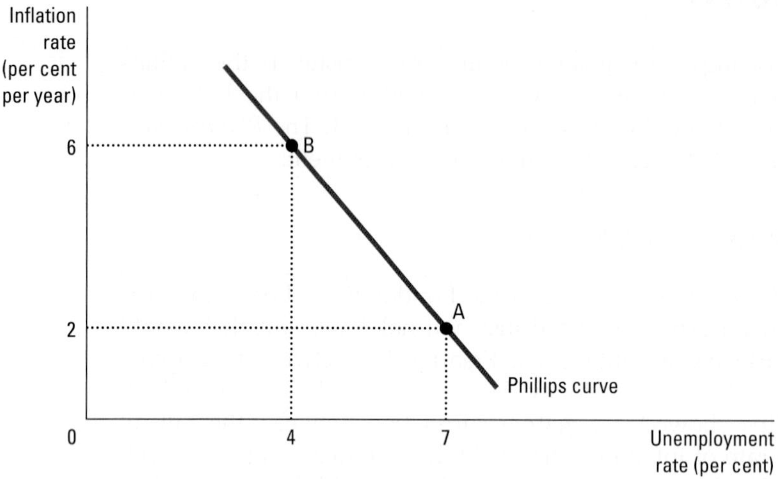

Phillips curve simply shows the combinations of inflation and unemployment that arise in the short run as shifts in the aggregate demand curve move the economy along the short-run aggregate supply curve. As we saw in Chapter 34, an increase in the aggregate demand for goods and services leads, in the short run, to a larger output of goods and services and a higher price level. Larger output means greater employment and, thus, a lower rate of unemployment. In addition, whatever the previous year's price level happens to be, the higher the price level in the current year, the higher the rate of inflation. Thus, shifts in aggregate demand push inflation and unemployment in opposite directions in the short run – a relationship illustrated by the Phillips curve.

To see more fully how this works, let's consider an example. To keep the numbers simple, imagine that the price level (as measured, for instance, by the consumer price index) equals 100 in the year 2012. Figure 36.2 shows two possible outcomes that might occur in year 2013. Panel (a) shows the two outcomes using the model of aggregate demand and aggregate supply. Panel (b) illustrates the same two outcomes using the Phillips curve.

In panel (a) of the figure, we can see the implications for output and the price level in the year 2013. If the aggregate demand for goods and services is relatively low, the economy experiences outcome A. The economy produces output of 7 500, and the price level is 102. By contrast, if aggregate demand is relatively high, the economy experiences outcome B. Output is 8 000, and the price level is 106. Thus, higher aggregate demand moves the economy to an equilibrium with higher output and a higher price level.

In panel (b) of the figure, we can see what these two possible outcomes mean for unemployment and inflation. Because firms need more workers when they produce a greater output of goods and services, unemployment is lower in outcome B than in outcome A. In this example, when output rises from 7 500 to 8 000, unemployment falls from 7 per cent to 4 per cent. Moreover, because the price level is higher at outcome B than at outcome A, the inflation rate (the percentage change in the price level from the previous year) is also higher. In particular, since the price level was 100 in year 2012, outcome A has an inflation rate of

FIGURE 36.2

How the Phillips Curve Is Related to the Model of Aggregate Demand and Aggregate Supply

This figure assumes a price level of 100 for the year 2012 and charts possible outcomes for the year 2013. Panel (a) shows the model of aggregate demand and aggregate supply. If aggregate demand is low, the economy is at point A; output is low (7 500), and the price level is low (102). If aggregate demand is high, the economy is at point B; output is high (8 000), and the price level is high (106). Panel (b) shows the implications for the Phillips curve. Point A, which arises when aggregate demand is low, has high unemployment (7 per cent) and low inflation (2 per cent). Point B, which arises when aggregate demand is high, has low unemployment (4 per cent) and high inflation (6 per cent).

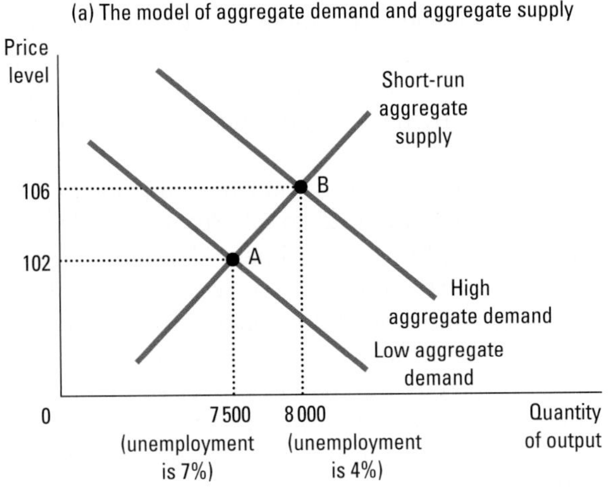

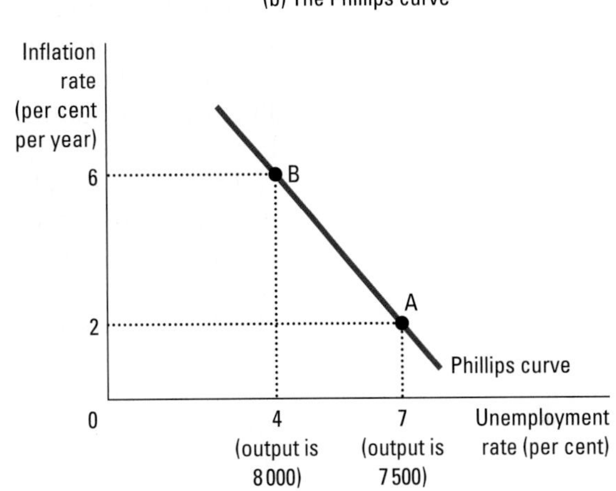

2 per cent, and outcome B has an inflation rate of 6 per cent. Thus, we can compare the two possible outcomes for the economy either in terms of output and the price level (using the model of aggregate demand and aggregate supply) or in terms of unemployment and inflation (using the Phillips curve).

As we saw in the preceding chapter, monetary and fiscal policy can shift the aggregate demand curve. Therefore, monetary and fiscal policy can move the economy along the Phillips curve. Increases in the money supply, increases in government spending, or cuts in taxes expand aggregate demand and move the economy to a point on the Phillips curve with lower unemployment and higher inflation. Decreases in the money supply, cuts in government spending, or increases in taxes contract aggregate demand and move the economy to a point on the Phillips curve with lower inflation and higher unemployment. In this sense, the Phillips curve offers policy makers a menu of combinations of inflation and unemployment.

Quick Quiz Draw the Phillips curve. Use the model of aggregate demand and aggregate supply to show how policy can move the economy from a point on this curve with high inflation to a point with low inflation.

SHIFTS IN THE PHILLIPS CURVE: THE ROLE OF EXPECTATIONS

The Phillips curve seems to offer policy makers a menu of possible inflation–unemployment outcomes. But does this menu remain stable over time? Is the Phillips curve a relationship on which policy makers can rely? Economists took up these questions in the late 1960s, shortly after Samuelson and Solow had introduced the Phillips curve into the macroeconomic policy debate.

The Long-run Phillips Curve

In 1968 economist Milton Friedman published a paper in the *American Economic Review,* based on an address he had recently given as president of the American Economic Association. The paper, entitled 'The Role of Monetary Policy', contained sections on 'What Monetary Policy Can Do' and 'What Monetary Policy Cannot Do'. Friedman argued that one thing monetary policy cannot do, other than for only a short time, is pick a combination of inflation and unemployment on the Phillips curve. At about the same time, another economist, Edmund Phelps, also published a paper denying the existence of a long-run trade-off between inflation and unemployment.

Friedman and Phelps based their conclusions on classical principles of macroeconomics, which we discussed in Chapters 25 to 32. Recall that classical theory points to growth in the money supply the primary determinant of inflation. But classical theory also states that monetary growth does not have real effects – it merely alters all prices and nominal incomes proportionately. In particular, monetary growth does not influence those factors that determine the economy's unemployment rate, such as the market power of unions, the role of efficiency wages, or the process of job search. Friedman and Phelps concluded that there is no reason to think the rate of inflation would, *in the long run,* be related to the rate of unemployment.

Here, in his own words, is Friedman's view about what the central bank can hope to accomplish in the long run:

> The monetary authority controls nominal quantities – directly, the quantity of its own liabilities [currency plus bank reserves]. In principle, it can use this control to peg a nominal quantity – an exchange rate, the price level, the nominal level of national income, the quantity of money by one definition or another – or to peg the change in a nominal quantity – the rate of inflation or deflation, the rate of growth or decline in nominal national income, the rate of growth of the quantity of money. It cannot use its control over nominal quantities to peg a real quantity – the real rate of interest, the rate of unemployment, the level of real national income, the real quantity of money, the rate of growth of real national income, or the rate of growth of the real quantity of money.

These views have important implications for the Phillips curve. In particular, they imply that monetary policy makers face a long-run Phillips curve that is vertical, as in Figure 36.3. If the central bank increases the money supply slowly, the inflation rate is low, and the economy finds itself at point A. If the central bank increases the money supply quickly, the inflation rate is high, and the economy finds itself at point B. In either case, the unemployment rate tends towards its normal level, called the *natural rate of unemployment.* The vertical long-run Phillips curve illustrates the conclusion that unemployment does not depend on money growth and inflation in the long run.

The vertical long-run Phillips curve is, in essence, one expression of the classical idea of monetary neutrality. As you may recall, we expressed this idea in Chapter 34 with a vertical long-run aggregate supply curve. Indeed, as Figure 36.4 illustrates, the vertical long-run Phillips curve and the vertical long-run aggregate supply curve are two sides of the same coin. In panel (a) of this figure, an increase in the money supply shifts the aggregate demand curve to the right from AD_1 to AD_2. As a result of this shift, the long-run equilibrium moves from point A to point B.

FIGURE 36.3

The Long-run Phillips Curve

According to Friedman and Phelps, there is no trade-off between inflation and unemployment in the long run. Growth in the money supply determines the inflation rate. Regardless of the inflation rate, the unemployment rate gravitates towards its natural rate. As a result, the long-run Phillips curve is vertical.

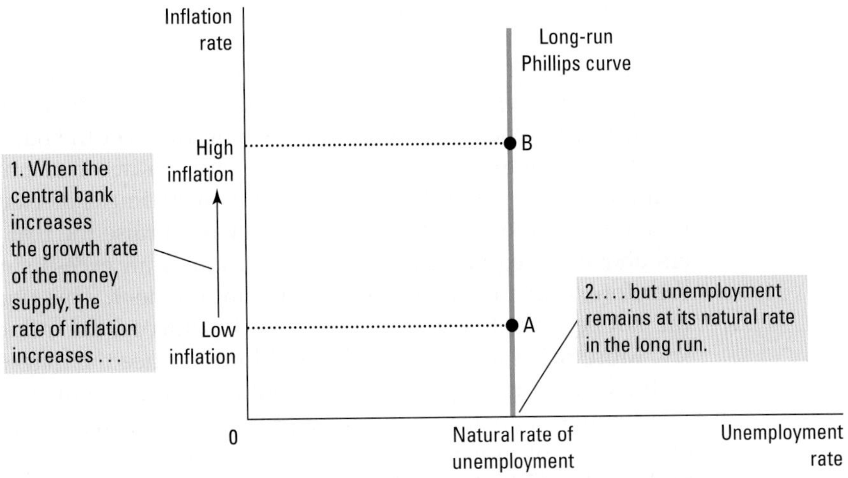

FIGURE 36.4

How the Long-run Phillips Curve Is Related to the Model of Aggregate Demand and Aggregate Supply

Panel (a) shows the model of aggregate demand and aggregate supply with a vertical aggregate supply curve. When expansionary monetary policy shifts the aggregate demand curve to the right from AD_1 to AD_2, the equilibrium moves from point A to point B. The price level rises from P_1 to P_2, while output remains the same. Panel (b) shows the long-run Phillips curve, which is vertical at the natural rate of unemployment. Expansionary monetary policy moves the economy from lower inflation (point A) to higher inflation (point B) without changing the rate of unemployment.

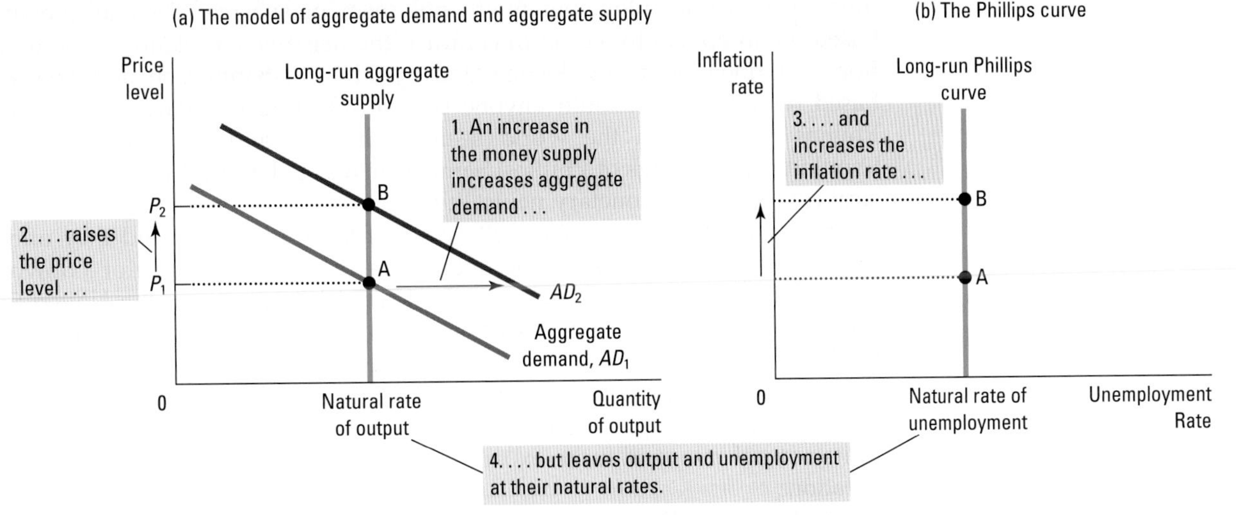

The price level rises from P_1 to P_2, but because the aggregate supply curve is vertical, output remains the same. In panel (b), more rapid growth in the money supply raises the inflation rate by moving the economy from point A to point B. But because the Phillips curve is vertical, the rate of unemployment is the same at these two points. Thus, the vertical long-run aggregate supply curve and the vertical long-run Phillips curve both imply that monetary policy influences nominal variables (the price level and the inflation rate) but not real variables (output and unemployment). Regardless of the monetary policy pursued by the central bank, output and unemployment are, in the long run, at their natural rates.

What is so 'natural' about the natural rate of unemployment? Friedman and Phelps used this adjective to describe the unemployment rate towards which the economy tends to gravitate in the long run. Yet the natural rate of unemployment is not necessarily the socially desirable rate of unemployment. Nor is the natural rate of unemployment constant over time. For example, suppose that a newly formed union uses its market power to raise the real wages of some workers above the equilibrium level. The result is an excess supply of workers and, therefore, a higher natural rate of unemployment. This unemployment is 'natural' not because it is good but because it is beyond the influence of monetary policy. More rapid money growth would not reduce the market power of the union or the level of unemployment; it would lead only to more inflation.

Although monetary policy cannot influence the natural rate of unemployment, other types of policy can. To reduce the natural rate of unemployment, policy makers should look to policies that improve the functioning of the labour market. Earlier in the book we discussed how various labour market policies, such as minimum wage laws, collective bargaining laws, unemployment insurance, and job-training schemes, affect the natural rate of unemployment. A policy change that reduced the natural rate of unemployment would shift the long-run Phillips curve to the left. In addition, because lower unemployment means more workers are producing goods and services, the quantity of goods and services supplied would be larger at any given price level, and the long-run aggregate supply curve would shift to the right. The economy could then enjoy lower unemployment and higher output for any given rate of money growth and inflation.

Reconciling Theory and Evidence

At first, the conclusion of Friedman and Phelps of a long-run trade-off between inflation and unemployment might not seem persuasive. Their argument was based on an appeal to *theory*. In contrast, the negative correlation between inflation and unemployment documented by Phillips, Samuelson and Solow was based on *data*. Why should anyone believe that policy makers faced a vertical Phillips curve when the world seemed to offer a downward sloping one? Shouldn't the findings of Phillips, Samuelson and Solow lead us to reject the classical conclusion of monetary neutrality?

Friedman and Phelps were well aware of these questions, and they offered a way to reconcile classical macroeconomic theory with the finding of a downward sloping Phillips curve in data from the United Kingdom and the United States. They claimed that a negative relationship between inflation and unemployment holds in the short run but that it cannot be used by policy makers in the long run. In other words, policy makers can pursue expansionary monetary policy to achieve lower unemployment for a while, but eventually unemployment returns to its natural rate, and more expansionary monetary policy leads only to higher inflation.

Friedman and Phelps reasoned as we did in Chapter 34 when we explained the difference between the short-run and long-run aggregate supply curves.

(In fact, the discussion in that chapter drew heavily on the legacy of Friedman and Phelps.) As you may recall, the short-run aggregate supply curve is upward sloping, indicating that an increase in the price level raises the quantity of goods and services that firms supply. In contrast, the long-run aggregate supply curve is vertical, indicating that the price level does not influence quantity supplied in the long run. Chapter 34 presented three theories to explain the upward slope of the short-run aggregate supply curve: sticky wages, sticky prices and misperceptions about relative prices. Because wages, prices and perceptions adjust to changing economic conditions over time, the positive relationship between the price level and quantity supplied applies in the short run but not in the long run. Friedman and Phelps applied this same logic to the Phillips curve. Just as the aggregate supply curve slopes upward only in the short run, the trade-off between inflation and unemployment holds only in the short run. And just as the long-run aggregate supply curve is vertical, the long-run Phillips curve is also vertical.

To help explain the short-run and long-run relationship between inflation and unemployment, Friedman and Phelps introduced a new variable into the analysis: *expected inflation.* Expected inflation measures how much people expect the overall price level to change. As we discussed in Chapter 34, the expected price level affects the wages and prices that people set and the perceptions of relative prices that they form. As a result, expected inflation is one factor that determines the position of the short-run aggregate supply curve. In the short run, the central bank can take expected inflation (and thus the short-run aggregate supply curve) as already determined. When the money supply changes, the aggregate demand curve shifts, and the economy moves along a given short-run aggregate supply curve. In the short run, therefore, monetary changes lead to unexpected fluctuations in output, prices, unemployment and inflation. In this way, Friedman and Phelps explained the Phillips curve that Phillips, Samuelson and Solow had documented.

Yet the central bank's ability to create unexpected inflation by increasing the money supply exists only in the short run. In the long run, people come to expect whatever inflation rate the central bank chooses to produce. Because wages, prices and perceptions will eventually adjust to the inflation rate, the long-run aggregate supply curve is vertical. In this case, changes in aggregate demand, such as those due to changes in the money supply, do not affect the economy's output of goods and services. Thus, Friedman and Phelps concluded that unemployment returns to its natural rate in the long run.

The Short-run Phillips Curve

The analysis of Friedman and Phelps can be summarized in the following equation (which is, in essence, another expression of the aggregate supply equation we saw in Chapter 34):

$$\begin{array}{c}\text{Unemployment} \\ \text{rate}\end{array} = \begin{array}{c}\text{Natural rate} \\ \text{of unemployment}\end{array} - a\left(\begin{array}{c}\text{Actual} \\ \text{inflation}\end{array} - \begin{array}{c}\text{Expected} \\ \text{inflation}\end{array}\right)$$

This equation relates the unemployment rate to the natural rate of unemployment, actual inflation and expected inflation. In the short run, expected inflation is given. As a result, higher actual inflation is associated with lower unemployment. (How much unemployment responds to unexpected inflation is determined by the size of a, a number that in turn depends on the slope of the short-run aggregate supply curve.) In the long run, however, people come to expect whatever inflation the central bank produces. Thus, actual inflation equals expected inflation, and unemployment is at its natural rate.

This equation implies there is no stable short-run Phillips curve. Each short-run Phillips curve reflects a particular expected rate of inflation. (To be precise, if you graph the equation, you'll find that the short-run Phillips curve intersects the long-run Phillips curve at the expected rate of inflation.) Whenever expected inflation changes, the short-run Phillips curve shifts.

According to Friedman and Phelps, it is dangerous to view the Phillips curve as a menu of options available to policy makers. To see why, imagine an economy at its natural rate of unemployment with low inflation and low expected inflation, shown in Figure 36.5 as point A. Now suppose that policy makers try to take advantage of the trade-off between inflation and unemployment by using monetary or fiscal policy to expand aggregate demand. In the short run when expected inflation is given, the economy goes from point A to point B. Unemployment falls below its natural rate, and inflation rises above expected inflation. Over time, people get used to this higher inflation rate, and they raise their expectations of inflation. When expected inflation rises, firms and workers start taking higher inflation into account when setting wages and prices. The short-run Phillips curve then shifts to the right, as shown in the figure. The economy ends up at point C, with higher inflation than at point A but with the same level of unemployment.

Thus, Friedman and Phelps concluded that policy makers do face a trade-off between inflation and unemployment, but only a temporary one. If policy makers use this trade-off, they lose it.

FIGURE 36.5

How Expected Inflation Shifts the Short-run Phillips Curve

The higher the expected rate of inflation, the higher the short-run trade-off between inflation and unemployment. At point A, expected inflation and actual inflation are both low, and unemployment is at its natural rate. If the central bank pursues an expansionary monetary policy, the economy moves from point A to point B in the short run. At point B, expected inflation is still low, but actual inflation is high. Unemployment is below its natural rate. In the long run, expected inflation rises, and the economy moves to point C. At point C, expected inflation and actual inflation are both high, and unemployment is back to its natural rate.

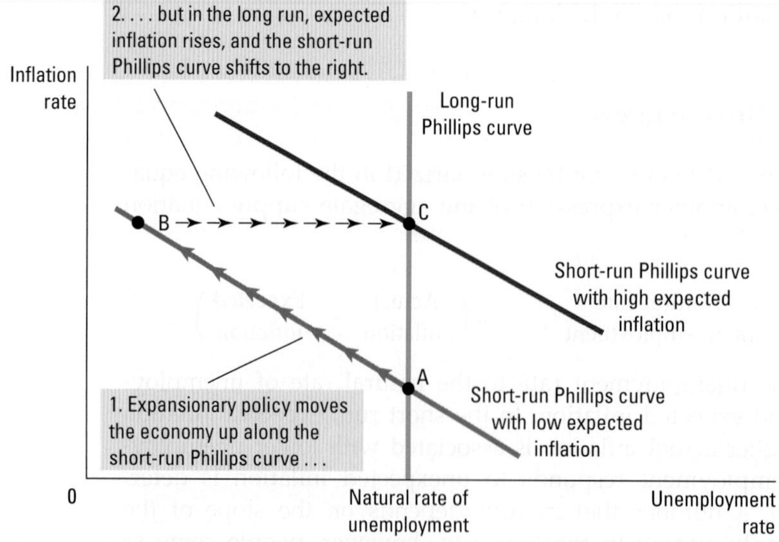

The Unemployment–Inflation Trade-off

Friedman and Phelps had made a bold prediction in 1968: if policy makers try to take advantage of the Phillips curve by choosing higher inflation in order to reduce unemployment, they will succeed at reducing unemployment only temporarily. This view – that unemployment eventually returns to its natural rate, regardless of the rate of inflation – is called the **natural-rate hypothesis**.

natural-rate hypothesis
the claim that unemployment eventually returns to its normal, or natural, rate, regardless of the rate of inflation

To some economists at the time, it seemed ridiculous to claim that the Phillips curve would break down once policy makers tried to use it. But, in fact, that is exactly what happened in both the UK and the United States. Beginning in the late 1960s, the UK government, for example, followed policies that expanded the aggregate demand for goods and services. On top of this, the UK and many other developed economies in the late 1960s and early 1970s experienced an increase in aggregate demand due to American involvement in the Vietnam War, which increased US government spending (on the military), which boosted US aggregate demand and so boosted net exports from other countries to the USA. In addition, in 1971, as a result of the relaxation of certain controls on bank lending, the UK experienced a major expansion in the money supply. In the following year, the government announced an extraordinarily expansionary fiscal policy, in terms of extra spending and tax reduction, and the economy began seriously to overheat and inflation started to rise. But, as Friedman and Phelps had predicted, unemployment did not stay low.

From the end of the Second World War through to the late 1970s, many governments in the Western world adopted Keynesian policies as the basis for managing the economy. There was an emphasis on attempting to keep unemployment low. The experience of mass unemployment and the rise in extremism in many parts of Europe and the misery caused by the Great Depression in the United States in the 1930s had persuaded policy makers that a focus on unemployment was vital to stable economic and political life. In the 20 years after the war, fiscal policy was dominant; in times of rising unemployment fiscal policy was loosened and tightened when inflation began to speed up. The government could pull its fiscal levers of tax and public spending to 'fine tune' the economy. The unusual circumstances of post-war reconstruction across Europe and the US meant that inflation did not seem to present a major problem.

Some economists argued that the focus on fiscal policy meant that not only did households form expectations about inflation but also about government policy. In the UK, many large industries were in public ownership including the railways, coal, electricity, airports and airlines, telecommunications and steel. In addition, trade unions enjoyed considerable power in many industries. Workers came to expect, it was argued, increases in real wages each year and that this would be accommodated by monetary expansion. In addition, the government would respond by loosening fiscal policy if the economy slowed down. This, it was argued, led to a fall in productivity and increased inflationary pressures as the government and industry accommodated wage increases. In the aggregate, UK industry became sluggish, lacked flexibility and lost competitiveness.

These conditions led to rising inflation and an inability of the government to reduce unemployment below the natural rate. After the oil crisis and miners' strike of the early 1970s and the fiscal boom produced by the government, stagflation took hold and the UK seemed to lurch from 'boom to bust'. Eventually the government was forced to borrow money from the International Monetary Fund (IMF) in 1976. In a famous speech to the Labour Party Conference in the same year, the then Prime Minister, James Callaghan, echoed Friedman and Phelps' theory to the nation when he said:

> We used to think that you could spend your way out of a recession and increase employment by cutting taxes and boosting government spending.

> I tell you in all candour that that option no longer exists, and in so far as it ever did exist, it only worked on each occasion since the war by injecting a bigger dose of inflation into the economy. And each time that happened, the average level of unemployment has risen. Higher inflation followed by higher unemployment. That is the history of the last 20 years.

This effectively saw a move away from Keynesian policies and a shift to monetary policy in the UK, while the US began to take greater steps to focus on the money supply. The focus of policy on the use of monetary and supply-side policies was seen as the way of keeping inflation under control and lowering the natural rate of unemployment. Throughout the 1980s, the UK and US governments trumpeted the benefits of supply-side policies. These looked at ways of expanding the productive capacity of the economy to shift the aggregate supply curve to the right. Such policies stressed the importance of enterprise, reducing business regulation, improving incentives through cutting taxes and benefits, reducing trade union power and investing in education and training to improve the workings and flexibility of the labour market in the long run.

Supply-side policies take some time to have an effect but structural economic reforms by the UK government throughout the 1990s led to a leftward shift in the Phillips curve. What caused this favourable shift in the short-run Phillips curve? Part of the answer lies in a low level of expected inflation. The policy of inflation targeting since 1992, combined with the independence of the Bank of England in 1997 created a credible policy framework in which workers and firms knew that interest rates would be raised if the economy began to overheat, and they tended to moderate their wage claims and price setting accordingly. Since the Bank of England now sets interest rates independently, people also know that there is no way in which politicians can use expansionary monetary policy for political reasons, such as to gain popularity before an election. This led to a period of relatively stable economic conditions in the UK with economic growth, low inflation and relatively low levels of unemployment right up until around 2008 when the financial crisis began to unravel.

In contrast, many European countries suffered relatively high levels of unemployment despite the European Central Bank having independence in the setting of monetary policy. Why was this? One argument that has been put forward to explain high European unemployment in the 21st century, and which seems to have some credibility, centres on the level of labour market regulation. As we pointed out above, the 1980s in the UK were characterized both by a weakening of the power of the trades unions and by a reduction in business regulation in general and in labour market regulation in particular. Whilst, for example, this had the effect of reducing job security for many people by making it easier for employers to terminate contracts, it also had the effect of making labour markets much more flexible. Thus, somewhat paradoxically perhaps, if it is harder to fire someone, firms will think hard before taking on new labour and unemployment may actually rise. Similarly, the minimum wage is typically set at a much higher level (relative to the average wage) in European countries like France and Germany, which again is a reason why the natural rate of unemployment might be higher in those countries.

Figure 36.6 displays the history of UK inflation and unemployment from 1971 to 2009. It shows very little evidence of the simple negative relationship between these two variables that Phillips had originally observed. In particular, as inflation remained high in the early 1970s, people's expectations of inflation caught up with reality, and the unemployment rate rose along with inflation. By the mid-1970s, policy makers had learned that Friedman and Phelps were right: There is no trade-off between inflation and unemployment in the long run. This is summarized in Figure 36.7 which summarizes the process.

FIGURE 36.6

The Breakdown of the Phillips Curve

This figure shows annual UK data from 1971 to 2009 on the unemployment rate and on the inflation rate (as measured by the RPI index). There is no obvious, stable negative relationship between inflation and unemployment.

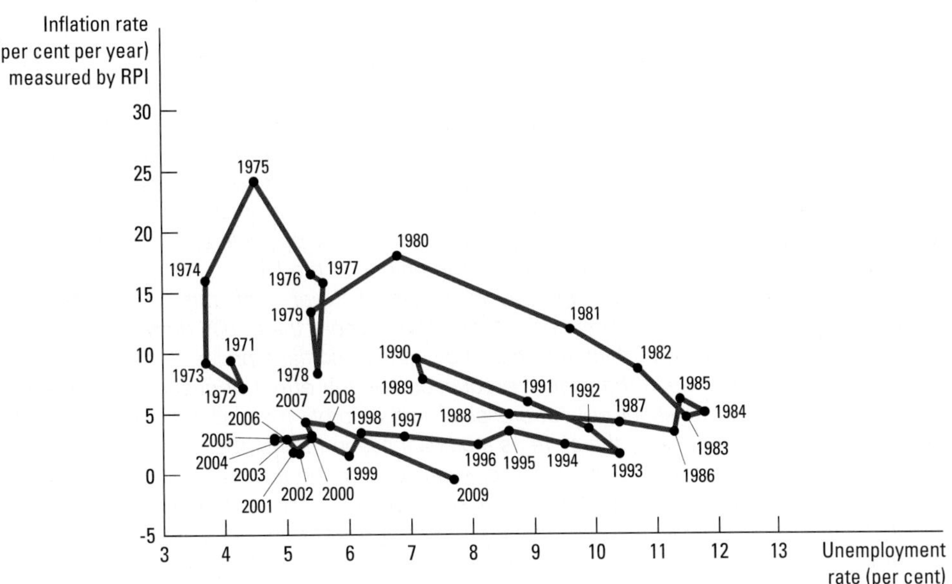

Source: UK Office for National Statistics.

Quick Quiz Draw the short-run Phillips curve and the long-run Phillips curve. Explain why they are different.

THE LONG-RUN VERTICAL PHILLIPS CURVE AS AN ARGUMENT FOR CENTRAL BANK INDEPENDENCE

Who would you rather was in charge of monetary policy – an elected government or an unelected central banker? Would it not be better to have the government in charge of the money supply and interest rates? After all, if they screw up, we can vote them out of office at the next election, while, on the other hand, the electorate has no such sanction over central bankers.

In fact, most economists – at least the majority of those who believe in a long-run vertical Phillips curve – would rather hand control of monetary policy to the central banker, particularly if the central banker in question had a reputation for being tough on inflation, and especially if he or she had a clear and publicly known target for the level of inflation to be achieved.

To see why, take another look at Figure 36.5. Suppose we're at point A, with the natural rate of unemployment and a low level of inflation, and that the government is in charge of monetary policy in the sense that they can just tell the central bank to change interest rates or the money supply and it is done. (This

FIGURE 36.7

Aggregate Demand/Aggregate Supply and the Phillips Curve: Two Ways of Telling the Same Story

1. *Assume that the economy is in equilibrium, with AS = AD at an inflation rate of 3 per cent and an unemployment rate of 7 per cent. The government believes that unemployment is too high and takes steps to boost demand through an expansionary fiscal policy.*
2. *What happens? The level of aggregate demand shifts to the right and there is a movement along the Phillips Curve to the left. The short-run outcome is that unemployment has fallen to 5 per cent but inflation has crept up to 4 per cent.*
3. *The next step is where the effect of expectations comes into the analysis. Given that unemployment has fallen, workers feel less threatened in their jobs, which affects how they negotiate pay awards. They will also anticipate that if inflation has risen to 5 per cent, it is entirely plausible that it could rise again next year. They then build this into pay claims. Part of the assumption now is that pay claims in excess of inflation will be met by employers. In the trade union-dominated world of the late 1970s, this was entirely possible and was one of the arguments Mrs Thatcher put forward for restricting the power of trade unions in the UK.*
4. *Let us assume that workers put in for average pay increases of 7 per cent: this represents a 'real' pay claim of 2 per cent given current inflation levels (5 per cent). If employers meet these pay demands (and in times of falling unemployment, they have no reason to think that that they cannot increase prices to the consumer) then they will experience additional costs. Any rise in the cost of production has the effect of pushing the AS curve to the left. For some businesses, the rising cost of labour will put pressure on their profit margins and some will be forced to shed labour in the process. What we now see, therefore, is a gradual rise in the number of unemployed people but a corresponding increase in the inflation rate as increased wage costs in the economy are passed on to the consumer.*
5. *The long-run situation sees the economy return to a situation of 7 per cent unemployment but in the process, experiencing an inflation rate now standing at 6 per cent. If the government perceived 7 per cent unemployment as unacceptable at the start of the analysis, there is no reason to assume that they will not do so at this stage and so the whole process starts again.*

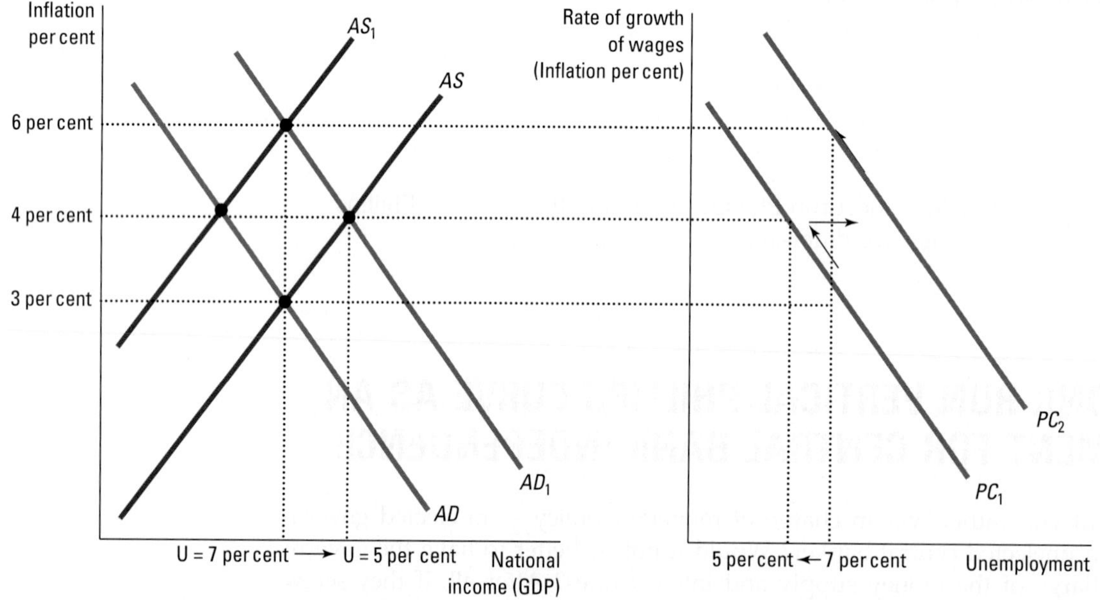

was in fact the case in the United Kingdom before 1997, when the Chancellor of the Exchequer, a member of the UK government, had control over monetary as well as fiscal policy.) Now imagine that we're just coming up to a general election in a few months time: what do you suppose the government will do? Since unemployment is never a vote winner, it is perhaps likely that they will be tempted to reduce interest rates and expand the money supply so that the economy moves from point A to point B and unemployment falls. (In reality, because of the uncertain lags in monetary policy that we discussed earlier, the government won't be able to guarantee that the economy will get to precisely point B just before the election, but it will certainly move along the short-run Phillips curve from point A towards point B, with actual inflation above expected inflation.) Of course, once people's expectations of inflation catch up with actual inflation, the short-run Phillips curve will shift up and the economy will move to point C. At point C there is the same rate of unemployment as in the first place (the natural rate) and a higher level of inflation, so in the long run the economy is in a worse state than if monetary policy had remained neutral and the economy had stayed at A. If the election takes place before inflationary expectations catch up, however, the government has a higher chance of being re-elected because, so long as the economy remains on the initial short-run Phillips curve at some point between A and B, inflationary expectations are low while unemployment is falling. Not only is this likely to lead to extra votes from people who were previously unemployed and now grateful to be in a job, economic activity in general will rise in the economy and people in general will experience an economic 'feel-good factor' and be grateful to the government for running the economy so well. Once inflationary expectations have finally caught up and we move to point C on the long-run Phillips curve with the same old level of unemployment and higher inflation, the feel-good factor will evaporate, but it's too late – the election is over and the same government is back in power.

Of course, the story we have just told implies a pretty cynical view of politics, and most governments would strenuously deny that they would carry out such tricks just to get re-elected. More importantly, however, the story also implies that people (workers and managers of firms) are pretty stupid. Why? Because everyone will know that the government has a strong incentive to pursue an expansionary monetary policy just before an election. In fact, firms and workers may begin raising prices and wages before the election in anticipation of the expansionary monetary policy, so we could end up jumping straight from point A to point C without any intervening fall in unemployment! This is an interesting result, and one worth stressing: if people believe that the government is about to pursue an expansionary monetary policy, then inflationary expectations will increase and inflation will rise but unemployment will not fall. In essence, the economy jumps immediately to the new long-run equilibrium.

But suppose that whoever is in charge of monetary policy issues a statement saying that she has no intention of pursuing an expansionary monetary policy. Should firms and workers believe her? Probably not. In fact, firms and workers might reason that if they really believed that no monetary expansion would take place, then that is when the politician would be most tempted to let rip with the money supply, since then they really would be taken by surprise by the monetary expansion and it would take a while for their inflationary expectations to catch up with actual inflation. In the meantime, the economy would move along the short-run Phillips curve to point B, unemployment would fall and the government would become more popular. So the more credible the politician's promise seems to be, the less you should believe her! Hence, it seems that if monetary policy is left to the politicians, we shall always end up with higher inflation but with no reduction in unemployment, even in the short run.

What if, instead, the government gave the governor of the central bank full control over monetary policy and told him that he would be fired unless he achieved a certain low level of inflation over a reasonable period of time, regardless of what happened to unemployment? Say, in fact, that this target level of inflation was the one at point A in Figure 36.5. Because the central banker has no incentive to reduce unemployment, the problem goes away: firms and workers believe that the economy will stay at point A and so it does, because inflationary expectations are exactly the same as actual inflation. Hence, by passing control over monetary policy to the central bank, the economy ends up with unemployment no different from when the government was in control of monetary policy, but with a lower level of inflation.

So what's in it for the government? Well, for a start we should not perhaps think that all politicians are necessarily as cynical as we have portrayed them. Perhaps they have the longer-run well-being of the economy at heart rather than just wanting to be re-elected at any cost. Or perhaps they are cynical, but just more sophisticated. A cynical government would clearly prefer point B (or somewhere near it) to point A at election time, since unemployment is lower than the natural rate and people still expect low inflation – a sure vote-winning combination. However, the government knows that firms and workers will factor the government's temptation into their price and wage setting, so that in fact the economy will jump to point C just before the election.

In fact, this situation is an example of a *Nash equilibrium*, which we discussed in Chapter 17. Remember that a Nash equilibrium is a situation in which economic actors interacting with one another each choose their best strategy given the strategies that all the other actors have chosen. Here, firms and workers know that if they don't raise inflationary expectations before an election, the government will most likely pursue an expansionary monetary policy and they will lose out because their prices and wages will be lower in real terms, and so they do raise inflationary expectations and the short-run Phillips curve shifts up and we move to point C in Figure 36.5. But doesn't the government still have the same temptation to inflate at point C? Well, possibly, but there will certainly be some point on the vertical, long-run Phillips curve where inflation is already so high that the government will not want to risk pushing it higher, even if it means a short-run reduction in unemployment. If firms and workers can guess roughly what this level of inflation is, they will set their wages and prices so that the economy will jump straight to that point – let's imagine that this is indeed point C. If, at point C, the government has no temptation to inflate the economy in order to gain popularity, and if firms and workers know this so that they have no incentive to change their price and wage setting behaviour, then we will have reached the Nash equilibrium.

Another way of thinking about this is to say that the Nash equilibrium (which we have assumed is at point C in Figure 36.5) represents the *time-consistent policy*. A time-consistent policy is simply one which a government does not have a temptation to renege on at some point in time and will usually represent a Nash equilibrium. In 2004, Finn Kydland and Edward Prescott jointly won the Nobel Prize in Economics partly for their work on the time-consistency of macroeconomic policy (see Chapter 34).

But take a look at point C: it may represent time-consistency in economic policy, but it is actually worse than point A for the government's electoral chances, since inflation is higher and unemployment is still at the natural rate. Hence, the best thing to do in order to maximize the chances of re-election is for the government to make the central bank independent in the sense of handing over control of monetary policy – providing of course that the central bank sees its role as the guardian of price stability; in other words, providing that the central bank is 'conservative' with respect to price stability. That way, the economy can just stay at A.

It is a testimony to the power of macroeconomic theory that this argument has persuaded many governments around the world to grant independence to their central bank in the conduct of monetary policy. The European Central Bank, for example, has been independent since its inception in 1998, and the Bank of England was granted independence in 1997. As we discussed in Chapter 29, in fact, the ECB both designs its monetary policy (e.g. decides what level of inflation in the Euro Area to aim for) and implements it. The Bank of England, on the other hand, has independence in the implementation of monetary policy but does not decide on the design of monetary policy – in particular, its inflation target is set by the UK Chancellor of the Exchequer. The US Federal Reserve is also independent in both the design and implementation of monetary policy. Although, unlike the ECB and the Bank of England, the Fed does not formally pursue an inflation target, it has a strong reputation for 'conservatism' with respect to inflation, so the overall effect is similar. A long-run vertical Phillips curve is a compelling case for taking control over monetary policy out of the hands of politicians and handing it over to a 'conservative central banker'.

SHIFTS IN THE PHILLIPS CURVE: THE ROLE OF SUPPLY SHOCKS

Friedman and Phelps had suggested in 1968 that changes in expected inflation shift the short-run Phillips curve, and the experience of the early 1970s convinced most economists that Friedman and Phelps were right. Within a few years, however, the economics profession would turn its attention to a different source of shifts in the short-run Phillips curve: shocks to aggregate supply.

This time, the shift in focus came not from two economics professors but from a group of Arab sheikhs. Conflict between Israel and its Arab neighbours triggered a series of oil price shocks as Arab oil producers used their market power to exert political pressure on western governments who supported Israel. In 1974, the Organization of Petroleum Exporting Countries (OPEC) also began to exert its power as a cartel in order to increase its members' profits. The countries of OPEC, such as Saudi Arabia, Kuwait and Iraq, restricted the amount of crude oil they pumped and sold on world markets. This reduction in supply caused the price of oil to almost double over a few years in the 1970s.

A large increase in the world price of oil is an example of a supply shock. A **supply shock** is an event that directly affects firms' costs of production and thus the prices they charge; it shifts the economy's aggregate supply curve and, as a result, the Phillips curve. Oil is constituent part of so many production processes that increases in its price has far reaching effects. For example, when an oil price increase raises the cost of producing petrol, heating oil, tyres, plastic products, distribution and many other products, it reduces the quantity of goods and services supplied at any given price level. As panel (a) of Figure 36.8 shows, this reduction in supply is represented by the leftward shift in the aggregate supply curve from AS_1 to AS_2. The price level rises from P_1 to P_2, and output falls from Y_1 to Y_2. The combination of rising prices and falling output is sometimes called *stagflation*.

supply shock
an event that directly alters firms' costs and prices, shifting the economy's aggregate supply curve and thus the Phillips curve

This shift in aggregate supply is associated with a similar shift in the short-run Phillips curve, shown in panel (b). Because firms need fewer workers to produce the smaller output, employment falls and unemployment rises. Because the price level is higher, the inflation rate – the percentage change in the price level from the previous year – is also higher. Thus, the shift in aggregate supply leads to higher unemployment and higher inflation. The short-run trade-off between inflation and unemployment shifts to the right from PC_1 to PC_2.

Confronted with an adverse shift in aggregate supply, policy makers face a difficult choice between fighting inflation and fighting unemployment. If they contract aggregate demand to fight inflation, they will raise unemployment further. If they expand aggregate demand to fight unemployment, they will raise inflation further. In other words, policy makers face a less favourable trade-off between inflation and unemployment than they did before the shift in aggregate supply: they have to live with a higher rate of inflation for a given rate of unemployment, a higher rate of unemployment for a given rate of inflation, or some combination of higher unemployment and higher inflation.

FIGURE 36.8

An Adverse Shock to Aggregate Supply

Panel (a) shows the model of aggregate demand and aggregate supply. When the aggregate supply curve shifts to the left from AS_1 to AS_2, the equilibrium moves from point A to point B. Output falls from Y_1 to Y_2, and the price level rises from P_1 to P_2. Panel (b) shows the short-run trade-off between inflation and unemployment. The adverse shift in aggregate supply moves the economy from a point with lower unemployment and lower inflation (point A) to a point with higher unemployment and higher inflation (point B) The short-run Phillips curve shifts to the right from PC_1 to PC_2. Policy makers now face a worse trade-off between inflation and unemployment.

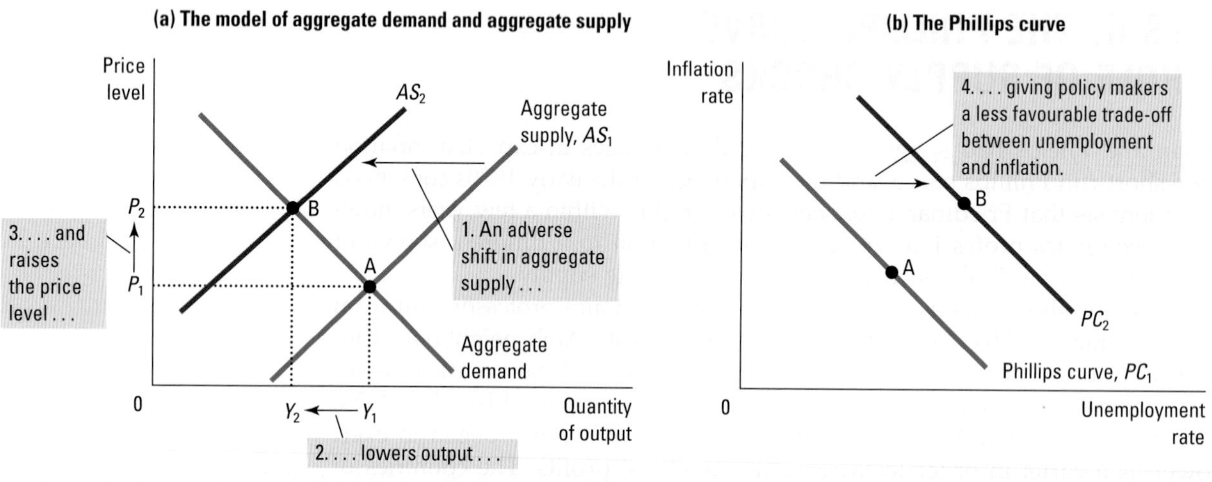

An important question is whether this adverse shift in the Phillips curve is temporary or permanent. The answer depends on how people adjust their expectations of inflation. If people view the rise in inflation due to the supply shock as a temporary aberration, expected inflation does not change, and the Phillips curve will soon revert to its former position. But if people believe the shock will lead to a new era of higher inflation, then expected inflation rises, and the Phillips curve remains at its new, less desirable position.

In the United Kingdom during the 1970s, expected inflation did rise substantially. In 1975 UK inflation, as measured by the RPI, rose above 24 per cent when just three years before it had been around 7 per cent. The problem was compounded in 1979, when OPEC once again started to exert its market power, more than doubling the price of oil. Figure 36.9 shows inflation and unemployment in the UK economy during this period.

In 1979, after the oil supply shocks, the UK economy had an inflation rate of around 14 per cent – nearly three times the inflation rate ten years earlier and an unemployment rate of over 5 per cent (more than double the 1969 level). This combination of inflation and unemployment was not at all near the trade-off that seemed possible in the 1960s. With the misery index in 1979 near an historic high, the UK electorate was widely dissatisfied with the performance of the economy. Largely because of this dissatisfaction, the Labour government led by James Callaghan lost its bid for re-election in 1979 and was replaced by a Conservative government under Margaret Thatcher, who proposed to bring in tough anti-inflationary monetary policy. (Callaghan had, in fact, already signalled a shift to monetary policy but the association of Labour with the challenging economic situation made it difficult for them to persuade the electorate that they could solve the problems the UK economy faced.)

"Barbara, which one is inflation and which one is wages?"

FIGURE 36.9

The Supply Shocks of the 1970s

This figure shows annual UK data from 1971 to 1980 on the unemployment rate and on the inflation rate (as measured by the RPI index). In the periods 1973–75 and 1978–80, increases in world oil prices led to higher inflation and higher unemployment.

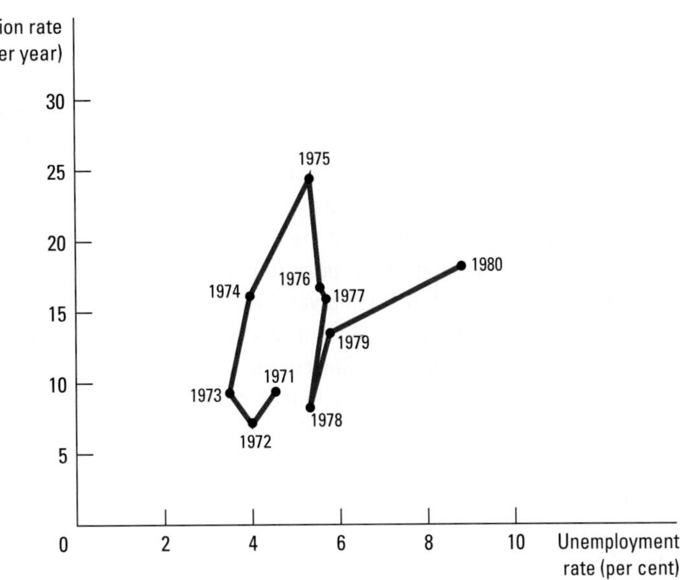

Source: UK Office for National Statistics.

Quick Quiz Give an example of a favourable shock to aggregate supply. Use the model of aggregate demand and aggregate supply to explain the effects of such a shock. How does it affect the Phillips curve?

THE COST OF REDUCING INFLATION

As we have seen, the primary focus of governments up to the Callaghan speech was on fiscal policy not monetary policy. By the mid-1970s, these policy measures appeared to be working very poorly. A condition of the financial support from the IMF required the UK government to pursue targets for monetary growth, although the Labour government's commitment to achieving these targets was not strong. In 1979, a new, Conservative government led by Margaret Thatcher was elected. The new government's policy framework was based on a more 'monetarist' view of the world which stressed the importance of controlling the money supply and which – although the politicians did not explicitly say so – was effectively rooted in the idea of a vertical long-run supply curve or vertical long-run Phillips curve.

Accordingly, within a few months of office, the new government announced the 'Medium-Term Financial Strategy' (MTFS): a five-year plan of annual targets for money supply growth that (since this was before the Bank of England had been granted independence) the government would require the Bank of England to implement. With inflation at this point above 20 per cent, the government

FYI

Wage Curve Theory

We have said that Phillips's research looked at the relationship between the rate of growth of wages and unemployment. The relationship of the wage rate to unemployment takes us a small step towards linking the level of inflation with unemployment. The rate of growth in wages is a factor that influences the overall level of prices in the economy. Wages represent a cost to employers; other things being equal, if they rise then employers might well seek to raise prices to cover the increased cost. If this happens throughout the economy on an aggregate level, wage growth leads to inflation. If the rate of growth of wages slows down, we might expect the labour market to be looser; in other words, the demand for labour in relation to the supply of labour is falling. Under normal market conditions, we would expect the wage rate to start to fall. In reality, this translates to the slowing down in the rate of growth of wages.

We then saw how further research into the Phillips curve led to the development of the so-called expectations augmented Phillips curve, captured in the following formula:

$$\Delta p_t = E_t \; \Delta p_{t+1} + (NR_t - RU_t)$$

This simply says that the change in the inflation rate in a time period (Δp_t) is equal to expected inflation in a time period ($E_t \; \Delta p_{t+1}$) and the natural rate of unemployment minus the national unemployment rate. This helped to explain what seemed to be happening in many Western economies in the 1970s. Households were *anticipating* inflation in the future and basing their behaviour and decision-making on those expectations: therefore, the Phillips Curve was shifting. This helped to explain how higher inflation might also be experienced at the same time as higher unemployment – so-called 'stagflation'.

There have, however, been a number of economists who have questioned the existence of the Phillips curve. One economist did pose that very question. David Blanchflower has worked at a number of institutions, including the University of Surrey and Warwick University. He is a former member of the Bank of England's Monetary Policy Committee and works at Dartmouth College in New Hampshire in the United States.

Remember that the assumption of the Phillips curve is that there is a relationship between the *rate of growth of wages* and unemployment. When unemployment rises, the rate of growth of wages falls and vice versa. This makes intuitive sense since if there is a large pool of unemployed workers, employed workers will be hesitant to push for higher wage claims for fear of joining the rank of unemployed.

Blanchflower has been quoted as suggesting that as a result of his work, 'the Phillips curve is wrong, it's as fundamental as that.' The following is a summary of his analysis in support of this view. The traditional Phillips curve relates the rate of growth of wages with the level of unemployment. Within this relationship, a higher level of unemployment is associated with a lower level of the rate of growth of wages. Conversely, if unemployment rates were low, the rate of growth of wages would be higher. Such a relationship is given as a macroeconomic one rather than microeconomic, i.e. it holds for the economy as a whole. If the level of unemployment increases, therefore, it suggests there will be excess supply in the labour market. In such cases, the labour market will adjust and the rate of growth of wages will fall to eliminate the excess supply.

Blanchflower and his colleague, Andrew Oswald, spent time researching links between unemployment and wage rates at a *microeconomic level* and found that the relationship between unemployment and wages might be different depending on the region that was being investigated. Their research looked at the *level of pay rather* than the rate of growth of wages. They argued that the *level* of pay was negatively related to the level of unemployment rather than the rate of growth in pay.

According to this argument, a worker in region A, which has a high level of unemployment, would earn lower wages than an equivalent worker in region B with lower levels of unemployment. Blanchard and Oswald's research casts doubt upon the standard explanation, in both regional economics and labour economics, that the wage rate in an area is positively linked to the level of unemployment in an area. In other words, the higher the level of unemployment, the higher the wage level needed to persuade someone to work in that area and vice versa.

Their work would tend to call into question some of the basic 'laws' of economics, particularly those related to something like the minimum wage. The conventional wisdom might be that if the minimum wage was introduced into an economy, the higher wage levels would be associated with a rise in unemployment. Blanchflower and Oswald's analysis suggests that this may not be the case and that in some areas there might even be a rise in the level of unemployment associated with a rise in wage levels.

FIGURE 36.10

The Traditional Explanation of the Effect of a Minimum Wage Set Above the Equilibrium Wage Level

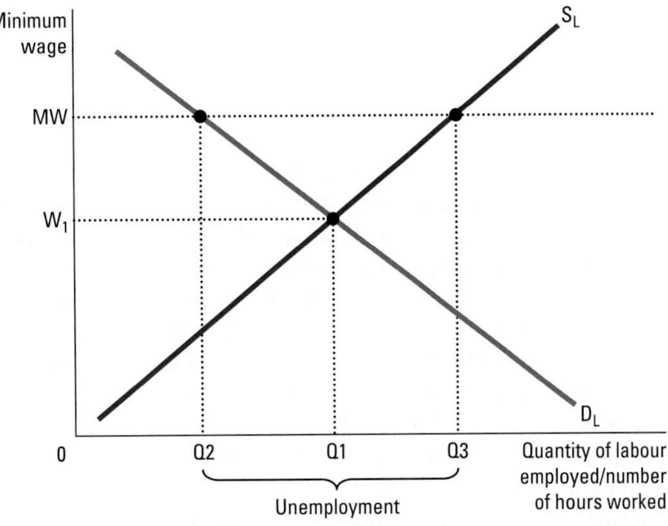

FIGURE 36.11

A Microeconomic Model of the Labour Market

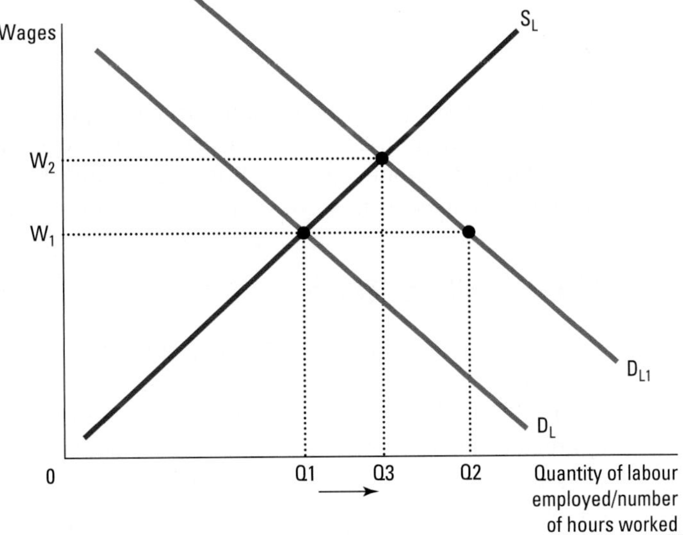

Figure 36.10 highlights the traditional view of the effect of the imposition of a minimum wage set above the market wage level (W_1) on the level of unemployment. The minimum wage causes a fall in the quantity of labour demanded and an increase in the quantity supplied of labour (a movement along the *D* and *S* curves for labour). The result is an increase in the amount of unemployment, shown by the distance *Q3* – Q2.

To understand this, it is important to refer back to the basic model of the labour market shown in Figure 36.11. If the demand for labour, for example, rose as indicated by a shift in the demand for labour curve to the right (D_L – D_{L1}), then there would be an excess demand for labour shown by the distance *Q2* – *Q1*. Wage rates would rise in response to this shortage of labour and as the shortage is competed away, more people would end up being employed (*Q3*) at higher wage rates (W_2). A rise in wage *rates*, therefore, is positively correlated with a fall in unemployment and vice versa.

Blanchflower and Oswald's research was based around millions of observations. They identified the existence of wage curves in 16 countries and since the publication of their research in 1994, a number of other researchers have confirmed their findings. Blanchflower and Oswald suggested that their wage curve would have an elasticity of –0.1. What this refers to is the responsiveness of rates of pay to changes in unemployment. An elasticity of –0.1, therefore, would suggest that if we took two regions within an economy, region A and region B, and if unemployment was 2 per cent in region B but 4 per cent in region A, we would expect wages to be around 10 per cent lower in region A than B. This suggests some sort of causal relationship stemming from the level of unemployment in an area feeding through to the level of wages in that area, rather than the other way round.

The suggestion that there is a relationship between the rate of growth of wages (and by implication, inflation) and unemployment, as we saw in the early part of this chapter, has implications for policy makers. This is based in part on the idea that controlling the rate of growth in wages (and hence inflation) is an important step in controlling unemployment. If, however, Blanchflower and Oswald's research on wage curves is correct, it changes the emphasis of policy making both at a macro and at a micro level. Let us assume that the government are looking at an unemployment rate that they consider too high, and so want to reduce that rate. If they refer to traditional macroeconomic models of the labour market, they might look at wages as being one way of reducing unemployment in that area – in other words, a fall in wages would help to bring about a reduction in unemployment.

If a wage curve does exist, then attempts to reduce unemployment in this way could backfire, since falling wages would be associated with higher unemployment! In addition, it might be believed that high unemployment in an area might be affected most dramatically by focusing on high unemployment groups in that area – those with low levels of education, for example. It might be expected that these groups of people will be most likely to take on jobs that are created at lower wages and as such, policies to reduce unemployment could be achieved without a major impact on inflation. Again, the existence of a wage curve would tend to provide an argument against doing this. This is partly because it is the *level* of wages that are important rather than the rate of growth of wages.

clearly felt that there was no alternative to a policy of *disinflation* – a reduction in the rate of inflation. Economic theory suggested how this could be done through controlling the money supply. But what would be the short-run cost of disinflation? The answer to this question was much less certain.

The Sacrifice Ratio

To reduce the inflation rate, the central bank has to pursue contractionary monetary policy. Figure 36.12 shows some of the effects of such a decision. When the central bank slows the rate at which the money supply is growing, it contracts aggregate demand. The fall in aggregate demand, in turn, reduces the quantity of goods and services that firms produce, and this fall in production leads to a fall in employment. The economy begins at point A in the figure and moves along the short-run Phillips curve to point B, which has lower inflation and higher unemployment. Over time, as people come to understand that prices are rising more slowly, expected inflation falls, and the short-run Phillips curve shifts downward. The economy moves from point B to point C. Inflation is lower, and unemployment is back at its natural rate.

Thus, if a nation wants to reduce inflation, it must endure a period of high unemployment and low output. In Figure 36.12, this cost is represented by the movement of the economy through point B as it travels from point A to point C. The size of this cost depends on the slope of the Phillips curve and how quickly expectations of inflation adjust to the new monetary policy.

FIGURE 36.12

Disinflationary Monetary Policy in the Short Run and Long Run

When the central bank pursues contractionary monetary policy to reduce inflation, the economy moves along a short-run Phillips curve from point A to point B. Over time, expected inflation falls, and the short-run Phillips curve shifts downward. When the economy reaches point C, unemployment is back at its natural rate.

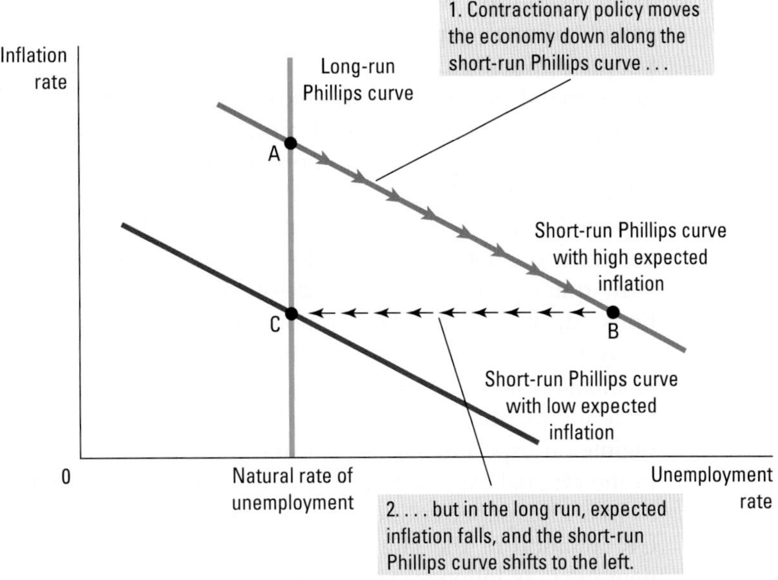

Many studies have examined the data on inflation and unemployment in order to estimate the cost of reducing inflation. The findings of these studies are often summarized in a statistic called the **sacrifice ratio**. The sacrifice ratio is the number of percentage points of annual output lost in the process of reducing inflation by 1 percentage point. A typical estimate of the sacrifice ratio is around 3 to 5. That is, for each percentage point that inflation is reduced, 3 to 5 per cent of annual output must be sacrificed in the transition.

sacrifice ratio
the number of percentage points of annual output lost in the process of reducing inflation by 1 percentage point

Such estimates surely must have made the UK government apprehensive as they confronted the task of reducing inflation in the early 1980s. Inflation was running at around 22 per cent per year in early 1980. To reach moderate inflation of, say, 5 per cent per year would mean reducing inflation by 17 percentage points. If each percentage point cost 3 per cent of the economy's annual output, then reducing inflation by 17 percentage points would require sacrificing over 40 per cent of annual output.

According to studies of the Phillips curve and the cost of disinflation, this sacrifice could be paid in various ways. An immediate reduction in inflation would depress output by 40 per cent for a single year, but that outcome would be extremely harsh even for the most hard-line inflation hawks. It would be better, many argued, to spread out the cost over several years. If the reduction in inflation took place over 5 years, for instance, then output would have to average only 8 per cent below trend during that period to add up to a sacrifice of 40 per cent. An even more gradual approach would be to reduce inflation slowly over a decade. Whatever path was chosen, however, it seemed that reducing inflation would not be easy.

Rational Expectations and the Possibility of Costless Disinflation

Just as policy makers were pondering how costly reducing inflation might be, a group of economics professors were leading an intellectual revolution that would challenge the conventional wisdom on the sacrifice ratio. This group included such prominent economists as Robert Lucas, Thomas Sargent and Robert Barro. Their revolution was based on a new approach to economic theory and policy called **rational expectations**. According to the theory of rational expectations, people optimally use all the information they have, including information about government policies, when forecasting the future.

rational expectations
the theory according to which people optimally use all the information they have, including information about government policies, when forecasting the future

This new approach has had profound implications for many areas of macroeconomics, but none is more important than its application to the trade-off between inflation and unemployment. As Friedman and Phelps had first emphasized, expected inflation is an important variable that explains why there is a trade-off between inflation and unemployment in the short run but not in the long run. How quickly the short-run trade-off disappears depends on how quickly expectations adjust. Proponents of rational expectations built on the Friedman – Phelps analysis argue that when economic policies change, people adjust their expectations of inflation accordingly. Studies of inflation and unemployment that tried to estimate the sacrifice ratio had failed to take account of the direct effect of the policy regime on expectations. As a result, estimates of the sacrifice ratio were, according to the rational expectations theorists, unreliable guides for policy.

In a 1982 paper entitled 'The End of Four Big Inflations' (one of which was the UK inflation of the late 1970s and early 1980s), Thomas Sargent described this new view as follows:

> An alternative 'rational expectations' view denies that there is any inherent momentum to the present process of inflation. This view maintains that firms and workers have now come to expect high rates of inflation in the future and that they strike inflationary bargains in light of these expectations. However, it is held that people expect high rates of inflation in the future precisely because the government's current and prospective monetary and fiscal policies warrant those expectations. … An implication of this view is that inflation can be stopped much more quickly than advocates of the 'momentum' view have indicated and that their estimates of the length of time and the costs of stopping inflation in terms of forgone output are erroneous. This is not to say that it would be easy to eradicate inflation. On the contrary, it would require more than a few temporary restrictive fiscal and monetary actions. It would require a change in the policy regime. … How costly such a move would be in terms of forgone output and how long it would be in taking effect would depend partly on how resolute and evident the government's commitment was.

According to Sargent, the sacrifice ratio could be much smaller than suggested by previous estimates. Indeed, in the most extreme case, it could be zero. If the government made a credible commitment to a policy of low inflation, people would be rational enough to lower their expectations of inflation immediately. The short-run Phillips curve would shift downward, and the economy would reach low inflation quickly without the cost of temporarily high unemployment and low output. The credibility of government policy is thus of prime importance.

The Thatcher Disinflation

Figure 36.13 shows UK inflation and unemployment from 1979 to 1988. As you can see, Prime Minister Margaret Thatcher did succeed at reducing inflation. Inflation came down from almost 20 per cent in 1980 to about 5 per cent in 1983

FIGURE 36.13

The Thatcher Disinflation

This figure shows annual UK data from 1979 to 1988 on the unemployment rate and on the inflation rate (as measured by the RPI index). The reduction in inflation during this period came at the cost of very high unemployment in 1982 and 1983. Note that the points labelled A, B *and* C *in this figure correspond roughly to the points in Figure 36.12.*

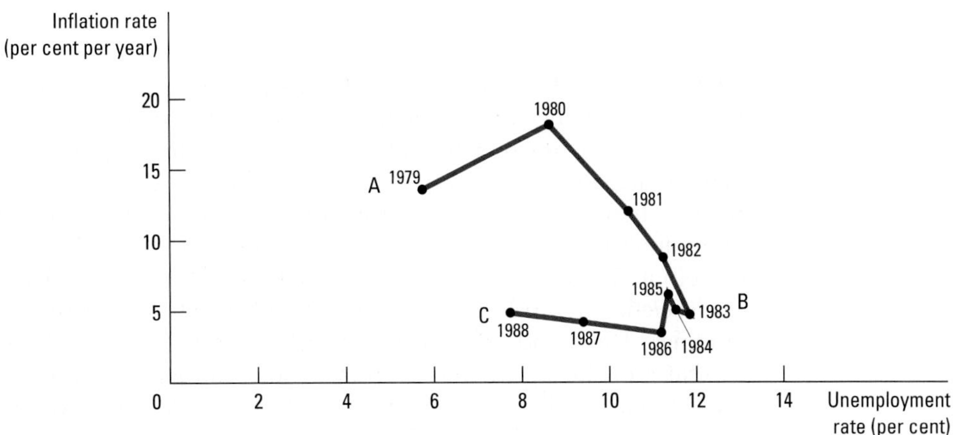

Source: UK Office for National Statistics.

and 1984. The figure shows that the Thatcher disinflation did, however, come at the cost of high unemployment. In 1982 and 1983, the unemployment rate was about 11 per cent – about double its level when the Thatcher government came to power. At the same time, the production of goods and services as measured by real GDP was well below its trend level. (See Figure 34.1 in Chapter 34.)

Does this experience refute the possibility of costless disinflation as suggested by the rational expectations theorists? Some economists have argued that the answer to this question is a resounding yes. Indeed, the pattern of disinflation shown in Figure 36.13 is very similar to the pattern predicted in Figure 36.12. To make the transition from high inflation (point A in both figures) to low inflation (point C), the economy had to experience a painful period of high unemployment (point B).

Yet perhaps there is good reason not to reject the conclusions of the rational expectations theorists so quickly. Even though the Thatcher disinflation did impose a cost of temporarily high unemployment, the cost was not as large as many economists had predicted. Most estimates of the sacrifice ratio based on the Thatcher disinflation are smaller than estimates that had been obtained from previous data. It seems that Prime Minister Thatcher's tough stand on inflation did have some direct effect on expectations, as the rational expectations theorists claimed.

INFLATION TARGETING

In many countries of the world today, including the UK and the Euro Area, the framework of monetary policy involves setting targets for inflation to be achieved over the medium run of two years or so, and then adjusting interest rates in order to achieve this objective. As we have pointed out in earlier chapters, setting interest rates is tantamount to setting the money supply if there is a stable and known relationship between the money supply and interest rates. However, the explicit focus on interest rates as the instrument of monetary policy, and medium-run inflation as the target of monetary policy, appears to have worked well for many economies. In the UK the move to the framework of inflation targeting arose as much out of the lessons of experience as out of the logic of economic reasoning.

The Path of UK Monetary Policy: From Monetary Targets to an Inflation Target

Although the UK government in the early 1980s announced a credible commitment to achieving targets for the growth of the money supply, it turned out in practice to be much more difficult to control the supply of money than had been anticipated. To a large extent this was due to a process of financial sector reforms that the Thatcher government also carried out. For example, the government abolished special taxes on high-interest rate bank deposits (known as 'the corset') and also introduced new legislation that allowed banks as well as building societies to lend money for the purposes of house purchase (i.e. mortgage lending). These and other financial sector reforms affected the money multiplier so that monetary growth was in fact much more difficult to predict and turned out to be faster than the government had targeted throughout the 1980s.

Towards the end of the 1980s, therefore, the government began to think of other indicators of the tightness of monetary policy. One such indicator is the exchange rate. In an open economy like the UK, the level of the exchange rate is very important. As we discussed in Chapter 35, if the UK currency has a high value in the foreign currency exchange market, then this will tend to depress aggregate demand by making exports more expensive to foreigners and imports cheaper to domestic residents, so that net exports fall. In addition, because domestic residents are effectively paying less money for their imports, this helps to keep the cost of imported goods like raw materials low and this also helps to keep down inflation. But the government began to think not only of a 'strong' exchange rate policy, but linking the value of sterling to other European currencies more formally by joining the European Exchange Rate Mechanism (ERM). Most of the European Union countries were already members of the ERM in the late 1980s. This was a 'semi-fixed' exchange rate system in which exchange rates between currencies of member countries were only allowed to fluctuate within small, pre-agreed bands, while their value against non-member currencies (like the US dollar) was allowed to be determined in the markets (i.e. to float freely). If there was a tendency for a currency to move out of an agreed band in the foreign currency exchange market – because there was an excess supply of a currency so that its foreign currency value was falling – then the government in question was obliged to take action to move it back inside. In the case of weak currency, this would usually take the form of raising interest rates so that net capital outflows diminished and the demand for the currency was restored. But it might also require temporary support for the currency in the form of official foreign exchange market intervention, where the government buys (or sells) its own currency in order to keep up (or keep down) its foreign currency value. Intervention can only be a temporary expedient where there is strong downward pressure on a currency, however, because the government needs reserves of foreign currency with which to buy its own currency and eventually it will, quite simply, run out of reserves.

The argument for joining the ERM was that it would provide a predictable element to UK monetary policy: if sterling weakened appreciably so that it began to edge out of its announced band of fluctuation, so that aggregate demand began to expand, interest rates would be raised in order to strengthen the currency and the effect would be to reduce aggregate demand. Also, because membership of the ERM constituted a formal arrangement, there would be a very big loss in the international prestige and reputation of a government if it were suddenly to leave the mechanism. In addition, maintaining the value of the pound within the ERM appeared to be a time-consistent policy, since although the government might be tempted to expand monetary policy before an election, the resulting reduction in interest rates would lead to the value of the currency falling out of the pre-agreed band of fluctuation.

The UK did in fact join the ERM in 1990. In 1992, however, it was forced to withdraw following a massive speculative attack on both sterling and the French franc.

The government was at this point forced to reassess the tools and indicators of monetary policy. Controlling the money supply through the setting of monetary targets had proven to be difficult during the 1980s. As we discussed above, this was probably largely due to various financial sector reforms and innovations that affected the money multiplier and made the money supply hard to predict. But having given up monetary targeting and replaced it with an exchange rate target (which the government had in turn been forced to abandon), to return to monetary targeting would have been risky. Instead, the government turned to a new framework for monetary policy: inflation targeting.

Targeting

The level of the money supply and the exchange rate can be thought of as intermediate targets of monetary policy. That is to say, they may be targeted in order to achieve certain other, policy targets, such as real GDP growth, employment and inflation. Now, an important principle that we have learnt in our study of monetary policy is that, in the long run, monetary policy cannot affect the real side of the economy – i.e. real GDP and employment. Therefore, in the long run, the only final target of monetary policy can be the inflation rate. Therefore, targeting the money supply or the exchange rate as a framework for monetary policy means that we are targeting those variables because it is felt that they will ultimately affect the rate of price inflation. Also, since neither the money supply nor the exchange rate is directly controllable, they cannot be instruments of monetary policy. In other words, the government cannot just set the level of the money supply it wants, it must attempt to bring about that level by open-market operations and other means, as we discussed in Chapter 29; similarly, it cannot just set the level of the exchange rate it wants, it must try to bring about that level by setting interest rates and by other means. Hence, the money supply and the exchange rate should really be viewed as intermediate targets that the government may aim for because it is believed that they will ultimately affect the final target of inflation. So why not just target the inflation rate? Interest rates (or at least some interest rates) are under the control of central banks, so they are definitely an instrument of monetary policy. And we know that raising interest rates reduces aggregate demand and so dampens inflation. So the government could just raise interest rates whenever inflation rose above a level that was considered desirable – say 2 per cent. This would be a crude form of inflation targeting.

There are two problems with this crude inflation targeting. First, changing (or not changing) interest rates today will not affect inflation today, it will only affect inflation in the future, since it takes time for the policy to have an affect on the economy. Secondly, there may be other factors that would affect inflation in the future. Suppose, for example, that inflation was at its target of 2 per cent per year. The central bank therefore decides not to change interest rates, since it is achieving its inflation target. However, suppose there was at the same time a wave of very high wage settlements in the economy, above any increases in labour productivity. Over the next six months to a year, this is expected to lead to a rise in price inflation in the economy as workers spend more and as firms pass on some of the wage increases in the form of higher prices. Should the central bank wait for the inflation to arrive, or should it act now by raising interest rates in anticipation of the inflationary pressures coming from higher wages? Clearly, the better policy is to target not today's inflation, which it is already too late to have any effect on, but future inflation. Of course, no one knows with certainty what future inflation is going to be, therefore a policy of inflation targeting generally involves targeting the forecast rate of inflation.

This is the policy framework that was adopted by the UK in late 1992. The inflation target is currently 2 per cent per year, as measured by the CPI, and to some extent, success in achieving the target is measured by whether the Bank of England's own inflation forecast up to two years ahead falls within 1 per cent of the target, above or below. Of course, it might be argued that the Bank of England is having it easy in the sense that it can judge itself whether or not it has achieved the target. However, an important element of successful inflation targeting is transparency: the Bank of England publishes detailed analyses of its forecasts and these are closely scrutinized. Secondly, if actual inflation does ever fall outside the range of plus or minus one per cent of the target, the Governor of the Bank of England is required to write a formal letter to the Chancellor of the Exchequer, explaining why inflation is out of the target range, what measures are being taken to get it back on course, and when it is expected to be back on target.

As we discussed in Chapter 29, both the Bank of England and the European Central Bank now pursue a policy of inflation targeting, and both target a level of inflation of 2 per cent. The country that pioneered inflation targeting was New Zealand, which adopted this policy in 1990. It was followed in 1991 by Canada, and in 1992 by the UK and Sweden. Like the UK, Sweden also adopted a policy of inflation targeting after it was forced to abandon its exchange rate peg in 1992. Other countries that have adopted inflation targeting in recent years include Norway and Switzerland.

Quick Quiz What is the sacrifice ratio? How might the credibility of the government's commitment to reduce inflation affect the sacrifice ratio?

IN THE NEWS

The financial crisis has led to economists and policy makers reassessing macroeconomic policy. Did policy makers become complacent and believe that they had found a way to control inflation and achieve growth at the same time? This interview with Olivier Blanchard, a member of the International Monetary Fund (IMF), proposes a view that lessons need to be learned from the crisis and that maybe policy objectives should be reassessed.

Rethinking Macroeconomic Policy

IMF Survey online spoke to Olivier Blanchard, one of the authors of *Rethinking Macroeconomic Policy*, about the reasons for publishing the paper and what he hopes to achieve. Blanchard, who joined the Fund in 2008 from the Massachusetts Institute of Technology, is Economic Counsellor of the IMF and head of the Research Department.

IMF SURVEY ONLINE: Why are you publishing this paper, which essentially attempts to lay out the contours of a new macroeconomic policy framework, now?

BLANCHARD: As the crisis slowly recedes, it's time for a reassessment of what we know about how to conduct macroeconomic policy. It was tempting for macroeconomists and policy makers to take much of the credit for the steady decrease in cyclical fluctuations from the early 1980s on and to conclude that we knew how to conduct macroeconomic policy. We did not resist temptation. The crisis naturally forces us to question our earlier conclusions and that's what we are trying to do in this paper.

IMF SURVEY ONLINE: So is this a mea culpa economists?

BLANCHARD: Well, macroeconomists clearly did not cause this crisis. But we now realize that economists and policy makers alike were lulled into a false sense of security by the apparent success of economic policy ahead of the crisis – a period known as the 'Great Moderation' when fluctuations in both output and inflation in most advanced economies were successfully reduced and living standards rose. The crisis has taught us a lot and we want to proactively draw lessons from the 'Great Recession.'

Our goal in this piece is to lay out some key questions about the design of macroeconomic policy frameworks. And to develop some ideas on how those frameworks might be strengthened. Looking ahead, we will need to consider in more depth how we should tailor our specific policy advice to advanced, emerging market and developing countries.

IMF SURVEY ONLINE: What are your conclusions so far?

BLANCHARD: The basic elements of the pre-crisis policy consensus still hold. Keeping output close to potential and inflation low and stable should be the two targets of policy. And controlling inflation remains the primary responsibility of the central bank. But the crisis forces us to think about how these targets can be achieved.

The crisis has made clear, however, that policy makers have to watch many other variables, including the composition of output, the behaviour of asset prices, and the leverage of the different participants in the economy. It has also shown that they have potentially many more instruments at their disposal than they used before the crisis. The challenge is to learn how to use these instruments in the best way. The combination of traditional monetary policy and regulatory tools, and the design of better automatic stabilizers for fiscal policy, are two promising routes.

IMF SURVEY ONLINE: What do you mean by combining monetary policy and regulatory tools?

BLANCHARD: Interest rates are a poor tool to deal with excess leverage, excessive risk taking, or apparent deviations of asset prices from fundamentals. We need a combination of monetary and regulatory tools.

For example, if leverage appears excessive, regulatory capital ratios can be increased; if liquidity appears too low, regulatory liquidity ratios can be increased; to dampen housing prices, loan-to-value ratios can be decreased; to limit stock price increases, margin requirements can be raised. These measures could be to some extent circumvented, but nevertheless are likely to have a more targeted impact than the policy rate on the variables they are trying to affect.

It's better to use the policy rate primarily in response to aggregate activity and inflation and to use these specific instruments to deal with specific output composition, financing, or asset price issues.

If monetary and regulatory tools are to be combined in this way, it follows that the traditional regulatory and prudential frameworks need to acquire a macroeconomic dimension. The main challenge, here, is to find the right trade-off between a sophisticated system, fine-tuned to each marginal change in systemic risk, and an approach based on simple-to-communicate triggers and easy-to-implement rules.

If one accepts the notion that, together, monetary policy and regulation provide a large set of cyclical tools, this raises the issue of how coordination is achieved between the monetary and the regulatory authorities, or whether the central bank should be in charge of both. Indeed, the trend toward separation of the two may well have to be reversed.

IMF SURVEY ONLINE: You argue that we should understand why, in many countries, central banks care more about the exchange rate than they admit, and we should draw policy conclusions. Can you explain?

BLANCHARD: In many emerging market countries, while monetary authorities describe themselves as inflation targeters, they clearly care about the exchange rate beyond its effect on inflation.

They probably have good reasons to do so. Isn't it time to reconcile practice with theory, and to think of monetary policy more broadly, as the joint use of the interest rate and sterilized intervention, to protect inflation targets while reducing the costs associated with excessive exchange rate volatility?

IMF SURVEY ONLINE: Central banks have chosen low inflation targets, around 2 per cent. In your paper, you argue that maybe we should revisit this target. Why?

BLANCHARD: The crisis has shown that interest rates can actually hit the zero level, and when this happens it is a severe constraint on monetary policy that ties your hands during times of trouble.

As a matter of logic, higher average inflation and thus higher average nominal interest rates before the crisis would have given more room for monetary policy to be eased during the crisis and would have resulted in less deterioration of fiscal positions. What we need to think about now if whether this could justify setting a higher inflation target in the future.

IMF SURVEY ONLINE: Isn't that risky?

BLANCHARD: The crisis has shown that large shocks to the system can and do happen. In this crisis, they came from the financial sector, but they could come from elsewhere in the future – the effects of a pandemic on tourism and trade or the effects of a major terrorist attack on a large economic centre. Maybe policy makers should therefore aim for a higher target inflation rate in normal times, in order to increase the room for monetary policy to react to such shocks. To be concrete, are the net costs of inflation much higher at, say, 4 per cent than at 2 per cent, the current target range? Is it more difficult to anchor expectations at 4 per cent than at 2 per cent?

At the same time, it is clear that achieving credible low inflation through central bank independence has been a historic accomplishment, especially in several emerging markets. Thus, answering these questions implies carefully revisiting the list of costs and possible benefits of inflation. Nevertheless, it is worth considering whether these costs are outweighed by the improved policy manoeuvrability that would be available in times of crisis from having slightly higher inflation.

IMF SURVEY ONLINE: Fiscal policy is back in fashion because of the crisis.

BLANCHARD: The crisis has returned fiscal policy to centre stage as a macroeconomic tool, for two main reasons: first, to the extent that monetary policy, including credit and quantitative easing, had largely reached its limits, policy makers had little choice but to rely on fiscal policy. Second, from its early stages, the recession was expected to be long lasting, so that it was clear that fiscal stimulus would have ample time to yield a beneficial impact despite implementation lags.

It has also shown the importance of having 'fiscal space,' again the room to manoeuvre during times of trouble. Some advanced economies that entered the crisis with high levels of debt and large unfunded liabilities have had limited ability to use fiscal policy, and are now facing difficult adjustments.

Those emerging market economies (some, for example, in Eastern Europe) that ran highly procyclical fiscal policies driven by consumption booms are now forced to cut spending and increase taxes despite unprecedented recessions. By contrast, many other emerging markets entered the crisis with lower levels of debt. This allowed them to use fiscal policy more aggressively without fiscal sustainability being called into question or ensuing sudden stops.

This suggests that we should revisit target debt to GDP ratios. Maybe we should aim for much lower ratios than before the crisis. This is a long way off, given where we start, but this is another issue we must revisit.

IMF SURVEY ONLINE: Can anything be done to make fiscal policy more effective during a crisis?

BLANCHARD: Discretionary fiscal policy measures usually come too late to fight the downturn because it takes time to put in place tax cuts or new spending measures. There is, therefore, a strong case for improving what are called the fiscal stabilizers. Our paper argues that we need to look carefully at measures that would automatically kick-in during a downturn and have a significant impact on the economy. For example, one could think of temporary tax policies targeted at low-income households, investment credits, or temporary social transfers that would be triggered by a macroeconomic variable crossing some threshold (the unemployment rate, say, rising above 8 per cent).

Source: http://www.imf.org/external/pubs/ft/survey/so/2010/INT021210A.htm "Interview with Olivier Blanchard: IMF Explores Contours of Future Macroeconomic Policy," by Jeremy Clift (February 12, 2010), *IMF Survey online* http://www.imf.org/external/pubs/ft/survey/so/2010/INT021210A.htm © International Monetary Fund, 700 19th Street, NW, Washington, DC 20431, USA. The views expressed in this paper belong solely to the authors. Nothing contained in this paper should be reported as representing IMF policy or the views of the IMF, its Executive Board, member governments, or any other entity mentioned herein.

CONCLUSION

This chapter has examined how economists' thinking about inflation and unemployment has evolved over time. We have discussed the ideas of many of the best economists of the 20th century: from the Phillips curve of Phillips, Samuelson and Solow, to the natural-rate hypothesis of Friedman and Phelps, to the rational expectations theory of Lucas, Sargent and Barro. Five of this group have already won Nobel prizes for their work in economics, and more are likely to be so honoured in the years to come. Our discussion has been based around the UK economy but the principles apply across other economies too – the UK is a convenient case study in the changing interpretation and application of economic theory.

Although the trade-off between inflation and unemployment has generated much intellectual turmoil over the past 40 years, certain principles have developed that today command consensus. Here is how Milton Friedman expressed the relationship between inflation and unemployment in 1968 (in an *American Economic Review* paper entitled 'The Role of Monetary Policy'):

> There is always a temporary trade-off between inflation and unemployment; there is no permanent trade-off. The temporary trade-off comes not from inflation per se, but from unanticipated inflation, which generally means, from a rising rate of inflation. The widespread belief that there is a permanent trade-off is a sophisticated version of the confusion between 'high' and 'rising' that we all recognize in simpler forms. A rising rate of inflation may reduce unemployment, a high rate will not.
>
> But how long, you will say, is 'temporary'? ... We can at most venture a personal judgment, based on some examination of the historical evidence, that the initial effects of a higher and unanticipated rate of inflation last for something like two to five years.

Today, nearly 40 years later, this statement still summarizes the view of most macroeconomists.

SUMMARY

- The Phillips curve describes a negative relationship between inflation and unemployment. By expanding aggregate demand, policy makers can choose a point on the Phillips curve with higher inflation and lower unemployment. By contracting aggregate demand, policy makers can choose a point on the Phillips curve with lower inflation and higher unemployment.
- The trade-off between inflation and unemployment described by the Phillips curve holds only in the short run. In the long run, expected inflation adjusts to changes in actual inflation, and the short-run Phillips curve shifts. As a result, the long-run Phillips curve is vertical at the natural rate of unemployment.
- The short-run Phillips curve also shifts because of shocks to aggregate supply. An adverse supply shock, such as the increase in world oil prices during the 1970s, gives policy makers a less favourable trade-off between inflation and unemployment. That is, after an adverse supply shock, policy makers have to accept a higher rate of inflation for any given rate of unemployment, or a higher rate of unemployment for any given rate of inflation.
- When the central bank contracts growth in the money supply to reduce inflation, it moves the economy along the short-run Phillips curve, which results in temporarily high unemployment. The cost of disinflation depends on how quickly expectations of inflation fall. Some economists argue that a credible commitment to low inflation can reduce the cost of disinflation by inducing a quick adjustment of expectations.

KEY CONCEPTS

Phillips curve, p. 783
natural-rate hypothesis, p. 791
supply shock, p. 797
sacrifice ratio, p. 803
rational expectations, p. 804

QUESTIONS FOR REVIEW

1. Draw the short-run trade-off between inflation and unemployment. How might the central bank move the economy from one point on this curve to another?
2. Draw the long-run trade-off between inflation and unemployment. Explain how the short-run and long-run trade-offs are related.
3. What's so natural about the natural rate of unemployment? Why might the natural rate of unemployment differ across countries?
4. Suppose a drought destroys farm crops and drives up the price of food. What is the effect on the short-run trade-off between inflation and unemployment?
5. The central bank decides to reduce inflation. Use the Phillips curve to show the short-run and long-run effects of this policy. How might the short-run costs be reduced?

PROBLEMS AND APPLICATIONS

1. Suppose the natural rate of unemployment is 6 per cent. On one graph, draw two Phillips curves that can be used to describe the four situations listed here. Label the point that shows the position of the economy in each case.
   a. Actual inflation is 5 per cent and expected inflation is 3 per cent.
   b. Actual inflation is 3 per cent and expected inflation is 5 per cent.
   c. Actual inflation is 5 per cent and expected inflation is 5 per cent.
   d. Actual inflation is 3 per cent and expected inflation is 3 per cent.
2. Illustrate the effects of the following developments on both the short-run and long-run Phillips curves. Give the economic reasoning underlying your answers.
   a. a rise in the natural rate of unemployment
   b. a decline in the price of imported oil
   c. a rise in government spending
   d. a decline in expected inflation.
3. Suppose that a fall in consumer spending causes a recession.
   a. Illustrate the changes in the economy using both an aggregate supply/aggregate demand diagram and a Phillips curve diagram. What happens to inflation and unemployment in the short run?
   b. Now suppose that over time expected inflation changes in the same direction that actual inflation changes. What happens to the position of the short run Phillips curve? After the recession is over, does the economy face a better or worse set of inflation–unemployment combinations?
4. Suppose the economy is in a long-run equilibrium.
   a. Draw the economy's short-run and long-run Phillips curves.
   b. Suppose a wave of business pessimism reduces aggregate demand. Show the effect of this shock on your diagram from part (a). If the central bank undertakes expansionary monetary policy, can it return the economy to its original inflation rate and original unemployment rate?
   c. Now suppose the economy is back in long-run equilibrium, and then the price of imported oil rises. Show the effect of this shock with a new diagram like that in part (a). If the central bank undertakes expansionary monetary policy, can it return the economy to its original inflation rate and original unemployment rate? If the central bank undertakes contractionary monetary policy, can it return the economy to its original inflation rate and original unemployment rate? Explain why this situation differs from that in part (b).
5. Suppose the central bank believed that the natural rate of unemployment was 6 per cent when the actual natural rate was 5.5 per cent. If the central bank based its policy decisions on its belief, what would happen to the economy?
6. The price of oil fell sharply in 1986 and again in 1998.
   a. Show the impact of such a change in both the aggregate demand/aggregate supply diagram and in the Phillips curve diagram. What happens to inflation and unemployment in the short run?
   b. Do the effects of this event mean there is no short-run trade-off between inflation and unemployment? Why or why not?

7. Suppose the central bank announced that it would pursue contractionary monetary policy in order to reduce the inflation rate. Would the following conditions make the ensuing recession more or less severe? Explain.
   a. Wage contracts have short durations.
   b. There is little confidence in the central bank's determination to reduce inflation.
   c. Expectations of inflation adjust quickly to actual inflation.
8. Some economists believe that the short-run Phillips curve is relatively steep and shifts quickly in response to changes in the economy. Would these economists be more or less likely to favour contractionary policy in order to reduce inflation than economists who had the opposite views?
9. Imagine an economy in which all wages are set in three year contracts. In this world, the central bank announces a disinflationary change in monetary policy to begin immediately. Everyone in the economy believes the central bank's announcement. Would this disinflation be costless? Why or why not? What might the central bank do to reduce the cost of disinflation?
10. Given the unpopularity of inflation, why don't elected leaders always support efforts to reduce inflation? Economists believe that countries can reduce the cost of disinflation by letting their central banks make decisions about monetary policy without interference from politicians. Why might this be so?
11. Suppose policy makers accept the theory of the short run Phillips curve and the natural-rate hypothesis and want to keep unemployment close to its natural rate. Unfortunately, because the natural rate of unemployment can change over time, they aren't certain about the value of the natural rate. What macroeconomic variables do you think they should look at when conducting monetary policy?

For further resources, visit
www.cengage.co.uk/mankiw_taylor2

13

TOPICS IN INTERNATIONAL FINANCE AND MACROECONOMICS

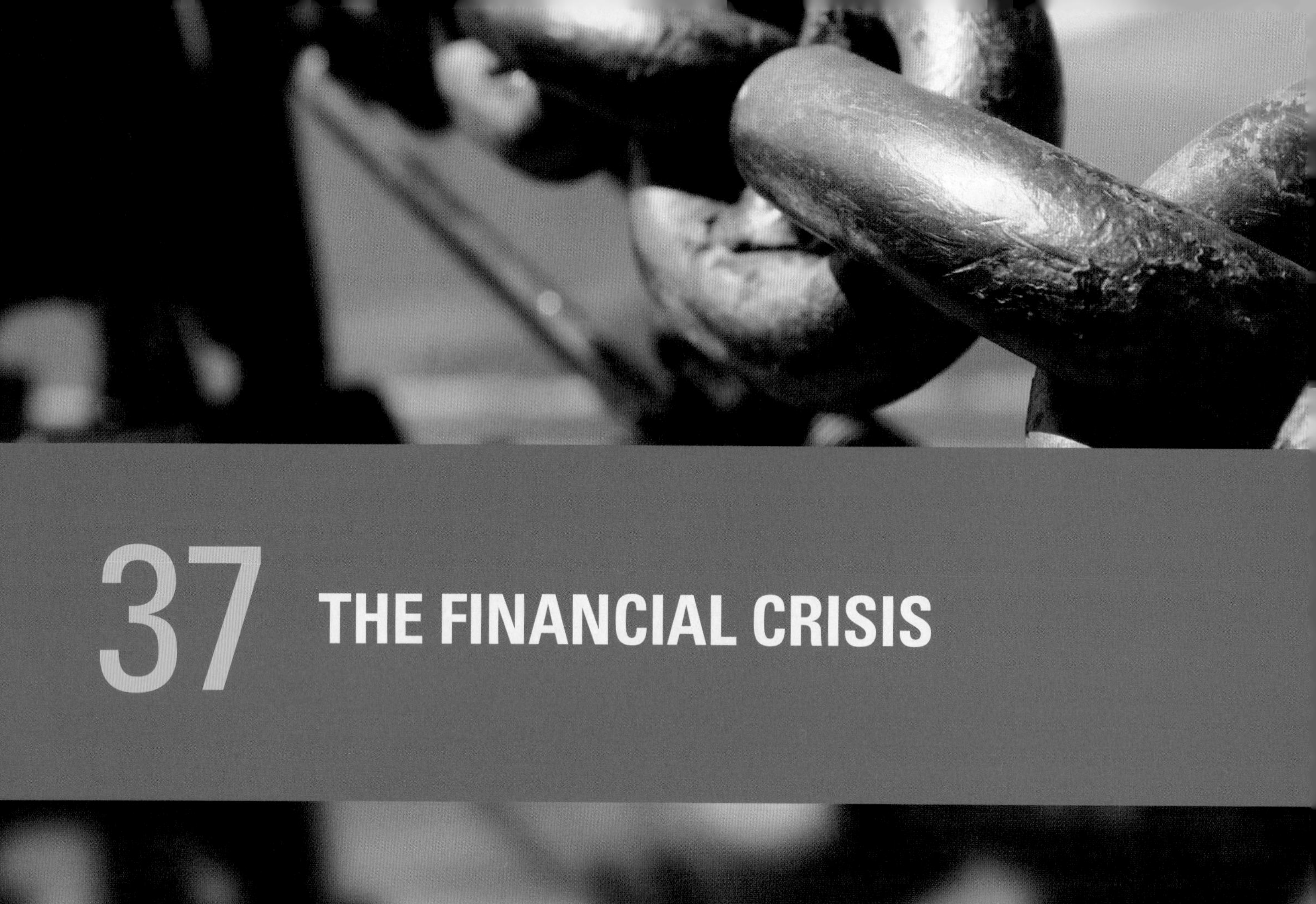

37 THE FINANCIAL CRISIS

One of the things that makes economics fascinating is the speed with which things can change. In 2005 few people predicted the calamitous events which would take place over the next four years. The financial crisis and the global recession that followed led to a reappraisal of some of the fundamental principles of economics and put macroeconomic policy and the issue of global financial regulation firmly on the agenda once again.

The origins of the crisis can be traced back to the deregulation of financial markets in the 1980s and 1990s. There was a belief that excessive regulation limited the ability of the supply side of the economy to operate efficiently and a series of legislative measures in both the US and UK dramatically changed the banking and financial landscape. Rules and regulations surrounding the activities of banks and building societies were abolished or relaxed. Various restrictions on bank lending were relaxed and as a result left the way open for financial institutions to develop new products and trading systems that resulted in a complex web of interdependent global financial markets. The innovation in the financial system was further enhanced by the developments in technology. We have already seen in Chapter 27 how an ability to manipulate statistics and be a mathematical wizard became important skills as the products being traded became more complex. Part of this innovation was a drive to find ever more sophisticated and 'risk-free' investments to generate profit and this would eventually embroil millions of people around the world, many with precious little understanding of what was happening to their money or how the system was working.

The deregulation of the financial markets has to be seen in conjunction with wider changes in society. The relative period of constant economic growth from the mid-1990s along with the (sometimes) spectacular rise in house prices led many to believe that the era of boom and bust had finally been relegated to history. For financial institutions the expectations of continued growth might also partly explain how attention turned from what might be termed 'prudent' lending to ever more risky investments on the back of new financial instruments. Banks, many of whom had been former mutual societies run for the benefit of their members, now had the pressure of generating returns for shareholders and in the search for ever larger returns, lending protocols were stretched to the limit and sometimes broken. These changes took place against an environment of relatively low real interest rates in the latter part of the 1990s and much of the early years of the first decade of the new century.

"Borrow 50p? Sorry, I'm staying out of the sub-prime lending market."

The prevalence of relatively low rates of interest meant the prospect of high-yield returns became even more attractive especially given the fact that such returns could be linked to bonuses for staff. Pension funds were being hit by changes to the way in which many corporate businesses managed their pension provision. The suspension of expensive final salary pension schemes along with cuts in contributions from government and employees meant that pension fund managers became eager to find investments that offered increased yields.

In the UK similar conditions enabled banks and mortgage lenders to compete for new custom through developing ever more attractive products including low-start mortgages, two-year fixed-rate deals, debt roll-up mortgages and mortgages based on an increasing proportion of the value of property and multiples of income. Across both sides of the Atlantic, borrowing to buy a house or, indeed many other 'luxuries' in life, was never easier. Deregulation and global trading meant that capital movements across national boundaries were much easier. Funds could be borrowed from countries with low interest rates (particularly Japan who experienced negative interest rates at times in the early 2000s) and invested in assets in countries with higher yielding currencies. The growth of hedge funds looking to secure high returns on investments for the clients whom they represented, along with the developments in IT which enabled them to exploit very small price differentials between markets, all combined to provide the background for a more risk-seeking mentality to pervade the financial markets.

BUBBLES AND SPECULATION

Alan Greenspan, the former Chair of the US Federal Reserve (Fed) commented in September 2009: 'That is the unquenchable capability of human beings when confronted with long periods of prosperity to presume that it will continue.' Greenspan was referring to the period when both credit and housing markets expanded in the latter part of the 1990s and into the new millennium. Total UK debt including credit cards and mortgages in 2006 was reported at being over £1.2 trillion and the Bank of England noted that outstanding balances on credit cards had risen by over 380 per cent since 1994. The thirst for credit on both sides of the Atlantic, particularly in the form of mortgage lending, has been cited as being one of the reasons for the financial crisis. Figure 37.1 shows UK house prices from 1983 to 2008. It can be clearly seen that the average house price rose dramatically from the late 1990s to 2007. This is also reflected by Figure 37.2 showing the index of house prices in the US. Between 2000 and 2009, house prices had risen by around 80 per cent.

It is at this point in the story that the effects of deregulation, the existence of relatively low interest rates, apparently stable economic conditions and the

FIGURE 37.1

UK House Prices, 1983–2008

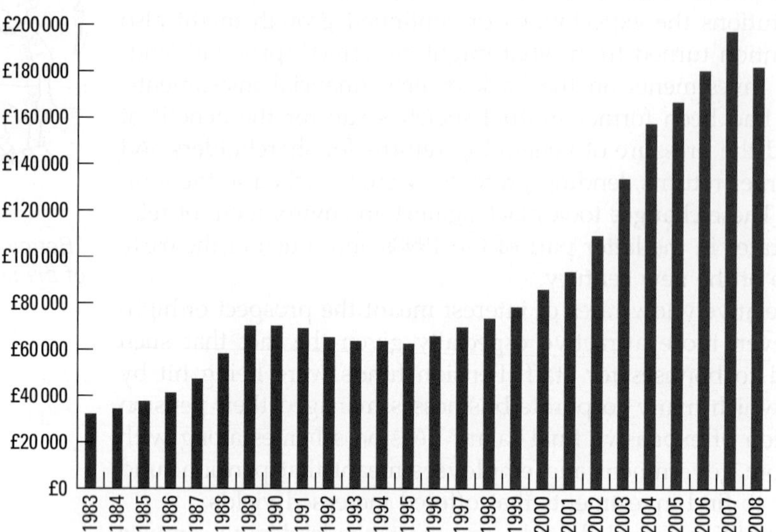

Source: Data from Halifax House Price Index.

FIGURE 37.2

S&P/Case-Schiller US National Home Price Index, 2000–09

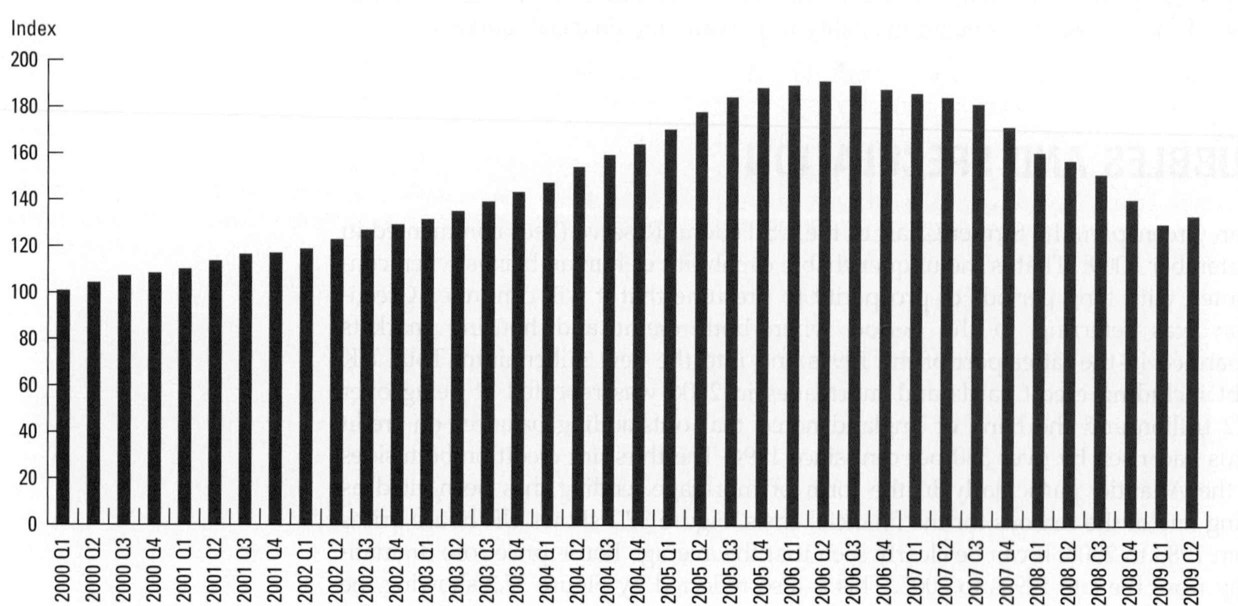

Source: Data from Standard and Poor's.

increase in risk-seeking activity amongst financial institutions all come together. The mixture generated a housing market bubble in both the UK and US. This bubble led to riskier loans being made accompanied at the same time with the growth of a market in which the increased risk could be sold off.

The Sub-prime Market

In the United States, extending mortgage opportunities to those not traditionally seen as being part of the market became part of the way in which banks and other lenders sought to increase their lending. Individuals seen as being a relatively low credit risk for mortgage lending were known as the prime market; the term is said to have derived from analogy with the best cuts of meat from an animal. It followed that there was a sub-prime group for whom access to mortgages was altogether more difficult. Some of these people had credit histories that were very poor; some did not have jobs but in an atmosphere of risk seeking and changed priorities this group provided lenders with a market opportunity because they were willing to pay higher rates of interest to secure a mortgage. Under 'normal' circumstances the bank would not only have acquired a liability but also an asset. The mortgage would generate a stream of cash flows in the form of the payment of the mortgage principal and interest over a period of years. Such an asset could be valuable in the new deregulated banking environment.

Securitization

The **securitization** of assets represented one of the innovations in banking that grew with the expansion of sub-prime lending. The basis of the process lay in the fact that the assets involved generated cash flows over a period of time. The practice of securitization enabled banks to increase the scope of their lending. Securitization takes loans off the balance sheet and so the bank does not have to set aside reserves to cover those loans (see special purpose vehicles (SPVs) in Chapter 29). Turning attention to lenders who would not normally be considered for loans represented not only a new departure in banking but encouraged the development of products and processes that would help to reduce the exposure to the additional risk that was clearly being entered into.

securitization the creation of asset-backed securities

Asset-backed securities (ABS) involved banks essentially putting together collections of debt and selling it on. These parcels of debt did have risk attached to them but this risk could be reduced by taking out insurance on them in the form of credit default swaps (see Chapter 26). These contracts were also traded to the extent that the owners of these contracts became far removed from the stream of income (i.e. the mortgage payments made by homeowners) on which the products being insured depended. In essence, the whole structure of mortgage lending was dependent on the ability of those who had taken out mortgages (including sub-prime) to be able to pay the principal and interest on their loans. When the number of borrowers defaulting on their repayments started to rise, the structure began to become unstable and the full extent of the interdependence began to reveal itself.

asset-backed securities (ABS) bonds or securities which form part of the securitization of assets. The bonds or securities issued by an SPV as part of a securitization

Collateralized debt obligations (CDOs) are one example of these asset-backed securities (see Chapter 26). The rise in the number of CDOs sold, based purely on sub-prime mortgage debt, increased dramatically from 2000 to 2007, from a few billion dollars to around $2 trillion. The web of financial institutions involved was global. The prudence which many financial institutions worked to in relation to spreading risks in portfolio management was now able to be set aside because investors could 'see' the risk almost disappear. CDO prices and the derivative CDS prices now had the risk factored in using sophisticated mathematical formulae developed by quantitative financial analysts (the quants – see Chapter 27). Historical data on which some of these formulae are based can be used to give an account of what happened in the past but this is not necessarily an indication of what will happen in the future. Formulae used to price CDOs were based on probabilities reflecting a period when house prices and stock markets were rising, economic growth was strong in a number of developed countries and times were 'good'. However, whether these were '*normal*' times was another matter.

The dramatic rise is house prices on both sides of the Atlantic helped to fuel a rise in bank lending against the background of a feel-good factor in the real economy and a confidence that risk could be managed effectively in the financial markets. There is some debate among economists as to whether the dramatic rise in house prices in the US and the UK during this period could be called a 'bubble'. The majority would probably say that it was a bubble, although some economists have argued that the rise in productivity and incomes led to sharply rising prices as demand for housing naturally outstripped supply. However, while rising productivity may explain part of the housing price boom, many people buying houses were doing so simply in the expectation that the price would continue to rise, and indeed many lenders were offering attractive mortgages to people with low credit ratings because they thought that the property on which the mortgage was secured would continue to rise in price. When people buy an asset not because of the flow of services it yields (a roof over one's head in the case of a house) but simply because they believe it is going to rise in price, we have the essential characteristic of a bubble. In any case, bubble or not, there is no doubting the fact that the housing market played a significant role in the financial crisis and the subsequent move to recession in many of the major economies of the world.

ASYMMETRIC INFORMATION, THE BONUS CULTURE AND RISK

With the benefit of hindsight it might seem rather foolish for anyone, let alone a bank, to have contemplated lending money to people with bad credit histories and low incomes. Surely banks knew the risk they were taking? Part of the answer is that they thought they did and whilst risk seeking might have been a more dominant behavioural trait than risk aversion, strategies had been put in place to limit the risks of the banks and other lenders to the exposure of lending to the sub-prime market – or so they thought.

In 2002, the financial corporation HSBC bought Household International, which specialized in providing financial products to individuals who would traditionally be described as being high credit risk. Household International dealt with some 50 million such customers. As these new banking processes gathered pace more banks became involved. To reduce risk, banks became involved in the CDS market. The first CDS was developed by the US investment bank JP Morgan in 1997 but since that time the market for this product increased to between $45 and $60 trillion. To put this into perspective, the US stock market is valued at around $22 trillion, the mortgage market in the US is around $7 trillion and the US Treasury bill market around $4.4 trillion. The top 25 banks between them held around $13 trillion in CDS with the key players being Bear Stearns, Lehman Bros, Merrill Lynch, Morgan Stanley, the German Deutsche Bank and the Swiss UBS.

The climate of persistent growth and reasonably stable interest rates and inflation (the so-called 'Great Moderation'), gave rise to the view that the risk involved was more limited than in reality, it was. After all, in the UK, for example, growth had been positive for almost 20 years. For the individual trader the focus was on generating sufficient returns to ensure substantial salary bonuses that were linked to their performance in generating those returns. For the senior executives in banks the generation of profit to satisfy shareholder demands was a key focus but few directly involved necessarily stood back from the situation to see what the big picture was. In 2007, for example, Morgan Stanley reported that its income had fallen by over $9 billion. Despite this, bonus payments had risen to $16.5 billion and represented 60 per cent of the bank's income. To an extent this was the role of the regulator and the central banks but, it seems, these were also not fully aware of the potential for the situation to become as serious as it did. The distinction between the retail and wholesale operations of banks became increasingly blurred. In the wake of the financial crisis questions were asked whether it was appropriate for a bank to conduct operations to improve its own profits using its clients' money rather than acting in the interest of its clients. This would provide a basis for proposed regulation to prevent further banking crises.

What is the relevance of asymmetric information in all this? Assume that a bank bundles up a collection of mortgages into a package which it then wants to sell. The bank must want to sell it for some reason and any potential buyer does not know for sure what the reason is. Is the reason because the bank wants to make more profit or because the bank knows that the loans are potentially 'bad' (i.e. that there is a high risk of the borrowers defaulting)? This is a classic situation of asymmetric information (see Chapter 22). In order for the bank to be able to sell off the debt it has to have some way in which it can show the investment is low risk.

To do this, banks employed credit ratings agencies to provide an independent analysis of the risk involved. Credit ratings agencies such as Moody's, Standard & Poor's, Egan-Jones and A.M. Best, analyse and present debt as a series of ratings relating to the extent of the risk associated with the debt. AAA is the least risky, moving down through AA, A and BBB – all of which would be considered reasonably good quality risk; BB, B and CCC would be ratings signifying much greater risk (referred to as 'below investment grade). There have been suggestions that there is a conflict of interest facing credit ratings agencies in that the groups asking them to provide the risk rating are the ones that are paying for the service whereas those who are affected by their analysis, the investor, is external. Credit ratings agencies, however, are in a position to access information that is highly complex or which is not widely available in the public domain and as a result provide a valuable service.

In addition to the credit rating on the package of loans, the bank selling the debt may assume some element of risk through taking a first-loss position. Mathematical and statistical analysis of the debt package may suggest that, based on the historical performance of similar loan packages, there is, say, a 1 per cent risk of default. If the bank agrees to assume the first 4 per cent of losses the buyer might be comforted in the fact that the bank is prepared to accept some of the consequences of the possibility of default. The position has been likened to a car dealer agreeing to pay the first two years of maintenance bills on a second hand car. In such a situation the buyer of the car might be reassured that they were not buying a 'lemon'. Past performance, however, may not be a reliable guide to future performance – if default exceeds the 4 per cent then serious problems can unravel. Given the performance of the economy over the past 20 years, however, there was no specific reason to expect that the detailed analysis of risk put together by the mathematicians and statisticians was anything but accurate. The assumption of first-loss position meant that confidence could be established in such transactions.

The incentives for those involved in banks and other financial institutions were to assume a risk-seeking approach, therefore. The demand by shareholders for better returns, the existence of a bonus culture which could provide some individuals with millions each year, the desire by individuals to get on the property ladder and, some argue, the lack of rigour in regulation and oversight by the central banks, all combined to provide a situation where the bubble could feed on itself and generate ever greater lending and a continuing search for ever more attractive investments.

THE BUBBLE BURSTS

CDS represent sound business principles when the risk of default is very low, which was the case when they were first developed in the late 1990s and when the bonds being insured were corporate bonds with a low risk attached to them. The expansion of CDS presented a different challenge to the financial markets when the housing market collapse came. It must be remembered that not only were these contracts taken out in relation to bonds linked to sub-prime loans but the trade of these contracts might mean that banks and other financial institutions might be buying the contract whilst not possessing the asset (the bond).

© STACY WALSH ROSENSTOCK / ALAMY

One of the other major problems with the CDS market is that it was not subject to any form of regulation. It is referred to as *'over the counter'*, a private financial transaction between the two parties. There is no official record, therefore, of who has made a trade with whom and whether the seller can actually meet the obligations it is entering into. The precise value of the CDS market is difficult to pinpoint for this reason. The number of CDS trades, the number of derivative trades and precisely who owns all these trades are not easy to identify. A number of major banks had exposure to CDS including Lehman Bros, Icelandic banks, Barclays and RBS, and in addition insurance companies like AIG were also heavily committed.

In 2006–07, the prevailing concern amongst central banks was the development of inflationary pressure. In the UK, for example, inflation as measured by the Consumer Prices Index rose to a high of 5.2 per cent by September 2008. The Bank of England had started to increase interest rates in June 2006 and in a series of quarter point rises saw Base Rate increase to 5.75 per cent by July 2007. In the US, the Fed raised interest rates for 16 consecutive months to June 2006 and the Federal Funds Rate reached 5.25 per cent by the autumn of 2006. As interest rates rose, borrowers, especially those on sub-prime mortgages, began to feel the pressure and reports of the number of defaults on sub-prime loans began to rise.

Once mortgage defaults began to rise to alarming numbers the number of financial institutions affected and their exposure became clearer. As mortgage rates rose borrowers found it increasingly difficult to meet their monthly payments. In some cases the difference between initial monthly payments and restructured payments based on new interest rates was very significant; many homeowners found their monthly mortgage payments more than doubling. The sub-prime market, remember, did contain a large number of people who were least able to cope with significant changes in monthly payments but in addition those that had taken out sub-prime mortgages for second homes and the buy-to-let market also found themselves stretched.

Faced with payments they could not afford, borrowers looked to sell their property or faced the prospect of foreclosure – the point where the mortgage lender seizes the property. As the number of foreclosures increased, house prices fell. As house prices fell, more and more people were caught in negative equity, where the value of their property was less than the mortgage secured on it. Thus, selling the house to get out of the debt was not an option for many; they would still be left with a large debt which they had no hope of paying off.

As mortgage payers began to default in increasing numbers, banks who lent money to SPVs had to call in the debt. Banks who set up the SPV then had to take the assets back onto their balance sheet. This not only limited their ability to lend further because they now have to put aside reserves to cover liabilities which are now on their balance sheet, but they may also have to write down the value of the assets, further damaging their balance sheet and ability to lend.

Moral Hazard

The flood of bad news from banks made it clear that the problems were significant. The authorities were faced with the challenge of intervening to help save banks from collapse. However, this prospect led to the problem of moral hazard. If banks knew that they would be bailed out by the government, then they would have less of an incentive to pursue prudential lending practices. In Chapter 22, when we introduced the concept of moral hazard, we gave the example of a homeowner buying too few smoke detectors because the homeowner bears the cost of the smoke detectors while the insurance company gets most of the benefit (it is less likely to have to pay out because there is less likelihood of the house burning down). In the same, way, in a government bail-out of a financial institution, the government is acting like an insurance company and there is less incentive for the bank to reduce its risks (and make less money) if it knows the government will always save it.

The prospect of simply saving a bank, who many people saw as having forsaken the prudence that for so long characterized these institutions, was something that stuck in the throat of 'Main Street' America. Millions of ordinary Americans were facing significant hardship and the loss of their homes; businesses were finding it increasingly difficult to access the funds that they needed to survive in the face of a growing threat of recession. Nobody was stepping in to help them, they argued. Bankers, who had caused the problems it was said, seemed to be getting off lightly. Governments stepped in to help them and those who had received salary bonuses of millions seemed to be the ones suffering least.

Global Problems

The effects of the unfolding crisis began to be felt across the world. Iceland's banks collapsed, in Eastern Europe the Ukraine applied for a $16.5 billion loan from the IMF after the currency, the hryvnia, fell by 20 per cent and around 80 per cent was wiped off stock market values. The Ukraine central bank was forced to use reserves to try to buy hryvnia in an effort to support the currency. Hungary asked for $10 billion (after receiving a €5 billion loan from the European Central Bank and raising interest rates by 3 per cent to 11.5 per cent). Turkey, Belarus and Serbia also sought financial assistance as credit dried up and banks around the world found they had increasing difficulties in meeting their liabilities. The Russian stock market fell by around 66 per cent between May and October 2008.

Put simply, most of these banks had lent too much money, had been exposed to the debts related to purchases of CDS and could not meet payments which were falling due. Without financial assistance these institutions could have collapsed and financial systems in these and associated countries would have ground to a halt.

Banking Collapse

The issue of moral hazard might be the reason why one of the most spectacular banking collapses in recent times occurred on 15 September 2008. The US investment bank Lehman Brothers had been at the forefront of the sub-prime and CDS market. It had built its business on leveraging – borrowing heavily to finance its activities. Over the weekend of 13 and 14 September, last ditch talks were convened to try and find a way of rescuing Lehman Brothers in the same way that Bear Stearns and Merrill Lynch had been rescued. The debts at Lehman and the extent of its exposure to sub-prime and CDS were too great, however, and Lehman Brothers filed for Chapter 11 bankruptcy protection on 15 September.

When Lehman collapsed it led to billions of dollars of claims on Lehman CDS – payments which had to be made by those who sold the protection. As a means of settling these claims, Lehman's bonds were sold via auction in early October 2008. The value of the bonds was set by the auction at around 8 cents to the dollar. So a $10 million bond would only be worth $800 000, meaning that protection sellers would have to make up the remaining $9 200 000 to meet the CDS obligation. With claims estimated at anything between $400 and $600 billion this put a massive strain on the financial system and many banks who had sold CDS on Lehman were now exposed and in danger of failing themselves which put further pressure on the system. Basically, banks found that they had to meet payment obligations and did not have the funds available in reserves to do so. Banks who were struggling to meet their obligations may have attempted to raise funds in the interbank money markets which, we have already seen, were almost at a standstill. Banks around the world found themselves in this difficult position as the extent of the web of securitization began to become clearer. The collapse of Lehman was seen as a spectacular event because it showed that central banks were not prepared to step in to help any bank that got into trouble.

Following the collapse of Lehman Brothers it become clear that the large insurance group, AIG, was in trouble. AIG had been an active seller of CDS and the collapse of Lehman had left it seriously exposed. The US government stepped in to support this company because so much of the rest of the economy and financial institutions would have been affected if AIG had been allowed to go to the wall. In the UK, Northern Rock, Royal Bank of Scotland (RBS) and Halifax Bank of Scotland (HBOS) were all subject to government support of various kinds, including the speeding up of permission for Lloyds TSB to take over HBOS before it collapsed. Some have suggested, however, that Lehman Brothers may have been a sacrificial lamb at the altar of moral hazard, in that the US government was sending a message that a government bail-out could not always be guaranteed.

THE PATH TO GLOBAL RECESSION

The problems in financial markets began to translate themselves to the real economy fairly quickly.

For many people, the problems in the housing market led to job losses. As mortgages became harder to access, demand for homes fell and many involved in real estate were affected. Jobs created in the US that were linked to the house price boom began to be reversed. With house prices falling, homeowners feel less secure and perceive the equity in their homes to be falling. The incentive to borrow against the positive equity in property therefore is reduced and homeowners may also feel a lack of confidence and decide to cut back on some of the luxuries they once enjoyed. These may be little things such as going to the cinema, taking weekend breaks, going to the pub or a restaurant. If restaurants suffer a fall in the number of weekly covers they take they may have to cut back on orders of ingredients which begins to affect suppliers and so on down the supply chain. For the owners of these businesses the effect can be significant as highlighted in the data from the British Beer and Pub Association quoted in the 'In the News' article on pages 351–352 of Chapter 16.

It was, however, the effect of the tight credit market that helped exacerbate the depth of recession in many countries. One of the causes of the downturn was due to the problems businesses had in accessing funds from banks. Businesses, especially small businesses, rely on cash flow for their survival. Many need flexibility and understanding from their banks when faced with shocks to their cash flow and the tight credit markets meant that many businesses found banks unwilling to lend to them and to extend overdrafts. Even if the bank was prepared to lend, the interest rate attached to the loan was often prohibitive. Faced with these problems many smaller businesses began to close. Larger businesses were not immune from the problems, either. The motor vehicle industry, in particular, suffered significant falls in sales. In January 2008, monthly production of vehicles in the US was 817 767; by February 2009 this had fallen to 388 267 – down 52.2 per cent in just over a year. The fall in production affected component suppliers and the negative multiplier effect worked its way through the economy.

As demand fell, businesses closed and unemployment rose. In the US, the unemployment rate rose from 6.2 per cent in August 2008 to 9.7 per cent a year later; the unemployment rate in the UK rose by 2.4 per cent over the same period and the EU predicted that unemployment would reach 11.5 per cent in 2010. An increase in unemployment impacts on business confidence. High street sales in many countries slowed, spending on goods and services with a relatively high income elasticity of demand also fell and as this happened business saw revenues falling with the resulting pressure on cash flow. Many businesses cut back on stocks and this further affected businesses along the supply chain.

SUMMARY: THE CAUSES OF THE FINANCIAL CRISIS

The events of 2007–09 raised a number of questions about assumptions in economic theory. The years since the recession of the early 1990s had been characterized by renewed focus on inflation, on improving the supply side of the economy and freeing monetary policy from government control. The role of the Fed, the Bank of England and the European Central Bank was clearly enshrined in their constitutions – to control inflation. Deregulation had created a new and evolving financial climate which, when mixed with the changes in technology and the ever expanding reliance of the major nations on the knowledge economy, led to new ways in which banks and other financial institutions could do business. In what might be described as a veneer of risk reduction, new products such as CDS seemed to provide a means for risk to be managed effectively. The expansion of lending to those who had previously not been a part of most banks' lending portfolios and ways in which this lending could be hedged, filtered through to the real economy on the back of increased housing prices. Once the assumptions that asset-backed securities would continue to be paid and the limited number of defaults broke down, the financial house of cards began to collapse. The unwinding of the liabilities banks faced in the wake of the sub-prime collapse eventually, and rather swiftly, found its way through to the real economy and to people losing their homes, jobs and livelihoods. The questions raised over the whole period were many and the challenge for policy makers and economists (see the interview with Olivier Blanchard on pages 808–809 of Chapter 36 on rethinking macroeconomic policy.) in the coming years was to learn from this experience and put in place structures that could help to give greater protection to banks and their customers. The role of government and central banks is crucial to the debate over such control.

THE CONDUCT OF MONETARY POLICY

As the financial crisis developed, focus centred on the response of central banks around the world. There were precedents of the effect on economies of crises in the banking sector; such crises tended to feed through to the real economy and result in a slowdown in economic activity that could be long-lasting and damaging to future growth potential. When recessions occur, firms cut back on investment and shed labour. These are two valuable resources that help to determine future growth potential. If labour remains unemployed de-skilling can mean it becomes harder to obtain jobs in future, especially for those who experience long-term unemployment. If firms cut back on investment then equipment and machinery suffers from depreciation and if the latest equipment is not purchased productivity can fall.

In addition, government resources are stretched as tax receipts tend to fall but government spending on welfare payments increase. If budget deficits widen it raises a debate about the state of public finances and the tax burden on future generations. Most countries in Europe have seen increased pressure on public finances with the fiscal stimulus programmes that have been put in place with many not expecting to see such pressure easing for many years. The opportunity cost of a deep and lasting recession can be significant.

The response of the authorities to the global financial crisis with regard to fiscal policy has been outlined in Chapter 34. The role of monetary policy in helping to alleviate the worst effects of the financial crisis and the resulting recession is seen as important and has since come under scrutiny with regard to the effectiveness of the action of key policy makers. The three major Western central banks, the Federal Reserve (Fed) under Ben Bernanke, the European Central Bank headed by Jean Claude Trichet and the Bank of England, headed by, Mervyn King, have come in for particular scrutiny.

Bernanke's predecessor, Alan Greenspan, tended to respond to economic crisis by lowering interest rates and flooding markets with liquidity. Indeed, it has been suggested that a low interest rate climate between 2002 and 2005 contributed to asset bubbles and the subsequent collapse. The search for yield created incentives to move into riskier assets and increased leverage, all fuelled by the availability of liquidity and cheap financing. Bernanke, in particular, with his background expertise in the 1930s depression, was looked to for decisive leadership in the early years of his tenure at the Fed.

The markets were looking for three key aspects of policy response from central banks: speed of intervention, innovation and coordination. There were aspects of each of these that have occurred since the crisis developed but there are also important differences in the degree to which each of the main central banks responded, partly because of the different levels of flexibility that each enjoyed. In the UK, for example, the Bank of England was given operational responsibility for monetary policy in 1997. The Bank of England Act 1998 states: 'the monetary policy objectives of the Bank: [are] to maintain price stability and, subject to that, to support the Government's economic policy, including its objectives for growth and employment.' The emphasis on maintaining price stability as its primary role is one that has been taken seriously by Mervyn King but there are those that believe that a central bank's role should also include a greater emphasis on watching over the financial community and maintaining a greater regulatory function. In the UK, the regulatory role is carried out by the Financial Services Authority (FSA) as part of the so-called 'tri-partite approach' which includes the Bank of England and the Treasury as well as the FSA. In the US the Securities and Exchange Commission (SEC) carries out the regulatory function although there are a number of other regulatory bodies, which some observers have claimed leads to confusion.

The Response to Crisis

The early signs of crisis emerged in 2007 when rumours of rising levels of default from sub-prime mortgages began to increase. In July, Standard & Poor's and Moody's downgraded ratings on bonds backed by sub-prime mortgages. In late July a German bank, IKB, said that it was in financial trouble as a result of its exposure to sub-prime and was swiftly taken over by German government owned bank, BKW. By early August the ramifications of the downgrading of funds related to sub-prime were starting to unravel and on 3 August Bear Stearns had to contact its shareholders following the collapse of two hedge funds that it managed and the subsequent fall in its share price. On 9 August, French bank BNP Paribas announced that it was ceasing trading three of its funds and with that credit markets effectively froze. Interbank lending ground to a halt as banks began to recognize that their exposure to sub-prime could be extensive. Mutual trust between banks is essential for the smooth operating of credit markets but with banks recognizing their own fragilities it was certain that others were also affected if not more so!

The freezing of credit markets effectively marked the start of intervention by central banks around the world. The ECB was one of the first to react with Trichet authorizing an injection of €95 billion into the financial markets to help ease overnight liquidity problems on 9 August. On the following day a further €61 billion was authorized. Soon after the ECB move the Fed announced that it would inject $38 billion to help ease liquidity; the Bank of England, however, did not follow suit. On 10 August the Bank was involved in the growing problems at Northern Rock which had expanded rapidly in previous years but now found its expansion based on leverage unsustainable and as credit markets froze it was struggling to continue. In the coming weeks the extent of the problems at Northern Rock became public and a run on the bank ensued. Moves to calm the situation did not seem to have too much effect and on 17 September the government, in consultation with the Bank, agreed to guarantee all existing Northern Rock deposits.

King was concerned with the problem of moral hazard. The Bank of England has a function as lender of last resort but King was keen to ensure that the words 'last resort' really meant that. As banks around the world began to falter over the coming months the question of which bank should be rescued and which left to fail had to be considered by central bank leaders. The Bank of England had issued warnings that it was concerned investors were not pricing risk appropriately. In the US, Ben Bernanke had made a number of statements attempting to calm the fears over the extent to which sub-prime would affect the real economy. In May 2007 he had given a speech at a conference in Chicago and said:

> We believe the effect of the troubles in the subprime sector on the broader housing market will likely be limited, and we do not expect significant spillovers from the subprime market to the rest of the economy or to the financial system.[1]

He reiterated this view a month later when he said:

> At this point, the troubles in the subprime sector seem unlikely to seriously spill over to the broader economy or the financial system.[2]

Whether this was an attempt to exert some psychological influence over decision-makers or a lack of information or understanding of the situation is still open to debate. In hindsight, it is easy to isolate quotes and point fingers at central banks.

---

[1] http://www.federalreserve.gov/newsevents/speech/bernanke20070517a.htm accessed 27 October 2009.

[2] http://www.federalreserve.gov/newsevents/speech/Bernanke20070605a.htm accessed 27 October 2009.

The reluctance of the Bank of England to inject funds into the markets was partly seen as the concern with moral hazard but also the subjugating of financial stability to a lesser role. It was reported that Governor King had privately admitted that financial stability had been lower down the list of priorities compared to the focus on inflation.[3] However, the Bank of England, at that time, had limited tools available to it to deal with the events that were unfolding in comparison to other central banks. It was not until the passing of the Banking Act in 2009 that the Bank of England was given additional powers and responsibilities that enabled it to improve its control of financial stability.

The new Banking Act provides a permanent set of tools that allows the tripartite authorities to resolve a distressed bank or building society in an orderly way. These powers should help reduce the impact of bank failure on financial stability and bank customers. The Act allows for:

- creation of a new Special Resolution Regime (SRR) for dealing with distressed banks
- giving the Bank of England a statutory financial stability objective and with it creating a Financial Stability Committee to advise on financial system matters
- formalizing the Bank of England's payment system oversight role
- the creation of a new framework for issuance of Scottish and Northern Ireland banknotes to be overseen by the Bank of England.[4]

In the event, the Bank of England eventually announced that it would provide financial help to institutions that needed overnight funds but that any such borrowing would incur a penalty rate. By April 2008 it had gained the authority to lend to banks against mortgage debt – something that the ECB could do which the Bank could not. The Bank was given authority to issue short-dated UK government bonds in exchange for mortgage securities. However, at the end of August 2007 it emerged that Barclays had asked the Bank for a loan of £1.6 billion and the news, which would not normally have made front page headlines, was interpreted as being another sign that a major bank was in trouble. Barclays needed the funds because of a malfunction in computer systems related to clearing and had tried borrowing from the wholesale markets. The Bank then removed the penalty rate since it seemed that far from calming nerves it merely served to increase the sense of panic.

As the months progressed and credit continued to be difficult to obtain, central banks began to ease monetary policy. However, given the concern over the prospect of inflation in Europe, the US and the UK, it was not until 2008 that concerted efforts to reduce interest rates were seen. King was concerned about inflationary pressures in the UK economy. Far from considering reducing interest rates, the expectation was that rates might rise above the 5.5 per cent that existed in January 2008. In the May 2008 *Quarterly Inflation Report*, the Bank had admitted that the Monetary Policy Committee was likely to have to write 'a number of explanatory open letters to the Chancellor' implying that the Bank expected inflation to rise above 3 per cent. It also said that it did not expect inflation to come back towards target until the latter part of 2009 and early 2010. The Report made it clear that the Bank expected 'less further policy easing than at the time of the February Report'[5]. By that time, the MPC had cut interest rates to 5.00 per cent.

The Fed had moved first, cutting rates by 0.75 per cent in January 2008; the ECB held its rate at 4.0 per cent. The Bank of England cut rates by a quarter

[3]See Brummer, A. (2008) *The Crunch: How Greed and Incompetence Sparked the Credit Crisis*. London: Random House Business Books, pp:120–122.

[4]http://www.bankofengland.co.uk/financialstability/role/risk_reduction/banking_reform_bill/index.htm accessed 26th October 2009.

[5]*Bank of England Quarterly Inflation Report*, May 2008.

point in February and April but by May the Fed had cut rates seven times in eight months with the Fed Funds Rate standing at 2.0 per cent. As 2008 progressed the financial situation did show clear signs that it was 'spilling over' to the economy and output levels began to contract in economies across the globe. The problems were such that in October, seven major economies, the UK, US, China, the EU, Canada, United Arab Emirates (UAE) and Sweden, announced a coordinated 0.5 per cent cut in interest rates. By then end of October the Fed cut again to 1 per cent.

In the US, discussions were taking place to set up the Troubled Asset Relief Plan (TARP), a $700 billion plan to support the banking system. In November the Fed announced a further $800 billion support fund. In that same month the Bank of England reduced rates by 1.5 per cent – the largest single change in rates since it was given independence in 1997. By March 2009 the MPC had cut interest rates in the UK to 0.5 per cent, the lowest since the Bank of England was established in 1694. The Fed cut its rates to a target of between 0 and 0.25 per cent and the ECB had cut rates to 1 per cent.

In addition to this considerable easing of monetary policy across the world, governments, in consultation with central banks, had stepped in to provide financial support for a wide range of businesses and financial institutions in addition to the fiscal stimulus described in Chapter 35. In most major economies, guarantees were given to protect bank deposits for 'ordinary' savers. In the UK the minimum guarantee was raised from £20 000 to £50 000 for one year; Spain increased its guarantees on deposits by five times, the United Arab Emirates (UAE) and Germany both guaranteed all private bank deposits. Italy pumped €40 billion worth of Treasury bills into the markets, France injected €10.5 billion into its top six banks, Iceland was forced to nationalize its three main banks and ask for a $4 billion loan from Russia who itself had injected $100 billion in extra liquidity and a further $37 billion in long-term loans to some of its largest banks.

The scale of the intervention by governments and central banks made it clear that the crisis was serious. As the recriminations began, the failure of banks and the extent to which governments had supported them became topical news. Greed, incompetence, a lack of understanding of the financial system and a very real anger that those who 'created' the crisis (bankers) seemed to be getting help and support whilst ordinary people lost their livelihoods was common. In particular, short-selling came in for some criticism and a number of countries including the UK, Germany, Italy, Greece, Spain, Austria, the Netherlands, Portugal and Switzerland all either imposed a temporary ban on short-selling or placed additional restrictions on the practice.

CASE STUDY

Short-selling

On the morning of the 19 September 2008, newspaper headlines in the UK were plastered with the sort of invective normally reserved for rapists, murderers and child molesters! This time, the anger of headline writers was directed at mostly highly educated and skilled people who had been going about their normal jobs and doing what they do rather well. The target for the anger was traders on the financial markets. 'Share sharks', 'rogue traders', 'spivs' and 'dodgy dealing' were all terms or phrases which appeared in the press as the fallout of the £12 billion merger between HBOS and Lloyds TSB started to unravel.

The problem, according to the press, was that traders on the financial markets brought HBOS to its knees through manipulation of the markets by short-selling stock. Without such a 'heinous practice' the bank would have survived intact and thousands of jobs across the country would have been saved. The whole practice of short-selling has been questioned and it seems that the conclusion was that it was immoral.

Short-selling is basically the practice of betting that a share price is going to fall. Here is how it works: an investor expects the price of shares (for example, in HBOS) to fall; they are currently priced at 250p. They contact a broker and arrange to 'borrow' 3 million shares; the investor sells the shares at 250p, therefore receiving a credit of £7 500 000. At some point in the future, the investor will close the deal by buying 3 million shares to pay back the broker. Let us assume that the buy-back price is now 200p. The investor has therefore made a profit of £1 500 000. Many short traders will pursue this option as a means of hedging against their long positions – a sort of insurance against losses they make elsewhere.

If the price had not fallen by as much as hoped, however, the profit would have been less and, if the price had risen during that time, the investor would have made a loss. The broker meanwhile gets interest on the value of the shares 'loaned' and if any changes occur during the period of the deal (for example if the company paid a dividend) or if the company announces some new share issue like a bonus issue (basically a two-for-one type issue), the investor must pay back the requisite number of shares – this could be 6 million shares at half the original value.

The argument put forward at the time was that short-selling was the reason for the dramatic fall in the share price of HBOS which prompted the merger talks. There was also concern that short-selling was behind other share price falls in banking companies and that further activities of this sort would lead to more instability in the financial markets. As a result, the City regulator, the Financial Services Authority (FSA) announced a ban on short-selling until 16 January 2009. The unprecedented move was greeted with mixed views by analysts and City insiders. Some believed that the action was a few days too late and others believed that the move was a knee-jerk reaction that did not take into account the widespread lack of confidence amongst investors – not just hedge funds – who were taking much of the blame for the uncertainty.

Source: Adapted from http://www.bized.co.uk/cgi-bin/chron/chron.pl?id=3181

The criticism that central banks kept interest rates too low for too long and tend to place more emphasis on price stability than on financial stability has been levied against a number of central banks. The Bank of England, for example, regularly comments on the housing market in the UK but the consumer price index (CPI), the governments preferred measure of inflation, does not take into consideration housing costs. The tendency, critics argue, is for monetary policy to ignore asset prices but when the fallout from a collapse in asset prices occurs, central banks are expected to respond to help alleviate the problems. The expectation that monetary policy would bail out investors creates incentives to become risk seeking.

However, it has been pointed out that whilst nominal rates had been low between 2002 and 2005, they merely reflected low real interest rates rather than any suggestion of a lax monetary policy stance by central banks. In 2004–05, central banks did start to increase rates in response to inflationary pressures, particularly rising energy prices, but real rates remained stable largely due to high levels of global saving particularly in emerging countries such as India and

China. The asset price bubbles which occurred were largely the result, it has been argued, of differences in the growth of emerging and developed economies. Global asset shortages means that the overall supply of liquid, safe financial instruments is less than demand and as a result capital flows to those countries, such as the US, where such assets reside. This further exacerbates the global imbalance of assets and the excess demand forces up prices triggering financial bubbles.

There are those who believe that, given the circumstances, central banks acted according to the three key aspects of policy response outlined on page 827. The speed with which central banks intervened and the extent of these interventions, including the asset purchasing programme or quantitative easing (see Chapter 29) did differ largely because of technical as well as ideological differences, but many see their role as having been decisive in exceptional circumstances. When inflationary pressures eased then central banks did relax monetary policy and acted in a coordinated way in October 2008 to bring down interest rates. Central banks have had to be flexible and innovative in dealing with the issues that were highly unusual. As with the Bank of England, central banks have expanded their roles and assumed new powers and responsibilities and introduced new tools and instruments. One such example has been the growth of bilateral swap agreements between central banks of different countries where local currencies can be swapped against the US dollar to enable trade to be financed and liquidity to be eased.

Price Stability or Financial Stability?

One key issue is the need to bridge the focus on price stability with financial stability. Central banks should, it is argued, have a vested interest in stability given that well functioning financial markets are crucial to the effective transmission of interest rate policy to the real economy. Central banks have a privileged position, it is argued, in that they are able to monitor financial markets and economic cycles and as a result have information which is valuable. Their continued independence allows them to be able to assess risk independently and their familiarity with the financial system provides them with a detailed knowledge of the system and thus put them in a position to advise and steer appropriately.

The response of central banks, and the concern about moral hazard, remains a topic for debate. The prospect of protecting bankers from the full consequences of their actions remains a contentious issue. Bank of England Governor, Mervyn King, has openly criticized plans to reform the banking system claiming that it creates a system whereby banks are regarded as being 'too big to fail' and as a result does not lead to the moderation of incentives and behaviour that may help to prevent future financial crises. Mr King has suggested that banks be broken up into different functions as a means of isolating the risk and reducing moral hazard.

CASE STUDY

The Volcker Rule

The debate about the future of the banking system in the wake of the financial crisis continues to be embroiled in claim and counter-claim as different perspectives on how banks should be regulated are aired. Many banks have grown and have been able to expand the ways in which they make profit.

These ways include the use of securitization, investing in hedge funds and private equity funds and using their own money to invest on their behalf not their clients; in some cases, this money has been borrowed which further increases the potential risk of default and financial problems. These activities come under the headings of 'principal investment activities' and 'proprietary trading'. These are activities that banks carry out that are not directly related to their relationship with their customers, those who deposit funds into a bank and use the services a bank provides.

Discussion over the cause of the financial crisis has focused on some of these outlying functions banks have engaged in. On both sides of the Atlantic, there have been calls for the activities of banks to be separated in order to protect customers and to reduce the systemic risk that banking activity has on the economy. By regulating banks in this way the idea is that no bank would become 'too big to fail' and thus avoid the problem of moral hazard. In February 2010 the US President, Barack Obama announced plans on banking reform. The President also brought back the octogenarian former Federal Reserve chair, Paul Volcker, to advise. The Economic Advisory Board chair has said: 'I favour a separation of commercial banking activities that are essential to the functioning of our financial system from more speculative trading-oriented capital markets activities that are not.' Mr Obama has dubbed this the 'Volcker rule'. Banks and other financial institutions have been pondering the implications of the rule. Many are concerned at the detail of any such new regulation and are also raising the point that the division of the two elements of banking is sometimes blurred. The idea has some intuitive appeal but would require a degree of global cooperation which is far from certain.

By the end of 2009, there were still a number of banks failing. Over 100 failed in the US up to the end of October 2009, for example, most relatively small. In May 2009, US authorities reported that as a result of so called 'stress tests' on leading US banks to see whether banks had sufficient capital to cope with the economic situation, 10 of the largest 19 banks, which together account for around two-thirds of the total assets of the US banking system, 'failed' the tests and needed additional funds to help them. The total amount of support needed was reported as being $74.6 billion. The bank landscape, post-crisis, looked very different with greater consolidation and fewer smaller banks in existence. Those that survived were potentially in a much stronger position to exploit the market and also so big that the accusations of 'being too big to fail' looked considerably more accurate. The G20 summit in Pittsburgh in September 2009 spent some time discussing bank remuneration and global regulation of financial markets. At the time of writing there are still negotiations continuing about bank regulation and the extent to which such regulation should be global in nature or left to individual countries.

LESSON LEARNED? THE ROLE OF THE REGULATORS

Was weak regulation to blame for the financial crisis and can stronger regulation help prevent a future financial crisis of this scale? Regulation refers to the rules and restrictions on financial institutions and the power to investigate the actions and behaviour of those institutions designed to create efficiency and equity in financial markets.

It is now widely accepted that there were a number of key issues that will need to be considered in any reforms of the regulatory system. The Organization for Economic Cooperation and Development (OECD) traced the development of the financial crisis through a series of four main stages:

1. A drive on the part of politicians to widen access to home ownership to the poor. Changes to regulations to facilitate this drive led to a growth in lending that was not prudent. This political impetus was evident through successive US Presidents from Clinton onwards and in the UK via New Labour. As a result the expansion of sub-prime lending in the US and cases of banks in the UK lending at 125 per cent of the value of homes, wider access to credit cards which built up debt and limited background checks for credit worthiness were not acted upon by regulators with sufficient vigour.
2. Changes in regulatory structures, particularly in the US, which allowed entry of new businesses into the mortgage market.
3. Basel II regulations which created incentives and the conditions for banks to develop off-balance sheet entities. (Basel II refers to a framework of regulations developed through discussions at the Bank for International Settlements (BIS).)
4. Changes in policy by national regulatory authorities such as the Securities and Exchange Commission (SEC) in the US and the Financial Services Authority (FSA) in the UK, which allowed banks to change leverage ratios from around 15:1 to 40:1. (Leverage ratios, such as debt-to-equity ratios, measure the proportion of debt to equity.)

The OECD was critical of national regulatory bodies suggesting that there were weaknesses in the way banks were regulated and that regulatory frameworks had not only failed to prevent the financial crisis but had been culpable in contributing to it. It identified a number of key causes which included:

- the bonus culture
- credit ratings agencies
- failures in corporate governance
- poor risk management strategies and understanding.

It is widely accepted that these are key factors that need to be addressed in any post-crisis regulatory framework. The International Monetary Fund (IMF) has broadly concurred with the OECD in its analysis of the key issues. It suggests that financial institutions and investors were both too bullish on asset prices and risk. The low interest rate environment and the extent of financial innovation (encouraged by changes in regulation) allowed excessive leverage to be carried out which increased the web of interconnectedness of financial products but at the same time rendered the inherent risks more opaque. It highlighted the lack of coordination between regulatory bodies and the legal constraints, which prevented information sharing to be more widespread as being factors helping authorities to be able to understand what was going on.

This fragmented approach meant that there were differences in the way in which national regulatory bodies dealt with bank failures and insolvency when in many cases these banks had a global presence not reflected by a global coordinated response by the regulators. The actions that were taken have been described as being 'piecemeal' and 'uncoordinated', which not only led to a weakening of the impact of the policy response but also to market distortion. It also pointed to the lack of appropriate tools available to some central banks to provide the necessary liquidity support in times of crisis, as outlined above.

Other criticisms of the regulatory regimes in place throughout the world highlight the fact that the rules that are in place may not be appropriate to deal with the pace of change in financial markets, that regulators spend too much time 'ticking boxes' rather than identifying poor practice and intervening. There have been accusations that the existence of rules means that regulators are able to hide behind them and shift blame. For example, there were a number of subsidiaries of three Icelandic banks operating in the UK but the FSA argued that these were, technically, outside its jurisdiction. In the US it has been estimated that the total assets of entities which are outside the banking system and the scope of regulation, but which act like banks, is as big as the 'official' banking system itself – a value of around $10 trillion in late 2007.

The complex nature of the interaction between regulated and non-regulated entities, such as SPVs, some types of insurance companies and loan originators, means that the scope of regulation may be more limited and contributes to the degree of opaqueness of the financial system. This was highlighted by the apparent lack of appreciation of the extent of the effects that the collapse of Lehman and two of the hedge funds managed by Bear Stearns had on the financial system globally. Equally, the responsibility of the banks themselves to act prudently can be taken away as managers can argue that it is up to the regulator to intervene when things go wrong rather than recognize themselves that actions may be imprudent. Too great a focus by regulators on process and box-ticking rather than principles and outcomes reduced the effectiveness of regulation.

Part of the reason for these problems stems from internal problems of the regulators themselves. To have a high level of understanding of the financial system and to be able to regulate it effectively, employees of the regulators have to be highly experienced and knowledgeable about the system. Overregulation, it has been argued, was partly responsible for creating the incentives for financial innovation to generate improved returns. Regulators and government financial departments had insufficient understanding of complex new products; it has been argued that a number of senior executives in banks did not fully understand the complexity of securitization models, lacked the skills in asset valuation techniques and risk models and were unaware of the extent to which 'tail losses' (the extremes of the normal distribution) could impact on their operations. If those at the forefront of such operations did not understand what they were dealing with is it possible to expect those working at the FSA, for example, to do so? Recruitment of the expertise and skills necessary to staff regulatory bodies effectively is a further issue. Why work for the FSA, for example, for a salary of £116 000 when the skills possessed by individuals of the calibre to work in the FSA could be sold to other sectors of the industry for many millions. Without the resources to do the job properly therefore, regulators will always be hampered.

The Financial Stability Forum (FSF) set up in 1999, has been liaising with working groups set up by the G20 nations to look at the global regulatory framework. It published a paper in April 2008 setting out an agenda for regulatory reform. Many of the items in that agenda relate to the perceived issues related to regulation outlined above. At the time of writing, many of these issues are the subject of ongoing discussion but there are a number of main areas where solutions are being considered:

- Greater clarity of roles between different parts of the regulatory framework. In the UK, for example, it has been suggested that the Bank of England should take responsibility for monitoring systemic risks (which affect the system as a whole) and the FSA (if it still existed) on risks in individual institutions. The alleged confusion over who was responsible for the financial stability of Northern Rock when it first reported difficulties has been highlighted as a case in point.

- Credit ratings agencies need to be overhauled. The potential for a conflict of interest to arise exists because the banks pay the fees to the agencies rather than the investors. The agencies have a vested interest in keeping their clients (the banks) happy because of their need for repeat business. It has also been argued that the methodology used by agencies to assess ratings needs to be made widely available and that some were not sufficiently aware of the existence of problems in some of the products they were rating and then overreacted at too late a stage which caused widespread panic.
- Improving transparency of operations in line with maintaining commercial sensitivities is necessary to help improve market discipline and prevent excessive risk taking.
- The consolidation in the industry which produces multinational massive institutions may increase the extent of the impact on the global system if one of those institutions fails. These institutions become 'too big to fail' and thus raise the problem of moral hazard. As a result it has been suggested that the growth of such institutions can be discouraged through setting up stricter capital requirements in proportion to the systemic risk that they impose.
- Regulators need better information on all financial institutions including off-balance sheet entities and how these interrelate.
- Legal, political and institutional barriers to closer cooperation need to be reduced so that appropriate action can be taken to deal with global financial institutions – global companies need global regulation. This may include the development of harmonized strategies to deal with banks and other financial institutions that become insolvent or fail. Closer cooperation may also enable regulators to step in before the problems become too big rather than waiting for the failure to occur and then stepping in.
- In 'good times' there should be a requirement on banks to set aside capital to provide a reserve that can be used when the economy suffers a downturn and credit is tight.

The actions of authorities can change incentives and thus behaviour. Some groups believe that whilst some rules may be necessary they need to be thought through very carefully so that incentives are not distorted and the outcomes undesirable. The free market think tank, the Adam Smith Institute, for example states: 'It is hardly news that legislation can have unintended consequences sometimes having the opposite effect to the desired objective.'[6]

It may be that the existing regulatory regime is satisfactory and that no new rules are needed. The IMF posed the question, 'is the existing regulatory model fatally flawed or simply poorly understood?' What may be needed is for the responsibilities of regulators to be more clearly defined so that all know where they stand. This is an important consideration since the establishment of the post-crisis regime will have to consider compliance and economic efficiency costs of any new regulation and what the consequences of it might be. If new regulation opens up unforeseen arbitrage opportunities, for example, that outcome may not be desirable. Any new regulation will also have to take into account any increase in moral hazard. Any reforms, therefore, need to consider the trade-offs that may exist – the benefits of reform set against excessive and inefficient regulation which could stifle financial innovation and lead to a flight from key financial centres if the reforms were not global.

---

[6]Tim Ambler, Regulation Fellow, Adam Smith Institute. http://www.adamsmith.org/publications/regulation-and-industry/the-financial-crisis:-is-regulation-cure-or-cause?-200811272506/ accessed 28 October 2009.

IN THE NEWS

Tobin Tax

Strategies to deal with the issues raised by the financial crisis have not been in short supply but the degree of consensus varies considerably. Some suggestions make use of well established economic theories and concepts but even so these are not always universally welcomed. The following article looks at the suggestion of a Tobin Tax to curb the excesses of the banking system which have, in part, been blamed for the financial crisis.

Those who have had the finger of blame pointed at them for the financial crisis have been senior bank officials and traders who have been accused of taking a cavalier approach to risk fuelled by the desire to generate 'profits' for the banks which in turn brought the reward of hefty bonuses. The bonus culture has been under considerable scrutiny and a number of suggestions have been put forward to try to change this culture or at least impose some sort of restriction on banks that offer bonuses that encourage excess and reckless risk taking that could be damaging to the wider economy.

In August 2009, Lord Turner, Head of the FSA (which was abolished in the UK Budget of June 2010), put forward his opinions on the issue in an interview with *Prospect* magazine. The FSA had been considering new rules which would mean that banks will not be able to guarantee bonuses for more than a year and senior employees' bonuses will have to be spread over a three-year period. In the interview, Lord Turner went further and suggested that a tax on banks would be a good way of curbing some of the excesses that have been witnessed in the past. The City has developed variations to the traditional ways of trading such as derivatives, fixed income securities and hedging, which might generate profit (and bonuses for workers) but played a limited role in financial markets. Lord Adair suggested some of these instruments represented 'socially useless activity'.

Lord Turner suggested that one way to reduce the attractiveness of such activities was to tax them. 'If you want to stop excessive pay in a swollen financial sector you have to reduce the size of that sector or apply special taxes to its pre-remuneration profit', he said. Lord Turner's suggestion drew on what is called a Tobin Tax, named after the Nobel Prize winning American economist who suggested that trade in currencies should be taxed to reduce excess short-term speculation following the collapse of the Bretton Woods system in 1971. That system had seen exchange rates fixed against the dollar whose value was based on gold. After the collapse of Bretton Woods, there followed a period of volatility in foreign exchange markets and Tobin's idea was to levy a small tax of the order of 0.1 per cent on every foreign currency transaction. The aim was to make the tax small enough so as not to disrupt trade but a sufficient penalty for short-term speculative trading. Tobin was clear that the tax was not meant to be a revenue raising device but a means of reducing the socially harmful effects of speculative trading.

Tobin's idea has resurfaced from time to time although rarely pursued with any conviction by policy makers. Lord Turner's suggestion, however, resurrected the debate on the value of the tax. Part of Lord Turner's thinking was based on the assumption that the belief in efficient markets and the moves to deregulation over a period of time had placed a considerable degree of power into the hands of banks. The financial crisis has shaken that underlying belief and as a result regulators around the world have to reconsider the assumptions under which regulatory regimes had operated.

Lord Turner also suggested other possible ideas for debate in the interview with *Prospect*. Included in these were restrictions on financial innovation, a review of pricing activity in wholesale markets and the competitive position of firms in financial markets.

The resurrection of a Tobin Tax certainly provoked reaction and debate. Representatives of banks have said that any new taxes on bank activities would have to be considered carefully. If London, for example, imposed this tax unilaterally it could lead to business being moved abroad as companies involved in financial activities seek to avoid taxes. This might result in London losing its place as a leading international finance centre. To be successful and to avoid capital flight it would be essential that the tax should not be unilaterally imposed.

Such a 'supra-national' tax would raise significant questions not least who would bring the legislation to introduce the tax, who would administer its collection and what would happen to any revenue collected – even if it was meant as a purely regulatory tax as Tobin originally saw his idea. The difficulties of getting a greater degree of harmonization between countries on global regulation seem challenging enough and the problems inherent in establishing and administering a global tax of this sort seem to suggest that the idea is stillborn. Lord Turner may have been fully aware of this but his interview certainly raised some important questions on the future of regulation of the financial services industry and set a tone for subsequent debate.

CONCLUSION

The assumptions of efficient markets provided a foundation for policy makers and regulators for a number of years. In hindsight, the catalogue of problems that built up and led to the financial crisis and subsequent deep global recession seem obvious. Economics may borrow some methodology from the hard sciences but as a science of human behaviour some of these methods are built on ever shifting sand. The ingenuity of human beings, allied to changes in technology and the effect of incentives means that any assumption may have to be changed in order to accommodate new landscapes.

The pain suffered by millions of people throughout the world who have lost savings, jobs, homes and more is a consequence of a severe and deep recession. Understanding what caused the financial crisis and how this feeds through to economic activity is a challenge for economists in the future. Whether it be devising new theories and a better understanding of how markets work, how central banks and those in authority can better manage events and crises as they occur, the role of regulation and the importance of information and knowledge in decision-making, the experiences of what has been a significant event have to be used to improve the welfare of future generations who may benefit from the suffering of those affected by the crisis.

SUMMARY

- Deregulation of financial markets encouraged new ways of lending and made it easier for lenders to access funds.
- The relatively benign economic climate of the early 2000s encouraged banks to become more risk seeking.
- Some of this risk could be insured against through new products such as credit default swaps.
- Banks in the US increased lending to the sub-prime market.
- The resulting effects on the housing market of easier access to mortgages increased demand and prices.
- Mortgage lending (along with other loans) were securitized by banks.
- Securitization in association with CDS increased the interdependency of the financial system globally.
- When interest rates started to rise to combat inflation, defaults in the sub-prime market began to grow.
- As the defaults increased the liabilities of banks to the debt which had been built up grew along with their liabilities to CDS claims.
- The banking crisis led to a sharp reduction in interbank lending as credit dried up.
- Tight credit along with the collapse of the housing market fed through to the real economy and unemployment began to grow and economic activity to slow.
- Most economies of the world experienced recession by 2008.
- The efficient market hypothesis formed the basis for policy making and regulation in many global financial markets.

- Efficient markets rely on high quality information and the ability of market participants to understand that information in pricing risk.
- Financial institutions developed a range of new products based on assumptions of limited risk.
- A lack of understanding of these models from bankers through to regulators and central bankers undermined a key basis of efficient markets.
- When the crisis hit, central banks responded by reducing interest rates and developing new techniques to complement fiscal stimuli.
- Both central banks and regulators have come in for criticism about their role in the crisis and their response after.
- Ongoing debate and discussions about how best to avoid such a financial crisis in the future will continue.

KEY CONCEPTS

securitization, p. 819

asset-backed securities (ABS), p. 819

QUESTIONS FOR REVIEW

1. What is meant by 'deregulation of the financial markets'?
2. Explain the different approaches to banking in the context of the concepts of 'risk-seeking' and 'risk-averse' behaviour.
3. How would a bank go about the process of securitizing a bundle of loans totalling $10 billion? What advantages would such a process bring to the bank?
4. What is meant by the term 'reverse multiplier'? What is the relevance of this concept to the slowdown in global economic activity experienced after 2008?
5. Why might the existence of asymmetric information in financial markets lead to market failure?
6. Explain how the rise in defaults on sub-prime mortgages fed though to increased risk of bank failures.
7. Should central banks place as much emphasis on financial stability as on price stability? Justify your answer.
8. Should financial markets be subject to more or less regulation if we are to avoid another financial crisis of the scale of that witnessed between 2007 and 2009? Justify your answer.

PROBLEMS AND APPLICATIONS

1. In the chapter attention was drawn to the following quote by Alan Greenspan, the former head of the Federal Reserve Bank: '. . . the unquenchable capability of human beings when confronted with long periods of prosperity to presume that it will continue'. What do you think he meant by this?
2. Newspapers often carry lurid headlines about the extent to which house prices are either rising or falling. During the financial crisis, there were regular reports headed 'House Prices Fall 50 Per Cent' and similar. Economists might view these headlines from a more critical perspective:
    a. What does 'House Prices Fall 50 Per Cent' actually mean? (This might sound a strange question but think about it from a homeowner's perspective.)
    b. Is the price of a house and its value the same thing? Explain.
    c. Is the value of a house only relevant to those who are actually buying and selling a property? Explain.

3. Why might 'sharply rising incomes and productivity' affect asset prices?
4. Explain why securitization is a good example of the principle of asymmetric information.
5. Explain why banks became reluctant to lend money to one another and thus created the credit crunch. To what extent does this show that the whole banking system is essentially based on trust and trust alone?
6. Lehman Brothers was allowed to fail but Fannie Mae, Freddie Mac and AIG were given government support. Was the US government right to make these decisions and does the support given to the three institutions show that moral hazard is a serious concern? Explain your answer.
7. Using the principle of the multiplier, explained in Chapter 33, explain how the collapse of the financial system fed through to the real economy.
8. What is meant by the term 'efficient' in the efficient markets hypothesis?
9. What are the signals that price sends to consumers in an asset market such as that for housing?
10. With reference to the concepts of present value and 'animal spirits', explain how an asset price bubble can develop and why such a bubble is unsustainable.
11. Explain why a serious and prolonged recession can damage long-term potential growth in an economy.
12. Outline the potential difficulties that arise with having a tripartite regulatory system such as that in the UK where the Financial Services Authority (FSA), Bank of England and HM Treasury each have a role to play in monitoring the financial system.
13. Is there a contradiction between the concerns of the Governor of the Bank of England, Mervyn King, during the financial crisis over moral hazard and the Bank's declared function of 'lender of last resort'? Explain your answer.
14. The chapter outlines some quotes from Ben Bernanke, the chair of the US Federal Reserve. Do you think that Mr Bernanke, was being naive in his view that the sub-prime crisis would be 'unlikely to seriously spill over to the broader economy or the financial system'? Explain.
15. Contrast the responses of the major central banks in the US, Europe and the UK to the financial crisis and comment on which you think acted most appropriately in the circumstances and why.
16. Should short-selling be outlawed? Explain your answer.
17. Would stronger regulation in the major economies of the world have helped prevent the financial crisis and subsequent recession?
18. Would a Tobin Tax help to 'curb bank excesses'? Explain.

For further resources, visit
www.cengage.co.uk/mankiw_taylor2

38 COMMON CURRENCY AREAS AND EUROPEAN MONETARY UNION

During the 1990s, a number of European nations decided to give up their national currencies and use a new, common currency called the *euro* by joining European Economic and Monetary Union (EMU). Why did these countries decide to do this? What are the costs and advantages of adopting a common currency among a group of countries? Is it optimal for Europe to have a single currency? In this chapter we'll look at some of these issues, drawing on our macroeconomics tool box that we've been developing over the past several chapters.

common currency area (or currency union or monetary union)
a geographical area throughout which a single currency circulates as the medium of exchange

First, a definition: a **common currency area** is a geographical area throughout which a single currency circulates as the medium of exchange. Another term for a common currency area is a *currency union*, and a closely related phenomenon is a *monetary union*: a monetary union is, strictly speaking, a group of countries that have adopted permanently and irrevocably fixed exchange rates among their various currencies. Nevertheless, the terms common currency area, currency union and monetary union are often used more or less interchangeably, and in this chapter we'll follow this practice.

Usually we speak of common currency areas when the people of a number of economies, generally corresponding to different nation states, have taken a decision to adopt a common currency as their medium of exchange, as was the case with the European monetary union. Let's start by taking a closer look at EMU and its currency, the euro.

THE EURO

There are currently 16 countries that have joined **European Economic and Monetary Union**, or EMU. (Note that 'EMU' stands for 'Economic and Monetary Union', not European Monetary Union, as is often supposed.) The countries that currently form the Euro Area are Belgium, Germany, Spain, France, Ireland, Italy, Luxembourg, the Netherlands, Austria, Portugal, Finland, Greece, Slovenia, Cyprus, Malta and Slovakia (informally known as 'Euroland' but more correctly as the Euro Area). The move towards a single European currency has a very long history and we do not have space to review it in detail here. We can, however, set out the main landmarks in its formation, starting in 1992 with the Maastricht Treaty (formally known as the Treaty on European Union), which laid down (among other things) various criteria for being eligible to join the proposed currency union. In order to participate in the new currency, member states had to meet strict criteria such as a government budget deficit of less than 3 per cent of GDP, a government debt-to-GDP ratio of less than 60 per cent, combined with low inflation and interest rates close to the EU average. The Maastricht Treaty also laid down a timetable for the introduction of the new single currency and rules concerning the setting up of a European Central Bank (ECB). The ECB actually came into existence in June 1998 and forms, together with the national central banks of the countries making up the common currency area, the European System of Central Banks (ESCB), which is given responsibility for ensuring price stability and implementing the single European monetary policy (as we discussed in Chapter 29).

European Economic and Monetary Union (EMU)
the European currency union that has adopted the euro as its common currency

The single European currency – the euro – officially came into existence on 1 January 1999 when 12 countries adopted it (although Greece did not join EMU until 1 January 2001). On this date, exchange rates between the old national currencies of Euro Area countries were irrevocably locked and a few days later the financial markets began to trade the euro against other currencies such as the US dollar, as well as to trade securities denominated in euros.

The period from the beginning of 1999 until the beginning of 2002 was a transitional phase, with national currencies still circulating within the Euro Area countries and prices in shops displayed in both euros and local currency. On 1 January 2002 the first euro notes and coins came into circulation and, within a few months, the switch to the euro as the single medium of exchange was complete throughout the Euro Area.

The formation of EMU was an enormously bold step for the 12 countries initially involved. Most of the national currencies that have been replaced by the euro had been in circulation for hundreds if not thousands of years. Why did these countries deem it so important to abandon these currencies and adopt a single, common currency? Undoubtedly, part of the answer to this question lies in the realm of politics as much as in the realm of economics. However, there was also a belief that having a common European currency would help 'complete the market' for European goods, services and factors of production that had been an ongoing project for much of the post-war period. More generally, the costs and benefits of adopting a common currency can be analysed within the framework of macroeconomic theory. Let's start by taking a look at the euro and its relationship to the Single European Market.

The Single European Market and the Euro

Following the devastation of two World Wars in the first half of the 20th century, each of which had initially centred on European conflicts, some of the major European countries (in particular France and Germany) expressed a desire to make further wars impossible between them through a process of strong economic integration that, it was hoped, would lead to greater social and political harmony. This led to the development of the European Economic Community (EEC) – now referred to as the **European Union**, or EU. Initially the EU consisted of just six countries: Belgium, Germany, France, Italy, Luxembourg and the Netherlands. In 1973, Denmark, Ireland and the United Kingdom joined. Greece joined in 1981, Spain and Portugal in 1986, and Austria, Finland and Sweden in 1995. In 2004 the biggest ever enlargement took place with 10 new countries joining. There are an additional three 'candidate countries' seeking membership at the time of writing. These are Turkey, Croatia and the Former Yugoslav Republic of Macedonia. The official website of the European Union defines the EU as 'a family of democratic European countries, committed to working together for peace and prosperity.'

European Union
a family of democratic European countries, committed to working together for peace and prosperity

MAP 38.1

Map of Europe

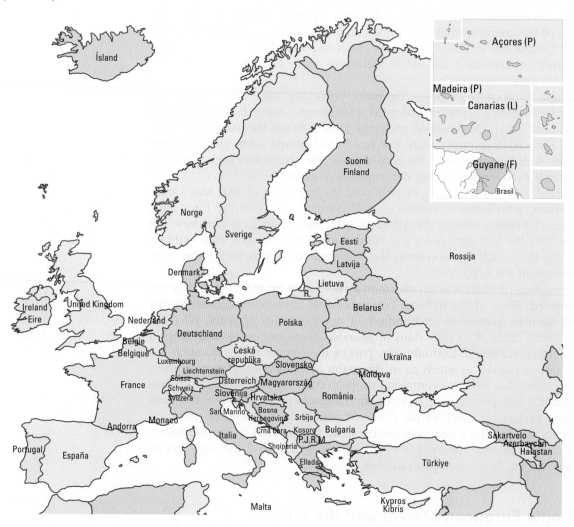

Source: http://europa.eu/abc/european_countries/index_en.htm

The EU has certainly been successful in its original central aim of ensuring European peace: countries such as France, England, Germany, Italy and Spain who have been at war with each other on and off for centuries now work together for mutual benefit. This has led to greater emphasis being given to the EU's second objective – namely prosperity – and, to this end, a desire to create a **Single European Market** (SEM) throughout which labour, capital, goods and services can move freely. As member states got rid of obstacles to trade between themselves, it was argued, companies would start to enjoy economies of scale as they expanded their market across Europe, just as US companies enjoy economies of scale as they expand across American states. At the same time, inefficient firms would be exposed to more cross-border competition, either forcing them out of business or forcing them to improve their efficiency. The aim was therefore to provide businesses with an environment of fair competition in which economies of scale could be reaped and a strong consumer base developed from which they could expand into global markets. Households, on the other hand, would benefit from lower prices, greater choice of goods and services, and work opportunities across a wide area, while the economy in general would benefit from the enhanced economic growth that would result.

Single European Market
a (still-not-complete) EU-wide market throughout which labour, capital, goods and services can move freely

Early steps towards the creation of the SEM included the abolition of internal EU tariff and quota barriers in 1968 and a movement towards greater harmonization in areas such as indirect taxation, industrial regulation, and in common EU-wide policies towards agriculture and fisheries.

Nevertheless, it proved difficult to make progress on the more intangible barriers to free movement of goods, services, capital and labour. For example, even though internal tariffs and quotas had been abolished in the EU, local tax systems and technical regulations on goods and services still differed from country to country so that it was in practice often difficult to export from one country to another. Thus, a car produced in the UK might have to satisfy a certain set of emission and safety requirements in one European country and another set of requirements in another EU country. Or a qualified engineer might find that her qualifications, obtained in Italy, were not recognized in Germany. The result was that during the 1970s and early 1980s, growth in the EU member states began to lag seriously behind that of international competitors – especially the United States and Japan. Therefore, in 1985 a discussion document (in the jargon, a 'White Paper') was produced by the European Commission that subsequently led to a European Act of Parliament – the 1986 Single European Act. This identified some 300 measures that would have to be addressed in order to complete the Single European Market and set 31st December 1992 as the deadline for completion. The creation of the SEM was to be brought about by EU Directives telling the governments of member states what changes needed to be put into effect in order to achieve four goals:

- The free movement of goods, services, labour and capital between EU member states.
- The approximation of relevant laws, regulations and administrative provisions between member states.
- A common, EU-wide competition policy, administered by the European Commission.
- A system of common external tariffs implemented against countries who are not members of the EU.

The EU Parliament building in Brussels.

Over 20 years on from the Single European Act, the SEM is still far from complete. In particular, there still exist between EU members strong differences in national fiscal systems, while academic and professional qualifications are not easily transferable and labour mobility across EU countries is generally low. Some of the reasons for this are hard to overcome: language barriers and relative levels of economic development hamper the movement of factors and member states continue to compete with one another economically, at times seeking their own national interest rather than the greater good of the EU.

Nevertheless, the years between 1985 and 1992 did see some important steps in the development of the SEM and the resulting achievements of the SEM project were not negligible: the European Commission estimates that the SEM helped create 2.5 million new jobs and generated €800 billion in additional wealth in the ten years or so following 1993.

In the context of the Single European Market project, therefore, the creation of a single European currency was seen as a final step towards 'completing the market', by which was meant two things: (a) getting rid of the transaction costs from intra-EU trade that result from different national currencies (and which act much as a tariff) and (b) removing the uncertainty and swings in national competitiveness among members that result from exchange rate movements. Before EMU, most EU countries participated in the Exchange Rate Mechanism (ERM), which (as we saw in Chapter 36) was a system designed to limit the variability of exchange rates between members' currencies. However, the ERM turned out not to be viable way of reducing volatility in the exchange rate and, in any case, had no effect on the transaction costs arising from bank charges associated with changing currencies when engaging in intra-EU trade.

It is clearly important, therefore, to see EMU within a broader European framework and, in particular, the Single European Market project. Nevertheless, the benefits of adopting a single currency across a geographical area can be analysed more generally using macroeconomic theory. Moreover, these benefits must be weighed against the costs of joining a common currency area.

THE BENEFITS AND COSTS OF A COMMON CURRENCY

Benefits of a Single Currency

Elimination of Transaction Costs One obvious and direct benefit of a common currency is that it makes trade easier between members and, in particular, there is a reduction in the transaction costs involved in trade between members of the common currency area. When a German company imports French wine, it no longer has to pay a charge to a bank for converting German marks into French francs with which to pay the wine producer, it can just pay in euros. Of course, the banking sector loses out on the commission it used to charge for converting currencies, but this does not affect the fact that the reduction in transaction costs is a net gain. This is because paying a cost to convert currencies is in fact a deadweight loss in the sense that companies pay the transaction cost but get nothing tangible in return. OK, so the banks were getting commission before and this was used to employ people who worked on currency transactions, but these people can now be used more productively in the economy, making everyone better off.

"I give you women – you give me weapons – why can't we have a common currency?"

Reduction in Price Discrimination It is sometimes argued that a second, albeit indirect gain to the members of common currency area results from the reduction in price discrimination that should ensue when there is a single currency. If goods are priced in a single currency it should be much harder to disguise price differences across countries. As we discussed in Chapter 15, price discrimination involves a deadweight loss to society, so this is a further gain from a single currency. This argument assumes that the transparency in prices that results from a common currency will lead to arbitrage in goods across the common currency area: people will buy goods where they are cheaper (tending to raise their price in that location) and reduce their demand for goods where they are more expensive (tending to reduce the price in that location).

Overall, however, EMU seems unlikely to bring an end to price discrimination across Euro Area countries. For items like groceries, having a single currency is unlikely to be much of an impetus to price convergence across the common currency area because of the large transaction costs (mainly related to travelling) involved in arbitraging, relative to the prices of the goods themselves. Would you travel to another country to do your grocery shopping if you knew the prices there were lower? Perhaps you might – when it is easy to travel this does happen as we saw in the Case Study in Chapter 31 on Ireland (p. 674). Doing so across the whole of the EU means that the effects are necessarily more limited. On the other hand, big ticket items like household appliances and electronic goods, where the transaction costs may be lower as a percentage of the price of the good in question, are also unlikely to be arbitraged heavily across national borders by consumers because of their durable nature and the need for confidence in after-sales service. Would you want to buy a fridge-freezer in a foreign country and run the risk of having to take it back or get someone from there to fix it for you if it goes wrong? (In addition, the fact that different countries in the EU still have different plugs and power systems, which are difficult to harmonize, might also reduce the overall impact!)

Reduction in Foreign Exchange Rate Variability A third argument relates to the reduction in exchange rate variability and the consequent reduction in uncertainty that results from having a single currency. Exchange rates can fluctuate substantially on a day-to-day basis. Before EMU, when a German supermarket imported wine from France to be delivered, say, three months later, it had to worry about how much a French franc would be worth in terms of German marks in three months time and therefore what the total cost of the wine would be in marks. This uncertainty might deter the supermarket company from importing wine at all, and instead lead them to concentrate on selling German wines, thereby foregoing the gains from trade (which we discussed in Chapter 9) and reducing economic welfare. The supermarket could have eliminated the uncertainty by getting a bank to agree to sell the francs at an agreed rate against marks to be delivered three months later (an example of a forward foreign exchange contract). But the bank would charge for this service, and this charge would be equivalent to a tariff on the imported wine and so, as we discussed in Chapter 9, this again would represent a deadweight loss to society.

The reduction in uncertainty arising from the removal of exchange rate fluctuations may also affect investment in the economy. This would clearly be the case for companies that export a large amount of their output to other Euro Area countries, since less uncertainty concerning the receipts from its exports means that it is able to plan for the future with less risk, so that investment projects such as building new factories appear less risky. An increase in investment will benefit the whole economy because it is likely to lead to higher economic growth.

Costs of a Single Currency

The major cost to an economy in joining a common currency area relates to the fact that it gives up its national currency and thereby gives up its freedom to set its own monetary policy and the possibility of macroeconomic adjustment coming about through movements in the external value of its currency. Clearly, if the nations of the Euro Area have only one money, they can have only one monetary policy, which is set and implemented by the European Central Bank. This must be the case because, since there is only one currency, it's not possible to have a different set of interest rates in different countries. Why is this a potential problem?

Suppose, for example, that there is a shift in consumer preferences across the common currency area away from goods and services produced in one country (Germany, say) and towards goods and services produced in another country (France, say). This situation is depicted in Figure 38.1, which shows a leftward shift in the German short-run aggregate demand curve and a rightward shift in the French short-run aggregate demand curve. What should policy makers in France and Germany do about this? As we discussed in Chapter 34 one answer to this is, nothing: in the long run, each economy will return to its natural rate of output. In Germany, this will occur as the price level falls and wages, prices and perceptions adjust. In particular, as unemployment rises in Germany, wages eventually begin to fall. Lower wages reduce firms' costs and so, for any given price level, the amount supplied will be higher. In other words, the German short-run aggregate supply curve will shift to the right, until eventually it intersects with the new short-run aggregate demand curve at the natural rate of output. The opposite happens in France, with the short-run aggregate supply curve shifting to the left. The adjustment to the new equilibrium levels of output are also shown in Figure 38.1.

Note that, if Germany and France had maintained their own currencies and a flexible foreign exchange rate, then the short-term fluctuations in aggregate demand would be alleviated by a movement in the exchange rate: as the demand for French goods rises and for German goods falls, this would increase the demand for French francs and depress the demand for German marks, making the value of francs rise in terms of marks in the foreign currency exchange market. This would make French goods more expensive to German residents since they now have to pay more marks for a given number of French francs. Similarly, German goods become less expensive to French residents. Therefore, French net exports would fall, leading to a fall in aggregate demand. This is shown in Figure 38.2, where the French aggregate demand schedule shifts back to the left until equilibrium is again established at the natural rate of output. Conversely – and also shown in Figure 38.2 – German net exports rise and the German aggregate demand schedule shifts to the right until equilibrium is again achieved in Germany.

In a currency union, however, this automatic adjustment mechanism is not available, since, of course, France and Germany have the same currency (the euro). The best that can be done is to wait for wages and prices to adjust in France and Germany so that the aggregate supply shifts in each country, as in Figure 38.1. The resulting fluctuations in output and unemployment in each country will tend to create tensions within the monetary union, as unemployment rises in Germany and inflation rises in France. German policy makers, dismayed at the rise in unemployment, will favour a cut in interest rates in order to boost aggregate demand in their country, while their French counterparts, worried about rising inflation, will be calling for an increase in interest rates in order to curtail French aggregate demand. The ECB will not be able to keep both countries happy. Most likely, it will set interest rates higher than the German desired level and lower than the French desired level. As we discussed in Chapter 29, the ECB pursues an inflation targeting strategy, and the inflation rate it targets is based upon a consumer price index constructed as an average across the Euro Area. If a country's inflation rate (or expected inflation rate) is below the Euro Area average, the ECB's monetary policy will be too tight for that country; if it is above the average, the ECB's monetary policy will be too

FIGURE 38.1

A Shift in Consumer Preferences Away from German Goods Towards French Goods

The German fall in aggregate demand leads to a fall in output from Y_1^G to Y_2^G, and a fall in the price level from P_1^G to P_2^G. The increase in French aggregate demand raises output from Y_1^F to Y_2^F. Over time, however, wages and prices will adjust, so that German and French output return to their natural levels, Y_1^G and Y_1^F, with lower prices in Germany, at P_3^G, and higher prices in France, at P_3^F.

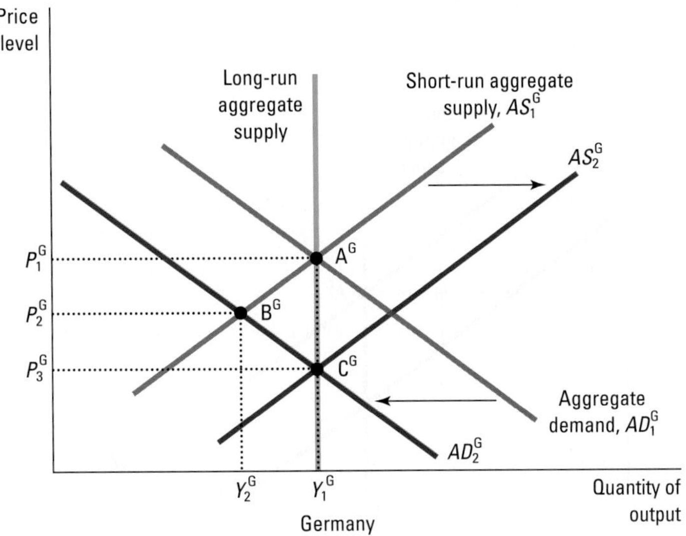

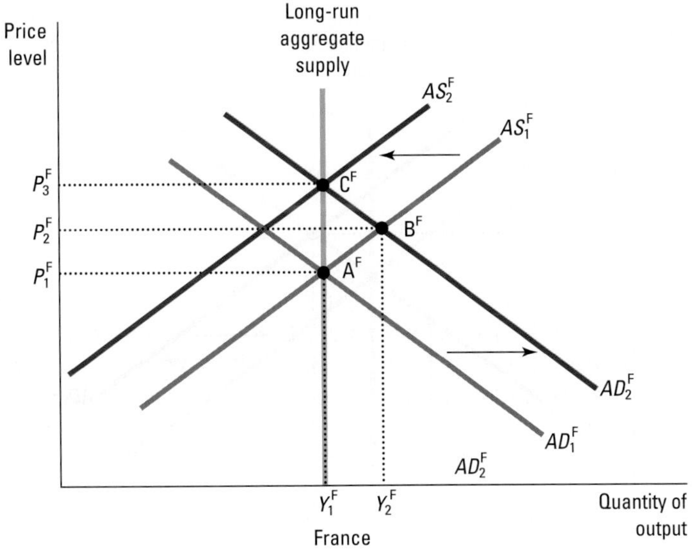

loose for it. All that is possible is a 'one size fits all' monetary policy. It is for this reason that entry to the eurozone is restricted to those countries that can meet the criteria outlined above where inflation and interest rates are close to the EU average.

FIGURE 38.2

A Shift in Consumer Preferences with Flexible Exchange Rates

The fall in German aggregate demand leads, before prices have had time to adjust, to a fall in output from Y_1^G to Y_3^G. However, because this is due to a fall in net foreign demand, the value of the German currency falls, making German goods cheaper abroad. This raises net exports and restores aggregate demand. The converse happens in France: the increase in net foreign demand raises the external value of the French currency, making French goods more expensive abroad and choking off aggregate demand to its former level.

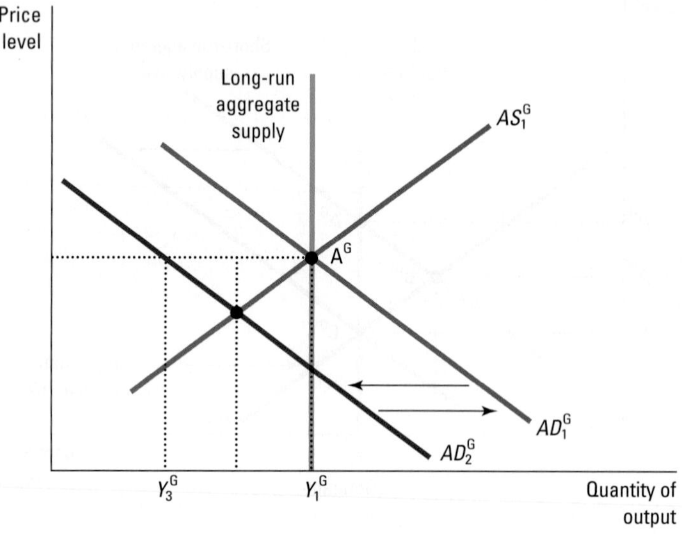

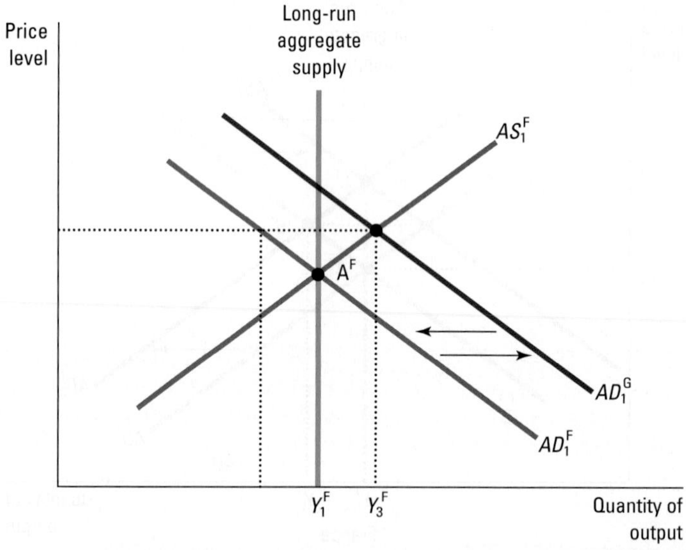

Quick Quiz List and discuss the key costs and benefits of joining a currency union.

THE THEORY OF OPTIMUM CURRENCY AREAS

Optimum currency area (OCA) theory attempts to set down a set of criteria for a group of countries such that, if the criteria were satisfied, then it would in some sense be 'optimal' for the countries to adopt a common currency. The qualifier 'optimal' here refers to the ability of each of the countries to limit the costs of monetary union and enhance the benefits. It is generally used loosely, since there is no way for certain of ensuring whether it is indeed optimal for a group of countries to form a currency union and, more often than not, countries will fulfil some but not all of the OCA criteria.

optimum currency area
a group of countries for which it is optimal to adopt a common currency and form a currency union

Characteristics that Reduce the Costs of a Single Currency

Consider first the characteristics of a group of countries that would reduce the costs of adopting a common currency. As we have discussed, the main cost to participating in a monetary union is the loss of monetary policy autonomy for the individual countries concerned, as well as ruling out the possibility of macroeconomic adjustment through exchange rate movements. One way in which the economic (and political) tensions arising from the loss of the exchange rate instrument and the imposition of a 'one-size-fits-all' monetary policy will be alleviated is if the economies in question move rapidly to long-run equilibrium following a macroeconomic shock: since we know there is only a short-run trade-off between inflation and unemployment, the faster the economies concerned can get to the long run – in other words, return to their natural rates of output and unemployment – the better. This speed of adjustment to long-run equilibrium will be high if there is a high degree of wage flexibility in the common currency area, and/or if there is a high degree of labour mobility.

Another way in which tensions across the common currency area would be alleviated would be if all countries in the currency union were prone to the same kind of demand shocks (e.g. if aggregate demand fell in all countries simultaneously), since then each would favour similar macroeconomic policy decisions (e.g. a reduction in interest rates).

We consider each of these types of characteristics in turn.

Real Wage Flexibility Suppose there is a high degree of wage flexibility in each of the member countries, so that wages respond strongly to rises and falls in unemployment. This means that the adjustment to long-run equilibrium, as shown in Figure 38.1, occurs very quickly. In our example, the shift in aggregate demand in Germany leads to falling wages, so that firms make more profit for any given level of prices and the aggregate supply curve shifts to the right and Germany returns to the natural rate of output. If wages are very flexible, this adjustment may be very rapid, so that the short run is very short indeed. Similarly for France: the rightward shift in aggregate demand leads to rapidly rising wages and firms find it less profitable to produce any given level of output, so that the supply curve shifts leftward and a new long-run equilibrium is established at the natural rate of output. Hence, by compressing the short run, tensions across the monetary union are ironed out very quickly.

Note that it is the real wage that is of importance here: it is real wages that must adjust in order to affect the aggregate supply curve by making it more (or less) profitable for firms to produce a given level of output at any given level of prices.

Labour Mobility Alternatively, suppose that labour is highly mobile between the member countries of the currency union: unemployed workers in Germany simply migrate to France and find a job. Again, the macroeconomic imbalance is alleviated, since unemployment in Germany will fall as many of the unemployed have left the country, and inflationary wage pressures in France decline as the labour force expands with the migrants from France. Therefore, it is clear that labour mobility may in some measure cushion a currency union from asymmetric shocks.

Capital Mobility Sometimes, economists argue that capital mobility can also compensate for the loss of monetary autonomy and the absence of exchange rate adjustment among the members of a common currency area. A distinction should be made here between physical capital (plant and machinery) and financial capital (bonds, company shares and bank loans). In terms of cushioning a currency union from asymmetric shocks, movements in physical capital can help by expanding productive capacity in countries experiencing a boom as firms in other member countries build factories there. However, given the long lags involved in the installation of plant and equipment, physical capital mobility is likely to be helpful mainly for narrowing persistent regional disparities rather than offsetting short-tem shocks.

The mobility of *financial* capital may be more useful in cushioning economies from short-term output shocks. For example, residents of a country experiencing a recession may wish to borrow money from the residents of a country experiencing a boom in order to overcome their short-term difficulties. In our two-country example, German residents would effectively borrow money from French residents in order to make up for their temporary fall in income. Clearly, this would require that German residents can easily borrow from French residents through the capital markets, so that financial capital mobility will be highest between countries whose capital markets are highly integrated with one another. For example, if a bank has branches in more than one country of a currency union, then borrowing and lending between boom and recession countries will be more or less automatic, as residents in the booming country increase the money they are holding in the bank as their income goes up and residents of the country in recession increase their overdrafts (or reduce their money holdings) as their income goes down.

We can relate this discussion back to the notion of permanent income, which we discussed in Chapter 20, and to the market for loanable funds, which we discussed in Chapter 26. Recall from Chapter 20 that a family's ability to buy goods and services depends largely on its permanent income, which is its normal, or average income, since people tend to borrow and lend to smooth out transitory variations in income. Now, when an aggregate demand shock adversely affects the German economy, a large amount of German households will see their transitory income fall and will want to borrow in order to increase income back up to the permanent or normal level. But since many German households are now doing this at the same time, if borrowing is restricted to German financial markets, this will tend to raise interest rates and generally make borrowing more difficult. In terms of the model that we developed in Chapter 26, if the market for loanable funds is restricted to the domestic market, then we might expect the supply of loanable funds to decrease in a recession and the demand to increase, raising interest rates. The resulting rise in interest rates may even make the recession worse by reducing investment.

On the other hand, in France, the economic boom means that many households are experiencing income levels above their permanent or average level, and so will tend to increase their saving. Now, if the German households can borrow from the French households – if the market for loanable funds covers both France and Germany – they can both consume at a level consistent with their normal or average levels of income with less of an effect on interest rates. There will be an increase in the supply of loanable funds because French residents are saving more and this will partly or even wholly offset the increase in the demand for loanable funds arising from German residents who want to borrow more. When the German economy comes out of recession and goes into recovery, German households can then repay the loans.

Of course, although we have discussed only bank loans, there are other forms of financial capital, such as bonds and company shares, but the principle of the recessionary economy being able to obtain funds from the booming economy remains the same. In effect, therefore, financial capital market integration across countries allows households to insure one another against asymmetric shocks so that the variability of consumption over the economic cycle can be reduced.

Symmetric Macroeconomic Shocks Note that, in describing the costs of belonging to a monetary union, we have used the example of a positive demand shock in one country and a simultaneous negative demand shock in another. A similar analysis would have followed if we had simply allowed either a positive or a negative demand shock in one country and no shock at all in the other country. The central point was that the demand shock was asymmetric in the sense that it impacted differently on different members of the currency union, requiring different short-run policy responses. Clearly, if the shock were symmetric there would be no problem. If, for example, aggregate demand rose simultaneously in all member countries, increasing expected future inflation, then a policy of raising interest rates would be welcomed by all members of the monetary union. This would be the case if the economic cycles of each of the countries making up the currency were synchronized in the sense that the various economies tended to enter recession at the same time and enter the recovery phase of the cycle at the same time, so that disagreements about the best interest rate policy are less likely to occur.

Characteristics that Increase the Benefits of a Single Currency

High Degree of Trade Integration The greater the amount of trade that takes place between a group of countries – i.e. the greater the degree of trade integration – the more they will benefit from adopting a common currency. One of the principal benefits of a currency union, and the most direct benefit, is the reduction in transaction costs that are incurred in trade transactions between the various countries when there is a constant need to switch one national currency into another on the foreign currency exchange market. Clearly, therefore, the greater the amount of international trade that is carried out between member countries – and therefore the greater the amount of foreign currency transactions – the greater the reduction in transaction costs that having a common currency entails.

The reduction in exchange rate volatility – another benefit of a currency union – will also clearly be greater the greater is the degree of intra-union trade, since more firms will benefit from knowing with certainty exactly the revenue generated from their sales to other currency union members, rather than having to bear the uncertainty associated with exchange rate fluctuations.

Quick Quiz What is meant by an optimum currency area? • List and discuss the key characteristics of an optimum currency area.

IS EUROPE AN OPTIMUM CURRENCY AREA?

Having determined what characteristics of a group of countries would make the benefits of a single currency stronger and the costs weaker, we can take a closer look to see whether Europe – and in particular the group of 16 countries that comprise the Euro Area – forms an optimum currency area.

Trade Integration

Table 38.1 shows the sum of intra-union imports and exports (i.e. imports from and exports to other European Union countries) for 15 EU countries, including the 12 countries that originally made up the Euro Area, for each year from 1995 to 2004, expressed as a percentage of GDP. Adding together intra-union imports and exports is appropriate here because transaction costs in trade between countries are incurred on both imports and exports. We can thus think of this percentage as an index of trade integration of each of the countries with the rest of Europe.

Consider first the 12 Euro Area countries of that time. In 2004, Belgium's intra-EU exports and imports added up to more than 100 per cent of its GDP, while Ireland, Luxembourg and the Netherlands also clearly benefited greatly from the reduction in transaction costs associated with the single currency, since the sum of intra-union exports and imports for these countries ranged from about 65 per cent to about 80 per cent of their GDP. Next in the list come Austria and Portugal, with indices of trade integration both over 40 per cent of GDP, while for France, Germany, Spain and Finland the corresponding figure is between around 25 per cent and 30 per cent. The trade integration index for Italy, however, amounted to only a little over 20 per cent, while Greece appeared to gain least from monetary union on this criterion, with combined European exports and imports amounting to only 13 per cent of GDP in 2004.

Among the three non-Euro Area countries for whom we have figures, Denmark and Sweden actually had combined European exports and imports as a percentage of GDP in the mid-30s – a higher figure than six of the 12 countries that have adopted the euro as their common currency, and around three times the corresponding figure for Greece. On the other hand, the UK's European trade integration index came to just over 21 per cent in 2004 – the lowest figure of any country in the table with the single exception of Greece.

TABLE 38.1

Imports Plus Exports of 15 European Countries From and To Other European Union Countries as a Percentage of GDP

	1995	1996	1997	1998	1999	2000	2001	2002	2003	2004
Euro Area										
Belgium	73.7%	73.8%	81.4%	88.0%	86.5%	87.3%	90.9%	90.8%	105.3%	105.3%
Germany	21.1	18.9	20.9	22.9	22.6	23.5	24.7	25.6	29.2	29.5
Greece	19.4	16.4	15.7	17.4	16.4	16.7	17.5	17.5	18.3	13.1
Spain	18.7	16.3	18.7	21.0	21.8	20.3	23.1	21.5	25.6	24.9
France	21.8	19.5	21.8	22.5	22.5	23.0	24.3	25.1	28.9	27.8
Ireland	57.8	52.3	49.9	53.1	50.4	52.1	55.0	55.6	64.8	65.3
Italy	21.0	16.3	17.4	18.5	19.0	19.7	20.2	20.3	22.4	22.1
Luxembourg	–	–	–	–	–	–	–	66.5	74.0	79.0
Netherlands	52.2	50.0	55.2	60.8	59.9	60.5	58.7	60.6	70.3	69.3
Austria	28.7	27.5	30.6	35.3	34.8	35.8	38.2	39.6	43.7	44.8
Portugal	35.5	29.4	30.7	32.3	34.0	35.2	36.7	37.7	41.1	40.7
Finland	21.9	20.1	23.1	28.1	28.2	28.7	30.4	30.4	35.5	32.8
Non-euro area										
Denmark	29.0	27.6	29.8	33.2	32.1	33.0	32.9	33.9	37.8	37.3
Sweden	26.9	22.5	16.3	32.0	31.5	30.7	35.1	35.1	38.7	33.2
UK	20.8	19.5	17.6	17.1	17.5	18.1	18.4	18.8	22.7	21.1

Source: Eurostat.

What does all this tell us? Well, firstly that the degree of trade integration across Europe is quite variable, but nevertheless on average quite high – with the notable exception of Greece.

Secondly, however, we can see from Table 38.1 that the degree of European trade integration appears to have been rising over time in nearly every country: comparing the index of trade integration in 1995 to its value in 2004, it has increased for every country in the table, again with the single exception of Greece. For some countries, such as Austria, this growth in European trade integration is very marked (an increase of around 16 percentage points), while for others, such as Italy and the UK, the increase over the ten-year period is only slight.

Looking at this measure of trade integration over the ten years, however, we can also see that it increased most strongly on average over the last five years or so of data. In Germany, for example, the index increases by only 1.5 percentage points from 1995 to 1999, but then rises by 6 percentage points from 2000 to 2004. In Ireland, the index actually drops by nearly 7.5 percentage points in the first 5 years and then increases by over 13 percentage points in the last 5 years. This has led some economists to argue that some of the criteria for an optimum currency area – such as a high degree of trade integration – may actually be endogenous: actually being a member of a currency union may enhance the degree of trade done between members of the union, precisely because of the decline in transaction costs in carrying out such trade.

Overall, the figures presented in Table 38.1 do suggest that many – if not all – European countries have gained a great deal from the reduction in transaction costs in international trade as a result of the single currency. Indeed, these gains have been estimated at about one quarter to one half of one per cent of Euro Area GDP. This may not sound massive, but remember that transaction costs are a deadweight loss. Moreover, the gains are not one-off: they accrue continuously so long as the single currency persists, since they would have to be paid in the absence of the currency union. They therefore become cumulative. In addition, if the degree of Euro Area trade integration tends to rise over time as a result of the single currency, as some economists have suggested, then the implicit gain from not having to pay transaction costs also rises over time.

The other, indirect benefit of a single currency when there is a high degree of trade integration follows from the reduction in uncertainty associated with doing away with the volatility in the exchange rates between members' national currencies (since those currencies are replaced with a common currency). These gains are hard to quantify, but the figures presented in Table 38.1 do again suggest that they are not negligible for the Euro Area.

Real Wage Flexibility

A great deal of research has been done on real wage flexibility in Europe and virtually all of it concludes that continental European labour markets are among the most rigid in the world, while the UK labour market, at least since the 1980s, has become one of the most flexible. One reason for this is the fact that all European Union countries have minimum wage laws, although this is not the whole story since the UK also has a minimum wage. Perhaps a more important reason is the high degree of collective wage bargaining that is common in continental Europe – i.e. wage agreements that cover a large number of workers. Figures on the degree of unionization of the labour force are quite deceptive in this sense: for example, in the early 2000s, in the UK, Italy and Germany about 30 per cent of the workforce belonged to a trade union, while in France the figure was around 10 per cent. Continental European unions, however, often have collective bargaining and other workplace rights that UK trade unionists can only envy. For example, in France there is a legal obligation for workers' representatives to bargain with employers and some 85–95 per cent of French workers are covered by collective agreements.

In addition, the introduction of the single European currency may also have had a negative effect on European wage flexibility, since many European collective wage agreements between workers and a firm in one country will also often extend to the firm's workforce in other European countries, and a single currency brings transparency in wage differences across countries, as well as price transparency. To return again to our example of a negative demand shock in Germany and a positive shock in France, a company with employees in both countries would find it hard to reduce real wages in Germany while raising them in France.

Furthermore, European labour law is generally very much more restrictive in many continental European countries than it is in the UK or the USA, as is the level of payroll taxes, so that a firm's costs of either reducing the workforce or increasing it can be very high. This means that, even if there were movements in the real wage, firms would be slow to expand or contract their output in response, so that shifts in aggregate supply will be slow to come about.

On the whole, therefore, adjustment to asymmetric shocks through real wage movements is unlikely to be significant in the Euro Area.

Labour Mobility

Labour is notoriously immobile across European countries, at least if one rules out migration from the new eastern European members of the EU such as Poland, and considers just the 16 Euro Area countries or these plus Denmark, Sweden and the UK. In part this may perhaps be attributed to differences in language, culture and other social institutions across Europe that make it difficult for workers to migrate. However, it seems that European workers are also very loath to move location even within their own countries. Indeed, the degree of labour mobility as measured by the percentage of the workforce that moves geographical location over any given period, is much lower within any particular European country than it is within the United States, and is even lower between the Euro Area countries. Europe therefore scores very low on this optimum currency area criterion.

Financial Capital Mobility

In discussing financial capital mobility, a distinction must be made between the wholesale and the retail capital markets. The wholesale financial markets are the capital markets in which only financial institutions such as banks and investment funds operate, as well as very large corporations, while the retail financial markets (such as high street banks) are those open to individual households and to small and medium-sized corporations. Prior to the introduction of the euro, financial integration among Euro Area countries was probably quite low, in both the wholesale and retail sectors. However, following the introduction of the euro, integration of the wholesale financial markets has increased dramatically. In particular, a liquid euro money market with single interbank market interest rates was established so that a bank in, say, Luxembourg can now borrow euros just as easily and at the same rate of interest from another bank in Frankfurt as it can from a bank located in the same street in Luxembourg. In the government bond market, the degree of market integration is also high, and this is shown by the fact that the interest rates on government bonds of the different Euro Area countries are very close to one another and tend to move very closely together. On the other hand, the integration of retail market products, such as loans to households and small and medium-sized enterprises, is lagging behind compared with the wholesale market products. This becomes evident from persistent cross-country differences in bank lending rates and the rather limited cross-border retail banking activity. Indeed, national banking sectors have remained largely segregated with only marginal cross-border penetration: in 2005, less than 5 per cent of total bank loans were granted across borders to customers in other Euro Area countries.

Symmetric Demand Shocks

The economic cycle across the countries of the Euro Area does appear to be positively correlated, in the sense that the timing of strong growth and downturns appear to be very close. In Figure 38.3, we have graphed data on annual growth rates in real GDP for France, Germany and the Euro Area as a whole for every year from 1999 to 2009. Clearly, the movements in growth rates over this period for France and Germany and for the whole Euro Area are very close. Even though Germany's growth performance has been slightly below that of France and the whole Euro Area since the mid-1990s, there is no clear example of asymmetric demand shocks impacting upon these countries as in the example we have

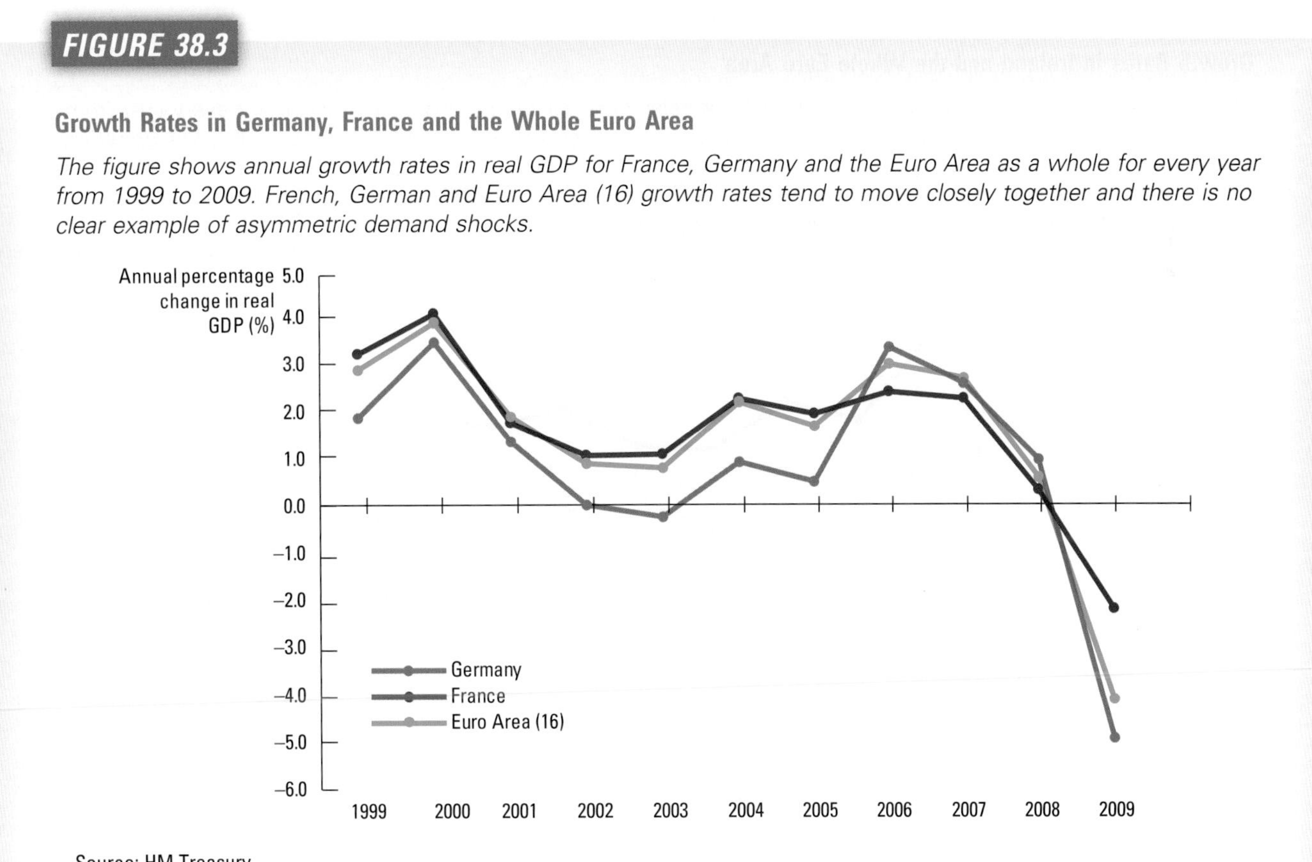

FIGURE 38.3

Growth Rates in Germany, France and the Whole Euro Area

The figure shows annual growth rates in real GDP for France, Germany and the Euro Area as a whole for every year from 1999 to 2009. French, German and Euro Area (16) growth rates tend to move closely together and there is no clear example of asymmetric demand shocks.

Source: HM Treasury.

used to illustrate the potential problems of a monetary union. In Figure 38.4, however, we have plotted real GDP growth rates for the Euro Area and Ireland over the same period. The problem that is evident from this graph is not so much that the turning points do not coincide, but that Ireland's growth rate has persistently outstripped the performance of the Euro Area as a whole, so that ECB monetary policy has arguably been far too loose for the Irish economy since the inception of EMU. On the other hand, the Irish economy, in terms of GDP, is still small as a proportion of total Euro Area GDP.

Overall, therefore, the evidence is a little mixed, although on the whole it suggests that the problem of asymmetric demand shocks is not a great one for the current member countries of EMU. The fact that there is not strong evidence of asymmetric demand shocks at the aggregate level, however, does not rule out the possibility that there may be asymmetric shocks at other levels in the economy. In fact, researchers have found that many of the shocks that impact upon European countries asymmetrically tend to be specific to a region or to an industry rather than to a country as a whole. This is not a problem made worse by joining a monetary union, however, since a country that experienced, say, a negative shock to one of its industries or regions would not in any case be able to deal with this using monetary or exchange rate policy without generating imbalances in its other regions or industries.

FIGURE 38.4

Growth Rates in Ireland and the Whole Euro Area

*The figure shows annual growth rates in real GDP for Ireland and for the Euro Area as a whole for every year from 2000 to 2010 (*estimate). The two growth rates do not move closely together and, in particular, Ireland's growth rate is persistently higher than that of the Euro Area as a whole up to 2007, but it slipped into recession first and the depth of its recession has been much worse than that of the Euro Area, so that ECB monetary policy has arguably been far too loose for the Irish economy in 'boom times' and too harsh in bad times.*

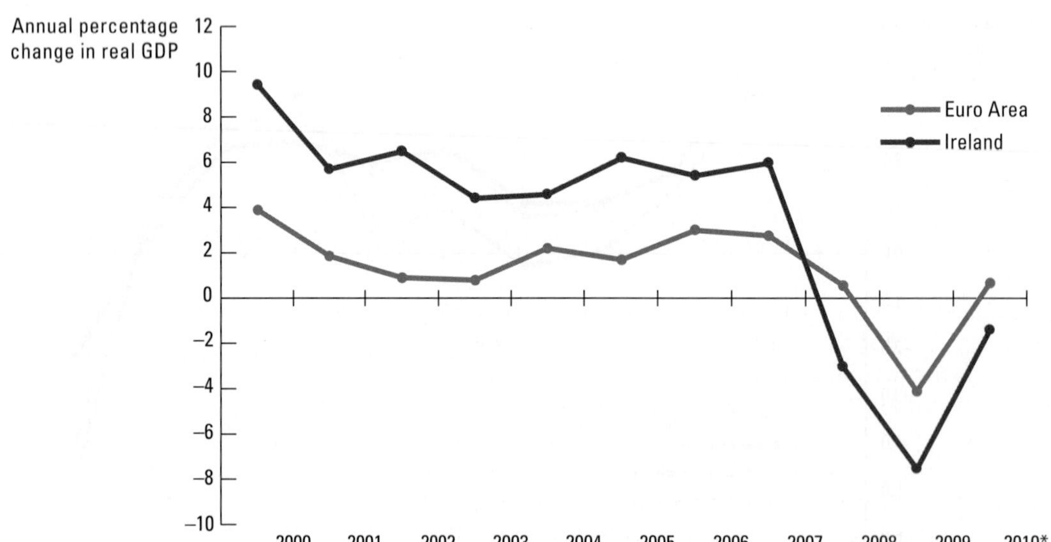

Source: Eurostat.

Summary: So Is Europe an Optimum Currency Area?

As in many policy debates in economics, there is no clear-cut answer to this question. Certainly, many European countries have a high degree of intra-union trade and have economic cycles that are more or less synchronized. However, labour mobility and wage flexibility (and labour market flexibility in general) are low in Europe, and while the euro has increased financial market integration in Euro Area's wholesale financial markets, the retail markets remain highly segregated at the national level.

Overall, therefore, if very strong differences in the economic cycle were to emerge across the Euro Area, the lack of independent monetary and exchange rate policy would be acutely felt. This could be a case argued in relation to the situation in Ireland as highlighted in Figure 38.4. For that reason, many economists argue that Europe – meaning the current Euro Area – is not an optimum currency area. Nevertheless, as we have noted in our discussion, it is possible that some of the optimum currency area criteria may be endogenous. In particular, the single currency is likely to generate even greater trade among EMU members. Given this, it is likely that the economic cycles of member currencies will become even more closely synchronized as aggregate demand shifts in one country have stronger and stronger spillover effects in other Euro Area countries. Moreover, the single currency may also raise labour mobility across Europe in the long run, since being paid in the same currency as in one's home country is one less issue to come to terms with when moving location to find a job. Also, with time, one would expect financial market integration to spread to the retail capital markets (indeed there is already strong pressure being exerted on the European banking industry by the European Central Bank and the European Commission for the introduction of new payment schemes for electronic credit transfers and direct debits between Euro Area banks, as well as for a unified framework for debit and credit cards).

Perhaps the only true test of whether the Euro Area is an optimum currency area (or can become one) is to see whether EMU survives in the long run. The difficulties experienced by the so-called PIIGS, (Portugal, Italy, Ireland, Greece and Spain) over the size and reliability of their sovereign debt in 2010 caused widespread problems in financial markets and led some to question whether any country defaulting on its debt would cause the destruction of the euro. At the time of writing this problem is a significant one and it is by no means certain that the euro can survive in the long term.

FISCAL POLICY AND COMMON CURRENCY AREAS

Our discussion so far has tended to centre on the loss of autonomy in monetary policy that is entailed in adopting a single currency among a group of countries. However, it is obvious that there is nothing in the adoption of a common currency that implies that members of the currency union should not still retain independence in fiscal policy. For instance, in our example of an asymmetric demand shock that expands demand in France and contracts aggregate demand in Germany, the French government could reduce government spending in order to offset the demand shock, while the German government could expand government spending. In fact, even if France and Germany did not make up an optimal currency because wages were sticky and labour mobility was low between the countries, national fiscal policy could, in principle, still be used to ameliorate the loss of monetary policy autonomy. Let's discuss further the issue of fiscal policy and currency unions.

Fiscal Federalism

Suppose that a currency union had a common fiscal policy in the sense of having a single, common fiscal budget covering tax and spending decisions across the common currency area. This means that fiscal policy in the currency union would work much as fiscal policy in a single national economy works, with a surplus of government tax revenue over government spending in one region used to pay for a budget deficit in another region. Return again to our example of an asymmetric demand shock that expands aggregate demand in France and contracts aggregate demand in Germany, as in Figure 38.1. Now recall from Chapter 36 that there are automatic stabilizers built into the fiscal policy of an economy that automatically stimulate aggregate demand when the economy goes into recession without policy makers having to take any deliberate action. In particular, since almost all taxes are closely related to the level of economic activity in the economy, tax revenue will automatically decline in Germany as a result of the aggregate demand shock that shifts it into recession. At the same time, transfer payments in the form of unemployment benefit and other social security benefits will also rise in Germany. The opposite will be true in France, where the automatic stabilizers will be operating in reverse as transfer payments fall and tax receipts rise with the level of economic activity. These changes will tend to expand aggregate demand in Germany and contract it in France, to some extent offsetting the asymmetric demand shock.

Now, if the governments of France and Germany have a common budget, then the increased net government revenue in France can be used to offset the reduction in net government revenue in Germany. If the resulting movements in aggregate are not enough to offset the demand shock, then the French and German governments may even go further and decide to increase government expenditure further in Germany and pay for it by reducing spending and perhaps raising taxes in France.

This kind of arrangement – a fiscal system for a group of countries involving a common fiscal budget and a system of taxes and fiscal transfers across countries – is known as **fiscal federalism**. The problem with it is that the taxpayers of one country (here France) may not be happy in paying for government spending and transfer payments in another country (in this example, Germany).

fiscal federalism
a fiscal system for a group of countries involving a common fiscal budget and a system of taxes and fiscal transfers across countries

National Fiscal Policies in a Currency Union: The Free Rider Problem

Assuming that, for political reasons, fiscal federalism is not an option open to the currency union, we still need to explore the possibility of individual members of the union using fiscal policy in order to offset asymmetric macroeconomic shocks that cannot be dealt with by the common monetary policy. In particular, in our example, what is wrong with Germany running a big government budget deficit in order to counteract the fall in aggregate demand and borrowing heavily in order to finance the deficit? One answer may lie in the effect on other members of the currency union of a rise in the debt of a member country.

Whenever a government raises its levels of debt to very high levels, there is always the possibility that the government may default on the debt. In general, this can be done in one of two ways. Where a country is not a member of a currency union and controls its own monetary policy, it can engineer a surprise inflation by a sudden increase in the money supply, so that the real value of the debt shrinks. In addition, as we discussed in Chapter 31, when there is a sharp rise in the price level, this will usually be accompanied by a sharp fall in the foreign currency value of the domestic currency. This means that, valued in foreign currency, the stock of government debt will now be worth far less. Thus, the government has in effect defaulted on a large portion of its debt by reducing its value both internally and externally.

If this is not possible – for example because, as in a currency union, the country no longer enjoys monetary policy autonomy and is not able to devalue the external value of its currency (since it uses the common currency) – then the only other way of reneging on the debt is through an outright default (e.g. stopping interest payments or failing to honour capital repayments when they fall due). Generally, the financial markets are good at disciplining governments that run up large debts, by charging them high rates of interest on the debt that the government issues – after all, if you thought there was even a slight possibility that you might not get your money back if you lent it, you would want to be paid a higher rate of interest in order to compensate for that risk. In the case of a monetary union, however, this means that excessive debt issuance by one member country will tend to force up interest rates throughout the whole of the common currency area. Although, as we discussed in Chapter 29, the ECB controls very short-term interest rates in the Euro Area through its refinancing operations, it does not control longer-term interest rates such as those paid on 10 or 20-year government bonds. Hence, fiscal profligacy by a government in the Euro Area will tend to push up the cost of borrowing for all members of the currency union.

On the other hand, interest rates may not be raised enough to discipline properly the high-borrowing government. This is because the markets feel that the other members of the monetary union would not allow the country concerned actually to default, and that if it threatened to do so the other members would probably rush in and buy up its government debt and 'bail out' the country concerned. If the markets believe in this possibility then the debt will not be seen as risky as it otherwise would be and so the interest rates charged to the debtor country on its debt will not be as high as they otherwise might be. The net effect is for that government to pay interest rates on its large stock of debt that are lower because of the implicit belief that it will be bailed out if it has problems servicing the debt, and for all other members of the currency union to pay higher interest rates on their government debt because the government has flooded the financial markets with euro-denominated government bonds. In essence, this is an example of the free rider problem that we discussed in Chapter 11: the government is enjoying the benefits of a fiscal expansion without paying the full costs.

In addition, if that government is using the proceeds of its borrowing to fund a strong fiscal expansion, this may undo or work against the anti-inflationary monetary policy of the ECB by stoking up aggregate demand throughout the whole of the Euro Area.

In order to circumvent some of these problems, the currency union members can enter into a 'no bail-out' agreement that states that member countries cannot expect other members to come to their rescue if their debt levels become unsustainable, as an attempt to convince the markets to charge profligate spend-and-borrow countries higher interest rates on their debt. In fact, exactly such a no bail-out agreement exists among members of EMU. Unfortunately, however, it seems clear that the no bail-out clause is not credible: if an EMU member were to default on its debt, this would have strong repercussions throughout the Euro Area as it would probably lead to the financial markets losing confidence in debt issued by other members and to strong selling of the euro in the foreign currency exchange market. In order to avoid this, it is likely that EMU members would in fact bail out a member country that was threatening to default on its debt.

For these reasons, the members of the currency union may wish to impose rules on one another concerning the conduct of national fiscal policies in order to avoid fiscal profligacy by any one member. At the outset of EMU, a set of fiscal rules was indeed drawn up and agreed to by EMU members. This set of rules was known as the Stability and Growth Pact (SGP) (see the case study). The SGP not only laid down strict rules on the maximum permissible budget deficit and debt-to-GDP ratio for EMU members, it also stipulated harsh punishments – fines amounting to as much as 0.5 per cent of GDP – for offenders. In the event, several countries, including France and Germany, breached the SGP but managed to persuade other members not to impose fines. In practice, national fiscal prudence is now ensured in the Euro Area by peer pressure.

Quick Quiz What is fiscal federalism? • How may it aid in the functioning of a common currency area?

CASE STUDY

The Stability and Growth Pact: A Ferocious Dog with No Teeth

The Stability and Growth Pact (SGP) was a set of formal rules by which members of EMU were supposed to be bound in their conduct of national fiscal policy. Its main components were as follows:

- Members should aim to achieve balanced budgets.
- Members with a budget deficit of more than 3 per cent of GDP will be subject to fines that may reach as high 0.5 per cent of GDP unless the country experiences exceptional circumstances (such as a natural disaster) or a very sharp recession in which GDP declines by 2 per cent or more in a single year.

Clearly, however, if EMU members adhered to the SGP, then it would rule out any free rider problems associated with excessive spending and borrowing in any one member country by forcing members to put a limit on the national government budget. The choice of a maximum budget deficit of no more than 3 per cent of GDP was related to a clause in the 1992 Maastricht Treaty that suggested that a 'prudent' debt-to-GDP ratio should be no more than 60 per cent. This itself was perhaps somewhat arbitrary – although it was very close to the actual debt-to-GDP ratio of Germany in 1992. To see, however, that a 60 per cent ratio of debt to GDP could entail 'prudent' budget deficits of no more than 3 per cent a year, let's do some simple budgetary arithmetic. Suppose a country is enjoying real GDP growth of 3 per cent a year and inflation of 2 per cent a year, so that nominal GDP is growing at the rate of 5 per cent a year. This means that the nominal value of its government debt can grow at a rate of 5 per cent a year and still be sustainable. But if the debt-to-GDP ratio is 60 per cent, this means that debt can increase by 5 per cent of 60 per cent, or 3 per cent of GDP a year while keeping the debt-to-GDP ratio constant. In other, words, it can run a budget deficit of 3 per cent of GDP a year.

While, however, there was some logic in setting a maximum budget deficit of 3 per cent a year (given a maximum prudent debt-to-GDP ratio of 60 per cent), it is not clear why the SGP suggested that members should aim for a balanced budget. The pros and cons of balancing the government budget are discussed at some length in the next chapter, but it should be clear from the budgetary arithmetic just discussed and our discussion in Chapter 12 that it is not imprudent for countries to run small budget deficits so long as they are enjoying sustained long-term growth in GDP. The effective straitjacketing of national fiscal policy that the SGP implied may have reflected a desire among the architects of EMU for the ECB to maintain an effective monopoly on demand management, so that its polices could not be countered by national fiscal policies.

The crucial question for the SGP, however, was whether or not the maximum allowable budget deficit would be enough for a country to let its automatic fiscal stabilizers come into play when it goes into recession. This is crucial in a monetary union because member countries will have already given up their right to pursue an independent monetary policy and they cannot use the exchange rate as an instrument of policy.

In practice, the SGP proved to be something of a toothless watchdog. As the Euro Area experienced sluggish growth in the early years of EMU, several member countries – and in particular France and Germany, two of the largest member countries – found themselves in breach of the SGP excessive deficit criteria. However, both France and Germany managed to persuade other EMU members not to impose fines and, in 2004, the European Commission drew up guidelines for softening the SGP. These guidelines included considering more widely the sustainability of countries' public finances on an individual basis, paying more attention to overall debt burdens and to long-term liabilities such as pensions, rather than to a single year's deficit.

Some critics of the new SGP guidelines argued that they were subjective and somewhat fuzzy. Yet perhaps fuzziness is the best solution. In effect, the commitment of an EMU member to maintaining fiscal prudence and not becoming a free rider now relies on peer pressure and national prestige: no country wants to have fingers wagged at them for spending and borrowing excessively. Most importantly, currency unions are, by definition, short on policy instruments – they require flexibility rather than rigidity in the conduct of fiscal policy. Having a system of rigid rules and draconian punishments and no credible way of enforcing the sanctions was not the correct way to ensure fiscal stability in the Euro Area.

IN THE NEWS

The discussion of the issues surrounding profligate versus prudent members of a currency area was highlighted in the latter part of 2009 and into 2010 when the financial crisis had a significant effect on the Greek economy. Fears that Greece would not be able to meet its debt obligations created significant tensions within the Euro Area and beyond.

The Greek Debt Crisis

The pressure on governments to provide financial support during the financial crisis led many to have to increase levels of public borrowing. The significant increase in borrowing led to some governments being at risk of default on the debt they have issued. There was particular concern over whether Greece would be able to meet its debt obligations. The credit default swap market for sovereign debt was more volatile in the latter part of 2009 and into 2010 with prices rising since September 2009.

In early 2010 it was reported that Greece owed €300 billion; this is more than the value of its gross domestic product (GDP); in fact its debt was 115.1 per cent of its GDP. The Greek government was also running a budget deficit of nearly 14 per cent – well beyond the 3 per cent required as the terms of membership of the European Monetary Union. Other members of the EU accused Greece of being 'profligate' and living beyond its means on the back of its membership of the Euro Area.

Greece had to raise around €50 billion in 2010 to meet its debt obligations; on 19 May 2010 it needed to pay €8.5 billion to bondholders. In April it seemed likely that it would find it difficult to raise the money to do so. In February and March of 2010, the Greek government tried to take a stance on public spending, proposing major cuts in jobs, pensions, wages and services. Greek workers took to the streets in protest. The potential difficulties the country faced in cutting spending affected financial markets who felt Greece was becoming too risky to invest in. Ratings agencies steadily cut the country's ratings until by late April, Greek debt was officially classed as 'junk'.

In the early part of 2010, the markets looked on as Greece sought to borrow money on international capital markets. On 25 January the Greek government went to the markets to borrow money in the form of its first bond issue of the year. In the event, the issue was oversubscribed as investors sought to pick up the bonds. Why? A simple reason, the interest on the bonds had to be high to persuade investors to take the risk. It was reported that the issue was valued at around €5 billion with a coupon of 6.12 per cent. Given that interest rates around the world at that time were at record low levels this was high. The spread between the interest Greece had to pay to borrow compared with the Germans was almost 4.0 per cent. The wider the spread on different financial instruments (the difference in the coupon of similar bonds in this instance), the more the market is factoring in the risk of default on the bonds considered more risky – the Greek bonds in this case.

The spread between Greek and German bonds continued to rise into April reaching 19 per cent on two-year bonds and 11.3 per cent on 10-year bonds. The nervousness on the financial markets over Greece's debt problems began to spread to other EU countries who were dubbed 'the Pigs' (Portugal, Ireland, Italy, Spain – and Greece). The fear that Greece would default led to concerns that the euro would fall sharply. If there is an expectation that the price of something is going to fall then there is a possibility of making some money and that is exactly what happened in February 2010. Data from the Chicago Mercantile Exchange (CME) showed that short positions against the euro from hedge funds and traders rose sharply. Traders took positions on the expectation that the euro would fall in value. Traders taking out contracts that the price of the euro would fall could exercise these contracts and make a profit if and when the euro fell in value. Data from the CME showed that over 40000 contracts had been taken out against the euro with a total value of around $8 billion.

The crisis began to gather momentum and the markets looked to other EU governments to organize a bail-out. On 10 April the 16 finance ministers of the eurozone [Euro Area] announced an agreement on a package of loans to Greece totalling €30 billion. Greece said that it did not intend to use the loans and instead rely on its 'austerity measures'. The extent to which Greece could deliver on these austerity measures was something the financial markets were not convinced about.

A week later the Greek Prime Minister, George Papandreou, finally bowed to what many thought was the inevitable and announced that Greece would take advantage of the emergency loans. Negotiations took place with the EU and the IMF on the structure of these loans, which were predicted to rise to €100 billion.

Whilst it was generally accepted that Greece needed the financial support there were questions raised about the terms under which the loans were to be given. The German government was financing a proportion of the loans with €8.4 billion being spoken of as a possible figure. In order to appease German taxpayers who were not supportive of bailing out the 'profligate Greeks', Chancellor Angela Merkel insisted on very strict terms and a condition that the Greek government make significant cuts to public spending. The Greek government was being squeezed from all sides. The financial markets were nervous that the problems in Greece would spread to other high debt countries (so-called 'contagion effect') and there were fears that the crisis could tip Europe back into recession.

CONCLUSION

This chapter has developed some of the main issues around common currency areas, focusing in particular on the European monetary union. Where there is a high degree of trade among a group of countries, there are benefits to be had from forming a currency union, largely arising from the reduction of transaction costs in international trade and reductions in exchange rate uncertainty. However, there are also costs associated with joining a monetary union, largely associated with the loss of monetary autonomy (member countries are no longer free to set their own interest rates) and the loss of exchange rate movements as a means of achieving macroeconomic adjustment. Any decision to form a currency union must weigh these costs and benefits against one another to see if there is an overall net benefit. Although, in the long run, the loss of exchange rate adjustment and monetary autonomy may have little effect on the equilibrium levels of output and unemployment in the economies involved, there may be substantial short-term economic fluctuations in these macroeconomic variables as a result of joining the currency union. This is particularly the case if there are asymmetric demand shocks impacting on the currency union so that it is impossible to design a 'one-size-fits-all' monetary policy to suit every country. Short-run adjustment will also be long and painful when wages do not adjust very quickly, although this problem may be overcome by labour mobility across the member countries.

A group of countries for which the benefits of monetary union are high and the costs are relatively low is termed an optimum currency area. Even though there is quite a high degree of trade integration among the member countries of the current European monetary union (with the notable exception of Greece), and their economic cycles do seem more or less synchronized and of a similar amplitude (with the notable exception of Ireland), labour mobility and wage flexibility in Europe are both notoriously low, and integration of Euro Area financial markets, although high in the wholesale sector, has so far been disappointing in the retail financial markets. Overall, therefore, the Euro Area is probably not an optimum currency area. Nevertheless, it is possible that some of these criteria may be endogenous: EMU may lead to increasing economic integration in the Euro Area that will in turn significantly raise the benefits and reduce the costs to each country of remaining in the monetary union.

SUMMARY

- A common currency area (a.k.a. currency union or monetary union) is a geographical area through which one currency circulates and is accepted as the medium of exchange.
- The formation of a common currency area can bring significant benefits to the members of the currency union, particularly if there is already a high degree of international trade among them (i.e. a high level of trade integration). This is primarily because of the reductions in transaction costs in trade and the reduction in exchange rate uncertainty.
- There are, however, costs of joining a currency union, namely the loss of independent monetary policy and also of the exchange rate as a means of macroeconomic adjustment. Given a long-run vertical supply curve, the loss of monetary policy and the lack of exchange rate adjustment affect mainly short-run macroeconomic adjustment, however.
- These adjustment costs will be lower the greater is the degree of real wage flexibility, labour mobility and capital market integration across the currency union, and also the less the members of the currency union suffer from asymmetric demand shocks.
- A group of countries with a high level of trade integration, high labour mobility and real wage flexibility, a high level of capital market integration and that does not suffer asymmetric demand shocks across the different members of the group, is termed an optimum currency area (OCA). An OCA is most likely to benefit from currency union.
- It is possible that a group of countries may become an OCA after forming a currency union, as having a common currency may enhance further trade integration, thereby helping to synchronize members' economic cycles, and having a single currency may also help foster increased labour mobility and capital market integration.

- While the current Euro Area displays, overall, a high degree of trade integration and does not appear to be plagued by asymmetric demand shocks, real wage flexibility and labour mobility both appear to be low. And while the introduction of the euro has led to a high degree of Euro Area financial market integration at the wholesale level, retail financial markets remain nationally segregated. Overall, therefore, the Euro Area is probably not at present an optimum currency area, although it may eventually become one.
- The problems of adjustment within a currency union that is not an OCA may be alleviated by fiscal federalism – a common fiscal budget and a system of taxes and fiscal transfers across member countries. In practice, however, fiscal federalism may be difficult to implement for political reasons.
- The national fiscal policies of the countries making up a currency union may be subject to a free rider problem, whereby one country issues a large amount of government debt and pays a lower interest rate on it than it might otherwise have paid, but also leads to other member countries having to pay higher interest rates. It is for this reason that a currency union may wish to impose rules on the national fiscal policies of its members.

KEY CONCEPTS

common currency area (or currency union or monetary union), p. 840
European Economic and Monetary Union (EMU), p. 841
European Union, p. 842
Single European Market, p. 843
optimum currency area, p. 849
fiscal federalism, p. 858

QUESTIONS FOR REVIEW

1. What are the main advantages of forming a currency union? What are the main disadvantages?
2. Are the advantages and disadvantages you have listed in answer to question 1 long run or short run in nature?
3. Is a reduction in price discrimination across countries likely to be an important benefit of forming a currency union?
4. What is an optimum currency area (OCA)? List the criteria that an OCA must satisfy.
5. Is EMU an optimum currency area?
6. What is fiscal federalism? How might the problems of macroeconomic adjustment in a currency union be alleviated by fiscal federalism?
7. Why might the members of a currency union wish to impose rules on the conduct of national fiscal policies?

PROBLEMS AND APPLICATIONS

1. Consider two countries that trade heavily with one another – Cornsylvania and Techoland. The national currency of Cornsylvania is the cob, while the Techoland national currency is the byte. The output of Cornsylvania is mainly agricultural, while the output of Techoland is mainly high-technology electronic goods. Suppose that each economy is in a long-run macroeconomic equilibrium.
   a. Use diagrams to illustrate the state of each economy. Be sure to show aggregate demand, short-run aggregate supply and long-run aggregate supply.

   b. Now suppose that there is an increase in demand for electronic goods in both countries, and a simultaneous decline in demand for agricultural goods. Use your diagrams to show what happens to output and the price level in the short run in each country. What happens to the unemployment rate in each country?
   c. Show, using your diagrams, how each country could use monetary policy to reduce the short-run fluctuation in output.
   d. Show, using your diagrams, how movements in the cob – byte exchange rate could reduce short-run fluctuations in output in each country.
2. Suppose Techoland and Cornsylvania form a currency union and adopt the electrocarrot as their common currency. Now suppose again that there is an increase in demand for electronic goods in both countries, and a simultaneous decline in demand for agricultural goods. As president of the central bank for the currency union, would you raise or lower the electrocarrot interest rate, or keep it the same? Explain. (Hint: you are charged with maintaining low and stable inflation across the electrocarrot area.)
3. Suppose that Techoland and Cornsylvania decide to engage in fiscal federalism and adopt a common fiscal budget.
   a. Show, again using aggregate demand/aggregate supply diagrams, how fiscal policy can be used to alleviate the short-run fluctuations generated by the asymmetric demand shock.
   b. Given the typical lags in the implementation of fiscal policy, would you advise the use of federal fiscal policy to alleviate short-run macroeconomic fluctuations? (Hint: distinguish between automatic stabilizers and discretionary fiscal policy.)
4. The United States can be thought of as a non-trivial currency union since, although it is a single country, it encompasses many states that have economies comparable in size to those of some European countries. Given that the USA has had a single currency for 200 years, it may be thought of as a successful currency union. Yet many of the American states produce very different products and services, so that they are likely to be impacted by different kinds of macroeconomic shocks (expansionary and recessionary) over time. For example, Texas produces oil, while Kansas produces agricultural goods. How do you explain the long-term success of the US currency union given this diversity? Are there any lessons or predictions for Europe that can be drawn from the US experience?
5. Explain, giving reasons, whether the following statements are true or false.
   a. 'A high degree of trade among a group of countries implies that there would be benefits from them adopting a common currency and forming a currency union.'
   b. 'A high degree of trade among a group of countries implies that they should definitely adopt a common currency and form a currency union.'
6. Do you think that the free rider problem associated with national fiscal polices in a currency union, as we discussed in the text, is likely to be a problem in actual practice? Justify your answer.
7. What is the function of the European Commission? What are the other five main institutions of the European Union and what are their respective roles? What are the other important EU bodies and what are their respective roles? (Hint: go to the European Union website: www.europa.eu.int.)
8. Explain how the Greek debt crisis threatened to cause a split in the Euro Area and even the possible demise of the euro.

For further resources, visit www.cengage.co.uk/mankiw_taylor2

14

FINAL THOUGHTS

39 FIVE DEBATES OVER MACROECONOMIC POLICY

It is hard to open up the newspaper without finding some politician or editorial writer advocating a change in economic policy. Economic issues are invariably central to the continuing political debate. The financial crisis and subsequent recession have raised even more questions about the way that markets operate, the role of government and regulators and how to prevent a recurrence of the problems that led to the crisis.

Previous chapters have developed the tools that economists use when analysing the behaviour of the economy as a whole and the impact of policies on the economy. This final chapter presents arguments on both sides in five current debates over macroeconomic policy. The knowledge you have accumulated in this course provides the background with which we can discuss these important, unsettled issues. It should help you choose a side in these debates or, at least, help you see why choosing a side is so difficult.

IF ONLY WE KNEW WHAT WE KNOW!

Information is a vital underpinning factor in economics. Economic agents make decisions based on information, whether this be a decision to buy an ice cream, invest in new plant and equipment, build new schools, invest in green technologies, purchase stock or cut back public spending. In making any decision we need to have information on the relative costs and benefits arising to make an informed decision. Our first policy debate looks at the role of information in economic decision-making in relation to the large government deficits facing many European countries. In the wake of the financial crisis and the recession, governments across Europe have imposed so-called austerity measures which have affected millions of people. Are such decisions justified on the basis of the information available?

Pro: Information Helps Make Accurate Decisions

Economic forecasting is not perfect but it helps governments and other agents make informed decisions that lead to more stable outcomes than if forecasting was not employed. The important thing about such forecasting is to ensure that the data is collected and analysed independent of any political interference. Data from organizations such as the International Monetary Fund (IMF), Organization for Economic Cooperation and Development (OECD) and central banks, as well as independent analysis, allow policy makers to collate, analyse and interpret data and put in place policy measures that can help stabilize the economy and improve welfare. The increasing sophistication of computers and the models developed by economists and others mean that our understanding is continuing to grow and this advances the discipline and improves decision-making.

We know a great deal more about economic change than at the time of the Great Depression in the 1930s and this knowledge has been put to good use in the last 30 years to create more stable economic conditions. Shocks to the system will occur but these shocks do not mean we should abandon the search to improve our understanding and the quality of the information gathered to aid decision-making. In the UK the new coalition government, formed following the general election in May 2010 set up the Office for Budgetary Responsibility (OBR) with a remit to produce independent forecasts for GDP growth. Its first report in June 2010 downgraded the forecasts for growth that had been made by the previous government, which it claimed had been too optimistic, and so has allowed the new government to take more effective decisions on reducing the budget deficit. It is exactly this sort of transparent data gathering and dissemination which helps build trust in governments, improves confidence that decisions are being taken in the light of the best information available and as a result allows the financial markets to operate more efficiently.

Con: Economic Forecasting is Nothing More than a Con-trick

The record of economic forecasters is not good – few, if any, were able to forecast the financial crisis and recession despite the sophisticated computers and complex mathematical models of the economy. The plain fact is that events are random and as such we never know when a 'Black Swan' is going to appear. Most forecasts are based on some form of extrapolation of past data and past events are no guide to the future. The 'experience of the turkey', originally outlined by Bertrand Russell and updated by Nassim Nicholas Taleb, highlights this perfectly. As a chick a turkey comes to appreciate that each day its owner visits to check on its welfare and provide it with food. As each day passes and the same thing happens; the turkey can build an understanding of past events which enable it to make a prediction about the future. The more days pass the more confidence the turkey has that tomorrow and future days will bring more of the same – food and care. Until one day a Black Swan arrives and the turkey is slaughtered for the dinner table. Nothing in the past experienced by the turkey prepares it for this event – it had no way of being able to see it coming.

Similarly, basing future economic forecasts on an analysis of past events does nothing to prepare us for Black Swans such as the financial crisis in 2007. The economy is simply too complex and too random to allow economists to impose any sort of order on events. The OBR is a case in point. It produced revised forecasts for UK economic growth soon after it was formed but noted that: 'The forecasts for the economy and public finances set out in this document represent the Budget Responsibility Committee's (BRC's) best view of future prospects. But we emphasize the inevitable uncertainties that apply to all forecasts at all times, and particularly to fiscal forecasts at the present time. The degree of uncertainty increases over the forecast horizon.' Later in the same section it said: 'It should be noted that the economic and fiscal shocks experienced in the recent past were beyond the outer limits of the probability distributions set out in the fan charts used by other forecasters.' In other words, no one saw the financial crisis coming and who knows what is round the corner. It later admitted: 'The…probability of growth in 2010 being within one percentage point of our central forecast (i.e. between ¼ per cent and 2¼ per cent) is 70 per cent. The probability of growth being within one percentage point of our central forecast in 2011 (i.e. between 1½ per cent and 3½ per cent) falls to below 40 per cent and to around 30 per cent in 2014.' This may serve to make the point of the BRC that they wish to be more transparent but such wide ranges and low probabilities do beg the question about just how valuable forecasting is when it is clearly open to such a margin of error.

As a result our understanding of risk and the potential for uncertainty must be improved and used so that we can take advantage of uncertainty rather than be surprised by it when it happens. We need to use models with care and not be blinded by the results they provide but try to consider how we might respond to the Black Swans when they arrive – to avoid trying to predict everything and to take advantage of uncertainty.

ARE STRUCTURAL DEFICITS REAL OR NOT?

The massive public sector deficits for many countries in Europe following the recession raised questions about the difference between cyclical and structural deficits. A cyclical deficit occurs when government spending and income is disrupted by the 'normal' economic cycle. In times of strong economic growth government revenue from taxes will rise and spending on welfare and benefits will fall and so public finances will move into surplus (or the deficit shrinks appreciably). In times of economic slowdown the opposite occurs and the size of the budget deficit will rise (or the surplus shrinks). A structural deficit refers to a situation where the deficit is not dependent on movements in the economic cycle but indicate that a government is 'living beyond its means' – spending what it has not got.

Pro: Policy Makers Need to Eradicate Structural Deficits

The existence of a structural deficit implies that the public finances will be even worse when entering a recession, necessitating increasing levels of borrowing which is unsustainable in the long term. Cyclical effects will merely serve to make the deficit worse. This is seen in examples of European government deficits in 2010 – some of the largest deficits in peacetime history and created in part by governments committing to spending too much in the 'good times'. Greece's public debt is estimated at around €300 billion or nearly 13 per cent of GDP; in Spain, debt represents around 11 per cent of GDP; Italy had a deficit around half of the other so-called PIIGS (Portugal, Italy, Ireland, Greece and Spain) at just over 5 per cent of GDP.

As a result of the size of these deficits, the risk of default by governments on their debt is greater; increasingly they will find it difficult to service their debt and the cost of so doing will rise. This also creates uncertainty in financial markets and threatens the survival of the euro. As a result fiscal consolidation is essential to reduce long-term interest rates and currency instability and help to promote economic growth. This fiscal consolidation should primarily be in the form of cuts in public spending rather than increases in taxes which may damage employment and investment.

Con: The Idea of a Structural Deficit is a Myth

The idea that government deficits are structural is unhelpful. The assumption is that governments have to borrow more because of the gap between income and expenditure but how certain can we be that the only reason governments are borrowing money is simply due to the changes to public finances wrought by the recession? The whole notion of a structural deficit assumes that it is the amount governments borrow when the economy is operating at its trend level. This implies that to measure it we need to know how far the economy is operating below trend – the output gap.

The problem is that there is considerable disagreement on the size of the output gap. It is accepted that the recession will have destroyed some potential output but how much is open to some interpretation. Dr Andrew Sentance, a member of the UK Monetary Policy Committee (MPC), suggested in June 2010 that the output gap in the UK was smaller than the Bank of England may have anticipated. To highlight the difficulties of measuring this gap, there have been a number of studies attempting to quantify the impact of economic downturns on the output gap and the outcomes vary significantly. In the UK the Institute for Fiscal Studies (IFS) has estimated that the output loss of the economic downturn from 2008 could be as much as 7.5 per cent whereas the Treasury estimates 5 per cent and other estimates put the gap as low as 2 per cent.

The size of the output gap is important because it has a direct effect on the cyclical component of the deficit – the larger the output gap the larger will be the cyclical component and the smaller the structural. This in turn affects any estimates of the size of borrowing when the economy does return to trend – in other words, the size of the structural deficit. Any calculations on the deficit would also be subject to assumptions about the sensitivity of taxes and spending to changes in GDP. How does tax revenue rise in relation to changes in GDP? This will depend in part on assumptions about the number of people who are able to find work as the economy expands but also on the extent to which potential output has been destroyed. How do changes in government spending vary in relation to changes in GDP? How many people will get off benefits and what effect will short-term fiscal stimulus measures have on spending (measures such as the car scrappage scheme which was adopted in several European countries).

As an increasing number of assumptions are made, calculations of the size of the structural deficit could be very different; which one should be used as the basis for policy decisions? In the light of this analysis is it useful to think of the idea of a structural deficit at all?

Quick Quiz Explain why inaccurate information might affect forecasts of economic growth and thus the size of government budget deficits.

SHOULD THE GOVERNMENT BALANCE ITS BUDGET?

A persistent macroeconomic debate concerns the government's finances. Whenever the government spends more than it collects in tax revenue, it covers this budget deficit by issuing government debt.

When we studied financial markets in Chapter 26, we saw how budget deficits affect saving, investment and interest rates. But how big a problem are budget deficits? As we saw in the debate above on structural deficits, the problem of deficits in Europe has caused considerable economic turmoil, so much so that many European countries have taken action to cut deficits and move towards 'balancing their budgets'. Our next debate concerns whether fiscal policy makers should make balancing the government's budget a high priority.

Pro: The Government Should Balance its Budget

When a government fails to balance its budget, it has to borrow money by issuing bonds in order to make up the shortfall. Many countries in Europe have had to increase borrowing in the wake of the financial crisis and the recession. The increase in debt placed some countries on the verge of bankruptcy. How to tackle the massive debt mountains has been a focus in recent years.

The most direct effect of high and rising government debt is to place a burden on future generations of taxpayers. When these debts and accumulated interest come due, future taxpayers will face a difficult choice. They can pay higher taxes, enjoy less government spending, or both, in order to make resources available to pay off the debt and accumulated interest. Or they can delay the day of reckoning and put the government into even deeper debt by borrowing once again to pay off the old debt and interest. In essence, when the government runs a budget deficit and issues government debt, it allows current taxpayers to pass the bill for some of their government spending on to future taxpayers. Inheriting such a large debt may lower the living standard of future generations.

In addition to this direct effect, budget deficits also have various macroeconomic effects. Because budget deficits represent *negative* public saving, they lower national saving (the sum of private and public saving). Reduced national saving causes real interest rates to rise and investment to fall. Reduced investment leads over time to a smaller stock of capital. A lower capital stock reduces labour productivity, real wages, and the economy's production of goods and services. Thus, when the government increases its debt, future generations are born into an economy with lower incomes as well as higher taxes.

There are, nevertheless, situations in which running a budget deficit is justifiable. Throughout history, the most common cause of increased government debt is war. When a military conflict raises government spending temporarily, it is reasonable to finance this extra spending by borrowing. Otherwise, taxes during wartime would have to rise precipitously. Such high tax rates would greatly distort the incentives faced by those who are taxed, leading to large deadweight losses. In addition, such high tax rates would be unfair to current generations of taxpayers, who already have to make the sacrifice of fighting the war.

Similarly, it is reasonable to allow a budget deficit during a temporary downturn in economic activity. When the economy goes into a recession, tax revenue falls automatically, because income tax and payroll taxes are levied on measures of income, and transfer payments such as unemployment benefit increase. People also spend less so that government income from indirect taxes also falls. If the government tried to balance its budget during a recession, it would have to raise taxes or cut spending at a time of high unemployment. Such a policy would tend to depress aggregate demand at precisely the time it needed to be stimulated and, therefore, would tend to increase the magnitude of economic fluctuations. When the economy goes into recovery, however, the opposite is true: tax receipts rise as the level of economic activity rises and transfer payments tend to fall. The government should therefore be able to run a budget surplus and use the money to pay off the debt incurred by the budget deficit it ran during the recession.

Wars aside, therefore, over the course of the business cycle, there is no excuse for not balancing the budget. If the government runs a deficit when the economy is in a recession, it should run a comparable surplus when the economy recovers, so that on average the budget balances.

Compared to the alternative of ongoing budget deficits, a balanced budget – or, at least, a budget that is balanced over the business cycle – means greater national saving, investment and economic growth. It means that future university graduates will enter a more prosperous economy. The government should balance its budget.

Con: The Government Should Not Balance its Budget

The problem of government debt is often exaggerated. Although government debt does represent a tax burden on younger generations, it is often not large compared with the average person's lifetime income. Often, the case for balancing the government budget is made by confusing the economics of a single person or household with that of a whole economy. Most of us would want to leave some kind of bequest to friends or relatives or a favourite charity when we die – or at least not leave behind large debts. But economies, unlike people, do not have finite lives – in some sense, they live forever, so there is never any reason to clear the debt completely.

Critics of budget deficits sometimes assert that the government debt cannot continue to rise forever, but in fact it can. Just as a bank evaluating a loan application would compare a person's debts to his income, we should judge the burden of the government debt relative to the size of the nation's income. Population growth and technological progress cause the total income of the economy to grow over time. As a result, the nation's ability to pay the interest on the government debt grows over time as well. Really, we should not be looking at the total amount of debt but at the ratio of debt to income. As long as this is not increasing, then the level of debt is sustainable. In other words, as long as the level of government debt grows more slowly than the nation's income, there is nothing to prevent government debt from growing forever. Some numbers can put this into perspective. Suppose the output of the economy grows on average about 3 per cent per year. If the inflation rate averages around 2 per cent per year, then nominal income grows at a rate of 5 per cent per year. Government debt, therefore, can rise by 5 per cent per year without increasing the ratio of debt to income.

Moreover, it is misleading to view the effects of budget deficits in isolation. The budget deficit is just one piece of a large picture of how the government chooses to raise and spend money. In making these decisions over fiscal policy, policy makers affect different generations of taxpayers in many ways. The government's budget deficit or surplus should be considered together with these other policies. For example, suppose the government reduces the budget deficit by cutting spending on public investments, such as education. Does this policy make young generations better off? The government debt will be smaller when they enter the labour force, which means a smaller tax burden. Yet if they are less well educated than they could be, their productivity and incomes will be lower. Many estimates of the return to schooling (the increase in a worker's wage that results from an additional year in school) find that it is quite large. Reducing the budget deficit rather than funding more education spending could, all things considered, make future generations worse off.

In fact, in the UK, the government's fiscal policy framework distinguished between government borrowing to finance investment and borrowing to finance current government expenditure. It also recognized the need to average out deficits and surpluses over the business cycle, and explicitly noted that the important aggregate in this context is the ratio of government debt to GDP. This was encapsulated in two fiscal rules, which the UK government called the 'golden rule' and the 'sustainable investment rule'. The golden rule was that, over the economic cycle, the government would borrow only to invest and not to fund current spending. In other words, the surplus on the current budget – the difference between government receipts and current public spending – would not be negative. The sustainable investment rule stated that, over the economic cycle, the ratio of government debt to GDP would be set at a 'stable and prudent' level, defined by the Chancellor as not more than 40 per cent of GDP. This rule had to be broken as a result of the financial crisis and the recession, and in the UK government debt was projected to peak at 74.9 per cent of GDP in 2014–15, according to the Budget of March 2010. You will be in a position to judge the accuracy of this forecast!

These rules meant that the UK government aimed to balance its budget (or not run a deficit) on current expenditure (i.e. ignoring investment) over the business cycle, but reserved the right to borrow in order to finance investment expenditure, so long as the debt-to-GDP ratio is kept at a stable level on average over the economic cycle. The qualification that the government budget on current expenditure will be balanced on average over the business cycle allows for the effect of automatic stabilizers, such as the increase in welfare expenditure and reduction in tax revenue that automatically occur in a recession (the opposite in a boom) and so helps flatten out economic fluctuations. Allowing a budget deficit on investment expenditure is sensible because, although it leads to rising public debt, it also leads to further growth opportunities through spending on education, roads and so on.

Just asserting that the government should balance its budget, irrespective of the economic cycle and irrespective of what kind of expenditures it is making, is overly simplistic.

Quick Quiz Why might we wish to distinguish between government current expenditure and government investment expenditure and take account of the economic cycle when judging whether the government should balance its budget?

IS MACROPRUDENTIAL POLICY THE 'MISSING INGREDIENT' FROM THE CURRENT POLICY FRAMEWORK?

In Chapter 37 we discussed the causes of the financial crisis and the response of regulators. The debate over the role of regulators continues to evolve as economists look to explain the reasons for the financial crisis and the problems that followed. One focus for policy makers has been the distinction between *systemic risk* – the effects on the whole banking and financial system of crises – and the risks posed by the failure of individual institutions. We have already seen that the collapse of Lehman Brothers bank precipitated a crisis in the banking system as a whole because of the interdependency of financial institutions in relation to borrowing, lending and new instruments such as collateralized debt obligations and credit default swaps.

One of the responses to this debate has been a focus on so-called *macroprudential policy*.

Pro: Macroprudential Policy Helps Bridge the Gap Between Macroeconomic Policy and the Regulation of Individual Financial Institutions

One of the characteristics of the financial crisis was the use of leverage (borrowing) by financial institutions to help drive yields. This led to a mismatch between leverage and liquidity in the financial system as a whole. When macroeconomic and market conditions changed (the rise in defaults on sub-prime mortgages, for example) the financial system as a whole came under strain. This exposed a gap between macroeconomic policy and the regulation of individual financial institutions with the result being that the shocks which occurred were more costly to the global economy than might have been the case.

One of the enduring problems of the crisis which has limited subsequent recovery has been the limitations in the availability of credit to businesses and individuals. This, in conjunction with the need to maintain payments services and insurance against risks should be the focus of macroprudential policy and regulation. At the same time, there may be the possibility of such regulation helping to prevent asset price bubbles, although this would not be a stated aim of any such policy. There is an increasing tendency for individual institutions to take greater risks in periods of economic growth which leaves them overexposed and then to become far more risk averse in any subsequent downturn. This is caused by moral hazard (the idea that some institutions become 'too big to fail') and a failure to recognize the external costs on other institutions of their behaviour.

Macroprudential policy would seek to deal with these two causes by assessing the level of capital ratios that financial institutions must keep as well as capital surcharges targeted at institutions that are deemed to be taking too many risks. These ratios and surcharges would act to create a greater degree of insurance against failure and allow regulators to deal more effectively with cases where banks or other institutions do collapse. The size of such surcharges could be dependent on the size and influence on the system as a whole so that it provides an incentive for these institutions to reduce the potential for their impact on the system.

Con: Macroprudential Policy Sounds Fine in Theory but the Practicalities are Overwhelming

By the very nature of asset price bubbles it is very difficult to be able to recognize when they are happening. Making judgements about which financial institutions are 'too big to fail' and the size of any capital ratio requirement and/or surcharge will be difficult to make and also subject to considerable resistance from banks and financial institutions. Discussions on such requirements as part of the Basel III negotiations in June 2010 led to a considerable watering down of the amount of capital required to be put aside after opposition from the industry. Without the cooperation of banks the chances of any such policy working would be limited. In addition, making any such policy on the basis of a set of rules applying to the global financial system is simply unrealistic. The other option would be that policy makers would have to make judgements and make these with some understanding of the effect on behaviour of the system as a result of their decisions. This is the idea that if a policy makes a decision then those affected by that decision will change their behaviour and policy makers do not have the capacity to accurately identify and model what that changed behaviour might be or how it would affect outcomes in the future.

There are also concerns about the degree of transparency and accountability of policy and policy makers. The objectives of macroprudential policy would have to be clearly set out so that all in the industry were aware of the role of policy and the extent to which policy makers can act. It would be important to get international cooperation on any such policy. Given the experience of the G20 countries in agreeing measures to impose a levy on banks as some form of payback to taxpayers as a result of being bailed out by those taxpayers, such international cooperation looks like a pipe dream. Countries who did have to use taxpayers money to bail out banks and who wanted an agreed levy to prevent banks moving operations to circumvent any such levy faced stiff opposition from countries whose banks had been less risk seeking and who did not require such large scale taxpayer support. If this relatively simple agreement was hard to get then how would policy makers hope to garner such widespread support for far more complex regulations? What this would mean is that individual countries might just go ahead and develop their individual macroprudential policies which would reduce the global effectiveness of any such policies. If this happened then the sophistication of international arbitrage would reduce the effectiveness of any differences in policy and requirements.

This, combined with the sheer complexity of getting agreement on exactly what levels of capital reserves are sufficient to help counter possible failure, what sorts of assets to include (some may not have been invented yet), how to estimate default probabilities of financial institutions, where in the economic cycle different economies actually are, how to get greater agreement on harmonizing international accounting standards, the extent to which short-term interest rates are an appropriate and adequate weapon to counter risk-seeking activity and counter perceived asset price bubbles and much more, means that whilst macroprudential policy makes sense in theory, in practice it is just not workable.

Quick Quiz Do you think that regulators will always be playing catch-up with financial institutions because the latter have an incentive to be creative and dynamic in increasing yields?

HOW DID ECONOMISTS GET IT SO WRONG?

The events from 2007 have once again raised fundamental disagreements between economists. The assumption of efficient markets underpinned claims that macroeconomic policy had solved the world's great problems. In a speech in 2004[1] Ben Bernanke, an acknowledged scholar of the Great Depression, said:

[1]http://www.federalreserve.gov/BOARDDOCS/SPEECHES/2004/20040220/default.htm accessed 1 July 2010.

'One of the most striking features of the economic landscape over the past 20 years or so has been a substantial decline in macroeconomic volatility.' He coined this 'The Great Moderation'. Bernanke put down the reduction in volatility to structural change, improved macroeconomic policies, in particular the focus on achieving stable and low inflation rates, and good luck!

The period 2007–10 can be described as anything but 'stable', so does that mean The Great Moderation was merely a myth or are the current difficulties merely a 'blip' in the process? Whatever it is deemed to be it has reopened the debate between supporters of Keynes who argue for a greater emphasis on fiscal policy and a renouncement of efficient markets and those who believe that efficient markets, whilst not being perfect, provide a better way of explaining events and understanding policy options. This debate will highlight some of the main arguments of both sides.

Pro: Economics Got it Wrong and it is Time to Return to the Ideas of the 'Master', J.M. Keynes

In the good times economists came to believe in the efficiency of markets; the Black Swans were not anticipated. If temporary shocks did occur central banks had it within their capacity to be able to correct these shocks primarily by injecting liquidity into the system and reducing interest rates. The ideas of Keynes were cast aside and economists went back to the idea that people essentially behaved rationally and that markets were the best way of allocating scarce resources for the benefit of all.

The developments in economics in the 1970s and beyond are largely a return to a neoclassical orthodoxy with monetarism the central weapon to help stabilize the economy. We have seen in Chapter 36 how attempts to push unemployment below its natural rate through fiscal policy would merely lead to inflation and a failure to achieve any long-term reduction in unemployment. Economists such as Kydland and Prescott as we noted in Chapter 34 offered an explanation of recessions not as an evil but as an adjustment to changes in the structure of the economy. Any attempt to fight recession could do more harm than good as a result. Not all economists took this view; so called 'New Keynesians' still maintained that there was a role for government in macroeconomic policy hand-in-hand with markets. So despite their reservations the fundamental beliefs in efficient markets and rational behaviour persisted.

The various shocks to the global economy throughout the 1980s, 1990s and in the first decade of the new Millennium were not enough to shake the belief in efficient markets. Stock markets crashed in 1973, 1987, 1997, 1998, 2000, 2002 and 2008, which should have raised concerns about the reliability of efficient markets. Keynes would have recognized these events as evidence of the unreliability of markets. The recession of 2008–09 is not simply an adjustment in the economy but an example of deficient demand. Those economists who support efficient markets will argue that if demand is deficient then prices will rise and the economy will return to balance. The very fact that economic growth has returned following stock market crashes in the last 30 years was support for this view. Recessions, according to Kydland and Prescott, were not the result of business cycles but adjustments to changes in technology; unemployment represented voluntary decisions by workers to drop out of the labour market until the economic good times returned.

New Keynesians (including Professor Mankiw) attempted to reconcile the Keynesian demand-side explanation of recession with imperfections in the market (the sticky wages and prices argument we presented in Chapter 34). The result was that macro policy was still dominated by an orthodoxy which believed central banks could utilize monetary policy in the fight against recession. Economists who warned against the rise in asset prices were largely ignored or at worst ridiculed for their view. The economy has paid a high price for ignoring these warnings.

This time round, monetary policy has failed to pull the economy out of recession; interest rates are at record lows and quantitative easing has pumped billions into the economy on both sides of the Atlantic. It was precisely because of this that Keynes argued for increased government spending to help stimulate the economy and this what is needed now. The upshot is that economics is in a position where it needs to reconcile its long-held belief in the efficiency of markets with the reality that such a theory contains fundamental flaws. Economics will have to confront those flaws and incorporate them into future research. It may be that behavioural economics has much to teach us about the way that economies operate and as a result improved ways to set and implement policy. What this means is that economists who rejected the ideas of Keynes will have to accept that he had an explanation of recessions that needs to be incorporated into this research.

Con: Efficient Markets Still Have Some Currency

The financial crisis was certainly a shock to the system. Does that mean that efficient markets are fundamentally wrong? Far from it – the central tenet of efficient markets is that it is not possible to predict the future and random walks mean precisely that. Spot a cow in a field and monitor its movements; it is simply not possible to plot the path of that cow in the next time period. Efficiency is not a synonym for stability; irrational optimism and pessimism can take over depending on the time period being analysed and how people perceive the risk environment.

There were indeed some economists who argued that asset prices were too high but equally there were other economists who put forward cogent arguments for the state of asset prices – which economist do you listen to? In hindsight it is always easy to pinpoint an individual who happened to make an accurate prediction but that ignores the fact that many others, who were not right this time round, were right on numerous occasions in the past – Alan Greenspan being one example. We have to recognize that there is unlikely to ever be one economic theory that can explain how markets work any more than there is unlikely to be one theory of the universe in physics. If it was possible to accurately price markets then it would have been done and we could plan our way out of all future problems.

Free marketers recognize that markets are not perfectly efficient; however, they are better than government intervention and the evidence of many years would give some weight to this argument. Just look at central planning in former communist countries, the nationalization of large swathes of industry in many parts of Europe as being examples of government failure. Any suggestion that financial markets cannot be trusted, and thus should come under far greater government regulation and scrutiny, is not the direction to go. Indeed, the failure of regulators to spot the financial crisis is as much a damning argument against government intervention as blaming the markets themselves. Behavioural economists are not suggesting that we jump from free markets to government intervention but that we might be able to develop more subtle ways of influencing behaviour and policy direction than what many would see as a clumsy attempt by government to recalibrate the economy.

Keynes may have had some useful ideas for his day but economics has moved on. If he were alive today, Lord Keynes may have had interesting and plausible contributions to make to how rational expectations can be built into Keynesian economics: the idea that people can come to expect over and over again that governments will intervene when the economy suffers downturns without changing their behaviour or how distortions to the economy through tax changes and spending decisions can be accounted for. There are simply too many assumptions and unknowns in simple Keynesian economic analysis; in its time it was revolutionary but that was 70 years ago. Few would argue that we should simply revert to the basis on which medical decisions were taken in the 1930s because we are experiencing difficulties with diagnoses and treatments in 2010; market and government failure as a result of government intervention cannot be ignored in policy making.

It is also important to remember that the financial crisis was caused in part by the behaviour of commercial banks that are part of some of the most strictly regulated markets anywhere in the world. The future lies in putting in place incentives so that banks and other financial institutions do not behave like they did in the past and so help prevent a recurrence of the events of 2007–08 (and probably before). Central banks have done far more than simply reduce base rates and expand the money supply and to suggest that these are the limits of monetary policy is to ignore some considerable work and activities of central banks across the world.

Economics as a discipline owes much to Keynes but the past 30 years have seen considerable changes and advances in the discipline which seeks to develop a more complex understanding of how the economy works and that process will continue. New Keynesians have been an example of how the discipline has sought to reconcile seemingly competing views and in so doing has come up with new ideas that some argue are radical and a departure from a simple confirmation of monetarism. The future for the subject continues to lie in trying to adopt scientific principles and analysis of data to help build understanding; to adopt rigour and objectivity in analysis, as far as humanly possible, and to present arguments for debate and discussion rather than simply reverting back to 70-year-old ideas.

Quick Quiz Give three examples of how government intervention to reduce unemployment by expanding government spending might not work.

CONCLUSION

This chapter has considered five debates over macroeconomic policy. For each, it began with a controversial proposition and then offered the arguments pro and con. If you find it hard to choose a side in these debates, you may find some comfort in the fact that you are not alone. The study of economics does not always make it easy to choose among alternative policies. Indeed, by clarifying the inevitable trade-offs that policy makers face, it can make the choice more difficult.

Difficult choices, however, have no right to seem easy. When you hear politicians or commentators proposing something that sounds too good to be true, it probably is. If they sound like they are offering you a free lunch, you should look for the hidden price tag. Few if any policies come with benefits but no costs. By helping you see through the fog of rhetoric so common in political discourse, the study of economics should make you a better participant in national and international debates.

SUMMARY

- Good decision-making relies on accurate and reliable information. The development of sophisticated models and tools of analysis have helped to improve the ability of policy makers to take informed decisions. Critics argue that many of the forecasting techniques currently in use are fundamentally flawed and that analysis of past events are not a guide to what may happen in the future – there is always the potential for a Black Swan.
- The financial crisis has left many countries with unsustainable budget deficits which are not determined by the normal economic cycle. As a result there is an imperative to implement significant austerity measures to improve confidence in government and in financial markets. Critics argue that structural deficits are very hard to calculate because of the lack of knowledge we have about how to measure output gaps. As a result, the idea of a structural deficit is unhelpful.
- Advocates of a balanced government budget argue that budget deficits impose an unjustifiable burden on future generations by raising their taxes and lowering their incomes. Critics of a balanced government budget argue that the deficit is only one small piece of fiscal policy. Single-minded concern about the budget deficit can obscure the many ways in which policy, including various investment spending programmes, affects different generations. It also ignores the important role of automatic fiscal stabilizers in ironing out economic fluctuations over the economic cycle.
- The financial crisis has highlighted gaps between the regulation of individual financial institutions and the financial system as a whole. Macroprudential policy can help to fill this gap by improving regulation and incentives for individual institutions to change their behaviour and thus reduce systemic risk. Critics point out that the idea might sound fine in theory but the practicalities of any sort of global macroprudential policy are simply so great that the idea will remain a pipe dream.
- The fallout of the financial crisis and the subsequent recession has highlighted flaws in the assumption of free markets and the idea of The Great Moderation. Economists fooled themselves into thinking that they had solved most of the problems of macroeconomic policy and placed too great a reliance on monetary policy for maintaining stable economic conditions. The crisis has revealed that there is still a role for Keynesian demand management in times of recession. Critics argue that simply reverting to ideas that were revolutionary 70 years ago is a retrograde step and ignores the considerable advance in economics since that time. Far from debunking the idea of efficient markets, the whole point of efficient markets is that it is impossible to predict what may happen in the future. The future for economics is to continue seeking to build our understanding and to use the wealth of ideas and rigorous research being carried out to help policy makers make more effective decisions.

QUESTIONS FOR REVIEW

1. Why might an analysis of past events provide an inaccurate forecast of the future?
2. What is the difference between a cyclical budget deficit and a structural budget deficit?
3. Explain how different assumptions of the size of the output gap in an economy could lead to a very different size of structural deficit.
4. Under what circumstances might a government budget deficit on current expenditure be justifiable?
5. Under what circumstances might a government budget deficit on investment expenditure be justifiable?
6. Some economists say that the government can continue running a budget deficit forever. How is that possible?
7. Incentives for financial institutions to price risk more accurately can help to reduce the potential for systemic failure in the banking system. Explain.
8. Is increased regulation in the financial services industry the best way of reducing the chances of another financial crisis? Explain your answer.
9. Ignoring the importance of demand deficiency in recessions leads to fundamentally flawed policies to deal with them. Explain.
10. Keynes' ideas were revolutionary 70 years ago but humans have developed such that they would now not be systematically fooled by repeated government intervention again. Do you agree? Explain your answer.

11. Bernard Madoff (see Chapter 27) was the ultimate Keynesian. He took money from savers and gave it to people who spent that money. Is the analogy of Madoff and Keynesianism a strong argument against the primacy of fiscal policy? Explain your answer.

PROBLEMS AND APPLICATIONS

1. The chapter suggests that the economy, like the human body, has 'natural restorative powers'.
   a. Illustrate the short-run effect of a fall in aggregate demand using an aggregate demand/aggregate supply diagram. What happens to total output, income and employment?
   b. If the government does not use stabilization policy, what happens to the economy over time? Illustrate on your diagram. Does this adjustment generally occur in a matter of months or a matter of years?
   c. Do you think the 'natural restorative powers' of the economy mean that policy makers should be passive in response to the business cycle?
2. Policy makers who want to stabilize the economy must decide how much to change the money supply, government spending or taxes. Why is it difficult for policy makers to choose the appropriate strength of their actions?
3. Why, given the sophistication of technology and the amount of information available to economists these days, is it so difficult to produce accurate forecasts of economic growth?
4. Should economists have seen the financial crisis coming or was it a 'Black Swan'? Explain.
5. Is there any meaningful difference between a cyclical deficit and a structural deficit? Explain your answer.
6. Governments across Europe have instituted austerity measures in an attempt to cut budget deficits which ballooned after the financial crisis. Are they right to do this at a time when the European economic recovery is acknowledged as being fragile.
7. Suppose the government cuts taxes and increases spending, raising the budget deficit to 12 per cent of GDP. If nominal GDP is rising 7 per cent per year, are such budget deficits sustainable forever? Explain. If budget deficits of this size are maintained for 20 years, what is likely to happen to your taxes and your children's taxes in the future? Can you do something today to offset this future effect?
8. The chapter says that budget deficits reduce the income of future generations, but can boost output and income during a recession. Explain how both of these statements can be true.
9. Given the difficulties of instituting a global macroprudential policy, should governments simply put aside any such attempt to develop such a policy and allow the invisible hand of free markets to regulate the global financial system? Explain.
10. Why might recessions be viewed simply as a 'necessary evil'? Explain.
11. Given what you have read in the relevant chapters of the book on the financial crisis would you agree that the global recession of 2008–09 was the result of deficient demand first and foremost? Explain.
12. '... the end result will not be an abandonment of the belief of many in the profession that the stock market is remarkably efficient in its utilization of information'. To what extent would you agree with this assessment of the value of the efficient markets hypothesis?
13. Most economists would pay tribute to the contribution that Keynes made in the wake of the publication of the 'General Theory' in 1936. Has the economy now changed to such an extent that Keynes' ideas are no longer relevant for policy makers? Explain your answer.

For further resources, visit
www.cengage.co.uk/mankiw_taylor2

GLOSSARY

ability-to-pay principle the idea that taxes should be levied on a person according to how well that person can shoulder the burden

abnormal profit the profit over and above normal profit

absolute advantage the comparison among producers of a good according to their productivity

absolute poverty a level of poverty where an individual does not have access to the basics of life – food, clothing and shelter

accounting profit total revenue minus total explicit cost

actual spending, saving or investment the realized or *ex post* outcome resulting from actions of households and firms

adverse selection the tendency for the mix of unobserved attributes to become undesirable from the standpoint of an uninformed party

agent a person who is performing an act for another person, called the principal

aggregate demand curve a curve that shows the quantity of goods and services that households, firms and the government want to buy at each price level

aggregate risk risk that affects all economic actors at once

aggregate supply curve a curve that shows the quantity of goods and services that firms choose to produce and sell at each price level

allocative efficiency a resource allocation where the value of the output by sellers matches the value placed on that output by buyers

appreciation an increase in the value of a currency as measured by the amount of foreign currency it can buy

Arrow's impossibility theorem a mathematical result showing that, under certain assumed conditions, there is no scheme for aggregating individual preferences into a valid set of social preferences

asset-backed securities (ABS) bonds or securities which form part of the securitization of assets. The bonds or securities issued by an SPV as part of a securitization

automatic stabilizers changes in fiscal policy that stimulate aggregate demand when the economy goes into a recession, without policy makers having to take any deliberate action

autonomous expenditure spending which is not dependent on income

average fixed cost fixed costs divided by the quantity of output

average revenue total revenue divided by the quantity sold

average tax rate total taxes paid divided by total income

average total cost total cost divided by the quantity of output

average variable cost variable costs divided by the quantity of output

balanced budget where the total sum of money received by a government in tax revenue and interest is equal to the amount it spends, including on any debt interest owing

balanced trade a situation in which exports equal imports

Bank of England the central bank of the United Kingdom

benefits principle the idea that people should pay taxes based on the benefits they receive from government services

bond a certificate of indebtedness

branding the means by which a business creates an identity for itself and highlights the way in which it differs from its rivals

budget constraint the limit on the consumption bundles that a consumer can afford

budget deficit an excess of government spending over government receipts

budget surplus an excess of government receipts over government spending

business cycle fluctuations in economic activity, such as employment and production

capital the equipment and structures used to produce goods and services

capital flight a large and sudden reduction in the demand for assets located in a country

cartel a group of firms acting in unison

catch-up effect the property whereby countries that start off poor tend to grow more rapidly than countries that start off rich

central bank an institution designed to regulate the quantity of money in the economy

circular-flow diagram a visual model of the economy that shows how money and production inputs and outputs flow through markets among households and firms

classical dichotomy the theoretical separation of nominal and real variables

closed economy an economy that does not interact with other economies in the world

Coase theorem the proposition that if private parties can bargain without cost over the allocation of resources, they can solve the problem of externalities on their own

collective bargaining the process by which unions and firms agree on the terms of employment

collusion an agreement among firms in a market about quantities to produce or prices to charge

commodity money money that takes the form of a commodity with intrinsic value

common currency area a geographical area, possibly covering several countries, in which a common currency is used

common currency area (or currency union or monetary union) a geographical area throughout which a single currency circulates as the medium of exchange

common resources goods that are rival but not excludable

comparative advantage the comparison among producers of a good according to their opportunity cost

compensating differential a difference in wages that arises to offset the non-monetary characteristics of different jobs

competitive market a market in which there are many buyers and many sellers so that each has a negligible impact on the market price

complements two goods for which an increase in the price of one leads to a decrease in the demand for the other (and vice versa)

compounding the accumulation of a sum of money in, say, a bank account, where the interest earned remains in the account to earn additional interest in the future

Condorcet paradox the failure of majority rule to produce transitive preferences for society

constant returns to scale the property whereby long-run average total cost stays the same as the quantity of output changes

consumer prices index (CPI) a measure of the overall prices of the goods and services bought by a typical consumer

consumer surplus a buyer's willingness to pay minus the amount the buyer actually pays

consumption spending by households on goods and services, with the exception of purchases of new housing

cost the value of everything a seller must give up to produce a good

cost–benefit analysis a study that compares the costs and benefits to society of providing a public good

credit default swaps (CDS) a means by which a bondholder can insure against the risk of default

cross-price elasticity of demand a measure of how much the quantity demanded of one good responds to a change in the price of another good, computed as the percentage change in quantity demanded of the first good divided by the percentage change in the price of the second good

crowding out a decrease in investment that results from government borrowing

crowding-out effect the offset in aggregate demand that results when expansionary fiscal policy raises the interest rate and thereby reduces investment spending

currency the paper banknotes and coins in the hands of the public

customs union a group of countries that agree not to impose any restrictions at all on trade between their own economies, but to impose the same restrictions as one another on goods imported from countries outside the group

cyclical unemployment the deviation of unemployment from its natural rate

deadweight loss the fall in total surplus that results from a market distortion, such as a tax

demand curve a graph of the relationship between the price of a good and the quantity demanded

demand deposits balances in bank accounts that depositors can access on demand by using a debit card or writing a cheque

demand schedule a table that shows the relationship between the price of a good and the quantity demanded

depreciation a decrease in the value of a currency as measured by the amount of foreign currency it can buy

depression a severe recession

diminishing marginal product the property whereby the marginal product of an input declines as the quantity of the input increases

diminishing returns the property whereby the benefit from an extra unit of an input declines as the quantity of the input increases

direct tax a tax that is levied directly on a person's income

discount rate the interest rate at which the Federal Reserve lends on a short-term basis to the US banking sector

discrimination the offering of different opportunities to similar individuals who differ only by race, ethnic group, sex, age or other personal characteristics

diseconomies of scale the property whereby long-run average total cost rises as the quantity of output increases

diversification the reduction of risk achieved by replacing a single risk with a large number of smaller unrelated risks

dominant strategy a strategy that is best for a player in a game regardless of the strategies chosen by the other players

economy a word to describe all the economic activity (buying and selling or transactions) that take place in a country or region

economic activity the amount of buying and selling (transactions) that take place in an economy over a period of time

economic growth the increase in the amount of goods and services in an economy over a period of time

economic profit total revenue minus total cost, including both explicit and implicit costs

economics the study of how society manages its scarce resources

economies of scale the property whereby long-run average total cost falls as the quantity of output increases

efficiency the property of a resource allocation of maximizing the total surplus received by all members of society

efficiency wages above-equilibrium wages paid by firms in order to increase worker productivity

efficient markets hypothesis the theory that asset prices reflect all publicly available information about the value of an asset

efficient scale the quantity of output that minimizes average total cost

elasticity a measure of the responsiveness of quantity demanded or quantity supplied to one of its determinants

equilibrium a situation in which the price has reached the level where quantity supplied equals quantity demanded

equilibrium price the price that balances quantity supplied and quantity demanded

equilibrium quantity the quantity supplied and the quantity demanded at the equilibrium price

equity the property of distributing economic prosperity fairly among the members of society

European Central Bank (ECB) the overall central bank of the 16 countries comprising the European Monetary Union

European Economic and Monetary Union (EMU) the European currency union that has adopted the euro as its common currency

European Union a family of democratic European countries, committed to working together for peace and prosperity

Eurosystem the system made up of the ECB plus the national central banks of each of the 16 countries comprising the European Monetary Union

excludability the property of a good whereby a person can be prevented from using it when they do not pay for it

explicit costs input costs that require an outlay of money by the firm

exports goods produced domestically and sold abroad

externality the uncompensated impact of one person's actions on the well-being of a bystander (a third party)

factors of production the inputs used to produce goods and services

Federal Reserve (Fed) the central bank of the United States

fiat money money without intrinsic value that is used as money because of government decree

finance the field of economics that studies how people make decisions regarding the allocation of resources over time and the handling of risk

financial intermediaries financial institutions through which savers can indirectly provide funds to borrowers

financial markets financial institutions through which savers can directly provide funds to borrowers

financial system the group of institutions in the economy that help to match one person's saving with another person's investment

fiscal federalism a fiscal system for a group of countries involving a common fiscal budget and a system of taxes and fiscal transfers across countries

Fisher effect the one-for-one adjustment of the nominal interest rate to the inflation rate

fixed costs costs that are not determined by the quantity of output produced

fractional-reserve banking a banking system in which banks hold only a fraction of deposits as reserves

free rider a person who receives the benefit of a good but avoids paying for it

frictional unemployment unemployment that results because it takes time for workers to search for the jobs that best suit their tastes and skills

fundamental analysis the study of a company's accounting statements and future prospects to determine its value

future value the amount of money in the future that an amount of money today will yield, given prevailing interest rates

game theory the study of how people behave in strategic situations

GDP deflator a measure of the price level calculated as the ratio of nominal GDP to real GDP times 100

Giffen good a good for which an increase in the price raises the quantity demanded

government purchases spending on goods and services by local, state and national governments

gross domestic product (GDP) the market value of all final goods and services produced within a country in a given period of time

gross domestic product per head the market value of all final goods and services produced within a country in a given period of time divided by the population of a country to give a per capita figure

horizontal equity the idea that taxpayers with similar abilities to pay taxes should pay the same amount

human capital the accumulation of investments in people, such as education and on-the-job training

idiosyncratic risk risk that affects only a single economic actor

implicit costs input costs that do not require an outlay of money by the firm

imports goods produced abroad and purchased for use in the domestic economy

import quota a limit on the quantity of a good that can be produced abroad and sold domestically

in-kind transfers transfers to the poor given in the form of goods and services rather than cash

income effect the change in consumption that results when a price change moves the consumer to a higher or lower indifference curve

income elasticity of demand a measure of how much the quantity demanded of a good responds to a change in consumers' income, computed as the percentage change in quantity demanded divided by the percentage change in income

indexation the automatic correction of a money amount for the effects of inflation by law or contract

indifference curve a curve that shows consumption bundles that give the consumer the same level of satisfaction

indirect tax a tax that is levied on goods and services bought

inferior good a good for which, other things equal, an increase in income leads to a decrease in demand (and vice versa)

inflation an increase in the overall level of prices in the economy

inflation rate the percentage change in the price index from the preceding period

inflation tax the revenue the government raises by creating money

informationally efficient reflecting all available information in a rational way

internalizing an externality altering incentives so that people take account of the external effects of their actions

investment spending on capital equipment, inventories and structures, including household purchases of new housing

investment fund an institution that sells shares to the public and uses the proceeds to buy a portfolio of stocks and bonds

job search the process by which workers find appropriate jobs given their tastes and skills

labour force the total number of workers, including both the employed and the unemployed

labour force participation rate (or economic activity rate) the percentage of the adult population that is in the labour force

law of demand the claim that, other things equal, the quantity demanded of a good falls when the price of the good rises

law of supply the claim that, other things equal, the quantity supplied of a good rises when the price of the good rises

law of supply and demand the claim that the price of any good adjusts to bring the quantity supplied and the quantity demanded for that good into balance

liberalism the political philosophy according to which the government should choose policies deemed to be just, as evaluated by an impartial observer behind a 'veil of ignorance'

libertarianism the political philosophy according to which the government should punish crimes and enforce voluntary agreements but not redistribute income

life cycle the regular pattern of income variation over a person's life

liquidity the ease with which an asset can be converted into the economy's medium of exchange

lump-sum tax a tax that is the same amount for every person

macroeconomics the study of economy-wide phenomena, including inflation, unemployment and economic growth

marginal changes small incremental adjustments to a plan of action

marginal cost the increase in total cost that arises from an extra unit of production

marginal product the increase in output that arises from an additional unit of input

marginal product of labour the increase in the amount of output from an additional unit of labour

marginal rate of substitution the rate at which a consumer is willing to trade one good for another

marginal revenue the change in total revenue from an additional unit sold

marginal tax rate the extra taxes paid on an additional unit of income

market a group of buyers and sellers of a particular good or service

market economy an economy that allocates resources through the decentralized decisions of many firms and households as they interact in markets for goods and services

market failure a situation where scarce resources are not allocated to their most efficient use

market for loanable funds the market in which those who want to save supply funds and those who want to borrow to invest demand funds

market power the ability of a single economic agent (or small group of agents) to have a substantial influence on market prices

maximin criterion the claim that the government should aim to maximize the well-being of the worst-off person in society

median voter theorem a mathematical result showing that if voters are choosing a point along a line and each voter wants the point closest to his most preferred point, then majority rule will pick the most preferred point of the median voter

medium of exchange an item that buyers give to sellers when they want to purchase goods and services

menu costs the costs of changing prices

microeconomics the study of how households and firms make decisions and how they interact in markets

model of aggregate demand and aggregate supply the model that most economists use to explain short-run fluctuations in economic activity around its long-run trend

monetary neutrality the proposition that changes in the money supply do not affect real variables

monetary policy the set of actions taken by the central bank in order to affect the money supply

money the set of assets in an economy that people regularly use to buy goods and services from other people

money market the market in which the commercial banks lend money to one another on a short-term basis

money multiplier the amount of money the banking system generates with each unit of reserves

money supply the quantity of money available in the economy

monopolistic competition a market structure in which many firms sell products that are similar but not identical

monopoly a firm that is the sole seller of a product without close substitutes

moral hazard the tendency of a person who is imperfectly monitored to engage in dishonest or otherwise undesirable behaviour

multiplier effect the additional shifts in aggregate demand that result when expansionary fiscal policy increases income and thereby increases consumer spending

Nash equilibrium a situation in which economic actors interacting with one another each choose their best strategy given the strategies that all the other actors have chosen

national saving (saving) the total income in the economy that remains after paying for consumption and government purchases

natural monopoly a monopoly that arises because a single firm can supply a good or service to an entire market at a smaller cost than could two or more firms

natural-rate hypothesis the claim that unemployment eventually returns to its normal, or natural, rate, regardless of the rate of inflation

natural rate of output the output level in an economy when all existing factors of production (land, labour, capital and technology resources) are fully utilized and where unemployment is at its natural rate

natural rate of unemployment the normal rate of unemployment around which the unemployment rate fluctuates

natural resources the inputs into the production of goods and services that are provided by nature, such as land, rivers and mineral deposits

negative income tax a tax system that collects revenue from high-income households and gives transfers to low-income households

net capital outflow the purchase of foreign assets by domestic residents minus the purchase of domestic assets by foreigners

net exports spending on domestically produced goods by foreigners (exports) minus spending on foreign goods by domestic residents (imports)

nominal exchange rate the rate at which a person can trade the currency of one country for the currency of another

nominal GDP the production of goods and services valued at current prices

nominal interest rate the interest rate as usually reported without a correction for the effects of inflation

nominal variables variables measured in monetary units

normal good a good for which, other things equal, an increase in income leads to an increase in demand (and vice versa)

normal profit the minimum amount required to keep factors of production in their current use

normative statements claims that attempt to prescribe how the world should be

oligopoly competition amongst the few – a market structure in which only a few sellers offer similar or identical products and dominate the market

open economy an economy that interacts freely with other economies around the world

open-market operations the purchase and sale of non-monetary assets from and to the banking sector by the central bank

opportunity cost whatever must be given up to obtain some item – the value of the benefits foregone (sacrificed)

optimum currency area a group of countries for which it is optimal to adopt a common currency and form a currency union

outright open-market operations the outright sale or purchase of non-monetary assets to or from the banking sector by the central bank without a corresponding agreement to reverse the transaction at a later date

perfect complements two goods with right-angle indifference curves

perfect substitutes two goods with straight-line indifference curves

permanent income a person's normal income

Phillips curve a curve that shows the short-run trade-off between inflation and unemployment

physical capital the stock of equipment and structures that are used to produce goods and services

Pigovian tax a tax enacted to correct the effects of a negative externality

planned spending, saving or investment the desired or intended actions of households and firms

positive statements claims that attempt to describe the world as it is

poverty line an absolute level of income set by the government below which a family is deemed to be in poverty. In the UK and Europe this is measured by earnings less than 60 per cent of median income

poverty rate the percentage of the population whose family income falls below an absolute level called the poverty line

present value the amount of money today that would be needed to produce, using prevailing interest rates, a given future amount of money

price ceiling a legal maximum on the price at which a good can be sold

price discrimination the business practice of selling the same good at different prices to different customers

price elasticity of demand a measure of how much the quantity demanded of a good responds to a change in the price of that good, computed as the percentage change in quantity demanded divided by the percentage change in price

price elasticity of supply a measure of how much the quantity supplied of a good responds to a change in the price of that good, computed as the percentage change in quantity supplied divided by the percentage change in price

price floor a legal minimum on the price at which a good can be sold

price level the price of a basket of goods and services measured as the weighted arithmetic average of current prices

principal a person for whom another person, called the agent, is performing some act

prisoners' dilemma a particular 'game' between two captured prisoners that illustrates why cooperation is difficult to maintain even when it is mutually beneficial

private goods goods that are both excludable and rival

private saving the income that households have left after paying for taxes and consumption

producer price index a measure of the change in prices of a basket of goods and services bought by firms

producer surplus the amount a seller is paid for a good minus the seller's cost

production function the relationship between quantity of inputs used to make a good and the quantity of output of that good

production possibilities frontier a graph that shows the combinations of output that the economy can possibly produce given the available factors of production and the available production technology

productivity the quantity of goods and services produced from each hour of a worker's time

profit total revenue minus total cost

progressive tax a tax for which high-income taxpayers pay a larger fraction of their income than do low-income taxpayers

property rights the exclusive right of an individual, group or organization to determine how a resource is used

proportional or flat tax a tax for which high-income and low-income taxpayers pay the same fraction of income

public goods goods that are neither excludable nor rival

public saving the tax revenue that the government has left after paying for its spending

purchasing power parity a theory of exchange rates whereby a unit of any given currency should be able to buy the same quantity of goods in all countries

quantity demanded the amount of a good that buyers are willing and able to purchase

quantity equation the equation $M \times V = P \times Y$, which relates the quantity of money, the velocity of money, and the euro value of the economy's output of goods and services

quantity supplied the amount of a good that sellers are willing and able to sell

quantity theory of money a theory asserting that the quantity of money available determines the price level and that the growth rate in the quantity of money available determines the inflation rate

random walk the path of a variable whose changes are impossible to predict

rational expectations the theory according to which people optimally use all the information they have, including information about government policies, when forecasting the future

real exchange rate the rate at which a person can trade the goods and services of one country for the goods and services of another

real GDP the production of goods and services valued at constant prices

real interest rate the interest rate corrected for the effects of inflation

real money balances what money can actually buy given the ratio of the money supply to the price level M/P

real variables variables measured in physical units

recession a period of declining real incomes and rising unemployment. The technical definition gives recession occurring after two successive quarters of negative economic growth

refinancing rate the interest rate at which the European Central Bank lends on a short-term basis to the Euro Area banking sector

regressive tax a tax for which high-income taxpayers pay a smaller fraction of their income than do low-income taxpayers

relative poverty a situation where an individual is not able to access what would be considered acceptable standards of living in society

repo rate the interest rate at which the Bank of England lends on a short-term basis to the UK banking sector

repurchase agreement (repo) the sale of a non-monetary asset together with an agreement to repurchase it at a set price at a specified future date

reserve ratio the fraction of deposits that banks hold as reserves

reserve requirements regulations on the minimum amount of reserves that banks must hold against deposits

reserves deposits that banks have received but have not loaned out

risk averse exhibiting a dislike of uncertainty

rivalry the property of a good whereby one person's use diminishes other people's use

sacrifice ratio the number of percentage points of annual output lost in the process of reducing inflation by 1 percentage point

scarcity the limited nature of society's resources

screening an action taken by an uninformed party to induce an informed party to reveal information

securitization the creation of asset-backed securities

shoeleather costs the resources wasted when inflation encourages people to reduce their money holdings

shortage a situation in which quantity demanded is greater than quantity supplied

signalling an action taken by an informed party to reveal private information to an uninformed party

Single European Market a (still-not-complete) EU-wide market throughout which labour, capital, goods and services can move freely

social security government benefits that supplement the incomes of the needy

stagflation a period of falling output and rising prices

standard of living refers to the amount of goods and services that can be purchased by the population of a country. Usually measured by the inflation-adjusted (real) income per head of the population

stock (or share or equity) a claim to partial ownership in a firm

store of value an item that people can use to transfer purchasing power from the present to the future

strike the organized withdrawal of labour from a firm by a union

structural unemployment unemployment that results because the number of jobs available in some labour markets is insufficient to provide a job for everyone who wants one

subsidy payment to buyers and sellers to supplement income or lower costs and which thus encourages consumption or provides an advantage to the recipient

substitutes two goods for which an increase in the price of one leads to an increase in the demand for the other

substitution effect the change in consumption that results when a price change moves the consumer along a given indifference curve to a point with a new marginal rate of substitution

sunk cost a cost that has already been committed and cannot be recovered

supply curve a graph of the relationship between the price of a good and the quantity supplied

supply schedule a table that shows the relationship between the price of a good and the quantity supplied

supply shock an event that directly alters firms' costs and prices, shifting the economy's aggregate supply curve and thus the Phillips curve

surplus a situation in which quantity supplied is greater than quantity demanded

tariff a tax on goods produced abroad and sold domestically

tax incidence the manner in which the burden of a tax is shared among participants in a market

technological knowledge society's understanding of the best ways to produce goods and services

the long run the period of time in which all factors of production can be altered

the short run the period of time in which some factors of production cannot be changed

theory of liquidity preference Keynes' theory that the interest rate adjusts to bring money supply and money demand into balance

total cost the market value of the inputs a firm uses in production

total expenditure the amount paid by buyers, computed as the price of the good times the quantity purchased

total revenue the amount received by sellers of a good, computed as the price of the good times the quantity sold

toxic debt mortgage-backed securities and other debt (such as bonds) that are not able to be repaid in many cases because the value of the assets against which they are secured have fallen significantly

trade balance the value of a nation's exports minus the value of its imports; also called net exports

trade deficit an excess of imports over exports

trade policy a government policy that directly influences the quantity of goods and services that a country imports or exports

trade surplus an excess of exports over imports

Tragedy of the Commons a parable that illustrates why common resources get used more than is desirable from the standpoint of society as a whole

transaction costs the costs that parties incur in the process of agreeing and following through on a bargain

transfer payment a payment for which no good or service is exchanged

unemployment insurance a government programme that partially protects workers' incomes when they become unemployed

unemployment rate the percentage of the labour force that is unemployed

union a worker association that bargains with employers over wages and working conditions

unit of account the yardstick people use to post prices and record debts

utilitarianism the political philosophy according to which the government should choose policies to maximize the total utility of everyone in society

utility a measure of happiness or satisfaction

value of the marginal product the marginal product of an input times the price of the output

variable costs costs that are dependent on the quantity of output produced

velocity of money the rate at which money changes hands

vertical equity the idea that taxpayers with a greater ability to pay taxes should pay larger amounts

welfare economics the study of how the allocation of resources affects economic well-being

well-being happiness or satisfaction with life as reported by individuals

willingness to pay the maximum amount that a buyer will pay for a good

world price the price of a good that prevails in the world market for that good

INDEX

F

N

O

P